# Pure Lands in Asian Texts and Contexts

**Pure Land Buddhist Studies**
a publication of the Institute of Buddhist Studies
at the Graduate Theological Union


**EDITORIAL BOARD**

Richard K. Payne
*Chair, Institute of Buddhist Studies at the Graduate Theological Union*

Carl Bielefeldt
*Stanford University*

Harry Gyokyo Bridge
*Buddhist Church of Oakland*

James Dobbins
*Oberlin College*

Jérôme Ducor
*Université de Lausanne, Switzerland*

Paul Harrison
*Stanford University*

Anne Klein
*Rice University*

David Matsumoto
*Institute of Buddhist Studies at the Graduate Theological Union*

Scott Mitchell
*Institute of Buddhist Studies at the Graduate Theological Union*

Eisho Nasu
*Ryukoku University, Kyoto, Japan*

Jonathan A. Silk
*Universiteit Leiden, Leiden, The Netherlands*

Kenneth K. Tanaka
*Musashino University, Tokyo, Japan*

PURE LAND BUDDHIST STUDIES

# Pure Lands in Asian Texts and Contexts

## *An Anthology*

Edited by Georgios T. Halkias
and Richard K. Payne

University of Hawai'i Press / Honolulu

Printed in the United States of America

24 23 22 21 20 19 6 5 4 3 2 1

**Library of Congress Cataloging-in-Publication Data**

Names: Halkias, Georgios, editor. | Payne, Richard K., editor.
Title: Pure Lands in Asian texts and contexts : an anthology / edited by
Georgios T. Halkias and Richard K. Payne.
Other titles: Pure Land Buddhist studies.
Description: Honolulu : University of Hawai'i Press, [2019] | Series: Pure
Land Buddhist studies series
Identifiers: LCCN 2018041487 | ISBN 9780824873097 (cloth : alk. paper) Subjects:
LCSH: Pure Land Buddhism—Literary collections—Translations into
English.
Classification: LCC BQ8514 .P87 2019 | DDC 294.3/926—dc23
LC record available at https://lccn.loc.gov/2018041487

The editors wish to thank BDK America for the generous subvention granted in support of this publication.

*Cover art*: Borobudur Temple Compound. Photo by Georgios T. Halkias.

The Pure Land Buddhist Studies series publishes scholarly works on all aspects of the Pure Land Buddhist tradition. Historically, this includes studies of the origins of the tradition in India, its transmission into a variety of religious cultures, and its continuity into the present. Methodologically, the series is committed to providing a venue for a diversity of approaches, including, but not limited to, anthropological, sociological, historical, textual, biographical, philosophical, and interpretive, as well as translations of primary and secondary works. The series will also seek to reprint important works so that they may continue to be available to the scholarly and lay communities. The series is made possible by grants from the Institute of Buddhist Studies.

University of Hawai'i Press books are printed on acid-free paper and meet the guidelines for permanence and durability of the Council on Library Resources.

# Contents

Series Editor's Preface ix
*Scott A. Mitchell*

Editors' Introduction 1
*Georgios T. Halkias and Richard K. Payne*

**I. Ritual Practices**

Overview 29

1 The Consecration Scripture Spoken by the Buddha on Being Reborn in Whichever of the Pure Lands of the Ten Directions You Wish 33
*Ryan Richard Overbey*

2 Esoteric Pure Land in Kakuban's Thought 56
*Anna Andreeva*

3 Akṣobhya *Homa*: Fire Offerings for the Buddha of the Eastern Pure Land 79
*Richard K. Payne*

4 *Nenbutsu* Practice in Genshin's *Ōjōyōshū* 115
*Robert F. Rhodes*

5 Visions of the Pure Land from the Mind Treasury of Namchö Migyur Dorje 139
*Georgios T. Halkias*

**II. Contemplative Visualizations**

Overview 157

1 Liberating Desire: An Esoteric Pure Land Text by Dīpaṃkaraśrījñāna 159
*Georgios T. Halkias*

2 Maitreya's Tuṣita Heaven as a Pure Land in Gelukpa Forms of Tibetan Buddhism 188
*James B. Apple*

3 Amoghavajra's Amitāyus Ritual Manual 223
*Thomas Eijō Dreitlein*

4 Dōhan's *Compendium on the Secret Contemplation of Buddha, Fascicle One* 269
*Aaron P. Proffitt*

**III. Doctrinal Expositions**

Overview 319

1 Answers to Forty-Eight Questions about Pure Land (Selections) 322
*Charles B. Jones*

2 The Role of Buddhism in Emperor Worship 349
*Fabio Rambelli*

3 "The Future of American Buddhism" 379
*Michihiro Ama*

4 Naikan's Path 396
*Clark Chilson*

5 Wŏnhyo's *Commentary on the Amitābha Sūtra* 420
*Richard D. McBride II*

**IV. Life-Writing and Poetry**

Overview 455

1 Biographies from *The Accounts of Those from Mount Kōya Who Have Attained Birth in a Pure Land* 457
*Ethan Lindsay*

2 Contemporary Pure Land Miracle Tales 477
*Natasha Heller*

3 In Praise of His Mighty Name: A Tibetan Poem on Amitābha from Dunhuang 496
*Jonathan A. Silk*

4 Pure Land Devotional Poetry by a Chan Monk 540
*Natasha Heller*

**V. Ethical and Aesthetic Explications**

Overview 551

1 Religion and Ethics in the Thought of Kiyozawa Manshi 554
*Jacques Fasan*

2 The Pure Land and This World in Hishiki Masaharu's Shin Buddhist Ethics 571
*Ugo Dessì*

3 Toward a Pure Land Buddhist Aesthetics: Yanagi Sōetsu on the Vow of Non-Discrimination between Beauty and Ugliness 587
*Elisabetta Porcu*

4 A Confucian Pure Land? *Longshu's Treatise on Pure Land* by Wang Rixiu 602
*Daniel Getz*

5 Tanaka Chigaku on "The Age of Unification" 631
*Jacqueline I. Stone*

**VI. Worlds beyond Sukhāvatī**

Overview 663

1 The Divine Scripture on the Rebirth in the Pure Land of the Highest Cavern Mystery of Numinous Treasure 665
*Henrik H. Sørensen*

2 A Manichaean Pure Land: The Buddhicized Description of the Realm of Light in the Chinese Manichaean *Hymnscroll* 707
*Gábor Kósa*

3 Śambhala as a Pure Land 744
*Vesna A. Wallace*

Contributors 763

Index 769

# Series Editor's Preface

Scott A. Mitchell

Buddhist studies has long been organized around the concept of the nation-state, privileging regional expressions of Buddhism over transcultural connections. Moreover, the field has been informed by modernist and Protestant understandings of religion that highlight, in turn, the heroic quest of personal religious or mystical experience, doctrinal orthodoxy, and the perspectives and practices of elite religious and scholarly experts. The sum total of these preconceptions, as editors Georgios T. Halkias and Richard K. Payne note in their introduction, "presumes to have already answered the question: What is important about Buddhism?" And that answer leaves little room for a full appreciation of Pure Land Buddhism. With this volume, then, the editors hope to provide us with a heuristic that will allow for new studies of Buddhism, studies that can reveal connections, relationships, and influences heretofore obscured.

*Pure Lands in Asian Texts and Contexts* is a collection of primary sources and commentaries from a wide range of languages, locations, and times across Buddhist Asia and North America, organized not by sect or geopolitical location but by genre. The editors' heuristic also examines Pure Land Buddhism through the lens of cult, drawing on the classic definition of the term as a "set of practices directed toward a particular figure." Understood in this way, Pure Land Buddhism becomes a more expansive term, referring to various collections of practices, texts, and doctrines focused on any particular buddha, bodhisattva, or other devotional figure. Such cults may foreground vows as well as a range of practices—from variations on the *buddhanusmṛti* theme (e.g., buddha-name recitation) and visualizations of buddhas and buddha realms to tantric empowerments. Pure Land cults, therefore, focus on specific figures and their associated lands but need not be confined to a specific sect, community, lineage, monastery, temple, or institution. Cultic practices transcend such categories, allowing us to see otherwise obscured connections between lineages, times, and locations. Moreover, because these practices are as likely to be taken up by elite masters as by the laity, cult-as-frame breaks down the distinction that invariably privileges the elite perspective. This volume then is obviously concerned with a far more expansive view of Pure Land Buddhism and is not confined to one Buddha (Amitābha) and one Pure Land (Sukhāvatī). A scholarly focus on the Japanese Pure Land traditions of Jōdo-shū and Jōdo Shinshū, leaving aside their obvious import, has limited the study of Pure Land Buddhism to the concerns of these schools, their founders, their practices, and their constructed linages and thus obscures Pure Land cults embedded in Buddhism writ large.

In support of a broader perspective, the editors have gathered an impressive array of material. Ritual texts from China, Japan, and Tibet demonstrate continuity rather than disjuncture between mainstream Mahāyāna and tantric practices. Visualization practices reveal perennial questions about the other-worldliness or immanence of various pure lands. As what the editors call a "pan-Asian and deeply entrenched religious phenomenon," it should be no surprise that Pure Land doctrines have long been in conversation with various Buddhist systems of thought, applied to changing political concerns, adapted to new cultural locations, or used as the basis for secular therapeutic practices. But unlike other forms of Buddhist ascetics, art, and poetry that have captured the Western imagination, Pure Land life-writing and poetry are often creative combinations of fictional and historical events and contain rich accounts of faith and longing for the Pure Land. And, importantly, the very idea of a pure land, ubiquitous across religious traditions, "both challenges and reinforces the uniqueness of Pure Land literature as a useful category," and so this book speaks to pure lands not only beyond Sukhāvatī, but beyond Buddhism itself.

*Pure Lands in Asian Texts and Contexts* advances Pure Land scholarship by extracting various pure lands from the margins of Buddhist studies. It joins a host of recent scholarship engaged, to varying degrees, in this same project. It is a welcome and much-needed contribution to the Pure Land Buddhist Studies series and to Buddhist scholarship generally.

Pure Lands in Asian Texts and Contexts

# Editors' Introduction

Georgios T. Halkias
Richard K. Payne

## Expanding Horizons of Pure Land Buddhist Studies

This collection of original sources, drawn from a wide range of traditional and contemporary Pure Land Buddhist cultures and translated here into English, is primarily organized according to a variety of genres shared throughout the entire Buddhist tradition. Each translation is introduced by an expository section providing historical, sectarian, and other contextualizing information written by the translator.

By organizing the material according to genre, common (and less common) issues of practice and doctrine can be explored more directly than if the collection were organized geopolitically, one of the organizing principles commonly employed in Buddhist studies today.[1] Buddhist studies continues to be largely organized by default according to modern nation-states in accord with how the field was established in the nineteenth century.[2] This collection, however, demonstrates the utility of an alternative framework for thinking about the benefits and limitations of the category "Pure Land Buddhism." The explicit theoretical principle is that there is an underlying coherence, or polythemic unity, to the thematics of pure lands across and beyond Buddhist Asia, a coherence that is only obscured by presuming that geopolitical categories deserve priority. Geopolitical categories, such as Indian Buddhism, Tibetan Buddhism, Chinese Buddhism, and so on, tend to essentialize national or even ethnic forms of Buddhism and to ignore cross-fertilization, intra-religious transfers (see Georgios Halkias, "Liberating Desire," in this volume), and shared practices among Buddhist and even non-Buddhist traditions in India and Central Asia (see Gábor Kósa and Henrik Sørensen in this volume).

Geopolitical frameworks originate in the concerns of modern imperialism and resistance to it. Those concerns include both direct political and economic control and the goals of religious missionizing that have motivated and justified imperialism. Two dimensions of this history of missionizing have been formative for the field of Buddhist studies as it is found today: the privileging of doctrine and the texts in which it is recorded,[3] and the privileging of intellectual and institutional elites. Proper belief, orthodoxy, has played a significant role for most missionary institutions in Christendom, as has a strategy of "top-down" conversion.[4] Though not without exception, the resulting intellectual project tended, therefore, to seek the most intellectually sophisticated streams of thought[5] within Buddhism[6] and the Buddhist leadership, both monastic and lay.[7] As a consequence, the intellectual profile of contemporary Buddhist studies has been informed by nineteenth-century theology and until relatively recently left little room for the practices and beliefs of a majority of Buddhist adherents throughout history. This intellectual profile presumes to have already answered the question: What is important about Buddhism? That question has, however, been again raised over the past few decades by several scholars, often those who have come to Buddhist studies after training in other disciplines. Gradually such scholarship has called attention to the limitations imposed by a geopolitical framework and a privileging of doctrine, despite which these organizing principles continue to be widely assumed as the most "natural" ways of organizing our understandings of Buddhist history, thought, and practice.

This being said, the geopolitical dimensions of Pure Land worship, teachings, and thought have contributed to the identification of distinct regional forms of practice and of interpretation.[8] By juxtaposing sources that would otherwise have been segregated from one another, a genre-based anthology brings this regional character into focus in ways that a geopolitical approach could not. This approach also lends itself to content-based comparisons between beliefs and practices among Buddhist traditions forming around conceptions and unique interpretations of "pure lands."

Though we do not follow a geopolitical arrangement of sources we have at the same time not underestimated the importance of taking geopolitical considerations into account. The collection also seeks to provide a wide selection of contributions that include but are not dominated by the Japanese Pure Land sects. By surveying a wide range of primary source material, we go beyond taking Japanese Pure Land as normative for the field of study while showing how the Buddhism of pure lands is not just an East Asian Buddhist orientation, but a pan-Asian and deeply entrenched religious phenomenon.

## Problematics of Defining "Pure Land Buddhism"

One of the goals of this collection is to provide an intellectual framework—a heuristic—that will allow for scholarly examination of the Buddhist tradition across its entirety in new ways. That is, a shift of perspective to one from which relationships, connections, influences, and patterns that are otherwise invisible can be revealed. For the purposes of this collection, therefore, the theme "Pure Land Buddhism" is understood broadly to include not only the forms of Buddhism in which Sukhāvatī (*bde ba can; jile jingtu; gokurakujōdo; kŭngnak chŏngt'o*) is the goal of practice, or Amitābha ('Od dpag med / Snang ba mtha' yas; Amituo fo / Wuliangguang fo; Amida butsu / Muryōkō butsu; Amit'a pul / Muryanggwang pul) is the main figure of devotion, even though admittedly a large number of scriptures are devoted exclusively to the vows he made when he was Dharmākara Bodhisattva (Chos kyi 'byung gnas; Fazang biqiu; Hōzō biku; Pŏpchang pigu) or to describing in detail the appealing features of his pure land. As used here, Pure Land Buddhism goes beyond the "three Pure Land scriptures" (*jingtu sanbu jing; jōdo sanbukyō; chŏngt'o sambu kyŏng*), in that it includes a range of *buddhakṣetra* (*sangs rgyas zhing; focha; bussetsu; pulch'al*), celestial, and even earthly pure lands associated with other buddhas, bodhisattvas, and devotional figures (see Wallace in this volume). More broadly, ideas of "hidden realms and pure abodes," as Ronald Davidson has called them, form part of the medieval Indian Buddhist *episteme* within which more specific conceptions of *buddhakṣetra* developed.[9] It is a coherent theme within the history of Buddhist praxis,[10] rather than a unique or special kind of Buddhism.

Galen Amstutz, Mark Blum, and Georgios Halkias have pointed to the *Vimalakīrtinirdeśa sūtra* as the *locus classicus* for the idea of a "pure land" as a "buddha-field" (*buddhakṣetra*) "that has been purified by the sacred presence of a buddha or bodhisattva," placing this understanding of a pure land in early Mahāyāna Buddhist thought.[11] In addition to this characteristic of buddha-lands as being purified by the presence of a buddha or bodhisattva, Amstutz and Blum also point out the defining role of vows taken during training. When the bodhisattva who has vowed to accomplish certain "specific religious skills . . . acquires a buddha-land into which sentient beings are born, both the bodhisattva/buddha and the sentient beings reborn there all acquire that same skill."[12] Sentient beings gain birth (*ōjō*) in such pure lands through any of the practices that involve "keeping the buddha in mind" (*buddhanusmṛti*; *nenbutsu*), which constitutes a wide range of practices including but not limited to rituals, meditation, visualization, austerities, recitation of scriptures, and chanting the Buddha's mantra. Amstutz and Blum also note the wide range of cosmological locations for various pure lands as given in the Indian materials. They note then that "there has always been a flexibility, variety, and even inconsistency in the concept of 'pure land' within Mahāyāna Buddhism as a whole," which is made even more complex by speculations regarding various different pure lands associated with individual buddhas developed in China, Korea, and Japan.[13] We also note that "pure lands associated with specific buddhas" are not restricted to East Asia, but can be found in Central Asia, Tibet, and Mongolia. As a matter of fact, in the Tibetan traditions of Buddhism, more than any other tradition, we find an explosion of buddhas and pure lands not limited to the figures Western scholarship has led us to expect (that is, Amitābha, Akṣobhya, Maitreya, and Bhaiṣajyaguru) but also to tantric deities (such as Vajrayoginī), Buddhist masters (such as PadmasambhavaB), and "hidden lands" (*sbas yul*), pristine physical places of spiritual accomplishment and renewal such as Pemako (Padma-bkod) in the far eastern borders of India with Tibet. Reflecting a broader theoretical issue in Buddhist thought, Amstutz and Blum also note that there are "two basic forms or expressions of belief in some kind of liminal *topos* contrasted with the all-too-obvious defiled land of our *saha* world: a pure land that is an *other world*, meaning an idealized environment not seen here in our experience, or a pure land that is *this world*, designating an idealized reconceptualization of this world that is experienced when religious awakening removes the defilements that limit our perception."[14] Georgios Halkias has similarly shown Pure Land Buddhism as an inner-visionary account of the path to enlightenment that has been enlivened by Tantric Buddhist iconography, ritual, and narrative while, as in Chan–Pure Land traditions, Sukhāvatī is stripped of all mental concepts and constructs in readings of Dzogchen, or the Great Perfection. There has never been any indication of doubt in the writings of Tibetan Buddhist scholars that Pure Land ritual practices and doctrines are a legitimate and integral part of Indian Mahāyāna Buddhism in its Vajrayāna formulations (see Halkias in this volume).

Although in decline, the bias against considering Pure Land beliefs and practices to be a valid form of Buddhism is found among some

Western academics and adherents of Buddhist modernism, notably those who have not taken the time to study these traditions carefully or who reject them for not fitting their own preconceptions about what Buddhism is and is not.[15] In addition to preconceptions about Buddhism, unexamined theoretical prejudices regarding the nature of religion have contributed to the marginalization of Pure Land Buddhism. Euro-American understandings of religion as grounded on special forms of experience (mystical experiences, conversion experiences, transcendent experiences, or religious experiences) dates to the eighteenth century. They were given particularly influential formulation in the theology of Friedrich Schleiermacher at the beginning of the nineteenth century[16] and were treated as foundational for the religious life by the new psychology of religion at the beginning of the twentieth century.[17] Such experiences are still privileged throughout the field of religious studies, which understands such experiences as private and individual, and often privileges them as sources of truth.[18] At the same time, the Romantic and neo-Romantic visions of heroic individuality valorized the idea of a religious quest for insight, awakening, enlightenment.[19] As formulated by Hōnen and Shinran, however, Pure Land employed the dichotomy of "path of sages" and "easy path" attributed to Nāgārjuna. As a result, austerities and yogic practices of all kinds were excluded in favor of the simple practice of *nenbutsu* as an expression of gratitude. Such devaluing of a heroic vision of an individual quest for awakening neither appeals to Romantic and neo-Romantic conceptions of "the religious quest" nor accords with the theoretical precommitment of religious studies regarding individual experience as the basis of religion.[20] As deeply entrenched as this complex of ideas is in Euro-American popular and academic religious culture, it is outside the traditions of Buddhist praxis. It is in other words an etic understanding, the imposition of which constitutes an act of cognitive imperialism.[21]

By taking instead the various emic understandings, that is, those in which the concept of pure land has been used over the entire course of the Buddhist tradition, we find that the category of "Pure Land Buddhism" can be used heuristically and geographically in an expansive fashion such that it makes available to scholarly reflection a wide range of phenomena that would otherwise be unavailable for comparative study and critical dialogue. In taking this expansive approach to the widespread phenomenon of Pure Land Buddhism, the collection seeks to further integrate its study into the field of Buddhist studies. The field has already been moving beyond the "problem" posed by Sir Charles

Eliot, who suggested that Pure Land Buddhism as he knew it in Japan should not be considered a form of Buddhism at all.[22] The presumption that Pure Land themes are somehow not authentically Buddhist seems to have contributed to looking for its origins outside the tradition. The predominant presumption held both popularly and (to only a slightly lesser extent) academically that Buddhism is a tradition of meditation is only partially accurate. Because the presumption is so pervasive, the question of Pure Land as a "legitimate" form of Buddhism continues to plague the field.

Examining the logical progression of Mahāyāna concepts, Jan Nattier has argued that the development of Pure Land is fully coherent with that history and that "there is no need to appeal to 'foreign influences' or 'non-Buddhist borrowings' to explain the rise of Amitābha in India."[23] And in another important piece of critical scholarship, Nattier has suggested understanding Pure Land as a historical movement within Buddhism that developed "ideas and practices related to Buddhas who are presently living in world-systems other than our own, a category which would include not only Amitābha but also Akṣobhya and the countless Buddha figures described in Mahāyāna texts as presiding over world-systems in all of the ten directions."[24] This is the case in Indian, Tibetan, and East Asian Mahāyāna traditions where the worship of pure lands is not limited to Buddha Amitābha and his buddha-field Sukhāvatī. For example, the earliest detailed presentation of the complex of ideas appears to be related to Buddha Akṣobhya (Mi bskyod pa; Achu fo; Ashuku butsu; Ach'ok pul) and his buddha-field of "wondrous joy" Abhirati (*mngon dga'*; *miaoxi / abiluoti*; *myōki / abiradai*; *myohŭi / abiraje*),[25] while the worship of Maitreya and Tuṣita Heaven as a pure land is attested throughout Asia, such as in the Tibetan traditions (see James Apple in this volume) and in both Paekche and early Silla periods of Korean history where "aspirants considered their own countries to be the Pure Lands where Maitreya would appear in the present."[26] In theory, every buddha has his own buddha-field (*buddhakṣetra*). The phrase "pure land," being a Chinese-coined term (*jingtu*; *jōdo*), is also found in Tibetan (*rnam dag zhing khams*) Buddhist manuscripts from Dunhuang (seventh to ninth century), which attests to either its direct borrowing from the Chinese *jingtu* or from a Central Asian tradition.

One of the things that has made it difficult to perceive Pure Land Buddhism as an integral part of the broader Buddhist tradition has been the tendency to essentialize the characteristics of Jōdo and Jōdo Shin thought and treat those as defining the category of Pure Land. We emphasize that we are here in no way intending to deny the importance of these traditions, for example in their popularization of hermeneutic juxtapositions between "self-power" (*rang stobs; zili; jiriki; charyŏk*) versus "other-power" (*dngos po'i nus pa; tali; tariki; t'aryŏk*) for Pure Land soteriology and modalities of faith. It is instead hoped that integrating them into a wider understanding of Pure Land thought and practice within Mahāyāna will actually better serve to legitimate them than has the exceptionalist rhetoric of some of their own apologists. One of the intentions of this collection is to expand the category of Pure Land beyond limiting sectarian formulations and make it available as an academic category appropriate for use in many different cultural contexts and in relation to a variety of different religious concerns and interpretations. Thus, rather than taking specific sectarian formulations as definitive of Pure Land Buddhism as such, any specific sectarian formulation is contextualized as part of the range of Pure Land Buddhisms.

The challenge of defining "Pure Land Buddhism" is in the ways we understand the term in its historical and contemporary formulations. As the diversity of this volume shows, there is no historically continuous, single, uniform lineage leading in a chronological arc from India through China, to Korea, to Japan, and recently on to the West, but rather there is a field of study. The field is constituted by a complex mix of visions, doctrines, metaphors, symbols, and practices crystallizing around the notion of a pure land (and also buddha realm more widely), but in each crystallization different local elements are involved. For example, the idea of the end of the dharma (*saddharmavipalopa; mofa; mappō; malpŏp*) was an element that played a particularly central role in the development of Pure Land Buddhisms in China, Japan, and Korea, while tantric methods for the swift transference of one's subtle consciousness to Sukhāvatī at the moment of death (*'pho ba*) remains central to all schools of Tibetan Buddhism and is one of the most popular funereal rituals across the Tibetan cultural world. Pure Land orientations offered a doctrinal basis for the joint cultivation with one or several other Buddhist traditions leading across Asia to the development of Tantra and Pure Land, Zen and Pure Land, Tiantai and Pure Land, and so forth.

Though as Charles Jones has noted, "there is a loose but self-conscious Pure Land 'lineage' (*zong*) or 'dharma-gate' (*famen*) with 'patriarchs' (*zu*) in China,"[7] use of the phrase "Pure Land" to identify a specific lineage institution derives from Hōnen, not earlier. And the lineage constructed by Shinran reflects the conceptual concerns he chose to emphasize and not an unbroken lineage of master-disciple teachings. This latter concept is itself of course an important part of any Buddhist rhetoric of legitimation. To point this out in relation to Pure Land Buddhism is, therefore, in no way pejorative, but rather makes it no different from every other Buddhist lineage. This does, however, highlight the problematics of taking Pure Land as formulated by Hōnen and Shinran, despite its importance, as determinative or normative.

Traditional conceptions of Pure Land Buddhism based on the Hōnen/Shinran formulation have generally identified it with "buddha-recollection" practice (*buddhānussati*; *buddhānusmṛti*; *nianfo*; *nenbutsu*; *yŏmbul*)—a pervasive practice of chanting Amitābha's name among lay and Chinese monastics during the Tang dynasty (618–907)—due to such proponents as Daochuo (562–645), Shandao (613–907), and Fazhao (fl. 762–804), and also a common cultic practice since the Unified Silla period (668–935).[28] While the Hōnen/Shinran formulation focuses on vocalization, there is a second kind of practice to keep the Buddha in mind: visualization. One of the ways this collection moves beyond the traditional formulation is by introducing additional kinds of Pure Land practices derived from Tantric Buddhism (see Halkias and Payne in this volume). Arguably, there are two Indian strands of Pure Land material, esoteric and exoteric, also noted in the Chinese, Japanese, and Tibetan material (see Halkias and Apple in this volume). One way of drawing a distinction between these two is to identify exoteric Pure Land as referring to practices that take Buddha Amitābha and his pure land as external supports for meditation, while Esoteric Pure Land strands take them as internal supports.[29]

Understood inclusively, Pure Land praxis evidences a dialectic oscillation between abstract and concrete understandings of the term. That is, pure lands as "real places" and after-death destinations are juxtaposed with metaphorical readings for Buddhist realization or, as in the case of tantric Buddhism, as internalized states of awareness brought about through the manipulation of subtle energies inside one's own body. These different readings are not incompatible with each other nor does belief in one preclude acceptance of the other. Indeed, in many cases they cross over such conceptual categories, highlighting various aspects of these descriptions. In Tibetan Pure Land commentarial literature such topics are discussed and explained through the union of sutra-type descriptions of the pure lands with tantric readings (the union of Pāramitāyāna and Vajrayāna in Tibetan Buddhism). Hence, a pure land may be both a place for rebirth brought about by the interdependence of the Buddha's aspirations and the merit of sentient beings aspiring for rebirth there (a classic Mahāyāna reading); it can refer to the purity of one's mind (*Vimalakīrtinirdeśa*, Vajrayāna) manifesting internally or externally as a pure land; and, from a humanistic perspective, it can inspire the making of this world into an enlightened paradise, a pure land. What runs through all these interpretations is their adherence to core Buddhist beliefs and doctrines that would endorse and legitimize these interpretations in the first place.

Comparative approaches to the study of religion have not infrequently either suggested or assumed that Sukhāvatī is a transcendent realm of postmortem existence and that it is therefore equivalent to Christian conceptions of Heaven.[30] The essays in this collection serve to problematize any presumption that the oppositional duality between immanent and transcendent is both "natural" and universal. Under the influence of Platonism, "Heaven" has been conceptualized as a transcendent realm of absolute existence, and any projection of Platonic philosophy onto Buddhist thought is at best an analogy of limited scope. More fundamentally, this also suggests that the very opposition between transcendent and immanent as formulated in much of the monotheistic traditions of the West is itself neither natural nor universal.[31] We therefore need to carefully nuance what we contrast with "immanent" (or any other term) when discussing the nature of a pure land, or even whether use of semiotic opposites is appropriate. In some cases, for example, the Western Pure Land was thought to be "otherworldly" in the sense of only being accessible across the divide of death, while in other cases it was instead thought to be a region of this world. Neither a metaphysically transcendent nor even an otherworldly conception of the Western Pure Land is universal; instead it is understood as a geographic location in this world (see also Sørensen) in many of the traditions examined in this collection, while in others, pure visions of the pure lands are synonymous with the realization of non-dual awareness.

## Cult as a Natural and Coherent Unit of Study

While most attention in both religious studies and Buddhist studies gives primacy of place to doctrine and belief, such approaches are tangential to questions regarding religious practices and the social forms that support those practices. What is integral to Buddhism across its history are lineages and practices.[32] The lineage provides a sense of membership in an ongoing continuity and a sense of inheritance of the practices.[33] The meaning of membership of course varied across time and religious culture, but in many tantric contexts initiation into a lineage of practice usually involves a complex of deity and practices related to that deity. For example, initiation—or "empowerment"—specifically authorizes a practitioner to perform a ritual practice (*sādhana*, *pūjā*, and so on) devoted to a particular buddha, bodhisattva, or protector. The way in which deity, practice, initiation, and lineage constitute a coherent whole suggests that in many cases the category of cult is not conceptually imposed by the artifice of definition, but rather a "natural" though socially constituted category. That is, while it is constituted as a social form, it has an integrity and coherence that does not simply derive from an academic act of definition. The term "cult," however, requires direct discussion, as it has three significantly divergent usages.

## *Three Usages*

Three significantly different usages of the term "cult"—pejorative, sociological, and classic—need to be distinguished from one another. The pejorative is all too familiar and has in many instances so dominated the meaning of the term that other meanings have been displaced. This usage of the term began at the end of the nineteenth century, but the proximate source of the pejorative sense is the emotionally and politically charged atmosphere of public discourse about the new religious movements in the 1970s.[34] At this time, "cult" became a popular term to identify all that was wrong with the new religious movements: brainwashing, sexual license, rejection of family, rejection of established beliefs, rejection of established authority, worship of false gods, guru devotion, and so on.[35] Although this use of the term "cult" remains in both the journalistic and some academic treatments of new religious movements, the pejorative meaning is distinct from its use as a category in the sociology of religion more generally.

As a sociological category, it is often part of a taxonomy of religious institutions. Weber and Troeltsch introduced a system of two institutions: church and sect. Other categories, including cult and denomination, were added in mid-twentieth-century works in the sociology of religions.[36] The difficulty with these categories is that they reflect the historical realities of Western Christendom. "In provenance the categories are ethnocentric, and hence their application outside a Christian context is problematic."[37] In the context of the sociology of religion, cults are characterized as loosely organized and often only engaging members on a temporary basis, as contrasted with the presumption that church membership is a lifelong and exclusive commitment. The temporary character corresponds to the characterization of cults as focusing on individual needs, such as for healing, or on personal ecstatic experience.[38] Use of the term "cult" in the sociology of religion seeks to identify a particular kind of social organization, in some cases by reference to style of membership. The classic usage focuses instead on a complex of activities and beliefs.

The classic meaning of "cult" is the set of practices directed toward a particular figure, such as the cult of Mithras or the cult of Heracles. The term itself is related to the Latin for "cultivate" and "culture" in the sense of caring for, specifically caring for a deity. As used here we intend it to identify the complex of deity and those practices considered either to care for the deity or to cultivate one's relation with the deity. Cults are not fixed and immutable, but rather changing and fluid, processes rather than entities, and therefore not definable by the itemization of parts. As Bernard Faure has noted, "When the cult of a deity takes off, it acquires a dynamics of its own. Its sum becomes greater than that of its elements, and it cannot be simply reduced to them without a loss."[39] The same practices may be found in different cults, directed toward different deities. Most categories used in the study of religion (including the category of religion itself) are social constructs, leading to the seemingly endless disputes over proper definition. Instead of attempting to define "cult" in a way that precludes debate, it is intended here as a heuristically valuable concept, an *upāya*.

An emphasis on cult does not mean, however, that it is the only institutional form that provides an understanding of the history of Buddhism. Drawing on the etymological descent in Tibetan of lineage (*brgyud*) from stream (*rgyud*), W. Blythe Miller has employed stream as a metaphor for lineage in contrast to sect (*chos lugs*).[40] As Miller notes in the case of premodern Tibet, there is a common Buddhist fiction of lineal coherence: "indigenous representations of lineage tend to emphasize diachronic lines of descent that sustain strong elements of stasis, cohesion and solidity, an emphasis that does not necessarily stand up under historical analysis."[41] What does constitute the unifying character of a lineage is "a fluid and adaptable collection of material and nonmaterial transmissions that are passed down from one generation to the next."[42] Miller contrasts lineage with sect, which "implies consolidation, a soteriology and set of practices distinct from other traditions, and bureaucratically linked institutions."[43] Sects can encompass several lineages, as well as being instantiated in several institutions, such as monasteries. In addition to monastic institutions, there has been a convergence toward institutions modeled on Protestant churches in the modernization of Buddhism as it has moved to Euro-American societies, where a particular understanding of religious institutions is enforced by juridical conceptions such as laws related to incorporating as a religious organization. In turn, cult is distinct from lineage, sect, monastery, and church.

Cult provides us with a coherent unit of inquiry, one value of which is that it is not identical with any of the other institutional forms. If we conceive of Buddhist institutions only within the categories of lineages, sects, monasteries, and churches, then the clustering of practices focused on an individual figure such as Amitābha or Akṣobhya—or Padmasambhava, or Dōgen, or whomever—is much more difficult to fit into our understanding. Cult, however, can be found in different lineages, sects, monasteries, and churches. It is, in other words, a category that crosses these institutional categories while having a coherence of its own. And, in this collection, we are seeking to understand the theme of pure lands, which in turn crosses cults, providing yet another dimension for understanding the history of Buddhist praxis.

Within Buddhist studies so much attention has been and continues to be paid to doctrines and doctrinal texts that the study of cults, as well as practices more generally, remains methodologically underdeveloped.[44] This is not unique to Buddhist studies, however. Writing on the study of ancient Israelite ritual, which is analogous to the study of Buddhist cults, Wesley Bergen has noted that "[a]rchaeological data is limited both in scope as well as in how much it can tell us. Textual evidence has its own limitations. The confluence of these two areas of study further complicates the task."[45] A full review of all of the points Bergen raises lies outside the scope of this introduction. In relation to a research program focusing on Pure Land Buddhism broadly conceived, however, two—present cultural presumptions and present ideological commitments—deserve mention.

Bergen notes that there are cultural difficulties in the study of historical rituals. Certainly the privileging of meditation in contemporary representations of Buddhism constitutes an impediment both to the study of Pure Land Buddhism and to the study of all cult and ritual other than meditation in Buddhist history. He also notes the retrospective influence of later interpretations on the understanding of earlier practices. When he says, "If we are attempting to grasp the social world of ancient Israel, ritual is more important than theology,"[46] the same can be applied *mutatis mutandis* to Buddhism at all periods in its history.

In Buddhist secondary literature, one finds several uses of the term "cult," including such well-known instances as the cult of the book, the cult of the stupa, and the cult of the relic. Such common usages identify the focus of ritual activity, but are at some variance with the more technical usage intended here. While a stupa may have been the site of cultic activity, it would seem not so much that the stupa per se was the object of cultic activity, but rather a buddha who is present in or as the stupa.[47] An interpretation of this kind is found, for example, in the *Bodhigarbhālaṅkāralakṣa-dhāraṇī*, that is, the *Dhāraṇī of the Hundred Thousand Ornaments of the Essence of Awakening.*

> If some monk or nun or lay man or woman, or some other son or daughter of good family, after writing this Dhāraṇī and making a *caitya*, were to put this Dhāraṇī into that *caitya*, although that person had made (only) one *caitya*, he would (in effect) have made a hundred thousand. He might also worship with heavenly flowers and perfumes and garlands, unguents, aromatic powders, cloths, umbrellas, flags and banners, but this is not the worshipping of only the *caitya*: the Jewel of the Buddha, the Jewel of the Dharma, and the Jewel of the Community would also (in effect) be worshipped with those articles of worship.[48]

Similarly, while books became common objects of veneration, David S. Ruegg notes that the cult was one of "the Sūtra as the 'body/icon of the Buddha' (*jinavigraha*)."[49] So it is not the book per se, but rather the book as the presence of a buddha as one who has accomplished that which is to be accomplished, and his teachings that are the intended object of veneration. The object as the manifest presence of a buddha or equivalently an awakened teacher is perhaps most clear in the case of relics.[50] This is not some ill-conceived apologetic attempt to protect Buddhism from accusations of idolatry, but rather is seeking closer terminological precision. The stupa, the book, the relic are part of cultic activity and need to be placed in a framework of the variety of cults that used such objects, just as those cults may have used other elements in the milieu such as meditation, chanting, and the *homa*, as seen in the contributions to this volume.

Another value in utilizing the category of cult is that it does not need to invoke the pseudo-explanatory power of the semiotic opposition of elite and popular. A not uncommon formulation along these lines is to regard monastics as religious elites primarily motivated by the quest for full awakening, contrasted with the "simple" needs of the laity for reassurance in the present life and hope for a better one in the future.[51] While such motivations and desires may be true of individuals, the semiotic opposition between elite and popular entails cultural presumptions. Although there are Buddhist analogues, the way the opposition is formulated in Euro-American religious discourse implicates presumptions based in the religious history of Europe and America. Not infrequently, Pure Land practitioners in East Asia formed mutual support societies that included both monks and laymen, and were in some cases led by laymen. The White Lotus Society founded by Huiyuan (334–416) of Lushan attracted some 123 or more members and is the basis for Huiyuan being considered the first "patriarch" of the Pure Land tradition in East Asia.[52] Similarly, in Heian, Genshin (942–1017) both established a Pure Land praxis by composing his *Ōjōyōshū* and was also central in the founding of the "samādhi society of twenty-five" (*nijūgo zanmaie*).[53] A looser network of Pure Land adherents, again comprising both monks and laymen, formed around Zhuhong (1535–1615) during the Late Ming era.[54]

## Many Buddhas, Many Cults

The turn to an inclusive sense of Pure Land Buddhism we intend here—a common theme shared across wide swaths of Buddhist history—creates a complex polysemy. In place of the familiar unitary sense of one buddha, Amitābha, and one pure land, Sukhāvatī, there are now many different buddhas, bodhisattvas, and protectors and many different pure lands. In order to avoid confusion, therefore, it is important to distinguish between Pure Land as a theme within Buddhism and the various cults that include that theme. This is an issue raised specifically by Silk in his essay included in this collection.

As discussed above, "cult" is being used here to identify a complex of practices and beliefs—and texts and institutions where appropriate—that center on one particular figure. As discussed above, this is the classic meaning within religious studies, and as used here it helps to make clear that Pure Land includes a wide variety of different cults. Effectively, in the past, what has been called Pure Land in anglophone scholarship has been the cult of Amitābha.[55] What provides coherence, not unity, to "Pure Land Buddhism" in this more expansive sense is the shared idea of a spatially located land, often identified as a postmortem goal of practice, and which is the special domain of a buddha or other similar figure. The second qualification here distinguishes Pure Land Buddhism from the more general bodhisattva vow to be born into the world for the sake of bringing living beings to awakening, which would include or would particularly seek birth in lands not having a resident buddha.

A cognate of "cult" is "cultivate," a term serendipitously often used in Buddhist hybrid English to describe maintaining a sustained practice, such as meditation or recitation. Sometimes in religious studies cult is used to refer to the outward practices, such as making offerings and preserving relics, and is contrasted with inner practices and experiences. The common source of both "cult" and "cultivate", however, suggests a more comprehensive understanding when we approach the variety of specific cults that fall under the more general category of Pure Land Buddhism. This collection refers to some of these including Mahāvairocana (Andreeva) and Akṣobhya (Payne).

## Future Directions

In working on this collection it has become clear to the editors that the book you now hold is a beginning and not an end. As suggested at various points in this introduction, one of the goals is to stimulate additional research that neither marginalizes the category of Pure Land Buddhism nor perpetuates preconceptions that question the validity of Pure Land as a form of Buddhist praxis. From this, one direction is expanding the range of inquiry into Pure Land traditions beyond the religious cultures represented here. One of the areas is in the Mahāyāna traditions of Southeast Asia, such as in Vietnamese culture. In the seventeenth century, Amitābha and his pure land played an important unifying focus for the religiosity of both commoners and royalty in Vietnam.[56] The importance of Pure Land praxis in modern Vietnamese Buddhism is evidenced in the work of Alexander Soucy. Although it is not the focus of his study, Soucy gives attention to Pure Land repeatedly in his work on Buddhism in contemporary Vietnam. A Đi Dà Phật (Buddha Amitābha) is part of the pantheon and is, naturally, appealed to for birth in his pure land, Cực Lạc.[57] Practice follows the injunctions of the sutras and comprises recitation of the buddha's name and the sutras themselves.[58] Although Pure Land is integrated into the Buddhist culture of modern Vietnam, it generally receives only occasional mention.

In addition to the cultural zones not included here, several important methodologies are not represented. These include material culture and the arts, including not only painting and the plastic arts privileging Pure Land themes such as the Sukhāvatī triad (*jingtu sansheng*; *jōdo no sanshō*; *chŏngt'o samsŏng*) for worship and edification, or for decoration, but also performing arts up to and including modern media representations. Architecture and archaeology also would be important contributors to future developments in the field. All these would need to be set in juxtaposition with the textual tradition, for as Lars Fogelin has shown for Buddhism in India,[59] and Nobuyoshi Yamabe has demonstrated for the Buddha Image cave and the *Ocean Sūtra*,[60] the two are necessary complements to one another.

## Structure of the Anthology

The anthology is organized into six thematic categories, which address different genres and topics of Pure Land thought, expression, and practice. A part overview introduces the category and summarizes each contribution. The six categories are: Ritual Practices, Contemplative Visualizations, Doctrinal Expositions, Life-Writing and Poetry, Ethical and Aesthetic Explications, and Worlds beyond Sukhāvatī.

## Notes

1 See Richard K. Payne, "Buddhist Studies beyond the Nation-State," in *Religion*, ed. Julia Kostova (New York: Oxford Handbooks Online, 2016, doi: 10.1093/oxfordhb/9780199935420.013.13).

2 Historiographic practice is, of course, never objectively neutral. That of the nineteenth century commonly reified race and ethnicity, conjoining those with language, thereby creating the concept of a nation, specifically one formed out of a mystical unity with the land, the mystique of "blood and soil" (Blut und Boden). In turn, nation was employed as a rationale for the creation of autonomous political states that would protect the rights of members of the nation. Not only did these discourses inflame much of the conflict from the end of the nineteenth century, but they continue to inform political discourse in the present.

3 Additionally, there was also a privileging of canonic languages over vernaculars. Charles Hallisey, "Roads Taken and Not Taken in the Study of Theravāda Buddhism," in *Curators of the Buddha: Buddhism under Colonialism*, ed. Donald S. Lopez Jr. (Chicago: University of Chicago Press, 1995), 31–61.

4 See, for one instance, Lionel M. Jensen, *Manufacturing Confucianism: Chinese Traditions and Universal Civilization* (Durham, NC: Duke University Press, 1998). This is not to say that missionary efforts were solely directed toward social elites, but rather that the effect on religious studies was the tendency to characterize traditions on the basis of how social elites understood them.

5 Or rather, what were judged to be the most intellectually sophisticated, generally on the basis of similarity to contemporaneous European and American philosophical and religious developments. While such apparent similarity eased the projects of comparison, judgments regarding similarity necessarily involved extracting parts of systems while ignoring the intellectual integrity of the systems as such. Jan Nattier has noted that "certain sūtras appear to have been highlighted above others not only due to the accident of their survival in Sanskrit or to their importance in Japan, but also as a result of their congeniality to contemporary western religious tastes." *A Few Good Men: The Bodhisattva Path according to* The Inquiry of Ugra (Ugraparipṛcchā) (Honolulu: University of Hawai'i Press, 2003), 7.

6 Narrative was likewise given little attention despite its philological value. As noted by Jonathan Silk, "narrative materials have often been ignored in the field of Buddhist Studies, a field which is biased toward doctrinal studies." "The Composition of the *Guan Wuliangshoufo-Jing*: Some Buddhist and Jaina Parallels to Its Narrative Frame," *Journal of Indian Philosophy* 25 (1997): 181–256, 191–192. Fortunately, the last two decades have seen increasing attention to narratological studies of Buddhist literatures.

7 This dimension is complicated by the tendency to devalue or even delegitimize "native informants," including monastic teachers, in favor of European mastery of the texts. See Donald S. Lopez Jr., "Foreigner at the Lama's Feet," in *Curators of the Buddha: Buddhism under Colonialism*, ed. Donald S. Lopez Jr. (Chicago: University of Chicago Press, 1995), 251–295.

8 For a discussion of the value of regional studies, see Jeff Wilson, *Dixie Dharma: Inside a Buddhist Temple in the American South* (Chapel Hill: University of North Carolina Press, 2012).

9 Ronald M. Davidson, "Hidden Realms and Pure Abodes: Central Asian Buddhism as Frontier Religion in the Literature of India, Nepal, and Tibet," *Pacific World: Journal of the Institute of Buddhist Studies*, third series, no. 4 (Fall 2002): 153–181.

10 For a discussion of the relations between various pure lands in Indic Mahāyāna, see Diwakar Acharya, "Evidence for Mahāyāna and Sukhāvatī Cult in India in the Middle Period: Early Fifth to Sixth Century Nepalese Inscriptions," *Journal of the International Association of Buddhist Studies* 31, no. 1–2 (2008 [2010]): 24–75.

11 Galen Amstutz and Mark L. Blum, "Pure Lands in Japanese Religion," *Japanese Journal of Religious Studies* 33, no. 2 (2006): 217; Georgios T. Halkias, *Luminous Bliss: A Religious History of Pure Land Literature in Tibet: With an Annotated Translation and Critical Analysis of the Orgyen-ling Golden Short Sukhāvatīvyūha-sūtra* (University of Hawai'i Press, 2013), 3–15.

12 Amstutz and Blum, "Pure Lands in Japanese Religion," 217–218.

13 Amstutz and Blum, "Pure Lands in Japanese Religion," 219. For the study of Pure Land Buddhism and the cult of Amitābha in Korea during the Three Kingdoms, Silla, Koryŏ, and Chosŏn periods, see special issue of the *Journal of Korean Religions* 6, no. 1 (April 2015), edited by Richard McBride II.

14 Amstutz and Blum, "Pure Lands in Japanese Religion," 219.

15 Galen Amstutz, "The Politics of Pure Land Buddhism in India," *Numen* 45 (1998): 69–96.

16 James L. Fredericks, "A Universal Religious Experience? Comparative Theology as an Alternative to a Theology of Religions," *Horizons* 22, no. 1 (1995): 67–87.

17 Roderick Main, "Psychology of Religion: An Overview of Its History and Current Status," *Religion Compass* 2, no. 4 (2008): 710.

18 See Matthew C. Bagger, *Religious Experience, Justification, and History* (Cambridge: Cambridge University Press, 1999), and Caroline Franks Davis, *The Evidential Force of Religious Experience* (Oxford: Oxford University Press, 1989).

19 According to M. H. Abrams, the idea of the quest is itself rooted in Christian imagery (*Natural Supernaturalism: Tradition and Revolution in Romantic Literature* [New York: W. W. Norton, 1971], 49–50). Also, "For the Romantics, the conceptual moves from the private self-individuated from family, political, and religious dependencies to the idea of the authority of the autonomous self over all previous grounds of authority and from there to the (problematic) infinity of the self were not illogical leaps." Gerald N. Izenberg, *Impossible Individuality: Romanticism, Revolution, and the Origins of Modern Selfhood, 1787-1802* (Princeton, NJ: Princeton University Press, 1992), 15. See also Elizabeth J. Harris, *Theravāda Buddhism and the British Encounter: Religious, Missionary and Colonial Experience in Nineteenth Century Sri Lanka* (Abingdon, UK: Routledge, 2006), 96–100.

20 Regarding the emphasis on experience vis-à-vis the study of Buddhism, see Robert H. Sharf, "Buddhist Modernism and the Rhetoric of Meditative Experience," *Numen* 42 (Oct. 1995): 228–283.

21 Timothy Fitzgerald, "Critical Religion: 'Religion' Is Not a Stand-Alone Category," in *Theory, Religion, Critique*, ed. Richard King (New York: Columbia University, 2017).

22 Sir Charles Eliot, *Japanese Buddhism* (1935, rprt. London: Routledge and Kegan Paul, 1959), 389–390.

23 Jan Nattier, "The Indian Roots of Pure Land Buddhism: Insights from the Oldest Chinese Versions of the *Larger Sukhāvatīvyūha*," *Pacific World: Journal of the Institute of Buddhist Studies*, third series, no. 5 (Fall 2003): 193. This position does not preclude foreign cultural elements finding expression within a Buddhist framework.

24 Jan Nattier, "The Realm of Akṣobhya: A Missing Piece in the History of Pure Land Buddhism," *Journal of the International Association of Buddhist Studies* 23, no. 1 (2000): 74.

25 Nattier, "The Indian Roots of Pure Land Buddhism," 185.

26 McBride, "Guest Editor's Introduction," in *Journal of Korean Religions* 6, no. 1 (2015): 7.

27 Charles B. Jones, "Review of Halkias, Georgios T., *Luminous Bliss: A Religious History of Pure Land Literature in Tibet*," H-Buddhism, H-Net Reviews, February 2014. http://www.h-net.org/reviews/showrev.php?id=40391.

28 McBride, "Guest Editor's Introduction," 5, 9.

29 This distinction parallels Chan–Pure Land debates in medieval China. In Tibetan exegesis, the exoteric-esoteric divide is further interpreted according to the three-bodies schema (*trikāya* doctrine): the *nirmanakāya* pure lands referring to actual *topoi* (manifest realms and after-death destinations); the *sambogakāya* pure lands pointing at archetypical dimensions (mystical visions of transcendental realms) accessible through the purification of energies in the subtle body; and the *dharmakāya* pure lands as metaphors for the awakened state of mind (i.e., emptiness, non-dual awareness) purified of all adventitious defilements.

30 A more general treatment of such analogies is Galen Amstutz, "Shin Buddhism and Protestant Analogies with Christianity in the West," *Comparative Studies in Society and History* 40, no. 4 (Oct. 1998): 724–747.

31 Contrary to the phenomenology of religion constructed by Mircea Eliade, with its claims of universality for his dichotomy of sacred and profane, see Timothy Fitzgerald, *The Ideology of Religious Studies* (Oxford: Oxford University Press, 2000), 41. Eliade's metaphysics has, of course, long been the object of critique within religious studies. The task here is to push for a Buddhist studies that does not default to such dichotomous categorization, recognizes the complex plurality of cosmologies within the Buddhist tradition, and does not attempt to reduce ambiguity by imposing any single harmonizing vision.

32 Frits Staal claimed that for traditions other than the Abrahamic monotheisms, the order of priority is practice, lineage, and doctrine. *Rules without Meaning: Ritual, Mantras, and the Human Sciences* (New York: Peter Lang, 1993), 335.

33 The language used here is perhaps a bit awkward, but it is a purposeful attempt to avoid the problematic conceptions of founders and their unique religious experiences, which is effectively the default for such discussions. See Tim Murphy, *Representing Religion: Essays in History, Theory and Crisis* (London: Equinox Publishing, 2007), 50–51.

34 J. Gordon Melton, "An Introduction to New Religions," in *The Oxford Handbook of New Religious Movements*, ed. James R. Lewis (Oxford: Oxford University Press, 2008), 17.

35 Melton, "An Introduction to New Religions," 20.

36 Lorne L. Dawson, "Church-Sect-Cult: Constructing Typologies of Religious Groups," in *The Oxford Handbook of the Sociology of Religion*, ed. Peter B. Clarke (Oxford: Oxford University Press, 2011), 525–544.

37 Dawson, "Church-Sect-Cult," 525.

38 Dawson, "Church-Sect-Cult," 528.

39 Bernard Faure, *Gods of Medieval Japan, Volume 1: The Fluid Pantheon* (Honolulu: University of Hawai'i Press, 2016), 18.

40 W. Blythe Miller, "The Vagrant Poet and the Reluctant Scholar: A Study of the Balance of Iconoclasm and Civility in the Biographical Accounts of Two Founders of the 'Brug pa bka' Brgyud Lineages," *Journal of the International Association of Buddhist Studies* 28, no. 2 (2005): 374.

41 Miller, "The Vagrant Poet and the Reluctant Scholar," 373–374.

42 Miller, "The Vagrant Poet and the Reluctant Scholar," 374–375.

43 Miller, "The Vagrant Poet and the Reluctant Scholar," 375.

44 There are exceptions, such as Stephan Beyer, *The Cult of Tārā: Magic and Ritual in Tibet* (Berkeley: University of California Press, 1973); Alan Sponberg and Helen Hardacre, eds., *Maitreya, the Future Buddha* (Cambridge: Cambridge University Press, 1988); John Clifford Holt, *The Buddha in the Crown: Avalokiteśvara in the Buddhist Traditions of Sri Lanka* (Oxford: Oxford University Press, 1991); John Clifford Holt, *The Buddhist Viṣṇu: Religious Transformation, Politics, and Culture* (New York: Columbia University Press, 2004); Elizabeth English, *Vajrayoginī: Her Visualizations, Rituals, and Forms* (Boston: Wisdom Publications, 2002); David Quinter, *From Outcasts to Emperors: Shingon Ritsu and the Mañjuśrī Cult in Medieval Japan* (Leiden: Brill, 2015), and Zhiru Ng, *The Making of a Savior Bodhisattva: Dizang in Medieval China* (Honolulu: University of Hawai'i Press, 2007).

45 Wesley Bergen, "Studying Ancient Israelite Ritual: Methodological Considerations," *Religion Compass* 1, no. 5 (2007): 579. This combination of archeology and philology is also taken by Lars Fogelin in his *An Archaeological History of Indian Buddhism* (Oxford: Oxford University Press, 2015).

46 Bergen, "Studying Ancient Israelite Ritual," 584.

47 Or, more radically, if the five elements of stupa symbolism together with either relics or texts of *buddhadharma* secured in the base indicate that it serves as a substitute body for the Buddha, then the cultic activity *is* toward the stupa, but as the physical presence of the Buddha. On related themes in East Asian Buddhism, Bernard Faure has noted that the sculp-

tures of Chan/Zen masters "are not portraits in the Western sense; like their aniconic counterpart, the *śarīra* [relic], they constitute 'substitute bodies.' In other words, they are not merely 'realistic,' they are *real*, pointing to no reality beyond themselves." "Substitute Bodies in Chan/Zen Buddhism," in *Religious Reflections on the Human Body*, ed. Jane Marie Law (Bloomington: Indiana University Press, 1995), 220.

48 Gregory Schopen, "The Bodhigarbālaṅkāralakṣa and Vimaloṣṇīṣa Dhāraṇīs in Indian Inscriptions: Two Sources for the Practice of Buddhism in Medieval India," *Wiener Zeitschrift für die Kunde Südasiens und Archi für Indische Philosophie* 29 (1985): 133–134.

49 David Seyfort Ruegg, "Aspects of the Study of the (Earlier) Indian Mahāyāna," *Journal of the International Association of Buddhist Studies* 27, no. 1 (2004): 19.

50 Cf. David Drewes, "Revisiting the Phrase '*sa pṛthivīpradeśaś caitybhūto bhavet*' and the Mahāyāna Cult of the Book," *Indo-Iranian Journal* 50 (2007): 101–143. We personally suspect that another factor involved in the difficulties of these analyses is the result of the desire for greater specificity on our part than was perhaps present on the part of those who created stūpas, caitya, books, statues, icons, etc. Drewes discusses the Kurram Casket (ca. 148 CE), saying, "Although it is fairly clear that in this case an actual relic contained in the reliquary was the stūpa's primary object of veneration, the [twelve *nidānas* of the *pratītyasamutpāda*] formula must also have been seen as sacred and may have been seen as consecrating the deposit" (127). Drewes' speculations cannot be confirmed, but the complex of conceptions that is involved in such a complementary presence of relic and inscription suggests that it is a mistake to impose a system of sharply delineated, mutually exclusive categories that are not supported by the evidence, despite the intellectual satisfaction of a clear system.

51 This semiotic opposition seems to have largely passed from Buddhist studies per se, but remains part of popular (mis)conceptions of the history of Buddhism.

52 Shinkō Mochizuki, *Pure Land Buddhism in China: A Doctrinal History*. 2 vols. (Berkeley, CA: Institute of Buddhist Studies and BDK America, 2016), 1:35.

53 Robert Rhodes, *Genshin's* Ōjōyōshū *and the Construction of Pure Land Discourse in Heian Japan* (Honolulu: University of Hawai'i Press, 2017), 9.

54 Jennifer Eichman, *A Late Sixteenth-Century Chinese Buddhist Fellowship: Spiritual Ambitions, Intellectual Debates, and Epistolary Connections* (Leiden: Brill, 2016).

55 An attempt to make this explicit was Richard K. Payne and Kenneth K. Tanaka, eds., *Approaching the Land of Bliss: Religious Praxis in the Cult of Amitābha* (Honolulu: University of Hawai'i Press, 2003).

56 Trian Nguyen, "Ninh Phúc Temple: A Study of Seventeenth-Century Buddhist Sculpture in Vietnam" (PhD diss., University of California, Berkeley, 1999), 35.

57 Alexander Soucy, *The Buddha Side: Gender, Power, and Buddhist Practice in Vietnam* (Honolulu: University of Hawai'i Press, 2012), 26.

58 Soucy, *The Buddha Side*, 121.

59 Fogelin, *An Archaeological History of Indian Buddhism*, 3.

60 Nobuyoshi Yamabe, "*The Sūtra on the Ocean-Like Samādhi of the Visualization of the Buddha*: The Interfusion of the Chinese and Indian Cultures in Central Asia as Reflected in a Fifth Century Apocryphal Sūtra" (PhD diss., Yale University, 1999).

## Bibliography

Abrams, M. H. *Natural Supernaturalism: Tradition and Revolution in Romantic Literature.* New York: W. W. Norton, 1971.

Amstutz, Galen. "The Politics of Pure Land Buddhism in India." *Numen* 45 (1998): 69–96.

———. "Shin Buddhism and Protestant Analogies with Christianity in the West." *Comparative Studies in Society and History* 40, no. 4 (Oct. 1998): 724–747.

Amstutz, Galen, and Mark L. Blum, "Pure Lands in Japanese Religion." *Japanese Journal of Religious Studies* 33, no. 2 (2006): 217–221.

Bagger, Matthew C. *Religious Experience, Justification, and History.* Cambridge: Cambridge University Press, 1999.

Bergen, Wesley. "Studying Ancient Israelite Ritual: Methodological Considerations." *Religion Compass* 1, no. 5 (2007): 579–586.

Beyer, Stephan. *The Cult of Tārā: Magic and Ritual in Tibet.* Berkeley: University of California Press, 1973.

Davidson, Ronald M. "Hidden Realms and Pure Abodes: Central Asian Buddhism as Frontier Religion in the Literature of India, Nepal, and Tibet." *Pacific World: Journal of the Institute of Buddhist Studies*, third series, no. 4 (Fall 2002): 153–181.

Davis, Caroline Franks. *The Evidential Force of Religious Experience.* Oxford: Oxford University Press, 1989.

Dawson, Lorne L. "Church-Sect-Cult: Constructing Typologies of Religious Groups." In *The Oxford Handbook of the Sociology of Religion*, edited by Peter B. Clarke, 525–544. Oxford: Oxford University Press, 2011.

Diwakar Acharya. "Evidence for Mahāyāna and Sukhāvatī Cult in India in the Middle Period: Early Fifth to Sixth Century Nepalese Inscriptions." *Journal of the International Association of Buddhist Studies* 31, no. 1–2 (2008 [2010]): 24–75.

Drewes, David. "Revisiting the Phrase '*sa pṛthivīpradeśaś caitybhūto bhavet*' and the Mahāyāna Cult of the Book." *Indo-Iranian Journal* 50 (2007): 101–143.

Eichman, Jennifer. *A Late Sixteenth-Century Chinese Buddhist Fellowship: Spiritual Ambitions, Intellectual Debates, and Epistolary Connections*. Leiden: Brill, 2016.

Eliot, Sir Charles. *Japanese Buddhism*. 1935, Reprint. London: Routledge and Kegan Paul, 1959.

English, Elizabeth. *Vajrayoginī: Her Visualizations, Rituals, and Forms*. Boston: Wisdom Publications, 2002.

Faure, Bernard. *Gods of Medieval Japan, Volume 1: The Fluid Pantheon*. Honolulu: University of Hawai'i Press, 2016.

———. "Substitute Bodies in Chan/Zen Buddhism." In *Religious Reflections on the Human Body*, edited by J. M. Law, 211–229. Bloomington: Indiana University Press, 1995.

Fitzgerald, Timothy. "Critical Religion: 'Religion' Is Not a Stand-Alone Category." In *Theory, Religion, Critique*, edited by Richard King. New York: Columbia University, 2017.

———. *The Ideology of Religious Studies*. Oxford: Oxford University Press, 2000.

Fogelin, Lars. *An Archaeological History of Indian Buddhism*. Oxford: Oxford University Press, 2015.

Fredericks, James L. "A Universal Religious Experience? Comparative Theology as an Alternative to a Theology of Religions." *Horizons* 22, no. 1 (1995): 67–87.

Halkias, Georgios T. *Luminous Bliss: A Religious History of Pure Land Literature in Tibet: With an Annotated Translation and Critical Analysis of the Orgyen-ling Golden Short Sukhāvatīvyūha-sūtra*. Honolulu: University of Hawai'i Press, 2013.

Hallisey, Charles. "Roads Taken and Not Taken in the Study of Theravāda Buddhism." In *Curators of the Buddha: Buddhism under Colonialism*, edited by Donald S. Lopez Jr., 31–61. Chicago: University of Chicago Press, 1995.

Harris, Elizabeth J. *Theravāda Buddhism and the British Encounter: Religious, Missionary and Colonial Experience in Nineteenth Century Sri Lanka*. Abingdon, UK: Routledge, 2006.

Holt, Clifford John. *The Buddha in the Crown: Avalokiteśvara in the Buddhist Traditions of Sri Lanka*. Oxford: Oxford University Press, 1991.

———. *The Buddhist Viṣṇu: Religious Transformation, Politics, and Culture*. New York: Columbia University Press, 2004.

Izenberg, Gerald N. *Impossible Individuality: Romanticism, Revolution, and the Origins of Modern Selfhood, 1787–1802*. Princeton, NJ: Princeton University Press, 1992.

Jensen, Lionel M. *Manufacturing Confucianism: Chinese Traditions and Universal Civilization*. Durham, NC: Duke University Press, 1998.

Jones, Charles B. "Review of Halkias, Georgios T., *Luminous Bliss: A Religious History of Pure Land Literature in Tibet*." H-Buddhism, H-Net Reviews. February 2014. http://www.h-net.org/reviews/showrev.php?id=40391.

Lopez, Donald S., Jr. "Foreigner at the Lama's Feet." In *Curators of the Buddha: Buddhism under Colonialism*, edited by Donald S. Lopez Jr., 251–295. Chicago: University of Chicago Press, 1995.

Main, Roderick. "Psychology of Religion: An Overview of Its History and Current Status." *Religion Compass* 2, no. 4 (2008): 708–733.

McBride, Richard D. II, ed. "Guest Editor's Introduction." *Pure Land Buddhism in Korea, Journal of Korean Religions* 6, no. 1 (April 2015): 5–11.

Melton, J. Gordon. "An Introduction to New Religions." In *The Oxford Handbook of New Religious Movements,* edited by J. R. Lewis, 16–31. Oxford: Oxford University Press, 2008.

Miller, W. Blythe. "The Vagrant Poet and the Reluctant Scholar: A Study of the Balance of Iconoclasm and Civility in the Biographical Accounts of Two Founders of the 'Brug pa bka' Brgyud Lineages." *Journal of the International Association of Buddhist Studies* 28, no. 2 (2005): 369–410.

Mochizuki, Shinkō. *Pure Land Buddhism in China: A Doctrinal History.* 2 vols. Berkeley, CA: Institute of Buddhist Studies and BDK America, 2016.

Murphy, Tim. *Representing Religion: Essays in History, Theory and Crisis.* London: Equinox Publishing, 2007.

Nattier, Jan. *A Few Good Men: The Bodhisattva Path according to* The Inquiry of Ugra (Ugraparipṛcchā). Honolulu: University of Hawai'i Press, 2003.

———. "The Indian Roots of Pure Land Buddhism: Insights from the Oldest Chinese Versions of the *Larger Sukhāvatīvyūha*." *Pacific World: Journal of the Institute of Buddhist Studies*, third series, no. 5 (Fall 2003): 179–201.

———. "The Realm of Akṣobhya: A Missing Piece in the History of Pure Land Buddhism." *Journal of the International Association of Buddhist Studies* 23, no. 1 (2000): 71–102.

Ng, Zhiru. *The Making of a Savior Bodhisattva: Dizang in Medieval China.* Honolulu: University of Hawai'i Press, 2007.

Nguyen, Trian. "Ninh Phúc Temple: A Study of Seventeenth-Century Buddhist Sculpture in Vietnam." PhD dissertation, University of California, Berkeley, 1999.

Payne, Richard K. "Buddhist Studies beyond the Nation-State." In *Religion*, edited by J. Kostova. New York: Oxford Handbooks Online, 2016. doi: 10.1093/oxfordhb/9780199935420.013.13.

Payne, Richard K., and Kenneth K. Tanaka, eds. *Approaching the Land of Bliss: Religious Praxis in the Cult of Amitābha.* Honolulu: University of Hawai'i Press, 2003.

Quinter, David. *From Outcasts to Emperors: Shingon Ritsu and the Mañjuśrī Cult in Medieval Japan*. Leiden: Brill, 2015.

Rhodes, Robert. *Genshin's* Ōjōyōshū *and the Construction of Pure Land Discourse in Heian Japan*. Honolulu: University of Hawai'i Press, 2017.

Ruegg, David Seyfort. "Aspects of the Study of the (Earlier) Indian Mahāyāna." *Journal of the International Association of Buddhist Studies* 27, no. 1 (2004): 3–62.

Schopen, Gregory. "The Bodhigarbālaṅkāralakṣa and Vimaloṣṇīṣa Dhāraṇīs in Indian Inscriptions: Two Sources for the Practice of Buddhism in Medieval India." *Wiener Zeitschrift für die Kunde Südasiens und Archi für Indische Philosophie* 29 (1985): 119–149.

Sharf, Robert H. "Buddhist Modernism and the Rhetoric of Meditative Experience." *Numen* 42 (Oct. 1995): 228–283.

Silk, Jonathan. "The Composition of the *Guan Wuliangshoufo-Jing*: Some Buddhist and Jaina Parallels to Its Narrative Frame." *Journal of Indian Philosophy* 25 (1997): 181–256.

Soucy, Alexander. *The Buddha Side: Gender, Power, and Buddhist Practice in Vietnam*. Honolulu: University of Hawai'i Press, 2012.

Sponberg, Alan, and Helen Hardacre, eds. *Maitreya, the Future Buddha*. Cambridge: Cambridge University Press, 1988.

Staal, Frits. *Rules without Meaning: Ritual, Mantras, and the Human Sciences*. New York: Peter Lang, 1993.

Wilson, Jeff. *Dixie Dharma: Inside a Buddhist Temple in the American South*. Chapel Hill: University of North Carolina Press, 2012.

Yamabe, Nobuyoshi. "*The Sūtra on the Ocean-Like Samādhi of the Visualization of the Buddha*: The Interfusion of the Chinese and Indian Cultures in Central Asia as Reflected in a Fifth Century Apocryphal Sūtra." PhD dissertation, Yale University, 1999.

# I

# Ritual Practices

## Overview

Pure Land Buddhist rituals have a long and intricate history that goes back to the earliest attestations of Sanskrit-Chinese translations of Pure Land texts, and possibly before that since they are indistinguishable from Mahāyāna rituals in general. Pure Land ritual texts are notably visible in cosmopolitan Central Asia between the eighth and tenth centuries CE, where they were subjected to Indo-Sino-Tibetan encounters, contestations, and fusions. Over millennia and across Asian contexts, Pure Land rituals have served as inclusive, performative, and instructive acts of faith and inspiration. These rituals centered on a variety of Buddhist deities and pure lands (beyond Amitābha and Sukhāvatī) and on funereal rites, esoteric traditions, and scriptures that reflect a cluster of related practices concerned with karma, birth, and rebirth, and which were developed for both monastic and lay settings. Contributions in this part come from the Japanese and Chinese cultural spheres and reveal a rich genealogy of Pure Land conceptions and practices. In some cases, such as tantric *homa* rituals for the purpose of protection, and mantric recitation of the *nenbutsu* as the sole requirement for accomplishing birth in Sukhāvatī, these ritual practices demonstrate continuities between mainstream and tantric Buddhist praxes.

Concentrating on a short part of a twelve-scroll anthology called the *Consecration Scripture* (chap. I.1), Ryan Overbey gives readers extraordinary insight into the early developments of Buddhist pure lands. The Buddha in this fifth-century text is aware of Amitābha's Pure Land, but claims that the Land of Bliss is merely an expedient device, a useful pedagogical trick for the greedy and confused denizens of our apocalyptic age. In fact, all the pure lands of the ten directions are precisely the same. Rebirth in the pure lands requires neither the recollection of names nor the saving grace of Amitābha; to gain rebirth in any of the pure lands the devotee must purchase merit-making rituals from monastic institutions. The text reveals important details concerning the role of the pure lands in the Buddhist funerary practices of the early medieval period.

Anna Andreeva's annotated translation of *Short Meditation on the Pure Land, Mysteriously Adorned* (chap. I.2), focuses on the ideas of the monk Kakuban (1095–1143), a pivotal figure in the history of medieval Japanese Buddhism. Although Kakuban remains understudied in the Western languages, his intellectual legacy greatly impacted religious expression in Japan. This work analyzes Kakuban's construction of the concept of Esoteric Pure Land (*mitsugon jōdo*) and his creation of a new form of religious practice that merged the Esoteric Buddhist and Pure Land imagery.

Richard Payne (chap. I.3) discusses Akṣobhya, the Buddha of the Eastern Pure Land, an important figure in the history of Pure Land Buddhism. Because he is a transitional figure between mainstream Buddhism and Amitābha Pure Land Buddhism, including him in the history obviates that apparent anomaly of the latter and portrays a more continuous historical development. By focusing on specific cults, we can see that a unifying characteristic of much of early medieval Buddhism is the belief in the existence of *buddhakṣetra* and other buddha realms where buddhas teach the dharma. The Shingon tradition can be seen not simply as having a pantheon displayed in the two maṇḍalas, but as a collection and systematization of cults, all of which remain viable options for ritual practice in present-day Shingon.

Robert F. Rhodes' translation (chap. I.4) of the *Ōjōyōshū* by Genshin (942–1017)—the first comprehensive outline of Pure Land Buddhism written in Japan, which played a crucial role in rooting this form of Buddhism in this country—focuses on the description of the *nenbutsu* found in this text. According to Genshin, the *nenbutsu* is the basic practice for attaining birth in the Pure Land and refers to a wide variety of spiritual exercises focused on Amida, from advanced meditation practices for contemplating the figure of this Buddha, down to the simple recitation of the phrase "Namu Amidabutsu" (Homage to the Buddha Amida). This reflects the various ways in which the *nenbutsu* is described in the sutras. Although the *nenbutsu* is now understood primarily as the recitation of "Namu Amidabutsu" in Japan, significantly, in the *Ōjōyōshū* it is understood as referring to a much wider range of practices than the simple *nenbutsu* recitation.

The most stunning and innovative Tibetan collection of Pure Land practices can be attributed to Namchö Migyur Dorje (Gnam chos Mi 'gyur rdo rje, 1645–1667) from the area of Ngom in Khams. Migyur Dorje is best known for a unique corpus of Esoteric Buddhist scriptures that originated from a series of mystical visions with the assistance of his teacher, the Kagyu hierarch Karma Chagme (Karma chags med, 1613–1678). This collection of revealed scriptures (*gter ma;* treasure literature), thirteen volumes in all, is known as the *Namchö* (*gnam chos*; lit. space-dharma). Georgios T. Halkias examines (chap. I.5) a representative work from the *Namchö* collection, the *Sādhana of the Pure Land Sukhāvatī.* According to the colophon, it was transmitted to Migyur Dorje by Buddha Amitābha in a luminous vision and includes several Esoteric practices contained in one *sādhana*-cum-empowerment.

## Chapter 1

# The Consecration Scripture Spoken by the Buddha on Being Reborn in Whichever of the Pure Lands of the Ten Directions You Wish

Ryan Richard Overbey

### Translator's Introduction

When we think about Pure Land Buddhism, our thoughts may go first to Amitābha (also known as Amitāyus) and his purified buddha-field called Sukhāvatī, the Land of Bliss. We may reflect on particular forms of Buddhist devotion (worship of Amitābha's image, recitation of Amitābha's name) orienting the practitioner toward rebirth in the Land of Bliss. In a Japanese or Japanese American Buddhist context, we may imagine that "Pure Land Buddhism" picks out a distinct set of independent traditions or "schools."

Scholarship over the past few decades has rendered this picture more complex. Gregory Schopen has shown that in the fifth- and sixth-century Buddhist communities that produced the Gilgit manuscripts, rebirth in Sukhāvatī was not associated with any distinct tradition, it was a "generalized religious goal."[1] Robert Sharf also argued that in Chinese Buddhism the recitation of Amitābha's name and aspiration to be reborn in the Land of Bliss is ubiquitous and not associated with any particular sectarian identity.[2] Sharf and Schopen show that when reading about Amitābha's pure land, we must be sensitive to ritual and institutional contexts.

Jan Nattier has explored Amitābha's cult and its relationship with other Pure Land discourses. Delving into the murky origins of the Land of Bliss, Nattier argued that the western land of Sukhāvatī likely emerged as a response to Akṣobhya's eastern land of Abhirati.[3] And in her work on the proto-*Buddhāvataṃsaka* literature, Nattier discussed an early system of the pure lands of the ten directions, a system that does not even include Amitābha, Akṣobhya, Abhirati, or Sukhāvatī.[4]

Nattier's work is valuable for giving us a glimpse of the practices and ideas of Pure Land Buddhism before the Amitābha's Land of Bliss became "generalized." Amitābha's pure land arose in conversation with other pure lands. On the way to becoming ubiquitous, advocates of Sukhāvatī surely engaged in some fierce debates. The translation below, from the *Consecration Scripture* (*Guanding jing*), reveals precisely such a moment of contestation, a clash between the cult of Amitābha and an alternative system of the pure lands of the ten directions.

The *Consecration Scripture* is an anthology of twelve distinct scriptures in twelve scrolls, possibly compiled around 457 CE.[5] The twelve scriptures in this collection address a wide range of topics, but the overarching concerns are practical and liturgical. Each of the scriptures focuses on rituals for healing, protection, prediction, and the generation of merit for the living and the dead.[6]

The eleventh scroll of the *Consecration Scripture* is titled *The Consecration Scripture Spoken by the Buddha on Being Reborn in Whichever of the Pure Lands of the Ten Directions You Wish*.[7] This scroll was particularly important; we have evidence that it circulated independently at Dunhuang,[8] and it was carved separately among the scripture tablets at Fangshan.[9] In Sichuan, at the Grove of the Reclining Buddha in Anyue County (Anyue Wofoyuan), a wall of Cave 33 features carvings of the *Consecration Scripture*. Only two scrolls were selected for this wall: the twelfth scroll discussing the powers of the Medicine Bodhisattva, and the eleventh scroll on rebirth in the pure lands of the ten directions.[10]

This scripture opens at the brink of the Buddha's *parinirvāṇa*. Śākyamuni offers his audience one final sermon, and he is questioned by the bodhisattva Puguang. Puguang wants to know what sorts of good works (*gongde*) one can perform to be reborn into one of the pure lands of the ten directions.[11] These pure lands are said to be absolutely identical to Sukhāvatī, the pure land of Amitābha. Indeed, the Buddha says that he has preached about Amitābha only for the pitiful, greedy beings inhabiting the semblance dharma. Śākyamuni responds with detailed instructions for merit making: reciting scriptures, lighting votive lamps, hanging pennants from reliquary shrines, repentance on behalf of the deceased, and even donations of real property. The scripture reads like a catalog of services offered by the Buddhist funeral industry. We learn that we may sponsor rituals for ourselves before our death, for our relatives on the verge of death, or for the recently dead who linger in purgatory. The scripture is refreshingly blunt in its calculations; sinful Buddhists receive only one-seventh the merit from these rituals, and for non-Buddhists only a donation of real property can guarantee a favorable rebirth.

The scripture closes with the moving story of Nāśa, a pious fellow with wicked parents. Nāśa's parents trick him into believing that they are decent people. When they pass away, Nāśa does the standard postmortem ritual, assuming that their good karma will lead to a happy rebirth. Only when Nāśa has a near-death experience does he learn that his parents suffer in the realm of hungry ghosts. Nāśa demands an explanation from the Buddha, who reveals to him the awful, hidden truth: his parents' predicament is indeed a just repayment for their evil deeds. Breaking down in tears, Nāśa desperately begs the Buddha for some ritual method to relieve their suffering. After Nāśa repents on their behalf and offers lavish gifts to the sangha, his parents are at last reborn in the heavenly realms.

What makes Nāśa's story so compelling is its ability to not only remind us of our anxieties about merit and rebirth, but also to *generate new anxiety* in ways that benefit the Buddhist order. Medieval Buddhists would have certainly worried about their own merit or the merit of their deceased relatives, but this story powerfully demonstrates that even if you think your parents were good people, they may hide dark secrets that render your own efforts at merit making ineffective. The scripture asks a compelling question: how can we ever *truly* know if our parents were virtuous or depraved?

What does this scripture tell us about Buddhism and the pure lands in the fifth century? The pure land of Amitābha addresses fundamental Buddhist anxieties about karma, death, and rebirth. This *Consecration Scripture* shows us that as late as the fifth century, at least in some Buddhist circles, Sukhāvatī was popular enough to require a strong response. The redactors of this scripture responded in two telling ways. First, they claimed that Sukhāvatī is not special and is in fact an *upāya*, a pedagogical trick for the benighted fools of our apocalyptic age. Second, they attempted to sow seeds of doubt about the karmic status of oneself and one's relatives. It may well be that in the centuries to come Amitābha's "other-power" would be able save us all from our depravity, but for these fifth-century Buddhists the performance of funerary rituals by monastic specialists was still the most important step one could take to ensure a favorable rebirth.[12]

## Translation

### Scroll 11: *The Consecration Scripture Spoken by the Buddha on Being Reborn in Whichever of the Pure Lands of the Ten Directions You Wish*

Translated by the Indian Trepiṭaka Bo Śrīmitra
of the Eastern Jin

Thus have I heard: Once upon a time the Buddha was between the twin *śāla* trees in the city of Kuśinagara. At that time, at the moment of the World-Honored One's *parinirvāṇa*, the eight kinds of beings (gods, dragons, etc.)[13] in boundless multitudes from the lands of the ten directions all wailed in grief and sighed in lamentation. The various sorts of birds and beasts all likewise came into the presence of the Buddha, bowed their heads to the ground, paid reverence, and finally withdrew and sat down.

The World-Honored One said, "All those with doubts should now ask! The Perfectly Awakened One is passing into final extinction. I have compassion for so many of you. If anyone has questions, I will give a final sermon."

At that time, there was from another land a bodhisattva named Puguang (Universally Extensive). He got up from his seat, bowed his head to the ground, made reverence, and addressed the Buddha, saying, "The disciples of the four groups,[14] whether they are on the day of their impending death or have already passed away, desire to be reborn in the lands of the ten directions. What good works should they cultivate in order to obtain rebirth?"

The Buddha said to the bodhisattva *mahāsattva* Puguang, "You take pity on the disciples of the four groups, and on all beings in generations to come. You have asked about the merit which causes one's desired birth. You should now listen carefully! I will preach about it in detail for you."

The Buddha said to the bodhisattva *mahāsattva* Puguang, "Suppose a disciple of the four groups, whether at the moment of impending death or not yet dead, wishes to be born in the Eastern Fragrant Grove *kṣetra*. Its Buddha is called Entering Vigor Bodhisattva. Boundless in number are the adornments of this land! If a person on the day of impending death wishes to be born there, then one will be reborn just as one wishes."

The Buddha said to the bodhisattva *mahāsattva* Puguang, "Suppose someone such as a gentleman or lady, on the day of impending death, wishes to be born in the Southeastern Golden Grove *kṣetra*. Its Buddha is called Consummate Vigor Bodhisattva. Boundless in number are the adornments of this land! If a person on the verge of death wishes to be born there, then one will be reborn just as one wishes."

The Buddha said to the bodhisattva *mahāsattva* Puguang, "Suppose someone such as a gentleman or lady, on the day of impending death, wishes to be born in the Southern Delight Grove *kṣetra*. Its Buddha is called Not Abandoning Delight Bodhisattva. Boundless in number are the adornments of this land! If a person whose life has ended wishes to be born there, then one will be reborn just as one wishes."

The Buddha said to the bodhisattva *mahāsattva* Puguang, "Suppose someone such as a gentleman or lady, on the day of impending death, wishes to be born in the Southwestern Gem Grove *kṣetra*. Its Buddha is called Highest Vigor Bodhisattva. Boundless in number are the adornments of this land! If at the moment of impending death one wishes to be born there, then one will be reborn just as one wishes."

The Buddha said to the bodhisattva *mahāsattva* Puguang, "Suppose someone such as a gentleman or lady, on the day of impending death, wishes to be born in the Western Flower Grove *kṣetra*. Its Buddha is called Cultivating Vigor Bodhisattva. Boundless in number are the adornments of this land! If a person on the verge of death wishes to be born there, then one will be reborn just as one wishes."

The Buddha said to the bodhisattva *mahāsattva* Puguang, "Suppose someone such as a gentleman or lady, on the day of impending death, wishes to be born in the Northwestern Adamantine *kṣetra*. Its Buddha is called One Vehicle Salvation Bodhisattva. Boundless in number are the adornments of this land! If a person on the verge of death wishes to be born there, then one will be reborn just as one wishes."

The Buddha said to the bodhisattva *mahāsattva* Puguang, "Suppose someone such as a gentleman or lady, on the day of impending death, wishes to be born in the Northern Grove of the Way *kṣetra*. Its Buddha is called Practicing Vigor Bodhisattva. Boundless in number are the adornments of this land! If a person on the verge of death wishes to be born there, then one will be reborn just as one wishes."

The Buddha said to the bodhisattva *mahāsattva* Puguang, "Suppose someone such as a gentleman or lady, on the day of impending death, wishes to be born in the Northeastern Blue Lotus *kṣetra*. Its Buddha is called Compassionate Vigor Bodhisattva. Boundless in number are the adornments of this land! If a person on the verge of death wishes to be born there, then one will be reborn just as one wishes."

The Buddha said to the bodhisattva *mahāsattva* Puguang, "Suppose someone such as a gentleman or lady, on the day of impending death, wishes to be born in the Lower Crystal *kṣetra*. Its Buddha is called Pure Livelihood Vigor Bodhisattva. Boundless in number are the adornments of this land! If a person on the verge of death wishes to be born there, then one will be reborn just as one wishes."

The Buddha said to the bodhisattva *mahāsattva* Puguang, "Suppose someone, such as a gentleman or lady, on the day of life's end wishes to be born in the Upper Desire Grove *kṣetra*. Its Buddha is called Utmost Sincerity Vigor Bodhisattva.[15] Boundless in number are the adornments of this land! If a person on the verge of death wishes to be born there, then one will be reborn just as one wishes."

The Buddha said to the bodhisattva *mahāsattva* Puguang, "If men and women of the four groups, on the day of impending death, wish to be born in the buddha *kṣetra*-lands[16] of the ten directions, they should thoroughly wash their bodies, put on fresh clean clothes, burn many good brands[17] of incense, hang up silk pennants and canopies, sing to the Three Gems, and read and recite the hallowed scriptures. For the sick I have broadly preached stories,[18] analogies, expressions, and the subtle and wondrous meanings of the scriptures: suffering, emptiness, and nonself; that the four elements are [merely] provisional combinations; and that the body is like a plantain tree, without anything substantial inside.[19] [The body] is also like a flash of lightning, never standing still for long. Therefore I say, 'Form is not fresh for long; it will return to ruin.' Those who practice the Way with pure sincerity can obtain salvation from suffering, and they will surely get whatever results their hearts desire."

The Buddha then said to bodhisattva *mahāsattva* Puguang, "Passing through the wondrous lands of the ten directions there is no end; they cannot be measured. The pure lands inhabited by the Buddha Thus Come Ones are also incalculable; one cannot articulate their number. Now I, in the midst of this great multitude, for the four groups, for the generations to come, and for all the beings in the semblance dharma,[20] preach about the buddha lands of the ten directions and the names of the buddhas. They cannot [all] be named, so I have briefly explained only a few."

The bodhisattva Puguang then addressed the Buddha, saying, "World-Honored One, are there any differences between the buddha *kṣetra*s of the ten directions, these pure and wondrous lands?"

The Buddha said to Puguang, "There are no differences."

Puguang then addressed the Buddha, saying, "World-Honored One, why in the scriptures do you praise Amitābha's *kṣetra*, with its trees of seven gems, its palaces and its tiered pavilions? [You say that] all who wish to be born there will contemplate it and then reach it just as their hearts desire."

The Buddha said to the bodhisattva *mahāsattva* Puguang, "You don't get my point. In the Sahā World people abound with the filth of greed. Those who have faith in me are few; those who cultivate false [views] are numerous. They do not believe in the True Faith,[21] and they are unable to concentrate. Their minds are confused and without resolve. While in truth there are no differences [between Buddha lands], I simply praise that land in order to cause beings to focus their attention on getting there. Those who are reborn will all surely get whatever results they wish."

The bodhisattva Puguang again addressed the Buddha, saying, "If there are men and women of the four groups, whether their lives have not yet ended or whether they have already passed away, I will now urge them to cultivate meritorious deeds and obtain birth in the Buddha *kṣetras* of the ten directions."

The Buddha said, "Excellent, bodhisattva *mahāsattva* Puguang! Instruct the people of the ten directions as you like."

The bodhisattva Puguang said to the four groups: "On a day when a person is on the verge of death or not yet dead, you should on their behalf burn incense, light lamps of enduring brightness, hang Passing-Away Pennants from the flagpole on a *stūpa* shrine, and chant hallowed scriptures for a full twenty-one days.

"The reason is this: people at the end of their lives dwell in liminal darkness.[22] Their bodies are like infants. Their sin and merit have not yet been determined, so you should cultivate merit for their sake. If you wish to cause the spirit of the deceased to be born in the incalculable *kṣetra*-lands of the ten directions, you should undertake these good works, and they will surely obtain rebirth.

"If the deceased did sinful deeds while alive, such that they should fall into the Eight Difficulties,[23] then with the good works of pennants and lamps they will surely obtain liberation.

"If they were good, and they wish to be reborn, but the parents are in different places and they do not obtain a speedy birth,[24] then with the good works of pennants and lamps they will obtain a speedy birth, and there will be no further difficulties remaining.

"If they have already been born, then this will create the seeds of meritorious virtue for that person. They will never be possessed by malevolent demons, and their clan will be prestigious and powerful. Therefore you should cultivate the good works of pennants and lamps.

"For those who have passed away, cultivate and practice meritorious deeds. With utmost sincerity and earnest remorse, you should act as a substitute for the deceased, repenting for errors and sins, and the impurity of their sin will disappear. Cultivating merit for the deceased is like sending provisions to a person from afar. Everyone will get results.

"It is like ordinary people who commit crimes. Thinking to themselves, they hope that their kin will seek great powers to rescue them from danger and distress. Today we burn incense in the hope of obtaining liberation. We cry out the name of the deceased and cultivate good works. Using the power of meritorious virtue and relying on it for liberation is just like this. Nobody will not obtain their wish to be reborn in the ten directions!"

The bodhisattva Puguang then addressed the Buddha, saying, "Suppose a person while alive did not take refuge in the Three Gems and did not practice the dharma and its precepts. When their life ends they should fall into the Three Mires[25] and experience suffering and torment. That person, on the verge of death, just then desires with absolute sincerity to take refuge in the Three Gems; to receive and practice the dharma and the precepts; to repent errors, sins, and offenses; to disclose them and apologize for them; and to reform themselves and then cultivate the good. At the moment of impending death they hear the preaching of the dharma of the scriptures, a good master converts and instructs them, and they get to hear the sounds of the dharma. If, on the very day they will die, they produce good thoughts, will they obtain liberation or not?"

The Buddha said to the bodhisattva *mahāsattva* Puguang, "If anyone such as a gentleman or a lady, at the moment of impending death, produces these thoughts, all of them will be liberated from suffering. It is just like when a debtor belongs to the house of the king; the lender will then be afraid, and will not come in search of the money. The Divine Thearch[26] will pardon them, King Yama will let them go, and his five officers and their attending spirits will on the contrary treat them with respect and will not think of them with evil thoughts. Because of this merit, they will not fall into the evil paths, they will be liberated from distress and difficulty, and they will all obtain rebirth just as their hearts wish."

The bodhisattva Puguang again addressed the Buddha, saying, "There are also beings who do not have faith in the Three Gems and do not practice the dharma and the precepts. Or sometimes they have faith, while other times they slander it. Sometimes their parents, siblings, and relatives are suddenly struck by sickness and suffering. Because of this, at the end of their lives, they will either fall into the Three Mires or the Eight Difficulties, and they will experience suffering and vexation without any respite. If their parents, siblings, and relatives cultivate merit for their sake, will they obtain the merit or not?"

The Buddha said to Puguang, "Cultivating merit for this person yields one-seventh [the normal rate]. Why is this so? Because in their previous life they did not have faith in the virtue of the Way, this causes the meritorious virtue to be one-seventh. If you make arrangements to ornament the body of the deceased, and if you give to the Three Gems halls and awnings, rooms and dwellings, gardens and pools, then the merit will at its most plentiful, and the strength of these good works will be able to rescue them from the catastrophe of hell. Because of this they will obtain liberation from the misery of sorrow and suffering, and for a long time they will obtain salvation and liberation and be reborn in the pure lands of the buddhas of the ten directions."

The bodhisattva Puguang again addressed the Buddha, saying, "Suppose a man or woman of the four groups well understands the dharma and the precepts, knows that the self is like an illusion, intently strives to cultivate and practice, and walks the path of *bodhi*. If before their death they perform in advance the twenty-one day [ritual], lighting lamps of enduring brightness, hanging up silk pennants and canopies, and inviting the sangha to chant hallowed scriptures, will the merit they obtain for cultivating meritorious deeds be numerous or not?"

The Buddha said to Puguang, "Their merit is incalculable and immeasurable. They will get whatever results their hearts desire."

The bodhisattva Puguang addressed the Buddha, saying, "World-Honored One, if a man or woman of the four groups, whether they are at the moment of impending death or they have already passed away, on the day of their death I now also will urge them to fashion yellow pennants and hang them up on the flagpole. This will cause them to get meritorious virtue, to be free from the sufferings of the Eight Difficulties, and to obtain birth in the pure lands of the buddhas of the ten directions.

"With the devotional offerings of pennants and banners they will ultimately attain *bodhi* just as their hearts wish. The pennants, flapping in the wind, will be worn down to nothing, ultimately becoming fine dust. When the wind blows this pennant dust, its merit is incalculable. The pennant flapping just once gives you the status of a Wheel-Turning King. Just a puff of dust gives you the status of a minor king. Its rewards are incalculable!

"Burning forty-nine lamps, one illuminates the impenetrable gloom. Suffering and sick beings are enveloped in their radiant brilliance, and all obtain sight of it. Because of this meritorious virtue one protects beings, and they all obtain respite."

The Buddha said to Puguang, "If a man or woman of the four groups practices the abstinence precepts,[27] they should fix their minds on the practice of inviting the sangha of the ten directions without discriminating between good or bad, between those who uphold the precepts or break the precepts, between high or low. When they travel to *stūpa* shrines to invite the monks, they should give devotional offerings to the sangha in sequence without any thoughts of discrimination or distinction. The merit from this is the most plentiful; it is incalculable and unlimited. Whether one encounters an arhat or someone with the four fruits of the [*śrāvaka*] path,[28] or someone with the Great Mind,[29] because of these good works one attains merit that is incalculable. Hearing them preach the dharma just once, one can attain entrance to the path to supreme nirvana."

The Buddha said to Puguang, and to all the eight classes of beings (humans, gods, dragons, etc.) as well to as the demons and spirits and such in the great multitude, "Each of you should listen carefully and think about what I say! I will now, amid this great multitude, preach about good and bad actions in the old story of the Elder Nāśa.[30]

"This elder lived in the city of Rājagṛha. He constantly cultivated benevolence and performed his duty. Whether to the hungry, the destitute, the needy, *śramaṇa*s and *brāhmaṇa*s, and all solicitors—he would give devotional offerings to them all, without a trace of reluctance. But his parents were very stingy and had no intention to give devotional offerings.

"The elder had some reason to travel to another place, so in the morning he bathed, put on clean clothes, tied the sacred thread. After this he knelt and prostrated to his parents, clasped his hands together, and addressed them, saying 'I have business to attend to in another place. There are a few belongings which I have divided into three portions. The first portion is a devotional offering for the support of my parents. Another portion is precious gems to be donated to the *śramaṇa*s and to the poor. The remaining portion I would like to keep and use for myself.'

"His parents said, 'We accept. After our child leaves, we shall cultivate meritorious virtues. If any people shall come soliciting, we will donate to them all.'

"Then the elder bid farewell to his parents and arrived at that distant place. After he left, his parents had wicked views, and they did not think about their child's intentions. When *śramaṇas* and the impoverished came to beg alms, thanks to their avarice and wicked views they had no intention to donate to them.

"After the child had been gone for some number of days, he was about to return back to his house. His parents calculated when he might return home, and they went off to the marketplace. They purchased pig and sheep bones, heads, hooves, fat, and blood, as well as fruits and various grains. Taking these, they scattered them around the home. The elder Nāśa returned from abroad, and upon seeing his parents his delight was incalculable. He touched their feet in prostration, and asked them how things were going.

"His parents were also delighted and exulted. They said to Nāśa, 'After you left we arranged merit offerings for your sake. To the *śramaṇas* and *brāhmaṇas*, to the solitary aged of our city, to the destitute beggars, we used your belongings to donate to them all!' When their son heard that they had arranged merit offerings and had given alms to the impoverished, his heart was greatly delighted.

"They said again to their son, 'We again just now invited the *śramaṇas* to an offering of merit. Today in our house everything is messy and cluttered, and we haven't yet swept and cleaned!' The son saw how the clutter looked, and believed that his parents had arranged offerings of meritorious virtue. He was doubly delighted, and his exultation was incalculable.

"Long afterward, his parents grew old and decrepit, they experienced the suffering of sickness and then passed away. Nāśa then put their corpses in coffins, prepared them for burial, and laid them to rest. After his parents passed away he chanted hallowed scriptures, burned incense, ritually prostrated, and sang songs of praise without stopping for a moment. After twenty-one days in which the sounds of the sutras never ceased, he thought to himself, 'In this life my parents thought about me with ultimate concern, and many times they cultivated meritorious virtue. Now I request that all the saints think about my parents. Because of their good works, may they be reborn in the *kṣetra*-lands of the ten directions, that they may give devotional offerings and worship in the presence of buddhas!'

"Then Nāśa abruptly became gravely ill; suddenly he was about to die. The only warmth [on his body] was above his heart. The elders and youngsters in his family had not yet placed him in a coffin and prepared him for burial when, after seven days had passed, he recovered. His family members asked him, 'Elder Nāśa, this is how bad your sickness and suffering were. You were actually dead, but now you have recovered. From where did you come?'

"The elder Nāśa said to his family, 'I come back after several days. A benevolent spirit guided me and showed me the unlimited bliss of the Hall of the Fortunate.[31] Then we arrived at the hells, and there was nothing we did not pass through. What my own eyes saw was only suffering and torment! And then I saw the home of the hungry ghosts, and my parents had been born there and were subject to its suffering! They saw me coming to look, and they wailed in grief and anguish! I wanted to rescue them, but was not able to secure their release. I thought my parents had cultivated a great deal of meritorious virtue while they were alive, with the expectation of being born in heaven. But instead they descended to the hell of the hungry ghosts, and experience suffering and vexation!'

"After he said these words, the elder Nāśa wept in anguish in front of his family. 'What devices, what powers of good works, can we now use in our family to rescue my parents and grant them liberation?'

"The elder Nāśa again thought to himself, 'When my parents were sick and suffering before, I cultivated a great deal of meritorious virtue. When they were about to die but not yet dead, and also after they died, I burned lamps of enduring brilliance, chanted scriptures, circumambulated,[32] and performed the abstinence precepts with singular focus, and for twenty-one days I was never once lazy or negligent. And yet now my parents are born in a hell of sin and suffering! There must be a reason for this.' So then he asked his relatives and the elder monks.

"The elder monks replied, 'We do not understand these profound and wondrous matters. Perhaps you should go and ask the Buddha World-Honored One?'

"Then the elder went to the Buddha, bowed his head, knelt on one knee, clasped his hands, and addressed the Buddha, saying, 'I would like to ask you a question. I only wish that the World-Honored One would have compassion and does not resent me.'

"The Buddha said, 'Go ahead and speak.'

"The elder Nāśa related the story above: 'My parents while alive were always cultivating meritorious virtue, and after they passed away, I made offerings for their sake for twenty-one days, until after they were laid to rest. This was all so they could be born in heaven, and yet they descended into hell. I asked the elder monks, but the elder monks could not understand. Therefore I now ask the Buddha, so that I can resolve my doubts. Because of my grave illness, I was suddenly about to die, and only after seven days did I recover. A benevolent spirit led me through the hells, and there was nowhere we did not travel. Because of this I was able to see my parents in the land of suffering and tribulation. They cultivated such merit as this, and yet they still fell into sin? I don't understand! This is why I am now asking the Buddha. I only wish that the World-Honored One would explain and free me from my doubts. What sorts of meritorious deeds could I and my parents cultivate that would liberate them from distress and difficulty, so they do not experience suffering and calamity, and so that we all could obtain birth in heaven, be bestowed with sovereignty and unlimited bliss, and obtain the path to nirvana?'

"The Buddha said to the elder, 'You should carefully hear what I have to say. You previously had to travel to another place, and you left your belongings and wealth with your parents, asking your parents to cultivate meritorious virtues. Your parents had wicked views and they deceived you. In truth they did not cultivate merit, but they lied and said that they had cultivated the conditions of merit. Because of their avarice they have fallen into that hell.'

"The elder heard what the Buddha said from his own divine mouth, and his doubts were forever eliminated. He said, 'This is my own fault. My parents are not to blame. In front of the Buddha I hereby act in place of my parents and repent for these sins, for the catastrophe of their avarice. May the elder's parents who are now in that hell obtain a little respite!'

"The Buddha said to Nāśa, 'Now I will lend you my divine eye, so that you may get to see your parents [obtaining] respite.'

"The elder then received the awesome divinity of the Buddha, and saw that his parents had both attained respite. The elder Nāśa then addressed the Buddha, saying, 'Now what other meritorious deeds should I do to cause my parents to be free of this suffering?'

"The Buddha said to the elder, 'Now you should ask permission of the saints to dwell in retreat for three months practicing the Way. When the retreat is over, you should return to your home and make provisions of hundreds of tasty food and drink and various sweets, and place them into nice clean dishes and hold them up as devotional offerings. You should also donate to the sangha nice clothes, various fragrant incenses, gold, silver, and precious gems, and other assorted offerings. This will allow you to obtain the merit to cause your parents to be free from their hardship and to never again receive the body of a hungry ghost.'

"The elder Nāśa then, just as the Buddha said, returned home and arranged the offering, without violating the Honored One's teaching. After he performed the devotional offering, because of this they were born in heaven and bestowed with sovereignty and the happiness of nonaction.

"[The Buddha said], 'Would you like to see the palace where your parents were born? I will use my awesome divinity to cause you to see that they no longer experience suffering.'

"The elder Nāśa received the power of the awesome divinity of the Buddha and saw that his parents were reborn in heaven above. Their heavenly amusements spontaneously arose as they desired, without any obstructions.

"The Buddha said to Nāśa, 'This is how it is with sin and merit. You cannot be incautious! Elder, just as your eyes see, your mind understands. Therefore we say, "You reap what you sow. You won't get anything from heaven."[33] Likewise with the elder's parents. Even if they were in [the realm of] hungry ghosts, their sin was still trivial. All the other hungry ghosts bear sins so grave I cannot fully describe them. Because the sin of the elder's parents was trivial, a small amount of meritorious virtue could bring assistance to them in this way. When the elder cultivates merit for a full twenty-one days, then the hungry ghosts will receive a lessening of their sin. This is the reason why, as I already made clear,[34] I said that if a person while alive does not know the Three Gems, does not perform the abstinence precepts, and has no teaching from an excellent teacher, then after they pass away their siblings, parents, relatives, and religious friends who cultivate merit for their sake will only obtain one-seventh [the normal rate]. Therefore, the elder's parents were sinful, and although they were living in hell in the bodies of hungry ghosts, and received a lightening of their sin due to the cultivation of merit, they obtained only one-seventh. Now you cultivate meritorious virtue and give devotional offerings to the sangha. Because of this they are freed from their hardships and obtain birth in heaven.'"

The Buddha said to the bodhisattva *mahāsattva* Puguang, "Either on the day impending the death of a person who has not yet died, or on the day of their death after they have passed away, their parents and relatives and religious friends should cultivate meritorious deeds for the sake of the deceased. They should sincerely perform the abstinence precepts. They should wash their bodies, put on fresh clean clothes, and sincerely worship the buddhas of the ten directions. They should also praise the names of the buddhas of the ten directions. In addition they should give fragrant incense as a devotional offering to the buddhas. They will obtain liberation from the calamity of sorrow and suffering, and they will be able to ascend to heaven above and realize the Way of nirvana."

The Buddha said to the bodhisattva *mahāsattva* Puguang, "When one has not yet died, one should ritually prostrate to the buddhas of the ten directions. When that person passes away, they will always encounter buddhas wherever they are born. For a thousand *kalpas*, myriad *kalpas*, billions of myriads of *kalpas*, there will be none who do not obtain liberation from the catastrophe of their grave sins. You should also for their sake utter these Supreme Passages of Consecration. The buddhas of the Three Times[35] and the god of gods all follow this text. The Thus-Come Ones of the Three Times preached these Supreme Passages of Total Grasping.[36]

"Bodhisattva *mahāsattva* Puguang, you should listen carefully! I act for your sake, and for the sake of all beings who are sick and suffer.[37] Whether they are on the verge of death, or if they have already died, or if they are on the day of their death, if they hear these passages, then they will get to see the Buddha wherever they are born. They will not descend into the Eight Difficulties. They will be far removed from the Evil Paths."

Then the World-Honored One, in the midst of the great multitude, expounded the Supreme Passages of the buddhas. He then sang in verse:[38]

*paripurṇa caryāsamanta daśanirāga mahāvihāra*
*gate samanta vitamogate mahākālīpa pativamita*
*sahālokate suparipurṇa ālīnadharma mahāvipate*
*trivibhāga surabhasaṅkhya hutisaṃbhakṣa mahāsamanta*
*atamaraṇe arimarata vijasamanta dhanikarata*

The Buddha said to the bodhisattva *mahāsattva* Puguang, "These Supreme Passages of Consecration are most certainly non-dual. They rescue the dead from the incalculable distress of sin, and they cause the deceased to obtain birth in heaven above, to be reborn in whichever of the ten directions their hearts wish. When these Great Passages are authentically spoken, wherever one is born one always sees the subtle and wondrous pure lands of the ten directions. While you are alive you should keep and uphold these passages. You should earnestly perform the abstinence precepts for the sake of the deceased for seven days and seven nights. You should receive and uphold the eight prohibitions, keep to a vegetarian diet for a long time, and ritually worship the Buddha

World Honored Ones of the ten directions. You will then make the Great Vow: 'I vow that I shall obtain the *saṃnāhasaṃnaddha*,[39] and I will cause the various classes of beings to attain the unsurpassed and authentic Great Way!'"

After the World-Honored One had spoken, he said to the gentlemen and ladies and such of the great multitude, to the eight classes of beings (gods, dragons, etc.), and to all the demons and spirits, "You all have heard me preach about the pure Buddha lands of the ten directions. You then heard me preach about the good and bad deeds in the story of the elder Nāśa. Are your minds faithful or not?"

The bodhisattva Puguang again rose from his seat and addressed the World-Honored One, saying, "You have preached about the happiness of the ornamentations of the incalculable good works of the pure lands of the buddhas of the ten directions. We also got to hear about the story of Nāśa. The World-Honored One then preached about the causes and conditions of various actions. How excellent! Our minds are greatly delighted! Our exultation is incalculable! The World-Honored One preaches these things, and so many benefit from it. Beings in their future lives will be liberated because of it. Taking up these rules, they will never again be greedy and stingy for material necessities. Hearing the words of this scripture, they will only have minds of charity, and there will be nothing they are reluctant to give up. Just as you intend they will donate to the impoverished and make them content. The state will become fertile and abundant, and thoughts of charity will be universal and equal. And so we will, little by little, plant down good works and accumulate virtue, until all attain the Buddha's Way."

The bodhisattva *mahāsattva* Puguang again addressed the Buddha, saying, "If men or women of the four groups want to cultivate and study the text of this *Consecration Scripture on Wishing to Be Born in the Pure Land*, how many sorts of practices can they do to obtain the teachings of this scripture?"

The Buddha said to Puguang, "There are twelve actions through which one may get to cultivate and study the text of this scripture:

1. Do not believe in the religions of the ninety-five types of wicked views.
2. Firmly uphold the prohibitions and precepts and never violate them.
3. Diligently study meditation, and teach it to those who have not yet studied it.

4. Have patient endurance and be free from anger, so if you encounter evil you will not be vexed by it.
5. Always delight in charity, and have compassion toward the solitary aged.
6. Always strive vigorously day and night without laziness.
7. Whether leaving, arriving, exiting, or entering, pay reverence to the *stūpa,* the images, and your honorable elders. Only then should you leave.
8. Gather together groups of people and preach to them, so that they all obtain faithful minds.
9. Do not covet worldly honor, clothes, entertainments, or material necessities. Always enjoy ascetic practice, and rely on the doctrine of the Four Necessities.[40]
10. Have no expectations when practicing the dharma. Only desire to benefit the various classes of beings, and do not hope for profit and gain among them.
11. When you approach death, do not deceive others and engage in wrong livelihood to make a living for yourself.[41]
12. When practicing this scripture, do not pick out the people who delight in wealth and power instead of the poor, the suffering, and the needy. You should view them all equally, regarding them as without differences.

These are the twelve actions of correct teaching."

When Puguang heard this, his mind was greatly delighted. "I will receive and practice them, and will never violate them!"

After the Buddha preached this scripture, among the great multitude there was none who was not delighted. Ānanda then rose from his seat, and asked, "Now that you have expounded this teaching, what shall we name it?"

The Buddha said to Ānanda, "This scripture is called *Puguang's Questions about Being Reborn in Whichever of the Pure Lands of the Ten Directions You Wish.* It is also called *The Story of the Good and Bad Deeds of Nāśa.* It is also called *The Supreme Passages of Consecration.*"

After the Buddha preached this scripture, the people of the four groups and the eight classes of beings (gods, dragons, etc.) heard what the Buddha preached, and they prostrated, received it, and practiced it.

## Notes

1 Gregory Schopen, "Sukhāvatī as a Generalized Religious Goal in Sanskrit Mahāyāna Sūtra Literature," *Indo-Iranian Journal* 19, no. 3–4 (September 1977): 177–210.

2 Robert H. Sharf, "On Pure Land Buddhism and Ch'an / Pure Land Syncretism in Medieval China," *T'oung Pao* 88 (2002): 282–331.

3 Jan Nattier, "The Realm of Akṣobhya: A Missing Piece in the History of Pure Land Buddhism," *Journal of the International Association of Buddhist Studies* 23, no. 1 (2000): 71–102. See also Jan Nattier, "The Indian Roots of Pure Land Buddhism: Insights from the Oldest Chinese Versions of the Larger *Sukhāvatīvyūha*," *Pacific World*, 3rd series, no. 5 (2003): 179–201. See also Payne in this collection.

4 This system appears as early as the second century CE. See Jan Nattier, "Indian Antecedents of Huayan Thought: New Light from Chinese Sources," in *Reflecting Mirrors: Perspectives on Huayan Buddhism*, ed. Imre Hamar, Asiatische Forschungen 151 (Wiesbaden: Harrassowitz Verlag, 2007), 115–118.

5 The scripture is attributed to Śrīmitra (fourth century CE), but this attribution is certainly false. Michel Strickmann has argued that if there were any credible attribution for the *Consecration Scripture* anthology as a whole, it might well be the work of Huijian 慧簡, who was said by the sixth-century cataloger Sengyou 僧祐 to have authored the twelfth scroll around the year 457 CE. See Michel Strickmann, "The *Consecration Sūtra*: A Buddhist Book of Spells," in *Chinese Buddhist Apocrypha*, ed. Robert E. Buswell (Honolulu: University of Hawai'i Press, 1990), 90–93; *T.* 2145.55:39a21–23.

6 Strickmann makes a strong argument for the thematic unity of the anthology, arguing that it was "constructed on a clear plan and had a unifying principle of order." See Strickmann, "The *Consecration Sūtra*," 84.

7 *T.* 1331.21:528c24–532b4.

8 There are at least four complete independent Dunhuang manuscripts (S. 1348, 2381, and 2484; BD3042), as well as numerous manuscript fragments. See Kokusai Bukkyōgaku Daigakuin Daigaku Fuzoku Toshokan (International College for Postgraduate Buddhist Studies Library), *Taishōzō Tonkō shutsudo butten taishō mokuroku* (A concordance to the Taishō Canon and Dunhuang Buddhist Manuscripts), 3rd ed., Daizōkyō taishō mokuroku (Taishō Canon Concordance Series) 2 (Tōkyō: Kokusai Bukkyōgaku Daigakuin Daigaku Fuzoku Toshokan [International College for Postgraduate Buddhist Studies Library], 2015), 207.

9 The Fangshan stone scriptures contain several carvings from this anthology. For an independent carving of the eleventh scroll dating to 831 CE, see

Zhongguo fojiao xiehui and Zhongguo fojiao tushu wenwu guan, eds., *Fangshan shijing* (Fangshan stone scriptures), 30 vols. (Beijing: Huaxia chubanshe, 2000), 3:387–388.

10 See Ryan Richard Overbey, "Scroll 12 and 11 of the *Consecration Sutra*," in *Buddhist Stone Sutras in China: Sichuan Province*, ed. Lothar Ledderose, Tsai Suey-Ling, and Sun Hua, vol. 2 (Wiesbaden: Harrassowitz Verlag, 2015), 28–34.

11 The names of these pure lands and their resident buddhas closely match the Chinese wording in the translation of the *Pusa benye jing* (*T.* 281), translated by Zhi Qian 支謙 (fl. third century CE). See Jan Nattier, "Indian Antecedents," 115–118; *T.* 281.10:446c17–447a6.

12 This scripture confirms Schopen's insight that Sukhāvatī was almost always mentioned in liturgical contexts, in the understudied world of *pūjā* and *puṇya*. See Schopen, "Sukhāvatī as a Generalized Religious Goal," 189.

13 Literally, "the eight kinds of beings [beginning with] gods and dragons." This refers to a common list of eight nonhuman beings: *devas*, *nāgas*, *yakṣas*, *asuras*, *gandharvas*, *garuḍas*, *kiṃnaras*, and *mahorāgas*.

14 The "four groups" are monks (*bhikṣu*), nuns (*bhikṣuṇī*), laymen (*upāsaka*), and laywomen (*upāsikā*).

15 The name of this Buddha differs slightly from the Buddha given in Zhi Qian's *Pusa benye jing*. Zhi Qian reads Zhijingjin 至精進, "Utmost Vigor." See *T.* 281.10:447a6.

16 The Chinese *chatu* 剎土 is a good example of transcription-cum-translation. The Sanskrit *kṣetra*, "land" may be phonetically transcribed with Chinese *cha* 剎, but here we see the transcription supplemented by its translation *tu* 土 "land." I try to preserve this effect in English with the admittedly awkward "*kṣetra*-land."

17 The Chinese *mingxiang* 名香 literally means "famed incense" or "incense of renown." The sense here is that various sorts of well-known, high-quality incense should be burned.

18 The Chinese *yinyuan* 因緣 literally means "causes and conditions." But in the context of Buddhist preaching this word often translates the Sanskrit words *avadāna* or *nidāna*, narrative tales demonstrating the workings of karma and rebirth.

19 This is a well-known metaphor for the emptiness of all phenomena. A plantain tree is simply layer after layer of leaves. You can peel away the outer leaves, but you will find only more leaves within. There is no "substance" or "core" of a plantain tree.

20 The concept of the "semblance dharma" (*saddharmapratirūpaka*; *xiangfa* 像法) has been explored in detail by Jan Nattier, *Once upon a Future Time:*

*Studies in a Buddhist Prophecy of Decline*, Nanzan Studies in Asian Religions 1 (Berkeley, CA: Asian Humanities Press, 1991), 65–89.

21 The Chinese *zhengfa* 正法 usually translates from the Sanskrit *saddharma*. It is not just any teaching or religion (dharma); it is the "true" or "real" (*sat*) teaching or religion. I translate this as "True Faith" to convey the provocative and polemical flavor of this term.

22 This "liminal darkness" refers to the *antarābhava*, an "intermediate state" after death in which the consciousness waits to be reborn into another womb. On the *antarābhava* see Bryan Jaré Cuevas, "Predecessors and Prototypes: Towards a Conceptual History of the Buddhist *antarābhava*," *Numen* 43, no. 3 (September 1996): 263–302.

23 The "Eight Difficulties" refer to the eight *akṣaṇas*, "inopportune" rebirths in which it is difficult to follow the teachings of a Buddha. These are birth (1) in hell, (2) as a hungry ghost, (3) as an animal, (4) as a god with a long life span, (5) in a remote frontier area, (6) as a disabled person with missing sense organs, (7) as a non-Buddhist, or (8) in a place without a Tathāgata. For a detailed note with canonical references on the eight *akṣaṇas* see Étienne Lamotte, *La Traité de La Grande Vertu de Sagesse de Nāgārjuna (Mahāprajñāpāramitāśāstra)*, 5 vols., Bibliothèque du Muséon 18 and Publications de l'Institut Orientaliste de Louvain 2, 12, 24 (Louvain: Bureaux du Muséon and Institut Orientaliste, Université de Louvain, 1944–1980), 1:479 note 2.

24 This gives us fascinating insight into the sales tactics of the early medieval Buddhist funeral industry. It is easy enough to sell pennant and lamp rituals when you know the dead were sinners. But how do you sell these services to the family of a virtuous person? Here the author invents an ingenious rationale. The intermediate state between death and rebirth might last as long as forty-nine days. So even if a virtuous person has died and their karma certainly assures them a wonderful rebirth, the author reminds us that the new parents may still take their time about engaging in sexual intercourse. Meanwhile the spirit of the deceased is waiting around in the gloomy *antarābhava*. Sponsoring the pennant and lamp rituals will ensure that the parents-to-be make love as soon as possible.

25 The "Three Mires" (*santu* 三塗) is the collective name for the three lowest realms of rebirth (*apāya* or *durgati*): hell-dweller, hungry ghost, and animal.

26 The "Divine Thearch" here means the god Indra. Just as the August Thearch (*huangdi* 皇帝)—the Chinese emperor—rules over the world under heaven (*tianxia* 天下), the divine Heaven of the Thirty-Three, Trāyastriṃśa, is ruled by the god-king Indra.

27 The rituals of "abstinence" or "fasting" (*zhai* 齋) were an important feature of Chinese Buddhist practice. See Sylvie Hureau, "Buddhist Rituals," in *Early Chinese Religion, Part Two: The Period of Division (220–589 AD)*, ed. John

Lagerwey and Lü Pengzhi, Handbuch Der Orientalistik, Section IV: China 21-2 (Leiden and Boston: Brill, 2010), 1213–1227.

28 The four fruits of the *śrāvaka* path are: (1) stream enterer, (2) once returner, (3) nonreturner, and (4) arhat.

29 The "Great Mind" is a gloss of *bodhicitta*, the profound aspiration undertaken by bodhisattvas. The scripture here is arguing that one should render devotional service to all Buddhist monks, Mahāyāna and non-Mahāyāna alike, regardless of their levels of attainment.

30 Although I use "elder" to translate *zhangzhe* 長者, it should be kept in mind that this term does not necessarily indicate old age. Often *zhangzhe* is used to describe a leader, be it a patriarch of a family or the head of a caravan. "Big Man" might capture the meaning most literally, but it sounds far too awkward in context. The name Nāśa is a tentative guess for the Indian name transcribed phonetically as *Nashe* 那舍.

31 "Hall of the Fortunate" translates *futang* 福堂, a place in the afterlife reserved for those who have performed merit-making activities. For this translation I am indebted to Robert Campany. For a detailed discussion of this term, and for the closely related "Lodge of the Fortunate" (*fushe* 福舍) and "Land of the Fortunate" (*fudi* 福地), see Robert Ford Campany, *Signs from the Unseen Realm: Buddhist Miracle Tales from Early Medieval China*, Kuroda Institute Classics in East Asian Buddhism (Honolulu: University of Hawai'i Press, 2012), 79 note 89; 122 note 285.

32 The Chinese here is *xing dao* 行道, which has a very broad meaning of "to practice the Way" or "to walk the path." It can also refer more narrowly to ritual circumambulation. In the context of Nāśa's performance of various ritual actions for the benefit of his dying parents, the narrower definition seems more appropriate.

33 Literally, "What one does onself, one obtains oneself. It is not the case that Heaven gives to humans." I have translated more freely to try to capture the sense of folksy wisdom conveyed here.

34 The most natural reading of the Chinese *qianzhangzhong* 前章中 is "in the preceding section [of text]." To make the phrase make sense in the context of a sermon uttered by the Buddha, I read *zhang* 章 verbally as "to set forth," "express," or "articulate."

35 That is to say, the buddhas of past, present, and future.

36 "Total grasping" (*zongchi* 總持) is the Chinese translation of *dhāraṇī*. For reflections on the meaning of this term, see Paul F. Copp, "Notes on the Term '*dhāraṇī*' in Medieval Chinese Buddhist Thought," *Bulletin of the School of Oriental and African Studies* 71, no. 3 (October 2008): 493–508; Ronald Mark Davidson, "Studies in *dhāraṇī* Literature I: Revisiting the Meaning of the Term *dhāraṇī*," *Journal of Indian Philosophy* 37, no. 2 (April 2009): 97–147.

37 The Chinese has a puzzling lacuna. We would normally expect something like "I shall preach . . ." here. But without this verbal phrase, we are forced to render the verb *wei* 為 as "to act for the sake of."

38 The Indic sounds here are transcribed into Chinese characters and arranged in five-character rhythm. The reader should note that the phonetic reconstruction here is necessarily tentative. The spell is found, with variations, elsewhere in the Chinese Buddhist canon, notably in the *Dhāraṇīsaṃgraha* of Atikūṭa. See *T.* 901.18.875a4–10; *T.* 1251.21.250b8–14.

39 The Sanskrit here means "Completely armored in the armor," an expression indicating full attainment of the bodhisattva vow. The phrase is often left transcribed in Chinese, which makes it sound like a mysterious invocation.

40 This may be variously interpreted, but here I read it as the four necessities of monastics: food, robes, shelter, and medicine.

41 "Wrong livelihood" here likely refers to a whole host of Buddhist monastic entrepreneurial ventures, such as fortune telling and divination.

## Bibliography

Campany, Robert Ford. *Signs from the Unseen Realm: Buddhist Miracle Tales from Early Medieval China*. Kuroda Institute Classics in East Asian Buddhism. Honolulu: University of Hawai'i Press, 2012.

Copp, Paul F. "Notes on the Term *'dhāraṇī'* in Medieval Chinese Buddhist Thought." *Bulletin of the School of Oriental and African Studies* 71, no. 3 (October 2008): 493–508.

Cuevas, Bryan Jare. "Predecessors and Prototypes: Towards a Conceptual History of the Buddhist *antarābhava*." *Numen* 43, no. 3 (September 1996): 263–302.

Davidson, Ronald Mark. "Studies in *dhāraṇī* Literature I: Revisiting the Meaning of the Term *dhāraṇī*." *Journal of Indian Philosophy* 37, no. 2 (April 2009): 97–147.

Hureau, Sylvie. "Buddhist Rituals." In *Early Chinese Religion, Part Two: The Period of Division (220–589 AD)*, edited by John Lagerwey and Lü Pengzhi, 2:1207–1244. Handbuch Der Orientalistik, Section IV: China 21-2. Leiden: Brill, 2010.

Kokusai Bukkyōgaku Daigakuin Daigaku Fuzoku Toshokan (International College for Postgraduate Buddhist Studies Library). *Taishōzō Tonkō shutsudo butten taishō mokuroku* (A concordance to the Taishō Canon and Dunhuang Buddhist Manuscripts), 3rd ed. Daizōkyō taishō mokuroku (Taishō Canon Concordance Series) 2. Tōkyō: Kokusai Bukkyōgaku Daigakuin Daigaku Fuzoku Toshokan (International College for Postgraduate Buddhist Studies Library), 2015.

Lamotte, Étienne. *La Traite de La Grande Vertu de Sagesse de Nāgārjuna (Mahāprajñāpāramitāśāstra)*. 5 vols. Bibliotheque du Museon 18 and Publications de l'Institut Orientaliste de Louvain 2, 12, 24. Louvain: Bureaux du Museon and Institut Orientaliste, Universite de Louvain, 1944–1980.

Nattier, Jan. "Indian Antecedents of Huayan Thought: New Light from Chinese Sources." In *Reflecting Mirrors: Perspectives on Huayan Buddhism*, edited by Imre Hamar, 109–138. Asiatische Forschungen 151. Wiesbaden: Harrassowitz Verlag, 2007.

———. "The Indian Roots of Pure Land Buddhism: Insights from the Oldest Chinese Versions of the *Larger Sukhāvatīvyuha*." *Pacific World*, 3rd series, no. 5 (2003): 179–201.

———. *Once upon a Future Time: Studies in a Buddhist Prophecy of Decline*. Nanzan Studies in Asian Religions 1. Berkeley, CA: Asian Humanities Press, 1991.

———. "The Realm of Akṣobhya: A Missing Piece in the History of Pure Land Buddhism." *Journal of the International Association of Buddhist Studies* 23, no. 1 (2000): 71–102.

Overbey, Ryan Richard. "Scroll 12 and 11 of the *Consecration Sutra*." In *Buddhist Stone Sutras in China: Sichuan Province*, edited by Lothar Ledderose, Tsai Suey-Ling, and Sun Hua, vol. 2, 28–34. Wiesbaden: Harrassowitz Verlag, 2015.

Schopen, Gregory. "Sukhāvatī as a Generalized Religious Goal in Sanskrit Mahāyāna Sutra Literature." *Indo-Iranian Journal* 19, no. 3–4 (September 1977): 177–210.

Sharf, Robert H. "On Pure Land Buddhism and Ch'an / Pure Land Syncretism in Medieval China." *T'oung Pao* 88 (2002): 282–331.

Strickmann, Michel. "The *Consecration Sutra*: A Buddhist Book of Spells." In *Chinese Buddhist Apocrypha*, edited by Robert E. Buswell, 75–118. Honolulu: University of Hawai'i Press, 1990.

Takakusu Junjirō and Watanabe Kaigyoku, eds. *Taishō shinshu daizōkyō*. 85 vols. Tōkyō: Taishō issaikyō kankōkai, 1924–1932.

Zhongguo fojiao xiehui and Zhongguo fojiao tushu wenwu guan, eds. *Fangshan shijing* (Fangshan stone scriptures). 30 vols. Beijing: Huaxia chubanshe, 2000.

### Works cited from the *Taishō shinshu daizōkyō*

*Chu sanzang jiji* (Collected notes on the translation of the Tripiṭaka), 15 scrolls. Compiled 502–557 by Sengyou 僧祐. *T.* 2145.

*Guanding jing* (Consecration Scripture). 12 scrolls. Compiled circa fifth century. *T.* 1331.

*Houjiatuoye yigui* (Ritual manual of Āṭānāṭīya). 3 scrolls. Attributed to Vajrabodhi (671–741). *T.* 1251.

*Pusa benye jing* (Scripture on the fundamental deeds of bodhisattvas). 1 scroll. Translated 222–229 by Zhi Qian 支謙. *T.* 281.

*Tuoluoni ji jing* (*Dhāraṇīsaṃgraha; Dhāraṇī collection scripture). 12 scrolls. Compiled 654 by Atikuṭa. *T.* 901.

## Chapter 2

# Esoteric Pure Land in Kakuban's Thought

Anna Andreeva

### Translator's Introduction

The twelfth-century monk Kakuban 覚鑁 (1095–1143) was one of the pivotal figures in the history of medieval Japanese Buddhism. Originally from Hizen Province, he entered the monastic training at an early age.[1] Brought to the Heian capital by a traveling Buddhist cleric who oversaw the local estates on behalf of their head temple, Ninnaji 仁和寺, young Kakuban was placed under the instruction of the princely abbot Kanjo 寛助 (1057–1125), a famous Esoteric master and a descendant of Japan's royal family, who had been instrumental in establishing several lineages of the Hirosawa branch of Shingon. After training initially at the Jōjuin 成就院 subtemple of Ninnaji and the Buddhist temples of Nara, Kakuban underwent a period of study at another major monastic center of Esoteric Buddhism, Mount Kōya. During the decade between 1115 and 1126, he studied and collected a variety of transmissions within the Ono and Hirosawa schools, while forming his own vision of the key Esoteric practice, "becoming the Buddha with this very body" (*sokushin jōbutsu*). Under the direction of the scholar-monk Meijaku 明寂 (or Myōjaku, ca. 1124), Kakuban also dedicated himself to seeking the elusive quality of *gen* 験, the special powers acquired by ascetics through the practice of the *gumonjihō*, an Esoteric ritual for acquiring the utmost lucidity of mind and perfect memory, as well as the performance of a thousand-day fire ritual, *homa*.[2]

Ninnaji played a significant role in Kakuban's education. As a young novice and a maturing monk repeatedly returning there, he must have witnessed the Denbōe 伝法会, a ritual assembly that focused on the lectures and debates discussing important Esoteric doctrines. It was established at Ninnaji by the scholar-monk Saisen 濟暹 (1025–1115), around the year 1109. These occasions of collegial study and scholarly debate, however still hierarchical or competitive, were clearly taken into consideration when Denbōe was later implemented by Kakuban at Mount Kōya; there, it marked the beginning of a new wave of Esoteric Buddhist scholarship. In the course of the 1120–1130s, after securing the patronage of the retired emperor Toba 鳥羽天皇 (1103–1156, r. 1107–1123), Kakuban rose to prominence at Kōya, where he was appointed the head of main temple, Kongōbuji 金剛峰寺. He managed to steer it away from the control of Tōji 東寺, the old fountainhead of Japan's Esoteric tradition located in the capital. Regrettably, the much-needed royal support also caused bitter property disputes between Kakuban's abode, Daidenbōin 大伝法院, and the main Kōya temple. Moreover, Kongōbuji's tensions with Tōji continued until the conflict finally culminated in 1140, when Kongōbuji monks burned down two of Kakuban's subtemples, Daidenbōin and Mitsugon'in 密厳院. Kakuban was forced to flee to Mount Negoro 根来, west of Kōya, where he spent his remaining years amidst continued military skirmishes.

Due to his efforts to infuse new meanings in the already established or discontinued practices, Kakuban came to be known as an early medieval reformer of Esoteric Buddhist practice in Japan. His role in introducing the new ideas and ways of Esoteric training can hardly be denied: his reconsideration of the importance of sound and voice, the contemplative technique focusing on the five viscera (*wuzang*, *gozō*), and, more recently, ritual discourse involving the embryological elements are among those already known.[3] No doubt, much more to learn still remains.

Kakuban's understanding of Esoteric Buddhist practice and doctrines included yet another vital aspect: he successfully reconciled the complex notions arising from Esoteric Buddhist practices, deities, and *maṇḍalas* with the ideas of Pure Land, proposing in effect a new conceptual construction of the latter. Although the ideas describing the pure lands occurred in Esoteric Buddhist scriptures that were recorded or taught even before his time,[4] these ideas were not consistently translated into the Esoteric Buddhist doctrine or visual vocabulary. Kakuban is thus remembered for outlining such ideas explicitly in a brief text titled *Short Meditation on the Pure Land, Mysteriously Adorned*. This text, or rather a concise ritual manual, lays out a step-by-step procedure for visualizing the Esoteric paradise, in a practice that Cynthea Bogel has described as "eidetic contemplation."[5] *Mitsugon jōdo ryakkan* (as Kakuban's manual is known in Japanese) thus provides a narrative that serves as locus for merging the Esoteric Buddhist and Pure Land *imaginaire* and facilitates a process of constructing a complicated, vivid, and clear mental image, in this case, of the cosmology of *mitsugon jōdo* ("mysteriously adorned pure land"), as if such an imagined world was actually visible and habitable. *Mitsugon jōdo ryakkan* may have been written during Kakuban's period of seclusion at Mitsugon'in on Mount Kōya between 1135 and 1141, when, besieged by the doctrinal and factional quarrels at Kōyasan temples, he retreated into a thousand days of keeping silent, or it may have been written at Mount Negoro, to where he was ousted before his death in 1143.[6]

The aforementioned meditation manual presents a synthetic vision of an Esoteric pure land that is presided over by the cosmic deity Mahāvairocana; this supreme land is said to encompass all other buddha-lands, including the Amida's Land of Ultimate Bliss (*gokuraku*). In his other treatises, Kakuban reveals a few more clues about his religious motivation. For example, in the *Secret Commentary on the Five Wheels and Nine Syllables* (*Gorin kujimyō himitsushaku*, *T.* 2514), he makes an appeal "to revere the wisdom of Mahāvairocana and to have deep faith in the basic vows of Amida."[7] This appeal had profound religious implications; by interweaving the two deities and doctrines in the performed contemplations, upon the moment of death, Esoteric practitioners who had achieved the internal authentication of the "three mysteries" by aligning their speech, body, and mind with those of Mahāvairocana could potentially be reborn in Mahāvairocana's pure land, Mysteriously Adorned. Kakuban thus indicates that for an Esoteric practitioner, this paradisiac destination reigns supreme, and yet all others who still lack faculties to be delivered to this land of Esoteric bliss can first be reborn into the provisional buddha-lands, such as that of Amida. Such doctrinal innovation allowed for a symbolic and physical inclusion of other types of Pure Land and *nenbutsu* practitioners under the arch of the all-encompassing epistemology of Esoteric Buddhism and asserted the spiritual dominance of the Shingon school. At the same time, it also became possible to scholastically develop, legitimize, and institutionalize within the Shingon milieu a new strand of Esoteric doctrine that was already becoming popular among the Esoteric Buddhist practitioners, including the Kōyasan monks, mountain recluses, and semi-itinerant holy men (*shōnin* 上人 and *hijiri* 聖).

## On *Mitsugon Jōdo* and Other Similar Notions

As has been pointed out by Jacqueline Stone earlier, *mitsugon jōdo*, the expression that Kakuban used to describe Mahāvairocana's pure land, was one of the whole cluster of similar terms mentioned in a variety of

Esoteric Buddhist scriptures that were introduced to Japan from Tang China.[8] In Esoteric Buddhist vocabulary, it represents the *dharmakāya* (J. *hosshin*, dharma body) of cosmic deity Mahāvairocana, who presides over the Two Maṇḍalas (that is, the Diamond-Vajra World, or the Kongōkai, and the Womb-Store World, or the Taizōkai). *Mitsugon jōdo* as a term does not occur within the Taishō Tripitaka too often: apart from Kakuban's own writings, such as the aforementioned *Mitsugon jōdo ryakkan* and *Gorin kujimyō himitsushaku*, it is encountered in another compendium titled *On the Meaning of the Four Kinds of the Dharma Body* (*Shishu hosshin gi*, *T.* 2346).[9] Unsurprisingly, this compendium was authored by the monk Saisen, Kakuban's predecessor at Ninnaji, who established the ritual of Denbōe in the first decade of the twelfth century. Perhaps, as a young novice, Kakuban witnessed some of Saisen's lectures using or explaining such a notion and it made a strong impression on him.

Other similar terms include the notions of "mysteriously adorned land," "buddha-land, mysteriously adorned," and "mysteriously adorned world." These have an older history and wider scope both in Chinese and Japanese Esoteric scholarship and may have preceded Saisen's and Kakuban's endorsement of *mitsugon jōdo* as a definitive Esoteric–cum–Pure Land concept.[10] Of the three aforementioned terms above, *mitsugon kokudo* seems to be the most frequently used term of all. Let us give a brief overview of it here.

Amoghavajra's (Bukong 不空, Fukū, 705–774) translation of the famous Buddhist tract known as *The Treatise on the Mind Aspiring for Enlightenment* (*Putixin lun*, *Bodaishinron*, *T.* 1665), placed this notion in the context of acquiring enlightenment, the ultimate goal for any Esoteric practitioner: "If one returns to the foundations, that is the mysteriously adorned land which does not arise in [any one] place but simply encompasses all phenomena. When praising the mind aspiring for enlightenment, it is said: if a person seeks Buddhist wisdom, he passes through [the certain stages of realization], achieves *bodhicitta*, and rapidly manifests the great state of awakening within the physical body beget by father and mother."[11] In his other translations of Esoteric sutras, such as *Dasheng miyan jing* (*Daijō mitsugonkyō*, Sūtra of the Mysterious Adornment of the Great Vehicle, *T.* 681), Amoghavajra used a similar expression, describing an Esoteric buddha-land, *mitsugon bukkoku*. He did so, perhaps, following another famous Chinese Buddhist translator, Yixing 一行 (Ichigyō, 683–727), who employed it in his *Commentary on the Mahāvairocana Sūtra* (*Darijing shu*, *Dainichikyō sho*, *T.* 1796).[12]

This Esoteric idea of rapid or sudden enlightenment propagated by the key historical figures involved in the processes of translating important Buddhist (most of all Esoteric) scriptures into Chinese made a strong impression in Heian Japan (784–1185). It was deemed important by the early systematizers of Esoteric Buddhism, the founder of the Shingon tradition, Kūkai 空海 (774–835), and the Tendai scholar Annen 安然 (841–?).[13] Kūkai cited this very passage in his *The Jeweled Key to the Secret Treasury* (*Hizō hōken*, *T.* 2426), whereas Annen noted that such an Esoteric buddha-land "does not arise in [any one] place, but comprises all Buddhist phenomena."[14] Elsewhere, quoting the above-mentioned passage on rapid enlightenment from the *Bodaishinron*, Annen added, "This is the Gate of Mantra [Shingon]: [it includes the notions of] the initial [stage of the] mind, sentient [unenlightened] beings, bodhisattvas of first abode, bodhisattvas in their final lifetime, buddhahood, inner realization, *samādhi*, the awakened mind, and the functions [of the body, speech, and mind]. The above phrase, in saying 'mysteriously adorned,' means 'this is the pure land of true retribution and wondrous enlightenment.'"[15]

Kakuban was keenly attuned to such discussions. He evidently considered the famous *Bodaishinron* passage cited above in minute detail, since he quoted or discussed it in several of his own works. These include a short contemplation manual, *Secret Commentary on Mind as a Moon Disk* (*Shingachirin hishaku*, ca. 1124, *T.* 2520), Kakuban's own *Secret Commentary* on the *Bodaishinron* (*Bodaishinron hishaku*, *T.* 2291), the aforementioned *Gorin kujimyō himitsushaku*, in which he interweaved the said passage with a discussion of the fivefold body and meditation on the five viscera, and his lectures on Kūkai's theory of the ten-stage enlightenment (*Jūjūshinron uchigikishū*, Collection of impressive teachings I heard, *T.* 2443). Evidently, Kakuban's own ideas were deeply rooted in the Esoteric Buddhist scholarly tradition, visual tropes, and language. For him, the idea of "enlightenment with this very body" was the point of both departure and arrival, as far as the methods of achieving such a coveted state were concerned. The idea of a place or an imagined cosmological destination where the physical body of an Esoteric practitioner could perfectly merge in seamless unity with Mahāvairocana was central to the Esoteric discourse on enlightenment. In addition to the Esoteric Buddhist scriptures, the descriptions of Esoteric pure land in Kakuban's manual resemble those in the famous treatise by the Tendai monk Genshin 源信 (942–107), the *Essentials of Rebirth in the Pure Land* (*Ōjōyōshū*, *T.* 2682).[16]

It seems that in the course of his intellectual quest to discover such an imagined locus, Kakuban briefly considered the use of other substitute terms that could describe the abode of Esoteric deities and wisdom. For example, in his short explication *Taizōkai sata* (On the substance of the Womb-store Realm, *T.* 2519), Kakuban employed the expression "secretly adorned Esoteric world" to explain one of the "pocket" realms carried by the deity Fudō Myōō on his head.[17] While this term continued to be used within the wider religious circles, he eventually chose to present a cosmology of Esoteric pure land, so necessary for the Esoteric Buddhist milieu in the mid-twelfth century, through a more precise and specific concept of *mitsugon jōdo.*

## Before and after Kakuban

Toward the second half of the twelfth century, the monastic complex at Kōyasan attracted the scores of *nenbutsu hijiri*, semilay religious practitioners who practiced the chanting of Amida's name in addition to collecting donations and pursuing other strands of religious practice. One should assume that such a trend must have emerged in the decades before, during Kakuban's time at Kōyasan. According to the Japanese scholar of religion Gorai Shigeru, the mountain itself was understood to be a special sacred place *and* a manifestation of pure land since the mid-Heian period. For example, a record in the *Kongōbuji kenritsu shūgyō engi* (Karmic origins of construction and Esoteric practice at Kongōbuji, ca. eleventh century) described Kōyasan's main temple as the "pure land of the previous buddha," while *Kōyasan ōjōden* (Records of rebirth at Kōyasan) composed during 1184–1193 included at least thirty-eight names of those Buddhist priests who practiced on the mountain and managed to attain rebirth in Amida's pure land.[18]

The activities of the *nenbutsu hijiri* on Mount Kōya can perhaps be traced back more precisely to the figure of Kyōkai 教懐 (1001–1093). He initially began to practice *nenbutsu* at a separate hall for study and practice (*bessho*) established by the Kōfukuji 興福寺 monks at Odawara 小田原 in Yamashiro Province in central Japan. He arrived at Kōyasan in his seventies and quickly attracted followers by chanting Amida's mantras, performing rituals dedicated to the Two Maṇḍalas and Esoteric deities, and making the offertory services to Amida.[19] Although the dating of these sources may be uneasy to juxtapose neatly with the events of Kakuban's life, they highlight the presence of groups of practitioners captivated by the ideas, imagery, and practices of pure land before his own arrival at Kōyasan in 1114, and they reveal valid historical reasons why Kakuban felt motivated to record his ritual manual on visualizing the pure land of Mahāvairocana. It was imperative for him to reflect the dominant religious mood prevailing among the Kōya *hijiri* throughout the eleventh and twelfth centuries and at the same time to proclaim the eminence of the doctrine and practice of rapid enlightenment, the major source of religious power for Esoteric Buddhists. Given the increasing numbers of *nenbutsu* and other kinds of *hijiri* residing at different subtemples of Kōyasan during the first half of the twelfth century, perhaps, outlining his vision of Esoteric pure land was a crucial means for Kakuban to consolidate the popular sentiment around his ideas and to secure his own position within the Kōyasan establishment.

Nevertheless, despite his moves to assert independence of the old monastic center vis-à-vis its then head temple Tōji, Kakuban met with fierce opposition at Kōyasan during the last years of his life. The tensions over the property as well as his leadership, and physical clashes between Kongōbuji monks and Kakuban's supporters were some of the reasons he chose to leave the mountain monastic complex and seek refuge at another location, Mount Negoro, in 1140. Not everyone, however, was opposed to his groundbreaking ideas. Some of the scholar monks and different groups of *hijiri* remaining at subtemples of Kōyasan preserved Kakuban's teachings and passed them on further, to the Buddhist practitioners who came to the mountain and joined others for private study in a bid to unlock the complex truths of Esoteric Buddhism and learn about its secret icons, deities, rituals, and cosmologies. Some of these individuals were fully ordained monks who came to seek legitimate transmissions of Esoteric teachings; oftentimes such monks went on to reside at major temples, and their names remain in the annals of Japanese Buddhist history. Others were semi-itinerant priests and holy men (*shōnin*) or different kinds of *hijiri* who pursued the study of Esoteric Buddhism and other strands of Buddhist practice at small countryside temples. After a period of study at Kōyasan, such men transported their ideas to other destinations.[20]

One of those who inherited Kakuban's ideas and spread them further was the Kōyasan monk Gochibō Yūgen 五智房融源 (ca. 1120–ca. 1218).[21] Like Kakuban, he was originally from Hizen Province. Because of this sense of proximity, he studied personally with Kakuban and later became the head of scholar-monks at Daidenbōin on Mount Kōya. Not much is otherwise known about Yūgen, except for his lectures given to one Hōkyō Rendōbō 寳篋蓮道房 (active ca. 1200–1235), who was extremely interested in the study of Esoteric Buddhism and later went to train at another Shingon stronghold, Daigoji 醍醐寺, near the Heian capital. Rendōbō was one of those semi-itinerant *shōnin* who flocked to the Buddhist communities at Kōyasan searching for access to qualified and credible teachers who could transmit secret Esoteric teachings. Based mostly at Miwa *bessho* in southeastern Yamato, he went on to become a founder of a local Buddhist lineage there called the Miwa-ryū 三輪流.[22]

In his lectures to Rendōbō explaining the complex truths of Esoteric Buddhist doctrine and ritual practice, Yūgen often refers to the times "when Kakuban was alive." As a result of this exchange (although it is not clear when exactly it took place), Rendōbō's personal study notes, known as *Kakugenshō* 覚源抄 (Brief account of lectures by Kakukai 覚海 and Yūgen, ca. early thirteenth century), contain a wealth of references to Kakuban's teachings, such as the contemplation on the five viscera and embryological theories, and they include the explanations of major scriptures and rituals of Esoteric Buddhism as taught at Mount Kōya by the end of the twelfth century.[23] Among this multitude, one also finds the references to "pure land of mysteriously adorned flower ornament," "wondrous pure land," and even a discussion on the true meaning of Shingon practice such as this one below.

> *Bodaishinron* already [says] that all sentient beings partially possess pure nature within the very intentions of their mind. Rotating within the wheel of six paths [of transmigration], there is no easy transformation. In truth, by revealing that "all phenomena are no different from reality" and that "current status equates to wondrous enlightenment," [we] thus [suddenly understand] the teaching that [says that] the heart-lotus of our own body is the lotus pedestal [of Mahāvairocana]. For this reason, the western pure land [of Buddha Amida] is the wondrous lotus of our own body. The inner chamber of Tuṣita Heaven [of Buddha Maitreya] is the cloud palace of one's own mind. The mysteriously adorned flower ornament is a pure land of one's own mind and one's own virtue.[24]

Kakuban's exposition of the Esoteric pure land of Buddha Mahāvairocana as seen in his *Mitsugon jōdo ryakkan* is based on the mandalic format; an Esoteric practitioner is invited to visualize such a wondrous realm picturing the sacred geography of pure lands of Amida, Maitreya, and other buddhas in his own mind, step by step. As will become evident from the following English translation of this text, Kakuban's search for such a pure land was initially positioned in a quasi-geographical, supramundane realm. Decades later, learning from the exchanges with Kakuban's disciple Yūgen and his lectures on the fundamental tenets of

Esoteric tradition seen in the *Bodaishinron* and other scriptures, the medieval holy man Rendōbō applied the mandalic categories of pure lands to the organic, physical bodies of Esoteric practitioners, perhaps reflecting on the theological trends proposed by Kakuban in the earlier years, for example his advocation of ritual meditation on the five viscera in the *Gorin kujimyō himitsushaku*.

Kakuban's most active supporter, the Shingon scholar-monk Raiyu 頼瑜 (1226–1304), who was instrumental in further settlement of Kakuban's lineage at Mount Negoro in 1288 and systematizing his ideas further, expressed the sentiment that prevailed among the followers and students of Kakuban's teachings. For example, in his treatise titled *Kinkai hatsueshō* (Short notes on arousing wisdom through the Diamond World, *T.* 2533), Raiyu summarized the perspective of both the scholar-monks and semi-itinerant *shōnin* such as the aforementioned Miwa *shōnin* Rendōbō, who chose to pursue their Esoteric studies and practices in self-imposed isolation at mountainous temples and countryside *bessho* halls: "when performing the *kaji* empowerment with that mudra and mantra, the polluted lands and desolate grass huts will transform into the pure land, mysteriously adorned. The mundane body of Esoteric practitioner will become the body of the Buddha. The *mudrā* [and mantra] represent the non-duality of principle and wisdom, and the three bodies [of the Buddha] and the three treasures will also appear."[25]

Indicative of the overall intellectual climate and Buddhist culture of exchange of ideas and oral transmissions, Kakuban's notions of Esoteric pure land traversed the different corners of Buddhist milieu regardless of sectarian affiliations (if such ever truly existed in medieval Japan). One of the major figures in the Jishū movement in medieval Kyoto, Takua Shōnin 託阿上人 (d. 1354), who was based at Konkōji 金光寺 on Shichijō, mentioned *mitsugon jōdo* in his treatise *Kibokuron* 器朴論 (Arguments of a rustic bowl, *T.* 2681).[26]

During the thirteenth and fourteenth centuries, Kakuban's ideas of *mitsugon jōdo* were known also on Mount Hiei, where they became recorded as part of descriptions of Kakuban's writings within the extensive encyclopedia *Keiranshūyōshū* (Collection of leaves gathered in stormy ravines, ca. 1349, *T.* 2410), compiled by the Tendai chronicler-monk Kōshū 光宗 (1276–1350) from the Kurodani Temple.[27] Even from this limited evidence, it becomes obvious that Kakuban's ideas, including his creative vision of Esoteric pure land, were attractive to an increasing number of religious practitioners in medieval Japan and had a significant impact on the development of the intellectual climate in medieval Buddhist milieu.

## Translation

### *Short Meditation on the Pure Land, Mysteriously Adorned* (*Mitsugon jōdo ryakkan* 密厳浄土略観, *T.* 2515)

Kakuban

That Mysteriously Adorned Pure Land is the lotus-capital of the King of Mind,[28] Mahāvairocana (*Dainichi shinnō no rento*). It is the golden land (*kṣetra; kinsetsu*) of the All-Illuminating Dharma Ruler, the place of abode for secret adornments, and the realm whose boundaries are demarcated by pure and subtle *maṇḍalas*. Its appearance is as broad and large as the cosmos. Its nature and characteristics are eternally unchanged and surpass the experiential realm (*dharmadātu*; *hokkai*).[29] The pure lands in ten directions make up its front gardens. The wondrous lands of various buddhas make up its back courtyard. Myriad worthies, with their buddha-bodies and buddha-lands, are laid out in *yin* and *yang*;[30] with their three bodies (*trikāya*),[31] they fill heaven and earth to the brim. [That pure land] consists of five wheels; the seed-wisdom is its self-nature,[32] and its appearance is adorned with three mysteries and myriad virtues.

On the ground of Single True Mind, there are seven golden mountains that surround [this ground] in enclosures. Between the seven peaks of the awakened dharma, there flows the sea of eight virtues. In the middle of this sea, there is a golden turtle of great compassion. On the turtle's back, there unfolds a treasure-lotus of pure consciousness. On this [lotus] pedestal rests Mount Sumeru (Shumi[sen] 須彌山). Its very peak is a *maṇḍala*. The mountain is, therefore, the pure and wondrous body of dharma in all its entirety, and the true form of the great *bodhicitta*.[33] It is high, wide, and limitless. [It views] the Mount Sumeru of [this] pitiful world as inevitably petty and small, with both its nature and its phenomenal manifestations permanently fixed. [Whoever is] regrettably born into this world [that is a] melting pot of delusion, will end up in change and demise.

The said form [of this *maṇḍala*] is octagonal. It reveals the triumph, rarity, and subtleness of the eight consciousnesses. In theory, it encompasses the four treasures that emit divine light of the four wondrous wisdoms. Innumerable wish-fulfilling trees[34] stretch out in lines. Countless chinaberry forests fill [this land] with fragrance from border to border. From their branches hang magnificent heavenly garments. From those trees hang beautiful bejeweled nets everywhere. The five-colored flowers of awakening blossom [bloom] on each tree; their hues are complicated. Throughout the six periods of the day, dharma-birds chirp in unison, all with different beaks. Sweet fruits weigh heavily on the tree branches. Golden flowers with silver calices cover up their leaves. When a light breeze blows on the bells, they produce soft chimes propagating the joy of the three golden dharmas. When flower birds twitter on the bejeweled trees, their echoing voices proclaim the bliss of meditation on the five stores.[35] The vast and abundant eight seas [of this pure land] are its treasure-ponds; the steep seven peaks impress as its treasured mansions. The lotus flowers of four colors blossom, floating in the midst of the sea. The five kinds of bejeweled trees [grow] thickly on mountain tops. The ebb and flow of tidal waves explains the teaching of the ten stages of mind.[36] The flower petals scatter [through the air] embellishing the meditation palaces on the five peaks. The pond of five wisdoms is selfless like a mirror; who can escape the myriad of shapes, colors, and forms of the dharma-world [reflected in it]? The lantern of five visions never grows dim; how can there remain any ignorance or darkness? The six great elements are akin to a fragrance that follows the wind of awakening and floats in all ten directions. The dharma-flavor of the four seasons matches the bliss desired by those inhabiting the three worlds. Peacocks and parrots in great numbers sing out reminding of the three treasures [of Buddhism]. Mallards, geese, and mandarin ducks from time to time cry out pining for the bliss of the three golden [dharmas]. The white crane of Thusness[37] dances on the waterside, the shore of nonduality. The dark blue mallards of three mysteries frolic in *maṇḍala* waters. The winds in the pine trees of three awakenings pick up eight tones of the lute. The ebb and flow of the fivefold [meditation][38] taps the drum of the four abilities of understanding and expression. The three equals[39] and the five notes [of the Buddha's teaching] vie to produce heavenly rhymes. [The seas of] the four mudras and eight virtues swaying from side to side replenish themselves. The heavenly beings (*devas*) of the upper and lower realms play music in the ten worlds. The deities of the inner and outer chambers fill the nine heavens with offerings.

The mountain summit and hilltops are wide and flat; their marvels and divine territories are truly without comparison. Surrounding [the mountain summit] is a vajra-fence. Each of its four sides has a gate open. In the east, there is a Vajra Gate that leads to the pure land of Akṣobhya (*Ashuku no jōsetsu* 阿閦淨刹). In the south, there is [Wish-Fulfilling] Gem Gate that encloses the mysterious land of Ratnasamḥbhava (*Hōshō no myōdo* 寶生妙土). In the west, there is the Lotus Gate that comprises the Amida's Land of Ultimate Bliss (*Mida no gokuraku* 彌陀極樂).[40] In the north, there is the Karma Gate, the pure land of Śākyamuni (*Shaka jōdo* 釋迦淨土) lies there. Each of these pure lands is subtle and wondrous [in every minute feature].

In the middle [of these pure lands], there is a palace of universal dharma (lit., dharma-world palace). It is wide, high, and its marvelous decoration glows in every detail. The lines of eight pillars stretch out to [each of] the four corners, with the four gates leading onto various distinct roads. Up and down the roads the ornate flowers bloom abundantly. To the left and right of the gates there are seven bejeweled auspicious banners. Precious and marvelous jewels constantly fall down like rain, and the divine offerings are left out day and night. Friendly rhymes and loving voices are set to various melodies. When appropriate, there is a chanting of Sanskrit syllables, and the singers sing hymns. Around the building there are solemnly decorated streams of cloths. On the ground level, there are four winding stair paths.

On top of the palace there are five towers, each adorned with a canopy of patterned banners suspended [from planks]. The flower garlands hang from bejeweled thin wire nets. Installed inside the palace are the earthen pots of pure and subtle wisdom [with the water from] the *argha* well. Near the altar platform burn the bright yet serene jeweled lanterns. The expedient means make various entertainers [appear], and benevolent guidance procures different kinds of musicians.[41] Singing and playing the sounds of wondrous dharma, they attend to and praise the pure *dharmakāya* [of Buddha Mahāvairocana]. When the eight inner and outer bodhisattvas of offerings line themselves on top of the platform,[42] the two marvelous qualities of merit and wisdom spread through the palace.

In the Buddhist realm, there is a distinction between the master [Buddha] and his attendants. Within the altar, there is a difference between the center and a periphery. The four extremities of the mind each count as a practice hall, while at the core there is the Mind King Maṇḍala. In the middle of it, there is a lotus pedestal. On top of it lies a lion skin seat. Upon all of those, there are the great treasure lotus and the pure full moon disk. In it [reflects] the king of eight-petal lotuses. On top of it there is a Sanskrit syllable of the *dharmakāya*. Its form and nature are luminous and pure. It is like a pool of light, clear and white. It realizes the numerous virtues and perfectly fulfills the two kinds of benefit. The Sanskrit syllable transforms into all-pervading five elements and becomes the stupa of the *dharmakāya*. Emitting the luminescence colored by the five wisdoms, this stupa illuminates the limitless Buddhist realms. It realizes the numerous virtues and supplies the three mysteries.

Then, the stupa transforms into the pure and subtle *dharmakāya* of Mahāvairocana tathāgata who pervades all extremities of the dharma-world. Inexhaustible are the various marks [of the Buddha]; one by one, [he possesses them] in abundance. [These marks] are innumerable (lit., exceed the number of seeds), each of them is auspicious and solemn.

With the crown of five wisdoms on top of his head, [this Buddha Mahāvairocana] is adorned with the necklace of myriad virtues and is dressed in a monastic robe made of fine patterned silk gauze. His body emits all-pervading wisdom light that purges any darkness. His hair is gathered on the top of his head; [his topknot] is so tall, that it cannot be fully seen. His dark blue hair is even and immeasurable. On the top of his head, there is the *uṣṇīṣa* pate[43] that fills skies with light. The tuft of white hair between his eyebrows illuminates the whole universe.

Adorned with hanging jewels, his earlobes are thick, broad, and long. Attracting the dew, his sublime forehead is smooth, straight, and broad. His face is round and perfect like a full lunar mansion in the autumn. Glowing in delight like a pool of light, his smile absorbs [the beauty from] the spring flowers. His even brows are clean and vivid; in smile [they acquire] a dark blue lapis lazuli gleam. Both eyes are bright and clear, surpassing the colors of a blue lotus. The cut of his nose is like a golden cane, high and complete with a straight tip. The nostrils hide from the human eye, they are clean and fresh both within and outside. The lips are red [like a fruit of the] *vimba* [red-gourd tree]; the upper and lower are perfectly symmetrical. His snow-white teeth are even and clean. The four fangs [emitting] the bright white light, are graceful and sharp. [His tongue of] three *sun*[44] is crimson red; it is thin and clean, broad, and long. Below it, there is a wish-fulfilling gem that sprinkles sweet dew (*amṛta*) on the tip of his tongue.

His throat is like a lapis lazuli cylinder that resembles a bundle of lotus flowers. The voice coming out of his throat is incredibly harmonious and graceful (lit., without any disharmony). Whoever hears his voice can but listen to it well. From his neck, he exhales halos of light. On his throat, there are markings, which leave no place unlit and nothing unrevealed. His shoulders and the back of his neck are rounded, his underarms are full. His forearms are long and smooth; their flesh is round like a rare jewel. The palms of his hands reveal a pattern of one thousand spoked wheels. His exquisite fingers are thin and long. Their tips reveal the auspicious marks of a swastika. The fingernails are shiny and even, and the finest stretches of skin connect [his fingers].

His chin and chest resemble those of a lion king. On his chest there is an auspicious swastika sign that reveals the seal of True Reality. His heart-mind is like a crimson lotus flower; his skin surpasses even the whitest of snows. His bodily luminescence pervades all realms in ten directions and shines throughout all natural constellations of the three times (past, present, and future). Solemn, marvelous, and unique, his body is all-pervading; it reaches any breadths and margins. His physical appearance is perfect in height, width, and volume. His facial expression is fulfilled, and his pose is upright. His hidden organ is pure and balanced. All seven parts [of his body] are perfect and could transfix [anyone's gaze] with loving bliss.

Both of his calves extend gradually, equally delicate and round. The soles of his feet are broad, long, and round, and they match his legs. He is sitting cross-legged, tall, agile, [and still]. On the soles of his feet there are inscriptions of thousand spoked wheels. His thighs are smooth and full.

From each of his pores (lit., hair follicles), one by one, he emits the five-wisdom radiance, and from each of his joints the light of *samādhi*. His necklace of Thusness and myriad virtues reflects pure light. The solemn adornments of the "three equals" and hundred prosperities merge together in complex patterns. All deities of the five families and the Two Realms reveal themselves at once in the great luminescence of Mahāvairocana (*Dainichi no kōmyō* 大日光明). All the principles and phenomena of the ten directions and three times at once manifest themselves in the pores of this All-Illuminating [Buddha]. The self-nature of his inner enlightenment, and his meritorious deeds are vast and profoundly deep. His external acts, empathy for others, and mercy pervade the universe and fill the realm to the brim. His dharma enjoyment of the three mysteries is eternal throughout the past, present, and future. His joy of meditation on the four *maṇ[ḍalas]* surpasses the four aspects[45] and is universal and unchanged. Emitting the radiance, he expounds the dharma, to benefit himself and others. His inner and outer actions are full of divine powers. Horizontally, he eliminates the ten worlds, so that the myriad dharmas could merge together. Vertically, he rises above the three times, so that all the buddhas may equally flock to him. Akṣobhya and Ratnasamḥbhava receive the offerings [from Mahāvairocana] via [the bodhisattvas] Joy and Garland. [A]mida and Amoghasiddhi (Fukū 不空) collect his cherishing praises from [the bodhisattvas] Song and Dance. Myriad buddhas thus receive [Mahāvairocana's] patronage, and [in response] they deepen their [filial] piety [toward him]. Myriad worthies, upon receiving his love and compassion, exponentially increase their respect and felicitations [toward him]. Following that, the four buddhas fold their palms in the *gasshō* gesture, and [bow low] bringing their foreheads to his feet. Then, myriad worthies, in deepest respect and sincerity, prostrate themselves [on the floor], lowering their heads toward the feet of the All-Illuminating One.

[Like an alchemist,] Tathāgata Akṣobhya fuses and melts the pure gold of the five wisdoms and offers it to the Dharmakāya [of Mahāvairocana] that dwells eternally in the past, present, and future. He burns the wondrous incense of Thusness and dedicates it to Nature Buddha who pervades the ten directions. The skillful Buddha Ratnasamḥbhava offers the myriad-virtue gems to the four *maṇḍalas*,[46] that are one with Mahāvairocana. He scatters the beautiful flowers [to honor] the two marvelous qualities [of prosperity and wisdom] and adorns the three mysteries who are none other than the All-Illuminating One.

[A]mida, who is the seed of awakening, lights up the seed-wisdom lotus torch and offers it to the Mind King of Yogic Meditation. He intones the verses in eight melodies in an accolade to the Lord Teacher of *Maṇḍalas*. Śākyamuni of Pervading Wisdom rotates the karma of the two kinds of benefits, aspiring [to serve] the Buddha of three golden dharmas. He devotes the five portions of unguent oil and incense [that cleanse away all transgressions] and lifts them up to the colossus of the six elements.

All these offerings are numerous and diverse. These [gifts by] the four buddhas are so limitless, that they exceed the number of particles in the earthly dust and the water drops in the sea. Each [of these four buddhas] encompasses limitless kindred and immeasurable assemblies of other divinities. Each constantly provides offerings of principles and phenomena and dutifully performs the acts of inner and outer piety. All the buddhas of the ten directions obediently surround and politely worship [their lord Mahāvairocana], and the four *pāramitā* bodhisattvas of *samādhi* affectionately reside at his side.[47] When the hymns of praise sung by the twenty-eight wheel-turning kings (*cakravartin*) reverberate throughout the dharma realm, the twelve heavenly consorts fill the vast space with their offerings. The ten thousand buddhas of inner enlightenment fold their arms in the seal of dharma and protect [Mahāvairocana]. In the outer chamber [of his *maṇḍala* palace], the twenty *devas* shake their adamantine *vajras* and guard their lord.

Some of these buddhas have received Mahāvairocana's permission to return to their own lands and practice the two kinds of benefits. Or, upon receiving the teaching and orders by the All-Illuminating One, they may circumambulate other buddha-lands and save the sentient beings there. As soon as a person takes refuge in Mahāvairocana and asks to be reborn in his pure land, the Mind King, Dharmakāya Mahāvairocana gathers all the buddhas who dwell as his manifestations in other realms, tugging them into his world and [merging them all into] the joint four-fold Dharmakāya. Then he rises from the ground in dharma bliss and meditative joy, heads toward the gate that matches the person's faculty [necessary for enlightenment], and fulfills that person's religious wishes.

At that time, riding the elephant king and leading the *sattvas*, the kings, bodhisattvas of Love and Joy, and other countless deities, Akṣobhya arrives from the eastern realm. Riding the jeweled horse and accompanied by the bodhisattvas of Treasures, Light, Banners, and Smile and his other eternal servants, Ratnasamḥbhava joins the meeting from the southern lands. Flying on his peacock, together with the bodhisattvas of Dharma, Benefit, Karmic Cause, and Speech as well as his innumerable manifestations, Amida pays homage from the west. Riding on the gold-feathered phoenix and leading the bodhisattvas of Karmic Deeds, Protection, Fangs, and Fists along with his eternal kin, Śākyamuni arrives from the northern direction, gathering clouds.

At that time, the *Uṣṇīṣa* of the Mind King, venerable Mahāvairocana, rides on the lion king of great awakening, attended by the deities produced from his own nature: the four buddhas and the four female *pāramitā* bodhisattvas, the sixteen rulers, the twelve heavenly consorts, the twenty-eight wheel[-turning] kings, the five great wisdom kings, the twenty *devas*, all arrive in inexplicable numbers like the minuscule particles of dust, all the various worthies and all the divine beings. He comes to greet the practitioner [who made the original vow to him] and takes him back to his original pure land.

What happens during this moment, it is difficult to describe. [At that time, Mahāvairocana] may reveal his limitless divine powers and clarify the most difficult ideas about the profound dharma. With the light of his Buddha wisdom, he may illumine any dark cavity of delusion. Or, through praising the divine dharma, the dancers and singers may purify the blind and clouded minds. At that very moment, the clouds of delusion will clear up at once, and the moon of awakening will suddenly appear where one stands. The wisdom eye will open for the first time, and the Buddhist realms will gradually reveal themselves. Then, the grass hut [of this practitioner] will turn into a golden hall. This worldly land of pollution will become the pure land. All the vegetation in the abundant forests will become the dharmakāya of the "three equals," and every wriggling species will equal the Nature Buddha of the six elements. All the resounding voices of sentient and nonsentient beings are akin to mantras.[48] The minds of those who are awakened and those who are not are inseparable from meditation and wisdom. The principal deity [Mahāvairocana] quietly seeps under the skin of the practitioner, and the practitioner crosses over and enters the principal deity. Together, they disperse into five parts (the five families of the Kongōkai) and manifest the lord and his assistants. Or, they return to the One Body and fuse the active and passive aspects. One single thought actualizes the myriad of virtues, and the two benefits are profoundly [realized] in a split second.

If the [practitioner's] religious vow and conduct are shallow and weak, and his faculties and karmic bonds are not yet ripe [for the immediate enlightenment], [Mahāvairocana] may soothe temporarily [by transporting him to] a provisional pure land. Eventually, he will meet [such a practitioner] in his wondrous [pure] land of dharma-nature. At the correct moment, he will [help to] transcend the karmic causes of delusion of the nine worlds and open up practitioner's physical body to the Buddha fruit of the three mysteries. So it is said.

## Notes

1 Nowadays, the Nagasaki Prefecture is in northern Kyushu.

2 *Mikkyō Daijiten*, the abridged edition, edited by Mikkyō jiten hensankai (Kyoto: Hōzōkan, 2007), 225–227. See also Donald Drummond, "Looking Back and Leaping Forward: Constructing Lineage in the Shingi Shingon Tradition of Japan," in *Esoteric Buddhism and the Tantras in East Asia*, ed. Charles D. Orzech, Henrik H. Sørensen, and Richard K. Payne (Handbook of Oriental Studies, Leiden: Brill, 2011), 817.

3 See the most recent analysis of Kakuban's contribution to the new trends in medieval Esoteric Buddhism in Lucia Dolce, "The Embryonic Generation of the Perfect Body: Ritual Embryology from Japanese Tantric Sources," in *Transforming the Void: Embryological Discourse and Reproductive Imagery in East Asian Religions*, ed. Anna Andreeva and Dominic Steavu (Leiden: Brill, 2016), 253–310. On the possible precursors to meditation on the five viscera, see Fabio Rambelli, "Tantric Buddhism and Chinese Thought in East Asia," in *Tantra in Practice*, ed. David Gordon White (Princeton, NJ: Princeton University Press, 2000), 361–380.

4 Marc Buijnsters has noted two of such possibilities: *Liqujing shu* (*Rishushaku*, Commentary on the Sūtra of Guiding Principle, *T.* 1003) and *Muryōju nyorai kangyō kuyō giki* (Ritual of contemplation and offerings to the Tathāgata Immeasurable Life, *T.* 930), both translated by the Indian monk Amoghavajra (Bukong 不空, Fukū, 705–774) and known in Japan since the early Heian period. These texts describe Buddha Amida as an Esoteric deity; the latter ritual manual proposes the possibility of a rebirth in Amida's Land of Ultimate Bliss (*gokuraku* 極楽) by the means of performing an Esoteric ritual. See Marc Buijnsters, "Jichihan and the Restoration and Innovation of Buddhist Practice," *Japanese Journal of Religious Studies* 26, no. 1/2 (1999): 39–82, especially 61–62.

5 *Kansō* 観想 or *kannen* 観念. See the discussion of Esoteric Buddhist visuality, in Cynthea J. Bogel, *With a Single Glance: Buddhist Icon and Early Mikkyō Vision* (Seattle: University of Washington Press, 2009), especially the sections "The *Dharmakāya* Buddha: *Mikkyō* Representation and Ritual," 34–36, and "*Mikkyō* Visuality," 36–38, and chapter 2, "A Religion of Images," 40–51.

6 Buijnsters, "Jichihan," 69. See also Jacqueline I. Stone, "The Secret Art of Dying: Esoteric Deathbed Practices in Heian Japan," in *The Buddhist Dead*, ed. Bryan Cuevas and Jacqueline I. Stone (Honolulu: University of Hawai'i Press, 2007), 134–174, especially 151. On the "double logic" in Kakuban's thought on Pure Land practice, see ibid., 155 onward.

7 English translation slightly modified from Dale A. Todaro, trans., "The Illuminating Secret Commentary on the Five Cakras and the Nine Syllables," in *Shingon Texts*, BDK English Tripitaka 98 (Numata Center for Buddhist Translation and Research, 2004), 257–328; here p. 311.

8 Jacqueline Stone has previously translated this term as "Pure Land of Esoteric Splendor." See Stone, "The Secret Art of Dying," 166 note 33.

9 *T.* 2346.77: 510c19–20.

10 *Mikkyō Daijiten*, 2107.

11 This treatise was attributed to the Indian master Nāgārjuna, while its Chinese translation is traditionally ascribed to Amoghavajra, one of the key figures in the development of Esoteric Buddhist tradition in East Asia. *T.* 1665.32: 574c20–22. 若歸本則是密嚴國土不起于座能成一切事。讃菩提心曰若人求佛慧通達菩提心父母所生身速證大覺位。All translations are mine unless otherwise stated.

12 Yet another term that proved meaningful and appealed to the medieval Japanese Buddhists was *mitsugon kaie* 密厳海會 (secretly adorned ocean-assembly). Kakuban's precedessor at Ninnaji, Saisen, first employed it in his notes on the *Mahavairocana sutra* (*T.* 2215); after him, it is mostly encountered in medieval Shingon commentaries on Yixing's *Darijing shu*, including the one penned by Kakuban's follower, the Negoroji monk Raiyu 頼瑜 (1226–1304) (*T.* 2217).

13 On Kūkai's systematization of Shingon doctrine and practice, see the classic study by Abé Ryūichi, *The Weaving of Mantra: Kūkai and the Construction of Esoteric Buddhist Discourse* (New York: Columbia University Press, 1999). On Annen's contribution to this process, see Lucia Dolce and Shin'ya Mano, "Godai'in Annen," in *Esoteric Buddhism and the Tantras in East Asia*, ed. Charles D. Orzech, Henrik H. Sørensen, and Richard K. Payne (Leiden: Brill, 2011), 768–775.

14 See, for example, Annen's *Shingonshū kyōjigi* (On the meaning of doctrine in Shingon School, *T.* 2396.75: 404b11–12).

15 Annen, *Taizō kongō bodaishingi ryaku mondōshō* (Short questions and answers on the principle of acquiring the mind aspiring for enlightenment through the Womb-store and Diamond Realms, *T.* 2397.75: 0480b13–18). 是眞言門初心凡夫初住菩薩後身菩薩佛地内證三摩地菩提心功用云々。此文云密嚴者是妙覺實報淨土。

16 See Robert F. Rhodes, chap. I.4.

17 See *T.* 2519.79: 0033c02–05.

18 Gorai Shigeru, *Kōya hijiri*, rev. ed. (Tokyo: Kadokawa shoten, 2005 [1975]), 71–73.

19 Gorai, *Kōya hijiri*, 98–105. Gorai also posits that the *hijiri* based at various "separate halls" (*bessho*) may have been one factor that played role in Kakuban's rise to prominence at Mount Kōya. Ibid., 106–114.

20 Anna Andreeva, *Assembling Shinto: Buddhist Approaches to Kami Worship in Medieval Japan* (Cambridge, MA: Harvard University Asia Center, 2017), chap. 3, "Miwa *Bessho*," 105–140.

21 *Mikkyō Daijiten*, 2194.

22 Anna Andreeva, "The Origins of the Miwa Lineage," in special issue "Rethinking Medieval Shintō," ed. Michael Como, Bernard Faure, and Nobumi Iyanaga, *Cahiers d'Extrême-Asie* 16 (2006–2007): 71–90, and more recently, Anna Andreeva, "'Lost in the Womb': Conception, Reproductive Imagery, and Gender in the Writings and Rituals of Japan's Medieval Holy Men," in *Transforming the Void: Embryological Discourse and Reproductive Imagery in East Asian Religions*, ed. Anna Andreeva and Dominic Steavu (Leiden: Brill, 2016), 420–478. See also note 20 above.

23 *Kakugenshō*, by Hōkyō Rendōbō, in *Shingonshū Zensho* [Complete collection of works of the Shingon School] (Kōyachō, Wakayamaken: Zoku shingonshū zensho kankōkai, 1977), 36:325–391.

24 For references to *mitsugon kezō jōdo* and *myō jōdo*, see, for example, *Kakugenshō*, *Shingonshū zensho*, 36:354–355. For the passage translated above, see ibid., 328. 菩提心論已一切衆生於心質中有一分浄性乃至輪廻六道無有變易。實開即事而真當位即妙之悟。顕我身心蓮華臺之教。去西方浄土己身妙蓮。都率内院自心雲閣、密厳華蔵自心自得浄土。

25 *T.* 2533.79: 122c23–26. 以此印言加持時。穢土草庵變成密嚴淨土。行者凡身即成佛體也。印即理智不二印明。又三身三寶等具足言也。

26 See *T.* 2681. 84: 13c03, where Takua attributes this term to the Shingon discourse.

27 On the contents of this encyclopedia, see Alan Grapard, "*Keiranshūyōshū*: A Different Perspective on Mt. Hiei in the Medieval Period," in *Re-Visioning "Kamakura" Buddhism*, ed. Richard K. Payne (Honolulu: University of Hawai'i Press, 1998), 55–69; or in Japanese, Tanaka Takako 田中貴子, *Keiranshūyōshū no sekai* [The world of the *Keiranshūyōshū*] (Nagoya: Nagoya daigaku shuppan, 2003).

28 The character *shin* 心 has been translated variously as the "heart" or "mind." The former reading is linked with the Sanskrit term *hṛdaya* meaning the "core," "heart" (both physical and symbolic), or "center." I adopt here the term "mind," as it best fits the meditative nature of Kakuban's writing. In many Esoteric commentaries after Kakuban, however, Esoteric practitioners often seem to imply the former meaning, especially in conjunction with the expressions such as "flesh ball in eight parts" (*hachibun nikudan* 八分肉団) or "eight-petal heart-lotus" (*hachiyō shinren* 八葉心蓮).

29 The dharma realm, the origins of all things.

30 That is, manifesting themselves in their stronger and weaker aspects.

31 The three bodies of the Buddha, namely the *dharmakāya* (*hosshin* 法身, the dharma body), the *saṃbhogakāya* (*hōshin* 報身, the reward body), and the *nirmāṇakāya* (*ōshin* 應身, the response or corresponding body).

32 That is to say, the very nature of this Esoteric pure land is to raise the potential for Buddhist enlightenment.

33 The mind aspiring for enlightenment.

34 According to the Hindu mythology, the *kalpavrikṣa* or *kalpataru* tree (*kōhaju* 劫跛樹) is a divine tree of life in Indra's garden that bears various fruits in different seasons.

35 The term *gozō zen* could be also possibly be understood as a meditation on the "five organs," which Kakuban described in his *Gorin kujimyo himitsushaku* (Secret treatise on the Five Wheels and Nine Syllables, *T.* 2514).

36 The ten stages of mind aspiring for enlightenment, as described in the *Mahāvairocana sūtra* (*Dari jing*, *Dainichikyō*, *T.* 848) and the subsequent Chinese and Japanese commentaries on it. In Heian Japan, the fundamentals of this concept were explained in the *Himitsu mandara jūjūshinron* (A treatise on the ten stages of mind aspiring for enlightenment according to the Secret Maṇḍalas, ca. 830, *T.* 2425), by the founder of Esoteric Buddhist tradition, the Shingon monk Kūkai (774–835).

37 *Yuru* 一如, *ichinyo*. Reality-nature, the essential principle of all existences.

38 *Gosō jōjinkan* 五相成身観, the fivefold meditation on achieving the body of Mahāvairocana as manifested in the Diamond Realm (Kongōkai).

39 In Esoteric doctrine, these "three equals" could be understood as "the principles of the three karmic agents of the body, the speech, and the mind, that are equal." This is explained in the *Mahāvairocana sūtra* (*Dari jing, Dainichi kyō*, *T.* 848); see, for instance, *T.* 848.18: 42b18–25, or *Mikkyō Daijiten*, 817 and 819.

40 The grammar here is unclear as the Taishō Daizōkyō version of this text reads "*koko ni dezu*"不出此, "does not come outside here." See *T.* 2515.79: 23b01.

41 The text here reads as follows: *hōben shūgi wo nasu, zenkō ha shoraku wo totonoeru* 方便作衆妓。善巧調諸樂. This phrase alludes to a set expression *zenkō hōben* 善巧方便, which means "to employ both expedient means and benevolent guidance in propagating the Buddhist teachings and saving sentient beings from ignorance and karmic debt, each according to their individual capacity."

42 *Hachiku* 八供, the eight bodhisattvas presenting the inner and outer offerings to Mahāvairocana (Dainichi) within the Diamond Realm Maṇḍala (the Kongōkai). The four inner offerings (*naiku* 内供) are performed by the bodhisattvas Joy, Garland, Song, and Dance; the four outer offerings (*geku* 外供) by the bodhisattvas of incense, flowers, lanterns, and unguent oil.

43 One of the thirty-two marks of the Buddha.

44 A measure of length. One *sun* is approximately 3.03 cm.

45 The four aspects in each phenomenon are emergence, development, change, and demise.

46 The four *maṇḍalas*, including the "great" (*dai* 大, or *maka* 摩訶), the *samādhi* (*sanmaya* 三摩耶), the "dharma" (*hō* 法), and the "karma" (*katsuma* 羯磨) *maṇḍalas* said to derive from the enlightened mind of Mahāvairocana and manifest the four aspects of different dharmas. *Mikkyō Daijiten*, 1024–1026.

47 The four female bodhisattvas giving birth to the Buddhas Akṣobhya (Ashuku), Ratnasamḫbhava (Hōshō), Amida, and Śākyamuni (Shaka).

48 The original sentence uses the term *manda* 曼荼, which can also be translated as a phonetic rendition of "*maṇḍala*." Since the sentence focuses on the description of voices, however, the "mantra" would be a far more appropriate translation here.

## Bibliography

### Primary Sources

*Kakugenshō*. By Hōkyō Rendōbō (active ca. 1200–1235). In *Shingonshū zensho* [Complete collection of works of the Shingon School], 36:325–391. Kōyachō, Wakayama-ken: Zoku shingonshū zensho kankōkai, 1977.

*Mikkyō Daijiten*, the abridged edition, edited by Mikkō jiten hensankai. Kyoto: Hōzōkan, 2007.

*Shingonshū zensho* [Complete collection of works of the Shingon School], 42 vols. Kōyachō, Wakayama-ken: Zoku shingonshū zensho kankōkai, 1977.

### Secondary sources

Abé Ryūichi. *The Weaving of Mantra: Kūkai and the Construction of Esoteric Buddhist Discourse*. New York: Columbia University Press, 1999.

Andreeva, Anna. *Assembling Shinto: Buddhist Approaches to Kami Worship in Medieval Japan*. Cambridge, MA: Harvard University Asia Center, 2017.

———. "'Lost in the Womb': Conception, Reproductive Imagery, and Gender in the Writings and Rituals of Japan's Medieval Holy Men." In *Transforming the Void: Embryological Discourse and Reproductive Imagery in East Asian Religions*, edited by Anna Andreeva and Dominic Steavu, 420–478. Leiden: Brill, 2016.

———. "The Origins of the Miwa Lineage." In special issue "Re-thinking Medieval Shintō," edited by Michael Como, Bernard Faure, and Nobumi Iyanaga, *Cahiers d'Extrême-Asie* 16 (2006–2007): 71–90.

Bogel, Cynthea J. *With a Single Glance: Buddhist Icon and Early Mikkyō Vision*. Seattle: University of Washington Press, 2009.

Buijnsters, Marc. "Jichihan and the Restoration and Innovation of Buddhist Practice." *Japanese Journal of Religious Studies* 26, no. 1/2 (1999): 39–82.

Dolce, Lucia. "The Embryonic Generation of the Perfect Body: Ritual Embryology from Japanese Tantric Sources." In *Transforming the Void: Embryological Discourse and Reproductive Imagery in East Asian Religions*, edited by Anna Andreeva and Dominic Steavu, 253–310. Leiden: Brill, 2016.

Dolce, Lucia, and Shin'ya Mano. "Godai'in Annen." In *Esoteric Buddhism and the Tantras in East Asia*, edited by Charles D. Orzech, Henrik H. Sørensen, and Richard K. Payne, 768–775. Handbook of Oriental Studies, Leiden: Brill, 2011.

Drummond, Donald. "Looking Back and Leaping Forward: Constructing Lineage in the Shingi Shingon Tradition of Japan." In *Esoteric Buddhism and the Tantras in East Asia*, edited by Charles D. Orzech et al., 815–826. Handbook of Oriental Studies, Leiden: Brill, 2011.

Gorai Shigeru. *Kōya hijiri*. Revised edition. Tokyo: Kadokawa shoten, 2005 [1975].

Grapard, Alan. "*Keiranshūyōshū*: A Different Perspective on Mt. Hiei in the Medieval Period." In *Re-Visioning "Kamakura" Buddhism*, edited by Richard K. Payne, 55–69. Honolulu: University of Hawai'i Press, 1998.

Rambelli, Fabio. "Tantric Buddhism and Chinese Thought in East Asia." In *Tantra in Practice*, edited by David G. White, 361–380. Princeton, NJ: Princeton University Press, 2000.

Stone, Jacqueline I. "The Secret Art of Dying: Esoteric Deathbed Practices in Heian Japan." In *The Buddhist Dead*, edited by Bryan Cuevas and Jacqueline I. Stone, 134–174. Honolulu: University of Hawai'i Press, 2007.

Tanaka Takako. *Keiranshūyōshū no sekai* [The world of the *Keiranshūyōshū*]. Nagoya: Nagoya daigaku shuppan, 2003.

Todaro, Dale A., trans. "The Illuminating Secret Commentary on the Five Cakras and the Nine Syllables." In *Shingon Texts*, BDK English Tripitaka 98, 257–328. Numata Center for Buddhist Translation and Research, 2004.

## Chapter 3

# Akṣobhya *Homa*

## *Fire Offerings for the Buddha of the Eastern Pure Land*

Richard K. Payne

### Translator's Introduction

Before considering the *homa* ritual manual translated below, we introduce the figure of Akṣobhya and discuss the historical relation between Akṣobhya and Amitābha, including the contrasting characteristics of their respective pure lands. Viewing the two buddhas as cultic figures means theorizing the concept of cult, and since the ritual considered is part of the Shingon tantric ritual corpus, the character of tantric thought and the pantheon of Shingon are also discussed.

## The Importance of Akṣobhya

Akṣobhya does not appear to have had any particularly significant following in East Asia. Despite this, he is important for our understanding of early Mahāyāna and the Indian development of Pure Land Buddhisms. Jan Nattier called attention to this importance in her pioneering essay "The Realm of Akṣobhya."[1] She noted that when she wrote that essay there was a paucity of study of Akṣobhya.[2] With three exceptions—Ingo Strauch's "More Missing Pieces of Early Pure Land Buddhism,"[3] Diwakar Acharya's "Evidence for Mahāyāna Buddhism and Sukhāvatī Cult in India in the Middle Period,"[4] and Charles Willemen's "Early Yogācāra and Visualization (*Bhāvanā*),"[5]—the situation has changed little since Nattier's evaluation in 2000.[6]

For the study of Pure Land Buddhism there are two aspects of Akṣobhya that are particularly significant: establishing points in the continuity of the development of Pure Land praxis; and the differences between the conception of Abhirati, the pure land of Akṣobhya, and

Sukhāvatī, the pure land of Amitābha. Looking more specifically at the question of how to think about praxis related to such figures in early Mahāyāna, we focus on the concept of cult. From this perspective the Akṣobhya *homa* translated below is one part of the corpus of cultic activities focused on figures from the Buddhist pantheon.

## *Continuum of Pure Land Development*

Nattier argued that representations of Amitābha and Sukhāvatī as unique and exceptional developments in the history of Indian Buddhism have served to disjoin this strain of Pure Land Buddhism from the rest of Mahāyāna.[7] Doing so has led to the not uncommon problem that Amitābha Pure Land praxis appears to many scholars—and their students—as something anomalous in comparison to the rest of the Buddhist tradition, that it is not "really" Buddhism.[8] A history of exceptionalist representations of Amitābha Pure Land as discontinuous from earlier forms, or as unique in contrast with the rest of the Buddhist tradition, reinforces the understanding that there is a gap between Pure Land and the rest of the Buddhist tradition.[9] This disjunction has been reified by explanations referencing Near Eastern solar cults or other influences extraneous to Buddhist tradition itself. Nattier suggests instead "a radically new way of understanding the emergence of so-called 'Pure Land' ideas in Indian Buddhism. No longer do these paradise-like realms appear as a concession to the needs of an under-achieving laity, much less as evidence for the incorporation of foreign (e.g., Iranian) or non-Buddhist (e.g., Hindu) ideas."[10] In Nattier's formulation, Pure Land conceptions are a logical development of ideas found in the Buddhist milieu in which Amitābha Pure Land praxis arose, specifically conceptions of what it means to be a bodhisattva who becomes a buddha.[11] The claim that there is necessarily only one buddha in any world-system at a time follows from the idea that a buddha, such as Śākyamuni, discovers the dharma in the absence of any other buddha from whom the dharma can be received.[12] If you learn from a buddha, you can be an arhat, but a buddha realizes awakening in isolation. Thus the logic of the path as described in mainstream Buddhist teachings means that for a bodhisattva to progress to being a buddha requires birth in a different world-system, which then becomes that buddha's realm. As Nattier summarized, "the existence of other Buddha-fields now appears as a logical necessity, elicited by the mainstream understanding of the requirements of the bodhisattva path itself. Whatever other factors in Indian culture at the time that might have contributed to this expanded vision of the cosmos, the idea of the bodhisattva path as a viable option for a small but significant minority within the Buddhist community virtually required that such a worldview be produced."[13]

Thus, placing Amitābha into a developmental sequence in which Akṣobhya is an earlier form of Pure Land praxis obviates the apparent disjunction between Pure Land Buddhism and "mainstream" Buddhism.[14] Instead of a sudden leap from early Buddhism to Pure Land Buddhism, "prior to the emergence of the belief in Amitābha several intermediate developments had taken place, and without a clear understanding of these prior stages the cultivation of devotion to Amitābha does indeed appear anomalous."[15] Acharya's investigation of fifth- and sixth-century inscriptions from Nepal similarly suggests a continuity, rather than the rupture many have seen between "mainstream" and Pure Land forms of Buddhism.[16]

Michael Radich has examined a specific dimension in which this continuity may be seen. The longevity and immortality of buddhas are motifs found in the late Pāli canonical period onwards.[17] He points out that Akṣobhya shares in the characteristic of longevity but eventually does enter *parinirvāṇa*, thus making way for another buddha to inherit his domain. Radich sees this as a kind of intermediary step toward the concept of buddhas who are characterized by immortality. "Extremely long life for cosmically remote Buddhas may thus be an earlier development than absolute immortality."[18] Such longevity also characterizes Amitābha and his successor, Avalokiteśvara. Avalokiteśvara's successor, Mahāsthāmaprāpta, however, does not enter *parinirvāṇa*, but is immortal.[19] In this particular instance, then, we see a specific characteristic in which there is continuity in the development from early Buddhist conceptions to Pure Land Buddhist conceptions.

Charles Willemen's examination of visualization texts from early Yogācāra also concludes that the order of development of the two is Akṣobhya first, with Amitābha as a response. Because of the closeness of his textual study, however, Willemen is able to fill in the steps in much greater detail, including the relation between the names Amitābha and Amitāyus. In his conclusion, Willemen proposes that

> Akṣobhya's Abhirati is of Gandhāran origin, to the east, and of Mahāsāṅghika affiliation. Amitābha's paradise is an immediate reaction to this development. It is of Bactrian origin, to the west, and of Sautrāntika Sarvāstivāda affiliation. Already in Kuṣāna times the two were combined in such texts as

> the *Karuṇāpuṇḍarīka*, and others. Amitābha's name may be explained as linked with the Gāndhāri for Ava(ābhā)lokitaśvara, as Dharmarakṣa's translations suggest. While the term Amitābha came to Luoyang and Chang'an via the Central Asian route, in southern China, in the fifth century, for example, the term Amitāyus is commonly used, and Daoist influence provides an explanation for this. Due to the prestige of Kumārajīva and Xuanzang, the term Amitābha became predominant in China during the Tang.[20]

In addition to providing a more continuous history than that of "Amitābha exceptionalism," adding Akṣobhya to the discussion also expands conceptions of what the concept "pure land" means.

## A Different Conception of Pure Land

This collection attempts to further Nattier's suggestion that the idea of a buddha pure land serves to identify a meaningful domain for understanding the history and development of Buddhist praxis. In this regard, it is worth noting some of the salient differences between Abhirati, the pure land of Akṣobhya, and Sukhāvatī, that of Amitābha. Tai-wo Kwan notes that the mythic northern country, Uttarakuru, serves as the model for Abhirati.[21] But "[a]lthough the pure land Abhirati resembles the Northern Country, especially with regard to the favorable conditions which endow people with freedom from want as well as from fear, Abhirati is a pure buddha land where people make conscious and rigorous effort to achieve what they consider most valuable."[22] Kwan sees a contrast between Abhirati as reflecting a rural ideal and Sukhāvatī as reflecting an urban one. "While the [*Akṣobhyavyūha*] takes a rural setting as the ideal condition of pure land and praises individual and ascetic mode of practice, the *Sukhāvatīvyūha*, in which the pure land of Buddha Amitābha is described, favors a pure land in which the social and cultic mode of practice is especially appropriate."[23] Kwan concludes that the practitioners portrayed as inhabiting Abhirati are forest dwellers, *aranya*,[24] which distinguishes them from the devotees who, born in Sukhāvatī, gaze upon the triad of Amitābha, Avalokiteśvara, and Mahāsthāmaprāpta.

The single most significant difference between Abhirati and Sukhāvatī is the difference between the two as goals for practitioners. The excellent qualities of Sukhāvatī are offered as a postmortem goal for anyone, birth there being placed within reach of anyone who can formulate ten thoughts of Amitābha.[25] The case with Abhirati is strikingly different. While the two realms are comparable in their excellent qualities, Nattier notes that "[c]ontrary to what we might expect, the sūtra does not use these attractive qualities . . . to encourage rank-and-file Buddhists to look forward to rebirth in Abhirati. Instead the delightful features of that land are marshaled to elicit a very different response: bodhisattvas are urged to study and emulate Akṣobhya's conduct so that they will eventually obtain such a world for themselves."[26] Sukhāvatī is represented in the sutras as a "karmic transit zone"[27] on the way to full awakening. In contrast Abhirati serves as an encouragement to bodhisattvas to pursue full buddhahood, encouragement that is needed because of the rigors of the bodhisattva path.[28]

In order to provide a general conception of what makes a pure land distinct from other realms in the Buddhist cosmos, Nattier suggests that pure lands are marked by the presence of a Buddha who teaches. "The essential feature of a Pure Land is thus not its physical attributes, lovely as they may be, but the opportunity to live in the presence of a Buddha."[29] This runs counter to many traditional discussions of what makes for a pure land, which themselves often define a pure land in contrast to this *sahā* world, which contains the three lower destinies—hungry ghosts, animals, and hell beings—while pure lands do not.

## Two Cults

This kind of interpretation seems to be at the base of Kwan's discussion regarding the relation between the two cults.[30] He suggests that since Abhirati is described as an ideal location for the pursuit of awakening in forests, the *Akṣobhyavyūha* would seem to have been directed more toward monastic Buddhists who might have themselves wished to pursue a more strenuous program of training as a forest dweller (*araññavāsi*).[31] The descripton of Sukhāvatī as an idealized parkland may suggest that Amitābha as portrayed in the *Sukhāvatīvyūha* is more oriented toward an urbanized audience. In this regard he suggests that the "unlimited and indescribable" pleasures ascribed to Sukhāvatī "would appeal to an audience whose desire for heavenly enjoyments is greater than their aspiration towards perfect enlightenment."[32] In the absence of other evidence, however, such associations remain speculative.[33]

Cult also gives us a way of thinking about similarities and differences in terms of practice rather than doctrine. These are clearly two different cults. Kwan tells us, for example, that although Akṣobhya and Abhirati are mentioned in the eight-thousand-line Prajñāpāramitā sutra (*Aṣṭasāhasrikāprajñāramitā sūtra*, *T.* 224, Lokakṣema translation, 179 CE), neither

Amitābha nor Sukhāvatī are. Likewise, the Akṣobhyavyūha sutra itself makes no mention of either Amitābha or Sukhāvatī. This is particularly striking given Sukhāvatī's later status as a "generalized religious goal" in Mahāyāna.[34] Kwan also tells us that the earliest Sukhāvatī sutra does not mention Akṣobhya. He considers this a puzzle, since both "were devoted to advocating pure land teachings."[35] He proposes that the solution to this puzzle is either geographic or chronological, preferring the geographic.

Thinking about this textual situation in terms of cults, however, allows us to see the extent to which this is a pseudo-problem. There is no "pure land teaching" that both texts are referring to and attempting to promote. Instead, we have two distinct cults, both of which employ the idea that the main buddha has his own pure buddha-land. Both are working with materials in their religious milieux, which includes the idea of a pure buddha-land, but they are only representatives of some broader "pure land teaching" when viewed retrospectively.

## Metonymic Character of Tantra

While not definitive, a characteristic of tantric praxis generally is that it is metonymic, that is, associative,[36] synthetic, or even synoptic. While individual cults were focused on specific deities, tantric practitioners often seem to be intent upon accumulating initiations into many such practices, which means conversely that there is no particular sense of exclusivity of affiliation. Admittedly speculatively, we might see the desire then to bring several such cults together into a more systematic formation, such as the *maṇḍala*. As Ronald Davidson has argued, the model for such a systematization is the political system of medieval India,[37] but the specific contents may well have been provided by pre-existing cults, such as those of Akṣobhya and Amitābha, particularly given their preexisting directional associations.

## Shingon Pantheon of Cult Figures

Specific practices, such as the *homa*, are themselves semiautonomous; that is, they can move between different doctrinal, lineal, and cultic contexts. What we find in contemporary Shingon is a plethora of different cults employing fundamentally the same ritual technologies, such as the *homa*, and understood as referring to individual figures found in the two *maṇḍalas* of the tradition: the *garbhakośadhātu maṇḍala* and the *vajradhātu maṇḍala*. For example, different temples have different main deities, sometimes reflected in the temple's name, and the different locations in the *maṇḍala* of such deities serves to also establish the relative ranking of temples. The pantheon was probably formulated in medieval India, systematized and then transmitted to China and on to Japan, along with the texts and ritual technologies. At each stage additional systematization contributed to the two *maṇḍala* forms we know today, such as the "well" pattern found in the *vajradhātu maṇḍala*. Each of the many figures of these *maṇḍala*s can be seen as at least potential cult deities. The *homa* manual translated below is a modern text, and therefore does not indicate that the cult of Akṣobhya was in some sense a single enduring entity across the centuries from medieval India to modern Japan. It is instead an instance of the endurance of cultic creativity within tantric Buddhism, drawing together a deity, Akṣobhya, and a ritual practice, the *homa*, to create a ritual form in the service of the cult of Akṣobhya.

## *Ashuku soku sai goma shiki shidai, Chūin*—Ritual Manual for the Protective Fire Offering Devoted to Akṣobhya, Chūin Lineage

The ritual manual translated here is for a tantric fire ritual (*homa*, *goma*) that is performed for protection (*śāntika*, *soku sai*). This kind of *homa* appears to be the most commonly performed in contemporary Japan. Also, the final of the four rituals that constitute the main part of the training of a Shingon priest is a protective *homa*. The main deity evoked in the training *homa* is Acalanātha Vidyārāja, the Immovable Lord of Wisdom, known in Japanese as Fudō Myōō (不動明王). Since the *Fudō soku sai goma* is one of the four training rituals, the protective form of the *homa* can be understood to function paradigmatically for all *homa*s a priest might engage in later. The *homa* manual translated here takes as its chief deity Akṣobhya, known in Japanese as Ashuku (阿閦), the Buddha of the Eastern Pure Land.

In this *homa*, as in most contemporary Shingon *homa*s, there are five sets of offerings made. The first is to Agni, the Vedic fire god who is almost invariably the first deity evoked in the *homa*s of the Shingon tradition. This is followed by a set of offerings to the Lord of the Assembly, a figure that, like the Chief Deity, can vary from *homa* to *homa*. In this case the Lord of the Assembly is Mahāvairocana of the Vajradhātu.

The central set of offerings is to Akṣobhya, who is the chief deity of this ritual. These are followed by sets of offerings to the bodhisattvas accompanying Akṣobhya, surrounding him in the *maṇḍala*, and to a set of Vedic deities and astral groupings. These five sets of offerings are structured similarly to one another. This systematic structure is also evidenced by the fact that the offerings prescribed here are to be embedded in a longer ritual. The only indication of this embedding found in the instructions themselves is the first line's reference to "the additional recitations." This refers to a particular point in the full ritual at which these offerings would be embedded. In public performances, the portion of the ritual preceding the start of the *homa* offerings per se—that is, where this manual begins—can be and apparently often is performed at some earlier time, perhaps the day before. Thus, for the observer, the ritual begins and ends with the actions prescribed here.

## Translation

### RITUAL MANUAL FOR THE PROTECTIVE FIRE OFFERING DEVOTED TO AKṢOBHYA, CHŪIN LINEAGE

First, following the additional recitations, hang the rosary on the left wrist, throughout the *homa*.

Next, empowerment of Mahāvairocana: form the wisdom fist *mudrā*, recite the mantra

ON BAZARA DATO BAN

[oṃ vajradhātu vaṃ]

Next, empowerment of the chief deity, outer fist, extend the two inner fingers like the point of a needle.

ON AKISYUBYA UN

[oṃ akṣobhya huṃ]

Next, visualize the three identities using the *dharmadhātu* meditation *mudrā*. Contemplate the following: the heart of the Tathāgata is identical with what actually exists, what actually exists is identical with the fire of wisdom; the hearth is identical with the body of the Tathāgata, the fire is identical with the Dharmakāya fire of wisdom; the mouth of the hearth is identical with the mouth of the Tathāgata; the fire is nothing other than the wisdom within the practitioner's body. Thus, the mouth of the Tathāgata's body, the mouth of the body of the hearth, and the mouth of the practitioner's body are all three the same.

Next, empower the poppy seeds.

Take the censer and place it in the left corner of the altar.

Next, take the bowl of poppy seeds from the left table and place it where the censer had been; empower using the single-pronged vajra, reciting the mantra of the Fire Realm seven times (there is an oral instruction: recite the single syllable chant twenty-one times); at the end scatter the poppy seed to the four directions, to the four corners, above and below, with the right hand. Beginning from the northeast corner, recite the chant of the Fire Realm once for each of the directions, throwing a total of ten times. Then return the bowl to its original location.

[1] The first section, for Agni.
Start with Agni's *mudrā* and name.

Grasp the right wrist with the left hand; bend the thumb of the right hand, placing it in the middle of the palm; the remaining fingers extend straight out. Empower the four places,

ON AGYANAU EI SENJIKYA SOWAKA
[oṃ agnaye śāntika svāhā]

Next, take the rosary and recite the short Agni mantra one hundred eight times.
Next, take the ball incense, chip incense, and flowers, placing them in order beside the hearth.
Next, take the vajra bell and place it where the ball incense had been on the left table.
Next, take the three-pronged vajra and hold it in the left hand.
Next, take the powdered incense and *puja* offerings from the right table and then place them beside the hearth.
Next, untie the string around the twenty-one pieces of sapwood, turn the base toward the practitioner and place on the vajra plate. Throw the string into the hearth.[38]
Next, take the pincers and insert the offering wood, piling it up in the hearth in sequence. From the orientation of the practitioner, in sequence from left to right place six sticks in line; eleven sticks total.
Next, with the pincers, insert a piece of pine into the flame of the lamp on the right and place it under the right corner of the firewood.
Next, take the fan and fan the flames.

Hold the fan partially open in the right hand, recite the mantra and fan three times; imagine a syllable KAN [*hāṃ*] on the surface of the fan; it changes, becoming a wind cakra, recite

ON BOKU JINBARA UN
[oṃ bhūḥ jvala hūṃ], three times.

Next, purification.

Sprinkle the wood in the hearth three times, sprinkle directly, the *kili kili* chant [ON KIRI KIRI BAZARA UN HATTA (oṃ kili kili vajra huṃ phaṭ)].

Next, empower the firewood on the hearth.

Using the three-pronged vajra, the *kili kili* chant three times.

Next, invite Agni.

First, visualize one's own body.

Form Amitābha's meditation *mudrā* [lit. *samādhi añjali*]. Visualize a syllable RAN [raṃ] above your heart moon cakra; this changes, becoming a triangular fire cakra. Your entire body becomes this fire cakra; the fire cakra changes, becoming the white body of the four-armed Agni, blazing flames completely surrounding his body; this is the great body of the vast *dharmadhātu*.

Next, empower oneself.

Form the *mudrā* of Agni, recite the short chant, adding the phrase of propitiation: SENJIKYA SOWAKA [śāntika svāhā]; empower the four actions.

Next, request Agni into the hearth.

Take one flower, the short chant of Agni three times, place it on top of the firewood in the hearth.

Next, visualize Agni in the middle of the hearth.

Form Amida's meditation *mudrā*. Visualize the flower going to the middle of the hearth, becoming a lotus leaf seat, over which is a syllable RAN [*raṃ*], which changes, becoming a wish-fulfilling jar; the wish-fulfilling jar changes, becoming the body of Agni, white in color, complete with four arms. His first right hand bestows fearlessness, his second holds a rosary. His first left hand grasps a sage's staff, his second grasps a water bottle. Blazing flames surround his body.

Next, request Agni to arise from the *maṇḍala*.

Form Agni's *mudrā* and recite his mantra, beckon three times with the wind finger. Next, form and recite the *mudrā* and mantra of the four wisdoms: recite

ON AGYANAU EI SENJIKYA EI KEI KI JYAKU UN BAN KOKU SOWAKA
[oṃ agnaye śāntika ehyehi jaḥ hūṃ baṃ hoḥ svāhā]

Next, contemplation.

Form Amida's meditation *mudrā*. Imagine inviting Agni, located in his original place in the *maṇḍala*, to mysteriously unite with the Agni in the hearth, forming a single body, not two.

Next, declaration, ring the gong.

"Only desiring that Agni descend to this seat
and compassionately accept this marvelous *homa* offering."

Next, rinse the mouth.

Sprinkle directly three times, imagine washing the mouth of Agni,

ON BARADA BAZARA DAN

[oṃ varada vajra dhaṃ]

Next, declaration, ring the gong.

"Sincerely offering perfumed water for rinsing the mouth,
only requesting that Agni accept this *homa*,
protect his disciple, and perfect *siddhi*."

Next, powdered incense, three times

ON AGYANAU EI SENJIKYA SOWAKA
[oṃ agnaye śāntika svāhā] each time.

Next, contemplation: form meditation *mudrā*. Imagine the incense entering Agni's mouth, going to the lotus blossom of his heart, becoming excellent offerings. Limitless, ocean-like clouds of powdered incense flow from his heart, through his body and out his pores, offered to all the buddhas, bodhisattvas, solitary enlightened ones [*pratyekabuddhas*], auditors [*śrāvakas*], and worldly deities.

Next, declaration, ring the gong.

"I now present the powdered incense offering,
only requesting that Agni accept this *homa*,
protect his disciple, and perfect *siddhi*."

Next, ghee.

Large and small ladles three times each; chant, visualization, and declaration as with the powdered incense; same with the sap wood and following; except contemplate "limitless ocean-like clouds of ghee flow out," and so on; change declaration to "ghee offering."

Next, sap wood.

Three pieces, "limitless, ocean-like clouds of pieces of wood flow out," and so on; "pieces of wood for the *homa*."

Next, food.

Three ladles, "limitless, ocean-like clouds of food offerings flow out," and so on; "food offering."

Next, five cereals.

Three ladles, "limitless, ocean-like clouds of the five cereals flow out," and so on; "five cereals offering."

Next, flowers.

Three times, "limitless, ocean-like clouds of flower offerings flow out," and so on; "flower offering."

Next, ball incense.

Three ladles, "limitless, ocean-like clouds of ball incense flow out," and so on; "ball incense offering."

Next, chip incense.

Three times, "limitless, ocean-like clouds of chip incense flow out," and so on; "chip incense offering."

Next, ghee.

Large and small ladles one time each, "limitless, ocean-like clouds of ghee flow out," and so on; "ghee offering."

Next, recite the universal offering and the three powers, ring the gong.

Next, vows, ring the gong.

"Sincerely requesting, and only desiring that Agni
compassionately accept this *homa* offering,
protect his disciple, and perfect *siddhi*."

Next, rinse the mouth.

Sprinkle directly three times, recite

ON BARADA BAZARA DAN SENJIKYA SOWAKA
[oṃ varada vajra dhaṃ śantika svāḥā]

Imagine washing Agni's mouth.

Next, declaration, ring the gong.

"Sincerely offering perfumed water for rinsing the mouth
only requesting that Agni accept this *homa*,
protect his disciple, and perfect *siddhi*."

Next, leave taking.

Take one flower, recite the short chant of the fire world and throw it to the original location in the *maṇḍala*: the northeast corner of the altar.

Next, contemplation.

Form Amida's meditation *mudrā*, and imagine that this flower, arriving at its original location, becomes a lotus leaf seat.

Next, form Agni's *mudrā*.

Press the empty finger against the back of the water finger, which is curled down; extend the wind finger sharply, recite

ON AGYANAU EI SENJIKYA GESSYA GESSYA BOKU
[oṃ agnaye śāntika gaccha gaccha muḥ]

Next, contemplation.

Form Amida's meditation *mudrā*, and imagine Agni returns to his original location in the *maṇḍala* from the middle of the hearth.

Next, declaration, ring the gong.

"Solely requesting Agni return to his original seat."

With the above the first section, the portion for Agni, is finished.

[2] Second section, for the Lord of the Assembly, Vajradhātu Mahāvairocana.

First, purify the offerings.

Repeat three times, wash clockwise, the *kili kili* chant. Wash the various offerings.
Next, karma empowerment.
Empower the various offerings clockwise and counterclockwise three times each,
ON BAZARA KYARAMA KEN
[oṃ vajra karma khaṃ]
Next, rinse the mouth and empower.
Sprinkle clockwise three times. Imagine washing the mouth of the hearth, recite
ON BARADA BAZARA DAN
[oṃ varada vajra dhaṃ]
Next, empower the hearth: three times, using the three-pronged vajra, the *kili kili* chant.
Next, pile the kindling: four pieces.
Next, take a flaming piece of pine and insert it.
Next, take the fan and fan the fire.
Imagine the syllable KAN [*haṃ*] on the surface of the fan; it changes, becoming a wind cakra,
ON BOKU JINBARA UN
[oṃ bhūḥ jvala hūṃ], three times
Next, purification.
Sprinkle the wood in the hearth three times, sprinkle directly, the *kili kili* chant.
Next, empower the kindling on the hearth.
Using the three-pronged vajra, the *kili kili* chant three times.
Next, invite the Lord of the Assembly.
First, visualize one's own body.
Form Amida's meditation *mudrā*. Visualize the syllable BAN [*vaṃ*] in the middle of the heart moon cakra; this changes, becoming a five-cakra stupa; this changes becoming Vajradhātu Mahāvairocana Tathāgata, wearing the jeweled crown of the five wisdoms, and jeweled necklaces, his body upright, holding the wisdom fist *mudrā*, his legs crossed in lotus posture.
Next, empower oneself.
ON BAZARA DATO BAN SENJIKYA SOWAKA
[oṃ vajradhātu vaṃ śāntika svāhā]
Next, request the Lord of the Assembly enter into the hearth.
Hold one flower cluster with both hands, insert it with the flower-holding *mudrā*; recite the mantra of the Lord of the Assembly three times, empower, offer on top of the kindling and make the request.

Next, visualize in the middle of the hearth.

Form Amida's meditation *mudrā*.

Visualize the flower going to the center of the hearth, becoming a jeweled lotus flower bud, above the bud is the syllable BAN [*vaṃ*]; this changes, becoming Vajradhātu Mahāvairocana Tathāgata, wearing the jeweled crown of the five wisdoms, and jeweled necklaces, his body upright, holding the wisdom fist *mudrā*, his legs crossed in lotus posture.

Next, request the Lord of the Assembly out of the *maṇḍala* and into the hearth.

Make the outer five-pronged [vajra] *mudrā*, then the *mudrā* and mantra to summon the four [Embracing Wisdom Bodhisattvas], hooking the right head finger, repeat three times.

ON BAZARA DATO BAN SENJIKYA EI KEI KI JYAKU UN BAN KOKU SOWAKA

[oṃ vajradhātu vaṃ śāntika ehyehi jaḥ hūṃ baṃ hoḥ svāhā]

Next, request the entourage of the Lord of the Assembly to come out of the *maṇḍala*. Form the great hook *mudrā* and recite the mantra, at the proper place form the *mudrā* and add the mantra of the four embracing deities, recite

NAUMAKU SANMANDA BODANAN AKU SARABA TARA HARA CHIKATEI TATAGYATA KUSYA BOJI SYARIYA HARI HORAKYA SENJIKYA EI KEI KI JYAKU UN BAN KOKU SOWAKA

[namaḥ samanta buddhānāṃ āḥ sarvatrā apratihata tathāgata ankuṣa bodhicarya paripūraka śāntika ehyehi jaḥ hūṃ baṃ hoḥ svāhā]

Next, contemplation.

Form Amitābha's meditation *mudrā*.

Imagine inviting the Lord of the Assembly, located in his original place in the *maṇḍala*, mysteriously unite with the Lord of the Assembly in the hearth, forming a single body, not two.

Next, declaration; ring the gong.

"Only desiring the Lord of the Assembly descend to this seat
and compassionately accept this marvelous *homa* offering."

Next, rinse the mouth: sprinkle directly, three times; imagine washing the mouth of the Lord of the Assembly, recite

ON BARADA BAZARA DAN

[oṃ varada vajra dhaṃ]

Next, declaration; ring the gong.

"Sincerely presenting perfumed water for washing the mouth
solely requesting the Lord of the Assembly accept this *homa*,

protect his disciple, and perfect *siddhi*."
Next, powdered incense, three times, recite
ON BAZARA DATO BAN SENJIKYA SOWAKA
[oṃ vajradhātu vaṃ śāntika svāhā]
Next, contemplation.
Form Amitābha's meditation *mudrā*.

Imagine the incense entering the Lord of the Assembly's mouth, going to his heart's lotus flower bud, becoming excellent offerings. Limitless, ocean-like clouds of powdered incense flow from his heart, through his body and out his pores, and are offered to all the buddhas, bodhisattvas, *pratyekabuddhas*, *śravakas*, and worldly deities.

Next, declaration; ring the gong.
"I now present the powdered incense offering
only requesting the Lord of the Assembly accept this *homa*,
protect his disciple, and perfect *siddhi*."
Next, ghee.

Large and small ladles three times each; chant, visualization and declaration as with the powdered incense; same with the sap wood and following, except contemplate "limitless ocean-like clouds of ghee flowing out," and change declaration to "ghee offering."

Next, sap wood.

Three pieces: "limitless, ocean-like clouds of pieces of wood flow out," "pieces of wood for the *homa*."

Next, food offerings

Three ladles: "limitless, ocean-like clouds of food offerings flow out," "excellent offerings of food."

Next, five cereals.

Three ladles: "limitless, ocean-like clouds of the five cereals flow out," "excellent offering of the five cereals."

Next, ball incense.

Three times: "limitless, ocean-like clouds of ball incense flow out," "excellent offerings of ball incense."

Next, chip incense.

Three times: "limitless, ocean-like clouds of chip incense flow out," "excellent offerings of chip incense."

Next, ghee.

Large and small ladles one time each: "limitless, ocean-like clouds of ghee flow out," "excellent offerings of ghee."

Next, recite the universal offering and the three powers, ring the gong.
Next, vows, ring the gong.

"Sincerely requesting and only desiring the Lord of the Assembly compassionately accept this *homa* offering,
protect his disciple, and perfect *siddhi*."

Next, rinse the mouth.

Sprinkle directly, and imagine washing the mouth of the Lord of the Assembly,

ON BARADA BAZARA DAN
[oṃ varada vajra dhaṃ]

Next, declaration, ring the gong.

"Sincerely offering perfumed water for rinsing the mouth
only requesting the Lord of the Assembly accept this *homa*,
protect his disciple, and perfect *siddhi*."

Next leave taking.

Take one flower cluster, recite the mantra of the Lord of the Assembly three times, and throw it to its original location in the *maṇḍala*, the northeast corner.

Next, contemplation: form Amitābha's meditation *mudrā*, and imagine this flower arriving at its original location in the *maṇḍala* and becoming a jeweled lotus flower seat.

Next, form the *mudrā* and recite the mantra of the Lord of the Assembly. Imagine escorting the deities.

Make the outer five-pronged [vajra] *mudrā*, and recite the mantra of the Lord of the Assembly. With the appropriate phrase from the *mudrā* for escorting.

ON BAZARA DATO BAN SENJIKYA GESSYA GESSYA BOKU
[oṃ vajradhātu vaṃ śāntika gaccha gaccha muḥ]

Next, send off the entourage of the Lord of the Assembly.

Form the great hook *mudrā* and recite the mantra, adding the phrase of propitiation at the end,

NAUMAKU SANMANDA BODANAN AKU SARABA TARA HARA CHIKATEI TATAGYATA KUSYA BOJISYA HARYA HARI HORAKYA SENJIKA GESSYA GESSYA BOKU
[namaḥ samanta buddhānāṃ āḥ sarvatrā apratihata tathāgata ankuṣa bodhicarya paripuraka śāntika gaccha gaccha muḥ]

Next, contemplation.

Form Amitābha's meditation *mudrā*, and imagine the Lord of the Assembly returns to his original location in the *maṇḍala* from the middle of the hearth.

Next, declaration, ring the gong.

"Solely requesting the Lord of the Assembly return to his original seat."

With the above, the second section, the portion for the Lord of the Assembly, is finished.

[3] Third section, portion for the chief deity, Akṣobhya.
First, purify the offerings.
Repeat three times: wash clockwise, the *kili kili* chant. Wash the various offerings.
Next, karma empowerment.
Empower the various offerings clockwise and counterclockwise three times each,
ON BAZARA KYARAMU KEN
[oṃ vajra karma khaṃ]
Next, rinse the mouth and empower.
Sprinkle clockwise three times, imagine washing the mouth of the hearth,
ON BARADA BAZARA DAN [oṃ varada vajra dhaṃ]
Next, empower the hearth.
three times using the three-pronged vajra, the *kili kili* chant.
Next, pile the kindling, six pieces: set six pieces as offering.
Next, take a flaming piece of pine and insert it.
Next, take the fan and fan the fire.
Imagine the syllable KAN [haṃ] on the surface of the fan, it changes, becoming a wind cakra,
ON BOKU JINBARA UN [oṃ bhūh jvala hūṃ], three times.
Next, purification.
Sprinkle the wood in the hearth three times, sprinkle directly, the *kili kili* chant.
Next, empower the kindling on the hearth.
Using the three-pronged vajra, the *kili kili* chant three times.
Next, invite the chief deity.
First, visualize one's own body.
Form Amitābha's meditation *mudrā*.
Visualize the syllable UN [huṃ] above the heart moon cakra; changes, becoming a five-pronged vajra (five prongs horizontally, this stands above that [image]), changes becoming Akṣobhya Tathāgata [Ashu Nyōrai], left hand holding two corners of his *kesa* below his navel touching, right hand making the *mudrā* of touching the earth, in just as the same way as the founder did.
Next, empower oneself.

Earth touching *mudrā*, left hand five fingers extended, right hand covering over the knee (outer tight, two middle pointed like needles), empower the four places [on the body].

ON AKISYUBYA UN SENJIKYA SOWAKA

[oṃ akṣobhya huṃ śāntika svāhā]

Next, request the chief deity onto the kindling on the hearth.

Hold one flower cluster with the hands in the flower-holding *mudrā*, empower, the chief deity's mantra three times into the *mudrā*. Invite by placing the flower on top of the kindling.

Next, visualization in the center of the hearth.

Form Amitābha's meditation *mudrā*.

Visualize the flower going to the center of the hearth, becoming a jeweled lotus flower throne, above which is the syllable UN [*huṃ*]; it changes, becoming a five-pronged vajra (five prongs horizontally, this stands above that [image]), changes becoming Akṣobhya Tathāgata [Ashu Nyōrai], left hand holding two corners of his kesa below his navel touching, right hand making the *mudrā* of touching the earth, in just as the same way as the founder did.

Next, request the chief deity at the head of the *maṇḍala*-assembly into the hearth. Mantra of the chief deity, add the phrase of propitiation [*śāntika*] at the end; then form the four wisdoms *mudrā*, summoning three times with the right head finger, while reciting the four wisdoms mantra:

ON AKISYUBYA UN SENJIKYA EI KEI KI JAKU UN BAN KOKU SOWAKA

[oṃ akṣobhya huṃ śāntika eihyehi jaḥ uṃ baṃ hoḥ svāhā]

Next, contemplation.

Form Amitābha's meditation *mudrā*.

Imagine inviting the chief deity, located in his original location in the *maṇḍala*, to mysteriously unite with the chief deity in the hearth, becoming one body, not two.

Next declaration, ring the gong.

"Only desiring the chief deity descend to this seat
and compassionately accept this excellent *homa* offering."

Next, rinse the mouth: sprinkle directly three times, imagine washing the mouth of the chief deity, recite

ON BARADA BAZARA DAN

[oṃ varada vajra dhaṃ]

Next, declaration, ring the gong.

"Sincerely presenting perfumed water for washing the mouth
solely requesting the chief deity accept this *homa*,

protect his disciple, and perfect *siddhi*."

Next, powdered incense: three times,

ON AKISYUBYA UN SENJIKYA SOWAKA

[oṃ akṣobhya huṃ śāntika svāhā]

Next, contemplation.

Form Amitābha's meditation *mudrā*.

Imagine the incense entering the chief deity's mouth, going to the lotus flower bud of his heart, becoming excellent offerings; limitless, ocean-like clouds of powdered incense flow from his heart, through his body and out his pores, offered to all buddhas, bodhisattvas, pratyekabuddhas, śravakas, and worldly deities.

Next, declaration, ring the gong.

"I now present the powdered incense offering,
only requesting that the chief deity accept this *homa*,
protect his disciple, and perfect *siddhi*."

Next, ghee.

Large and small ladles three times each; chant, visualization and declaration as with the powdered incense; same with sap wood and following, except contemplate "limitless, ocean-like clouds of ghee flowing out," change declaration to "ghee offering."

Next, sap wood.

One hundred eight pieces: take three pieces at a time, put the ends into the ghee, turning the wood over, and offer up, chanting three times; burn thirty-six sets [of three] for a total of one hundred eight pieces. Throw the binding string into the middle of the hearth.[39] In the contemplation, "limitless, ocean-like clouds of pieces of wood flow out," in the declaration, change to "pieces of wood for the *homa*."

Next, food offerings.

Three ladles; "limitless, ocean-like clouds of food offerings flow out," "excellent offerings of food."

Next, five cereals.

Three ladles; "limitless, ocean-like clouds of the five cereals flow out," "excellent offerings of the five cereals."

Next, flowers.

Three times; "limitless, ocean-like clouds of flowers flow out," "excellent offerings of flowers."

Next, ball incense.

Three times; "limitless, ocean-like clouds of ball incense flow out," "excellent offerings of ball incense."

Next, chip incense.

Three times; "limitless, ocean-like clouds of chip incense flow out," "excellent offerings of chip incense."

Next, mixed offerings.

First, take the chip incense, put it into the flowers cup; next, take the ball incense, put it into the same cup; next, take the ball incense cup and put it on top of the chip incense cup; next, take the flowers cup and put it into the food offerings cup; next, put the flowers cup on top of the ball incense and chip incense cup; next, take the five cereals cup and put it into the food offerings cup and mix thoroughly; next, separate the two cups and divide evenly; next, return each cup to its original place.

Next, ghee.

Large and small ladles one time each; "limitless, ocean-like clouds of ghee flow out," "excellent offering of ghee."

Next, *mudrā* and mantra of universal offering, one repetition, adding the phrase of propitiation [*śāntika*] as usual; the two head fingers are jewel-shaped.

Next, sap wood.

Take six pieces together from the bundle of twenty-one, offer together into the hearth; "limitless, ocean-like clouds of pieces of wood flow out," "excellent wood for the *homa*."

Next, medicinal herbs.

Seven times: take the cup and place it where the censer had been; the offering done, return the cup to its original place: "limitless, ocean-like clouds of medicinal herbs flow out," "excellent offerings of medicinal herbs."

Next, *pūjā* offerings.

Take the cup and place it where the censer had been; holding the three-pronged vajra, take up the single-pronged vajra and empower with the Fudō one-syllable mantra

NAUMAKU SANMANḌA BAZARA DAN KAN SENJIKYA SOWAKA

[oṃ amṛtodbhava hūṃ phaṭ śāntika svāhā], twenty-one times.

Next, offer the mantra of the chief deity one hundred eight times—holding the rosary on the left, count one hundred eight times, recite

ON AKISYUBYA UN SENJIKYA SOWAKA

[oṃ akṣobhya huṃ śāntika svāhā]

Next, contemplation.

Form Amitābha's meditation *mudrā*.

Imagine these *pūjā* offerings enter the mouth of the chief deity, going to the lotus blossom of his heart, becoming vast numbers of brightly shining cakras; then from each and every one of his pores these brightly shining cakras flow out through the entirety of empty space; next, the various buddhas and bodhisattvas of the world, having received the *pūjā*, these brightly shining cakras return, entering one's own and the donor's heads; the evil consequences of greed, hatred and ignorance are completely erased from our bodies, the calamities and unhappiness caused by evil people and evil destinies are destroyed, vitality and lifespan increase, and peace and tranquility are attained.

Next, declaration, ring the gong.

"I now present *pūjā* offerings
only requesting that the chief deity accept this *homa*
protect his disciple, and perfect *siddhi*."

The offering finished, return the cup to its original location.

Next, recite the universal offering and the three powers, ring the gong.

Next, vows.

Put down the three-pronged vajra, rub the rosary and when finished make the pledge; ring the gong.

"Sincerely request and only asking the chief deity
compassionately accept this excellent *homa* offering,
protect his disciple, and perfect *siddhi*."

Next, take up the three-pronged vajra.

Next, rinse the mouth: sprinkle three times directly, and imagine washing the mouth of the chief deity, recite

ON BARADA BAZARA DAN
[oṃ varada vajra dhaṃ]

Next, declaration, ring the gong.

"Sincerely presenting perfumed water for washing the mouth
solely requesting that the chief deity accept this *homa*,
protect his disciple, and perfect *siddhi*."

Next, leave taking.

Holding one flower cluster, recite the mantra of the Chief Deity, throw to the northeast corner of the altar.

Next, contemplation.

Form Amitābha's meditation *mudrā*.

Imagine this flower arriving at its original position in the *maṇḍala*, becoming a jeweled lotus flower throne.

Next, form the *mudrā* and recite mantra of the Chief Deity, imagine escorting the deities. Extend the right head finger three times.

ON AKISYUBYA UN SENJIKYA GESSYA GESSYA BOKU
[oṃ akṣobhya huṃ śāntika gaccha gaccha *mūḥ*]

Next, contemplation.

Form Amitābha's meditation *mudrā*.

Imagine the chief deity returns from the middle of the hearth to his original location in the *maṇḍala*.

Next, declaration, ring the gong.

"Solely requesting that the chief deity return to his original seat."

With the above, the third section, the portion for the chief deity, is finished.

[4] Fourth section, portion for the various deities: the thirty-seven deities.

First, purification.

wash the various offerings three times, wash clockwise, the *kili kili* chant.

Next, karma empowerment.

Empower the various offerings, clockwise and counterclockwise three times each,

ON BAZARA KYARAMA KEN

[oṃ vajra karma khaṃ]

Next, rinse the mouth and empower: wash clockwise three times, and imagine washing the mouth of the hearth, recite

ON BARADA BAZARA DAN

[oṃ varada vajra dhaṃ]

Next, empower the hearth.

Three times, using the three-pronged vajra, the *kili kili* chant.

Next, pile the kindling, ten pieces: on top of a square of four, set six pieces in order from the left.

Next, order the offerings in place.

Next, take a flaming piece of pine and insert it.

Next, take the fan and fan the fire.

Imagine the syllable KAN [*haṃ*] on the surface of the fan, it changes becoming a wind cakra, recite

ON BOKU JINBARA UN

[oṃ bhūḥ jvala hūṃ], three times.

Next, purification.

Sprinkle the wood in the hearth three times, sprinkle directly, the *kili kili* chant.

Next, empower the kindling on the hearth.

Using the three-pronged vajra, empower by reciting the *kili kili* chant three times.

Next, invite the various deities.

First, visualize one's own body.

Form Amitābha's meditation *mudrā*.

Visualize the five syllables BAN, UN, TARAKU, KIRIKU, AKU [vāṃ, hūṃ, trāḥ, hrīḥ, aḥ] above the heart moon cakra; these change, becoming first like a stūpa, the five wisdoms, a jewel, a lotus, a karma-sign, these change into the five buddhas: Mahāvairocana [Dainichi], together with Akṣobhya [Ashuku], Ratnasambhava [Hossho], Amitābha [Mida], and Śākya [Shakka] with perfected features; the four pāramitā bodhisattvas, sixteen great-, eight *pūjā*- and four embracing wisdom-bodhisattvas all surround them.

Next, empower oneself.

Outer five-pronged vajra *mudrā*, empower the four locations,

ON BAZARA DATO BAN UN TARAKU KIRIKU AKU SENJIKYA SOWAKA

[oṃ vajradhātu vāṃ hūṃ trāḥ hrīḥ aḥ śāntika svāhā]

Next, invite the various deities onto the kindling in the hearth.

Invite by offering five flower clusters onto the kindling,

ON KYARAMA SENJIKYA SOWAKA

[oṃ kamala śāntika svāhā], three times.

Next, visualize in the hearth.

Form Amitābha's meditation *mudrā*.

Visualize these flowers going to the middle of the hearth, becoming unlimited lotus blossom seats; on top of the seats are the five syllables BAN, UN, TARAKU, KIRIKU, AKU [vāṃ, hūṃ, trāḥ, hrīḥ, aḥ]; these change, becoming first like a stūpa, the five wisdoms, a jewel, a lotus, a karma-sign, these change into the five buddhas: Mahāvairocana [Dainichi], together with Akṣobhya [Ashuku], Ratnasambhava [Hossho], Amitābha [Mida], and Śākya [Shakka] with perfected features; the four *pāramitā* bodhisattvas, sixteen great-, eight *pūjā*- and four embracing wisdom-bodhisattvas all surround them.

Next, invite the various deities from the *maṇḍala* assembly.

Form the inner five-pronged vajra *mudrā*. At the end of the mantra for the various deities add the phrase of propitiation and the beckoning phrase, beckon three times with the right head finger.

Next, form the *mudrā* and recite the mantra of the four wisdoms,

ON BAZARA DATOBAN UN TARAKU KIRIKU AKU SENJIKYA EI KEI KI JAKU UN BAN KOKU SOWAKA

[oṃ vajradhātu vāṃ hūṃ trāḥ hrīḥ aḥ śāntika eihyehi jaḥ uṃ baṃ hoḥ svāhā]

Next, contemplation.

Form Amitābha's meditation *mudrā*.

Imagine inviting the various deities, located in their original places in the *maṇḍala*, to mysteriously unite with the various deities in the hearth, becoming one body, not two.

Next, declaration, ring the gong.

"Only desiring that the various deities descend to this seat
and compassionately accept this excellent *homa* offering."

Next, rinse the mouth.

Sprinkle directly three times, imagine washing the mouths of the various deities.

ON BARADA BAZARA DAN
[oṃ varada vajra dhaṃ]

Next, declaration, ring the gong.

"Sincerely offering perfumed water for washing the mouth
solely requesting the various deities accept this *homa*,
protect their disciple, and perfect *siddhi*."

Next, powdered incense.

Three times, recite

ON BAZARA DATO BAN UN TARAKU KIRIKU AKU SENJIKYA SOWAKA
[oṃ vajra dhātu vāṃ hūṃ traḥ hrīḥ aḥ śāntika svāhā]

Next, contemplation.

Form Amitābha's meditation *mudrā*.

Imagine the incense enters the mouths of the various deities, going to the lotus blossoms of their hearts, becoming vessels with offerings of delicacies; limitless, ocean-like clouds of powdered incense flow from their hearts, through their bodies and out their pores, offered to all the buddhas, bodhisattvas, pratyekabuddha, śravaka, and worldly deities.

Next, declaration, ring the gong.

"I now present the excellent offering of powdered incense
only requesting that the various deities accept this *homa*
protect their disciple, and perfect *siddhi*."

Next, ghee.

Large and small ladles three times each; chant, visualization and declaration as with the powdered incense, same with sap wood and following, except contemplate "limitless, ocean-like clouds of offerings of ghee flow out," change declaration to "excellent offering of ghee."

Next, sap wood, three pieces, "limitless, ocean-like clouds of pieces of wood flow out," "pieces of wood for the *homa*."

Next, mixed offerings.

First, Mahāvairocana, three ladles.

ON BAZARA DATOBAN SENJIKYA SOWAKA
[oṃ vajradhātu vaṃ śāntika svāhā]
Next, Akṣobhya, three ladles.
ON AKISYUBYA UN SENJIKYA SOWAKA
[oṃ akṣobhyam hūṃ śāntika svāhā]
Next, Ratnasambhava, one ladle.
ON ARATANAU SENBANBA TARAKU SENJIKYA SOWAKA
[oṃ ratnasambhava traḥ śāntika svāhā]
Next, Amitāyus, one ladle.
ON ROKEI JINBARA ARANJA KIRIKU SENJIKYA SOWAKA
[oṃ lokeśvararāja hrīḥ śāntika svāhā]
Next, Amoghavajra Siddha, one ladle.
ON ABOKYA SHIDDEI AKU SENJIKYA SOWAKA
[oṃ amoghasiddhe aḥ śāntika svāhā]
Next, the thirty-two deities.
Three ladles; the universal offering mantra.
Next, the deity who extinguishes evil destinies.
Three ladles.
NAUMAKU SANMANDA BODANAN DOBO SENAN ABITA RAN JISE TOBA DATON SENJIKYA SOWAKA
[namaḥ samanta buddhānāṃ dhvaṃsanaṃ abhud dhāraṇī sattva dhātuṃ śāntika svāhā]
Next, for the chief deity of the temple.
Three ladles, add the phrase of propitiation [*śāntika*] to the recitation.
Next, for the Great Teacher Kūkai.
One ladle, same as above.
Next, for the clear light mantra which when practiced extinguishes sins.
One repetition, same as above.
Offering to the sacred spirits of the site.
Three ladles, same as above.
Next, retinue of this group.
Recite the universal offering mantra, at the end offer all of the remaining mixed offerings.
Next, declaration, ring the gong.
"I respectfully offer these excellent mixed offerings
only desiring that the various deities accept this *homa*,
protect their disciple, and perfect *siddhi*."
Next, ghee.
Large and small ladles one time each, "limitless, ocean-like clouds of ghee flow out," "excellent offerings of ghee."

Next, recite the universal offering and the three powers, ring the gong.
Next, vows, ring the gong.

"Sincerely requesting and only desiring that the various deities
compassionately accept this excellent *homa* offering,
protect their disciple, and perfect *siddhi*."

Next, rinse the mouth.

Three times, sprinkle directly, and imagine washing the mouths of the various deities,

ON BARADA BAZARA DAN
[oṃ varada vajra dhaṃ]

Next, declaration, ring the gong.

"Sincerely offering perfumed water for rinsing the mouth
only requesting that the various deities accept this *homa*
protect their disciple, and perfect *siddhi*."

Next, leave taking: take five flower clusters and offer to the northeast corner of the altar, recite

ON KYAMARA SENJIKYA SOWAKA
[oṃ kamala śāntika svāhā]

Next, contemplation.

Form Amitābha's meditation *mudrā*.

Imagine these flowers arrive at their original location in the *maṇḍala*, becoming jeweled lotus blossom thrones.

Next, recite the mantra of the various deities together with the leave-taking mantra, and form the inner five-pronged [vajra] *mudrā*.

ON BAZARA DATO BAN UN TARAKU KIRIKU AKU SENJIKYA GESSYA GESSYA BOKU
[oṃ vajra dhātu vaṃ hūṃ traḥ hrīḥ aḥ śāntika gaccha gaccha muḥ]

Next, contemplation: form Amitābha's meditation *mudrā* and imagine the various deities return to their original locations in the *maṇḍala* from the middle of the hearth.

Next, declaration, ring the gong.

"Solely requesting that the various deities return to their original seats."

With the above, the fourth section, the portion for the various deities is finished.

[5] Fifth section, portion for the worldly deities: Acala [Fudō] and the twelve *devas*.

First, purification.

Wash the various offerings three times, wash clockwise, the *kili kili* chant.

Next, karma empowerment.

Empower the various offerings clockwise and counterclockwise three times each,

ON BAZARA KYARAMA KEN

[oṃ vajra karma khaṃ]

Next, rinse the mouth, and empower.

Wash clockwise three times, imagine washing the mouth of the hearth,

ON BARADA BAZARA DAN

[oṃ varada vajra dhaṃ]

Next, empower the hearth.

Three times using the three-pronged vajra, the *kili kili* chant.

Next, pile the kindling: set five pieces in order from the left.

Next, take a flaming piece of pine and insert it.

Next, take the fan and fan the fire.

Imagine the syllable KAN [haṃ] on the surface of the fan, changes becoming a wind cakra,

ON BOKU JINBARA UN

[oṃ bhūḥ jvala hūṃ], three times.

Next, purification.

Sprinkle the wood in the hearth three times, sprinkle directly, the *kili kili* chant.

Next, empower the kindling on the hearth.

Using the three-pronged vajra, empower by reciting the *kili kili* chant three times.

Next, invite the worldly *devas*.

Take three flower clusters, break the stems off by twisting, take one more leaf and wrap around the rest, recite the one syllable mantra of Acala, and invite the worldly *devas* onto the kindling on the hearth.

Next, visualize [the worldly deities] in the hearth.

Form Amitābha's meditation *mudrā*.

Visualize one's own body as the class of worldly *devas*; empowering oneself is usually omitted. Visualize these flowers arriving at the center of the hearth, becoming a flower throne for the Vidyārāja and lotus leaf thrones for the *devas*; above the flower throne is the syllable KAN [*hāṃ*] which changes, becoming Acala Vidyārāja [Fudō Myōō] complete with four arms; further, above each of the lotus leaf thrones is the syllable UN [*hūṃ*], which change, becoming the twelve *devas*, the seven celestial lights, and the twenty-eight lunar mansions; the dignified bearing and appearance of each and every one is clearly evident.

Next, invite the worldly *devas* from their assembly in the *maṇḍala.*

At the end of the great hook *mudrā* and mantra say the phrase of propitiation, together with forming and reciting the four embracing wisdoms *mudrā* and mantra.

NAUMAKU SANMANDA BODANAN AKU SARABA TARA HARACHI KATEI TATAGYATA KUSYA BOJISYARIYA HARI HORAKYA SENJIKYA EI KEI KI JYAKU UN BAN KOKU SOWAKA

[namaḥ samanta buddānāṃ āḥ sarvatrā paratihata tathāgata açkuṣa bodhicarya paripuraka śāntika eihyehi jaḥ uṃ baṃ hoḥ svāhā]

Next, contemplation.

Form Amitābha's meditation *mudrā.*

Imagine inviting the worldly *devas*, located in their original places in the *maṇḍala*, to mysteriously unite with the worldly *devas* in the hearth, forming one body not two.

Next, declaration, ring the gong.

"Only desiring that the worldly *devas* descend to this seat
and compassionately accept this excellent *homa* offering."

Next, rinse the mouth.

Sprinkle directly three times, imagine washing the mouths of the worldly *devas*,

ON BARADA BAZARA DAN

[oṃ varada vajra dhaṃ]

Next, declaration, ring the gong.

"Sincerely offering perfumed water for washing the mouth
solely requesting that the worldly *devas* accept this *homa*,
protect their disciple, and perfect *siddhi*."

Next, powdered incense.

Three times, recite

NAUMAKU SANMANDA BAZARA DAN KAN SENJIKYA SOWAKA

[namaḥ samanta vajrānāṃ hāṃ śāntika svāhā]

Next, contemplation.

Form Amitābha's meditation *mudrā.*

Imagine the incense enters the mouths of the worldly *devas*, going to the lotus blossoms of their hearts, becoming vessels with offerings of delicacies, limitless, ocean-like clouds of powdered incense flow from their hearts, through their bodies and out their pores, being offered to all the buddhas, bodhisattvas, pratyekabuddhas, śravakas, and worldly deities.

Next, declaration, ring the gong.

"I now present the excellent offering of powdered incense
only requesting that the worldly *devas* accept this *homa*,
protect their disciple, and perfect *siddhi*."

Next, ghee.

Large and small ladles three times each; chant, visualization, and declaration as with powdered incense, same with the sap wood and following, except contemplate "limitless, ocean-like clouds of ghee flow out," change declaration to "excellent offering of ghee."

First, Acala.

Three pieces with the one-syllable mantra; as above, but alter contemplation: "limitless, ocean-like clouds of pieces of wood flow out," and so on.

Declare:

"I now present pieces of wood for the *homa*
only requesting that Acala accept this *homa*,
protect his disciple, and perfect *siddhi*."

Next, Agni.

Three pieces, short Agni chant, the following as above—this is to be done as in the previous Agni section.

"I now present pieces of wood for the *homa*
only requesting that Agni accept this *homa*,
protect his disciple, and perfect *siddhi*."

Next, mixed offerings.

First, Acala.

Three ladles, compassion chant—with the phrase of propitiation added.

Next, Īśana.

One ladle.

NAUMAKU SANMANDA BAZARADAN ISYANAYA SENJIKYA SOWAKA
[namaḥ samanta vajradhāṃ īśanāya śāntika svāhā]

Next, Indra.

One ladle.

NAUMAKU SANMANDA BAZARADAN INODARAYA SENJIKYA SOWAKA
[namaḥ samanta vajradhāṃ indrāya śāntika svāhā]

Next, Agni.

Three ladles.

NAUMAKU SANMANDA BAZARADAN AGYANAU EI SENJIKYA SOWAKA
[namaḥ samanta vajradhāṃ agnaye śāntika svāhā]

Next, Yama.

One ladle.

NAUMAKU SANMANDA BAZARADAN ENMAYA SENJIKYA SOWAKA
[namaḥ samanta vajradhāṃ yamāya śāntika svāhā]

Next, Rākṣasa.

One ladle.

NAUMAKU SANMANDA BAZARADAN JIRICHIEI SENJIKYA SOWAKA
[namaḥ samanta vajradhāṃ nirṛtye śāntika svāhā]

Next, Varuṇa.

One ladle.

NAUMAKU SANMANDA BAZARADAN BARODAYA SENJIKYA SOWAKA
[namaḥ samanta vajradhāṃ varuṇāya śāntika svāhā]

Next, Vāyu.

One ladle.

NAUMAKU SANMANDA BAZARADAN BAYABEI SENJIKYA SOWAKA
[namaḥ samanta vajradhāṃ vāyave śāntika svāhā]

Next, Vaiśravana.

One ladle.

NAUMAKU SANMANDA BAZARADAN BEISHIRAMANDAYA SENJIKYA SOWAKA
[namaḥ samanta vajradhāṃ vaiśravanāya śāntika svāhā]

Next, Brahma.

One ladle.

NAUMAKU SANMANDA BAZARADAN BORAKANMANEI SENJIKYA SOWAKA
[namaḥ samanta vajradhāṃ brahmane śāntika svāhā]

Next, Pṛthivī.

One ladle.

NAUMAKU SANMANDA BAZARADAN BIRICHIBIEI SENJIKYA SOWAKA
[namaḥ samanta vajradhāṃ pṛthiviye śāntika svāhā]

Next, Āditya.

One ladle.

NAUMAKU SANMANDA BAZARADAN ANICHYA SENJIKYA SOWAKA
[namaḥ samanta vajradhāṃ ādhityāya śāntika svāhā]

Next, Candra.

One ladle.

NAUMAKU SANMANDA BAZARADAN SENDARAYA SENJIKYA SOWAKA
[namaḥ samanta vajradhāṃ candrāya śāntika svāhā]

Next, the seven celestial lights.

One ladle.

NAUMAKU SANMANDA BAZARADAN GYARAKEI JINBARIYA HARA HATA JYU CHI RAMAYA SENJIKYA SOWAKA

[namaḥ samanta vajradhāṃ grahеśvarya prāpata jyotirmaya śāntika svāhā]

Next, the twenty-eight lunar mansions.

One ladle and the *dhāraṇī*.

NAUMAKU SANMANDA BAZARADAN DAKISYA TARA JIRINDANI EI SENJIKYA SOWAKA

[namaḥ samanta vajradhāṃ nakṣatra nirnādaniye śāntika svāhā]

Next, for the practitioner or the donor, the four sets of constellations.

One ladle each:

1. birth star,[40]
2. birth celestial light,[41]
3. birth lunar mansion,[42] and
4. birth constellation.[43]

Next, retinue of the worldly *devas*.

Recite the clear light mantra, at the end offer the entirety of the remaining offerings.

Next, ghee.

Large and small ladles, one time each, "limitless, ocean-like clouds of ghee flow out," "excellent offering of ghee."

Next, recite the universal offering and the three powers, ring the gong.

Next, vows, ring the gong.

"Sincerely requesting and only desiring that the worldly *devas*
compassionately accept this excellent *homa* offering,
protect their disciple, and perfect *siddhi*."

Next, rinse the mouth.

Sprinkle directly three times, and imagine washing the mouths of the worldly *devas*,

ON BARADA BAZARA DAN

[oṃ varada vajra dhaṃ]

Next, declaration, ring the gong.

"Sincerely offering perfumed water for rinsing the mouth
only requesting that the worldly *devas* accept this *homa*,
protect their disciple, and perfect *siddhi*."

Next, leave taking.

Take three flower clusters, break the stems off by twisting, take one more leaf and wrap around the rest; recite the one-syllable mantra of Acala—throw to the northwest corner of the altar.

Next, contemplation.

Form Amitābha's meditation *mudrā*.

Imagine these flowers arrive at their original location, becoming a flower throne and lotus blossom seats.

Next, form Acala's single-pronged vajra *mudrā*.

Next, reciting the mantra, open the wind fingers of the *mudrā*, extending them out three times,

NAUMAKU SANMANDA BAZARADAN KAN SENJIKYA GESSYA GESSYA BOKU

[namaḥ samanta vajradhāṃ hāṃ śāntika gaccha gaccha muḥ]

Next, snap the fingers of the right hand three times,

ON BAZARA BOKISYA BOKU

[oṃ vajra mokṣa muḥ]

Next, contemplation.

Form Amitābha's meditation *mudrā*.

Imagine the worldly *devas* return to their original location in the *maṇḍala* from the middle of the hearth.

Next, declaration, ring the gong.

"Solely requesting that the worldly *devas* return to their original seats."

The above finishes the *homa*.

## Notes

1 Jan Nattier, "The Realm of Akṣobhya: A Missing Piece in the History of Pure Land Buddhism," *Journal of the International Association of Buddhist Studies* 23, no. 1 (2000): 71–102.

2 Nattier, "The Realm of Akṣobhya," 72–73.

3 Ingo Strauch, "More Missing Pieces of Early Pure Land Buddhism: New Evidence for Akṣobhya and Abhirati in an Early Mahayana Sutra from Gandhāra," *The Eastern Buddhist* 41, no. 1 (2010): 23–66.

4 Diwakar Acharya, "Evidence for Mahāyāna Buddhism and Sukhāvatī Cult in India in the Middle Period: Early Fifth to Late Sixth Century Nepalese Inscriptions," *Journal of the International Association of Buddhist Studies* 31, no. 1/2 (2008 [2010]): 24–75.

5 Charles Willemen, "Early Yogācāra and Visualization (*Bhāvanā*)," in *Wading into the Stream of Wisdom: Essays in Honor of Leslie S. Kawamura*, ed. Sarah F. Haynes and Michelle J. Sorenson (Honolulu: University of Hawai'i Press, 2013), 211–227.

6 Akṣobhya does receive mention in several studies, such as Hiram W. Woodward Jr., "Tantric Buddhism at Angkor Thom," *Ars Orientalis* 12 (1981): 57–67.

7 Personally, I believe that the relative "invisibility" of the Buddhist Churches of America on the religious landscape of the United States is in part explained by what might be called "Pure Land exceptionalism."

8 This evaluation evidences the problems created by the tendency toward essentializing both Buddhism and Pure Land. Reduced to doctrinal formulae, particularly under the dubious paradigm that "Pure Land Buddhism = Protestant Christianity," the two do appear incompatible with one another. The need to move from essentialized and static conceptions to historical and dynamic ones is part of what motivated this collection.

9 This disjunction continues to be reinforced by Buddhist modernist claims that the essence of original Buddhism is a rational program of individual mental and moral development.

10 Nattier, "The Realm of Akṣobhya," 90.

11 While the emphasis here is on the continuity of development, it is not intended to reinforce the idea that the Buddhist tradition was a closed system. Such container metaphors (what is inside or outside Buddhism) are generally dysfunctional impositions of forms of affiliation presumed by Christian institutional history.

12 According to Paul Griffiths, there are different understandings concerning the number of buddhas in a cosmos at one time. Paul Griffiths, *On Being Buddha: The Classical Doctrine of Buddhahood* (Albany: State University of New York Press, 1994), 120.

13 Nattier, "The Realm of Akṣobhya," 90–91.

14 Galen Amstutz has suggested a five-stage development. Galen Amstutz, "The Politics of Pure Land Buddhism in India," *Numen* 45, no. 1 (1998): 71.

15 Nattier, "The Realm of Akṣobhya," 72.

16 Diwakar Acharya, "Evidence for Mahāyāna Buddhism and Sukhāvatī Cult in India in the Middle Period," 63.

17 Michael Radich, "Immortal Buddhas and Their Indestructible Embodiments: The Advent of the Concept of *Vajrakāya*," *Journal of the International Association of Buddhist Studies* 34, no. 1/2 (2011 [2012]): 227–290.

18 Radich, "Immortal Buddhas and Their Indestructible Embodiments," 234.

19 Radich, "Immortal Buddhas and Their Indestructible Embodiments," 235.

20 Willemen, "Early Yogācāra and Visualization," 221.

21 Tai-wo Kwan, "A Study of the Teaching Regarding the Pure Land of Akṣobhya Buddha in Early Mahāyāna" (PhD diss., University of California, Los Angeles, 1985), 69ff.

22 Kwan, "A Study of the Teaching Regarding the Pure Land of Akṣobhya Buddha in Early Mahāyāna," 78.

23 Kwan, "A Study of the Teaching Regarding the Pure Land of Akṣobhya Buddha in Early Mahāyāna," 82.

24 Kwan, "A Study of the Teaching Regarding the Pure Land of Akṣobhya Buddha in Early Mahāyāna," 144.

25 Conditions for birth in Sukhāvatī can be even looser. Amstutz, "The Politics of Pure Land Buddhism in India," 72.

26 Nattier, "The Realm of Akṣobhya," 82–83.

27 Amstutz, "The Politics of Pure Land Buddhism in India," 72.

28 This idea that early Mahāyāna is rooted in the greater rigor of the bodhisattva path than monastic Buddhism is also explored by Jan Nattier in her *A Few Good Men: The Bodhisattva Path according to* The Inquiry of Ugra *(Ugraparipṛcchā)* (Honolulu: University of Hawai'i Press, 2003). On the forest-dwelling monks in the early Mahāyāna, see Daniel Boucher, *Bodhisattvas of the Forest and the Formation of the Mahāyāna: A Study and Translation of the Rāṣṭrapālaparipṛcchā-sūtra* (Honolulu: University of Hawai'i Press, 2008).

29 Nattier, "The Realm of Akṣobhya," 75.

30 Kwan traces the image of Abhirati from both the 8,000 Line Perfection of Wisdom Sutra, and the *Akṣobhyavyūha*. See Kwan, "A Study of the Teaching Regarding the Pure Land of Akṣobhya Buddha in Early Mahāyāna," 144–145.

31 Regarding the importance of more strenuous practice, such as the "qualities of purification" (*dhutaguṇas*) in the formation of Mahāyāna, see Nattier, *A Few Good Men*; and Boucher, *Bodhisattvas of the Forest and the Formation of the Mahāyāna*.

32 Kwan, "A Study of the Teaching of the Pure Land of Akṣobhya Buddha in Early Mahāyāna," 166.

33 Willemen's inquiry referred to above makes more specific suggestions as to the venues from which the two cults arose.

34 Gregory Schopen, "Sukhāvatī as a Generalized Religious Goal in Sanskrit Mahāyāna Sūtra Literature," *Indo-Iranian Journal* 19, no. 3 (1977): 177–210.

35 Kwan, "A Study in the Teaching regarding the Pure Land of Akṣobhya Buddha in Early Mahāyāna," 151.

36 Laurie L. Patton, *Bringing the Gods to Mind: Mantra and Ritual in Early Indian Sacrifice* (Berkeley: University of California Press, 2005), 2, introduces this term as a means of avoiding the pejorative characteristics of "magic." It is equally useful for the study of tantric praxis.

37 Ronald M. Davidson, *Indian Esoteric Buddhism: A Social History of the Tantric Movement* (New York: Columbia University Press, 2002), chap. 4.

38 If the bundle has been tied with plastic string, as is often the case in contemporary Japan, the string is set aside and discarded later.

39 Again, if the binding string is plastic, then it is set aside.

40 That star of the seven stars that applies to the year of birth.

41 That star of the seven celestial lights that applies to the year of birth.

42 That star of the twenty-eight lunar mansions that applies to the day of birth.

43 That star of the twelve constellations that applies to the month of birth.

## Bibliography


Amstutz, Galen. "The Politics of Pure Land Buddhism in India." *Numen* 45, no. 1 (1998): 69–96.

Boucher, Daniel. *Bodhisattvas of the Forest and the Formation of the Mahāyāna: A Study and Translation of the Rāṣṭrapālaparipṛcchā-sūtra.* Honolulu: University of Hawai'i Press, 2008.

Davidson, Ronald M. *Indian Esoteric Buddhism: A Social History of the Tantric Movement.* New York: Columbia University Press, 2002.

Diwakar Acharya. "Evidence for Mahāyāna Buddhism and Sukhāvatī Cult in India in the Middle Period: Early Fifth to Late Sixth Century Nepalese Inscriptions." *Journal of the International Association of Buddhist Studies* 31, no. 1/2 (2008 [2010]): 24–75.

Griffiths, Paul. *On Being Buddha: The Classical Doctrine of Buddhahood.* Albany: State University of New York Press, 1994.

Kwan, Tai-wo. "A Study of the Teaching Regarding the Pure Land of Akṣobhya Buddha in Early Mahāyāna." PhD dissertation, University of California, Los Angeles, 1985.

Nattier, Jan. *A Few Good Men: The Bodhisattva Path according to* The Inquiry of Ugra *(Ugraparipṛcchā).* Honolulu: University of Hawai'i Press, 2003.

———. "The Realm of Akṣobhya: A Missing Piece in the History of Pure Land Buddhism." *Journal of the International Association of Buddhist Studies* 23, no. 1 (2000): 71–102.

Patton, Laurie L. *Bringing the Gods to Mind: Mantra and Ritual in Early Indian Sacrifice.* Berkeley: University of California Press, 2005.

Radich, Michael. "Immortal Buddhas and Their Indestructible Embodiments: The Advent of the Concept of *Vajrakāya.*" *Journal of the International Association of Buddhist Studies* 34, no. 1/2 (2011 [2012]): 227–290.

Schopen, Gregory. "Sukhāvatī as a Generalized Religious Goal in Sanskrit Mahāyāna Sūtra Literature." *Indo-Iranian Journal* 19, no. 3 (1977): 177–210.

Strauch, Ingo. "More Missing Pieces of Early Pure Land Buddhism: New Evidence for Akṣobhya and Abhirati in an Early Mahayana Sutra from Gandhāra." *The Eastern Buddhist* 41, no. 1 (2010): 23–66.

Willemen, Charles. "Early Yogācāra and Visualization (*Bhāvanā*)." In *Wading into the Stream of Wisdom: Essays in Honor of Leslie S. Kawamura*, edited by Sarah F. Haynes and Michelle J. Sorenson, 211–227. Honolulu: University of Hawai'i Press, 2013.

Woodward, Hiram W., Jr. "Tantric Buddhism at Angkor Thom." *Ars Orientalis* 12 (1981): 57–67.

# Chapter 4

# *Nenbutsu* Practice in Genshin's *Ōjōyōshū*

Robert F. Rhodes

## Translator's Introduction

The *Ōjōyōshū* (Collection of Essential Passages concerning Birth [into the Pure Land of the Buddha Amida]), composed by the Japanese Tendai monk Genshin (942–1017), is a pivotal text in the formation of Japanese Pure Land Buddhism. Although Pure Land commentaries and treatises had been written earlier in Japan, the systematic and comprehensive account of Pure Land worldview and practice found in the *Ōjōyōshū* proved extremely influential, and it was largely thanks to this work that the Pure Land teaching became firmly rooted in Japan. The following selection is taken from its discussion on the method of contemplating the Buddha Amida, which constitutes the central element in the *Ōjōyōshū*'s understanding of the *nenbutsu*.

Genshin was born in the Katsuragi-shimo county in the southern part of the Nara basin. His father was apparently not particularly religious but his mother was a devout Buddhist. Genshin became a monk of the Enryakuji, the head temple of the Tendai school, at an early age. A brilliant student, he quickly became recognized as a promising young scholar-monk and steadily advanced up the Tendai monastic hierarchy. But suddenly, around 980, Genshin secluded himself at Yokawa in the northernmost corner of the Enryakuji temple complex, refusing all further participation in the public functions of the temple. Subsequently, he turned to Pure Land Buddhism and, after just a few years of intense study, completed the *Ōjōyōshū* in the fourth month of 985.

It may not be out of place here to recount the famous story concerning how Genshin came to seclude himself in Yokawa. According to this account, Genshin was invited to a Buddhist service at the imperial court and received a number of precious gifts in return. He sent the most valuable gift to his mother, but instead of the thanks he expected, his mother sent him a letter of admonishment, saying in effect, "Although I appreciate your gift, it is my wish that you sever all ties with secular affairs and concentrate on your cultivating your spirituality." Chastised by his mother's words to stop hobnobbing with the nobility and focus on his practices, Genshin subsequently secluded himself in Yokawa.

This story is already found in Genshin's earliest biography, which is included in the *Nijūgo zammmai kakochō*, a registry of the deceased members of the *nenbutsu* association to which Genshin belonged. Since the biography was in all likelihood written shortly after his death, it is not improbable that his mother's words served as the direct cause of his retirement to Yokawa. It must be noted, however, that the Enryakuji was at this time embroiled in a serious power struggle between the so-called Enchin faction, which had long dominated the Tendai sect, and the newly emergent Ennin faction, led by Genshin's master Ryōgen (912–985). After Ryōgen became the chief abbot of the Enryakuji in 966, he worked systematically to remove members of the Enchin line from positions of influence in the Enryakuji, thus exacerbating the factional rivalry within the monastery. Around this time, too, both factions had begun to employ armed monks to settle their disputes. Ultimately, in 993, after the halls of the Enchin faction were attacked and destroyed by the armed monks of the Ennin faction, the former were expelled from the Enryakuji, resulting in a permanent split within the Tendai school. Genshin's decision to hide away in Yokawa may have been the result of his disgust with the factional strife brewing in his monastery.

The *Ōjōyōshū* was written under these unsettling circumstances. It teaches that we should quickly turn our backs on this defiled world of birth-and-death, seek birth in Amida's Pure Land and practice the *nenbutsu* in order to reach Amida's world. The *Ōjōyōshū* is a lengthy work consisting of ten chapters. The first chapter, titled "Despising the Defiled World," is taken up with a description of the suffering inherent in the world of transmigration. In this section, Genshin examines each of the six realms of transmigration (the realms of hell, hungry ghosts, animals, asuras, human and heavenly being) and declares that there is no place within these six realms that is free of suffering. It is in this chapter that we find the most famous section of the *Ōjōyōshū*: the terrifying description of the torments experienced by the beings of hell as retributions for their evil actions in previous lifetimes.

In contrast, the second chapter, "Seeking the Pure Land," focuses on the splendors of the Pure Land. In this chapter, Genshin enumerates ten blissful features that characterize Amida's realm. For example, he states that on his or her deathbed, the dying Pure Land devotee is greeted by Amida and his retinue and is spontaneously transported to the Pure Land. Genshin also emphasizes that the Amida's realm is an extremely splendid place and that everything there is pleasing to the senses. Perhaps more important for him, however, are those features that make the Pure Land an unexcelled location for practicing the Buddhist path. Those beings born in the Pure Land can gain instruction from the great bodhisattvas residing in that land, not to mention from the Buddha Amida himself, thereby ensuring that they will attain buddhahood quickly and effortlessly.

The fourth chapter, "Proper Practice of the *Nenbutsu*," is the central chapter of the *Ōjōyōshū*, inasmuch as this chapter delineates the method for attaining birth in the Pure Land. Here Genshin argues that the *nenbutsu* is the central practice for achieving birth in the Pure Land. But it needs to be underscored that unlike later Japanese Pure Land thinkers like Hōnen (1133–1212), the founder of the Pure Land school, and his disciple Shinran (1173–1262), the founder of Shin Buddhism, Genshin does not limit the *nenbutsu* simply to the practice of reciting the phrase "*Namu Amidabutsu*." Rather, he understands it as an entire range of practices focused on the Buddha Amida, from sublime contemplation of the Buddha's figure undertaken in *samādhi*, down to the simple recitation of "*Namu Amidabutsu*." Reflecting the great emphasis traditionally placed on meditation in Tendai discourse, Genshin highlights the literal meaning of the word *nenbutsu*—to remain mindful of the Buddha—and stresses that the *nenbutsu* is first and foremost a meditative practice focused on Amida.

Genshin describes the *nenbutsu* practice using the scheme of the five gates of mindfulness that first appeared in Vasubandhu's *Treatise on Birth in the Pure Land* (*Wangshenglun*).[1] These five gates, as described in the *Ōjōyōshū*, can be summarized as follows.

1. The gate of veneration: to pay obeisance to the Buddha Amida by undertaking the *gotai tōchi* prostration, that is, the act of prostrating oneself in front of the Buddha so that the five parts of the body (the arms, legs, and forehead) touch the ground.
2. The gate of praise: to praise Amida by reciting laudatory verses addressed to this Buddha.
3. The gate of vow: to arouse the aspiration for enlightenment (*bodhicitta*).

4. The gate of contemplation: to practice the *nenbutsu*.
5. The gate of merit transference: to transfer all the merits gained from one's practice in order to achieve one's own birth, as well as the birth of all other beings, in the Pure Land, even while realizing the emptiness of oneself, the Pure Land, and the merits that one has accrued.

The passage translated below corresponds to the gate of contemplation above. Even though Genshin explicitly states that, provided they are done with utmost sincerity, it is possible to gain birth in the Pure Land just by venerating Amida or by reciting verses in praise of this Buddha (i.e., just by undertaking the practices enumerated in the first or second gates above); the central practice among the five gates is contemplation. Significantly, Genshin distinguishes the act of contemplating Amida into the following three types:

1. Contemplation of the individual marks of Amida.
2. Contemplation of the comprehensive mark of Amida.
3. Mixed and abbreviated contemplation.

First, the contemplation of the individual marks of Amida means to contemplate the figure of this Buddha by visualizing in succession the thirty-two marks (*lakṣaṇa*) adorning his body. Starting from the prominent round lump of flesh on the top of the Amida's head (*uṣṇīṣa*), the practitioner visualizes each of the marks individually, down to the lotus blossoms that appear under the Buddha's feet. Then the practitioner visualizes these marks in reverse order (i.e., from the lotus blossom to the *nikkeisō*). This process is repeated sixteen times until one can visualize Amida's figure perfectly. Interestingly, the *Ōjōyōshū* lists not thirty-two but forty-two marks of the Buddha, including several features that are classified as secondary characteristics in Buddhist texts.

The contemplation of the comprehensive mark of Amida refers to the practice of visualizing Amida either as a brilliant luminous figure of gigantic proportions or as the embodiment of all three buddha bodies: the response body, the recompense body, and dharma-body. For Genshin, this represents the most sublime form of Amida contemplation. For those people who feel incapable of undertaking such lofty contemplative exercises, though, Genshin permits simpler forms of Amida visualization. These practices constitute the third type of *nenbutsu* listed above: the mixed and abbreviated contemplation. Although Genshin gives several forms of this contemplation of different levels of difficulty, particularly noteworthy here is the practice of visualizing the white tuft of hair between Amida's brows and the salvific light emanating from it.

Finally, for those people who feel unable to pursue even these simplified forms of visualization, Genshin recommends the recitative *nenbutsu*, or the single-minded recitation of "*Namu Amidabutsu*." He states,

> If you are incapable of contemplating the marks and secondary characteristics (of Amida), you should remain mindful (of the Buddha) by single-mindedly reciting (the name of the Buddha Amida, i.e., recite "*Namu Amidabutsu*") while imagining yourself taking refuge (in Amida), while imagining yourself being led to the Pure Land at death, or while imagining yourself attaining birth in the Pure Land.

Here Pure Land practitioners are encouraged to recite "*Namu Amidabutsu*" while imagining themselves taking refuge in the Buddha, being led to the Pure Land at death or being born in the Pure Land.

To conclude, in the *Ōjōyōshū*, Genshin provided a systematic and comprehensive account of the various types of *nenbutsu* practices found in Buddhist texts. Reflecting his background as a Tendai monk, he considered the contemplative forms of the *nenbutsu* to be the higher form of this practice. For those who are unable to undertake these lofty practices, however, he declared that the recitative form of the *nenbutsu* suffices to attain birth in Amida's Pure Land.

## Translation

### *Ōjōyōshū*

Genshin

Fourth, the gate of contemplation. A beginner is incapable of undertaking the most profound contemplation. As the *Daśabhūmika-vibhāṣā-śāstra* says, "Bodhisattvas who have newly aroused the aspiration for enlightenment, should first remain mindful of the Buddha's physical marks" and so forth. Moreover, the merits of (contemplating) the marks and secondary characteristics are frequently taught within many sutras. Therefore you should now cultivate the contemplation of the physical marks. This is divided into three: (1) contemplation of the individual marks, (2) contemplation of the comprehensive mark, and (3) mixed and abbreviated contemplation.

First, the contemplation of the individual marks consists of two sections. First, contemplation of the flower throne. The *Contemplation Sūtra* says,

> Those who wish to contemplate that Buddha should form the following image in their minds. Contemplate a lotus flower on the ground made of the seven jewels. Make it so that each lotus petal has the colors of a hundred jewels and has eighty-four thousand veins like a heavenly painting. Each vein emits eighty-four thousand rays of light, all distinct from one another and clearly visible. The smaller petals are two hundred and fifty *yojanas* in both length and breadth. The blossom has eighty-four thousand such petals. Between each petal are ten billion kingly *maṇi* jewels as illuminating ornaments. Each *maṇi* jewel emits a thousand rays of light. The light resembles a canopy made from the seven jewels and covers the entire earth. The dais is made of Śakra's pendent *maṇi*-gems and is decorated with a net made of eighty thousand diamonds, *kiṃśuka* gems, Brahma's *maṇi* gems and exquisite pearls. Atop the dais, there are four pillars with jeweled banners. Each jeweled banner is as large as a thousand million *koṭi* Mount Sumerus. Atop the banners are jeweled canopies like those in the palace in Yāma's heaven. They all have fifty billion sublime gems as illuminating ornaments. Each gem emits eighty-four thousand rays of light and each ray of light is made up of eighty-four thousand different hues of golden color. Each golden light pervades the jeweled ground and in various places transform themselves into such things as diamond dais, pearl nets and clouds consisting of various flowers. They appear as they wish in the ten directions to perform the work of the buddhas.[2] This is called the contemplation of the flower throne.
>
> This sublime blossom was originally produced by the power of the *bhikṣu* Dharmākara's vows. Those who wish to remain mindful of that Buddha should first form the image of the flower throne. When forming this image, they should not undertake any other contemplation. They should visualize all objects one by one. Each petal, each gem, each ray of light, each dais and each banner should be seen clearly and distinctly as if they are looking at their own image in a mirror. To practice in this way is called the correct contemplation and to contemplate otherwise is called the incorrect contemplation. [End of quote. When contemplating this mark of the throne, the (karmic effects of) transgressions committed during fifty thousand *kalpas* of birth and death will be extinguished and you will surely be born in the World of Supreme Bliss.]

Next, properly contemplate the marks and secondary characteristics. That is to say, the body of the Buddha Amida seated on the flower dais is adorned with resplendent marks and secondary characteristics.

1. No one can perceive the lump of flesh on top of the head. It is tall and round like a heavenly parasol. If you wish to contemplate it in detail,

you should next contemplate it as follows. A great thousand-colored halo shines forth from the top of the lump of flesh. Each color (of the halo) is divided into eighty-four thousand branches. Within each branch are eighty-four thousand transformed buddhas. Rays of light are also emitted from the top of the transformed buddhas' heads. One after another, these rays of light reach innumerable worlds in the zenith. From these worlds in the zenith, transformed bodhisattvas descend like clouds to circumambulate the Buddha. [The *Great Collection Sūtra* says, "This mark of the lump of flesh was gained by being respectful toward one's parents, monastic teachers, and masters" and so forth. If people experience joy upon seeing this mark, they will eliminate extremely weighty evil karma created over a period of one hundred billion *kalpas* and will never fall into the three evil paths.[3]]

2. The eighty-four thousand strands of hair on the top of the head all grow upward and curl to the right. They never fall out and they are not disheveled. The hair is deep blue in color, luxuriant, fragrant, and extremely soft. If you wish to contemplate them in detail, you should contemplate them as follows. Each strand of hair is surrounded by a vortex of a five-colored ray of light. When extended to full length, the hair is impossible to measure. [In Śākyamuni's case, his hair was long enough to stretch from Nikurodha monastery[4] to his father's palace and further encircle the city seven times.] It gives off innumerable all-illuminating rays of light that change their color into that of a deep blue lapis lazuli. Within this color are transformed buddhas, so numerous as to be uncountable. After manifesting this mark, (the light) all return to the top of the Buddha's head where they spin to the right and create a vortex. [The *Great Collection Sūtra* says, "The mark of his hair being gold and fine was gained by not committing any evil acts toward sentient beings."]

3. Five thousand rays of light shine forth from the hairline. Although intertwined, the rays of light are distinct from each other. The light all sways upward, forming a vortex around the hair. The light circles the Buddha's head five times and is just like a painting made by a heavenly artist. The rays of light are round in shape and are as fine as a thread. Within the threads (of light), there appear numerous transformed buddhas, surrounded by transformed bodhisattvas serving as their attendants. All forms and images also appear there as well. [Those who wish to contemplate in detail should employ this contemplation.]

4. The ears are thick, wide, and long and form a plump oval. Moreover, you should contemplate them in detail as follows. Each ear has seven strands of hair growing in a curl, each of which emits five rays of light.

Each ray of light is made up of a thousand colors. Within each color resides a thousand transformed buddhas and each buddha in turn emits a thousand rays of light, illuminating innumerable universes in the ten directions. [The karmic cause for attaining this mark needs to be investigated. The *Buddha Contemplation Samādhi Sūtra* says, "Those who contemplate this mark will extinguish (the karmic effects of) transgressions committed during eighty *kalpa*s of birth-and-death. In lives to come, they will become attendants of those who uphold *dhāraṇī*s" and so forth. Notes concerning the various benefits found below are all based on the *Buddha Contemplation Samādhi Sūtra*.]

5. The forehead is wide, flat, and splendid in shape. [The karmic causes for attaining this secondary characteristic and its benefits need to be investigated.]

6. The face is perfectly round, radiant, and gentle. It is dignified and luminous as the autumn moon. The two eyebrows, distinct and clear, are shaped like Indra's bow. They are incomparable in color and shine like a deep blue lapis lazuli. [Because he experienced joy upon seeing people come to him to seek (the Dharma), his face is perfectly round. Those who contemplate this mark will eliminate (the karmic effects of) transgressions committed during one hundred million *kalpa*s of birth and death and will meet the buddhas face to face when they are reborn in the next life.]

7. There is a white tuft of hair, curling to the right, between the brows. It is as soft as *tūla* cotton and whiter than snow. Moreover, you should next contemplate them in detail as follows. When this hair is pulled, it becomes as straight and long like a white lapis lazuli pipe and when it is released, it forms a curl like a crystal jewel. [The length of the white tuft of hair of a sixteen-foot-tall buddha[5] is fifteen feet. It is two inches in diameter and six inches in circumference.] From it shine forth toward the ten directions innumerable rays of light as bright as ten trillion suns. It is impossible to perceive this light completely. Moreover, numerous lotus blossoms appear in the light. These blossoms are stacked up on each other until they pass beyond worlds in the zenith as numerous as countless numbers of dust particles. These blossoms form a round pillar. On each blossom sits a transformed buddha adorned with the marks and secondary characteristics and surrounded by attendants. Each transformed buddha also emits innumerable rays of light and within each of these rays of light, there are again innumerable transformed buddhas. Among these world-honored ones, those who are walking are innumerable, those who are standing are innumerable, those who are sitting are

innumerable, and those who are lying down are innumerable. Some of them preach great compassion and great friendliness, some of them preach the thirty-seven aids to enlightenment,[6] some of them preach the six perfections, and some of them preach the various special merits possessed by the buddhas. Even if this (mark) were to be preached at length, no sentient being, even those up to the bodhisattvas of the tenth stage, can comprehend it. [The *Great Collection Sūtra* says, "This mark was gained by not hiding but praising the virtues of others." The *Buddha Contemplation Samādhi Sūtra* says, "This white tuft of hair was attained by striving day and night, by not being negligent, and by diligently practicing, as if their heads were on fire, various virtues such as the six perfections, thirty-seven aids to enlightenment, the ten powers,[7] fearlessness,[8] great compassion and great friendliness over a period of innumerable *kalpas*. Those who contemplate this mark will eliminate (the karmic effects of) transgressions committed during numerous lifetimes extending over a period of nine billion six hundred million *nayutas* of *kalpas* multiplied by the number of grains of sand in the Ganges."]

8. The Tathāgata's eyelashes are like those of a bull king. They are deep blue in color, even in length, and not disheveled. Moreover, you should next contemplate it in detail as follows. Five hundred strands of hair grow above and below the eyes. They are soft as the fuzz of the *udumbara* blossom[9] and quite pleasing. Crystal-colored rays of light shine forth from the tips of the five hundred strands of hair. They circle the head once and produce perfectly sublime blue lotus blossoms. Upon each blossom dais is the god Brahmā holding a blue parasol. [The *Great Collection Sūtra* says, "The mark of the bull king's eyelashes was gained by seeking supreme enlightenment in sincerity." The *Mahāparinirvāṇa sūtra* says, "It is because he gave rise to a virtuous mind upon seeing something hateful."]

9. The Buddha's eyes are blue and white. Both the top and bottom eyelids move when blinking. The whites of the eyes are whiter than a white jewel, while the irises are bluer than a blue lotus blossom. Moreover, you should next contemplate them in detail as follows. Rays of light shine forth from the eyes. They divide into four branches and illuminate innumerable worlds in the ten directions. Within the blue light are blue transformed buddhas, while in the white light are white transformed buddhas. These blue and white transformed buddhas manifest various supernatural powers. [The *Great Collection Sūtra* says, "This mark of the blue eyes was gained by cultivating a mind of compassion and viewing sentient beings with love" and so forth. Those who contemplate this

mark even for a short while will always have pure eyesight wherever they may be reborn in the future. Their eyes will be free from disease, and (the karmic effects of) transgressions they have committed during numerous lifetimes extending over a period of more than seven *kalpas* will be eliminated.]

10. The nose is long, prominent, and straight. The nostrils are hidden from view. It is shaped like a parrot's beak or a metal hooks at the tips of a bow (used for attaching a bowstring). It is clean, both inside and out, and is free from impurities. Two rays of light issue forth from it to illuminate the ten directions. The lights transform themselves and perform the work of innumerable buddhas. [Those who contemplate this secondary characteristic will extinguish (the karmic effects of) transgressions committed during a thousand *kalpas*. They will be able to smell exquisite perfume wherever they may be reborn in the future and they will always have the perfume of the precepts (i.e., the fragrance arising from the merits of having kept the precepts) as their bodily adornments.]

11. The color of the lips is crimson and pleasant like a *bimba* fruit. The top and bottom lips are balanced like a scale and are very attractive. Moreover, you should next contemplate it in detail as follows. Spherically shaped globes of light, strung together like a hundred thousand crimson pearls, are emitted from the Buddha's mouth. They flow in and out of the nose, the white tuft of hair (between the brows) and the hair on the head and finally merge with the halo (around the Buddha's head). [The karmic cause for attaining this mark of the lips needs to be investigated.]

12. The forty teeth are clean and uniform. There is no space between them and they have deep roots. They are whiter than snow and constantly emit light. The light is red and white in color and its radiance is brilliantly reflected in the eyes of those who behold them. [The *Mahāparinirvāṇa sūtra* says, "This mark of the forty exceedingly white and uniform teeth with no space between them was gained by refraining from lying, slandering, and expressing anger" and so forth.]

13. The four canine teeth are exceedingly white. They gleam immaculately and are sharp like a crescent. [The *Great Collection Sūtra* says, "This mark of the two white canine teeth was gained because the physical, mental, and vocal actions were pure" and so forth. Those who contemplate the marks of the lips, mouth, and teeth will eradicate (the karmic effects of) transgressions committed over a period of two thousand *kalpas*.]

14. The World-Honored One's tongue is thin, pure, broad, and long. It can cover the entire face and can reach to the ears, to the hairline and so

on up to Brahmā's heaven. In color, it is reddish gold. Moreover, you should next contemplate it in detail as follows. On the tongue are five images resembling seal impressions. When (the Buddha) laughs and moves his tongue, they emit five-colored rays of light. The light circles the Buddha seven times and re-enters his body through the top of his head. The acts of supernatural powers that they perform are innumerable and limitless. [The *Great Collection Sūtra* says, "The mark of the broad and long tongue was gained by refraining from the four vocal misdeeds"[10] and so forth. Those who contemplate this mark will eliminate (the karmic effects of) transgressions committed during one hundred billion eighty-four thousand *kalpas* and will meet eight billion buddhas residing in other worlds].

15. There are two jewels, one each under both sides of the tongue. They secrete *amṛta*[11] that flows to the top of the tongue. No heavenly being, worldly person or bodhisattva of the tenth stage is endowed with such a tongue, nor do they experience such sweet taste. [A different description is given in the *Mahāprajñāpāramita sūtra*. It needs investigation. The *Mahāparinirvāṇa sūtra* says, "The mark of the supreme taste was gained by providing offerings of drink and food."]

16. The Tathāgata's throat is like a lapis lazuli pipe and is shaped like lotus blossoms piled up on each other. The voice that comes forth from it is harmonious and elegant and it can be heard equally by everyone. It resounds far and wide like a heavenly drum, and the words that issue from it are refined and graceful like the song of a *kalavinka*.[12] The voice can be heard effortlessly throughout the great thousand-fold universe but if (the Buddha) so wills it, its reach can be incalculable and limitless. However, in order to benefit sentient beings, the voice never increases nor decreases in accordance with the capacities of the listeners. [The *Mahāparinirvāṇa sūtra* says, "The mark of the noble sound of the voice was gained by not criticizing the shortcoming of others and by not slandering the true Dharma." The *Great Collection Sūtra* says, "It was by being always gentle toward sentient beings" and so forth.]

17. The neck emits a circle of light. Dotted marks are distinctly visible at the top of the throat and each of these dots emits a ray of light. Each of these rays of light makes a total of nine circuits around the former circle of light. The rings made from the light are clearly distinguished from each other. Sublime lotus blossoms are found between each of the rings. Atop the blossoms are seven buddhas. Each of these transformed buddhas has seven bodhisattvas as their attendants. Each of these bodhisattvas holds a wish-fulfilling gem and each gem glows with golden

light. The gem is also endowed with such colors as green, yellow, red, white, and *mani* and they all encircle the rays of light. The light is one fathom in both height and width. It circles the Buddha's neck and is distinct as a painting. [The *Unsurpassed Basis Sūtra* says, "The Buddha gained the marks of the ten-foot-long circle of light and golden colored body by joyfully providing offerings of clothes, food and drink, carriages, bedding, and ornaments."]

18. From the neck shine forth two rays of light. They are endowed with ten thousand colors and illuminate all the universes in the ten directions. Everyone touched by the light becomes a *pratyekabuddha*. The light illuminates the neck of these *pratyekabuddhas*. When this mark appears, the practitioners (contemplating Amida) see all the *pratyekabuddhas* of the ten directions throw their begging bowls upward toward the sky. The begging bowls perform eighteen miracles. The soles of each (of the *pratyekabuddhas'*) feet are inscribed with letters and these letters proclaim the twelve-fold chain of dependent origination.

19. The Buddha does not have an Adam's apple and the place where it is usually found is smooth. The light from this place illuminates the ten directions and is amber in color. A *śrāvaka*'s mind arises in everyone who encounters this light. When these *śrāvaka*s behold the light, it divides into ten branches. Each branch consists of a thousand strands of colors, resulting in ten thousand strands of light. There is a buddha in each strand of light. Each buddha has four *bhiksus* as his attendant and each of these *bhiksus* preaches (the truth concerning) suffering, emptiness, impermanence, and non-self. [The three marks above should be employed by those who wish to undertake more detailed contemplation.]

20. The Tathāgata's shoulders and nape are round and quite exquisite. [The *Fahua wenju* says, "This mark was gained by undertaking, and continually deepening, the practice of charity."]

21. The Tathāgata's armpits are full.[13] They emit a reddish-purple light which performs the work of the buddhas to benefit all beings. [The *Unsurpassed Basis Sūtra* says, "The marks of both shoulders being flat and the armpits being full were gained by engaging in activities to benefit sentient beings, cultivating the four right efforts[14] and being free from all fear."]

22. Both of the Buddha's arms are exceedingly straight. They are equal in length and slightly rounded like the nose of an elephant king. When standing upright, they touch the knees. Moreover, you should next contemplate them in detail as follows. Lines forming an image of a thousand-spoked wheel are found on the palms. Each (of the wheels)

emits a hundred thousand rays of light that illuminate the ten directions and transform themselves into streams of golden water. Among the streams of golden water is a sublime stream of crystal-colored water. Hungry ghosts who see this stream are freed from fever; animals (who see it) gain knowledge of their past lives; crazed elephants perceive it as a lion king; lions perceive it as a *garuḍa* king; and dragons also perceive it as a *garuda* king. These animals all perceive (the stream) as something they respect. Fear arises in their hearts and they put their palms together to pay obeisance to it. As a result of their paying obeisance, they are born in heaven after they die. [The *Great Collection Sūtra* says, "The arms being equal in length were gained by saving and protecting those in fear. The mark of the arms touching the knees was gained by seeing the actions of others and helping them."]

23. The fingers are round and there is no space between them. They are slender, long, and adorable. A swastika appears at the tip of each finger. The clean and radiant nails resemble a bronze flower. [The *Yogācārabhūmi* says, "The mark of the slender and long fingers was gained by paying obeisance to, venerating, putting the hands together in respect to, and standing up with respect in the presence of worthy elders."]

24. Between all of the fingers, there is a web like those of a goose king. They are interlaced with gold forming a design identical to that of twilled fabrics. It is one hundred trillion times superior to the gold taken from the Jambu River. The color is exceedingly luminous and is too bright to see. The web can be seen when the fingers are stretched apart but they cannot be seen when the fingers are placed together. [The *Mahāparinirvāṇa sūtra* says, "This mark is gained by cultivating the dharmas of the four modes of encompassing (sentient beings)[15] and by embracing sentient beings."]

25. The hands are soft and pliant like *tūla* cotton and surpass those of all other beings. It is possible to grasp things both with the front and back of the fingers.[16] [The *Mahāparinirvāṇa sūtra* says, "The mark of the pliant hand is gained by using one's own hands to bathe, dry, care for, and massage one's parents and teachers when they are suffering from illness."]

26. The World-Honored One's jaws, chest, and torso are broad and imposing like that of a lion king. [The *Yogācārabhūmi* says, "This mark is gained because, even though he serves as a leader when sentient beings undertake activities in accordance with the Dharma, he helps others and is free of arrogance and violent behavior."]

27. On the chest, there is a swastika called the "seal of reality." It emits a great light. Moreover, you should next contemplate it in detail as

follows. Within the light are countless hundreds of thousands of blossoms, and upon each blossom are innumerable transformed buddhas. These transformed buddhas send forth a thousand rays of light that benefit sentient beings and so on. (Ultimately the light) enters into the buddhas residing in the ten directions through the tops of their heads. At that time, the buddhas send forth a hundred thousand rays of light from their chests and each of these rays of light preaches the six perfections. Each of the transformed buddhas also dispatches an attractive and good-looking transformed person resembling Maitreya to comfort the practitioners. [Those who behold this light will eliminate (the karmic effects of) transgressions committed during twelve billion *kalpas* of birth and death.]

28. The Tathāgata's heart is shaped like a red lotus blossom. Sublime purple-gold rays of light twine around it and it is suspended in the Buddha's chest like a lapis lazuli pipe. The blossoms are neither open nor closed and they are round like the heart. Ten trillion transformed buddhas sport around the heart. In addition, transformed buddhas as numerous as the countless number of grains of sand in the Ganges multiplied innumerable times also reside in the Buddha's heart. They sit on a diamond dais and emit innumerable rays of light. Within each ray of light also reside transformed buddhas as numerous as innumerable particles of dust. They stick out their long broad tongues and emit ten trillions rays of light to undertake the work of the buddhas. [Those who remain mindful of the Buddha's heart will eliminate (the karmic effects of) transgressions committed during twelve billion *kalpas* of birth-and-death and meet innumerable bodhisattvas in each of their future lives, and so on. Those who wish to undertake more detailed contemplation should undertake this contemplation.]

29. The skin on the Tathāgata's body is everywhere pure gold in color. It is as clear and radiant as an exquisite golden dais. It is adorned with numerous jewels and is just what many people wish to behold. [The *Mahāparinirvāṇa sūtra* says, "This mark is gained by providing offerings of clothes and bedding."]

30. The light from Amida's body can spontaneously illuminate three thousand world systems and, if the Buddha so wills it, it can illuminate countless, limitless numbers of world systems. However, because he feels compassion for sentient beings, the Buddha holds back his light and it usually only reaches one fathom from his face. [The *Mahāparinirvāṇa sūtra* says, "This mark is gained by giving incense, flowers, and lamps to people" and so forth. Those who contemplate this great light, just by

arousing the desire to see it in their hearts, will have (the karmic effects of their past) transgressions eliminated.]

31. Physically, the Tathāgata is tall, broad, and splendid. [The *Great Perfection of Wisdom Treatise* says, "The mark of the upright and broad body is gained by respecting one's venerable elders, by welcoming and seeing them off, and by waiting on them."].

32. The World-Honored One's body is as tall as it is wide. It is round like a banyan tree. [The *Great Perfection of Wisdom Treatise* says, "This mark is gained by continually encouraging sentient beings to practice *samādhi*." The *Sūtra on Requiting Favors* says, "The mark of the perfectly round body is gained because he cures sentient beings whose four elements[17] are out of harmony." The *Fahua wenju* says, "This mark is gained by (treating all beings) equally with a mind of friendliness."]

33. In both appearance and deportment, the Buddha is magnificent and upright. [The *Yogācārabhūmi* says, "The mark of the body not slouching is gained because he humbles himself to care for people with illnesses and provides them with good medicine."]

34. The Tathāgata's genital is concealed and (the place where it should be) is flat like the full moon and glows with a golden light. It is like a sun disk or a diamond-like organ. It is pure both inside and out. [The *Mahāparinirvāṇa sūtra* says, "The mark of the genital concealed like that of a horse is gained by seeing a naked person and offering him clothing." The *Great Collection Sūtra* says, "It was by not publicizing the faults of others." The *Great Perfection of Wisdom Treatise* says, "It was by frequently undergoing repentance and refraining from illicit sex." Master (Shan-) dao says, "The Buddha declared, 'When a person who covets sex reflects upon the Tathāgata's mark of the concealed genital, his covetousness ceases, the obstructions arising from his evil actions are eradicated and he will gain innumerable virtues.'"]

35. The World-Honored One's feet, palms, nape, and shoulders—these seven places are plump. [The *Mahāparinirvāṇa sūtra* says, "The mark of the plumpness of the seven places is gained by giving up and not regretting valuable things when conducting acts of charity and not considering whether those receiving the offerings are merit-fields or not."]

36. Both of the World-Honored One's legs are round and tapered. They are like those of Aiṇeya, the hermit deer king. A golden light shines forth from the spaces between the bones that make up the knees. [The *Yogācārabhūmi* says, "This mark of the legs being like Aiṇeya's is gained by accepting the true Dharma in accordance with reality, preaching it widely to others, and serving others."]

37. The World-Honored One's heels are broad, long, and rounded. It is balanced with the tops of the feet. They are superior to those of all sentient beings.

38. The insteps are long and tall like the back of a tortoise. They are pliant and well-shaped and balanced with the heels. [The *Yogācārabhūmi* says, "The actions that result in the acquisition of the three marks of the sole being flat, of the feet being endowed with an image of the thousand-spoked wheel and having thin, long fingers also, as a rule, results in the acquisition of the two marks concerning the heels and insteps. This is because the latter (two) are based upon the former three marks."]

39. Eighty-four thousand soft and deep blue strands of hair, all curling to the right, grow from the front, back, sides, and top of the Tathāgata's body. Moreover, you should next contemplate them in detail as follows. On the tip of each strand of hair are lotus blossoms as numerous as particles of dust multiplied a hundred, thousand, and ten thousand times. Each lotus blossom produces countless transformed buddhas and each transformed buddha recites various verses. Their voices continue unabated like rainfall. [The *Unsurpassed Basis Sūtra* states, "The mark of the hair on the body swaying upward and curling to the right is gained by cultivating excellent virtuous dharmas without being satisfied with lower or middling levels of attainment but always seeking to gain the highest level (of attainment)." The *Sūtra of the Upāsaka's Precepts* says, "It is because he approaches the wise, takes pleasure in listening to them, takes pleasure in debating with them, takes pleasure in putting what he has heard into practice, cultivates the path, and eliminates the thorns of defilements."]

40. An image of a thousand-spoked wheel adorns the soles of the Tathāgata's feet. There is no part of a wheel, such as the spokes and hub, which is not completely found on it. [The *Yogācārabhūmi* says, "This mark is gained through the act of venerating one's parents in various ways, helping and protecting sentient beings suffering in various ways, and through the actions coming and going to do it" and so forth. Those who perceive the mark of the thousand-spoked wheel will remove extremely weighty evil karma created over a period of a thousand *kalpas*.]

41. The soles of the Tathāgata's feet are endowed with the mark of flatness. It is sublime and stable like the bottom of a comb box. Although the ground may not be level, wherever he steps, the ground will become flat so that every part of the sole will touch the ground. [The *Mahāparinirvāṇa sūtra* says, "This mark is gained by being steadfast in keeping the precepts, unwavering in practicing charity, and abiding in true speech" and

so forth. The karmic causes for gaining this mark of the feet being pliant and having long, narrow, webbed fingers that can grasp things both with the front and back of the fingers, are the same as in the case with the hands above.]

42. If you wish to contemplate in detail, you should contemplate (as follows). (With each step) a blossom appears below each foot and heel. They are surrounded by light that encircle them ten times. The blossoms appear one after another. On each of the blossoms are five transformed buddhas, all having fifty-five bodhisattvas as attendants. On the top of each bodhisattva's head is a light-emitting *maṇi* jewel. When this mark appears, eighty-four thousand extremely slender rays of light shine forth from each pore on the Buddha's body, adding further splendor to the Buddha's light-bathed body. The light is extremely lovely. The light is one fathom in length but is endowed with numerous marks, and so on. When the various great bodhisattvas of other worlds perceive this light, the light grows correspondingly larger. [End.]

The texts differ in their description of the forms, benefits, and the methods for attaining these marks and secondary characteristics. However, the brief description of the thirty-two marks here is mostly based on the *Mahāprajñāpāramitā sūtra*, while the detailed descriptions of the marks and the description of the secondary characteristics as well as their various benefits are based on the *Buddha Contemplation (Samādhi) Sūtra*.

Moreover, the karmic actions leading to the attainment of the marks can be divided into the general and specific (causes). As for the general cause, it is stated in fascicle 49 of the *Yogacarabuhmi*, "Beginning from the stage of the pure unsurpassed mental intention,[18] each one of the aids to enlightenment (*saṃbhāra*) can equally lead to the acquisition of all marks and secondary characteristics" and so forth.

The treatise divides the specific cause into three types. The first are the sixty-two causes. They are discussed in detail in the treatise. The second are the pure precepts. If bodhisattvas break the pure precepts, they will be unable to gain even the body of a lowly menial person (in the next lifetime). How much less can they acquire the marks of a great person (i.e., a buddha). The third are the four kinds of virtuous practices: (1) to practice acts of virtue, (2) to (instruct sentient beings) through skillful expedients, (3) to benefit sentient beings, and (4) to transfer merits without holding wrong views. [End.]

Although further distinctions can be made among the specific causes, I have, for the time being, given above the causes that (most directly) correspond to the effect.[19] The order in which (the marks) are listed differs from one text to another. I have followed the most appropriate order in listing them here. Furthermore, I have followed the example of the *Buddha Contemplation (Samādhi) Sūtra* in including the secondary characteristics along with the marks as objects of contemplation.

The proper order in which to contemplate the marks is as given above. The reverse order is the opposite, starting from the feet and ending with the top of the head. The *Buddha Contemplation (Samādhi) Sūtra* says,

> When (you are able to perceive Amida's marks) with your eyes closed, use the imaginative power of your mind and (contemplate the marks until you can perceive) the Buddha as distinctly and clearly as when he was in the world. Even though you contemplate these marks, do not (contemplate) many marks (all at once). Begin with one and envision (only) that one. After envisioning one (mark), envision another. Repeat (the contemplation) in proper order and (then) in reverse order sixteen times. In this way, make the mental image (of the Buddha's marks) extremely sharp and clear. After that, still your mind and focus your thoughts on one place (i.e., on one mark). At this time, gradually raise your tongue and press it against your palate. Rest the tongue at the proper place and continue this (contemplation) for two weeks. Afterwards both your mind and body will be at peace.

Master Shandao says, "After sixteen times, focus your mind and contemplate the mark of the white tuft of hair. Keep your mind from wandering."

Second, the contemplation of the comprehensive mark. First, as in the previous section, contemplate the large lotus blossom adorned with manifold jewels and next contemplate the Buddha Amida seated atop the flower dais. The color of his body is like that of a hundred trillion grains of gold taken from the Jambu River. His height is six hundred thousand *koṭis* of *nayutas* of *yojanas* multiplied by the number of grains of sand in the Ganges. The white tuft of hair curling to the right between his brows is as large as five Mount Sumerus. His eyes are like the waters of the four great oceans, and their blue irises and whites are distinct. The pores of his body emit light as large as Mount Sumeru and the aureole it creates is as broad as ten billion great world systems. Within the light are transformed buddhas as numerous as the number of grains of sand in the Ganges multiplied innumerable number of times. Each transformed buddha has countless bodhisattvas as attendants. (The Buddha) has eighty-four thousand marks such as these and each mark has eighty-four thousand secondary characteristics. Each secondary characteristic emits eighty-four thousand rays of light. Each ray of light illuminates all the lands in the ten directions, embracing sentient beings who remain mindful of the Buddha, never to abandon them.

You should know that within each mark are found rays of light numbering seven hundred five *koṭis* multiplied six million times. They are brilliant and their spiritual merits are glorious, like a golden mountain king towering in the midst of a great ocean. Innumerable transformed buddhas and bodhisattvas fill the light, manifesting supernatural powers and surrounding the Buddha Amida.

In this way, that Buddha possesses countless merits, marks, and secondary characteristics. Surrounded by a host of bodhisattvas, he preaches the right Dharma. At this time, the practitioner does not perceive any other form (besides the figure of Amida). Mount Sumeru, Encircling Adamantine Mountain, and other large and small mountains all disappear. The great oceans, rivers, the earth, and forests all disappear. Only the marks and secondary characteristics fill the eyes. Light of the color of gold taken from the Jambu River pervades the world. For example, when the flood at the time of the destruction of the universe[20] fills the world, everything is submerged and disappears. As far as the eyes can see, there is nothing but a vast expanse of water. The light of that Buddha is also like this. (The Buddha Amida) towers high above the entire world and there is nothing that his marks and secondary characteristics with their light do not illuminate. When the practitioner looks upon himself with his mental eye, he finds himself illuminated by that light. [The above is based on the *Contemplation Sūtra*, the *Two Fascicles Sūtra*, the *Pratyutpanna sūtra*, and the *Great Perfection of Wisdom Treatise*. After completing this contemplation, you can undertake the following contemplations as you wish.]

Or perhaps you should contemplate (as follows): the body of that Buddha (i.e., Amida) is three bodies in one. His single body can be perceived differently. He can be seen as being sixteen feet tall, eight feet tall, or exceedingly tall, and the body he manifests is golden in color. It benefits (beings) in innumerable ways. He is identical in phenomenon with all buddhas. [Response body]

Neither common beings nor sages can fathom any of his marks and secondary characteristics. The god Brahma cannot perceive the crown of his head. Nor can Mahāmaudgalyāyana fully fathom his voice.[21] His is the supreme formless body. It is adorned without being adorned. He is fully and completely endowed with the ten powers, four fearlessness, three stations of mindfulness,[22] great compassion, eighty-four thousand gates of *samādhi*, eighty-four thousand perfections and dharma-gates as numerous as the number of grains of sand in the Ganges. He is identical in his thoughts to all buddhas. [Recompense body]

The sublime pure dharma-body completely possesses the various marks and secondary characteristics. Each of these marks and secondary characteristics are reality itself. The dharma-realm of reality is complete in itself and does not diminish. It neither arises nor passes away; it neither comes nor goes; it is neither identical nor different; it is neither annihilated nor eternal. All virtues, both created (*saṃskṛta*) and uncreated (*asaṃskṛta*), are eternally pure since they are based on this dharma-body. He is identical in substance with all buddhas. [Dharma-body]

Hence the three bodies of the buddhas of the three periods of time and ten directions, the countless all-pervading dharma-gates innumerable as particles of dust, the dharma-ocean of the buddhas' assemblies, the myriad perfectly fused virtues, as well as the inexhaustible dharma-realm, are fully present in the one body of Amida. They are neither vertical nor horizontal, neither identical nor different, neither real nor false, neither existent nor nonexistent. They are pure in their original nature; they are beyond thought and verbal expression. For example, it is like the wish-fulfilling gem, which neither contains nor does not contain treasures. The myriad virtues of the buddha body are also like this.

Moreover, the Tathāgata is not said to be identical to the *skandhas*, *ayatanas*, and *dhātus*. This is because sentient beings all consist of them (i.e., *skandhas*, *ayatanas*, and *dhātus*). The Tathāgata is not said to exist apart from the *skandhas*, *ayatanas*, and *dhātus*. This is because (dharmas that) exist apart from them (i.e., *skandhas*, *ayatanas*, and *dhātus*) are dharmas that do not exist through causes and conditions. (The Tathāgata) is neither identical to nor apart from (*skandhas*, *ayatanas*, and *dhātus*). He is quiescent and exists only in name.

Therefore you should know that the various marks that are contemplated are the marks and light of (Amida's) three bodies (seen as being) identical with each other. Since form is emptiness, we can speak of the true marks of suchness. Since emptiness is form, we can speak of marks and light. There is not a single sight or smell that is not the middle way. The same is true of sensation, perception, mental formation, and consciousness. (Both) the three (evil) paths to which I belong and the myriad virtues of Amida are originally empty and quiescent. They are of one substance and interpenetrate each other. I vow to become a buddha and become equal to the sagely Dharma king. [The above is based on the *Contemplation Sūtra, Mind Ground Contemplation Sūtra, Golden Light Sūtra,*

*Buddha Mindfulness (Samādhi) Sūtra, Prajñāpāramitā sūtra, Mohe zhiguan,* and so forth.]

Third, the mixed and abbreviated contemplation. There is a white tuft of hair between the Buddha's brows. It curls to the right and is as large as five Mount Sumerus. Within it are eighty-four thousand secondary characteristics. Each secondary characteristic has eighty-four thousand rays of light. This light is sublime and is endowed with the color of myriad jewels. In a word, there are seven hundred five million *koṭi* rays of light. They brilliantly illuminate the ten directions like one hundred billion suns and moons. Within this light are manifested all buddhas, surrounded by an assembly of innumerable bodhisattvas. (Each buddha) emits a sublime voice and preaches various oceans of Dharma. Each ray of light illuminates all the worlds in the ten directions, embracing sentient beings who remain mindful of the Buddha, never to abandon them. I, too, am within its embrace. Even though defilements obstruct my vision and I am unable to perceive it, (Amida's) great compassion shines on me at all times without tiring.

Or else, you should arouse your mind and imagine yourself seated with legs crossed in a lotus blossom and, with the blossom closed, being born in the Land of Supreme Bliss. Subsequently, when the lotus blossom opens, you gaze up to the august face (of Amida) and contemplate the mark of the white tuft of hair between the brows. At that time, it emits a light consisting of five hundred colors that shines upon your body. You see innumerable transformed buddhas and bodhisattvas filling the sky. The sound of the waterfowl and the (breeze blowing through) the trees and forests, as well as the voice emitted by the buddhas all preach the sublime Dharma. Imagine in this way and fill your heart with bliss. I vow that, with various sentient beings, I may gain birth in the Land of Peace and Happiness. [The above is based on the *Contemplation Sūtra, Huayan Sūtra,* and so forth. Details can be found in a separate volume.]

If you wish to do the extremely abbreviated (contemplation), you should concentrate your thoughts in the following way. The mark of the white tuft of hair between the brows forms a curl and is like a crystal. Its light illuminates the entire world and embraces us. I vow to be born (in the Pure Land) together with (other) sentient beings.

If you are incapable of contemplating the marks and secondary characteristics (of Amida), you should remain mindful (of the Buddha) by single-mindedly reciting (the name of the Buddha Amida, i.e., recite "*Namu Amidabutsu*") while imagining yourself taking refuge (in Amida), while imagining yourself being led to the Pure Land at death, or while imagining yourself attaining birth in the Pure Land. [End. Because different people have different desires, various types of contemplation are explicated.] Whether you are walking, standing, sitting, lying down, speaking, or remaining silent—no matter what you are doing—always remain mindful (of Amida) in your heart, just as a starving person thinks of food and a thirsty person thinks of water. You may lower your head and raise your arms, or raise your voice and recite (Amida's name). Although your outward actions may differ, always keep the thought in mind. Keep it (in mind) continuously from one instant to the next, and do not forget it, no matter whether you are awake or asleep.

## Notes

1 This treatise, which is extant only in Chinese, is also known as the *Jingtulun* (Pure Land treatise). For a translation of this text, see Minoru Kiyota, "Buddhist Devotional Meditation: A Study of the *Sukhāvatīvyūhôpadeśa*," in *Mahāyāna Buddhist Meditation: Theory and Practice*, ed. Minoru Kiyota (Honolulu: University Press of Hawai'i, 1978), 274–290.

2 I.e., they function like buddhas to instruct living beings in various ways to lead them to enlightenment.

3 The three evil paths refer to the realms of hell, hungry ghosts, and animals. They constitute the first three of the six realms of transmigration.

4 A Buddhist monastery in the city of Kapilavastu.

5 Refers to a body that a buddha manifested in order to instruct sentient beings. A representative example is the body of the Buddha Śākyamuni.

6 The thirty-seven aids to enlightenment are (1) four stations of mindfulness (to remain mindful of the fact that the body is impure, that sensation is suffering, that the mind is impermanent, and that dharmas are without self), (2) four right efforts (to prevent evil that has not yet arisen from arising, to eradicate evil that has already arisen, to arouse virtues that have not yet arisen, and to increase the virtues that have already arisen), (3) four bases of supernatural powers (energy from the conscious cultivation of will, mind, effort, and analysis), (4) five faculties (faith, effort, mindfulness, *samādhi,* and wisdom), (5) five powers (same as the five faculties but developed further), (6) seven factors of enlightenment (mindfulness, discrimination between teachings, effort, joy, ecstasy, *samādhi,* and equanimity) and (7) the eight noble paths.

7 The ten powers of a buddha. They are (1) power to know right from wrong, (2) power to know the consequences of actions, (3) power to know the vari-

ous meditations, (4) power to know the capacities of sentient beings, (5) power to know the desires of sentient beings, (6) power to know the natures of sentient beings, (7) power to know the destinies of sentient beings, (8) power to know his former lives, (9) power to know where sentient beings will be reborn, and (10) power to know that his defilements have been eradicated.

8 Refers to the fourfold fearlessness or the fearlessness that comes from the knowledge that (1) all dharmas have been realized, (2) all defilements have been eradicated, (3) all obstruction to practice have been eliminated, and (4) the path to liberation has been preached.

9 A blossom that blooms just once in three thousand years.

10 Lying, equivocation, slander, and frivolous speech.

11 An elixir of immortality.

12 A bird with a beautiful voice said to be found in the Pure Land.

13 I.e., they are not hollow.

14 The four right efforts are included among the thirty-seven aids to enlightenment. See note 6 above.

15 Charity, loving words, other-benefiting practice, and sympathetic understanding.

16 In other words, it is possible to arch the fingers backwards and grasp things with the back of the hands.

17 The four elements from which sentient being are constituted: earth, water, fire, and wind.

18 The third of the seven stages of the bodhisattva enumerated in the *Yogācārabhūmi*. It corresponds to the first of the ten bodhisattva stages.

19 As seen above, the passages describing Amida's marks above are also frequently accompanied by descriptions of the actions that serve as the cause for acquiring them. Genshin explains here that the actions leading to the attainment of the marks described above are those that are most directly related to the attainment of the marks in question. Hence it is possible that other actions may, on occasion, result in the attainment of that particular mark.

20 According to the cyclical Buddhist view of history, the universe never ends but eternally undergoes alternating periods of growth and decline. The duration of the universe is divided into four periods: (1) the period of its creation, (2) the period of its duration, (3) the period of its destruction, and (4) the period of its disappearance. In the final period, the universe is destroyed by fire, flood, and wind.

21 Allusion to a story in the *Great Perfection of Wisdom Treatise* (*T.* 1509.25:127c–8a). Mahāmaudgalyāyana traveled to innumerable buddha realms in the

universe to see how far away Śākyamuni's Buddha's voice can be heard. But no matter how far Mahāmaudgalyāyana went, he heard Śākyamuni's voice clearly, as if the Buddha was speaking close by.

22 A set of virtuous qualities of the buddhas. The buddhas remain calm and unperturbed (1) when their disciples correctly understand the Dharma and act accordingly, (2) when their disciples do not understand the Dharma correctly and act incorrectly, and (3) when there are both kinds of disciples.

## Bibliography

Kiyota, Minoru. "Buddhist Devotional Meditation: A Study of the *Sukhāvatīvyūhôpadeśa*." In *Mahāyāna Buddhist Meditation: Theory and Practice*, edited by Minoru Kiyota, 274–290. Honolulu: University Press of Hawai'i, 1978.

Chapter 5

# Visions of the Pure Land from the Mind Treasury of Namchö Migyur Dorje

Georgios T. Halkias

## Translator's Introduction

Tibet's encounter with Indian Buddhism was neither a singular historical event nor a one-way process. Buddhism spread to Tibet from India, Central Asia, and China over several centuries starting roughly in the eighth century CE and continuing well into the thirteenth century.[1] As has been recently argued, the Buddhist conversion of Tibet did not imply "a violent rupture with the past, but a selective mirroring and reworking of what has been there before, albeit reconfigured over time."[2] The official sanction of Buddhism by Trisong Detsen (Khri srong lde btsan, 742–ca. 800 CE) was followed by a protracted course of conversion during which time Buddhism acquired distinct native cultural and spiritual elements, becoming "Tibetanized" in the process. Natural landscapes inhabited by Tibetan *genii of loci* (*sa bdag*) were culturally and ritually transformed into icons of Buddhist soteriology and cosmology. Mahāyāna pure lands imported from India to Tibet came to accord with pre-Buddhist narratives of the first Tibetan kings descending from heavenly beings, the gods of the realm of clear light. Over time, "pure abodes" came to be seen as quintessential after-death destinations for the faithful and a euphemism for the timeless resting place of deceased Tibetan Buddhist masters. In their polysemic use, pure lands featured in national myths of Tibet as a sacred land and became synonymous for physical sites of Buddhist pilgrimage (*gnas skor*), sanctified locales, "hidden valleys" known as *beyül* (*sbas yul*) tucked in the Himalayas, and the residence or hermitage of any Tibetan saint.

## Tibetan Orientations of Pure Land

Among all the Mahāyāna pure lands that translocated from India to Tibet, none attained the religious prominence and popular acceptance of Sukhāvatī.[3] Possibly one of the reasons for this selection was the identification of the territory of Tibet as the pure land of the Bodhisattva Avalokiteśvara, the Regent of Sukhāvatī. The story of the conversion of the Tibetan empire to the Buddhist faith through the enlightened activities and emanation of Avalokiteśvara as the first Tibetan emperor Songtsen Gampo (Srong btsan sgam po, ca. seventh century CE) constitutes a well-known state myth and literary trope recounted in Tibetan Buddhist histories and revitalized through the rule-by-incarnation institutions of the Karmapa and the Dalai Lama.

Another reason for the Tibetan assimilation of Sukhāvatī (*bde ba can*) is that it featured both as a generalized and as a specific soteriological goal in Indic Mahāyāna texts translated into Tibetan during the first and second transmissions of Buddhism. There is a copious variety of works of Tibetan authorship—classified according to emic divisions as *sutra* (exoteric), *tantra* (esoteric), and *terma* (revealed)—which take Sukhāvatī as the "ground" (*gzhi*), "path" (*lam*) and "fruition" (*'bras bu*) of Buddhist meditative practice. In fact, Tibetan compositions focusing on Amitābha/Amitāyus and his pure land constitute a distinctive literary category in Tibet known as the *demön* (*bde smon*) that includes works from several genres such as "aspiration prayers" (*praṇidhāna*; *smon lam*), "commentaries" (*'grel ba*), tantric meditations including "*sādhana*" (*sgrub thabs*), the "transference technique" (*'pho ba*), and "cremation rituals" (*ro sreg*), among others.

Chronologically, we can roughly divide contemplative texts with an undeniable Pure Land orientation into Indo-Tibetan translations dating from the eighth century onwards and indigenous Tibetan compositions from at least the fourteenth century, if not well before then. Despite unique and sophisticated trends and interpretations of Sukhāvatī in Tibetan religious and secular contexts, sectarian Pure Land movements never formed in Tibet as they did in Japan for example, inspired by Hōnen (1133–1212), Shinran (1173–1262), and Ippen (1239–1289). Kapstein described accurately the Tibetan situation when he wrote that "to the extent that rebirth in Sukhāvatī was emerging as a soteriological goal for Tibetan Buddhists, it was by no means an exclusive goal or one that was decisively preeminent in relation to other important Buddhist ends."[4]

## The Ecstatic Yogi and the Scholar Monk

Arguably, the most stunning and innovative collection of Tibetan Pure Land practices is attributed to the child prodigy Namchö Migyur Dorje (Gnam chos Mi 'gyur rdo rje, 1645–1667) and his middle-aged Buddhist teacher, the Kagyu hierarch Karma Chagme (Karma chags med, 1613–1678). Born in the area of Ngom in the Nangchen region of Khams, Migyur Dorje is best known for a unique corpus of occult Buddhist scriptures originating from a series of mystic visions filling a total of thirteen volumes.[5] We can presume that most of Migyur Dorje's numinous encounters with Buddhist deities and past Buddhist masters were written down with the support of Karma Chagme, a prolific scholar familiar with the old and new Tantras and founder of the Nëdo (*gnas mdo*) monastic lineage.[6] There are many influential texts attributed to Chagme, but probably none as widely known and recited as his *Aspiration Prayer to the Pure Land Sukhāvatī* (*Rnam dag bde chen zhing gi smon lam*).[7] There is no doubt that he was a devout believer in Amitābha's pure land, for an anecdotal story relates that when he was allegedly asked about the efficacy of pure land he replied, "May this old monk Chagme eat shit if his mother doesn't end up in Sukhāvatī."[8]

Migyur Dorje's collection of preternatural revelations known as the *Namchö* (*gnam chos*; lit. space-dharma) is said to have arisen from the aspirations and pure minds of beings. For the Nyingma school, Buddhist literature that is distinguished for its mode of revelation and visionary inspiration is classified as "pure vision treasure" (*dag snang gter*)[9] and generally falls into the following categories: (a) scriptures that have fallen from the sky (*gnam mkha' nas glegs bam bab*); (b) teachings from apparitions of Buddhist masters (*bla ma*), tutelary deities (*yi dam*), or space travelers (*ḍākinī*) (*bla ma yi dam mkha' 'gro'i tshogs zhal gzigs nas des gsung*); (c) teachings from an imperceptible presence (*zhal ma mthong chos kyi sgra*); (d) from emanated letters (*sprul pa'i yi ge*); and (e) from scriptures appearing in space (*gnam yig*).[10]

As stated in Migyur Dorje's "liberation-narrative" (*rnam thar*), it did not take long for his master and tutor Karma Chagme to realize that the five-year-old child entrusted to him was extraordinary and unusually drawn toward reading, writing, art, and Esoteric rituals, which appears to have been among his favorite subjects. After completing a three-year retreat in the hermitage of Muksang (*rmugs sangs*), the fifteen-year-old siddha began to give teachings and empowerments to a multitude of disciples. His fame spread across eastern Tibet and he became renowned as a Buddhist master who opened hidden lands (*sbas yul*), revealed treasures (*gter ma*), and ripened the minds of many sentient beings with whom he was karmically connected.[11] Karma Chagme recounts that when his apprentice reached the appropriate age and yogic mastery to take a consort he stopped a lunar eclipse while practicing the yoga of sexual reversal, that is, holding back his semen (*khams dkar po*) and forcing the vital energy to enter into (*'jug*) the central channel (*dbu ma*).[12] His popularity brought him repeated invitations from religious leaders and the governors of the principalities of Chamdo (Chab mdo) and Derge (Sde dge) in Khams.

His transmission of the *Namchö* treasures was upheld by one of his principal students, Rigzin Kunsang Sherab (Rig 'dzin Kun bzang shes rab, 1636–1698), who consolidated most of the *Namchö* texts into one collection and composed commentaries that later became an integral part of the monastic curriculum and training of the Payül (Dpal yul) lineage of the Nyingma School institutionalized in 1665. The successful assimilation of *siddha* scriptures by the monastic fold revitalized the monastic curriculum with novel and fresh teachings, allowed for the creation of new monastic lineages, and offered institutional confirmation to wandering ascetics whose local popularity with the Tibetan population warranted a symbiotic relationship between monks and lay tantric teachers rather than an antagonistic coexistence.[13]

## Contents of the *Sādhana of the Pure Land Sukhāvatī*

There are several works of the Tibetan Pure Land genre attributed to Migyur Dorje and in this chapter we will examine a representative work from the *Namchö* collection, the *Sādhana of the Pure Land Sukhāvatī* (*Bde chen zhing sgrub thabs*). According to the text's colophon it was transmitted to Migyur Dorje by Buddha Amitābha as he appeared to him in a luminous vision. To facilitate a quick overview of the structure of the *Sādhana of the Pure Land Sukhāvatī*, I have introduced the following nine headings (I–IX) not found in the Tibetan text.

I. Titles
  - I.1. Caption Title
  - I.2. Manuscript Titles

II. Deity Generation
  - II.1. Tantric Refuge
  - II.2. Self-Generation as Lokeśvara

II.3. In-Front Generation of Amitābha and Retinue
II.4. Invitation of Wisdom Beings

III. Mantra Recitations
III.1. Extensive Mantra
III.2. Medium-Length Mantra
III.3. Short Mantra
III.4. Condensed Mantra
III.5. Shorter Mantra
III.6. Shortest Mantra
III.7. Additional Mantra

IV. Dream-Yoga Meditation

V. Long-Life Meditation

VI. Transference Meditation

VII. Prayers
VII.1. Supplication Prayer for Accomplishing the *Sādhana*
VII.2. Supplication Prayer for Accomplishing Dream-Yoga
VII.3. Supplication Prayer for Accomplishing the Empowerment
VII.4. Supplication Prayer for Accomplishing Long Life
VII.5. Supplication Prayer for Accomplishing the Transference
VII.6. Aspiration Prayer for Taking Rebirth in Sukhāvatī

VIII. Empowerment

IX. Colophon

Section I provides the long and short titles of the text as they appear in the manuscript and the index (*dkar chag*) of the *Namchö* collection. In section II the practitioner of the *sādhana*, the *sādhaka*, is instructed to take tantric refuge to one's own teacher (*guru*; *bla ma*), the tutelary deity (*deva*; *yi dam*), and the sky-goers (*ḍākinī*; *mka' gro*). There is no requirement to draw a *maṇḍala* or prepare a ritual cake (*torma*) for this *sādhana*-cum-empowerment. The meditation begins by visualizing oneself in the translucent semblance of Avalokiteśvara, white in color and sitting on a lotus. In front of oneself the visualization consists of the Sukhāvatī triad, with Buddha Amitābha in the center sited on a lotus and moon seat with his two hands in meditation mudra and his two acolyte bodhisattvas, the bodhisattva of compassion, Avalokiteśvara, to his right and the bodhisattva of power, Vajrapāṇi, to his left. Light rays extend from the principal figures towards the wisdom beings (*jñānasattva*) imagined to reside in Sukhāvatī. Section III consists of mantras of different lengths starting with Amitābha's extensive root mantra and concluding with the recitation of the shortest root-syllable mantra *hrīḥ*. The long-life mantra is listed last. This and all subsequent sections are sealed with the vow of concealment. Section IV contains abridged instructions for the "dream-yoga meditation" (*rmi lam*) performed for the purpose of visiting Sukhāvatī in one's dreams and beholding the principal deities. During the day one is trained to perceive all events as unreal, having an insubstantial, dream-like quality, and before falling asleep one should visualize a red lotus with four petals and the four-syllable mantra *oṃ āḥ hrīḥ svāhā* at one's subtle energy center located at the throat. Then one should visualize Sukhāvatī in one's heart center, manifesting from a red lotus flower. Section V offers brief instructions for performing the long-life meditation while reciting the long-life mantra *oṃ bhrūṃ svāhā* and visualizing Buddha Amitāyus holding a vase filled with long-life nectar that dissolves into oneself. Section VI provides a brief account of the performance of the transference technique *phowa* usually done at the moment of death for the purpose of bypassing the intermediate state (*bar do*) following death and taking rebirth in Sukhāvatī. During this meditation one trains to block the doors of possible rebirths in the six realms and generates a strong aspiration to take birth in Amitabhā's pure land by directing one's subtle mind to the heart of Buddha Amitābha, visualized as a white drop in the shape of the syllable *hrīḥ* ejected from the crown of one's head. Section VII is a collection of supplication prayers for accomplishing the *sādhana* of Amitābha and all the different meditation practices contained in the previous sections (i.e., dream-yoga, long-life, transference) and the tantric empowerment section. Section VIII consists of a vase empowerment ritual for taking rebirth in the Pure Land Sukhāvatī and meeting face to face Buddha Amitābha. The last section consists of a colophon informing us that this *sādhana* was revealed to Migyur Dorje when he was thirteen years of age submerged in an extended vision of luminosity in the guise of Buddha Amitābha and his retinue, who instructed him to meditate on places in all directions as Sukhāvatī.

## A Pure Land *Sādhana* from the Mind's Treasury

The *Sādhana of the Pure Land Sukhāvatī* is located in the *Namchö* collection (vol. 1. pp. 14–21; ff. 5v–9r).[14] In the following Tibetan-English translation the use of notes is meant to provide explanatory references to difficult passages. Section divisions, headings, and insertions in square brackets are not found in the Tibetan text and are introduced for the purpose of providing clarification when needed. The Tibetan is provided in parentheses for a few specialized terms in anticipation of potential interest by the readers.

## TRANSLATION

### *Sādhana of the Pure Land Sukhāvatī*

Migyur Dorje

[I. Titles]
[I.1. Caption Title]
*The Sādhana of the Pure Land Sukhāvatī: From the Mind Treasury of the Space-Dharma, the Cycle of the Profound Whispered Lineage*
[I.2. Manuscript Titles]
*The Sādhana of the Pure Land Sukhāvatī*
*The Empowerment to Accomplish the Pure Land Sukhāvatī: A Collection of Oral Instructions*
[II. Deity Generation]
[II.1. Tantric Refuge]
[Namo] Guru, *deva, ḍākinī.* Hūṃ.
[II.2. Self-Generation as Lokeśvara]
In this Amitābha *sādhana* there is no requirement for [preparing] a maṇḍala and a torma. Transform yourself into a white bodhisattva [sited] on a flower-lotus.[15]
[II.3. In-front Generation of Amitābha and Retinue]
[Visualize] in front of you the Protector Amitābha on a moon seat on a lotus sited in meditative equipoise [arising from the syllable] oṃ. His body is of red color with one face and two arms. He is seated cross-legged holding a begging bowl and wearing the robes of a monk. To his right stands the Lord of the World [Avalokiteśvara], of white [color] with one face and four arms. He is standing on a moon seat on a lotus and his two palms are joined together. With his [other] right hand he holds a rosary and with his [other] left a lotus. To his left stands Mahāsthāmaprāpta Vajrapāṇi holding a bell and standing on a lotus and moon seat. They are surrounded by countless buddhas, bodhisattvas, śrāvakas, and arhats.
[II.4. Invitation of Wisdom Beings]
Light rays emanate from three syllables [oṃ āḥ hūṃ] [located] in the three places [head, throat, and heart][16] of "three principal figures" [Amitābha, Avalokiteśvara, Vajrapāṇi]. Contemplate that these [rays of light] are extending an invitation to Sukhāvatī.[17]

[III. Mantra Recitations]
Then recite these [root] mantras as much as possible:

[III.1. Extensive Mantra]
First, the extensive mantra: oṃ āḥ hūṃ amidheva āyuḥ siddhi hūṃ
[III.2. Medium-Length Mantra]
Then, the medium-length mantra: oṃ amidheva hrīh
[III.3. Short Mantra]
Then, the short mantra: oṃ āḥ hrīḥ svāhā
[III.4. Condensed Mantra]
Then, the condensed mantra: oṃ hrīḥ svāhā
[III.5. Shorter Mantra]
Alternatively, an even shorter mantra: hrīḥ svāhā
[III.6. Shortest Mantra]
Then, enumerate the shortest mantra: hrīḥ until it is sufficient.
[III.7. Additional Mantra]
Then recite an adequate number of the mantra: oṃ bhrūṃ svāhā.[18]
This is the practice of Amitābha.
[seal of commitment] ཿ sa ma ya ཿ rgya rgya rgya ཿ [19]

[IV. Dream-Yoga Meditation]
For the practice of dream-yoga (*rmi lam*) experience [events] during the day as [if they are] a dream. At the throat center, visualize a four-petaled red lotus on which [the syllables] oṃ āḥ hrīḥ svāhā are arranged. At the centre of the syllable hrīḥ appears the syllable oṃ. Then visualize in your heart center a red lotus flower and on top of this the pure-land Sukhāvatī.[20] Imagine it appearing very clearly as if (you are) there. Direct your concentration like this while falling asleep and in your dreams you will behold the pure-land Sukhāvatī. You will also directly encounter Avalokiteśvara, Amitābha, and Vajrapāṇi.
ཿ sa ma ya ཿ rgya rgya rgya ཿ

[V. Long-Life Meditation]
After that follow the activities of the long-life *sādhana*; otherwise, you do not need to change the visualization. The [long-life] vase [of Amitāyus] is filled with [long-life] nectar.[21] Think that [the nectar] dissolves into yourself as you recite: oṃ brhūṃ svāhā twice, or as much as you wish.
ཿ sa ma ya ཿ rgya rgya rgya ཿ

[VI. Transference Meditation]
Then follow the stages of *phowa* (*'pho ba*). Visualize with intensity in your heart center a red hrīḥ with a long *visarga*. Six light rays emanate from the syllable hrīḥ and block the doors of six kinds of rebirth [god, demigod, hu-

man, animal, *preta*, hell-being]. Next contemplate the opening of the aperture of Brāhma on the crown of your head. Then, visualize on the crown of your head Amitābha, as explained before, with his retinue of two [bodhisattvas]. Meditate that your consciousness, a white drop in the shape of the [syllable] hrīḥ, is ejected into Amitābha's heart center. Then, without the slightest doubt, generate the aspiration to be reborn in Sukhāvatī.

༔ sa ma ya ༔ rgya rgya rgya ༔

[VII. Prayers]
Next follows the stages of the supplication prayer.
[VII.1. Supplication Prayer for Accomplishing the *Sādhana*]
First is the supplication prayer of accomplishment. "Emaho! With one-pointed devotion I supplicate and pray to Amitābha the supreme, to Avalokiteśvara and Vajrapāṇi, and to the rest of immeasurable buddhas and bodhisattvas. Bestow upon me the supreme *siddhi*, bestow upon me the blessings to accomplish the *sādhana* of Amitābha."
[VII.2. Supplication Prayer for Accomplishing Dream-Yoga]
Next follows the supplication prayer for the dream-yoga meditation. "Emaho! One-pointedly, I supplicate Amitābha the incomparable *dharmakāya*, Avalokiteśvara, and Vajrapāṇi. After traveling to Sukhāvatī in my dreams, [grant me your] blessings to meet Amitābha."
[VII.3. Supplication Prayer for Accomplishing the Empowerment]
Then follows the empowerment supplication prayer. "Lama and Protector Amitābha, Lord Avalokiteśvara and Vajrapāṇi, and immeasurable buddhas and bodhisattvas I make this supplication: confer upon me the tantric empowerment."
[VII.4. Supplication Prayer for Accomplishing Long Life]
"Emaho! With a devoted mind, I prostrate, offer praise, and make supplication prayers to the impeccable Buddha Amitābha, Avalokiteśvara, and Vajrapāṇi and to the limitless buddhas and bodhisattvas, Bestow upon me the *siddhi* of [long] life."
[VII.5. Supplication Prayer for Accomplishing the Transference]
After is the transference supplication prayer. "Emaho! Single-minded I supplicate the most remarkable protector Amitābha, Mahākāruṇika [Avalokiteśvara], and Vajrapāṇi; bless me so that I may transfer my mind-stream to Sukhāvatī.

༔ sa ma ya ༔ rgya rgya rgya ༔

[VII.6. Aspiration Prayer for Taking Rebirth in Sukhāvatī]
Then follows the aspiration prayer. Recite the following. "Emaho! Splendid Buddha Amitābha of infinite light to your right is the Lord of Great

Compassion [Avalokiteśvara] and to your left the Bodhisattva Lord of Powerful Means [Vajrapāṇi], surrounded by countless buddhas and bodhisattvas. In the pure land known as Sukhāvatī there is immeasurable joy and happiness. May I, after passing away in this and in all my future lives, immediately take rebirth there. Having been born there, may I meet Amitābha face to face, and having recited this aspiration prayer may the buddhas of the ten directions bless me to achieve this without obstacles." [Recite the mantra for accomplishing the aspiration] tadyathā pañcendriya avabhodhanāya svāhā.
ཿ sa ma ya ཿ rgya rgya rgya ཿ

[VIII. Empowerment]
Successively take the empowerment. Recite going for refuge in the three jewels and then hold the vase with your hands. "The vase is one with the syllable hūṃ, it is Sukhāvatī, Buddha Amitābha's pure land. By placing it above my head may I behold a vision of the Buddha Infinite Light" [Amitābha]. At this time recite the root mantra as much as you aspire. Then hold the vase [transformed into the body of Amitābha] and recite, "This hūṃ is Amitābha the Conqueror. By placing it on my crown may I take rebirth in Sukhāvatī and behold face to face the Buddha Infinite Light."[22] Recite the root mantra as many times as you wish. Then pick up the *torma*. "This hūṃ is the Buddha of Infinite Light, encircled by buddhas and bodhisattvas. By placing it on my crown may I take rebirth in Sukhāvatī and behold Amitābha." Recite again the root mantra as much as you want. Then take the vajra in your hands. "This hūṃ is the Protector Amitābha, encircled by buddhas and bodhisattvas. I place it on my crown and having attained the empowerment of Amitābha may I take rebirth in Sukhāvatī." Then recite the root mantra as many times as you wish. "This hūṃ is Amitābha the Protector. Placing it above my crown may I take rebirth in Sukhāvatī and meet Amitābha." Recite like this the root mantra as many times as you desire.

[seal of commitment] sa ma ya ཿ rgya rgya rgya ཿ
[sealed in secrecy] kha tham gu hya ཿ xx ཿ xx ཿ

[IX. Colophon]
On the seventh day of Saga Dawa (Vesak) in the year of the Fire Female Bird (1657) Tulku Migyur Dorje was thirteen years of age when he was graced with the triad, Amitābha and his retinue, in an incomprehensible vision of light the size of a mountain who instructed him thus: "The oral

instruction thereafter is to meditate on places in all directions as the field of Sukhāvatī. If this [teaching] spreads to all migrating sentience, it will be suitable. If it doesn't that is all right as well. But if it spreads there will be great benefit. One does not need to meditate on Avalokiteśvara. If one does, that is fine. If one were to perform the long-life rituals, the gathering of the essence of the elements, etc., in a different way, it is all right. If one doesn't, it is fine as well."

sa ma ya ༔ rgya rgya rgya ༔

Furthermore it is said that in the evening once again he encountered Amitābha and retinue in their original form and received the oral instructions and supplication prayer for the practice of dream-yoga.

## Notes

1 Tibetan historiography refers to two major religious transmissions: the early transmission (*bstan pa snga dar*) and later transmissions of the Buddha's doctrine (*bstan pa phyi dar*). While the bulk of translations of Buddhist texts occurred during these times, there are documented translation activities well beyond that date; see for example Lobsang Shastri, "Activities of Indian Panditas in Tibet from the 14th to the 17th Century," in *Proceedings of the 9th Seminar of the International Association for Tibetan Studies, 2000: Volume 1: Tibet, Past and Present*, ed. Hank Blezer (Leiden: Brill, 2002), 129–145.

2 See Georgios T. Halkias, "The Mirror and the Palimpsest: The Myth of Buddhist Kingship in Imperial Tibet," in *Locating Religions: Contact, Diversity and Translocality*, ed. Reinhold Glei and Nikolas Jaspert (Leiden: Brill, 2017), 130.

3 For an extended discussion on the cult of Sukhāvatī in Tibet, see Georgios T. Halkias, *Luminous Bliss: A Religious History of Pure Land Literature in Tibet: With an Annotated Translation and Critical Analysis of the Orgyen-ling Golden Short Sukhāvatīvyūha-sūtra* (Honolulu: University of Hawai'i Press, 2013).

4 Matthew Kapstein, "Pure Land Buddhism in Tibet? From Sukhāvatī to the Field of Great Bliss," in *Approaching the Land of Bliss: Religious Praxis in the Cult of Amitābha*, ed. Richard Payne and Kenneth Tanaka (Honolulu: University of Hawai'i Press, 2004), 20.

5 For biographical information about Namchö Migyur Dorje in Tibetan and Western sources, see Georgios Halkias, "Pure-Lands and Other Visions in Seventeenth-Century Tibet: A *Gnam-chos sādhana* for the Pure-Land Sukhāvatī Revealed in 1658 by Gnam-chos Mi-'gyur-rdo-rje (1645–1667)," in *Power, Politics and the Reinvention of Tradition: Tibet in the Seventeenth and Eighteenth Century*, ed. Brian Cuevas et al. (Leiden: Brill, 2006), 109 note 11.

6 For a brief history on the Nëdo lineage, see Kong sprul blo gros mtha' yas, *Shes bya kun khyab mdzod* (Delhi: Shechen publications, 1997), fols. 16, 186, 193.

7 For an English translation, see Tadeusz Skorupski, "A Tibetan Prayer for Rebirth in the Sukhāvatī," *The Pure Land*, New Series No. 12, 1995. Chagme's work inspired a number of commentaries that revitalized Tibet's Pure Land literature; see Halkias, *Luminous Bliss*, 101–136.

8 *a ma bde ba can du ma 'khyol na / ban rgan chags med skyag pa zos pa yin*; in Guru bkra shis, *Gu bkra'i chos 'byung* (Pe cin: krung go'i bod kyi shes rig dpe skrun khang, 1990), 630.

9 Concerning this genre of revealed Buddhist literature Janet Gyatso explains in "Genre, Authorship, and Transmission in Visionary Buddhism: The Literary Traditions of Thang-stong rGyal-po," in *Tibetan Buddhism: Reason and Revelation*, ed. Steven D. Goodman and Ronald M. Davidson (Albany: State University of New York Press, 1997), 98: "A Pure Vision is an experience in which the visionary meets directly with a celestial Buddha or teacher of another era who preaches a special sermon. This may occur in a worldly setting or in one of the Buddhist Pure Lands. Pure Visions are variously said to occur while the visionary is in the state of meditative absorption (*nyams*), in the dream state (*rmi-lam*), or in the 'reality' (*dngos*) of the waking state. Unlike a treasure teaching, a Pure Vision is not said to have been hidden previously. Rather, there is a presupposition which draws on the tantric idea that any advanced practitioner with developed 'pure vision' would for that reason experience and participate in a pure world. Here 'pure' is reminiscent of 'Pure Land', where Buddhas live and advanced teachings are given."

10 *Gnam chos, Nang gi rnam thar* (fol. 15–19), in *Gnam chos thugs kyi gter kha snyan brgyud zab mo'i skor*, vol. 11. For a description of the contents of this collection, see Halkias, "Pure-Lands and Other Visions," 121–151. Much of this chapter is based on the above-cited work, but the current version includes a new introduction, additional material, and a revised Tibetan-English translation. For a detailed index of the first ten volumes of the Migot collection, see Von R. O. Meisezahl, "gNam čhos, Die Schriften des Mi 'gyur rdo rĵe (1646–1667)," *Ural-Altaische Jahrbücher*, Neue Folge Wienbaden, Harrassowitz 1 (1981): 195–226, and "Die Schriften des Mi 'gyur rdo rĵe (1646–1667)," *Ural-Altaische Jahrbücher*, Neue Folge, Wienbaden, Harrassowitz 2 (1982): 245–272. I am most grateful to the late Gene Smith for sharing with me an updated compilation of the *Gnam chos* cycle that includes three additional volumes (11–13), not included in the Migot collection, as well as providing some missing pages in Meisezahl's index (Band XXXV).

11 Guru bkra shis, *Gu bkra'i chos 'byung*, 625, 628.

12 Guru bkra shis, *Gu bkra'i chos 'byung*, 626. Tsering Lama Jampal Zangpo, *A Garland of Immortal Wish-Fulfilling Trees: The Palyul Tradition of Nyingmapa*

(Ithaca, NY: Snow Lion Publications, 1988), 49, recounts the same event without going into any details.

13 Sensitive to their heterodox inception, monastic factions that wished to adapt the *Namchö* texts and put them to ritual use classified them according to Buddhist scriptural divisions and situated them in a semihistorical context. Anticipating perhaps a reaction from Tibetan skeptics and conservative scholars, Mi 'gyur Dorje's inner biography classifies the *Scriptures of the Kadampa* (*Bka' gdams glegs bam*) as *gnam chos* (folio 18). Furthermore, examples of scriptures having fallen from the sky are cited for each class of Nyingma *tantras* (*kriyā*, *caryā*, *yoga*, *mahāyoga*, *anuyoga*, *atiyoga*). The section concludes that all *tantras* are space-dharma (*des na rgyud thams cad gnam chos lags so*); cf. ibid., folio 16.

14 *Bde chen zhing sgrub thabs* in *Gnam chos thugs kyi gter kha snyan brgyud zab mo'i skor*, vol. 1.

15 An oral commentary to this practice by contemporary Tibetan Buddhist master and Pure Land specialist H. E. Choeje Ayang Rinpoche (1942–present) recommends the visualization of a four-armed white Avalokiteśvara.

16 According to tantric physiology, these places correspond to the three upper *cakra* or energy nodes (*rtsa 'khor*) stimulated simultaneously by word, color, and sound frequency (oṃ-white, āḥ-red, hūṃ-blue). The syllables are visualized across internalized body locations: the "dharma-cakra" at the heart, (*chos kyi 'khor lo*), the "pleasure-cakra" (*longs spyod kyi 'khor lo*) at the throat, and the "cakra of great bliss" (*mahāsukha*) at the fontanel (*bde chen gi 'khor lo*). The cakra at the fontanel is utilized during the practice of *phowa* (*'pho ba*) or transference and also serves as a point of entry for the wisdom-beings (*ye shes pa*) that are invited during this visualization.

17 This section refers to the triad of Amitābha, Avalokiteśvara, and Vajrapāṇi, known as the "pledge-beings" (*samayasattva*; *dam tshig pa*), inviting the "awareness-beings" (*jñānasattva*; *ye shes pa*), that is, their enlightened counterparts who are residing in Sukhāvatī, to come and merge with them. The symmetrical correspondence between the "structured-imaginary" (the pledge-beings in the visualization) and the "expansive-real" (the wisdom-beings localized in Sukhāvatī) is established through word, color, and sound visualized as the inseparability of the three emanating outwards as white, red, and blue light rays. The response of the wisdom-beings is one of empowering the tantric practitioner whose pledge to attain enlightenment merges and becomes indivisible with the state of enlightenment represented by the wisdom beings.

18 The term *bsgrangs* refers to counting or enumerating, and *chog pa* means sufficiency, or when a prespecified number of mantra recitation is reached.

19 These mantras are now sealed by the tantric vows of concealment. The term *rgya* may be an abbreviation of *phyag rgya* (*mudrā*) where a particular hand mūdra is expected, or it may be derived from the verb *rgya ba* and used to indicate "extent" but also meaning "area" or "region." More generically, it is affixed after other words to indicate something that seals something else to keep the contents hidden, as in a seal on an envelope.

20 The original text renders *bde chen* (*mahāsukha*) instead of *bde can* that translates Sukhāvatī.

21 Long-life practices usually involve Amitābha visualized in the *sambhogakāya* form of Amitāyus.

22 Concerning the consecration of ritual objects in "Literature on Consecration (rab gnas)," in *Tibetan Literature, Studies in Genre*, ed. José Cabezon and Roger R. Jackson (Ithaca, NY: Snow Lion, 1996), 291–292, Yael Bentor explains:

> Not only is the consecration performed within the frame of the sādhana, it is, in fact, a special application of the sādhana. Having completed the generation process (*utpatti, bskyed pa*), one can apply one's powers to the generation of a receptacle as a deity (*rten bskyed*) through a similar method. The main components at the core of the consecration ritual, common to almost all consecration manuals I have been able to examine, are as follows: (1) Visualizing the receptacle away (*mi dmigs pa*), always performed in conjunction with meditation on emptiness (*stong pa nyid*). (2) Generation of the receptacle as the *dam tshig sems dpa'* (*samayasattva*) of one's *yi dam* (*rten bskyed*). (3) Invitation of the *ye shes sems dpa'* (*jñānasattva*) into the receptacle (*spyan 'dren*) and its absorption (*bstim*) into the *dam tshig sems dpa'* (*dam ye gnyis su med pa*). (4) Transformation of the receptacle back into its conventional appearance of an image, stūpa, book, etc. (*rten bsgyur*). (5) Requesting the *ye shes sems dpa'* to remain in the receptacle as long as saṃsāra lasts (*brtan bzhugs*).

## Bibliography

### Primary Sources

Gu ru bkra shis (eighteenth century). *Gu bkra'i chos 'byung*. Pe cin: krung go'i bod kyi shes rig dpe skrun khang, 1990.

Kong sprul blo gros mtha' yas (1813–1899). *Shes bya kun khyab mdzod*. Delhi: Shechen Publications, 1997.

Mi 'gyur rdo rje (1645–1667). *Gnam chos thugs kyi gter kha snyan brgyud zab mo'i skor*. Paro Kyichu: Dilgo Khyentsey Rinpoche; Bylakuppe, India: Pema Norbu Rinpoche, 1983.

## Secondary Sources

Bentor, Yael. "Literature on Consecration (rab gnas)." In *Tibetan Literature, Studies in Genre,* edited by José Cabezon and Roger R. Jackson, 290–312. Ithaca, NY: Snow Lion, 1996.

Gyatso, Janet. "Genre, Authorship, and Transmission in Visionary Buddhism: The Literary Traditions of Thang-stong rGyal-po." In *Tibetan Buddhism: Reason and Revelation*, edited by Steven D. Goodman and Ronald M. Davidson, 95–106. Albany: State University of New York Press, 1997.

Halkias, Georgios T. *Luminous Bliss: A Religious History of Pure Land Literature in Tibet: With an Annotated Translation and Critical Analysis of the Orgyen-ling Golden Short Sukhāvatīvyūha-sūtra*. Honolulu: University of Hawai'i Press, 2013.

———. "The Mirror and the Palimpsest: The Myth of Buddhist Kingship in Imperial Tibet." In *Locating Religions: Contact, Diversity and Translocality*, edited by Reinhold Glei and Nikolas Jaspert, 123–150. Leiden: Brill, 2017.

———. "Pure-Lands and Other Visions in Seventeenth-Century Tibet: A *Gnam-chos sādhana* for the Pure-Land Sukhāvatī Revealed in 1658 by Gnam-chos Mi-'gyur-rdo-rje (1645–1667)." In *Power, Politics and the Reinvention of Tradition: Tibet in the Seventeenth and Eighteenth Century*, edited by B. Cuevas et al., 121–151. Leiden: Brill, 2006.

Kapstein, Matthew. "Pure Land Buddhism in Tibet? From Sukhāvatī to the Field of Great Bliss." In *Approaching the Land of Bliss: Religious Praxis in the Cult of Amitābha*, edited by Richard Payne and Kenneth Tanaka, 1–16. Honolulu: University of Hawai'i Press, 2004.

Lobsang Shastri. "Activities of Indian Panditas in Tibet from the 14th to the 17th Century." In *Proceedings of the 9th Seminar of the International Association for Tibetan Studies, 2000: Volume 1: Tibet, Past and Present*, edited by Hank Blezer, 129–145. Leiden: Brill, 2002.

Meisezahl, R. O. "Die Schriften des Mi 'gyur rdo rǰe (1646–1667)." *Ural-Altaische Jahrbücher*, Neue Folge, Wienbaden, Harrassowitz 2 (1982): 245–272.

———. "gNam čhos, Die Schriften des Mi 'gyur rdo rǰe (1646–1667)." *Ural-Altaische Jahrbücher*, Neue Folge, Wienbaden, Harrassowitz 1 (1981): 195–226.

Skorupski, Tadeusz. "A Tibetan Prayer for Rebirth in the Sukhāvatī." *The Pure Land*, New Series no. 12 (1995): 375–409.

Tsering Lama Jampal Zangpo. *A Garland of Immortal Wish-Fulfilling Trees: The Palyul Tradition of Nyingmapa.* Ithaca, NY: Snow Lion Publications, 1988.

# II

# Contemplative Visualizations

## Overview

There is much to be said about the formation and transmission of Buddhist esoteric practices incorporating Pure Land imagery and ideology. Marketed under an Indian proliferation of name-descriptors like "Esoteric Buddhism," "Tantra," "Vajrayāna," the "Path of the Results," the "Mantra Vehicle," and so on, we find a plethora of esoteric Pure Land texts in circulation for practice by a specialized and general audience across East Asia and the highlands of Southeast Asia. Works of the esoteric Pure Land genre are innovative in their understanding of Pure Land symbology, and they challenge rigid distinctions between esoteric and exoteric Buddhism, be it academic or indigenous. They also reveal an ubiquitous Mahāyāna discourse on otherworldly realms accessible in the present moment, at the moment of death, and more commonly in the future as the result of internalized contemplations of the deity and its pure abode, and in venerations of the tantric teacher in the form of Maitreya or Buddha Amitābha.

Georgios T. Halkias (chap. II.1) focuses on an Indo-Tibetan esoteric work with Pure Land references, the *Quintessence of Amitābha: Means for Realizing the Yamāntaka of Passion* (*Amitābhā-hṛdaya-rāga-yamāri-sādhana-nāma*). The author is Atīśa Dīpaṃkaraśrījñāna (982–1054 CE), a famous Buddhist scholar and notable scholar of the Mahāvihāra Vikramaśilā, a prominent monastic university and center of Tantric Buddhism during the Pāla Empire that held close ties with Tibetan Buddhists and flourished after the finest days of Nālandā. Though Atīśa is revered as one of the greatest scholars ever to visit Tibet, modern scholarship has focused on his scholastic achievements and less so on his esoteric works. There are several Vajrayāna lineages in Tibet that can be traced to Atiśa, while many of his works in the Tengyur include ritual texts and meditation manuals belonging to the highest tantric classes of the Guhyasamāja and Cakrasaṃvara deities (Anuttarayoga). In the *Quintessence of Amitābha: Means for Realizing the Yamāntaka of Passion*, Atiśa weaves Mahāyāna pure land stereotypes with a creative process of self-transformative practices exemplified in tantra.

James Apple (chap. II.2) furnishes for the first time in English a brief eighteenth-century Tibetan prayer manual for reciting the *Hundred Deities of Tuṣita* (*Dga' ldan lha brgya ma'i rnal 'byor gyi sgo nas mdo sngags kyi lam gyi lus yongs su rdzogs pa la bag chags 'jog tshul nyams len snying por dril ba*) by the tutor to the eighth Dalai Lama, Yeshé Gyeltsen (Ye shes rgyal mtshan, 1713–1793). The prayer manual elucidates the Gelukpa (*dge lugs pa*) sect's understanding of Tuṣita Heaven as a pure land within the context of venerating the "root" guru Tsongkhapa Losang Drakpa (1357–1419). The introduction to the translation describes the historical conditions that develop for the Gelukpa veneration of Tsong-kha-pa as well as the conditions for the emergence of Maitreya's Tuṣita Heaven as a pure land in Tibetan forms of Buddhism.

Thomas Eijō Dreitlein (chap. II.3) presents a full annotated translation of the text of the *Amitāyus Ritual Manual* (*Wuliangshou yigui*), an important esoteric ritual practice manual in East Asian Buddhism, probably translated from an unknown Indic original with additions by Amoghavajra. It was significant in Tang Chinese Buddhism as an esoteric ritual for birth in Sukhāvatī, and is also an important source for the Jūhachidō ritual format that developed in Japanese esoteric Buddhism and for the esoteric Amida practices that later appeared in Japan. Dōhan (1179–1252) was a scholar-monk on Mount Kōya and lived during a time of turbulence and social upheaval.

Aaron Proffitt (chap. II.4) examines the *Himitsu nenbutsu sho* (Fascicle 1), which represents Dōhan's effort toward a synthesis of the diversity of approaches to rebirth in the Pure Land, a goal which many people at the time believed to be their only possible means of salvation. As a scholar of the Esoteric Buddhist lineage of Kūkai (774–835), Dōhan employed a wide variety of sutras, ritual texts, and commentaries to make the case that though beings may aspire for the Pure Land, Amitābha Buddha is actually as close as one's own speech and breath.

# Chapter 1

# Liberating Desire

## *An Esoteric Pure Land Text by Dīpaṃkaraśrījñāna*

Georgios T. Halkias

### Translator's Introduction

The Indian Buddhist scholar Dīpaṃkaraśrījñāna (982–1054 CE), hereafter Atiśa,[1] is one of the most revered *paṇḍitas* ever to cross the Himalayas to Tibet. His reputation as a notable teacher at the Mahāvihāra Vikramaśilā[2] earned him a generous invitation to western Tibet by the monk-prince of the royal house of Ngari, Lha Lama Yéshé Ö (Lha bla ma ye shes 'od, 947–1019/24), who sought an expert's authority to rectify the spread of spurious tantric practices across his kingdom.[3] Atiśa traveled more than a thousand kilometers to reach western Tibet from India via Nepal, arriving in Ngari in the summer of the Tibetan year of the Water Horse with an entourage of Indian and Tibetan disciples and a bundle of Sanskrit Buddhist manuscripts.

Not long after settling at Tholing vihāra in 1042, his royal host Jangchup Ö (Byang chub 'od, 984–1078) asked him to compose a treatise that reconciles the teachings of the Buddhist sutras with the tantras. In what may be one of his most widely read works composed in Sanskrit, the *Lamp for the Path to Enlightenment* (*Bodhipathapradīpa*; *Byang chub lam gyi sgron ma*), Atiśa offers a structured outline of the different phases of Indian Buddhism, which he relates to the teachings of the Buddha skillfully delivered in accordance with the mental development of people of "three disciplines" or capacities (*trisaṃvara*): beginning, intermediate, and superior. This ingenious threefold division enabled Tibetans to make sense of Buddhism's intricate ritual and doctrinal corpus that had developed more than a millennium ago since the times of Śākyamuni.[4] It was also used to explain why some of the so-called "higher teachings" of

Buddhism promising swift liberation had an effect on some people but not on others. Atiśa not only positioned tantric Buddhism firmly within the doctrinal and soteriological fold of Mahāyāna, but he elevated the fruitional path of Tantra or "vehicle of results" (*'bras bu'i theg pa*), above the so-called "vehicle of characteristics" (*mtshan nyid theg pa*) acknowledged as the Buddha's exoteric teachings (sūtra) delivered to an audience of hearers (*śrāvaka*), solitary realizers (*pratyekabuddha*), and certain bodhisattvas.

The impact of Atiśa's life and work on the development of Buddhism in Tibet should not be underestimated. This is evident when it comes to aspects that are well entrenched in Tibetan Buddhism, such as a professed doctrinal compatibility and integration of Vajrayāna practices with Mahāyāna tenets, and a hierarchized distribution of Buddhist practices. Though some scholars have downplayed Atiśa's influence in central Tibet, pointing out that he belonged to the Mahāsāṃghika (a vinaya lineage different from the Mūlasarvāstivāda followed by the Tibetans), there is little doubt that his works introduced new important trends in Tibetan literature and gave Tibetan Buddhism its distinctive flavor as the "union of the three vehicles."[5] Notable Tibetan developments in hagiographical writing (*rnam thar*) are traceable to his disciples, while the popular *lam rim* genre focusing on a gradual course of awakening was greatly influenced by his *Bodhipathapradīpa*. Furthermore, the spread of "mind training" (*blo byong*) manuals were to a large extent inspired by his *Bodhisattva's Garland of Jewels* (*Bodhisattvamaṇyāvalī*; *Byang chub sems nor bu'i 'phreng ba*), a short text containing pithy instructions on what needs to be cultivated and what ought to be abandoned on the bodhisattva's path.[6] Last but not least, his emphasis on the strict observance of "karma and its effects," the *prātimokṣa* vows, and monastic rules (*vinaya*) were important elements that characterized the ethos of the School of the Kadampa (*bka' gdams pa*), the first distinctive Tibetan Buddhist order he established with his devoted Tibetan disciple Dromtön ('Brom ston rgyal ba'i byung gnas, 1008–1064). The Kadampa and many of its distinct features were eventually absorbed into the School of the Gelukpa (*dge lugs pa*) founded under the direction of Tsongkhapa Lozang Drakpa (Tsong kha pa Blo bzang grags pa, 1357–1419), who maintained a close affinity with the teachings of the Kadampa masters.[7]

During his stay in Tibet, Atiśa taught widely on Indian Buddhist classics, favoring philosophical works by Candrakīrti (ca. 570–650 CE) and Bhāviveka's authoritative commentary on the essence of the Middle Way, the *Blaze of Reasoning* (*Tarkajvāla*; *Rtog ge 'bar ba*) (ca. 490/500–570

CE). He was a charismatic teacher who trained many Tibetan masters and was also an industrious scholar, translator, and author of philosophical works. More than one hundred translations from Sanskrit to Tibetan attributed to him are preserved in the Tengyur (*bstan 'gyur*).[8] His *Entry in the Two Truths* (*Satyadvayāvatāra*; *Bden pa gnyis la 'jug pa*), a terse work twenty-nine verses long, is considered a significant contribution to the formation of early Madhyamaka in Tibet. It inspired a short commentary, the *Collection of Instructions on the Middle Way* (*Dbu ma man ngag gi 'bum*) that "provides clear evidence of an active teaching lineage of Chandrakīrti's Madhyamaka . . . brought to Tibet by Atiśa."[9]

Atiśa's erudition extended well into Esoteric Buddhist tenets and practices. From biographical accounts we learn that in his early years he embraced the life of a tantric yogi and received the secret tantric name Jñānaguhyavajra after receiving initiation and teachings on the Hevajra by Rāhulagupta. He spent several years in Uḍḍiyāna, a flourishing Indian center of Buddhist Esotericism, where he apparently joined in "tantric feasts in the company of *ḍākinī*."[10] According to *The Jewel Garland of Buddhist History* (*Chos 'byung jin bris nor bu 'phreng ba*), he studied the tantras for nine years and trained under renowned tantric adepts or Mahāsiddhas like Jetāri, Kāṅha, Avadhūtipa, Dombhipa, and Nāropa, from whom he learned the *Kalachakra Tantra* (*Dus kyi 'khor lo rtsa rgyud*).[11] Remembered by the Tibetans with "a smile ever present on his face and Sanskrit mantras always on his lips," it is recounted that he held numerous visions of Buddhist deities during his life and attained supernormal powers (*siddhi*).[12] We may come to better appreciate hagiographical references to his mystical experiences if we bear in mind that during his times the model of the "scholar-cum-adept" (*paṇḍita-siddha*; *mkhas grup*) played an integral part in the self-definition of elite scholars in Indian Buddhist universities, as it did later for teachers in monastic establishments across Tibet.

In the *Summary of All Pledges* (*Sarvasamayasaṃgraha*; *Dam tshig thams cad bsdus pa*) Atiśa reiterates traditional Indian arguments for the superiority of Vajrayāna over the "Perfection Vehicle" (*Pāramitāyāna*).[13] His *Summary* inspired the prodigious Tibetan compiler Butön (Bu ston rin chen grup, 1290–1364) to write on the contemplative and efficacious advantages of Tantra, contributing his own views to a debated topic in Indo-Tibetan Buddhism.[14]

There are several Vajrayāna lineages and practices in Tibet that could be linked to Atiśa. His tantric works preserved in the Tengyur feature Guhyasamāja and Cakrasaṃvara ritual texts and meditation manuals belonging to the highest tantric class (Anuttarayoga; *bla na med pa'i rgyu*). Some of his other works center on Mahāyāna and Vajrayāna deities like Hayagrīva, Vajrayoginī, Vajrapāṇi, Achala, Avalokiteśvara, and Tārā, who is reported to have accompanied him in mystical visions throughout his life.[15] According to some counts, given the charged climate in western Tibet he was not permitted to translate tantric texts during his three-year stay there. Whatever may have been the extent or truth of this prohibition, he was not deterred from devising a unique version of the *Guhyasamāja Tantra* (*Gsang ba 'dus pa rtsa rgyud*), with Lokeśvara as the central deity, while residing at Guge.[16]

Contemporary scholarship has focused for the most part on Atiśa the philosopher-cum-scholar, ignoring or rationalizing the more mystical and subjective sides of Tibetan Buddhism. There is, however, an undeniable mystical side to his life that is not missed by Tibetan hagiographical traditions. Here we read that he relied on liminal visions to prophesy the founding of Sangphu Neuthok (Gsang phu ne'u thog) and to discover a hidden "treasure-text" (*gter ma*) buried in a pillar in the Jokhang Temple, the main cathedral of Lhasa. These tenuous associations with the new Tantric schools (*gsar ma*) and the imperial treasure tradition upheld by the Nyingma (School of the Old Tantras) are not incidental. They seem to reflect a creative social milieu where nascent Tibetan Buddhist orders vied for ways to legitimize and secure their diverse teaching lineages and practices by tracing their origins to authoritative Indian antecedents. It is of no small importance to Tibet's intellectual history that his alleged discovery of three manuscripts known as the *Pillar Testament* (*Bka' chems ka khol ma*) are considered a main historical source for conceptualizing Buddhism during the imperial period and for anticipating the subsequent development of the treasure tradition.[17]

## The *Quintessence of Amitābha*

The *Quintessence of Amitābha: Means for Realizing the Yamāntaka of Passion* (*Amitābhā-hṛdaya-rāga-yamāri-sādhana-nāma*; *'Od dpag tu med pa'i snying po 'dod chags gshin rje gshed sgrub pa'i thabs*) offers us a glimpse into Atiśa's tantric legacy in Tibet. It is unclear if this work preserved in the Tengyur was among the Sanskrit manuscripts he brought from India or if it was composed during his stay in Tibet over a period of twelve years until his death in 1054. The *Quintessence of Amitābha* is a terse *sādhana* in which Atiśa integrates Pure Land views and imagery with the subtle practices of Tantra. Long before Atiśa's time, soteriological beliefs associated with the contemplation of pure lands (or buddha-fields) were made popular with the advent of Mahāyāna and the pan-Asian spread of Pure Land scriptures, like the short and long *Sukhāvatīvyūha* sutras, the *Ārya-aparimitāyur-jñāna-nāma-mahāyāna-sūtra*, and the *Ārya-aparimitāyur-jñāna-hṛdaya-nāma-dhāraṇī.*[18]

The *Quintessence of Amitābha* is a thought-provoking text in that it reflects both late tenth-century Indian perspectives on pure lands orientations and on Esoteric Buddhism. There is no indication in Atiśa's biography that he composed the *Quintessence of Amitābha* motivated by a personal aspiration for rebirth in Sukhāvatī.[19] It may very well be that he utilized pure lands aspirations and related conceptions in predictable and expected ways that seem to support Schopen's hypothesis of the generic function of Sukhāvatī across Indian Mahāyāna literature.[20] In fact, there seem to be several compatible and complementary ways to read the *Quintessence of Amitābha*. It is an Esoteric manual for contemplative practice, a historical document for the development of Indo-Tibetan Buddhism in the eleventh century, and more generically an exercise that establishes correspondences across conceptual boundaries that accord with Esoteric texts in general and with Atiśa's integration of the two vehicles in particular.[21]

Arguably, correlative schemes are commonplace in the tantras. They instigate a higher order of mutual interconnectedness between Buddhist orientations, philosophical doctrines, meditative experiences, and other concept clusters including activities, perceptual states and ways of knowing related to the Buddhist path. In his study of Japanese Esoteric traditions, Rambelli notes that in both Indian and Chinese tantric systems correlative thought elements are "organized in closed series regulated by a rigorous combinatory logic. Correlative thinking makes the entities 'consubstantial' and 'interchangeable' with each other."[22] This seems to be the case with Buddha Amitābha, a popular Mahāyāna deity that has been interpreted in a variety of ways across Indo-Tibetan tantric literature. In all classes of Tantra (i.e., *Kriyā, Caryā, Yoga, Anuttarayoga*) he is the main buddha figure of the "Lotus Family" (*padmakula; pad ma'i rigs*) and is conceptually linked with the aggregate of discrimination (*saṃjñā; 'du shes*).[23] At the same time, he is phenomenologically associated with speech, communication, longing, and desire, and he is commonly supplicated during the "awareness empowerment of the vajra," one of "five knowledge empowerments" (*rig pa'i dbang lnga*) in Vajrayāna.[24] In the *Cloud of White Lotus Offerings*, Könchok Tsültrim (Dkon mchog tshul khrims, 1892–1972) explains that during this initiation, vajra is the empowering object, the faculty of discrimination is the aggregate blessed, desire is the affliction purified, and pristine wisdom of individual analysis is the resultant state.[25] Thus, while Amitābha signifies on an elemental level the primacy of fire with its properties of consumption and luminosity and figures in a variety of gnoseological processes, all these threads may be read from the perspective of the path of mental training as hermeneutic methods leading individually and in unison toward an awareness that discerns the transient nature and insubstantiality of phenomena in their reification through a number of language registers and speech acts.

## *The* Sādhana *of Deity Yoga*

The *sādhana* (*sgrub thabs*), or "means of accomplishing" spiritual or mundane aims is a common genre of Indo-Tibetan Vajrayāna literature. Works of this type tend to be similar in their structure but differ in their selection of tantric deities, their length, details of their composition, and the attainments (*siddhi*) associated with the central deity.[26] The ultimate aim of "deity-yoga" (*devatāyoga*; *lha'i rnal 'byor*) is coemergent union with the "tutelary deity" (*yi dam*) understood in progressively more subtle ways. At a basic level of interpretation, deity-yoga stands for the "skill-in-means" (*upāya*; *thabs*), or method of associating the "deity of primordial wisdom" (*ye shes pa'i lha*) with one's self-arising "wisdom or awareness" (*prajñā*; *shes rab*).

There is a great variety in the sequence of practices within these texts, depending on which level of tantra and which tradition they belong to. Different relationships with the deity are cultivated, such as that of the lord, friend, sibling, and then total identification through visualization of oneself as the deity.[27] A series of interiorized visualizations are said to produce a radical and transformative recognition of the tripartite aspects of identification of one's body, speech, and mind as "self" with a selfless state of awareness exemplified by the archetypal deity.

From one perspective it is a transformation of the practitioner's body, speech, and mind (*lus ngag yid*) into enlightened body, speech, and mind (*sku gsung thugs*) of a chosen buddha (*yi dam*). The transformation of the body is performed through generating oneself as the *yidam* and taking up its pride (*nga rgyal*); the transformation of the speech through the recitation of the *yidam*'s mantra; and the transformation of the mind through gathering back the visualization of the *yidam* and dissolving it into non-dual emptiness.[28]

There is considerable complexity and subtlety in the practice of *sādhanas*, and a detailed treatment would take us far beyond the scope of the present study. That being said, a few remarks may be useful. An important side of correlative thinking in the *sādhanas* lies in the supposition of a unifying field between modalities of knowing, perception, and expression. Hence, one's own subjective condition is reconstituted through a series of correspondences, functions, and associations that mirror seemingly differentiated aspects of a singular reality. The visualized deity forms (*yi dam*) and the "vajra body" (*rdo rje lus*) are seen both as modalities of perception and as expressions of timeless awareness manifesting through a series of symbolic, psychological, and cosmological actions embodied during the *sādhana*. Although deities, like the practitioners who invoke them, are not meant to be treated as substantial self-existing objects in the world, in tantric commentaries we are told that they are "not merely one's fabrication" either, but the "progressive manifestation of *one's own mind* that realizes emptiness."[29]

## *The Sublimation of Desire and Death*

For the nonsectarian (*ris med*) Tibetan Buddhist scholar Jamgön Kongtrul Lodrö Thaye ('Jam mgon kong sprul blo gros mtha' yas, 1813–1899), "the uncommon approach of mantra is to transform afflictive emotions." When desire toward another arises, this transformation is attained either by conceptually inhabiting the luminous form of Amitābha, or a ferocious deity such as Heruka in a sexual merging with his consort. The same applies to all other deluded emotions that can be treated in related ways.[30] It may seem inconsistent with the sobriety and self-restraint of early Buddhist scriptures that later Indo-Tibetan tantric literature abounds with vivid references to desire and sexuality. Buddhist traditions acknowledge the illusive power of desire as the driving force that fuels the world of becoming and turns, metaphorically speaking, the interminable wheel of craving and becoming. The view that desire is the source of one's experience in the world recalls a passage from the *Upanisads*: "As one desires, so does one become, for the person is made of desire. As he desires, so does his will become; as his will is, so is the action he does."[31]

For the *Hevajra Tantra* (*Kye'i rdo rje'i rgyud*), desire is the origin of all things that manifest either as differentiating mind (*saṃsāra*) or unifying awareness (*nirvāṇa*), while the potential for liberation lies in the recognition of the dependent arising nature of both as displays of our own subjectivity. Thus, we read, "That by which the world is bound, by the same things it is released from bondage. But the world is deluded and does not understand this truth, and one who does not possess this truth cannot attain perfection."[32] For Snellgrove, pleasure and desire should not be avoided since tantra "recognizes the powerful energy aroused by our desires to be an indispensable resource for the spiritual path."[33] He explains: "Because the goal is nothing less than the realization of our highest human potential, tantra seeks to transform every experience—no matter how 'unreligious' it may appear—into the path of fulfilment. It is precisely because our present life is so inseparably linked with desire that we must make use of desire's tremendous energy if we wish to transform our life into something transcendental."

In the sixth chapter of *Outline of the Jewel Mound of Instructions* (*Man ngag rin chen spungs pa'i dkar chag*) the Tibetan author Chégompa (Lce sgom pa; twelfth–thirteenth centuries) divides Mahāyāna into the paths of sutra and tantra and argues that the Buddha taught the path of the sutra "for people who are only slightly afflicted by desire and who are able to renounce the world." But for most people, who are greatly afflicted by desire and can't renounce the world, he taught the Mantra path.[34] The Indian master Tripiṭakamāla echoed similar views when he said that "desire is brought to the path only by those whose meditation is disturbed by lustful thoughts," a position that had its share of criticism in the Gelukpa School.[35]

In fact, spiritual responses to desire (sexual and otherwise) vary according to the Buddhist tradition or vehicle. For the so-called early teachings of the *śrāvakas*, desire is a source of suffering and countermeasures and contemplative antidotes are prescribed against it. On the other side of the spectrum, for tantric Buddhism the arising of desire is concomitant with awakening and this understanding may serve as an impetus for enhancing the awareness of one's insubstantial condition. We can appreciate the function of symbols and correlative associations in our tantric manual as the "skillful means" for channeling desire in the deity-form Yamāntaka, located in the west where the sun sets and the ensuing darkness serves as the background against a stunning state of luminosity in the shape of Amitābha.[36] In time, our conventional ideations and habitual illusions of familiarity are challenged through an intricate series of intra- and extratextual configurations of signification (in the form of sounds, symbols, and language) that point simultaneously to something within and beyond ourselves.

Not unlike other Indo-Tibetan tantric texts, the *Quintessence of Amitābha* aims at the most basic level to induce a cognitive-emotive break from ordinary modes of self-fixation during the deity-generation stage into another shape and form (*utpattikrama*; *bskyed rim*). The conceptualization of desire as a dynamic process of birth, life, and sexual union is followed by an eventual exhaustion of theoretical elaborations and dissociations between self and other during the perfection stage (*utpanakrama*; *rdzogs rim*) of deity-yoga, a process akin to orgasm, death, and liberation.[37]

The creation stage undermines attachment to the solid, impure phenomenal world, but it can still leave us with traces of attachment to this new manifestation we have created or perceived. So in the completion stage, the whole new wonderful world dissolves back into basic ground, from which it never really departed. In the context of relationship with life cycles mentioned above, this stage corresponds to death. Recognizing that the visualization was created in the first place by mind, empty and radiant, and dissolves back to it purifies or prepares us for the process of actual death, when this realization can result in full awakening.[38]

As in mystery cults, the *sādhaka* undergoes a symbolic yet just as genuine initiatory process from anxiety-ridden states of routine mental confinement and dimmed perceptual visibility to the liberating expanse of omnidirectional awareness, during which time his habitual divisions and engagements with things, oneself, and others are channeled into a translucent and noncorporeal deity-form endowed with exalted qualities and nonlocalized attributes. In due course, the *sādhaka* dissolves the deity-form into "emptiness," or non-dual awareness. During this transition from duality to non-duality and back he experiences a profound sense of liberation from solid enactments of individuality even at the subtlest level of his identification with the deity. Through repetitive practice and adaptation he is said to arrive at an experiential understanding of the arising of desire, deity, and the dissolution of deity as expressions and experiences of motion and stillness, resonance and intensity emanating from an all-encompassing field of timeless awareness.

In the twilight language (*sāṃdhyā-bhāṣā*; *dgongs pa'i skad*) of mysticism and layered signification that characterizes tantric texts, we are confronted with a timeless contest between desire for birth, becoming, and sexual union with another (*ἔρως*; *eros*), and of death personifying the ultimate fear of separation, singularity, destruction, and undoing (*θάνατος*; *thanatos*). These themes are brought forward, enacted, and sublimated, if not in a strict Freudian sense, certainly within a Buddhist soteriological framework where one's dualistic imaginings and projections are transformed through their inherent potential for liberation from fixation in the unfathomable state of insubstantiality from which they have never departed.

## Contents and Summary of the *Quintessence of Amitābha*

To facilitate a better understanding of the contents and structure of the *Quintessence of Amitābha*, the Tibetan-English translation has been divided into the following nine headings (I–IX) not found in the Tibetan text.

I. Title in Sanskrit and Tibetan
II. Homage to Vajrasattva and Yamāntaka
III. Statement of Purpose
IV. Mahāyāna Intention and the Six Perfections
  IV.1. Aspiring for Two Benefits (Self and Others)
  IV.2. Practicing the 'Six Perfections'
V. Preparatory Rituals and Practices
  V.1. Mantra Recitation and Ablution Ritual
  V.2. Purification (Meditation on Emptiness)
  V.3. Prostrations, and so forth
  V.4. Four Mahāyāna Rituals
  V.5. Meditation on the Emptiness of Self
  V.6. Meditation on Amitābha
    V.6.a. For Protection
    V.6.b. For Purifying the Buddha-Fields
VI. Deity Generation and Empowerment
  VI.1. Visualization of Seed Syllables
  VI.2. Recitation of Amitābha's Mantra
  VI.3. Meditation on Emptiness
  VI.4. Self-Generation as Vajra-Amitābha with Companions
  VI.5. Other-Base Generation as Yamāntaka
  VI.6. Contemplation of the Five Elements
  VI.7. Identification with the Deity
  VI.8. Above-Generation of Yamāntaka
  VI.9. Offerings to Carcikā
  VI.10. Identification with the Essence of the Deity
  VI.11. Visualization of Syllables and Mantra Recitation
  VI.12. Meditation on Emptiness
VII. Post-meditation Session
  VII.1. Releasing the Mudra
  VII.2. Awakened Dignity
VIII. Pure Lands Dedication Prayer
IX. Coda

As in most Sanskrit-Tibetan translations in the Tibetan canon, section I contains the Sanskrit and Tibetan titles of the *Quintessence of Amitābha*. In section II homage is given to the peaceful Vajrasattva[39] and the wrathful deity Yamāntaka conceptually invoked but with indivisible nonconceptual attributes of mind, speech, and body. Yamāntaka, also known as Bhairava, is a furious bull-headed form of the celestial bodhisattva of wisdom Mañjuśrī. He is commonly visualized in several modifications with "one, three or nine" heads, with "two, six, fourteen or thirty-four" arms, and "two or sixteen" legs. The etymology of his name gives "the destroyer of the lord of death," and in this capacity he personifies the forceful overcoming of all obstructing forces to realization, understood here as a compulsive process of differentiation, of becoming self and other, and of experiencing death and life as a pair of irreconcilable opposites (*saṃsāra*).[40] Section III states that the purpose of the *Quintessence of Amitābha* is to provide an explanation of the *sādhana* of Vajra-Yamāntaka for devotees of Bhairava (i.e., Yamāntaka). Section IV reinforces the ideal of a bodhisattva who cultivates a mind that aspires to awakening (*bodhicitta*; *byang chub*) for the benefit of oneself and others, and suggests prior familiarity with the training of a bodhisattva in the practice of giving (*dāna*; *sbyin pa*), the first of the so called "six perfections" (*ṣaṭpāramitā*; *pha rol tu phyin pa drug*). The other five are not listed but implied, namely: discipline (*śīla*; *tshul khrims*), patience (*kṣānti*; *bzod pa*), diligence (*vīrya*; *brtson 'grus*), meditation (*dhyāna*; *bsam gtan*), and wisdom (*prajñā*; *shes rab*). Section V introduces purification and apotropaic rituals including the performance of ablution with mantra recitation, contemplation of one's own inner essence, prostrations, and the four rituals of Mahāyāna, that is, the cultivation of the so-called four immeasurable aspirations. The practitioner is asked to "meditate on the Protector of the Lotus [i.e., Hayagrīva] to pacify negative forces and purify the buddha-fields,"[41] for the sake of dispelling interferences from negative forces and for "purifying the buddha-fields." The conception of "purifying the buddha-fields" is a recurrent motif in Indian Mahāyāna literature and symbolizes the bodhisattva's ethical and meditative training that goes into the purification of his mind from the root *kleśas*, or "three poisons" (*dug gsum*), namely aggression, desire, and ignorance.[42] In section VI we encounter the main practices of the *sādhana* starting with the self-generation of the "empty deity" (*stong pa'i lha*), called in our text "*the mother of self-awareness*" (i.e., meditation on emptiness). This is followed with the "deity of sound" (*sgra'i lha*) and the "deity of letters" (*yi ge'i lha*) and finally one's "self-generation" (*bdag bskyed*) into the "deity of form" (*gzugs kyi lha*), that of Vajra-Amitābha (*rdo rje snang ba mtha' yas*) and his two pure land bodhisattva acolytes, Avalokiteśvara and Vajrapāṇi.[43] After this, one engages in the generation of Yamāntaka visualized clearly in his wrathful aspects on top of one's head and receives empowerment. Meditation of the five elements (*'byung ba lnga*), earth, water, fire, air, and space, is the method hinted for the manipulation and transformation of karmic wind movements and their corresponding elements that go into the formation of the physical experience of one's body.

Atiśa admonishes that even if the *sādhaka* has been initiated to different levels of tantric exegesis, he should continue to propitiate Carcikā[44] and other tutelary gods and goddesses. The eventual synthesis between the generation and perfection stages parallels the union of life and death, the inseparability of method and wisdom, desire and its consummation. "The absolute cannot be understood independently of general [Buddhist] practice (vyavahāra). Without the ladder of genuine relativity a wise man cannot ascend to the top of the palace of reality (tattva)," Atiśa explains elsewhere.[45] In line with the presentation of other *sādhanas*, the *Quintessence of Amitābha* does not end with a dissolution meditation in emptiness. At the end of the session, the *sādhaka* returns to conventional reality, "emerging from a compassionate awakening" (*snying rje sad pas langs nas*)[46] with the "pride of the deity" (*lha'i nga rgyal*), or the confidence and certainty that stems from preserving the insights gained during meditation in daily life.[47] Section VIII concludes with a typical Pure Land aspiration: "through the sādhana of these potent teachings of the Buddha, may all migrating beings [arise] on a most stainless lotus." While "birth on a stainless lotus" can be read as a generic Mahāyāna metaphor for attaining liberation from *saṃsāra*, there are additional hermeneutic layers to the rich symbolism of Buddha Amitābha and his western field in tantric literature. Section IX confirms that we have reached the end of our text composed by Ācāraya Dīpaṃkara.

## The *Quintessence of Amitābha*: A Tibetan-English Translation

The following English translation of the *Quintessence of Amitābha: Means for Realizing the Yamāntaka of Desire* is based on the Tibetan text published in the Tengyur Pedurma.[48] According to the colophon, the *Quintessence of Amitābha* was originally written in Sanskrit by Dīpaṃkaraśrījñāna and translated in Tibetan after his death by Prajñāśrījñānakīrti (1062–1102), a scholar whose name is attested in several Sanskrit-Tibetan translations in the Tengyur.

The *Quintessence of Amitābha* is a tantric practice manual that would have been accompanied by Atiśa's oral instructions given to his initiated disciples for whom this *sādhana* was originally intended. In the absence of a commentary, the following translation reflects an attempt to make sense of an arcane system of tantric teachings originally written in Sanskrit and imparted in an outline form nearly a millennium ago. For my understanding and interpretation of this text I am indebted to later Tibetan exegetical literature on tantra, which may or may not reflect Atiśa's own original predilections. Hence any unresolved ambiguities, errors, and misunderstandings burden the present translator. The use of notes is meant to provide explanatory references to difficult passages. Section headings and insertions in square brackets are not found in the Tibetan text and are introduced for the purpose of making the text more readable. The Tibetan is provided in parentheses for a few specialized terms in anticipation of potential interest by the readers.

## Translation

### *Quintessence of Amitābha: Means for Realizing the Yamāntaka of Desire*

Ācārya Dīpaṃkara

[I. Title in Sanskrit and Tibetan]
In the language of India: *Amitābhā-hṛdaya-rāga-yamāri-sādhana-nāma*
In the language of Tibet: *'Od dpag tu med pa'i snying po 'dod chags gshin rje gshed sgrub pa'i thabs*

[II. Homage to Vajrasattva and Yamāntaka]
I pay homage to the magnificent Vajrasattva and to the supreme Yamāntaka, undivided in their awakened body, speech, and mind.

[III. Statement of Purpose]
For whomever is devoted to Bhairava I will explain the *sādhana* of *Adamantine Passion* (Vajra-Yamāntaka; *'Dod chags rdo rje*).[49]

[IV. Mahāyāna Intention and the Six Perfections]

[IV.1. Aspiring for the Two Benefits (Self and Others)]
Uphold the benefit of yourself and others.

[IV.2. Practicing the "Six Perfections"]

Properly train in generosity, and so forth [the other five perfections] to gain trust, wisdom, and compassion.

[V. Preparatory Rituals and Practices]

[V.1. Mantra Recitation and Ablution Ritual]

At the beginning apply this "mantra" for the protection of [your] mind and perform [rituals] of "ablution" (*khrus*).[50]

[V.2. Purification (Meditation on Emptiness)]

[Then] sit on a cloth spread [on the ground] and "arouse the utmost essence of your being" (*rang gi snying nyid bskul bar bya*).

[V.3. Prostrations, and so forth]

Perform the collection [of practices] comprising prostrations and so forth.

[V.4. Four Mahāyāna Rituals]

[Perform] the "four rituals of Mahāyāna" (*theg chen cho ga bzhi*).[51]

[V.5. Meditation on the Emptiness of Self]

In the very condition of your "empty nature" (*stong pa'i rang bzhin de nyid*) the [illusion] of the "continuity of self" (*bdag rgyud*) will be purified.

[V.6. Meditation on Amitābha]

Meditate on the *Protector of the Lotus*, [Amitābha/Hayagrīva]

[V.6.a. For Protection]

with the resolve to subdue obstructing forces

[V.6.b. For Purifying the Buddha-Fields]

and to "purify the buddha-fields" [V.6.b].

[VI. Deity Generation and Empowerment]

[VI.1. Visualization of Seed Syllables]

Receive consecration from various light rays darting forth like weapons from the "seed syllables" (*sa bon*) *baṁ* and *raṁ* blazing on a sun disk,[52] the gathering of "sixteen arrows" (*bcu drug mda'*) together with five light rays.[53]

[VI.2. Recitation of Amitābha's Mantra]

[while reciting the mantra] oṁ amitābhā hrīdaya rāga yamāri ātma konya haṁ.

[VI.3. Meditation on Emptiness]

With the method of the "mother of self-awareness" (*rang rig yum*),[54]

[VI.4. Self-Generation as Vajra-Amitābha with Companions]

Transform into Vajra-Amitābha [sited] on a lotus with radiance similar to a ruby, and a blue and a white presence on his two sides [Vajrapāṇi and Avalokiteśvara].[55]

[VI.5. Other-Base Generation as Yamāntaka]
[Meditate] on the upper and lower forces causing fright on your skin, [as you visualize the deity] with a hooked knife, skull and sword, and a precious wheel of fierce destruction, [wearing] a serpent and skeletons as various ornaments, with raised hair, threatening fangs, and raging eyes staring out of a blazing fire.
[VI.6. Contemplation of the Five Elements]
Meditate on your vajra eyes, ears, nose, and tongue as they relate to the elements of your body starting with the nature of earth and so forth [the elements of water, fire, air, space].
[VI.7. Identification with the Deity]
Contemplate that your vajra body, speech, and mind (*rdo rje lus dang ngag yid*) is the Buddha's vajra body, speech, and mind (*rdo rje sku gsung thugs*).[56]
[VI.8. Above-Generation of Yamāntaka]
Abide in an "immutable state" (*mi bskyod*)[57] to receive the empowerment of the "Destroyer of Death" [Yamāntaka] visualized above your head.
[VI.9. Offerings to Carcikā]
Even if you have entered the "four gates of mantra" (*sgo bzhi'i sngags*),[58] raise various offerings to Carcikā[59] and others [i.e., goddesses, gods, etc.].
[VI.10. Identification with the Essence of the Deity]
You are of the nature of vajra-passion and the most horrific "Destroyer of Death."
Realize desire as the source of [all] phenomena. Make obeisance and praise these exalted teachings!
[VI.11. Visualization of Syllables and Mantra Recitation]
[Perform] the consecration with [the syllables] oṁ āḥ huṁ, emanating from and gathering into the taste of nectar.[60] For as long as the yogi remains unwary he should emanate, absorb, and spread the field of recitation: oṁ ā ro līk rā ga ti huṁ huṁ huṁ paṭ paṭ sva hā.[61]
[VI.12. Meditation on Emptiness]
Recollect all kinds of desires and attachments up until the contemplation of excessive passion. Give up the continuous recitation of mantras and meditate instead on the unfathomable [state of the] "unborn" (*a don*).[62]

[VII. Post-Meditation Session]
[VII.1. Releasing the Mudra]
Having emerged from a compassionate awakening, take on the activity of releasing the mudra.[63]

[VII.2. Awakened Dignity]
If you abandon the pride of one who is awakened toward all [phenomena] your *samaya* (*dam tshig*) will deteriorate.[64]

[VIII. Pure Land Dedication Prayer]
Through the *sādhana* practice of these powerful teachings may numerous passions decline as you sail across the ocean of *saṃsāra* on a boat of bliss. May all migrating beings [arise] on a stainless lotus.

[IX. Coda]
The so-called *Quintessence of Amitābha: Means for Realizing the Yamāntaka of Desire* by Ācāraya Dīpaṃkara has been completed.

## Notes

1 According to Helmut Eimer, "The Development of the Biographical Tradition concerning Atiśa Dīpaṃkaraśrījñāna," *Journal of the Tibet Society* 2 (1982): 47 note 1, the name Atiśa derives from the Sanskrit *atiśaya,* meaning "eminent, superior" (*phul du byung ba*), but this name is not attested in any of the Sanskrit sources.

2 A prominent monastic university and center of tantric Buddhism during the Pāla Empire that held close ties with Tibetan Buddhists and flourished after the finest days of Nālandā University.

3 In "Problems in the Transmission of Vajrayāna Buddhism in the Western Himalaya about the Year 1000," in *The Medieval Period: c. 850–1895, The Development of Buddhist Paramountcy*, ed. Alex Mckay (London: RoutledgeCurzon, 2003 [1984]), 123–133, David Seyford Ruegg argues that the syncretism between Śaivism and Buddhist Vajrayāna in the Himalayas explains the controversial tantric practices of "union" and "liberation" or "mactation" (*sbyor grol*) that were widespread in western Tibet and which forced the king of Purang, *lha bla-ma* Ye-shes-'od, to issue an ordinance against them; see Samten Karmay "The Ordinance of lHa Bla-ma Ye-Shes-'od," in *The Arrow and the Spindle: Studies in History, Myths, Rituals and Beliefs in Tibet,* ed. Samten Karmay (Kathmandu: Mandala Book Point, 1998 [1980]), 3–16. In *Tibetan Renaissance: Tantric Buddhism in the Rebirth of Tibetan Culture* (New York: Columbia University Press, 2005), 79, Ronald Davidson similarly notes that according to the *Pillar Testament*, said to have been discovered by Atiśa, Ngakpas, or village tantric lamas, were granting consecrations without having received them, "deceiving people by singing mantras as if they were songs, and offering sexual congress during *abhiṣeka* rituals for a fee, a form of ritualized prostitution."

4 According to the qualifications of practitioners, tantric practices were relegated to those Mahāyāna aspirants of the highest capacity. In *Indo-Tibetan Buddhism: Indian Buddhists and their Tibetan Successors* (Boston: Shambhala, 2002), 483, David Snellgrove notes that "this famous little work of Atiśa's seems to be conceived as a kind of accommodation to the wishes of his host," for there seems to be a conflict of priorities between his praising of monastic virtues on the one hand and tantric initiations on the other, since the latter are reserved for those of higher capacity but not accessible for those with monastic vows.

5 See Davidson, *Tibetan Renaissance*, 110–111, and John Powers, *Introduction to Tibetan Buddhism* (Ithaca, NY: Snow Lion Publications), 157–158. For a discussion of the *triyāna*, see Georgios T. Halkias, "Buddhist Meditation Traditions in Tibet: The Union of the Three Vehicles," in *Buddhist Meditation: An Introduction*, ed. Sharah Shaw (New York: Routledge Press, 2008), 159–186.

6 In his biography we read that Atiśa studied in the monastic university of Odantapurī with Dharmarakṣita, the author of the famous mind-training manual, *The Wheel of Sharp Weapons*; see Alaka Chattopadhyaya, *Atīśa and Tibet: Life and Works of Dīpaṃkara Śrījñāna in Relation to the History and Religion of Tibet* (Delhi: Motlilal Banarsidass, 1981 [1967]), 378. For a landmark *lam rim* text that is based on the *Bodhipathapradīpa,* see Tsongkhapa's *The Great Treatise on the Stages of the Path to Enlightenment* (*Byang chub lam rim chen mo*).

7 In fact most of our information of the history of the Kadampa school and its main agents are from systematic collections by scholars of the Gelukpa tradition composed from the late fifteenth century onwards; see Ulrike Roesler, "On the History of Histories: The Case of the bKa' gdams pa-s," in *Contributions to Tibetan Buddhist Literature. Tibetan Studies: Proceedings of the Eleventh Seminar of the International Association for Tibetan Studies*, ed. Orna Almogi (Halle: International Institute of Tibetan Studies, 2008), 393–413.

8 Chattopadhyaya, *Atīśa and Tibet*, appendix B, classifies a large number of texts in the Tibetan canon where Atiśa is listed as author and translator (section 2); author only (section 3); translator only (sections 4 and 7). Though this work contains much useful biographical information, it is also ridden with inaccurate interpretations and it should be consulted with caution.

9 James Apple, "An Early Tibetan Commentary on Atiśa's *Satyadvayāvatāra*," *Journal of Indian Philosophy* 41, no. 3 (2013): 265. For Atiśa's contributions to Madhyamaka philosophy in Tibet, see James Apple, "An Early Bka'-gdams-pa Madhyamaka Work Attributed to Atiśa Dīpaṃkaraśrījñāna," *Journal of Indian Philosophy* 44, no. 4 (2016): 619–725. Karen Lang, "Spa-tshab nyi-ma grags and the introduction of Prasaṅgika Madhyamaka into Tibet," in

*Reflections on Tibetan Culture: Essays in Memory of Turrell Wyllie* (New York: Mellen Press, 1990), 132, has argued that "Atiśa established the works of Bhāviveka and Chandrakīrti as the basis of Madhyamaka study."

10 Chattopadhyaya, *Atīśa and Tibet*, 74–75. In the absence of Indian literary sources, we have to rely exclusively on Tibetan sources for biographical information on Atiśa; see Eimer, "The Development of the Biographical Tradition concerning Atīśa Dīpaṃkaraśrījñāna," 41–51.

11 See Snellgrove, *Indo-Tibetan Buddhism*, 480. This being said, he doesn't seem to have authored or translated any works on this subject.

12 See Das Sri Sarat, *Indian Pandits in the Land of Snows* (Calcutta: Baptist Mission Press, 1893), 74, and Lobsang Norbu Tsonawa, *Indian Buddhist Pandits from "The Jewel Garland of Buddhist History"* (Dharamsala: Library of Tibetan Works and Archives, 1985), 67. Additional hagiographical information is in George N. Roerich, *The Blue Annals* (Calcutta: Royal Asiatic Society of Bengal, 1949–1953), 241–261.

13 Atiśa the Indian master Indrabhūti listed seven reasons for the superiority of Tantra: (1) the guru (*bla ma*), (2) vessel or disciple (*snod*), (3) rite (*cho ga*), (4) activity (*las*), (5) pledge (*dam tshig*), (6) view (*lta ba*), and (7) practice (*spyod pa*). In the same work he explains that the vow taken by tantric practitioners is to work for the benefit of oneself and others and this differs from the *pratimokṣa* pledges of individual liberation for the sake of oneself, and the bodhisattva vow that is taken for the benefit of others; see Peking Kangyur 4547, vol. 81, 209.5.5–209.5.5 and 211.5.5–211.5.6 respectively.

14 In his work Butön solicits supporting views from nine Indian scholars: Tripiṭakamāla, Jñānashrī, Ratnākarashānti, Nāgārjuna, Indhrabhūti, Jñānapāda, Ḍombhīheruka, Vajraghaṇṭapāda, and Samayavajra; see *Extensive Presentation of the General Tantra Sets: Ornaments Beautifying the Precious Tantra Sets* (*Rgyud sde spyi'i rnam par gzhag pa rgyud sde rin po che'i mdzes rgyan*) translated in English by Jeffrey Hopkins, *Tantric Techniques* (Ithaca, NY: Snow Lion Publications, 2008), 205–242. Arguably, for the Tibetan tradition the most influential has been Tripiṭakamāla's views for the superiority of tantra discussed in the *Nayatrayapradīpa* (Lamp for the three modes): "Even if the aim is the same [between the two vehicles], the Mantra Vehicle is superior due to non-obscuration, many skillful methods, non-difficulty, and being designed for those of sharp faculties"; see Donald Lopez in *Elaborations on Emptiness: Uses of the Heart Sūtra* (Princeton, NJ: Princeton University Press, 1993), 90 note 20, who notes that the above verse by Tripiṭakamāla (Toh. 3707; rgyud tsu, 16b3ff.) has been widely cited on Tibetan discussions about the difference between sutra and tantra and has been forcefully criticized by Tsongkhapa.

15 Achala, Avalokiteśvara, and Tārā, along with Śākyamuni, are the four main meditation deities of the Kadampa School (*bka' gdams lha bzhi*). It would ap-

pear that Tārā was Atiśa's main meditational deity. A north Indian work by Vāgīśvarakīrti on delaying or "cheating death" was translated into Tibetan by him and Rinchen Zangpo (958–1055) and was destined to become a primary source for White Tārā practices in Tibet; see Johannes Schneider, *Vāgīśvarakīrtis Mṛtyuvañcanopadeśa, eine buddhistische Lehrschrift zur Abwehr der Todes*, Beiträge zur Kultur-und Geistesgeschichte Asiens, 66, Denkschriften der philoso-phisch-historischen Klasse, 394 (Vienna: Verlag der Österreichischen Akademie der Wissenschaften, 2010), 68.

16 The prohibition is mentioned by Luciano Petech, "Western Tibet: Historical Introduction," in *Tabo: A Lamp for the Kingdom*, ed. Deborah Klimburg-Salter (Milan: Skira, 1997), 237. David Snellgrove and Hugh Richardson, *A Cultural History of Tibet* (Bangkok: Orchid Press), 130, write that Atiśa devised a special version of the *Guhyasamāja Tantra*, "making instead [of the set of the Five Buddhas], Lokeśvara . . . its central divinity, a subtle change from dependence on an accepted Buddhist symbolic arrangement to devotional allegiance to a divine being conceived as a god in the Hindu pattern."

17 His discovery of an imperial testament said to have been issued by the first Tibetan Emperor Srong btsan sgam po is significant for Tibetan historiography, not least because the emperor was considered an emanation of the Bodhisattva Avalokiteśvara, the patron deity of Tibet. For a pertinent discussion see Georgios T. Halkias, "The Mirror and the Palimpsest: The Myth of Buddhist Kingship in Imperial Tibet," in *Locating Religions: Contact, Diversity and Translocality*, ed. Nikolas Jaspert and Reinhold Glei (Leiden: Brill, 2017), 123–150. For an introduction to the *Pillar Testament* see Andrei Ivanovich Vostrikov, *Tibetan Historical Literature* (London: RoutledgeCurzon, 1994 [1970]), 28–32.

18 For the spread of Pure Land orientations in Tibet and Central Asia, see Georgios T. Halkias, *Luminous Bliss: A Religious History of Pure Land Literature in Tibet: With an Annotated Translation and Critical Analysis of the Orgyen-ling Golden Short Sukhāvatīvyūha-sūtra* (Honolulu: University of Hawai'i Press, 2013), 35–83. For a list of Indian texts dedicated to Amitābha in the Kangyur, see Halkias, "With and without Titles in Sanskrit: Indo-Tibetan Pure Land Texts in the Kangyur," *Journal of Buddhist Studies* 9 (2014): 195–206, and for a translation and discussion of the *Ārya-aparimitāyur-jñāna-hṛdaya-nāma-dhāraṇī*, see Halkias, "Aspiring for Sukhāvatī in Indo-Tibetan Buddhism: Entering the dhāraṇī and buddhakṣetra of Buddha Aparimitāyus." *Journal of Buddhist Studies* 9 (2013): 77–110.

19 On the contrary, according to hagiographical accounts he espoused for rebirth in Tuṣita Heaven; see Chattopadhyaya, *Atīśa and Tibet*, 305 and 330.

20 Gregory Schopen, "Sukhāvatī as a Generalized Religious Goal in Sanskrit Mahāyāna Sūtra Literature," *Indo-Iranian Journal* 19 (1977): 177–210.

21 Without delving into comparisons between analytic (dialectical/analogical) and correlative thinking and without arguing that they are incompatible processes, the use of the term "correlative" here suggests an instructive way to interpret layered Esoteric textual traditions that developed over extended periods of time. For an illuminating discussion on religion and correlative thinking, see Steve Farmer, John Henderson, and Michael Witzel, "Neurobiology, Layered Texts, and Correlative Cosmologies. A Cross-Cultural Framework for Premodern History," *Bulletin of the Museum of Far Eastern Antiquities* 72 (2000): 48–90.

22 Fabio Rambelli, *A Buddhist Theory of Semiotics: Signs, Ontology, and Salvation in Japanese Esoteric Buddhism* (London: Bloomsbury Publisher, 2013), 14.

23 For the Anuttarayoga tantras, the contemplation of the "Five Buddha Families" (*pañcakula; rigs lnga*) conceptually correspond to the "five aggregates" (*pañcaskandha; phung po lnga*) that constitute the individual; see Alex Wayman, *The Buddhist Tantras: Light on Indo-Tibetan Esotericism* (Delhi: Motilal Banarsidass, 1990 [1970]), 223. The other lineages in the group are the Buddha Family (*tathāgatakula; de bzhin gshegs pa'i rigs*); the Vajra Family (*vajrakula; rdo rje'i rigs*); Ratna or Jewel Family (*Ratnakula; rin chen rigs*); Karma or Action Family (*Karmakula; las kyi rigs*). Kirti Tsenshap Rinpoché, in *Principles of Buddhist Tantra* (Boston: Wisdom Publications, 2011), 160, cites that in this process of transformation the five aggregates are the five *sugatas*, the five constituents the four consorts, while the "bases, channels, sinews, and joints are actually bodhisattvas." He explains that "according to this verse, each of the five aggregates is associated with one of the five male tathāgatas . . . (1) Akṣobhya is the purifying agent of the aggregate of consciousness; (2) Vairocana is the purifying agent of the aggregate of form, (3) Ratnasambhava is the purifying agent of the aggregate of feeling, (4) Amitābha is the purifying agent of the aggregate of discrimination, and (5) Amoghasiddhi is the purifying agent of the aggregate of formation."

24 These five "awareness empowerments" serve as an entry to the practices of "Performance Tantra" (*Charyatantra*) in the sense of empowering one to listen, explain, and practice mantras of action and performance tantras. Elsewhere it has been shown that tantric rituals and contemplative practices associated with Pure Land Buddhism came to Tibet via the lineages of Jetāri and Jñānaḍākinī Siddharājñī; see Georgios T. Halkias, "Fire Rituals in the Tibetan Tengyur: The *Aparimitāyur-homa-vidhi-nāma* by the Queen of Siddhas," in *Homa Variations: The Study of Ritual Change across the Longue Durée*, ed. Richard Payne and Michael Witzel (Oxford University Press, 2015), 227–228.

25 Kirti Tshenshap Rinpoché, *Principles of Buddhist Tantra,* 387.

26 Daniel Cozort, "Sādhana (*sGrub thabs*): Means of Achievement for Deity Yoga," in *Tibetan Literature: Studies in Genre*, ed. José Cabezon and Roger

Jackson (Ithaca, NY: Snow Lion, 1996), 334, writes, "The particular *sādhana* one practices, and hence, the deity one achieves, is related to the guidance one receives in the choice of a type of Tantra—from the classes of Action (*bya*), Performance (*spyod*), Yoga (*rnal byor*) or Highest Yoga (*rnal 'byor bla med*)—and in the choice of the deity that is its focus, which may very well be affected by the religious order to which one belongs." In the *Sādhanamāla,* compiled sometime in the early twelfth century, *sādhanas* are retroactively ascribed to the famous Indian Buddhist scholars Asaṅga and Nāgārjuna, and to king Indrabhūti of Uddiyāna; see Maurice Winternitz, *A History of Indian Literature: Buddhist Literature and Jain Literature*, vol. II (Delhi: Motlilal Banarsidass, 1983), 378–379.

27 Sarah Harding, *Creation and Completion: Essential Points of Tantric Meditation* (Boston: Wisdom Publications, 2014), 14.

28 Yael Bentor, *Consecration of Images and Stūpas in Indo-Tibetan Tantric Buddhism* (Leiden: Brill, 1996), 1.

29 Cozort, "Sādhana (*sGrub thabs*)," 331–343.

30 Harding, *Creation and Completion*, 37.

31 See Valerie Roebuck, *The Upanisads* (London: Penguin, 2003), 70.

32 David Snellgrove, *The Hevajra Tantra: A Critical Study,* vol. I (London: Oxford University Press, 1959), 200. Similarly, in the *Ḍākinī Vajrapañjara Tantra* (*Mkha' 'gro ma rdo rje gur gyi rgyud*) it says, "by passion the world arises and down-cast by passion, it goes to its end." Wayman, *The Buddhist Tantras,* 203. Wayman explains that the tantric use of passion "stems from the old Buddhist term *pañcakāmaguṇa* (the five strands of desire), which stands for the five sensory objects constituting the 'knowables' (*jñeya)* that unexamined for what they are, also constitute the 'obscuration of the knowable' (*jñeya-āvaraṇa),* the last impediment to enlightenment."

33 Snellgrove, *The Hevajra Tantra*, 200.

34 Yael Bentor, "The Tibetan Practice of the Mantra Path According to Lce-sgom-pa," in *Tantra in Practice*, ed. David Gordon White (Princeton, NJ: Princeton University Press, 2000), 327.

35 For Tripiṭakamāla the employment of desire on the Buddhist path with a physical partner is for practitioners of lower capacity, a view not held by Tsongkhapa, who argued that the use of an actual consort is "needed even by the very best of trainees in order to bring about a withdrawal of the grosser levels of consciousness as in the process of dying"; see Hopkins, *Tantric Techniques*, 283. More extensive critiques of his views are to be found in Bo dong Phyogs las rnam rgyal's *Rgyud sde spyi'i rnam par gzhag pa'i zin bris* and by the first Pan chen Lama Blo bzang chos kyi rgyal mtshan; see Lopez, *Elaborations on Emptiness*, 90 note 20.

36 According to the consecration manual studied by Yael Bentor in *Consecration of Images and Stūpas in Indo-Tibetan Tantric Buddhism* (Leiden: Brill, 1996), 98, the "Yamāntaka of Passion" ('Dod chags gshin rje gshed) is located in the west. He is known in Tibetan as Vajrabhairava (Rdo rje 'jigs byed) and is listed as one of four Yamāntakas occupying the four directions in the thirteen-deity Yamāntaka-maṇḍala.

37 For a detailed discussion see Lati Rinpoche and Jeffrey Hopkins, *Death, Intermediate State and Rebirth in Tibetan Buddhism* (Ithaca, NY: Snow Lion, 1981).

38 Harding, *Creation and Completion*, 17.

39 Vajrasattva may feature as the lord of the sixth enlightened family when he is not incorporated into the Vajra Family. According to Tsongkhapa's *Great Treatise on the Stages of Mantra (Sngags rim chen mo)*, in the *Anuttarayoga Tantra* he features as its own family that symbolizes the passion toward the Buddhas in sexual union (*yab yum*); Wayman, in *The Buddhist Tantras*, 47, explains "that is the meaning of the lord who has passion in order to produce 'materializations' (*nirmita*) from the *bodhicitta* of the Father-Mother pairs of the retinue deities."

40 The juxtaposition of the Lord of Death with Amitābha's buddha-field populated with residents in the afterlife makes an analogy between these two deities symbolically consistent and potent. Yamāntaka's appearance is told in a passionate tale of a spiritual quest overcoming death. According to the story, "there was once a hermit who lived in a cave for a long time. He needed to contemplate there for a full fifty years to attain *nirvāṇa*. There was just one day to go when two robbers entered the cave. They were dragging a stolen bull which they then killed by cutting off his head. But when they saw the hermit they decided to kill him as well because he had witnessed their crime. They cut off his head, although he begged them not to. But the hermit had already acquired supernatural powers. He placed the bull's head on his shoulder and turned into the terrible deity Yama. Yama killed both robbers and drank their blood. Thus he lost any hope for reaching *nirvāṇa*. Infuriated, he threatened to kill all Tibetans. The Tibetans asked the bodhisattva Mañjuśrī to help them. Mañjuśrī assumed the terrifying figure of Yamāntaka (which also had a bull's head) and drove Yama into subterranean domains"; see Linnart Mäll, *Studies in the Aṣṭasāhasrikā Prajnāpāramitā and Other Essays* (Delhi: Motilal Banarsidass, 2005), 165. For the association of Mañjuśrī with Buddha Amitābha, see Alex Wayman, *Chanting the Names of Mañjuśrī: The Mañjuśrī-Nāma-Saṃgīti* (Delhi: Motilal Banarsidass, 1985), 3.

41 According to Panchen Sonam Drakpa's *General Presentation of the Tantra Sets*, the enlightened family of the lotus has five divisions comprising tantric texts of (a) the principle of the lotus lineage (Amitāyus), (b) the lord of the lotus lineage (Avalokiteśvara), (c) the mother of the lotus lineage (Ārya

Tārā), (d) the fierce males and females of the lotus lineage (Hayagrīva), and (e) the group of messengers of the lotus lineage; see Tsongkhapa, *Deity Yoga*, 243–244.

42 For a discussion of the Mahāyāna training of bodhisattvas in the purification of buddha-fields, see Halkias, *Luminous Bliss*, 6–7.

43 Kirti Tshenshap Rinpoché, in *Principles of Buddhist Tantra*, explains that the self-generation stage (*bdag bskyed rim*) is accomplished by "relying on the six deities: (1) the empty deity, (2) the sound deity, (3) the letter deity, (4) the form deity, (5) the seal deity, and (6) the sign deity." In this context, Vajra-Amitābha stands just as much as for the ideal of liberation in the Pure Land Sukhāvatī as he does for the indestructible and diamond-like quality of awareness (vajra; *rdo rje*) that discerns phenomena in their insubstantial mode of arising. The etymology of Amitābha's name invokes a sense of "unlimited luminosity" that makes the world of appearances visible without confusion or distortion. Hence Atiśa advises the *sādhaka* to generate himself in the likeness of Amitābha's translucent form and recite his mantra.

44 Carccā or Carcikā often depicted in frightening form, emaciated and wearing a garland of skulls, is a Hindu goddess also enlisted as the consort of Yamantāka in the inner southeast direction; see Bentor, *Consecration of Images*, 145. It shows that her worship was prevalent or at least important in the region where Atiśa preached. For evidence of her worship in Bengal, see Gouriswar Bhattacharya, "Inscribed Image of a Śaivācārya from Bengal," in *South Asian Archeology 1993: Proceedings of the Twelfth International Conference of the European Association of South Asian Archaeologists*, ed. Asko Parpola and Petteri Koskikallio (Helsinki: Helsinki University 1994), 93–99. According to David Gordon White, *Kiss of the Yogini: "Tantric Sex" in its South Asian Contexts* (Chicago: Chicago University Press, 2003), 291, Carcika was also a Kushan deity that had the form of a cat while she is identified with Kubjikā in the "Kumārikākhaṇda" of the *Manthānabhairava Tantra*. Carcika is also the form assumed by the goddess Cāmuṇḍā.

45 See Bentor, *Consecration of Images*, 1996, 17.

46 Section VII points to the fact that "not only wisdom, but compassion as well, plays an important role in Buddhist *sādhanas*"; see Bentor, *Consecration of Images*, 4.

47 According to Harding, *Creation and Completion*, 16, "a sense of confidence in being the actual deity counteracts one's sense of ordinariness and frees one from all the limitations usually imposed by our mundane sense of self." It is not to be confused "with its opposite: ordinary, ego-oriented pride."

48 *Bstan 'gyur dpe bsdur ma*. 1994–2008. Beijing: krung go'i bod rig pa'i dpe skrun khang, vol. 24, 268–270.

49 Unbeknown to us to what extent this was intended or not, the term *'dod chags rdo rje* conjures up several associations to the mind of an informed reader. It literally means "vajra passion," which is an important theme that runs throughout our text. It is also used for the Tibetan name for Vajra-Yamāntaka ('Dod chags rdo rje) and another Buddhist deity, the Bodhisattva Vajrarāga, a white form of one-faced Mañjuśrī depicted in meditation *mudra* with two arms holding a bow and arrow and sited in cross-legged posture (*vajraparyaṅka āsana*). Vajrarāga Mañjuśrī is known by the "two names of Vāk and Amitābha *Mañjuśrī* showing his allegiance to . . . Buddha Amitābha"; see Benoytosh Bhattacharyya, *The Indian Buddhist Iconography: Mainly Based on the Sādhanamālā and Cognate Tāntric Texts of Rituals* (Calcutta: Firma K. L. Mukhopadhyay, 1958), 102. Vajrarāga typically belongs to a group of sixteen bodhisattvas in the *Vajradhātu-maṇḍala* of the *Sarvatathāgata-tattvasaṁgraha-tantra* and is seated on the left of Akṣobhya; see Thomas E. Donaldson, *Iconography of the Buddhist Sculpture of Orissa*, vol. 1 (Delhi: Indira Gandhi National Centre of the Arts, 2001), 171.

50 Ablution rituals usually constitute an important part in the class of *Action Tantras* (*Kriya*). The specific mantra is not given in the text and it probably refers to the purification mantra: oṃ svabhāva śuddhāḥ sarvadharmāḥ svabhāva śuddho haṃ.

51 The four Mahāyāna rituals (*cho ga*) probably refer to the cultivation of the "four boundless attitudes" (*apramāṇa*; *chad med bzhi*): the wish that others be happy (*maitrī*), the wish that they don't suffer (*karuṇā*), the joyful desire that they never lose their happiness (*muditā*), and relating to them without partiality (*upekṣā*).

52 The syllable *raṁ* corresponds to the fire element and *baṁ* to the water element.

53 The meaning of this sentence eludes me. There may be some connection between the symbolism of the sixteen arrows and the distinct Kadampa meditation practice of the "sixteen spheres" (*thig le bcu drug*) said to have originated with Atiśa. That being said, I can't discern an immediate connection between the arrows and sixteen levels of teachers and deities represented in spheres of light; see Franz-Karl Ehrhard, "The Transmission of the *Thig-le Bcu-Drug* and the *Bka' gdams glegs bam*," in *The Many Canons of Tibetan Buddhism*, ed. Helmut Eimer and David Germano (Leiden: Brill, 2002), 29–56. Other speculative readings may suggest the sixteen spokes of the throat chakra or perhaps the sixteen Sanskrit vowels visualized across different parts of one's body in coordination with the five elements; see Wayman, *The Buddhist Tantras*, 210.

54 The reference to the "mother of self-awareness" or "self-aware mother" is the deity exemplifying the sutras on *prajñā* in *Prajñāpāramitā*. She is commonly referred to as the "mother" of the buddhas and bodhisattvas and is a personification of emptiness; see Edward Conze, *Thirty Years of Buddhist*

*Studies: Selected Essay by Edward Conze* (Oxford: Bruno Cassirer, 1967), 207–208. The actual method of the "self-knowing mother" refers to meditation on emptiness.

55 The visualization that entails the so-called Sukhāvatī triad featuring Buddha Amitābha in the center of his Pure Land and *Vajrapāṇi* and *Avalokiteśvara* to his left and right respectively, may refer to perfection stage practices where the three channels in the subtle body are visualized. The attainment of Vajra-Amitābha is in reference to the "*vajra* initiation of Amitābha" that "purifies the defilements of passion [*'dod chags*]." In the process of self-generation the aggregate of perception [*'du shes kyi phung po*] is transformed and the "enlightened wisdom of discrimination is actualized"; see Bentor, *Consecration of Images*, 31.

56 The three aspects of differentiated reality are symbolized by Buddha Vairocana who represents the "vajra-body," Buddha Amitābha "vajra-speech," and Buddha Aksobhya "vajra-mind"; see Alex Wayman, *Yoga of the Guhyasamājatantra: The Arcane Lore of Forty Verses* (Delhi: Motilal Banarsidass, 1977), 106, 118. These vajra-states are accomplished during physical isolation (vajra body), verbal isolation (vajra speech), and mental isolation (vajra mind). For Kirti Tshenshap Rinpoché, *Principles of Buddhist Tantra*, 152, "the completion stage concentrations pertaining to the three isolations refers to concentrations producing the three vajras." He explains that "we attain the vajra body, vajra speech, and vajra mind of the resultant state of Buddha Vajradhara through first meditating on corresponding causal states in the generation stage."

57 The term *mi bskyod* may also refer to Vajrasattva-Akṣobhya, in which case the instructions would be suggesting that one transforms in the form of Vajrasattva or Akṣobhya to receive the empowerment.

58 For Tsongkhapa the "four doors of entry to the secret mantra" are discussed from the viewpoint of different grades corresponding the four sets of tantras, namely "Action Tantras," "Yoga Tantras," "Supreme Yoga," and "Highest Yoga"; see Tsong-ka-pa, *Tantra in Tibet: The Great Exposition of Secret Mantra*, ed. and trans. Jeffrey Hopkins (London: Allen and Unwin, 1977).

59 Carcikā (Carccā) is one of the well-known mothers (*mātṝkā*) of the Hindu pantheon that also goes by the name Cāmuṇḍā.

60 The mantra *oṁ* is sacred to Vairocana, *āḥ* to Amitābha, and *huṁ* to Akṣobhya. In chapter 12 (38–49) of the *Guhyasamājatantra* the pledge *oṁ āḥ huṁ* is the supreme vajra-method through which one becomes equal to Vajrasattva. Having meditated on Aksobhya of the syllable *huṁ*, "the best pledge-diamond of the tongue, and having enjoyed by the praxis of the five ambrosias [nectar], on may obtain the triple vajra"; see Wayman, *Yoga of the Guhyasamājatantra*, 32–33.

61 According to the *Guhyasamāja Tantra* (168a) when the Blessed One entered the fourth *samādhi* called "Vajra birth of the great passion of all the Tathāgatas" he "brought forth from his vajra body, speech, and mind this mantra, the supreme innermost essence of the Family of Passion" (Amitābha), the sacred sound: Ā-ro-lik; see Francesca Fremantle, "A Critical Study of the Guhyasamāja Tantra" (PhD diss., University of London, 1971), 30; Bhattacharyya, *Indian Buddhist Iconography*, 45; and Wayman, *Yoga of the Guhyasamājatantra*, 125.

62 The vowel "a" is the mother of all phonemes, for it is the beginning of the Sanskrit alphabet and it is the most elementary articulation inherent in all Sanskrit consonants. It is also a negative particle (in Greek and Sanskrit) and symbolizes a fundamental negation and thus symbolizes the process of creation and nonproduction.

63 The phrase *phyag rgya bkrol* usually refers to the mudra of releasing the hands with a click of the fingers. I surmise that here it alludes to the end of the formal meditation practice.

64 In the context of Tantra, *samaya* has the implication of law and/or command not to be transgressed, a "sacred promise." Divine pride (*lha'i nga rgyal*) is the nonafflictive orientation held by a tantric practitioner who identifies with a tantric deity. Though this seems to contradict the central Buddhist teaching of not-self (*annatā*), Daniel Cozort, *Highest Yoga Tantra* (Ithaca, NY: Snow Lion), 58, explains that "divine pride is cultivated only after meditation on emptiness, which negates the false conception of I; hence, the I of deity yoga is not conceived to inherently exist, as is the ordinary I, but rather is understood to be only nominally existent, even when one is completely focused on the thought that one is the deity."

## Bibliography

Apple, James B. "An Early Bka'-gdams-pa Madhyamaka Work Attributed to Atiśa Dīpaṃkaraśrījñāna," *Journal of Indian Philosophy* 44, no. 4 (2016): 619–725.

———. "An Early Tibetan Commentary on Atisa's *Satyadvayāvatāra*." *Journal of Indian Philosophy* 41, no. 3 (2013): 263–329.

Bhattacharya Gouriswar. "Inscribed Image of a *śaivācārya* from Bengal." In *South Asian Archaeology 1993, Proceedings of the Twelfth International Conference of the European Association of South Asian Archaeologists*. vol. I, edited by Asko Parpola and Petteri Koskikallio, 93–99. Helsinki: Helsinki University, 1994.

Bhattacharyya, Benoytosh. *The Indian Buddhist Iconography: Mainly Based on the Sādhanamālā and Cognate Tāntric Texts of Rituals*. Calcutta: K. L. Mukhopadhyay, 1958.

Bentor, Yael. *Consecration of Images and Stūpas in Indo-Tibetan Tantric Buddhism.* Leiden: Brill, 1996.

——. "The Tibetan Practice of the Mantra Path According to Lce-sgom-pa." In *Tantra in Practice*, edited by David Gordon White, 326–346. Princeton, NJ: Princeton University Press, 2000.

*Bstan 'gyur dpe bsdur ma* [Tengyur Bedurma]. 1994–2008. Beijing: krung go'i bod rig pa'i dpe skrun khang.

Chattopadhyaya, Alaka. *Atīśa and Tibet: Life and Works of Dīpaṃkara Śrījñāna in Relation to the History and Religion of Tibet.* Delhi: Motlilal Banarsidass, 1981 [1967].

Conze, Edward. *Thirty Years of Buddhist Studies: Selected Essay by Edward Conze.* Oxford: Bruno Cassirer, 1967.

Cozort, Daniel. *Highest Yoga Tantra.* Ithaca, NY: Snow Lion, 2005.

——. "Sādhana (*sGrub thabs*): Means of Achievement for Deity Yoga." In *Tibetan Literature: Studies in Genre*, edited by J. Cabezon and R. Jackson, 331–343. Ithaca, NY: Snow Lion, 1996.

Das Sri Sarat. *Indian Pandits in the Land of Snows.* Calcutta: Baptist Mission Press, 1893.

Davidson, Ronald. *Tibetan Renaissance: Tantric Buddhism in the Rebirth of Tibetan Culture.* New York: Columbia University Press, 2005.

Donaldson, Thomas E. *Iconography of the Buddhist Sculpture of Orissa*, vol. 1. Delhi: Indira Gandhi National Centre of the Arts, 2001.

Ehrhard, Franz-Karl. "The Transmission of the *Thig-le Bcu-Druk* and the *Bka' gdams glegs bam*." In *The Many Canons of Tibetan Buddhism*, edited by Helmut Eimer and David Germano, 29–56. Leiden: Brill, 2002.

Eimer, Helmut. "The Development of the Biographical Tradition concerning Atīśa Dīpaṃkaraśrījñāna." *Journal of Tibet Society* 2 (1982): 41–51.

Farmer, Steve, John Henderson, and Michael Witzel. "Neurobiology, Layered Texts, and Correlative Cosmologies. A Cross-Cultural Framework for Premodern History." *Bulletin of the Museum of Far Eastern Antiquities* 72 (2000): 48–90.

Fremantle, Francesca. "A Critical Study of the Guhyasamāja Tantra." PhD dissertation, University of London, 1971.

Halkias, Georgios T. "Aspiring for Sukhāvatī in Indo-Tibetan Buddhism: Entering the *dhāraṇī* and *buddhakṣetra* of Buddha Aparimitāyus." *Journal of Buddhist Studies* 9 (2013): 77–110.

——. "Buddhist Meditation Traditions in Tibet: The Union of the Three Vehicles." In *Buddhist Meditation: An Introduction*, edited by S. Shaw, 159–186. New York: Routledge Press, 2008.

——. "Fire Rituals in the Tibetan Tengyur: The *Aparimitāyur-homa-vidhi-nāma* by the Queen of Siddhas." In *Homa Variations: The Study of Ritual Change across the Longue Durée*, edited by Richard Payne and Michael Witzel, 225–245. Oxford: Oxford University Press, 2015.

——. *Luminous Bliss: A Religious History of Pure Land Literature in Tibet: With an Annotated Translation and Critical Analysis of the Orgyen-ling Golden Short Sukhāvatīvyūha-sūtra*. Honolulu: University of Hawai'i Press, 2013.

——. "The Mirror and the Palimpsest: The Myth of Buddhist Kingship in Imperial Tibet." *Locating Religions: Contact, Diversity and Translocality*, edited by Nikolas Jaspert and Reinhold Glei, 123–150. Leiden: Brill, 2017.

——. "With and without Titles in Sanskrit: Indo-Tibetan Pure Land Texts in the Kangyur." *Journal of Buddhist Studies* 9 (2014): 195–206.

Harding, Sarah. *Creation and Completion: Essential Points of Tantric Meditation*. Boston: Wisdom Publications, 2014.

Hopkins, Jeffrey. *Tantric Techniques*. Ithaca, NY: Snow Lion Publications, 2008.

Kirti Tsenshap Rinpoché. *Principles of Buddhist Tantra*. Boston: Wisdom Publications, 2011.

Lang, Karen. "Spa-tshab nyi-ma grags and the Introduction of Prasaṅgika Madhyamaka into Tibet." In *Reflections on Tibetan Culture: Essays in Memory of Turrell Wylie*, edited by L. Epstein and R. Sherburne, 127–141. New York: Mellen Press, 1990.

Lati Rinpoche and Jeffrey Hopkins. *Death, Intermediate State and Rebirth in Tibetan Buddhism*. Ithaca, NY: Snow Lion, 1981.

Lobsang Norbu Tsonawa. *Indian Buddhist Pandits from "The Jewel Garland of Buddhist History."* Dharamsala: Library of Tibetan Works and Archives, 1985.

Lopez, Donald. *Elaborations on Emptiness: Uses of the Heart Sūtra*. Princeton, NJ: Princeton University Press, 1993.

Mäll, Linnart. *Studies in the Aṣṭasāhasrikā Prajnāpāramitā and Other Essays*. Delhi: Motilal Banarsidass, 2005.

Petech, Luciano. "Western Tibet: Historical Introduction." In *Tabo: A Lamp for the Kingdom*, edited by Deborah E. Klimburg-Salter, 229–255. Milano: Skira, 1997.

Powers, John. *Introduction to Tibetan Buddhism*. Ithaca, NY: Snow Lion Publications, 2007.

Rambelli, Fabio. *A Buddhist Theory of Semiotics: Signs, Ontology, and Salvation in Japanese Esoteric Buddhism*. London: Bloomsbury Publisher, 2013.

Roebuck, Valerie. *The Upanisads*. London: Penguin, 2003.

Roerich, George N. *The Blue Annals*. Calcutta: Royal Asiatic Society of Bengal, 1949–1953.

Roesler, Ulrike. "On the History of Histories: The Case of the bKa' gdams pa-s." In *Contributions to Tibetan Buddhist Literature. Tibetan Studies: Proceedings of the*

*Eleventh Seminar of the International Association for Tibetan Studies*, edited by Orna Almogi, 393–413. Halle: International Institute of Tibetan Studies, 2008.

Ruegg, Seyford D. "Problems in the Transmission of Vajrayana Buddhism in the Western Himalaya about the Year 1000." In *The Medieval Period: c. 850–1895, The Development of Buddhist Paramountcy*, edited by A. Mckay, 123–133. London: RoutledgeCurzon, 2003 [1984].

Samten Karmay. "The Ordinance of lHa Bla-ma Ye-Shes-'od." In *The Arrow and the Spindle: Studies in History, Myths, Rituals and Beliefs in Tibet*, edited by Samten Karmay, 3–16. Kathmandu: Mandala Book Point, 1998, [1980].

Schneider, Johannes. *Vāgīśvarakīrtis Mṛtyuvañcanopadeśa, eine buddhistische Lehrschrift zur Abwehr der Todes.* (Beiträge zur Kultur- und Geistesgeschichte Asiens, 66; Denkschriften der philoso-phisch-historischen Klasse, 394) Vienna: Verlag der Österreichischen Akademie der Wissenschaften, 2010.

Schopen, Gregory. "Sukhāvatī as a Generalized Religious Goal in Sanskrit Mahāyāna Sūtra Literature." *Indo-Iranian Journal* 19 (1977): 177–210.

Snellgrove, David. *The Hevajra Tantra: A Critical Study.* London: Oxford University Press, 1959.

——. *Indo-Tibetan Buddhism: Indian Buddhists and their Tibetan Successors.* Boston: Shambhala, 2002.

Snellgrove, David, and Hugh Richardson. *A Cultural History of Tibet.* Bangkok: Orchid Press, 2003.

Tsong-kha-pa Blo-bzang-grags-pa. *Deity Yoga: In Action and Performance Tantra.* London and Boston: Snow Lion, 1987.

——. *Tantra in Tibet: The Great Exposition of Secret Mantra.* Edited and translated by Jeffrey Hopkins. London: Allen and Unwin, 1977.

Vostrikov, Andrei Ivanovich. *Tibetan Historical Literature.* London: RoutledgeCurzon, 1994 [1973].

Wayman, Alex. *The Buddhist Tantras: Light on Indo-Tibetan Esotericism.* Delhi: Motilal Banarsidass, 1990 [1970].

——. *Chanting the Names of Mañjuśrī: The Mañjuśrī-Nāma-*Saṃgīti. Delhi: Motilal Banarsidass, 1985.

——. *Yoga of the Guhyasamājatantra: The Arcane Lore of Forty Verses.* Delhi: Motilal Banarsidass, 1977.

White, Gordon David. *Kiss of the Yogini: "Tantric Sex" in its South Asian Contexts.* Chicago: Chicago University Press, 2003.

Winternitz, Maurice. *A History of Indian Literature: Buddhist Literature and Jain Literature*, vol. II. Delhi: Motlilal Banarsidass, 1983.

## Chapter 2

# Maitreya's Tuṣita Heaven as a Pure Land in Gelukpa Forms of Tibetan Buddhism

James B. Apple

### Translator's Introduction

An overlooked aspect in the study of Tibetan Buddhism is the Gelukpa (*dge lugs pa*) understanding of Tuṣita Heaven as a pure land (*dag pa'i zhing khams*).[1] Ever since Tsongkhapa Losang Drakpa (Tsong kha pa blo gzang grags pa, 1357–1419) founded the monastery of Ganden (*dga' ldan*, Tuṣita, "Heaven of Joy") his Gelukpa followers have placed devotional emphasis on creating merit to form links with the Buddha Maitreya, and Maitreya's pure land within Tuṣita Heaven.

The Gelukpa understanding of Tuṣita Heaven as a pure land develops based upon a long history of Maitreya worship in Tibet, upon the aspirations for rebirth in Tuṣita by previous Indian and Tibetan scholars, and in relation to events during and after Tsongkh-pa's life that are connected to Maitreya and Tuṣita Heaven. The practices and devotions surrounding the understanding of Tuṣita Heaven as a pure land are interconnected with the history of the institutional development among those who follow Tsongkhapa and are centered around the Ganden monastery he founded, an institution that has the very name of the heaven itself. Practices and beliefs related to Tuṣita were developed among Tsongkhapa's immediate followers and over the course of several centuries and were exported to wherever the Gelukpa tradition thrived, which included areas throughout Tibet, a vast area from Kalmuck Mongolian regions, Inner and Outer Mongolia, the Buriat Republic of Siberia, and even temples in China. The later popularity of these beliefs and practices was also related to the ascendancy of political power of the Gelukpa school in Tibet, particularly from the seventeenth century, and contributed to social cohesion among Gelukpa followers.[2] With its affilations to the monastery Tsongkhapa founded and the name of the tradition itself,[3] the Gelukpa orientation toward Tuṣita must also have had sectarian ramifications, as most other "schools"[4] of Tibetan Buddhism shared and continue to have a Pure Land orientation toward Sukhāvāti (*bde ba can*).[5]

The following sections provide a brief historical background to Maitreya and Tuṣita in the life of Tsongkhapa, describe the context for the understanding of Tuṣita Heaven as a buddha-field among Tsongkhapa's followers, and conclude with a description of the characteristics of Maitreya's field as a pure land.

## Maitreya and Tuṣita in the Life of Tsongkhapa

The venerable Maitreya-nātha (Rje btsun byams pa mgon po) played an important role throughout Tsongkhapa's life, particularly in his youth and during the phase of his life when he first studied the Mahāyāna practice of the perfections (*phar phyin*). One of Tsongkhapa's teachers, the Kadampa master Lhodrag Namkha Gyeltsen (Lho brag nam mkha' rgyal mtshan, 1326–1401), considered him an emanation of Maitreya and advised Tsongkhapa to study first the "five texts of Maitreya" (*Byams gzhung sde lnga*)[6] at the beginning of his textual studies. Most importantly for the later Gelukpa orientation toward Tuṣita, Tsongkhapa was predicted by Mañjuśrī through the intermediary of Lama Umapa Tsöndrü Sengé (Bla ma dbu ma pa brtson 'grus seng ge, fourteenth century) to be reborn in Tuṣita Heaven as the Bodhisattva Mañjuśrīgarbha ('Jam dpa'i snying po).[7] As discussed below, Tsongkhapa also received during a question-and-answer session a prediction that he would be reborn in Tuṣita through the medium of Namkha Gyeltsen.

When Tsongkhapa was around the age of thirty-eight, and after spending several years in retreat with eight of his disciples, he engaged in a project to refurbish a rundown statue of Maitreya at Dzingji ('Dzing ji).[8] The refurbishment of this statue came to be regarded by later biographers as the first of Tsongkhapa's four great deeds in Tibetan Buddhist culture. Tsongkhapa's secret biography mentions he had a direct vision of Maitreya during this time and soon after composed several devotional poems to Maitreya.[9] These poems express devotion to Maitreya but do not directly mention Tsongkhapa's aspiration for rebirth in Tuṣita. During this time in Dzingji, Tsongkhapa also composed a devotional prayer for rebirth in Sukhāvāti, the *Bde ba can du skye ba'i smon lam* (An aspirational prayer for rebirth in Sukhāvāti), as well as a longer work that comments upon the basis for the aspiration to take rebirth in the supreme field of Sukhāvāti.[10]

Tsongkhapa founded the Great Prayer Festival (smon lam chen mo) in Lhasa in 1409, another of his great deeds, which also had connections with Maitreya. The Great Prayer Festival concludes with the invitation of Maitreya (*Byams pa gdan 'dren*) procession, and Maitreya connects with the overall purpose of the festival, which according to George Dreyfus was "a celebration of Maitreya, the future Buddha, a means to accelerate his coming, but also a way to assert the centrality of monasticism."[11] After the first Great Prayer Festival, Tsongkhapa's disciples offered to build a monastery for him. Tsongkhapa agreed, and this led to the building of Riwo Ganden Nampar Gyelwé Ling (Ri bo dga' ldan rnam par rgyal ba'i gling), the first monastery of the Gelukpa school and traditionally said to be named after Tuṣita (Dga' ldan), the "Joyous" Heaven of Maitreya. In brief, three of the four great deeds in Tsongkhapa's life were connected in some manner with Maitreya and Tuṣita. Tsongkhapa's collected works, as far as I can currently locate, contain five small prayers dedicated to Maitreya.[12] In one of these prayers Tsongkhapa states, "When body and mind come to part, I pray to be spared the sufferings of death and behold regent Maitreya and entourage. Reborn in the realm of Tuṣita, I pray to be at once in his disciple circle, there to receive a prediction for awakening."[13]

Tsongkhapa's stated aspiration for rebirth in Tuṣita was to receive a prediction for achieving buddhahood. He did not provide any further details regarding his cosmological understanding of Tuṣita, either as a heaven or a special pure land.

## *Tuṣita Heaven as a Pure Land among Tsongkhapa's Followers*

The emergence of Tuṣita Heaven as a "pure land" (*dag pa'i zhing khams*) in Gelukpa forms of Tibetan Buddhism therefore developed within the context of a long history of Maitreya veneration in Tibet and was intimately related to the life of Tsongkhapa and the historical formation of what became the Gelukpa order. The beginning practices that later developed into visualizing Tsongkhapa and his two main disciples, Gyeltsab Darma Rinchen (Rgyal tshab dar ma rin chen, 1364–1432) and Khedrubje Gelek Pelzang (Mkhas grub rje dge legs dpal bzang, 1385–1438), emanating from Maitreya bodhisattva in Tuṣita Heaven start during the life of Tsongkhapa himself and with practices developed by his immediate disciples. These practices were shaped by the orientation toward Tuṣita exhibited in Tsongkhapa's life and the devotional practices by his disciples that focused upon Tsongkhapa and his rebirth in Tuṣita after his death.

The primary practices that gradually develop and shape the followers of Tsongkhapa and the later Gelukpa orientation toward Tuṣita as a pure land are guru-yoga (*bla ma'i rnal 'byor*), the "Objectless Loving-Kindness" Prayer (*Dmigs brtse ma*), and, perhaps most importantly, the "Hundred Deities of Tuṣita" (*Dga' ldan lha brgya ma*). The two latter practices are distinctive forms of guru-yoga that focus on Tsongkhapa. In the following translation of Yeshé Gyeltsen's text, all these practices are integrated into the meditation session.

The practice of guru-yoga or guru devotion is central to tantric practices in Tibetan Buddhism and has a long history in India and Tibet. Guru-yoga is a ritual practice where one meditates on one's own root spiritual teacher (*bla ma*) as an embodiment of buddhahood.[14] In this practice, a practitioner meditates on the inseparable nature of one's own mind and the guru's awakened mind. As mentioned by the twentieth-century Tibetan scholar Pabongkhapa Dechen Nyingpo (Pha bong kha pa bde chen snying po, 1878–1941), the nineteenth-century Tibetan scholar Sherap Gyatso (Shes rab rgya mtsho, 1803–1875), as well as noted by Alex Wayman,[15] the beginnings of guru-yoga practices that focus on Tsongkhapa are to be found in the instructions on guru-yoga that Tsongkhapa himself supposedly gave directly to his disciples Khedrubje (Mkhas grub rje, 1385–1438) and Baso Chöjé (Ba so chos rje, 1402–1473). These instructions are preserved in two texts found at the beginning of Tsongkhapa's collected works.[16] Both of these texts are made up of technical esoteric instructions of visualizing Tsongkhapa in the form of Mañjuśrī that are patterned upon ritual structures found in the *Guhyasamāja Tantra*.[17] These texts indicate the importance of guru-yoga for Tsongkhapa and his followers and also demonstrate that Tsongkhapa received special veneration during his lifetime as an embodied tantric buddha-deity.

The "Objectless Loving-Kindness Prayer" (*Dmigs brtse ma*)[18] was traditionally based upon a verse that was originally composed and presented by Tsongkhapa to his teacher Rendawa Zhonnu Lodro (Red mda' ba gzhon nu blo gros, 1349–1412). Rendawa skillfully returned the praise from his student into a verse of veneration to Tsongkhapa. The verse in praise of Tsongkhapa is as follows:

> You are Avalokiteśvara, great treasure of objectless compassion.
> Mañjuśrī, lord of stainless knowledge
> Master of the Secret Ones (Vajrapāṇi), destroyer of the armies of Māra
> Tsong-kha-pa, crown ornament of the scholar-masters of the Land of Snows
> Losang drakpa, to your feet I direct my prayer.[19]

This verse will become a type of mantra for Tsongkhapa's followers and is recited by devotees of Tsongkhapa to the present day. This verse shows that Tsongkhapa was seen as an embodiment of three types of bodhisattvas and is a vital component of guru-yoga practice related to Tsongkhapa. The verse is recited for purposes ranging from protecting against malevolent forces to compelling rainfall.[20] This verse will be incorporated into the main ritual practice that invokes Tsongkhapa from Tuṣita Heaven and contributes to the Gelukpa understanding and vision of Tuṣita Heaven, or at least, a special area of Tuṣita, as a pure land associated with the Buddha Maitreya.

The prayer that involves the Gelukpa orientation toward Tuṣita Heaven is known as "Hundred Deities of Tuṣita," which is attributed to Dülnakpa Palden Sangpo ('Dul ngag pa dpal ldan bzang po, 1402–1473). Dülnakpa Palden Sangpo, originally from Tsangtanak (Gtsang rta nag), was a Vinaya master and student of Sherap Sengé (Shes rab seng ge, 1383–1445) and Gendün drup (Dge 'dun grub, 1391–1475), the post facto first Dalai Lama.[21] According to Thuken Losang Chökyi Nyima (Thu'u bkwan blo bzang chos kyi nyi ma, 1737–1802),[22] while staying in Sengé Tsé (Seng ge rtse), Sherap Sengé advised Dülnakpa to give tantric teachings. After receiving a copy of Tsongkhapa's commentary on the *Guhyasamāja Tantra*, a book carrier, and a begging bowl from Sherap Sengé, Dülnakpa went to the Sé (*srad*) valley region and founded the Sé Gyü Dratsang (Srad rgyud grwa tshang), the oldest tantric monastery of the Gelukpa sect along with its tradition of tantra (*srad rgyud lugs*).[23] It is not clear when Dülnakpa wrote the text of "Hundred Deities of Tuṣita" but he composed the work as a form of "guru-yoga" (*bla ma'i rnal 'byor*) to Tsongkhapa based on the oral lineage transmission of guru-yoga that he received from Sherap Sengé.[24] The text is made up of ten verses patterned along the lines of the Seven-Limbed Prayer[25] liturgy and infused with Mahāyāna and Tantric Buddhist imagery. Jamyang Dewai Dorjé ('Jam dbyangs bde ba'i rdo rje, 1682–1741) and the Seventh Dalai Lama Kalsang Gyatso (Bskal bzang rgya mtsho, 1708–1757) describe a story where Dülnakpa combined the "Hundred Deities of Tuṣita" and the "Objectless Loving-Kindness Prayer" together in order to gain protection from a spirit that was causing great harm in the Sé valley.[26] The "Hundred Deities of Tuṣita" and the "Loving-Kindness Prayer" are recited together in Gelukpa monasteries and temples up to the present day. The "Hundred Deities of Tuṣita" title comes from the opening verse, which invokes Tsongkhapa to appear in one's vision. The opening verse of the prayer states:

From the heart of the Lord Protector among the hundreds of Tuṣita's gods,
emerges a brilliant white cloud, like a great mass of fresh yoghurt.
Here comes the Omniscient Lord of Dharma, Losang drakpa
Please come down to us, together with your Sons![27]

Here Tsongkhapa, along with his two main disciples, Gyeltsab Darma Rinchen to his right and Khedrubje Gelek Pelzang to his left, is visualized emerging from the heart of Maitreya, the leader of the deities in Tuṣita, who is surround by hundreds of bodhisattva deities. Tsongkhapa and his two disciples, known as Jey Yab Sey Sum (*rje yab sras gsum*), "The Trio of the Precious Master and (his two chief) Disciples," come down before the meditator on billows of clouds visualized sitting on lotus thrones placed upon sun and moon disks indicating their status as tantric Buddha-deities. The meditator praises them as a supreme field of merit and then goes through a sequence of ritual offerings, confessions, rejoicing, and dedication in relation to Tsongkhapa and his two disciples' perceived presence and centered around Tsongkhapa's deeds. The "Objectless Loving-Kindness Prayer" is repeatedly recited in the ninth verse.

The "Hundred Deities of Tuṣita" invocation recalls the belief among Tsongkhapa's immediate followers, and later widespread in the Gelukpa tradition, that Tsongkhapa, at the end of his life, was reborn in Tuṣita Heaven as a bodhisattva. That Tsongkhapa would be reborn in Tuṣita was predicted during his lifetime by Vajrapāṇi through the medium of the Kadampa (*bka' gdam pa*) teacher and tantric master Namkha Gyeltsen. When the medium was asked by Tsongkhapa concerning his life and destiny, the response was that Tsongkhapa "will be born in Tuṣita, in the presence of Maitreya, in the form of the Bodhisattva Mañjuśrīgarbha. Then from Tuṣita he will wish to accomplish beings' aims in another human universe, and he will be reborn there in the form of a Dharmarāja, an Enlightened King."[28]

The "secret" biographies composed by Tsongkhapa's immediate disciples will also mention that he was reborn in Tuṣita Heaven as the Bodhisattva Mañjuśrīgarbha. Along these lines, the practice manuals and commentaries associated with the "Hundred Deities of Tuṣita" invocation and visualization also mention prophecies of Tsongkhapa's rebirth in Tuṣita by his teacher and by Tsongkhapa himself.

In combination with the practices and devotions of guru-yoga and the "Objectless Loving-Kindness Prayer," the invocation and visualization practices involved in the practice of Dülnakpa's "Hundred Deities of Tuṣita" were initially centered at the tantric monastery of Sé and became known as the "exclusive guru-yoga of the Sé tantric lineage" (*srad brgyud lugs kyi bla ma'i rnal 'byor*). The earliest extant lineage lists for the practice of "Hundred Deities of Tuṣita" are found in the commentaries of such figures as Dewai Dorjé (1682–1741), Yeshé Gyeltsen (Ye shes rgyal mtshan, 1713–1973), and Losang Gyeltsen Sengé (Blo bzang rgyal mtshan seng ge, 1757–1849). These lists contain the same sequence of names and are provided in table 1.

**Table 1. Tuṣita's Hundred Deities Lineage According to Yeshé Gyeltsen (1713–1793) (*Sol 'deb dang bsdus don*)**

| | |
|---|---|
| Tsongkhapa<br>(1357–1419) | Dorjé Sangpo<br>(Rdo rje bzang po, b. 16th century) |
| Sherap Sengé<br>(Shes rab seng ge, 1383–1445) | Sangyé Gyatso<br>(Sangs rgyas rgya mtsho, b. 16th/17th) |
| Dülzin Palden Sangpo<br>('Dul 'dzin dpal ldan bzang po, 1402–1473) | Könchok Gyatso<br>(Dkon mchog rgya mtsho, 1558–1628) |
| Jamyang Gendün Phel<br>('Jam dbyang dge 'dun 'phel, 15th century) | Könchok Yarphel<br>(Dkon mchog yar 'phel, b. 1602) |
| Tashi Phak<br>(Bkra shis 'phags) | Ngawang Lodrö<br>(Ngag dbang blo gros, b. 17th) |
| Samdrup Gyatso<br>(Bsam grub rgya mtsho) | Ngödrup Gyatso<br>(Dngos grub rgya mtsho, b. 17th) |
| Tsöndrü Phak<br>(Brtson 'grus 'phags, b. 15th) | Dönyö Khedrup<br>(Don yod mkhas grub, 1631–1737) |
| [up to top right] | Ngawang Jampa<br>(Ngag dbang byams pa, 1682–1762) |

The earliest extant commentary on the "Hundred Deities of Tuṣita" is by Jamyang Shepai Dorjé ('Jam dbyangs bzhad pa'i rdo rje, 1648–1721), who received the teaching from Könchok Yarphel (Dkon mchog yar 'phel, b. 1602). Jamyang Shepa took the lineages affiliated with these practices from Drepung Gomang monastery back to his home province in Amdo and to the monastery of Tashi khyil (Bkra shis 'khyil), which he founded in 1710.[29] The practice and visualization of the "Hundred Deities of Tuṣita," although involving tantric elements, does not require a tantric initiation and focuses on the guru devotion to Tsongkhapa. The teaching must have easily spread throughout the seventeenth and eighteenth centuries as Gelukpa forms of Buddhism gained patronage and spread throughout areas of Tibet, Mongolia, and later Buryatia and even China. Many historical documents and works of art demonstrate the popularity of this practice in areas of Tibet and Inner Asia during this time.[30]

## The Characteristics of Maitreya's Field of Tuṣita as a Pure Land

For Tsongkhapa's followers, the "field" (*kṣetra*) where the future Buddha Maitreya resides within Tuṣita is considered a so-called pure land, or purified field (*dag pa'i zhing khams*). It is important to note that not all of Tuṣita Heaven is considered a pure land for followers of Tsongkhapa. As is well known within Buddhist cosmology, the heaven of Tuṣita is fourth among the six heavens of the "realm of desire" (*kāmadhātu*), and all Buddhists recognize that Bodhisattva Maitreya, as the next buddha-to-be, currently resides in Tuṣita Heaven. The *Abhidharmakośa* (3.69–71) provides only a brief account of the characteristics of beings in Tuṣita and other desire realm heavens. Nevertheless, based upon a great amount of lore related to Tuṣita or other heavenly realms found in the *Abhidharmakośa,* Mahāyāna sutras such as the *Lalitavistara, Maitreyapraṇidhana, Sukhāvatīvyūha,* and other texts, early Gelukpa scholars provide a description of Tuṣita and the pure field of Maitreya within it. The earliest extant description is found in the work of Jamyang Shepai Dorjé (1648–1721). Jamyang Shepa's description is too brief, but the description of the Tuṣita pure land by one of his students, Jamyang Dewai Dorjé ('Jam dbyangs bde ba'i rdo rje, 1682–1741),[31] who received the Sé (*srad*) lineage of "Hundred Deities of Tuṣita," provides an early detailed example of how Gelukpas visualized Tsongkhapa and his two main disciples coming down from Tuṣita Heaven. The description of the "supreme pure field" (*dag pa'i zhing mchog*) of Maitreya's area of Tuṣita is relatively consistent across the extant commentaries on "Hundred Deities of Tuṣita," although several authors mention extra details in their visualization instructions. Along these lines, the descriptions of visualization found in the commentaries corresponds to extant Tibetan artwork. A good example is a mislabeled piece from the Musée National des Arts Asiatiques-Guimet known as the "Apparition de *Tsong-kha-pa*,"[32] which closely follows the following description. Jamyang Dewai Dorjé's description, found in his *Srad brgyud lugs kyi zab lam bla ma'i rnal 'byor thun mong ma yin pa'i khrid yig tsit ta ma ni'i phreng ba* (A garland of wish-fulfilling jewels, an extraordinary practice manual for the profound path of guru-yoga of the Sé tantric tradition), is as follows:

> In this regard, generally, the sovereign or king of the Tuṣita gods is known as *Devaputra Endowed with Happiness* (*saṃtuṣita; lha'i bu rab dga' ldan*), and from his palace, in a way that a monastery has superior qualities from being far from a city, is the palace of the Foremost Venerable [Maitreya] known as "Exalted Victory Banner." Furthermore, all of the ground is made from a variety of precious stones that are smooth like the palm of one's hand, soft when pressed down upon and comfortable to walk on. It has lakes, water fountains, waterfalls, grassy meadows, and so forth which produce pleasure to touch and has various types of birds who happily float about and coo sweet sounds. There are wish-fulfilling trees, whose branches are made from various kinds of jewels, that produce whatever one wishes such as clothes of the gods and so forth. In the center of that is the palace of the Foremost Venerable [Maitreya] known as "Exalted Victory Banner," being a three-tiered mansion with a gilded roof and having ornamental silken latticework of jewels and auspicious symbols, adorned by various ornaments of jewels such as the jeweled fan of a yak tail (*camararatna*), in brief, a hundred thousand times more beautiful than Shakra, lord of the gods' mansion in the Heaven of the Thirty-Three, captivating and beautiful. In front of that palace is the place where the Foremost Venerable [Maitreya] teaches dharma known as the "Pleasant doctrine-bearing Joyous Place," on golden ground partitioned like a chess board with *vaiḍūrya*, soft when pressed upon and easy to walk on. In the center of the pleasant and amazing place ornamented with various jeweled trees, on top of a seat of lotus and moon disk of a jeweled throne atop eight great lions facing outward, is the Foremost Venerable Ajitanātha, whose body color is like heaps of gold, having an overwhelming majestic brilliance (*gzi brjid dang ldan pa*) like being embraced by ten million suns [5a5]. His body is adorned with the three-fold saffron monastic robes, completely endowed with the major and minor marks of a Buddha, with his two hands in the upper and lower gesture of teaching the dharma and his two legs in a beautiful sitting posture, his face looking to beings in [5b1] Jambudvīpa and radiating limitless light from his body. In the midst of being surrounded by various offering clouds with a retinue that includes the

> Lord [Atiśa] and his sons, the holy guru [Tsong kha pa], master with his sons, as well as immeasurable groups of tenth stage bodhisattvas and fortunate devaputras, he speaks the distinct sound of the holy dharma beginning with *Perfection of Wisdom*. Out of his heart center, from a crystal clear diagram like an endless knot design, on white billowing clouds like yoghurt, elevated in the middle with two [5b3] above who are to his right and left is the holy guru Tsongkhapa, the color of his body white with a tinge of red, adorned with a golden *paṇḍita*'s hat on his head, wearing the three dharma robes, sitting in the vajra crossed-legged posture his hands in the gesture of teaching the dharma that also hold above a book and a sword that are on lotus stalks. On top of a cloud to his right side is Gyeltsab Darma Rinchen, his bodily complexion bright with white color tinged with red, smiling, and his head slightly tilted, and on the left side is the Omniscient Khedrup, his bodily complexion white with a slight tinge of red, his body posed in a wrathful manner (*khro tshul*). Both of their right hands are in the gesture of teaching the dharma and their left hands are holding a book.[33]

This visualization of Maitreya's Field (*Maitreyakṣetra*) as a part of Gelukpa "Hundred Deities of Tuṣita" practices and guru devotions focused upon Tsongkhapa indicates the special orientation that the Gelukpa tradition has toward Tuṣita Heaven. The Tibetan commentaries related to these practices repeatedly mention that the supreme "pure field" is a specific area within Tuṣita that contains Maitreya's palace and pleasure grove. The commentaries use the analogy of the relation between a monastery and a city to explain how this area of Tuṣita is not part of saṃsara, "just as monasteries are within cities but at a distance from them."[34] Commentators such as Dechen Nyingpo (Bde chen snying po, 13b3) will emphasize that this area of Tuṣita "possesses all the qualities of a buddha-field" (*sang rgyas kyi zhing gi yon tan phun sum tshogs pa dang ldan pa*) and will add details that parallel the descriptions of Sukhāvāti so that the various birds in this area of Tuṣita sing songs containing the Nobles' Four Truths and that there are ponds containing water of eight special qualities. The textual sources for the visionary accounts of Maitreya's palace and pleasure grove are not fully clear. The lord of Tuṣita, Saṃtuṣita, is found in a number of Nikāya suttas and Mahāyāna sutras, as well as in the *Lalitavistara*.[35] The name of Maitreya's palace, "Exalted Victory Banner" (*rgyal mtshan mthan po*; *uccadhvaja*), is the name of the palace where Śākyamuni taught as a bodhisattva in Tuṣita Heaven before descending to this world in the *Lalitavistara*.[36] I am, however, currently unable to locate the source for the name of the pleasure grove (*kun dga' ra ba*; *ārāma*) "Pleasant doctrine-bearing Joyous Place" (*kun dga' ra ba yid dga' chos 'dzin*).

As previously mentioned, the visualization and orientation toward Tuṣita takes place within a broader context of visualizing Tsongkhapa in association with guru-yoga practices. These practices have multilevel correlations with Mahāyāna and especially Vajrayāna symbols and meanings. The practices are engaged in to generate merit, to purify negativities, and to gain spiritual attainments and realizations that are embodied in the visualized presence of Tsongkhapa. But what do these practices have to do with Tuṣita Heaven and why invite Tsongkhapa from the special area in Tuṣita Heaven? In response to these questions we may think with Jan Nattier's typology for understanding the Maitreya myth and transpose her categories to understanding the visualization of Tsongkhapa and his disciples from Tuṣita. Nattier outlines a fourfold typology for the Maitreya myth:

> (1) *Here and Now*: In this version of the myth, the believer expects to meet Maitreya on earth, during his or her present lifetime. (2) *Here and Later*: The believer expects the meeting to take place on earth, but at some time after the believer's death (i.e., in a future rebirth). (3) *There and Now*: In this "visionary" recension of the Maitreya myth, the believer strives for an immediate encounter with Maitreya, who is currently residing in the Tuṣita Heaven. (4) *There and Later*: The believer may aspire to a rebirth in Maitreya's other worldly paradise, the Tuṣita Heaven, after this present lifetime.[37]

The practices affiliated with "Hundred Deities of Tuṣita" involve all four of these aspects for followers of Tsongkhapa. The primary orientation is toward (1) *Here and Now* and (3) *There and Now* through the visualization of Tsongkhapa and his two main disciples coming from Tuṣita. As previously mentioned, Tsongkhapa is considered to be currently residing in the pure land of Tuṣita in the form of the Bodhisattva Mañjuśrīgarbha. Meditators cultivate a clear vision of Tsongkhapa in his form as a scholar-monk coming down from Tuṣita on a carpet of clouds. Along these lines, the practices also have a (4) *There and Later* orientation. The commentaries discuss that by the repeated visualization of Tuṣita one will create the karmic seeds and links to easily take rebirth in Tuṣita and be among the retinue of bodhisattvas residing there together with such figures as Tsongkhapa and Atiśa. Commentators generally consider that the practices of the "Hundred Deities of Tuṣita," "Objectless Loving-Kindness Prayer," and other practices related to Tsongkhapa lead to easy rebirth in the special area of Tuṣita. The pure land of Tuṣita is also thought to be within part of this world system (*lokadhātu*; *'jigs rten kyi khams*) and therefore easier to reach than the western paradise of Sukhāvāti (*bde ba can*). Finally, these visualization practices also involve the (2) *Here and Later* orientation and another orientation that I call *Beyond Here and There and Much Later.* The *Here and Later* orientation is based on the Tibetan Buddhist cosmological understanding that all Buddhas of the Fortunate Aeon (*bhadrakalpika; bkal pa bzang po*) descend from Tuṣita Heaven. This aspect is related to Maitreya and establishing the karmic connections to take rebirth in this world when Maitreya, as the fifth Buddha of the Fortunate Aeon, becomes the future Buddha in the distant future. The *Beyond Here and There and Much Later* orientation involves the devotee to Tsongkhapa creating karmic links to take rebirth in the pure land of the "Marvelous Array" (*ngo mtshar rmad byung bkod pa'i zhing*) in the even more distant future when Tsongkhapa becomes the Buddha Seng ge'i nga ro (Siṃhasvara).[38]

In sum, the Gelukpa orientation toward Tuṣita Heaven as a pure land develops among Tsongkhapa's followers within the context of Buddhist tantric practices of guru-yoga and the role of Maitreya and Tuṣita Heaven in the cultural memory of Tsongkhapa's life. The practices of guru-yoga with Tsongkhapa as the central buddha-deity started in his lifetime among his closest disciples. The practices were taken up and developed by Dülnakpa Palden Sangpo (1402–1473), and a lineage of these teachings was transmitted through the Sé tradition of tantric practice. These practices then spread out among Gelukpa-based individuals and institutions throughout Tibet. As the Gelukpas gained political power in the seventeenth century, the "Hundred Deities of Tuṣita" and its related practices were exported to areas where Gelukpas received patronage and support. The relations of Tsongkhapa to Tuṣita Heaven and Maitreya play an important part in the beliefs and practices of Gelukpa practitioners up to the present day.

## Translation

### *An Essential Condensed Practice and Meditation Technique for Creating Karmic Propensities for a Completely Perfect Body of the Path of Sutra and Tantra by Means of the Yoga of the Hundred Deities of Tuṣita*

Yeshé Gyeltsen

Tibetan title: *Dga' ldan lha brgya ma'i rnal 'byor gyi sgo nas mdo sngags kyi lam gyi lus yongs su rdzogs pa la bag chags 'jog tshul nyams len snying por dril ba.* Folio numbers and roman numeral page numbers added to the text in square brackets.

[1 (92)] I pay homage with great respect through the three doors [of body, speech, and mind] to the Lord Losang Drakpa (Blo bzang grags pa), [embodiment of the] protector Mañjuśrī, who singly embodies the three qualities of wisdom, loving kindness, and spiritual power of all the buddhas of the three times. Please take care of us with great compassion at all times. Here is a method to practice the great treasure of blessings renowned as the hundred deities of Tuṣita, the profound path of guru deity-yoga. In a trustworthy and clean place, sweep and clean nicely and then set out representations of body, speech, and mind with the principal [representation] being an image of the Lord guru [Tsongkhapa]. Prepare a beautiful arrangement of undeceitfully acquired offerings. Sit on a comfortable seat with correct body posture. Internally draw the frame of mind without becoming subjected [2a (93)] to the afflictions, disturbances, appearances of this life and so forth and distinguish a clear sense of whether impurities are present. Then, contemplate on the difficulty of finding the freedoms and endowments, the unpredictability of the time of death, the infallibility of cause and effect, and the sufferings of *saṃsāra*.[39] Strongly produce a determination to be free [from *saṃsāra*] having a sense of disgust with the world. Recognize all sentient beings, equally and impartially, as one's mother. Remember their kindness and express gratitude to repay their kindness. Cultivate as much as one is able the thought of love, compassion, and the aspiration for awakening. Based on the nature of that precious aspiration for awakening one should cultivate the profound path of guru deity-yoga. Think to receive the blessings produced by realization of this [and] supplicate the root gurus of the lineage with great reverence.

[2b (94)] I supplicate the venerable Mañjuśrī, Tsongkhapa,
Sherap Sengé, Dülzin Palden Sang,
Jamyang Gendün Phel, and Tashi Phak,
Please bless my mental continuum.
I supplicate the great lineage holders Samdrup Gyatso, Tsöndrü Phak,
at the feet of Dorjé Sang and Sangyé Gyatso,
to Könchok Gyatso, and Könchok Yarphel,
Please bless my mental continuum.
I supplicate for the oral stream of this dharma to Ngawang Lodrö,
the holder of the treasure of this close lineage Ngödrup Gyatso,
and the one who has attained an integrated body Dönyö Khedrup,
Please bless my mental continuum.
I supplicate Ngawang Jampé pal,
the single grouped compassion of all the Victorious Ones

> who has incomparable kindness,
> to the spiritual teacher with kindness who clarified this path,
> Please bless my mental continuum.

Through the force of supplicating with single pointedness to the source of all attainments, the root lineage of the gurus, the light rays of the compassionate knowledge of the divine guru purify the darkness of delusion, misknowlege. [3a (95)] [Recite:]

> May I quickly attain the final achievement, the single pointed aim and the status of a divine guru. May I gain certainty in the knowledge not dependent upon others found in the accumulated well-spoken and expansive teachings.

Thus, one should resolutely supplicate and contemplate that the root spiritual teachers of the lineage bless one's continuum by dissolving into oneself.

Then, in the space before one, [visualize] a vast and expansive wish-fulfilling tree with hundreds of thousands of leaves, on top of which is the reverend father spiritual teacher [Tsongkhapa] and his spiritual sons [Gyeltsab and Khedrup] surrounded by the spiritual teachers of the attainment lineage along with tutelary deities, buddhas, bodhisattvas, *dakiṇīs*, and dharma protectors who are to be supplemented as objects of refuge.[40] With intense faith and reverence for their extensive qualities of body, speech, and mind, supplicate the parent-like sentient beings of the six lineages of transmigration[41] in the periphery around you and contemplate them proclaiming in a single voice with yourself and all sentient beings equivalent to the ends of space,

> I take refuge in the precious holy spiritual teachers. [3b (96)] I take refuge in the Bhagavans, the fully awakened buddhas. I take refuge in the holy dharma. I take refuge in the spiritual community of Noble beings.

State this many times. Then proclaim multiple times and cultivate resolutely to produce the aspiration for awakening by stating,

> I take refuge until attaining awakening in the precious Buddha, Dharma, and Spiritual Assembly. May I, through the merit collected through giving and so forth, achieve buddhahood in order to benefit beings.

Next, utter many times while resolutely invoking one's personal sacred deity (*yi dam*),

> May all sentient beings have happiness and the causes of happiness. May all sentient beings be free from suffering and the causes of suffering. May all

> sentient beings not be separated from the happiness that is without suffering. May all sentient beings abide in equanimity that is free from proximate hatred and attachment. In particular, may I quickly attain in all ways the precious status of a completely and fully awakened buddha for the benefit of all sentient beings. For this purpose, I will practice the profound path of guru deity-yoga.

After this, contemplate that the objects of refuge grouped above you bless you by descending into you.

Then, [4a (97)] visualize the buddha-field of Tuṣita: North of Jambudvīpa there is beautiful Mount Meru. On top of this is the heaven of the thirty-three gods.[42] In the space above this is the celestial realm of the Land Without Combat.[43] In the space above this is Tuṣita Heaven. In a region within the celestial realm of Tuṣita, in the manner that a monastery resides away from a city, dwells the venerable protector Maitreya. That pure realm (*zhing khams*) is covered with earth made from a variety of precious stones, soft when pressed down upon and comfortable to walk on. It is full of many wish-fulfilling trees. Any object that one desires comes down from these trees. Furthermore, the lakes, ponds, and flower gardens have various divinely emanated birds that sing the melodious songs of Dharma. In the center of that pure realm is the palace of the Foremost Venerable [Maitreya] known as "Exalted Victory Banner," a fabulous mansion made from various precious jewels whose light outshines even the light rays of the sun and the moon. The exterior of the palace is adorned with the latticework of jewels, different precious substances, bells, and various ornaments such as the jeweled fan of a yak tail (*camararatna; rnga yab*). There are gods in the sky who hold many objects of offering and offer them. In front of the palace is the place where the Foremost Venerable Maitreya teaches dharma to followers vast like the ocean known as the "Pleasant doctrine-bearing Joyous Place," a pleasure grove having golden ground partitioned with *vaiḍūrya* like a chess board. [4b (98)] In the midst of inconceivable clouds of offerings, upon a precious jeweled throne lifted up by lions, dwells the foremost venerable Maitreya, the protector, whose face looks toward Jambudvīpa and whose legs and feet sit in a majestic pose. His body, like a Mount Meru of gold, emanates light rays that surpass even the radiance of one hundred thousand suns in the ten directions. At his heart the spiritual father [Tsongkhapa] and his two spiritual sons [Gyeltsab and Khedrup] reside appearing like a reflection in a mirror. One should visualize a limitless retinue of emanations like the *devaputras* Vimalākāśa (Nam mkha' dri ma med pa) and Mañjugarbha ('Jam dpal snying po),[44] along with countless bodhisattvas who reside as if they are ready to explain the dharma of the great vehicle (Mahāyāna). Invite the spiritual father [Tsongkhapa] and his two spiritual sons [Gyeltsab and Khedrup] from the heart of the venerable [Maitreya], and when they arrive in the space before one, think how nice it is by means of fervent devotion.

From the heart of the Lord Protector among the hundreds of Tuṣita's gods,
emerges a brilliant white cloud, like a great mass of fresh yoghurt.
Here comes the Omniscient Lord of Dharma, Losang Drakpa
Please come down to us, together with your Sons!

By uttering, the spiritual father [Tsongkhapa] and his two spiritual sons [Gyeltsab and Khedrup] gradually arrive from the heart of the Protector Maitreya. When they are nearly in the space in front of you, visualize a large throne of precious jewels upheld by eight great lions along with two smaller thrones [5a (99)] to the left and right of the large throne and imagine that the spiritual father [Tsongkhapa] and his two spiritual sons sit on top of each throne. Furthermore, one should invocate on top of the central throne, the great Tsongkhapa, who is the venerable Mañjuśrī manifested as a saffron-robed [monk], religious king of the three worlds, who has a white body with reddish hue. He wears the three kinds of religious robes and dons a golden *paṇḍita*'s hat on his head. He sits in the vajra cross-legged posture. His hands at his heart are in the gesture of teaching the dharma; they also hold the stems of blue lotuses whose blossoms open above his right and left shoulders and support a sword of wisdom and a book of the *Perfection of Wisdom* (*prajñāpāramitā*; *sher phyin*). From his heart emanations radiate outwards scattering in the ten directions doing whatever is necessary to tame any being in any way. He resides as the essence gathered together of wisdom, compassion, and power of all the Victorious Ones. Visualize sitting to his right the all-knowing Gyeltsab and sitting to his left the all-knowing Khedrup.

In the sky before me, on a lion throne with a lotus and moon seat,
Sits the holy guru cheerful with delight.
O supreme field of merit for my mind of faith,
Please stay for a hundred aeons to spread the teachings.

Then, emanate many hundred of thousands of emanations of your own body prostrating and offering assemblies of visualized offerings that correspond nicely [5b (100)] with the arrangement of actual offerings.[45]

His heart-mind comprehends the extent of the objects of knowledge
His speech of eloquent elucidation adorns the ears of the fortunate.
His beautiful body radiates with fame's glory.
I bow to you so meaningful to see, hear, and remember.

Various delightful offerings of flowers, perfumes,
Incense, bright lights, and pure sweet waters: This ocean of
Offering-clouds presented and imagined,
I offer to you, O highest field of merit.

Whatever nonvirtues of body, speech, and mind
I have accumulated since time without beginning,
especially transgressions of my three vows,
I confess each one with fierce remorse from the depths of my heart.

In this dark age, you strove for knowledge and realization,
Abandoned the eight worldly concerns[46]
and realized the great value
Of the human life with freedom and opportunity.

O Lord, we rejoice sincerely in your prodigious deeds.
Pray, O holy perfect lamas, in the Dharma Body's sky,
From the billowing clouds of wisdom and compassion, Pour down a rain of vast and profound Dharma Upon the deserving disciples of this world.

By whatever virtue I have gathered here,
May the teachings and all living beings receive every benefit,
and especially may the essence of the teaching
of holy Losang Drakpa shine forever.

Thus, one gradually observes each of the seven limbs of prayer.

Next, offer an extensive *maṇḍala*.[47] With folded hands negate all perverted awarenesses—from having disrespect to the spiritual friend through to apprehension of signs as the two postulated entities [6a (101)] of the self of individuals and the self-nature of phenomenal things—and happily generate all the various unmistaken awarenesses such as respecting the spiritual teacher and so forth, [then recite:]

Please bless us by pacifying all inner and outer conditions of hindrance.
State this three times with fierce devotion. Then,
I supplicate the supreme spiritual teacher, unrivaled,
compassionate, all-surpassing Victorious One

Unsurpassable protector of those who wish to be liberated,
the glorious one who is the single eye among beings of the three realms.

Supplicate to attain the supreme attainment, gradually reciting. The venerable spiritual teacher [Tsongkhapa], who, ever since previously developing the aspiration for awakening and having arrived here, accomplished deeds equivalent to a buddha arriving in this world, and having manifested the luminous dharma-body (*dharmakāya*; *chos sku*) arrived in Tuṣita Heaven and then displayed emanations; contemplate and resolutely request that all his exemplary holy emanations pervade all the buddha-fields such as Tuṣita Heaven and so forth. Furthermore, resolutely supplicate to arouse compassion:

I pray to honorable Jamgön Lama ('Jam mgon bla ma)
Compassionate protector whose superior kindness
For beings who spread the five kinds of corruption[48]
Cannot be tamed by the Victorious One and his sons.

Please grant your blessings by maturing [6b (102)] and liberating my mind-stream.

I pray to Jamgön Lama who takes up the burden
Promising to liberate all beings without exception
Before the top faculty eyes of the Victorious one
From the ocean of countless aeons of previous existences

Please grant your blessings by maturing and liberating my mind-stream.

I pray to honorable Jamgön Lama
Who from that time in as many buddha-fields
As the sands of the Ganges River makes offerings to the Victorious Ones
Setting on the path of maturation and liberation countless beings to be tamed.

Please grant your blessings by maturing and liberating my mind-stream.

I pray to honorable Jamgön Lama
At the moment when the sun of the Buddha's teaching appears in this field
Your mind, with the fragrance of a perfect one-thousand petaled lotus,
Pleases all the bee-like wise ones.

Please grant your blessings by maturing and liberating my mind-stream.

I pray to honorable Jamgön Lama
Who through immeasurable emanations of body, speech, and mind
Based on the aspirational prayers of previous lifetimes
Spreads the doctrine of the Buddha throughout all of India and Tibet.

Please grant your blessings by maturing and liberating my mind-stream.

I pray to honorable Jamgön Lama
Who, in Tibet appears among many learned scholars and accomplished practitioners
As the moon among a constellation of stars
A Matchless leader in all aspects

Please grant your blessings by maturing and liberating my mind-stream.

I pray to honorable Jamgön Lama
Who is given the confident approval of the Protector Maitreya
Who stated that you are equivalent to the Lord of Subduers [7a (103)]
In disseminating the speech of the Subduer, [comprising] all of the sutras and tantras.

Please grant your blessings by maturing and liberating my mind-stream.

I pray to honorable Jamgön Lama
A vajra who is born from a lake taming
The mass of evil doers, malicious demons here in the country of Bhoṭa [i.e., Tibet]
The protector is your magical emanation net itself.

Please grant your blessings by maturing and liberating my mind-stream.

I pray to honorable Jamgön Lama
Compassionate one who disseminates here in this northern land
All the special instructions and teachings of the land of Noble Ones
You are renowned as the honorable eminent one

Please grant your blessings by maturing and liberating my mind-stream.

I pray to honorable Jamgön Lama
Compassionate one who lights the lamp of the Buddha's teaching
Here in the northern land that is covered with the darkness of delusion
Unchallenged by the Victorious One's sunlight

Please grant your blessings by maturing and liberating my mind-stream.

I pray to the compassionate Jamgön Lama
Here in the pure realm which surrounds the courtyard of Mount Meru
The precious teachings of the Victorious One, the source of benefit and happiness
We wish your true words will abide for a long time.

Please grant your blessings by maturing and liberating my mind-stream.

I pray to the honorable Jamgön Lama
Master composite of the spiritual teacher, tutelary deity, and three jewels
Displaying the magical emanation net of the three families unified [7b (104)]
The wisdom, compassion, and power of all the Victorious Ones

Please grant your blessings by maturing and liberating my mind-stream.

O Protector, may we attain illumination in the knowledge that does rely on another
in the entire expansive and profound scriptures
cleansing the darkness of my mind's delusion
with the light of your compassion.

Hearing many teachings from the holy spiritual friend and
Gaining certainty by reflecting on their meaning
Please grant to me the wisdoms of hearing, reflection, and meditation[49]
That are able to single-pointedly engage the meaning of reality

Please grant your blessings spiritual teacher
To liberate all the beings whether wealthy
or without resources by all the virtuous qualities
such as memory, eloquence, supersensory powers, concentration, and so forth

Thus, fervently request with great devotion. Then, [recite the "Objectless Loving-Kindness Prayer" (*Dmigs brtse ma*):]

You are Avalokiteśvara, great treasure of objectless compassion
Mañjuśrī, lord of stainless knowledge
Master of the Secret Ones (Vajrapāṇi), destroyer of the armies of Māra
Tsongkhapa, crown ornament of the scholar-masters of the Land of Snows
Losang Drakpa, to your feet I direct my prayer.

By uttering hundreds of thousand of times, while resolutely supplicating and requesting, a white shaft of light arises from the heart of the spiritual father [Tsongkhapa] and his two spiritual sons. From within that, a stream of nectar descends down to one's head and spreads throughout the interior of one's body. [8a (105)] All evil deeds, obscurations, illnesses, or negative influences that have accumulated from beginningless time are purified through cleansing. One should fervently imagine that one's body becomes the nature of clear light, transparent and clear like pure crystal. Then one should visualize the expansion of one's awareness with wisdom: By way of an orange stream of nectar arising and descending into your body from the heart of the venerable spiritual father [Tsongkhapa] and his two spiritual sons, firmly visualize that you obtain the blessings of the body, speech, and mind of Mañjuśrī. An empowering flow of great wisdom blesses by means of the body, clear wisdom by means of speech, profound wisdom by means of the mind, quick wisdom through the doorway of hand gestures, and the empowering of teaching, debating, and writing blesses through the book and the sword, and so forth. One should understand the special instructions of this practice from the oral transmission of a spiritual teacher. Then at the time of concluding the session, recite

> Precious root glorious guru,
> Please grant attainments of body, speech, and mind
> And protect by means of your great kindness
> in dwelling at the lotus seat of my heart.

Having made the supplication, the two sons dissolve into the venerable [Tsongkhapa]. The venerable guru [Tsongkhapa] then proceeds to the space above your head and as he dissolves into your head, you should fervently visualize a continuous stream of blessings. One should recite, "From this point forward in all my lives, I" and so forth. In times between sessions one should recite *The Foundations of All-Good Qualities* (*Yon tan gzhi gyur ma*)[50] [8b (106)] and recite aspirational prayers to quickly produce in one's continuum a complete perfect body of the path of sutra and tantra. Furthermore, one should recite the following aspirational prayer:

> May this virtue in all my lifetimes
> Without departure of being cared for
> by the spiritual friend of the supreme vehicle
> accomplish the oceanic depth and breadth of Dharma.

May I fulfill the commands through relying on the spiritual friend
Even completely giving away my own life and body
Just as the youthful Manibhadra relied on the Protector Maitreya and
Sadaprarudita relied on Dharmodgata.[51]

Please quickly empower my continuum to produce
Aversion to samsaric states,
Mastery of love, compassion, the aspiration for awakening,
The correct view, and the profound path of the two stages [of generation
and completion].

Immediately after the appearances of this life
May I be nourished by the nectar of the supreme vehicle
By taking rebirth at the holy palace of Dharma in Tuṣita Heaven
In the presence of Ajita [Maitreya] and Mañjugarbha.

At the time that I am reborn in the pure realm
among the foremost of his retinue
May I attain the prediction for highest awakening
From the Tathāgata Siṃhasvara (Seng ge'i nga ro).[52]

Recite and make aspirational prayers. Then, in the period of time between one session and another, one should establish mindfulness in the three doors [of body, speech, and mind] and especially protect the basic and corollary rules of the three vows [of pratimokṣa, bodhisattva training, and vajrayāna samaya) [that include] the 36 rules of a novice, the 253 [9a (107)] monk precepts, the root downfalls and misdeeds of a bodhisattva, and the number of tantric root downfalls. Repeatedly review one's conduct and strive to be unpolluted by downfalls and if sometimes a downfall occurs, do not become indifferent but regret it like expelling poison and with great fear quickly confess [the faults] and vow to refrain striving as much as one is able. One should do this every day, putting meaning into the leisure one has attained and at the time before death, one should make effort in the yoga of transference by means of the five powers. Moreover, by means of deity-yoga, one should make an effort to be reborn in a pure realm or, based on the mind training of both the precious aspiration for awakening and the view of the profound Middle Way according to the spiritual biographies of earlier Kadampa masters, when one is subdued by death one should purify accordingly by not transferring from that [mind training] when death occurs. In brief, always in every situation establish as much karmic propensity as one can toward a completely perfect body of the path of sutra and tantra by means of the deity-yoga of the guru.

This, for the faithful, is "An Essential Condensed Practice and Meditation Technique for Creating Karmic Propensities for a Completely Perfect Body of the Path of Sūtra and Tantra by means of the *Yoga of the Hundred Deities of Tuṣita* of the Noble Profound Scholar-Monk Losang" (*Blo bzang mkhas mchog gi dga' ldan lha rgya ma'i rnal 'byor gyi sgo nas mdo sngags kyi lam gyi lus yongs su rdzogs pa la bag chags 'jog tshul nyams len snying por dril ba zhig dgos*). Based on being requested with great insistence again and again together with flowers of precious substances, the holder of the oral instructions of the Ganden whispered lineage, [9b (108)] the monk Yeshé Gyeltsen (Ye shes rgyal mtshan), composed this in the Sukhāvatī chamber of the Great Palace.

## Notes

1 For instance, neither Alan Sponberg and Helen Hardacre's edited volume on Maitreya, *Maitreya, the Future Buddha* (Cambridge: Cambridge University Press, 1988), nor Lewis Lancaster's (1987; revised 2005) encyclopedia entry on Maitreya, "Maitreya," in *Encyclopedia of Religion, Second Edition,* ed. Lindsay Jones (Detroit: Macmillan Reference USA, 2005 [1987]), 5618–5623, include any discussion of the veneration and worship of Maitreya in Tibetan Buddhist culture. On the bodhisattva and future Buddha Maitreya see Louis Latourette, *Maitreya, le Bouddha futur* (Paris: Libraire Lemercier, 1926); W. Baruch "Maitreya d'après les sources de Sérinde," *Revue de l'Histoire des Religions,* Tome 132 n°1–3 (1946): 67–92; and Etienne Lamotte, *History of Indian Buddhism: From the Origins to the Saka Era* (Louvain-la-Neuve: Université catholique de Louvain, Institut orientaliste, 1988), 699–710. See Paul Demiéville, "La Yogācārabhūmi de Sangharaksa," *Bulletin de l'Ecole française d'Extrême-Orient.* Tome 44 N°2, (1951): 376–397, on Maitreya and the paradise of Tuṣita Heaven, and Luboš Bělka "Maitreya in Tibetan Buddhism: Image and Myth," *Studia Asiatica* 7, no. 1 (2006): 55–73, for Maitreya in Tibetan Buddhism.

2 See Donald Lopez, "A Prayer to the Lama," in *Religions of Tibet in Practice*, ed. Donald Lopez Jr. (Princeton, NJ: Princeton University Press, 1997), 376–386; and Martin Mills, *Identity, Ritual and State in Tibetan Buddhism: The Foundations of Authority in Gelukpa Monasticism* (London: RoutledgeCurzon, 2003) for the social cohesion formed by the practices of guru-yoga in Tibetan Buddhist culture.

3 The followers of Tsongkhapa traditionally are thought to have referred to themselves as Dga' ldan pa, "those of Dga'-ldan monastery." But a number

of early sources (Mkhas grub, *Dad pa'i 'jug ngogs* 2012, 79.2; Mkhas grub, *Gsang ba'i rnam thar*) refer to the monastery as *dge ldan rnam par rgyal ba'i gling*, "dge ldan" meaning "those who have virtue." The earliest sources for the term Gelukpa are found in seventeenth-century sources. See Roger Jackson et al., *The Crystal Mirror of Philosophical Systems: A Tibetan Study of Asian Religious Thought* (Boston: Wisdom Publications, 2009), and Lhundub Sopa and Paul Donnelly, *Like a Waking Dream: The Autobiography of Geshe Lhundub Sopa* (Boston: Wisdom Publications, 2012).

4 Although the classification of "schools" has been problematic in the history of Tibetan Buddhism, I provisionally use the term to refer to a religious identity based on shared institutional affiliation (*chos lugs*) with interrelated "lineages of attainment" (*grub rgyud*) and doctrinal ways of thinking (*grub mtha'*); see Matthew Kapstein, *The Tibetans* (Malden, MA: Blackwell Publications 2006), 231–233.

5 A number of major studies on pure lands in Tibetan forms of Buddhism have emphasized aspirations and practices associated with Sukhāvāti and not other pure lands such as Abhirati, Mount Potalaka, Copper-Colored Mountain, or Tuṣita; see Tadeusz Skorupski "A Prayer for Rebirth in the Sukhāvatā," *The Buddhist Forum, Vol. III (Papers in Honour of Prof. David Syfort Ruegg)* (London: School of Oriental and African Studies, 1994), 373–409; Matthew Kapstein, "Pure Land Buddhism in Tibet? From *Sukhāvatī* to the Field of Great Bliss," in *Approaching the Land of Bliss: Religious Praxis in the Cult of Amitābha*, ed. R. Payne and K. Tanaka (Honolulu: University of Hawai'i Press, 2013), 16–51; and Georgios Halkias, *Luminous Bliss: A Religious History of Pure Land Literature in Tibet: With an Annotated English Translation and Critical Analysis of the Orgyan-gling Gold Manuscript of the Short Sukhāvatīvyūha-sūtra* (Honolulu: University of Hawai'i Press, 2013).

6 The "Five Texts of Maitreya" (*Byams gzhung sde lnga*) in Tibetan Buddhism are the *Abhisamayālaṃkāra*, *Mahāyānasūtrālaṃkāra*, *Madhyāntavibhāgakārikā*, *Dharmadharmatāvibhāgakārikā*, and *Mahāyānottaratantra-śāstra*.

7 See Mkhas grub, *Dad pa'i 'jug ngogs*, 37–38.

8 See Mkhas grub, *Dad pa'i 'jug ngogs*, 51; Robert Thurman, *The Life and Teachings of Tsong Khapa*, rev. ed. (Dharamsala, India: Library of Tibetan Works and Archives, 2006 [1982]), 186; Gavin Kilty, trans., *The Splendor of an Autumn Moon: The Devotional Verse of Tsongkhapa* (Boston: Wisdom Publications, 2001), 292.

9 See Mkhas grub, *Gsang ba'i rnam thar rin po che'i snye ma*, 141–143; Thurman, *Life and Teachings of Tsong Khapa*, 198–206; Kilty, *The Splendor*, 115–149.

10 See Mkhas grub, *Gsang ba'i rnam thar rin po che'i snye ma*, 143. For an English translation see Kilty, *The Splendor*, 83–95.

11 George Dreyfus, *Drepung: An Introduction,* Section 3, 2006, The Tibetan and Himalayan Library, http://www.thlib.org/places/monasteries/drepung/essays/#!essay=/dreyfus/drepung/intro/s/b1.

12 These are: *Rgyal ba byams pa'i bstod pa, Rgyal ba byams pa mgon po la smre sngags kyi sgo nas bstod pa tshangs pa'i cod pan, Rje btsun byams pa mgon po la bstod pa gser bzang btso ma, Rje btsun byams pa mgon po la bstod pa rin po che gsal ba'i sgron me,* and *Rje btsun byams pa mgon po la bstod pa zab yangs mkhyen pa ma,* found in volume Kha, *Bka' 'bum thor bu* (2012) in Tsongkhapa's collected works.

13 *Rgyal ba byams pa'i bstod pa* (in collected works, volume kha, *Bka' 'bum thor bu,* 2012: 603.13–16): *lus sems so sor 'bral ba na // gnad gcod sdug bsngal med pa dang // rgyal ba'i rgyal tsab mi pham mgon // 'khor dang bcas pa mthong bar shog / de nas dga' ldan gnas su ni // skyes ma thag tu 'khor dbus su // mi pham mgon la byang chub tu // lung bstan bdag gis thob gyur cig /.* English translation in Kilty, *The Splendor,* 276–278, where he refers to this prayer as "Twenty-One Verse Rosary Prayer" (*phreng ba'i gsol 'debs tshigs bcad nyer gcig ma*).

14 *Bod rgya tshigs mdzod chen mo* (1998:1984): rang gi rtsa ba'i bla ma sang rgyas kun 'dus kyi ngo bor sgom pa'i cho ga zhig; see also Lopez, "Prayer to the Lama" on the practice of guru-yoga.

15 Alex Wayman, *Untying the Knots in Buddhism: Selected Essays* (Delhi: Motial Banarsidass Publishers, 1997).

16 These two works are *Bla ma'i rnal 'byor zab khyad can chos kyi rgyal po tsong kha pa chen pos mkhas grub thams cad mkhyen pa la gcig brgyud kyi tshul du gnang ba zhugs so,* pages 177–181 in *Rje tsong kha pa chen po'i gsung 'bum bzhugs so,* volume 1 [ka], and *Rje rin po ches ba so chos rje la gcig brgyud kyi tshul du gnang ba'i bla ma'i rnal 'byor bzhugs so,* pages 182–184 in *Rje tsong kha pa chen po'i gsung 'bum bzhugs so,* volume 1 [ka].

17 Note also that in Tsongkhapa's *The Fulfillment of All Hopes,* a commentary to the *Gurupañcāśikā* attributed to Aśvaghoṣa, viewing the guru as awakened is based on the *Guhyasamājatantra;* see Gareth Sparham, *The Fulfillment of All Hopes: Guru Devotion in Tibetan Buddhism* (Boston: Wisdom Publications, 1999), 59–60.

18 The title *dmigs brtse ma,* as pointed out by Daniel Berounsky, "Tibetan 'Magical Rituals' (*las sna tshogs*) from the Power of Tsongkhapa," *Revue d'Etudes Tibétaines* 31 (2015): 97, is untranslatable and derived from the first verse of the prayer (syllables of the title in bold print): **mig mey tse**wey terchen chenrezik (***dmigs med brtse*** *ba'i gter chen spyan ras gzigs*) with the particle "ma" added to titles of works. For studies on this verse, see Carola Roloff, *Red mda'ba, Buddhist Yogi-Scholar of the Fourteenth Century: The Forgotten Reviver of Madhyamaka Philosophy in Tibet* (Wiesbaden: Reichert, 2009), 77, 203, 336 note 192); Anne-Marie Blondeau, "Défense de Tsong kha pa: À propos d'un texte polémique attribué à mKhas grub rje,"

in *Tibetan Studies. Proceedings of the 7th Seminar of the International Association for Tibetan Studies*, Graz 1995, vol. I, ed. Helmut Krasser et al. (Wien: Verlag der Österreichischen Akademie der Wissenschaften, 1997), 70; and Elena de Rossi Filibeck, "Sul commento alle parole 'dMigs brtse ma," in *Indo-Sino-Tibetica: Studi in onore di Luciano Petech*, ed. P. Daffina (Roma: Bardi editore, 1990), 103–115.

19 *dmigs med brtse ba'i gter chen spyan ras gzigs / dri med mkhyen pa'i dbang po 'jam pa'i dbyangs / bdud dpung ma lus 'joms mdzad gsang ba'i bdag / gang can mkhas pa'i gtsug rgyan tsong kha pa / blo bzang grags pa'i zhabs la gsol ba 'debs //*

20 See Berounsky, "Magical Rituals," and L. A. Waddell, *Tibetan Buddhism: With its Mystic Cults, Symbolism and Mythology, and in Its Relation to Indian Buddhism* (New York: Dover Publications, 1972 [1895]) 499, for apotropaic functions of this verse.

21 Weirong Shen, *Leben und historische Bedeutung des ersten Dalai Lama dGe 'dun grub pa dpal bzang po: (1391–1474): Ein Beitrag zur Geschichte der dGe lugs pa-Schule und der Institution der Dalai Lamas* (Sankt Augustin: Institut Monumenta Serica, 2002).

22 Jackson, *The Crystal Mirror*, 287–289.

23 Byams-pa-thub-bstan, and Tenzin Dorjee, *The History of Segyu Gaden Phodrang Monastery (1432–1959): A Wonderful and Meaningful Religious History of the Glorious Segyu Gaden Phodrang Monastery—The Fountain-Head of Great Secret Tantric Teachings* (Sebastopol, CA: Healing Buddha Foundation, 1999).

24 *phur bu lcog bla ma byams pa, dmigs brtse ma'i chos skor las par bla rgyud rnam thar don ming gis bsgrigs pa dga' ldan lha brgya ma 'dul nag pas mdzad pa bcas*, 5b2: *rje'i snyan rgyud shes seng la gnang ba bla ma'i rnal 'byor gyi zhal shes bstsal ba 'dul ngag pas yi ge bkod pa dga' ldan lha brgy ma yin no /.*

25 The seven-limbed prayer, or seven-branch service (*saptāṅgavidhi; yan lag bdun pa*) is a liturgy of worship made up of seven parts: (1) prostration (*vandanā; phyag 'tshal ba*), (2) offerings (*pūjana; mchod pa phul ba*), (3) confession (*pāpadeśana; sdig pa bshags pa*), (4) rejoicing in merit (*anumodanā; rje su yi rab ba*), (5) requesting the teaching (*adhyeṣaṇā; bskul ba*), (6) begging [the Buddhas not to abandon beings] (*yācanā; gsol ba*), and (7) dedication of merit (*pariṇāmanā; bsngo ba*). This form of worship, possibly having fewer or more than seven parts, is found in early Mahāyāna sutras from the first century; see Kate Crosby and Andrew Skilton, *The Bodhicaryāvatāra* (Oxford: Oxford University Press 2008), 9–13.

26 'Jam dbyangs bde ba'i rdo rje (1682–1741), Srad brgyud lugs kyi zab lam bla ma'i rnal 'byor thun mong ma yin pa'i khrid yig tsit+ta ma Ni'i phreng ba, 10a1–11a4. bsKal bzang rgya mtsho (7th Dalai lama, 1709–1757), Dga' ldan lha brgya ma'i khrid yig dngos grub kun 'byung, 2b6–3a3. Berounsky, "Magical Rituals," 99, translates the 7th Dalai Lama's account.

27 *dga' ldan lha brgya ma* (9b1–2) *in Dmigs brtse ma'i chos skor las / bla ma'i rnal 'byor gyi brgyud 'debs bde ba'i rdo rdes mdzad pa: dga' ldan lha brgya'i dgon gyi thugs ka nas / / rab dkar zho gsar spungs 'dri'i chu 'dzin rtser / / chos kyi rgyal po kun mkhyen blo zang grags / /sras dang bcas pa gnas 'dir gshegs gsol /* Translations based on Thurman, *Life and Teachings of Tsong Khapa*, 246.

28 Tsongkhapa, Zhu lan sman mchog bdud rtsi'i 'phreng ba (2012:249): *blo bzang grags pa 'di nyid skye ba rting ma gar 'khrungs zhus pas / dga' ldan du byams pa'i drung du byang chub sems dpa' 'jam dpal snying po zhes bya bar skye / de nas dga' ldan nas 'dzam bu sling gzhan du sems can gyi don la dgongs te / chos rgyal nyid du skyes ba bzhes te sems can gyi don dpag du med pa 'byung /* See Thurman, *Life and Teachings of Tsong Khapa*, 229; Sparham, *The Fulfillment of All Hopes*, 22.

29 See Jeffrey Hopkins, *Maps of the Profound: Jam-yang-shay-ba's Great Exposition of Buddhist and Non-Buddhist Views on the Nature of Reality* (Ithaca, NY: Snow Lion Publications, 2003), 14–15, on the life of 'Jam dbyangs bzhad pa ngag dbang brtson grus (1648–1721).

30 See Gilles Béguin and Sylvie Colinart, *Les Peintures du Bouddhisme Tibétain* (Paris: Réunion des musées nationaux, 1995), and Claus Deimel, Ingo Nentwig, and Hermann Speck von Sternburg, *Buddhas Leuchten and Kaisers Pracht: die Pekinger Sammlung Hermann Speck von Sternburg* (Leipzig: Grassimuseum, 2008). The Himalayan Art website (www.himalayanart.org) contains images of this practice in, for example, Tibet eighteenth century (items no. 18, 65799, 69912), China (item no. 58974), Mongolia (items no. 50052, 50057, 50498), and Buryatia (item no. 74206).

31 Jamyang Dewai Dorjé (1682–1741) was an important Geluk master of the seventeenth century who was born in Lhasa and connected with Ri bo dge 'phel, where he received the teachings of the *srad brgyud* from 'Jam dbyangs bzhad pa'i rdo rje in 1691. He also received teachings of the Gelukpa tradition from Blo bzang tshul khrims, Thang sag pa dngos grub rgya mtsho, and 'Khrul gzhi mang thos rgya mtsho.

32 Béguin and Colinart, *Les Peintures du Bouddhisme Tibétain*, 404–406, items no. 312, 313, and 314.

33 For transcribed text, see appendix 1.

34 The commentaries use the abbreviated phrase *grong las dgon pa'i tshul du yod*. Modern Tibetan Gelukpa teachers use the same analogy, for instance, in describing Maitreya's place in the Joyous Land called "Pleasant Doctrine-bearing Joyous Place" (*dga' ldan yid dga' chos 'dzin*). Gedün Lodrö states that "it is in the Joyous Land but away from it, just as monasteries are within cities but at a distance from them" (Dge 'dun blo gros et al., *Walking through Walls: A Presentation of Tibetan Meditation* (Ithaca, NY: Snow Lion Publications, 1992), 262.

35 Monier Monier-Williams, *Sanskrit English Dictionary* (1899), s.v. *saṃtuṣita*, T. W. Rhys Davids, William Stede, editors (1921–1925), *The Pali Text Society's Pali-English dictionary*, s.v. deva: *santusita.*

36 Franklin Edgerton, *Buddhist Hybrid Sanskrit Dictionary* (1953:118), s.v. uccadhvaja; Lalitavistara (29.14 Parivarta 4) *dharmālokamukhaparivartaścaturthaḥ / iti hi bhikṣavo bodhisattvo janmakulaṃ vyavalokya* ***uccadhvajaṃ*** *nāma tuṣitālaye mahāvimānaṃ catuḥṣaṣṭiyojanānyāyāmavistāreṇa yasmin bodhisattvaḥ saṃniṣadya tuṣitebhyo devebhyo dharmaṃ deśayati sma.*

37 Jan Nattier, "The Meanings of the Maitreya Myth: A Typological Analysis." In *Maitreya, the Future Buddha*, ed. Alan Sponberg and Helen Hardacre (Cambridge: Cambridge University Press, 1988), 25–32.

38 The biographies of Tsongkhapa and related prayers provide the name of Tsongkhapa's future Buddhahood as the Tathāgata Seng ge'i nga ro (Siṃhasvara) in the field of "Marvelous Array" (*ngo mtshar rmad byung bkod pa*). The scholar 'Jigs med dam chos rgya mtsho (1898–1946) wrote a guidebook for this buddha-field titled *Ngo mtshar rmad byung bkod pa'i zhing gi bshad pa smon lam dang bcas pa rmad byung bkod par 'jug pa'i them skas.* Some sources state that Tsongkhapa will become the eleventh Buddha in the *Bhadrakalpika sutra.* The eleventh Buddha in the Tibetan version of the *Bhadrakalpika sutra,* however, is named Sunetra (*spyan legs*). See translation below and James B. Apple, "Where and When Does Tsong-kha-pa Become a Buddha? Notes on His Future Buddhahood," forthcoming.

39 These are topics within the "Stages of the Path" (*lam rim*) literature. See Tsong-kha-pa Blo-bzang-grags-pa, *The Great Treatise on the Stages of the Path to Enlightenment* (Ithaca, NY: Snow Lion Publications, 2000).

40 See Jackson, *The Crystal Mirror,* on the function, structure, and content of the Tibetan "field of assembly."

41 Six lineages of transmigration are gods (*deva; lha*), humans (*manuṣya; mi*), demigods (*asura; lha ma yin*), animals (*tiryañc; dud 'gro*), hungry ghosts (*preta; yi dwags*), and hell denizens (*nāraka; dmyal ba*).

42 *Sum cu rtsa gsum gyi lha gnas, Trāyastriṃśa; Tāvatiṃsa.*

43 *'Thab bral gyi lha gnas*, Yāma.

44 Vimalākāśa (Nam mkha' dri ma med pa) is thought to be the rebirth of Atiśa and Mañjugarbha; ('Jam dpal snying po) is the rebirth of Tsongkhapa.

45 The following verses are also found in Thurman, *Life and Teachings of Tsong Khapa*, 275–276.

46 The eight worldly concerns (*aṣṭalokadharma; 'jig rten rgyi chos brgyad*) are gain (*lābha; rnyed pa*), loss (*alabha; ma rnyed pa*), pleasure (*sukha; bde ba*), misery (*duḥkha; sdug bsngal*), praise (*praśamsā; bstod pa*), degradation (*nindā; smad pa*), fame (*yaśa; snyan grags*), and infamy (*ayaśa; ma grags*). *Mahāvyutpatti*, 2341–2348.

47 See John Powers, *Introduction to Tibetan Buddhism*, rev. 2nd ed. (Ithaca, NY: Snow Lion Publications, 2007), 306–309, on maṇḍala offerings in Tibetan Buddhism, and Wayman, *The Buddhist Tantras: Light on Indo-Tibetan Esotericism* (New York: S. Weiser, 1973), 82–109, on the components of the *maṇḍala* offering.

48 The five corruptions or impurities (*pañcakaṣāya; snyigs ma lnga*) are: (1) decrease in lifespan (*āyuskaṣāya; tshe snyigs ma*); (2) increase of wrong views (*dṛṣṭikaṣāya; lta ba snyigs ma*); (3) increase of negative emotions or the five poisons (*kleśakaṣāya; nyon mongs snyigs ma*); (4) mental and physical corruption of living beings (*sattvakaṣāya; sems can snyigs ma*); (5) corruption of the age (*kalpakaṣāya; dus kyi snyigs ma*).

49 The three successive kinds of wisdom (*thos sam sgom gsum kyi shes rab*) are wisdoms arising from study (*śrutamayī; thos byung*), reflection (*cintāmayī; bsam byung*), and meditation (*bhāvanāmayī; sgom byung*).

50 *The Foundations of All Good Qualities* (*Yon tan gzhi gyur ma*) is found in Tsongkhapa's collected works, *Rje tsong kha pa chen po'i gsung 'bum bzhugs so*, volume 2 [kha]. For an English translation, see Geshe Wangyal, "The Foundation of All Excellence," in *The Door of Liberation* (New York: Maurice Girodias Associates, 1973), 255–257, rev. ed. (Boston: Wisdom Publications, 1995), 183–185.

51 The story of Sadaprarudita and Dharmodgata is found in the *Eight Thousand Verse Perfection of Wisdom* (*Aṣṭasāhasrikāprajñāpāramitā, Shes rab kyi pha rol tu phyin pa brgyad stong pa*).

52 Yeshé Gyeltsen mentions in this verse the aspiration for rebirth during the time of Tathāgata Siṃhasvara (Seng ge'i nga ro). Presumably this refers to the time of Tsongkhapa's future buddhahood. Mkhas grub's *Dad pa'i 'jug ngogs*, 106–107, mentions Tsongkhapa's awakening in the intermediate state (*bar do*) and subsequent emanation body (*sprul pa'i sku*) rebirth in Tuṣita heaven as Mañjuśrīgarbha ('Jam dpal snying po). No other Tathāgatas are mentioned. Robert Thurman (*The Central Philosophy of Tibet: A Study and Translation of Jey Tsong Khapa's Essence of True Eloquence* [Princeton, NJ: Princeton University Press, 1991]) mentions that Tsongkhapa receives a prediction to become the Buddha Siṃhanada in the universe Adbhutavyuha ("Miraculous Array"). The earliest source I can currently locate that mentions a similar prediction is in George N. Roerich, trans., *The Blue Annals* (New Delhi: Motilal Banarsidass, 1976 [1949]), 1079; Chengdu 1257.3–5), composed by 'Gos lo tsā ba gzhon nu dpal (1392–1481), which states that Tsongkhapa will be awakened as the Tathāgata Siṃhasvara (Seng ge'i nga ro). A later hagiography of Tsongkhapa by Cha har dge bshes Blo bzang tshul khrims (1740–1810), *Rje tsong kha pa'i rnam thar chen mo*, 308, mentions Tsongkhapa's rebirth as Mañjuśrīgarbha, rebirth as the eleventh Buddha of the fortuate Aeon Sunetra (*spyan legs*), 316–317, and as the Tathāgata Siṃhasvara (Seng ge'i nga ro), 481. As noted by

John Powers and David Templeman, *Historical Dictionary of Tibet* (Lanham, MD: Scarecrow Press, 2012), 644, "A special tree at sKu 'bum monastery in Amdo has leaves which bear the seed syllables and outlines of hand implements of the Buddha Seng ge sgra (Siṃhanāda), the 11th of the 1,000 buddhas who will appear during the present 'fortunate eon.'" In the Tibetan version of the *Bhadrakalpita sūtra* (Fortunate aeon, vols. 1–4, 1986), however, the eleventh Buddha is Sunetra (*spyan legs*), while Seng ge sgra, is number 160. The Tathāgata Siṃhasvara (Seng ge'i nga ro) in the *Bhadrakalpita sūtra* is number 843. A seventeenth-century Tibetan painting in Musée National des Arts Asiatiques-Guimet known as the "Apparition de *Tsong-kha-pa*" (Béguin and Colinart, *Les Peintures du Bouddhisme Tibétain,* 404–406) labels the future buddha as Sangs rgyas spyan mdzes (Cārulocana), but this is tathāgata number 522. See Apple, forthcoming, on this issue.

## Bibliography


Apple, James B. "Where and When Does Tsong-kha-pa Become a Buddha? Notes on His Future Buddhahood." Forthcoming.

Baruch, W. "Maitreya d'après les sources de Sérinde." *Revue de l'Histoire des Religions* 132, no. 1–3 (1946): 67–92.

Béguin, Gilles, and Sylvie Colinart. *Les Peintures du Bouddhisme Tibétain.* Paris: Réunion des musées nationaux, 1995.

Bělka, Luboš. "Maitreya in Tibetan Buddhism: Image and Myth." *Studia Asiatica* 7, no. 1 (2006): 55–73.

Berounsky, Daniel. "Tibetan "Magical Rituals" (*las sna tshogs*) from the Power of Tsongkhapa." *Revue d'Etudes Tibétaines* 31 (2015): 95–111.

Blo bzang 'phrin las rnam rgyal (19th century). *'Jam mgon chos kyi rgyal po tsong kha pa chen po'i rnam thar thub bstan mdzes pa'i rgyan gcig ngo mtshar nor bu'i 'phreng ba dang mdzad rnam zhal thang bzhugs so.* Lhas sa: Bod-ljongs mi dmangs dpe skrun khang, 2009.

Blo bzang tshul khrims, cha har dge bshes (1740–1810). *Rje tsong kha pa'i rnam thar chen mo.* Pe cin: Krung go'i bod rig pa dpe skrun khang, 2010.

Blondeau, Anne-Marie. "Défense de Tsong kha pa: À propos d'un texte polémique attribué à Mkhas grub rje." In *Tibetan Studies. Proceedings of the 7th Seminar of the International Association for Tibetan Studies*, Graz 1995, vol. 1, edited by Helmut Krasser, Michael Torsten Much, Ernst Steinkellner, and Helmut Tauscher, 59–76. Wien: Verlag der Österreichischen Akademie der Wissenschaften, 1997.

Bskal bzang rgya mtsho (1708–1757, 7th Dalai Lama). *Rgyal ba kun gyi mkhyen brtse nus gsum gyi bdag nyid rje btsun tsong kha pa chen po la dmigs brtse ma'i gsol 'debs dang 'brel ba'i bla ma'i rnal 'byor dga' ldan lha brgya ma'i 'khrid yig dngos grub kun 'byung*. In *Bskal bzang rgya mtsho'i gsung 'bum*, vol. 1 (ka), 11–44. Buddhist Digital Resource Center, https://www.tbrc.org/#!rid=W2623.

Byams pa thub bstan, and Tenzin Dorjee. *The History of Segyu Gaden Phodrang Monastery (1432–1959): A Wonderful and Meaningful Religious History of the Glorious Segyu Gaden Phodrang Monastery—The Fountain-Head of Great Secret Tantric Teachings*. Sebastopol, CA: Healing Buddha Foundation, 1999, 1.

Crosby, Kate, and Andrew Skilton. *The Bodhicaryāvatāra*. Oxford: Oxford University Press, 2008.

Deimel, Claus, Ingo Nentwig, and Hermann Speck von Sternburg. *Buddhas Leuchten and Kaisers Pracht: Die Pekinger Sammlung Hermann Speck von Sternburg*. Leipzig: Grassimuseum, 2008.

Demiéville, Paul. "La Yogācārabhūmi de Sangharaksa." *Bulletin de l'Ecole française d'Extrême-Orient* 44, no. 2 (1951): 339–436.

Dge 'dun blo gros, Jeffrey Hopkins, Leah Zahler, and Anne C. Klein. *Walking Through Walls: A Presentation of Tibetan Meditation*. Ithaca, NY: Snow Lion Publications, 1992.

Dharma Publishing. *The Fortunate Aeon: How the Thousand Buddhas Become Enlightened*. Volumes I–IV. Berkeley, CA: Dharma Publishing, 1986.

Dreyfus, George. *Drepung: An Introduction*. The Tibetan and Himalayan Library. http://www.thlib.org/places/monasteries/drepung/essays/#!essay=/dreyfus/drepung/intro/s/b1, 2006.

Edgerton, Franklin. *Buddhist Hybrid Sanskrit Grammar and Dictionary*. New Haven, CT: Yale University Press, 1953.

Filibeck, Elena de Rossi. "Sul commento alle parole 'dMigs brtse ma.'" In *Indo-Sino-Tibetica: Studi in onore di Luciano Petech*, edited by P. Daffina, 103–115. Roma: Bardi editore, 1990.

Halkias, Georgios. *Luminous Bliss: A Religious History of Pure Land Literature in Tibet: With an Annotated English Translation and Critical Analysis of the Orgyan-gling Gold Manuscript of the Short Sukhāvatīvyūha-sūtra*. Honolulu: University of Hawai'i Press, 2013.

Hopkins, Jeffrey. *Maps of the Profound: Jam-yang-shay-ba's Great Exposition of Buddhist and Non-Buddhist Views on the Nature of Reality*. Ithaca, NY: Snow Lion Publications, 2003.

Jackson, Roger. "The Tibetan Tshogs Zhing (Field of Assembly): General Notes on Its Function, Structure, and Contents." *Asian Philosophy* 2, no. 2 (1992): 157–172.

Jackson, Roger R., et al., trans. *The Crystal Mirror of Philosophical Systems: A Tibetan Study of Asian Religious Thought*. Boston: Wisdom Publications, 2009.

’Jam dbyangs bde ba’i rdo rje (1682–1741), Mkhyen rab bstan pa chos ’phel (1840–1907/8). *dmigs brtse ma’i chos skor stod smad kha skong dang bcas pa* [Buddhist Digital Resource Center, https://www.tbrc.org/#!rid=W1KG9980]. 3 vols. [s.l.]: [s.n.], [n.d.].

——. *Srad brgyud lugs kyi zab lam bla ma’i rnal ’byor thun mong ma yin pa’i khrid yig tsit+ta ma Ni’i phreng ba (bla rnal khrid ga)*. In *Ggsung 'bum, 'jam dbyangs bde ba'i rdo rje* [Buddhist Digital Resource Center, https://www.tbrc.org/#!rid=W7797]: 51- 80. [lha sa]: [zhol bka' 'gyur pa khang], [1999?].

’Jigs med dam chos rgya mtsho (1898–1946). *Ngo mtshar rmad byung bkod pa’i zhing gi bshad pa smon lam dang bcas pa rmad byung bkod par ’jug pa’i them skas*. In *gsung ’bum; ’jigs med dam chos rgya mtsho* [Buddhist Digital Resource Center, https://www.tbrc.org/#!rid=W00EGS1017401]. 3: 679–618. null: [rong bo dgon chen], [2006?].

Kapstein, Matthew. “Pure Land Buddhism in Tibet? From *Sukhāvatī* to the Field of Great Bliss.” In *Approaching the Land of Bliss: Religious Praxis in the Cult of Amitābha*, edited by Richard Karl Payne and Kenneth Ken’ichi Tanaka, 16–51. Honolulu: University of Hawai‘i Press, 2004.

——. *The Tibetans*. Malden, MA: Blackwell Publications, 2006.

Kilty, Gavin, trans. *The Splendor of an Autumn Moon: The Devotional Verse of Tsong-khapa*. Boston: Wisdom Publications, 2001.

Lamotte, Etienne. *History of Indian Buddhism: From the Origins to the Saka Era*. Louvain-la-Neuve: Université catholique de Louvain, Institut orientaliste, 1988.

Lancaster, Lewis. “Maitreya.” In *Encyclopedia of Religion, Second Edition*, edited by Lindsay Jones, 5618–5623. Detroit: Macmillan Reference USA, 2005.

Latourette, Louis. *Maitreya, le Bouddha futur*. Paris: Libraire Lemercier, 1926.

Lopez, Donald S. “A Prayer to the Lama.” In *Religions of Tibet in Practice*, edited by Donald S. Lopez Jr., 376–386. Princeton, NJ: Princeton University Press, 1997.

Mills, Martin A. *Identity, Ritual and State in Tibetan Buddhism: The Foundations of Authority in Gelukpa Monasticism*. London: RoutledgeCurzon, 2003.

Mkhas grub rje dge legs dpal bzang (1385–1438). “Rje btsun bla ma tsong kha pa chen po’i ngo mtshar rmad du byung ba’i rnam par thar pa dad pa’i ’jug ngogs.” In *Rje tsong kha pa chen po’i gsung ’bum bzhugs so*, vol. 1 [ka], 1–114. Pe cin: krung go’i bod rig pa dpe skrun khang, 2012.

——. “Rje rin po che’i gsang ba’i nram thar rgya mtsho lta bu las cha shas nyung ngu zhig yongs su brjod pa’i gtam rin po che’i snye ma bzhugs so.” In *Rje tsong kha pa chen po’i gsung ’bum bzhugs so*, vol. 1 [ka], 133–160. Pe cin: krung go’i bod rig pa dpe skrun khang, 2012.

Monier-Williams, Monier. *A Sanskrit-English Dictionary*. New York: Oxford University Press, 1988 [1989].

Nattier, Jan. "The Meanings of the Maitreya Myth: A Typological Analysis." In *Maitreya, the Future Buddha*, edited by Alan Sponberg and Helen Hardacre, 23–47. Cambridge: Cambridge University Press, 1988.

Phur bu lcog Bla ma byams pa. *Bla rgyud rnam thar don ming gis bsgrigs pa / dga' ldan lha brgya ma 'dul nag pas mdzad pa bcas*. In *dMigs brtse ma'i chos skor*, vol. one, part kha, 12–29 (Buddhist Digital Resource Center, https://www.tbrc.org/#!rid=W1KG9980, n.d., written down by Lha ye shes bstan pa'i mgon po (1760–1810)).

Powers, John. *Introduction to Tibetan Buddhism*. Rev. 2nd ed. Ithaca, NY: Snow Lion Publications, 2007.

Powers, John, and David Templeman. *Historical Dictionary of Tibet*. Lanham, MD: Scarecrow Press, 2012.

Rhys Davids, T. W., and William Stede, eds. *The Pali Text Society's Pali-English Dictionary*. Chipstead: Pali Text Society, 1921–1925. http://dsal.uchicago.edu/dictionaries/pali.

Roerich, George N., trans. *The Blue Annals*. New Delhi: Motilal Banarsidass, 1976 [1949].

Roloff, Carola. *Red mda'ba, Buddhist Yogi-Scholar of the Fourteenth Century: The Forgotten Reviver of Madhyamaka Philosophy in Tibet*. Wiesbaden: Reichert, 2009.

Schwieger, Peter. *Ein tibetisches Wunschegebet um Wiedergeburt in der Sukhavati*. Beitrage zur Zentralasienforschung, Band 1. St. Augustin: VGH Wissenschaftsverlag, 1978.

Shen, Weirong. *Leben und historische Bedeutung des ersten Dalai Lama dGe 'dun grub pa dpal bzang po (1391–1474): ein Beitrag zur Geschichte und der Institution der Dalai Lamas*. Sankt Augustin: Institut Monumenta Serica, 2002.

Skorupski, Tadeusz. "A Prayer for Rebirth in the Sukhāvatā." *The Buddhist Forum, Vol. III (Papers in Honour of Prof. David Syfort Ruegg)*, 373–409. London: School of Oriental and African Studies, 1994.

Sopa, Lhundub, and Paul Donnelly. *Like a Waking Dream: The Autobiography of Geshe Lhundub Sopa*. Boston: Wisdom Publications, 2012.

Sparham, Gareth, trans. *The Fulfillment of All Hopes: Guru Devotion in Tibetan Buddhism*. Boston: Wisdom Publications, 1999.

Sponberg, Alan, and Helen Hardacre. *Maitreya, the Future Buddha*. Cambridge: Cambridge University Press, 1988.

Thurman, Robert A. F. *The Central Philosophy of Tibet: A Study and Translation of Jey Tsong Khapa's Essence of True Eloquence*. Princeton, NJ: Princeton University Press, 1991.

———. *The Life and Teachings of Tsong Khapa*, rev. ed. Dharamsala, India: Library of Tibetan Works and Archives, 2006 [1982].

Tsering Namgyal, "Sherab Gyatso," Treasury of Lives. http://www.treasuryoflives.org/biographies/view/Drungchen-Sherab-Gyatso/2495. Accessed May 4, 2013.

Tsong-kha-pa Blo-bzang-grags-pa. *The Great Treatise on the Stages of the Path to Enlightenment.* Ithaca, NY: Snow Lion Publications, 2000.

Tsong kha pa blo bzang grags pa (1357–1419). "Bla ma'i rnal 'byor zab khyad can chos kyi rgyal po tsong kha pa chen pos mkhas grub thams cad mkhyen pa la gcig brgyud kyi tshul du gnang ba zhugs so." In *Rje tsong kha pa chen po'i gsung 'bum bzhugs so*, vol. 1 [ka], 177–181. Pe cin: krung go'i bod rig pa dpe skrun khang, 2012.

———. "Rgyal ba byams pa'i bstod pa." In *Rje tsong kha pa chen po'i gsung 'bum bzhugs so*, vol. 2 [kha], 601–604. Pe cin: krung go'i bod rig pa dpe skrun khang, 2012.

———. "Rgyal ba byams pa mgon po la smre sngags kyi sgo nas bstod pa tshangs pa'i cod pan." In *Rje tsong kha pa chen po'i gsung 'bum bzhugs so*, vol. 2 [kha], 211–217. Pe cin: krung go'i bod rig pa dpe skrun khang, 2012.

———. "Rje btsun byams pa mgon po la bstod pa gser bzang btso ma." In *Rje tsong kha pa chen po'i gsung 'bum bzhugs so*, vol. 2 [kha], 222–223. Pe cin: krung go'i bod rig pa dpe skrun khang, 2012.

———. "Rje btsun byams pa mgon po la bstod pa rin po che gsal ba'i sgron me." In *Rje tsong kha pa chen po'i gsung 'bum bzhugs so*, vol. 2 [kha], 218–222. Pe cin: krung go'i bod rig pa dpe skrun khang, 2012.

———. "Rje btsun byams pa mgon po la bstod pa zab yangs mkhyen pa ma." In *Rje tsong kha pa chen po'i gsung 'bum bzhugs so*, vol. 2 [kha], 223–224. Pe cin: krung go'i bod rig pa dpe skrun khang, 2012.

———. "Rje rin po ches ba so chos rje la gcig brgyud kyi tshul du gnang ba'i bla ma'i rnal 'byor bzhugs so. In *Rje tsong kha pa chen po'i gsung 'bum bzhugs so*, vol. 1 [ka], 182–184. Pe cin: krung go'i bod rig pa dpe skrun khang, 2012.

———. *Rje tsong kha pa chen po'i gsung 'bum bzhugs so*, vols. 1–18 [ka-tsha]. Pe cin: krung go'i bod rig pa dpe skrun khang, 2012.

———. "Yon tan gzhir gyur ma." In *Rje tsong kha pa chen po'i gsung 'bum bzhugs so*, vol. 2 [kha], 178–179. Pe cin: krung go'i bod rig pa dpe skrun khang, 2012.

———. "Zhu lan sman mchog bdud rtsi'i 'phreng ba bzhugs so." In *Rrje tsong kha pa chen po'i gsung 'bum bzhugs so*, vol. 1 [ka], 231–250. Pe cin: krung go'i bod rig pa dpe skrun khang, 2012.

Waddell, L. A. *Tibetan Buddhism: With Its Mystic Cults, Symbolism, and Mythology, and in Its Relation to Indian Buddhism.* New York: Dover Publications, 1972 [1895].

Wangyal, Geshe. "The Foundation of All Excellence." In *The Door of Liberation.* New York: Maurice Girodias Associates, 1973, 255–257. Revised edition, Boston: Wisdom Publications, 1995, 183–185.

Wayman, Alex. *The Buddhist Tantras: Light on Indo-Tibetan Esotericism*. New York: S. Weiser, 1973.

———. *Untying the Knots in Buddhism: Selected Essays*. Delhi: Motial Banarsidass Publishers, 1997.

Ye shes rgyal mtshan (1713–1793). "Dga' ldan lha brgya ma'i rnal 'byor gyi sgo nas mdo sngags kyi lam gyi lus yongs su rdzogs pa la bag chags 'jog tshul nyams len snying por dril ba." In *Gsung 'bum, ye shes rgyal mtshan*. [Buddhist Digital Resource Center, https://www.tbrc.org/#!rid=W1022], vol. 14:108–124 [1–9 ff, 92–108]. New Delhi: Tibet House Library, 1974–1977.

Zhang Yisun et al., eds. *Bod rgya tshigs mdzod chen mo*. Beijing: mi rigs dpe skrun khang, 1998 [1984].

# Chapter 3

# Amoghavajra's Amitāyus Ritual Manual

Thomas Eijō Dreitlein

### Translator's Introduction

The *Ritual Manual on Cultivating the Visualization of and Making Offerings to Amitāyus Tathāgata* (*Wuliangshou rulai xiu guanxing gongyang yigui*[1] 無量壽如來修觀行供養儀軌, hereafter *Wuliangshou yigui*)[2] is an important Esoteric ritual practice manual in East Asia stated as a translation of Amoghavajra (705–774). It is significant in Chinese Buddhism as an Esoteric ritual for birth in Sukhāvatī, and it is also an important source for the Eighteen Methods (*Jūhachidō*) ritual format that developed in Japanese Esoteric Buddhism and for the Esoteric Amida practices that later appeared in Japan.

## The *Wuliangshou Yigui* and Related Ritual Manuals

This text may be classified according to its ritual format as belonging to a group of Tang ritual manuals inclusive of the following texts.[3] These texts all follow, to varying degrees, the ritual format later called Jūhachidō in Japan, and they make up the sources of that format. The deities vary among the following, and only the *Wuliangshou yigui* is a practice of Amitāyus.

1. *Wuliangshou yigui* (Amitāyus ritual manual), *T.* 930, trans. Amoghavajra.
2. *Ruyilun yigui* (Cintāmaṇicakra ritual manual), *T.* 1085, trans. Amoghavajra.
3. *Ganlu Juntuli yigui* (Amṛta-Kuṇḍalī ritual manual), *T.* 1211, trans. Amoghavajra.
4. *Wuchusemo yigui* (Ucchuṣma ritual manual), *T.* 1225, trans. Amoghavajra.

5. *Achu fa* (Akṣobhya method), *T.* 921, trans. Amoghavajra.
6. Vajrabodhi's *Zhunti jing* (Cundī sūtra), *T.* 1075, trans. Vajrabodhi.
7. Amoghavajra's *Zhunti jing*, *T.* 1076, trans. Amoghavajra.

## The *Wuliangshou Yigui* in China

The *Wuliangshou yigui* contains several passages suggestive of the Pure Land sutras popular in Chinese Buddhism, including the *Amitāyus Visualization Sūtra*,[4] but the basic ritual structure of the *Wuliangshou yigui* is clearly related to the above Tang Esoteric ritual manuals.[5] In translating an Indian tantric manual on Amitāyus ritually belonging to the above grouping—or possibly in creating an original one based on that format—Amoghavajra seems to have intentionally added a number of passages reminiscent of the Pure Land sutras influential in China and may have also redefined the purpose of the practice as birth in Sukhāvatī, in order to produce an Esoteric ritual of Amitāyus that would be of particular interest to many Chinese.[6]

Because it consistently focuses on the goal of birth in Sukhāvatī,[7] it is possible to say that the *Wuliangshou yigui* has adopted an Esoteric ritual format for an exoteric goal.[8] This text offers an interesting combination of Esoteric practices with Pure Land teachings, with birth in Sukhāvatī as the purpose of its practice. For example, at the beginning of the *Wuliangshou yigui* (1.1) Vajrapāṇi tells the Buddha that, "for the sake of beings with evil karma in the coming defiled world of the Dharma-ending age, I will preach the *dhāraṇī* of Amitāyus Tathāgata. By cultivating the gate of the three mysteries and attaining the *samādhi* of recollecting the buddha, they will attain birth in the pure land and [there] enter the ranks of the bodhisattvas on the *bhūmis*." The "defiled world of the Dharma-ending age"[9] and the goal of birth in Sukhāvatī are mentioned here, but the means to achieve that goal are the esoteric three mysteries practice and the "*samādhi* of recollecting the buddha." The recollection mentioned here is not the repetition of the buddha's name (*nianfo*)—which is nowhere recommended in the *Wuliangshou yigui*—but is the *buddhānusmṛti* known from many non-Esoteric texts.[10]

The *Wuliangshou yigui* then goes on to say that "with few merits and no wisdom, birth in that world cannot be readily attained." This passage is suggestive of a passage in the Smaller *Sukhāvatīvyūha sūtra*, namely "with the merits of only a few good roots one cannot achieve birth in that world."[11] It may be significant that in the Smaller *Sukhāvatīvyūha Sūtra* the lack of good roots is why holding Amitāyus' name is recommended for birth into Sukhāvatī, while in the *Wuliangshou yigui* the lack of merits and wisdom is the reason this Esoteric practice leading to birth in Sukhāvatī is taught.

The brief description of Sukhāvatī given in the *Wuliangshou yigui* echoes the Pure Land sutras. The *Wuliangshou yigui* has the following (2.12), which seems to be a paraphrase of either the Smaller *Sukhāvatīvyūha sūtra* or *Amitāyus Visualization Sūtra*.[12] "The ground is made of the seven precious substances. The waters, birds, trees, and forests there all preach the sounds of Dharma.[13] There are countless adornments, as explained in the [Pure Land] sūtras." No description of the appearance of Amitāyus himself appears in this text, and we are instead referred to the *Amitāyus Visualization Sūtra* by name for details (3.3). The *Wuliangshou yigui* closes by recommending the practitioner to regularly read Pure Land sutras (5).[14]

Since no Indian or Tibetan version of the *Wuliangshou yigui* is extant for comparison, the degree that Amoghavajra may have adjusted his Chinese version of an Indic text to suit Chinese audiences, or indeed whether he created one himself based on a familiar format, remains uncertain.[15] The *Wuliangshou yigui* has a clear Indic ritual core, but it defines a purpose and uses language that would have resonated with a general Chinese audience.

## The *Wuliangshou Yigui* in Japan

The *Wuliangshou yigui* was probably practiced in Japan more or less as it stands through the ninth century, but during the tenth century and later it may have been gradually replaced in Japanese Esoteric Buddhism by edited practice manuals based on it. The texts in the list above, to varying degrees, have a common format that was later called Jūhachidō in Japanese Esoteric Buddhism, referring to the first portion of the ritual in each text consisting of a basic ritual format with eighteen *mudrās* (and the corresponding mantras).[16] The concept of Jūhachidō is based on a list apparently written by Kūkai while still in China[17] giving a Jūhachidō template consisting of eighteen *mudrās*.[18]

The outline in table 1 is most clearly in debt to the *Ruyilun yigui* and *Wuliangshou yigui*. The basic concept of the Shingon Jūhachidō is a streamlined template for the opening section of an Esoteric deity yoga practice that can easily be applied to any deity.[19]

The template concept of the Jūhachidō was further developed in Japan into the Eighteen Methods Recitation Sequence manuals (*Jūhachidō nenju shidai*, 十八道念誦次第), which in several versions has remained a

**Table 1. Outline of the Jūhachidō Sequence (*Jūhachidō kubi shidai*, 十八道頚次第), or the "Eighteen Methods" (**Aṣṭadaśa-naya*)**

| | |
|---|---|
| (1) Purify the three actions | (10) Send out the carriage |
| (-) Universal prostration | (11) Receive the carriage |
| (2) Buddha family *samaya* | (12) Welcome [the deity] |
| (3) Lotus [family *samaya*] | (13) Hayagrīva |
| (4) Vajra [family *samaya*] | (14) Spread the net-boundary |
| (5) Protect the body | (15) Fire-enclosure |
| (6) Earth-boundary | (16) *Argha* |
| (7) Fence-boundary | (17) Lotus-throne |
| (8) Great treasury of space | (18) Offering |
| (9) *Tathāgata*-fist | |

standard in Japanese Esoteric Buddhist practice to this day. In the Shingon School, a full ritual manual called *Jūhachidō nenju shidai Daishi Chūin* (attributed to Kūkai) was composed later, possibly sometime in the late ninth to tenth centuries. It owes its format perhaps mostly to the *Ruyilun yigui* and is also thoroughly indebted to the *Wuliangshou yigui* for wording and other details.[20]

Besides having an important influence on the creation of the Jūhachidō format, the *Wuliangshou yigui* was a major source for the creation of Esoteric Amida practices in Japan. Two early Shingon *shidai* attributed to Kūkai quote sections of the *Wuliangshou yigui* and even illustrate the main visualizations, suggesting that these two texts were conceived of as edited versions of the *Wuliangshou yigui* with certain Japanese additions.[21] The later Shingon Amida practice in *Hishō*, for example, is deeply indebted to the *Wuliangshou yigui*.[22]

## Structure of the *Wuliangshou Yigui*

As with the *Ruyilun yigui*, the structure of the ritual in the *Wuliangshou yigui* is quite clear and precise. The text can be divided into three main sections: an introductory section (I), the ritual practice in three parts (2, 3, 4), and a concluding section (5, 6).

The introductory section first gives the purpose of the practice (1.1), which is to "attain birth in the pure land and [there] enter the ranks of the bodhisattvas on the *bhūmis*" through the given Esoteric practice. Next the necessity of first receiving *abhiṣeka* and receiving direct instructions from the master is underlined (1.2), a feature common to most Esoteric ritual manuals.[23] After receiving *abhiṣeka* and personal instruction in the ritual, the practitioner is ready to begin the practice, and so details on the selection of the site, the preparation of the shrine, and the arrangement of the altar and offerings are given (1.3), another feature found in many manuals.

After these preliminaries, the description of the practice begins. The ritual practice may be further divided into three main sections: the opening rituals (2), which generally follow the Jūhachidō template explained below, the main practice (3) involving three important meditations, and the concluding rituals (4), which repeat the opening rituals in a reverse sequence. The structure of the practice is in the manner of inviting the deity as if an honored guest to a feast, followed by three mantra and meditation practices, and finally the concluding rituals to return the deity whence it came.

The steps of the Jūhachidō template all appear in the first opening section (2) and consist of eighteen *mudrās* with their corresponding mantras, in the later Shingon tradition divided up into six methods. The following chart shows the eighteen *mudrās* and mantras as taught in the Shingon tradition, with the corresponding sections in the *Wuliangshou yigui* given in the third column.

"Purifying the three actions" (2.1) explains a ritual ablution using *mudrā* and mantra performed before entering the shrine, after which the practitioner enters the shrine and visualizes Amitāyus before him in Sukhāvatī, and then prostrates to him and his retinue (2.2). After kneeling and performing rites for repentance, raising joy, requesting the buddhas to turn the wheel of Dharma and remain long in the world, and dedicating merit (2.3), the practitioner sits in a cross-legged meditation posture before the altar and rubs purifying perfume (such as sandalwood powder) on his hands (2.4).

The practitioner then forms the *mudrās* and mantras and engages in the visualizations of the *samayas* of the three families: Buddha, Lotus, and Vajra (2.5–7), a standard practice in this type of ritual manual. For the Buddha family he visualizes Amitāyus before him, for the Lotus family he visualizes Avalokiteśvara, and for the Vajra family Vajragarbha (Vajrapāṇi). These are the representative deities of the three families of

**Table 2. The Jūhachidō Template and Its Correspondence with the *Wuliangshou yigui*.**

| Six Methods | Eighteen *Mudrās* | *Wuliangshou yigui* correspondence |
|---|---|---|
| (1) Methods for adorning the practitioner | 1. Purify the three actions | 2.1 |
| | 2. Buddha family | 2.5 |
| | 3. Lotus family | 2.6 |
| | 4. Vajra family | 2.7 |
| | 5. Wear armor | 2.8 |
| (2) Methods for binding the area | 6. Bind the earth | 2.9 |
| | 7. Bind the four directions | 2.10 |
| (3) Methods for adorning the *bodhimaṇḍa* | 8. Visualize the *bodhimaṇḍa* (Tathāgata-fist *mudrā*) | 2.12 |
| | 9. Great treasury of space | 2.11 |
| (4) Methods for inviting the deity | 10. Jeweled carriage | 2.13 |
| | 11. Receive the carriage | 2.14 |
| | 12. Welcome the main deity | 2.15 |
| (5) Methods for protecting the area | 13. Trailokyavijaya[a] | 2.16 |
| | 14. Vajra-net | 2.17 |
| | 15. Fire-enclosure | 2.18 |
| (6) Methods for making offerings | 16. *Argha* | 2.19 |
| | 17. Lotus-throne | 2.20 |
| | 18. Universal offering | 2.21 |

[a]Trailokyavijaya is used for a Vajraśekhara or a Vajra family practice. The *Wuliangshou yigui* and *Ruyilun yigui* give a Lotus family deity practice, so the wrathful deity of the Lotus family, Hayagrīva, is used in those texts.

the *Mahāvairocanābhisaṃbodhi sūtra*, with the important exception that Amitāyus has been substituted for Mahāvairocana. These three steps are intended to purify the practitioner's actions of body, speech, and mind respectively.[24] After that, the practitioner ritually girds himself with the armor of great compassion to prevent evil influences from interfering with the practice (2.8). This completes the section described in the Shingon tradition as the "methods for adorning the practitioner."

Next, the practitioner prepares the ritual area where the deity will be invited by first making the ground impenetrable to evil influences from below. This is done by "binding the earth" (2.9) through raising and lowering a *mudrā* and then "binding the four directions" (2.10) by revolving the *mudrā* clockwise three times to make the sides of the area impervious in the four directions. At this point, the space above the ritual area remains ritually open. This completes the "methods for binding the area."

Next, offerings are visualized as emerging from the *mudrā* of Ākāśagarbha (2.11) and becoming real offerings. After that, in the section on "visualizing the *bodhimaṇḍa*" (2.12), Amitāyus' seed-letter *hrīḥ* is visualized as emitting a red, crystal-like light that extends in the ten directions, eliminating the transgressions of all beings who encounter it. The shrine is then transformed into Sukhāvatī with *mudrā* and mantra, and a *gāthā* is repeated.[25] The *Wuliangshou yigui* then states that by practicing the above *samādhi* of visualizing the letter *hrīḥ*, one can enter Sukhāvatī at the end of one's life. This completes the "methods for adorning the *bodhimaṇḍa*."

Next, an emanation of the deity is invited to enter the ritually prepared space now adorned with both physical and visualized offerings. First a carriage is sent to Sukhāvatī for Amitāyus and his retinue (2.13), then the carriage returns (2.14), remaining in space above the altar, and finally Amitāyus is invited to descend into the ritual space from above (2.15). This completes the "methods for inviting the deity."

After Amitāyus enters the ritual space, the *mudrā* and mantra of Hayagrīva, the wrathful deity particular to the Lotus Family, is used to first expel any loitering evil influences from the ritual area by revolving the *mudrā* counterclockwise three times, and then to seal the area again by revolving it clockwise three times (2.16). After that, the opening above the altar is closed off with a vajra-net (2.17), and a barrier of flames is established to further prevent any unwanted intruders (2.18), with both *mudrās* revolved clockwise three times. This completes the "methods for protecting the area."

The last part of the opening section is to offer various offerings to Amitāyus in the ritual space. First, *argha*-water for washing, physically placed on the altar, is presented (2.19), then lotus-thrones are visualized and given to Amitāyus and his retinue to sit on (2.20), and finally, many kinds of offerings are visualized together and offered through a *mudrā* and mantra (2.21). This concludes the "methods for making offerings," and also concludes the opening section and the eighteen *mudrā*s and mantras in six methods.

Next, the main section of the practice, consisting of three mantra and meditation practices, begins (3).[26] The first of these meditations (3.1) begins with the practitioner visualizing Amitāyus and his retinue "with perfect clarity as if directly before your eyes" (3.1.1), and then repeating a Sanskrit *gāthā* of praise to draw the attention of Amitāyus to him, eliminate karmic obstructions, and calm the mind (3.1.2). Next, the practitioner enters the *samādhi* of Avalokiteśvara (3.1.3) by first visualizing a brilliant letter *hrīḥ* on a moon disc at the heart, transforming it into an eight-petaled lotus with Avalokiteśvara sitting in the center. Avalokiteśvara holds a lotus bud in his left hand in the gesture of opening it with his right hand, signifying the opening of the inherent awakening possessed by sentient beings. On the eight petals of the lotus eight buddhas are seated facing inwards toward Avalokiteśvara. The lotus then expands to an infinite size as an infinite offering to all the buddhas and relieves the suffering of all beings illuminated by the brilliance of the lotus. The lotus then contracts to its original size.

After this, the practitioner forms the *mudrā* and mantras of the two deities visualized (3.1.4). First, a *mudrā* and mantra of Avalokiteśvara is used to achieve yogic identity with that bodhisattva (3.1.4.1), and then the root *dhāraṇī* of Amitāyus is repeated with a *mudrā* (3.1.4.2). We are told that repeating this *dhāraṇī* just once removes all kinds of transgressions, and repeating it ten thousand times gives the practitioner a firm *bodhicitta* that manifests as a brilliant moon disc in the chest. At the end of the practitioner's life he will see Amitāyus and "receive a birth at the highest level of the highest grade in the world of Sukhāvatī, and will attain the state of a bodhisattva."

Next, the root *dhāraṇī* of Amitāyus is recited a minimum of 108 times while visualizing Amitāyus in Sukhāvatī (3.2). The practitioner empowers the *mālā* to multiply the recitation, then, after making a prayer to benefit all beings, the root *dhāraṇī* is repeated. This is conducted with concentration "allowing no break in its continuity and without distraction."[27] Through this recitation one gains purity in body and mind "even to the extent that you constantly see Amitāyus Tathāgata whether your eyes are open or shut. Then in *samādhi* you will hear him preach the profound and sublime Dharma. . . . Your body becomes identical with [that of] Avalokiteśvara Bodhisattva, and you can rapidly enter that world (Sukhāvatī)." Then a concluding prayer that all beings may attain birth in Sukhāvatī and hear Amitāyus' preaching is made.

The third part of the main section of the practice (3.3) consists of visualizing *bodhicitta* in the heart as a "brilliant and pure luminous disc like a full moon." After a meditation on emptiness, a radiant letter *hrīḥ* is visualized on the moon disc, and the radiance of the letter transforms into Sukhāvatī. Amitāyus and his entourage are visualized there. No details are given, and instead the text says that they are "as explained in the *Amitāyus Visualization Sūtra*." After this, the root *dhāraṇī* and *mudrā* of Amitāyus are repeated (3.3.1) to complete the main practice section.

After that, the concluding rituals (4), consisting of a simplified version of the opening section in reverse sequence, begin. First, the praise section is repeated (4.1), then the universal offering *mudrā* and mantra (4.2), the offering of *argha*-water (4.3), prayers (4.4), and then the various boundaries established earlier are all removed together with the fire-enclosure *mudrā* and mantra revolved once counterclockwise (4.5). Next, the deity and his retinue are sent off (4.6) with the *mudrā* that was previously used to receive the deity (2.14) with an appropriately adjusted mantra. Then the *samaya* of the three families is repeated (4.7), followed by the wearing of armor (4.8) as before, then the practitioner prostrates before Amitāyus (4.9) and leaves the shrine (4.10). This concludes the ritual practice.

Next there is a brief concluding section (5), consisting of recommendations to the practitioner about how to occupy his time outside of the three practice sessions per day called for in the text (1.3). Besides walking, the instructions include reading Pure Land sutras, practicing the six *pāramitās*, dedicating merit so that all beings can enter the Pure Land, and so on. This section ends with the statement that "this practice may be used for any Lotus family [deity]." Finally, there is a brief supplement to the text (6) giving the heart-mantra of Amitāyus and stating that by repeating this mantra one hundred thousand times the practitioner will see Amitāyus during his life and will be born in Sukhāvatī without fail.

## TRANSLATION

### *Wuliangshou rulai xiu guanxing gongyang yigui:* The Ritual Manual on Cultivating the Visualization of and Making Offerings to Amitāyus Tathāgata

Tang Tripiṭaka Master Śramaṇa Amoghavajra,
of Great and Wide Wisdom, at Imperial Request[28]

[1. Introduction][29]
[1.1. Purpose of the Practice]
At that time, Vajrapāṇi Bodhisattva was in the great assembly of Vairocana Buddha. He arose from his seat, held his palms together in respect, and said to the Buddha, "Lord, for the sake of beings with evil karma[30] in the coming defiled world of the Dharma-ending age, I will preach the *dhāraṇī* of Amitāyus Tathāgata.[31] By cultivating the gate of the three mysteries and attaining the *samādhi* of recollecting the Buddha, they will attain birth in the pure land and [there] enter the ranks of the bodhisattvas on the *bhūmis*."
With few merits and no wisdom, birth in that world cannot be readily attained.[32] That is why, by relying on this teaching to cultivate the correct recollection of the Buddha, one will definitely be born in the highest level of the highest grade in the world of Sukhāvatī, and [there] attain the first *bhūmi*.

[1.2. The Need for *Abhiṣeka* Followed by Personal Instruction]
Whether a householder or a renunciant, anyone who wishes for birth in the pure land should first enter the *maṇḍala* to receive *abhiṣeka*. After that, receive instructions from the master on this mantra recitation ritual.

[1.3. The Site and Preparation of the Shrine]
Either in a superior place[33] or wherever you reside, spread [*gomayī* on the ground[34]] to purify [in a pure room,[35]] and build [there] a square altar. Above it hang a parasol, and around it hang banners. On the surface of the altar demarcate an eight[-petaled lotus] *maṇḍala*.[36] Grind sandalwood incense [into a powder] and spread it at the deity's position [in the center].
On the western side of the altar place a statue of Amitāyus Tathāgata.[37] The mantra holder sits to the east of the altar facing the statue to the

west, either laying out a grass mat or sitting on a small low-legged sitting platform.[38]

Three times every day scatter various kinds of flowers [on the altar, burn various kinds of incense,[39]] and place two [cups of] *argha*[-water on the altar],[40] using either conch-shell bowls, or cups made of precious stone, gold, silver, or copper, or of stone, ceramic, earthenware, and so on that have never been used before.[41] Fill [the two cups] with perfumed water and place them on the altar.

On the four corners of the altar place four auspicious jars. Prepare [offerings of] incense, lamps, perfume, and food according to your ability.[42] Empower them one by one and offer them respectfully.

[2. The Opening Rituals]
[2.1. Before Entering the Shrine: Purifying the Three Actions] (1/18)[43]
The practitioner[44] performs daily ablutions and puts on new, pure robes. Or else he may perform an ablution through mantra empowerment.[45]

Then contemplate and observe that all sentient beings are pure in their fundamental nature, but due to invasive afflictions (*āgantukakleśa*) that [fundamental nature] is obscured and they do not realize what is real. [Confused, they lose the aspiration to *bodhi*, sinking and drowning in the sea of *saṃsāra* to experience limitless suffering.[46]] Therefore, this *adhiṣṭhāna* of the three mysteries is taught, which can[47] lead both the self and others to the attainment of purity.

Then[48] hold both hands in a lotus-*añjali* and repeat the mantra for purifying the three actions, three times.[49] The mantra is:
[1] oṃ svabhāva śuddhāḥ sarva dharmāḥ svabhāva śuddho 'ham.[50]
By the *adhiṣṭhāna* of this mantra, an ablution of the pure inner mind is accomplished.

[2.2. After Entering the Shrine: Universal Prostration][51]
Every time you enter the shrine (*bodhimaṇḍa*), stand upright and properly before the main deity (Amitāyus). Form a lotus-*añjali*, close your eyes, and mentally visualize [that you are] in the world of Sukhāvatī facing Amitāyus Tathāgata and his retinue of bodhisattvas. Then [prostrate by] touching the five parts of your body[52] to the ground, visualizing that you reverently prostrate before each buddha and bodhisattva. Then repeat this mantra of universal prostration:
[2] oṃ sarva tathāgata pāda vandanaṃ karomi.[53]
[2.3. Repentance, Joy, Requesting, and Dedication][54]
[2.3.1. Repentance]

Then touch your right knee to the ground as you hold an *añjali* at your heart. Sincerely confess and repent all the wrongdoings [you have committed] throughout beginningless time.

[2.3.2. Joy]

Then take joy in the meritorious actions cultivated by the buddhas, bodhisattvas, *śrāvakas*, *pratyekabuddhas*, and all sentient beings.

[2.3.3. Requesting]

Next, visualize in all worlds in the ten directions the *tathāgatas* who attain supreme and perfect awakening, and ask them to turn the wheel of Dharma. Request all the *tathāgatas* who are at the point [of entering] nirvana to remain long in the world and not enter into *parinirvāṇa*.

[2.3.4. Dedication]

Next, make this vow, "I dedicate the good roots I have amassed,[55] and this accumulation of merits through prostrating to the buddhas, repenting, rejoicing, and requesting [the buddhas to turn the wheel of Dharma and to remain in the world] to all sentient beings. May they all attain birth in the world of Sukhāvatī, see the Buddha and hear his Dharma, and rapidly attain supreme and perfect *bodhi*."

[2.4. Take Your Seat and Rub Perfume on Your Hands]

After that, sit in the full cross-legged position (*paryaṅka*), or the half cross-legged position (*ardha-paryaṅka*) with the right leg over the left. Rub perfume on your hands.

[2.5. Buddha Family *Samaya-Mudrā*] (2/18)

First, form the Buddha family *samaya-mudrā*. Hold[56] both hands in a hollowed-palm *añjali*. Open the two forefingers, bend them slightly, and touch both of them to the upper joints of the middle fingers. Next, open the two thumbs and touch both of them to the lower phalanges of the two forefingers. This completes the *mudrā*.

Visualize the thirty-two major and eighty minor marks of Amitāyus Tathāgata clearly and distinctly. Then repeat the Buddha family *samaya-mantra*:

[3] oṃ tathāgatodbhavāya svāhā.[57]

Repeat this either three or seven times, place the *mudrā* on the crown of your head, and then[58] dissolve it.

By forming this *mudrā* and repeating this mantra, you awaken all of the noble deities[59] of the Buddha family [from *samādhi*]. They all come [and gather[60]] to empower and protect the mantra cultivator and lead him to rapidly attain purity in his physical actions. Obstacles arising from past wrongdoing are eliminated,[61] and merits and wisdom are increased.

[2.6. Lotus Family *Samaya-Mudrā*] (3/18)
Next, form the Lotus family *samaya-mudrā*. Form a hollowed-palm *añjali* with both hands. Hold[62] the two thumbs and the two little fingers together, bend the other six fingers slightly, shaped like the [eight] petals[63] of a lotus in bloom, and [the *mudrā*] is complete.

After forming the *mudrā*, visualize Avalokiteśvara Bodhisattva, beautiful and majestic, and accompanied by infinite *koṭīs* of the noble deities of the Lotus family sitting around him in a circle. Then repeat the Lotus family *samaya-mantra*:
[4] oṃ padmodbhavāya svāhā.[64]
Empower by repeating this [mantra] either three or seven times, place the *mudrā* to the right of the crown of your head, and then dissolve it.

By forming this *mudrā* and repeating this mantra, you awaken Avalokiteśvara Bodhisattva and the noble deities of the Lotus family [from *samādhi*]. They all come to empower the practitioner, who attains purity in his speech actions. His words and speech are powerful but modest, and people enjoy listening to him. He has unobstructed eloquence, and is able to[65] preach the Dharma masterfully.

[2.7. Vajra Family *Samaya-Mudrā*] (4/18)
Next, form the Vajra family *samaya-mudrā*. Hold both hands with the left turned down and the right turned up, and with their backs touching. Cross the right thumb with the left little finger. Cross the left thumb with the right little finger. Spread[66] the six fingers in between, touch them to the wrists in the shape of a three-pointed vajra, and [the *mudrā*] is complete. Form the *mudrā* at the heart.

Visualize Vajragarbha (Vajrapāṇi) Bodhisattva,[67] beautiful and radiant, surrounded by his retinue of uncountable vajra-holders. Then repeat the Vajra family *samaya-mantra*:
[5] oṃ vajrodbhavāya svāhā.[68]
Empower by repeating this [mantra] either three or seven times, place the *mudrā* to the left of the crown of your head, and then dissolve it.

By forming this *mudrā* and repeating this mantra, awaken Vajragarbha (Vajrapāṇi) Bodhisattva and the noble deities of the Vajra family [from *samādhi*]. They all come to empower the practitioner, who attains purity in his mental actions. He attains *bodhicitta*, *samādhi* is fully realized, and he rapidly gains liberation.

[2.8. *Mudrā* of Wearing Armor to Protect the Body] (5/18)
Next, form the *mudrā* of wearing armor to protect the body. Interlace the two little fingers and the two ring fingers inside [the palms], with the right [fingers] pressing[69] on the left. Extend the two middle fingers with their tips supporting each other. Bend the two forefingers in the shape of hooks. Hold them at the backs of the middle fingers, but do not make contact. Hold the two thumbs side by side touching the ring fingers, and [the *mudrā*] is complete. Form the *mudrā* at your heart.

Repeat the mantra and seal the five places of the body, repeating the mantra once for each. First, seal the forehead. Next, the right shoulder. Next, the left shoulder. Seal the heart and the throat. These are the five places.

Then raise the thought of great compassion.[70] Observe all beings everywhere, [contemplating] "May they all may wear armor adorned with great goodwill and compassion to rapidly be freed from obstacles and realize the best and superior[71] mundane and transcendent accomplishments." After visualizing in this way, you then perfect the wearing of vajra-armor. No *māras* will dare to obstruct you. The mantra for protecting the body is:
[6] oṃ vajrāgni pradīptāya svāhā.[72]
Because of the power of goodwill and sympathy [achieved] through forming this *mudrā* and repeating this mantra, all *deva-māras* and obstructers will see the practitioner's[73] sun-like[74] radiant brilliance. Each will give rise to thoughts of goodwill and will be unable to cause obstructions. Those with malicious intent will be unable to gain an advantage over you. The afflictive (*kleśāvaraṇa*) and karmic obstructions (*karmāvaraṇa*) will no longer affect you. Also, you will be freed[75] from future sufferings in the evil destinies (*durgati*) and will rapidly attain supreme and perfect[76] *bodhi*.

[2.9. Mudrā of Vajra-Stakes for Binding the Earth] (6/18)
Next, form the *mudrā* of vajra-stakes (*vajra-kīla*) for binding (*sīmābandha*) the earth. First, place the right middle finger between the left forefinger and middle finger. Place the [right] ring finger between the left ring finger and little finger. The tips of the fingers are all outside. Wrap the left middle finger around the back of the right middle finger, and insert it between the right forefinger and middle finger. Wrap the left ring finger around the back of the right ring finger, and insert it between the right ring finger and little finger. The tips of the two little fingers and the two

forefingers each support the other. Hold the two thumbs together pointing down, and [the *mudrā*] is complete.

After forming this *mudrā*, visualize that the *mudrā* is shaped like a vajra. The two thumbs point to the earth and touch it. Repeat the mantra once and seal the earth once. Do this three times, perfecting a solid vajra-throne (*vajrāsana*). The mantra for the earth-boundary[77] is:

[7] oṃ kīli-kīli vajra vajri bhūr bandha bandha hūṃ phaṭ.[78]

By [the power of[79]] the *adhiṣṭhāna* of forming this *mudrā* and repeating this[80] mantra, [the ground] below as far as the edge of the adamantine-disc (*kāñcana-maṇḍala*) an indestructible vajra-boundary is created. It cannot be disturbed by even powerful *māras*. Through expending a small amount of effort, great success can be achieved. The impure and unwholesome[81] things in the earth are all purified by the power of this *adhiṣṭhāna*. The size of the boundary may be as large or small as you like, and is thus completed.

[2.10. Vajra-Fence *Mudrā*] (7/18)

Next, form the vajra-fence (*vajra-prākāra*) *mudrā*. Use the previous earth-boundary *mudrā*, but open the palms and stretch[82] the two thumbs extending them shaped like a fence, and [the *mudrā*] is complete.

Visualize that brilliant flames flow out from the *mudrā*. Revolve the *mudrā* around your body to the right three times. Complementing the previous earth-boundary, a vajra-firm wall is completed. The fence-boundary mantra is:

[8] oṃ sāra-sāra vajra prākāra hūṃ phaṭ.[83]

By the power of forming this *mudrā*, repeating this mantra, and practicing this visualizing, a brilliant vajra-flame fence-boundary in all directions is created, which may be as large or small as you like. No *māras*, persons of malicious intention, tigers, wolves, lions, or poisonous insects can approach.[84]

[2.11. Great *Mudrā* of Ākāśagarbha Bodhisattva] (9/18)[85]

Next, form the great *mudrā* of Ākāśagarbha Bodhisattva. Hold both hands in *añjali*, with the two middle fingers interlaced on the outside [of the hands] and with the right [finger] over the left. Extend[86] them to touch the backs of the hands. Bend the two forefingers together in the shape of a jewel, and [the *mudrā*] is complete.

Visualize that limitless offerings of all kinds flow out from the *mudrā*, specifically garments, food, palaces, towers, and so on, as discussed at length in the [Vajraśekhara] yoga [manuals]. Then repeat the mantra of great Ākāśagarbha Bodhisattva[87]:

[9] oṃ gagana sambhava vajra hoḥ.[88]

Even if the cultivator's power of visualization is slight, by the power of the *adhiṣṭhāna* of this *mudrā* and mantra, the offerings all become real. You are just like someone making vast offerings in the world of Sukhāvatī.[89]

[2.12. Visualize the *Bodhimaṇḍa*] (8/18)

Next, visualize that in the center of the altar there is the letter *hrīḥ*.[90] It emits a great radiance the color of red *sphaṭika*[91] (crystal) that illuminates all the worlds in the ten directions. Among sentient beings in those worlds who encounter this radiance, there is not one whose obstacles caused by wrongdoings are not eliminated.[92]

Next, form the *tathāgata*-fist *mudrā*.[93] Hold the four fingers of the left hand in a fist, and extend the thumb out straight. Make a vajra-fist with the right hand and grip the nail of the left thumb,[94] and [the *mudrā*] is complete. Use this fist-*mudrā* to seal the earth. Empower by repeating the mantra seven times, transforming [this place] into that world (Sukhāvatī). The *tathāgata*-fist mantra is:

[10] *oṃ bhūḥ khaṃ*.[95]

By the strength of the *adhiṣṭhāna* of forming this *mudrā* and repeating this mantra, this great trichiliocosm is transformed into the world of Sukhāvatī. The ground is made of the seven precious substances. The waters, birds, trees, and forests there all preach the sounds of Dharma.[96] There are countless adornments, as explained in the [Pure Land] sutras. Then repeat this *gāthā*:[97]

> Through the power of my merits,
> The power of the Tathāgata's *adhiṣṭhāna,*
> And the power of the *dharmadhātu,*
> May [this shrine] transform into the world of Sukhāvatī.[98]

By constantly practicing this *samādhi,* in the present lifetime whenever in *samādhi* the practitioner will see Amitāyus Tathāgata among the great assembly of bodhisattvas in the world of Sukhāvatī, and will hear the preaching of limitless sutras. When your life is about to come to its end, your mind will not be confused.[99] *Samādhi* is fully realized, and in an instant (*kṣaṇa*) you will be rapidly born into that world. You will be miraculously born on a lotus [there] to attain the state of a bodhisattva.[100]

[2.13. Jeweled-Carriage *Mudrā*] (10/18)
Next, form the jeweled-carriage *mudrā*. Turn the palms up and interlace [the fingers of] both hands[101] with the right [fingers] over the left. The sides [of the tips] of the two forefingers support each other. The two thumbs touch the lowermost phalanges of the two forefingers, and [the *mudrā*] is complete. The mantra for sending off the carriage is:
[11] oṃ turu turu hūṃ.[102]
Form[103] this *mudrā* and visualize that a carriage adorned with the seven precious substances is perfected. It travels to that world of Sukhāvatī. Request that Amitāyus Tathāgata and his retinue of bodhisattvas ride on this carriage.

[2.14. Receive the Carriage] (11/18)
Do not dissolve the [previous] *mudrā*. Using it,[104] brush the two thumbs against the tips of the two middle fingers toward your body, and repeat the mantra for receiving[105] the carriage:
[12] namas try adhvikānāṃ tathāgatānāṃ oṃ vajrāgny ākarṣaya svāhā.[106]
Then visualize that the carriage arrives at the *bodhimaṇḍa* and abides in the space [above].

[2.15. *Mudrā* for Welcoming] (12/18)
Next, form the *mudrā* for welcoming the noble assembly. Interlace both hands inside [the palms] with the right [fingers] over the left. Form a fist with the palms together. Bend the left thumb inside the palms, and bend the right thumb [outside] like a hook, and beckon toward your body. Repeat the mantra of welcoming:
[13] oṃ ārolik ehy ehi svāhā.[107]
Because of your respectful request made by forming this *mudrā* and repeating the mantra, Amitāyus Tathāgata does not abandon his vow of compassion, and comes to this *bodhimaṇḍa* that is a pure land created in *samādhi*. Together with the great assembly of limitless *koṭīs* of bodhisattvas, he receives the offerings of the cultivator and is a witness to his merits.[108]

[2.16. Expel and Form a Boundary with Hayagrīva] (13/18)
Next, form the *mudrā* of Hayagrīva Avalokiteśvara Bodhisattva[109] to expel [*māras*] and form a boundary. Hold both hands in *añjali*, and bend the two forefingers and two ring fingers into the palms with their backs touching. Hold the two thumbs side by side, bend them slightly without

touching them to the forefingers, and [the *mudrā*] is complete. Repeat the mantra of Hayagrīva Vidyārāja:

[14] oṃ amṛtodbhava hūṃ phaṭ svāhā.[110]

Repeat this three times and revolve the *mudrā* three times to the left to expel all *māras*, who all scatter of their own accord. [Then[111]] revolve the *mudrā* to the right three times to form a great and firm boundary.

[2.17. Vajra-Net *Mudrā*] (14/18)

Next, form the vajra-net (*vajra-pañjara*) *mudrā*. Using the previous earth-boundary *mudrā*, touch the two thumbs to the lower phalanges of the two forefingers, and [the *mudrā*] is complete. Repeat the mantra three times. As you repeat the mantra, revolve [the *mudrā*] to the right[112] over the crown of your head, and then dissolve it. The net-boundary mantra is:

[15] oṃ visphurād rakṣa vajra pañjara hūṃ phaṭ.[113]

By the power of the *adhiṣṭhāna* from forming this *mudrā* and repeating this[114] mantra, the space overhead is covered with a vajra-firm net. Even the *devas* of the Paranirmitavaśavartina heaven are unable to [cross over it to create[115]] obstructions. The practitioner can dwell at ease in body and mind, and *samādhi* is easily accomplished.

[2.18. Vajra Fire-Enclosure Boundary *Mudrā*] (15/18)

Next, form the vajra fire-enclosure boundary *mudrā*. Cover the palm of the left hand with the back of the right hand, with both hands touching. Stretch[116] and extend the two thumbs, and [the *mudrā*] is complete.

Visualize that limitless brilliant flames flow out from the *mudrā*. Revolve the *mudrā* to the right three times.[117] The outside of the vajra-fence is ringed in flame, thus forming a firm and pure great fire-boundary.[118] The fire-enclosure mantra is:

[16] oṃ asamāgni hūṃ phaṭ.[119]

[2.19. Present Perfumed *Argha*-Water] (16/18)

Next, present perfumed *argha*-water.[120] With both hands raise the *argha* cup, holding it at the forehead to respectfully present it. Repeat the mantra three times.

Visualize that you bathe both feet of [each member of the] noble assembly. The *argha* mantra is:

[17] namaḥ samanta buddhānāṃ gagana samāsama svāhā.[121]

By presenting an offering of perfumed *argha*-water, the three actions of the cultivator are purified, and all the afflictions and the defilements of wrongdoings are washed away. [Going] from the stage of resolute practice[122] on to the ten *bhūmis* and the stage of a *tathāgata,* when you finally realize the *bhūmis* and *pāramitās*, you will receive *abhiṣeka* by the deathless (*amṛta*) water of Dharma from all the *tathāgatas*.[123]

[2.20. Lotus-Throne *Mudrā*] (17/18)
Next, form the lotus-throne[124] (*kamalāsana*) *mudrā*. The *mudrā* is like the previous Lotus family *samaya-mudrā*. Bend the fingers somewhat to make them rounded. This is [the *mudrā*].

After forming the *mudrā,* visualize that limitless vajra-lotuses flow out from the *mudrā*. These fill the world of Sukhāvatī and Amitāyus Tathāgata, the great bodhisattvas, and all of the noble assembly [there] each receives a lotus as a seat. The lotus-throne mantra is:
[18] oṃ kamala svāhā.[125]
By the *adhiṣṭhāna* of forming this lotus-throne *mudrā* and repeating the mantra, the practitioner will achieve the completion of the ten *bhūmis* and will attain the vajra-throne (*vajrāsana*). His three actions will be as firm as a vajra.[126]

[2.21. Universal Offering *Mudrā*] (18/18)
Next, form the vast and infallible *maṇi*-jewel offering *mudrā*. Hold both hands in *vajrāñjali*. Hold the two forefingers together[127] and bend them in the shape of a jewel. Extend the two thumbs side by side, and [the *mudrā*] is complete. Repeat the vast and infallible *maṇi*-jewel offering *dhāraṇī*:
[19] oṃ amogha pūjā maṇi padma vajre tathāgata vilokite samanta prasara hūṃ.[128]
By repeating this vast and infallible *maṇi*-jewel offering *dhāraṇī* just three times, in the assembly of Amitāyus Tathāgata and in limitless[129] worlds as numberless as the particles of dust in the world an immeasurably vast offering rains down, consisting of clouds and seas of all kinds of perfume, clouds and seas of all kinds of flower garlands, clouds and seas of all kinds of incense, clouds and seas of all kinds of sublime heavenly food, clouds and seas of all kinds of sublime heavenly garments, clouds and seas of all kinds of *maṇi*-jewel radiant lamps and torches,[130] clouds and seas of all kinds of banners, flags, jeweled curtains, and jeweled parasols, and clouds and seas of all kinds of sublime heavenly music. In all the assemblies of the buddhas and bodhisattvas everywhere these become a real and vast offering.

Because you make offerings by forming this *mudrā* and repeating this *dhāraṇī*,[131] you receive an immeasurable accumulation of merits as limitless as unobstructed space. In every future life you will always be born into the great assemblies of all the *tathāgatas*. You will be miraculously born on a lotus, attain the five superpowers, divide your body into ten million emanations, and be able to save suffering beings in this defiled world to give them all ease[132] and benefit. In the present lifetime you will receive countless fruits, and in the future you will attain a birth in the pure land.

[3. The Main Practice]
[3.1. Visualization of Amitāyus and Avalokiteśvara][133]
[3.1.1. Visualize the Main Deity, Amitāyus]
Next, you should clear your thoughts and settle your mind, and concentrate in one-pointedness. Visualize Amitāyus Tathāgata with perfect clarity as if directly before your eyes, fully possessing the excellent marks, along with his countless retinue and his world. If you long[134] [to see Amitāyus constantly] from moment to moment, you will fully attain accomplishment in *samādhi*. Sincerely and single-mindedly wish for birth in his world. Allow no other objects in mind continuously from moment to moment.

[3.1.2. Praise Amitāyus]
Then repeat the praise of Amitāyus Tathāgata three times. The praise is: [20]namo'mitābhāyanamo'mitayuṣe|namonamo'cintya-guṇākarātmane || namo 'mitābhāya jināya te mune | sukhāvatīṃ yāmi tavānukampayā || sukhāvatīṃ kanaka-vicitra-kānanāṃ | manoramāṃ sugata-sutair alaṃkṛtāṃ || tavāśrayāt prathita-guṇasya dhīmataḥ | prayāmi tāṃ bahuguṇa-ratna-saṃcayām ||[135]

Three times every day the cultivator constantly repeats this praise of the Buddha's virtues to awaken Amitāyus Tathāgata [from *samādhi*], who, not abandoning his vow of compassion, illuminates the practitioner with an immeasurable radiance. Karmic obstructions and serious wrongdoings are all eliminated, and your body and mind become peaceful, calm, and joyous. If you can sit for a long time doing mantra recitation without getting fatigued, your mind will become pure and you will rapidly attain *samādhi*.[136]

[3.1.3. Enter the *Samādhi* of Avalokiteśvara[137]]
Then enter the *samādhi* of Avalokiteśvara Bodhisattva. Close your eyes and clear your thoughts. Visualize in your body a perfect circle of pure white, like a pure moon, lying face up[138] within your heart. Above the pure moon [disc] visualize the letter *hrīḥ*[139] emitting a great radiance. The letter transforms into an eight-petaled lotus. On the center[140] of the lotus is Avalokiteśvara Bodhisattva. His beautiful appearance is distinct.

In his left hand he holds a lotus, and with his right hand he makes the gesture of opening the petals of the lotus.[141]

Have this thought,[142] "All sentient beings fully possess within their bodies this lotus of awakening. The pure *dharmadhātu* is not tainted by afflictions."

On each of the eight petals of the lotus is a *tathāgata*, sitting in *samādhi* in the full cross-legged position. Their faces are turned toward Avalokiteśvara Bodhisattva. Behind their heads are radiant haloes. Their bodies are golden in color and are dazzlingly brilliant.[143]
Then visualize that this eight-petaled lotus gradually expands and enlarges, [until it becomes] the same in extent as unobstructed space (*ākāśa*).

Then have this thought, "With this lotus of awakening I illuminate the oceanic assembly of the *tathāgatas*; may this become a vast offering." When your mind becomes imperturbable in this *samādhi*, then raise a profound compassion and sympathy for limitless sentient beings. Those who are illuminated by this lotus of awakening are all liberated from suffering and the afflictions, and become identical with Avalokiteśvara Bodhisattva.[144]
Then visualize that the lotus gradually contracts [until it becomes] equal in size to your body.[145]

[3.1.4. Empowerment by the Main Deity]
[3.1.4.1. *Mudrā* and Mantra of Avalokiteśvara]
Then form the *mudrā* of Avalokiteśvara Bodhisattva, and empower the four places. They are: the heart, forehead, throat, and the crown of your head. For the *mudrā* interlace both hands [with the fingers] outside [the hands]. The two forefingers support[146] each other [shaped] like a lotus petal. Extend the two thumbs alongside each other, and [the *mudrā*] is complete. Then repeat the mantra of Avalokiteśvara Bodhisattva:
[21] oṃ vajradharma hrīḥ.[147]
By empowering your heart, forehead, throat, and the crown of your head[148] through forming this *mudrā* and repeating this mantra, your body then becomes identical[149] with Avalokiteśvara Bodhisattva, [identical and with no difference[150]].

[3.1.4.2. Root *Mudrā* and *Dhāraṇī* of Amitāyus]
Next, form the root *mudrā* of Amitāyus Tathāgata. Interlace both hands [with the fingers] outside [the hands] to make a fist. Extend the two middle fingers with the tips supporting[151] each other in the shape of a

lotus petal.[152] After forming this *mudrā*,[153] repeat the *dhāraṇī* of Amitāyus Tathāgata seven times, and dissolve the *mudrā* at the crown of your head. The root *dhāraṇī* of Amitāyus Tathāgata is:
[22] namo ratna-trayāya namaḥ āryāmitābhāya tathāgatāyārhate samyak-sambuddhāya tad yathā oṃ amṛte amṛtodbhave amṛta-sambhave amṛta-garbhe amṛta-siddhe amṛta-teje amṛta-vikrānte amṛta-vikrānta-gāmine amṛta-gagana-kīrtikare amṛta-dundubhi-svare sarvārtha-sādhane sarva-karma-kleśa-kṣayaṃ-kare svāhā.[154]

By repeating this *dhāraṇī* of Amitāyus Tathāgata just once, the ten unwholesome actions (*daśākuśalakarmapatha*),[155] four serious (*pārājika*) offenses,[156] and the five crimes with immediate retribution (*pañcānantarya*)[157] you have committed will be eliminated. All karmic obstructions will be extinguished. If you are a *bhikṣu* or *bhikṣuṇī* and have committed a root offense, after repeating this seven times you will immediately regain purity in the moral discipline.

If you repeat this [*dhāraṇī*] a full ten thousand times you will attain the *samādhi* of never abandoning *bodhicitta*. *Bodhicitta* will manifest in your body as a brilliant and pure luminous disc like a pure moon. When your life is about to come to its end, you will see Amitāyus Tathāgata and the countless *koṭī*s of his assembly of bodhisattvas encircling the practitioner, welcoming and comforting you [in mind and body[158]]. You will then receive a birth at the highest level of the highest grade in the world of Sukhāvatī and will attain the state of a bodhisattva.

[3.2. Mantra Recitation]
Then take a lotus-seed *mālā* and hold it between your palms. Raise the *mālā* with both hands in an *añjali* shaped like an unopened lotus bud. Empower [the *mālā*] with the mantra for revolving a *mālā* a thousand-fold.[159] The mantra is:
[23] oṃ vajra guhya jāpa samaye hūṃ.[160]
After empowering it, then raise the *mālā* to the crown of your head and make this prayer, "May all sentient beings rapidly accomplish the superior and great vow [to accomplish] the mundane and transcendent *siddhis* they seek."

Then with both hands at your heart gather together the five fingers of both hands like an unopened lotus bud. Hold the *mālā* in your left hand, and move it with the thumb and ring finger of your right hand. Repeat the *dhāraṇī* once, and at the sound of the word *svāhā* advance the *mālā* one bead each time.

Make your voice for mantra repetition neither slow nor fast, and neither rising nor falling. Do not [repeat the mantra] in a loud voice. Articulate the letters of the mantra distinctly one by one.

Mentally visualize the Pure Land created in this *samādhi* and Amitāyus Tathāgata invited earlier, perfectly possessing the excellent marks and sitting in the center of the altar. Visualize in this way with perfect clarity, and concentrate on the mantra recitation, allowing no break in its continuity and without distraction.

During one sitting recite [the *dhāraṇī*] either one hundred (i.e., 108) or one thousand (i.e., 1080) times. If you do not complete 108 repetitions [during one practice session], then you will not fulfill the number of repetitions [necessary for realizing your] prayers.

Because of the *adhiṣṭhāna* of Amitāyus Tathāgata, your body and mind become pure, even to the extent that you constantly see Amitāyus Tathāgata whether your eyes are open or shut. Then in *samādhi* you will hear him preach the profound and sublime Dharma.

From each letter and each phrase [of the *dhāraṇī*] you realize countless *samādhi*-gates, countless *dhāraṇī*-gates, and countless liberation-gates. Your body becomes identical with [that of] Avalokiteśvara Bodhisattva, and you can rapidly enter that world (Sukhāvatī).

When the number of mantra repetitions is complete, hold the *mālā* and raise it to the crown of your head and make this prayer, "May all sentient beings attain birth in the world of Sukhāvatī, see the Buddha and hear his Dharma, and rapidly realize supreme and perfect[161] *bodhi*."

[3.3. Visualize a Letter-Disc]

Next, form the *dhyāna-mudrā*. Interlace [the fingers of] both hands on the outside [of the hands]. Hold the backs of the two forefingers together, and make them vertical from the middle joints up [to the tips]. Extend the two thumbs straight, touch them to [the tips of] the two forefingers, and [the *mudrā*] is complete.[162]

Then visualize *bodhicitta* within your body. It is a brilliant and pure luminous disc like a full moon. Then meditate in this way. The essence of *bodhicitta* is free of all material things. It is free[163] of the aggregates (*skandhas*), fields (*āyatanas*), realms (*dhātus*), and [distinctions of] subject and object. Because dharmas are without a self, they are of a single mark and are identical. Because the mind is fundamentally non-arising and own-nature is empty,[164] thus on the luminous disc of the pure moon disc visualize the gate of the letter *hrīḥ*. An immeasurable light flows out from the letter.[165] Visualize that one by one the rays become the world of

Sukhāvatī [where] the noble assembly encircles Amitāyus Buddha, as explained in the *Amitāyus Visualization Sūtra*.[166]

[3.3.1. Root *Mudrā* and *Dhāraṇī* of the Deity]
After finishing this mantra recitation and *samādhi* cultivation, when you wish to leave the *bodhimaṇḍa* form the *mudrā* of the main deity (Amitāyus), repeat the root *dhāraṇī* seven times, and dissolve it over the crown of your head.

[4. The Concluding Rituals]
[4.1. Praise]
Then repeat the [previous] praise.[167]

[4.2. Universal Offering]
Next, form the universal offering *mudrā* and repeat the vast and infallible *maṇi*-jewel offering *dhāraṇī* [as before].

[4.3. *Argha*]
Again offer *argha*[-water].

[4.4. Prayers]
Declare all the prayers in your heart to the noble assembly, [saying] "May the noble ones not transcend their root vows, and fulfill my prayers."

[4.5. Dissolve the Boundaries]
When the mantra recitation, offering, and prayers are concluded, then form the previous fire-enclosure *mudrā*.[168] Revolve it to the left once to dissolve the boundaries created earlier.

[4.6. Send Off the Main Deity]
Next, form the jeweled-carriage *mudrā* and repeat the previous jeweled-carriage mantra.[169] Brush the two thumbs against the tips of the two middle fingers outward, and repeat the original mantra to respectfully send off the noble assembly. Remove the word *ākarṣaya*[170] in the mantra and add the words *gaccha-gaccha*[171] to complete the sending-off.[172]

[4.7. *Samaya-Mudrā*s of the Three Families]
Next, form the *samaya-mudrā*s of the three families and repeat each mantra three times.

[4.8. *Mudrā* for Wearing Armor to Protect the Body]
After that, form the *mudrā* for wearing armor to protect the body and seal the five places of the body.

[4.9. Prostrate to the Buddhas]
Then, before the main deity, sincerely make prayers and prostrate to the buddhas.

[4.10. Leave the Shrine]
Leave the *bodhimaṇḍa* at will.
[5. Activities Outside of the Ritual Practice]
Walk about as you like.[173] You should constantly read and recite the *Amitāyus Sūtra.*[174] Cherish in your heart the superior intention,[175] and carefully practice mantra recitation. Seal buddhas and seal *stūpas*,[176] take joy in giving charity, and cultivate morality, patience, vigor, meditation, and wisdom. Dedicate the merit of all the wholesome qualities you cultivate, so that together with all beings you can attain the same birth in the highest level of the highest grade in Pure Land, [there to] realize the [first] *bhūmi* of joy (*pramuditā*), and receive the prediction (*vyākaraṇa*) of [attaining] supreme *bodhi*. This practice may be used for any Lotus family [deity].[177]

[6. Supplement]
The heart (*hṛdaya*) mantra of Amitāyus Tathāgata is:[178]
[24] oṃ amṛta teje hara hūṃ.[179]
By repeating this [mantra] one hundred thousand times, you will be able to see Amitāyus Tathāgata, and when your life comes to its end you will definitely attain a birth in the world of Sukhāvatī.[180]

The Ritual Manual on Cultivating the Visualization of and Making Offerings to Amitāyus Tathāgata[181]

## Notes

1 This text is *T.* 930 in the Taishō Edition, *Koryo taejanggyong* (hereafter *K*) 1312 in the Korean Buddhist canon, and appears in the *Dai-Nihon kōtei shukusatsu daizokyo* (*Dai-Nihon kotei shukusatsu daizōkyō*, hereafter *SD*) in the volume labeled 閏五. It is included in an important Japanese xylographic edition, Jōgon's (淨嚴, 1639–1702) early Edo period *Himitsu giki*. The readings

in *K* and *T.* for the *Wuliangshou yigui* and many other ritual manuals often are at variance with the original imported texts handed down in the Japanese esoteric traditions. In *T.* the preferred readings often appear in the footnotes. The present translation is from *SD*, with careful reference to the copy of the *Himitsu giki* (Jōgon's xylographic edition, hereafter *HG*), in the volume labeled 兊一) in the library of Kōyasan University with emendations in Jōgon's hand, and notes the areas of divergence with the *T.* and *K* editions.

2 The title of the text is given in *SD* and *HG* as *Wuliangshou rulai xiu guanxing gongyang yigui* (The ritual manual on cultivating the visualization of and making offerings to Amitāyus Tathāgata, abbreviated herein as *Wuliangshou yigui*). The *T.* and *K* give the title as *Wuliangshou rulai guanxing gongyang yigui*, omitting the character 修 ("cultivating"). Only the *Kaiyuan shijiao lu* (730, *T.* 2154.55:700b) gives a similar title, "*Wuliangshou rulai guanxing yigui*, in one fascicle of twelve sheets."

In the Tang *Dai Zong chao zengsi Kong dabianzheng guangzhi sanzang heshang biaozhi ji* (*T.* 2120.52:839c) the title of this text is listed as "*Wuliangshou rulai niansong yigui*, one fascicle" (*Amitāyus Tathāgata Mantra Recitation Ritual Manual*, one fascicle). The text seems to have historically had a shorter title on the outside of the original scroll, with the longer title on the inside immediately preceding the text. In the *Da Tang zhenyuan xu kaiyuan shijiao lu* (794, *T.* 2156.55:767b) the same title is given, with an explanation that the inner title of the text is *Xiu guanxing gongyang yigui* (again giving the length of the scroll as twelve sheets). The comment about the inner title is repeated in the *Zhenyuan xinding shijiao lu* of 800 in the fifteenth fascicle *T.* 2157.55:879c, and also 924c, 1028c. With *Wuliangshou rulai* added before *Xiu guanxing gongyang yigui*, that is the title as given in *SD* and *HG* (and in *Mikkyō daijiten*, 2148b). *Wuliangshou rulai niansong yigui* is thus the outer title of the text.

This text was imported to Japan no less than five times, by Saichō (最澄, 767–822), Kūkai (空海, 774–835), Ennin (圓仁, 794–864), Eun (惠運, 798–869), and Enchin (圓珍, 814–891). In his *Shōrai mokuroku* (*TKZ* 1.9, *T.* 2161.55:1061b) Kūkai gives the title of this text as "*Wuliangshou rulai niansong yigui*, one fascicle," which is the outer title appearing in the Tang catalogs (while in his *Sangaku-roku* he adds 經 after 儀軌, i.e., 無量壽如來念誦儀軌經一卷, *TKZ* 1.45). Annen (安然, 841–?) gives the same outer title in his *Sho-ajari shingon mikkyō burui sōroku* (*T.* 2176.55:1117c), and the inner title of the text as *Wuliangshou rulai xiu guanxing gongyang yigui* (無量壽如來念誦儀軌一卷　內云修觀行供養儀軌不空譯貞元新入目錄　澄海仁運珍云無量壽如來修觀行供養儀軌一卷). Therefore, the text is here titled *Wuliangshou rulai xiu guanxing gongyang yigui*, including the character 修.

3 These are abbreviated titles, for the full titles see the bibliography. The *Wuliangshou yigui* and *Ruyilun yigui* are the most closely related in content.

The *Ganlu Juntuli yigui*, *Wuchusemo yigui*, and *Achu fa* have some additional features not found in the *Wuliangshou yigui* and *Ruyilun yigui*, many of which are based on the Vajraśekhara ritual manuals. The two *Zhunti jing* texts begin as *dhāraṇī* scriptures and append ritual manuals similar to the other texts mentioned. These seven texts have ritual consistency and were all imported to Japan by Kūkai in 806 or were already in Japan by that date.

4 Charles Orzech has noted that "Although obviously dependent upon the *Guan jing*, the *Wuliangshou yigui* does not borrow significantly from it but is content to evoke it"; see "A Tang Esoteric Manual for Rebirth in the Pure Land: Rites of Contemplation of and Offerings to Amitāyus Tathāgata," in *Path of No Path: Contemporary Studies in Pure Land Buddhism Honoring Roger Corless*, ed. Richard K. Payne (Berkeley, CA: Institute of Buddhist Studies and Numata Center for Buddhist Translation and Research, 2009), 35. There are no outright quotations from that text in the *Wuliangshou yigui*. But while the *Wuliangshou yigui* does indeed seem to make use of the *Amitāyus Visualization Sūtra* in the few places noted below, that dependency does not seem to influence the actual ritual format that forms the core of the text, but it does extend to the purpose of the practice in the text. The present author reads these points as intentional additions to an Indic Esoteric ritual manual (or format) to enhance receptivity with a Chinese audience.

5 Besides the relationships among the above texts, they also have partial connections with the *Susiddhikara* and *Suxidijielo gongyang fa*, the *Mahāvairocanābhisaṃbodhi sūtra*, and Vajraśekhara texts.

6 Amoghavajra even goes so far as to mention the *Amitāyus Visualization Sūtra* by name (3.3) once, a text not known in India. Amoghavajra may have edited or embellished other Indian Esoteric manuals to enhance receptivity in China, or to put it differently, to answer the specific needs of Chinese Buddhists. For example, the *Guanzhi yigui* (*T.* 1000) is a ritual manual for an Esoteric practice of the *Lotus Sūtra*, which he may have compiled or edited for Chinese audiences. The *Dafangguang fo Huayan-jing Rufajie-pin dunzheng Piluzhena fashen zilun yujia yigui* (*T.* 1020) and *Dafangguang fo Huayan-jing Rufajie-pin sishierzi guanmen* (*T.* 1019) are two Esoteric manuals dealing with the *Gaṇḍavyūha* which he may have also taken a more direct hand in composing.

7 As Orzech, "A Tang Esoteric Manual," 32, has noted, "the *Wuliangshou yigui* is unusual in the degree of integration of that [exoteric Chinese] material into its esoteric program." While many Esoteric manuals mention birth in Sukhāvatī, none do so to the degree of the *Wuliangshou yigui*, and not as the primary aim of the practice. For example, the closely related *Ruyilun yigui* says that the practitioner "will be spontaneously born on a lotus [in Sukhāvatī], and will rapidly realize supreme and perfect *bodhi*" as part of the text for the Buddha family *samaya*, but otherwise does not mention

birth in Sukhāvatī. The idea of using Esoteric ritual means for attaining exoteric or even mundane goals is not, however, unknown in Esoteric texts. For example, both *Zhunti jing* translations give lists of both mundane and transcendent benefits attainable from reciting Cundī's *dhāraṇī*. The *Wuliangshou yigui*, nevertheless, is unique in stating no purpose other than birth in Sukhāvatī.

8 The aim of Esoteric ritual practice is often explained in other ritual manuals as the rapid or accelerated attainment of awakening. To use examples from the above list, the *Ganlu Juntuli yigui* (*T.* 1211.21:42b) mentions the "rapid path to *bodhi*" and to "rapidly gather the accumulation of merit and wisdom to attain the perfect and pure *dharmakāya*." The *Ruyilun yigui* clearly defines the purpose of its ritual as nothing less than the rapid attainment of full buddhahood to give ease to suffering beings, and is thoroughly consistent with what might be called typical Esoteric discourse: "Raise the thought of great goodwill and compassion, [thinking] 'Cultivating this practice, for the sake of all beings I will rapidly realize supreme and perfect *bodhi*.'" (*T.* 1085.20:204a).

An interesting point of contrast is that while the *Wuliangshou yigui* opens with the statement that the purpose of the practice is to "attain birth in the Pure Land and [there] enter the ranks of the bodhisattvas on the *bhūmis*" (1.1) and closes with the suggestion that one can attain the first *bhūmi*, or *pramuditā*, in Sukhāvatī after achieving birth there (5), the thoroughly Esoteric *Ganlu Juntuli yigui* says that "[i]n the present life you will become a bodhisattva of the first *bhūmi*, the stage of joy (*pramuditā*). After a further sixteen births, you will attain supreme and perfect *bodhi*" (*T.* 1211.21:49a). See Shingen Takagi and Thomas Eijō Dreitlein, *Kūkai on the Philosophy of Language* (Tokyo: Keio University Press, 2010), 31, on the matter of sixteen births.

9 This is not often mentioned in Esoteric texts, which generally do not accept the idea that spiritual progress is impossible in the present age.

10 The "*samādhi* of recollecting the buddha" appears in many exoteric Mahāyāna texts where it is not specific to Amitāyus. In the *Pratyutpanna-samādh sūtra*, however, the *samādhi* of recollecting or visualizing Amitāyus in particular is linked with birth in Sukhāvatī. The Chinese translation by Lokakṣema (*T.* 418.13:905b; see also *T.* 417.13:899a, *T.* 416.13:876a–b, and *T.* 419.13:922b) has:

> By practicing this recollection of the buddha, a bodhisattva will attain birth in Amitāyus' world. He constantly recollects in this way: the buddha's body fully possesses all the thirty-two major marks, gives off a penetrating radiance, and is beautiful beyond compare. . . . By recollecting the buddha, you attain the *samādhi* of emptiness. This is the recollection of the buddha.

Later Shingon commentators have gone to some length to make the point that the *nenbutsu* is not intended here. Among the Shingon commentaries on this text, the *Shogiki ketsuei* (*ZSZ* 1.215a) says that here "the *samādhi* of recollecting the buddha is visualizing Amitāyus Buddha on a lotus." The *Himitsu giki denju kuketsu* (*SZ* 3.393a–b) says:

> The [Esoteric] "*samādhi* of recollecting the buddha" has two meanings. The first is not [the exoteric practice] of holding the (Amitāyus') name, but is visualizing the buddha's true body, meaning visualizing eight Amitāyus Buddhas on the eight petals of a lotus (see 3.1.3). The second is indeed holding the name, but in this case [the Siddham letters] *amṛte* (repeated ten times in the root *dhāraṇī*, 3.1.4.2) in the mantra are the name. [The difference is] simply one of knowing the three mysteries [practice] and not knowing it.

The *Shoki honjō roku* (*ZSZ* 3.396a) makes the above two points and then says, "Both thoroughly possess the three mysteries. The recollection of the buddha explained in the *Pratyutpanna-samādhi sūtra* (see previous note) is not the repetition of the (Amitāyus') name [taught by] the Pure Land masters."

11 The Smaller *Sukhāvatīvyūha sūtra* passage is (*T.* 366.12:347b) (cf. Fujita Kōtatsu, *Bonbun Muryōju-kyō, Bonbun Amida-kyō* (The Larger and Smaller *Sukhāvatīvyūha* sutras) (Kyoto: Hōzōkan, 2011), 89):

> Śāriputra, with few good roots or merit, one cannot attain birth in that world (nāvaramātrakeṇa śāriputra kuśalamūlenāmitāyuṣas tathāgatasya buddhakṣetre sattvā upapadyante). Śāriputra, if there is a man or woman of good family who hears of Amitāyus Buddha, and who holds his name for either one day, or two days, or three days, or four days, or five days, or six days, or seven days single-mindedly and without confusion, then when that person's life is about to come to its end, Amitāyus Buddha will appear before him or her with his noble assembly. When that person's life is at its end, his mind will not be confused and he will be born immediately in Amitāyus Buddha's world of Sukhāvatī.

12 The Smaller *Sukhāvatīvyūha sūtra* (*T.* 366.12:347a, cf. Fujita, *Bonbun Muryōju-kyō*, 89) has:

> These birds [in Sukhāvatī] are all magically created by Amitāyus Buddha to preach the sounds of Dharma (*dharmaśabdaṃ niścārayanti*). Śāriputra, when a light breeze blows in this buddha-field, it sways the rows of jeweled trees and jeweled nets. They give off a marvelous sound like a hundred thousand kinds of musical instruments played together. All those who hear this sound spontaneously recollect the Buddha (*buddhanusmṛti*), Dharma (*dharmānusmṛti*), and Saṃgha (*saṃghānusmṛti*).

The *Amitāyus Visualization Sūtra* (*T.* 365.12:343b, 344b) similarly has:

> The practitioner will hear [the sounds of] flowing water, the light, the jeweled trees, the mallards, geese, and paired mandarin ducks all as preaching the excellent Dharma. . . . See the buddhas and bodhisattvas filling space. The waters, birds, and forests, and the voices of the buddhas, all preach the excellent Dharma.

13 This sentence is also quoted in the *Liqu shi* (*T.* 1003.19:612b) in the section on Avalokiteśvara. Kūkai seems to allude to this sentence in his *Chūju kankyō no shi* (*TKZ* 8.43, Takagi and Dreitlein, *Kūkai on the Philosophy of Language*, 240, but with an emphasis on the immanency of the Pure Land: "The [sounds of the] birds and animals, and plants and trees all are the sound of the Dharmakāya's preaching, and Sukhāvatī and Tuṣita are originally within our hearts."

14 See note 174.

15 Besides the ritual format, the praise section (3.1.2) of the *Wuliangshou yigui* gives a Sanskrit *gāthā* found in a Sanskrit version of the Larger *Sukhāvatīvyūha sūtra* (Fujita, *Bonbun Muryōju-kyō*, 3, see also note 135) but apparently never translated into Chinese, suggesting that Amoghavajra used Sanskrit materials in translating the *Wuliangshou yigui.* The preparation of the shrine, the ritual format, the Sanskrit mantras, the *mudrās*, and all the other esoteric features of the text are clearly not the creations of Amoghavajra.

16 These eighteen are present in the *Ruyilun yigui* most clearly and in the *Wuliangshou yigui* with one inversion in the sequence. The other texts listed above have greater degrees of variation along with various additions and omissions.

17 This list is appended to the ninth fascicle of Kūkai's copy of the texts he imported, the *Sanjūjō sakushi*, see *KZ* 2.611. It seems possible that Kūkai received this format as an oral teaching from Huiguo and wrote it down, which is the opinion of Raiyu (in *Jūhachidō kuketsu, T.* 2529.79:71c), for example. Kakuban has noted, however, that it is the creation of Kūkai (*Jūhachidō sata, T.* 2517.79:26c) on the basis of the *Wuliangshou yigui* to use with any deity (*T.* 2517.79:27b). Besides the above list, in fascicle 29 of his *Sanjūjō sakushi* (see *KZ* 2.613–614) Kūkai wrote out mantras for the above nineteen in Siddham script.

18 In Kūkai's list there are actually nineteen steps with the addition of "universal prostration," which is strictly speaking not the name of a *mudrā.* The Sanskrit title **aṣṭadaśa-naya* in Siddham script is certainly a reverse translation from the Chinese.

19 The first section of the *Ruyilun yigui* along with some of the introductory verses from the *Ruyilun yujia* were combined in a text, probably in Japan, called *Jūhachi geiin* to flesh out the bare list in the *Sanjūjō sakushi.* Most passages from the *Ruyilun yigui* specific to Cintāmaṇicakra were removed or

altered in creating the *Jūhachi geiin* to make it applicable to other deities. There is a debate over whether Kūkai compiled this text himself or received it from Huiguo. Nevertheless, the *Jūhachi geiin* is a compilation of two Tang ritual manuals as noted. Kūkai alone claims to have imported this text, and it does not appear in any Chinese catalogs.

20 The *Jūhachidō nenju shidai Daishi Chūin* was adopted into the Hirosawa-ryū schools (and also exceptionally into Chūin-ryū), with the main deity as Mahāvairocana of the Vajradhātu. The Ono-ryū and Daigo-ryū schools, however, developed a different and expanded format *Jūhachidō nenju shidai* with Cintāmaṇicakra as the main deity, closely based on the *Ruyilun yigui,* while also using aspects of the longer *Ganlu Juntuli yigui* ritual format. See *Mikkyō daijiten* (890–891) under *Jūhachidō nenju shidai* for a full list of *Jūhachidō nenju shidai.*

21 The texts are the *Sahō shidai* and *Muryōju nyorai kuyō sahō shidai.* The dates and authors of these two texts remain uncertain, and the purpose for which they are to be practiced is not given, whether exclusively or primarily for birth in Sukhāvatī as in the *Wuliangshou yigui,* or for buddhahood in this lifetime as the developed Shingon tradition would claim.

22 *T.* 2489.78:485b–487b. The *Hishō* practice includes the praise *gāthā*, the visualization of Avalokiteśvara, the *mudrās* of Avalokiteśvara and Amitāyus, and so on verbatim. It is practiced to this day in the Sanbōin-ryū (三寶院流) lineage of Shingon practice. The Chūin-ryū (中院流) Amida practice, for example, is in turn a simplification of the *Hishō* Amida practice. *Hishō* (*T.* 2489.78:486c) and other important ritual collections including *Takushō* (*T.* 2488.78:424a) also include esoteric practices for rebirth in Sukhāvatī, such as the *mudrā* and mantra for "attaining birth in Sukhāvatī without fail." However, Amitāyus/Amitābha practices in Shingon *hōryū* from the mid-Heian period on usually have as their main purpose the attainment of buddhahood in this lifetime, and secondarily birth in Sukhāvatī, typically for the deceased. For example, the *Sahō-shū* (作法集) of the Sanbōin-ryū lineage includes a set of additions to the *Hishō* Amida practice for practicing it for the deceased to attain birth in Sukhāvatī.

23 Similar comments on the need for receiving *abhiṣeka* and direct instruction before practicing a *sādhana* such as this appear in the *Ruyilun yigui* (*T.* 1085.20:203c), the *Ganlu Juntuli yigui* (*T.* 1211.21:42b–c), and so on.

24 The general format for ritual steps in the opening section is established here. First, the name of the ritual step is introduced, and the *mudrā* explained. After the description of the *mudrā* is completed, a visualization is given. Then the mantra is given, followed by the number of repetitions, and any actions for dissolving the *mudrā* at the end of the section. The intention is that the *mudrā* is formed and the visualization done while repeating the mantra, thus constituting a practice simultaneously involving

body (*mudrā*), speech (mantra), and mind (visualization). Finally, the effectiveness of that step in the ritual is described.

25 In the *Wuliangshou yigui*, the "great treasury of space" (2.11) comes before "visualiz[ing] the *bodhimaṇḍa*" (2.12). In the *Ruyilun yigui* the *bodhimaṇḍa* is first visualized filled with offerings, and then the *mudrā* of the "great treasury of space" (Ākāśagarbha) is used to make those offerings "no different from real ones" (*T.* 1085.20:205a). The sequence of these two steps in the *Ruyilun yigui* is the basis for the Jūhachidō template. All the other related ritual manuals follow the sequence in *Ruyilun yigui.*

26 In other ritual manuals these three practices are for the purpose of accomplishing yogic identity with the main deity. For example, for the practices corresponding to the first meditation of this section the *Ruyilun yigui* has "visualize your own body in the image of the main deity, with six arms and beautiful in appearance" (*T.* 1085.20:206a, the preferred *SD* and *HG* reading in the footnotes), the *Ganlu Juntuli yigui* has "by this *samādhi* of arranging letters [in your body], your body transforms into the main deity" (*T.* 1211.21:47c), and so on. In the developed Shingon tradition, these three sections are sometimes explained as practices for integration with the main deity through body, speech, and mind, respectively. The *Wuliangshou yigui* says that by the *mudrā* and mantra of Avalokiteśvara the practitioner's "body then becomes identical with Avalokiteśvara" (3.1.4.1), but does not explicitly mention yogic integration with the main deity Amitāyus, instead seemingly focusing on attaining the necessary qualities for birth in Sukhāvatī. But since the *Wuliangshou yigui* claims at the end of the text that "[t]his practice may be used for any Lotus family [deity]" (V), the text could be considered a deity yoga practice for identification with Avalokiteśvara at the least. See also notes 133 and 143.

27 Similar expressions occur in nearly all the texts listed above.

28 *SD, HG*唐三藏沙門大廣智不空奉　詔譯; *T., K* 開府儀同三司特進試鴻臚卿肅國公食邑三千戸賜紫贈司空謚大鑒正號大廣智大興善寺三藏沙門不空奉詔譯.

29 These sections headings are added based on Jōgon's marginalia in red in the edition of *HG* in the library of Kōyasan University.

30 *K, T., SD* 惡業; *HG* 惡趣.

31 *SD, HG* 如來; *K, T.* 佛.

32 See note 11.

33 A "superior place" for Esoteric practice is discussed in detail in chapter 6 of the *Susiddhikara* (*T.* 893.18:363c ff; Rolf W. Giebel, *Two Esoteric Sūtras* (Berkeley, CA: Numata Center for Buddhist Translation and Research, 2001), 143–144.). The *Fantian zedi fa* (*T.* 910) consists of a list of forty-two locations suitable for Esoteric practice. The *Ruyilun yigui* (*T.* 1085.20:203c), *Ganlu Juntuli yigui* (*T.* 1211.21:42c) and others also provide details.

34 This interpretation is based such related texts as the *Ruyilun yigui* (*T.* 1085.20:203c), "spread *gomayī* (cow dung) on the ground," the *Ganlu Juntuli yigui* (*T.* 1211.21:42c), "Purify and clear the ground, spreading it with *gomayī*. Then smear sandalwood perfume on the maṇḍala[-altar]," and similar passages in Vajrabodhi's *Zhunti jing* (*T.* 1075.20:175a), Amoghavajra's *Zhunti jing* (*T.* 1076.20:180b), and so on. The *Mahāvairocanābhisaṃbodhi sūtra* (*T.* 848.18:5a) says, "Take *gomayī* and *gomūtra* (cow urine) before they touch the ground, mix them, and spread them [on the altar]."

35 *T., K, SD* 塗拭清淨 (spread [*gomayī*] to purify); *HG* 塗拭淨室 (spread [*gomayī*] in a pure room).

36 An "eight[-petaled] lotus maṇḍala" appears in several of the ritual manuals related to the *Mahāvairocanābhisaṃbodhi sūtra* practice in reference to the eight-petaled lotus at the core of the Mahākaruṇāgarbhodbhava Maṇḍala, and from other ritual manuals such as *T.* 1146.20:603a, the *Liqu shi* (*T.* 1003.19:613c), and so on. Here it may also refer to the visualization described below of Avalokiteśvara seated on a lotus with eight buddhas on the eight petals of the lotus: see 3.1.3.

37 *SD, HG* 如來; *T., K* omit.

38 Kūkai mentions an ivory sitting platform that he brought back from China in his *Shōrai mokuroku* (*TKZ* 1.33, Takagi and Dreitlein, *Kūkai on the Philosophy of Language*, 219).

39 *T., K* 燒種種香 (burn various kinds of incense); *SD, HG* omit.

40 The *Wuliangshou yigui* explicitly calls for only two offering cups unlike the later Shingon practice of six. This is also seen in other related ritual manuals such as the *Ruyilun yigui* (*T.* 1085.20:203c), the *Ganlu Juntuli yigui* (*T.* 1211.21:46b), and the *Wuchusemo yigui* (*T.* 1225.21:135c).

41 *T., K, SD* 或用盆盃及金銀銅器石瓷瓦等器未經用者 (using either basins or bowls, or cups made of gold, silver, or copper, or cups made of stone, ceramic, earthenware, and so on that have never been used before). *HG* has 或用螺盃及寶金銀銅器石瓷瓦等未經用者 as translated as above. The *Ganlu Juntuli yigui* (*T.* 1211.21:46b) mentions similar materials including *śaṅkha* (商佉, conch shell), and says to "float seasonal flowers on the water."

42 The six kinds of offerings in these texts are typically *argha*, perfume, flowers, incense, food, and lamps. In the *Wuliangshou yigui* and *Ruyilun yigui* the *argha* is offered later with a mantra, and the rest of the offerings are offered together with a "vast and infallible *maṇi*-jewel offering *mudrā*" and mantra (2.21), or a "universal offering" *mudrā* and mantra (*Ruyilun yigui*, *T.* 1085.20:206a). Besides an *argha mudrā* and mantra and a universal offering *mudrā* and mantra, other related texts such as the *Ganlu Juntuli yigui* (*T.* 1211.21:46b–47b29), *Achu fa* (*T.* 921.19:18b–19a), Vajrabodhi's *Zhunti jing*

(*T.* 1075.20:176b–c), and Amoghavajra's *Zhunti jing* (*T.* 1076.20:182b–c) add five separate *mudrās* and mantras for the remaining five offerings.

43 These numbers indicate the sections corresponding to the eighteen *mudrās* of the Jūhachidō template mentioned above.

44 *SD, HG* 行者; *T., K* 行人.

45 *SD, T., K* add 著新淨衣或用真言加持以為澡浴; *HG* omits and has only "The practitioner performs daily ablutions." The idea is that either a physical ablution or a notional (nonphysical) ablution by means of mantra and visualization are acceptable, as in the *Ruyilun yigui* (*T.* 1085.20:203c), the *Wuchusemo yigui* (*T.* 1225.21:135c). The *Ganlu Juntuli yigui* (*T.* 1211.21:43b) warns the practitioner not to "cling to ideas of external purity. Always use the Dharma water of the ultimate truth of inherent purity to wash your body and mind, thus harmonizing with the truth of suchness." However, the *Zhunti jing* (*T.* 1075.20:175a, *T.* 1076.20:180b) requires the ritual purity of physical ablutions.

46 *T., K* 迷失菩提淪溺生死受無量苦; *SD, HG* omit.

47 *SD, HG* 能; *T., K* omit.

48 *HG* omits 以.

49 This *mudrā* and mantra is combined with the four in 2.5–8 in Shingon practice as the "method for protecting the body," but in this text and in the *Ruyilun yigui* the first *mudrā* and mantra is used for ritual ablution before prostrating and is not organic with the other four. In the *Ganlu Juntuli yigui* this is used after the prostrations and after taking the seat for practice, and so seems more integrated with the other four in that text. *Shogiki ketsuei* comments (*ZSZ* 1.215a), "This is purifying the three actions as an ablution. It is not purifying the three actions [as part of] the method for protecting the body." *Himitsu giki denju kuketsu* says (*SZ* 2.360a), "this is a notional ablution," which is "used as a method for ablution before entering (sitting at) the altar" (*Shoki honjō roku ZSZ* 3.7a). In the *Jūhachi geiin* this comes after the prostration section taken from *Ruyilun yujia,* and so immediately precedes the other four *mudrās* and mantras (separated from them only by the application of perfume to the hands, as in the *Ganlu Juntuli yigui*). The aim of the notional or visualized ablution is as given below, an "ablution of the pure inner mind" rather than of the physical body.

50 Yukio Hatta, *Shingon jiten* (Tokyo: Hirakawa Shuppansha, 1985) no. 1808. "*Oṃ*, all dharmas are pure in their own-nature. I too am pure in my own-nature."

51 This and the following sections concern the ritual actions after entering the shrine.

52 The five parts of the body meant are the two arms, two legs, and the head.

53 Hatta, *Shingon jiten,* no. 1644. "*Oṃ*, I prostrate to the feet of all the *tathāgatas*." This paragraph and mantra corresponds in meaning to the first stanza of Gokai.

54 The *Ruyilun yigui* (*T.* 1085.20:204a, see also the *Lianhuabu xin yigui T.* 873.18:300a–b) has the Five-Part Repentance here, a set of verses for recitation used in most Shingon practices (other than the Taizōkai-related practices). The five sections are known as (1) Sincere Refuge, (2) Sincere Repentance, (3) Sincere Joy, (4) Sincere Request (that the buddhas remain in the world and preach the Dharma), and (5) Sincere Dedication, and they are said to be derived from the ten great vows of Samantabhadra in the *Gaṇḍavyūha* chapter (*T.* 293.10:844b ff.) of the *Avataṃsaka*. The present text does not use the verses, instead presenting briefer material of similar content including visualizations. The use of visualizations rather than verses is also seen in the *Ganlu Juntuli yigui* (*T.* 1211.21:43a–b) and in an expanded form with mantras added in the *Achu fa* (*T.* 921.19:15c–16b, where the universal prostration functions as Sincere Refuge as it does in the present text) and others.

55 *SD, HG* 我所積集善根禮佛懺悔隨喜勸請以此福聚廻施一切有情 (as above). *T., K* 我所積集禮佛懺悔隨喜勸請無量善根以此福聚廻施一切有情 ("The immeasurable good roots I have amassed through taking refuge in the buddhas, repenting, rejoicing, and requesting: this accumulation of merits I dedicate to all sentient beings").

56 *HG* omits 以.

57 Hatta, *Shingon jiten,* no. 309. "*Oṃ*, to the arising of the Tathāgata! *Svāhā*."

58 *SD, HG* 便; *T., K* omit.

59 *SD, HG* 聖衆; *T., K* 諸佛.

60 *T., K* 集會; *SD, HG* omit.

61 *T., SD, T, K* 消; *HG* 銷.

62 *SD, HG* 著; *T., K* 捻.

63 *SD, HG* 菓; *T., K* omit.

64 Hatta, *Shingon jiten,* no. 559. "*Oṃ*, to the arising of the lotus! *Svāhā*."

65 *T., K, SD* 得; *HG* omits.

66 *SD, HG* 博; *T., K* 縛.

67 The *Mahāvairocanābhisaṃbodhi sūtra* (*T.* 848.18:7a) and other texts at times refer to Vajrapāṇi as Vajragarbha (金剛藏). The *Ruyilun yigui* (*T.* 1085.20:204b) also has Vajragarbha in this context, meaning Vajrapāṇi. Amoghavajra's *Zhunti jing* (*T.* 1076.20:181a) has Vajrapāṇi (金剛手) in the same context, as does the *Jūhachidō geiin* (*T.* 900.18:782b) that is based on the *Ruyilun yigui*.

68 Hatta, *Shingon jiten,* no. 1501. "*Oṃ*, to the arising of the vajra! *Svāhā*."

69 *SD, T., K* 壓; *HG* 押.

70 *SD, HG* 大悲心; *T., K* 大慈悲心.

71 *SD, T., K* 上上殊勝; *HG* 殊勝.

72 Hatta, *Shingon jiten,* no. 1422. "*Oṃ*, to the brilliance of the vajra-fire! *Svāhā*."

73 *SD, HG* 行者; *T., K* 行人.

74 Following *HG* 猶如; *SD, T., K* 由如.

75 *SD, HG* 離; *T., K* 護.

76 *SD, HG* 無上正等菩提; *T., K* 無上菩提.

77 *SD, HG* 地界; *T., K*下方.

78 Hatta, *Shingon jiten,* no. 150. "*Oṃ*, stake, stake, O *vajra-vajrī*-earth! Bind, bind, *hūṃ phaṭ*!"

79 *SD, HG* 加持; *T., K* 加持力.

80 *T., K, SD* 及誦; *HG* omits.

81 *SD, HG* 穢惡; *T., K* 惡穢.

82 *SD, HG* 磔; *T., K* 搩.

83 Hatta, *Shingon jiten,* no. 1766. "*Oṃ*, firm, firm, O vajra-fence, *hūṃ phaṭ*!" Or: *oṃ sara-sara vajra-prākāra hūṃ phaṭ* ("Oṃ, move, move, O vajra-fence, *hūṃ phaṭ*!").

84 *SD, HG* 附; *T., K* 輔.

85 The *Wuliangshou yigui* inverts the sequence of the eighth and ninth steps in the standard Jūhachidō sequence, as in the *Ruyilun yigui* and others. See note 28.

86 *SD, HG* 愽; *T., K* 縛.

87 *T., K, SD* 菩薩; *HG* omits.

88 Hatta, *Shingon jiten,* no. 179. "*Oṃ*, O vajra born from space, *hoḥ*!"

89 *HG, SD* 之; *T., K* omits.

90 The *bīja*-mantra of Amitāyus is *hrīḥ* in the Vajraśekhara. In the *Mahāvairocanābhisaṃbodhi sūtra* (*T.* 848.18:37a) his seed-letter is *saṃ*, and the *Darijing shu* (*T.* 1796.39:788b) also gives *aṃ*. Red is the color of the Lotus family.

91 *SD, T., K* 紅頗梨, *HG* 紅頗瓈. 頗梨 is the transliteration of Skt. *sphaṭika* (*phalika, phaḷiha, phāḷiya*).

92 *SD, HG* 無有不得; *T., K* 無不皆得.

93 The *Wuliangshou yigui* is one of the very few ritual manuals that gives the *tathāgata*-fist *mudrā* and the above mantra that is standard in Shingon *shidai.*

94 *T., K, SD* 左大指甲; *HG* omits 甲.

95 Hatta, *Shingon jiten,* no. 640. "*Oṃ*, *bhūḥ* (earth), *khaṃ* (space)!"

96 This sentence seems to be a paraphrase of the *Amitāyus Visualization Sūtra* (*T.* 365.12:343b, 344b), or of the Smaller *Sukhāvatīvyūha sūtra* (*T.* 366.12:347a, cf. Fujita, *Bonbun Muryōju-kyō*, 89). See note 12.

97 *SD, HG* 伽陀; *T., K* 伽他.

98 This verse, often called the "*gāthā* of the three powers" (三力偈) appears in many ritual manuals. The final line given above is unique to the *Wuliangshou yigui*. The *Ruyilun yigui* (*T.* 1085.20:205a), *Ganlu Juntuli yigui* (*T.* 1211.21:45a), *Achu fa* (*T.* 921.19:17c), Amoghavajra's *Zhunti jing* (*T.* 1076.20:181b), and other texts all have as their final line "May this offering be given universally and endure" (普供養而住), which is also the standard phrase used in Shingon ritual practice.

99 *SD, HG* 散動; *T., K* 散亂.

100 The *Dazhidu lun* (*T.* 1509.25:262a) explains the "state of a bodhisattva" (菩薩位) as meaning *anutpattikadharmakṣānti*, or the conviction of the non-arising of dharmas (無生法忍). See the entry for *anutpattikadharmakṣānti* in Buswell and Lopez, *The Princeton Dictionary of Buddhism*, 55.

101 *SD, HG* 以二頭指; *T., K* omit 以.

102 Hatta, *Shingon jiten*, no. 327. "*Oṃ*, hasten, hasten! *Hūṃ*!"

103 *SD, T., K* 由; *HG* omits.

104 *SD, T., K* 以; *HG* 便以此.

105 *SD, HG* 請; *T., K* omit.

106 Hatta, *Shingon jiten*, no. 428. "I take refuge in the *tathāgatas* of the three times. *Oṃ*, bring the vajra-fire near! *Svāhā*."

107 Hatta, *Shingon jiten*, no. 63. "*Oṃ*, O gentle one! Come near, come near! *Svāhā*."

108 *HG* 證明功德; *SD, T., K* 速令得上上成就 (leads him to rapidly attain the best of the best accomplishments).

109 Hayagrīva is used in this capacity for all the deities of the Lotus family, while the other families employ different main *vidyārājas*.

110 Hatta, *Shingon jiten*, no. 42. "*Oṃ*, O born from the deathless, *hūṃ phaṭ*! *Svāhā*."

111 *HG* 便; *SD, T., K* omit.

112 *SD, T., K* 旋; *HG* 旋轉.

113 Hatta, *Shingon jiten*, no. 1536. "*Oṃ*, open wide and protect, O vajra-net! *Hūṃ phaṭ*!"

114 *SD, T., K* 及誦; *HG* omits.

115 *T., K* 違越而生; *SD, HG* omit.

116 *SD, HG* 磔; *T., K* 搩.

117 *T., K* 火; *SD, HG* omit.

118 *SD*, *HG* 大界火界; *T.*, *K* 火院大界.

119 Hatta, *Shingon jiten*, no. 71. "*Oṃ*, O fire with no equal, *hūṃ phaṭ*!"

120 *SD*, *HG* 獻閼伽香水; *T.*, *K* 結獻閼伽香水印 ("form the *mudrā* of offering perfumed *argha*-water").

121 Hatta, *Shingon jiten*, no. 178. "I take refuge in all the buddhas. O that like space, with no equal! *Svāhā*."

122 *Shoki honjō roku* (*ZSZ* 3.396b) explains that the "the stage of resolute practice" (勝解行地, *adhimukti-caryā-bhūmi*) here has possible two meanings. The first is that it is the bodhisattva stages prior to the ten *bhūmis*, and thus ten *bhūmis* (十地) means from the first *bhūmi* to the tenth *bhūmi*. The second is that it is the first *bhūmi*, and so 十地 means the tenth *bhūmi*. Shinjō says the first interpretation is preferred.

123 *T.*, *K* 得一切如來甘露法水受與灌頂; *SD*, *HG* 得一切如來受與甘露法水灌頂.

124 *SD*, *HG* 蓮華座; *T.*, *K* 華座.

125 Hatta, *Shingon jiten*, no. 123. "*Oṃ*, O lotus! *Svāhā*."

126 *SD*, *T.*, *K* 若, *HG* 如.

127 *SD*, *HG* 捻; *T.*, *K* omit.

128 Hatta, *Shingon jiten*, no. 50. "*Oṃ*, O infallible offering, in the sight of the Tathāgata [possessing] the jewel, lotus, and vajra, extend everywhere! *Hūṃ*!"

129 *SD*, *HG* 無邊微塵剎土; *T.*, *K* 微塵剎.

130 *SD*, *HG* 光明燈燭; *T.*, *K* 燈燭光明.

131 *T.*, *K* add 皆; *SD*, *HG* omit.

132 *SD*, *HG* 安隱; *T.*, *K* 安樂.

133 In Shingon practice, a meditation in this position used for interpenetration and identification with the main deity is called *nyūga-ga'nyū* (lit. "[you] enter me, and I enter [you]"); this term is unknown in any of the ritual manuals translated into Chinese, so it may be a coinage of Huiguo or Kūkai. Kūkai mentions this term in his *Himitsu mandara jūjūshin ron* (*TKZ* 2.4) etc., and so can at least be dated to him. As mentioned above (see note 26), yogic identification seems to be limited to Avalokiteśvara in the *Wuliangshou yigui*. See also note 143.

134 *SD*, *HG* 欣慕; *T.*, *K* 忻慕.

135 No reference in Hatta, *Shingon jiten*. "I take refuge in Amitābha. I take refuge in Amitāyus. I take refuge in your mine of inconceivable merits. I take refuge in Amitābha, the Jina and Muni. Through your compassion I go to Sukhāvatī. There are golden multicolored groves in Sukhāvatī, and it is beautifully adorned by the sons of the Sugata. To your abode of the well-known intelligence of your merits, where abundant merit-jewels are

accumulated, I go forth." A similar *gāthā* appears in *T.* 875.18:326b in Siddham script. Fujita's Sanskrit Larger *Sukhāvatīvyūha sūtra*; see Fujita, *Bonbun Muryōju-kyō*, 3, has this as its opening *gāthā* with some minor differences.

136 In most ritual manuals the praise section comes immediately after the universal offering and before the meditation for integration with the main deity.

137 This section is quoted nearly in full in *Hishō* (*T.* 2489.78:486a), and is there called "visualizing the self."

138 This is the standard understanding of the orientation of a moon disc in the ritual manuals; see for example also the *Jin'gang wang yigui* (*T.* 1132.20:571c), "Place [Vajrasattva's] body on a pure moon disc, as if seated on a bright mirror lying flat."

139 *SD, HG* 呬哩; *T., K* 日哩.

140 *HG* 臺; *SD, T., K* omit.

141 *SD, HG* 開華葉勢; *T., K* 開敷葉勢.

142 Based on *HG* and the Ninna-ji manuscript cited in *T., SD, T., K* have 是菩薩作是思惟"this bodhisattva has this thought."

143 Regarding these eight buddhas, the *Hishō mondō* (*T.* 2536.79:308a) says regarding this passage as quoted in *Hishō* (*T.* 2489.78:486a) that these eight buddhas are all Amitāyus. Usually Avalokiteśvara, Mahāsthāmaprāpta, and the other bodhisattvas sit around Amitāyus, but here the situation is reversed. The idea is that the resultant stage that is Amitāyus is dependent on the causal stage of Avalokiteśvara's great compassion. The *Hishō mondō* also notes that these may be the buddhas and bodhisattvas of the central eight-petaled lotus of the Mahākaruṇāgarbhodbhava Maṇḍala. Another interpretation is that the buddhas on the eight petals represent all buddhas in the ten directions.

The *Hishō kuketsu* (*SZ* 28.27b–28b) says that Avalokiteśvara is the causal stage and Amitāyus the resultant stage, so Avalokiteśvara is visualized in the center of the lotus, and the eight buddhas are Amitāyus. This is because the resultant stage is "peripheral" to the causal stage, with the causal stage being primary; therefore, the resultant buddhas are placed peripherally. Avalokiteśvara reveals great compassion, which is the basis for liberating beings. Therefore, Avalokiteśvara is placed in the center of the lotus. The eight buddhas face the center of the lotus because they rely on great compassion. Great compassion is primary, and all the other virtues of the resultant stage are secondary to it. Therefore Avalokiteśvara sits in the center of the lotus, and the other virtues (the eight buddhas) are placed on the petals.

In this connection it is interesting to note that the *Liqu shi* (*T.* 1003.19:612a) explains that Lokeśvararāja/Amitāyus is the same deity as Avalokiteśvara, and is Lokeśvararāja/Amitāyus in his pure land of Sukhāvatī and Avalokiteśvara in our Sahā world:

> "The Tathāgata who attains the reality of the purity of own-nature" is another name for Lokeśvararāja Tathāgata. This buddha is also called Amitāyus. When in his pure and splendid buddha-field, he manifests a buddha's body [as Amitāyus]. When he abides in the defiled world of the five corruptions, he is Avalokiteśvara Bodhisattva.

144 Or possibly, the practitioner becomes identical with Avalokiteśvara Bodhisattva.

145 A similar practice is also given in a simple form in the *Liqu shi* (*T.* 1003.19:612b) for Avalokiteśvara/Vajradharma, "Visualize your body as the *hrīḥ* letter-gate. It becomes an eight-petaled lotus. In the center of the lotus is Vajradharma. On the eight petals visualize eight buddhas." This practice is also briefly mentioned in other ritual manuals (e.g., *T.* 1041.20:32b and *T.* 1040.20:31b). Note that this visualization is illustrated in *Sahō shidai* (*KZ* 2.502) and *Muryōju nyorai kuyō sahō shidai* (*KZ* 2.515), with the *Wuliangshou yigui* text quoted nearly in full (*KZ* 2.501–503, 514–516).

146 *SD, HG* 拄; *T., K* 柱.

147 Hatta, *Shingon jiten*, no. 1069, "*Oṃ*, O Vajradharma, *hrīḥ*. This is the *mudrā* of Vajradharma (Avalokiteśvara) in the Samaya-assembly and the mantra of Vajradharma in the Karma-assembly of the Vajraśekhara.

148 *SD, HG* 心額喉頂; *T., K* omit.

149 *SD, HG* 等同; *T., K* 同.

150 *T., K* 等無有異; *SD, HG* omit ("identical and with no difference").

151 *SD, HG* 拄; *T., K* 跓.

152 This is the *mudrā* of Amitāyus in the Samaya-assembly of the Vajraśekhara.

153 *SD, HG* 結此印已; *T., K* 結成印已.

154 Hatta, *Shingon jiten*, 246. "I take refuge in the Triple Jewel. I take refuge in Ārya-Amitābha, the Tathāgata, Arhat, and Samyaksaṃbuddha. Thus: *Oṃ*. O deathless! O born from the deathless! O producer of the deathless! O holder of the deathless within! O accomplisher of the deathless! O deathless light! O deathless courage! O deathless courage that attains! O famed of deathless space! O thundering voice of the deathless! O accomplisher of all aims! O destroyer of all karma and afflictions! *Svāhā*."

155 These are the inverses of the ten paths of wholesome conduct (*daśakuśalakarmapatha*): (1) to take life, (2) to take what is not given, (3) sexual misconduct, (4) false speech, (5) slanderous speech, (6) harsh speech, (7) divisive or useless speech, (8) greed, (9) animosity, and (10) false views. See the entries for *ten unwholesome courses of action* (1086) and also *karmapatha* (422–423) in Buswell and Lopez, *The Princeton Dictionary of Buddhism.*

156 The four serious offenses for monastics requiring expulsion from the community are taking life, taking what is not given, sexual activity, and lying

(specifically about attainments). See the entries for *four "defeat" offenses* (1069) and *pārājika* (621–622) in Buswell and Lopez, *The Princeton Dictionary of Buddhism*.

157 These are matricide, patricide, killing an *arhat*, shedding the blood of a buddha with malicious intent, and causing a schism in the monastic community. See the entry for *five acts that bring immediate retribution* in Buswell and Lopez, *The Princeton Dictionary of Buddhism*, 1073.

158 *SD, HG* 安慰行者則; *T., K* 行者安慰身心即.

159 This means multiplying the mantra recitation a thousandfold. The *Ganlu Juntuli yigui* calls this mantra the mantra of Vajrabhāṣa, and explains that by its power "when you repeat one mantra and move [the *mālā*] one bead, it has become the repetition of 1,000 mantras" (*T.* 1211.21:48b).

160 Hatta, *Shingon jiten*, no. 975. "*Oṃ*, O *samaya* of vajra secret mantra recitation! *Hūṃ*!"

161 *SD, HG* 無上正等菩提; *T., K* 無上菩提.

162 *T., K* omit twenty-eight characters: 以二手外相叉二頭指背相著從中節已上直豎二大指捻二頭指即成.

163 *SD, HG* 離; *T., K* 無.

164 *T., K* repeat 自性空, *SD, HG* omit.

165 This visualization is illustrated in the Heian *shidai* attributed to Kūkai titled *Sahō shidai* (*KZ* 2.506) and *Muryōju nyorai kuyō sahō shidai* (*KZ* 2.519).

166 Orzech, "A Tang Esoteric Manual," 35, translates this as indicating plural Sukhāvatīs: "Each ray of light becomes a Sukhāvatī with its retinue surrounding Amitāyus Buddha, just as described in the *Guan jing*."

167 *T., K* 真言讚歎真言已, *SD, HG* omit.

168 Using the fire-enclosure *mudrā* and mantra alone to dissolve the barriers is common in these ritual manuals, while the Shingon tradition repeats each of the *mudrā*s and mantras used for creating barriers, one time each in reverse.

169 *SD, HG* 誦前寶車輅真言; *T., K* omit.

170 Second person singular imperative causative of *ākṛṣ*, "bring near."

171 Second person singular imperative of *gam*, "go, go."

172 *T., K* omit these twenty-three characters: 於真言句中除迦囉灑二合野句加蘗蹉蘗蹉句即成奉送 translated above. Mantra no. 12 in 2.14 is meant with the substitution mentioned: *namas try adhvikānāṃ tathāgatānāṃ oṃ vajrāgny gaccha gaccha svāhā*.

173 A ritual method for slow walking with mantras and visualizations to be done after an esoteric ritual practice is found in the *Wuwei sanzang chanyao* (*T.* 917.18:946a).

174 According to *Shogiki ketsuei* (*ZSZ* 1.215b), *Amitāyus Sūtra* here means the *Amitāyus Visualization Sūtra,* but the Larger *Sukhāvatīvyūha sūtra* certainly seems equally possible. Instructions to read sutras in the intervals between the specified number of daily ritual practices are common. The *Ruyilun yigui* (*T.* 1085.20:206c), *Ganlu Juntuli yigui* (*T.* 1211.21:49a), *Wuchusemo yigui* (*T.* 1225.21:139a), and *Achu fa* (*T.* 921.19:20a) all simply say to read the Mahāyāna sutras. The *Ruyilun yujia* (*T.* 1086.20:211b) specifies the *Laṅkāvatāra, Avataṃsaka, Prajñāpāramitā,* and *Adhyardhaśatikā-prajñāpāramitā,* Vajrabodhi's *Zhunti jing* (*T.* 1075.20:178a) says to read the *Large Prajñāpāramitā, Avataṃsaka, Anantamukha, Lotus, Laṅkāvatāra, Mahāparinirvāṇa,* and other Mahāyāna sutras and treatises, and Amoghavajra's *Zhunti jing* (*T.* 1076.20:184a) gives the *Avataṃsaka* and *Large Prajñāpāramitā.* The *Wuliangshou yigui* recommendation to read only Pure Land *sutras* is thus unusual.

175 *SD, HG* 心懷增上意樂; *T., K* 勿懷上慢意樂 ("do not cherish pride in superior intentions").

176 This refers to practices still transmitted in Shingon Buddhism using a seal or stamp with the image of a buddha, *stūpa,* etc. which is "impressed" on incense smoke as it expands as a way of extending the merit of the practice.

177 *SD, HG* 此法通一切蓮華部; *T., K* the same after an insertion, see the following note.

178 *T., K* have a different mantra and insert additional text, *SD, HG* omit:

> *Oṃ lokeśvararāja hrīḥ.* (Hatta no. 884, "*Oṃ,* O Lokeśvararāja, *hrīḥ!*") Repeating this mantra once is equal to reading the Smaller *Sukhāvatīvyūha sūtra* once, or an inexpressible number of times. It is secret and superior, and thus can eliminate obstacles. This cannot be explained in full. This practice may be used for any Lotus family [deity]. The Mantra Recitation Method of Amitāyus Tathāgata.

179 Hatta, *Shingon jiten,* no. 39. "*Oṃ,* O deathless light, dispel! *Hūṃ!*" In the Shingon tradition this mantra is considered a short version of Amitāyus' long *dhāraṇī* given above.

180 *T., K* add here an otherwise unknown "Amitāyus Tathāgata vow *dhāraṇī*"; *SD, HG* omit.

181 *SD, HG* 修; *T., K* omit.

## Bibliography

### Primary Sources

*Achu fa.* Full title: *Achu rulai niansong gongyang fa* (Mantra recitation and offering method of Akṣobhya Tathāgata), *T.* 921, trans. Amoghavajra.

*Amitāyus Visualization Sūtra*. Chinese: *Guan Wuliangshou-fo jing* (**Amitāyurdhyāna-sūtra*), *T*. 365, trans. Kālayaśas, 424–442.

*Avataṃsaka*. Chinese translations: (1) *Dafangguang fo Huayan jing* (*Mahā-vaipulya Buddhāvataṃsaka-sūtra*), *T*. 278, trans. Buddhabhadra in 60 fascicles, 418–422; (2) same title *T*. 279, trans. Śikṣānanda in 80 fascicles, 695–699.

*Chūju kankyō no shi narabi ni jo* (A poem in reflection on my fortieth birthday, with an introduction), in Shōryō shū, *Teihon Kōbō Daishi zenshū* (hereafter *TKZ*) 8.43–44, by Kūkai, 813 (Kōnin 4.11, age 40).

*Da Tang zhenyuan xu kaiyuan shijiao lu* (Great Tang Zhenyuan Era continuation of the Kaiyuan Catalog of Śākyamuni's teachings), *T*. 2156, compiled by Yuanzhao (圓照), 794.

*Da Xukongzang pusa niansong fa* (Mantra recitation method of Great Ākāśagarbha Bodhisattva), *T*. 1146, trans. Amoghavajra.

*Dafangguang fo Huayan-jing Rufajie-pin dunzheng Piluzhena fashen zilun yujia yigui* (Ritual manual of the letter-wheel yoga of instant realization of the Dharmakāya Vairocana in the *Gaṇḍavyūha* Chapter of the *Mahā-vaipulya Buddhāvataṃsaka-sūtra*), *T*. 1020, trans. Amoghavajra.

*Dafangguang fo Huayan-jing Rufajie-pin sishierzi guanmen* (The gate of the visualization of the forty-two letters in the *Gaṇḍavyūha* Chapter of the *Mahā-vaipulya Buddhāvataṃsaka-sūtra*), *T*. 1019, trans. Amoghavajra.

*Dai Zong chao zengsi Kong dabianzheng guangzhi sanzang heshang biaozhi ji* (Collected documents of Tripiṭaka Master Amoghavajra), *T*. 2120, by Yuanzhao (圓照).

*Darijing shu* (Commentary on the Mahāvairocana[-abhisaṃbodhi]-sūtra), abbreviated title of *Da-Piluzhena-chengfo-jing shu* (Commentary on the *Mahāvairocanābhisaṃbodhi-sūtra*), *T*. 1796, by Śubhakarasiṃha and Yixing (一行), 725.

*Dazhidu lun* (**Mahāprajñāpāramitopadeśa*, a commentary on Kumārajīva's translation of the *Pañcaviṃśatisāhasrikā-prajñāpāramitā*, *T*. 223), *T*. 1509:25, attributed to Nāgārjuna, trans. Kumārajīva, 402–406.

*Fantian zedi fa* (Brahma-deva's method for selection of the site), *T*. 910:18.

*Gaṇḍavyūha*. Chinese translation: *Dafangguang fo Huayan jing*, *T*. 293 trans. Prajña, in 40 fascicles, 795–798. Also the *Rufajie-pin* 入法界品 chapter in *T*. 278 and *T*. 279.

*Ganlu Juntuli yigui*. Full title: *Ganlu Juntuli pusa gongyang niansong chengjiu yigui* (The ritual manual for accomplishment through the offering and mantra recitation of Amṛta-Kuṇḍalī Bodhisattva), *T*. 1211, trans. Amoghavajra.

*Guanzhi yigui*. Full title: *Chengjiu Miaofa-lianhua-jingwang yujia guanzhi yigui* (Ritual manual of yogic meditation for attaining wisdom to perfect the king of sutras, the *Saddharmapuṇḍarīka*), *T*. 1000, trans. Amoghavajra, 773.

*Himitsu giki* (The Esoteric ritual manuals), xylographic edition published by Jōgon in the Jōkyō and Genroku eras (1684–1703) in 74 volumes, with 187 texts in 324 fascicles, and is the basis of the Esoteric manuals printed in *Dai-Nihon kōtei shukusatsu daizōkyō*.

*Himitsu giki denju kuketsu* (Transmitted oral teachings of the Esoteric ritual manuals), *Shingon-shū zensho* (hereafter *SZ*) 2, by Shinjō (真常, 1719–1802).

*Hishō* (The Esoteric collection), *T.* 2489, by Shūkaku (守覺, 1150–1202) based on the teachings of Shōken (勝賢, 1138–1196).

*Hishō kuketsu* (Oral teachings on the Esoteric collection), *SZ* vol. 28, a commentary on *Hishō* (*T.* 2489), by Kyōjun (教舜, ca. 1264).

*Hishō mondō* (Questions and answers on the Esoteric collection), *T.* 2536, a commentary on *Hishō* (*T.* 2489), by Raiyu (頼瑜, 1226–1304), 1297.

*Jin'gang wang yigui*. Full title: *Jin'gang wang pusa mimi niansong yigui* (Secret mantra recitation ritual manual of Vajrarāja Bodhisattva), *T.* 1132, trans. Amoghavajra.

*Jūhachi geiin* (Eighteen mudrās), *T.* 900, compilation based on the *Ruyilun yigui* (*T.* 1085) with some of the introductory verses from *Ruyilun yujia* (*T.* 1086).

*Jūhachidō nenju shidai Daishi Chūin* (Eighteen methods recitation sequence, by Kōbō Daishi of the Chūin Monastery), *Kōbō Daishi zenshū* (hereafter *KZ*) 2.616–628, attributed to Kūkai.

*Kaiyuan shijiao lu* (Kaiyuan era catalog of Śākyamuni's teachings), *T.* 2154, compiled by Zhisheng (智昇), 730.

*Larger Sukhāvatīvyūha Sūtra.* Chinese translation: *Fo shuo Wuliangshou jing*, *T.* 360, trans. Saṅghavarman, 252.

*Lianhuabu xin yigui*. Full title: *Jin'gangding lianhuabu xin niansong yigui* (Ritual manual of the mantra recitation of the heart of the Lotus family in the Vajraśekhara), *T.* 873, written or trans. Amoghavajra.

*Liqu shi* (Commentary on the Prajñāpāramitā path to truth, the sūtra of the infallible and true samaya of the Great Bliss Vajra [*Dale jin'gang bukong zhenshi sanmaye jing*, *T.* 243]), abbreviated title of *Dale jin'gang bukong zhenshi sanmeiye jing bore boluomiduo liqu shi*, *T.* 1003, a commentary on Amoghavajra's translation (*T.* 243) of the *Adhyardhaśatikā-prajñāpāramitā-sūtra*, trans. Amoghavajra.

*Mahāvairocanābhisaṃbodhi-sūtra*. Chinese translation: *Da Piluzhena chengfo shenbian jiachi jing* (The sūtra of the miraculously transformative Adhiṣṭhāna of the Mahāvairocana's attainment of Buddhahood, full title: *Mahāvairocanābhisaṃbodhi-vikurvitādhiṣṭhāna-vaipulya-sūtrendra-rāja*), *T.* 848, trans. Śubhakarasiṃha and Yixing (一行), 724–725.

*Muryōju nyorai kuyō sahō shidai* (Ritual sequence for making offerings to Amitāyus Tathāgata), *KZ* 2.511–520, alternate title *Guhari hihō* (Secret method of red crystal), attributed to Kūkai.

*Pañcaviṃśatisāhasrikā-prajñāpāramitā*. Chinese translation: *Mohe bore boluomi jing*, *T.* 223, trans. Kumārajīva, 404.

*Pratyutpanna-samādhi-sūtra*. Chinese translation: *Bore sanmei jing*, *T*. 418, trans. Lokakṣema.

*Ruyilun yigui*. Full title: *Guanzizai pusa Ruyilun niansong yigui* (Avalokiteśvara Bodhisattva Cintāmaṇicakra mantra recitation ritual manual), *T*. 1085, trans. Amoghavajra.

*Ruyilun yujia*. Full title: *Guanzizai pusa Ruyilun yujia* (Avalokiteśvara Bodhisattva Cintāmaṇicakra yoga), *T*. 1086, trans. Amoghavajra.

*Sahō shidai* (The ritual sequence), *KZ* 2.495–508, attributed to Kūkai.

*Sangaku roku* (Catalog of the three trainings), *TKZ* 1.41–61 (full title: *Shingon-shū shogaku kyō-ritsu-ron mokuroku*, Catalog of the sūtras, vinaya, and treatises to be studied in the Shingon School), by Kūkai, 823 (Kōnin 14.10.10).

*Sanjūjō sakushi* (Thirty notebooks), by Kūkai.

*Sho-ajari shingon mikkyō burui sōroku* (General catalog of the mantra Esoteric collections of the Ācāryas), *T*. 2176, by Annen (安然, 841–?).

*Shogiki ketsuei* (Secrets of the ritual manuals), *Zoku Shingon-shū zensho* (hereafter *ZSZ*) 1, by Jōgon (浄嚴, 1639–1702).

*Shoki honjō roku* (Catalog of the ritual manuals received), *ZSZ* 3, by Shinjō (真常, 1719–1802).

*Shōrai mokuroku* (A list of texts and items brought from China, also *Goshōrai mokuroku*), *TKZ* 1.1–39, by Kūkai, 806 (Daidō 1.10.22, age 33).

*Smaller Sukhāvatīvyūha Sūtra*. Chinese translation: *Fo shuo Amituo jing*, *T*. 366, trans. Kumārajīva, 402.

*Susiddhikara*. Chinese translation: *Suxidijieluo jing*, *T*. 893, trans. Śubhakarasiṃha, 726.

*Suxidijielo gongyang fa* (Susiddhikara offering method), *T*. 894, trans, Śubhakarasiṃha.

*Takushō* (The Hirosawa-ryū collection), *T*. 2488, by Shūkaku (守覺, 1150–1202) based on the teachings of Kakuzei (覺成, 1126–1198).

*Wuchusemo yigui*. Full title: *Da weinu Wuchusemo yigui* (The ritual manual of Great Wrathful Ucchuṣma), *T*. 1225, trans. Amoghavajra.

*Wuliangshou yigui*. Full title: *Wuliangshou rulai xiu guanxing gongyang yigui* (The ritual manual on cultivating the visualization of and making offerings to Amitāyus Tathāgata), *T*. 930, trans. Amoghavajra.

*Wuwei sanzang chanyao* (Tripiṭaka Master Śubhakarasiṃha's essentials of Dhyāna), *T*. 917, ascribed to Śubhakarasiṃha.

*Zhunti jing*. Full title: *Fo shuo qijuzhi fomu Zhunti daming tuoluoni jing, guangxing fa fu* (The sūtra preached by the Buddha on the Great Vidya Dharaṇī of Cundī, mother of seven koṭīs of Buddhas, with an attached visualization practice), *T*. 1075, trans. Vajrabodhi.

*Zhenyuan xinding shijiao lu* (Zhenyuan era new and definitive catalog of Śākyamuni's teachings), *T.* 2157, compiled by Yuanzhao (圓照), 800.

*Zhunti jing.* Full title: *Qijuzhi fomu suoshuo Zhunti tuoluoni jing* (The sūtra on the Dhāraṇī of Cundī, preached by the mother of seven koṭīs of Buddha), *T.* 1076, trans. Amoghavajra.

## Secondary Sources

Buswell, Robert E., Jr., and Donald S. Lopez Jr. *The Princeton Dictionary of Buddhism.* Princeton, NJ: Princeton University Press, 2014.

Fujita Kōtatsu. *Bonbun Muryōju-kyō, Bonbun Amida-kyō* (The larger and smaller Sukhāvatīvyūha sūtras). Kyoto: Hōzōkan, 2011.

Giebel, Rolf W. *Two Esoteric Sūtras.* Berkeley, CA: Numata Center for Buddhist Translation and Research, 2001.

Hatta, Yukio. *Shingon jiten* (Mantra encyclopedia). Tokyo: Hirakawa Shuppansha, 1985.

Orzech, Charles D. "A Tang Esoteric Manual for Rebirth in the Pure Land: Rites of Contemplation of and Offerings to Amitāyus Tathāgata." In *Path of No Path: Contemporary Studies in Pure Land Buddhism Honoring Roger Corless*, edited by Richard K. Payne. Berkeley, CA: Institute of Buddhist Studies and Numata Center for Buddhist Translation and Research, 2009.

Takagi, Shingen, and Thomas Eijō Dreitlein. *Kūkai on the Philosophy of Language.* Tokyo: Keio University Press, 2010.

# Chapter 4

# Dōhan's *Compendium on the Secret Contemplation of Buddha*, Fascicle One

Aaron P. Proffitt

## Translator's Introduction

The *Himitsu nenbutsu shō* (Compendium on the secret contemplation of Buddha), made up of three fascicles, was written by the Kōyasan scholar-monk Dōhan (道範, 1178–1252) around 1223 or 1224. During his lifetime, Dōhan was a well-known scholar of the works of Kōbō Daishi Kūkai (774–835), the monk commonly regarded as the founder of the Shingon School of Japanese Esoteric Buddhism. In addition to his scholarship on Kūkai and East Asian Esoteric Buddhist texts, Dōhan was also well-versed in Tendai, Kegon, Hossō, and Sanron, and he even wrote about the early Zen and Pure Land movements of his day. The *Himitsu nenbutsu shō* represents Dōhan's attempt to account for the diversity of approaches to Pure Land rebirth within the context of late twelfth- to early thirteenth-century Japan. Even though Pure Land Buddhism and Esoteric Buddhism are often thought to function as two mutually exclusive spheres of activity, through the study of this text in its broader ritual and soteriological contexts, a more complex picture emerges.[1]

Pure Land thought and practice was a major area of concern for Shingon thinkers in Japan during Dōhan's lifetime. Dōhan entered the priesthood at the age of fourteen at the Kōyasan temple Shōchi-in, under the direction of Myōnin (1148–1229). The central object of devotion (*honzon*) at Shōchi-in is the Buddha Amitābha. Dōhan also studied at Daigoji, and under Shukaku Hōshinnō (1150–1202)[2] of Ninnaji, both major temples associated with the imperial family and the lineage of Kūkai. Like Shōchi-in, Ninnaji also possesses Amitābha as its central object of devotion. Later, Dōhan returned to Kōyasan and studied under a monk named Kenchō (?–1202) at Hōkō-in. Myōnin and Kenchō studied under the same master, and both of their temples had as their central object of devotion the Buddha Amitābha.

Dōhan also studied under Kakukai (1142–1223) of the Keō-in temple on Kōyasan and Jōhen (1166–1224) of Kyoto's Zenrinji, who relocated to Kōyasan toward the end of his life. Kakukai was an early critic of the Pure Land movement and emphasized the non-duality of this world and the pure land,[3] taking a position that might be considered more in line with the present-day Shingon School orthodoxy. Jōhen, an important scholar of Kūkai's works, on the other hand, while initially a critic of the Pure Land movement, was later inspired by Hōnen's *Senchaku hongan nenbutsu shū* (*T.* 2608), which he purportedly received from Hōnen's disciple Ryūkan (1148–1227),[4] and wrote a "continuation" of Honen's famous text, the *Zoku senchaku mongi yōshō*.[5] I would suggest that Dōhan's *Himitsu nenbutsu shō*, written close to the time of the deaths of both Kakukai and Jōhen, may represent Dōhan's attempt to encompass the "Esoteric Pure Land" thought of his two most influential teachers.

Arguably the most significant event in Dōhan's monastic career was his exile to Sanuki on the island of Shikoku (present-day Kagawa Prefecture) after a dispute between Daidenbō-in and Kongōguji factions on Kōyasan turned violent. In 1243, Dōhan and a number of high-ranking scholars and administrators associated with the Kongōbuji side were found guilty by the *bakufu* (samurai government) court at Rokuhara and exiled. Dōhan took up residence at Zentsūji, a temple built at the purported birthplace of Kūkai, and recorded his time in exile in the *Nankai rurōki*,[6] a diary in which Dōhan employs mixed *kanbun-kana* (using Chinese and Japanese script). Dōhan's dual devotion to Kūkai as a bodhisattva-like savior and Amitābha Buddha are represented in this diary as well. While based in Zentsūji, Dōhan made pilgrimage to sites associated with the early biography of Kūkai, and upon hearing that Hōshō (d. 1245), his close associate with whom he studied under Kakukai, had died in exile, Dōhan performed a fifty-day-long Amitābha fire ritual, *Amida goma*,[7] resulting in a vision of Amitābha.

Dōhan was a prolific scholar who composed many commentaries, subcommentaries, lectures, and treatises and was an active ritual master. Therefore, his *Himitsu nenbutsu shō* must be situated within his broader oeuvre and ritual career. Dōhan wrote on the works of Kūkai, including the *Shakumakaenron ōkyōshō* (*T.* 2288),[8] *Hizōhōyaku mondanshō*,[9] *Sokushin jōbutsugi kikigaki*,[10] *Shōji jissōgi shō*,[11] *Hannya shingyō hiken kaihō shō*,[12] *Kongōchōgyō kaidai kanchū*,[13] and so on. Other works on the major texts now associated with the East Asian Esoteric Buddhist tradition include *Jōōshō* (*T.* 2447),[14] *Yugikyō kuketsu*,[15] *Dainichikyōsho joanshō*,[16] *Dainichikyōsho henmyō shō*,[17] *Bodaishinron dangiki*.[18] Dōhan also composed shorter works on Shingon practice, such as the *Dōhan shōsoku*,[19] *Aun gōkan*,[20] *Shoshin tongaku shō*,[21] *Kōmyō shingon shijū shaku*,[22] *Unjigi shakukanchū shō*,[23] *Dōhan nikka rinjū higi*,[24] and *Rinjū yōshin ji*.[25]

## The *Himitsu Nenbutsu Shō*

The *Himitsu nenbutsu shō* constitutes an effort by Dōhan to consider the diversity of approaches to Pure Land rebirth during his time, focusing in particular upon the recitation of the name of Amitābha Buddha, or *nenbutsu* (*nianfo*): "Namu Amida Butsu." This text also actively engages such questions as the relationship between this world and the Pure Land Sukhāvatī (Jile jingtu; Gokuraku jōdo) and the nature of the Buddha Amitābha and this Buddha's relationship to the Buddhist practitioner. While focused on Dōhan's vision of the mantra practitioner (*shingon gyōnin*) and devotion to the cult of Kōbō Daishi Kūkai, Dōhan also drew upon the works of Chinese thinkers like Shandao (613–681), Zhiyi (538–597) and Yuanzhao (1048–1116), and Japanese thinkers like Annen (841–915?), Kakuban (1095–1143), Jōhen (1165–1223), Jippan (d. 1144), and so on.

It is often the case that scholars of Esoteric Buddhism or Pure Land Buddhism employ contemporary sectarianism in their interpretation of premodern Buddhism. The *Himitsu nenbutsu shō*, however, frustrates such efforts. Dōhan's view of the *nenbutsu* is not the syncretism of Pure Land and Esoteric Buddhisms, nor is it merely the Shingon School's orthodox view of Pure Land practice. Rather, as I have argued elsewhere, Dōhan's view may be better understood as a *kenmitsu nenbutsu*, a perspective that accounts for the diversity of "revealed" and "hidden" (exoteric and esoteric) meanings present within the *nenbutsu*.[26]

Dōhan upholds the notion that all Buddhas are expressions of one ultimate reality, the dharmakāya (*fashen*; *hōsshin*), represented in the form of the Buddha Mahāvairocana, and that all buddha lands ("pure lands") are dimensions of the pure land of Mahāvairocana, the *mitsugon jōdo*, or "Pure Land of Mystical Splendor." The Buddha Amitābha is therefore conceived as one modality of this cosmic reality working to guide beings to awakening, a modality that is simultaneously rooted in the subjective and physical realities of beings.

The *nenbutsu* is the vehicle by which the Buddha Amitābha works within the world. Through a detailed exegesis of the three- and five-syllable *nenbutsu*-mantra, *A-MI-TA* and *NAMO-A-MI-TA-BU*, written in the

Sanskrit script known as Siddhaṃ (*shittan*),[27] Dōhan states that the mystery of speech (*kumitsu*), wherein the speech acts of sentient beings are revealed to be the speech acts of the Buddha, was chosen by Amitābha because it encompasses the very body-mind of sentient beings. The *nenbutsu* is the organs of speech (throat, tongue, lips = A-MI-TA) and the vital breath that makes life and speech possible. Through the mystical union of *nenbutsu*/speech/breath, speech is reinscribed, encompassing body and mind, just as the *nenbutsu* collapses the binaries between enlightened buddhas and ordinary beings, awakening and illusion, self and other, the pure land and saṃsāra, and so on. Each pair stands together in a productive tension, unified in a single reality, but in this unification difference is not necessarily negated.

Scholars have often viewed "Esoteric Pure Land" thinkers as "syncretizing" Esoteric Buddhism and Pure Land Buddhism. Others, however, recognize that Pure Land thought and practice are a major part of Japanese Shingon and Esoteric Buddhism more broadly and argue that Dōhan, Kakuban, and others represent the Shingon School's orthodox stance on Pure Land. Both perspectives, however, are to be found lacking because Esoteric Buddhism and Pure Land Buddhism had not by this time come to be imagined as two distinct "kinds," sects, or schools of Buddhism. Rather, during Dōhan's time various doctrinal and ritual lineages were interwoven and competed with one another through the simultaneous study of multiple areas of specialization (*kengaku*), including mastery of "Esoteric" rituals for "this worldly benefits" (*genze riyaku*) and the purification past karmic deeds, up to and including the attainment of rebirth in the pure land of a Buddha, and even buddhahood. In other words, "Esoteric Buddhism" and "Pure Land Buddhism" functioned as overlapping and fluid areas of concern and specialization within a heterogeneous East Asian Mahāyāna Buddhist environment. This is the intellectual, ritual, and soteriological context within which the *Himitsu nenbutsu shō* should be read.

## Manuscripts and Print Editions

There are several printed versions of the *Himitsu nenbutsu shō*, but according to the *Nihon Bukkyō tenseki daijiten*,[28] while it is not clear whether or not an original version still exists, a manuscript version (*shahon*) may be found in the archive of Hōjō-in temple on Kōyasan dating from 1606 (Keichō 11), and printed editions (*kanpon*) dating from 1645 (Shōhō 2, the first printed edition), 1686 (Jōkyō 3), and 1907 (Meiji 40) are also in circulation.

At present, the most authoritative edited *kanbun* edition of the first fascicle is Takeuchi Kōzen, "Dōhan cho, 'Himitsu nenbutsu shō,' honbun kōtei (ichi)," *Kōyasan daigaku ronsō* 20 (1985): 13–71, which was edited based on the Jimyō-in edition, dating from the Muromachi period (1392–1573), as well as editions from 1548 (Tenmon 17), and the Hōjō-in version. This *kanbun* edition was used to produce a classical Japanese version by the *Himitsu nenbutsu shō kenkyūkai,* ed., "Dōhan cho 'Himitsu nenbutsu shō' no kenkyū—honbun kōtei to kaki kudashi gochū," *Buzan gakuhō* 39 (1996): 105–131. Both Takeuchi and the "Buzan-ha" edition note the existence of an early version titled *Amidajō* dating from 1391 (Meitoku 2). This edition, however, is identified by the Buzan-ha *Himitsu nenbutsu shō kenkyūkai* as belonging to Hōbodai-in, while Takeuchi identifies it as being held at Tōji Kanchi-in.

Other versions may be found at the Eizan bunko archive, dating from 1616 (Genwa 2). The *Kokusho sōmokuroku,* vol. 6, indicates that editions dating from early and mid-Tokugawa may be found in the archives of Ryūkoku University, Ōtani University, Kōyasan University, Taishō University, Tōyō University, and so on.

More recently published versions may also be found in *Dai Nippon Bukkyō zenshō* (*DNBZ*), 70:51–82, *Zoku jōdoshū zenshō* (*ZJZ*), 15:79–110, and *Shingonshū anjin zensho* (*SAZ*), 2:225–266. Among these, the *SAZ* edition has been recognized as most authoritative, as evidenced by its usage as the base text by the Buzan-ha edition. For the translation of fascicle one that follows, I have referenced the versions produced by Takeuchi, Buzan-ha, *SAZ, DNBZ,* and *ZJZ,* but I have largely followed the *SAZ.*

## Description of Fascicle One

The *Himitsu nenbutsu shō*'s three fascicles are divided into a number of subsections. Here I will provide a brief description of the subsections of fascicle one so that the reader may acquire a general picture, before reading the translation below.[29] The *Himitsu nenbutsu shō* follows a question-and-answer (*mondō*) format, with Dōhan engaging a hypothetical interlocutor. Dōhan employed this writing style in his work training students in debate contests on Kōyasan and in Kyoto, and many of his extant works were clearly composed for an educational context.[30]

### *On the Name*

Dōhan begins with a rhetorical question: "Why is it that virtually all monks in the present age rely upon the *nenbutsu*?" Dōhan answers with a four-fold secret explication (*shijū hissaku*) on the nature of Amitābha Buddha and how this Buddha relates to various sutras and practices in the Mahāyāna tradition. Ultimately, Dōhan suggests that the true nature of the Buddha Amitābha, as well as the *nenbutsu* and the pure land, is revealed to abide within the body-mind of ordinary beings.

Drawing upon Jippan's *Byōchū shugyōki,*[31] Dōhan investigates the inner meaning of the three letters of the name *A-MI-TA*. This exegetical technique is known as *Amida-santai-setsu,* or "explanation of the three truths of *A-MI-TA*." Stone and Sueki have examined this practice, noting that it constitutes an early form of Tendai *hongaku,* "original enlightenment" thought.[32] The three syllables of the name of the Buddha are used to explain the relationship between the "three truths": *kū, ke, chū,* or emptiness, provisionality, and the middle, respectively. The three truths are part of the foundation of Chinese Tiantai and Japanese Tendai thought, exerting considerable influence in medieval Japan. Dōhan begins with an explanation of the Contemplation of the Letter *A* (*ajikan*), a central contemplative practice in the Shingon tradition. The Sanskrit syllable "A" signifies the original non-arising of all *dharmas* as well as *śūnyatā,* or emptiness, the concept that all things lack an inherent unchanging essence. "A" initially corresponds to emptiness, the "MI" corresponds to the non-duality of ultimate and provisional realities, the so-called "middle path," and "TA" corresponds to the provisional reality. Using this three truths structure, Dōhan establishes that A-MI-TA as well correspond to the three bodies of the Buddha, the relationship between buddhas and beings, this world and the pure land, and so on. In this way, dualistic views (this world and the pure land are distinct) and nondualist views (this world and the pure land are one) are placed in productive tension with one another.[33]

Next, Dōhan employs a five-syllable *nenbutsu* "maṇḍala," with *NAMO* in the center, and the Sanskrit syllables *A-MI-TA-BU,* in the four directions (*A* in the bottom position, and progressing clockwise). Here again, each syllable is used in a complex system of correspondences, encompassing the five buddhas, the forms of wisdom associated with each buddha, the five elements, five hindrances, and so on. Dōhan argues that even the various afflictions associated with the human condition are fundamentally oriented toward the wisdom of the buddhas. In other words, the "base" faculties are not simply flaws, but seeds that will grow into expressions of the highest wisdom.[34]

### *On the Primordial Vow of the Calling of the Name*

In the next section, Dōhan begins by asking why the Buddha chose the *nenbutsu* as the object of his "primal vow." According to Dōhan, because the *nenbutsu* is an act of speech, it is an expression of the "mystery of speech" (*gomitsu*). Drawing upon the *Amida santai setsu* again, Dōhan notes that because speech occupies the middle position between the mysteries of body and mind (*shinmitsu* and *imitsu*, respectively), it is through speech that they are unified. Likewise, Amitābha Buddha unifies Śākyamuni and Mahāvairocana, just as the pure land serves as the bridge between saṃsāra and the *mitsugon jōdo*.[35]

### *On the* Nenbutsu Samādhi

In the next section, Dōhan examines the *nenbutsu samādhi* (*nenbutsu sanmai*), first systematized by Chinese Tiantai and Japanese Tendai thinkers. By Dōhan's time, the *nenbutsu samādhi* had become an important form of practice on Kōyasan and other major monastic centers. In this section, Dōhan reveals new layers to the *nenbutsu samādhi*, that the Buddha Amitābha permeates all corners of the universe like a divine wind. This breath-wind is the vital breath that sustains and enlivens all sentient beings and creates the potential for speech: the *nenbutsu*. Dōhan also argues against distinguishing between the so-called vocal and meditative *nenbutsu*, based on this notion that the true *nenbutsu* is inextricably linked to the very life force of sentient beings.[36]

### *On the Ten-Thought Moments*

In the next section, Dōhan considers the "ten-thought moments," the ten utterances of "Namu Amida Butsu" said to render pure land rebirth possible. According to the *Sukhāvatīvyūha sūtra*, the Dharmakāra Bodhisattva vowed that if sentient beings think upon him or call his name even ten times, they will be reborn in his pure land. The "ten-thought moments" are discussed also in the *Contemplation Sūtra*.[37] Dōhan uses the "ten-thought moments" as an exegetical tool for re-evaluating the relationship between practice and attainment. Ultimately, the ten-thought moments are but one moment, the initial aspiration for awakening. Furthermore, the ten bodhisattva stages are likewise collapsed. There is neither high nor low. The first stage, the initial aspiration for awakening, or even one moment of Buddha contemplation, are fundamentally equal to the attainment of buddhahood itself.[38]

## Translation

*The Compendium on the Secret Contemplation of Buddha*

This should not be shown to those
who have not yet received *abhiṣeka*[39]

Śramaṇa Dōhan (1179–1252)
of Vajra Peak Temple [Kongōbuji]

### On the Name[40]

Question: It is widely known that these days among practitioners of mantra and *śamatha-vipaśyanā*[41] there are many who rely upon the practice of chanting the name of Amitābha hoping to be reborn in Sukhāvatī. As for the [widely practiced] *nenbutsu samādhi,*[42] it does not depend upon the various conditions of time or place [into which sentient beings are born, and may thus be cultivated by all].[43] But why have so many taken refuge in the primal vow? Is it perhaps because [the *nenbutsu*] is an easy practice that possesses the virtues of uninterrupted cultivation? Or is it perhaps that the chanting of the name has superficial and profound, apparent and hidden meanings?

Answer: Practitioners of *śamatha-vipaśyanā* rely in particular upon the *nenbutsu samādhi* of the four-fold *samādhi* [described within] the *Mohezhiguan* (*T.* 1911), and their main practice is the chanting of the name of Amitābha.[44] [In addition] the practitioner of mantra employs the purport of this four-fold secret explication[45] in their contemplative cultivation of the buddha bodies, names, and lands, etc.:

One, long ago, before the Buddha Amitābha attained awakening, he first set out on the [Buddhist] path as King Araṇemin,[46] giving rise to the mind that seeks enlightenment before the Buddha Ratnagarbha.[47] Then, as the *bhikṣu* Dharmākara he made the forty-eight vows before the Buddha Lokeśvararāja. Having become a Buddha as a result of these vows, he is thus called Amitābha. These and other things are explained in the *Karuṇā-puṇḍarīka sūtra* (*T.* 157)[48] and the *Contemplation Sūtra* (*T.* 365), among others. This may be regarded as the shallow-abbreviated [meaning].

Two, the Buddha Amitābha, is among the manifold virtues of the universal gate of the Dharmakāya Mahāvairocana. In the *Vajradhātu-maṇḍala*, he is recognized among the five wisdoms as the wisdom of sublime discernment,[49] and within the eight petals of the *Mahākaruṇā-garbhodbhava-maṇḍala*,[50] he is understood to be the gate of realizing awakening, as is explained in the two great sutras [*Mahāvairocana sūtra* (*T.* 848)[51] and *Vajraśekhara sūtra* (*T.* 874)[52]]. This may be taken to be the deep secret [meaning]. In general, within the exoteric teachings, the buddhas of the ten directions are produced of the bodhisattva's practice and awakening. In the mantra path, the *tathāgatas* of the ten directions and the fourfold *maṇḍala*[53] are the manifold virtues of the practitioner that are revealed and attained.

Three, the Buddha Amitābha, is the living wisdom[54] of Mahāvairocana Dharmakāya, ever abiding in the three worlds [of past, present, and future]. This is called "Limitless Life" (Amitāyus). Therefore, Amitābha is none other than Mahāvairocana. One gate is all gates. This may be taken to be the secret within the deep secret.

Four, the Buddha Amitābha is realized to be the true nature of the body-mind of all sentient beings, the essentially pure, perfectly bright, embodiment of the wisdom that sees all things as equal. That which is referred to as the eight-petal heart lotus of sentient beings[55] is the three-point *maṇḍala* of Amitābha.[56] Though submerged in the muck of ignorance, [this enlightened mind] is neither defiled nor hidden. Though revealed by the Buddha's light of initial awakening, it is neither arisen nor made manifest. In the past, present, and future, it is unchanging. The manifold virtues are thusly steadfast. This may be taken as the deepest secret within the deep secret.

When contemplating the name of Amitābha, his land, etc., one should immerse one's thoughts deeply in the four levels. In the examination that follows, one should rely upon these four levels. In accordance with one's capacities, one may see that this deep and profound name is in fact a secret mantra.[57] Though it too is called "the chanted name" it is wholly different than the shallow understanding of the ordinary path.[58]

Jippan Shōnin's (d. 1144) *Byōchū shugyō ki*[59] states: "Using the empowerment[60] of the three mysteries,[61] attain [liberation through] *siddhi*.[62] One must assume the fundamental *mudrā* of the object of devotion, recite the fundamental mantra of that object of devotion, and in your mind contemplate the meaning of the mantra's characters.

"The character *A* is the essence of mantra.[63] The three doctrines [inherent in] the character *A* are emptiness, being, and original non-arising. You should contemplate the three meanings as [having] one essence, and take it to be the Dharma-body [the *dharma-kāya*, ultimate reality] of the object of worship. That Dharma-body is not different from one's very mind. That mind is the essence of the three meanings. In accordance with the mystery of emptiness, the obstructions [to rebirth in the pure land] that arise from the sins one has committed are extinguished in accordance with the teaching [of the Dharma]. In accordance with the mystery of substance, the pure land that is sought after is attained in accordance with the vow.

"That which is referred to as 'original non-arising' is none other than the middle way. [Through following] this middle way, the fixed characteristics of both the pure land and the obstruction of sin are 'nonexistent.'[64] Because there are no fixed characteristics, the practice is in accordance with principle. Because the practice accords with principle, the highest accomplishment is thusly attained. (Every day, one should practice like this three or four times.)

"Whenever there is free time, or during a time when your body is weak [from illness], one should arrange one's body in a reverential posture; this is regarded as the mystery of the body. The mouth intones the name of the object of worship; this should be regarded as the mystery of speech. Of all movements, there is not that which is not a *mudrā*. How much more so those reverential postures? Of all speech acts, there is not that which is not a mantra. How much more so the intoning of the name of [Amitābha] Buddha? The mind, relying upon the [deep] meaning of the name, is taken to be the mystery of mind. As for this [deep] meaning, the three characters of the Buddha's name [encompass] all mantras. If you understand the [fundamental] meaning of the name of [Amitābha Buddha], it means 'ambrosia' (*amṛta*), [because] the Buddha separates [beings] from all bile and poison, obstacles, and confusion, [so that they may] realize the cooling serenity of nirvana. Moreover, the Buddha causes sentient beings that keep this mantra in mind to [realize that they are non-dual with the Buddha]. This is called *amṛta*.

"If you rely upon the [inner] meaning of the characters, they constitute a three-character mantra. First, *A* is taken to be the essence. The rest is a developed exegesis.

*A* is the doctrine of non-arising, and is none other than the middle path.
*MI* is the self, and the doctrine of *jizai*.[65]
*TA* is suchness, and the doctrine of extinction.

"The manifold virtues of the Buddha's middle path of the unborn are free from all extremes: there is not 'this,' there is not 'that.' In the great-self of no-self,[66] there is not that which is not *jizai*. Upon being able to understand the *jizai* of no-self, the mind is awakened and grasps thusness. This is none other than extinction.

. . . .

"[Finally,] when the end [of one's life] has come, and one's eyes are beginning to close, abide in the meditative mudra of the object of worship, intone the name [of Amitābha Buddha], and with one mind, take refuge in the manifold virtues of the middle path."

Kakuban's (1095–1143) [*Gorinkujimyō himitsu shaku*] (*T.* 2514) states: "Practitioners of the mantra path, as for the Buddha's Name, '*NAMO AMITA* Buddha,'[67] do not establish a shallow understanding. If one enters the Mantra Gate,[68] all speech and all words are in all cases Mantra. How much more so the [mantra] *A-MI-TA*?"[69]

The *Mahāvairocana sūtra*, Fascicle Seven, states, "The *Vajraśekhara sūtra* explains that the lotus blossom eyes of Avalokiteśvara embody limitless adornments equal to that of all the buddhas."[70] (Take this passage as a model for how to understand the name of Amitābha.)

For the mantra practitioner, it is precisely the shallow [understanding] that penetrates [and is not separate from] the most profound secret, and it is precisely the easy [practice] that immediately attains [and is not separate from] awakening. Therefore,[71] the name of the Buddha in which monks and lay alike have taken refuge is none other than the primal vow of chanting Amitābha's name.

Question: What about the profound secret meaning of the name [of the Buddha]?

Answer: A mantra is something that in "one character can encompass one-thousand principles, and in its very form, realizes the thusness of dharmas."[72] Therefore, the name in three characters possesses countless virtues. That which is called the three characters of *A-MI-TA*, as described below, are like the *bija* mantras for the three divisions of [the maṇḍala]: Buddha, Vajra, and Lotus.[73]

*A* is the fundamentally uncreated middle way, it is therefore the Buddha division.
*MI* is the ungraspable meaning of the self. When the self is transcended it becomes the wisdom that beings and dharmas are both empty, it is therefore the Vajra division.
*TA* is the teaching of the ungraspable doctrine of suchness. This is the principle of thusness as fundamentally pure, it is therefore the Lotus division.

In general, regarding these three divisions [of the *maṇḍala*]:

The Lotus is the principle of originally pure self-nature.
The Vajra is indestructible wisdom.
The Buddha is the Dharma-body in which principle and wisdom are mutually joined.

Principle universally pervades all of existence, and is therefore taken to be wondrous being (the five elements: [earth, water, fire, wind, and space]). Wisdom severs the attachment to the [mistaken view that] self and dharmas possess "self," and is therefore taken to be true emptiness. ([the sixth] element: consciousness) In the Buddha division [of the maṇḍala], principle and wisdom, being and emptiness, are wholly embodied, and it may therefore be taken to be the Middle Way. For this reason, *A*, *MI*, and *TA*, are also the three truths.[74]
. . . .
Also, the three divisions [of the *maṇḍala* (Buddha, Vajra, Lotus)] are none other than the Three Bodies of Dharma-body, reward-body, and response-body.
The Buddha division may be taken to be the response body. This is because meditation and wisdom are non-dual, and principle and wisdom [or reality and knowing reality] are bound to one another. (*A*)
The Vajra division may be taken as the reward-body. This is because of the wisdom of the emptiness of beings and dharmas. (*MI*)

The Lotus division may be taken as the Dharma-body. This is because of the principle of the fundamentally pure self-nature. (*TA*)

Also, these three characters correspond to the dharma-reward-response [bodies].
*A* is the principle of original non-arising, and may therefore be taken to be the Dharma-body.
*MI* is the wisdom of great emptiness, and may therefore be taken to be the reward-body.
*TA* is thusness, and may therefore be taken to be the response-body. In this way it possesses the meaning of establishing a connection with the response [body].

Also, these three letters may be taken to represent the three points [principle, wisdom, and phenomena].
*A* may be taken as the Dharma-body, this is because it represents the principle that universally [penetrates] every corner [of the universe].
*MI* may be taken as wisdom, this is because it represents the wisdom that is indestructible like a vajra.
*TA* may be taken as liberation.[75]
. . . .

Also, the three characters are the three mysteries [of body, speech, and mind].
*A*, and the Buddha division [of the *maṇḍala*], may therefore be taken to be the mystery of body.
*MI*, and the Vajra division, may therefore be taken to be the mystery of mind.
*TA*, and the Lotus division, may therefore be taken to be the mystery of speech.

These three characters are also the three jewels [of Buddha, Dharma, and Sangha].
*A* is the mystery of body, and may therefore be taken to be the Buddha jewel.
*MI* is the mystery of mind, and may therefore be taken to be the Sangha jewel.
*TA* is the mystery of speech, and may therefore be taken to be the Dharma jewel.
. . . .

These three characters may also be taken to be the three [forms of] wisdom.
*A* is unimpeded wisdom, the wisdom of [realizing] that initial and inherent awakening are not two. (Middle.)
*MI* is all knowing wisdom, the wisdom of initial awakening. (Emptiness.)
*TA* is the wisdom of spontaneous arising, the wisdom of inherent awakening. (Being).

These three characters are also the three organs of speech: throat, tongue, and lips.[76]
*A* is the throat, which is none other than the voice of the Buddha division [of the *maṇḍala*].
*MI* is the lips, which are none other than the voice of the Vajra division.
*TA* is the tongue, which is none other than the voice of the Lotus division.
. . . .
These also have an extremely deep meaning.

These three organs are the beginning, middle, and end of the voice's outward production.
*A* is the throat because it abides within the throat, having not yet arisen as speech.
*TA* is the tongue because it is produced by the tongue touching the roof of the mouth.
*MI* is the lips because it is produced by the meeting of the lips.
In this way, the order of throat, tongue, and lips [correspond] to the inner, middle, and outer [components] of the voice.
. . . .

These three characters are also the three honored ones of Sukhāvatī.
*A* is the Dharma-body and Amitābha.
*MI* is the reward-body and Avalokiteśvara.
*TA* is the response-body and Mahāsthāmaprāpta. Therefore, one Buddha is three honored ones, and the three honored ones are of one body.
. . . .

These three characters not only wholly embody nirvana and bodhi. They are also the true nature of *saṃsāra* and the afflictions. The three characters constitute the true nature of the three poisons [delusion, anger, and greed].

*A* is the true nature of delusion.
*MI* is the true nature of anger.
*TA* is the true nature of greed.

Greed is the attachment to favorable objects and is therefore the nature of being. This is the essence of the Tathāgata's great compassion and is of the same essence as the Lotus division and principle.

Anger is the rejection of unfavorable objects, and because it [expresses] the desire to do away with those phenomena, it is therefore the nature of emptiness. This is the nature of the Tathāgata's great wisdom and is of the same nature as the Vajra division and wisdom.

Delusion neither attaches to nor rejects the various objects of sense perception, being the nature of foolishness; for this reason it is of the same essence as the non-duality of the Buddha division [neither grasping nor rejecting].

For this reason, these three characters are the true nature of the three poisons. These three poisons are of the same essence as the three bodies [of the Buddha]. Therefore, by means of the causes and conditions [that give rise] to the chanting and contemplation of these three characters, the nature of "delusion is bodhi" is revealed. In this way, the three fundamental poisons of sentient beings [afflicting them] throughout beginningless transmigration are none other than the attainment of pure self-nature,[77] and the resultant virtues of the fundamental nature of the heart-lotus.

According to the [*Dale jin'gang bukong zhenshi sanmeiye jing banruo boluomiduo liqushi* (*T.* 1003) (hereafter the *Rishushaku*), drawing upon the *Dalejin'gangbukong zhenshisanmoye jing* (*T.* 243) (hereafter the *Rishukyō*)], "The attainment of pure self-nature is a level of the *maṇḍala*. The three gates establish the form of the three poisons and are established in the three gates of the *maṇḍala*. This northern gate establishes the form of the Lotus. This indicates the originally pure self-nature of the three poisons."[78]

These three characters are also the true nature of the three [evil] paths of the afflictions, karma, and suffering.
*A*, the Dharma-body, is therefore the [true nature of the] path of suffering.
*MI*, wisdom, is therefore the [true nature of the] path of the afflictions.
*TA*, liberation, is therefore the [true nature of the] path of karma.

The three paths have the meaning of the three points, which is the same as the Tendai interpretation, which is concerned with the nature of principle, the characteristics of phenomena. The three paths are the three characters, and the three characters are the three points, and therefore, the true virtue of "*saṃsāra* is none other than nirvana" is revealed within the *qi* [or "breath"] of the chanting of the name in three characters. The Buddha's intention in teaching about the attainment of pure land rebirth by those who have committed the [five] evil sins in the [*Contemplation Sūtra* (*T.* 365)[79]], and so on, is like this.

Also, the three characters not only universally pervade the world of sentient beings, but also the nonsentient grasses and trees. That which is referred to as the six elements become the four *maṇḍalas* and three types of worlds [sentient, insentient, enlightened].[80] Therefore, the collected aggregates and phenomenal world are composed of these six elements. [Moreover,] these six elements are the three mysteries.

Earth, water, and fire may be taken to be the mystery of body.
Wind[81] and space may be taken to be the mystery of speech.
The element of consciousness may be taken to be the mind.

According to the *Unjigi* (*T.* 2430): "The three mysteries of the Dharma-body may fit into something the size of a mustard seed, and yet they cannot be shrunken. They encompass the great void, and yet it cannot be expanded. They make no distinction between clay tiles and grasses and tree, nor the realms of humans, gods, hungry ghosts, or animals. There is nothing that is not illumined by them? There is nothing that they do not embrace? They are therefore known as *samādhi*. The three mysteries of the Dharma-body pervade the universe. There is not that which the three characters '*A-MI-TA*' do not reach."[82]

The body is the mudra, speech the mantra, and mind, the object of devotion.

This is the general outline of the inner and outer meaning of the three characters. If one were to explain in fine detail, even in the passing of a kalpa, it would be difficult to [explain] it fully

. . . .

Next, concerning the six characters of [the *nenbutsu*], *na-mu a-mi-da-butsu*, [I will here] reveal their meaning. These six characters [encompass] the five wisdoms and five buddhas, and so on.

In constructing this kind of *maṇḍala* for the mantras of all objects of devotion, use *OṂ* as the central dais.[83] This is common for all mentally constructed *maṇḍala*. *NA-MO* and *OṂ* both [serve as phrases for] taking refuge. Therefore, *NA-MO* is to be established in the central position. Moreover, in the [*Dainichikyō kaidai*,[84]] it says: "At the beginning of all sutras, before the two characters '*ru-shi*,' the two character *NA-MO* may appear, but the translators abbreviate this. If we follow the Sanskrit text, then these two characters *NA-MO* should be present."
The word Refuge (*ki-myō*) [is composed of two characters that together may be read as "return to life"]; this refers to the Buddha of Limitless Life. Refuge [includes as well] the one who relies [on the Buddha]. Limitless Life has the virtue of the eternally indestructible Dharma-body, and this body pervades the infinite space of the Dharma-realm. Its mind mixes in the

"Na-mo A-mi-ta-bu" in the Siddham script for writing Sanskrit mantras. From the Shōhō 2 (1645) edition of the *Himitsu nenbutsu shō*. Image courtesy of Ryūkoku University

essence and appearance of principle and phenomena. This body, this mind, where is it not present? What is not included in it? Therefore [taking refuge may be understood as returning to the source of life.]

For this reason one uses this refuge [*NAMO*] and establishes it on the central dais as the totality of the infinitely abiding life of the Dharma-body. The four wisdoms of the four directions return to this center, the fundamental basis for the Dharma-body of Limitless Life.

*A*, to the East [bottom position], gives rise to the bodhi mind and the wisdom [that is like a] great round mirror.
*MI*, to the South [left side], is the seventh consciousness, the self. East and Center are the harmonious unity of principle and wisdom, joined together in the noble one. This is the wisdom of the nature of equanimity.
*TA*, to the West [upper position] is the wisdom of the lotus of thusness [the wisdom of subtle discernment[85]].
*BU* [Buddha] in the North [right side] is the wisdom of the karma-body that performs actions.
. . . .
The [*Kongōchōkyō kaidai* (*T.* 2221)] elaborates: "The buddhas of the five wisdoms are all Tathāgatas. Gathering together all dharmas, they collectively constitute the bodies of these five buddhas, these five buddhas are seen to be the fundamental essence, the source of all the myriad buddhas, and the primordial origin of all dharmas."[86]

The [*Benkenmitsu nikyōron* (*T.* 2427) (hereafter, *Nikyōron*)], says: "The five wisdoms are the wisdoms attained by the five great [elements]."[87]

There are two explanations for the way in which the five elements may be taken to be the five wisdoms.

The first one takes earth as the middle, [followed by] wood (void) fire, metal (wind), water. The order is east, south, west, north [down, and clockwise]. This is the order according to five phases [Chinese five-phases (*wuxing*) theory]. The essence of wood is sky [or void], and the essence of metal is wind. (This is Amoghavajra's explanation, wherein earth may be taken as the center of the *maṇḍala*.)

And the second takes void as the center, [followed by] earth, water, fire, and wind. The order is north, west, south, and east [center, right, and counterclockwise]. This is the order of the Four Continents. (This is Śubhakarasiṃha's explanation.)

The five wisdoms and five buddhas are positioned according to these two explanations, with the same center, east, south, west, north [center, down, and clockwise], in the following order: Mahāvairocana, Akṣobhya, Ratnasaṃbhava, Amitābha, and Amoghasiddhi.

The five phases, the five elements, and moreover, the five sense faculties of all sentient beings, coursing without beginning through *saṃsāra,* are the five wisdoms and the five elements. Eye, ear, nose, tongue, and body correspond, in order, to wood, water, metal, fire, and earth. These are [also] the five wisdoms of hūṃ, aḥ, hrīḥ, traḥ, and vaṃ [the seed syllables of the five buddhas].

The five viscera within the body are also the five buddhas: liver, heart, spleen, lungs, kidney, corresponding, in order, to wood, fire, earth, metal, and water, which has the order of the five buddhas of the east, south, center, west, and north [respectively].

That which is bound to the five objects of perception is also the five wisdoms. The [perception of] form [or sight], sound, scent, flavor, and touch, correspond to wood, water, metal, fire, and earth.

The five wisdoms are distributed in the following way:

Perception of form/sight in the eastern direction is the wisdom like a perfectly round mirror, because myriad forms are reflected therein.

Sound in the northern direction is the wisdom of unencumbered accomplishment of all things, because it is the sound of the Dharma being preached like the heavenly drum and the conch shell.

Scent employs the power of the wind to be able to reach everywhere. This is in the western direction, the wisdom of the subtle discerning wisdom that has the meaning of preaching the Dharma, which is compared with fragrant wind. Therefore, fragrance and wind are together in the western direction.

Taste in the southern direction is the wisdom of equanimity, perceiving all things as being the same and having one taste.

Touch is the object of the bodily sense organs. The body employs the four faculties (site, sound, smell, taste), and feeling possesses the four great elements (earth, water, fire, wind). Touch may be taken as the center.

(As outlined above, the five wisdoms, the five viscera, and five phases are distributed in accordance with the explanation in the *Mohezhiguan*.[88] The five wisdoms, five buddhas, according to the Mantra teaching. Also, *kaji-shin*,[89] five accomplishments,[90] and five wisdoms, etc., are not included here because their meanings are manifold.)

The five sense fields give rise to the five desires, and the desires are related to the five objects of sense perception, which are also, in essence, the five wisdoms. They should be known in accordance with the realm of perception (referring to the previous section). Moreover, the five fundamental afflictions of the five faculties that are the cause of the suffering of beginningless transmigration in *saṃsāra* are also these five wisdoms.

That which is referred to as greed, anger, and ignorance, in the order of center, east, and south, are the three points, and the three wisdoms. Doubt is based in wisdom, and corresponds to the western direction (wisdom of subtle discrimination). Because pride is in its essence the ability to accomplish all things, it is in the north.

The activities of sentient beings that result in the five rebirths are also the embodiments of the five wisdoms.

The fruits of anger is hell.
Greed results in the preta realm.
Ignorance results in the animal realm.
Doubt results in the human realm.
Pride results in the heavenly realm.

The five wisdoms correspond to the above [mentioned] afflictions. In this way, the resultant virtues of the five wisdoms pervade all places, and therefore the six characters of the name also pervade the universe. This is because when these six characters are intoned, [it is equal to] the attainment of the manifold virtues of the five wisdoms, five buddhas, and so on. The manifestation of the innate virtues of "birth and death is nirvana," and "the afflictions are awakening," etc., should be understood in accordance with these three characters discussed above.

. . . .
The three characters grasp the doctrine of thirteen, revealing the thirteen pavilions of the *Mahākaruṇā-garbhodbhava maṇḍala*.[91] They also correspond to the [first] thirteen virtuous meditations of the [*Contemplation Sūtra*.][92] The six characters grasp the doctrine of nine, revealing the nine assemblies of the *Vajradhātu-maṇḍala* and the nine levels [of rebirth in the pure land] in the *Contemplation Sūtra*.[93]

However [just as] body and mind are non-dual, the [*maṇḍalas*] are of one essence. Therefore, the three characters [*A-MI-TA*] and the six characters [*NA-MO-A-MI-TA-BU*] together encompass the manifold virtues of the principle and wisdom of both *maṇḍalas*. . . .

The dual *maṇḍala* is all buddhas and bodhisattvas of the ten directions and three times [past, present, and future], the two vehicles,[94] eight [kinds of beings: *devas, nāgas, yakṣa, gandharva, asura, garuḍa, kiṃnara, mahoraga*], etc.,[95] and the round wheel of the ten worlds, inner realization and outer application, the perfectly round altar of the *dharma-dhatū*. This is because when one is chanting the name of one Buddha, [one is in fact] chanting the names of all the buddhas of the ten directions.

Therefore, the *Mahāvairocana sūtra* states, "The lotus eyes of Avalokiteśvara are equal to all buddhas."[96] Accordingly, the one name is taken up, and identified as the *kaji* of fundamental nature [which reveals the fundamental non-duality between buddhas and beings and that the mind of the Buddha is none other than the mind of sentient beings].

Tiantai [Zhiyi's] *Mohezhiguan* states, "When one chants [the name of] Amitābha, it is equal in virtue to chanting the names of the buddhas of ten directions. Solely take Amitābha to be the Lord of this Dharma gate."[97]

Also, according to [Kūkai's *Shōji jissō gi* (*T.* 2429)], the voice that intones the three characters or six characters is called *Voice* [*shō*]. The three or six characters, Amitābha Tathāgata, the three bodies, the name [received by the bodhisattva upon the attainment of awakening], the five wisdoms, [and so on are] called *Letter* [*ji*]. This is because the name is letter [or sign]. This *Voice-Letter* [*shōji*] is the embodiment of the buddhas and may be taken as *Reality* [*jissō*]. . . . This *Voice-Letter* is *Reality*. This is because intoning the *Voice-Letter* of the six characters is the embodiment of Tathāgata *Reality*. Therefore, the transformation-buddha that Shandao encountered within the *qi* ("breath") of his *nenbutsu* is the "truth-body," the *Voice* that is *Reality*. For this reason, [because the Buddha is fully present in the act of chanting his name] therefore, there is no sense in merely constructing a vision coming from the western direction.

Moreover, as for the meaning of the phrase, there are three levels of the translation of the name A-MI-TA. The first is called Limitless Life, this is the eternally abiding life of the Dharma-body. The second is called Limitless Light, this is the luminous [supernatural cognition] wisdom of the reward-body. The third is called Lord of Amṛta this is the response-body, whose teachings are like medicine. Moreover, as for the name Limitless Life, this possesses three bodies. This is like the Tendai scholar [Zhanran's (711–782) explanation in the *Fahua wenjuji* (*T.* 1719)] [based on Zhiyi's *Miaofa lianhuajing wenju* (*T.* 1718) (hereafter, *Hokke mongu*) commentary on the *Tathāgata's Lifespan* chapter (*T.* 262, 9.42a29) in the *Lotus Sūtra*.[98]]

Our tradition explains as well that Limitless Life has the meaning of inner realization and outer application.

The [*Dapiluzhena chengfo jingshu* (*T.* 1796; hereafter, *Dainichikyōsho*)] says, "In the western direction, contemplate [the Buddha] Limitless Life. This is the *upāya* wisdom of the Tathāgata. Because the realms of beings are without limit, therefore, the *upāya* of Buddha is also without end. For this reason, it is named 'Limitless Life.' This interpretation refers to the extent of the [Buddha's ability] to convert beings. This is called 'Limitless Life.'"[99]

The *Dainichikyō-kaidai* states, "[The Buddha of] Limitless Life, is the eternally indestructible virtue of the Dharma-body, whose body pervades the space of the universe and whose mind is mutually [inner] nature and [outer] characteristics of principle and phenomena."[100] According to this, inner realization is called "Limitless Life."

Exoteric scholars regard Amitābha as having a [limited lifespan, at the end of which he will be succeeded by his attendant bodhisattvas], and therefore, as a result they establish names that have limit, or do not have limit. This is the shallow, abbreviated, view.

There is also the deep and profound meaning, whereby Amitābha is taken to be the life force of sentient beings and called Limitless Life. Amitābha is referred to as the essence of the Lotus of the mysteries of speech. Therefore, the language and speech of beings of the six realms . . . and the sounds of the words of the enlightened and deluded beings of the ten realms, they are, without exception, in essence the *dharma-dhatū* of Amitābha. The sound and speech of [these beings], among the six elements, [may be taken to be] the element of wind, which is the in and out breath of all sentient beings. This "breath-wind" may be taken as the fundamental life force of sentient beings.

The *Mahāvairocana sūtra* explains, "life is that which is called wind (*prāṇa*)."[101] The [*Jin'gang fengluoge yiqie yujia yuqijing* (*T.* 867) (hereafter, *Sōōkyō*)] declares, "the fundamental basis of life is vajra."[102] In all cases, the breath-wind is taken to be the basis of life. Accordingly, Amitābha is the life of sentient beings, and taking the realms of beings to be without limit, he is called Limitless Life . . .

## On the Primal Vow of the Calling of the Name

Question: Why does this Buddha use the calling of the name for the primal vow?

Answer: This revered one is the Buddha of the mystery of speech within the universal gate of the three mysteries. Name is speech, and therefore [the Buddha] employs the chanting of the name [as the object of] the primal vow.

Question: As for this mystery of speech, what efficacy does it possess? What efficacy does the *nenbutsu* possess that this particular Buddha's name is taken to be the object of reverence for freeing oneself from birth and death and the attainment of awakening?

Answer: Speech possesses the efficacy of the middle way. This is because the middle way is the true road for entering the stage of the buddhas. That which is referred to as speech abides in the center of the three sites of karmic production [mental, vocal, physical], and is also endowed with the body and mind, prior and subsequent. Vocal utterances give rise to speech-karma, the movement of the tongue gives rise to bodily karma, and mental karma arises from the cogitation of the mind. ([This accords with the interpretation of] Jiaxiang (549–623) (aka Jizang, the Sanlun scholar). The body is something that can be seen and takes up space, and the mind is something that cannot be seen and takes up no space, and the voice cannot be seen and yet takes up space. Thus, the voice joins being and nonbeing, grasping both, yet ungrasped by either. It is nonbeing and yet not nonbeing. This is the meaning of the central [position of the mystery of speech].

According to [Kūkai's *Nikyōron*, where he quotes the *Sōōkyō*, aka, *Yugikyō*[103]], "That which is referred to as the indestructible vajra is extolled as the eternally abiding body, and that which is known as the mind of brilliant light is praised as the awakened virtue of the mind. That which is referred to as the palace is revealed to be the place where in turn the body and mind become both abode and that which abides [mind arising from body, and body arising from mind]. The middle, is the mystery of speech, which moreover has the significance of being unattached to either extreme."

According to the *Rishushaku,* "Take the mystery of speech to be the virtue of the middle."[104] The intent of this teaching is that the buddha-bodies and buddha-lands of the *tri-kāya* are the three mysteries.

Śākyamuni is the mystery of the body (the ordinary world).
Amitābha is the mystery of speech (the Pure Land Sukhāvatī).
Mahāvairocana is the mystery of mind (the Pure Land of Mystical Splendor).

This central Buddha Amitābha abides in the Pure Land [Sukhāvatī], [between] this [defiled] world and the Pure Land of Mystical Splendor, rescuing sentient beings from the muck of *saṃsāra* and [placing them on] the pure lotus dais of perfect quiescence. In this way, speech possesses the efficacy of the middle way, penetrating inner realization and outer application. In the [*Hokke mongu*], the notion of "abiding by the side of the gate" is explained as follows: "The practitioner of the perfect middle [way], arrives at the gate and correctly sees the *samādhi* of emptiness. The wisdom eye of the [path] of partial truth perceives but one side of the Dharma-body."[105]

. . . .

Question: Amitābha is the Buddha of the mystery of speech and therefore has taken the calling of the name as the primary object of devotion. However, what about those within this world who are deaf or unable to speak and cannot call upon the name; can they not attain awakening, or attain rebirth in that land?

Answer: If one considers the details closely, each of the three actions have the aspects of body, speech, and mind. As with the karma accrued from the act of murder, there is [karma accrued in body, speech, and mind]. In contemplative chanting, there is Lotus, Vajra, and Samādhi, and so on. Therefore, for those who lack the capacity to hear or speak, if they learn of the Primal Vow of the Buddha Amitābha, and in their minds rejoice deeply in great faith, and contemplate NAMU AMIDA BUTSU in their mind, this is precisely [the intent] of the term "vocal recitation." Because [vocal recitation] can grasp the karma of speech, the name takes speech to be its basis. In general, the three mysteries are used together. You should inquire into this further.

## On the *Nenbutsu Samādhi*

The *nenbutsu samādhi* has three levels:

First is the *samādhi* of the response-body. This is the first among the 84,000 Dharma gates of the many [exoteric teachings].[106] [In the *Avataṃsaka sūtra*] Sudhana received the *nenbutsu samādhi* from Meghaśrī bhikṣu.[107] This was the initial Dharma gate [that he attained].

Second is the *nenbutsu samādhi* of the reward-body. This is what is referred to as the *samādhi* of contemplating Amitābha Buddha and calling his name. In the [*Banzhou sanmei jing* (*T.* 418–419)] it says, "Whoever desires to be born in my land, if they constantly contemplate my name without rest, they will attain birth there."[108]

Third is the *nenbutsu samādhi* of the Dharma-body, the all-encompassing *dhāraṇī* gate. This is also called the mantra [gate]. There are many different kinds of mantra. [There are] the *dhāraṇī* in the sutras, the names [of buddhas and bodhisattvas] that may be used as mantras, single *bija* ("seed syllables") that may be used as mantra. In the [*Wuliangshou rulai guanxing gongyang yigui T.* 930[109]], and others, [it says that]: "through cultivation of the gate of the three mysteries, one attains the *nenbutsu samādhi*." This is the third: the *dhāraṇī* gate.[110]

However, these three kinds of *samādhi* are merely differences of teaching. In reality the name of Amitābha is a mantra, and therefore, the *samādhis* of chanting the name are in fact [forms of] the secret *dhāraṇī nenbutsu samādhi.*

. . . .

As for the pure bodhi mind, according to the *Mahāvairocana sūtra,*[111] "What is bodhi? It is truly knowing one's own mind as it is." The [*Dainichikyōsho*] states, "It is precisely that which reveals the place of the treasure of the Tathāgata's virtue. It is like if a person gives rise to the intention to open a treasure storehouse, but does not know where it is located, they will not progress [toward that goal]. For this reason, I will indicate again, [bodhi] is none other than the practitioner's very mind. If one truly knows one's mind, it is none other than the attainment of awakening immediately upon first giving rise to the mind that seeks awakening. By way of a metaphor, it is like the prodigal son of the householder [in the *Lotus Sūtra* (*T.* 262, 16b25–19a11)], from the moment the son recognized his father, how could he have been an impoverished guest again?"[112]

"To truly know one's mind" [means] to know that in fact one's very own mind is none other than bodhi. "One's [own] mind" is the heart-lotus. By means of the Lotus Samādhi, when this heart-lotus opens, the myriad virtues of the *maṇḍala* of the eight petals and nine objects of reverence are revealed and attained. [And this] is the awakening to the originally unborn nature of one's own mind, and this is called "bodhi." This is because the pure bodhi mind and the *nenbutsu samādhi* are unified ("yoga"). If one believes deeply in this way, one moment of mindful recollection and intoning of the name [of the Buddha] is none other than the opening of the inherent virtue of the lotus dais. Therefore, it is the attainment of awakening immediately upon the initial arousal of the mind that seeks awakening.[113]

Question: What is the difference between *shō* (intoning the name) and *nen* (mindful recollection, contemplation, of the name)?

Answer: Tiantai [Zhiyi's] *Mohezhiguan* states, ". . . with the voice, constantly intone the name of the Buddha Amitābha, and with the mind constantly contemplate the Buddha Amitābha, [and with the body, constantly embody the Buddha Amitābha[114]], or alternate chanting and contemplating together, or first contemplate and then chant, or first chant and then contemplate."[115] This is the difference between *shō* and *nen.*

According to the purport of Shandao's explication, ten-thought moments are ten vocal acts. This is the ordinary, or common teaching. The purport of the mantra teachings is that the three mysteries are equal, and universally pervade the *dharma-dhatū*. Because the three mysteries are bound together. The body is the embodiment of all three. Speech is the vocalization of all three. Mind is the conception of all three.

Therefore, in the [*Dainichikyōsho*], it says, "body is equal to speech, speech is equal to mind, thus, like the great ocean, they universally pervade all places, and together they are all of one taste. Therefore, they are called equal."[116]

The [*Mahāvairocana*] *sūtra* states, "Life is that which is called the wind."[117]

The [*Dainichikyōsho*] elaborates, "Wind is ideation, and ideation is contemplation."[118]

. . . .

In fact, when one [chants the name of the Buddha] with one mind, body-mind-speech are of one essence, therefore vocal recitation and contemplation are one. Though, according to this teaching, the three mysteries are equal and pervade all places, and therefore the three mysteries mutually embrace one another and are mixed, they not disordered. Therefore, vocal recitation and contemplation are the same but different. . . . . But, with the Amitābha *samādhi*, contemplation is vocal recitation; this is because Amitābha is the embodiment of voice-speech.

## On the Ten-Thought Moments

The *Hizōki* says, "According to the secret teaching, the accomplishment of ten-thought moments is [the same as] the full accomplishment of the ten perfections [of the bodhisattva path]. Or, to put it in more detail, the *Sūtra* states, 'through the accomplishment of ten-thought moments one may attain rebirth in the Western Pure Land, the land into which bodhisattvas of the first stage are born. The ten perfections are cultivated according to each stage, and completed according to each stage. Therefore, taking the accomplishment of the ten-thought moments as the grasping of the ten perfections, when one is born into the pure land, one will surely realize the tenth stage'

"For what reason is this land referred as a place where bodhisattvas of the first stage are born? The answer may be stated as follows: that which is referred to as the secret teaching is referred to as the 'horizontal teaching.' This is because between the first stage and tenth stage, there is neither high nor low. Therefore, it is only the doctrine of progression [or gradual enlightenment] that you [should] criticize. Regarding the exoteric teaching of progression through stages, according to the secret teaching, that which is referred to as the bodhisattva stages is [but] one's mind. It is the Dharma gate, the buddhas, the bodhisattvas. In general other teachings differ on these matters."[119]

Question: Regarding the matter of the ten-thought moments as it appears in the *Contemplation Sūtra,* therein, the ten-thought moments are said to result in rebirth in the lowest of the lowest grade [of the pure land]. Now, in the *Hizōki,* Sukhāvatī is generally taken to be the land into which bodhisattvas of the first stage are born. The ten-thought moments are taken to be the cause of this. According to the *Contemplation Sūtra,* the nine levels [are as follows], the upper division [levels 7–9] is for bodhisattvas, the middle division [4–6] is for those who believe in the two vehicles, and the lower division [1–3] is for ordinary beings. According to this, how [is one to understand] the similarities and differences between the *Contemplation Sūtra* and the *Hizōki*?

Answer: For the mantra practitioner, to be born into Sukhāvatī is the "first stage." In the [*Wuliangshou rulai guanxing gongyang*] *yigui,* it says, "Through this Dharma teaching, if one practices diligently with a focused mind, one will certainly be born in the highest level of the realm of Sukhāvatī and assuredly achieve the first stage."[120]

In our tradition, this "first stage" is the first stage of the fundamental stage of the *buddha-yāna.* This is different from the "stage of bliss" which is referred to [as the "first stage"] in the exoteric teachings because this "first stage" is none other than the stage of buddhahood itself. For this reason, in reality, in Sukhāvatī there is only the highest level of rebirth as the first stage.

. . . .

The ten-thought moments of birth in the lower level [may be understood to possess] the following three meanings:[121]

One, according to the superficial [reading], ten-thought moments may be taken to be [the cause of] the lowest stage [of rebirth].

Two, the people who receive rebirth in the lowest stage of the lowest level are those who have committed the extremely evil acts, and therefore, they enter the ten-thought moments of secret *aṃṛta*. This is the precious elixir [they require]. This accords with the explanation in the *Liuduji jing*.[122]

As explained in the [*Hizō*]*ki*, the secret [meaning] of the ten-thought moments may be taken to be the cause of the first stage, and in the [*Wuliangshou rulai guanxing gongyang*] *yigui* rebirth in the highest level in one lifetime, which is in contrast to the common interpretation of the nine levels. The subtle practice of mantra may be taken to be the highest level, and the highest level may be taken to be the teachings of the incomparable unsurpassable [truth]. [However,] that which is highest is not in opposition to the lower eight levels. Therefore, the *Hizōki* states, "abiding within the most wonderful bliss, it is therefore called Sukhāvatī"; this is its intended [meaning].[123]

Three, the nine levels [as described in the] *Contemplation Sūtra* in reality are all the true causes of the ten-thought moments. . . . The nine levels of the *Contemplation Sūtra* possess exoteric and esoteric, "horizontal and vertical" meanings. In the *Hizōki*, relying on the "horizontal (esoteric) teachings," the ten-thought moments may be taken to be the common cause of [rebirth in] Sukhāvatī, possessing bliss, it may be taken as the first stage. The superficial aspects of the *Contemplation Sūtra* explain the ten-thought moments to those of the lowest level in accordance with the vertical (exoteric) teaching.

[Fascicle 1 (*SAZ* Edition) ends here][124]

## Notes

This introduction to the translation of the first fascicle of the *Himitsu nenbutsu shō* is an adaptation and summary of sections of my dissertation. See Aaron P. Proffitt, "Mysteries of Speech and Breath: Dōhan's (1179–1252) *Himitsu nenbutsu shō* and Esoteric Pure Land Buddhism" (PhD diss., University of Michigan, 2015), introduction, esp. 1–12, 26–42; chap. VI, esp. 401–417. For a full description of all three fascicles that make up the *Himitsu nenbutsu shō*, see 414–428, and for further analysis of the contents of fascicle one, see 428–463. A fully annotated and unabridged version of fascicle one appears on pages pages 464–500, accompanied by the original *kanbun* text.

For further discussion of some of the major themes in the first fascicle, see also Aaron P. Proffitt, "Dōhan no himitsu nenbutsu shisō: Kenmitsu bunka to mikkyō jodokyō," *Journal of World Buddhist Cultures* 1 (2018): 117–138. This translation was completed thanks to generous support from the Fulbright Foundation. Thanks to Professor Eishō Nasu for his assistance in acquiring the "Na-mo A-mi-ta-bu" image and the Shōhō 2 (1645) edition of the *Himitsu nenbutsu shō.*

1 See: Proffitt, "Mysteries of Speech and Breath," 290–345, for a more sustained engagement with Dōhan's biography and the Esoteric Pure Land culture of medieval Kōyasan. Regarding Dōhan's prolific scholastic output, see 382–400.

2 Brian Ruppert, "Dharma Prince Shukaku and the Esoteric Buddhist Culture of Sacred Works (Shōgyō) in Medieval Japan," in *Esoteric Buddhism and the Tantras in East Asia,* ed. Charles D. Orzech, Henrik H. Sørensen, and Richard K. Payne (Leiden: Brill, 2011), 794–802.

3 Robert Morrell, "Shingon's Kakukai on the Immanence of the Pure Land," *Japanese Journal of Religious Studies* 11, no. 2–3 (1984): 195–220.

4 Nasu Kazuo, "Jōhen to Hōnen Jōdokyō," *Indogaku Bukkyōgaku kenkyū* 106 (2005): 80–85; Yamaguchi Shikyo, "Dōhan cho Himitsu nenbutsu shō no hihan taishō nitsuite," *Buzankyōgaku taikaikiyō* 30 (2002): 102–103.

5 Jōhen, *Zoku Senchaku mongi yōshō* (Tokyo: Kokusho Kankōkai, 1984).

6 *GR* (*Gunsho ruiju*) 19:468–476.

7 *GR* 19:472b–473a.

8 *T.* 2288; *BKD* (*Bussho kaisetsu daijiten*) 5:25b; *MD* 176c.

9 Mori Shigeki, ed., *Toganō korekushon kenmitsu tenseki monjo shūsei,* vol. 5 (Tokyo: Hirakawa shuppansha, 1981); *BKD* 9:110a; *MD* 1862a.

10 *ZSZ* (*Zoku Shingonshū zensho*) 17; *BKD* 7:76d; *ZSZ* 42:68

11 *SZ* (*Shingonshū zensho*) 14; *BKD* 5:401b–d, *MD* 403b; *SZ* 43:61; Nakamura Honnen, "'Shōjijissōgi shō' (Dōhan ki) ni tokareru nyogi gensetsu ni tsuite-sono ichi, 'Shaku makaen ron' to Kūkai no chosa ni miru nyogi gensetsu wo chūshin to shite," *Mikkyō bunka* 203 (1999): 1–20.

12 *ND* (*Nihon daizōkyō*) 10 (1916 edition), 20 (1975 edition); *BKD* 9:73d; *MD* 1836a.

13 *ZSZ* 7; *BKD* 3:478b; *ZSZ* 42:37; Nakamura Honnen, "Dōhan sen 'Kongōchōkyō kaidai kanchū' ni tsuite," *Kōyasan daigaku Mikkyō bunka kenkyūjo kiyō* 21 (2008): 29–52.

14 *T.* 77:2447; *BKD* 8:88b; *NBTD* (*Nihon bussho tenseki daijiten*) 386.

15 *SZ* 5; *ZSZ* 7 (*ZSZ* 42:40); *BKD* 11:84a, *NBTD* 525c–d; *MD* 2206b–c; *SZ* 43:11.

16 *BT* 19; *ZSZ* 5:1–97; *BKD* 5:287c; *BKD* 7:400c; *NBTD* 368b; *MD* 1516a; *ZSZ* 42:29–34.

17 *ZSZ* 5:99–444; *BKD* 7:403c; *NBTD* 369c; *MD* 1517b; *ZSZ* 42:34–35.

18 *ND* 24 (1916 edition), 47 (1975 edition); *BKD* 9:427d–428a; Nakamura Honnen, "Dōhan ki Bodaishinron dangiki ni tsuite," in *Mandara no shoos to bunka: Yoritomi Motohiro hakushi kanshiki kinen ronbunshū,* ed. Yoritomi Motohiro hakushi kanshiki kinen ronbunshū kankōka (Kyoto: Hōzōkan, 2005), 395–430.

19 *NKBT* (*Nihon koten bungaku taikei*) 83:76–83; translated in full by Pol Van den Broucke, "Dōhan's Letter on the Visualization of Syllable A," *Shingi Shingon kyōgaku no kenkyū* 10 (2002): 65–87, (as *Shōsoku ajikan*) *BKD* 5:346d.

20 Translated by Richard K. Payne, "Ajikan: Ritual and Meditation in the Shingon Tradition," in *Re-visioning "Kamakura" Buddhism,* edited by Richard K. Payne (Honolulu: University of Hawai'i Press, 1998), 232–233; based on the edition printed in Mitsuun, Moriyama Kamon, ed. *Ajikan hiketsushū* (Jōkō-in, 1912; repr., Moriyama Kamon, 2010), 19–20.

21 *SZ* 22; *BKD* 5:246c; *NBTD* 298; *MD* 1226c; *SZ* 43:142; Tanaka Hisao, "Dohan no Shoshin tongaku shō ni tsuite," *Nihon rekishi* 172 (1962): 87–89; Nakamura Honnen, "Dōhan ki Shoshintongaku shō ni tsuite," in *Mikkyō to shobunka no kōryū: Yamasaki Taikō kyōju koki kinen ronbunshū,* ed. (Kyoto: Bunkōdo, 1998), 151–184.

22 *SAZ* 2:74–81; *NBTD* 165; *BKD* 3:338c.

23 3 fasc., *SZ* 7; *BKD* 1:230a; *NBTD* 68.

24 *Mikkyō bunka kenkyūjo seikyō bunsho chosahan,* Kōyasan shinnō seikyō bunsho chosa gaiyō—suke, shiryō kaishō 'Dōhan nikka rinjū higi," *Kōyasan daigaku mikkyō bunka kenkyūjo kiyō* 16 (2003): 79–92.

25 1 fasc., *SAZ* 2:792–795; printed edition available at Kyoto University; 11:277c.

26 Proffitt, "Mysteries of Speech and Breath," 4, notes 7–8; I also suggest that the context wherein exoteric (revealed) and esoteric (secret) practices and doctrinal interpretations functioned together, allowing "multiple visions of reality . . . to stand together in a productive tension that is not necessarily resolved," 39. See also 401–402, 426–429.

27 Here and throughout the translation I have used capital Roman letters to rendered words and mantras that appear as Siddhaṃ in the source text.

28 *NBTD* (*Nakamura Kōsetsu Bukkyō daijiten*), 446.

29 *SAZ* 2:226–266.

30 Proffitt, "Mysteries of Speech and Breath," 346–400, esp. 382–400.

31 *SAZ* 2.

32 Proffitt, "Mysteries of Speech and Breath," 437 note 1403. For an examination of the Amida santai setsu see, Sueki Fumihiko, "Amida santai-setsu o megutte," *Indogaku Bukkyōgaku kenkyū* 28, no. 1 (Dec. 1979): 216–222; Jacqueline I. Stone, *Original Enlightenment and the Transformation of Medieval Japanese*

*Buddhism* (Honolulu: University of Hawai'i Press, 1999), 162; for an examination of Dōhan's views on the *nenbutsu*, see James Sanford, "Breath of Life: The Esoteric Nembutsu," in *Tantric Buddhism in East Asia*, ed. Richard Payne (Boston: Wisdom Publications, 2006), 177–179.

33 *SAZ* 2:226–231.

34 *SAZ* 2:231–235.

35 *SAZ* 2:235.

36 *SAZ* 2:235–237.

37 The ten-thought moments are discussed in the *Sukhāvatīvyūha sūtra* (*T.* 360, 268a26–28) and *Contemplation Sūtra* (*T.* 365, 346a18–20).

38 *SAZ* 2:237–238.

39 This line is omitted in the *DNBZ* edition.

40 *SAZ* 2:226.

41 *Shikan* (*zhiguan*) refers to the forms of meditation associated with the Tendai lineages, and scholars of Zhiyi's (538–597) *Mohezhiguan* (*T.* 1911; Makashikan). See *NKBD* 949.

42 By this time, the *nenbutsu samadhi* possessed a "tantric" connotation in Japan.

43 *NKBD* 571c.

44 *T.* 1911, 46.1a–140c, esp. 4a11–12, 12b24–25.

45 *Shishu hishaku* is an exegetical technique that Dōhan's uses to account for religious diversity, examining teachings believed to function on the shallow-abbreviated level, the deep secret level, the secret within the deep secret level, and the deepest secret within the deep secret level. The first level may be thought of as the literal understanding. The second is what we may think of as the preliminary esoteric level. The third level grasps the fundamental nature of dharmas. The fourth level reveals the fundamental reality of things as they are, and seems to redeem the first level. See *MD* (*Mikkyō Daijiten*), 931.

46 Ujitani Yūken, "Hikekyō no Amidabutsu honjō setsuwa," *Indogaku bukkyōgaku kenkyū* 33, no. 1 (1968): 74–80.

47 Ratnagarbha is the Buddha who inspired both Amitābha and Śākyamuni (*MBD*, 72c).

48 *T.* 157, 3.185a24–186a24, and so on.

49 Five wisdoms (*pañca-jñānāni*, *gochi*), five buddhas, etc.: (1) *Dharmadhātu-svabhāva-jñāna* (*hōkaitaishōchi*) is the wisdom that comprehends reality and all things in their essential nature as they truly are, and corresponds to Mahāvairocana in the Center, and the ninth consciousness, *amala-vijñāna*, or pure consciousness. (2) *Ādarśa-jñāna* (*daienkyōchi*) is wisdom that com-

prehends all things simultaneously like a great round mirror, and corresponds to Akṣobhya in the East, the eighth consciousness, *ālaya-vijñāna*, or store consciousness where experiences give rise to a unified consciousness. (3) *Samatā-jñāna* (*byōdōshōchi*) is the wisdom that perceives the inherent non-duality between all things, and corresponds to Ratnasaṃbhava, the seventh consciousness, *manas-vijñāna*, or the consciousness that gives rise to the erroneous sense of self. (4) *Pratyavekṣaṇā-jñāna* (*myōkanzatchi*) is the wisdom of subtle discrimination, and corresponds to Amitābha in the West, the sixth consciousness of mind *mano-vijñāna*, which unifies the five consciousnesses of eye, ear, nose, tongue, and body. (5) *Kṛtya-anuṣṭhāna-jñāna* is the wisdom to accomplish all things for the benefit of self and others, and corresponds to Amoghasiddhi in the north, the first five consciousnesses of eye, ear, nose, tongue, and body. See also Thomas Eijō Dreitlein and Takagi Shingen, *Kūkai on the Philosophy of Language* (Tokyo: Keio University Press, 2010), 361–362; *NKBD* 493b–c and *MD* 620c–621a.

50 *Vajradhātu-maṇḍala* (Kongōkai mandara), or Vajra Realm Maṇḍala, is one of two main maṇḍala in the Japanese Shingon tradition, the other one being the *Mahākaruṇā-garbhodbhava maṇḍala* (sometimes rendered as Garbhadhātu Maṇḍala, or "Womb Realm Maṇḍala") (Taizōkai mandara). These two *maṇḍalas* are understood to represent two non-dual aspects of reality, the fundamental Buddhahood of reality (Taizōkai), what actually exists, and the wisdom through which this reality is grasped (Kongōkai). See Dreitlein and Takagi, *Kūkai on the Philosophy of Language*, 374, 401–402, 356: Dharmakāya of Truth and Dharmakāya of Wisdom.

51 *T.* 848, *Darijing*, *Dainichikyō*, full title: *Mahāvairocanābhisaṃbodhi sūtra* (*Dapiluzhena chengfo shenbian jiachi jing*, *Daibirushana jōbutsu jinben kaji kyō*).

52 *Vajraśekhara sūtra* is a commonly used abbreviation for the longer Sanskrit title: *Sarva-tathāgata-tattva-saṃgrahaṃ nāma mahāyāna-sūtram*. This text was translated by Vajrabodhi (671–741) as *Jingangding yuqie zhong lüechu niansong jing* (*T.* 866), by Vajrabodhi's student Amoghavajra (705–774) as *Jingangding yiqie rulai zhenshi shedasheng xianzheng dajiaowang jing* (*T.* 874), and by Dānapāla (ca. early eleventh century) as *Yiqie rulai zhenshi shedasheng xianzheng sanmei jiaowangjing* (*T.* 882).

53 Four-fold Maṇḍala (*shishu mandara*) could be conceived as reality seen from four different perspectives: (1) *Mahā-maṇḍala* (*daimandara*) is constituted by all embodied beings composed by the five elements including all buddhas, bodhisattvas, gods, humans, etc., and the totality of all of the *maṇḍalas* below. (2) *Samaya-maṇḍala* (*sanmaya mandara*) is composed of the mudras and handheld implements of the buddhas and bodhisattvas and other beings in the *maṇḍala*, signifying their great vows. (3) *Dharma-maṇḍala* (*hō mandara*) signifies the inner realization of all buddhas and bodhisattvas and is represented by the Sanskrit seed-syllables, *bīja* (*shuji*), encompassing all of the

teachings of the buddhas up to and including all written and spoken speech. (4) *Karma-maṇḍala (katsuma mandara)* signifies the activities of buddhas and bodhisattvas in the world working toward the benefit of all beings, but also includes the activities of all beings as well. (*MD* 943b, 1024b–1026a; *NKBD* 664b; Dreitlein and Takagi, *Kukai on the Philosophy of Language*, 363–364).

54 *Emyō* 慧命 signifies that Buddha nature and life itself are connected (*NBD* 134a–b).

55 The chambers of the heart were traditionally believed to resemble the eight petals of the lotus. The spiritual heart and the physical heart are one and the same (*MD* 1818).

56 The *santen* may refer to the "three points of the Sanskrit letter 'I,'" which is written with three small circles in the form of a triangle. Because neither a horizontal nor vertical line may encompass them all, it signifies the multiplicity of reality, neither one, nor not one. In the *Mahāparinirvāṇa sūtra* (*T.* 374) it signifies the non-duality of *dharmakāya, prajñā, mokṣa*. See also Dōhan's *Dainichikyōsho henmyō shō* (*ZSZ* 5) and *Yugikyō kuketsu* (*SZ*) established a standard understanding of the non-dual relationship between principle 理, wisdom 智, and phenomena 事 (*NKBD* 598a; *MD* 817a, 58).

57 This passage is omitted in the *SAZ* edition: 常途念佛祖師。唯依初重意。立乘祕往生之義。大智律師等。雖立自性彌陀之義。是理性之一門。非事相之眞說。今眞言行人。具在四重祕意。顯密兼通。四身圓證。[As for the common path of the *nenbutsu* patriarchs and teachers, they rely only upon the intent of the first level, and establish the vehicle of the doctrine of the secret of going for rebirth. Vinaya Master Dazhi大智律師 [Yuanzhao 元照, aka Zhanran 湛然 (1048–1116)] and others, even though they establish the self-nature of Amitābha, this is the one gate of the essence of principle, but this is not the true teachings of phenomenon/ritual. The practitioners of mantra wholly inhabit the four-fold secret meaning, penetrate both the revealed and secret [teachings], and perfectly realize the four bodies [of the *dharmakāya*].] See *DNBZ* 51b.

58 *SAZ* 2:227.

59 *SAZ* 2.

60 Empowerment (*adhiṣṭhāna, jiachi, kaji*) achieved through yogic practice (union of body, speech, and mind) wherein one attains the abilities (*siddhi*) to harness the power of the Buddha through devotion and the attainment of the realization of one's fundamental always-already manifest non-duality with the Buddha. This response by the Buddha is referred to as "empowerment." This term has also at times been translated as "grace" (*MD* 234a–b; *NKBD* 203d–204a; Dreitlein and Takagi, *Kukai on the Philosophy of Language*, 346–347).

61 Three Mysteries (*sanmi*; *sanmitsu*) are realized through the coordinated practice of *mudrā* (body), mantra and *dhāraṇī* (speech), and visualization and contemplative practices with an object of devotion such as a buddha image or a *maṇḍala* (mind). Through this form of practice one realizes that the body, speech, and mind of beings (the three sources of karma, *sangō* (*MD* 788a), are in fact united with the body, speech, and mind of the particular object of reverence (such as Amitābha, or Śākyamuni) as well as the Dharma-body (ultimate reality) itself (*MD* 839b–840b).

62 "Accomplishment" (*siddhi*; *xidi*; *shijji*): it has long been noted that certain powers arise from the mastery of deep states of concentration. These "powers" or accomplishments are referred to as *siddhi*. While often associated with magic or supernormal powers (avoidance of disaster, good luck, acquisition of wealth, success in love, etc.), it is often the case that the power attained is the power to attain awakening, rebirth in a pure land, heaven, or the [Pure] Land of Mystical Splendor, *Mitsugon kokudo*, and ultimately, awakening (*MD* 984b–c).

63 The Sanskrit syllable *A* is an important object of reverence and contemplation in the Shingon tradition. A is the negative prefix in Sanskrit and the first letter of the alphabet. Contemplation of the character *A* (*ajikan*) is an important form of contemplative practice in Shingon Buddhism (Dreitlein and Takagi, *Kukai on the Philosophy of Language*, 344–345). Here, and throughout, *DNBZ* uses the Chinese characters *A-mi-da* 阿彌陀, while *SAZ* and other manuscripts use Siddhaṃ letters, *A-MI-TA*. To represent Siddhaṃ letters, I will be using capital Roman letters, as there is as of yet no standardized font available.

64 In the *DNBZ* edition, this four-character phrase appears before the preceding four character phrase as 定相浄土. Placement here seems correct when compared to following line.

65 *Jizai* 自在, which means something close to "sovereign," refers to the ability to accomplish tasks unimpeded. Having realized the fundamental emptiness of all things, one is able to do anything (*NKBD* 648a–b).

66 Kūkai discusses the concept of *muga daiga* ("the great self of nonself") in the *Hokke kaidai* (*T.* 2190, 56.182a01–04) and the *Dainichikyō kaidai* (*T.* 2211, 58.07a03–05).

67 *SAZ* has "*Namu Amita*," but the Buzan edition gives "*NAMO AMṚTA*."

68 *DNBZ* addition 門.

69 See *T.* 2514, 79:22b10–12. The reason Siddhaṃ is used here is to render each syllable of the *nenbutsu* as a mantra unto itself. In this way, the *nenbutsu* contains infinite meanings. See Kukai's commentary on the *Heart Sūtra*, *Hannya shingyō hiken ryakuchū* (*T.* 2203B), One character encompasses one thousand principles (*T.* 2203B.57.0018a08).

70 *T.* 848, 18.53c14–17.

71 *SAZ* 2:228.

72 *T.* 2203B.57.18a08.

73 Three divisions (*sanbu*), or three families, of the *Mahākaruṇā-garbhodbhava-maṇḍala* are: (1) Buddha division, led by Mahāvairocana and represented by the mystery of body, (2) Lotus division, led by Avalokiteśvara (who is closely connected with Amitābha) and represented by the mystery of speech; (3) Vajra division, led by Vajrapaṇi and represented by the mystery of mind. See Dreitlein and Takagi, *Kukai on the Philosophy of Language*, 396–397.

74 In the *Mohezhiguan* Zhiyi developed the three truths (*santai*) exegetical strategy as a way to imagine a position whereby Nāgārjuna's two truths (emptiness and provisionality, or ultimate and apparent reality) could be understood together: emptiness, provisionality, and the middle 空假中 (*ku-ke-chū*).

75 *SAZ* 2:229.

76 See *MD* 1695; see other related concepts through 1693–1697. See also Kukai *Shōjissōgi* (*T.* 2429, 77.0402b28).

77 *SAZ* 2:231.

78 While referencing *Dalejin'gangbukong zhenshisanmoye jing* (*T.* 243, 8.784c), the quote actually appears to come from the *Rishukyō* commentary, *Dale jingang bukong zhenshi sanmeiye jing banruo boluomiduo liqushi* (*T.* 1003, 19.612a10–b06).

79 *T.* 365, 12.341a25, 345b10–c, and 346a13.

80 *NKBD* 1004.

81 See also, Jippan's *Ajigi* (*T.* 2438, 77.0521a26).

82 *T.* 2430, 77.406c29–407a03; *TKDZ* 3:65, 10–12; Yoshito S. Hakeda, *Kūkai: Major Works. Translated with an Account of His Life and a Study of His Thought* (New York: Columbia University Press, 1972), 258–259.

83 *SAZ* 2: 232.

84 *T.* 2211, 58.3a6–8; *TKDZ* 4:34.

85 *Nyonyo rengechi*, another name for *Myōkanzatsuchi*; *MD* 1744.

86 *T.* 2221, 61.02c25–27; *TKDZ* 3:77–78.

87 *T.* 2427, 77.380b23; *TKDZ* 3:105.

88 *T.* 1911, 46.107a–108b.

89 *MD* 236 explains that the *kajishin* signifies the body of the *dharmakāya* that manifests for the benefit of sentient beings.

90 *MD* 607.

91 On the thirteen pavilions (*jūsan-in*) of the *Mahākaruṇā-garbhodbhava maṇḍala*, see: *MD* 863c.

92 The *Contemplation Sūtra* (*T.* 365) describes sixteen aspects of the pure land that one who intends on seeking rebirth there should contemplate: (1) the setting sun (*T.* 365, 12.341c27–342a06), (2) the water of the pure land (342a06–a23), (3) the land (342a23–b01), (4) the jeweled trees (342b01–b23), (5) the jeweled ponds (342b23–c06), (6) the jeweled towers (342c06–c14), (7) the lotus throne of the Buddha (342c14–343a18), (8) the marvelous body of the Buddha (343a18–b15), (9) the light of the Buddha (343b15–c12), (10) Avalokiteśvara Bodhisattva (343c12–344a18), (11) Mahāsthāmaprāpta Bodhisattva (344a18–b14), (12) envision your own rebirth in the pure land (344b14–24), (13) the extent of the Buddha's influence and various aspects of the pure land (344b24–c08), (14) beings of the highest capacity (344c09–345b07), (15) beings of middling capacities (345b08–c09), (16) beings of lower capacities (345c10–346a26).

93 On the nine assemblies of the *Vajra-dhatū-maṇḍala*, see *MD* 663–664, 668–669; The pure land is divided into three grades, each of which is divided into three levels, making nine levels total. See previous note.

94 Two vehicles: *śrāvakas* and *pratyekabuddhas*.

95 *NKBD* 1357.

96 *T.* 848, 18.53c14.

97 *T.* 1911, 46.12b22–24.

98 *T.* 1719, 34:328b. I would like to thank Robert Rhodes for helping me find this reference.

99 *T.* 1796, 39.622c20–23.

100 *T.* 2211, 58.6c15–17; *TKDZ* 4:35.

101 *T.* 848, 18.17b29.

102 *T.* 867, 18.267a03–04.

103 *Nikyōron* (*T.* 2427, 380a18–c01); *TKDZ* 3:104, quoting the *Sōōkyō* (*T.* 867, 18.253c19–254a17). See also Kūkai's *Himitsu mandara jūjūshinron* (*T.* 2425, 77.360c29–b09).

104 *T.* 1003, 19.608B3.

105 Passage notes Zhanran's commentary, but this quote actually comes from Zhiyi's text: *T.* 1718, 34.82b10–15: 見父之處者即是門側。二觀爲方便即門二邊。圓中之機當門正見。二乘偏眞故言門側。但空三昧偏眞慧眼。傍窺法身耳。遙見其父。正見有二種。一近見。二遠見。今言大機始發扣召事遠。是故言遙。又機微非應赴。名之爲遙也。*Tankū* 但空 (*NKBD* 1157), is contrasted with *fudankū* 不但空 (*NKBD* 1449). According to Tendai doctrine, the perfect middle path (*enchū* 圓中, *NKBD* 143) is able to perceive both the essential emptiness and being of things simultaneously. This text is quoting the famous *Lotus Sūtra* parable about the prodigal son who, upon seeing his father, becomes scared and runs from the middle path to the side of the gate.

Noticing this, the father dons humble robes so that he can reach out to his son. This illustrates the two teachings. Biased views are understood to perceive the truth from a limited perspective, and thus only perceive the dharma body from one side. Attached to the truth of emptiness, they only see part of the truth, whereas those within the perfect teaching [correctly] see the nature of emptiness and substance.

106 *MD* 1562 explains that the revealed teachings present many words, discourses, and concepts to establish a doctrine, whereas the secret teachings use a single letter to encompass all meanings. This entry cites the following passage from the *Hannya shingyō hiken* 般若心經祕鍵 (*T.* 2203A, 12b22–12c10).

107 *T.* 278, 689c17–690b25. "Virtuous Cloud" Bhikṣu is the first teacher that Sudhana encounters on the bodhisattva path.

108 *T.* 417, 899a09–899c03, *T.* 418, 904b24–906a07.

109 See the translation of this text by Rev. Thomas Eijō Dreitlein, chap. II.3.

110 *T.* 930, 19.67b29–67c22.

111 *T.* 848, 18.01c01–03.

112 *T.* 1796, 39.587b11–22.

113 This phrase, 初發心時便成正覺, is an important concept in the *Avataṃsaka sūtra* (*T.* 278, 449a13–0449c15) and is quoted in numerous other texts that Dōhan draws upon, such as the Yijing's *Dapiluzhena chengfo jingshu* (*T.* 1796, 579a07–0593a25); Zhiyi's *Mohezhiguan* (*T.* 1911, 59b14–69c27, 94a16–0097a10, 97a15–0101c22); Kūkai's *Himitsu mandara jūjūshinron* (*T.* 2425, 353b05–356c25), *Hizohō yaku* (*T.* 2426, 371c24–0372b08), *Unjigi* (*T.* 2430, 406c11–408a29); Saisen's *Benkenmitsu Nikyōron kenkyōshō* (*T.* 2434, 444c16–446c25), *Kenmitsu shabetsu mondō* (*T.* 2435, 484c19–485c2, 491a22–0492a29, 497c01–0498b15); and Dōhan's *Jōōshō* (*T.* 2447, 706b05–706c01).

114 This phrase is not present in all manuscripts.

115 *T.* 1911, 12b18–22.

116 *T.* 1796, 39.583a15–16.

117 *T.* 848, 18.17b29.

118 *T.* 1796, 39.689b08.

119 *TKDZ* 5:148.

120 *T.* 930, 19.67c5–6.

121 *DNBZ* edition says "two" and therefore does not contain the third section present in the *SAZ* edition.

122 *T.* 152, 8.868b.

123 *TKDZ* 5:144–145.

124 *TKDZ* 5:148.

## Bibliography

(*BKD*) *Bussho kaisetsu daijiten*. Edited by Ono Gemmyō. Tokyo: Daitō shuppansha, 1999.

(*BT*) *Bukkyō taikei*, 63 vols. Edited by Bukkyō taikei henseikai. Tokyo: 1917–1938.

(*DDB*) *Digital Dictionary of Buddhism*. Edited by Charles A. Muller. http://buddhismdict.net/ddb. Edition of 12/31/2014.

(*DNBZ*) *Dai Nihon Bukkyō zensho*. 100 vols. Edited by Suzuki Gakujutsu zaidan. Tokyo: Kōdansha, 1970–1973.

(*GR*) *Gunsho ruijū*. 19 vols. Edited by Hanawa Hokiichi. Tokyo: Keizai zasshisha, 1898–1902.

(*KDS*) *Kōgyō Daishi senjutsushū*, 2 vols. Edited by Miyasaka Yūshō. Tōkyō: Sankibō Busshorin, 1977.

(*MBD*) *Mochizuki Bukkyō daijiten*. 10 vols. Edited by Mochizuki Shinkō et al. Tokyo: Sekai seiten kankō kyōkai, 1974.

(*MD*) *Mikkyō daijiten* (revised and expanded, small edition). Edited by Mikkyō jiten hensankai. Kyoto: Hōzōkan, 1983.

(*NBTD*) *Nihon Bukkyō tenseki daijiten*. Edited by Kanaoka Shūyū. Tokyo: Yūsankaku, 1986.

(*ND*) *Nihon daizōkyō*. 100 vols. Edited by Suzuki Gakujutsu Zaidan. Tokyo: Suzuki gakujutsu zaidan, 1973–1978.

(*NKBD*) *Nakamura Kōsetsu Bukkyō daijiten*. Edited by Nakamura Hajime. Tokyo: Tokyō shoseki, 2001. Revised small edition, 2010.

(*NKBT*) *Nihon koten bungaku taikei*. 102 vols. Tokyo: Iwanami shoten, 1968–1978.

(*SAZ*) *Shingonshū anjin zensho*. 2 vols. Edited by Hase Hōshū. Kyoto: Rokudai shinpōsha, 1913–1914.

(*SZ*) *Shingonshū zensho*, 44 vols. Edited by Kōyasan Daigaku Mikkyō bunka kenkyūjo. Wakayama: Kōyasan Daigaku, 1977.

(*TKDZ*) *Teihon Kōboō Daishi zenshū*. 10 vols. Edited by Mikkyō bunka kenkyūjo. Wakayama-ken Kōyasan: Mikkyō bunka kenkyūjo, 1991–1997.

(*T.*) *Taishō shinshū daizōkyō*. 100 vols. Edited by Takakusu Junjirō et al. Tokyo: Taishō Issaikyoō Kankōkai, 1924–1935.

(*ZJZ*) *Zoku Jōdoshū zenshō*. 15 vols. Tokyo: Shusho hozonkai, 1974.

(*ZSZ*) *Zoku Shingonshū zensho*. 42 vols. Edited by Zoku Shingonshū ZenshoKankōkai, Nakagawa Zenkyō. Wakayama: Zoku Shingonshū zensho kankōkai, 1975–1988.

## Dōhan's Major Works (Selected)

*Aun gōkan*. Edited by Mitsuun, Moriyama Kamon. *Ajikan hiketsushū*. Jōkō-in, 1912. Reprint, Moriyama Kamon, 2010, 19–20.

*Benkenmitsu nikyōron shukyō shō* (*ZSZ* 18:273–323), Jōhen (1165–1223). Compiled by Dōhan.

*Bodaishinron dangiki* (*ND* 24 [1916 ed.], 47 [1975 ed.]).

*Chō kaishō*. 2 fascicles, Kakukai (1142–1223). Compiled by Dōhan. Kanayama Bokushō,

"Chōkaishō (Dōhan ajari ki)," *Mikkyō kenkyū* 10 (1922): 167–228.

*Dainichikyōsho henmyō shō* (*ZSZ* 5:99–444).

*Dainichikyōsho joanshō* (*ZSZ* 5:1–97).

"Dōhan nikka rinjū higi." *Kōyasan daigaku mikkyō bunka kenkyūjo kiyō* 16 (2003): 79–92.

*Dōhan shōsoku* (*NKBT* 83:76–83).

*Gyōhō kanyō shō* (*SZ* 23:147–178).

*Hannya shingyō hiken kaihō shō* (*ND* 10 (1916); *ND* 20 (1975).

*Himitsu nenbutsu shō* (*DNBZ* 70:51–82; *ZJZ* 15:79–110; *SAZ* 2:225–266); *Himitsushū nenbutsu shō* (Kyoto: Nagata chōbe, 1686); *Himitsu shū nenbutsu shō* (Rokudai shinhōsha insatsubu, 1907); Himitsu nenbutsu shō kenkyūkai. "Dōhan cho 'Himitsu *nenbutsu* shō' no kenkyū—honbun kōtei to kaki kudashi gochū." *Buzan gakuhō* 39 (1996): 105–130.

*Hizōhōyaku mondanshō*. Edited by Mori Shigeki. *Toganō korekushon kenmitsu tenseki monjo shūsei*, vol. 5. Tokyo: Hirakawa shuppansha, 1981.

*Hizōki shō* (*ZSZ* 15:35–58).

*Joōshō* (aka *Teiōshō*) (*T.* 2447).

*Kakua mondō shō*. Edited by Mori Shigeki. *Toganō korekushon kenmitsu tenseki monjo shūsei*, vol. 1. Tokyo: Hirakawa shuppansha, 1981.

*Kōmyō shingon shijū shaku* (*SAZ* 2:74–81).

*Kongōchōgyō kaidai kanchū* (*ZSZ* 7:1–18).

*Nankai rurōki* (*GR* 18:468–476).

*Nanzan hiku* (*ZSZ* 41:99–102).

*Nichi sotsu toba daiji*. Edited by Kōyasan Hachiyō Gakkai. *Chūinryū sakuhōshū* (Kōyasan: 1918), 27–29.

*Rinjū yōshin ji* (*SAZ* 2:792–795).

*Rishushaku hidenshō* (*ND* 17).

*Shakumakaenron ōkyōshō* (*T.* 2288).

*Shōji jissōgi shō* (*SZ* 14:9–36).

*Shoshin tongaku shō* (*SZ* 22:149–175).

*Sokushin jōbutsugi kiki gaki* (*ZSZ* 17:1–37).

*Unjigi shakukanchū shō* (*SZ* 15:11–54), Dōhan's oral transmissions, later compiled by Ryūgen (1342–1426).

*Yoga sūtraṃ kuden* (*ZSZ* 7:91–134).

*Yugikyō kuketsu* (*SZ* 5:27–136).

## Premodern Sources

*Ajigi* (*T.* 2438), Jitsuhan/Jippan (d. 1144).

*Amida hisshaku* (*T.* 2522), Kakuban (1095–1143).

*Amituo gu yinsheng wang tuoluoni jing* (*T.* 370).

*Banzhousanmei jing* (*T.* 418).

*Beihua jing* (*T.* 157), Dharmakṣema (385–433).

*Benkenmitsu nikyōron* (*T.* 2427), Kūkai (774–835).

*Benkenmitsu Nikyōron kenkyōshō* (*T.* 2434), Saisen (1025–1115).

*Byōchū shugyō ki* (*SAZ* 2), Jippan/Jitsuhan.

*Da banniepan jing* (*T.* 374), Dharmakṣema.

*Dafangguangfo huayan jing* (*T.* 278), Buddhabhadra (early fifth century).

*Dafangguangfo huayan jing* (*T.* 279), Śikṣānanda (652–710), Yijing (635–713).

*Dafangguangfo huayan jing* (*T.* 293), Prajñā (early ninth century).

*Dainichikyō jūshinbon shoshiki* (*T.* 2215), Saisen.

*Dainichikyō kaidai* (*T.* 2211), Kūkai.

*Dale jin'gang bukong zhenshi sanmeiye jing banruo boluomiduo liqushi* (*T.* 1003).

*Dalejin'gang bukong zhenshisanmoye jing* (*T.* 243).

*Dapiluzhena chengfo jingshu* (*T.* 1796), Yixing.

*Dapiluzhena chengfo shenbian jiachi jing* (*T.* 848), Śubhakarasiṃha and Yixing (683–787).

*Dasheng qixin lun* (*T.* 1666) Aśvaghoṣa (second century).

*Dazhidulun* (*T.* 1509), attr. Nāgārjuna (ca. second century). Translated by Kumārajīva (344–413).

*Fahua wenjuji* (*T.* 1719.34.151), Zhanran (711–782).

*Fanwangjing* (*T.* 1484.24.997), attr. Kumārajīva.

*Foshuo wulianqshou jinq* (*T.* 360.12.265), Buddhabhadra.

*Foshuo yiqie rulai zhenshi shedashengxianzheng sanmei jiaowangjing* (*T.* 882), Dānapāla.

*Gorin kuji myō himitsu shaku* (*T.* 2514), Kakuban.

*Guanfo sanmei hai jing* (*T.* 643), Buddhabhadra.
*Guanwuliangshuo jing* (*T.* 365), Kālayaśas.
*Hannya shingyō hiken* (*T.* 2203), Kūkai.
*Hannya shingyō hiken ryakuchū* (*T.* 2203B), Kakuban.
*Himitsu mandara jūjushinron* (*T.* 2425), Kūkai.
*Hishūnongiyō* (*SZ* 22), Jōhen.
*Hizōhōyaku* (*T.* 2426), Kūkai.
*Hizōki* (*TKDZ* 5), Kūkai.
*Hokkekyō hishaku* (*T.* 2191), Kakuban.
*Hokkekyō kaidai* (*T.* 2190), Kūkai.
*Hōkōin sekifuki, Kongōbuji shoinke sekihushū* (*ZSZ* 34).
*Honchō kōsōden* (*DNBZ* 103).
*Ichigo taiyō himitsu shū* (*KDS* 1), Kakuban.
*Jike Shōchiin, Kii zokufūdoki* (*ZSZ* 37).
*Jin'gangding yiqierulai zhenshishe dacheng xianzheng dajiaowangjing* (*T.* 865), Amoghavajra (705–774).
*Jin'gang fengluoge yiqieyujia yuqijing* (*T.* 867), Vajrabodhi.
*Jin'gangding yujia zhong luechu niansong jing* (*T.* 866), Vajrabodhi (671–741).
*Kakukai hokkyō hōgo* (*NKBT* 83:55–58), Kakukai (1142–1223).
*Kenmitsu shabetsu mondō* (*T.* 2435), Saisen.
*Kongōchō kaidai* (*TKDZ* 4).
*Kongōchō mujōshū dendōroku zokuhen* (*ZSZ* 33).
*Kongōchōgyō kaidai* (*T.* 2221), Kūkai.
*Kongōkai daihō taijuki* (*T.* 2391), Annen.
*Kōsō gōjō Shōchiin Dōhan den, Kii zokufudōki*, fasc. 10 (*ZSZ* 39).
*Kōya ōjōden* (*ZJZ* 6).
*Kōya shunjū hennen shūroku* (*DNBZ* 131).
*Miaofa lianhua jing* (*T.* 262), trans., Kumārajīva.
*Miaofa lianhua jing wenju* (*T.* 1718), Zhiyi (538–597).
*Mohezhiguan* (*T.* 1911), Zhiyi.
*Muryōju nyorai sakuhō shidai* (*KDZ* 2:495–521), attr. Kūkai.
*Nanzan chūin shingon hihōshoso denpu* (*ZSZ* 32).
*Ōjōyōshū* (*T.* 2682), Genshin (942–1017).
*Sanzhong xidi podiyuzhuanyezhang chusanjie mimituoluonifa* (*T.* 905), Śūbhakarasiṃha.

*Senchaku hongan nenbutsu shū* (*T.* 2608.83.1), Hōnen.

*Shimoheyanlun* (*T.* 1668.32.591), attr. Nāgārjuna.

*Shōchiin ruiyō senshi meibo*, in *Kongōbuji shoinke sekihushū* (*ZSZ* 34).

*Shōjijissōgi* (*T.* 2429), Kūkai.

*Tuoluoni ji jing* (*T.* 901), Atikuta (seventh century).

*Unjigi* (*T.* 2430), Kūkai.

*Wuliang rulai guanxing gongyang yigui* (*T.* 930), Amoghavajra.

*Yahō meitokuden* (*DNBZ* 106).

*Zoku senchaku mongi yōshō*, Jōhen, *Zoku Senchaku mongi yōshō* (Tokyo: Kokusho Kankōkai, 1984).

## Secondary Sources

Abé, Ryūichi. *The Weaving of Mantra: Kūkai and the Construction of Esoteric Buddhist Discourse*. New York: Columbia University Press, 1999.

Buijnsters, Marc. "Jichihan and the Restoration and Innovation of Buddhist Practice." *Japanese Journal of Religious Studies* 26, no. 1–2 (1999): 39–82.

Dreitlein, Thomas Eijō, and Takagi Shingen. *Kūkai on the Philosophy of Language*. Tokyo: Keio University Press, 2010.

Endō Isami. "Kamakura ki ni okeru himitsu nenbutsu shisō no kōsatsu—Jōhen, Dōhan wo chūshin toshite." *Taishō daigaku daitaku-in kenkyū ronshū* 38 (2014): 206–234.

Gorai Shigeru. *Kōya hijiri*. Tokyo: Kadokawa bunko, 1975. Reprint 2011.

Hakeda, Yoshito S. *Kūkai: Major Works. Translated with an Account of His Life and a Study of His Thought*. New York: Columbia University Press, 1972.

Hasuzawa Jojun. "Kakkai sonshi no monka." *Mikkyō bunka* 10 (1922): 151–166, 167–228.

Hinonishi Shinjō. "The Appearance and Evolution of the Hōgō of Kōbō Daishi." Translated by William Londo. *Japanese Religions* 27, no. 1 (2002): 1–18.

———. "Kōbō daishi no hōgō no rekishi to sono shūkyō teki imi." *Indogaku bukkyōgaku kenkyū* 90 (1997): 142–146.

———. "Kōyasan no jōdoshinkō." *Indogaku bukkyōgaku kenkyū* 70 (1987): 227–230.

Inagaki Hisao. "The Esoteric Meaning of 'Amida.'" In *Kōgyō daishi Kakuban kenkyū*, 1104–1095. Tokyo: Shujūsha, 1992.

Kameyama Takahiko. "Chūsei Shingonshū ni okeru myōsoku shisō no tenkai—Shūkotsushō wo chūshin ni." *Indogaku Bukkyōgaku kenkyū* 59 (2011): 651–654.

Kanayama Maboku. "Chōkaishō (Dōhan ajari ki)." *Mikkyō kenkyū* 10 (1922): 167–228.

Kitagawa Masahiro. "*Keiran shūyōshū* niokeru jōdo shisō." *Mikkyō bunka* 207 (2001): 1–32.

Kōda Yūun. "Dōhan ajari no jagi sōden ni tsuite." *Mikkyō-gaku kaihō* 19–20 (1981): 36–47.

Kōyasan Reibōkan. *Kōya Shōchi'in no rekishi to bijutsu*. Wakayama: Kōyasan Reibōkan, 1998.

Kūkai and Kakuban. *Shingon Texts: On the Differences between the Exoteric and Esoteric Teachings, the Meaning of Becoming a Buddha in This Very Body, the Meanings of Sound, Sign, and Reality, the Meanings of the Word Hūṃ, the Precious Key to the Secret Treasury*. Berkeley, CA: Numata Center for Buddhist Translation and Research, 2004.

Kushida Ryōkō. "Himitsu *nenbutsu* shisō no bokkō." *Taishō daigaku kenkyū kiyō tsūgō* 48 (1963): 43–80.

——. *Shingon mikkyō seiritsu katei no kenkyū*. Tokyo: Sankibō busshorin, 1964.

Londo, William. "The Other Mountain: The Mt. Kōya Temple Complex in the Heian Era." PhD dissertation, University of Michigan, 2004.

Morita Kaneyoshi. "Nankai ruroki kō." *Nihon bungaku ronkyū* 39 (1979): 32–39.

Morrell, Robert. "Shingon's Kakukai on the Immanence of the Pure Land." *Japanese Journal of Religious Studies* 11, no. 2–3 (1984): 195–220.

Motoyama Kōju. "Himitsu nenbutsu ni tsuite." *Gendai mikkyō* 11/12 (1999): 35–48.

Nagasaki Ken. "Nankai rurōki." *Kokubungaku kaishaku to kanshō* 54, no. 12 (1989): 82–86.

Nakamura Honnen. "Dōhan ki 'Bodaishin ron dangi ki' nitsuite." In *Mandara no shosō to bunka: Yoritomi Motohiro hakase kanreki kinen ronbunshū*, edited by Yoritomi Motohiro hakushi kanshiki kinen ronbunshū kankōka, 395–430. Kyoto: Hōzōkan, 2005.

——. "Dōhan ki 'Shoshintongaku shō' ni tsuite." In *Mikkyō to shobunka no kōryū: Yamasaki Taikō kyōju koki kinen ronbunshū*, edited by Yamasaki Taikō kyōju koki kinen ronbunshū kankōkai, 151–184. Kyoto: Bunkōdo, 1998.

——. "Dōhan no Jōdo kan." *Kōyasan daigaku ronsō* 29 (1994): 149–202.

——. "Dōhan sen 'Kongōchō kyō kaidai kanchū' ni tsuite." *Mikkyō bunka kenkyūjo kiyō* 21 (2008): 29–52.

——. "Jōhen sōzu no shinkō no ichi sokumen nitsuite." *Mikkyō gakkaihō* 31 (1992): 1–49.

——. "Shingon kyōgaku ni okeru shōshikan." *Nihon Bukkyōgaku nenpō* 75 (2010): 169–184.

——. *Shingon mikkyō ni okeru anjinron*. Wakayama Prefecture: Kōyasan University, 2003.

——. "'Shōji jissō gi shō' (Dōhan ki) ni tokareru nyogi gensetsu nitsuite—sono ichi, 'Shaku makaen ron' to Kūkai no chosaku ni miru nyogi gensetsu wo chūshin toshite." *Mikkyō bunka* 203 (1999): 1–20.

——. "Zenrinji Jōhen no teishōshita kyōgaku nitsuite." *Kōyasan daigaku ronsō* 26 (1991): 73–97.

Nasu Kazuo. "Hōnen to sono monka ni okeru 'senju' 'zasshu' rikai—tokuni Ryūkan, Shōkū, Jōhen nitsuite." *Shinshū kenkyū* 52 (2008): 42–62.

——. "Jōhen to Hōnen Jōdokyō." *Indogaku Bukkyōgaku kenkyū* 106 (2005): 80–85.

——. "Myōhen kyōgaku to Jōhen kyōgaku." *Shūkyo kenkyū* 363 (2010): 359–360(R).

Ōshika Shinō. "Chūsei Tōmitsu kyōgaku ni okeru sankōdan kaishaku: Dōhan ni okeru daisankōdan kaishaku wo chūshin ni." *Indogaku Bukkyōgaku kenkyū* 60, no. 1 (2011): 115–118.

——. "Chūsei Tōmitsu kyōgaku ni okeru shohōmyōdō no hensen: Daihachi jushin to no kankei wo chūshin ni." *Indogaku Bukkyōgaku kenkyū* 61, no. 1 (2012): 40–43.

——. "Chūsei Tōmitsu kyōgaku ni okeru shukuzen kaishaku no tenkai: Dōhan no shukuzen kaishaku wo chūshin ni." *Chizan gakuhō* 63 (2014): 131–149.

——. "Tōmitsu ni okeru shochisokugyokusetsu no tenkai." *Tōyō no shisō to shūkyō* 29 (2012): 71–89.

Ōyama Kōjun. "Dōhan daitoku no 'Kōya hiji." *Mikkyō bunka* 11 (1923): 116–135, 136–154.

Payne, Richard K. "*Ajikan*: Ritual and Meditation in the Shingon Tradition." In *Re-visioning "Kamakura" Buddhism,* edited by Richard K. Payne, 219–248. Honolulu: University of Hawai'i Press, 1998.

——. "Aparamitāyus: '*Tantra*' *and* 'Pure Land' in Late Medieval Indian Buddhism?" *Pacific World,* third series, no. 9 (2007): 273–308.

——. "The Cult of Arya Aparamitayus: Proto-Pure Land Buddhism in the Context of Indian Mahayana." *The Pure Land, Journal of Pure Land Buddhism* 13–14 (1997): 19–36.

——, ed. *Re-Visioning "Kamakura" Buddhism.* Honolulu: University of Hawai'i Press, 1998.

——. "The Shingon Subordinating Fire Offering for Amitābha: 'Amida Kei Ai Goma,'" in *Pacific World: Journal of the Institute of Buddhist Studies,* third series, no. 8 (2006): 191–236.

Payne, Richard K., and Kenneth Tanaka, eds. *Approaching the Land of Bliss: Religious Praxis in the Cult of Amitābha.* Honolulu: University of Hawai'i Press, 2004.

Proffitt, Aaron P. "Dōhan no himitsu nenbutsu shisō: Kenmitsu bunka to mikkyō jodokyō." *Journal of World Buddhist Cultures* 1 (2018): 117–138.

——. "Mysteries of Speech and Breath: Dōhan's (1179–1252) *Himitsu nenbutsu shō* and Esoteric Pure Land Buddhism." PhD dissertation, University of Michigan, 2015.

——. "Nenbutsu Mandala Visualization in Dōhan's *Himitsu nenbutsu shō*: An Investigation into Medieval Japanese Vajrayāna Pure Land." *Pacific World: Journal of the Institute of Buddhist Studies*, third series, no. 15 (2013): 153–170.

Ruppert, Brian D. "Dharma Prince Shukaku and the Esoteric Buddhist Culture of Sacred Works (Shōgyō) in Medieval Japan." In *Esoteric Buddhism and the Tantras in East Asia*, edited by Charles D. Orzech, Henrik H. Sørensen, and Richard K. Payne, 794–802. Leiden: Brill, 2011.

Sanford, James H. "Amida's Secret Life: Kakuban's Amida hishaku." In *Approaching the Land of Bliss*, edited by Richard K. Payne and Kenneth K. Tanaka, 120–138. Honolulu: University of Hawai'i Press, 2004.

——. "Breath of Life: The Esoteric Nembutsu." In *Tantric Buddhism in East Asia*, edited by Richard Payne, 161–190. Boston: Wisdom Publications, 2006.

Satō Mona. "Chūsei Shingonshū ni okeru jōdo shisō kaishaku: Dōhan *Himitsu nenbutsu shō* o megutte." *Indo tetsugaku bukkyōgaku kenkyū* 9 (2002): 80–92.

——. "Dōhan cho Himitsu nenbutsu shō inyō bunken shutten chūki." *Bukkyō bunka kenkyū ronshū* 4 (2000): 130–141(L).

——. "Dōhan ni kan suru kisoteki kenkyū—denki shiryō wo chūshin toshite." *Bukkyō bunka kenkyū ronshū* 7 (2003): 85–95 (L).

Scheid, Bernhard, and Mark Teeuwen, eds. *The Culture of Secrecy in Japanese Religion*. London: Routledge, 2006.

Stone, Jacqueline I. "By the Power of One's Last Nenbutsu: Deathbed Practices in Early Medieval Japan." In *Approaching the Land of Bliss: Religious Praxis in the Cult of Amitābha*, edited by Richard K. Payne and Kenneth Tanaka, 77–119. Honolulu: University of Hawai'i Press, 2004.

——. "Deathbed Practices in Medieval Japan, Developments after *Ōjō yōshū*." *Indogaku Bukkyōgaku kenkyū* 50, no. 1 (2001): 528–524 (L).

——. *Original Enlightenment and the Transformation of Medieval Japan*. Honolulu: University of Hawai'i Press, 1999.

——. "The Secret Art of Dying, Esoteric Deathbed Practices in Heian Japan." In *The Buddhist Dead: Practices, Discourses, Representations*, edited by Bryan J. Cuevas and Jacqueline I. Stone, 134–174. Honolulu: University of Hawai'i Press, 2007.

Sueki Fumihiko. "Amida santai-setsu o megutte." *Indogaku Bukkyōgaku kenkyū* 28, no. 1 (1979): 216–222.

Tachikawa Musashi and Yoritomi Motohiro, eds. *Nihon Mikkyō*. Tokyo: Shunjūsha, 2000. Reprint 2005.

Tanabe, George, J. "Kōyasan in the Countryside: The Rise of Shingon in the Kamakura Period." In *Re-Visioning "Kamakura" Buddhism*, edited by Richard Payne, 43–54. Honolulu: University of Hawai'i Press, 1998.

Tanaka Hisao. "Dōhan no Shoshin tonkaku shō' ni tsuite." *Nihon rekishi* 172 (1962): 87–89.

——. *Kamakura Bukkyō*. Tokyo: Kyōiku sha, 1980. Reprint, Kōdansha gakujutsu bunko, 2009.

Tanaka Kenji. "Komonjo kaitoku kōza, Kamakura jidai no ryūjin no nikki, 'Nankai rurōki' ni miru Sanuki no sugata." *Kagawa kenritsu monjokan kiyō* 15 (2011): 1–13.

Tinsley, Elizabeth. "Jūsan seiki Kōyasan no den Dōhan cho 'Henmyō-in daishi myōjin go takusen ki' no kōzō to seisaku katei ni tsuite 13." *Indogaku bukkyōgaku kenkyū* 53, no. 3 (2010): 1284–1287.

Toganoo Shōun. *Himitsu Bukkyōshi*. Kōyasan: Kōyasan Daigaku shuppanbu, 1933.

——. *Nihon Mikkyō gakudōshi*. Kōyasan: Kōyasan Daigaku Shuppanbu, 1942.

Tomabechi Seiichi. "Guhari shoku Amidazō wo megutte." *Chizan gakuhō* 44 (1995): 53–79.

——. *Heianki shingonmikkyō no kenkyū: Heianki no shingonmikkyō to mikkyōjōdokyō*, vol. 2. Tokyo: Nonburusha, 2008.

Ueda Shinjō. "Hairyū no Ajari Dōhan." *Misshū gakuhō* 161 (1912): 617–642.

Ujitani Yūken. "Hikekyō no Amidabutsu honjō setsuwa." *Indogaku bukkyōgaku kenkyū* 33, no. 1 (1968): 74–80.

Van den Broucke, Pol K. "Dōhan's Letter on the Visualization of Syllable A." *Shingi Shingon kyōgaku no kenkyū* 10 (2002): 65–87.

Van der Veere, Hendrick. *A Study into the Thought of Kōgyō Daishi Kakuban with a Translation of His* Gorin kuji myō himitsushaku. Leiden: Hotei, 2000.

Wada Ujō. "Kōyasan ni okeru Kamakura Bukkyō." *Nihon Bukkyō gakkai nenpō* 34 (1969): 79–96.

Yamaguchi Shikyo. "Dōhan cho Himitsu nenbutsu shō no hihan taishō nitsuite." *Buzan kyōgaku taikaikiyō* 30 (2002): 81–122.

Yamamoto Nobuyoshi. "Kōyasan Shōchi'in shozō Ajari Dōhan jihitsubon (nishu)." In *Kodai chūsei shiryō kenkyū*, vol. 2, edited by Minagawa Kanichi, 342–375. Tokyo: Yoshikawa Kōbunkan, 1998.

——, ed. *Shōchiin monjo*. Tokyo: Yoshikawa Kōbunkan, 2004.

# III

# Doctrinal Expositions

## Overview

While doctrinal interpretations of Pure Land concepts centering on a salvific Buddhist deity and an idealized afterlife world had been commonplace themes in Indian Mahāyāna literature, the dissemination of such clusters of concepts, practices, and texts to other lands have often given rise to distinct regional transformations, internal critiques, and elaborate commentaries that endure into our present times. Pure Land doctrines have been interpreted in a variety of ways and often under the guise of a singular soteriological aim expressed as birth in Sukhāvatī. Contributions in this section challenge common assumptions by identifying instances where Pure Land doctrines are interpreted without explicit reference to their soteriological contents. In radically innovative contexts, Pure Land ideology has been interpreted to serve nationalist interests in twentieth-century Japan (observed also in other parts of the world, such as Tibet); as a means to spread Buddhism to an American audience; and as Naikan psychotherapy, a form of therapy for people suffering with mental illnesses.

Charles B. Jones (chap. III.1) describes how, from its first formulation during the fifth to seventh centuries, Pure Land teaching and practice elicited protest and criticism for its seeming dualism and lack of rigorous practice. In response, Pure Land advocates wrote a number of texts answering questions and providing explanations for the tradition. Zhuhong, wishing not to duplicate previous texts, collaborated with an educated lay follower to come up with a new set of questions, and these, along with his answers, which he called "Answers to Forty-Eight Questions about the Pure Land," shed light not only on Pure Land thought as such, but also on the Three Teachings movement and the religious concerns of literate elites during the late Ming dynasty.

Itō Shōshin (1876–1963), influential Buddhist intellectual of Pure Land modernism, is best known as the proponent of the idea of "selfless love" (*mugaai*) and as an unrepentant supporter of Japanese emperor worship and imperial policies in the first half of the twentieth century. In "The Role of Buddhism in Emperor Worship," translated by Fabio Rambelli (chap. III.2), Itō addresses an early twentieth-century religious crisis (which is also a crisis of traditional religiosity fostered by modernization) through a radical critique of Buddhism. In particular, he argues that the Japanese ought to discard from their own form of Buddhism all those Indian and Chinese elements that are not in conformity with Japanese spirit, which emphasizes devotion to the emperor and the country and values elements such as harmony and mutual aid. Thus Itō proposes a reformulation of Buddhism in light of State Shinto and emperor worship; in this context, his most radical and controversial step is the identification of the Buddha Amida with the Japanese emperor and of the pure land with present-day Japan. This text is an example of Japanese attempts to come to terms with the dramatic transformations brought about by modernization, which also affected religiosity in numerous and important ways.

Michihiro Ama (chap. III.3) examines "The Future of American Buddhism," by Tana Daishō (1901–1972). Tana was an active minister of the Buddhist Churches of America and contributed to the development of its Sunday School program. He also wrote and compiled a set of books in Japanese as a doctrinal exegesis of Shin Buddhism and expressed his concerns and ideas about the future of Shin Buddhism in the United States. In "The Future of American Buddhism," he redefines Shin Buddhism as a family religion and suggests implementing at home a variety of Buddhist practices that originated in Japan. In his mind, those practices would replace and simultaneously enhance American customs, such as Thanksgiving and Christmas, if properly transformed to American cultural contexts. His work testifies to an instance of Americanization and Japanization of Shin Buddhism.

Although psychological studies of Buddhism in English typically focus on Zen or Theravada traditions, the most common Buddhist-inspired psychotherapy in Japan, Naikan, originated in Shin Pure Land Buddhism. In the autobiographical account translated here by Clark Chilson (chap. III.4), the founder of Naikan, Yoshimoto Ishin (1916–1988), describes his experiences doing *mishirabe,* which was a self-reflection practice promoted by a Shin organization based in Osaka. During *mishirabe,* practitioners were required to fast and stay awake, usually for days, while reflecting on the wrong they had done in life. If successful, *mishirabe* led to an enlightenment experience in which practitioners realized the saving grace of Amida. Yoshimoto modified *mishirabe* to create

Naikan, which psychiatrists started to use in the 1960s as a therapy for patients with a variety of mental illnesses. The translation ends with Yoshimoto addressing basic questions about Naikan and how it is done.

Wŏnhyo's (617–686) *Pulsŏl Amita-gyŏng so* (Commentary on the *Amitābha Sūtra Spoken by the Buddha*), translated here by Richard D. McBride II (chap. III.5), is one of only a handful of surviving medieval Sinitic scholarly analyses on the Smaller *Sukhāvatīvyūha sūtra* (called the *Amituo jing* in East Asia). It is the only remaining treatment of this sutra from the Korean kingdom of Silla (ca. 300–935). Wŏnhyo's commentary draws heavily from the *gāthā* attributed to Vasubandhu (ca. 400–480) in the *Wangsheng lun* (*Sukhāvatīvyūhopadeśa*) and Tanluan's (ca. 488–554) *Wangsheng lun zhu* (*Wuliangshou jing yubotishe yuansheng jie zhu* [Commentary on the *Sukhāvatīvyūhopadeśa*]). Although Wŏnhyo draws great inspiration from Tanluan's categories and diction, the commentary still bears the unmistakable mark of Wŏnhyo's scholarly essays: It alludes to his inclusive and comprehensive approach to doctrinal classification, it displays a creative and profound understanding of works in the commentarial tradition, and it stresses Wŏnhyo's overriding exhortation to all living beings to arouse the *bodhicitta*.

## Chapter 1

# Answers to Forty-Eight Questions about Pure Land (Selections)

Charles B. Jones

### Translator's Introduction

Yunqi Zhuhong (雲棲袾宏, 1535–1615) stands among the "four eminent monks" of the late Ming dynasty and was acclaimed early as the eighth "patriarch" of the Chinese Pure Land tradition.[1] As a man who pursued success in the civil examination system and entered the Buddhist monastic order later in life than most of his fellow monks at age thirty-one, he was sought out by the literati as someone with whom they could talk. He understood their life in "examination hell" and spoke Mandarin, the official language of the examination compound. One such gentry follower, Yu Chunxi 虞淳熙 (1553–1621), provided the impetus for the production of this text. He wanted Zhuhong to formulate responses to various questions and objections related to Pure Land practice arising from his background in gentry life and learning.

Zhuhong and his collaborator worked within a genre of Buddhist literature that utilized the question-and-answer format to settle doubts and objections to Pure Land concepts and practices. The introduction specifically names two previous examples of this genre, the *Discourse on Ten Doubts about Pure Land* (*Jingtu shi yi lun*, *T.* 1961) attributed to Tiantai Zhiyi 天台智顗 (538–597), and *Questions about Pure Land* (*Jingtu huowen*, *T.* 1972) by Tianru Weize 天如惟則 (1286–1354). Zhuhong followed their examples but modestly claimed to have nothing to add to the work of his predecessors. Thus, he and Yu spent time thinking up questions that had not been previously addressed in this genre.

The result is a text that speaks very much to the interests of Buddhist gentry of the late Ming dynasty. The questions contain more than strictly Buddhist objections and questions; they refer to many works outside the Buddhist canon, including Daoist, Confucian, and White Lotus texts. One of the great challenges facing this translation was to learn enough about the references contained within the questions and answers to understand their points and make sense of Zhuhong's answers.

In calling this work "Answers to Forty-Eight Questions about Pure Land," Zhuhong is relating the booklet to the forty-eight vows undertaken by the bodhisattva Dharmākara as he set out upon the path that would lead him to buddhahood as Amitābha and would provide the rationale for the practice of *nianfo*. The number is purely symbolic; in fact, there are many more than forty-eight questions here, since each of the forty-eight sections contains multiple (and sometimes unrelated) questions.

I have used the following versions of the text for this translation: Online version at the Chinese Buddhist Electronic Text Association: CBETA X.1158; *Lianchi dashi quanji yunqi fahui*. 8 vols. Taipei: Zhonghua fojiao wenhuaguan, 1983, 3:1525–1582; and Zhuhong. 1584. *Da jingtu sishiba wen* (Answers to forty-eight questions about Pure Land). XZJ 108:383–399.

## Translation

*Answers to Forty-Eight Questions about Pure Land*

Yunqi Zhuhong

### Preface to *Answers to Forty-Eight Questions*:

The Pure Land teaching has its causal basis in Dharmākara and its point of departure in Vaidehī. It was explained in the golden words of the Master of the Teachings of Vulture Peak (i.e., the Buddha Śākyamuni) and flowed out through the Lotus Society of the great master [Huiyuan] of Kuanglu (*Kuang Lu dashi* 匡廬大士, i.e., Lushan Huiyuan 廬山慧遠, 334–416). By single-mindedly setting one's hopes [on rebirth in the pure land], one passes straight out of the triple world. This truly is the essential ford for the age of the end of the dharma!

However, those of superior capacities [understand that] phenomena themselves are principle; firm in truth, they believe and do not go back. Fools hear and follow but give rise to baseless delusions. Only those who are neither superior nor inferior, who occupy the middle stream, who could be swayed either to follow along or to fight against, and whose intention is not set, can penetrate to [Tiantai] Zhizhe [by reading] his *Ten Doubts* or be inspired by [Tianru] Zegong (則公) from his *Questions*. Their

Celestial Drum[2] [sounds] in earnest; their merciful hearts are fervent. Why expend more words? It is for that which their words do not already contain.[3] As the shadows deepen we add more oil;[4] when the illness worsens we increase the medicine. How could there be nothing further to say beyond these two works?

It was the layman [Yu] Deyuan [虞] 德園居士 who, on the strength of his long-standing vows, gave rise to the great mind of compassion on behalf of hundreds and thousands of living beings, and sent around sixty-eight[5] difficult questions; I could not avoid resolving the issues in accordance with the questions. Taking them in order to settle his doubts would bring him across the river of suffering; directly resolving his qualms would bring him out of the cave of death and birth. Quickly putting aside mouse-like timidity and in the company of these[6] sages of old, [I] assisted the common work of these prior sages.

Regarding the [pure] land's absence outside the enlightened mind, the whole of reality becomes clear and the myriad dharmas vanish. Who is the west [i.e., the pure land]? Penetrating the lack of a mind outside the land, then the seven jewels adorn [the pure land] and the nine lotuses open.[7] What obstruction is there to original quiescence? Nevertheless,

> From his broad and doubt-free abode
> the layman conjured questions like wind on the water's face.
> I, from my silently unquestioning place
> dreamed up replies like the sound of valley springs.[8]

Although the "clouds fly and the bottle empties,"[9] we do not presume to be the peers of the ancient sages in their grand plan to shine a light, dispel the darkness, and remove at least a little of the film clouding the eyes of people today. Perhaps they have minds with the capacities of *icchantikas* and are stubborn as in the past, decidedly lukewarm toward Pure Land and not practicing [it]. They hold to a one-sided view of emptiness and are complacent; they do not even ask about it! What a pity!

Signed by the Monk Zhuhong of Hangzhou in the winter of Wanli 20 (1584)

## Question 1

*Question*: People of the world hear the words "to contemplate the Buddha is to contemplate the mind" and "as the mind is pure the land will be pure," and because they adhere to the interior mind and try to dust it off and make it pure, they incline toward [the teaching of] emptiness and are pleased with themselves. They deny the western quarter and say that the mind and the land are the same in principle. Thus they say, "My mind is firm; what is served by longing for the land? The worm truly eats through mud; how could yellow dirt be the equal of the diamond realm [or *vajradhātu*]; the great sea turtle truly bears mountains; how is holding the earth like wheeling in the sky?" Now they also make further analogies such as comparing an alchemical furnace [or immortal's hermitage] to the lotus-calyx, or the forty pulse meridians to the interconnected jewel-net, or the one numinous inner brightness to Amitābha's peaceful abiding. The lungs approximate to the west; crossing through the tongue is taken as the pools [of the pure land]. These are only metaphors for the dharma; there is no question of their [external] reality. This being so, they draw in everything from the inauspicious and auspicious readings of geomancy to the flourishing or decline of posterity as examples of the interpenetration of dependent and proper recompense and demonstrate the unchanging nature of [the Buddha's] response to beings' capacities. This does not get to the direct cause [of a buddha's attainments] nor does it exhaust the ten marvels [of a buddha's capabilities]. One must seek further for clear teachings and set these evil views to one side.

*Answer*: The expression "as the mind is pure the land is pure" is quite correct. However, this expression has two senses. The first relates to principle. This means that the mind is that land. Outside of a pure mind, there is no pure land. The second relates to phenomena. This means that the mind is the basis of the land. The purity of the mind is the purity of the land. If one grasps at principle but discards phenomena, then would this not be like the world affirming that pure leisure is this very immortal, with the result that outside of pure leisure there is no true immortal? Now suppose one takes up parts of the body and says [it is the] pure land. This is a most pernicious view, and the suffering it brings is most profound. We Buddhists only illuminate the unified mind, but obstinate people constantly grasp at the four elements [of the body]. For this reason, they hold the network of flesh to be the jeweled net and point at vain imaginings as the real Buddha. The lungs are subsumed under the western direction and so are easy to designate as the golden earth [of the pure land]. The tongue secretes saliva and so is called the flowered pools. This is vulgar and false in a thousand ways; one cannot begin to enumerate them! How could one not know that the human body is impure? Its substance is illusory, not real. One wastes efforts on it, but in the end it turns to corruption and decay. Still, one is fascinated with it in ignorance. People overhear the phrase "as the mind is pure the land is pure," and not only are the ignorant masses misled by it, even the literati are led to harm. Well might one heave a sigh at this!

## Question 2

*Question*: The fact that merchants who go to sea and gentry who go to court do not need to be urged beforehand is so because the caps and carriages fill the eyes [of the latter] and goods and money move the hearts [of the former]. When Śākyamuni appeared in the land, he led people to choose for themselves. Sudhana ascended the tower and all the buddhas circulated the light for him to contemplate; he did not await encouragement. Making a good friend work hard (lit. "get calluses on his feet") to intercede and lead one to faith is not as good as the light that came from Shandao's mouth; "good guidance" indeed! I have heard that [if one] practices *nianfo* in this way then the flower of the pure land flourishes; if one practices *nianfo* with a lax mind, then the flower of the pure land withers. The Buddha [Amitābha] has broadly opened expedient means; why would he not have placed this flourishing or withering of the flower right before people? In the event that they remain in the world, then whether they open or close their eyes, the lotus will be with them. When their time comes, then they can mount this lotus-wheel and catapult to rebirth there. [. . .] Why would this not be as good as expedient means?

*Answer*: Seeking reputation and pursuing profit are functions of this world; therefore, anyone can see them. Invoking the Buddha and attaining rebirth [in the pure land] is actually a cause and its effect [transpiring in] adjacent lifetimes; therefore, it is difficult for people to know it. Although the real flourishing or withering of the lotus flower takes place before people's eyes, those who are lost are not conscious of it. A purified mind does what is good, and so the spirit is clear and the *qi* is bright. The will thus grows and extends. A defiled mind does evil, and the *qi* is thus violent and the spirit is coarse, and one's inner state is dispirited. Is it not obvious that the flower is flourishing or withering? Moreover, the [living] eye does indeed approach the holy images in Master [Hui]yuan's sincere words, or when the silver dais alights on the pool as in the story of Master [Dao]zhen, and so on up to the perception of one's own body floating on the red lotus like Gao Haoxiang. So past generations have had such people; why say that the present generation is without [such] signs?

## Question 3

*Question*: The [practice] which the Daoists refer to as the "silent approach" resembles contemplation of a buddha. Their "heavenly sovereign" is a bodhisattva, and approaching the bodhisattva [stage] could be the stage of nonretrogression. Confucius is the Bodhisattva Rutong (儒童). Having thought of King Wen [of the Zhou dynasty] to the extent of dimly seeing his physical form is actually similar to contemplating a buddha. King Wen is on the right or left of the [heavenly] sovereign; Confucius should abide with them. Nowadays [one] uses the thought of King Wen and turns to the thought of Confucius. To think of Confucius is to think of the bodhisattva, and to approach Confucius is to approach the bodhisattva. One ought thereby to attain the stage of nonretrogression. Thus, why is it necessary to draw these two figures to the west?

*Answer*: Although the "heavenly sovereign" might be called a bodhisattva, the bodily form one observes is that of a king within the desire realm. Even if Confucius is called [the Bodhisattva] Rutong, he only manifests as a superior man in the human realm. To use an analogy, when a high official temporarily transfers [to a local post], the [local] examination selectees submit [to him]. When the sovereign suddenly goes abroad incognito, those who would go for an audience do not attend court. Thus we know that the Buddha is the only compassionate father of those born in the four ways, the great master of the three realms, the god among gods, the sage among sages, without peer. How can one make a "silent approach" to the desire realm or continue longing for the human realm? One must set one's intentions on the western [pure land] beyond the myriads of [other] buddha-lands, and on the one who is the Lord of Conversion [i.e., the Buddha] from among sages and worthies [as numerous as] the sands of the Ganges. If it is not the Buddha whom the [other] two teachings reverence, then who is it that they reverence?

## Question 4

*Question*: Perhaps one might assert that the Buddha parted from sentient beings, forsaking bone and flesh and abandoning his human body to go to another home and establish himself in another land with his spirit clear and profound. He enters the realm of dreams, and within the dream he obtains a treasure. The forms [of the treasure] are not real, and he hears this with sadness; what "utmost bliss" is this? Or one could say that being born is also a dream, and since everything is a dream, it is all the more lamentable. One might say that the bodhisattva wakes up first, but practices the six perfections as if in a dream. Thus as the true recompense is arrayed, it becomes more indistinct. Do I not [ultimately] revert to the eternally quiescent light? The quiescent light is formless. Does one depend only on that which is vast and indistinct? This would not be as good as residing within the world among dreams so as to contribute to good fortune and repudiate evil.

*Answer*: Vainly floating in the world is a dream; it is not real. The eternally quiescent light is reality; it is not a dream. People of the world mistake dreams for reality and reality for dreams. This is how they get all mixed up. It really is lamentable. How does one know that bone and flesh are the enemies, that the body is a fetter? Attain rebirth in the pure land and one is freed from sinking in disease and one can recover one's allotted life span. One is freed from prison and returns in splendor to one's old home. This is called the "utmost bliss" (another name for the pure land), and is it not indeed so? Although the bodhisattva's practice of this way is said to be like a dream, it should really be understood as something whose approach brings great joy and as an auspicious domain during the night. How can this compare with the heavy drowsiness and loss of mental clarity [in dreams] in which the spirit draws fierce and evil omens? Now a bodhisattva comes back from the dream, while worldlings leave one dream to enter another. As to [the land of] Quiescent Light, that is clearly an awakening from a deep slumber!

## Question 6

*Question*: With regard to separating from the deluded body and seeking the dharma-body: There is no extra dharma-body; this very present deluded body itself is the dharma-body, [which means that] the Buddha [Amitābha] takes this body to the pure land. Isn't that right? If in the pure land one should [be able to] manifest the body of one *zhang* and six, etc., without bringing the old substance of the leather bag (i.e. the present human body), then this would be a change as extensive as if a star fell as a stone, or a dove changed into a hawk. Isn't that right? Ah, me; to drift in the dark of the predawn hours and still have the bright sun fly up. The Land of Bliss and its domain of peace and calm allows for the secret escape of the ghost from the world's random flow; those who neglect the nine grades [of rebirth in the pure land] in favor of the seven paths [of rebirth in *saṃsāra*] are beyond astonishing!

*Answer*: On the basis of his divine power, the Buddha [Amitābha] takes up the great chiliocosm and brings it to the pure land as if it were [as light as] goose down. How much easier must it be, then, for him to gather in the form-body? To the contrary, those in the school of spirits and immortals (i.e., Daoists) do not achieve liberation because of their infatuation with spirits of form. The form-body is like bubbles and dew; this is not what goes to rebirth [in the pure land]. Dharma-nature pervades all of space; why would it need to go anywhere to be transformed? Now this mysterious transfer of the worldling's substance surpasses the realm of the sages to get to the same result. How does this compare with the secret escape of ghosts or doing the work of the school of demons? Just seek to be reborn there [in the pure land], and don't bother discussing body and mind.

## Question 7

*Question*: Those in the world who seek rebirth [in the pure land] are not the ones who really want to be reborn. Even when they contemplate (or recite) [the Buddha] with correct ritual and the Buddha appears before them to conduct them to the West, they decline on the grounds that their alms-rounds are unfinished or their weddings have not been concluded, and they hope to forestall death a little while longer. Then there is a person who is different from these previously [mentioned]. He vigorously cultivates *samādhi* all hours of the day and night but after some consideration he grows weary and gives it up, losing this critical opportunity. Then he goes so far as to throw his own body to destruction, burning himself up in the fire. Since he did not abandon the results [of his previous practice] and remained serene as if entering into meditative stability, then would the Buddha take pity on his stupidity [at committing suicide] and lead him by the hand [to the pure land]?

*Answer*: This is the wise person's practice of Pure Land: In life they purify their own minds, and when their results are fulfilled they attain rebirth by the conditions [created by their practice]. Those who do not wish to attain rebirth because of attachments to the conditions of the world are arrogant. Those who wish to hasten their rebirth and commit suicide are stupid. This kind of habit, if light, leads one into the horde of *māras,* and if heavy, will keep one drifting in the evil paths of rebirth. The light of the sun shines everywhere, but it cannot reach into a covered basin. Although the Buddha's compassion is great, he cannot rescue these people.

## Question 9

*Question*: [Let's say that] a person is diligent and heroic in this [practice] and for a day or a week or a full month or a whole year has the single, unperturbed mind. Later he is seized by another teacher who leads him into the two gates of Chan and doctrine. Although he does not accomplish either of these, he still has not left Buddhism. When the end comes, would the Buddha [Amitābha] still be willing to have mercy on him? Also, suppose he is diligent at the outset but slacks off midway, but on his deathbed repents and resumes as at the beginning, or is diligent at the outset but then turns to evil midway, but on his deathbed repents and resumes as at the beginning. Should this person enter into a lower grade (*xia pin*) or into the "City of Doubt" (*yicheng*)?

*Answer*: The thought of the Buddha is the Buddha (*ji nian ji fo*), so in what respect is *nianfo* not Chan? Contemplation through analysis of emptiness is the *tripiṭaka* teaching, contemplation through the intuitive grasp of emptiness is the common [teaching], contemplation through the stages is the separate [teaching], and contemplation through the one mind is the perfect [teaching], so in what respect is *nianfo* not doctrine? Two birds with one stone! Who asserts that these are not completed? The former [Chan] penetrates and the latter [doctrine] dissolves. This cannot be called "being seized." There is no doubt that one may be reborn in the pure land like this. The only thing to fear is that one will give rise to distinctions and hang up the mind on two paths. This fault is produced from the self; the Buddha-dharma is not to blame. As to the matter of repentance, that is hard to say. Śākyamuni practiced diligently for seven days and brought his prior practice to completion in enlightenment. [The butcher] Wide Forehead (*Guang'e*) laid down his cleaver and was immediately established in *bodhi*. Neither a lower grade nor the "City of Doubt" proved an obstacle.

## Question 12

*Question*: When releasing birds, fish, and turtles, one chants mantras and recites the Buddha's name for their sakes, wishing that they may attain rebirth [in the pure land]. Are these animals supposed to attain rebirth or abandon this karmic reward to be born among human beings? And would not the master and those who release living beings go to rebirth [in the pure land] by their diligent practice of recitation [rather than the animals]?

*Answer*: Even the birds and beasts [on behalf of whom] these mantras and vows are made can attain rebirth [in the pure land] by assuming the power of this dharma if their karma is light and conditions mature. If their karma is heavy and the conditions are insufficient, then they stop short [of the pure land] and have their guilt extinguished so as to change their form and attain a better path [as a human or *deva*]. However, even if the birds and beasts do not necessarily attain rebirth, the merit earned by those who recite mantras, make vows, and release living beings is not wasted. In future lives they will be liberated and finally have all of their past karma come to fruition. The [story of] Maudgalyāyana liberating the bees is [an instance of this] as clear as a bright mirror.

## Question 13

*Question*: To entice people with the comparative superiority and inferiority of pure and impure lands is to entice ordinary worldlings. What worldlings find supremely blissful (*jile* 極樂) is women; what they find extremely not blissful is no women as well has having to part from family members. Now you would have [me] abandon family and enter a country without women, and all [I] can do is flatly refuse to enter. How can the Buddha be so lacking in skillful means? Or one could say that with rebirth in that land one attains the six supernatural powers. The divine eye can penetrate into the women's quarters, so how is one free from this anxiety? Even though one is lodged in the pure land, one still sees women all the time. How would this differ from having women in that land? Does that really amount to an absence of women? Also, refined gentlemen are by nature inclined toward the plain and simple and do not treasure gold and jade. Therefore, it often happens that they reject jade disks and throw away pearls, scatter gold and burn fine brocades. Without being dazzled by hearing the name of this jeweled field [i.e., the pure land], won't they fail to make vows [to seek rebirth there]?

*Answer*: Although the pure land provides enticements for ordinary worldlings, the first time its enticements were presented, the obstructions caused by the female form had aleady been explained in detail through such metaphors as "flowered arrows" and "leather bags." It is proper to say that women are taken as impure and the absence of women is taken as pure, or that women are considered as not pleasant while the absence of women is considered the supreme bliss. How could one turn around and flatly refuse to be reborn and take refuge in the west? Now as to the six supernatural powers and the ability to penetrate to a distance, these all stem from the enlightenment of the mind-ground, and the [salvation of the] nine degrees of relation have been laid out in detail. This is more than just sky flowers and glitter. Why would it be that just the sight of women would constitute an obstruction? Coming to the principled non-acquisitive gentlemen who do not hanker after the jeweled land, they have not yet found out that [the term] "jewel" has more than one meaning. It is not really a single physical substance. Here [in the Sahā world] "jewel" means the accumulation of good fortune, something one sees and for which one then develops greed. There [in the pure land] "jewel" indicates something that matures from pure virtue. One abides with it for a long time without being tainted. Holding fast to the trifling matter of leading a life of few desires, one loses the glorious prospects of [gaining] the domain of the enlightened. This would be like detesting lewd songs by nature but giving them up together with the lute and zither, or hating the unofficial histories in one's mind but then burning them together with the *Counsels of Yao* (*Yao Mo*) and the *Canon of Shun* (*Shun Dian*). How is deprecating gold and jade and forsaking the western [pure land] different from these?

## Question 15

*Question*: [The bodhisattva] Dharmākara feared that because people would be afraid to go to any trouble they would not seek rebirth [in the pure land], so he said ten recitations would be enough. Śākyamuni feared that people would be afraid to go to any trouble and would not seek rebirth [in the pure land], so he said that seven days would be enough. He saw the man and wife using grains of rice to count their recitations and taught them to join up the 360,000 times 100,000,000 names, and Śākyamuni also enticed people [by saying] "hearing even the name of the Buddha's *ūrṇā*" and "invoking the name just once." The intention was the same [in each case]. When we come to Masters [Hui]yuan and [Zun]shi, then we hear that it takes six periods [i.e., all day and all night] and rituals of repentance to prepare [for rebirth]. Would a gentleman scowl [at this] and leave? So this makes the "seven days" and the "ten recitations" incorrect. The Buddha's words are false, and that is that! Why would the walls around the Pure Country be so high as to repel people?

*Answer*: When great sages [work to] convert people, their skillful teaching will not be all of one kind. They will give elaborate teachings for the sake of those who are sophisticated and give simple teachings for the sake of the simple. The "seven days" and the "ten recitations" were not said to be easy in order to flatter people. With proficiency [in the practice] increased a hundredfold, seven days is superior to seven days [*sic*][10] and ten recitations surpasses 10,000 recitations. The "six periods" and the "rituals of repentance" were not said to be difficult in order to obstruct people. When one brings strong conditioning from past lives, than in just a short time one cannot scrape and grind it all away. If there is any gap then the *samādhi* will be difficult to achieve. Longshu (i.e. Wang Rixiu, ?–1173) practiced a thousand prostrations daily and Yongming recited [Amitābha's name] 10,000 times through the day and night. Scowl and leave? Not for me just yet.

## Question 18

*Question*: I could imagine the six words [of the invocation of Amitābha] on the parts of my body, contemplating them one by one. This concentrates the mind just as much as *ānapāna* or counting breaths, so why do you not permit it but dismiss it as heterodox? Also, nowadays the Pure Land tradition is worse than teachings such as the White Lotus. It only has two or three of [the practices] recorded in the *Precious Mirror* (*Baojian*); it does not bring them up exhaustively. Suppose that when the Buddha was preaching the [Smaller *Sukhāvativyūha*] *sūtra*, authenticated as it was by [the Buddhas of] the six directions extending their broad and long tongues, he had then [also] expounded the hundred varieties of demon-kings with numerous auguries like the *ding*-vessel of Yu. Evil spirits came to rest in Jambudvipa, but we do not consider this. What then is there to say? Moreover, right at this moment their talk is most fierce, the harm they do is profound. Should we consider it a heretical teaching of that sort?

*Answer*: *Ānapāna* is using breath to focus the mind. It is completely different from refining *qi*. Successive contemplations [of the bodily visualizations described in the question] seek results through attachment to the body. It is definitely a heretical tradition. The *Precious Mirror* criticizes it and other books strive to refute it in a thousand forms and myriad states; there is no way to describe them all. The dharma is weak but the demons are strong. This is how it should be [when the age] turns toward its end; the Buddha predicted it. It is not something he had not considered. If nowadays there is something blazing hot and doing damage, then it is the so-called *Scripture in Sixteen Words* and [its teaching of] sending each breath to the navel and expending one's power directing it to the [lower] field of cinnabar; its misconstrual of the word "who"; its silly understanding of "*namo*"; things of this nature are like evil spirits and demons and are all without content. [Not even the] ninety-five [heretical teachings] of India would receive them, and here [in China] they are not included in the two schools of Confucianism and Daoism. It blazes fiercely to the skies but will go out after a while. Why bother even labeling it as a heretical path?

## Question 19

*Question*: Those who are lost these days seem like they are sitting with their backs to a candle. No one who turns his head would fail to see the candle. [Similarly] as soon as one contemplates (or invokes) the Buddha with whom one shares an affinity, this should cause one to see the Buddha. If one must wait until one's contemplation has ripened and only then see [the Buddha], then one who turns his head to the candle would likewise have to stare for a while until his eye ripened enough to see it. Would he only see it after a long period [of staring]? Suppose that the Buddha had set forth a skillful expedient so that when [someone] contemplated (or invoked) the Buddha, he should thereupon see the Buddha. [It would follow that] when one stopped this mind and cut off the contemplation, and when one has mixed thoughts, then one becomes muddled. This is everyone who practices *nianfo*; are they *icchantikas*?

*Answer*: Every day the sun mounts the sky, but with a basin on your head you're not aware of it. A blind person would not know if there were a bright mirror constantly before his face. If a person practices *nianfo* and connects with Amitābha thought after thought, but he obscures and deludes himself, then how is this any different? If the Buddha-moon fails to appear because the mind-water is not clear, then sentient beings themselves are to blame; what fault is there with the Buddha? Moreover, [even] with a bright candle at their backs, how many people will turn their heads? Giving guidance is futile to the stiff and stubborn. Why blame only the Buddha for being hard to see?

## Question 20

*Question*: The *Yellow Emperor's Classic of Internal Medicine* (*Huangdi nei jing* 黃帝內經) elucidates the "sickness of great delusion" as suddenly seeing something for no reason. These days student-practitioners will suddenly see something in the midst of basic nonbeing; how is this any different from seeing a ghost? It also says that at the time of death they are met and led along. What it describes as devils beguiling one to abandon one's body and follow then when fortune ebbs—is this not also great delusion? Moreover, these are called delusions of views or mental disturbances. Could all delusions be broken by this [medical teaching]? How could anyone not be deluded?

*Answer*: How could suddenly seeing something for no reason not be heterodox? How could the present accomplishment of long-standing contemplation not be orthodox? This is the constant principle of cause and effect. The student-practitioner of pure karma (or Pure Land practice) ought daily to consider the source of cause and effect and make a fine distinction between the errant and the proper. As to what is seen at the last moment of life, it is obvious when it is a demon and when it is the Buddha; who would be deluded? If you are contemplating a standing Buddha but what appears is a seated Buddha, then it is a demon. If the [Buddha's] proper attributes and the surrounding manifestations do not match the descriptions in the sutras, then it is a demon. If one contemplates emptiness via emptiness but it is obscured, then it is a demon. If it is none of these, then the purity of the mind will mature and the pure domain will manifest before one, and one will be conducted to rebirth and receive teaching from [the Buddha's] golden mouth. Can this really be compared with a sudden groundless vision?

## Question 24

*Question*: The Tuṣita Heaven is the dwelling of [the future Buddha] Maitreya. In the past, people often took vows to seek rebirth there and they had ceremonies for it. Then the Tang [dynasty monk] Dao'ang (道昂) focused on cultivating the western direction, but at the time of his death [a retinue from the] Tuṣita Heaven came to welcome him. Can one not vow [rebirth in] the Tuṣita Heaven but arrive [there] anyway? Likewise, can one not vow [rebirth in] Sukhāvatī but arrive [there] in spite of that? Again, one might vow to obtain [the realm of a] Copper-wheel [king] but attain [the realm of an] Iron-wheel [king], or vow to attain the golden dais but instead attain a silver dais. Thus, one might choose the Western Pure Land but receive the Eastern Pure Land. It remains unknowable.

*Answer*: The ten kinds of virtuous behavior, precepts, and *samādhi* are the causes by which one is reborn in a heaven; generating vows and dedicating merit are the causes by which one is reborn in a pure land. Thus, those born in a heaven can include those not qualified by vows, but birth in the pure land cannot be accomplished without vows. Now [birth in] the pure land is not [accomplished] without the power of merit, but vows must come first. Furthermore, one seeks birth in a heaven based on yearning, and virtue is most important for it. In the world there are those who begin cultivating practices leading to heaven, but later realize their mistake and devote themselves to the western [Pure Land]. Therefore, at death the Jade Capital appears and they quickly go into seclusion there, but then it becomes apparent that it would have been proper to seek a buddha-land exclusively. How can one practice casually and accomplish it? Now the copper and iron [wheels] are a different matter. The golden and silver daises are just a little off; they deal with seeking the superior but only attaining the middling. However, in the end they must accord with one's vows. If one makes resolutions [to attain] the West but one's merit falls short, then one attains rebirth in the good paths of humans and *devas*. If one is single-minded and generates firm and sincere vows, then [if it is for] the West then one will of necessity [attain] the West; why would one even consider birth in the East?

## Question 26

*Question*: When Avalokiteśvara succeeds [Amitābha], those in later worlds will of course know to recite the name of that Buddha. I do not know what buddha's name the monk Dharmākara recited in order to establish his pure land. Assuming he had no [buddha's name] to recite (or buddha to contemplate), then he should not force that which he himself did not follow on other people. Assuming that he recited (or contemplated) all the buddhas universally, then he especially should not make others focus only on him. Again, the opening of this gate began with Amitābha, so why should all [other] buddhas only know to admire this and close their [own] gates. Did they have no regard for the place of living beings?

*Answer*: When the ancient buddhas emerged in the world they were already beyond number, so who could count the number of former buddhas that later buddhas would have contemplated? Nevertheless, a teacher inaugurates a dharma-gate according to [beings'] capacities, and of necessity it must come from the mouth of only one buddha, as when rites, music, and military expeditions come only from the Son of Heaven. It is not that all the [other] princes did not speak of *nianfo*. Moreover, the sea of dharma is boundless. It is not that it stops at *nianfo* and there are no other teachings available. Do not grasp at the [various] gates of conversion (*huamen* 化門); why would one need to practice them all oneself and [only] then go and teach others? Even though Amitābha did not recite (contemplate) some other ancient buddha, why should he not direct beings to recite (contemplate) him? It is analogous to Confucius, who had no constant teacher himself; did that get in the way of him being the ancestral teacher for ten thousand generations? One need only focus one's contemplation. Why raise so many doubts?

## Question 27

*Question*: The Buddha [Amitābha's] lifespan is said to be like the sands of the river [Ganges] and like the *kalpas* of stone, tremendous and remote, and not something that the two vehicles can know. [However,] if one says that the Bodhisattva Avalokiteśvara will succeed (*shaotong* 紹統) that Buddha, then it is both immeasurable and measurable. Will the Buddha have had enough of living beings? Will living beings be fed up with the Buddha? A Buddha who has had it with living beings is *ipso facto* not a Buddha. [If] living beings become fed up with the Buddha, the *Lotus Sūtra* says that Avalokiteśvara's universal gate will not open for a long time. It does not seem that those who delight in the new will be pleased to go along with this. [Also,] after the final nirvana of Amitābha, won't there once again be a period of the Correct Dharma, a period of the Counterfeit Dharma, and a period of the Final Dharma just as when [the future Buddha] Maitreya descends to take birth?

*Answer*: There are two [kinds of] immeasurability. First is immeasurable immeasurability. This is the dharma-nature (*dharmatā*) that is equivalent to space. Second is measurable immeasurability. This is something that continues on, but humans and *devas* cannot calculate it. A doubt claims that Śākyamuni taught all his disciples by "leaving the land in confusion" (*mibang* 迷邦) and so manifested impermanence while Amitābha, the lord of all the worthies in the pure land, was right in that his nirvana involves eternal life. This looks like dissatisfaction with living beings, but the beings in the pure land are already awakened to the eternally abiding body of the Buddha. One cannot compare them to the ordinary beings of the Sahā world, who generally take any disappearence of the [Buddha's] traces as a real death. There is no going or coming, nor is [the Buddha] new or old. How could those born in that land not be clear about this teaching? On this principle, when a son takes over [as head of] a household, the father retires and when a minister has the virtue then the prince abdicates [in favor of him]. Since living beings do not doubt they might be without a Buddha, the Buddha can provisionally appear to abandon them (or abandon his own life) to enter into nirvana. How could this be called "being fed up [with them]"? As to [Avalokiteśvara] filling in [Amitābha's] place and thus impeding the Dragon-Flower [Assembly], the dharma [taught in the pure land] has no Correct, [Counterfeit], or Final, and thus it radically differs from the Sahā world.

## Question 28

*Question*: The bliss of the [Land of] Utmost Bliss is produced from sentiments and consciousness. [Beings] above the third *dhyāna* [heaven] have already stopped indulging in pleasure, but those in the nine grades [of rebirth in the pure land] return to the pursuit of pleasure. Why is this? If you say that the tranquility of extinction is the highest bliss, then why set up the condition that clothing and food be provided spontaneously and that the various forms of suffering are not even named? If you say that the pure land is mind only, then [I counter that] the fundamental mind is [characterized by] constant bliss. Why say in addition that "the contemplation of the buddha-mind is great compassion"?

*Answer*: Although [the Land of] Utmost Bliss connects to ordinary feelings, its reality is of two sorts. The first opposes suffering by explaining pleasure. It is devoid of all suffering, and so one calls it "Utmost Pleasure." The second designates its nature by saying "bliss." Because it lacks both suffering and pleasure, it is called "Utmost Bliss." How can this true bliss be compassed by a deluded consciousness? Furthermore, *śrāvakas* take extinction to be bliss; the bodhisattvas take compassion to be bliss, so would the mind of great compassion not be constantly blissful? But people of the world say "compassion" when they mean worry. How petty!

## Question 30

*Question*: When a person engages in worship of the Buddha, every one of the buddhas knows; the buddhas of the ten directions come in welcome. Why does that person have a direction to face? All buddhas are identical in their fundamental natures, and identical in their particular manifestations. They are identical in everything. The one invoking (or contemplating) the Buddha accords with all the buddhas of the ten directions who come to meet him or her. He or she meets and welcomes only the three holy ones of a single direction. It must be that what he or she sees in the time of invocation (or contemplation) is one-sided and shallow.

*Answer*: The buddhas can know everything, but they do not go forth in an unruly crowd. Since one assiduously concentrates on one Buddha, then [that Buddha] is automatically in accordance through sympathetic resonance. A practitioner of Pure Land causes all the buddhas to manifest equally, but there must be a main [Buddha] and attendant [buddhas]. Amitābha manifests alone, with clouds of transformation-buddhas following. The principle of cause and effect is like this; it is not that the attainment is one-sided and shallow.

## Question 33

*Question*: Purity is defilement, and defilement is purity. The west[ern Pure Land] and this [Sahā world] are not even an inch from each other. Birth [there] is no-birth; going there is really nongoing. [However], now we say "in a finger snap," or "in a single thought [-moment]," or "[in the time it takes to] flex and straighten your arm." These too are approximations of time, and so it still seems one lifts a foot and then takes a step. Though we could say it is extremely fast, it still is a double path (i.e., dualistic).

*Answer*: When grasping is dispelled and delusions dissolved, though a thousand mountains obstruct the road, they interpenetrate in nonduality. When feelings are closed and consciousness locked, one judges the separation to be surpassingly profound even at the speed of a fingersnap. These days people of learning attempt nothing more than novelty in their speech. They love to say "defilement is purity" without knowing that their heads are submerged in the deepest (lit. ninth) abyss. They aver that there is no distinction between sky and dirt. Their bodies sink into an abalone latrine; they say there is no difference between fragrance and stench. This is pathetic!

## Question 34

*Question*: Stop people on the road and ask them, and they all say, "*Nianfo*. One hears it, so it is an oral recitation, not mental contemplation." Ask further, and they say mind and mouth are mutually responsive in speech. The mutual response of mind and mouth becomes sound. Because the mind moves this is considered thought. Could sound be considered thought? Some say that the myriad things are mind only. How is sound not mind? If that were the case, then wouldn't the sound of bells, drums, and the *qin* (琴) and *se* (瑟) also be thought? How confusing!

*Answer*: Bells and drums may contain rich harmonies, but unstruck they do not sound. The *qin* and *se* may have marvelous sound, but unplucked it does not emerge. Bells and drums, *qin* and *se* are analogous to the outward extension of lips and tongue. The beating and the plucking are like the inward movements of the mind. Cut off thought, and how could they produce sound? Hence mumbling in your bed comes from dreaming. How then could the sound of "Buddha" come pouring out if not from the mind-source? However, people of the world resign themselves to just calling out [the name] without focus and without zeal. First they play on thought which becomes sound, and in the next moment sound is followed by disordered thoughts. They call this "mutual response," but it is not really mutual response. [Master] Tianru had a saying: "Mouth and mind mutually respond recitation after recitation; mind and Buddha keep pace together with no distance [between them]." Practice *nianfo* like that. Wouldn't that be nearer the mark?

## Question 36

*Question*: Gathering all of the six sense-faculties into the practice of *nianfo* is the speech of greatest power. Since contemplation is what is produced from mind and intention, then vows, transfer of merit, worship, and repentance are all summed up in this one word "*nian*." Nowhere in the world are there vows outside of mind, or transfer of merit, worship, or repentance outside of mind. Now then, single-minded *nianfo* (recollection or invocation of a buddha) and the wisdom generated by that buddha [together] are vows. Being exclusively focused on that buddha is transfer of merit. [Saying the word] "*namo*" is worship. That one thought cancels the guilt of *saṃsāra* is repentance. The rest can be known by these examples. Where is there any deficiency in *nianfo* that would keep the mind continuously in turmoil?

*Answer*: Single-mindedness and purity are regarded as the inner illumination of the contemplation of principle. The raising and moving of the five limbs are said to be the external auxiliaries of phenomenal repentance. It is not that direct contemplation of the fundamental mind is not the quintessence, but beings in the Final Dharma period have meager wisdom and heavy defilements and must avail themselves of [both] the contemplation of principle and phenomenal repentance. The inner and the outer must both be deployed together for the attainment of *samādhi*, the maturation of wisdom, and rapid liberation from *saṃsāra*. However, people nowadays retain only phenomenal repentance; contemplation of principle is completely deserted. Moreover, [even this phenomenal repentance] is external decoration and empty formality with no actual regret in it. Rather, it just causes men and women of pure belief to have continuously turbulent minds. They turn their backs on the royal vows of Samantabhadra and act contrary to the basic strictures of compassion. [One] sighs at this loss; it is a malady of long standing!

## Question 37

*Question*: The *Contemplation Sūtra* says, "The contemplation of the Buddha's mind is great compassion." If people of the world can release living beings and refrain from killing, be kind to people and love animals, proceeding up to bringing the nine types of living beings to nirvana without having any thought of nirvana, their minds would then be equal to that of Dharmākara. As well, they would not be in violation of Śākyamuni's instructions on mind-contemplation. So why choose such coarse traces as contemplation of [the Buddha's] body or vocal invocation of his name, turning away from the Buddha's mind as [if it were] an auxiliary cause?

*Answer*: There are two kinds of *nianfo*. The first is to think of the Buddha's [pure] mind-nature, and the second is to contemplate his physical body or recite his name. To contemplate the Buddha's [pure] mind-nature is to see the *saṃbhogakāya*. It does not impede one's approach to the Buddha possessed of the luminous major and minor marks in the west. Contemplating the body or reciting the name is seeing the *nirmāṇakāya*, but one can also see the Buddha as he is in himself outside of all imagery. The fundamentals and the traces are mutually supportive; principle and phenomena have the same source. The mind-nature is not an auxilliary condition at all; how can body and name be coarse traces? Nowadays, followers of the "Five Books in Six Volumes" (*Wubu liuce*) borrow the term "nonaction" and push "emptiness" and "cause and effect." They keep people from worshipping images and sneer at those who invoke the name. The ancients had a saying: "Everyone is a Danxia; only thus can they chop up a buddha [image]; each and every [would-be] Baizhang can say '*wu*' at the outset." Those who are not [at their level] yet will enter the hells like arrows shot forth.

## Question 39

*Question*: [When] contemplating the Buddha as one's own mind, [if] one uses a deluded mind to contemplate a delusory buddha, [then] the buddha one sees is a delusion. Enlightenment is like a reflection in a mirror or like empty space. The substance of this illusion is completely real and one realizes entrance into the lotus ranks. But suppose a demon transforms its body to that of a buddha. That would be a delusion too. Between this illusion and the foregoing one there is no duality and no distinction. Therefore, how could this delusion not be the same as [the Tiantai three concepts of] emptiness, the provisional, and the middle? The basic essence is completely real, but we must desire to dispel it. How does one drive out attachment to the very activity of dispelling?

*Answer*: Distinguishing the real from the illusory and discriminating demons from buddhas would take a lifetime of teaching; it could not be otherwise. To speak in accordance with the truth, though, if the real is not established, then where is delusion? Moreover, if buddhas are lacking, then who should we consider a demon? If one does not see an existent demon, why bother to drive it out? When one's deluded consciousness is still blocked, one cannot yet do anything that is without demonic activity. One should carefully consider what the *Śūraṅgama sūtra* teaches.

## Question 41

*Question*: I am afraid this business of having no women in the pure land will perplex practitioners. [The Bodhisattva] Guanyin emerges from the pure land frequently in female form, as in that form which we call Lady Malang and so on. The [*Huayan Sūtra*] *With Commentary* points out that young girls of the type that Sudhana saw are also "marks of compassion." Now a bodhisattva already on the [ten] grounds (*bhūmi*) begins to practice the compassionate deliverance of people. Since the buddha-mind is compassionate, then to turn back to his own [buddha-]land [is just to] manifest his own splendor and not to display any "mark of compassion." What about this?

*Answer*: The Sahā world is particularly stained by desire, so Guanyin turns the minds [of those within it] as a female. Sudhana had not yet clarified his ability to differentiate, and so Vasumitrā (婆須[達多) manifested as a female to impart her wisdom. It is not what one would call a transformation of compassion. One practices compassion and manifests as female. One who has not yet practiced the transformation of compassion must first cauterize the stains of desire. [Even] the best practitioner of the nine lotuses will lose some of his good sprouts if there is a female [present] when he begins to purify his mind. How inappropriate!

## Question 43

*Question*: Ciyun divided the "one mind of principle" from the "one mind of phenomena." Now the one mind exhausts principle and the one mind creates phenomena; these two minds give rise to each other. They are like the two poles on a scull. If they flail in the water without rest, how could one say this is not chaotic? If principle is like phenomena and phenomena are like principle, then that mind is this mind, and as a result one has only a single mind to use. How could one deny it? As Master [Zhi] li said, "Principle manifests phenomena." Also, this single type of contemplation does not accord with so-called "contemplation of principle" and "contemplation of phenomena." The whole teaching tradition of Tiantai holds firmly to this; why are Ciyun and his successors the only ones who do not?

*Answer*: Wisdom is one but illuminates both the provisional and the real. One does not crack wisdom in two. The mind is one but is explained in terms of delusion and reality. One does not break the mind into two pieces. In contemplation there is both principle and phenomena; what is the obstruction? For example, a mirror and the images [reflected in it] are distinct but not separate. The moon can be reflected in several bodies of water without itself being divided. Phenomena lead one to think of their principle; principle resides within phenomena. One infers phenomena from principle; phenomena are not outside of principle. Why expect thought to arise from two places? As to what you said about principle and phenomena being chaotic like the poles of a scull being tossed about wildly, the one is the two and the two are the one. They are neither the same nor are they cut off from one another. Since [Zhili] says "Principle manifests through phenomena," one gets two uses from one planting. This is both clear and profound. How does Ciyun go contrary to Tiantai teachings?

## Question 45

*Question*: In the pure land the water, birds, and trees proclaim the teachings of impermanence, suffering, emptiness, and no-self. This cannot be a definitive teaching. Since that Buddha [Amitābha] wishes the sounds of the dharma to flow forth, why not let them flow in one perfect sound that would enable any kind of being to attain liberation? Why must it be these [kinds of] sounds? Supposing that anyone whose nature is fixed as a *śrāvaka* were to be drawn to refuge in this land and it were to continue producing these sounds. Would that not just increase the severity of their malady?

*Answer*: The dharmas of impermanence, suffering, and emptiness are not limited to the small [vehicle]. They extend to the most superior and the most inferior; they are both one-sided and perfect. To contemplate that there is neither arising nor extinction is called impermanence. The non-arising of the five aggregates is considered real suffering. When bodhisattvas hear these [teachings] their minds are further expanded. When *śrāvakas* understand these sounds, then they quickly lose their small [vehicle status]. If we do not call this "perfect sound," then what shall we call it?

## Question 46

*Question*: Those who are closed up in a lotus calyx for six *kalpas* or twelve *kalpas* cannot hear the dharma-preaching of the three holy ones [during that time]. Within [the distance of] one *yōjana* there is no lack of water, birds, and trees. [Thus,] those worldlings of the lower grades [of rebirth] have only the doctrines of impermanence, suffering, emptiness, and no-self. External manifestations are before their eyes, [but] they do not grasp at them. Not having grasped at them for a long time, they should dissolve away. Why should the substance of the chariot-wheel[-sized] lotus alone remain? Also, it says that [the lotus-calyx] is as blissful as the Heaven of the Thirty-Three. Since it grants the bliss of this heaven, how does one keep from backsliding? Moreover, if at this time one does not backslide, then why not just cultivate the karma leading to [rebirth in] this heaven?

*Answer*: That the lotus is slow to open comes about precisely according to the days of this world; one has not yet arrived at the principles of impermanence, suffering, and emptiness. If one comes to the illumination of these principles sooner, then why would one remain long within the lotus calyx? Thus, one knows that once one stops grasping at manifestations, the golden [lotus] flower will open. Once one stops grasping at its features, the Buddha with his wondrous features appears. The doctrine that one is born in the lotus still abides; what is the point of explaining that the lotus is dissolved? I am afraid that if one says that its bliss compares to that of the heavens, one will slip back and fall. You don't know that this is only playing on the heavens as a metaphor. Those who are reborn in the pure land do not hanker after celestial palaces, so even though they are in a blissful setting, they are not led astray. Why would a person whose mind is set on the great Way agree to then engage in practices leading to the pleasures of the heavens? Alternatively, one might answer that since what one receives is equal to the higher heavens, how could it be that one's status is among the lower grades [of rebirth]. Strictly speaking, this would indicate that the very highest parts of the triple world are not as good as the lowest of the low among the nine lotuses. This shows that even though the karmic reward is inferior, the recompense is superior. A crown prince still in swaddling clothes is still very different from the many officials; the sound of a *kalaviṅka* that has not yet emerged from its womb excels that of all birds. For this reason, [even] birth in the lower grades is superior to the palaces of heaven. The teaching of the ancients is evident; there is no room for argument!

## Question 47

*Question*: People's fear of *saṃsāra* is great and impermanence moves swiftly along. Therefore, at the outset their wish to seek liberation is fierce; they dare not stop for a moment. [However,] once they hear the teaching of the "lateral exit from the triple world," the explanation of the quick path of practice, [see] the literature on how *nianfo* eliminates guilt, about ten oral invocations of the aspiration to attain rebirth [in the pure land], then many say there is a buddha upon whom they can lean and that no karma suffices to produce dread. They become more leisurely and do not put in the effort, and many fall into the old hands of Yama. Thus, the Pure Land tradition holds them back. That tradition teaches about the two gates. The two paths of Chan [meditation] and doctrinal study are extremely difficult to master and do not allow one to see quick results. Having the two words "birth and death" always on one's mind is the only way to achieve this.

*Answer*: Among ordinary practitioners of the Way, there are some who hear the word "difficult" and give up, or hear the word "easy" and go on. There are others who hear the word "difficult" and get moving, but hear the word "easy" and become lazy. When the ancient sages dispensed the teachings, they did what was appropriate to the time. The ability to to put one's mind to work well rests solely with the individual. The path of *nianfo* directly transcends the triple world; they opened this path out of the height of their compassion. If [living beings] become degraded out of idleness, then the error is theirs; it is not that the buddhas lead living beings astray. "I wish to be virtuous, and lo! Virtue is at hand." Virtue is right before one's eyes. "The mad overcome their thoughts and thus become sages." Sagehood is not distant. Are [the Confucian classics] also leading people astray by the word "easy"? With respect to "sudden enlightenment with one word" and "become a buddha instantly," these represent the Chan school using the word "easy," but it is very profound. Would you also call this an error?

## Notes

I am fortunate to have been able to consult several scholars in preparing this translation. I owe a debt of gratitude to the many scholars and graduate students who responded to queries on the Scholars of Buddhist Studies Facebook group and the Digital Dictionary of Buddhism forum. In particular, however, I wish to thank Natasha Heller, Charles Muller, Dan Lusthaus, Chü-fang Yü, Charles Patton, Tom Newhall, Achim Beyer, Jean Soulet, and Bhikkhu Nyanatusita.

1 For example, an encomium written upon the death of Zhuhong in 1615 by his follower Wu Yingbin (1565–1634) is titled "Stupa Inscription with Preface of Master Lianchi, the Eighth Patriarch of the Lotus School

and Restorer of the Ancient Yunqi Temple of Hangzhou" (Lianzong bazu Hangzhou gu yunqisi zhongxing zunsu Lianchi dashi taming bing xu). See Wu reprint, n.d., 8:5135–5157.

2 According to the Digital Dictionary of Buddhism (http://www.buddhism-dict.net/ddb/), *tiangu* 天鼓 is a drum that sounds of itself in the Heaven of the Thirty-Three to warn gods of their impending death and is in other contexts an epithet of the Buddha himself. In more ordinary usage, it can simply mean thunder, or the thundering of gods.

3 The Ten Doubts of Zhiyi and the Questions of Tianru both served to answer questions and settle doubts about Pure Land thought and practice, just as the present work, and Zhuhong had worked to ensure that both works circulated in his day. Given the parallelism of this passage, he appears to be equating Zhiyi with the drum of heaven and Tianru with the compassionate mind, and asking what more needs to be said. He then answers that there are things not yet addressed in their works, justifying the need for his forty-eight questions.

4 This phrase may be a reference to Han Yu's essay *Jinxue jie*, which contains the phrase 焚膏油以繼晷, "to burn more oil in order to extend the day." Many thanks to Corey Byrnes of the Facebook Sinologists group for the pointer.

5 六八難問. Shengyan interprets this as sixty-eight difficult questions rather than six or eight. See Shengyan, *Mingmo fojiao yanjiu*, 119.

6 I use the phrase "these sages" here because I presume Zhuhong is putting himself in the company of Zhiyi and Tianru.

7 According to the DDB, the phrase "nine lotuses" is an abbreviation for the nine grades of rebirth in the pure land. However, Zhuhong's assertion that they "open" seems to indicate a more literal reading of the phrase simply as "nine lotuses."

8 This is very poetic. Removing the "nevertheless," we get two perfectly parallel lines:
居士於廓爾無疑之鄉。而幻出問端。似風來水面。
山僧於默然無問之地。而夢酬答語。若谷和泉聲。

9 *Yun xing ping xie* 雲興瓶瀉. This phrase occurs from time to time in Chinese Buddhist sources. It is explained in a commentary on the *Lotus Sūtra* in this way: 雲興瓶瀉者。言二菩薩。問者。如雲興長空。答者。 如倒瓶瀉水。 "As for [the phrase] 'the clouds fly and the bottle empties,' this is said of the two bodhisattvas. The one who asks is like clouds flying in the open sky. The one who answers is like a bottle pouring out water." See *Fahua dacheng yinyi* 法華大成音義, CBETA X.620, 32:554c10–c12.

10 A later edition of the text has "Seven days is superior to an entire lifetime," which makes more sense and parallels the next clause more exactly. See CBETA X.1172, 62:73c17–74a2.

## Bibliography

*Fahua dacheng yinyi* 法華大成音義, CBETA X.620.

*Jingtu chenzhong* 淨土晨鐘, CBETA X.1172.

Shengyan. *Mingmo fojiao yanjiu* (Studies in Late Ming Buddhism). Zhihui hai 9. Taibei: Dongchu Publications, 1992.

Tianru 天如. *Questions about Pure Land* (*Jingtu huowen* 淨土或問), *T.* 1972.

Tiantai Zhiyi 天台智顗 (attrib.). *Discussion of Ten Doubts about Pure Land* (*Jingtu shi yi lun* 淨土十疑論), *T.* 1961.

Zhuhong 袾宏. *Answers to forty-eight questions about Pure Land* (*Da jingtu sishiba wen* 答淨土四十八問). In *Xu zang jing* 續藏經. 750 vols. in 150 cases. Kyōto: Zōkyō Shoin, 1905–1912. Reprint: 151 vols. Taipei, Xinwenfeng, 1993. 108:383–399.

——. *Answers to forty-eight questions about Pure Land* (*Da jingtu sishiba wen* 答淨土四十八問). CBETA X.1158.

——. *Answers to forty-eight questions about Pure Land* (*Da jingtu sishiba wen* 答淨土四十八問). In *Lianchi dashi quanji yunqi fahui* 蓮池大師全集雲棲法彙. 8 vols. Taipei: Zhonghua fojiao wenhuaguan 中華佛教文化館, 1983, 3:1525–1582.

## Chapter 2

# The Role of Buddhism in Emperor Worship

Fabio Rambelli

### Translator's Introduction

Itō Shōshin 伊藤証信 (1876–1963) was an influential Buddhist intellectual in the first half of the twentieth century. It is not an exaggeration to say that he addressed in his thought and activity most, if not all, new developments that Japanese Buddhism faced during modernization.[1] Itō, who studied at Shinshū University (now Ōtani University) under Kiyozawa Manshi 清沢満之 (1863–1903), the great Buddhist modernizer, was deeply influenced by the late Meiji-Taishō religious developments, in which the Japanese religious world had to confront itself with various Christian denominations, spiritualism, new religions, atheism (the latter, especially, in socialist and anarchist movements) and the newly arising cult of the Japanese emperor (also known as Mikadoism). In 1904, Itō had a religious experience that profoundly marked his entire life and career, a revelation of what he came to call "selfless love" (*mugaai* 無我愛). Itō had grown increasingly dissatisfied with established Buddhism and decided to abandon the Jōdo Shinshū sect in the same year. In 1905 he established his own organization called Mugaen 無我苑 (Garden of selflessness), to practice and spread the content of that revelation. Itō also began an active career as a public intellectual and proselytizer that lasted until after World War II. Initially, Mugaen arose the interest of leading figures of the Japanese socialist movement, such as Kōtoku Shūsui 幸徳秋水, Sakai Toshihiko 堺利彦, and Kawakami Hajime 河上肇,[2] which led to Itō's arrest in 1908. In prison, he went through a phase of "conversion" from his leftist leanings to support for the imperial state policies. As a consequence, Itō began to combine his ideas about selfless love as a universal cosmic principle with radical strains of emperor worship, or Mikadoism. After the end of World War II, Itō did not publish much, but he never renounced his wartime positions. In fact, in one of his last articles he claimed that Japan's lost war generated a new impulse for the realization of selfless love through pacifism. Let us now look at Itō's thought in some detail.

The term "selfless love" is an explicit combination of a Buddhist concept (*muga* 無我) with a Christian one (*ai* 愛), a clear indication of the intellectual climate of the time, but Itō emphasized that selfless love itself, as the absolute truth of the universe, was independent of any established religion or philosophical system. Following his religious experience, Itō claimed that "selfless love" (*mugaai*) is the fundamental essence of the universe, "when each single entity within the universe completely entrusts its own whole life to the love of every other individual entity and at the same time it loves all other individual entities with all its capacity."[3] Here the expression "each single entity" refers not only to human beings, but to any entity in the whole universe, from astral bodies down to subatomic particles. For Itō, understanding this absolute truth enables one to overcome suffering and anxiety, because all that happens can be understood as a manifestation of this universal love-force. We are all destined to eventually experience and practice selfless love in all aspects of our life.[4]

Itō's idea of selfless love contains elements of communal sharing and mutual aid that characterized the early socialist movement in Japan. After his "conversion," however, Itō began to attempt to relate selfless love to what he calls "Japanese Spirit" (*Nippon seishin* 日本精神), an idea he identifies with the Way of the Gods (*kannagara no michi* 神ながらの道) of Shinto-based radical nationalism and which was based on a modernist and authoritarian reading of the ancient myths of *Kojiki* 古事記 (712). For Itō, the Japanese nation under the benevolent and magnanimous rule of the emperor was in the process of a complete implementation of selfless love. Actually, Itō claimed that the Japanese Spirit is universal in its essence and underlies all religions and philosophies of the world, which in truth aspire to attain the central values of Shinto, that is, harmony and selflessness. The historical mission of Japan, as the ultimate realization of the Way of the Kami, is the establishment of a new world order based on ideals of cooperation and harmony under the enlightened guide of the emperor, whom Itō envisioned as a divine being, the personification of entire universe. (This bloated idea of the emperor's divinity was quite common at the time.) Itō's claim that the ideals of Shinto underlie all religions and philosophies is a sinister echo of analogous statements by authors such as D. T. Suzuki, for whom Zen was also the basis for all and any religious experience. In fact, Itō provides us perhaps with the full implications of the meaning of those positions at the time, as not mere attempts to deprovincialize the Japanese religious experience, but rather as ideological supports for Japan's imperialistic agenda.

Itō's interest in right-wing interpretations of Japanese myths brought him to formulate a radical critique of the meaning and usefulness of Buddhism in contemporary Japan. He argued that Buddhism had serious flaws because it departed in important ways from the imperial ideology (*kōdō* 皇道) and the Japanese national essence (*kokutai* 国体). Accordingly, Itō came to the conclusion that only those elements of Buddhism that could be harmonized with the Japanese Spirit had to be preserved; everything else should be eliminated without regret.[5]

After the war, Itō became a pacifist but remained unrepentant of his support for wartime Japan's imperialist policies. He wrote that although Japan's utmost defeat prevented the realization of this plan as he had conceived of it, the promulgation of Japan's new peace constitution could still become the foundation for world peace; this was indeed the result of Japan's transformation in light of selfless love.[6]

The text translated here, "Where Is the Living Buddha Amida?" is a short book written and published by Itō in 1937.[7] It takes the form of a dialogue between the author (indicated here as character "A") and a lay member of the Jōdo Shinshū sect (character "B"); still, the reader has the impression that both characters in the text represent phases of Itō's own spiritual and political development. The style is informal and colloquial, and the text does read like a transcription of a conversation. The text covers many aspects that preoccupied Itō's thought and activities: dissatisfaction with established religious teachings and practices (the lay person is no longer able to worship Amida in his family shrine, as it can't relate it to his own spiritual needs); a new interpretation of Amida as identical with nature and the universe, which turns Amida into an element of a spiritualist worldview; the idea that Amida and the chief Shinto deity, the sun goddess Amaterasu, are the same entity; the claim that the Japanese emperor is in fact the living Amida Buddha in this world (as opposed to a "dead," Indian-style Amida who has abandoned the real world to retreat to a distant world-system) and, more precisely, the personification of the divinity of the entire universe; the theme of self-dedication to the others (family, society, the nation, the emperor, the world, and all sentient beings in the universe), in which Itō combines Buddhist ideas with ideological impositions to uncritically serve authoritarian state policies; the critique of Buddhism as not fully appropriate to the new Japanese nation (the metaphor of the "Indian smell" that ought to be eliminated); and a fully secular reinterpretation of rebirth in the pure land as rebirth in Japan in order to forever continue to serve the emperor and the state.

This text is an interesting example of the general religious discourse in the early Shōwa period, in which many authors decided to write and publicize their own individual theorizations of the emperor's divine nature. They normally did so not under state coercion, but out of their own will, perhaps in order to contribute to shaping the emperor's cult. These individual interventions, while using widespread and state-controlled themes—such as the divinity and superiority of Japan, the fundamentalist (and unquestioning) literal reading of portions of ancient myths, the idea of a unique essence to the Japanese national polity (*kokutai*), the promotion of loyalty and service to the emperor and the state—also included their own theories, which often bordered on heresy. For instance, Itō's interpretation of the present emperor as the personification of the divine essence of nature and the entire universe (which is the fundamental cosmic principle), and of the Shinto sun goddess Amaterasu 天照皇大神 as identical with the Buddha Amida, run counter to official versions of State Shinto.

### Translation

### "Where Is the Living Buddha Amida?"

Itō Shōshin

## Preface

One evening, I met with a lay member of the Shinshū sect, and our conversation also touched upon the problem of religious belief. This man was dissatisfied with traditional Shinshū doctrines; he had developed fundamental doubts about the true identity of the Buddha Amida and the location of the Pure Land of Bliss and was experiencing deep anxiety about his present life.

I understood that this man was as serious a seeker of the truth as is rarely found today and let him ask questions freely and answered him honestly about my own beliefs without hiding anything. We both came to be immersed in a deep intellectual excitement and a rich pleasure of the Dharma and did not realize that the night had passed and a new day was now dawning.

Digressions aside, when we parted, the man asked me to write down the content of that night's conversation lest he forgot it, and I readily consented. When the draft was ready I showed it to him. The man read it and said, "This is excellent! It would be a pity to leave this to sit deep inside a drawer." He printed it and gave it to a friend of his recommending him to read it, saying, "There's nothing like sharing this emotion together!" Another friend also read it and again praised it much and encouraged me, saying "This text is an excellent work that satisfies the broad religious needs of our age; it should be put on sale and made available to the general reader."

Encouraged by the words of this friend, I agreed to publish many copies of the printed text that the initial person had given to his friend. This is how this book came about. It started as a conversation with a lay follower of the Shinshū sect, but the content and meaning of this book can also be applied to all beliefs in both already established and newly created religions. I hope readers will understand it and savor the purport of this book as it relates to the religious beliefs of each individual.

February 17, 1937
Mugaen, Tokyo branch
The author

## First Chapter

### *1. The Buddha Amida in the Family Shrine and at Temples Deserves Our Gratitude and One Feels Bad when Not Worshiping Him*

A: I find it very admirable that you always worship the Buddha Amida. There are many people who, because they don't have anything to worship or don't believe in anything, have sad lives; in fact, the great majority of people are like that. I think you are a happy and noble person.

B: Thank you. To tell you the truth, though . . . actually, I feel strange these days. In the past it was nothing like this, but recently I found myself in this situation, and to be honest, I am a bit troubled by it. I still worship like before, but I'm not sure why I'm doing it.

A: Is it so? What do you mean by feeling strange?

B: I feel ashamed and it's not easy for me to talk about it, but please listen. These days, when I sit there in front of the family shrine (*butsudan* 仏壇)

and worship the Buddha Amida,[8] I no longer feel that sense of gratitude . . . Before, I used to think without problems that the Buddha Amida would save me, this wretched guy—only the Buddha Amida could do it. . . . Every time I felt sad or lonely, I thought about Buddha Amida's help, and in tears I chanted the *nenbutsu* out of gratitude, and sadness and loneliness would disappear, and I was just happy in that state of adoration. But lately, I can't simply think with docility and feel happy like that anymore.

A: Since when do you feel like that? And is there a reason for this change?

B: I don't remember very well, but two or three years ago, little by little, I began to feel this way. I can't think of any specific reason, but one day I heard one young monk talking to someone. He was saying, "These images and statues in the family shrine—they can't possibly save us. For that, we really must encounter the living Buddha Amida." I too felt strongly in that way: "That's right, I thought, that's my impression too . . ." And after that, I came to think that the Buddha Amida in the family shrine was unreliable. However, since I don't know where to find the living Buddha Amida, I have no choice but to worship at the family shrine. I still worship it because I have no other choice, but to tell you the truth, these days I can't even feel nostalgia when I look at my parents' picture in the shrine, and because of that I feel terribly sad. Is there anything I can do?

A: So, until two or three years ago, you did think that the wooden statue of Buddha Amida in the family shrine could help you?

B: If you ask me so directly, I am not so sure that I can answer yes without hesitation, but somehow, when I looked intently at that beautiful image of the Buddha while worshiping on my knees with joined hands in front of the open shrine, I forgot everything else and felt like I was becoming one with it. But that has kind of dried out, and I can't get that feeling anymore.

A: How about Buddha images at temples? And how about the Buddha Amida at the main temple of the sect?

B: Before, I felt gratitude for the Buddha in my shrine at home, and much more so for the Buddhas at temples. Since I visit there only once in a while, there is the added factor that it's a rare, unusual view. As for the main temple, I have been there only very rarely, and thus I felt that its Buddha deserved my gratitude even more, and every time I sat in front of the portrait of the Founder (Shinran) I cried tears of gratitude. Now, when I go to Kyoto once a year, I do feel a sense of nostalgia, but it's not like before. I feel sorry about it, but there's nothing I can do about it.

## 2. *The Existence of the Buddha Amida and the Signs of His Help*

A: In other words, do you now think that the Buddha Amida isn't anywhere, and therefore you can no longer experience his help at all?

B: Well, actually it's not quite like that. You see, I'm sure that in the past, when I didn't know the Buddha and the Dharma, every day of my life was full of anxiety. Always hesitant, I felt as though things were always going to get to me; and nonetheless, I was also afraid of death. What's more, when I thought about what happens after death, I was in complete darkness. Now, when I think back about that time, I can still feel that anguish so strong as to make me shudder. But now, in contrast, I no longer feel such anguish and anxiety. Perhaps, I am being helped, isn't it? And if I am being helped, there is no doubt that the Buddha Amida is somewhere, right? I don't doubt that. It's just that I no longer feel that sense of gratitude for the Buddha Amida in my family shrine or at the temple as I used to feel in the past. I feel sad and unsatisfied, and I wish I could somehow recover that simple and docile feeling I had in the past.

A: I see. Now I understand your feelings much better. Actually, I have been through a similar path myself. But now I can worship the Buddha Amida with a much more lively sentiment than I used to. When I saw you earlier kneeling in front of the Buddha in worship, I thought you were experiencing the same feelings I have and I expressed my joy at it, but then you told me that it was not like that, and when I asked you why, you explained in detail your circumstances; now I understand you very well. However, you can't go back to your old feelings. Since your state of mind has advanced so much, you can't go back. In fact, there is no need for you to go back; rather, you should advance even further. If you advance further, you will find yourself in a place where you will no longer feel sad and helpless, and you will be able to worship enthusiastically the truly living Buddha Amida in a very different way than today.

## 3. *Liberation from Life's Anxieties and Troubles*

B: Well, then, please teach me how to worship the living Buddha Amida.

A: You said that in the past you were full of unbearable anxiety about life and death but now you no longer feel it. Well, who do you think you have to thank for this? But before we get into this, I'd like to ask you why you think you used to feel such unbearable anguish and anxiety.

B: Mmm . . . I can't really feel that sensation anymore even if I try to, but everything felt hopelessly unstable, dangerous, unreliable, and untrustworthy. For example, I felt like I was going to get sick, or that people were making fun of me, or that friends were going to betray me, or that I was going to lose my job the next day—I was always full of this stressful and depressing sensation. How strange!

A: So, now you don't feel that sensation at all? After all, the things you were worried about were not wrong. Both of us can get sick, even right now—it's a real danger. Also, the fact that we don't know when people are going to make fun of us, or that we don't know when we are going to get fired and lose our jobs—aren't these real possibilities? Isn't it like that even now?

B: Well, yes, it is. However, now, for some strange reason I don't understand, I don't feel anxious like I used to. In the past I used to worry about each of all those things, and it didn't really feel like living. But now, I don't worry. It's true that I could get sick any time even now, but now I don't think about what's going to happen if I get sick. If I do get sick I'll think about it when it happens and I'll take care of that then. If there is nothing I can do about it, well, so be it. With this kind of realization, I don't worry. In the same way, I don't know when I will be fired, but if I am, so be it; I'll do something about it when that happens, isn't it? So, I am calm and don't worry. In the past, I was always worried about being fired, so I couldn't focus on my job, and in that way it was more likely that I would actually get fired. Because of that, it was more and more difficult to do my job, and I almost got fired eventually. Now, I think that if I must get fired so be it, I'll worry about it when that happens. So, now I am focused and work well. And since I work well, it's very unlikely that I'll be fired. With illness it's the same. In the past, I was always thinking about what would happen if I got sick; I was always worried and couldn't sleep well at night. And since I didn't get enough sleep, in the morning I was tired, and so I thought even more about getting sick, so I got more and more worried, I slept less and less, and I was getting weaker and weaker, to the point that I could no longer stand up in the morning. Now, I think that if I get sick, so be it, I'll take care of that when it happens. So I'm very calm and sleep well at night, and since I sleep well, when I wake up in the morning I feel good, and since I feel good, I am more and more calm and focused and do my best at work, and therefore I can sleep better and better at night, and in the morning I feel better and better. This is how I am now. If only I could worship the Buddha Amida with gratitude, then there would be nothing to complain; this is the only thing that is no longer like in the past that I am unhappy about.

## 4. *The Power of Experience Is a Blessing from Nature*

A: Why is it that you don't worry anymore about illness and unemployment, in spite of the fact that in the past you were so anguished about those things?

B: Mmm. Well, perhaps it's because I came to understand, after a long experience, that even if you worry about those things, there is nothing you can do about them. Not only that. If you do worry about them, everything gets much worse. Illness, unemployment, and all other disasters in one's life, they just can't be solved by simply worrying about them. Or perhaps, it's because I came to realize that they are not easy things that can be easily solved by people worrying and trying to tinker about them. These things are very big and complex and are caused by nature; therefore, there's nothing else to do than giving up human artificial tinkering and abandoning oneself to nature.

A: Well, if you put it that way, then it gets a bit too superficial, but in any case, it is clear that you, after a long experience, were able to escape the anxiety and anguish you used to feel about life. However, I think that that long experience you mention is not only limited to your own life, but encompasses heredity and disposition handed down from our ancestors. This is because heredity and disposition can be understood as the results of experiences accumulated by our ancestors, perhaps even dating back to the time of primitive life organisms. By the way, experience refers to the capacity to modify one's attitude according to the stimuli coming from one's environment; so we can say that being able to escape one's life anxiety thanks to experience means that you were able to save yourself thanks to all stimuli from your environment. In this sense, we can say that this happened thanks to nature.

B: Thanks to nature—it's exactly so. But then the Buddha Amida has no longer anything to do with it?

A: No, no. Thanks to nature actually means thanks to the Buddha Amida.

## 5. *Nature Is No Other than the Buddha Amida*

B: Wait a moment. I don't really understand when you say that "Thanks to nature actually means thanks to the Buddha Amida." I have heard that Amida is the substance of awakening (*kakutai* 覚体) characterized by infinite light and endless life (*kōmyō muryō jumyō muryō* 光明無量寿命無量), and is full of compassion and wisdom. But in nature there is light and darkness, long life and short life, compassion and lack of compassion, wisdom and stupidity—everything in the world is part of it. But then isn't there a big difference between Amida and nature?

A: Well, yes, at first sight Amida and nature seem to be vastly different, but if one pays attention well, it's not like that. One clearly realizes that both are exactly the same thing.

B: Well, then, please explain that to me.

A: One minute ago, you said that out of a long personal experience you were able to no longer feel anxiety for petty things, and that was thanks to nature. That is clear, right?

B: Yes, I understand that.

A: Then my question is, that nature you talk about, is it made only of things you like, or does it also include things you dislike?

B: Of course, there are also bad things in it. In fact, there are probably more bad things in it than things I like.

A: OK. When you say that nature saved you (from your anxiety), do you mean that the things you like in nature saved you? Or the bad things? Which is it?

B: Mmm. . . . If I think of it, I would say both. If only things we like existed in this world, it would be easy and comfortable, but our life would be too carefree; actually, it would not be interesting, we would spend our days doing nothing, and would not become human beings endowed with intelligence and depth. On the other hand, if only bad and painful things happened day and night, one could not endure it and would end up exhausted. One could say that good things and bad things happen alternately, they make us happy and they make us suffer, and they teach us the sweet and the sour of this world; that becomes our experience, that's what saves us. If I no longer feel anxiety for petty things, nor feel slighted, nor worry like I did in the past, it's thanks to all of that.

A: Then, because in nature there are both sweet and sour things, we can understand the sweet and sour things in life, and we are really able to find peace. In other words, for us in order to really find peace and to be fundamentally saved, there have to be not just sour things, of course, and not just sweet things, but sweet and sour things have to happen alternately to offer us various experiences. But then, we should be grateful for the sweet things, but shouldn't we be equally grateful for the sour things too? As you say, in nature there is light and darkness, long life and short life, good things and bad things, but aren't all those things together materials that offer us experience, that really give us peace, and enlighten us? Thus, the totality of nature is in fact the activity (*hataraki* 働き) of a great wisdom that gives us peace of mind and enlightenment; this great wisdom is an operation that fundamentally saves us, and therefore it is also a form of great compassion. Moreover, this is an activity of the universe itself—which is spatially infinitely vast and temporally eternal; because of that, one can call it the Lord Tathāgata (*nyoraisama* 如来様) of infinite light and infinite life. Once we have reached this point, do you now understand that Amida is no other than nature itself?

## 6. Personified Nature and Human Beings' Efforts

B: But . . . Amida is a majestic being, and like human beings he has eyes, a nose, hands, and feet, but nature is a vague and random conglomerate of all kinds of things, right? I cannot really understand when you say that the two are the same.

A: You are wrong because when you say "Amida" you immediately think of the wooden statue in the family shrine, and when you say "nature" you think about mountains, rivers, and plants without human beings and without the Buddha. The true nature is the body of the Buddha, and the true Buddha is the brain of nature. That's why, to be saved by nature and to be saved by Amida, is ultimately the same thing.

B: I think that in order to be saved by nature, human effort is useless and one doesn't have to do anything. But in order to be saved by Amida, I have the impression that one has to somehow show gratitude for his activity, one has to help Amida. But because I no longer feel a sense of gratitude for him, like in the past, I am at a loss.

A: It looks like you still don't understand how grateful you have to be toward nature and its personified essence; because of that, you think of it as distinct from Amida. When I told you that your concept of nature is a bit superficial, that's what I meant. When you said that mere human concerns and efforts cannot solve problems such as illness and unemployment, and therefore you gave up on that because the only way is to follow nature's course—that is the sketchy part. Why do you say that illness and unemployment cannot be solved by human efforts? Of course, right now, illness cannot be cured only by human effort, but it's not true that human effort is completely useless. Recent developments in medicine are truly remarkable, and certain injections work like magic; the results of surgery are also very impressive. As for unemployment, with the right mental attitude a person can really help himself well. Also, you certainly know that unemployment relief activities play an important role in society. Furthermore, how great is the impact of modern science, with its progress, toward eliminating disasters and improving human life? Even just by looking at the airplanes or the radio, one understands how great is the effect of human creativity and effort. The power of human wisdom and will, if compared with the power of nature, is still small, but one can imagine that in the future, after an infinite amount of time, there will be an infinite progress, and human power will be able to do everything. Perhaps, nothing will be impossible for humans, even moving the entire universe at will. One should at least have such far-reaching ideals, and plan the progress of human life onwards from today.[9] Instead, you think that nature cannot be affected by human concerns and creativity, and say that one should simply let oneself go and follow nature's course. What is this if not superficial? I'd say that this shows a high degree of lack of knowledge about human power and the essence of nature.

B: But if you say those things, I'll end up once again worrying about illness, unemployment, and death, and it'll make me anxious and troubled again. I won't be able to tolerate to go back to a life of agony as before. And even if I'd go back to it, that won't happen again. That stupid anxiety won't come back; no matter what people tell me, there is no other way than to let nature follow its course and find peace of mind in it.

A: So, if you get sick, you will not see a doctor, or take medicines? If your children start binge eating, or catch a cold, or if they are lazy and miss school—you'll give up and let it all be, leaving it all to nature's course because human power can't do anything about any of it?

B: No, of course I won't do that. I pay a lot of attention to health, more than usual, and when I or my children catch even a little cold, I immediately see a doctor and take, or have them take, medicine. I also think that education is very important, and won't absolutely let them skip classes; if I see them slacking just a bit, I yell at them and make them study.

A: I thought so. If you pay attention to health, and if you are committed to education—that will have an effect.

B: Yes, it's true. That's why I will keep up with my efforts to improve my lifestyle by paying careful attention to all kinds of things.

## 7. *The Cause of All Kinds of Anguish is Petty Egoism*

A: Do you have any worries or anxiety, even though you are so careful and resourceful?

B: Worries and anxiety? No, on the contrary. All that is above all a source of pleasure.

A: Then why did you say that in the past you felt this enormous anxiety because you worried about illness, about losing your job, about death?

B: Well, I was worrying about things there was no use worrying about. And because of that, I was neglecting my health, I was neglecting my job . . . I was doing all kinds of things that would shorten my life. If I think about it now, I stuck my head in a tight place. In one word, I was petty. I was spineless. I only cared about myself in the present moment. Even now, when I suddenly think selfishly about my own immediate interests, I get anxious about a lot of things, and I get confused, and nothing seems to make any sense. In those moments, I try to become broad minded; I forget myself and try to ignore my immediate interests and to follow the universal principle, and I tell myself that if something is good for all, that is the best thing. Even when I do small things, I try to do it with a big feeling. Then, anxiety immediately goes away, and out of somewhere energy arises, and I get a strong feeling that I can do anything.

A: That's precisely it! That is the most important thing! If you only think about your immediate interests, it's obvious that everything becomes dark. That's because each of us does not exist alone, but is born and lives thanks to everybody else. Therefore, each of us does not live only for himself, but for everybody else. But when one wrongly thinks only about himself, that does not match reality, and one falls into fantasy or delusion; then, of course, nothing seems to make sense, and everything becomes pitch dark. But now you, differently from the past, don't worry about unnecessary things and have reached peace of mind by entrusting everything to nature, and that's because you have abandoned your previous state of mind that brought you to consider yourself separate from nature and society at large, to have a conflicting relation with the others, and to only care about yourself. Now you consider yourself as directly related to nature. Since each of us is originally one component of nature, it is utterly unreasonable to think about separating oneself arbitrarily, isolating oneself, and only concerning oneself with one's individual interests. And since one keeps pushing forward this unnatural attitude, it becomes a source of agony, and there certainly is nothing more painful than that. This was your agony in the past. But now you have overcome that terrible agony, you are really a fortunate man. How many people in the world are still drowning in that terrible agony? In fact, the majority of humankind, especially all those people who have misunderstood western culture, with its individualism and egoism, and have been negatively impacted by it—many of them have fallen into that agony. I only wish that those people would free themselves quickly from that disastrous condition.

### *8. The Realization, Based on Experience, That Self and Others Are One and the Salvation Offered by Amida*

B: Me too. I escaped narrowly and I am very grateful for it. But how is all this related to being saved by Amida?

A: This is exactly what being saved by Amida is about. Amida becomes all kinds of lights and colors and enters inside us through our eyes, becomes our experiences, and opens up our wisdom. Also, Amida becomes all kinds of sounds and enters inside us through our ears, becomes our experiences, and opens up our wisdom. Moreover, Amida becomes various kinds of smells, various kinds of flavors, various kinds of tactile sensations, various kinds of thoughts, and enters inside us through our nose and mouth and body and mind, and opens up our wisdom. In this way, colors, sounds, smells, flavors, heat, light, movements—they are all the body of Amida, and his august body embraces all of us completely, and nurtures our souls (*tamashii*) night and day. That's why it is said that our experiences are reared by Amida. You and I and all human beings—no, all living beings, since the moment they are born in this world—no, since the beginning of the world, are being nurtured by Amida. The fact that you are no longer afflicted, like you were in the past, by petty concerns, is a sign that Amida's nurturing has manifested its effect on your soul. In the past, you focused only on your immediate little self, separated yourself from all others and saw the others as enemies, and tried to create your own destiny, but since things did not turn out the way you wanted, you suffered—but as I said before, that was a big delusion that does not match reality. After a long time of experiences (observations and reflections)—that is, thanks to Amida's nurturing—you awakened from that delusion and entrusted everything to him. Now, for you nature is no longer the other, much less the enemy, and society, the nation, mountains, rivers, heaven, and earth—they are all connected to you, they are one with you. In fact, they were one with you since the beginning, but in the past you didn't know, you thought they were all separate entities, and so you had an unhappy life. But now you understand that oneself and Amida are originally one (*ittai*), they have never been separate and will never be. Because of that, you have attained great peace of mind.

## Second Chapter

### 1. *A Life of Service to the Others Based on the Identity of Self and Others Eventually Turns into a Life of Loyalty toward Our Noble Country*

B: I see. If you put it that way, I totally agree with you. Does it mean that it is no longer necessary to worship the Buddha in the family shrine or at the temple?

A: No, that's not what I mean. Didn't you say that you are troubled because you no longer feel gratitude toward Amida in your family shrine?

B: Yes, I'm very troubled by that. I wish I could feel that gratitude again and were able to passionately worship Amida again, like in the past.

A: But of course you won't be able to go back to the past. Plus, there is no need for that. Until two or three years ago you may have been able to worship with gratitude the wooden statue of Amida, according to the old custom. Later, you came to be nurtured more and more by Amida as nature, and as a result you now feel that a wooden statue of Amida is no longer enough, but that is actually a good thing.

B: What do you suggest I do?

A: I repeat myself, but I think you should understand well that nature is Amida.

B: I understand that.

A: Because you were saved by Amida as nature, you were able to free yourself from useless and stupid anxiety. Now you forget about your little self's immediate interests and treat everything, even each little thing, as something that concerns everyone. For example, when you care for your personal health, it's no longer, as in the past, out of petty individualistic thoughts, such as concern for your personal death or regret for your individual life. And that's because the belief that your body is no longer your personal property, but something that belongs to all, to society (*ōyake* 公), to nature, to Amida—this belief has become unquestionable. From the perspective of this belief, wealth, health, progeny, family, society, politics, war—they are no longer causes for suffering and anxiety, but the seeds of everyone's joy and ways to express one's gratitude and carry out one's public duties. I think that the words you said before also meant this.

B: That's exactly true.

A: Everything is a way to carry out one's public duties, everything is a way to express one's gratitude—if we Japanese are to say this in our own language, this means that everything is a way to manifest our loyalty to His Majesty the Emperor and to contribute to the imperial destiny of our endless dynasty, which also amounts to serving our nation and our people.

B: I see. Because of nature, that is, Amida's nurturing, one overcomes all petty attachments to one's little self and is freed from all worries and anxieties, and full of joy one does all he can for everyone else. This I understand well. But you say that for us Japanese, this amounts to carrying out our public duty to serve His Majesty the Emperor.

A: Yes, that's correct.

B: I think I understand most of it, but I'd like to ask you to explain that last point a little more.

## *2. Translating the Term "Buddha Amida" into Chinese and Japanese*

A: I want you to understand this point well, so I'd like to go back and begin with the name "Amida Buddha."

B: Please do.

A: As you know very well, the term "Amida Buddha" comes from Sanskrit. Translated into Chinese, it has been rendered as encompassing the two meanings of "Awakened one of infinite light" and "Awakened one of infinite life." Infinite light refers to a light that shines everywhere, even in the most recondite corners of the world and operates to destroy all darkness. This activity, and the fact that it continues without interruption as long as time exists, from an infinite past until an infinite future, is called "infinite life." Therefore, infinite life is a function of wisdom; it continues tenaciously forever; infinite light is a function of compassion, which patiently destroys the darkness of ignorance. The term "awakened one" (*kaku* 覚) refers to the personification (*jinkakusha* 人格者) of perfect wisdom. Therefore, one understands that Amida Buddha is the same thing as nature, as I explained before. However, nature is normally envisioned not as a personified entity, in which wisdom and compassion operate, but as a cold and confused aggregation that keeps transforming through new births and extinctions simply in accordance with the law of cause and effect, in a blind and mechanistic way. This is a superficial point of view that observes nature nonreligiously (*hi-shūkyōteki* 非宗教的) as unrelated to our human soul; this is not the true way to observe nature as it is, so as to grasp its real essence. If we observe the real essence of the universe and nature, correctly and clearly, as centered on our human soul, we will understand in it the functions of light and life that stimulate and awaken our soul and will see in it an immense personal entity full of wisdom and compassion. Buddhism variously calls this Suchness (*shinnyo* 真如), Dharma-essence (*hosshō* 法性), Dharmakāya (*hosshin* 法身), Tathāgata (*nyorai* 如来). Christianity calls this God (*goddo* ゴッド), and Shinto calls it *kami* 神.

B: As you just explained, I've heard that Amida Buddha was translated into Chinese as Awakened one of infinite light and Awakened one of infinite life. However, how can we translate it into Japanese?

A: This is certainly a problem, isn't it? In the past, there were also other Chinese translations, such as "Tathāgata of unobstructed light pervading the ten realms," or "Tathāgata of wondrous light," but it would seem that people didn't think much about a Japanese translation. In the past, people highly esteemed the Chinese language and so Chinese translations were enough, but now, at the time when the Japanese spirit is surging and Japan is autonomously acquiring self-awareness, Chinese translations are no longer satisfactory and we do need a Japanese translation. This is perfectly reasonable. For example, a foreign commodity that does not exist in Japan, most likely will not have a Japanese name; either its foreign name will be used as its Japanese name, or a new Japanese word for it will be created; there is no other possibility. However, if the same commodity also exists in Japan, it must have a Japanese name, so that its original Japanese name will also be used to render the imported commodity. This is fairly obvious. Now, if we investigate to see whether an entity of the same nature as what is called in Sanskrit Amida Buddha also exists in Japan, I would immediately say that, appropriately, Amaterasu Ōmikami has the same nature as the Buddha Amida, and thus I have no hesitations to feel that her august name is the most appropriate Japanese translation for Amida Buddha. The reason is that Amaterasu means "shines over heaven and earth" and is a perfect synonym for "infinite light"; "*ōmi*" in "ōmikami" is an honorific expression, and "kami" is an abbreviation of "*kagami*." The term *kagami,* similarly to the word "kagami" 鏡 (mirror) is the nominal form of the verb *kangamiru* 鑑みる (to reflect, to think), and refers to wisdom. Wisdom (*chie* 智恵), differently from knowledge (*chishiki* 知識), is not attained logically by inference or conceptualization, but intuitively, like a mirror reflects reality, and is an activity that grasps the totality of things at once. This is called *kangamiru* (to reflect), and when it is nominalized we have *kagami,* which, abbreviated, gives us *kami*; the latter was given the Chinese character for "god." Thus, *kami* means a wise being, a perfect synonym for the term Buddha as "Awakened one."[10] Therefore, we can say that choosing Amaterasu Ōmikami as the Japanese translation for Amida Buddha is unquestionably the best translation both in terms of words and in terms of essence. Anybody, when thinking about the Japanese translation of Amida Buddha, would see that this is self-evident, but since no one until now has ever attempted to translate the name Amida Buddha into Japanese, no one has ever noticed this self-evident fact.

B: I agree with you when you say that Amaterasu Ōmikami refers to the Buddha of infinite light, but that only refers to one of the two meanings of the term Amida Buddha; isn't the other meaning, Buddha of infinite life, left out by this translation?

A: No, that's not true. Since Amaterasu Ōmikami is the great goddess shining over heaven and earth, her august name means that she, her august being of perfect wisdom, will continue to illuminate our body and mind as long as heaven and earth exist, from a beginningless beginning to an endless end. Clearly, this also expresses the meaning of Buddha of infinite life.

### *3. Amaterasu Ōmikami and the Buddha Amida*

B: There is no need to mention it here, but Amaterasu Ōmikami is the august ancestor of our imperial family and the deity who established

Japan. On the other hand, the Buddha Amida was once the king of a certain country; he abandoned the profane world and became the monk Hōzō (Dharmakāra). He made a vow and practiced asceticism, and ten kalpas ago he became a Buddha and established the Land of Bliss in the west, past one trillion Buddha-lands away from us; he is the lord of that realm where he presently preaches the Dharma, and in order to save sentient beings in all lands in the ten directions he is causing them to be reborn there. In this way, their names are very similar, but aren't their respective natures profoundly different?

A: I see. The Buddha Amida is said to have become a Buddha ten kalpas ago, but in fact he was already a Buddha since an infinite and incommensurable past time, and thus was already existing at the beginning of heaven and earth, precisely like the first Shinto god Ame no minaka nushi 天御中主. This Buddha, existing since the remotest past, has changed many times his appearance, and has manifested himself as many different Buddhas; in particular, the Buddha Amida, in which the monk Dharmakāra achieved his path, is the figure (*okata* お方) with whom we are most familiar today and have the closest connection. Also, it is said that he established his realm far away to the west, but his realm is vast and limitless and extends in the ten directions; the light of that Buddha is infinite and encompasses the ten directions, so that there is no place that is not his Land of Bliss, and there is nothing that is not under Amida's light. However, if we look at Amaterasu Ōmikami, she is the august child of the gods Izanagi and Izanami, direct descendants of the god Ame no minaka nushi, who appeared at the beginning of heaven and earth;[11] as is clear from her name, she shines forever everywhere in heaven and earth. She dispatched to this country (Japan) the imperial ancestor god Ninigi, saying, "The land of fecund rice-ears and reed-plains of the one-thousand-five-hundred autumns should be ruled by my descendants. You, imperial descendant, rule it! Go, and prosper there forever!"[12] and gave him the three imperial regalia. "The land of fecund rice-ears and reed-plains" should be understood as the entire world, and the eternal imperial rule (*tenjō mukyū* 天壌無窮) refers to the infinite life (*muryōju* 無量寿) of the emperor. The three imperial regalia are, as is well known, the jewel, the mirror, and the sword, and should be interpreted as symbols of compassion, wisdom, and power. Ruling the world by means of these three regalia is the august destiny of our emperors, beginning with the god Ame no minaka nushi, continuing with Amaterasu Ōmikami, until our present emperor. One cannot say that the Buddha

Amida's deeds recorded in India, and the august traces of Amaterasu Ōmikami, which constitute the roots of our country's history, are perfectly identical to the smallest detail, but their natures are essentially very much similar enough that it is not difficult to infer that the same universal truth has been expressed in slightly different hues according to each respective national style.

## *4. The Imperial Family of Our Country as the August Descendants of Amaterasu Ōmikami and Śākyamuni as a Manifestation of the Buddha Amida*

B: From what you say, I understand that Amida and Amaterasu Ōmikami are the same entity, and one would think that the only difference between them is that the former has an Indian name, whereas the latter has a Japanese name. However, there is a fundamental difference: while I have never heard that the descendants of Amida reside in some country on earth, the noble descendants of Amaterasu Ōmikami are the imperial family in its uninterrupted and eternal lineage, the historical emperors of our Japan. How do you explain this?

A: You point out an essential issue here. Amida Buddha is presently in the Pure Land of Bliss (Gokuraku Jōdo), past one trillion buddha-lands to the west, exactly in the same way as Amaterasu Ōmikami resides in Takamagahara.[13] However, the noble descendant in the direct lineage of Amaterasu Ōmikami is now His Majesty the Emperor of Japan, but the descendants of Amida Buddha are nowhere to be found. Śākyamuni, born in India in the royal family of the country of Kapilavastu, is said to be a manifestation of the Buddha Amida, and in this aspect, he resembles our Imperial Majesty, who is the noble descendant of Amaterasu Ōmikami. But in many other important aspects, the two are completely different. First of all, the country of Kapilavastu in India was not established by the descendants of Amida Buddha, and therefore is incomparably inferior to our country of Japan, which was established by Emperor Jinmu, the noble descendant in the direct lineage of Amaterasu Ōmikami. Indeed, the country of Kapilavastu was utterly destroyed by a neighboring country during Śākyamuni's lifetime. Because his was such a lowly country, Śākyamuni knew that he could not realize his own ideal to make it a powerful country worthy of the manifestation of Buddha Amida; accordingly, he abandoned his country, gave up his royal title and his royal family, and became an ascetic and went to practice in the mountains. After six years of ascetic practice, he was eventually able to establish his ideal country in the world of Dharma and ascended to the throne as Dharma King—as appropriate for a manifestation of the Buddha Amida; throughout his life he preached the Dharma and saved many sentient beings. However, Śākyamuni entered nirvana already 2,400 years ago, and does not live in this world now.

### 5. *Why Buddhism, Which Originated in the Lost Kingdom of Kapilavastu, Is Beneficial to Our Country, Which Is Characterized Instead by the Eternal Rule of the Emperors as Sanctioned by the Gods*

B: But then, Amida Buddha and Amaterasu Ōmikami are the same being; Śākyamuni the manifestation of Amida Buddha is already dead and his country of Kapilavastu in India no longer exists, whereas our imperial family—the descendants of Amaterasu Ōmikami, as living gods, have been more prosperous each generation, and the noble country they rule, our country of Japan, will continue to prosper forever together with heaven and earth, and we, its citizens, as babies born from the various generations of these living gods, should be nice to each other and should always be loyal to our noble country. In this way, Śākyamuni's ideals will be very much realized in our own country. Does this mean that we no longer need Buddhism?

A: No, that's not true. Since our country is originally the "country in which people do not state their individual will" (*kotoage senu kuni*, 言上げせぬ国), we are not used to express things theoretically, but instead we have been realizing and implementing in practical terms the ideas of kami and buddhas. In other words, we are a nation which can realize those ideals in the real world, and because of that, since ancient times our citizens have devoted their efforts exclusively toward the implementation of those ideals, without spending much time honing abstract ideas. However, we have imported and learned those aspects from countries with a long history of honing ideals, mastering scientific principles, and perfecting theories, such as China, India, and the West; thus, we have become able to present the foundations of our own practices, explain them, and savor their ideas. This will be very important also in the future. Without theory, one cannot understand the actual meaning of things; without a grasp of scientific principles one cannot clarify universality; and without honing ideals, it is possible to lose track of the course of action. Since its establishment, our country has learned religion and science from other countries, and they have had a large impact as the basic elements for our life. Buddhism, in particular, has contributed, and will keep contributing, a great deal to the growth and development of our country.

B: The country of Kapilavastu in India no longer exists, and Śākyamuni was the prince of that lost country. For what reason does Buddhism, taught by the king of an extinct country, contribute to the growth and development of our own country of Japan, which is not only endless like heaven and earth but will also continue to prosper forever?

A: The direction of wind has changed dramatically, hasn't it? Aren't you a Buddhist believer? Don't you feel the acute desire to worship again Amida in your family shrine with gratitude? In spire of that, you suddenly change your attitude, and attack Buddhism with a vilifying way of speaking.

B: That's not what I meant, but listening to you, I have gradually begun to think that Buddhism is actually quite meaningless and useless for us Japanese. Nonetheless, I do believe in Buddhism and would like to worship Amida with gratitude. Please, teach me how to do that.

A: Anyway, Śākyamuni was a noble man born with a status that would bring him to become the king of his country. I am sure that at the beginning he wanted to make his country into a splendid, ideal country, that he wanted to become an excellent king of that country, and that he wanted to make his citizens happy. However, as I said before, that country was hopeless, and eventually he became an ascetic, abandoned the profane world, and entered the realm of Dharma.

## 6. Śākyamuni's Motivations to Become an Ascetic and Prince Shōtoku's Noble Activities in the Profane World

B: Sorry to interrupt you, but I've heard that Śākyamuni's motivation to become an ascetic was the desire to escape the four or eight forms of suffering (*shiku hakku* 四苦八苦), that is, birth, old age, illness, and death, the pain caused by the fact that one must eventually be separated from the persons one loves, or by the fact that at some point one must deal with something one hates, or that one cannot get what one desires; not only that, he also wanted to help other sentient beings to escape such suffering. But you are saying that he became an ascetic out of pessimism because his country in India was hopeless and could not become an ideal country. Which version is true?

A: Of course, since Śākyamuni was also a human being, it is possible that, like all human beings, he was afflicted by the four or eight forms of suffering, and decided to become an ascetic in order to escape them. However, I don't think that this was the only source of Śākyamuni's suffering. In addition to types of suffering he had in common with all human beings, there must have been something particular that afflicted him alone. I haven't studied the life of the Buddha in detail, so I don't know how standard hagiographies put it, but no matter what later people wrote, someone like Śākyamuni, as heir to the throne, must certainly have felt a responsibility to improve his country and bring happiness to its citizens. I cannot even begin to understand the pessimism he must have felt when looking with that state of mind at the reality of that Indian country of his. He understood that he could not establish his ideal country in the real world, became an ascetic and entered the world of Dharma, and eventually discovered the country of the Buddha Amida which met his ideals.[14] In this regard, I'd like to consider what Śākyamuni would have done if he had been born in Japan, whether he would have become an ascetic or not. What do you think?

B: Well, perhaps he would not have become an ascetic. In this respect, that reminds me of Prince Shōtoku 聖徳太子. He is called the Buddhist master of Japan; he deeply believed in Buddhism and spread it in Japan and put it in practice in his government. In a sense, we could say that he is Śākyamuni born in our imperial family. Prince Shōtoku did not become an ascetic. He lectured about Buddhist scriptures at court and practiced Buddhism as a lay person.[15]

A: This is an important point. I'm glad you noticed it! It is exactly as you say. As it is also stated in the Imperial Rescript on Education (*Kyōiku chokugo* 教育勅語), the imperial ancestor Amaterasu Ōmikami, out of her boundless virtues, created our country of Japan and subsequently our imperial family inherited it forever in a continuous and uninterrupted line; its citizens, throughout all generations, have been loyal and filial, and each of them has been of the same mind in joining together to realize the essence of our national polity (*kokutai*).[16] The country of the Buddha Amida which Śākyamuni discovered upon entering the world of Dharma has been clearly and splendidly developed here in Japan in the real world. Therefore, in Japan, it's not necessary to abandon the profane world in order to enter the Dharma; instead, it is possible to realize the Dharma within the profane world and as a lay person; in fact, the Dharma has been steadily realized and will continue to be also in the future. For this reason, all the sutras that Buddha taught after entering the world of Dharma and attaining enlightenment are very useful as reference materials in order to establish the theoretical, religious, and philosophical foundations of Japan's national polity (*kokutai*). However, we cannot deny the fact that, since those sutras were taught in India, are expressed in an Indian language and their audience was composed of Indians, they smell of India—they contain elements of the Indian style which is different from our national style. We have to be careful with them. If we strip them without hesitation of their Indian smell and perfume them instead with our national style, Buddhism will be the best source to foster our national system of thought.

## *7. Which Sacred Image Should Be Worshiped by Japanese Buddhists*

B: Now I understand much better. Regarding Amida in the family shrine, how should I understand it? How should I think of it when I worship?

A: As I said before, the Buddha Amida is the deified form of the universe and of nature, pervaded by wisdom and compassion, which Śākyamuni discovered when he entered the world of Dharma; it has been sculpted in a form that resembles Śākyamuni in the Indian style. I guess this is the reason why it no longer fits your sentiments. Your long experience makes you understand the great debt of gratitude (*daion* 大恩) toward Amida Buddha, the deified form of the universe and nature—in Japanese language, Amaterasu Ōmikami; you believe in it, you have entrusted yourself to it, and you have begun a new life of service to it. For a while, you worshiped with gratitude the anthropomorphic image of the Buddha Amida in your family shrine, but after all you are not Indian, you are Japanese, and with age your essence has become manifest, and at a certain point, you felt dissatisfied with the Indian-style Amida. In addition, a wooden statue or a painting, no matter how well made, lacks the blood of living human beings. In order to express the deified form of the living universe and nature, the form of a living human being is necessary, otherwise it will feel unsatisfactory; this is perfectly reasonable. The fact that you feel that the Indian-style wooden Amida in your family shrine is not enough, and that you are seeking a more living sacred image to worship, is because your faith has deepened and you have come to realize the obvious way of life for a Japanese. This is excellent! Our august object of worship, a living manifestation of both Amida Buddha and Amaterasu Ōmikami, who are the deified forms of the universe and nature, is presently in the Imperial Palace in Tokyo. It is no else than His

Majesty the Emperor! You should know that Amida in your family shrine is no other than His Majesty the Emperor, in the Indian style and with the shape appropriate to the world of Dharma, whom you placed there and worship.

B: That's very convoluted! If I want to pay respect to and worship His Majesty the Emperor, I don't need that wooden statue in Indian style resembling Śākyamuni; isn't it better to worship directly His Majesty the Emperor by turning oneself toward the Imperial Palace? Or, if one wishes to worship the august image of His Majesty the Emperor day and night, one should place his august portrait in the alcove (*tokonoma*) and worship him at heart's content.[17]

A: If you feel like doing so, that's excellent, please go ahead and do it. But since you said that you wanted to be able to worship more dearly and in a more meaningful way the wooden image of Amida you have in your family shrine, I simply told you the way to do it. Furthermore, while it is true that Buddhism—its teachings, images, and scriptures—come from India and their Indian smell has somewhat affected our national style, the system of thought, philosophy, and religion coming out of its profound path to enlightenment have significantly nurtured the intellectual life of our nation and cultivated the foundation of our national polity; it is not meaningless, then, to worship an Indian-style image of the Buddha Amida to express one's gratitude for all that. Therefore, if I may suggest it, the most appropriate thing to do for a Buddhist believer would be, as a Japanese, to worship everyday the august portrait of His Majesty the Emperor, who is an august expression of the divine essence of the universe and nature, and at the same time worship every day the venerable image in Indian style of the Buddha Amida out of gratitude for nurturing our intellectual system over many years. On the first day of this year I have myself begun, albeit belatedly, to perform my morning devotions according this method.

## *8. The Question of the Survival of Individual Consciousness after Death*

B: Thank you very much for all this. You have dispelled doubts that I had been harboring for many years, and now my heart feels suddenly lighter. I would like to ask you one last important question . . .

A: Please, go ahead, feel free to frankly ask anything you wish.

B: What happens to our consciousness after death?

A: What a difficult question! That is a troubling issue. However, if your motivation in asking this question lies in your worries about your happiness after death, I would prefer not to answer, because if you are concerned about this matter it means that you are still prisoner of a petty spirit as before, when your anxiety made you suffer, being only concerned about your little individual self. So, if I got involved in it and told you that if you do this, after death you will be happy, but if you do that after death you will be unhappy, you would end up more deeply immersed into it, and I'm afraid you'd fall again into anxiety about your individual fate after death, like a little, petty ghost. What is your motivation for asking this question?

B: Please don't get back to me so aggressively. Let me confess honestly. At some point I did fall prey to selfish, petty anxiety. I understand very well what you said before, that in this present existence, it is good enough to devote one's life out of utter loyalty to His Majesty and to our country. If one spends one's life earnestly in this way, in the next existence one should expect to be reborn in a good place such as the Land of Bliss, but is it really so? Since this thought came to my mind, I decided to ask you. Well, let me change completely the motivation for my question, and ask you instead what are the results of scientific studies about the world after death. This is just out of my desire for knowledge.

A: If it is so, I am afraid I can only tell you that I don't know. First of all, whether individual mental phenomena continue to exist in some way after death is an issue that cannot be explained scientifically. Even the academia is divided about this, and they still haven't come up with a definitive answer. I think that this will be clarified in the future, but right now to say that this is unknown is the best scientific answer. And if we don't know whether individual mental phenomena continue or not after death, one's destiny after death is an even more intractable question.

B: Then, it is possible that individual mental phenomena will continue, right?

A: That's right.

## *9. The Japanese's Obvious Desire concerning What Happens to the Souls in the Next Life*

B: If they do continue, what should I do?

A: In the hypothetical case that each individual's free will should determine whatever happens, right?

B: Yes.

A: In that case, shouldn't we expect that it will be the same as one wishes in this present existence? If it is true that in the present world one wants to work with all one's force and dedicate one's life to the country, the sovereign, and society, one would certainly want the same also after death. If one changes one's ideas after death, that means that one's ideas in the present existence were just provisional and temporary.

B: I see. But then, the traditional desire of the Buddhists to be reborn after death in the splendid pure land, after having done good things and having had faith in Amida in this world, is wrong, isn't it?

A: That also depends on motivations. The idea of leaving Japan, leaving the earth to be reborn in a distant buddha-land and attain individual peace there after death, is a cold, selfish, and stingy idea; it doesn't fit the Japanese Spirit, but neither does it fit Mahāyāna Buddhism. It is more like the temper of the Lesser Vehicle's Śravaka (direct disciples of the Buddha) or even the hungry ghosts. The Pure Land teachings also say that rebirth in the Land of Bliss is not in order to enjoy oneself there as an individual, but to become able to save sentient beings. But even so, "saving sentient beings" is a vague expression. For us Japanese, the place with which we have the strongest ties is of course our country of Japan. Even if by hypothesis one should be reborn in the Land of Bliss, it is sure that one would certainly return immediately to Japan, to continue to devote all one's power to loyally serve His Majesty, protect one's country, serve one's parents and siblings both in flesh and spirit, support one's fellow citizens, help our neighboring country China, and contribute to the realization of the harmonization of all countries in the world beginning with peace in East Asia. I think that this should be the vision of the future for a Japanese citizen who has acquired true awareness.

B: Is there any Buddhist in the past who taught such a thing?

A: Not many. I think that the vision of the future of Kusunoki Masashige 楠木正成, who was a deep believer of Buddhism, corresponds to my teaching I just expounded. Masashige, when he was mortally injured at Minatogawa, said that he wanted to be reborn seven times in Japan to serve his imperial country.[18] Here, "seven times" does not mean "one time less than eight times," it means "always." Kasunoki Masashige, as a Japanese Buddhist, wished from the bottom of his heart to remain for ever in this country to serve it in the future, and through the activities of the country, to serve all humanity in the world and all living beings in

the universe. I think we all should follow Masashige and desire to serve our imperial country throughout life and death in our respective status and profession. This is the what the practitioner of the living *nenbutsu,* the true person to be reborn in the Land of Bliss, would do today.
B: Thank you very much!

A: Thank you for listening with attention.

## Notes

1 Fabio Rambelli. "Buddhism and the Capitalist Transformation of Modern Japan: Sada Kaiseki (1818–1882), Uchiyama Gudō (1874–1911), and Itō Shōshin (1876–1963)," in *Buddhist Modernities: Reinventing Traditions in the Globalizing Modern World,* ed. Hanna Havnevik et al. (London and New York: Routledge, 2017), 33–50.

2 See Fabio Rambelli, *Zen Anarchism: The Egalitarian Dharma of Uchiyama Gudō* (Berkeley, CA: Institute for Buddhist Studies, 2013).

3 Itō Shōshin, "Waga mugaai seikatsu shinjō," *Daisekai* 11, no. 7 (July 1956): 63.

4 Ibid., 62.

5 Itō Shōshin, *Shinsei bukkyōgaku* (Tokyo: Dōshi dōkōsha, 1942).

6 Itō, "Waga mugaai seikatsu shinjō," 65.

7 Itō Shōshin, *Ikita Amida-sama wa izuko ni gozaru ka* (Aichi: Mugaen hakkō, 1937).

8 The family shrine (*butsudan*) is still present in the vast majority of Japanese households, where is used to memorialize the family's deceased members.

9 Despite his pantheistic spiritualism, Itō is clearly a champion of scientific and technological progress.

10 Of course, this etymology of *kami* is far-fetched, but helps Itō to show nominalistically that Amida and Amaterasu are two designations of the same entity.

11 Ame no minaka nushi is the first god in Shinto mythology.

12 This is a reference to a section of the *Kojiki* (712), in which Amaterasu orders her grandson Ninigi to take possession of Japan, after which the first emperor, Jinmu, was sent down to earth to rule Japan. See Basil Hall Chamberlain, *The Kojiki: Records of Ancient Matters* (Rutland, VT: Tuttle, 2005), 112, 127–133.

13 Takamagahara 高天原, lit. "high heavenly plains," is the heavenly realm in which, according to Shinto ancient mythology, the heavenly gods reside

(as opposed to the earthly gods, who were native to Japan before the descent and rule of the first emperor, Jinmu).

14 This interpretation of Śākyamuni's life and his motivations seems to be unique to Itō, who also wrote about it in other works. He clearly sees a political dimension in Śākyamuni's thought and activity, namely, the desire to establish an "ideal country" on earth, a desire that was fatally thwarted by the "hopeless" nature of Śākyamuni's own state. Itō does not state explicitly what he means by "ideal country," but we can infer it from his description of Japan, where a divine emperor is dedicated to the welfare of his subjects and engaged in establishing an eternal world harmony, and its citizens are constantly devoted to serving the emperor, the state, and the common good.

15 Prince Shōtoku (Shōtoku Taishi, 572–622) was the regent under Empress Suiko (554–628, r. 593–628); he is traditionally considered responsible for the diffusion of Buddhism into Japan.

16 "National polity" (*kokutai*) was one of the central keywords of imperial ideology and propaganda until the end of World War II. The official definition of this term can be found in the *Kokutai no hongi,* a text published by the Japanese Ministry of Education in 1937. See *Kokutai no hongi. Cardinal Principles of the National Entity of Japan* (Cambridge, MA: Harvard University Press, 1949).

17 This passage refers to two common ways to pay respect to the emperor that developed in modern Japan and were promoted by official propaganda: turning toward the direction of Tokyo, where the imperial palace was located, and bow; or bowing in front of a portrait of the emperor located in the alcove (*tokonoma*), traditionally the most symbolically important part of a private house.

18 Kusunoki Masashige (1294–1336) was a warrior fighting for Emperor Go-Daigo in his attempt to overcome the Kamakura military government of the Shogun. He died in the battle of Minatogawa in present-day Kobe. He and his brother, a fellow samurai, exchanged vows to be reborn again in Japan for seven more lives in order to serve the emperor. In the Edo period, Masashige came to be considered a model of samurai values; until the end of World War II, the modern Japanese state adopted and amplified Masashige's symbolism.

## Bibliography

Chamberlain, Basil Hall, trans. *The Kojiki: Records of Ancient Matters.* Rutland, VT: Tuttle, 2005.

Itō Shōshin 伊藤証信. *Ikita Amida-sama wa izuko ni gozaru ka* 生きた阿弥陀様は何処に御座るか. Aichi: Mugaen 無我苑, 1937.

———. *Shinsei bukkyōgaku* 真正仏教学. Tokyo: Dōshi dōkōsha 同士同行社, 1942.

———. "Waga mugaai seikatsu shinjō" 我が無我愛生活信条, *Daisekai* 大世界 11, no. 7 (July 1956): 61–65.

*Kokutai no hongi. Cardinal Principles of the National Entity of Japan*. Cambridge, MA: Harvard University Press, 1949.

Rambelli, Fabio. "Buddhism and the Capitalist Transformation of Modern Japan: Sada Kaiseki (1818–1882), Uchiyama Gudō (1874–1911), and Itō Shōshin (1876–1963)." In *Buddhist Modernities: Reinventing Traditions in the Globalizing Modern World*, edited by Hanna Havnevik et al., 33–50. London: Routledge, 2017.

———. *Zen Anarchism: The Egalitarian Dharma of Uchiyama Gudō*. Berkeley, CA: Institute for Buddhist Studies. 2013.

# Chapter 3

# "The Future of American Buddhism"

Michihiro Ama

## Translator's Introduction

"The Future of American Buddhism" (*Amerika bukkyō no shōrai*) is written by Tana Daishō (1901–1972), a Shin Buddhist minister affiliated with the Buddhist Churches of America (BCA). Tana is best known as the author of *A Diary of An Enemy Alien in Santa Fe and Lordsburg Internment Camps* (*Santa Fe, Lordsburg, senji tekikokujin yokuryūsho nikki*, 1976–1989), written in Japanese in four volumes, about his experience while interned during the Pacific War (1941–1945). The BCA is the oldest ethnic Buddhist organization in the United States and is part of the Nishi Honganji organization, a dominant branch of Jōdo Shinshū, with headquarters in Kyoto, Japan. In the West, Jōdo Shinshū is known as Shin Buddhism founded on the teaching of Shinran (1173–1263).

Tana was born in the city of Sapporo on the island of Hokkaidō in March 1901. Because of his family's poor economic situation, he was raised by his grandparents. After Tana completed elementary school, his grandparents sent him to a Shin Buddhist temple in Astubetsu in Hokkaidō, where the old and childless resident priest made him his apprentice. Tana received ordination at the age of seventeen. Because he decided to stay on in Kyoto, the resident priest in Atsubetsu arranged for Tana to work at the Nishi Honganji headquarters. Later, after being assigned to the Sunday School Department at the age of twenty-four, he qualified as an overseas minister (*kaikyōshi*). In 1924, the headquarters sent him to Taiwan, transferred him to the Berkeley Buddhist Temple in the United States in 1928, and brought him back to Japan two years later. He was sent to Korea in 1934 and then reassigned to Berkeley in 1936. He returned to Japan the next year and married Tomoe at the age of thirty-eight. Tomoe was born in a temple family in Hokkaidō and was a sister of Tana's fellow minister, Hayashima Daitetsu, who also came to the United States as *kaikyōshi* in 1937. Tana returned to Berkeley with Tomoe in 1938 and had two sons, Yasuto and Shibun. Their other sons, Chinin and Akira, were born during the internment and postwar period, respectively.

When the Japanese navy attacked Pearl Harbor, Tana was serving in Lompoc, California. The Federal Bureau of Investigation arrested him immediately. After the attack, Tana was first detained at the Santa Barbara County jail, transferred to a Civilian Conservation Corp camp in Tujunga, outside Los Angeles, and then to the Santa Fe internment camp (New Mexico) in March 1942. The War Relocation Authority transferred him to the army's Lordsburg internment camp (New Mexico) about three months later but then returned him to the Santa Fe internment camp in 1943. In Santa Fe, Tana suffered recurring bouts of tuberculosis, which he had developed in Taiwan, and was hospitalized until the War Relocation Authority released him in April 1946, approximately seven months after the war had ended. In the meantime, after his arrest, Tana's wife and children were forced to move to Tulare Assembly Center and then to the Gila Relocation Center, Arizona, as a result of Executive Order 9066.

After the war, Tana and his family moved to Richmond, California, and then to Hawaii. He worked in Nishi Honganji's Hawaii District, known as the Honpa Hongwanji Mission of Hawaii, for about three years. He then returned to the Buddhist Churches of America in 1951. After serving at the Palo Alto and San Mateo Buddhist Temples as resident minister, he became head of the BCA Sunday School Department in 1955. Illness forced him to resign from the BCA in 1959. He died in 1972 in Palo Alto.

In 1955, the BCA Sunday School Department commissioned Tana to initiate a project to compile textbooks in commemoration of Shinran's seven hundredth year. Tana collected materials and wrote on four separate topics in Japanese: "Introduction to Buddhism" (*Bukkyō nyūmon*), "The Teaching of Buddha" (*Hotoke no kyōbō*), "The Buddha's Salvation" (*Hotoke no kyūsai*), and "The Life of Buddhists" (*Busshi seikatsu*). After a textbook advisory committee's review, three Nisei ministers used his writings as references, and the BCA published *Buddhism for Youth, Part One: Buddha and His Disciples* in 1962 and *Buddhism for Youth, Part Two: The Teaching of Buddha* in 1965, both of which discuss the basic principles of Buddhism but not of Shin Buddhism.

Tana later wrote a set of three books in Japanese. They were on the same themes as his earlier works but more intensive and written in a "question and answer" style: *The Buddha's Salvation* (*Hotoke no kyūsai*) in 1966, *The Life of Buddhists* (*Busshi seikatsu*) in 1969, and *The Teaching of Buddha* (*Hotoke no kyōbō*) in 1972. Each volume contains a collection of his correspondence to his former Sunday school students during his internment.

The section translated as "The Future of American Buddhism" is included in *The Life of Buddhists*. In this book, Tana aimed to explain the basic teachings of Śākyamuni and Shinran to BCA Sunday school children, the ideal Buddhist way of life for children, and the future of Shin Buddhism in the United States. Like his predecessors before the war, Tana diverged from Shin Buddhist practices in Japan and catered to the Nisei laity's demands, while re-evaluating traditional values and reapplying Japanese practices to their current situation. In "The Future of American Buddhism," Tana identified the presence of diverse Buddhist practices as one of the challenges that Shin Buddhists faced in the United States. Unlike in Japan, where established Buddhist denominations created their own boundaries within the setting of Mahāyāna Buddhism and remained indifferent to Southeast Asian Buddhist practices, Euro-American sympathizers began their studies of Buddhism following the Theravada tradition. Tana thus explained the importance of bridging differences between Shin Buddhism and other forms of Buddhism in the United States and advised young Shin Buddhists not to engage in denominational competition as Buddhists did in Japan.

Tana also defined Shin Buddhism as a family religion and suggested ways Sunday school children could adapt traditional Shin Buddhist practices to their religious climate in the United States. In particular, he aimed to integrate Japanese Buddhist practice at home into the conventions of households in the United States. He argued that Shin ministers in the United States conducted memorial services mainly at temples for more than seventy years, even though their Japanese counterparts performed such services at the homes of temple members. Reflecting on this Japanese custom, Tana proposed to make each household in the United States a center of Buddhist activity. He felt that what Shin Buddhists observed at temple needed to be extended to their private spheres so they could practice Buddhism at home. For example, Tana suggested Thanksgiving as a day to commemorate the passing of Shinran, who died on November 28,[1] and Christmas as a day to celebrate Gautama Siddartha's enlightenment. Instead of a Christmas tree, Tana suggested a bodhi tree with a statue of the Buddha underneath. Tana thus attempted to relocate

Buddhist practice from the temple to the home and adapt Christian American household practices to Shin Buddhist life.

Tana's vision for American Buddhism is perceived exclusively from the lens of Shin Buddhism. He does not discuss the future of American Buddhism from a broader perspective nor make concrete suggestions for young American Shin Buddhists to consider Theravāda practice. His suggestions are not doctrinal but social and conventional. His approach is Japan-centered because his primary concern was how to educate BCA Sunday school children within an American Buddhist context and stimulate their interest in the religion of their parents. It is, however, unclear how much the BCA Sunday school children and members of the BCA's Young Buddhist Associations actually put Tana's suggestions into practice.

In fact, according to Michael Masatsugu, during the 1950s a number of Nisei Shin Buddhists participated in the Berkeley Buddhist Study Group, which was affiliated with the BCA.[2] This group engaged in a transsectarian Buddhist dialogue with Euro-American Buddhists, including the Beats, Asians, and Asian Americans. These people sought a universal Buddhism; their discussions included different Buddhist practices, reflecting on their racial and ethnic backgrounds.[3] For those Nisei Shin Buddhists, Tana's exclusive focus on Shin Buddhism might have appeared too sectarian, even though he had proposed that Shin Buddhists adopt broader Buddhist practices.

"The Future of American Buddhism" suggests how Shin Buddhism could be transformed in American society. Tana discusses a Japanese perception of the religious climate of the United States, evaluates Shin Buddhist practice in particular and Japanese Buddhist practices in general vis-à-vis the rise of Euro-American interest in Buddhism, and demonstrates a development of the BCA Sunday school curriculum. It is a testimonial to the transpacific development of Japanese Buddhism.

For this translation, some of the words Tana used are translated slightly differently, depending on context. *Bukkyōkai* is translated as either a Buddhist temple or Buddhist church, reflecting the name of the Buddhist Churches of America (BCA). This organization started out as the Buddhist Mission of North America (BMNA) but changed its name to the BCA shortly after BMNA issued a statement pledging loyalty to the government of the United States at the beginning of the Pacific War. For the translation of *beikoku*, both America and the United States are used, even though "America" in English is a broad term suggesting North, Central, and South America and various countries included in those regions.

**TRANSLATION**

"The Future of American Buddhism"

Tana Daishō

## Implications for the Future of American Buddhism

There are great expectations for what is referred to as American Buddhism. The Buddhism we have heard till today in our Japanese American communities in the United States is brought by Japanese immigrants. It is thus natural that the children of those immigrants—the Nisei and Sansei (second and third generation of people of Japanese ancestry)—hear about Buddhism in the same way their parents did. Buddhism was introduced into Japan from China and assimilated into Japanese society, after which it came to be known as Japanese Buddhism.

And it is that form of Buddhism that has been introduced into the United States. In order for Japanese Buddhism to be accepted, not only by Japanese Americans, but also by the people of the United States in general, it needs to be integrated into American customs, habits, and moral standards. By discussing what those of us living during the pioneering era of American Buddhism can do at this moment, the maturity of American Buddhism is anticipated.

Question: What is the attitude we must have concerning the future of American Buddhism?

Answer: According to Euro-Americans who study Buddhism, no religion is more religiously tolerant than Buddhism. They give as proof the fact that it originated in India, spreading to China and then to Japan, demonstrating the peaceful transmission of Buddhism from one country to another. Accordingly, we should not try to make the United States a Buddhist country by religiously conquering it.

Question: What do you mean by integrating Buddhism into American customs and moral standards and way of doing things?

Answer: After the Pacific War, Japanese styles seem to have become popular in American music and architecture. The eaves of houses seem to be getting long as in Japanese houses. The roofs of some libraries look just like those Buddhist temples in Japan. It is in subtle ways like those, Buddhism should contribute to spiritual culture in the United States.

Question: What is the first thing we must do?

Answer: The spirit of freedom of religion, which was sought by European immigrants to the United States, is still strong in this country. While valuing their own religion, Americans respect the religion of others. Ignoring this religious attitude and asserting only the excellence of Buddhism will be counterproductive. Buddhism should be as salt is in cooking and blend into American religious consciousness.

Question: Why is such caution necessary in the United States where freedom of religion is guaranteed?

Answer: A hundred years have passed since Japan opened up to the Western world. Japan was flooded with a myriad of Western cultural influences. Propagation of Christianity, which had been banned during the Tokugawa period (1603–1867), also began. Especially immediately after the Pacific War, American missionaries spread the Christian teaching enthusiastically by taking advantage of the US occupation of Japan. Despite all that activity, according to a survey in 1961, there are only 727,445 Christians in Japan, which has a population of ninety million. That low rate of success shows that American missionaries ignored traditional Japanese religious sentiments, including the practice of ancestor worship, and attempted to make Christianity in Japan the way it is in Europe and the United States.

Consider this. Four hundred years ago, European missionaries introduced the Blessed Virgin Mary to the Japanese as a "child-caring bodhisattva" (*kosodate kannon*) as an object of worship. The result was an unprecedented number of Christian converts, many of whom died in Japan as martyrs when national unifiers of Japan [such as Toyotomi Hideyoshi (1536–1598) and Tokugawa Ieyasu (1542–1616)] banned Christianity. Buddhist propagation in a new land must be peaceful and not disturb the religious sentiment of the people you wish to convert.

Question: What else should we be careful about when introducing Buddhism to the United States?

Answer: The Japanese Buddhist denominations have mutually excluded themselves from each other, and unfortunately Japanese immigrants have carried this practice to the United States. Here in America, however, religions are mutually respected. As followers of the same Mahāyāna Buddhist traditions, we should not engage in doctrinal debates, arguing about which Buddhist denomination is superior. We can start this lesson with our Sunday schools. About forty or fifty years ago, Sunday schools of different Buddhist denominations in Japan began celebrating Hanamatsuri together and now in the United States the Hanamatsuri celebration is being held jointly by the Federation of Japanese Buddhist denominations. This is where the spirit of Sangha, represented by the saying "There is absolutely nothing that can obstruct a crowd that is united," can be seen.

## The Past and the Present of American Buddhism

When we speak of "American Buddhism" in the Buddhist Churches of America (hereafter the BCA, *beikoku bukkyōdan*), we point only to the Mahāyāna Buddhist tradition that was brought to the United States from Japan, where the relationship between the Mahāyāna and Theravāda Buddhist traditions is not considered seriously. That is because the Japanese do not have a history of practicing Theravāda Buddhism. In the United States, however, the Theravāda Buddhism [of Ceylon] has been introduced through the English language and practiced. That is what has made it easy for Americans to accept and practice Zen, when Daisetz Suzuki (1870–1966) promoted it. As the result of the World Buddhist Conference, the term Hinayāna Buddhism (*shōjō* in Japanese, meaning "small vehicle") is no longer used because of its association with inferiority, compared to Mahāyāna Buddhism, seen as "larger vehicle."

Question: How was the Buddhism of Ceylon [Sri Lanka] introduced in the United States? How does it differ from Japanese Buddhism?

Answer: Christian missionaries introduced Southern Buddhism to Europe. During the seventeenth and eighteenth centuries when Western imperialism reached Asia, Southern Buddhism became a subject of academic inquiry. It was then introduced to the United States. Henry Steel Olcott (1832–1907), who had served in the Civil War with the rank of colonel, and others organized the Theosophical Society and began promoting Ceylonese Buddhism. Buddhist monks in Ceylon observe the same precepts from the time of Śākyamuni Buddha, including not eating after the noon hour. This must have appealed to puritanical American Christians.

In contrast, Japanese Buddhism is mixed in various cultural colors. The Buddhism originated in India moved to China where it acquired Chinese customs and then to Japan, reflecting diverse cultural backgrounds and conventions of different time periods. Accordingly, Japanese Buddhism is very different from Ceylonese Buddhism.

For American Buddhism to prosper, the Northern and Southern traditions of Buddhism should not compete with each other, but rather reinforce each other by mutually adopting the positive aspects of their different traditions.

Question: Does that mean we must change the meaning and significance of *shinjin* based on *nenbutsu* as used in our Shin Buddhist tradition?

Answer: No. *Shinjin* based on the *nenbutsu* is the eternal Dharma that allows us to attain buddhahood. We should adapt the Buddhist way of life to American society with *shinjin*. In other words, it is a matter of how we organize Buddhist events in the United States.

Question: What do you mean?

Answer: The day Buddha died is very important in Northern Buddhism. Similarly, the day Shinran Shōnin died is important in our tradition. We conduct a *Hōonkō* service every year to commemorate his passing. Further, every Buddhist family observes memorial services for their deceased loved ones. In the United States, however, birthdays of political leaders are considered important. The birthdays of George Washington and Abraham Lincoln are celebrated as national holidays, and birthdays are celebrated for babies and elders alike in every household. In the state of Hawaii, as a result of a state legislature's resolution during 1962, the governor announced that the week of April 8 as the Buddha Day Week. Americans are used to celebrating birthdays but not the days of death. That is why we should consider how to observe *Hōonkō* so it fits smoothly with other celebrations in the United States.

Question: How are Southern Buddhists coping with this matter?

Answer: In general, Southern Buddhists celebrate the so-called Vesak Day on the day of the full moon in May. It commemorates the day the

Buddha was born and his enlightenment and entry into nirvana, and it is called Buddha Day. It is also observed in India and by the Vedanta society in the United States in which many Americans participate.

Question: Wouldn't it be more proper for us to faithfully follow customs of Japanese Buddhists?

Answer: It would be all right for us as individuals, but that would go against the principle of Mahāyāna Buddhism, expressed as "Becoming aware yourself and then leading others to that same awareness" (*jishin kyōninshin*). Bhiksu in Southern Buddhism correctly observe the precept of not eating after noon. But this practice is not for everyone everywhere. This form of precept-centered Buddhism was introduced into Japan about fourteen hundred years ago and developed as the Kosa school (*kusha-shū*) and the Satyasiddhi school (*jōjitsu-shū*). These forms of Buddhism are valuable as schools to study even today, but they have not become denominations for the general public. From this Japanese experience, we must consider how to promote Buddhism from a larger perspective.

## The Way American Buddhism Should Be

Since its inception in 1899, the Buddhist Churches of America has called affiliated temples "XXX Buddhist organization" (temple name *bukkyōkai*). This way of naming should be maintained as an ideal convention in the United States.

In our BCA Sunday schools, Śākyamuni Buddha's teachings are taught together with his life, beginning with his birth, which we celebrate as Hanamatsuri. That is how our students understand Theravāda Buddhism, which was introduced into the United States from western Europe. The BCA's challenge is how to relate *shinjin* based on the *nenbutsu* to the teachings of Theravāda Buddhism as the Dharma that allows us to attain Buddhahood. Jōdo Shinshū, as a form of Japanese Buddhism, has never experienced this problem and this is where American Buddhism differs from Japanese Buddhism.

Following in the footsteps of the BCA, other Japanese Buddhist denominations have established themselves in the United States. The relationship between these Japanese denominations is unfortunately the same as in Japan. They are not friendly with each other and not unified in propagating Buddhism as a whole. We live in the United States. We should, therefore, remove the denominational barriers developed in Japan, because we are all Buddhists who follow the same Mahāyāna tradition and build the future of American Buddhism.

Question: But shouldn't we concentrate on only Shinran Shōnin's Jōdo Shinshū teaching?

Answer: That would be all right if this concerned only those who grew up reciting the *nenbutsu* in Japan. In the United States, however, there is what might be called state religion, loosely based on Christianity. Further, there is the tradition of Southern Buddhism, which has been studied in Europe for more than 120 years. The Southern Buddhist tradition is considered to be basic Buddhism (*konpon bukkyō*) and has been studied as Indian philosophy. Scholars today have investigated the development of Mahāyāna Buddhism from basic Buddhism. If we ignore that research and simply emphasize Amida Buddha's salvation, we will not be able to explain the differences between Shin Buddhist soteriology and Christian salvation. In other words, the reason why Shin Buddhists are Buddhists will not be understood.

Fortunately, the BCA has taught about Śākyamuni's life and basic teaching in Sunday schools. We can thus explain that the basic Buddhist teaching developed into the great tradition of Mahāyāna Buddhism from which the teaching of *shinjin* based on the *nenbutsu* bloomed.

Question: That explanation relates Śākyamuni's teachings taught as United Buddhism (*tsūbukkyō*) and what Śākyamuni Buddha taught about Amida Buddha and the *nenbutsu,* doesn't it? Śākyamuni Buddha and Amida Buddha are not unrelated as we used to be taught, are they?

Answer: In Southern Buddhism, only Śākyamuni Buddha is considered to be a Buddha. In Mahāyāna Buddhism, various activities of Śākyamuni Buddha became distinct and various buddhas came to be considered to embody them. This is like a single ray of sunlight being divided as the colors of a rainbow appearing to us. Just as we perceive the sunlight through the various colors of a rainbow, the teaching of *shinjin* based on *nenbutsu* helps us understand the primary aspect of the Buddha—that is, nirvana—and allow us to entrust the salvific power of Amida Buddha through Śākyamuni Buddha's teachings. In our tradition, the relationship between Śākyamuni and Amida Buddha is indicated by the figure of the baby Buddha and that of Amida Buddha—that is, both are standing.

In his *Hymns of the Pure Land* (*Jōdo wasan*), Shinran shōnin explains their relationship:

> Amida, who attained buddhahood in the infinite past,
> Full of compassion for foolish beings of the five defilements,
> Took the form of Śākyamuni Buddha
> And appeared in Gaya.[4]

Question: How should we understand Bodhisattva Dharmākara (*hōzō bosatsu*) from the standpoint of today's world?

Answer: Most of the world religions consider that there is only one God. That is why Western scholars understand the Theravāda Buddhist position that Śākyamuni Buddha is the sole Buddha. Our religion becomes problematic in the United States, because we treat Amida Buddha existentially, which leads to the question of whether Dharmākara exists or not, and doubts about Bodhisattva Dharmākara arise. Dharmākara is like a single color of a rainbow whose appearance helps us understand the importance of sunlight in general. Amida Buddha's salvation is the working of the primary Buddha in the world of nirvana, which is shown to us by Śākyamuni Buddha. In order to make this clear, the sutra explains that once upon a time a king abandoned the world with the intention of creating a land where all sentient beings are embraced. That king came to be known as Bodhisattva Dharmākara, whose story is similar to the story of Gautama Siddhārtha, who left his kingdom and became an ascetic. In Shin Buddhism, this story is known as the origin of Amida Buddha or the origin of Original Vow that saves all sentient beings.

Question: How did Japanese Buddhist denominations become separated from each other as they are now?

Answer: Most Japanese Buddhist denominations were founded by the political authority of the day. In the beginning of the seventeenth century, the Tokugawa shogunate, for instance, divided the former Honganji into East Honganji (Higashi Honganji) and West Honganji (Nishi Honganji) to weaken the Honganji's influence. Therefore, even though Buddhist monks and priests were supposedly in accord with each other, denominational leaders competed with other denominations. Such competition gradually affected each denomination's local temples and also the attitude of the members. As the result, only few visit temples other than those of their own denomination. This kind of background, created before the Meiji era, continues to persist in Japan. That is why even though Japan is often seen as a Buddhist country, the opinions of Buddhists as a whole are not reflected on the politics of Japan. It will be troublesome if Japanese Buddhist denominations continue this practice in the United States.

Question: When would a Buddhist consensus be needed in America?

Answer: Religion is respected in the United States. Americans as a whole expect religious leaders to be the leaders of society and morality. In March 1966, Reverend Doctor Hanayama Shōshin, then bishop of the BCA, attended the National Inter-Religious Conference on Peace in Washington at the invitation of the secretary of state, Dean Rusk.[5] Bishop Hanayama was selected as the Buddhist representative because the BCA was the largest Buddhist organization in the United States. In the future, however, the Buddhist delegate should represent all American Buddhists.

## A Move for American Buddhism to Be Practiced at Home

Seventy years have passed since Japanese Buddhism was introduced into the United States. Buddhist temples are the centers of Buddhist activities here, which include conducting services that in Japan are usually performed at home. Thus, Buddhist followers in the United States attend temples frequently. I believe, however, that those who are considered American Buddhists should be those who practice Buddhism at home. To bring this change about, the services conducted at a temple should be conducted at home.

Question: What are the services that can or should be performed at home?

Answer: Hanamatsuri, one of the three main Buddhist service events held at every temple, began forty or fifty years ago in Japan, and is now widely celebrated in Japanese American temples in the United States.

Question: How should that be done at home?

Answer: We shall let the children who come to Sunday schools handle it, but it would be easy. On April 8, place a basin on a coffee table, arrange a few small branches to form a halo in the basin, and decorate it with a spring flower on the top. That would a splendid Lumbini garden. Then have the children place a figure of an infant Buddha in the middle.

A temple often does not celebrate Hanamatsuri exactly on April 8. Mindful Buddhist families, however, can commemorate the Buddha's birthday on the exact date at home. Further, they can invite children of other races who have not attended Buddhist Sunday schools to this celebration where they can pour sweet tea on an image of the baby Buddha. Such childhood experiences can serve as a cause for them to learn about Buddhism when they grow up.

Does that day seem far in the distance? Well, if temples continue organizing Hanamatsuri the way they presently do, there will be students who, even though they attend Sunday schools for many years, will never experience pouring sweet tea over an image of an infant Buddha. But if each household treats the Buddha as a family member and holds the Hanamatsuri as his birthday celebration that will be flower buds of American Buddhism. Children like to celebrate birthdays.

Question: What if we don't have a statue of a baby Buddha? What do you suggest?

Answer: Why not use a birthday cake with a single candle in the center? That candle will be born in the minds and hearts of the children as the infant Buddha.

Question: After the autumn harvest, Shin Buddhists in Japan conduct a *Hōonkō* service at home. How should we observe *Hōonkō* at home in the United States?

Answer: Thanksgiving, which is celebrated throughout the United States, would be a good time for it. We can make that day the observance of *Hōonkō*, not just a time when we eat a filling turkey dinner. Incidentally, November 28 is the day Shinran Shōnin passed away. In addition to paying our indebtedness to his teaching, we can conduct a Buddhist service to show our gratitude to our parents, the king, sentient beings, and the Three Treasures—the so-called four kinds of indebtedness (*shion*). If we do that, a Buddhist thanksgiving will be integrated naturally into American life.

Question: What about Christmas?

Answer: The entire United States celebrates Christmas with Christmas trees and colorful decorations; all children become excited about it. Telling our children, "We Buddhists do not celebrate Christmas" will prevent the seeds of Buddhism from sprouting.

Question: Then how should we Buddhists celebrate Christmas?

Answer: We can set up a bodhi tree with a statue of Śākyamuni Buddha underneath in our homes on December 8. That is the day of *Jōdō-e,* the day Gautama Siddhārtha attained buddhahood. Children will be excited because Christmas will have arrived in their homes before anyone else's in the United States.

Question: But aren't Christmas trees associated with celebrating Christ's birth?

Answer: No. Christmas did not begin as a celebration of Christ's birth. Nor is December 25 as the date of his birth historically true. Further, there are no Christmas trees covered with snow in the place where he was born.

Question: Then, how did Christmas come to take its present form?

Answer: The custom of decorating a tree with snow seems to have started in Scandinavia as part of a winter solstice festival. Christians later began associating that with the celebration of Christ's birth, and that is how Christmas spread all over the world.

Question: Are you saying that therefore it is all right for us to consider a bodhi tree to be similar to a Christmas tree and celebrate the *Jōdō-e* at home?

Answer: Yes. Americanization of Buddhism does not mean changing our traditions, but it does encourage us to integrate Buddhist events into the American lifestyle by not disrupting American livelihood, customs, and annual events.

We, Buddhists, should not be discouraged because of Christmas and its association with Christianity. Christmas is what exhilarates all children. We should, without hesitation, celebrate Christmas as *Jōdō-e.* Children can dance around a bodhi tree just as they do during Bon dances.

Throughout its history, from India to China and from there to Japan, Buddhism adapted to the country in which it was introduced. Japanese Buddhists should also adapt to American ways boldly and patiently. That is where the future of American Buddhism lies.

Question: Is there anything else you can say about promoting Buddhist activities at home?

Answer: Sundays are holy days in the United States. Unlike our counterparts in Japan, Buddhists cannot conduct memorial services during weekdays. In the United States, almost all major Buddhist services are held on Sundays at temples, but unfortunately, services are often divided by groups, such as Sunday school children, members of the Young Buddhist Association, and adults. Accordingly, the closeness of participating as a family is often lost. Both children and adults should gather together, at least to honor the Buddha.

Question: How should we do that?

Answer: Today, children reluctantly attend Sunday schools because their parents send them to the temple. What parents should do is attend Sunday schools with their children. That would make their small children happy. When both parents and children bow together before the Buddha and listen to a Sunday school Dharma talk together, that is when Buddhism comes alive.

Question: How can children be taught to recite the *nenbutsu,* which they learn at Sunday schools, at home?

Answer: Have the entire family recite the *nenbutsu* before the home altar morning and evening and before each meal.

This is a story I heard at the BCA National Council Meeting held at Monterey Buddhist Church on November 5, 1967. Mr. Yamashita Iwao said that when he came home hungry after school as a child, his mother always said, "Say namu-amida-butsu and then eat a bowl of rice offered to the Buddha." Iwao's mother had educated him this way since he was a child. That kind of interaction in daily life is much more effective than merely telling our children to recite the *nenbutsu* in front of the family altar. Today, no matter how busy he is, Mr. Yamashita never fails to personally bring his three children to Sunday school.

Question: Anything else?

Answer: A Buddhist temple needs to be connected to the larger society within which it exists. Our temples have been peculiar places where only people of Japanese ancestry gather. In Japan, a long time ago, in addition to the mail worship hall, Shitennō temple was equipped with a hospital, pharmacy, and orphanage to help the sick and those in trouble. A Buddhist temple in America should not become a "mystery house" isolated from society, where temple members associate only with themselves through the *nenbutsu* teaching. The temples should be recognized for their contributions to society. That is what makes our children proud of them.

Question: How can Buddhist temples contribute to society?

Answer: A temple must contribute to the welfare of the community in which it is located. As an example, with the assistance of a local health administration office, a temple can become a place to donate blood. There are many such activities that can be provided by temples. The important point is that we, American Buddhists, should not remain complacent about how admirably temples function in Japan and merely copy what they do. Rather, we should be forward looking and make American temples a point of departure from the Japanese Buddhist tradition, and carry the torch of the Buddhist teachings here and now where we live. That is how the children of the Buddha, who bear the future of American Buddhism, should conduct themselves.

## Acknowledgments

The author wishes to thank Ken'ichi Yokogawa for editing the introduction and translation.

## Notes

This explanatory introduction primarily derives from Michihiro Ama, "A Transnational Development of Japanese Buddhism during the Postwar Period—The Case of Tana Daishō." *Pacific World*, third series, no. 14 (2012): 1–26.

1 Shinran is considered to have passed away on the 28th of the eleventh lunar month, which was converted to January 16 according to the Western calendar. Higashi Honganji retains the November 28 date.

2 The Berkeley Buddhist Study Group provided a basis for the later development of the Institute of Buddhist Studies in the 1960s.

3 Michael K. Masatsugu, *Reorienting the Pure Land: Japanese Americans, the Beats, and the Making of American Buddhism, 1941–1966* (PhD diss., University of California Irvine, 2004), 12.

4 Dennis Hirota, Hisao Inagaki, Michio Tokunaga and Ryushin Uryuzu, trans., *The Collected Works of Shinran,* vol. 1 (Kyoto: Jōdo Shinshū Hongwanji-ha, 1997), 349.

5 According to Tana's source language, Hanayama attended *Zenkoku kaku shūkyo daihyō kaigi* on March 15, 1967. It is, however, likely that what he attended was the National Inter-Religious Conference on Peace held in Washington in March 1967. See Swarthmore College Peace Collection, World Conference on Religion and Peace Records, 1967–1995, http://www.swarthmore.edu/library/peace/DG051-099/DG078WCRP.html.

## Bibliography

Ama, Michihiro. "A Neglected Diary, a Forgotten Buddhist Couple: *Tana Daishō's Internment Camp Diary* as a Historical and Literary Text." *Journal of Global Buddhism* 14 (2013): 45–62.

——. "A Transnational Development of Japanese Buddhism during the Postwar Period—The Case of Tana Daishō." *Pacific World,* third series, no. 14 (2012): 1–26.

Hirota, Dennis, Hisao Inagaki, Michio Tokunaga, and Ryushin Uryuzu, trans. *The Collected Works of Shinran.* 2 vols. Kyoto: Jōdo Shinshū Hongwanji-ha, 1997.

Masatsugu, Michael K. *Reorienting the Pure Land: Japanese Americans, the Beats, and the Making of American Buddhism, 1941–1966.* PhD diss., University of California Irvine, 2004.

Tana, Daishō. *Hotoke no kyōbō.* Kyoto: Hyakkaen, 1972.

——. *Santa Fe Rōzubāgu senji tekikokujin yokuryūsho nikki.* 4 vols. Edited by Tomoe Tana. Tokyo: Sankibō busshorin, 1976–1989.

——. *Sunday school text nukigaki: Busshi seikatsu hen.* Palo Alto, CA: Buddhist Horin Society, 1969.

——. *Sunday school text nukigaki: Hotoke no kyūsai hen.* Palo Alto, CA: Buddhist Horin Society, 1966.

# Chapter 4

# Naikan's Path

Clark Chilson

## Translator's Introduction

In the Larger *Sukhāvatīvyūha sūtra,* Gautama Buddha recalls for his disciple Ananda how eons ago the monk Dharmākara sought to establish a buddha-field, a pure land. Dharmākara vowed that when he attained buddhahood he would bring to his buddha-field those who entrusted themselves to him, thus allowing them to escape *saṃsāra*. Millions of years later, his vows fulfilled, Dharmākara became Amitābha, the Buddha of the Western Pure Land, a realm of bliss.

For Shinran, the reputed founder of Shin Pure Land Buddhism, having a heart that trusts Amitābha (or Amida in Japanese) was essential for liberation from *saṃsāra* for those like himself who were filled with afflicting passions (*bonnō*). His ideas about an entrusting heart (*shinjin*) became central for understanding rebirth in Amida's Pure Land. Yet in his writings he did not give clear instructions for what to do to get *shinjin* or to verify that one had it. Some claimed that as a gift bestowed by Amida, nothing could be done to get it, and they saw any attempt to obtain it as an illegitimate self-power practice. Although many among the Shin clergy promoted this line of thinking, lay people outside the temple walls formed organizations that conducted rites in homes and elsewhere that they said induced experiences of receiving *shinjin*.

These emotional, even ecstatic, rituals of receiving *shinjin* fostered a strong belief among their participants that they were guaranteed rebirth in Amida's Pure Land. Because clergy at mainstream Shin Buddhist institutions during the Edo period (1603–1868) adamantly condemned such rituals as heretical, groups that practiced them did so in secrecy to avoid persecution from both Shin temples and local authorities, who saw the rites as based on dangerous teachings. Some who were caught practicing them were sent to prison, or into exile, or in rare cases were executed. Despite efforts to eradicate such rites, they endured. By the late nineteenth and early twentieth centuries we have evidence that they were being done in the Kanto, Kansai, Hokuriku, and the Tohoku regions. Among those who did such rites was D. T. Suzuki, who as a boy was taken by his mother to a secretive Shin Buddhist lay group that practiced them.

It is within this larger historical background of distinctive rites practiced by lay Shin Buddhist groups that we can position the contemplative practice of *mishirabe* 身調べ and the Taikan-an 諦観庵 group described by Yoshimoto Ishin (1916–1988) in the excerpted sections of an autobiography translated below. As a source that gives us a glimpse into the activities of a lay Shin Buddhist group in the early twentieth century that had followers in Osaka and Nara, the text has value for our understanding of Pure Land Buddhism in two ways. First, it contributes to our knowledge of the range in which lay Shin Buddhists interpreted Shin scriptures and developed Shin practices that were distinctive from what was found at mainstream Shin temples. By doing so it enhances our knowledge of the wide diversity within Shin, the most popular type of Buddhism in Japan. Second, the texts shows us the origins of Naikan, a practice developed by Yoshimoto based on *mishirabe* that has been used as a self-cultivation practice and, since the 1960s, as a psychotherapeutic intervention used by mental health professionals in Japan to treat addictions and mood disorders, among other things.

Unlike the ecstatic rites to receive *shinjin* practiced by secretive Shin groups (*hiji bōmon*) that involved calling out to Amida over and over again *tasuketamae, tasuketamae, tasuketamae,* ("save me, save me, save me"), *mishirabe* involved examining one's past for instances of wrongdoing, while abstaining from sleep, food, and drink. Those doing *mishirabe* were called "the sick" (*byōnin* 病人) and those guiding them "the enlightened" (*kaigoin* 開悟人). "The sick" would sit behind a folding screen (*byōbu*) contemplating what they did in life. About every two hours one of "the enlightened" would go listen to what "the sick" had discovered about themselves. To prompt "the sick" into deeper reflection, "the enlightened" would ask them questions such as "If you died now, would you go to the land of bliss or hell?" or "Do you understand your sins?" At some point, "the sick" would either quit or have an awakening into the insurmountable depths of their depravity or afflicting passions, thus becoming aware of their powerlessness to save themselves and of Amida's mercy.

*Mishirabe* served as the core practice of the Taikan-an, a lay temple in Fuse, Osaka, named after its founder Nishimoto Taikan (1849–1912), a former Honganji-ha priest. As with other lay Shin organizations, its members regarded textual knowledge as inferior to experiential knowledge. The difference between the two types of knowledge was analogously explained as the difference between knowing that fire is hot from hearing about it and knowing it is hot by burning a hand in it.

At age nineteen Yoshimoto became interested in doing *mishirabe*. He grew up in an affluent Shin Buddhist family that had its own fertilizer business. His mother in particular became devout after her daughter died when still a toddler on May 12, 1924. As a child Yoshimoto did daily worship with his mother at home and learned to recite Shin scripture from memory. As a teenager he aspired to be a calligrapher and read about Buddhism. Yoshimoto remembers himself as a self-satisfied youth. His confidence was shaken, however, by an interrogation on the meaning of Shin scripture by his uncle Fukumoto, who was a member of the Taikan-an. Yoshimoto attempted *mishirabe* but quit after a few days. He tried again and failed again. A third time he tried to do it alone in a cave without success. His father, who feared that his son was going mad due to religious fervor, became critical of the Taikan-an group, calling it a "Say-nothing confraternity" (Iwazukō 言わず講), a phrase used to refer to secretive Shin organizations.

On his fourth attempt at *mishirabe,* about a year after his first one, Yoshimoto had an awakening that changed his life. He describes losing consciousness and then waking in a state of extreme joy, full of energy despite his lack of sleep and not having eaten in days. Yoshimoto characterized his awakening as one of transformation from a state of confusion to one of enlightenment (*tenmei kaigo* 転迷開悟).

Inspired by his *mishirabe* awakening, he wanted others to experience the joy he did. He feared, however, that the physical deprivations the Taikan-an required would prevent others from engaging in deep self-reflection. So with the support of his teacher Komatani, who was later killed in a US air raid in 1945, Yoshimoto began to allow people to sleep, eat, and drink while he guided them in intense self-reflection. By 1941, Yoshimoto distinguished the self-reflection he was teaching from *mishirabe* by referring to it as Naikan, which literally means "introspection." Although intensive Naikan, like *mishirabe,* would always involve concentrated self-reflection while sitting behind a screen alone and multiple daily visits from someone who went to listen to what the person doing self-reflection was finding, Naikan would become distinct from *mishirabe* by not only becoming less ascetic, but also by being restricted to set periods of time, usually seven days, rather then until some dramatic awakening occurred. Over time the use of Shin Buddhist language to explain Naikan or to guide others doing it diminished in importance.

Yoshimoto discovered in the 1940s that the desire to become established in faith in Amida or to understand Shin teachings was not necessary for Naikan to have life-changing outcomes. While running his wife's family's leathercloth business, he had some of his employees do a week of Naikan in 1943. He found that his employees who had done Naikan started to complain less and get along better with others. The change in these employees, who had not done Naikan for religious reasons, led him to conclude that religious motivations were not necessary for Naikan to have a positive effect.

Although Yoshimoto became a Shin priest of the Kibe-ha and then established a Naikan temple in 1955 where he guided people in Naikan, after the 1940s he commonly presented Naikan as a nonreligious practice that did not require faith. This made it easier for him to introduce Naikan into prisons in the 1950s and 1960s because, as publicly funded institutions, they could not legally endorse any religious activities. In addition to guiding prisoners in Naikan himself, he also trained correctional officers to serve as Naikan guides for prisoners who wanted to do it. While most prisoners had little interest in Naikan, those who volunteered to do it had a much lower rate of recidivism.

In the 1960s Naikan started to attract the attention of psychiatrists, particularly those in the psychiatry departments at Okuyama University and Jikei University in Tokyo. At that time, Dr. Ishida Rokurō, who was in private practice, combined Naikan with autogenic training to treat those suffering from various forms of neurosis and psychosomatic illnesses. Other psychiatrists, such as Suwaki Hiroshi and Takemoto Takahiro in the 1970s, found that Naikan was more effective for getting their alcoholic patients to stop drinking than any other treatment they had tried.

As a result of Naikan's success in various settings and Yoshimoto's tireless promotion of it, Naikan received considerable media attention in newspapers and on TV. This led to hundreds of people flocking to Nara each year to do Naikan with Yoshimoto in the 1970s and 1980s. Yoshimoto's disciples also began to establish their own training centers, which attracted a steady stream of clients. In 1978, to promote the practice and study of Naikan, Yoshimoto's disciples created the Japan Naikan Association, and two decades later, in 1998, they formed the Japanese Naikan Medical Association to support research on the applications of

Naikan for medicinal purposes. Both associations now have annual conferences and publish annual academic journals. A survey of Naikan in 2003 by the psychiatrist Kawahara Ryūzō reported that there were twenty-seven medical institutions that used Naikan in Japan and five in China. As for Naikan training centers, the survey indicated that there were thirty-two in Japan, one in the United States, two in Germany, and three in Austria.

Naikan today is done intensively in retreat-like, weeklong sessions or as part of one's daily activities. Since 1968, it has primarily focused on meditating on three "themes," which are formulated as questions: (1) What did I receive [from a specific person during a specific time period]? (2) What did I give back [to that person during that time]? (3) What troubles did I cause [that person during that time period]? During intensive Naikan, which is commonly done at training centers (*kenshūjo*), those doing Naikan, called Naikansha, will meditate on these questions in relation to various people to whom they are close for seven days for fifteen to sixteen hours a day. During that time, except for going to the toilet, bathing, and perhaps a thirty-minute cleaning period that provides exercise, the Naikansha will sit behind a screen doing Naikan. Throughout the week no activity is done—such as reading, talking to other Naikansha, or using a cell phone—that would distract from doing Naikan.

During intensive Naikan at training centers, meals are placed in front of the Naikansha's screen three times a day. About every two hours, eight or nine times a day, an "interviewer" (*mensetsusha*) will open the Naikansha's screen, bow, and ask ritualistically, "During this time, who have you been examining yourself in relation to and for what time period?" If the Naikansha has been doing Naikan on his mother when he was between the ages of twelve and fourteen, he might respond as follows: "I have been examining myself in relation to my mother when I was between the ages of twelve and fourteen. What I received from my mother was a basketball for my twelfth birthday and help on a homework assignment on photosynthesis. As for what I gave back to her, I went to get her cough medicine when she was sick one winter day. I caused her trouble by yelling that she was a stupid old woman and slamming the car door in her face one morning when she dropped me off at a friend's house."

Interviews are typically kept to less than five minutes. They end by the interviewer asking the Naikansha what he or she will do Naikan on next and with the Naikansha answering that question. If the Naikansha's answers to the three questions are vague (e.g., "My mother gave me love" or "I caused my wife trouble by not being considerate"), the interviewer might suggest that the Naikansha give more concrete answers that can be visualized. In general, however, the interviewer just prompts the Naikansha with predetermined language and avoids counseling. It is considered best that the Naikansha come to realizations about themselves on their own. In addition to the three questions, Naikansha might also be invited to reflect on their lives in one- to three-year increments to find and examine times when they lied or stole something.

In contrast to intensive Naikan, daily Naikan involves contemplating the three questions from a few minutes to a couple of hours a day. Although many who go to do intensive Naikan have never done daily Naikan, at hospitals it is often assigned before having patients try intensive Naikan. Daily Naikan does not involve interviews, but some people write down their answers to the questions in a diary. Daily Naikan may involve contemplating the three questions or instances of lying or stealing at times in the distant past, but it is frequently done on the previous twenty-four hours, or previous week, or some other short time period in the recent past. Yoshimoto regarded daily Naikan as complementing intensive Naikan and as vital for living happily no matter what happens.

For most people, a week of intensive Naikan is needed to have an experience that changes how they view their lives. Testimonies of those who have done intensive Naikan often indicate that after struggling for the first few days, memories start to become vivid around the fourth day. Naikansha commonly report having insights into both how selfish they have been and into how much love they received. Because Naikan leads people to see situations and events from the perspective of others, the remorse that Naikansha feel rarely threatens their self-esteem and usually results in empathy for others (often others they were angry with), which improves their social relationships. After a week of intensive Naikan, Naikansha commonly say they feel a profound sense of gratitude.

The experiences that Naikansha have, and their consequences, provide fertile ground for research for those interested in Buddhist-inspired therapies. Because most studies in English that investigate how Buddhist meditative practices can improve psychological well-being focus on Zen or Theravada Buddhism, Naikan, with its roots in Pure Land Buddhism, can offer new understandings on how different meditative practices can produce different psychological outcomes. In particular, a comparison of Naikan with the mindfulness meditation made popular in North America by Jon Kabat-Zinn, Thich Nhat Hanh, and others can reveal how different secularized meditative practices that grew out of Buddhism can have different effects.

When comparing Naikan and mindfulness, we should recognize their similarities: both were inspired by Buddhist practices but are now commonly presented as nonreligious; both train the mind to focus attention in particular ways; and both have been used for medicinal purposes to enhance well-being. But investigating their differences is even more important: while mindfulness meditation used in therapeutic contexts in North America focuses on paying attention to the present moment, Naikan gives attention to the past; while mindfulness emphasizes what the individual meditator is experiencing, Naikan emphasizes social relations; while mindfulness teachers advocate for not evaluating one's experience as good or bad, Naikan involves evaluating one's own actions to see how they affected others. These differences lead to different results. Understanding how they complement each other, how they conflict, and how they have distinctive strengths to relieve suffering in the various contexts in which they are done would add to our knowledge on the effects of different meditative practices.

To understand Naikan, and other secularized, Buddhist-inspired practices, we must also look beyond just how they work in the present. We can learn much about how the relationship between the form and the context of a practice matters by studying the history of Buddhist types of meditation that have been reformulated as nonreligious. The form of a meditation (that is, the methods for doing it) in a religious context may be similar to that in a secular one, even as the reasons vary greatly for doing the meditation. A meditative practice done to achieve an awakening is different in orientation, if not form, from one done to treat stress, addiction, or mood disorders. While there are differences in form between Naikan and *mishirabe*, the differences in the motivational and social contexts between Naikan as a psychotherapy and *mishirabe* as a Pure Land Buddhist practice are even greater. By learning the origins of Naikan's methods and the contexts in which they were done, we can better understand the significance of religious contexts and how they differ from secular ones for both understanding and effecting a sense of well-being.

The text translated below is excerpted from three places in a much longer autobiography by Yoshimoto Ishin titled *Naikan no Michi.*[1] It provides a primary source for understanding Naikan and the Shin Buddhist context that gave rise to its methods. The first section describes Yoshimoto's encounter with Taikan-an members and his first failed attempt at *mishirabe.* The second provides a description of Yoshimoto's fourth attempt at *mishirabe,* which was successful. The third section gives answers by Yoshimoto to frequently asked questions on Naikan, and in doing so shows how it is different from *mishirabe.* The three sections are taken from pages 28–35, 61–65, and 153–159 of *Naikan no Michi.* The first two sections also appear almost verbatim in Yoshimoto's book *Naihanhō.*[2]

## Translation

*Naikan's Path*

Yoshimoto Ishin

### Yoshimoto's Encounter with the Shin Buddhism of Taikan-An

On our way to Fuse, we stop at my uncle Fukumoto's house. After performing the daily evening worship and having dinner, we sat around a brazier encased in a wooden box. I became serious and opened my mouth first. I asked, "What kind of instructional place is Fuse? Is it like a lodging place that a middle school would use for its kendo club's practices?"

My uncle responded, "Instead of talking about that, tell me what you think is meant in the *Shōshinge* by 'Nothing exceeds the difficulties of the most difficult.'" His question confused me. Then from the side, Yonesawa, who seemed to be a Buddhist priest, answered, "It is an admonition to not treat the holy name of Amida lightly."

Then my uncle asked, "Do you understand the meaning of 'The *nenbutsu* has no self'? What do you feel is the meaning of that?"

Silence. Not having the skill to answer this, I remained silent for a while.

Then my uncle asked, "In the *Ryōgebun* of Shinshū, it says 'Discarding the self-power mind of the various practices and disciplines.' Have you ever had the experience of 'discarding'?"

I kept silent.

"It also says 'In what is most important, the afterlife, we trust [Amida] to save us.' How have you ever trusted? When and where did you trust?" my uncle asked.

Thinking it strange to remain silent, after some time passed I said, "In Ishimaru Gohei's book it says, 'The Shinshū of today lacks power to save people. Only those who experience the feeling that Shinran felt when he left Mount Hiei will be saved.' Is Fuse a place that puts people in such a state of mind?"

My uncle slowly responded, "Well, I guess you could say that."

"Then how about going tomorrow?"

"At this point you would probably be sent home as soon as you got there as someone who is 'still far, far away' from where he needs to be. So first go to Inoue Yasuyuki's place in the first block of Maruyama Street in Abeno ward of Osaka." My uncle then drew me a map, saying, "If you walk a block west from the bus stop at Matsumushi, there is a small shop that sells sweets. You'll see it there."

I showed my uncle part of an article that I wrote titled "Buddhism and Calligraphy," which appeared in the calligraphy magazine I was on the editorial board of titled *Essence* (*Seika*), published by the Essence Calligraphy Institute. He only gave it a sidelong glance while eating a tangerine, then said, "There is a huge gap between knowing that fire is hot from hearing about it and actually putting your hand in a fire and then pulling it out shaking it saying 'ouch, that's hot!' Learning 'I am a bad person; I am going to hell' from reading and listening to others is very different from experiencing the immense depths of one's sins that comes from the self-awareness of examining the truth of your past.

"Telling yourself 'Lying can be a skillful means,' you casually lie in your business transactions. You say it is wrong to kill mosquitoes and flies but that we just can't go about not killing them. What about those sins? The sins we commit will eternally haunt us. The law of cause and effect cannot be bent. The cause for going to hell, however, is not sin per se; it is having a self-centered mind. In other words, ignorance (*mumyō*) is the cause. If you eradicate the darkness of ignorance, sins become the material for self-reflection and a source of gratitude."

"How can we shed light on the darkness of ignorance?" I asked.

"When you do self-reflection you come to know your sins and, as a result, death becomes terrifying. If one deeply enters into self-reflection (*naikan*),[3] the self-centered mind naturally disappears."

"How should we think about the problem of sexual lust, which is a serious problems for humans?" I asked.

"People commonly think about this in two types of ways. First there are those who see it as a natural biological phenomenon and necessary for the survival of the species. For them it is a basic instinct, so it is understandable that people will make their way to red light districts. Then there are those of the other type, who think sexual lust is a terrible, perverse sin. So they denounce those who go to red light districts as evil others. They see only themselves as pure and grow increasingly arrogant from suppressing their sexual desires. Following this way of thinking, there are only two types of people: those who commit such sins and those who do not. But Shinran was neither one of these.

"There is a story—it might just be a legend and not historically accurate—that when Saint Shinran was at the prestigious temple Shōgoin he saw the princess Tamahi, daughter of the emperor's chief minister, Kujō. No matter how much he tried to expel her looks from his mind, he could not do so. The burning of lust in his heart caused him sadness and anguish. But the saint deeply reflected on himself and discovered the truth that his lust was a karmic condition that allowed him to know his sin and acknowledge his foolish self. His self-centered mind then left him.

"Old proverbs say 'the more fruit an ear of rice bears, the lower it bows' and 'The wisteria flower looks up most to those who lower themselves.' Refinement and the beauty of humility are natural results from realizing our sins."

"I knew that story," I said.

"Even if you knew it, without having the experience of what it meant, your knowledge of it was merely intellectual. It is *nenbutsu* without substance."

"I also believe in Amida's salvation and do not doubt it. Is there something wrong with that?" I protested.

My uncle said, "A long time ago my father, Denjūrō, guided many people to Taikan-an. There were two women who heard rumors about it and came from far away. One was forty years old and the other sixty. After listening to a common sermon, the older one said joyfully, 'Thank you. The compassion of the Buddha is precious. Even a dirty, ordinary person like me lives by his grace.' Her gratitude was authentic and sincere. The other woman with a despondent tone and a lonely expression lamented, 'Even if the trees on the peak of the mountain move, the earth is still and doesn't budge a bit for me. I am horrid.' When my father noticed this, he supposedly uttered 'Even when people hear the same sermon, their reactions differ greatly.' Of these two, who do you think is more admirable?"

"The younger is the more admirable," I answered quickly. My uncle got the gist of what I meant and smiled. In my heart I felt, "This guy might have hope in me."

My sense of things was completely off. It was like a chair that I safely sat in was all of a sudden pulled out from under me. I became embarrassed about myself, my conceit and arrogance. With my thin mustache, wearing a traditional Japanese overcoat with white socks and a white collar, I put on airs of a calligraphy teacher and a Buddhist. I was the epitome of vanity.

I felt like the earth beneath my feet was cracking and about to give way. I was twenty-one by the old way of counting, but by current measures, I had yet to turn twenty years old, not even old enough to take part in today's coming-of-age ceremony. All that I had written and said was not based on any experience but things I had heard secondhand. I appeared to myself as someone playing the part of a ridiculous clown.

I spent the night at my uncle's home, but had no desire to sleep. I was wide awake all night. Before that night I had felt like a capable evangelist, but I went home with complicated feelings. I felt down but also that I had been warned that I was in the midst of walking down a dangerous path. When I told my mother what happened, she said, "We have harvested the persimmons, but haven't yet finished with the rice. Why don't you go to Fuse after we are done harvesting the rice." But my personality was such that I wanted to do something as soon as I thought of it. So the next day I went to Inoue's place in Osaka. He was not home but his wife let me in and showed me a copy of the *Ōjōyōshū*. She talked with me about various things until evening. When her husband came home, he talked to me until the next morning. He agreed to introduce me to Okayama Eijirō, who lived in Kibi in Kakuyama village in the Shiki district of Nara Prefecture.

Then Mrs. Inoue took me to the bus stop because it was raining. She was a person of pure kindness who gave me guidance until just before I got on the bus.

I got to Mr. Okayama's place around 10 a.m. Until evening we talked and I encountered the dharma that led to my destiny. During that time, members of the Taikan-an group who had heard I was there started to slowly gather in the adjacent room. One by one, they came into the room where I was. To test to see if I had come to listen to theory or whether I actually wanted to do the practice, they asked me, "Did you come out of concern for the afterlife? Did you come wanting to be told the teachings? This is about what is most important, the afterlife. There is no point in just hearing about it with your ears." In this manner everyone earnestly instructed me. It was a mixed group that included both an illiterate, uneducated old woman and an intellectual who graduated from an elite girl's school. I heard people whisper, "Is he a teacher? It is rare to have someone so young."

At that time, before anyone did intensive self-reflection behind a screen, there were one or two days of "solidifying the ground" (*chi katame*), which was a custom that involved repeating stories to strengthen people's resolve and to emphasize some things.

During the discussions and debates that occurred at this stage, some seekers went home; but I was eager to start. I thought that the verbose sermons, formally delivered, were a waste of precious time. (Later I consulted with my beloved teacher Komatani about this point, and [when we started spreading Naikan together] we changed the length of the preparation stage based on how mentally ready a person was.)

In the evening my uncle Fukumoto arrived from Gojō. In the next room I heard people quietly saying things like, "He looks much better than he did two days ago when he came from Ōshima." That night as a result of a discussion between my uncle and Mr. Okayama, it was decided that I would be instructed at Morikawa's place. I imagine that this probably had two purposes: First Grandpa Zenkichi (my wife's grandfather) had done intensive self-reflection half a year ago, but later he failed to do it on a regular basis. So he required some follow-up instruction. Second, it allowed them to foster a relationship with the head of the household, Morikawa Minojirō (my wife's father). In addition to these aims, the home was also probably chosen because it was the residence of my elder sister-in-law, so I was a relative of the family.

At the time I used to call my wife's mother "elder sister." When I stayed over at her home, I used to pretentiously give sermons to her despite the fact that she was already quite superior to me in understanding the truth. When I later realized this, I wept and apologized for my constant rudeness to her.

Within the Taikan-an, those who were knowledgeable from reading and listening to others were called the "scattered" (*jōsan*) type and those who knew through experience were called the "authentic" (*shinjitsu*) type. In today's parlance, I think we might render them as "theory type" and "practice type." The word *mishirabe* (self-examination), not Naikan, was used then. Those doing *mishirabe* were called "the sick" (*byōnin*).

The sermons given during the "solidifying-the-ground" stage suggested that one should not eat, drink, or sleep. But having slept little in the previous two days and lacking zeal, I soon started to nod off during *mishirabe*. I could not bear it anymore so I lay down. When I suddenly woke up, I saw my "elder sister" [i.e., mother-in-law] sitting next to me. She had tears in her eyes. With a lump in her throat, she encouraged me saying, "We said no sleeping. I know it is hard but I beg you to pull yourself together."

In addition to sermons, some secret stories were told. One was about how my uncle Fukumoto's deceased father, who in search of the immutable law used to cross the Yoshinokawa [Ki no River] every night in the winter cold to go hear sermons. Another story related how my uncle Fukumoto had been preparing himself from his youth. Way back four generations ago when there were no means of convenient transportation, my uncle, inspired by the travels of the twenty-four disciples of Shinran, used to put on his straw sandals and go searching for a teacher of truth. He did so because he thought that the true immutable law could not be heard in the sermons being given at regular temples.

Okayama Eijirō was from Muro in Gose, Nara, which was the hometown of my uncle Fukumoto's wife, who had the same surname as him. Okayama took my teacher Komatani Taishin and Inoue Yasuyuki to Fukumoto's place, who then took them to Fuse, where they were taken care of.

My uncle then thought of his sister Riu. He went to visit her at the home of the family she married into, which was the Morikawa family of the Takada region. He first encouraged the head of the household, Minojirō, to be initiated into the Taikan-an, but he showed no interest in doing so. So my uncle settled with just taking his sister to the group. While she was there undergoing the initiation [i.e., doing *mishirabe*], Grandpa Zenkichi's blind mother (Minojirō's grandmother), Kito, started to cry saying, "Where did sister Riu go? Maybe she ran away because I am here?" Kito had many great grandchildren who were still small, and when evening came everyone missed Riu and became sad. So my father-in-law, Minojirō, went to Fuse to get his wife. At the time, however, the custom was not to allow anyone—even spouses—who had not done *mishirabe* to meet with those in the midst of intense self-reflection. The reason for this was not so much to protect secrets, but rather to not discourage those who came to see the person from wanting at some later point to do the rite. It was similar to the reason why some were kept from seeing a woman give birth to a child [if they saw it, they might not want to have children themselves].

Minojirō pleaded at the door of the Taikan-an, "Please let me take my wife home. Her absence for several days is causing trouble in my household. The old people and the kids are crying all day. I need to take her home." The person who came out to see him was my uncle Fukumoto.

"I beg you, please be patient for two or three more days," he said in a tone of sadness with his palms pressed together. "We're not going to do anything bad to her."

"Brother, didn't you give her to me in marriage? She is my wife. It causes problems if she just selfishly leaves the house for days. I want to take her home today. Please let me see her."

"Come now, don't say that. Please trust me. I am sure she will leave happy. I beg you."

At the end of this tense exchange, my good-natured father-in-law succumbed to the pleadings and went home empty-handed. Shortly after my father went to visit him at the Morikawa's business office in the third district of Osaka's Nihonbashi.

My father thought a heresy was eating away at my wife's household, and this was of the utmost concern to him. He said to my father-in-law, "Brother, this is bad. You need to bring sister home as soon as possible. It is a cult of the 'Say-Nothing Confraternities.' Those who enter it eat extravagantly everyday. The 'companions' do not work. They get together to 'encounter their destinies.' It's an organization in which members play all day and bit-by-bit waste away their wealth. They are also near Koriyama. It's concerning."

My father-in-law was disturbed. Because my father-in-law's elder sister was the daughter-in-law of my father, he called my father "father." He trusted my father and was stirred up because of his respect for him.

My mother-in-law had great expectations related to my spiritual pursuits. She thought, "If Ishin gets initiated, we can bring in his father. If that happens, my beloved husband, who looks up to him, will be encouraged by him and might also enter the group." Taikan-an members were resolute about converting all their relatives, so naturally trouble frequently occurred.

It is worth mentioning that the name "Say-Nothing Confraternities" is not used by members of those confraternities. Rather it is a phrase used pejoratively by outsiders who would use it when mentioning a rumor, such as "That person is one of those in the 'Say-Nothing Confraternity.'" There are innumerable types of those confraternities, large and small, which vary in content. With each passing year they seem to be diminishing in strength, but they still exist in various regions. Members of those confraternities believe and say that "It is our Shinshū that is correct (orthodox)."

The Taikan-an in Fuse that I was led into was absolutely not a cult. Even my father, who later was embarrassed by his lack of self-understanding, wound up knocking on its door and receiving its teachings. But the apparent confining of people led to misunderstandings and suspicion, so it is understandable why my father at the time saw it as a cult.

## A Description of Yoshimoto's Final *Mishirabe*

[After several failed attempts] one year later, my decisive *mishirabe* began. Because it was not known whose words would have a strong effect on the seeker doing *mishirabe,* many people took turns acting as guides and came to do interviews. Anyone who had the experience of successfully doing *mishirabe* was qualified to serve as one of the enlightened (*kaigoin*), [who every couple of hours went to listen to what people doing *mishirabe* were discovering about themselves and to guide them].

During my prior attempts at *mishirabe* various people came to listen to me and give me guidance, but this time my teacher Komatani made the wise decision that the *kaigoin* for me would only be Okayama and Fukumoto, while others would listen outside the screen (*byobu*). This was done because it was difficult to communicate with whoever the next *kaigoin* might be, and because with a *byōnin* who was too clever or talked carelessly a misunderstanding might arise that would cause trouble.

With an anxious expression on my face, I asked Okayama, "In case like last time, calculating thoughts arise that say that even if I do not do this the Buddha will save me, what should I do?" He answered, "Please thoroughly shake it off."

The next day Komatani came and encouraged me by saying, "Think of this as your time. Stay strong." His attitude had completely changed from a year ago when I visited Fuse.

Before me was the seat of dharma (*hōza*) to which I aspired! It was the place of meditation that I dreamed about for a year with nostalgia. My uncle of Gojō said, "This place of *mishirabe* has been passed down for 2,600 years. It is a sacred place of repentance and self-reflection similar to the place Śākyamuni sat under the bodhi tree. Do not defile it."

I responded, saying, "I will not move, even if I die. Be assured that I will absolutely not leave."

I slowly began examining myself. It was four months after the Sino-Japanese war started on July 7 [1937]. While my friends obeyed their orders to go to war and were suffering, I wondered if what I was doing was okay. I thought to myself, "It is thanks to the sacrifices of many around me that I am living today. For those going off to war, leaving their wives and parents, I will persevere this time even if I die."

Here are some of the recollections I had during self-examination (*mishirabe*): After the summer, when Japan was focused on national loyalty, my father gave bronze statues of Ninomiya Kinjirō and Kusunoki Masashige to Katakiri Elementary School. I gave a speech on the day at the unveiling ceremony. I remember how I, the least filial and loyal person in the world who lacked any training, gave an arrogant, drawn-out talk without any amplifying speakers to eight hundred children lined up in rows for a long time in the school yard, which was roasting in blazing heat. In the manner of a know-it-all, I gave a talk that weaved together things I heard or read. I must have looked like a comical pitchman.

Even if I said I would throw away my body, life, and wealth, that was just lip service. This was evident to me when I asked myself if I could throw away my award from a calligraphy exhibition. I realized that it would be difficult, even though it was far less valuable than my body, life, or wealth. It was just foolish talk.

Two or three days into *mishirabe,* I began to give in to the desire to sleep. When I was nodding off in the middle of the night, [a *kaigoin* named] Nami encouraged me. With her head scraping the tatami floor, she said, "Please, pull yourself together! I beg you."

"Okay, okay," I said, reviving myself.

All of a sudden I noticed the sound of a waterfall coming from the cliff behind the house. Under normal circumstances it might have just been something unpleasant to my ears. But instead I wondered on what day the drops of water that flowed and flowed, pouring into the sea, then evaporating and becoming rain an incalculable number of times over and over again, would eventually become the flowing waterfall again.

I told myself "Don't fall asleep! Hang in there!" On the 11th, the fourth day, real pain started to set in. (I omit the details of my self-examination here because I have written about them elsewhere and I could go on forever about them.) It became so painful that I got up and wanted to go home. But when I remembered the previous year, I sat back down.

Every two hours my uncle came in, opened the screen and sat in front of me, saying, "Where would you go if you died now?"

"To hell," I said.

"It would not be like you're going to look at flowers, you know."

Silence. My disposition was not progressing as was expected.

My uncle who thought this strange asked, "How are you feeling?"

"I feel like I have no way out, no options. I feel resignation, like someone in mortal danger under a sharp sword."

"You are still getting caught up in that type of intellectualization. Focus more earnestly!"

After about two hours had passed, my teacher Komatani came to interview me.

Komatani (K): "Have you been able to completely focus?"

Yoshimoto (Y): "No."

K: "Do you understand your sins?"

Y: "I understand them on the surface, but do not feel them deep in my heart."

K: "I wanted you to be saved this time. I wanted you to be helped. Everyone helped you day and night but your bad karma is too strong. There is nothing that can be done for you."

Y: "Teacher, help me!"

K: "All methods have been exhausted. Those who do not have the correct karmic disposition can't be helped."

Y: "Please, I beg you!" I said clinging on to him.

K: "Nothing can be done. I have neither the virtue nor confidence to help you."

He brushed my hands away that were clinging to him. As he got up to leave and was on his way out, I grabbed on to his knees. Shuddering with guilt and fear of death, I gasped for breath in the depths of despair.

After that, I fell face down unconscious. I do not know how long I was like that; it might have been minutes or hours, but when I came to I was so full of joy all I could do was cry. Beyond this, I cannot write because it is hard to describe in words. Like when the samurai Araki Mataemon transmitted the ultimate meaning of his tradition to Yagyū Minefuyu, he challenged him to a contest using actual skills, because if Minefuyu would have merely answered questions one way or another, he would have been relying on logic. A lineage from teacher to student cannot be simply transmitted in words. You cannot know the taste of water or rice unless you put it in your mouth.

The time was 8 p.m. on November 12, 1937. Although the year and month were different, at 8 p.m. on the twelfth of the month my deceased younger sister Chieko began her journey to the other world. I also at the same time achieved rebirth in the pure land, albeit without the death of my body. It was the time I was liberated from confusion, and it is worthy of memorializing as such. If I were to give an analogy for what happened, it was like teetering on the lip of the mouth of an active volcano, and then suddenly being rescued. That profound feeling and joy I wanted to share with people throughout the world. I became convinced that this was the ultimate joy and purpose of life.

The passion for this practice has burned in me continuously since that time thirty-five years ago. From the night of the eighth, I went without sleep for four days and nights. I should have been sleepy, but I was so excited I could not sleep on the night of the 12th. It was completely mysterious, as was my lack of hunger despite not eating. It was very strange that I had no sense of having an empty stomach. I discovered that during the twenty-four hours of the day, the best time to do *mishirabe* was between 3 and 4 in the morning. I had realized this the previous year when I did *mishirabe* in Fuse, but I forgot to write that so I add it here.

Just before my moment of awakening, I got up to urinate. I was so weak I could hardly walk and leaned on the shoulders of two people to go to the toilet. Less than an hour after that, I was immersed in joy and was able to walk easily. I felt like I was walking a foot above a cloud. Just before this, my face had a horrifying look, like I had just crawled out of the bottom of hell. But then with a joyful feeling, I smiled and a loud laughter rose up from the bottom of my belly that I could not suppress. My drawn face suddenly turned into a round happy one.

It had been one year, a long, long year. It was a year that had the suffering typical of ten years. The desire to want to save one's eternal life cannot be compared to anything, not going to war for one's country, not a once in a lifetime marriage, or anything else. Yes, now I was saved! I could die at any time satisfied. I achieved my purpose. I could achieve the ultimate and final purpose for why I was born in this world. Joy. Complete joy. It was what flying must feel like, with hands flapping and feet off the ground.

Inoue Yasuyuki was so worried when he heard my laughing that he came running in. After my awakening to faith, he continued to teach me things in detail. Twenty-eight years have passed since then,[4] but I will write what he told me that I recall.

1. Do not forget one's debt to one's teacher. He emphasized this point in detail by using the old story of "The Five-Colored Deer." ("The Five-Colored Deer" is a Buddhist legend in which a hunter who got lost and was saved by a five-colored deer. The hunter repaid the deer's good deed with evil when he sold it to the king.)
2. During Buddhist guidance (what is now called "counseling"), do not open your mouth until the other person is finished talking.
3. Today is an initiation, not a graduation. The point being that one has only taken on ears to hear and eyes to see.
4. From now on, sin will be a source for examining yourself and an element for ecstasy. If you neglect self-reflection, you will be whipped in hell, so pay greater attention than before and devote yourself to examining yourself.

5. [According to Rennyo's Letter (2.1)],[5] "If neglected, even one's faith (*shinjin*) will vanish. It is said that by continually cleaning out the channels of faith, we let the water of Amida's dharma flow." How are the channels cleaned out? By not neglecting self-reflection and deepening it.

In addition to these points, he conveyed important knowledge to me throughout the night.

During those four days of *mishirabe* there were times of wailing and times when I cried until no more tears would come, and then spent half a day just sitting there in a daze. On the second day the face of my lovely wife would appear before my eyes, and I thought that I would like to embrace her once more before I died. But after the third day, my body was so weak that even that thought vanished. It was a long and painful four days. I will never forget my indebtedness to my teacher, to Okayama, to Inoue, my uncle, my mother in-law, my father in-law, Ganshōji, Kinuko, sister Nami, Kita Genbei, and my numerous friends who guided me to the Buddha. Thank you! Thank you!

Also, with regards to my father in Koriyama, I bow down to the sky in the distant north and with palms together I apologize, beg forgiveness, and thank him. If my father had not tried to stop me, I would have treated lightly the sacred, immutable dharma. This did not happen thanks to my father's opposition. There is a saying that there is much water in much ice and much merit in many obstacles. Suffering leads to even greater joy.

I believe that the best and most certain way to repay my debt is to share this knowledge with people throughout the world. I vow to spend the rest of my days, without wasting a moment and without concern for my life or body, leading the way to save people with Naikan.

## Yoshimoto's Answers to Questions about Naikan

Question: Please tell me the purpose of Naikan?

Answer: Naikan aims to change one's state of mind so that no matter what happens you can live with feelings of gratitude, and say "Thank you. I am happy." I think it is also the purpose for which we were born in this world.

To put this simply using Buddhist language, it is *tenmei kaigo* 転迷開悟, which means moving out of a state of confusion to a state of enlightenment. When I put it this way, however, people might say, "That's religious, isn't it?" It is true that the foundation out of which the Naikan method was born contains Buddhist teachings, but now it has no connection with Buddhism. It should be thought of rather as reflection on the self that leads to feelings of indebted gratitude.

It is because of this that Naikan has been widely accepted at prisons in different regions. It does not push any particular religion. Clause three of article twenty of the Japanese Constitution says, "The State and its organs shall refrain from religious education or any other religious activity." So prisons have incorporated it as a nonreligious practice for inmates to reflect on themselves and feel grateful, which in turn prevents recidivism.

### *The Purpose of Naikan's Themes*

Q: Please explain the method for presenting Naikan's themes.

A: First, at the foundation of Naikan is examining yourself in relation to your mother. Look at what you received from her, what you gave back, and what troubles you caused. This is done by closely examining yourself chronologically up to recent times. Then you do the same with your father, then your spouse. Then you closely examine the times you lied and stole in life.

Sometimes, however, depending on what brings a person to do Naikan, special topics need to be assigned. This is why when people come to do Naikan, they are asked their reasons for coming to do it. If someone is having a hard time getting along with his boss at work, he will do Naikan on his boss, examining himself thoroughly. If someone is having a hard time getting along with her mother-in-law, she will examine herself in relation to her. If a high school student has a problem with attending school, listen to what the situation is. If the student is getting scolded in his school club by an upperclassman and wants to quit because of the strict treatment, he will be guided to examine himself in relation to the upperclassman.

Among the various purposes for which people do Naikan, we find not only social anxiety, but also problems with alcohol. A person becomes physically ill with *saké,* yet still cannot quit. If he wants to stop drinking, he closely investigates how much he lost due to alcohol.

Here is an example of such a dialogue:

Naikansha [N]: How many years has it been since you started drinking?

Mensetsusha [M]: Twenty years.

N: Okay, closely examine each year of those twenty years. Make a chart of how much money you spent on alcohol and how much you spent on snacks at the bar.

M: Okay.

N: In addition to that, please write down the costs of hospitalizations when your liver was bad, how much you lost in daily wages, and all other financial losses.

After spending three or four days examining these things, the person might say,

N: Wow. This is amazing!

M: How much did you lose altogether?

N: Hmm. I drank up more than all the land and fields that were passed down by my ancestors.

M: In today's money, how much was it?

N: One hundred million yen. This is truly shocking.

When they do this every day and their self-reflection becomes deeper, just the "sa" sound of "*saké*" will make them shiver. They say, "I know, but I just can't quit." In fact, however, they do not know.

I tell them, "But if you think this will make you quit, you are sorely wrong. Please continue doing Naikan daily for about two hours a day. Then you will really be able to quit."

For those who can't quit gambling, they examine themselves in the same way.[6]

## *The Personal Problems of Those Doing Naikan*

Q: Some who do Naikan examine themselves in relation to their mother two or three times. What is the point of that?

A: Naikan questions cannot be presented to everyone in the same way. If it is determined that what is most important for a particular person is that he examine himself in relation to his mother, than we will have him do it three or four times. Do not think of the questions as a set. You need to see what questions are perfect for the person.

For example, a long time ago at a prison, there was a guy who was hated in his family and everyone in his family was an enemy. He was treated as the rascal of the family, so it could not be figured out whom in the family would be good to begin his Naikan on. The correction officer who was leading Naikan thought at length about this, and had the prisoner do Naikan on his victims. But his victims were just people he encountered. He did not know those to whom he did bad things, so there was no point in having him reflect on himself in relation to them. The officer, who was at a loss as to what to do, said, "Well, examine how it would be if you were in the place of your victims." After the officer assigned that topic, the prisoner was finally able to start to do Naikan. Next he was able to examine himself in relation to his mother.

Leading Naikan in a prison does not necessarily mean starting with the issues of victims because inevitably some will think, "Oh, this Naikan guide is trying to get me to confess. I can't do that." It was just for this particular person, who thought of his relatives as his enemies, that starting with his victims was successful.

The Naikan guide has to accurately discern the problems and troubles burdening the person doing Naikan, then pick an appropriate theme for him or her to self-reflect on.

### *Start with Something Easy*

Q: What should you do if you cannot order your thoughts or cannot remember?

A: When people start self-reflection in relation to their mothers, they might not be able to immediately do it by examining how they were with their mother during the first years of elementary school. In those cases, they can start by focusing on the previous month. It is like when you learn to swim, you start practicing with the easy exercise of grabbing on to the pool's rail and kicking your feet.

There are also those that say they did not really receive anything from their mothers. In those cases, you have them examine times that they lied and stole. If they still are unable to examine themselves and it is hopeless, then all you can do is let them go home. There are also those who have particular ailments that are hard to deal with, such as those with germ phobias who are constantly going to the sink to wash their face or who do not get out of the bathtub for more than two hours. Because there is nothing that can be done with these cases, they are requested to leave.

Q: Please explain intensive Naikan and daily Naikan.

A: The intensive Naikan method takes a week. The person doing Naikan gets up at 5 a.m. and until 5:30 cleans and washes up. Then until 9 p.m. he sits in one place doing Naikan. This is fundamental for understanding how to do Naikan and is an initiation to it. After this, it is important that the person continue to do Naikan for at least two hours daily so he does not lose what he gained. This is called daily Naikan or intermittent Naikan. For daily Naikan, during the first of the two hours, you examine yourself in relation to your mother, then for the second hour, if done at night, you examine yourself for that day, and if done in the morning, you examine yourself on the previous day. Intensive Naikan sessions are like telephone poles and daily Naikan the wires that connect them. Putting up telephone poles is pointless unless the wires with electric current are linked to them.

## *The Efficacy of Naikan*

Q: With regards to Naikan's efficacy, does it help raise someone's productivity at work?

A: The efficacy is not limited to productivity at work, but appears in many areas of life. It is applied in psychiatry. Many psychiatrists have told me about cases in which it has had great therapeutic efficacy. There are also reports of the differences of those in prison who have done Naikan compared to those who have not, and that the recidivism rate for those who have done Naikan is much lower.

I have also heard from five high schools around the country where teachers have been diligently teaching Naikan for one or two years. I was told that misbehaving students got better and that Naikan works to prevent students from becoming delinquent.

With regards to productivity at companies, I can mention the company Banyū, whose employees would soon quit after starting there. Since its enthusiastic president started practicing Naikan eight or nine years ago, the retention rate of the company's employees has gotten better. Every year he comes to my Naikan training center. He is very happy because about half of his employees are quite serious practitioners and the friendships among them have greatly deepened.

It is not just these particular cases. There are innumerable examples of regular people suffering with relationship problems, such as those between spouses, mother- and daughter-in-law, parent and child, who found happiness after doing Naikan. As a result of doing Naikan, people start to feel gratitude toward others, even when they can see wrong in them, and those other people also change as a result.

## Notes

1 Yoshimoto Ishin, *Naikan no Michi* 内観の道 (Koriyama: Naikan kenshūjo, 1977).

2 Yoshimoto Ishin, *Naihanhō* (Tokyo: Shunjusha, 2000 [1965]), 42–52 and 93–101.

3 Yoshimoto uses the term *naikan* frequently when referring to this time period, although the term was not yet used when he was still doing *mishirabe*.

To avoid confusion with Naikan, which developed later, I translate *naikan* here and elsewhere as "self-reflection."

4 This inconsistency with the "thirty-five years" mentioned earlier is probably due to revisions made for a later publication date. In fact, the publication date of *Naikan no michi* that this text is based on was forty years after 1937. On pages 98 and 99 of *Naikanhō*, published in 1965, twenty-eight years is listed for both times.

5 Rennyo was a fifteenth-century Shin Buddhist leader who is sometimes referred to as the "restorer of Jōdo Shinshū." His letters are regarded as scripture by Shin Buddhists.

6 Two charts of actual cases of calculations for the cost of alcohol consumption are omitted here.

## Bibliography

Chilson, Clark. *Secrecy's Power: Covert Shin Buddhists and Contradictions of Concealment.* Honolulu: University of Hawai'i Press, 2014.

Kawahara Ryūzō. "Naikan ryōhō no kokusaika no genjō" [The current situation of the internationalization of Naikan therapy]. *Seishin Shinkeigaku Zasshi* 105, no. 8 (2003): 988–993.

Yoshimoto Ishin. *Naihanhō.* Tokyo: Shunjusha, 2000 [1965].

——. *Naikan no Michi* 内観の道. Koriyama: Naikan kenshūjo, 1977.

# Chapter 5

# Wŏnhyo's *Commentary on the Amitābha Sūtra*

Richard D. McBride II

## Translator's Introduction

Wŏnhyo's 元曉 (617–686) *Pulsŏl Amita-gyŏng so* (佛說阿彌陀經疏, Commentary on the *Amitābha Sūtra* spoken by the Buddha) is a curious and instructive example of a work in the conventional category of Buddhist commentarial literature. Wŏnhyo's commentary is one of only a handful of surviving medieval Sinitic scholarly analyses on the Smaller *Sukhāvatīvyūha sūtra*, which is better known in East Asia as the *Amituo jing* (*Amitābha Sūtra*), and it is the only remaining treatment of this sutra from Wŏnhyo's homeland, the early Korean kingdom of Silla 新羅 (ca. 300–935). The most distinguishing characteristic of Wŏnhyo's commentary is that it draws heavily from the *gāthā* attributed to Vasubandhu (ca. 400–480) in the *Wangsheng lun* ([*Wuliangshou jing yubotishe yuansheng jie* (*Sukhāvatīvyūhopadeśa*)], *T.* 1524) and Tanluan's (ca. 488–554) *Wangsheng lun zhu* ([*Wuliangshou jing yubotishe yuansheng jie zhu* (Commentary on the *Sukhāvatīvyūhopadeśa*)], *T.* 1819). Although Wŏnhyo draws great inspiration from Tanluan's categories and diction, the commentary still bears the unmistakable mark of Wŏnhyo's scholarly essays: It alludes to his inclusive and comprehensive approach to doctrinal classification (*p'an'gyo*; *panjiao*), it displays a creative and profound understanding of works in the commentarial tradition, and it stresses Wŏnhyo's overriding exhortation to all living beings that they should arouse the *bodhicitta*.

The most widely used scripture of the cult of Amitābha in East Asia from the early medieval period was the *Amituo jing*, which was translated into Chinese by Kumārajīva (Jiumoluoshi 鳩摩羅什, 344–413) about 402 CE. The short length and elegant prose of this sutra made it a classic that was widely adored and much used for devotional purposes.[1]

The sutra introduces the merits of the Buddha Amitābha and his Pure Land Sukhāvatī (Kŭngnak; Jile, "Extreme Bliss"). It encourages people to aspire for rebirth in the pure land and informs them that if they maintain Amitābha's name in their minds for from one to seven days he will appear to them before they die and enable them to be reborn in the pure land.[2] It teaches that if good people adhere to the discourse recorded in the scripture, reflect upon it, and bear it in mind, they will be protected and remembered by all buddhas. They will also make irreversible progress toward enlightenment if they believe these things and practice with faith. Furthermore, the scripture teaches that those who vow to be born in Sukhāvatī will not regress in their journey on the path toward complete enlightenment and will be born in that land.[3] The other longer scriptures related to the cult of Amitābha developed these themes more fully.[4]

Only five commentaries on the *Amituo jing* have been preserved from the medieval period of Sinitic Buddhism.[5] Each of these commentaries portrays conventional characteristics of the genre of Buddhist exegetical literature as well as possessing distinctive features. The conventional traits of commentaries on the *Amituo jing* that date to the medieval period are placing the sutra within the larger context of the Mahāyāna tradition, typically within the hierarchical system of doctrinal taxonomy that the author advocates. These articulate the core teachings of the sutra and excerpt and analyze selected passages from the sutra, usually to point out similarities and differences with passages from the seminal sutras and commentaries of the leading doctrinal traditions. Few modern scholars have been drawn to the extant commentaries on the *Amituo jing* as a topic of academic inquiry although these works contain instructive but typically brief explications of such doctrinal issues as the one mind (*ilsim*, *yixin*) and the theories of buddha-bodies and buddha-lands.[6] To some extent, the composition of a commentary on the *Amituo jing* was probably a recommended or required exercise for a monastic exegete in medieval East Asia. Although their works have been lost, most of the foremost exegetes from Wŏnhyo's home country of Silla in the seventh and eighth centuries are reported to have written commentaries on the *Amituo jing*.[7] Selected passages from some of the early Korean commentaries on the *Amituo jing* have been preserved in later Korean and Japanese sources.[8]

Wŏnhyo's Pure Land views have been studied in detail by many scholars, but most scholars have focused on his more detailed treatment of similar issues in his *Muryangsu-gyŏng chongyo* 無量壽經宗要 (Doctrinal essentials of the *Wuliangshou jing*) and typically refer to *Amit'a-gyŏng so* to either introduce or supplement material in the former commentary.[9] Most modern scholarly treatments of Wŏnhyo's commentary on the *Amituo jing* consist primarily of brief summaries of the commentary and graphic outlines of its structure.[10] I am only aware of a few article-length treatments of Wŏnhyo's *Amit'a-gyŏng so.*[11]

As I mentioned previously, the structure of Wŏnhyo's commentary on the *Amitābha Sūtra* is that of a conventional scholarly commentary on a Buddhist sutra in East Asia. Wŏnhyo organizes his essay into (1) an articulation of the sutra's great intent (*taeŭi* 大意), (2) a discussion of its core teachings (*chongch'i* 宗致), and (3) an explication of passages from the text (*munsŏk* 文釋). Wŏnhyo conveys his view that the great intent of the sutra is that the mind of living beings is separate from characteristics and nature and is like the ocean and empty space. Defiled lands, such as the world of living beings, and pure lands, such as Amitābha's Sukhāvatī, are originally the one mind. Hence, *saṃsāra,* the cycle of rebirth and death, and nirvana, great peace and tranquility, are, in the end, not two ultimate limits or polar opposites. In this connection, Wŏnhyo asserts the ultimate unity between Śākyamuni's advising people in a "defiled land" on why they should abide in the mundane world as bodhisattvas and Amitābha's ultimate purpose in drawing living beings to him out of the mundane world into the pure land. In other words, Wŏnhyo makes the case that the *Amituo jing* encapsulates the great intent of both of these buddhas by making it accessible to both the monastic and lay communities. He substantiates the core devotional practices of the cult of Amitābha by asserting that when one hears the title of the sutra with one's ears one enters the one vehicle and when one intones the Buddha's name with one's mouth one transcends the three realms of existence. These benefits and more are available to people who offer ritual obeisance to Amitābha, solely recollect that Buddha, worship with praise and song, and engage in meditative visualization.

In the section outlining the core teachings of the sutra, Wŏnhyo supports the position that the sutra establishes two kinds of purity that transcend the three realms of existence: (1) the purity of the material world and (2) the purity of the world of living beings. In this connection, Wŏnhyo briefly lays out his general system of doctrinal classification and the place of this sutra within it. Wŏnhyo uses descriptive concepts as well as sutras and treatises to anchor his taxonomy, referring to them as "approaches": (1) the approach of perfection and fullness (*wŏnmanmun* 圓滿門), as explicated in the *Pusa yingluo benye jing* (Sūtra on the original acts that serve as a bodhisattva's adornments); (2) the approach of being fixed in one direction (*irhyangmun* 一向門), as described for advanced bodhisattvas in the *Mahāyāna-saṃgraha*; (3) the approach of simple purity (*sunjŏngmun* 純淨門), as explained for entry-level bodhisattvas in the *Saṃdhinirmocana sūtra*; and (4) the approach of the group of those assured of certain success (*chŏng chŏngch'wimun* 正定聚門), as articulated in the Larger *Sukhāvatīvyūha sūtra* (*Wuliangshou jing*). Wŏnhyo admits that a comprehensive discussion of Sukhāvatī would be permeated with these four approaches. Simply stated, Wŏnhyo's fundamental doctrinal taxonomy is manifest through these four approaches. The most superior doctrinal position is that of what scholars would refer to as the nascent Hwaŏm/Huayan tradition, with the view of a comprehensive path of bodhisattva practice in which all the states interfused and interconnected. The second and third positions are from the standpoints of Yogācāra texts, here differentiated because Wŏnhyo sees the *Mahāyāna-saṃgraha* as being for advanced bodhisattvas above the eighth stage and the *Saṃdhinirmocana-sūtra* as being for bodhisattvas at the early stage of extreme joy. The fourth position is that of sutras that are intended for people who have not yet become bodhisattvas.

The third and final section, comprising an analysis of the original text, is divided into three parts that treat the conventionally accepted tripartite structure of Mahāyāna sutras: the preface section (*sŏ* 序), the core teachings section (*chŏng* 正), and the propagation section (*yut'ong* 流通). Of these, the core teachings section is the most developed and instructive. Wŏnhyo returns to the concept of purity and both draws heavily from and reformulates conceptualizations of the fulfillment of meritorious virtues (*kongdŏk sŏngch'wi* 功德成就) articulated in great detail in the *Wangsheng lun* attributed to Vasubandhu and Tanluan's *Wangsheng lun zhu*. In describing the adornments of Sukhāvatī and its lord Amitābha, the *Wangsheng lun* lists the fulfillment of seventeen different meritorious virtues, which is linked to a *gāthā* praising the purity and merits of Sukhāvatī. Tanluan's *Wangsheng lun zhu* reproduces and amplifies a discussion on these meritorious virtues and makes explicit their connection to the decorations of the Pure Land, although meritorious virtues nos. 8, 11, and 17 exhibit slight variations from the received text of the *Wangsheng lun* (see table 1).

Wŏnhyo approaches this same material creatively. As the notes to the translation show more clearly and specifically, Wŏnhyo deploys several couplets from Vasubandhu's *gāthā* as well as short passages from Tanluan's commentary to validate his description of the meritorious virtues of the pure land and Amitābha. He reorganizes the received meritorious virtues into a new configuration and formulates nine new meritorious virtues that more lucidly express his vision. The order Wŏnhyo presents in the text is provided in parentheses in the column treating the *Amit'a-gyŏng so* in table 1. Considering that Tanluan's Pure Land writings on the whole tend to exhibit a desire to be compatible with the *Avataṃsaka sūtra* and the doctrinal positions of the nascent Huayan tradition,[12] in this commentary I see Wŏnhyo communicating a comprehensive Huayan-esque analysis of the adornments of Sukhāvatī that distinguishes between the individual parts (nos. 1–14) and the whole (no. 15). This refocuses the discussion of the meritorious virtues of the various kinds of adornments of the pure land around their universal purity. Wŏnhyo then advances his analysis of purity to include an examination of the direct reward (nos. 16–19), making in all nineteen meritorious virtues of purity.

The last topic treated with robust discussion in Wŏnhyo's commentary is the direct cause of rebirth in the Pure Land. Simply stated, to Wŏnhyo, if someone really wants to obtain rebirth in the Pure Land, one can do nothing better than to arouse the *bodhicitta*. Wŏnhyo boils away all the elaboration surrounding the doctrine of the nine grades of rebirth, questions regarding backsliding, and even famous qualifications regarding heinous crimes and slandering the true dharma described in the eighteenth vow found in the *Wuliangshou jing*, to get at the heart of the matter. Ultimately none of these matter if someone arouses the great aspiration, because arousing the *bodhicitta* is precisely the direct cause of rebirth in the pure land. For those who do not arouse the *bodhicitta*, there is no direct cause of rebirth in the pure land. Those beings must rely on ancillary causes such as reciting the name of the Buddha Amitābha. Emphasis on arousing the *bodhicitta* is quintessentially Wŏnhyo's approach to the overarching unity of Buddhist doctrine and practice. It illustrates how Wŏnhyo is able to demonstrate that a comprehensively harmonious thread is woven through the often distinct strands of Mahāyāna Buddhist doctrine.

**Table 1 The Meritorious Virtues of Amitābha's Pure Land**

| | *Wangsheng lun*[a] | *Wangsheng lun zhu*[b] | *Amit'a-gyŏng so* |
|---|---|---|---|
| 1. | fulfillment of the meritorious virtue of purity (清淨功德成就) | fulfillment of the meritorious virtue of the purity of the adornments (莊嚴清淨功德成就) | (15) fulfillment of the meritorious virtue of the purity of the adornments (莊嚴清淨功德成就) |
| 2. | fulfillment of the meritorious virtue of measurements (量功德成就) | fulfillment of the meritorious virtue of the measurements of the adornments (莊嚴量功德成就) | |
| 3. | fulfillment of the meritorious virtue of nature (性功德成就) | fulfillment of the meritorious virtue of the nature of the adornments (莊嚴性功德成就) | (14) meritorious virtue of the nature of the adornments (莊嚴性功德) |
| 4. | fulfillment of the meritorious virtue of form (形相功德成就) | fulfillment of the meritorious virtue of the form of the adornments (莊嚴形相功德成就) | |
| 5. | fulfillment of the meritorious virtue of varied kinds of phenomena (種種事功德成就) | fulfillment of the meritorious virtue of the varied kinds of phenomena in the adornments (莊嚴種種事功德成就) | (4) fulfillment of the meritorious virtue of various kinds of phenomena (種種事功德成就) |
| 6 | fulfillment of the meritorious virtue of subtle form (妙色功德成就) | fulfillment of the meritorious virtue of the subtle form of the adornments (莊嚴妙色功德成就) | (5) meritorious virtue of the fulfillment of the sublime form of the adornments (莊嚴妙色成就功德) |
| 7. | fulfillment of the meritorious virtue of touch (觸功德成就) | fulfillment of the meritorious virtue of the touch of the adornments (莊嚴觸功德成就) | |

**Table 1 (*continued*)**

| | *Wangsheng lun*[a] | *Wangsheng lun zhu*[b] | *Amit'a-gyŏng so* |
|---|---|---|---|
| 8. | fulfillment of the meritorious virtue of the adornments (莊嚴功德成就) | fulfillment of the meritorious virtue of the three kinds of adornments (莊嚴三種功德成就) | |
| 9. | fulfillment of the meritorious virtue of the rain (雨功德成就) | fulfillment of the meritorious virtue of rain in the adornments (莊嚴雨功德成就) | (8) meritorious virtue of raining flowers (雨華功德) |
| 10. | fulfillment of the meritorious virtue of the glory (光明功德成就) | fulfillment of the meritorious virtue of rain in the adornments (莊嚴光明功德成就) | |
| 11. | fulfillment of the meritorious virtue of sound (聲功德成就) | fulfillment of the meritorious virtue of the sublime sound of the adornments (莊嚴妙聲功德成就) | |
| 12. | fulfillment of the meritorious virtue of the lord (主功德成就) | fulfillment of the meritorious virtue of the lord of the adornments (莊嚴主功德成就) | (16) meritorious virtue of the lord (主功德) |
| 13. | fulfillment of the meritorious virtue of the entourage (眷屬功德成就) | fulfillment of the meritorious virtue of the entourage in the adornments (莊嚴眷屬功德成就) | (17) meritorious virtue of the companions (伴功德); fulfillment of the meritorious virtue of the entourage in the adornments (莊嚴眷屬功德成就) |
| 14. | fulfillment of the meritorious virtue of enjoyment (受用功德成就) | fulfillment of the meritorious virtue of the enjoyment of the adornments (莊嚴受用功德成就) | (10) meritorious virtue of enjoyment (受用功德) |

**Table 1 (*continued*)**

| | *Wangsheng lun*[a] | *Wangsheng lun zhu*[b] | *Amit'a-gyŏng so* |
|---|---|---|---|
| 15. | fulfillment of the meritorious virtue of being devoid of all difficulties (無諸難功德成就) | fulfillment of the meritorious virtue of being devoid of all difficulties in the adornments (莊嚴無諸難功德成就) | (1) fulfillment of the meritorious virtue of being devoid of all difficulties (無諸難功德成就) |
| 16. | fulfillment of the meritorious virtue of the approach of great meaning (大義門功德成就) | fulfillment of the meritorious virtue of the approach of great meaning in the adornments (莊嚴大義門功德成就) | (12) meritorious virtue of the great meaning (大義功德) |
| 17. | fulfillment of the meritorious virtue of all that has been sought (一切所求功德成就) | fulfillment of the meritorious virtue of all that has been sought is sufficient in the adornments (莊嚴一切所求滿足功德成就) | |
| | | | (2) fulfillment of the meritorious virtue of the land in the adornments (莊嚴地功德成就) |
| | | | (3) fulfillment of the meritorious virtue of water in the adornments (莊嚴水功德成就) |
| | | | (6) meritorious virtue of the musical performers (妓樂功德) |
| | | | (7) meritorious virtue of the jeweled land (寶地功德) |
| | | | (9) meritorious virtue of self-existence (自在功德) |

Table 1 (*continued*)

| *Wangsheng lun*[a] | *Wangsheng lun zhu*[b] | *Amit'a-gyŏng so* |
|---|---|---|
| | | (11) meritorious virtue of transformation (變化功德) |
| | | (13) fulfillment of the meritorious virtue of the emptiness of the adornments (莊嚴虛空功德成就) |
| | | (18) meritorious virtue of the great assembly (大眾功德); fulfillment of the meritorious virtue of the great assembly in the adornments (莊嚴大眾功德成就) |
| | | (19) meritorious virtue of the supreme head (上首功德); fulfillment of the meritorious virtue of the supreme head of the adornments (莊嚴上首功德成就) |

[a]*Wangsheng lun, T.* 1524.26.231b24–c8.

[b]*Wangsheng lun zhu* 2, *T.* 1819.40.830b25–26. For an English translation of the entire section of the *Wangsheng lun zhu* dealing with this material, see Roger Corless, "T'an-luan's Commentary on the Pure Land Discourse: An Annotated Translations and Soteriological Analysis of the *Wang-shêng-lun chu* (*T.* 1819)" (PhD diss., University of Wisconsin–Madison, 1973), 239–256. Revised and updated version of Corless' translation: Roger Corless, trans, "A Commentary on *The Upadeśa on the Sutras of Limitless Life with Gāthās on the Resolution to be Born* Composed by the Bodhisattva Vasubandhu: Expository Commentary by the Monk Tanluan," *Pacific World: Journal of the Institute of Buddhist Studies*, third series, no. 17 (2015): 69–233. Available online at: http://www.shin-ibs.edu/publications/pacific-world/pacific-world-third-series-number-17-2015, accessed June 9, 2017.

## Translation

*Commentary on the Amitābha Sūtra Spoken by the Buddha*
*(Amit'agyŏng so)*

Wŏnhyo, Śramaṇa in the State of Silla,
Haedong 海東 in the Tang Empire

I will analyze this sutra by differentiating three approaches: first, I will narrate its "great intent"; second, I will explain its core teachings; and third, I will enter into an analysis of the text.

## I. Narration of the Great Intent

Now the mind of living beings, being "mind," is separate from characteristics and nature, and is like the ocean and empty space. Because it is like empty space, there are no characteristics that are not interfused. How could it occupy such locations as east and west? Because it is like the ocean, there is no nature that is kept [unchanging]. How could there be a moment devoid of motion or calm?

This being the case, sometimes, as a result of impure actions, [the mind] flows in an everlasting manner in compliance with the five impurities.[13] Sometimes [the mind] avails itself of pure conditions and becomes eternally quiescent by severing the four streams.[14] If one considers this motion and calm to be all a great dream, then one sees them from the vantage point of awakening and there is neither streams nor quiescence. Defiled lands and pure lands are originally the one mind. *Saṃsāra* and nirvana are, in the end, not two ultimate limits.

Nevertheless, grasping the awareness of non-duality is very difficult, and leaving behind the delusion that presumes they are one is not easy. For this reason, the great saints left behind traces that are both far and near, and that which they laid out are verbal teachings that sometimes praise and sometimes disparage. Arriving at this point, the Sugata Śākyamuni manifests in this defiled land and advises abiding while admonishing against the five impurities. The Tathāgata Amitābha dwells in his pure land, drawing in the three classes of beings to seek rebirth there.

Presently, this sutra articulates the great intent of both of these honored ones' appearing in the mundane world and the essential approaches for the four classes of followers[15] to enter into the Way to enlightenment. It instructs that one can desire [rebirth in] the pure land

and praises that one can take refuge in sublime virtue. "Being able to take refuge in sublime virtue" means that when one hears the title of the sutra with one's ears, one enters the one vehicle and does not turn away from it, and when one intones the Buddha's name with one's mouth, one transcends the three realms[16] and does not return to them. How much more so should one who offers ritual obeisance, solely recollects, worships with praise and song, and engages in meditative visualization! "Being able to desire [rebirth in] the pure land" means that when one bathes in the sublime golden lotus pond one forsakes the defiled causes of conditioned rebirth. Wandering through trees of jade and forests of sandalwood, one heads toward the holy results of the deathlessness. In addition, seeing the Buddha's light, one enters into marklessness [that which is devoid of characteristics], and listening to Brahmā sounds, one awakens to nonproduction.

Afterwards, one transcends in accordance with the fifth approach [returning to the mundane world to teach and guide other living beings], returns bridled in the garden of life and death, and rests in the forest of defilements. Not taking a step, one wanders widely in the world systems of the ten directions, and not relaxing for one thought-moment, one manifests everywhere in the three boundless realms.[17] What bliss could be superior to this? How can the term "extreme bliss" be void!

The expression "Spoken by the Buddha" (*Pulsŏl* 佛說) is that which comes out of his golden mouth, which teachings have been unaltered for a thousand generations. "Amitābha" (Amit'a) is a name that has been established to imply real virtue and has not been exhausted in a myriad eons. Subject and object are combined together, being signified in the title, so it is called *The Amitābha Sūtra Spoken by the Buddha*.

## II. Core Teaching

I will classify the core teachings of the sutra. This sutra sets up two kinds of purity that transcend the three realms of existence as its core teachings, and causing all living beings to be able to not backslide on the Way to unsurpassed enlightenment is its core ideal. What are the names of the two kinds of purity? As has been discussed and explained, there are two kinds of this purity: first, purity of the material world; and second, purity of the world of living beings.[18] Because there is a more extensive explanation, nevertheless in entering this purity there are four approaches. First is the approach of perfection and fullness. Only buddhas and tathāgatas are able to enter through this approach, as explained in the *Original Acts Sūtra*.[19] Second is the approach of being fixed in one direction. Bodhisattvas above the eighth stage are able to enter through this approach, as explained in the *Mahāyāna-saṃgraha*.[20] Third is the approach of simple purity. Only bodhisattvas above the third stage of extreme joy[21] are able to enter through this approach, as explained in the *Saṃdhinirmocana sūtra*.[22] Fourth is the approach of the group of those assured of certain success. Only those who do not backslide are able to enter through this approach, [as well as] the group of those who are lost and the group of those not assured of certain success,[23] as explained in the two-rolled *[Sukhāvatīvyūha] sūtra* in two rolls.

A comprehensive discourse on the world system of Extreme Bliss (Sukhāvatī) would be endowed with these four approaches. Now, the core teaching of this sutra, these two kinds of purity, correctly displays the fourth, the approach of the group of those assured certain success, because *śrāvakas* not assured of certain success and ordinary people are able to be reborn [in the pure land]. The treatise explains that adherents of the Two Vehicles will not be reborn [there], and that those with seed-natures are completely determined will not be able to be reborn [there].

The *Sound King Sūtra* (*Shengwang jing*) explains that Amitābha in the world system of Peace and Bliss has a father and a mother. [His mother] is a transformation woman and not a woman [with a body produced due to] real reward.[24] The treatises explain that women are not reborn there.[25] Because there are no real women, we know that the transformation birds are also like this.

Also, although he is said to have a father and mother, he is not a womb-born being. Indeed, transformation beings pretend to be his father and mother. Thus, the sutra [*Sound King Sūtra*] says, "If [a living being in] the four assemblies is able to correctly receive the name of that buddha, by means of this meritorious virtue, when he is on the verge of death, Amitābha, along with his great throng, will go to where this person is and cause [the aspirant] to see him. Upon seeing him [the aspirant] will seek rebirth with felicitous joy, and he will double his meritorious virtue. By means of this causal connection, the place where he is reborn will eternally forsake the forms of wombs and polluted desires, and he will have a transformation birth spontaneously in the midst of a beautiful, sublime, jeweled lotus flower in a pure place. [The aspirant] will be endowed with the great spiritual penetrations,[26] and bright light will shine forth brilliantly."[27] One should know that his father and mother only pretend to lodge there.

In addition, that sutra [*Sound King Sūtra*] says: "Amitābha and the *śrāvakas*, furnished with *tathāgatas*, *arhats*, and those attaining complete and universal wisdom, that land is called 'Clear and Great' (*chŏngt'ae* 清泰), sage kings dwell there, and the length and width of their castles are tens of thousands of *yojanas*."[28] Furthermore, the *Visualization Sūtra* explains that "The height of the Buddha's body is sixty ten-thousands of *koṭis*[29] of *nayutas*[30] of *yojanas* as the sands of the Ganges River."[31]

With respect to the incongruity that the castles are small and the bodies are large, one should know that that Buddha [Amitābha] has numerous castles, and that in accordance with the largeness or smallness of the assembly the castle is either large or small. He displays [himself] in a large body in large castles, and he manifests himself in a small body in small castles. The *Sound King Sūtra* says that tens of thousands of *yojanas* is [the size] of the castles where he dwells along with *śrāvakas*. One should know that the Buddha's body is befitting for where he dwells. The *Visualization Sūtra* explains that since the height of his body is great, one should know that his castles are also extremely large because all the assemblies dwell together in those places. As in the [*Sukhāvatīvyūha*] *sūtra* in two rolls and this [*Visualization*] *Sūtra*, the differences in size of lotus flowers in the pond accord with the size of the flowers and the size of the pond. One should know that the castle and the [buddha's] body are also just so. The remaining discrepancies correspond to this and are thus brought into agreement.

Some hold that since a father and mother are described in the *Sound King Sūtra*, this shows that the place where that buddha dwells is a defiled land,[32] but this meaning is not the case. That sutra previously explained that [an aspirant] will enjoy a transformation birth spontaneously in a jeweled lotus flower, he will be endowed with the great spiritual penetrations, and bright light will shine forth brilliantly. In addition, the passage below says that there are two bodhisattvas: first, one called Avalokiteśvara, and second, one called Mahāsthāmaprāpta. These two bodhisattvas stand in attendance on his left and right. These things, being all characteristics of the pure land, are because they are not different than what is explained in the *Visualization Sūtra*.

One should know that what in that sutra are explained as Devadatta, demon kings, and so forth, are all constructions brought about by transformations in the pure land, which do not cause these things not to be pure lands, just as [the existence] of transformation beasts does not mean something is a defiled land. I will stop here and return to the discussion of analyzing the original text.

## III. Analysis of the Original Text

### A. *Preface Section*

Here follows the third section; we will enter the text and analyze it. The text is made up of three sections: preface, core teaching, and propagation. There are six phrases in the preface section, and among these the first two mark the meaning of the phrase and the latter four provide evidence of the meaning of the first two.

The expression "Thus" (*yŏsi* 如是) means to wholly raise the dharma that was heard and marks a mind that is believing and obedient. The expression "have I heard" (*amun* 我聞) means to specifically lead and enable one to hear and marks a will lacking contrariness and quarrelsomeness. The latter four then draw evidence of two responses and clarify the aspirant's remembering the times and places he has heard and bring about the ability to hear it without mistakes. Inasmuch as there is a great master and a great assembly, they validate the believability of what has been described. Among those, indeed, all can be known as if it were common.

There are three great assemblies in the sixth preface: first, the assembly of the *śrāvakas*; next, the assembly of the bodhisattvas; and after that, the assembly of miscellaneous sorts [of living beings].

In the assembly of the *śrāvakas*, Śāriputra in this [language (literary Chinese)] is called "Son of the Body" (Sinja 身子). Maudgalyāyana is called "Praising and Chanting" (Ch'ansong 讚誦). Kāśyapa is called "Drinking Light" (Ŭmgwang 飲光). Kātyāyana is called "Door Rope" (Sŏnsŭng 扇繩). Mahākauṣthila is called "Big Knees." Revata is called "Provisional Accord" (Kahwahap 假和合). Śuddhi-panthaka [Cūḷapanthaka] is called "Snake Slave" (Sano 蛇奴), and sometimes he is called "Small Path" (Sado 小道). Nanda is called "Felicitous Joy" (Kyŏnghŭi 慶喜). Ānanda is called "Joyous Delight" (Hwanhŭi 歡喜). Rāhula is called "Hindrance" (Pokchang 覆障), and sometimes he is called "Palace-Born" (Kungsaeng 宮生). Gavāṃpati is called "Ruminating Ox" (Usi 牛呞). Piṇḍola is called "Elder" (Kinyŏn 耆年). Bharadvāja is called "Sharp Intellect" (Rigŭn 利根). Kālōdayin is called "Black Superior" (Hŭksang 黑上), and he was a master in the time before Siddhārtha left the householder way of life. Kapphiṇa is called "Lodging for the Night in the Room" (Pangsuk 房宿). Vakkula is called "Wholesome Countenance" (Sŏnyong 善容). Aniruddha is called "No Craving" (Mubin 無貧), and sometimes he is called "As One Wishes" (Yŏŭi 如意). Among the assembly of bodhisattvas, Ajita is called

"Unconquerable" (Munŭngsŭng 無能勝), and Gandhahastin is called "Red One" (Chŏksaek 赤色). The rest [of the figures appearing in the sutra] can be known.

## B. Core Teaching Section

The section after "At that time the Buddha spoke"[33] is the second section that explains the core teaching of the sutra. There are three parts to this section: first, correctly showing the fruits of the two kinds of purity; second, encouraging the cultivation of the two kinds of direct causes;[34] and third, drawing examples to validate [the aspirant's practice].

In the first part [on the fruits of purity], there are two: brief statement and detailed explanation. Among these there are two paragraphs, first marking the dependent result and second signaling the direct reward. In analysis, there are also two: first analyzing the dependent result and second analyzing the direct reward.

In the purity of the dependent result, there are two approaches to meaning. There are six distinctive features of the text, and with respect to the meritorious virtues of the parts and whole, there are fifteen meanings. The two approaches are first, the approach of analyzing the name [of the sutra]; and second, the approach of differentiating the distinctive features. The six [distinctive features] are because that the approach of [analyzing the name] is unpacked in two, and the approach of [differentiating] the distinctive features is separated into four. The fifteen [meritorious virtues] of parts and whole are because there are fourteen dealing with the parts and one that completes the whole. Regarding the fourteen dealing with the [meritorious virtues] of the parts, there are four examples in the six passages: in the former, each one has one; in the latter, each two has two; in the third passage three are unpacked; and in the fourth passage five are distinguished. For this reason, all together there are fourteen meritorious virtues.

The first passage says, "[the living beings in that land] suffer no pain, but only enjoy all manner of pleasures."[35] This is the fulfillment of the meritorious virtue of being devoid of all difficulties, as discussed in the song, which says, "Eternally forsaking the vexations of body and mind / one receives pleasure constantly without interruption."[36]

The second passage refers to seven rows of railings, decorative nets, and rows of trees. This is the fulfillment of the meritorious virtue of the land in the adornments, as discussed in the song, which says, "Assorted flowers of different bright colors / bejeweled railings surround it."[37]

In the third passage there are three meritorious virtues: the gold sand in the pond water. This is the fulfillment of the meritorious virtue of water in the adornments, as discussed in the song, which says, "All the ponds are girded with the seven treasures; the clear water contains the eight virtues; below amasses yellow gold sand; and above glitters the color of blue lotus flowers. The stairways and pavilions are made of gold and silver, and so forth. This is the fulfillment of the meritorious virtue of various kinds of phenomena, as discussed in the song, which says, "Prepared with the properties of all jewels / and endowed with sublime ornaments."[38] The lotus flowers are like wheels, blue in color, [radiating] blue light, and so forth; the meritorious virtue of the fulfillment of the sublime form of the adornments are as discussed in the song: "Immaculate light blazes / brilliant purity glitters in the world."[39]

In the fourth passage there are five meritorious virtues. First is the meritorious virtue of the musical performers because they constantly abide in celestial music. Second is the meritorious virtue of the jeweled land because the land is yellow gold. Third is the meritorious virtue of raining flowers because it rains flowers in the six time periods [of the day],[40] as discussed in the song, which says, "The golden lands makes celestial musicians / raining flowers disperse in their midst. / The joyful musicians do not grow weary / day and night they never sleep." Fourth is the meritorious virtue of self-existence because [the beings there] ride, comprehend, and wander [wherever they will]. Fifth is the meritorious virtue of enjoyment because after their meal they take a stroll, as discussed in the song, which says, "Making offerings to the buddhas of the ten directions / as a reward they obtain the penetrations and make wings. / Loving and taking pleasure in the taste of the Buddha-dharma / *dhyāna* and *samādhi* are their food."[41]

Nevertheless, there are two kinds of food in that land: first is food for the inside, as explained in this treatise; second is food for the outside, as explained in other sutras, like the *[Sukhāvatīvyūha] sūtra* in two rolls, which says, "If they desire for a mealtime, bowls made of the seven jewels spontaneously appear before them [. . .] filled over spontaneously with food and drink of a hundred tastes. Although the food is offered, they do not eat it. Once the sight has been seen and the aroma smelt, one naturally feels that he is satisfied."[42] Now, this sutra says that "after their meal they take a stroll,"[43] so the distinctive feature harmonizes with the food for the outside that is received for use.

In the fifth passage there are two meritorious virtues. First is the meritorious virtue of transformation because it describes the sublime dharma that flocks of birds are created by transformation, as discussed in the song, which says, "All manner of birds of diverse colors / each and every one emits elegant sounds. / Those who hear it think of the three jewels / forget their delusions and enter the one mind."

Second is the meritorious virtue of the great meaning because there is no name or substance to such things as the evil paths,[44] as discussed in the song, which says, "Men with wholesome roots in the Mahāyāna / universally do not hold in contempt the name [of the pure land]. / Women and people with deficient senses / and those of the ilk of the two vehicles are not reborn [there]."[45] A case in point: The sutra says that there are no evil paths and contempt, and the treatises manifest that there is no contempt for the human path of rebirth. Mutually they raise [points] as such, and their meaning is just as explained.

In the sixth passage there are two meritorious virtues. [First,] as has been discussed and explained, it is the fulfillment of the meritorious virtue of emptiness of the adornments. A *gāthā* says, "Limitless treasures are entwined with each other / a net set amidst empty space. / All manner of bells make sounds / issuing forth the sound of the sublime dharma."[46]

Second is the meritorious virtue of the nature of ornamentation. As has been discussed and explained, it is the fulfillment of the meritorious virtue of the nature of ornamentation. A *gāthā* says, "The Way to complete enlightenment is great compassion / and the production of wholesome roots."[47]

Now, it is said that those who spontaneously and intermittently think thoughts of the three jewels are precisely the mind of [pure] nature. By relying on the seeds of supramundane wholesome roots they do not wait for meritorious functioning[48] and spontaneous production; hence, correct recollection of the three jewels forsakes the heterodox and takes refuge in the right. Because it ties the Way to enlightenment to a host of practices, it is called the Way to complete enlightenment. The superior and sublime meritorious virtue of recollecting these three jewels, transferring and giving [the merit] to all [living beings], is called great compassion.

The above, all together, are fourteen meritorious virtues, which invariably transcend the three realms of existence and six paths of rebirth. For this reason, comprehensively it is called the world system of purity. As has been discussed and explained, it is the fulfillment of the meritorious virtue of the purity of the adornments. A *gāthā* says, "When visualizing the characteristics of that world system / it is superior to transcending the way of the three realms of existence."[49] Or, if one discusses and explains the eighteen perfections of [Amitābha's *saṃbhogakāya*], now in this sutra the purity of the dependent result is explained as these fifteen [meritorious virtues]. If one adds the four passages on the direct reward, which were explained later, then there are nineteen meritorious virtues of purity. Nevertheless, the sutras and treatises have similarities and differences. Among these, indeed all things corresponding to that can be known.

### *The Purity of the Direct Reward*

The passage after "Śāriputra, what do you think?"[50] is about the second purity of the direct reward. The passage manifests four kinds of meritorious virtues: first, the meritorious virtue of the lord [Amitābha]; second, the meritorious virtue of the companions; third, the meritorious virtue of the great assembly; and fourth, the meritorious virtue of the supreme head.

In the meritorious virtue of the lord [Amitābha], roughly two kinds [of meritorious virtues] appear: first, limitlessness of light; and second, limitlessness of life. If we analyze "Amitābha" corresponding to this passage of the sutra, this land is interpreted as and corresponds to "limitless." Furthermore, referring to "since he has attained buddhahood, ten *kalpas* have passed,"[51] one should know that it is because he has been abiding for limitless *kalpas* after this time.

Second, the meritorious virtue of the companions is because the disciples of the *śrāvakas* are all arhats. The treatise says, "It is the fulfillment of the meritorious virtue of adorning the entourage."[52] A *gāthā* says, "It is because the assembly of the pure flowers of the Tathāgata / blooms in the flower complete enlightenment."[53]

This case means that this "assembly of pure flowers" is called the assembly of those who attain the seven kinds of pure flowers. What are these seven? First is the purity of precepts; second is the purity of mind; third is the purity of sight; fourth is the purity of overcoming doubt; fifth is the purity of informed views on the Way to enlightenment and wrong paths; sixth is the purity of informed views on practice; and seventh is the purity of informed views on the cessation of practice. A detailed explanation of these appears in the *Yogācārabhūmi*.[54] This assembly of the seven kinds of pure[55] flowers [correspond to] the transformation beings born from the flowers of the buddha's complete enlightenment.

Third, the meritorious virtue of the great assembly is because beings born from living beings are all *avaivartika* [nonregressing]. Those who for up to ten thought moments recollect the meritorious virtues [of Amitābha] and are reborn in that realm [do so] because they enter the group of those assured of certain success and eternally do not backslide. The treatise says, "What is the fulfillment of the meritorious virtue of the adorned great assembly? A *gāthā* says, 'The immovable assembly of men and gods / is because it is born of the ocean of pure knowledge.'"[56] A case in point: All rely on being contained and enriched by the ocean of the Tathāgata's knowledge because they enter the group of those assured of certain success and are immoveable and nonchanging.

Fourth, the meritorious virtue of the supreme head, since many among those are bodhisattvas who will succeed to buddhahood in one lifetime,[57] is because such are explained as being at least *asaṃkhyeya*.[58] What is the fulfillment of the meritorious virtue of adorning the supreme head? A *gāthā* says, "Just as Mount Sumeru is the king [of mountains] / its superiority and sublimity are unsurpassed";[59] a case in point is that bodhisattvas who will succeed to buddhahood in one lifetime are superior among the ten stages because they are like the king of a sublime mountain.

Eight kinds of adornments are fully manifested in the treatise,[60] and this sutra displays, in summary, the four kinds of meritorious virtues. The above two passages together are the first, and the section on manifesting the fruits of the two kinds of purities is finished.

### *The Two Kinds of Direct Causes*

From the passage "those living beings that hear [of that land] should make a vow"[61] on afterward is the second [cause], encouragement to cultivate the two kinds of pure causes, which in particular there are four: first, encouragement to make a vow; second, clearly cultivating the cause; third, displaying the reception of effects; and fourth, the concluding encouragement.

Two kinds of causes are clarified in the second passage: first, direct causes; and second, ancillary causes. Among the direct causes, words are unable to express how those who attain rebirth in that realm by means of the causal connections of the blessed virtues of a few wholesome roots are because they manifest the aspiration to great *bodhi* and embrace many wholesome roots in order to attain rebirth there by means of causal connections, just like the text of "The Chapter on Bodhisattva Stages and Arousing the Mind."

In addition, since all bodhisattvas initially arouse the mind and they are able to embrace all the factors of enlightenment, because the surpassing wholesome roots are the supreme head, they are able to disregard unwholesome acts of the three kinds of karma in the places of all sentient beings and mutually resonate with the meritorious virtues.

A case in point: When a bodhisattva initially arouses the *bodhicitta,* he is able to embrace all the surpassing wholesome roots; he is able to cut off unwholesome karma and mutually resonate with the meritorious virtues. For this reason, it is explained as attaining rebirth there by means of the causal connections of the blessed virtues of a few wholesome roots. For this reason, we can know that these causes embrace the causes of the nine grades [of rebirth], by means of the three groups, in the [*Sukhāvatīvyūha*] *sūtra* in two rolls. These three are all those who have aroused the *bodhicitta.*

The meaning of this passage is only manifested in the treatises, which says "men and so forth, who have wholesome roots in the Mahāyāna, do not slander the name."[62] This means, and precisely says, that those who are reborn in that realm, although they are in the nine grades [of rebirth], because the causes are equal for the wholesome roots that arouse the mind of the Mahāyāna, as a result and so forth, they do not slander the name.

Someone may raise an objection: If one needs to arouse a great aspiration to be reborn directly in the pure land, he does not resonate with being reborn there and realizes the lesser result because they do not backslide at all. If they had backslid from that great [place], they would realize the lesser result because this place is neither existent nor nonexistent.

Furthermore, among the forty-eight vows articulated in the [*Sukhāvatīvyūha*] *sūtra* in two rolls, "If, when I attain buddhahood, living beings in the ten directions produce an utmost mind and believe and rejoice, and desire to be reborn in my land for up to ten thought moments; if they are not reborn there, may I not lay hold of complete enlightenment, save for those who commit the five heinous crimes[63] and slander the true dharma."[64] If they do not arouse a great aspiration and do not attain rebirth [in the pure land], then they should also choose to not arouse the mind because they did not choose to do so. One should clearly know that it is not necessary. With respect to the non-utmost mind as the utmost mind, to articulate what is chosen; for this reason, still more it is not necessary to choose. Although there is this disruption, all do not comply with principle.

The reason why is that if one arouses the *bodhicitta,* it is already the direct cause; and for those who do not arouse the mind, there is immediately no cause [for rebirth in the pure land]. Hindrances are nonexistent, so why does one need to choose and differentiate? The five heinous crimes and slandering the dharma really are hindrances, but they are not immediately without cause; hence, one needs to choose and differentiate. For this reason, this difficulty is unheard of.

Furthermore, if one is not reborn there and backslides from the *bodhicitta,* only while residing in here [in this life] will one first arouse a great aspiration and be perfumed with seeds, and at a later time backsliding from his aspiration and [being reborn] in lower levels will be his manifest practice. For good reason, if one first arouses the great aspiration and his seeds do not fail, he will be able to construct the causes to be reborn in that realm, and he will backslide from his manifest practice of the aspiration for the Mahāyāna; hence, one is reborn in that realm and chooses the lesser result. For this reason, that difficulty returns [to nothingness] and manifests its own limitation.

### *Ancillary Causes*

Second, I will clarify ancillary causes. The one mind that grasps at the name [of the Buddha Amitābha] is not perplexed because the name is brought about by the inconceivable meritorious virtue of the Tathāgata Amitābha. Regarding from one day to seven days, it is because a superior person brings it about quickly and inferior people mature slowly. The *Sound King Sūtra* explains that those who recite the name for ten days are because it takes inferior people ten days to bring it about.[65] Or, it is because if they are able to recite it for one or two days, or so forth, it is the cause for rebirth in the lowest grade; for those who are able to recite it for five, six, or seven days, it is the cause of the middle grade; and those who are able to recite it for up to ten days achieve the cause of the highest grade.

The section after "those people"[66] is the third on receiving and grasping.

The section after "I perceive"[67] is the fourth on concluding encouragement. The above four passages together are the second, encouragement to cultivate the ultimate end of the cause.

The section after "just as I now praise,"[68] for the most part, provides evidence of the third cited example. There are four of these: first, drawing explanations from other buddhas, its testimony is believable; second, analyzing the name of this sutra, it achieves superior benefits; third, raising a vow that is infallible, it strongly encourages arousing the mind; and fourth, praising the rarity of the dharma, one may have confidence in its concluding encouragement.

### *Structure and Contents*

Among the first, the former is to differentiate by praising by oneself, and the latter is citing that all the buddhas of the ten[69] directions offer praise together.

The section after "why do you think"[70] is the second passage. There are three questions, and next is the third encouragement to believe.

The section after "if there are people who make a vow"[71] is the third passage. The former manifests the power of the vow, and the latter encourages making the vow.

The section after "just as I now"[72] is the fourth passage. There are three parts: first, one praises other [buddhas]; next, other [buddhas] praise one; and third, concluding praise and encouragement to believe. The foregoing three sections are the conclusion of the text explaining the core meaning of the sutra.

### *C. Propagation Section*

The section after "The Buddha explained"[73] is the propagation section.
The end of the *Commentary on the Amitābha Sūtra Spoken by the Buddha.*

## Notes

1 Luis Gómez, *The Land of Bliss: The Paradise of the Buddha of Measureless Light* (Honolulu: University of Hawai'i Press, 1996), 125–126.

2 *Amituo jing*, *T.* 366.12.347b; Hisao Inagaki, *The Three Pure Land Sutras*, rev. 2nd ed. (Berkeley, CA: Numata Center for Buddhist Translation and Research, 2003), 123.

3 *Amituo jing*, *T.* 366.12.348a7–17; Gómez, *The Land of Bliss*, 150–151.

4 Gómez, *The Land of Bliss*, 126–127.

5 The five medieval commentaries are one by Tiantai Zhiyi (538–597), *T.* 1755; one by Huijing (578–645), *T.* 1756; two by Cien Kuiji (632–682), *T.* 1757 and *T.* 1758; and Wŏnhyo's commentary. Two other commentaries remain from the Song period (960–1279) and one from the Ming period (1368–1644): Zhiyuan (976–1022), *T.* 1760; Lingzhi Yuanzhao (1048–1116), *T.* 1761; and Ouyi Zhixu (1599–1655), *T.* 1762.

6 See, for instance, Saitō Shunken, "Den Jion Daishi sen Amidakyō sho no busshin · butsudoron," *Indogaku Bukkyōgaku kenkyū* 43, no. 2 (December 1994): 218–221; Han Pogwang, *Shiragi Jōdo shisō no kenkyū* (Osaka: Tōhō Shuppan 1991); and Iida Motoki, "Gangyō *Amidakyō sho* ni tsuite," *Bukkyō ronsō* 49 (March 2005): 90–99.

7 See Tongguk Taehakkyo Pulgyo Munhwa Yŏn'guwŏn, 東國大學校佛教文化研究院, ed. *Kankoku Bussho kaidai jiten* (Tokyo: Kokusho Kankōkai, 1982), 7, 10, 19, 33, 35, 38, 52, 61, 66; Pulgyo Munhwa Yŏn'guwŏn, 東國大學校佛教文化研究院, 453–454.

8 For a brief accounting of such excerpts, see An Kyehyŏn, *Silla chŏngt'o sasangsa yŏn'gu* 新羅淨土思想史研究 (Seoul: Asea Munhwasa, 1976), 214–216 note 4.

9 See, for instance An, *Silla chŏngt'o sasangsa yŏn'gu,* 11–68; Kwŏn Kijong, "Wŏnhyo ŭi chŏngt'o sasang yŏn'gu: Muryangsu-gyŏng chongyo rŭl chungsim ŭro," *Pulgyo yŏn'gu* 11–12 (1995): 401–424; and Kim Yŏngt'ae, *Silla Mit'a chŏngt'o sasang yŏn'gu* (Seoul: Minjoksa, 1988).

10 See, for instance, An, *Silla chŏngt'o sasangsa yŏn'gu,* 14–15; Kim Chinhwan "Silla sidae ŭi chŏngt'o sasang: Wŏnhyo Taesa chungsim," in *Un'gyŏng Ch'ŏn Okhwan Paksa hwagap kinyŏm nonmunjip* (Seoul: Samhwa Ch'ulp'ansa, 1979), 295–296, is practically a verbatim copy of An, *Silla chŏngt'o sasangsa yŏn'gu*; and Jang Hwee-ok, "Wŏnhyo ŭi chŏngt'o sasangi Ilbon e mich'in yŏnghyang," *Ilbonhak* 12 (1993): 82–83, includes a précis of the opening section of the sutra, the "Great Intent."

11 Han Pogwang, *Shiragi Jōdo shisō no kenkyū* (Osaka: Tōhō Shuppan 1991), 111–125; Han Pogwang, "Gangyō no Amidakyō sho ni tsuite isshin furan no mondai," *Indogaku Bukkyōgaku kenkyū* 51, no. 1 (December 2002 [101]): 1–9(R); and Iida Motoki, "Gangyō *Amidakyō sho* ni tsuite," *Bukkyō ronsō* 49 (March 2005): 90–99.

12 See Ōtani Kōshin, "Donran to Kegon shisō," in *Jōdokyō no kenkyū: Ishida Mitsuyuki hakushi koki kinen ronbun* (Kyōto: Nagatabunshōdō, 1982).

13 The five impurities (*ot'ak; wuzhuo; panca-kaṣāya*) are the impurities of lifespan (*sut'ak; shouzhuo*), kalpas (*kŏpt'ak; jiezhuo*), defilements (*pŏnnoet'ak; fannaozhuo*), views (*kyŏnt'ak; jianzhuo*), and those with feelings (*yuch'ŏngt'ak; youqingzhuo*). *Apidamo jushelun* (*Abhidharmakośabhāṣya*) 12, *T.* 1558.29.64a21–22.

14 The four streams (*saryu; siliu*), or four raging streams (*sa p'ongnyu; si baoliu*) are the four defilements that torment the mind that is originally quiescent: desire (*yok p'ongnyu* 欲暴流), existence (*yu p'ongnyu* 有暴流), opinion (*kyŏn p'ongnyu* 見暴流), and ignorance (*mumyŏng p'ongnyu* 無明暴流). See *Yuga shidi lun* (*Yogācārabhūmi*) 8, *T.* 1579.30.314c17–19.

15 The four classes of followers (*sabae* 四輩) refers to the four-fold congregation (*sajung; sizhong*), which is made up of monks (*pigu* 比丘; *bhikṣu*), nuns (*puguni* 比丘尼; *bhikṣuṇī*), the male laity (*up'asae* 優婆塞; *upāsaka*), and the female laity (*up'ai* 優婆夷; *upāsikā*).

16 The three realms of existence (*samgye; sanjie; triloka*) are the desire realm (*yokkye; yujie*), the realm of form (*saekkye, sejie*), and the formless realm (*musaekkye, wusejie*). See *Chang ahan jing* (*Dīrghāgama sūtra*) 8, *T.* 1.1.50a26–28.

17 For Wŏnhyo, the expression "three boundless realms" (*mubyŏn samse* 無邊三世) probably derives from his familiarity with the *Avataṃsaka sūtra*. See,

for instance, *Dafangguangfo huayan jing* 9, *T.* 278.9. 452c2–3; roll 30, *T.* 278.9.590c17, and roll 31, *T.* 278.9.599c26.

18 Purity of the material world (*kisegan ch'ŏngjŏng* 器世間清淨) refers to purity in the realm of things, the world containing countries and peoples. What I have translated as the "material world" is literally the "world as a vessel" (*kisegan* 器世間, also *kisegye* 器世界, *kise* 器世; *bhajanaloka*). Purity of the world of living beings (*chungsaeng segan ch'ŏngjŏng* 眾生世間清淨) refers to the purity of the beings that reside in material worlds.

19 The *Original Acts Sūtra* (*Benye jing*) is short for the *Sūtra on the Original Acts That Serve as a Bodhisattva's Adornments* (*Pusa yingluo benye jing*, *T.* 1485). The existing recension was translated in two rolls by the monk Zhu Fonian of the Yao-Qin dynasty between 376 and 378. Divided into eight chapters, it describes pure precepts of the three groups of beings (*samch'wi chŏnggye* 三聚淨戒) of the Mahāyāna and the fifty-two stages of the bodhisattva path of practice—the mind of the ten faiths (*sipsin sim* 十信心), the mind of the ten abodes (*sipchu sim* 十住心), the mind of the ten practices (*siphaeng sim* 十行心), the mind of the ten transferences (*siphoehyang sim* 十迴向心), the mind of the ten stages (*sipchi sim* 十地心), the mind that enters the dharma realm (*ip pŏpkye sim* 入法界心), and the mind of quiescence (*chŏngmyŏl sim* 寂滅心)—which are the original acts of the bodhisattvas. With respect to the concept of "original acts that serve as adornments," when seen from the standpoint that the sutra's name is a term related to the *Avataṃsaka* and to the forty-two levels that are included in the bodhisattva stages, and to the narrative contents from the preaching in the *Avataṃsaka sūtra* are contained in the seventh chapter, "The Great Throng Receives Instruction" chapter (*Dazhong shouxue pin*), the two sutras share a profound relationship. Also, along with the *Sūtra on Brahmā's Net* (*Fanwang jing*), it is considered to be one of the most important sutras on the Mahāyāna precepts in East Asian Buddhism.

20 The title *Mahāyāna-saṃgraha* (*She dasheng lun*) means it is a treatise that embraces or subsumes the full range of meaning of the Mahāyāna. It was composed by the Indian scholar Asaṅga (Wuzhuo, active ca. fourth–fifth century), who divided the most superior teachings of the Mahāyāna into ten sections. This treatise is one of the foundational exegeses of consciousness-only thought (*yusik sasang*; *weishi sixiang*). Although no Sanskrit edition of the work is extant, there is one Tibetan translation and three Chinese translations: Buddhaśanta's (Fotuoshanduo) translation (*T.* 1592) in two rolls completed in 531, Paramārtha's (Zhendi, 499–569) translation (*T.* 1593) in three rolls completed in 563, and Xuanzang's (ca. 602–664) translation (*T.* 1594) in three rolls completed in 649. The most representative commentaries on the *Mahāyāna-saṃgraha* for the case of India are those composed by Vasubandhu and Asvabhāva (Wuxing) (*T.* 1595–1598). There are many commentaries in East Asia. The Shelun school was

established after Paramārtha translated the *Mahāyāna-saṃgraha* in China. The Shelun and Dilun schools mutually influenced each other, and the Shelun school exerted much influence in the formation of the doctrines of the Huayan tradition.

21 Although Wŏnhyo says "the third stage of extreme joy" (*chesam kŭkhwanhŭi chi* 第三極歡喜地), the joyous stage is usually considered the first of the ten stages of the bodhisattva. The ten stages (*sipchi, shidi; daśabhūmi*) are (1) the joyous stage (*hwanhŭi chi; huanxi di; pramuditā-bhūmi*), (2) the immaculate stage (*igu chi; ligou d; vimalā-bhūmi*), (3) the light-giving stage (*yŏm chi; yandi, palgwang chi; faguang di; prabhākari-bhūmi*), (4) the brilliant stage (*myŏng chi; ming di* or *chohye chi; zhaohui di; arciṣmatī-bhūmi*), (5) the stage that is very difficult to conquer (*nansŭng chi; nansheng di; sudurjayā-bhūmi*), (6) the stage that is face-to-face (*hyŏnjŏn chi; xianqian di; abhimukhī-bhūmi*), (7) the far-reaching stage (*wŏnhaeng chi; yuanxing di; dūraṁgamā-bhūmi*), (8) the immovable stage (*pudong chi; budong di; acalā-bhūmi*), (9) the stage of wholesome wisdom (unerringly effective intentions) (*sŏnhye chi; shanhui di; sādhumatī-bhūmi*), and (10) the stage of the cloud of dharma (*pŏbun chi; fayun di; dharmameghā-bhūmi*).

22 *Jieshenmi jing* (*Saṃdhinirmocana sūtra*) 2, *T.* 676.16. The *Saṃdhinirmocana sūtra* (*Jieshenmi jing, T.* 676) is one of the seminal sutras of the Yogācāra tradition. It is a sutra divided into eight chapters that explains the deep meaning of "consciousness-only." It belongs to the middle period of the Mahāyāna sutras. Although the exact date of his compilation is unknown, since it is cited in Asaṅga's (Wuzhao, 385–480) *Mahāyāna-saṃgraha* (*She dasheng lun*), it was probably compiled and composed before that time. The sutra clarifies the boundaries of consciousness-only, the visualization methods (*kwanbŏp; guangfa*), and the fruits of practice/functioning (*haenggwa; xingguo*); it also clarifies the appearance of the *ālayavijñāna* (immaculate consciousness) and the nature of the mind in three aspects. The sutra also explains that the Buddha "turned the wheel of the dharma" (*chŏn pŏmnyun; zhuan falun*) three times: the first being the Hīnayāna teaching of the four noble truths in Deer Park, the second being the early Mahāyāna teaching of "emptiness" (*kong; śūnyatā*) of the Prajñāpāramitā sutras, and the third and final teaching being the advanced Mahāyāna teaching that "all dharmas lack substantial marks (*ch'esang; tixiang; svabhāva-lakṣaṇa*), are neither produced nor destroyed but are in quiescence and that their self-nature is *nirvāṇa*." *Shenmi jietuo jing* (*Saṃdhinirmocana sūtra*) 2, *T.* 675.16.673c; see John Powers, *Wisdom of Buddha: The Saṃdhinirmocana Mahāyāna Sūtra* (Berkeley, CA: Dharma Publishing, 1995), 138–141.

23 Wŏnhyo terms "the group of those assured of certain success" (*chŏng chŏngch'wi* 正定聚), "the group of those not assured of certain success" (*pulchŏng ch'wi* 不定聚), and "the group those who are lost" (*musajŏng ch'wi* 無邪定聚) as the three groups of beings (*samch'wi chungsaeng; sanju zhong-*

*sheng*). Analogous terms are the group of those completely assured of certain success (*p'ilchŏng ch'wi*; *biding ju*), the group of those who are completely lost (*p'ilsa ch'wi*; *bixie ju*), and the group of those with no assurance (*pulchŏng ch'wi*; *buding ju*). See *Mohe bore boluomi jing* (*Pañcaviṃśatisāhasrikāprajñāpāramitā sūtra*) 17, *T.* 223.8.348a13–14.

24 Cf. *Amituo guyin shengwang tuoluoni jing*, *T.* 370.12.352b24–27. Wŏnhyo is providing a paraphrastic explanation of a passage that provides names for Amitābha's father and mother and others.

25 *Wangsheng lun* [*Wuliangshou jing yubotishe yuansheng jie* (*Sukhāvatīvyūhopadeśa*)], *T.* 1524.26.231a13–14; cf. *Wangsheng lun zhu* [*Wuliangshou jing yubotishe yuansheng jie zhu* (Commentary on the *Sukhāvatīvyūhopadeśa*)] 1, *T.* 1819.40.830c4–14; roll 2, *T.* 1819.40.838b14–15.

26 The great spiritual penetrations (*taesint'ong*; *dashentong*) come in lists of five or six. The five spiritual penetrations (*o sint'ong*; *wu shentong*; *ot'ong*; *wutong*; *pañca-abhijñāḥ*) are the (1) divine eye (*ch'ŏnan t'ong*; *tianyan tong*; *divyacakṣus*), (2) divine ear (*ch'ŏni t'ong*; *tianer tong*; *divya-śrotra*), (3) knowledge of the thoughts of others (*t'asim t'ong*; *taxin tong*; *para-citta-jñāna*), (4) recollection of former incarnations (*sukchu t'ong*; *suzhu tong*; *pūrvanirvāsānusmṛti*), (5) "deeds leading to magical power and release" (*ṛddhivimokṣakriyā*) or "direct experience of magical power (*sin'gyŏng t'ong*; *shenjing tong*; *ṛddhisākṣakriyā*). See *Apidamo da piposha lun* ([Abhidharma-] *Mahāvibhāṣā*) 141, *T.* 1545.27.728b12–24; 727b22–24. The six spiritual penetrations (*yuk sint'ong*, *liu shentong*; *ṣaḍ-abhijñāḥ*) are (1) psychic power (*sinjok t'ong*; *shenzu tong*; *ṛddhi-vidhi-jñāna*), magical power; (2) heavenly ear (*ch'ŏni t'ong*; *tianer tong*; *divya-śrotra-jñāna*), supernormal hearing; (3) cognition of others' thoughts (*t'asim t'ong*; *taxin tong*; *para-citta-jñāna*), the ability to read minds; (4) recollection of past lives (*sungmyŏng t'ong*; *suming tong*; *pūrva-nirvāsānusmṛti-jñāna*), (5) heavenly eye (*ch'ŏnan t'ong*; *tianyan tong*; *divya-cakṣus-jñāna*), the ability to discern the previous lives of others; and (6) cognition of the extinction of outflows (*nujin t'ong*; *loujin tong*; *āsrava-kṣaya-jñāna*), a state in which one is no longer plagued by any form of defilement. See *Apidamo da piposha lun* 102, *T.* 1545.27.530a18–b10; and *Dazhidu lun* 28, *T.* 1509.25.264a–266b; see also Étienne Lamotte, trans., *Le traité de la grande vertu de sagesse de Nāgārjuna*, 5 vols. (Louvain: E. Peerters, 1949–1980), 4:1809–1838. By means of the spiritual penetrations a bodhisattva purifies his *buddhakṣetra*; see *Mohe zhiguan* 2a, *T.* 1911.46.14a–b.

27 *Amituo guyin shengwang tuoluoni jing*, *T.* 370.12.352b13–17.

28 *Amituo guyin shengwang tuoluoni jing*, *T.* 370.12.352b21–23. A *yojana* (*youxun* 由旬, also *yushanna* 踰繕那, *yuzhena* 踰闍那, and *youyan* 由延) is a length of measurement commonly used in traditional Indian religious literature. One definition is that one *yojana* is the distance that yoked oxen can plow in one day. The Chinese Yogācāra monk Xuanzang, however, defined a

*yojana* as the distance a *cakravartin* king can march his armies in a day, 40 *li*, or about 19.5 km. See *Da Tang xiyuji* 2, *T.* 2087.51.875c4–6.

29 There were four primary definitions of *koṭi* among Wŏnhyo's contemporaries in medieval East Asia: one *koṭi* equals one hundred thousand (*simman* 十萬), one *koṭi* equals one million (*paengman* 百萬), one *koṭi* equals ten million (*ch'ŏnman* 千萬), and one *koṭi* equals one hundred million (*manman* 萬萬). These four were known to the Faxiang monk Kuiji (Cien, 632–682) and the Huayan monk Fazang (643–712); see *Yuga shidi lun lüezuan* 1, *T.* 1829.43.17b23–c3; *Huayan jing souxuan ji* 4, *T.* 1719.35.174c15–18.

30 A *nayuta* (*nayut'a*; *nayouta*) is the name of a type of measurement in ancient India and was translated into Chinese as "a million" or "a billion" (*cho*; *zhao*). Some opine that ten *ayutas* (*ayuta*) are one great *ayuta*, and ten great *ayutas* is one *nayuta*. Since one *ayuta* is said to be ten *koṭis* (*ŏk* 億), one *nayuta* may be a thousand million (*chŏnŏk* 千億). Although there are lots of theories on the meaning of the term, regardless of its precise meaning it is used to mean an extremely large number, much like a zillion. *Nayuta* (*nayut'a*, *nayoutuo*; also *nayuda*, *nayuduo*; *nayuda*, *nayouduo*; *niyuda*, *niyouduo*; and *nasul*, *nashu*) means an exceedingly large amount or unit of time and has been translated as ten thousand (*ilman* 一萬), a million (*simman* 十萬), a billion (*ilch'ŏnŏk* 一千億), a trillion (*ilcho* 一兆), and a gazillion (*ilgu* 一溝). The *Abhidharmakośabhāṣya* says that one *nayuta* is a billion. See *Apidamo jushe lun* (*Abhidharmakośabhāṣya*) 12, *T.* 1558.29.63b14–19; cf. *Apidamo dapiposha lun* (*Mahāvibhāṣya*) 177, *T.* 1545.27.890c15–891a20.

31 *Guan Wuliangshou jing*, *T.* 365.12.343b17–18.

32 A defiled land (*yet'o*; *huitu*), sometimes rendered as "dusty path" (*chindo*; *zhendao*), refers to world systems that are filled to the brim with defilements and are places where living beings are subject to the five sense desires. The five sense desires and pleasures (*oyongnak*; *wuyule*), usually called either the five sense desires (*oyok*; *wuyu*) or the five pleasures (*orak*; *wule*), refer to the sense desires of sights, sounds, smells, tastes, and touches, which are experienced through the five sense organs of the eyes, ears, nose, tongue, and body. See *Chang ahan jing* (*Dīrghāgama*) 13, *T.* 1.1.74c11–23; *Liuduji jing* 4, *T.* 152.321a11–17. Another list of sensory pleasures is material possessions, sights, food and drink, fame, and sleep.

33 *Amituo jing*, *T.* 366.12.346c10.

34 A direct cause (*chŏngin*; *zhengyin*) is a true cause as compared to an indirect or contributory cause (*yŏnin*; *yuanyin*).

35 *Amituo jing*, *T.* 366.12.346c13.

36 From "This fulfillment" until end of sentence, cf. *Wangsheng lun zhu* 2, *T.* 1819.40.838b10–11; the *gāthā* is from *Wangsheng lun*, *T.* 1524.26.231a12.

37 *Wangsheng lun*, *T.* 1524.26.231a3.

38 From "This is the fulfillment" to the end of the sentence, cf. *Wangsheng lun zhu* 2, *T.* 1819.40.837a13–14; the *gāthā* is from *Wangsheng lun*, *T.* 1524.26.230c25.

39 From "The sublime colors of ornaments" to the end of the sentence, cf. *Wangsheng lun zhu* 2, *T.* 1819.40. 837a18–19; the *gāthā* is from *Wangsheng lun*, *T.* 1524.26.230c26. Wŏnhyo's text is different from Tanluan's because he transposes the compounds *kongdŏk* 功德 (meritorious virtues) and *sŏngch'wi* 成就 (fulfillment), thus altering the grammar of the passage.

40 The six time periods (*yuksi* 六時) are the six divisions (roughly four-hour periods) of the day and night in premodern Korea. The day is divided into three periods: early morning (*sinjo* 晨朝), daytime (*ilchung* 日中), and sundown (*ilmol* 日沒); and night is divided into three time periods: early evening (*ch'oya* 初夜), midnight (*chungya* 中夜), and the dead of night (*huya* 後夜).

41 The first line is found in many sutras, such as the *Avataṃsaka*. See *Huayan jing* 27, *T.* 278.9.577b5. The second line is found only in Wŏnhyo's commentary. The last two lines are from the received recension of *Wangsheng lun*, *T.* 1524.26.231a11.

42 Cf. *Wuliangshou jing* 1, *T.* 360.12.271b28–c3.

43 *Amituo jing*, *T.* 366.12.347a10.

44 The evil paths (*akto* 惡道) refer to the three unwholesome rebirths (*samdo*; *santu*, also *samakto*; *sanedao*) are rebirth as a beast, as a hungry ghost, or as a denizen of hell. *Zengyi ahan jing* (*Ekottarāgama*) 31, *T.* 125.2.717c12–13.

45 Cf. *Wangsheng lun*, *T.* 1524.26.231a13–14.

46 From "it is the fulfillment" to the end of the sentence, cf. *Wangsheng lun zhu* 2, *T.* 1819.40.837c14–15; the *gāthā* is from *Wangsheng lun*, *T.* 1524.26.231a4–5.

47 From "it is the fulfillment" to the end of the sentence, cf. *Wangsheng lun zhu* 2, *T.* 1819.40.837a2–3; the *gāthā* is from *Wangsheng lun*, *T.* 1524.26.230c23–24.

48 Meritorious functioning (*kongyong*; *gongyong*) refers to the functioning of body (*sin*; *shen*), speech (*ku*; *kou*), and mind (*ŭi*; *yi*). With respect to the first to seventh stages, although bodhisattvas realize true thusness, because they must amass the merit of the aids to penetration (*kahaeng*; *jiaxing*), this is called the stage of meritorious functioning (*kongyong chi*; *gongyong di*).

49 From "it is the fulfillment" to the end of the sentence, cf. *Wangsheng lun zhu* 2, *T.* 1819.40.836c18–19; the *gāthā* is from *Wangsheng lun*, *T.* 1524.26.230c21.

50 *Amituo jing*, *T.* 366.12.347a25.

51 *Amituo jing*, *T.* 366.12.347a29.

52 See *Wangsheng lun zhu* 1, *T.* 1819.40.830b3–4; *Wangsheng lun zhu* 2, *T.* 1819.40.836c13–14 and 838a28–b5.

53 *Wangsheng lun*, *T.* 1524.26.231a10.

54 The *Yogācārabhūmi* (*Yuga lun*, short for *Yuga shidi lun*, *T.* 1579) is believed to have been composed by Maitreya and transposed by Asaṅga. Xuanzang executed the translation into Chinese between 646 and 648 CE. This work is one of the representative works of the Yogācāra tradition and provides a detailed discussion of the spheres, practices, and fruits of the practitioner of Yogācāra, the theory of the *ālayavijñāna*, the theory of the three natures (*samsŏngsŏl* 三性說), the theory of the three nonnatures (*sammusŏngsŏl* 三無性說), the theory of consciousness only, and so forth. It served as the basis for the Consciousness-Only school's theory of the Middle Way, the theory of dependent arising, and the teaching of the three vehicles. It was one of the seminal treatises of the Faxiang school 法相宗 (K. Pŏpsangjong).

55 Reading *pu* 浮 as *chŏng* 淨.

56 *Wangsheng lun zhu* 2, *T.* 1819.40.840a1–2; the *gāthā* is from *Wangsheng lun*, *T.* 1524.26.231a21. These received texts have "gods and men" (*tianren*), whereas Wŏnhyo transposes the words.

57 [Bodhisattvas] who will succeed [to buddhahood] in one lifetime (*ilsaeng poch'ŏ [posal]*; *yisheng buchu [pusa]*), also called "succeeding bodhisattvas" (*poch'ŏ posal*; *buchu pusa*) refer to a person bound to this world of delusion for only this one lifetime. In his next life such a person will cast off delusion and will attain Buddhahood. It is also a reference to "equal enlightenment" (*tŭnggak*; *dengju*), the highest level attainable by a bodhisattva. The Bodhisattva Maitreya, who presently resides in meditation in Tuṣita Heaven and who will descend to the human world in the future when his life there ends and attain buddhahood, is commonly held as an example of this kind of bodhisattva who assists individuals to reach the level of buddhahood. See *Dafangguang fo huayan jing* 4, *T.* 278.9.418b1, and roll 41, *T.* 278.9.759c18.

58 *Asaṃkhyeya* (*asŭnggi* 阿僧祇) is translated into Chinese as "a limitless number" (*muangsu* 無央數). This designation was created to differentiate the limitlessly long length of time it takes for one to complete and fulfill the bodhisattva practices and attain the fruit of Buddhahood into three periods. During the first limitless *kalpa*, a bodhisattva courses in the ten faiths, the ten abidings, the ten practices, and the ten transferences, the first forty stages of the bodhisattva's path of practice. During the second limitless *kalpa*, the bodhisattva courses in the first seven stages of the ten stages of the bodhisattva path. During the third limitless *kalpa*, the bodhisattva courses in stages eight through ten and achieves Buddhahood.

59 *Wangsheng lun zhu* 2, *T.* 1819.40.840a2–3; the *gāthā* is from *Wangsheng lun*, *T.* 1524.26.231a22.

60 The eight kinds of adornments (*p'alchong changŏm*; C. *bazhong zhuangyan*) are referred to in *Wangsheng lun zhu* 2, *T.* 1819.40.841c9–11.

61 *Amituo jing*, *T.* 366.12.347b7.

62 *Wangsheng lun, T.* 1524.26.231a13–14; cf. *Wangsheng lun zhu* 1, *T.* 1819.40.830c4–14; roll 2, *T.* 1819.40.838b14–15.

63 The five heinous crimes (*oyŏk; wuni*) are (1) patricide, (2) matricide, (3) killing an arhat, (4) shedding the blood of a buddha, and (5) destroying the harmony of the *saṃgha*. See *Apidamo jushe lun* (*Abhidharmakośabhāṣya*) 17, *T.* 1558.29.926b27–29.

64 *Wuliangshou jing* 1, *T.* 360.12.268a26–28.

65 Cf. *Amituo guyin shengwang tuoluoni jing, T.* 370.12.352b28–c11.

66 *Amituo jing, T.* 366.12.347b13.

67 *Amituo jing, T.* 366.12.347b15.

68 *Amituo jing, T.* 366.12.347b18.

69 Reading *yuk* 六 as *sip* 十.

70 *Amituo jing, T.* 366.12.347a25.

71 *Amituo jing, T.* 366.12.348a13.

72 *Amituo jing, T.* 366.12.348a18.

73 *Amituo jing, T.* 366.12.348a26.

## Bibliography

An Kyehyŏn 安啓賢. *Silla chŏngt'o sasangsa yŏn'gu* 新羅淨土思想史研究 (Research on the history of Pure Land thought in Silla). Seoul: Asea Munhwasa, 1976. Reprint, Seoul: Hyŏnmunsa, 1987.

Coreless, Roger Jonathan. "T'an-luan's Commentary on the Pure Land Discourse: An Annotated Translations and Soteriological Analysis of the *Wang-shêng-lun chu* (*T.* 1819)." PhD dissertation, University of Wisconsin–Madison, 1973.

Gómez, Luis O., trans. *The Land of Bliss: The Paradise of the Buddha of Measureless Light*. Honolulu: University of Hawai'i Press, 1996.

Han Pogwang 韓普光 (Han T'aesik 韓泰植). "Gangyō no Amidakyō sho ni tsuite isshin furan no mondai" (The issue of the one mind that is undisturbed in Wŏnhyo's *Commentary on the* Amitābha Sūtra). *Indogaku Bukkyōgaku kenkyū* 51, no. 1 (December 2002 [101]): 1–9(R).

——. *Shiragi Jōdo shisō no kenkyū* (Research on Pure Land thought in Silla). Osaka: Tōhō Shuppan, 1991.

Iida Motoki. "Gangyō *Amidakyō sho* ni tsuite" (On Wŏnhyo's *Commentary on the Amitābha Sūtra*). *Bukkyō ronsō* 49 (March 2005): 90–99.

Inagaki, Hisao, trans. *The Three Pure Land Sutras*. Rev. 2nd ed. Berkeley, CA: Numata Center for Buddhist Translation and Research, 2003.

Jang Hwee-ok (Chang Hwiok) 章輝玉. "Wŏnhyo ŭi chŏngt'o sasangi Ilbon e mich'in yŏnghyang" 元曉의 淨土 思想이 日本에 미친 影響 (The influence of Wŏnhyo's Pure Land thought on Japan). *Ilbonhak* 日本學 12 (1993): 77–92.

Kim Chinhwan 金鎭煥 (Ch'ŏrin 哲印). "Silla sidae ŭi chŏngt'o sasang: Wŏnhyo Taesa chungsim" 新羅時代의 淨土思想: 元曉大師中心 (Pure Land thought in the Silla period: Centered on Great Master Wŏnhyo). In *Un'gyŏng Ch'ŏn Okhwan Paksa hwagap kinyŏm nonmunjip* 雲耕千玉煥博士華甲紀念論文集 (Festschrift commemorating the sixtieth birthday of Un'gyŏng Ch'ŏn Okhwan), comp. Ch'ŏn Okhwan Paksa Hwagap Kinyŏm Nonmunjip Wiwŏnhoe 千玉煥博士華甲紀念論文集發刊委員會 (Committee for the Festschrift commemorating the sixtieth birthday of Ch'ŏn Okhwan), 289–311. Seoul: Samhwa Ch'ulp'ansa, 1979.

Kim Kyŏngjip 김경집. "Wŏnhyo ŭi chŏngt'ogwan yŏn'gu" 元曉의 淨土觀 研究 (Research on Wŏnhyo's view of the Pure Land). *Pojo sasang* 普照思想 11 (1998): 367–393.

Kim Yŏngt'ae 金煐泰, ed. *Silla Mit'a chŏngt'o sasang yŏn'gu* 新羅彌陀淨土思想研究 (Research on Amitābha and Pure Land thought in Silla). Seoul: Minjoksa, 1988.

Kwŏn Kijong 권기종. "Wŏnhyo ŭi chŏngt'o sasang yŏn'gu: Muryangsu-gyŏng chongyo rŭl chungsim ŭro" 元曉의 淨土思想 研究: 無量壽經宗要를 中心으로 (Research on Wŏnhyo's Pure Land thought: Centered on *Doctrinal Essentials of the Wuliangshou jing*). *Pulgyo yŏn'gu* 佛教研究 11–12 (1995): 401–424.

Lamotte, Étienne, trans. *Le traité de la grande vertu de sagesse de Nāgārjuna*. 5 vols. Louvain: E. Peerters, 1949–1980.

Ōtani Kōshin. "Donran to Kegon shisō" (Tanluan and Huayan thought). In *Jōdokyō no kenkyū: Ishida Mitsuyuki hakushi koki kinen ronbun* (Studies on Pure Land Doctrine: Festschrift in commemoration of the 77th birthday of Dr. Ishida Mitsuyuki), comp. Ishida Mitsuyuki Hakushi Koki Kinen Ronbunshū Kankōkai (Committee for the Compilation of the Festschrift in Commemoration of the 77th Birthday of Dr. Ishida Misuyuki), 121–138. Kyōto: Nagatabunshōdō, 1982.

Powers, John, trans. *Wisdom of Buddha: The Saṃdhinirmocana Mahāyāna Sūtra*. Berkeley, CA: Dharma Publishing, 1995.

Pulgyo Munhwa Yŏn'guwŏn 佛教文化研究院 (Buddhist Culture Research Center), ed. *Han'guk Chŏngt'o sasang yŏn'gu* 韓國淨土思想研究 (Research on Korean conceptions of the Pure Land). Seoul: Tongguk Taehakkyo Ch'ulpanbu, 1985.

Saitō Shunken. "Den Jion Daishi sen Amidakyō sho no busshin · butsudoron" (The theories of the buddha body and buddhaland described in the *Commentary on the Amitābha Sūtra* traditionally ascribed to Dharma Master Cien). *Indogaku Bukkyōgaku kenkyū* 43, no. 2 (December 1994): 218–221.

Tongguk Taehakkyo Pulgyo Munhwa Yŏn'guwŏn 東國大學校佛教文化研究院 (Institute for Buddhist Culture at Dongguk University), ed. *Kankoku Bussho kaidai jiten* (Dictionary of Synopses of Korean Buddhist Books). Tokyo: Kokusho Kankōkai, 1982.

## Selected Primary Sources

*Amituo guyin shengwang tuoluoni jing* (*Aparimitāyurjñānahṛdaya-dhāraṇī*). One roll. Translator unknown, Liang dynasty (502–557). *T.* 370.12.352b–353a.

*Amituo jing* (Smaller *Sukhāvatīvyūha sūtra*). One roll. Translated by Kumārajīva (343–413) in 402. *T.* 366.12.346b–348b; *Han'guk Pulgyo chŏnsŏ* (Complete works of Korean Buddhism). 14 vols. Seoul: Tongguk Taehakkyo Ch'ulpansa, 1979[–2004], 1:562c–566a.

*Dafangguang fo huayan jing* (*Buddhāvataṃsaka sūtra*; flower garland sūtra). 60 rolls. Translated by Buddhabhadra (Juexian, 359–429) between 418 and 422. *T.* 278.9.395a–788b.

*Guan Wuliangshou jing* (Book on the visualization of Amitāyus). One roll. Translation attributed to Kalayaśas (Jiangliangyeshe) between 422 and 442. *T.* 365.12.340b–346b.

*Muryangsu-gyŏng chongyo* 無量壽經宗要 (Doctrinal essentials of the *Wuliangshou jing*). One roll. By Wŏnhyo (617–686). *T.* 1747, 37.125b–131c; *Han'guk Pulgyo chŏnsŏ* (Complete works of Korean Buddhism). 14 vols. Seoul: Tongguk Taehakkyo Ch'ulpansa, 1979[–2004], 1:553c–562b.

*Pulsŏl Amit'a-gyŏng so* 佛說阿彌陀經疏 (Commentary on the *Amitābha Sūtra* spoken by the Buddha), One roll. By Wŏnhyo (617–686). *T.* 1759.47.348a–350b; *Han'guk Pulgyo chŏnsŏ* (Complete works of Korean Buddhism). 14 vols. Seoul: Tongguk Taehakkyo Ch'ulpansa, 1979 [–2004], 1:562c–566a.

*Wangsheng lun* (*Wuliangshou jing yubotishe yuansheng jie* [*Sukhāvatīvyūhopadeśa*]). One roll. Attributed to Vasubandhu (Tianqin or Shiqin, ca. 400–480) and translated by Bodhiruci (Putiliuzhi, fl. 508–540). *T.* 1524.26.231a–233a.

*Wangsheng lun zhu* (*Wuliangshou jing yubotishe yuansheng jie zhu* [Commentary on the *Sukhāvatīvyūhopadeśa*]). Two rolls. By Tanluan (ca. 488–554). *T.* 1819.40.826a–844b.

*Wuliangshou jing* (Larger *Sukhāvatīvyūha sūtra*). Two rolls. Translated by Kang Sengkai (Saṃghavarman) in 252. *T.* 360.12.265c–279a.

# IV

# Life-Writing and Poetry

## Overview

The advent of Pure Land Buddhist orientations in India and beyond have never been solely about texts and doctrines, as unique as these may have been in their formulation in certain geographical contexts and times. Serving as personal spiritual orientations, they have promoted a certain ascetic and/or philosophical stance toward life's ephemeral phenomena, and in some cases they have been subsumed under more inclusive Buddhist traditions like Chan. Pure Land as a social orientation features shared practices and beliefs among adherents aspiring to meet in the pure land after death. Nowhere do we find such rich accounts of faith, longing, depictions of the afterlife, and tales of the supernormal as in the contributions of life-writing and poetry celebrating Pure Land ideals. As we will see in this section, these narratives often blend historical occurrences with fictional episodes and serve as a culture of testimonies of practitioners aspiring for the pure land at their moment of death and envisioning immortality beyond.

Ethan Lindsay (chap. IV.1) examines the *Kōyasan ōjōden* (Accounts of those from Mount Kōya who attained birth in a pure land, late twelfth century), one of the most revealing texts about religious life at Japan's Mount Kōya in the medieval era. This collection of thirty-eight biographies belongs to the *ōjōden* genre of religious literature, a genre of religious biographies of Buddhist practitioners who have purportedly been born in a pure land at death. Showing a great range of practices, objects of devotion, and postmortem destinations, this text is one of the most important early sources about devotees at Mount Kōya who were aspiring for a variety of types of *ōjō*, or birth in a pure land at death.

Contemporary miracle tales from the first volume of *Nianfo ganying lu* (Records of the sympathetic resonance of recollecting the Buddha's name) reflect Pure Land practice in modern China and Taiwan and promote the efficacy of recitation to a transnational audience. The anecdotes, translated here by Natasha Heller (chap. IV.2), show the interaction of traditional beliefs, such as the appearance of Amitābha at a believer's deathbed, with institutional medicine and other contemporary phenomena. These tales also illustrate Pure Land social practice: how people come to their faith, groups that gather around the sick, and the circulation of the testimony of believers.

Among the treasures yielded by the cave-library of Dunhuang are many texts that had remained otherwise unknown, apparently never transmitted in canonical collections or otherwise. Jonathan A. Silk (chap. IV.3) looks at one of these texts, a poem in fifty-nine verses in the Tibetan language dedicated to the Buddha Amitābha and the wonders of his land, the Western Paradise. Replete with imagery adopted from the Pure Land sutras, it shows evidence of its composition in an environment in which Tibetan was a sacred religious language, but in which the influence of Chinese forms of Buddhist practice were nevertheless important, and perhaps even dominant. The present contribution begins with an exploration of the ways in which some definitions of "Pure Land Buddhism" may mislead us by reifying what is best identified only retrospectively as a "tradition," and it gives an analysis of the poem. It then presents a translation, followed by notes that clarify the imagery and influences on the poet.

Zhongfeng Mingben (1263–1323) was a prominent Chan monk who also advocated the practice of *nianfo* recitation and the aspiration for rebirth in the Western Pure Land. He became closely identified with the dual practice of Chan and Pure Land, and late Ming Buddhists would point to him as an exemplary figure from the Yuan dynasty. Mingben was also an accomplished poet and wrote two sets of poems on the Pure Land; selected verses from one of these sets are translated here by Natasha Heller (chap. IV.4). These poems talk about Pure Land practice for those of different social background and practice on traditional feast days. Another key theme is the relationship between Chan and Pure Land, and Mingben uses verse to advocate for treating recitation of Amitābha's name as an opportunity for Chan practice.

# Chapter 1

# Biographies from *The Accounts of Those from Mount Kōya Who Have Attained Birth in a Pure Land*

Ethan Lindsay

## Translator's Introduction

Mount Kōya (Kōyasan in Japanese), or the High Plains Mountain, is one of Japan's enduring sacred sites, a mountain where one of Japan's most famous Buddhist monks, Kūkai (774–835), established a Buddhist monastery in 816. According to the traditions of faith pertaining to this mountain, after a life of teaching, writing, performing miracles, and establishing a number of temples in Japan, Kūkai "entered meditation" on this mountain in 835 and has remained there in this state of meditation until the present day. This mountain, which rises more than 2,500 feet above sea level south of Ōsaka in present-day Wakayama Prefecture, Japan, is renowned as a place of breathtaking natural beauty. A popular destination for pilgrims from medieval times to the present day, it is also the site of a large Shingon Buddhist religious complex with more than a hundred temples.

Strongly associated with Kūkai's life and teachings, Mount Kōya has long been one of the major centers of Shingon Esoteric Buddhism in the Japanese islands. In the medieval era, however, this complex and multivalent sacred site housed Buddhist practitioners aiming to attain numerous different religious goals, including birth in a variety of pure lands. We see this Pure Land devotion portrayed in a vivid fashion in the *Kōyasan ōjōden* (Accounts of those from Mount Kōya who attained birth in a pure land, late twelfth century), one of the most revealing documents about religious life at Mount Kōya in the medieval era.

The *Kōyasan ōjōden* belongs to the *ōjōden* genre of religious literature, a genre of religious biographies of Buddhist practitioners who have purportedly been born in a pure land at death. This text is one of the most important sources about devotees at Mount Kōya who were aspiring for some type of *ōjō*, or birth in a pure land at death. The practitioners represented in this collection were believed to have achieved birth in the Western Pure Land of Amida Buddha or some other superior realm. Many world-spheres away to the west, the Pure Land of Amida Buddha (Amitābha), or "Utmost Bliss" (Sukhāvatī; Gokuraku), lies completely outside *saṃsāra*, the cycle of rebirth and suffering from which Buddhists hope to escape. Being born in Amida's Pure Land meant that one had escaped deluded rebirth and would never regress on the path of awakening. In early medieval Japan, Buddhists aspired to a range of postmortem destinations, including the Tosotsu (Tuṣita) Heaven, where the future Buddha Miroku (Maitreya) resides; Mount Fudaraku (Potalaka), the paradise of the bodhisattva Kannon (Avalokiteśvara); or Vulture Peak (Ryōjusen), where the eternal Śākyamuni Buddha preaches the Dharma. But by far the most popular postmortem destination at this time was Amida's Pure Land of Utmost Bliss.[1]

*Ōjōden*, or "accounts of birth in the Pure Land," played a key role in the spread of beliefs about birth in Amida's Pure Land, in particular for promoting the ideal of dying in a state of right mindfulness.[2] *Ōjōden* collections feature biographies of monks, nuns, and lay men and women of a variety of social classes who were believed to have been born in a pure land, usually Amida's Pure Land. In most cases, *ōjōden* describe the final hours of the individual and, in so doing, provide models for what a death with right mindfulness should be. The devotees usually are expecting death, sometimes even predicting the day and hour at which they will die. These practitioners bathe, put on clean clothes, and sit upright in a posture of meditation or lie down in the "nirvāṇa position" in which they face west and position their head to the north. Extraordinary signs (*isō*) usually demonstrate the liberative aspect of their death. Signs that Amida has already descended to welcome the person in his pure land include strange music, unearthly fragrance in the death chamber, and five-colored clouds that appear in the west. In some cases, the bodies of the deceased emit fragrance rather than decaying, or the bodies remain in the meditation posture even after entering crematory fires. In addition, relatives, close associates, and sometimes even complete strangers have dreams revealing the person's birth in Amida's Pure Land. The hagiographical portrayals in *ōjōden* spread a normative ideal about how one should die.

Prior to the *Kōyasan ōjōden*, in addition to several *ōjōden* collections written in China, six previous *ōjōden* collections had been compiled in

Japan, beginning with Yoshishige no Yasutane's *Nihon ōjō gokurakuki* (A record of Japanese who attained birth in [the Pure Land of] Utmost Bliss, ca. 985). Yasutane (ca. 931–1002) is known for his Chinese learning, and he was closely associated with Genshin (942–1017), another monk on Mount Hiei, the large Tendai center northeast of the imperial capital. Around the same time that Yasutane compiled the inaugural collection of *ōjōden* in Japan, Genshin completed *Ōjō yōshū* (Essentials of birth in the Pure Land), a seminal religious treatise that had a deep impact on the emergence of Japanese Pure Land thought and practice. *Ōjōyōshū* provides instructions for practice to gain birth in the pure land, in particular emphasizing the value of the contemplative *nenbutsu,* or the visualization of Amida Buddha. In compiling his collection of *ōjōden,* Yasutane also attempted to lead others to practice Buddhism in such a way as to gain entry into Amida's Pure Land. Yet he chose to instruct practitioners with hagiographic images of exemplary deaths that had purportedly been successful. Prior to Yasutane, in China Jiacai's *Jingtu lun* (Treatise on the Pure Land, ca. seventh century) presented twenty similar biographies of both clergy and laity. In addition, Wenshen (n.d.) and Shao Kang's (d. 805) collection, *Wangsheng xifang jintu ruiyang zhuan* (Accounts of auspicious responses accompanying birth in the Western Pure Land), contains forty-eight such biographies. The seminal early Japanese collection of *ōjōden,* Yasutane's *Nihon ōjō gokurakuki* is a collection of forty-two accounts that he found in previous records and through personal inquiry, about Buddhist devotees who were regarded as successfully attaining birth in the pure land. Following Yasutane's compilation, five other major *ōjōden* collections were produced in Japan in the twelfth century prior to the composition of the *Kōyasan ōjōden.* These collections included Ōe no Masafusa's *Zoku honchō ōjōden,* Miyoshi no Tameyasu's *Shūi ōjōden* and *Goshūi ōjōden,* Renzen's *Sange ōjōki,* and Fujiwara no Munetomo's *Honchō shinshū ōjōden.*[3]

Beginning with Inoue Mitsusada's scholarship on Pure Land Buddhism in Heian-era Japan, which made use of the *Kōyasan ōjōden* as an illuminating document about Pure Land practices on Mount Kōya, a number of scholars have studied this text with an eye to the ways in which it reveals the Pure Land faith of the monks of Mount Kōya.[4] These scholars have also used the text because of its valuable information about the formation of Mount Kōya as a sacred place more generally. Recent scholarship about the authorship of the text has added much to our understanding of this collection and the circumstances in which it was compiled.

This text was composed by a monk the text identifies as Nyojaku, an author who reveals only a very small amount of information about himself in the preface. For many years, the identity of Nyojaku was unclear, but several scholars have recently shown that he was Fujiwara no Sukenaga (1118–1195).[5] Like many of the men of the renowned Fujiwara family, Sukenaga was active as a courtier in the government. He ascended through various court ranks, including head chamberlain (Kurōdo no Tō), consultant (Sangi), major controller of the left (Sadaiben), and counselor (Nagon).[6] Sukenaga states in the preface that he maintained his aspiration to be born in the pure land even while being busy in his duties as a government official. Sukenaga himself claims to be a serious person of faith who has engaged in the practice of chanting Amida Buddha's name for many years, hoping to be born in Amida's Pure Land after death. Eventually, in 1181 he decided to seclude himself from the secular world and to single-mindedly engage in Buddhist discipline.

The preface states that Sukenaga first visited Mount Kōya in 1184. He left the seclusion of the Hōkaiji temple and climbed Mount Kōya. He then engaged in a one-hundred-day period of intense prayer. He met an elderly monk, who encouraged Sukenaga to compile a literary collection of the stories about the men who had obtained birth in a pure land when they died at Mount Kōya. According to Sukenaga's preface, this monk had witnessed the deathbed rituals (*rinjū gyōgi*) of many men at Mount Kōya. A number of monks at this mountain were reported to have achieved *ōjō,* and devotees on the mountain and elsewhere claimed to have witnessed various extraordinary signs (*isō*) confirming the deceased monks' births in a pure land. Monks on Mount Kōya encouraged Sukenaga to make a record of the practitioners who they believed had actually achieved birth in a pure land after death, so that these accounts would be left to later generations. This he attempted to do in the manner of Yoshishige no Yasutane and Ōe Masafusa, who had compiled similar collections prior to this time. In contrast to the previous collections, however, the *Kōyasan ōjōden* includes monks of only one place, Mount Kōya. This collection is thus unusual among *ōjōden* in that it focuses upon a single temple complex instead of featuring people who achieved *ōjō* at a number of different places.[7]

By compiling this collection of *ōjōden,* Sukenaga hoped to secure religious benefits, including his own successful entry into the pure land. We should note that Sukenaga did not compile this text until near the end of his life, when he was becoming increasingly aware of his approaching death. In the preface he writes, "If I transmit [these stories] to later generations, I will plant good karmic roots. . . . I have chanted Amida Buddha's name for many years. . . . What day will the Buddha [come and] welcome me? By all means I will be born in the pure land in my next rebirth."[8]

Sukenaga probably wrote the *Kōyasan ōjōden* in a short period of time after 1187. The thirty-eight biographies in this collection for the most part are presented in chronological fashion. They cover about one hundred years from Kyōkai's death in 1094 to Shōin's passing in 1187. The monk of the thirty-third account passed away the year that Sukenaga arrived on Mount Kōya. The final five monks were probably still alive when Sukenaga came. It is possible that Sukenaga witnessed the deaths of these five monks still living at Mount Kōya during his stay on the mountain. Six of the men included in the *Kōyasan ōjōden* had been included in previous *ōjōden* collections. For example, in compiling his collection, Sukenaga appropriated the biographies of Kyōkai, Kiyohara Masakuni, Yuihan, and Rentai from the *Shūi ōjōden* and the biographies of Keisen and Shinmyō from the *Sange ōjōki*.[9] Sukenaga included these prior stories but also added his own editorial remarks to these tales.

Reflecting the social realities on the mountain at the time, the practitioners portrayed in this collection display a variety of geographical and religious backgrounds. Many came from nearby. The *Kōyasan ōjōden* introduces as many as thirteen men from Kii province, where this sacred peak was located. Yet several of those included came from faraway locales such as Kyūshū, Tosa, and Shinano. Rentai moved to Mount Kōya from Tosa; Minami Chikushi and Kita Chikushi from Kyūshū, and Sainen from Shinnō. There are also a fairly large number of monks who moved to Mount Kōya in middle age after studying a range of Buddhist traditions. For example, Kyōkai had previously lived at Kōfukuji, one of the Seven Great Temples of Nara and the headquarters of the Japanese Hossō school. Rinken came from Tōdaiji, the enormous Nara temple that had been the center of the "provincial temples" system (*kokubunji*). Rentai and Shōyo had been monks at Ninnaji, a temple in the northwestern area of the capital city of Heiankyō and the headquarters of the Omuro lineage of the Shingon Esoteric Buddhist tradition. Kyōjin and Shinkaku began their monastic careers at Onjōji, the headquarters of the Jimon branch of the Tendai Buddhist tradition.

Despite this variety in geographical and religious background, the practitioners in this collection are primarily male monastics. Kiyohara

Masakuni is the only lay person included, suggesting that most of the practitioners on the mountain who were seeking *ōjō* were monks. In addition, the exclusion of all nuns from the collection is in accord with the prohibition against women on Mount Kōya.

Not only do the devotees discussed in the *Kōyasan ōjōden* exhibit devotion to a number of different sacred beings, but they also seek a number of different postmortem destinations. In this, the men featured in this collection probably were not unique. In fact, hagiographical literature of the same era presents a range of postmortem destinations and a number of different practices to achieve those goals. Nevertheless, the range of possible postmortem destinations available at Mount Kōya indicates what Sukenaga perceived as the great soteriological potency of this particular place. In addition, it is a sign of the broad, accommodating religious faith of Sukenaga and other like-minded devotees. He himself was clearly seeking birth in Amida's Pure Land, but he had no problem imagining the possibility of other forms of salvation and other possible wondrous lands in which to be born at death.

The *Kōyasan ōjōden* is truly one of the most informative collections of literature about religious devotion on Mount Kōya in eleventh- and twelfth-century Japan. In order to understand this text, scholars today need not read it with the hope of finding unambiguous historical facts about the men who are memorialized in these stories. In fact, in many cases it is impossible to separate history from sacred myth in these narratives. Rather, it is best to understand these accounts as hagiography, that is, attempts to memorialize what are seen as hallowed lives of revered monks who have lived and died on Mount Kōya. Nevertheless, even if one does not approach these biographies as transparent, entirely factual representations of what exactly transpired in these men's lives, the biographies remain valuable primary sources. In fact, from these stories, we learn about the range of religious practices on this mountain and other similar sacred sites, the variety of sacred objects who were being worshiped in medieval Japan, and the major religious goals including birth in a number of different pure lands. In fact, these hagiographical narratives convey much about the general contours of religious devotion at Mount Kōya in the eleventh and twelfth centuries. In addition, they add to an understanding of the diverse forms of Pure Land Buddhist devotion displayed more broadly in medieval Japan.

## Translation

### *Kōyasan ōjōden* (Accounts of those from Mount Kōya who attained birth in a pure land)

Fujiwara no Sukenaga

## Biography 1, Kyōkai

The Buddhist monk Kyōkai was a person from the capital city [of Heian-kyō]. In his youth he renounced the householder's life and lived at Kōfukuji. In the prime of his life, he left this Buddhist temple and lived at Odawara. As a result of this, he became known as the Holy Man of Odawara. After this, he moved to Mount Kōya.

For a span of over twenty years, on a daily basis he conducted the religious disciplines connected to the Dual Maṇḍalas and the Buddhist rites of Amitābha Buddha, chanted the Spell of the Augustly Victorious One, and recited the mantra of Amitābha Buddha. People were not aware that he did any other religious disciplines. On the twenty-seventh day of the fifth month of Kanji 7, he became somewhat sick even though he was not yet old and frail.

On the following morning, with his own hands he copied hundreds of images of the Immovable One (Acalanātha; Fudō Myōō) and then conducted the eye-opening consecration ritual for these images. Around 10:00 a.m. Kyōkai and a group of monks that he had summoned together chanted the name of Amitābha Buddha and sang the name of the Buddha with the same tune in their different voices. Kyōkai had turned the right side of his body toward the western direction and passed away peacefully. At that time he was ninety-three years old. By the power of his religious virtue and karmic merit, he had known the time of his death in advance.

At the time of his death, auspicious signs [of his birth in the pure land] appeared. Late in the afternoon, auspicious clouds suddenly covered [the sky], and the sky was filled with music. Sometime later, when it had become dark at night, monks Enjitsu and Keinen, who dwelled on the mountain, were each in their own living quarters and heard heavenly music in the distance. These monks then went to tell the other monks [on the mountain] about this occurrence. Another group of monks also clearly heard the music, and some other people in a similar manner listened very intently to this music. By the time of the wee hours of the morning, again there was more music. Little by little, the music went toward the western direction in the distance and then it abated.

Although these auspicious signs appeared from time to time, it was certainly difficult to know which person [had been born in the pure land]. However, it has been reported that on the night that Esoteric Master Yuihan passed away, Eminent Monk Keinen had a dream in which a retinue of countless holy beings came to welcome the Esoteric Master [to the pure land]. Eminent Monk Kyōkai came riding on a cloud amid those holy beings. If Kyōkai had not attained birth in the pure land, how could he have been positioned amid the retinue of holy beings [from the pure land]?

Around the fourth month of Genryaku 1 (1184), I made a pilgrimage [to Mount Kōya] in order to visit this eminent monk's sacred traces. I climbed up to the Odawara clerical retreat, and an elderly monk who lived there came out [to meet me]. While I was speaking with him, this monk informed me that Eminent Monk Kyōkai's father had been a government official. While he was the provincial governor of Sanuki Province, Kyōkai's father summoned a criminal and gave the man the death penalty.

Kyōkai was only a young boy at this time and the criminal had pity on him even though the criminal could not bear the death penalty. After the criminal died, he became an evil spirit that was profoundly resentful. As a result of this hatred, the criminal's evil spirit killed Kyōkai's father and the rest of his family. Only Kyōkai's life was spared.

This evil spirit did not express any remorse, and his crimes and curses continued to appear again and again. Thus, Kyōkai escaped his mountain dwelling and moved to this mountain [Mount Kōya]. This place [on Mount Kōya] is still named Odawara. The relics of the thatched hermitage where Kyōkai normally lived are still here.

Someone drew his true likeness and enshrined the portrait in this hall. Those who see it are choked with tears, and those who hear about it feel their entrails rent by grief. I (Sukenaga) wholeheartedly worshiped this portrait in order to establish the [auspicious] karmic conditions of my next rebirth. Although the drawing is old, the appearance is fresh. Kyōkai's tongue hangs down in a slanted fashion and his eyes seem as if they are blinking. His neck leans to the right. His body is sitting in the lotus meditation position. He is chanting and [in the process of] dying.

Kyōkai had tied a protective Buddha to his monastic robe. He covered this protective Buddha with paper and twisted it up and down. A monk who lived nearby came and told me, "Eminent Monk Kyōkai was afraid of the evil spirit that harbored resentment toward him. After Kyōkai moved to this numinous land, the evil spirit still appeared here and publicly announced his black magic. However, because Kyōkai possessed the protective Buddha, he permanently put an end to this problem [and truly escaped]. He faced death with right mindfulness and achieved birth in the pure land. We truly know that the Buddha Realm and the Demon Realm are one, not two [separate realities]."

## Biography 2, Kiyohara Masakuni

Kiyohara Masakuni, a man with a court rank but no official government position, was a person from Katsuge County in Yamato Province. From a young age, he loved the military arts. There was no evil that he did not commit. When he was sixty-one years old, suddenly he renounced the householder's life [and took the Dharma name Kakunyū].

After this, every day he chanted the name of Amitābha Buddha one hundred thousand times. This lasted for twenty-seven years. He earnestly sought birth in the pure land and did not think about anything else.

He dreamed that Holy Man Nichien, who had traveled from Japan to Tang China, came to him. Nichien stated, "If you want to be born in the land of Supreme Bliss, you should live on Mount Kōya."

Masakuni took this dream to heart, and on the twenty-third day of the ninth month of Kanji 7 (1093), he left his home province and moved to Mount Kōya. After this, his spirit became disturbed and he was attacked by illness. One of his neighbors, the eminent monk [Shinmyō] who was called the Holy Man of Kita Chikushi, then came to Kiyohara Masakuni. This man stated, "I dreamed that Amitābha Buddha and a countless number of holy beings came to welcome you [in the pure land]. You should know that your illness now marks the very end of your life [on earth] and your victorious birth in the pure land. Please do not have any resentment or regret."

Kiyohara Masakuni then gradually was cured of his sickness. One day, all of a sudden, he decided to take a purifying bath. On the same day, the eleventh day of the tenth month of the same year, he straightened his robes and lifted an incense censer in his hand. He faced the west and passed away. At the time of his death, he was eighty-seven years old.

At this time, there was an eminent monk who was spending the night praying at the Hinokuma shrine to the local deity Kunikakasu in Kii province. On that night, this man had an auspicious dream in which a retinue of countless holy beings came from the west. These holy beings were accompanied by heavenly music. They welcomed the elderly monk [Kiyohara Masakuni] and then returned [to the pure land].

This dream revelation occurred on the exact day of Kiyohara Masakuni's death. I have very little doubt that it indicated the monk's birth in the pure land.

## Biography 3, Yuihan

Esoteric Master Yuihan was a person from the Soga village in Ito County in Kii Province. His family name was Ki. He studied both exoteric and esoteric Buddhism, and he meditated in the mountains. Eventually, he left the capital and for a long time entered the clouds of Mount Kōya. He was often referred to as the Esoteric Master of the Southern Temple. From that time onward, he became entirely weary of this world, and he single-mindedly longed for the Western Land (the Pure Land).

In the third year of the Kahō era (around 1096), on the twenty-eighth day of the first month, suddenly Yuihan contracted a small illness. For two or three days, until the first day of the second month, Yuihan performed a ritual offering in which he made a copy of the complete *Lotus Sūtra* as well as ten thousand copies of an image of the "Immovable One" (Acalanātha; Fudō Myōō). In the early morning of the third day of the second month, Yuihan bathed and dressed in pure clothes. He had Eminent Monk Son'en carry out the fire ritual in which the Buddha attendant named Augustly Victorious (Sonshō) was the main Buddha image.

The purpose of this fire ritual was so that Yuihan could face death with right mindfulness. On this day, Yuihan faced the fire ritual platform. He reverently worshiped the west [the pure land], stating, "My whole life will end tonight. Now is the only time to view the maṇḍalas."

He then returned to his room, where he sat upright facing the west. With his hands he formed the "Meditation *Mudrā* of Marvelous Penetrating Wisdom." He chanted the Treasure Name of Amitābha Buddha. Furthermore, he connected a string of five colors to his own hands, forming the meditation *mudrā,* and to a Buddha statue. Around midnight he passed away as if he were sleeping and attained birth in Amitābha Buddha's Pure Land.

On the fifth day of the month, some people dressed his corpse for burial and sent it to a mausoleum. For the next ten days, Yuihan's disciples came to view the body but the appearance had not changed from Yuihan's living body. In addition, his meditation *mudrā* had not shifted in any way. His hair on his head was still growing a little, and the corpse was not emitting any rotten odor. Therefore, both monastics and laity gathered at the door of the tomb, making karmic connections and forming a community.

On the thirty-fifth day after Yuihan's death, the death anniversary on which Buddhist memorial services were usually conducted for the deceased, when Yuihan's disciples opened the door of the tomb and looked inside, Yuihan's meditation *mudrā* and the appearance of his body were just as they were before, without any change. The disciples were surprised and frightened by this very strange occurrence. They closed the tomb and did not open it anymore.

At the time of Yuihan's death, there were many auspicious signs [indicating his birth in the pure land]. For example, Meditation Monk Shinmyō [also known as the Holy Man of Kita Chikushi] of Yuihan's Southern Temple for a long time had shut himself in a grass hut and did not open the door. At the time of Yuihan's death, Shinmyō heard a voice in the sky, stating, "[The monk of the] Southern Temple just now has died."

In addition, at the same time, Eminent Monk Keinen had a dream in which he saw a large castle. A community of Buddhist monks had assembled there. The Esoteric Master of the Southern Temple was engaged in the Meditation on the Setting Sun.

At that time, music in the west could be heard, and a retinue of holy beings was coming [from the western Pure Land] to the east. First, six heavenly bird people who normally live in the pure land descended, fluttering their dance clothes. Next, (Monk) Kyōkai of Odawara came riding on a cloud. Keinen inquired about the meaning of this dream. A person there answered, "The meaning is that the Esoteric Master of the Southern Temple has been born in the pure land."

In addition, Eminent Monk Zenjō was a monk who had lived on Mount Kōya in the past. For some months, he had performed a variety of religious practices, but on this day he returned to the mountain. Eminent Monk Zenjō had heard about Yuihan's death, and he was crying and prostrating himself. That night, he dreamed that it became clear high in the western sky. Purple clouds were rising diagonally in the sky. A countless number of holy beings formed a Buddhist assembly amid the purple clouds. Yōko Bodhisattva by himself alone came out from the purple clouds.

In addition, before this time Holy Man Yuishō had copied a Buddhist scripture in accordance with ritual regulations. He gave this scripture as an offering to Yuihan. He buried the text at Kōbō Daishi Kūkai's tomb at Mount Kōya's Inner Sanctum. On the day of Yuihan's death, Eminent Monk Yuishō conducted the Rishu Sanmai ceremony at the Inner Sanctum. While Yuishō was neither dreaming nor completely awake, he heard a voice in the sky. This voice exclaimed, "Yuihan, the best Buddhist monk to emerge in a thousand years, just now has died."

We have omitted thousands of examples of auspicious signs [of Yuihan's birth in the pure land] that were very similar to these examples. We needed to compile a unified account [of his life].

## Biography 4, Rentai

The Buddhist monk Rentai was a person from Tosa Province. At an early age he left his father and mother's house and then lived for many years at the Ninnaji temple. His teacher was Esoteric Master Eisan. After reaching the prime of his life, his resolve to follow the Buddhist path strengthened. He decided to live in a thatched hut. He also changed his name to Rentai, and people called him Stone Treasury Eminent Monk. Day and night he engaged in rigorous Buddhist practices, and he rested very rarely. He also lived on Kinpusen and stopped eating salt and grain. His body withered, and all of his muscles and bones were exposed.

Various monks spoke to him, saying, "When the Holy Man dies, this sacred land will be polluted." Thus, on the basis of the consensus opinion he left that place. But Zaō Gongen made a pronouncement [of permission to live at Kinpusen], so Rentai again returned to live [at Kinpusen]. After some time, Rentai even more sought a secluded dwelling place and moved far away to Kōya. After many years, an aspiration arose in his heart to serve the people from poor families. All at once he decided to depart from this mountain. Although a group of people detained him, he forced his way out of the mountain. He vowed to return [to Koya] at the end of his life when facing death. After this, he conducted Buddhist discipline. Without deciding whether to stay or leave, he eventually reached Kongōchōji in Tosa Province.

On the nineteenth day of the fifth month of Jōtoku 2, he departed from the Western Sea and returned to Mount Kōya. Then he spoke to the assembly of monks, saying, "Lately there has been unease in my heart. I have not been able to sleep or eat very well. Thus I thought of my promise from long ago and returned to this mountain from far away."

One person then asked him, "As for the Land of Supreme Bliss or the Tuṣita Heaven, to which one do you aspire?" Rentai replied, "The religious discipline of my predecessors is not necessarily in accordance [with mine]. The Dharma Realm is all Thusness. To which place should I aspire?"

Solely for the purpose of [amassing] provisions for the next life, he chanted the *Lotus Sūtra* ten thousand times. After that, he did not memorize any more religious texts. He always admonished his disciples, saying, "At the time of my death, you should not bury [my body]. Just put it in a field, giving it to the birds and the beasts."

Someone answered, "If we do that, will your decomposed bones be scattered and pollute the pure ground?" Rentai sadly replied, "Yes, that is right. That is right."

Rentai had already become very sick, and he wanted to leave [Mount Kōya]. Although some other monks refused to let him leave, he shook his head and did not listen. Finally, the group gave into his wishes and sent Rentai away in a palanquin.

On the seventh day of the sixth month, Rentai shaved his own head and straightened his robes. It was as if he was not worried at all. He left the mountain gates and proceeded to Tosa Province. He left the sacred land [of Mount Kōya] and traveled far away from human society. On a distant path, he got out of the palanquin.

Rentai was under a tree and straightened his robe. He faced the western direction and his hands formed the meditation *mudrā*. He raised his voice, chanting, "Hail Three Bodies in One Amitābha Thus-Come One! Hail Great Teacher Who Spreads the Dharma (Kōbō Daishi)! Hail Universally Luminous Diamond Bodhisattva!" In this way he worshiped. He was sitting on ground covered with dew, and his breathing ceased.

The people who were watching [this scene] were wiping the tears from their eyes. At this time clouds were rising in the western sky. In the forest before [these onlookers] the wind was terrible. There were sounds of thunder above the clouds.

However, beneath the wind there was a pleasant fragrance. Suddenly the sky became clear. The clouds in the sky had become thin, wispy clouds [associated with fair weather].

At this time, Rentai was eighty-six years old.

At daybreak on the following morning, one of Rentai's disciples had a dream. A Diamond World maṇḍala was hanging in the middle of the sky. Rentai was sitting upright in the Perfected-Body Assembly, the central assembly of the entire maṇḍala. He was seated in the position of the

Diamond Cause Bodhisattva, one of the four attendant bodhisattvas that normally surround Amitābha Buddha in the Western Lunar Disk in this section of the maṇḍala.

At this time Rentai spoke in verse, exclaiming, "We aspired for Awakening and pursued the four immeasurable minds (love, compassion, sympathetic joy, and impartiality). Now I have traveled to the west. I rose to the rank of Diamond Cause Bodhisattva."

## Biography 8, Kyōtoku

Eminent Monk Kyōtoku was a person who for years and years lived in the Jimyō In on this mountain (Mount Kōya). He built a small Buddhist temple in this place. He cultivated wisdom and virtuous behavior in this temple, and people called him the Holy Man of the Small Dwelling.

Whenever a young boy nearby grew prejudiced and even scorned Kyōtoku, Kyōtoku always spoke to this boy, saying, "I have read the *Lotus Sūtra* six thousand times, and my body will never enter the dark paths of rebirth of the hell beings, hungry ghosts, and animals. You must not disparage me, or you will encounter destruction."

At the time of his death . . . Kyōtoku summoned disciples who could perform Buddhist rites. He enshrined an image of Amitābha Buddha and faced the west in the correct manner. He chanted the name of Amitābha Buddha in a loud voice, and he wholeheartedly adhered to right mindfulness. He died while chanting. The group of those who were either peaceful or acrimonious [toward Kyōtoku] formed karmic connections with him through their encounters with him.

At this time, Archbishop Shūgyō of the Kezō In was staying on Mount Kōya for a period of prayer. Esoteric Master Shūkan of Ōmi Province lived at the Ninnaji temple. He spoke to Archbishop Shūgyō, stating, "I had a dream revelation that there was a figured silk banner that came flying from the west and went toward Mount Kōya. Very soon later, this flag flew back to the west in the same manner as before. In all likelihood, someone on Mount Kōya has achieved birth in the pure land."

They then inquired about the date that this dream occurred and discovered that it was the very night that Kyōtoku died. The monks of Mount Kōya suddenly broke out into tears with sadness. However, Archbishop Shūgyō rejoiced to an unusual extent and conducted the Buddhist rites normally held over the forty-nine day period between the death and the next rebirth.

## Biography 11, Ryōzen

Superintendent Monk and Esoteric Master Ryōzen was a person from the town of Kanzaki in Naka County in Kii Province. His family name was Sakagami. His mother dreamed that a moon disk entered her chest, and then she became pregnant. Ryōzen was born in Eishō 3 (1049).

When he was six and seven years old he constantly spoke about how a moon disk was manifesting itself before him. His parents thought this was strange. Eventually, he entered the Buddhist order. At the age of eleven, for the first time he ascended to the Kongōbuji temple on Mount Kōya.

His teacher was the Monk of Mountain Meditation Ninson. At the age of fourteen, after he had renounced the householder's life and taken the precepts, Ryōzen met [the Monk of the] Northern Room Gyōmyō and received the "Spell That Makes Things in Accord with One's Wishes" (Daizuigu darani), the Spell of the Augustly Victorious One, and the Great Rite of the Two Maṇḍalas.

For a long time, Ryōzen shut himself within Mount Kōya's mountain gates. He did not look back upon the impurity and suffering of the lay world. He longed to be released from the impure land [of earth]. This is what his heart desired. Ryōzen also was seeking the pure land, and he took this to be his personal religious discipline.

A group of people practicing near Ryōzen called him the Little Holy Man. Later, Ryōzen became a disciple of Superintendent Monk and Esoteric Master Meizan of the Central Temple. He bathed in the waters of the Five Wisdoms that the buddhas possess.

Ryōzen was truly a monk with exceptional ability who towered above most others in the meditation grove. He was a pillar of the Buddhist community.

Those who had received the transmission of the Esoteric Buddhist teaching, the group who had been initiated into the Womb Maṇḍala with its three groups of holy beings and the Diamond Maṇḍala with its five groups of holy beings, now extended to thirty-five men. In addition, the group of people who had received the transmission of a single buddha and a single *mudrā* numbered over one hundred people.

While Ryōzen was alive, he performed many good karmic actions. For example, he built a mantra hall and enshrined various sacred beings. He summoned Abbot Archbishop Kanjo to this hall and appointed him to preside as the head preaching monk. He also placed three attendant monks at this hall and initiated a Buddhist rite that was conducted over many days.

In addition, Ryōzen built a Maitreya hall and conducted the Lotus Rite (Hokke hō). Great Archbishop Jōkai served as the officiant for this ritual offering. Ryōzen also built a Stūpa of Many Treasures that was about fifteen meters in height. We know that as a matter of course the various buddhas enshrined in this stūpa have achieved awakening and that these buddhas are those who turn the Wheel of the Dharma [and guide sentient beings to awakening].

Apart from these structures, he established a bell tower and a scripture repository, which were lined up [at the central monastic complex] one after another. Ryōzen lived on Mount Kōya for a span of eighty-one years.

On the twenty-first day of the second month of the fifth year of Hōen (1139), Ryōzen put on pure robes and spread out a mat. He worshiped the Immovable One (Fudō Myōō; Acalanātha). Above all, this was an act of prayer and petition. Next, he faced the south and worshipped Kūkai's Portrait Hall. Then, Ryōzen faced the west and yearned for the Land of Bliss. Finally, as his body and mind remained still, without moving, he passed away.

Ryōzen was ninety-two years old when he died. He had been a monk for seventy-nine years. People witnessed miraculous signs and experienced dream revelations about Ryōzen's birth in the pure land, but they did not have the spare time to record these miracles.

Someone reported that after Ryōzen's death, some people constructed a stūpa and enshrined his body in this structure. This place is named Taniue. The religious structures that Ryōzen built at Mount Kōya have been handed down to his disciples generation after generation. The light of the Dharma has not ceased.

## Biography 13, Kyōjin

Hōshōbō Kyōjin's family name was Taira. He originally lived at Onjōji but later moved to Mount Kōya. During his life, he continued to advance [along the Buddhist path] while conducting Buddhist discipline. He studied broadly in the eight main traditions of Buddhism in Japan (the six Nara schools, Tendai, and Shingon). He also quickly mastered the Diamond World maṇḍala with its five groups of sacred beings. He took Mañjuśrī Bodhisattva to be his main sacred icon. He conducted Esoteric consecrations and transmitted many schools of teachings.

Kyōjin was facing death in the late afternoon of the twentieth day of the third month of Eiji 1 (1141). Mañjuśrī Bodhisattva suddenly appeared before him in a body that was about one meter in height. Mañjuśrī Bodhisattva spoke to the eminent monk, saying, "Three days later, around 4:00 a.m., I will come with ten thousand other bodhisattvas. We will lead you to the Golden-Hued World (Mañjuśrī's heaven)."

At that time, Eminent Monk Kyōjin joined his hands before his chest and worshiped the bodhisattva. In verse, he stated, "I only wished for a marvelous sign, and your golden-hued body appeared. You did not cast away your original vow and became a teacher and guide. After doing this, you return to your heaven."

Long ago Meditation Teacher Hōshō met a bodhisattva in human form who told him that he would be born in the moonlight of the Western Pure Land. Now, a bodhisattva has appeared to Eminent Monk Kyōjin and promised that he will be transported to the clouds of the Golden-Hued World. In both of these cases, long ago and right now, Mañjuśrī assumed a form appropriate to the circumstances and appeared in the human world.

On the twenty-third day of the same month, around 4:00 a.m., suddenly an unusual aroma was emitted. [As a result] some people were awakened to the heart of faith [in the Three Treasures of Buddhism]. At this time, Eminent Monk Kyōjin instructed his disciples, saying, "Please read the Devadatta chapter of the *Lotus Sūtra* (chapter 12), and please chant the mantra of Mañjuśrī." Eminent Monk Kyōjin then formed an esoteric *mudrā* and, as if he were entering meditation, suddenly departed this world.

After he died, Kyōjin remained seating upright [in the meditation posture] for a day, and he did not move. His hands formed the *mudrā* just like before.

Butsugonbō Shōshin was the head of academic studies (*gakutō*) at the Denbō'in on Mount Kōya. He was living on the mountain during a period of lectures on Buddhism, around the time [that this incident occurred]. The teacher [Kyōjin] and student [Butsugonbō Shōshin] had a close relationship. Butsugonbō Shōshin knew the details [about Kyōjin's life]. Thus I asked Butsugonbō Shōshin about these matters and recorded them as I have done here.

## Biography 14, Rinken

Superintendent Monk and Esoteric Master Rinken was a person from Kii Province and Naka County. While he was a lay person, his family name was Taira. In the beginning [of his Buddhist training], he encountered Junkai of Tōdaiji and studied the Kegon tradition. Later, he followed

Keishun of Mount Kōya and received the rites of various buddhas. In addition, he was a disciple of Esoteric Master Ryōzen, who transmitted the "Consecration of the Two Maṇḍalas" to him.

Rinken made votive offerings of money and built temple buildings. He also supplied provisions for making and copying Buddhist scriptures. He lived a long life of seventy-seven years. Rinken displayed diligence in Buddhist discipline that was truly limitless, an aspiration to cut through karmic afflictions and manifest the fruit of Awakening, and a desire to make the Dharma flourish and to benefit sentient beings. Judging the wholehearted way in which he did these things, we see that Rinken's diligence and aspirations were worthy of the sages of antiquity.

In the middle third of the eighth month of Kyūan 6, suddenly he contracted a minor illness. He enshrined a statue of Maitreya Bodhisattva, and he hung a five-colored banner to this statue. He formed an esoteric *mudrā* with his hands and chanted the name of Maitreya Bodhisattva. His breathing stopped, and his life suddenly was extinguished.

People that Rinken knew and those that he did not know very well came to visit. They rejoiced and became choked with tears. They did not know if he, with Amitābha's guidance, was born in Amitābha's Pure Land or if he had gone to dwell in the Tuṣita Heaven before Maitreya Bodhisattva's descent to Earth [in the distant future]. Where karmic connections will lead one is something that people cannot fathom.

## Notes

1 Jacqueline Stone, "By the Power of One's Last Nenbutsu," in *Approaching the Land of Bliss*, ed. Richard Karl Payne and Kenneth K. Tanaka (Honolulu: University of Hawai'i Press, 2004), 78.

2 Frederic J. Kotas, "Ōjōden: Accounts of Rebirth in the Pure Land" (PhD diss., University of Washington 1987), 32–33.

3 These collections are all contained in Inoue Mitsusada and Oosone Shōsuke, eds., *Ōjōden, Hokke genki*, vol. 7 of *Nihon shisō taikei* (Tokyo: Iwanami Shoten, 1974), as is the *Dainihonkoku Hokkekyō genki*, which contains many *ōjōden* even though it is not exclusively an *ōjōden* collection.

4 See especially Inoue Mitsusada, "Inseiki ni okeru Kōyasan no jōdokyō," *Nihon Jōdokyō seiritsushi no kenkyū* (Tokyo: Yamakawa Shuppan, 1975), and Gorai Shigeru, *Kōya hijiri* (Tokyo: Kadokawa Sensho, 1975).

5 See Murakami Hiroko, "*Kōyasan ōjōden* sensha Nyojaku ni tsuite—sono shinkō to senjutsu ishiki o chūshin ni," *Sundai shigaku* 115 (March 2002):

1–24; Shimura Kunihiro, "Ōjōden no keifu—gokuraku ganbō," *Kokubungaku: kaishaku to kanshō* 52, no. 11 (November 1987): 148–150; and *Nihon setsuwa densetsu daijiten*, s.v. "*Kōyasan ōjōden*" and "Nyojaku."

6 Murakami, "*Kōyasan ōjōden* sensha Nyojaku ni tsuite—sono shinkō to senjutsu ishiki o chūshin ni," 13.

7 *Mii ōjōden* is another *ōjōden* collection focusing on residents of a single place. Its chief editorial principle is to highlight the spiritual attainments of Onjōji monks, in contrast to earlier collections, whose biographies of Tendai clerics were largely limited to monks of Mount Hiei. In this regard, *Mii ōjōden*'s focus differs from *Kōyasan ōjōden*, even though they both deal with a single place.

8 Fujiwara no Sukenaga, *Kōyasan ōjōden*, in *Ōjōden, Hokke genki*, ed. Inoue Mitsusada and Oosone Shōsuke, vol. 7 of *Nihon shisō taikei* (Tokyo: Iwanami Shoten, 1974), 695.

9 Murakami Hiroko, *Kōyasan shinkō no seiritsu to tenkai* (Tokyo: Yuzankaku, 2009), 22.

## Bibliography

### Primary Sources

Fujiwara no Sukenaga. *Kōyasan ōjōden*. In *Ōjōden, Hokke genki*, edited by Inoue Mitsusada and Oosone Shōsuke. Vol. 7 of *Nihon shisō taikei*. Tokyo: Iwanami Shoten, 1974.

Inoue Mitsusada and Oosone Shōsuke, eds. *Ōjōden, Hokke genki*. Vol. 7 of *Nihon shisō taikei*. Tokyo: Iwanami Shoten, 1974.

### Secondary Sources

Gorai Shigeru. *Kōya hijiri*. Tokyo: Kadokawa Sensho, 1975.

Inoue Mitsusada. "Inseiki ni okeru Kōyasan no jōdokyō." In *Nihon Jōdokyō seiritsushi no kenkyū*. Tokyo: Yamakawa Shuppan, 1975.

Kotas, Frederic J. "Ōjōden: Accounts of Rebirth in the Pure Land." PhD dissertation, University of Washington 1987.

Murakami Hiroko. "*Kōyasan ōjōden* sensha Nyojaku ni tsuite—sono shinkō to senjutsu ishiki o chūshin ni." *Sundai shigaku* 115 (March 2002): 1–24.

———. *Kōyasan shinkō no seiritsu to tenkai*. Tokyo: Yuzankaku, 2009.

Nara Hiromoto. "Kōgyō Daishi Kakuban izen no Kōyasan jōdokyō." In *Kōgyō Daishi Kakuban kenkyū: Kōgyō Daishi happyaku-gojūnen goonki kinen ronshū*, edited by Kōgyō Daishi Kenkyū Ronshū Henshū Iinkai. Tokyo: Shunjūsha, 1992.

Shimura Kunihiro. "Ōjōden no keifu—gokuraku ganbō." *Kokubungaku: kaishaku to kanshō* 52, no. 11 (November 1987): 148–150.

Shirai Yūko. *Inseiki Kōyasan to Kūkai nyūjō densetsu*. Tokyo: Dōseisha, 2002.

——. *Kūkai densetsu no keisei to Kōyasan*. Tokyo: Dōseisha, 1986.

Stone, Jacqueline I. "By the Power of One's Last Nenbutsu." In *Approaching the Land of Bliss*, edited by Richard Karl Payne and Kenneth K. Tanaka. Honolulu: University of Hawai'i Press, 2004.

——. "The Secret Art of Dying: Esoteric Deathbed Practices in Heian Japan." In *The Buddhist Dead: Practices, Discourses, Representations*, edited by Brian J. Cuevas and Jacqueline I. Stone. Honolulu: University of Hawai'i Press, 2007.

Wada Shūjō. "Kōyasan no rekishi to shinkō." In *Kōyasan: sono rekishi to bunka*, edited by Matsunaga Yūkei et al. Kyoto: Hōzōkan, 1984.

Weinstein, Stanley. "Aristocratic Buddhism." In *Cambridge History of Japan*, vol. 2, edited by John W. Hall et al. New York: Cambridge University Press, 1999.

## Chapter 2

# Contemporary Pure Land Miracle Tales

Natasha Heller

### TRANSLATOR'S INTRODUCTION

Miracle tales have long been an important genre of Chinese Buddhist literature, taking as their focus a particular scripture, a Buddhist image, or a practice such as sutra recitation. Narratives centered around the effectiveness of the scripture, image, or practice in calling forth the protection and aid of buddhas and bodhisattvas. Some miracle tales might also focus on bodily transformations effected by Buddhist practice, as in tongues and lips that did not decay because of their many years reciting the texts of scriptures or intoning the names of buddhas. Another common theme in miracle tale stories is the response of nature; unusual smells and phenomena of light attested to the power of Buddhist objects and practices.

Miracles like those that appear in Buddhist tales were usually explained through *ganying*, a key term for Chinese religions that has been translated by Robert Sharf as "sympathetic resonance."[1] In Chinese cosmological understanding, phenomena in the same category are connected in such a way that when one provides a stimulus (*gan*), another will respond (*ying*). In these tales, the practices of pious Buddhists could elicit the response of buddhas and bodhisattvas, and so the tale served to demonstrate the compassionate care of Buddhist deities as well as to affirm the effectiveness of sutra chanting, reverence to images, *nianfo* (buddha-name recitation), and other devotional activities. Many of these stories included near-death experiences or dreams; real or oneiric journeys offered the opportunity to confirm scriptural accounts of other realms, and those who had such experiences served as witnesses to the joys or horrors there.

Miracle tales were key forms of testimony (or propaganda) for a developing religion, and they were not only recorded but also circulated.

By reading about miracles that happened to Buddhists in other times and places—yet most often still within China—people were encouraged to take up or persevere in their own religious devotions. When these stories circulated in print far beyond those who might have known about them firsthand, it became important to signal the veracity of the stories. Authors did so by including details, giving the tales a specificity that served to locate them in space and time and to align them with other types of historical accounts. Names of people, toponyms, and references to temples were all ways of helping a reader or hearer to better imagine the tale, and they served as evidence that the account had been passed down by those with intimate knowledge of the occurrences described therein.

For Pure Land tales, the miracles often centered on episodes near death that could affirm someone's postmortem destiny. The appearance of Amitābha during a person's final moments, as was promised in *Foshuo guan wuliangshoufo jing* (The scripture on the contemplation of the Buddha of Infinite Life spoken by the Buddha), served to confirm that the practitioner would soon be born in the western paradise. Details about that rebirth could even confirm that the person had been assiduous enough in recollecting Amitābha's name to merit one of the higher levels of rebirth.[2]

The tales translated below are from the first volume of *Nianfo ganying lu* (Records of the sympathetic resonance of recollecting the Buddha's name). This collection includes some traditional tales but also gathers contemporary accounts of Pure Land practice and its efficacy. Longstanding beliefs are reflected in these tales—for example, that Amitābha appears at the time of death to escort the deceased to the pure land—but the tales also revise generic conventions and reflect contemporary concerns. For example, most of the tales include names and locations with even greater specificity than their premodern forerunners. Going beyond the name of a village, the tales give names and sometimes numbers of streets, farms, work units, and prisons; people in the stories are also identified with names and titles. These details reflect a culture of testimony among Pure Land believers and create a community of those believers in China and Taiwan.

The tales themselves reflect a community of believers in other ways, describing those who come to assist the very ill in reciting Amitābha's name, noting people who served as teachers to others, and referring to families who share their Pure Land practice. These groups of believers are embedded within a modern world, with its institutions like work units, prisons, and, especially in these stories, hospitals. The interaction between modern medicine and faith is a key aspect of these tales, as many of the protagonists are gravely ill and beyond the help of doctors. Instead, they find comfort and at times healing through the invocation of Amitābha's name. Amitābha can also keep people safe from other kinds of dangers, like accidents and ghosts.

These tales can be read as a contemporary continuation of the collection and circulation of religious miracle tales. *Nianfo ganying lu* also represents one part of the religious landscape of China and Taiwan. The first volume was edited by the Taiwanese Buddhist monk Huijing (b. 1950) and the next two volumes were put together by his disciple Jingzong (b. 1966). A fourth volume was published in late 2014. Huijing took vows under Xingyun (b. 1927). Xingyun is the founder of Foguangshan, one of the most important Buddhist organizations in Taiwan; through Xingyun, Huijing is in a lineage of "Humanistic Buddhism." Huijing's own prominence owes a great deal to the charismatic Buddhist leader Li Yuansong (1957–2003), a self-taught lay Buddhist, who, after his own awakening experience, began teaching Chan in Taibei. As his followers grew in number, Li eventually established a year-round community of believers at Xiangshan. After falling ill, Li had several pivotal conversations with Huijing in 2003 and came to place all his faith in the Pure Land tradition. From Li's perspective it was not possible to practice Chan and Pure Land together, so he made a radical change. His community at Xiangshan became one of Pure Land copractitioners headed by Huijing.[3]

Some years before, in 1996, Jingzong had become a disciple of Huijing. Over the next decade he built a following in mainland China and established Hongyuan Temple at Mount Jingting in Anhui. In 2012, Jingzong became abbot of Wuzhen Monastery outside of Xi'an, where he continues to promote a tradition he traces back to Shandao (613–681).[4] The Pure Land tradition of Huijing and Jingzhong spans both sides of the Taiwan Straits, and the personal accounts they collect also come from both Taiwanese and mainland Chinese believers. The organization that publishes these miracle tales also publishes reprints of Pure Land scriptures and premodern and modern Buddhist writings ranging from Daochuo (562–645) to Yinguang (1862–1940). The works are published in both traditional and simplified characters and are distributed for free by the Pure Land Culture and Education Foundation. These are also made available online, through web pages and downloadable PDFs, and the organization maintains a Facebook page that often includes accounts of sympathetic resonance connected to Pure Land practice.[5] The circulation of these texts helps to build the community of Pure Land believers and to introduce newcomers to the faith, just they did centuries ago, but incorporating the technologies and socioeconomic realities of the modern world.

## Translations

*Nianfo ganying lu*
Huijing

### Recollecting the Buddha to Save One's Life, Radiating Light

Extracted from "Returning to My Hometown of Hualian," by Zhang Xiren of Zhanghua County, Yuanlin township, 65 Zhongshan Road, 1st section. Huijing, *Nianfo ganying lu,* vol. 1, 79–82.

For me, the saying "the impermanence of human life lies in the space of a breath" is not the least false, because I have suffered a heart attack twice in the last two years. Afterward, I reflected carefully: Was the pain I experienced the same as the pain experienced by pigs when I was helping my family to slaughter them?

In the eighty-second year of the Republic (1993), Zhang Jinwen—who at that time was serving as representative of Puxin township—asked me to help push his car. However, I was already sick with a cold and not up to my usual strength, and after exerting myself to push the car I experienced a stabbing pain in my heart and fell down. According to what Representative Zhang told me later, at that time I already seemed to be in a state of shock, and if I had not gotten immediate help I probably would have died. At that time my outward appearance was that of death, but my feeling of consciousness was still there, and as the pain increased it felt like the elements of my body were splitting apart. It was just like the Buddha had once likened to "a live turtle having its shell pulled off," with pain suffusing my whole body. I recommend that everyone, when in this situation, recollect the name of the Buddha, so that at the approach of death one is able to avoid losing proper mindfulness (*zhengnian*).

When Representative Zhang carried me into his house to wait for the ambulance, I could hear clearly the sound of him calling to his family and their conversation. Because I had previously explained to them the practice of recollecting the Buddha, Mrs. Zhang and her mother came to assist me in calling his name.

A miraculous thing happened at that moment: each name of the Buddha that they recited suddenly became a wave of light in the air, and I immediately felt at ease and without pain. I also noticed that the light produced by each person's recitations different in brightness and duration. Given her practice of morning and evening devotions, Mrs. Zhang's recitations were somewhat brighter and lasted longer. Led by them, I was able to recollect the Buddha's name in my mind, and I noticed that the light from my own recitations was the brightest and most enduring. The *Dizang Sūtra* says that one is only able to obtain one part out of seven when people create merit on our behalf, and this is entirely true.

At a time when my body and mind were in duress, I was fortunate that the light from their assisted recitation, along with guidance of the proper thought of reciting the Buddha's name, allowed me not to lapse into pain and bewilderment. The ambulance took me to the cardiac hospital, but because my condition was so severe the hospital did not want to admit me. Then I was taken to Wulun Hospital where a doctor declared me already beyond saving. He told Representative Zhang, who had accompanied me, that my next-of-kin would need to sign an affidavit before the hospital would be willing to administer aid. Representative Zhang, after hearing this, furiously tried to reason with the doctor, saying that if they waited until my family came, the possibility of saving my life would grow uncertain.

At this moment I could hear their conversation, and with the urgency of the situation I forgot to concentrate on recollecting the Buddha's name. Also, only Representative Zhang had accompanied me to the hospital, and there was no one to help recite Amitābha's name in support, and so I lost the protection of the Buddha's power. This was very unfortunate, because I then immediately felt like I was falling somewhere deep, and the speed was like a roller-coaster going directly down, seemingly headed for a cold hell. As I went down, it got darker and colder, and it felt like knives were cutting me, all over my body. When the Buddhist scriptures refer to "the wind knife cutting apart the body," it is probably describing what I experienced at that moment.

Fortunately, the seeds from my common practice of reciting the Buddha's name came into use during this urgent moment. In great pain, this very thought occurred to me and in distress I called out, "Amitābha!" (Afterwards, I learned that everyone in the hospital heard my loud cry of the Buddha's name.) Unimaginably, right at that very moment, a small dot of brightness appeared before my eyes, and when I persisted in reciting "Namo Amitābha," the radiating light immediately enlarged in front of me. I relaxed, my eyes opened, and I woke up. Everyone was staring at me, not yet understanding that I had done a turn in front of the gate of ghosts, and escaped with my life!

## Ceaselessly Reciting the Name of the Buddha, Ghosts Retreat and Illness Is Cured

From Chen Hailiang, *Kexu ze xu,* reprinted in Huijing, *Nianfo ganying lu,* vol. 1, 107–109.

For most people, illness is connected to karma. When karmic retribution is completely finished, if one were to seek an early recovery, it would not be possible without asking for the protection of the Buddha's power. There are many cases in which famous doctors of both Chinese and Western medicine had no means to cure serious illness, but through prayer to buddhas and bodhisattvas recovery was possible. One such recent case is that of Mr. Shao Lian'e, who was saved by reciting the Buddha's name.

Mr. Shao was from Hangzhou, and at age nineteen suffered a serious illness in Shanghai. He went to Baolong Hospital for treatment. After seeing a doctor the diagnosis was that there was no hope for recovery. On the seventh night after entering the hospital, he suddenly saw Ox-Head, Horse-Face, *yakṣas,* and demons swaying back and forth at the head of his bed. At that time the lights were on, and he was fully conscious. He knew that they were coming for him and that he was about to die. He drew up his courage and sat up in bed. Then he thought, if there are ghosts, then certainly there are buddhas and bodhisattvas. And what came to mind were the six syllables "Namo Amitābha," which he began to recite in a loud voice.

After the first intonation of the Buddha's name, many of the ghosts startled him by retreating several steps, and they no longer dared approach him. Mr. Shao felt that with the inconceivable efficacy of these six syllables he would be able to turn back the ghosts' attack. Thereupon, with a sincere mind he began the chant the Buddha's name without cease. Because the ghosts were not able to apprehend him, King Yama personally arrived on the scene. He was wearing a green robe, and was wearing a tasseled crown. He also was turned back by the name of the Buddha and could not draw near.

Mr. Shao saw the magnitude of the Buddha's power, and with even more confidence recited the Buddha's name in a loud voice. The doctors in the hospital thought the sound of his voice would disturb the other patients, and they urged him to stop reciting. But how could Mr. Shao stop, standing as he was at the brink of death! The doctors could only move him to another hospital room, and Mr. Shao just kept on chanting. In this way, he passed almost five days, whereupon he suddenly saw an orb of golden light. It was like a shooting star and fell from in front of his face toward the ground, gradually becoming larger. After a moment, its illumination filled the room, and in the middle was a golden Buddha, standing still in splendor with a golden cloud beneath his feet. His left hand held a rosary and held it with fingers joined to the right hand, in front of his chest. Smiling at Mr. Shao, he was kindly and joyous, with an amiable attitude; this was none other than Amitābha! At that point the ghosts had already disappeared, and then the Buddha became hidden.

Mr. Shao, since he had personally seen Amitābha appear, became even more excited. The pain of his illness had already abated, and the next day he left the hospital, lively and healthy and completely returned to his former state.

## End-Stage Cancer Completely Cured through the Recitation of the Buddha's Name

From Dharma Master Guozhen, *Wo yuan nian mituo* (I vow to recite Amitābha's name), in Huijing, *Nianfo ganying lu,* vol. 1, 134–137.

In Sanzhong, Taiwan, there is a certain Chen Rongming who was forty years old when this happened in 1995. For the previous three years, he frequently suffered from a bloody nose. He didn't pay it much attention, just rubbing on ointments to stop the bleeding or taking a pain killer, but during the summer it gradually got worse, and he sought treatment at Rongmin Hospital. His illness had already worsened to the point where he had headaches, was blind in both eyes, and couldn't even eat. After a biopsy and CT scan, they confirmed that it was end-stage nose and throat cancer, and the cancer cells had already spread throughout his entire head. The doctor advised Mr. Chen that he would need to undergo radiation and chemotherapy, and to take morphine to control the pain. Even so, his life expectancy was only two months, and he was told to put his affairs in order.

His wife was devastated, and because Mr. Chen had no worker's insurance, he had to borrow money to go to the hospital and couldn't stay there any longer. So he resolved himself to go home and quietly wait for death's approach. Not wanting to cause trouble for his wife, he attempted suicide by cutting his wrists, but was rescued. This unhappy piece of news came to the notice of Layman Huang of Taibei's Daily Good Deed Society, who immediately expressed his care for the Chen family by sending them sympathy money. Huang sincerely encouraged Mr. Chen, telling him that the best thing to do in order to ease his pain and be reborn in the pure land was to single-mindedly recollect the name of Amitābha. At the beginning Layman Chen had his doubts, but later he was moved by Huang's sincere encouragement and began to recollect Amitābha's name.

"Amitābha" is only four syllables, so everyone can recollect it, but for someone with a terminal illness on the brink of death, with an illness that makes it hard to make any sound, it is truly not easy to recite the Buddha's name. Day by day, he went from mentally reciting the name to reciting it with lips and teeth,[6] and then to reciting it with a soft voice. After more than ten days, he started to feel his spirit and energy returning a bit. He already had begun to believe, and under the compassionate guidance of Layman Liao, who had sent statues of the Pure Land triad,[7] he concentrated his mind even more on the name, reciting it several tens of thousands of times each day. He did not return to his bedroom but spent the whole day sitting in a rattan chair reciting Amitābha's name. The more he recited, the more he felt the joy of the dharma, and slowly, without his being aware of it, his appetite increased, his pain lessened, and his strength made obvious progress.

He did nothing besides reciting the name of the Buddha, resting only a bit before beginning to recite again. He had already been out of the hospital over four months, and during this time he did not take any medicine or receive shots, but just recited "Amitābha" over and over again, doing so until his efforts became concentrated and self and object were forgotten, approaching the state in which the mind cannot be disturbed, and life and death are transcended to be reborn again.

Layman Chen says that now reciting the Buddha's name is his greatest pleasure, full of dharma-joy. Amitābha is truly a great doctor, with compassion that is hard to measure, rescuing him from the brink of death. This is like someone having his hands and feet cut apart at the joints, and his body sliced into bits, but still not being willing to submit, instead happily reciting with a unified mind the meritorious vast names—Namo Amitābha!

Now Layman Chen's strength is the same as anyone else's, even to the point where he can do twenty pushups without shortness of breath. Moreover, sight gradually returned to his left eye, to the amazement of his doctors, who treated this as a medical miracle.

Layman Chen Rongming's arising from near death and returning to life is a rare example of stimulus and response (*ganying*), and truly this had two special causes: First, when his eyes lost sight all the varied rights and wrongs of the external world no longer had any connection with him, and so his eyes could not be polluted again, completely cutting off external conditions. This can be called obtaining good fortune through misfortune; his mind was internally pure, making it easy to reach the *samādhi* of recollecting the Buddha's name. Second, because his household was poor and he had no way to go to the hospital, he was, on the contrary, able to relinquish sensory emotions and the grasping of the flesh, wishing to entirely entrust himself to the holy Amitābha, single-mindedly seeking birth in the pure land. If he had had financial resources, then he would have lusted after life and feared death; unable to set aside fame and wealth, he would have sought famous doctors everywhere, and made a great mistake by trying to be clever. By obstructing the mind of the Way, he would have lost a great benefit.

## With One Sound of Amitābha's Name, Children Avoid a Car Accident

From *Lianhe Bao,* November 13, 1992, reprinted in Huijing, *Nianfo ganying lu,* vol. 1, 189–191.

*Apologies to the evil spirits! The day after he saved a chivalrous man, a truck without a driver lost control and charged toward a little girl and boy . . .*

A few days ago, when Uncle and Auntie came back home to visit grandma, they told us about a strange thing they had personally experienced, and as everyone listened it sent chills up their spines.

A bit ago, Uncle got a construction job near Mount Yangming [north of Taibei]. One Saturday, because progress had been delayed he worked until after 8 p.m. He was driving a small commercial truck back home, going from Mount Yangming to Beitou on mountain roads. On the road he saw a motorbike speeding ahead, wavering on the turns as they descended the mountain. Because it was already dark, and Uncle was concerned about blurred vision, he stopped the car after he had passed a bend. Then, without hearing any sound, the air suddenly filled with the smell of gas. Fearing for someone's life, he took a flashlight and went down the slope. He found a smashed motorbike on top of a man. Uncle called out to him, but the driver had no strength to lift his head, dripping with fresh blood. Suddenly, his whole face trembling with fear, he called out mournfully: "No! I beg you not to come near!" And then he fell unconscious.

After he had been sent to the emergency room, with a quavering voice he told Uncle that at that time he heard someone calling, lifted his head, and then saw a troop of demons with claws extended rushing toward him. Therefore he called out in fear, and a ray of bright light shot towards him, and he didn't know what happened after that.

The next day, bright and early on Sunday morning, Uncle took his wife and children to Mount Yangming to enjoy the scenery. They stopped at a waterfall, and Uncle and Auntie were talking about the strange events of the previous night while the two children played nearby. Suddenly he caught sight of a driverless truck rushing out of control at his daughter and son. He shouted "Amitābha," and the truck sped by his children, gradually coming to a stop. Uncle and Auntie ran over to help up their children who were sprawled on the ground. It was truly a miracle that the two children were not harmed in the least, and were just very frightened.

When they returned home, some elderly neighbors advised Uncle that the day's events were probably due to the incident with the motorbike driver, because he had created enmity with the demons. Thereupon he went directly to the temple to ask a senior monk to hold a Buddhist service so he could transfer the resulting merit and dissolve the enmity with the ghosts. His circumstances should change after the incident was over, but when Uncle narrated his experience, he still had some lingering fear.

## Pursued by a Vengeful Spirit, Reciting the Buddha's Name Brings Down a Fever

From Lin Kanzhi, *Nianfo ganying jianwen ji* (Records of experiences of miraculous response from reciting the name of the Buddha), reprinted in Huijing, *Nianfo ganying lu,* vol. 1, 198–200.

Ten years ago, there was a woman who taught at the Institute for Spreading the Teachings in Wufeng (Taizhong). She lived on Zhongzheng Road in Wufeng, and was over seventy years old. Everyone called her "Sister," and she was one of disciples of the three treasures who most faithfully and devoutly recited the name of the Buddha. One day, this teacher told me about her grandson, who was nine years old. Several days before he had gone out on an excursion; when he left in the morning he was very happy, but when he came back in the afternoon he wasn't feeling well. He didn't eat dinner, and went right to bed, which he usually shared with his grandmother.

Now the old have more experience, and so when she saw her grandson come home and collapse into a deep sleep, she felt very uneasy and was unable to sleep herself. She stayed by his side, often touching her grandson's forehead to check his temperature. At two in the morning, her grandson started to run a fever. Reverently she went to get a glass of *Great Compassion Dhāraṇī* water to have her grandson drink. After he drank the *dhāraṇī* water, he told her: "Grandma! When I was out today, I ate lunch under a tree, and then played a bit. I started to feel bad because a kid came home with me. He told me that he was nine years old and last year he fell to his death at that place. He was wearing his school uniform and said he was really lonely. He wants me to be his friend! Grandma, right now he's standing at the head of the bed, and he wants me to go play."

When Sister heard her grandson say this, she couldn't help but shiver and get goose pimples. She worked up her courage and said, "My family has no grudge with you. If you bear someone ill will you should release it, and not keep these ties. I will recite the *dhāraṇī* of rebirth on your behalf, so that you can be reincarnated and escape your suffering. Now listen carefully!"

Sister then recited for three circuits of the rosary, over three hundred times, and then recited the holy name of Amitābha thousands of times. Then her grandson called out, "Grandma! When you recited the *dhāraṇī* of rebirth, he went out the door and waved to me, calling me to come with him. When you were reciting the name of Amitābha, he disappeared."

## Before Going to Be Reborn, Great Happiness Has Already Appeared

Recorded by Han Fujun on June 21, 2000, Huijing, *Nianfo ganying lu,* vol. 1, 275–283.

Laywoman Huang Xiagui was seventy two years old and was a member of the production team on a farm in Qianjiang, Hubei. She was just an old villager who didn't even know one character, and she had suffered from rectal cancer for four years. Laywoman Huang started studying Buddhism in the fall of 1998, and in the following spring made a vow to recite the name of the Buddha. In April of 2000, she heard Master Jingzong's tape, "Great Master Shandao's Essential Points."[8] She passed on to be reborn on June 17, 2000, at seven in the morning. After she went to be reborn her face was still rosy, and she wore a smile. She was cremated forty-nine hours later, and her body was still pliant.

In May of that year, Laywoman Huang's illness had begun to get gradually worse, and she no longer got out of bed. On the 10th of June, Laywoman Huang's daughter, He Yizhen—who also recited the name of the Buddha—called to tell me (they were at the farm, and I was in Qianjiang, about twenty kilometers away) that her mother had already lost her appetite. The next day she called me again to tell that her mother was completely refusing food, didn't want to drink water, had lost control of her bowels, and was leaking blood and black liquid from her rectum. (These conditions persisted until she died.)

On the 12th, she again called to tell me that her mother was calling, "Mama Amitābha, come soon to meet me!" The next morning, I went to He Yizhen's house on the farm (which was half a kilometer from Laywoman Huang's house), and He told me that when she saw that her mother had closed her eyes she said to her, " Ma, why are you always closing your eyes? Open your eyes!" Her mother had said, "When my eyes are closed I see beautiful things. The ground is multicolored, red, green, blue, and yellow, producing rays of light, very round, and which flow like water. It was so beautiful, I ran barefoot across it very quickly, and it was wonderful. [Laywoman Huang's feet had corns on the bottom, and she usually wore soft-soled shoes.] When I open my eyes, I just see that worn-out table, that worn-out bench, that worn-out cupboard—all these worn-out things! I don't like them, and I don't want to see them. When I close my eyes, I see beautiful things emitting light; when my eyes are open I just see black things—I won't look at them!"

I followed He Yizhen to her mother's house, and when I came to stand by her bed, she was very happy to see me, calling me her great benefactor, because I had introduced her to Buddhism, to reciting the name of the Buddha, and to the original vow of Amitābha. She very happily told me herself of all the things she had seen with her eyes closed. Then she said, "A month ago, I couldn't give this up, I couldn't give that up [she was talking about her children and grandchildren]. Now I'm not worried about anything, I don't want anything, I just want Amitābha to quickly come and meet me. I'll happily go with him!"

On the morning of the 14th, Laywoman Huang's sons, daughters, daughters-in-law, and grandchildren were with me in her room. She waved her hand and said, "Since you are all here, I want to tell you that you shouldn't cry for me. If you cry, you will just holding me back. I don't want to be held back at all; you should all just happily send me off!"

Laywoman Huang had a sister who lived in the same unit, and she often came to weep at her sister's bed about leaving the world behind, and that the love of her children would endure. Laywoman Huang told her to leave, saying, "I don't want to hear this kind of stuff; it makes my heart uneasy. I just want to hear the recording of 'Namo Amitābha.'"

On the afternoon of the 14th, I went with her daughter to Laywoman Huang's bedside, and she said to us, "I just now saw him come." At the same time, we both asked her, "Whom did you see?" She replied, "He was just like the statue on the table." (On her table there was a statue of Amitābha as he had appeared in America, something I had given her when she first started to study Buddhism.) The two of us asked her again, "Where was he?" She said, "He was in midair, and I tried to grab him, but my hands couldn't reach. I wanted to grab on and not let go, so I could go with him."

That evening, He Yizhen stayed behind to take care of her mother, and I went to He's house to rest. On the morning of the 15th I was bowing before the statue of the Buddha at He's house, and I thought of how Laywoman Huang was bleeding and leaking foul fluids, which had to be very painful. So in front of the Buddha, I entreated him, saying, "Amitābha! Since you are great and compassionate, saving even those who commit the five great crimes and the ten evil deeds,[9] please quickly come to meet Laywoman Huang. Soon, soon, soon—come to meet her!"

I lifted my head from where I lay prone on the floor, with my eyes closed. Suddenly it was if my spirit had left my body, and it seemed like Amitābha was transporting me. I saw myself at once reach Laywoman Huang's bedside, and saw an enormous Amitābha extending his right hand and taking her arm, lifting her up and flying off. Laywoman Huang grasped his hand, as small as a little dot, like a little swallow. I immediately thought of the phrase "to take up and not let go" from the scriptures, and my heart was filled with emotion and gratitude. I knew with certainty that Laywoman Huang would be reborn without obstruction.

When I saw Huang Xiagui [in the vision], she was wearing a jade-white jacket and a deep blue skirt, and I only saw her from behind. Later I asked He Yizhen what Huang Xiagui was wearing, and what He told me matched what I had seen.

That same morning, I was just about to leave He Yizhen's house to go see Laywoman Huang when I received a phone call from her granddaughter, who was calling from abroad. She said that in her dream she had seen a sign that her grandmother wanted to leave, so she got out of bed and read the forty-eight vows (of Amitābha) and then recited, "Namo Amitābha." When she had made one recitation there was a beam of golden light, and when she said his name again there was another beam of light. She could see them even when she closed her eyes. She asked Amitābha to let her grandmother live a little longer. I said, "Oh no, you need to change your thinking and ask Amitābha to quickly greet your Grandma and take her to be reborn, because your grandma cannot return to health, and is suffering a lot! If you don't, and you are asking Amitābha to let her live a little longer, and we are asking him to quickly come to meet her, what will Amitābha do?" She replied that given the circumstances she would just go along with what we were doing. (I was very familiar with all three generations of the family.)

Because Huang Xiagui had not said which day she was going to be reborn, I went back to Qianjiang on the afternoon of the 15th. The events between the evening of the 15th and the morning of the 17th were told to me by He Yizhen.

He Yizhen said, "On the morning of the 16th, Huang Xiagui asked me what time it was. I told her it was 9 a.m. She said 'Oh no! If it is past 9 a.m. I won't be able to go today, and will have to wait until tomorrow.'" (She said she had been born at nine in the morning and wanted to leave before nine in the morning, so she talked about the time and not which day.)

Her daughter told me that when it got light on the morning of the 17th, it was just after 4 a.m. She had her eyes closed but she saw golden light. In the light there was a Buddha on a throne on a lotus, approaching from afar, getting bigger and bigger, until he was just outside the window. She immediately opened her eyes, and then couldn't see him. She thought to herself, this is certainly the Buddha who is coming to meet my mother. After it was completely light, at 7:40 a.m., Laywoman Huang went to be reborn.

After this, her daughter called me to come over. When I got there it was about 10 a.m., and her body was still on the bed with yellow paper covering her face. I lifted the paper and recited "Namo Amitābha" three times and discovered that Huang's right eyelid lifted up so that it appeared half open, and I could see her eyeball. After this I again closed her eyes, and her face wore a smile.

Laywoman Huang's face was full of wrinkles when she was alive, but after she had gone to be reborn, the wrinkles unfolded and her face was smooth.

There was a small incident on the 18th, the day after Laywoman Huang had gone to be reborn. The mother of Huang's daughter-in-law blamed everyone for not putting something frozen under the corpse, and said that there would certainly be rancid water dripping, so someone should quickly get a pot to catch the water.

On the morning of the 19th, the third day after Laywoman Huang had gone to be reborn, I went from He Yizhen's house to Huang's house and there encountered a moving scene. Laywoman Huang's body was on the east side of the room, and to her west was filled with kneeling people. With a glance, I could tell that most of them were not Buddha reciters. In that work group, there were originally only nine people who recited the name of the Buddha. After Laywoman Huang's passing, there were only eight. There were over four hundred people in the work group, so those who recited the name of the Buddha were very few. Normally there were a few good mourners, but this time many people came to see her body. The 19th, the third day after rebirth, the body was still soft and with no decay. When people saw this kind of thing, they were shocked, and said, "This is truly rare! How can there be someone who dies and does not get stiff! And with such warm weather (it was about 35 degrees Celsius), after three days, how could the body not change color! There's no decay!" With this, those who saw her naturally felt respect, and together bowed to her. There were even manual laborers who brought their work tools, and when they saw the situation also bowed down. (There were over twenty people.)

## A Felon Recollects the Buddha, and Amitābha Comes to Greet Him

From *Minglun yuekan* 156 (1985), reprinted in Huijing, *Nianfo ganying lu,* vol. 1, 303–306.

I am the manager of the guard section at the Taizhong prison and also a lay disciple who has taken refuge in the Three Jewels of the Buddhist teaching. Two years ago, our prison extended a formal invitation to Teacher Jiang of the Taizhong Lotus Society to come to the prison to spread the teachings of the Pure Land. Thereupon the habit of reciting the name of the Buddha spontaneously began to grow, and the dharma-joy of Amitābha spread to every corner of the prison.

In December of last year, there was a prisoner Lin Yisi, seventy years old, from Houli. When he was young, he entered into the wrong path, and spent most of his life behind bars. His crimes included murder, theft, obscene acts, and so forth, and one could say that his criminal record was piled up with felonies. At that time, because he had committed a crime against public decency, he was serving a sentence of several years. When he came to prison, because he was old and weak, he was suffering from serious kidney disease. Warden Hu has a bodhisattva's heart and assigned me to escort him to Taizhong hospital for treatment. His fees were paid by the prison, and the warden exhorted the guards to take good care of him.

Our fellow sufferer Lin, although he had not taken refuge in the Buddha, because the Lotus Society had spread the dharma at the prison, had had his eyes and ears filled with the teaching. When people met each other, they joined their hands together in salutation and said "Amitābha!" There is a saying, "The Buddha-dharma is like honey, sweet all the way through," and it fits here.[10]

One day at noon I was tasked with going to Taizhong Hospital to watch fellow sufferer Lin. The nurse told me that his illness had taken a turn for the worse, his life was in danger, and the family should be informed so they could take care of him. Lin was alone without wife or children, so there was just me to wholeheartedly take care of him, to help him change his clothes and to feed him, and serve him medicinal decoctions. I also recited the name of the Buddha on his behalf, and dedicated my merit to him. Around one o'clock, Lin revived a bit and returned to consciousness. According to the method in the Lotus Society's book *Chizhong xuzhi* (What one must know when approaching the end), I taught him to recite the name of the Buddha and seek rebirth. When I told him the story of how the butcher Zhang Shanhe of the Tang dynasty gained rebirth,[11] and about Amitābha, king of the forty-eight vows, this increased his faith.

At first, Lin's karmic obstructions were considerable, and because his family did not come to visit, for a while sadness welled up in his heart, his eyes brimmed with tears, and he cried without stopping. After a while, I suddenly heard him shout out, "There's a ghost! There's a ghost! I won't go, I won't! Don't grab me!" I personally saw this, and knew that his karma was coming to fruition right then, as the gates of hell opened. Thereupon I solemnly told him in a loud voice, "Throughout your life you did many bad things, and now your evil karma is upon you, even to the point where the demons of hell have come to grab you before your death. If you don't now quickly repent and recite the name of Amitābha, and implore Amitābha to compassionately come and lead you to the Western Pure Land, when will you do so? I will recite on your behalf (*zhunian* 助念), but if you don't wake up again, then the ghosts have tied you up and there will be no escape." I instructed him to recite the name of the Buddha, but also took out the small image of the Three Sages of the Pure Land from the Lotus Society that I carried with me, and placed in front of Lin's face, in order to help him recollect the Buddha.

The Buddha-dharma is inconceivable, and Lin's good roots from a former life miraculously appeared at the key moment of his death and in the end he was able to follow my exhortations and murmur the name of Amitābha. His personality was such that he could not refuse, and as I led him and assisted his recitation, the sound of Amitābha filled the room, entirely harmonious.

After about a stick of incense, I asked him how he was. He answered me slowly: "I don't see the demon . . . Amitābha has come! Amitābha has come!" At the end I saw his face fill with a smile, and knew that he had left the world without pain. After he died, his face was vivid, as if alive. His body was soft and pliable, and these auspicious omens made one sigh in amazement.

When most prisoners go to the hospital for treatment, they have to wear shackles, and Lin was no exception. When another guard, surnamed Cai, was taking off the shackles, I said a silent prayer: Lin, if you have been reborn in the Western Pure Land, let the shackles come off at once as proof. The response of reciting the Buddha's name is really inconceivable! Normally it takes a great deal of strength to support the prisoner in a sitting position, and then one must use a iron hammer and a steel knife, unceasingly going at the shackles until they come off. In the end, it didn't even take the strength of blowing a feather—with just a couple of taps, the shackles came off the dead man's body.

No wonder the guard Cai said, "This is the merit of Amitābha." Also, there was an older gentleman who worked in the morgue and was charged with handling the body, and he clicked his tongue in astonishment: "I've never seen a dead person so good looking! And even more, he's a prisoner! This is really due to Amitābha's protection."

This is a true story about someone doing bad things his whole life, repenting and reciting Amitābha's name when he approached death, and then being led by the Buddha to be reborn. Therefore those who deeply believe in the path of Pure Land Buddhism, and cultivate myriad good practices and encourage others, should not harbor any doubt or feel inferior for getting caught up in ordinary words, let alone words about the pure land. One should sincerely promote copractitioners and not look down on the wonderful Pure Land teaching of "the three roots are all covered" and "carrying karma to be reborn."[12]

## Notes

1 Robert Sharf, *Coming to Terms with Chinese Buddhism: A Reading of the Treasure Store Treatise* (Honolulu: University of Hawai'i Press, 2002), 82–88.

2 For example, see the account of Lady Yueguo, translated in Daniel Stevenson, "Death-Bed Testimonials of the Pure Land Faithful," in *Buddhism in Practice*, ed. Donald S. Lopez Jr. (Princeton, NJ: Princeton University Press, 1995), 598–600.

3 Zhe Ji, "Expectation, Affection, and Responsibility: The Charismatic Journey of a New Buddhist Group in Taiwan," *Nova Religio: The Journal of Alternative and Emergent Religions* 12, no. 2 (2008): 59–63. See also Chinese Pure Land Buddhist Association, "Dharma Master Huijing," http://purelandbuddhism.org/About/DHuijing.htm, accessed July 30, 2015.

4 A brief biography of Jingzong can be found at Chinese Pure Land Buddhist Association, "Dharma Master Jingzong," http://purelandbuddhism.org/About/DJingzong.htm, accessed July 30, 2015.

5 For discussion of the distribution of free materials, especially morality books, see Gareth Fisher, "Morality Books and the Regrowth of Lay Buddhism in China," in *Religion in Contemporary China: Revitalization and Innovation*, ed. Adam Yuet Chau (London: Routledge, 2011).

6 Although this may not be implied here, "adamantine recitation" (*jingang nian*金剛念) is listed among four types of recitation.

7 The triad is made up of Amitābha, Avilokatêśvara, and Mahāsthāmaprāpta.

8 Shandao (613–681) was a dedicated practitioner of veneration of Amitābha and promoted Pure Land practices widely. He is recognized as a patriarch of the Pure Land tradition by both Chinese and Japanese Pure Land traditions.

9 The five great crimes are acts for which one would be expelled from the Buddhist community: killing one's father, killing one's mother, killing an arhat, harming the Buddha, or destroying monastic harmony. The ten evil deeds are killing, stealing, licentious behavior, lying, flattery, insult, treachery, covetousness, anger, and wrong views.

10 This phrase appears in *Sishierzhang jing* (Scripture in forty-two sections), *T.* 17, no. 784, 724a9.

11 Told in many sources, the story of Zhang Shanhe recounts that as he approached death the butcher was confronted by the cattle he had killed. A

monk told Zhang that he was destined to fall into one of the evil paths, but that this could be avoid by reciting Amitābha's name ten times. Zhang did so, and was rewarded with a vision of Amitābha coming to escort him to the pure land. For one version of the story, see Peng Xisu (d. 1793), *Jingtu shengxian lu* (Record of the sages and worthies of the Pure Land). Shinsan Dai Nihon zokuzōkyō 新纂大日本續藏經. Edited by Kawamura Kōshō 河村孝照. Tokyo: Kokusho Kankōkai, [1975–1989], 78, no. 1549, 304c.

12 "Three roots" (*sangen*) refers to the three levels of capacity of human beings, and the phrase indicates that reciting the name of Amitābha is salvific for all of them. Here the phrase means that one should not look down on people of lower capacity. Those who "carry karma" (*daiye*) of evil deeds need Amitābha to escort them to the pure land, while those who have rid themselves of their karma (*xiaoye*) are spontaneously born there.

## Bibliography

Chinese Pure Land Buddhist Association. "Dharma Master Huijing (慧淨法師)." http://purelandbuddhism.org/About/DHuijing.htm. Accessed July 30, 2015.

———. "Dharma Master Jingzong (淨宗法師)." http://purelandbuddhism.org/About/DJingzong.htm. Accessed July 30, 2015.

Fisher, Gareth. "Morality Books and the Regrowth of Lay Buddhism in China." In *Religion in Contemporary China: Revitalization and Innovation,* edited by Adam Yuet Chau. London: Routledge, 2011.

Huijing, comp. *Nianfo ganying lu* (Records of the sympathetic resonance of recollecting the Buddha's name), vol. 1. Taibei: Jingtuzong wenjiao jijin hui, 2004.

Ji, Zhe. "Expectation, Affection, and Responsibility: The Charismatic Journey of a New Buddhist Group in Taiwan." *Nova Religio: The Journal of Alternative and Emergent Religions* 12, no. 2 (2008): 48–68.

Jones, Charles B. "Foundations of Ethics and Practice in Chinese Pure Land Buddhism." *Journal of Buddhist Ethics* 10 (2003): 2–20.

Sharf, Robert H. *Coming to Terms with Chinese Buddhism: A Reading of the Treasure Store Treatise.* Honolulu: University of Hawai'i Press, 2002.

Stevenson, Daniel B. "Death-Bed Testimonials of the Pure Land Faithful." In *Buddhism in Practice*, edited by Donald S. Lopez Jr., 592–602. Princeton, NJ: Princeton University Press, 1995.

Sun Yanfei. "The Chinese Buddhist Ecology in Post-Mao China: Contours, Types and Dynamics." *Social Compass* 58, no. 4 (2011): 498–510.

## Chapter 3

# In Praise of His Mighty Name

## *A Tibetan Poem on Amitābha from Dunhuang*

Jonathan A. Silk

Nothing, it is obvious to say, is meaningful or valuable in isolation, and the significance, and subsequently the value, of something can only be determined by a context. Nor is it surprising that cultural artifacts, like any other objects, have significance only in context, at a particular location at a particular time, and to a particular person or persons, a community. From this it follows that if we choose to view an object in a decontextualized frame—without reference to any specific community—we surrender any chance to discern the object's value, since this can only be assigned by some person or persons. But the matter is not entirely simple, since traditions are by definition nonspecific, nonparticular, and nonlocal, and the generalization inherent in the formation of tradition requires an easing, or even erasure, of local distinctions, a glossing over of the individual in favor of the generic. As a result of this simple reasoning, we are compelled to conclude that our appreciation of, for instance, a religious text must balance its specific and generic loci. This is a balance that is often difficult to achieve.

Religious traditions are communities of individuals. We know—or persuade ourselves that we know—what these individuals thought and did on the basis of evidence produced by these individuals, evidence such as texts and physical objects. From an examination of this evidence we form a picture of the worldview of, let us say, "Tibetan Buddhism" or "Pure Land Buddhism," while knowing full well from the outset that there has never existed one, single Tibetan or Pure Land Buddhism, abstracted from time and place. What exists is particular evidence, local in time and place, and an abstraction that ties multiple instances together over space and time. Whether a particular piece of evidence—a certain scripture, let us say—is also found in some form in other times and places as well does not materially alter the fact that each instance is in itself local to begin with.

Traditions, by virtue of their translocal and universalizing nature, have a tendency to erase the local, due in part to the fact that the authority, legitimacy, and vitality of traditions stem from their very (claim to) universality. When we consider texts belonging to—in the sense of "honored by"—traditions, it follows that such texts both are inherently local, being used by individuals in specific times and places, and general, being shared across diverse times and place, with the result that they are simultaneously the property of all, but when considered in the abstract, the property of none, of no particular individual or community.

It is not difficult to locate individual objects, such as manuscripts or paintings. What is harder is to set them in a meaningful contextual frame. The literary antecedents of a text or the stylistic antecedents of a painting are just as important for its understanding as the social, political, or historical circumstances of its production, and this type of context might be termed "original." Another type of context is one imposed on objects by a later community retrospectively, a point to which I will return below.

In addition to a tremendous treasure of visual documentation painted on the walls themselves, the sealed repository of discarded documents found early in this century in the cave-temples of Dunhuang in western China has provided us with a huge amount of manuscript material, of interest to political and social historians, to linguists, and to scholars of religion. Much is already known about Dunhuang during its cultural heyday until the ninth or tenth century, and the documents recovered from the "sacred dust heap" continue to be studied by a growing legion of specialists. For readers of the present book, the documents of greatest interest are likely to be those that deal most directly with Buddhism. These make accessible, among many other things, Chinese and Tibetan manuscript versions of texts frequently far older than the versions preserved in standardized canonical collections, first of all in the Tibetan Kanjurs and the Chinese *Dazangjing*. All these materials are by definition local, although they may be related to traditions defined by other objects as well. But in addition to manuscripts containing versions of known and translocal texts, there are many others that contain texts entirely unknown to the canonical traditions. These texts are deeply interesting in that we recognize them as inherently particular, since they were apparently local products that were never generalized and never universalized.[1] Part of the effort to provide an "original" context for such works within the world of Dunhuang involves the attempt to read them in light of the entire library of Dunhuang Buddhist culture. Subsequently, one might also seek to understand such texts in the broader context of, respectively, the Chinese and Tibetan Buddhist cultures, not to mention the cultural history of humanity. But the initial task must be to edit the texts, reconstruct them where necessary, and read them in a much more limited, even minimally contextualized, frame.

The text I call "The Praise of the Name of the Tathāgata Amitābha" is one example of this local literature, a hymn written in the Tibetan language, of which only six fragmentary manuscripts from Dunhuang are known to exist.[2] Since my earlier publication in 1993 I have identified an additional leaf of one of the manuscripts then used, now edited in the appendix to this chapter.[3] No other Tibetan version, nor model in any other language, has yet been identified. The poem of fifty-nine verses, each consisting of four seven-syllable lines, must be reconstructed from these six fragmentary manuscripts, none of which contains the complete set of verses.[4] Most of the manuscripts also contain exclamations to *Amita, that is to the Buddha Amitābha / Amitāyus,[5] written after each quarter of each verse. I believe these are not integral to the text, but rather a part of the liturgical instructions for its recitation, similar to the "Amen" that in Jewish or Christian prayer books indicates the proper congregational response. One of the things that is so interesting about these exclamations is their language. The poem itself is in Tibetan, and naturally the manuscripts are written in Tibetan script. The exclamations are also written in Tibetan script: *a myi ta pur, na mo a myi ta pur.* But this is not understandable as Tibetan language; the language is in fact Chinese, a transcription of 阿彌陀佛 南無阿彌陀佛, the medieval pronunciation of which was something like ʔâ-mjie-dâ-bjwət nậm-mju ʔâ-mjie-dâ-bjwət (Modern Standard Chinese: *amituofo nanwu amituofo*),[6] "Amita Buddha! Namo [Homage to] Amita Buddha!" This suggests that the manuscripts, if not also the text they contain, may date to the time of the Tibetan occupation of Dunhuang, the period of roughly 780–850, although the manuscripts might also be later, even as late as the tenth or eleventh century.[7]

It is virtually certain that this text as presented by its manuscripts was intended for recitation in a community in which Tibetan-Chinese bilingualism was common, if not the norm. Those manuscripts that accompany the text with interjections after each quarter verse seem to present the poem as something like a mantric composition, intended for rhythmical recitation in a cultic setting, rather than for primarily literary enjoyment, or at least they present it *also* as a mantric composition.[8] But a text may simultaneously have more than one function. The *Heart Sūtra,* for example, was and continues to be widely used for virtually mantric recitation in many cultural contexts, but at least one of its functions was, and perhaps still is, also to serve as a precis of the doctrine of the Perfection of Wisdom. In the same way, while *stotra,* or praise literature—one genre into which our poem falls—is surely designed not only, and probably not primarily, for study or poetic appreciation but rather for oral recitation, the type of recitation that was intended seems unlikely to have been the mantric, meditative, or ecstatic type.[9] In general, poetry is designed to be recited or read as poetry, rather than, for example, as mantra. If one does not, therefore, pay attention to the poetic qualities of the verses, an important facet of their "meaning" goes unnoticed. That our text may in fact be understood as poetry or song is strongly suggested not only by its form, including a number of structural rhythmical repetitions in the final quarters of verses, but also by its imagery, some of which is shared not only with the *Sukhāvatīvyūha* (Pure Land) sutras and other classical scriptural literature, but even with the highly literary poems of Mātr̥ceṭa and other Buddhist poets.[10] Some of the images are stereotypical in Buddhist literature, such as the image of a Buddha worshipped by Brahma and other gods (vs. 7), and the flowers of the limbs of awakening (vs. 8), common in the Avadāna literature. Striking however is the analogy (vs. 46) between one dwelling in the jungle as an ascetic, like a lion, and the man-lion, who is the Buddha. Equally striking is the pun in the following verse between the ascetic sitting at the foot of a tree and sitting at the foot of the bodhi tree in order to reach the seat of awakening, with its play on the meanings of the term *bodhimaṇḍa,* the physical seat beneath the bodhi tree in Bodh Gaya and the metaphorical spot of awakening, which is Awakening itself.

A complication in our appreciation of the poetic qualities of the work is the question of the language in which it was originally written. While there are a few examples of uncomfortable phrasing that could suggest it as a translation, there are also puns or apparent puns in the Tibetan that would argue for its original composition in that language. A not unlikely possibility is that within the multicultural and multilingual context of Dunhuang the poet was influenced from different quarters, melding both Tibetan and Chinese elements in an almost seamless fabric.

The overall structure of the poem is very clear and has been analyzed in the following way:[11]

| Verse | | |
|---|---|---|
| 1–11: | Reverence | |
| and | | Fruit of the Buddha |
| 12–19: | Array of the buddha-field | |
| 20–25: | Six Perfections and the land | Cause of the Buddha |
| 26–30: | Sentient beings in the land | Fruit of Rebirth |
| 31–59: | Practice for Rebirth | Cause of Rebirth |

This structure elegantly divides the text into two halves: Buddha and sentient beings, cause and effect. In more detail, the fifty-nine verses may also be analyzed as follows:

Verses 1–11: All read in the last line "Thus I devoutly pay homage to him."

1–5: Praise of the "mighty name."

1: A general praise of Amitābha, mentioning that name.

2–5: Begin with "If one were to hear this mighty name,"[12] and continue with the various benefits that come from that practice.

6–10: Praise of various aspects of Amitābha's powers continues.

Verse 11: Transitional. This verse contains the stock line of homage, but begins the praise of the pure field that follows.

Verses 11–19: Description of the pure field.

Verses 20–25: The pure field is perfected by correct practice of the six perfections, each perfection being given a verse. The six verses are almost identical, only the name of the perfection and the verb vary.

Verses 26–30: Description of the state of beings born in the pure field.

Verse 31: Transitional. What happens at the time of death.

Verses 32–59: All are constructed with a condition expressed in lines a–c, "if such-and-such practices are carried out," then in line d: "One will be born in that pure field."

32–39: Various practices are listed, including practicing the ten virtuous acts (*daśakuśala*), cultivating the four infinitudes (*brahmavihāras*), reverencing one's parents, keeping the precepts, and producing the aspiration for awakening. Many of the practices seem monastic.

40–51: Advocacy of the cultivation of the twelve ascetic purification practices (*dhūtaguṇa*), each practice described in its own verse.

52–59: Advocacy of the cultivation of abstruse philosophical doctrines as a path to the pure field.

Doctrinally the text spans a broad spectrum. It advocates the mere hearing of the name of Amitābha, and details the fruits that flow from this—at least superficially passive—act. But at the same time it praises the generic Mahāyāna Buddhist practice of cultivating the six perfections, presumably performed by Amitābha himself (though this is not clear), and goes on to the rigorous monastic, renunciant practices of the twelve ascetic purification practices, the *dhūtaguṇas.* Finally, the last portion of the poem concerns the correct understanding of rather abstruse philosophical doctrines, including abandoning being and nonbeing (52), the Buddha's *dharmatā* (53), nonapprehension of the two extremes (54), the lack of self-nature even in illusions (56), the not-one-not-many (57), and even some ideas reminiscent of the Rdzogs chen, such as the use of the deeply resonant term *gzhi.* The doctrinal content, then, is vastly inclusive, if anything tending toward the philosophical and monastic or renunciant, rather than the devotional.

Many of the ideas and images in the poem, especially those that characterize the pure land and its inhabitants, can be found already expressed in the Larger and Smaller *Sukhāvatīvyūha* sutras, and to a lesser extent in the *Guan Wuliangshoufo jing* (Sūtra of contemplation on the Buddha of Immeasurable Life), although such ideas and descriptions, it should be noted, are by no means limited to those texts. Despite the final third of the poem, from verse 40 onwards, which is thoroughly unrelated to them, the Pure Land scriptures do seem to be the direct inspiration for at least major parts of the poem. No doubt influenced at least in part by this, Akamatsu presented the poem as an example of "Tibetan literature related to the Pure Land teachings."[13]

Given the general tendency to see literature that deals in any way with the Buddha Amitābha as "Pure Land" literature, it will be helpful to inquire about the senses in which we can speak of something as being "related to the Pure Land teachings." In other words, what is the justification for our placing objects entirely unknown to later tradition within the context of that tradition? Are we justified in expanding the canon of a tradition, in deciding that the implicit definitions of canonicity we derive from a tradition's choices may be further applied to enter new objects into the canon of that tradition?[14]

In ordinary modern Japanese the term *jōdokyō* is used with a strong resonance of the doctrines and teachings of Hōnen (1133–1212) and

Shinran (1173–1262) and their schools, respectively the Jōdoshū (Pure Land Sect) and the Jōdo Shinshū (True Pure Land Sect).[15] If by "Pure Land" is meant, however, that system of beliefs and resultant practices which emphasizes exclusively, or almost exclusively, the saving power of the Buddha Amitābha / Amitāyus (hereafter only Amitābha, for the sake of brevity), requiring of the devotee faith in that buddha's power for the purpose of obtaining not direct buddhahood but rather rebirth in Sukhāvatī, and moreover to a great extent rejecting the viability of traditional elite Buddhist practices, then we must reach two main conclusions.

First, the Pure Land devotionalism just described arose only in medieval Japan, specifically under the influence of Hōnen and Shinran. It has antecedents, to be sure, in some writings of Dao'an (313–385), Shandao (613–681) and others, but the Chinese versions of Pure Land faith were not nearly as exclusivistic and single-minded as the Japanese. That Indian texts like the Larger and Smaller *Sukhāvatīvyūha* sutras represent Pure Land thought as a uniquely identifiable system or creed in the Indian milieu can be maintained only by denying these scriptures their context within the whole of Mahāyāna Buddhist literature.[16] The second conclusion we can draw is that the version of Pure Land thought that we find in our poem has as much affinity with generalized medieval Mahāyāna doctrines as it does with anything justifiably labeled Pure Land in the aforementioned exclusivistic sense.[17]

Akamatsu has also suggested that our text is related to texts like the *Aparimitāyurjñāna Sūtra* on the one hand, and the hymns of Tanluan (476–542), Shandao, and Fazhao (d. ca. 820) on the other.[18] This is apparently based on his assumption that the repetition of the phrase *A mi ta pur, namo a mi ta pur* is an integral part of the text. The texts of Tanluan and the others are praises of Amitābha that actually contain the same or similar interjections as those in our manuscripts, that is *nanwu amituofo* (Homage to Amita Buddha), *nanwu zhixin guimingli xifang amituofo* 南無至心歸命禮西方阿彌陀佛 (Homage, I wholeheartedly take refuge in Amita Buddha of the western quarter), and so forth. And in many manuscripts of the *Aparimitāyurjñāna Sūtra* we find the frequent repetition of a *dhāraṇī* interspersed with the text. Since I consider the interjections in our poem to be additions, appended for the purposes of cultic recitation, I do not believe that conclusions can be drawn about the genre of the text on this basis. The connection of our poem with Chinese hymns should, however, be further investigated.[19]

At the same time, and perhaps even more directly, an attempt must be made to examine all similar literature in Tibetan from Dunhuang, which ultimately must include an effort to understand this literature in light of Chinese materials as well. So far, apparently the only scholar to have approached this subject seriously is Akamatsu.[20] In addition to the poem studied here and research on Dunhuang Tibetan versions of the two *Sukhāvatīvyūha* sutras,[21] he has published an edition and translation of a poem of uncertain title concerning Amitābha,[22] and he has examined, but not published an edition or translation of, a poem called *Snang ba mtha' yas kyi [zhing gi] yon tan la rnal 'byor pas bstod pa* (The Yogin's praise of the virtuous qualities of [the land of] Amitābha).[23] In a further work, Akamatsu introduced a number of Dunhuang manuscripts that mention Amitābha in one way or another, but almost none of them have Amitābha or Sukhāvatī as a central theme and, as Akamatsu points out, most of them are in fact tantric.[24]

Forty years ago, Gregory Schopen argued for the generalization of the ideal of Sukhāvatī, which becomes a reward not only for acts of devotion or practices connected with Amitābha, but for Buddhist religious practices in general, wherever they be directed.[25] This raises the question why acts directed toward Amitābha and leading toward the reward of rebirth in Sukhāvatī should have a historically special status. Schopen does not address this question, and in fact seems to assume that the direction of influence is from a specialized Amitābha cult toward a more generalized cultic doctrine. Without denying the pervasive role of the Pure Land Sukhāvatī in Indian Buddhist literature, it is equally plausible to maintain that the particular cultic connection between Amitābha and Sukhāvatī has taken on a special, exaggerated importance only in the light of later sectarian developments in the Far East, and specifically in Japan from the medieval period on, and that such a connection is not a central element of Indian Buddhism.[26] This raises the historical question of the causes of the rise of Pure Land devotionalism in the Far East, but frees us from the responsibility of seeking everywhere in Indian Buddhism for Pure Land elements. The reason, I would suggest, why documents such as the present poem are distinguished from other types of praises lies more in modern Japanese sectarianism than in the historical situation of the texts themselves. We have, after all, no specific "Mañjuśrī Buddhism," despite the widespread popularity of texts such as the *Mañjuśrī-nāmasaṁgīti*. It is not that our poem and other texts like it do not contain Pure Land type doctrines, for obviously they do. Rather, these elements do not necessarily indicate any exclusively Amitābha-directed cultic activity, nor do they indicate by their doctrines a special historical connection with Pure Land proper, that is (as I suggest above), with specifically medieval Japanese Buddhist concerns.

Our poem focuses primarily on Amitābha and on the goal of rebirth in his land. Whether in the full context of Dunhuang Buddhism this might make it a "Pure Land" text as defined above remains for me unclear. But there is little to lead us to place it in a doctrinal continuum with the thought of Hōnen or Shinran, and from this point of view it seems misleading as well as historically anachronistic and unjustifiable to assign it to the category of "Pure Land thought."[27] In addition, as mentioned above, the poem also contains some highly philosophical sections. The ideas mentioned there are not, so far as I know, specific to any one school, but they evidence a familiarity on the part of the author with the main topics of Mahāyāna Buddhist philosophical dogmatics. Likewise, the exposition of the ascetic purification practices shows a familiarity with a topic of general concern in generic Buddhist literature, especially that dealing with the proper renunciant life. From this point of view, it should be emphasized that despite some sections that clearly presuppose a nonmonastic audience, the poem as a whole cannot properly be interpreted as an expression of lay piety; the discussion of the ascetic purification practices and of the meditation on advanced topics of Buddhist dogmatics strongly suggests an intended audience of—or at least prominently including—professional monastics.

Despite a widespread, although perhaps vague, awareness of the influences China has had on Tibetan Buddhism, in general there still seems to be a presumption that when we look for antecedents of Tibetan practices and ideas we should turn to India. The present poem serves as an example perhaps suggesting that, at least in part, the genre of prayers for rebirth in the pure land of Amitābha so common in later Tibetan Buddhism might owe some of its inspiration not directly, for example, to the basic scriptures of the Pure Land traditions, the so-called Larger and Smaller *Sukhāvatīvyūha* sutras—although they are frequently cited—but rather to earlier Chinese models, perhaps by way of texts such as that studied here. At this stage in the investigation of Tibetan Buddhist history, we are unable to specify in detail possible influences of this type. In fact, until recently, most research on Pure Land traditions in Tibet—almost all of which has been done by Japanese scholars—concentrated on the Tibetan translations of the two Sanskrit *Sukhāvatīvyūha* sutras. Such investigations, however, clearly tell us very little about Tibetan traditions per se.[28] Rather more meaningful in this regard are the studies of

Onoda Shunzō, Kajihama Ryōshun, and others,[29] which have paid attention primarily to prayers for rebirth in Sukhāvatī (*bde smon*).

Onoda, for example, identifies two traditions of Pure Land type materials in Tibetan literature. One he locates in the Dge lugs pa, particularly in a text of Tsong kha pa (1357–1419), the *Bde ba can gyi zhing du skye ba 'dzin pa'i smon lam zhing mchog sgo 'byed* (Opening the door to the best land: A prayer to obtain birth in the Land of Bliss),[30] and in a later commentary on Tsong kha pa's text by the first Lcang skya Ngag dbang blo bzang chos ldan dpal bzang po (1642–1714), his *Zhing mchog sgo 'byed kyi dmigs rim mdor bsdus* (Summary of the stages of visualization according to "Opening the Door to the Best Land").[31] The same author has also written the *Bde ba can gyi zhing du bgrod pa'i myur lam gsal bar byed pa'i sgron me* (The clarifying lamp: A quick path for travel to the Land of Bliss).[32] The list of similar texts could easily be multiplied to include such texts as the *Bde ba can gyi smon lam dag zhing nye lam* (A shortcut to the Pure Land: A vow for the Land of Bliss)[33] by Sum pa mkhan po Ye shes dpal 'byor (1704–1788), and many others.[34]

Another tradition, of course not unrelated, is that of the Karma Bka' brgyud scholar Karma chags med, who probably belongs to the seventeenth century, and his *Rnam dag bde chen zhing gi smon lam* (A vow for the Land of Highest Bliss), with its commentary *Rnam dag bde chen zhing gi smon lam gyi 'byed 'grel bde chen zhing du bgrod pa'i them skas bzang po* (A wonderful staircase for ascension to the Land of Great Bliss: Commentary to a vow for the Land of Highest Bliss). This text has been examined a number of times by modern scholars, even as long ago as 1932, and translated into Japanese, German, and English.[35]

Other texts that have been translated so far into Japanese include a *'Pho ba* text of the eighteenth century Chu bzang bla ma Ye shes rgya mtsho,[36] the *Bde ba can gyi zhing du thogs pa med par bgrod pa'i myur lam* (An unhindered quick path to the Land of Bliss) of the first Panchen Lama Blo bzang chos kyi rgyal mthan (1567–1662),[37] the *Bde ba can gyi zhing sbyong ba'i dad pa gsal bar byed pa drang srong lung gi nyi ma* (The sun of the sage's instruction called clarification of faith [leading to] cultivation of the Land of Bliss) of Mi pham 'Jam dbyangs rnam rgyal rgya mtsho (1846–1912),[38] and parts of the *Bde ba can gyi zhing las brtsams pa'i gtam dge ba'i lo tog spel byed dbyar skyes sprin chen glal ba'i sgra dbyangs* (A talk on the Land of Bliss: Thundering sound from the big bursting summer clouds which nourish the Crops of Good Qualities) of the third Rdo Grub chen Rinpoche (1865–1926).[39]

A determination of the relation of such texts to the so-called Pure Land materials in Tibetan from Dunhuang, which by way of illustration probably predate Tsong kha pa's time by as much as five or six centuries, and that of Karma chags med by perhaps nine, must be a task for the future. But in addition to their intrinsic interest and their value for an investigation of local Buddhism in Dunhuang, one of the things Tibetan materials such as the poem presented here do is remind us that our search for sources of later Tibetan traditions must encompass not only Indian but also Chinese antecedents as well, despite the well-known official history that holds that the so-called Council of Bsam yas set Tibetan Buddhism on an unalterable course blown by Indian winds alone. Without any doubt, some, at least, of the gentle, cool breezes which always blow in the Land of Bliss also blew, across the Tibetan plateau, from east to west.

The translation offered here remains tentative; there are more than a few verses I only poorly understand. Following the translation, a section of commentary provides notes on the individual verses. Verse numbers, not found in the original, have been added to the translation.

## Translation

### *The Praise of the Name of the Tathāgata Amitābha*

1 The Sugata Amitābha
Possesses masses of infinite merit.
His mighty name is famous throughout the ten directions.
Thus I devoutly pay homage to him.

2 If someone were to hear this name of his
He would obtain even the stage of nonreturn.
Thus I devoutly proclaim his name and
Placing my hands together I pay homage.

3 If one were to hear this mighty name
All obscurations without exception would be cleansed, and
Defilements without exception would be thoroughly purified.
Thus bowing my head I pay homage.

4 If one were to hear this mighty name
He would obtain the great buddha stage, and

He would exhaust the suffering of birth and death.
Thus bowing my head I pay homage.

5 If one were to hear this mighty name
Terrifying to Māra and false teachers
He would attain the stage of victory.
Thus bowing my head I pay homage.

6 Since he possesses the marvelous, immeasurable double accumulation,
His highest dharma of control is limitless, and
He is praised by all the buddhas of the ten directions.
Thus bowing my head I pay homage.

7 Brahma and Devendra Śakra and
All the many groups of gods mentally
Touch their jeweled crowns to his feet.
Thus bowing my head I pay homage.

8 Through the flowers of the limbs of awakening
Restrained sentient beings are variously adorned and
Elevated to the level of the best awakening.
Thus bowing my head I pay homage.

9 [Amitābha's] clear wisdom is limitless and
Removes the darkness of delusion.
He teaches countless bright dharma doors.
Thus bowing my head I pay homage.

10 He is the great transformation, the man-lion.
His bodily marks are limitless.[40]
Hearing his name the buddha's mastery is purified.
Thus bowing my head I pay homage.

11 Everywhere in that purified buddha-field
The teaching shines like the rays of the sun,
And the flowers of auspiciousness bloom.
Thus bowing my head I pay homage.

12 That buddha-field is established by those conditions, and
Its multitudinous jewels are causally arisen.[41]
Vast, flat, clear and pure,
Its jeweled tree trunks are crowded together.

13 Its paths are covered with jeweled paving stones,
A web of jewels is spread as an ornament.
The various garments of the gods are scattered.
The sweet smell of the best perfume arises everywhere.

14 Various types of music from sweet voices
Proclaim the names of the three jewels.
The hindrances of all those who hear [the music] are cleared.
All evil paths are cut off.

15 The bathing pools are established by great merit.
Their sides are built up from the seven jewels.
They are scattered with golden pebbles and sand, and
Filled full with the water possessing eight virtuous qualities.

16 [This land is] ornamented by lovely divine flowers, and
Various heavenly birds soar and wander about.
They send forth sweet sounding voices, incomparably lovely.
They possess ten types of lovely sweet-sounding voices according to their inclinations.

17 The palaces of jewels are built up and
The fine and lovely symmetry is seen.
The divine banners are raised and fixed;
Perfume and flowers fall like rain.

18 The hosts of gods worship for a great aeon.
From many and various buddha-fields
Many sons of the conqueror gather there.
They honored that conqueror and entreated him.

19 The sky is covered by a divine canopy
Floating ensigns are fixed in space
Those born from the best fortunate lotus
In order to honor the Sugata gaze intently at his face.

20 Since the ten types of gifts are correctly given
With regard to the pure triple sphere,
Those buddha virtues and
That pure field are completely perfected.

21 Since the ten types of discipline are correctly preserved
With regard to the pure triple sphere,

Those buddha virtues and
That pure field are completely perfected.

22 Since the ten types of patience are correctly cultivated
With regard to the pure triple sphere,
Those buddha virtues and
That pure field are completely perfected.

23 Since the ten types of energy are correctly diligently initiated
With regard to the pure triple sphere,
Those buddha virtues and
That pure field are completely perfected.

24 When the ten types of meditation are correctly cultivated
With regard to the pure triple sphere,[42]
Those buddha virtues and
That pure field are completely perfected.

25 When the ten types of wisdom are correctly manifested
With regard to the pure triple sphere,
Those buddha virtues and
That pure field are completely perfected.

26 If one wants to be born in that buddha field[43]
One must call to mind the three jewels.
All who will be born in that buddha field
Will be possessed of lovely golden color.

27 In full possession of the thirty-two major marks,
Adorned by the eighty minor marks,
Their life span will be immeasurable.
Common people are not born there.

28 Possessing the five superknowledges[44]
They will clearly remember their former existences.
They will also know other minds.
They will display limitless varieties of magical powers.

29 Their divine eye will see infinite fields.
Their magic ear will hear the sound of dharma too.
When protected by the Sugata, one dwells happily.
One practices happily the varieties of great magic.

30 Honoring all the limitless buddhas,
Before the morning is past they return again, [and]
Happily go to their individual places.
They gather at the feet of that buddha.

31 Some hearing the mighty name
Always see the Buddha, the protector.
At the time of [their] death the Sugata shows [them] his face[45]
And they will receive the prophecy of their future joy.

32 Producing the oceanic aspiration for awakening and
Practicing the ten virtues and the pure triple sphere,
If one has honored all the jewels
One will be born in that pure field.

33 One should completely practice the six perfections and
Cultivate the four immeasurables.
If one transfers one's merit in common with all beings
One will be born in that pure field.

34 [One should] reverently pay homage to the supreme ācārya and[46]
Honor one's parents with deference.
If one abandons all haughtiness and pride
One will be born in that pure field.

35 Having served learned people,
Copied and listened to the Good Law,[47]
If understanding its intent one teaches it to others,
One will be born in that pure field.

36 Although one preserves the best eight-part precepts
For a mere day or for a whole lifetime,
If one preserves one's promises insofar as one is able,[48]
One will be born in that pure field.

37 On the six days of the *upoṣadha,* or
During the three-month festivals,
If one produces the aspiration for awakening and preserves the discipline
One will be born in that pure field.

38 If those who received the teachings thusly
Vow to become unimpaired faultless sages and

Preserve [their vows] for as long as life,
They will be born in that pure field.

39 If in order to perfect the unexcelled awakening
The nobles have correctly cultivated
The three doors of liberation,
They will be born in that pure field.

40 If one has cultivated pure discipline
Taking the vow to do the ascetic practices,
Doing the difficult practice of wearing refuse rags,
One will be born in that pure field.

41 If one abandons other worldly possessions, contented,
Having taken hold of the three best robes,
The banner praised by the Sage,
One will be born in that pure field.

42 If one has cultivated the vow of wearing felt,
Having completely abandoned all notions,
Being without a haughty or arrogant mind
One will be born in that pure field.

43 If one has undertaken to live on alms food
In order to benefit all sentient beings and
In order to illuminate all the directions,
One will be born in that pure field.

44 If, in accord with being immovable from the highest awakening,
One has cultivated the vow of one sitting,
In order to attain the state of an unexcelled buddha,
One will be born in that pure field.

45 If one has cultivated the vow of not taking [food] late,
Passionless, abandoning greed, holding fast to discipline
In order to obtain the best stage of nonreturn,
One will be born in that pure field.

46 If one has kept to dwelling in a jungle
As the lion, king of beasts,
In order to become the man-lion,
One will be born in that pure field.

47 If one has cultivated the vow of dwelling at the foot of a tree
By sitting at the foot of the bodhi tree
In order to travel to the seat of awakening,
One will be born in that pure field.

48 If one has cultivated the vow of dwelling without a roof
Intrepid, not relying on a refuge,
In order to perfect excellent awakening,
One will be born in that pure field.

49 If one has cultivated the vow of frequenting cemeteries,
Mediating extensively on compassion and love
In order to cultivate natural purity,
One will be born in that pure field.

50 If one has cultivated the vow of sleeping in a sitting posture
In order, having accumulated masses of merit and wisdom,
To manifest them with a single pointed mind,
One will be born in that pure field.

51 In order not to fall away from the *dharmadhātu* basis
And to understand it perfectly just as it is,
If one has preserved the taking of any seat which is offered
One will be born in that pure field.

52 If one has meditated on the teaching which has passed beyond thought
and reasoning,
Not dwelling in all dharmas,
Abandoning being and nonbeing,
One will be born in that pure field.

53 If one has meditated on this *dharmatā* of buddhas,
Without ends or middle, true reality,
Which passes beyond the three times,
One will be born in that pure field.

54 If one has meditated on the nonapprehension of the two extremes,
Passing beyond the aggregates and components,
Liberated from the spheres,
One will be born in that pure field.

55 If one has meditated without discrimination
On the teaching of equality, beyond thought,

True by its intrinsic nature,
One will be born in that pure field.

56 All dharmas are like an illusion and
Those illusions too are empty of self-nature.
If one meditates on this very fact of things,
One will be born in that pure field.

57 If one has meditated on the natural purity
Of the teaching that, being not one, not many,
Is non-dual with regard to what is to be rejected and what is to be adopted,
One will be born in that pure field.

58 If one has meditated on the dharma without marks,
Unproduced, without defects,
Without fictional human ideas, without appearances,
One will be born in that pure field.

59 If one has meditated on the reality that
The Tathāgata's nature is unproduced and
All dharmas are, in this, like the Sugata,
One will be born in that pure field.

## Commentary

All translations in the following (which are my own unless otherwise noted) are made from the Sanskrit, if this is available. I do not wish to imply by this that the author or authors of our text knew the Sanskrit versions (or any version, for that matter) of the texts I cite as parallels. The materials are provided for the light they shed on the poem's meaning, and in the hope that they will spur further research into its sources. More detailed notes, including many of a philological nature, are found in my earlier publication.[49]

Verse 1 evokes the Larger *Sukhāvatīvyūha Sūtra* (LSV) §39-a: "The Tathāgata Amitābha . . . whose unhindered name is proclaimed aloud in the worlds of the ten directions," and the following verse LSV §9-a, vs. 3:

If when I have attained the seat of awakening
[My] name would not instantly reach the ten directions,
The many wide endless buddha fields,
May I not be a powerful lord of the world.

Verse 2 reminds one of LSV §29: Those beings who bring to mind the Tathāgata Amitābha gain various fruits including "They will be irreversible from unexcelled perfect awakening," and the following verses LSV §31-f, vss. 17–18:

> Then the Buddha Amitāyus preaches:
> This [what precedes these verses] was my former vow.
> Sentient beings hearing [my] name in whatever manner
> Shall absolutely always come to my field.
> This splendid vow of mine has been fulfilled,
> And sentient beings come from many world spheres,
> And having come before me in an instant
> They are irreversible here, bound to only one more birth.

With 3 we may compare the *Ajitasenavyākaraṇanirdeśa,* which says that when one hears the name of Śākyamuni, "Whatever evil they have done, either then or in the past, will all quickly be destroyed."[50]

Verse 4 is similar to an expression in another Dunhuang poem to Amitābha, in which we read, "Whichever beings hear the famous name will be released from all the various sufferings."[51] It also suggests the Smaller *Sukhāvatīvyūha Sūtra* (SSV) §2: "In that world sphere Sukhāvatī sentient beings have no bodily suffering or mental suffering . . ." "The suffering of birth and death," of course, refers to all sufferings of *saṁsāra.* The *Guan-jing* repeatedly contains the expression that a certain act or practice will lead to the elimination of the extremely heavy karma binding one to birth and death. In the *Ajitasenavyākaraṇanirdeśa* it is said that the relevant result of hearing the Buddha's name is that "He who hears, indeed, the name of the Lord of the World will never be destined for an evil state."[52] These quotations from the *Ajitasenavyākaraṇanirdeśa* establish that these types of notions are at least not limited to "Pure Land" texts.

In verse 5 there seems to be a reference to the fifth stage of the bodhisattva's course (*sudurjayā-bhūmi*). The *Madhyamakāvatāra* of Candrakīrti says, "At the stage called 'The Unconquerable,' the mighty one cannot be subdued even by all the forces of Māra," and the commentary explains, "A bodhisattva abiding at the fifth bodhisattva stage cannot be subdued even by the *devaputramāras* found in all world systems, to say nothing of their servants and minions."[53]

In 6, the double accumulation consists of merit (*puṇyasambhāra*) and wisdom (*jñānasambhāra*). In the *Mañjuśrī-nāmasaṁgīti* verse 57 we read, "Possessed of merit, with accumulated merit, he is knowledge and the great source of knowledge. Possessed of knowledge in knowing the real and unreal, he has accumulated the two accumulations."[54] In 6b we have only one manuscript, and the reading may be corrupt. I do not understand the line very well. Samten Karmay suggests, "He possesses limitless power [to teach] the Dharma."

To 7 we may compare the *Munayastava* 10: "Worshipped by Brahma, Indra, Varuṇa, Āditya, Yakṣas, Asuras, men and snakes, homage to him, the famous!"[55] Compare also *Ārya-Mañjuśrī-nāmāṣṭaśatakam* 12ab: "Hero made of all the gods, you are paid homage by all the gods."[56]

In 8 again we may recall the *Ārya-Mañjuśrī-nāmāṣṭaśatakam* 15: "[You are] clever and intelligent, and wise and clear sighted. [You are] virtuous and a wish-fulfilling tree adorned with the flowers of the limbs of awakening."[57] The key term also appears in the *Mañjuśrī-nāmasaṁgīti* 128, whose metaphor is close to ours: "Fragrant from the blossoms of the limbs of enlightenment, being the ocean of qualities of the Tathāgata, in knowing the practice of the eight-limbed path, he knows the path of the perfect complete awakening."[58] A half verse from Mātṛceṭa's *Varṇārhavarṇa Stotra* VIII.21ab may also be cited: "Strewn with the flowers of the limbs of awakening, fragrant and free from the outflows."[59] The expression is a stock one in Buddhist narrative literature (*avadāna*).[60] Verse 9 evokes LSV §9-b, vs. 6b: "Having removed the darkness of all men . . ."

With 11, the *Varṇārhavarṇa Stotra* I.22 also has the term "flowers of auspiciousness" (*guṇapuṣpāṇi*).[61] Nāgārjuna's *Niraupamya-stava* 25b has a similar expression.[62] Whether these terms carry the same sense as that in our text I am not sure.

With reference to 12, LSV §16-1-b-c has a lengthy discussion of the jeweled trees in Sukhāvatī, too long to quote here. Another similar passage, again too long to quote, is *Guan-jing* II.8–12 (*T.* 365 [XII] 342b1–22).

13a is a bit difficult, but a hint is given by another Dunhuang manuscript poem about Amitābha: "In that land of Amitābha the ground is strewn with golden sand, a jeweled web canopy is spread out, a multitude of garlands branch off from silk tassels, and all the directions without exception are decorated with ornaments."[63] In 13d, LSV §8-n, vow 31, describes how Amitābha vows his land to be filled with vases of fragrant perfumes. See also §16-1, and passim in LSV.

For 14, see LSV §8-n, vow 32: "And pleasant-sounding musical clouds always playing . . ." Again SSV §7: "In that buddha field when those [previously mentioned] rows of palm trees and nets of bells are blown by the wind they put forth a sweet and pleasing sound, like for example the sweet and pleasing sound put forth by a heavenly musical instrument consisting of hundreds of thousands of myriads of elements played together by nobles. Just thus is the sweet and pleasing sound put forth when those rows of palm trees and strings of bells are blown by the wind. And when the people there have heard those sounds the recollection of the buddha arises in them, the recollection of the dharma arises in them, the recollection of the saṁgha arises in them." LSV §18-e describes the sounds that the rivers in Sukhāvatī produce, namely whatever sound one wishes to hear, including a long list of doctrinal terms beginning with buddha, dharma, and saṁgha. At *Guan-jing* II.16 (*T.* 365 [XII] 342b8–10) we read: "Again [in the pure land] there are musical instruments suspended in the sky like heavenly jeweled banners. Unstruck they sound by themselves, and all of these sounds proclaim the mindfulness of the buddha, the mindfulness of the dharma, and the mindfulness of the bhikṣusaṁgha." See also verse 19.

To verse 15 we may compare SSV §4: "There are lotus pools in the world sphere Sukhāvatī made of the seven jewels, namely gold, silver, lapis, crystal, red pearls, emeralds, and the seventh jewel coral. They are full of the water of the eight excellent qualities, filled up to their banks so that even a crow would be able to drink from them, and they are strewn with golden sands. And all around those lotus pools on four sides there are four staircases colorful and beautiful with four jewels [list omitted]." See also the parallel quoted above under verse 13.

To verse 16 we may compare SSV §6: "In that buddha field there are geese, herons, and peacocks. Three times during the night and three times during the day they come together and sing, and they sing each their own songs. And from their singing issues forth the sound of the [five] powers, the [five] strengths, and the [seven] limbs of awakening. The people there having heard that sound produce mindfulness of the buddha, mindfulness of the dharma, and mindfulness of the saṁgha." And to verse 17 LSV §19-c: "They desire such a palace, of such a color, sign and appearance, height, breadth, with hundreds of thousands of turrets made of a multitude of jewels, covered with heavenly canopies, with jeweled couches arranged with variegated pillows, and just such a palace appears before them. And in these mentally arisen palaces they dwell, play, sport and frolic honored and surrounded by seven thousands of heavenly maidens." We also recall SSV §5: "And in that buddha-field three times at night and three times during the day a rain of heavenly *mandarava* flowers rains down." At 19 we think of LSV §31-c, vs. 7ab: "Those flowers thrown there stood as an umbrella then one hundred leagues in size."

In verses 20–25 we find the six perfections enumerated, and their cultivation suggested as practices leading to rebirth in a pure buddha-field.[64] In verse 20 and the following, the purity of the so-called three spheres probably refers to giver, gift, and receiver, but might also refer to the doer, the action, and the receiver of the action. It is also possible, though less probable, that it refers to the triad of body, speech, and mind. In general, then, this grouping should likely refer only to charity, the first of the perfections here enumerated. But in fact it is extended to refer to all of them.

In verse 20, the ten types of gift are alternately explained in various sources. Das gives one list, the source of which is not clear.[65] In verse 21, it is probable that the ten types of discipline refers to the ten rules of moral behavior (*daśa-śīla*), not killing, and so on. In verses 22–23, no list of ten types of patience (*kṣānti*) or energy (*vīrya*) is known to me.

To 26 we can compare LSV §8-a, vow 3: "If, Blessed One, those sentient beings born in that buddha-field of mine should not all be of one color, namely of a golden color, may I not attain unexcelled perfect awakening." At 27 see LSV §35: "And, Ānanda, the bodhisattvas who are born in that buddha-land are all possessed of the thirty-two characteristic marks of a great man." See also SSV § 8: "The extent of the lives of his followers and of that Tathāgata will be infinite." This passage is not in the canonical Tibetan translation, but is in both Chinese versions. Again, compare LSV §8-e, vow 14: "If, Blessed One, when I have attained to unexcelled perfect awakening there is any sentient being in my buddha-field whose life span would be measurable, excepting by the power of a vow, may I not attain to unexcelled perfect awakening."

For 28 and 29, compare LSV §31-f, vs. 16:

> And having come here to the best field
> They quickly obtain magical powers,
> And the divine eye and the divine ear,
> The memory of former births and knowledge of the thoughts of others.

For 28 compare LSV §8-b, vow 6: "If, Blessed One, there should be born in my buddha-field any sentient being who would not have the power to recall his former births, [even] so far as recalling hundreds of thousands of myriads of aeons, may I not attain unexcelled perfect awakening." Again, LSV §36: "And from that moment on none shall ever be without the power to recall their former births,"[66] and LSV §8-c, vow 9: "If, Blessed One, the sentient beings who would be born in my buddha-field would not all be skillful in knowing the thoughts of others, [even] knowing the thoughts and deeds of beings throughout hundreds of thousands of millions of myriads of buddha-fields, may I not attain to unexcelled perfect awakening." See also LSV §8-b, vow 5: "If, Blessed One, there should be born in that buddha-field of mine sentient beings who would not all obtain the highest perfections consisting of magical powers, so far as the ability to pass over hundreds of thousands of millions of myriads of buddha-fields in a fraction of an instant of thought, may I not attain unexcelled perfect awakening."

To verse 29 compare LSV §8-b, vow 7: "If, Blessed One, all the beings who would be born in my buddha-field would not have obtained the divine eye, such that they might see even hundreds of thousands of millions of myriads of world spheres, may I not attain unexcelled perfect awakening." Compare too LSV §8-b, vow 8: "If, Blessed One, all the beings who would be born in my buddha-field would not have obtained the divine ear, such that they could hear the preaching of the True Dharma simultaneously from even hundreds of thousands of myriads of buddha-fields, may I not attain unexcelled perfect awakening."

For verse 30, see SSV §5: "Those sentient beings born there once before the [morning] meal go to other world spheres and worship hundreds of thousands of myriads of buddhas there. And having bestrewn each Tathāgata with a rain of hundreds of thousands of myriads of flowers, they return again to their proper world sphere for their daily rest." And LSV §8-i, vow 22: "If, Blessed One, when I have attained awakening, all the bodhisattvas who would be born in that buddha-field should, having gone once before their [morning] meal to other buddha-fields, not serve, with all things that cause happiness, many hundreds of buddhas, many thousands of buddhas, many hundreds of thousands of buddhas, many myriads of buddhas, even up to many hundreds of thousands of millions of myriads of buddhas, this by means of the buddha's power, then may I not attain unexcelled perfect awakening." A further discussion of this process, in considerable detail, is given at LSV §37-a-b-c, but it is too long to quote here. In 30d, which buddha is being referred to is not quite clear, but probably the buddha of the field in which they dwell, which would presumably be Amitābha.

For 31, any buddha can be referred to as protector (*mgon po*). Amitābha refers to himself as *lokanātha* in LSV §9-a, vs. 3d. It is not really clear whether the present verse refers specifically to Amitābha, although this seems the most likely explanation. Compare LSV §8-g, vow 18: "If, Blessed One, when I should attain awakening, those sentient beings who have raised the thought directed toward unexcelled perfect awakening in other world spheres, having heard my name might bear me in mind with serene thoughts, and if as the time of their death approaches I would not stand before them, surrounded and honored by the community of monks, in order to calm their minds, may I not attain unexcelled perfect awakening." LSV §27 and 28 also relate the same material, but are too long to quote here. See also SSV §10 (202.11–19): "And whatever son of good family or daughter of good family, Śāriputra, who will hear the name of the Blessed One, Tathāgata Amitāyus, and having heard it will be mindful of it for one night, or for two nights, or for three nights, or for four nights, or for five nights, or for six nights, or for seven nights, mindful of it with mind undisturbed, when that son of good family or daughter of good family will die, at his death that Tathāgata Amitāyus, accompanied by his retinue of Śrāvakas and honored by the group of bodhisattvas, will be present before him and he will die with a calm mind. Having died he will be reborn in the buddha-field of that Tathāgata Amitāyus, in the world sphere Sukhāvatī." See also *Guan-jing* IV.8, 12, 20 (*T.* 365 [XII] 345a8–11; a24–27; b21–27), for similar passages.

This kind of passage is certainly not limited to the LSV, the SSV, and the *Guan-jing*, even when the place of rebirth is to be Sukhāvatī. This has been shown by Schopen,[67] quoting from the *Ekādaśamukham*, and the *Sarvatathāgatādhiṣṭhānasattvālokanabuddhakṣetrasandarśanavyūha Sūtra*: Both passages say, "And at the time of death he will see the Tathāgata, and having died he will be reborn in the world sphere Sukhāvatī." The latter text contains another similar passage as well: "And at the time of death he will see the buddha and he will see bodhisattvas . . . and having died he is reborn in the world sphere Sukhāvatī." See also the passage from the *Bhaiṣajyaguru* translated by Schopen,[68] "to them at the time of the moment of death eight bodhisattvas, having come through magic power, will make visible their way." Note of course that the object of veneration here in the first set of these passages is not Amitābha / Amitāyus, but rather Śākyamuni. In the *Bhaiṣajyaguru* the object of veneration is the Buddha Bhaiṣajyaguruvaiḍūryaprabha.

To verse 32 compare *Guan-jing* I.18 (*T.* 365 [XII] 341c10): Those who desire to be born in the pure land should, among other practices, "practice the ten virtuous acts."

The reference in 33 is to the four immeasurables (*apramāṇa*, also known as the four *brahmavihāras*), namely loving kindness, compassion, sympathetic joy and impartiality (*maitrī, karuṇā, muditā,* and *upekṣā*).

For 36, compare the *Bhaiṣajyaguru*, which makes the connection of the eight-fold fast (*aṣṭāṁgasamanvāgata-upavāsa*) with Sukhāvatī: With regard to the four assemblies and good sons and daughters, if they "fast the fast possessed of eight limbs [that is, keep eight out of ten *śīla* rules], for one year or three months uphold the foundation of training . . . ," then they vow to gain birth in Sukhāvatī.[69] Further note that the *Bhaiṣajyaguru* directly connects this with a deathbed appearance guarantee. See the remarks to verse 31 above.

In 37 the reference is to the 8th, 14th, 15th, 23rd, 29th, and 30th of the month, and to the rain retreats. Compare also the *Guan-jing* I.18 (*T.* 365 [XII] 341c11): Among other practices leading to rebirth in the pure land is "producing the aspiration for awakening."

In 39 the three doors are emptiness, signlessness, and wishlessness.

Verses 40 and following deal with the *dhūtaguṇas*. The order in which they are presented agrees with that in the *Mahāvyutpatti* §1127–39, which is not a common ordering.[70] It is interesting to note that in the *Xu Gaoseng zhuan, T.* 2060 (L) 606a15–16, a seventh-century text, the monk Faxiang is said to have practiced the *dhūtaguṇas* while also praying to Amitābha.

In verse 42, with regard to abandoning all notions being connected with going to Sukhāvatī, the *Samādhirāja* says, "One who abandons all notions possesses infinite samādhis. . . . He, passing over world spheres, goes to Sukhāvatī."[71]

In 44, one tradition understands this to mean staying on one seat for eating and for sleeping (or meditating). But the original meaning may rather be that one eats only once in a day.[72] This is close to the sense in our Pāli sources, for example *Visuddhimagga* (Ñyāṇamoli 1956) II.35, that one eats in one session, and if one rises the meal is over. This does not imply that one cannot eat again later at a different meal. The imagery in the present verse, that of staying in one place immovably, does not firmly indicate one way or the other which meaning is the one being adopted here.

In verse 46 one may particularly note the poetical imagery, highlighted in the introduction above. One dwells in the forest or jungle, like a lion, in order to become the man-lion, that is, a buddha. Again in verse 47 the punning is clear. One sits at the foot of a tree (the ascetic purification practice) by sitting at the foot of the bodhi tree, the spot where the Buddha sat, in order to reach the seat of awakening, the *bodhimaṇḍa,* both the literal seat beneath the bodhi tree and the metaphorical ground of awakening.

In verse 48, there is evidently a pun on *skyabs la mi rten,* not relying on a refuge or shelter, both metaphorical and literal, and the ascetic purification practice of dwelling outside without a (literal) roof.

*Dhutaguṇanirdeśa* §13.2.v lists among the advantages of this practice *rten pa med pa nyid,* rendered by Bapat "One has not to depend upon anything." It could as easily, and perhaps more literally, be translated "Being without a refuge."

It might be possible to render the whole of verse 51 as follows:

> If one has observed that basis correctly,
> In order to manifest perfectly just as it is
> The *dharmadhātu* not deprived of a basis,
> One will be born in that pure field.

At 52 begins a new theme, the discussion of abstract philosophical points. The doctrines seem to be more or less Madhyamaka flavored, but it is not possible to identify any exact possible sources. It is also possible that the Madhyamaka-type ideas owe something to Chan influence.

For verse 54, see *Niraupamyastava* 8ab.[73]

As seen in verse 57, the "neither one nor many" argument (**ekānekaviyogahetu*) is a common one. See for example Śāntarakṣita's *Madhyamakālaṁkāra,* verse 1 and following.

## Appendix

In my 1993 work I edited all known manuscript witnesses for the poem presented above. However, upon reading Halkias' *Luminous Bliss,* I realized that the material he presented on pages 75–83 is in fact a previously unrecognized portion of the same poem. Now preserved in the British Library under the shelfmark IOL Tib J 310.1207, its dimensions are 8.5 × 26 cm, it follows every line with the interjection *a myi ta pur,* and it shares the paleography of the manuscript preserved in Paris as Pelliot tibétain 761. It must be considered a leaf of the same original. One leaf in between this and the previously known portion is still missing, and other leaves at the beginning and end are also not yet discovered. I present below a new reading, based on the fine color photographs presented on the website of the International Dunhuang Project. I have added the verse numbers, which do not appear in the manuscript.

48 a myi ta pur ||
rnam dag zhing der skye bar +gyur || a myi ta pur ||

49 snying rje byang cub cher bsgoms te || a myi ta pur ||
rang bzhi̇n dag par bsgoms ba'i phyi̇r || a myi ta pur ||

dur khrodu pa+ï sdom byas na || a myi ta pur ||
rnam dag zhing der skye bar ~~sa~~ +gyur || a myï ta pur ||

50 bsod nams $_{\text{ye}}$ shes tshogs bsags te || a myi ta pur ||
rtse gcig sems kyis mngon bya+ ba+ï phyir || a myï ta pur ||
cog bu pa+ï sdom sbyangs na+ || a myi ta pur ||
rnam dag zhing der skye bar +gyur || a myi ta pur ||

51 chos $_{\text{kyi}}$ dbyings la myi nyams shing || a myi ta pur ||
yang dag ji bzhïn mngon ba+i phyir || a myi ta pur ||
gzhi bzhïn som ba+ [*verso*] bsrungs byas na || a myi ta pur ||
rnam dag zhing der skye bar +gyur || a myi ta pur ||

52 tham cad chos la myi gnas shing || a myi ta pur ||
yod dang myed pa rnams spang st[e] || a myi ta pur ||
bsam rtogs +das pa+i chos bsgoms na+ || a myi ta pur ||
rnam dag zhing der skye bar +gyur || a myi ta pur ||

53 sangs $_{\text{rgyas}}$ rnams ky[i] chos nyid de || a myi ta pur ||
mtha+ dang dbung myed yang dag nyid || a myi ta pur ||
dus gsum +das pa+ï sgom byas na+ || a myi ta pur ||
rnam dag zhing der skye bar +gyur || a myi ta pur ||

phung po khaṁs las +das pa ste || a myi ta pur ||
skye mche[d] rnams las | rnam par grol || a myï ta pur ||
mtha gnyis dmyïgs

## Notes

Much of this chapter is based on my 1993 work, "The Virtues of Amitābha: A Tibetan Poem from Dunhuang," *Ryūkoku Daigaku Bukkyō Bunka Kenkyūjo Kiyō* 32: 1–109, which contains a full transcription of manuscript sources (but see the appendix above for an important addition), a normalized transcription of the Tibetan text, and extensive commentary on the verses, all omitted here. The present version contains a new introduction and additional material. I extend my deep thanks to Professor Oka Ryōji and the authorities of the Bukkyō Bunka Kenkyūjo of Ryūkoku University for their permission to make use of some of my earlier material here.

The text translated here was published for the first time by Akamatsu Kōshō in his 1987 essay "Tonkō Chibetto Bunken no Jōdokyō Kankei Tekisuto" [Dunhuang Tibetan texts related to Pure Land Buddhism], *Indotetsugaku Bukkyōgaku* (Hokkaidō Indotetsugaku Bukkyō Gakkai) 2: 195–220.

Akamatsu's article was brief, but thanks to the great kindness of Mr. Akamatsu, I obtained photocopies of the Dunhuang manuscripts and was able to present a fuller study in "The Virtues of Amitābha." I express once again my great debt to Mr. Akamatsu and my gratitude for the help his studies have given me. In addition, I thank Cristina Scherer-Schaub and the late J. W. de Jong for suggestions in correction of a few points in my earlier publication, and Nobuyuki Yamagiwa for some remarks on this revision, which I first worked on in 2001, though it could not then be published.

1 At least this is how they present themselves to us; it may be that we see things this way simply as a result of our ignorance of their larger context. Of course, every text was at some point in its history a local product, so it is chiefly the afterlife of the text that is of primary interest to us in this context.

2 The actual title of the text remains unknown. The head title of the manuscript called Pelliot tibétain (hereafter P. tib.) 112 would seem to indicate that *de bzhin gshegs pa snang ba mtha' yas gyi mtshan brjod pa* is a title, "The Praise of the Name of the Tathāgata Amitābha." The end title of this same manuscript gives an (abbreviated?) title of *snang ba mtha' yas*, corresponding simply to Amitābha. The latter at least looks more like a generic label than a title. P. tib. 6 contains the end title (?) *snang ba mtha' yas mtshan*, perhaps something like **Amitābha-nāma*? I do not believe that our text ever had a title in Sanskrit or any Indic language, and I offer this Sanskrit equivalent merely as a tool for understanding.

3 In his *Luminous Bliss: A Religious History of Pure Land Literature in Tibet: With an Annotated English Translation and Critical Analysis of the Orgyan-gling Gold Manuscript of the Short Sukhāvatīvyūha-sūtra* (Honolulu: University of Hawai'i Press, 2013): 75–83, Georgios Halkias publishes what he was able to identify only as a portion of an "aspiration poem," found in the British Stein collection as IOL Tib. J 310.1207. This leaf is in fact a further portion of the manuscript noted as Pelliot tibétain 761. See the appendix above.

4 The physical descriptions that follow are based on Marcelle Lalou, *Inventaire des Manuscrits tibétains de Touen-houang conservés à la Bibliothèque Nationale*, 1 (Paris: Adrien Maisonneuve, 1939), on Akamatsu's remarks, and on my own examination of the photocopies available to me. Neither Akamatsu nor I were able to examine the actual manuscripts. Color photographs are now available via the Artstor website. In "The Virtues of Amitāba" I have presented further details, including those concerning other texts copied in the same manuscripts.

(1) P. tib. 6: Twelve leaves, 8.5 × 25.7 cm, in concertina format, evidently incomplete. The whole verso (arbitrarily so named) contains verses 7 to 48 of our text, and on the recto the ninth leaf contains verses 57 to 59. The colophon on this leaf reads: *snang ba mtha' yas mtshan rdzogs so || dpal gyi shes rab kyis bris ste || zhus nas tshang ma mchis ||*. This might be

rendered, "The [text praising the] names of Amitābha is completed. Written by Dpal gyi shes rab, and having been corrected it is complete." I do not know of the name of this copyist appearing in other Dunhuang manuscripts. The manuscript is fairly carefully written with some corrections. The manuscript does not contain the evocation to Amita found in other manuscripts after each foot.

(2) P. tib. 105: A roll 25 × 578 cm. In total it contains 421 lines, of which the first four are fragmentary. From the first extant line to the 65th line we find from verse 12 (fragment only) to the end of our text. There is a notation at the end of the text that reads, *tshigs bcad dang po la a myi da phur gcig 'bod || 'og ma la gnyis 'bod ||*. We might render this as "One exclaims 'A myi da phur' once after the first line, and twice after the second." We see in P. tib. 516 what this should mean: the first and third lines have *a mye tha bur* (or *phur*), the second and fourth *a mye tha bur na mo a mye tha bur.*

(3) P. tib. 112: A fragmentary roll 30.5 × 110 cm, of which 100 lines remain. Lines 1–32 of this manuscript contain verses 1–14 of our text. Before the first verse there is a sentence that reads, *de bzhin gshegs pa | snang ba mtha yas gyi mtshan brjod pa'o || legs pa dang sangs rgyas gyi zhing gyi yon tan thob pa || mdor smos pa ||*. We may render this as "The Praise of the Names of the Tathāgata Amitābha. The acquisition of the good and the virtues of the buddha-field, briefly stated." And even though the text seems to cut off at verse 14c, a colophon is added that reads, *snang ba mtha yas rdzogs so || gtsang mas bris*. We may render this as "[This text concerning] Amitābha is finished. Written by Gtsang ma." This copyist's name is also found on P. tib. 1597 (Lalou, *Inventaire des Manuscrits tibétains de Touen-houang,* 96), where it is written *ban de gtsang ma*. The manuscript is not clearly written, and perhaps the paper was overly absorbent.

(4) P. tib. 516: Two leaves in poṭhi-format 8.8 × 27.5 cm, styled A and B. The first verse to the 5th of our text is written on the lower half of the recto and the full verso of 516B, and the 22nd to the 29th on both sides of 516A.

(5) P. tib. 760: A horizontal roll measuring 25 × 83 cm, containing verses 26 to 51, without anything else on the roll. It is not well written, with *da* and *nga*, for example, being more than usually indistinguishable.

(6) P. tib. 761: Two leaves in poṭhi format, 8.5 × 25.5 cm, called 761 A and B. The right edge of A is missing, probably five or six letters being lost per line. These leaves contain the 30th to the 41st verses. See the appendix for a further portion of this manuscript.

Charts illustrating graphically which manuscript contains what text are found in Jonathan Silk, "The Virtues of Amitābha: A Tibetan Poem from Dunhuang," *Ryūkoku Daigaku Bukkyō Bunka Kenkyūjo Kiyō* 32 (1993): 6;

and Akamatsu Kōshō, "Tonkō Chibetto Bunken no Jōdokyō Kankei Tekisuto" [Dunhuang Tibetan texts related to Pure Land Buddhism], *Indo-tetsugaku Bukkyōgaku (Hokkaidō Indotetsugaku Bukkyō Gakkai)* 2 (1987): 198.

5 Manuscripts P. tib. 6 and 105 aside, the other manuscripts contain the interjection after each verse. P. tib. 105 contains, at the end, an instruction to insert these interjections after every verse.

6 The phonology of this exclamation is discussed in Silk "The Virtues of Amitābha," 17–19. (In that discussion I overlooked the relevant remarks of Berthold Laufer, "Loan-words in Tibetan." *T'oung-pao,* second series, 17, no. 4 (1916): 423.) The *-t* final often became *-l/-r* in Middle Chinese, as reflected clearly in the Korean pronunciation of "buddha," *bul.*

7 Tokio Takata, "Multilingualism in Tun-huang," *Acta Asiatica* 78 (2000): 65, points out that Chinese was being written in Tibetan script in Dunhuang as late the tenth century; his article is an excellent overview of the multilingualism of Dunhuang generally. See also Tsugihito Takeuchi, "Sociolinguistic Implications of the Use of Tibetan in East Turkestan from the End of Tibetan Domination through the Tangut Period (9th–12th c.)," in *Turfan Revisited: The First Century of Research into the Arts and Cultures of the Silk Road,* ed. Desmond Durkin-Meisterernst, Simone-Christiane Raschmann, Jens Wilkens, Marianne Yaldiz, Peter Zieme, et al. (Berlin: Dietrich Reimer Verlag, 2004), and Tsugihito Takeuchi, "Old Tibetan Buddhist Texts from the Post-Tibetan Imperial Period (mid-9th c. to late 10th c.)," in *Old Tibetan Studies: Dedicated to the Memory of R. E. Emmerick,* ed. Cristina Scherrer-Schaub (Leiden: Brill, 2012). Halkias, *Luminous Bliss,* 77, unfortunately misunderstood the transcribed Chinese *a myi ta pur* as Tibetan, or even Sanskrit, overlooking Laufer's work pointed out in the previous note.

8 Of course, religious poetry by definition has a religious locus, but it is fair to assume that the works of, for example, a religious poet like Mātṛceṭa were often appreciated from an aesthetic point of view, rather than merely from a religious one. The same must hold for the religious poems included in the Sanskrit anthology titled *Subhāṣitaratnakoṣa,* which, by including them in what is by definition a collection of fine literature, contextualizes the poems primarily from the point of view of their literary qualities.

9 The same is true for the genre of *nāmasaṁgīti,* or "lauds of the names," which celebrates the good qualities of a deity or object of worship. The purpose of such literature, a genre within which our text may also be included, cannot be served unless the text is in some way understood on a literal level.

10 It is the limitations of my knowledge that lead me to point mostly to Indian parallels; no doubt those knowledgeable in Chinese and Tibetan traditions will be able to bring forth other valuable relevant materials.

11 By Akamatsu, "Tonkō Chibetto Bunken no Jōdokyō Kankei Tekisuto," 201.

12 Verse 2 omits "mighty" because it introduces the subject, "someone."

13 *jōdokyō ni kansuru chibettobun shiryō.*

14 By framing the question in this way I do not intend to preclude the addition of any new materials, previously unknown, to a canon. I do not doubt that one would be justified in considering a newly discovered work by Hōnen, Shinran, or Rennyo as a perfectly acceptable Pure Land text. One modern example of just such a process might be the letters of Eshinni, Shinran's wife, discovered only in 1921. It is another question who might have the authority to enter such objects into a canon; in any case, surely the outside scholar has no authority to do so, nor is this action appropriate or meaningful from a disinterested academic viewpoint.

15 The *Kōjien* (Shinmura Izuru, ed., *Kōjien*, 2nd ed. [Tokyo: Iwanami shoten, 1980]: 1103, s.v. jōdo-kyō), a standard Japanese dictionary, defines the term as "The teaching of the Pure Land Way. In opposition to the Way of the Nobles in which one practices in the present life and attempts to obtain Buddhahood, it is the teaching in which one expects, after death, to be reborn in the pure land, and there obtain Buddhahood. To it belong in India Aśvaghoṣa, Sthiramati, Nāgārjuna, and Vasubandhu, in China Huiyuan, Shandao, and Cimin, and in Japan Kūya, Genshin, Ryōnin, Hōnen of the Jōdoshū, Shinran of the Jōdo Shinshū, Ippen of the Jishū, and so on." Needless to say, this view of the Indian and Chinese lineage of Pure Land Buddhism is an entirely emic and Japanese one.

16 It is very questionable whether these two scriptures had much impact on Indian Buddhism at all. It is worthwhile noting that neither is, as far as is yet known, ever quoted by an Indian author. One may contrast this, for example, with the *Saddharmapuṇḍarīka,* which is relatively well-known in Indian texts (on which see Jonathan Silk, "The Place of the *Lotus Sūtra* in Indian Buddhism," *Journal of Oriental Studies* 11 [2001]). In addition, there are also considerable questions as to whether the commentary to the Larger *Sukhāvatīvyūha,* the so-called **Sukhāvatīvyūhopadeśa* (*T.* 1524), is really an Indian work, much less by Vasubandhu. On the Larger *Sukhāvatīvyūha* in India, see Gérard Fussman, "La place des *Sukhāvatī-vyūha* dans le Bouddhisme Indien," *Journal Asiatique* 287, no. 2 (1999).

17 It is, however, a little difficult to leave the point here because Akamatsu, strictly speaking, suggests not that this text is a Pure Land text, but rather that it is "related to Pure Land." It is unclear to me precisely what this means. In the sense that temples belonging to the Shingon monastic center on Kōyasan are filled with images of Amida, one could say that at least some Shingon is "related to Pure Land," and some do seem willing to accept that there are elements "related to Pure Land" even in Shingon Buddhism. If this is the case, and a particular claim is being made for a Pure Land identification rather than the notice of one among many generic

Buddhist elements, I cannot help but think that the term "Pure Land" is being used in an overly broad sense such that one can never be quite sure what it means.

I incidentally find my own concerns echoed by Charles Jones in his review of Halkias, *Luminous Bliss* (H-Buddhism, H-Net Reviews, February 2014; http://www.h-net.org/reviews/showrev.php?id=40391, 2), when he says, "The reason Western scholars refer to 'Pure Land Buddhism' at all is that there is a loose but self-conscious Pure Land 'lineage' (*zōng* 宗) or 'dharma-gate' (*fǎmén* 法門) with 'patriarchs' (*zǔ* 祖) in China and a strong set of Pure Land institutions in Japan. . . . Why characterize *any* Tibetan literature or practice as 'Pure Land' at all? Why segregate out texts dealing with Sukhāvatī and Amitābha from, say, other instances of *dhāraṇī* or *gter-ma* literature? Has the strong presence of a Pure Land tradition in East Asia led to the reification of an etic category in the Tibetan materials that would not have emerged without it?"

18 Akamatsu points to *T.* 1978, 1980, 1983 as his examples. It is possible Akamatsu associates the *Aparimitāyurjñāna* here because he connects the buddha of that text, Aparimitāyus, with Amitābha. At least from an Indian perspective, this is an error, as these buddhas are distinct. We may note that such apparent confusion is frequent in the scholarship; see for instance Alex Wayman, *Chanting the Names of Mañjuśrī* (Boston: Shambala, 1985), 3; and Shunzō Onoda, "*Amida Kuon Jōō Darani-kyō* ni motozuku Chibetto Mandara" [A Tibetan maṇḍala based on the *Aparimitāyurjñānahṛdaya-dhāraṇī*], *Nihon Bukkyō Gakkai Nenpō* 52 (1987). On the other hand, there is some indication that an association was made by traditional exegetes as well, at least in Tibet. I will address these issues in a study of the *Aparimitāyurjñāna,* now in preparation.

19 I believe Akamatsu is wrong to associate the *Aparimitāyurjñāna* and its *dhāraṇī* with tantra, but I will discuss this point also in the study mentioned in the previous note.

20 His most recent publication of which I am aware, however, is from 1991, and he does not seem to be active in the field.

21 Akamatsu Kōshō, "Chibetto-yaku Amidakyō no Ihon: Tonkō Shahon P tib 758 ni tsuite" [A variant Tibetan version of the Smaller *Sukhāvatīvyūha*: Dunhuang manuscript P. tib 758], *Indogaku Bukkyōgaku Kenkyū* 33, no. 1 (1984), and Akamatsu Kōshō, "Chibetto-yaku Muryōjukyō no Tonkō Shinshutsu Iyakuhon" [A variant Tibetan translation of the Larger *Sukhāvatīvyūha* from Dunhuang], *Ryūkoku Daigaku Bukkyō Bunka Kenkyūjo Kiyō* 23 (1984). I have prepared an edition of the Dunhuang text of the Smaller Sūtra, translated from Chinese into Tibetan (roughly two-thirds of the text remains), and I am in the course of preparing an edition of the Larger Sūtra translated from Chinese, of which we have slightly more than half the text.

22 Akamatsu Kōshō, "Tonkō Chibetto Bunken no Jōdokyō Kankei Shiryō: P. tib. 153 ni tsuite," P. tib. 153 [Dunhuang Tibetan materials related to Pure Land Buddhism: P. tib. 153], *Indotetsugaku Bukkyōgaku (Hokkaidō Indotetsugaku Bukkyō Gakkai)* 3 (1988). The unique manuscript of the poem translated by Akamatsu is P. tib. 153. I have referred to this occasionally below when it contains parallels to the poem studied here.

23 See Akamatsu Kōshō, "Tonkō Shahon yori mitaru Chibetto no Jōdo Shisō Juyō," [The Tibetan reception of Pure Land Buddhism in the light of the Dunhuang documents], *Indogaku Bukkyōgaku Kenkyū* 35, no. 1 (1986). Five manuscripts have been identified, P. tib. 67, 99, 158, 759, and Stein 452.

24 Akamatsu Kōshō, "Amidabutsu ni genkyū suru Tonkō Chibetto-bun Shiryō Gaikan" [An outline of Dunhuang Tibetan materials concerning Amida Buddha], *Indotetsugaku Bukkyōgaku (Hokkaidō Indotetsugaku Bukkyō Gakkai)* 5 (1991), particularly 205. An exception is Stein 724, which was subsequently studied, although inadequately, in Silk, "Virtues of Amitābha," 71–72. See now my re-edition, "The Ten Virtues of Loudly Invoking the Name of Amitābha: Stein Tibetan 724 and an Aspect of Chinese *Nianfo* Practice in Tibetan Dunhuang," *Journal of the American Oriental Society* 137, no. 3 (2017): 473–482. The reference to Amitābha's "magical nail" is due to a misunderstanding (apparently of Louis de La Vallée Poussin, *Catalogue of the Tibetan Manuscripts from Tun-Huang in the India Office Library* [Oxford: Oxford University Press, 1962], 232) that *A mye da phur kyi yon tan bcu* is purely Tibetan; as discussed above, *a mye da phur* is Chinese; there is nothing here about a nail (*phur*), a fact which was noted already by Akamatsu, "Amidabutsu ni genkyū suru Tonkō Chibetto-bun Shiryō Gaikan," 209 note 43.

25 Gregory Schopen, "Sukhāvatī as a Generalized Religious Goal in Sanskrit Mahāyāna Sūtra Literature," *Indo-Iranian Journal* 19 (1977).

26 Cf. Fussman, "La place des *Sukhāvatī-vyūha* dans le Bouddhisme Indien," 577.

27 The same type of critique can be applied to Akamatsu's arguments that Pure Land thought is part of the doctrinal position of Tsong kha pa and other Tibetan thinkers. We might refer, for example, to statements in the first few cantos of the *Padma thang yig,* the hagiography of Padmasambhava, which continually praise Amitābha. That text, however, is far from being a Pure Land document in any meaningful sense.

28 I think there is little point in spending time on such exercises in cultural comparison as the attempts of Nakamura Hajime, "Gokuraku Jōdo no Kannen no Indogaku-teki Kaimei to Chibetto-teki Hen'yō" [Studies on the idea of Pure Land in the perspective of Indian cultural history and the modification of the idea by Tibetans], *Indogaku Bukkyōgaku Kenkyū* 11, no. 2 (1963) (largely repeated by Kagawa, *Jōdokyō no Seiritsushiteki Kenkyū*, 331–352), to assert the Tibetan understanding of Pure Land Buddhism on the basis of

translation equivalents in the Tibetan translations of the *Sukhāvatīvyūha* scriptures. Aside from the probability, which is often not fully considered by such authors, that the Indic originals from which the translators worked were not identical with the extant Indic texts, the overall project to determine cultural characteristics from random uncontextualized word choices is, I believe, essentially pointless. (On the other hand, Nakamura Hajime, "Amidakyō Chibetto-yaku ni tsuite" [The Tibetan translation of the Smaller *Sukhāvatīvyūha sūtra*], in *Iwai Hakase Koki Kinen Tenseki Ronshū*, ed. Iwai Hakase Koki Kinen Jigyōkai [Shizuoka: Kaimeidō, 1963], some of which is repeated in the notes to his translation of the sūtra in *Jōdo Sambukyō* [*ge*] [Tokyo: Iwanami shoten, 1964], 133–141, shows a much more sober approach to the Tibetan translation.)

29 Onoda Shunzō, "Chibetto Senjutsu no Jōdokyō-kei Butten" [Pure Land Buddhist scriptures compiled in Tibet], *Bukkyō Daigaku Daigakuin Kenkyū Kiyō* 7 (1979); Onoda Shunzō, "Tsonkapa-zō *Saijōkoku Kaimon* Shiyaku" [A tentative translation of Tsong kha pa's *Zhing mchog sgo 'byed*]. *Bukkyō Bunka Kenkyū* 27 (1981); Onoda Shunzō, "Chibetto-shoden no Jōdo Kansō Shūhō: Aoki Bunkyō-shi Shōrai Shiryō Nos. 103, 104, 107, 108, 109 ni tsuite no Kanken' Nos. 103, 104, 107, 108, 109 [Tibetan Pure Land visualization manuals: Items from the Aoki Bunkyō collection], *Kokuritsu Minzokugaku Hakubutsukan Kenkyū Hōkoku* Bessatsu 1 (1983); Onoda Shunzō, "Chibetto Bukkyō no Jōdokyō Rikai" [The Tibetan understanding of Pure Land Buddhism], *Chūgai Nippō* 24152 (Jan. 19, 1990); Kajihama Ryōshun, "Tsonkapa-cho *Gokuraku e no Seiganmon* no Kenkyū" [A study of a prayer book on rebirth in the Land of Bliss (Sukhāvatī) written by Tsong kha pa], *Ōsaka Kodai Setsunan Daigaku Chūken Shohō* 23, no. 3 (1991); Kajihama Ryōshun, "Mi pham no Jōdo Shisō" Mi pham [Mi pham's Pure Land thought], *Indogaku Bukkyōgaku Kenkyū* 41, no. 1 (1992); Kajihama Ryōshun, "Panchen Rama Issei-cho *Gokuraku no Kokudo ni Shōgai naku iku tame no Jinsoku na Michi* no Kenkyū" [A study of the quick path for going to the Land of Bliss (Sukhāvatī) without obstruction written by the 1st Panchen Lama], *Setsudai Gakujitsu* ser. B, no. 10 (1992); Kajihama Ryōshun, "Tsonkapa no Jōdo Shisō no Kenkyū" [Tsong kha pa's Pure Land thought], *Ōsaka Kodai Setsunan Daigaku Chūken Shohō* 24, no. 3 (1992); Kajihama Ryōshun, "Mipamu no Jōdo Shisō no Kenkyū " [Mi pham's Pure Land thought], *Setsudai Gakujitsu* ser. B, no. 11 (1993); Kajihama Ryōshun, "Chankya Issei no Jōdo Shisō" [Lcang skya I's essay on Pure Land thought], *Ōsaka Kodai Setsunan Daigaku Chūken Shohō* 25, no. 3 (1993); Kajihama Ryōshun, "Chankya Issei no Ichishōron ni tsuite" [Lcang skya's Essay on Amitābha]. *Shūkyō Kenkyū* 66, no. 4 (1993); Kajihama Ryōshun, "Chankya Issei no Ōjō Shisō no Kenkyū" [Lcang skya's ideas on rebirth in the Pure Land ], *Setsudai Jinbun Kagaku* 1 (1994); Kajihama Ryōshun, "Chankya Issei no Shōgai" [The life of Lcang skya I]. *Ōsaka Kodai Setsunan Daigaku Chūken Shohō* 26, no. 3 (1994); Kajihama Ryōshun, "3rd rDo Grubchen Rinpoche's

Pure Land Thought (I)," *Indogaku Bukkyōgaku Kenkyū* 43, no. 1 (1994); Kajihama Ryōshun, "Chankya Issei no Ōjō Shisō" [Lcang skya's ideas on rebirth in the Pure Land ], *Shūkyō Kenkyū* 67, no. 4 (1994); Kajihama Ryōshun, "Dotsupuchen Rinpoche Sansei no Ōjō Shisō no Kenkyū (I)" (I) [3rd Rdo Grub chen Rinpoche's ideas on rebirth in the Pure Land ], *Setsudai Jinbun Kagaku* 2 (1995); Kajihama Ryōshun, "3rd rDo Grubchen Rinpoche's Pure Land Thought (II)," *Indogaku Bukkyōgaku Kenkyū* 44, no. 2 (1995); Kajihama Ryōshun, "Tsonkapa no *Saikō no Kokudo no Kaimon* no Ichikaisetsusho ni tsuite" [Dpal Sprul Rinpoche's Explanation of Tsong kha pa's *Prayer for Entrance into the Best Land*], *Shūkyō Kenkyū* 68, no. 4 (1995); Kajihama Ryōshun, "Dotsupuchen Rinpoche Sansei no Ōjō Shisō no Kenkyū: *Gokuraku no Kokudo ni tsuite Chosaku sareta Shomotsu* no Dai-ni-shō o chūshin toshite" [3rd Rdo Grub chen Rinpoche's ideas on rebirth in the Pure Land: The second chapter of the *Book on the Land of Bliss*], *Setsudai Jinbun Kagaku* 3 (1996); Kajihama Ryōshun, "Peruturu Rinpoche no Shōgai to Jōdo Shisō" [The life of Dpal Sprul Rinpoche, and his Pure Land thought], in *Watanabe Takao Kyōju Kanreki Kinen Bukkyō Shisō Bunkashi Ronsō,* edited by Watanabe Takao Kyōju Kanreki Kinenkai (Kyoto: Nagata Bunshōdō, 1997); and now, Kajihama Ryōshun, *Chibetto no Jōdo Shisō no Kenkyū* (Kyoto: Nagata Bunshōdō, 2002); Kajihama Ryōshun, "3rd rDo Grubchen Rinpoche's Pure Land Thought (III)," *Indogaku Bukkyōgaku Kenkyū* 50, no. 2 (2002); and Kajihama Ryōshun, "Chibetto no gokuraku no kokudo" [The Land of Bliss (Sukhāvatī) in Tibetan Buddhism], *Shūkyō Kenkyū* 75, no. 4 (2002). See also the translations by Tshul khrims skal bzang and Odani Nobuchiyo, "Chibetto no Jōdokyō: Minshū no Shinkō" [Tibetan Pure Land Buddhism: Faith of the people], *Jōdo Bukkyō no Shisō* 3: *Ryūju, Seshin, Chibetto no Jōdokyō, Eon* (Tokyo: Kōdansha 1993), and Tokiya Kōki, "Muryōkōbutsu Raisanmon o megutte (josetsu): Sono Kaisetsu to Wayaku [Introduction to the Praise of Amitābha Buddha: Interpretation and translation], *Takata Tanki Daigaku Kiyō* 3 (1985). See now also Ryoshun Kajihama, *Amitābha in Tibetan Buddhism* (Takatsuki-city, Osaka: The Author, 2016), a collection of his studies in English.

30 Ōtani University, ed., *Catalogue of Tibetan Works Kept in Ōtani University Library* (Kyoto: Otani University Library, 1973), no. 10018 (hereafter Ōtani). Translated in full in Onoda, "Tsonkapa-zō *Saijōkoku Kaimon* Shiyaku," Kajihama, "Tsonkapa no Jōdo Shisō no Kenkyū," and Tshul khrims skal bzang and Odani, "Chibetto no Jōdokyō: Minshū no Shinkō," 233–267, and in Kajihama, "Tsonkapa-cho *Gokuraku e no Seiganmon* no Kenkyū," with the Tibetan text, and both Japanese and English translations of the verses and vows only. Tokiya, "Muryōkōbutsu Raisanmon o megutte (josetsu)," contains the Tibetan text and Japanese translation of the verses and vows, along with the corresponding translation into Chinese completed by the monk Dalama Gabochusamudandaerji 達喇嘛嘎卜楚薩木丹達爾吉 in 1829, titled *Jile yuanwen* (*T.* 935). As far as I know, Tokiya is the first to have identi-

fied this work as a translation of Tsong kha pa's text. (According to the kind information of Leonard van der Kuijp, the name of this monk is probably Tibetan, Dka' bcu Bsam gtan rdo rje, though this does not necessarily make him a Tibetan.) The text was recently translated into English by Halkias *Luminous Bliss,* 107–108. The same author, in the pages that follow, refers to a number of other texts as well, offering tables of contents for several.

31 Translated in Onoda, "Chibetto-shoden no Jōdo Kansō Shūhō," and Kajihama, "Chankya Issei no Ōjō Shisō no Kenkyū."

32 Ōtani 11910, translated in Kajihama "Mipamu no Jōdo Shisō no Kenkyū."

33 Ōtani 11101.

34 Probably in the same general class belongs the text translated in Gelong Karma Khechong Palmo, with Thranggu Rimpoche and Cho kyi Nyma Tulku, "Translation of 'Byang chub ltung bshags,'" *Bulletin of Tibetology* 10, no. 2 (1973).

35 Translated by Munekawa Shūman, "Kanzen Shōjō Gokuraku Kokudo Seigan" [A Prayer for rebirth in the Land of Perfect Bliss], in *Imaoka Kyōju Kanreki Kinen Ronbunshū,* edited by Taishō Daigku Jōdogaku Kenkyūkai, *Jōdogaku* 5, no. 6 (1932), translated and edited by Peter Schwieger, *Ein tibetisches Wunschgebet um Wiedergeburt in der Sukhāvatī* (St. Augustin: VGH Wissenschaftsverlag, 1978), and translated by Tadeusz Skorupski, "A Prayer for Rebirth in Sukhāvatī," *The Buddhist Forum* 3 (1994).

36 Tshul khrims skal bzang and Odani, "Chibetto no Jōdokyō: Minshū no Shinkō," 267–277. The authors inexplicably fail to note anywhere the name of the text they are translating, or its source.

37 Ōtani 10432; Kajihama, "Panchen Rama Issei-cho *Gokuraku no Kokudo ni Shōgai naku iku tame no Jinsoku na Michi* no Kenkyū."

38 Kajihama, "Mipamu no Jōdo Shisō no Kenkyū."

39 Kajihama, "Dotsupuchen Rinpoche Sansei no Ōjō Shisō no Kenkyū (I)," and Kajihama, "Dotsupuchen Rinpoche Sansei no Ōjō Shisō no Kenkyū."

40 P. tib. 112, "the size of his body."

41 P. tib. 112 has something like "arisen from change," or "transformationally arisen."

42 P. tib. 516, "When one [correctly] practices the cultivation [of the ten types of meditation] with regard to the pure triple sphere."

43 P. tib. 105, "pure field."

44 P. tib. 516, six superknowledges. Lists with both five or six superknowledges are equally well known; see Robert E. Buswell Jr. and Donald S. Lopez Jr., eds., *The Princeton Dictionary of Buddhism* (Princeton, NJ: Princeton University Press, 2014), s.v. *abhijñā.*

45 P. tib. 6, entails a change in subject: "they see the Sugata's face at the time of their death." This may be better.

46 P. tib. 761, "pay homage to the ācāryas," which agrees better with the passage from the *Guan-jing* I.18 (*T.* 365 [XII] 341c9): Those who desire to born in the Pure Land should, among other practices, "filially nourish their father and mother, and serve their teachers and elders."

47 P. tib. 760, 761, "enquire about."

48 P. tib. 6, "If one preserves them in so far as one is able," "them" referring back to the eight-part precepts which are also the antecedent of the expression "one's promises." The two readings are therefore equivalent in meaning.

49 See Silk, "The Virtues of Amitābha, 1–109.

50 Jiro Hirabayashi, William B. Rasmussen, and Safarali Shomakhmado, "The *Ajitasenavyākaraṇa* from Central Asia and Gilgit," in *Buddhist Manuscripts from Central Asia: The St. Petersburg Sanskrit Fragments*, ed. Seishi Karashima and Margarita I. Vorobyova-Desyatovskaya, vol. I: 85–143 (Tokyo: The Institute of Oriental Manuscripts of the Russian Academy of Sciences, and The International Research Institute for Advanced Buddhology, Soka University, 2015): 100–101.

51 Akamatsu, "Tonkō Chibetto Bunken no Jōdokyō Kankei Shiryō: P. tib. 153 ni tsuite," 223.9–10.

52 Hirabayashi, Rasmussen, and Shomakhmado, "The *Ajitasenavyākaraṇa* from Central Asia and Gilgit": 93–94.

53 C[laire] W. Huntington Jr., with Geshé Namgyal Wangchen, *The Emptiness of Emptiness: An Introduction to Early Indian Mādhyamika* (Honolulu: University of Hawai'i Press, 1989), 156, and 225 note 2.

54 Ronald M. Davidson, "The *Litany of Names of Mañjuśrī*: Text and Translation of the *Mañjuśrīnāmasaṁgīti*," in *Tantric and Taoist Studies in Honour of R. A. Stein*, ed. Michel Strickmann (Brussels: Institut Belge des hautes Études Chinoise, 1981), text, 26, translation, 53; and Wayman, *Chanting the Names of Mañjuśrī*, 78.

55 Dieter Schlingloff, *Buddhistische Stotras aus ostturkistanischen Sanskrittexten* (Berlin: Akademie Verlag, 1955), 86.

56 Ryūjō Kambayashi, "Laudatory Verses of Mañjuśrī," *Journal of the Taishō University* 6–7, no. 2 (1930), reprint in *Wogihara Hakase Kanreki Kinen: Shukuga Ronbunshū* (Tokyo: Sankibō, 1972), 284, 289.

57 Kambayashi, "Laudatory Verses of Mañjuśrī," 284, 290.

58 Davidson "The *Litany of Names of Mañjuśrī*," 34, 59; see also Wayman, *Chanting the Names of Mañjuśrī*, 102.

59 D. R. Shakelton Bailey, "The Varṇārhavarṇa Stotra of Mātṛceṭa (I) & (II)," *Bulletin of the School of Oriental and African Studies* 13 (1950–1951): 974; Jens-Uwe Hartmann, *Das Varṇārhavarṇastotra des Mātṛceṭa* (Göttingen: Vandenhoeck & Ruprecht, 1987), 244.

60 See Étienne Lamotte, *Histoire du Bouddhisme Indien, des Origines à l'ère Śaka* (Louvain: Institut Orientaliste, Université Catholique de Louvain, 1958), 715–716, and note.

61 Shakelton Bailey, "The Varṇārhavarṇa Stotra of Mātṛceṭa (I) & (II)," 676; Hartmann, *Das Varṇārhavarṇastotra des Mātṛceṭa*, 81.

62 Giuseppe Tucci, "Two Hymns of the Catuḥ-stava of Nāgārjuna," *Journal of the Royal Asiatic Society* (1932): 320.

63 Akamatsu, "Tonkō Chibetto Bunken no Jōdokyō Kankei Shiryō," 222.4–8.

64 In the Dunhuang Amitābha text found in Akamatsu, "Tonkō Chibetto Bunken no Jōdokyō Kankei Shiryō," 224.9–225.10, the ten perfections are listed, along with their particular contributions to salvation.

65 Rai Sarat Chandra Das, *A Tibetan-English Dictionary* (Calcutta: Bengal Secretariat Book Depot, 1902), 939.

66 See Gregory Schopen, "The Generalization of an Old Yogic Attainment in Medieval Mahāyāna Sūtra Literature: Some Notes on *Jātismara*," *Journal of the International Association of Buddhist Studies* 6, no. 1 (1983), esp. 119–121, on obtaining *jatismāra* through acts connected with sacred names.

67 Schopen, "Sukhāvatī as a Generalized Religious Goal in Sanskrit Mahāyāna Sūtra Literature," 187–198.

68 Schopen, "Sukhāvatī as a Generalized Religious Goal in Sanskrit Mahāyāna Sūtra Literature," 177.

69 Schopen, "Sukhāvatī as a Generalized Religious Goal in Sanskrit Mahāyāna Sūtra Literature," 177–178.

70 For discussion of these so-called ascetic purification practices, see Miyamoto Shōson, *Daijō Bukkyō no Seiritsushiteki Kenkyū* (Tokyo: Sanseidō, 1954), 302–310, and especially the chart on 304, and Jean Dantinne, *Les Qualities de l'Ascete (Dhutaguṇa): Etude sémantique et Doctrinale* (Brussels: Thanh-Long, 1991).

71 Schopen, "Sukhāvatī as a Generalized Religious Goal in Sanskrit Mahāyāna Sūtra Literature," 189, quoting *Samādhirāja*, chap. 32, vs. 268cd & 270ab.

72 So Nakamura Hajime, *Bukkyōgo Daijiten* (Tokyo: Tōkyō Shoseki, 1981), 803a.

73 Tucci, "Two Hymns of the Catuḥ-stava of Nāgārjuna," 314.

## Bibliography


Akamatsu Kōshō."Amidabutsu ni genkyū suru Tonkō Chibetto-bun Shiryō Gaikan" [An outline of Dunhuang Tibetan materials concerning Amida Buddha]. *Indotetsugaku Bukkyōgaku (Hokkaidō Indotetsugaku Bukkyō Gakkai)* 5 (1991): 191–209.

——. "Chibetto-yaku Amidakyō no Ihon: Tonkō Shahon P tib 758 ni tsuite" [A variant Tibetan version of the Smaller *Sukhāvatīvyūha*: Dunhuang manuscript P. tib 758]. *Indogaku Bukkyōgaku* 33, no. 1 (1984): 150–151.

——."Chibetto-yaku Muryōjukyō no Tonkō Shinshutsu Iyakuhon" [A variant Tibetan translation of the Larger *Sukhāvatīvyūha* from Dunhuang]. *Ryūkoku Daigaku Bukkyō Bunka Kenkyūjo Kiyō* 23 (1984): 2–7.

——. "Tonkō Chibetto Bunken no Jōdokyō Kankei Shiryō: P. tib. 153 ni tsuite," P. tib. 153 [Dunhuang Tibetan materials related to Pure Land Buddhism: P. tib. 153]. *Indotetsugaku Bukkyōgaku (Hokkaidō Indotetsugaku Bukkyō Gakkai)* 3 (1988): 216–228.

——."Tonkō Chibetto Bunken no Jōdokyō Kankei Tekisuto" [Dunhuang Tibetan texts related to Pure Land Buddhism]. *Indotetsugaku Bukkyōgaku (Hokkaidō Indotetsugaku Bukkyō Gakkai)* 2 (1987): 195–220.

——."Tonkō Shahon yori mitaru Chibetto no Jōdo Shisō Juyō" [The Tibetan reception of Pure Land Buddhism in the light of the Dunhuang documents]. *Indogaku Bukkyōgaku Kenkyū* 35, no. 1 (1986): 57–61.

Bapat, P. V. *Vimuktimārga Dhutaguṇa-nirdeśa.* Bombay: Asia Publishing House, 1964.

Buswell, Robert E., Jr., and Donald S. Lopez Jr., eds. *The Princeton Dictionary of Buddhism.* Princeton, NJ: Princeton University Press, 2014.

Dantinne, Jean. *Les Qualities de l'Ascete (Dhutaguṇa): Etude sémantique et Doctrinale.* Brussels: Thanh-Long, 1991.

Das, Rai Sarat Chandra. *A Tibetan-English Dictionary.* Calcutta: Bengal Secretariat Book Depot, 1902.

Davidson, Ronald M. "The *Litany of Names of Mañjuśrī*: Text and Translation of the *Mañjuśrīnāmasaṁgīti.*" In *Tantric and Taoist Studies in Honour of R. A. Stein*, edited by Michel Strickmann, 1–69. Brussels: Institut Belge des hautes Études Chinoise, 1981.

Edgerton, Franklin. *Buddhist Hybrid Sanskrit Dictionary.* New Haven, CT: Yale University Press, 1953.

Fussman, Gérard. "La place des *Sukhāvatī-vyūha* dans le Bouddhisme Indien." *Journal Asiatique* 287, no. 2 (1999): 523–586.

*Guan-jing*: *Guan Wuliangshoufo-jing. Taishō* 365. Edited and translated in Yamada Meiji, *The Sūtra of Contemplation on the Buddha of Immeasurable Life.* Kyoto: Ryukoku University, 1984.

Halkias, Georgios T. *Luminous Bliss: A Religious History of Pure Land Literature in Tibet: With an Annotated English Translation and Critical Analysis of the Orgyan-gling Gold Manuscript of the Short* Sukhāvativyūha-sūtra. Honolulu: University of Hawai'i Press, 2013.

Hartmann, Jens-Uwe. *Das Varṇārhavarṇastotra des Mātṛceṭa.* Göttingen: Vandenhoeck & Ruprecht, 1987.

Hirabayashi, Jiro, William B. Rasmussen, and Safarali Shomakhmado. "The *Ajitasenavyākaraṇa* from Central Asia and Gilgit." In *Buddhist Manuscripts from Central Asia: The St. Petersburg Sanskrit Fragments*, edited by Seishi Karashima and Margarita I. Vorobyova-Desyatovskaya, vol. I: 85–143. Tokyo: The Institute of Oriental Manuscripts of the Russian Academy of Sciences, and the International Research Institute for Advanced Buddhology, Soka University, 2015.

Huntington, C[laire] W., Jr., with Geshé Namgyal Wangchen. *The Emptiness of Emptiness: An Introduction to Early Indian Mādhyamika.* Honolulu: University of Hawai'i Press, 1989.

Jones, Charles B. Review of Georgios Halkias, *Luminous Bliss.* H-Buddhism, H-Net Reviews. February 2014. http://www.h-net.org/reviews/showrev.php?id=40391.

Kagawa Takao. *Jōdokyō no Seiritsushiteki Kenkyū.* Tokyo: Sankibō Busshorin, 1993.

——. *Muryōjukyō no Shohon Taishō.* Kyoto: Nagata Bunshōdō, 1984. [The paragraphs agree with those of Max Müller's edition, but are further subdivided.]

Kajihama Ryōshun. "3rd rDo Grubchen Rinpoche's Pure Land Thought (I)." *Indogaku Bukkyōgaku Kenkyū* 43, no. 1 (1994): 498–492 (27–33).

——. "3rd rDo Grubchen Rinpoche's Pure Land Thought (II)." *Indogaku Bukkyōgaku Kenkyū* 44, no. 2 (1995): 952–948 (29–33).

——. "3rd rDo Grubchen Rinpoche's Pure Land Thought (III)." *Indogaku Bukkyōgaku Kenkyū* 50, no. 2 (2002): 987–984 (50–53).

——. *Amitābha in Tibetan Buddhism.* Takatsuki-city, Osaka: The Author, 2016.

——. "Chankya Issei no Ichishōron ni tsuite" [Lcang skya's essay on Amitābha]. *Shūkyō Kenkyū* 66, no. 4 (1993): 172–174 (770–772).

——. "Chankya Issei no Jōdo Shisō" [Lcang skya I's essay on Pure Land thought]. *Ōsaka Kodai Setsunan Daigaku Chūken Shohō* 25, no. 3 (1993): 121–151.

——. "Chankya Issei no Ōjō Shisō" [Lcang skya's ideas on rebirth in the Pure Land]. *Shūkyō Kenkyū* 67, no. 4 (1994): 185–186 (759–760).

——. "Chankya Issei no Ōjō Shisō no Kenkyū" [Lcang skya's ideas on rebirth in the Pure Land]. *Setsudai Jinbun Kagaku* 1 (1994): 5–12.

——. "Chankya Issei no Shōgai" [The life of Lcang skya I]. *Ōsaka Kodai Setsunan Daigaku Chūken Shohō* 26, no. 3 (1994): 181–195.

——. "Chibetto no gokuraku no kokudo" [The Land of Bliss (Sukhāvatī) in Tibetan Buddhism]. *Shūkyō Kenkyū* 75, no. 4 (2002): 215–216 [not seen].

——. *Chibetto no Jōdo Shisō no Kenkyū*. Kyoto: Nagata Bunshōdō, 2002.

——. "Dotsupuchen Rinpoche Sansei no Ōjō Shisō no Kenkyū: *Gokuraku no Kokudo ni tsuite Chosaku sareta Shomotsu* no Dai-ni-shō o chūshin toshite" [3rd Rdo Grub chen Rinpoche's ideas on rebirth in the Pure Land: The second chapter of the *Book on the Land of Bliss*]. *Setsudai Jinbun Kagaku* 3 (1996): 67–92.

——. "Dotsupuchen Rinpoche Sansei no Ōjō Shisō no Kenkyū (I)" [3rd Rdo Grub chen Rinpoche's ideas on rebirth in the Pure Land]. *Setsudai Jinbun Kagaku* 2 (1995): 189–216.

——. "Mi pham no Jōdo Shisō" Mi pham [Mi pham's Pure Land thought]. *Indogaku Bukkyōgaku Kenkyū* 41, no. 1 (1992): 390–384 (151–157).

——. "Mipamu no Jōdo Shisō no Kenkyū " [Mi pham's Pure Land thought]. *Setsudai Gakujitsu* ser. B, no. 11 (1993): 23–48.

——. "Panchen Rama Issei-cho *Gokuraku no Kokudo ni Shōgai naku iku tame no Jinsoku na Michi* no Kenkyū" [A study of the quick path for going to the Land of Bliss (Sukhāvatī) without obstruction written by the 1st Panchen Lama]. *Setsudai Gakujitsu* ser. B, no. 10 (1992): 9–28.

——. "Peruturu Rinpoche no Shōgai to Jōdo Shisō" [The life of Dpal Sprul Rinpoche, and his Pure Land thought]. In *Watanabe Takao Kyōju Kanreki Kinen Bukkyō Shisō Bunkashi Ronsō*, edited by Watanabe Takao Kyōju Kanreki Kinenkai, 1192–1173 (263–282). Kyoto: Nagata Bunshōdō, 1997.

——. "Tsonkapa no Jōdo Shisō no Kenkyū" [Tsong kha pa's Pure Land thought]. *Ōsaka Kodai Setsunan Daigaku Chūken Shohō* 24, no. 3 (1992): 263–296 (1–34).

——. "Tsonkapa no *Saikō no Kokudo no Kaimon* no Ichikaisetsusho ni tsuite" [Dpal Sprul Rinpoche's explanation of Tsong kha pa's *Prayer for Entrance into the Best Land*]. *Shūkyō Kenkyū* 68, no. 4 (1995): 206–207 (898–899).

——. "Tsonkapa-cho *Gokuraku e no Seiganmon* no Kenkyū" [A study of a prayer book on rebirth in the Land of Bliss (Sukhāvatī) written by Tsong kha pa]. *Ōsaka Kodai Setsunan Daigaku Chūken Shohō* 23, no. 3 (1991): 293–322 (1–30).

Kambayashi Ryūjō. "Laudatory Verses of Mañjuśrī." *Journal of the Taishō University* 6–7, no. 2 (1930): 243–297. Reprint in *Wogihara Hakase Kanreki Kinen: Shukuga Ronbunshū*. Tokyo: Sankibō, 1972.

Lalou, Marcelle. *Inventaire des Manuscrits tibétains de Touen-houang conservés à la Bibliothèque Nationale*, 1. Paris: Adrien Maisonneuve, 1939.

——. *Inventaire des Manuscrits tibétains de Touen-houang conservés à la Bibliothèque Nationale*, 3. Paris: Bibliothèque Nationale, 1961.

——. "Notes à propos d'une amulette de Touen-houang." *Mélanges chinois et bouddhiques* 4 (1936): 135–149.

Lamotte, Étienne. *Histoire du Bouddhisme Indien, des Origines à l'ère Śaka*. Louvain: Institut Orientaliste, Université Catholique de Louvain, 1958.

Laufer, Berthold. "Loan-words in Tibetan." *T'oung-pao*. Second series, 17, no. 4 (1916): 403–552.

La Vallée Poussin, Louis de. *Catalogue of the Tibetan Manuscripts from Tun-Huang in the India Office Library*. Oxford: Oxford University Press, 1962.

LSV. Larger *Sukhāvatīvyūha sūtra*. In Kagawa Takao, *Muryōjukyō no Shohon Taishō*. Kyoto: Nagata Bunshōdō, 1984.

Miyamoto Shōson. *Daijō Bukkyō no Seiritsushiteki Kenkyū*. Tokyo: Sanseidō, 1954.

Mochizuki Shinkō. *Bukkyō Daijiten*. Tokyo: Sekai Seiten Kankō Kyōkai, 1932–1936.

Munekawa Shūman. "Kanzen Shōjō Gokuraku Kokudo Seigan" [A prayer for rebirth in the Land of Perfect Bliss]. In *Imaoka Kyōju Kanreki Kinen Ronbunshū*, edited by Taishō Daigku Jōdogaku Kenkyūkai. *Jōdogaku* 5, no. 6 (1932): 643–670.

Nakamura Hajime. "Amidakyō Chibetto-yaku ni tsuite" [The Tibetan translation of the Smaller *Sukhāvatīvyūha sūtra*]. In *Iwai Hakase Koki Kinen Tenseki Ronshū*, edited by Iwai Hakase Koki Kinen Jigyōkai. Shizuoka: Kaimeidō, 1963.

——. *Bukkyōgo Daijiten*. Tokyo: Tōkyō Shoseki, 1981.

——. "Gokuraku Jōdo no Kannen no Indogaku-teki Kaimei to Chibetto-teki Hen'yō" [Studies on the idea of Pure Land in the perspective of Indian cultural history and the modification of the idea by Tibetans]. *Indogaku Bukkyōgaku Kenkyū* 11, no. 2 (1963): 131–153 (509–531).

——. *Jōdo Sambukyō (ge)*. Tokyo: Iwanami shoten, 1964.

Ñyāṇamoli [*sic*], Bhikkhu. *The Path of Purification (Vissudhimagga)*. Two volumes. 1956, 1964. Reprint: Berkeley, CA, and London: Shambala, 1976.

Onoda Shunzō. "*Amida Kuon Jōō Darani-kyō* ni motozuku Chibetto Mandara" [A Tibetan maṇḍala based on the *Aparimitāyurjñānahṛdaya-dhāraṇī*]. *Nihon Bukkyō Gakkai Nenpō* 52 (1987): 87–99.

——. "Chibetto Bukkyō no Jōdokyō Rikai" [The Tibetan understanding of Pure Land Buddhism]. *Chūgai Nippō* 24152 (January 19, 1990): 1.

——. "Chibetto Senjutsu no Jōdokyō-kei Butten" [Pure Land Buddhist scriptures compiled in Tibet]. *Bukkyō Daigaku Daigakuin Kenkyū Kiyō* 7 (1979): 1–21.

——. "Chibetto-shoden no Jōdo Kansō Shūhō: Aoki Bunkyō-shi Shōrai Shiryō Nos. 103, 104, 107, 108, 109 ni tsuite no Kanken' Nos. 103, 104, 107, 108, 109 [Tibetan Pure Land visualization manuals: Items from the Aoki Bunkyō collection]. *Kokuritsu Minzokugaku Hakubutsukan Kenkyū Hōkoku* Bessatsu 1 (1983): 184–192.

——. "Tsonkapa-zō *Saijōkoku Kaimon* Shiyaku" [A tentative translation of Tsong kha pa's *Zhing mchog sgo 'byed*]. *Bukkyō Bunka Kenkyū* 27 (1981): 141–156.

Ōtani University, ed. *Catalogue of Tibetan Works Kept in Otani University Library.* Kyoto: Otani University Library, 1973.

Palmo, Gelong Karma Khechong, with Thranggu Rimpoche and Cho kyi Nyma Tulku. "Translation of 'Byang chub ltung bshags.'" *Bulletin of Tibetology* 10, no. 2 (1973): 18–34.

Sakaki Ryōsaburō. *Mahāvyutpatti.* Kyoto: Kyōto Teikoku Daigaku Bunka Daigaku Sōsho 3, 1916.

Schlingloff, Dieter. *Buddhistische Stotras aus ostturkistanischen Sanskrittexten.* Berlin: Akademie Verlag, 1955.

Schopen, Gregory. "The Generalization of an Old Yogic Attainment in Medieval Mahāyāna Sūtra Literature: Some Notes on *Jātismara.*" *Journal of the International Association of Buddhist Studies* 6, no. 1 (1983): 109–147.

——. "Sukhāvatī as a Generalized Religious Goal in Sanskrit Mahāyāna Sūtra Literature." *Indo-Iranian Journal* 19 (1977): 177–210.

Schwieger, Peter. *Ein tibetisches Wunschgebet um Wiedergeburt in der Sukhāvatī.* St. Augustin: VGH Wissenschaftsverlag, 1978.

Shakelton Bailey, D. R. "The Varṇārhavarṇa Stotra of Mātṛceṭa (I) & (II)." *Bulletin of the School of Oriental and African Studies* 13 (1950–51): 671–701, 947–1003.

Shinmura Izuru, ed. *Kōjien.* 2nd ed. Tokyo: Iwanami shoten, 1980.

Shiraishi, Shindō. "Bhadracarī: ein Sanskrittext des heiligen Jiun. Abdruck im Jahre 1783." *Yamanashi Daigaku Gakugei Gakubu Kenkyū Hōkoku / Memoirs of the Faculty of Liberal Arts and Eduction, Yamanashi University* 13 (1962): 1–18. Reprinted in *Shiraishi Shindō Bukkyōgaku Ronbunshū*, edited by Shiraishi Hisako, 444–461. Sagamihara-shi, Japan: Kyōbi shuppansha, 1988.

Silk, Jonathan. "The Place of the *Lotus Sūtra* in Indian Buddhism." *Journal of Oriental Studies* 11 (2001): 89–107.

——. "The Ten Virtues of Loudly Invoking the Name of Amitābha: Stein Tibetan 724 and an Aspect of Chinese *Nianfo* Practice in Tibetan Dunhuang," *Journal of the American Oriental Society* 137, no. 3 (2017): 473–482.

——. "The Virtues of Amitābha: A Tibetan Poem from Dunhuang." *Ryūkoku Daigaku Bukkyō Bunka Kenkyūjo Kiyō* 32 (1993): 1–109.

Skorupski, Tadeusz. "A Prayer for Rebirth in Sukhāvatī." *The Buddhist Forum* 3 (1994): 375–409. http://www.shin-ibs.edu/publications/the-buddhist-forum/the-buddhist-forum-volume-iii.

SSV. Smaller *Sukhāvatīvyūha sūtra.* In Wogihara Unrai, *Bonzō Waei Gappeki Jōdo Sambukyō: Jōdoshū Zensho* 23. Tokyo: Sankibō Busshorin, 1972.

Takata, Tokio. "Multilingualism in Tun-huang." *Acta Asiatica* 78 (2000): 49–70.

Takeuchi, Tsuguhito. "Old Tibetan Buddhist Texts from the Post-Tibetan Imperial Period (mid-9th c. to late 10th c.)." In *Old Tibetan Studies: Dedicated to the*

*Memory of R. E. Emmerick*, edited by by Cristina Scherrer-Schaub, 205–214. Leiden: Brill, 2012.

——. "Sociolinguistic Implications of the Use of Tibetan in East Turkestan from the End of Tibetan Domination through the Tangut Period (9th–12th c.)." In *Turfan Revisited: The First Century of Research into the Arts and Cultures of the Silk Road*, edited by Desmond Durkin-Meisterernst, Simone-Christiane Raschmann, Jens Wilkens, Marianne Yaldiz, Peter Zieme, et al., 341–348. Berlin: Dietrich Reimer Verlag, 2004.

Tokiya Kōki. "Chibetto-yaku Sanshu no Sangan ni tsuite" [Three types of confession prayers in Tibetan translation]. *Nihon Chibetto Gakkai Kaihō* 23 (1977): 1–5.

——. "Muryōkōbutsu Raisanmon o megutte (josetsu): Sono Kaisetsu to Wayaku [Introduction to the praise of Amitābha Buddha: Interpretation and translation]. *Takata Tanki Daigaku Kiyō* 3 (1985): 25–47.

Tshul khrims skal bzang, and Odani Nobuchiyo. "Chibetto no Jōdokyō: Minshū no Shinkō" [Tibetan Pure Land Buddhism: Faith of the people]. In *Jōdo Bukkyō no Shisō* 3: *Ryūju, Seshin, Chibetto no Jōdokyō, Eon*. Tokyo: Kōdansha 1993: 187–278.

Tucci, Giuseppe. "Two Hymns of the Catuḥ-stava of Nāgārjuna." *Journal of the Royal Asiatic Society* (1932): 309–325.

Wayman, Alex. *Chanting the Names of Mañjuśrī*. Boston: Shambala, 1985.

Wogihara Unrai. *Bonzō Waei Gappeki Jōdo Sambukyō: Jōdoshū Zensho* 23. Tokyo: Sankibō Busshorin, 1972. [Originally 1931. This contains, unchanged, Max Müller's editions of the SSV and the LSV and Tibetan editions of both.]

Yamada Meiji. *The Sūtra of Contemplation on the Buddha of Immeasurable Life*. Kyoto: Ryukoku University, 1984.

# Chapter 4

# Pure Land Devotional Poetry by a Chan Monk

Natasha Heller

## Translator's Introduction

Zhongfeng Mingben (1263–1323) was one of the most prominent monks during the Yuan dynasty (1271–1368), and in many ways exemplified Chinese Buddhism of this period. He lived in the area around Hangzhou and Suzhou, a region with a vigorous economy and the center of cultural life in China at the time. Little is known about Mingben's early years, but he became the disciple of a monk known for his stern demeanor. After years of study and meditation in the Chan tradition, Mingben had an awakening and was acknowledged by his teacher as his heir. Mingben's teacher headed a temple, funded by local elites, on Mount Tianmu, and later Mingben himself would be asked to take over leadership. But Mingben only reluctantly served in positions within the monastic administration, and he refused the abbacies of major monasteries. He preferred to live in relative isolation in simple dwellings and also spent time traveling the region by boat. Mingben was very well connected, receiving frequent letters and visits both from officials and from cultured elites. He left behind a considerable body of writing in different genres, and these writings were collected by his disciples, who successfully appealed to the emperor for their inclusion in the Buddhist canon shortly after Mingben's death.

Although he was identified primarily with the Chan tradition, Mingben also advocated the practice of *nianfo* recitation and the aspiration for rebirth in the Western Pure Land. He became closely identified with the dual practice of Chan and Pure Land, and late Ming Buddhists would point to him as an exemplary figure from the Yuan dynasty. Indeed, there are even Pure Land ritual texts that are attributed—posthumously and dubiously—to Mingben. In advocating for the dual practice of Chan and Pure Land, he followed in the tradition of Yongming Yanshou (904–

975). In his work *The Collection of the Shared Source of the Myriad Good Deeds* (*Wanshan tonggui ji*), Yanshou argued that the Pure Land should be seen as a state of mind, rather than a geographic destination. Yanshou also promoted good works such as repairing roads and helping the poor, and he assumed that all Buddhists would engage in repentance, ritual offerings, sutra chanting, and other long-standing practices.[1] Writing in the tenth century, Yanshou was reacting in part to Chan monks who argued that conventional religious practices were just another form of attachment and who at times behaved in startling ways in an attempt to free students from such fetters. Although the most radical of such positions—which might include advocating smashing statues of the Buddha—were largely rhetorical, Chan discourse did prompt a new examination of Buddhist practices and what they were meant to achieve.

Given Yanshou's influence on the later monk, we might well consider Mingben an inheritor of his approach to understanding Buddhist practices within the context of Chan doctrine. Yet Mingben's commitment to the religious goal of awakening—understood as a fundamental change in one's perception of the world—meant that practice should be centered on that goal and that dedication to a single form of practice was the most effective way of reaching it. Mingben's primary framework for Buddhist practice was drawn from the Chan tradition of *kanhua*, or contemplation of the "key phrase" (*huatou*) of the public cases (*gongan*) of past masters. This approach to meditation arose in the Song dynasty as Chan monks grappled both with how to explain meditation and how to engage with the words of past Chan masters. The *kanhua* approach promoted by Dahui Zonggao (1089–1163) and others sought to unify the mind through focus on a key phrase. The intention was to bring about a radical change in perspective, or an awakening to the true nature of reality. Mingben wrote extensively on *kanhua* practice and clearly believed that *kanhua* was the most expedient practice for both clergy and lay Buddhists. To aid them in their practice, Mingben recommended specific phrases for his disciples to take up, often telling them to contemplate "the great matter of birth-and-death" (*shengsi dashi*). One should hold this or another phrase in mind during meditation, focusing one's attention on the phrase so that the whole mind was unified. Nor was this an easy process: Mingben told his disciples that they should not expect immediate success in their efforts and that they might need to continue with their practice for years or decades. Perhaps because this approach to Chan could seem so arduous, he also encouraged lay disciples by telling them *kanhua* practice was compatible with their worldly obligations. Such persuasion was necessary because not all lay people seemed to have confidence that they could take on the same practice as Chan monks. Instead, they may have seen *nianfo* or other forms of recitation as more suitable to lay life. Mingben was well aware of the popularity of Pure Land practice among lay Buddhists, and explained that *nianfo*, or the recitation of the Buddha's name, could be integrated within the framework of *kanhua* practice. For example, when one recited the Buddha's name, one could also take a key phrase used for *kanhua* and contemplate it during recitation. Mingben advised one lay Buddhist, "You have long been intimate with the study of Pure Land, but also admire the purport of Shaolin. You just need to take the phrase 'before my father and mother were born, that is my original face,' and put it in your mind when you recite the Buddha's name, keeping it in mind from moment to moment without setting aside, and being diligent about it without leaving it behind."[2] Mingben was building on earlier teachings that advocated contemplating who is doing the reciting when one is engaged in *nianfo*.[3]

Reading further in Mingben's writings, we find that this combined practice is not one in which Chan and Pure Land are on equal footing. Rather, for Mingben the use of a key phrase alongside *nianfo* might be understood as Chan *through* Pure Land practice. Chan retains priority, and the spiritual goal Mingben has for his followers is not rebirth in the pure land but awakening. Writing to a fellow monk, he makes the point that both practices should be motivated by the goal of escaping the cycle of transmigration: "If one does not truly become awakened with one's whole body, how could there be a principle of liberation? When engaging in Chan one wants to put an end to birth and death; in reciting the Buddha's name and cultivating the Pure Land, one also wants to put an end to birth and death."[4] Comparing Yanshou with Mingben, the later monk placed more emphasis on a single practice. In part this was due to Mingben's deeper connection to the Chan tradition, but it also grew out of his emphasis on intense practice with the goal of awakening. Mingben might have agreed with Yanshou that all Buddhist practices were ultimately one, but as a practical matter it was best to focus one's energies on a single method of contemplation.

Mingben communicated his ideas on the relationship between Chan and Pure Land in a number of ways, from letters to sermons to poems. Like most Buddhist monks, Mingben wrote for many different audiences, and did so in different registers. Writing to his disciples, both lay and ordained, Mingben's prose often takes an approach that fuses practice with doctrine. Poems could be doctrinal as well, but they might also offer praise for Buddhist figures and themes, promote Buddhist practices, or provide a link between other poets, both living and dead. Mingben wrote two sets of poems on the Pure Land. One was written in response to a set of poems on the Pure Land by a monk whose biography has been lost to history. In Mingben's preface to his own poems, he writes of the identity of Pure Land and Chan, even though "it seems as if a single dharma peak has become two," and he credits Yongming Yanshou with this teaching.[5]

Selections from the other set of poems on the Pure Land written by Mingben are translated below. These devotional poems on the Pure Land seem to have been composed to encourage Pure Land practice among the laity, perhaps especially those with the financial means to support Buddhist institutions. Besides the poems themselves, a preface and an afterword by prominent lay disciples provide the best clues for Mingben's intentions in writing this set of poems. Mingben had very prominent lay followers, including the statesman, painter, and calligrapher Zhao Mengfu (1254–1322). Zhao wrote both an afterword and a verse encomium, emphasizing in both that the poems numbered 108, like a Buddhist rosary, and that Mingben had written these poems out of compassion for lay followers. Mingben hoped, according to Zhao, to inspire practitioners by describing the great happiness of the Western Pure Land. Another literati follower, Feng Zizhen (1253–1348), wrote a preface to the poems, again emphasizing that they numbered 108 and so were like beads on a rosary. Feng encourages readers to always keep Amitābha in mind so that they can become like great lay Buddhists of the past who established Pure Land societies for collective practice.[6] That Feng and Zhao were involved in promoting Mingben's collection of poems suggests that the audience for the poems was likely other intellectual elites of the age. Poems were an important mode of communication between friends and also a way for educated men to demonstrate their mastery of the literary tradition. Indeed, Mingben and Feng Zizhen cultivated their relationship through a long exchange of poems about plum blossoms. Poems of that type are often filled with allusions to earlier verses on the same topic. The poems on the Pure Land, in contrast, are in a far simpler style and draw on general knowledge of Buddhist history in China and Pure Land teachings. For example, references to white lotuses would be easily understood as indicating rebirth in the pure land. The poems are straightforwardly didactic in many cases, and they openly urge readers to behave in certain ways.

It is significant that both Zhao and Feng emphasized the number of poems; that Mingben chose to write 108 poems shows that he intended these as a devotional exercise. Instead of—or perhaps parallel with—counting the beads on a rosary, Mingben wrote poems; reading these poems likewise might have been an alternative to counting rosary beads. The poems situate Pure Land practice within a variety of social settings, making the point that *nianfo* is possible within daily life. Mingben writes verses that chastise the wealthy for not engaging in *nianfo* and praise those of lower classes who practice assiduously. Mingben takes as topics for verses the different holidays of the year, suggesting that these feasts may be apt opportunities to contemplate Amitābha or that Pure Land thought could substitute for non-Buddhist practices. Yet a dominant theme is also the relationship between Chan and Pure Land. Mingben also hopes that readers will go beyond a simple devotion to the Pure Land and also treat recitation of Amitābha's name as an opportunity for Chan practice. He writes of becoming a Buddha as the goal of recitation, and talks about the Amitābha within, both ways of viewing Pure Land practice as consonant with Chan. Mingben also refers to "two kinds of *gongan*," treating both Pure Land and Chan accounts as sources for contemplation and verification of one's own experience.

## Translation

### "Seleted Verses from Cherishing the Pure Land"

Zhongfeng Mingben

In the eastern sea a red orb,
Its rays everyday reach the western grove.
How many exceptional men are in this world,
And who has ever been able to cherish their brief time?

[Just as] squinting one's eyes produces flowers in the sky,
One mistakenly takes the triple realm [of *saṃsāra*] as one's home.
The chiliocosm of eternally quiescent pure lands,
Not separated by even a mote of dust, but always obscured.

When in delusion there is no awakening, and in awakening there is no
  delusion
At the moment delusion is exhausted, there is awakening.
When you have gotten free of both delusion and awakening,
Then the cauldrons of hell are originally lotus ponds.

Ten thousand *kalpas* of transmigration are like a severe illness,
One sound of the Buddha's name is a good doctor.
In the end, both medicine and illness are forgotten,
No need to again proclaim that a mother remembers her child.[7]

Don't again speak of the Pure Land outside of Chan,
You must know that outside of the Pure Land there is no Chan.
Take up both sorts of *gongan,*
At Xionger peak a five-petaled lotus opens.[8]

There is not a single dharma in Brahma's abode,
But within the place of no dharmas there are a thousand distinctions.
Looking around, one's own nature is separate from all discrimination,
With every thought, simply open a white lotus.

In the lotus pond there is not a day when flowers do not open,
Four-colored light shines on the jeweled tower.
Golden arms extend to show care,
Why do sentient beings not think of coming?

Where the Blood Pond dries out, the Lotus-Root Pond is pure;
When the Tree of Knives withers, the Treasure Tree blooms.
If you delight in the original marks of non-abiding,
Then in a place of non-abiding you will be perfectly complete.

Buddhas and sentient beings long have had a connection,
But sentient beings show no inclination toward their Buddha-nature.
How can they readily accept the suffering of the Sāhā realm,
And be unwilling to turn their heads at a painful lash?

Mindfulness is a strand of rosary beads,
A painful lash compels one to make a far-reaching plan.
Recite until recitation is empty, and recitation is cast off,
Not knowing that one dwells in a white lotus.

In the world, which conditions are called the most happy?
Just those where the myriad types of suffering cannot encroach.
If people of the Way wish to seek a road home,
They should simply understand their own minds amid the dust.

You are an Amitābha Buddha,
Over long *kalpas,* when have you opened your eyes?

Today you spin around, following sound and appearance,
Now when you want to see, it is still difficult.

Celebrating the new spring, looking at the lanterns;
The candles of ten thousand households illumine the golden lotus.
Unfolding the shining land of eternal quiescence,
How could the Buddha-dharma not be before you?

On the cold food festival the remote suburbs are filled with wailing,
Who is there to distantly recollect the ancient golden immortal?
Since the beginning of the *kalpa* buried in the Lotus Land,
No need for people to come burn paper money.

Climbing a tower to enjoy the mid-autumn moon together,
Turning back, who thinks of the country of one's parents?
Don't ask how many lifetimes one has fled,
Even today still showing concern and not yet forgetting each other.

Sincerely discuss the apparent *gongan,*
The morning chime sounds again, the candles burn long;
Throughout the day and night, the sound unceasing
Filling the gate, the scent of wind-blown white lotus.

Reciting the Amitābha's name one intends to be a Buddha
If one does not intend to be a Buddha, why recite?
It is just those who are sentient beings
All possess a simple lotus root.

If you want to form a Lotus Society as a contributing condition [for rebirth],
Is it that self and other are completely overturned, or not?
Not a moment one does not form rare thoughts,
Delightedly boarding together the boat of liberation.

Morning meditation and evening rites are diligent endeavors,
The lotus-womb in the golden pond frequently enters one's dreams.
One's body shattered, sacrificed over millions of *kalpas*
It is not easy to requite one's compassionate parents.

All suffering arises from craving and anger,
But you do not know from where craving and anger arises:
It is because you have forgotten the Amitābha of your own nature,
The various thoughts running about in confusion—all are demons.

The elder brother calls and the younger responds, recollecting Amitābha,
Hoping that the whole family will escape the river of desire.
Discerning that the mind is constant like this,
Just teaching buddhas—there's nothing to be done.

Morning and evening, making confession,
Bowing one's head, weepingly address old Amitābha.
How many times have you revolved through the six paths?
Vow this time to escape the net!

Amitābha dwells in the west, and Bodhidharma came from the west;
Recollecting the Buddha, engaging in Chan—both modes together.
The ball of doubt from myriad *kalpas* is about to break,
And at the same time the flowers of the mind all open.

Recitation of the Buddha's name does not obstruct daily life;
People, in their daily life, obstruct themselves.
Who is able to preserve the illusory shadows of a hundred years?
Do not abandon the venerable King of Vows of the Western Heaven!

Wealthy, powerful people should recite Amitābha's name.
Gold fills their vaults and grain fills their storehouses,
In their worldly possessions they have no lack,
Yet at death they will not see the "King of Vows."

When the poor recite the Buddha's name,
Although without family goods, they are immersed in thought.
Naked and with empty hands,
They will directly ascend the lotus platform to be reborn.[9]

It is fitting to recollect the Buddha when one grows old,
In the past, there were not many days when it was not temporarily forgotten.
The six syllables of "Namo Amitābha"
Are the boat of compassion to cross the sea of suffering.

## Notes

1 Albert Welter, *The Meaning of Myriad Good Deeds: A Study of Yung-ming Yen-shou and the Wan-shan t'ung-kuei chi* (New York: Peter Lang, 1993), 132–137, 149–154, 157–160.

2 *Tianmu Zhongfeng Heshang guanglu,* in *Zhonghua Dazang jing* 1:74 ([Taibei]: Xiuding Zhonghua Dazang jing hui, 1965), 5b: 11a; 32106b.

3 Heng-ching Shih, *The Syncretism of Ch'an and Pure Land Buddhism* (New York: Peter Lang, 1992), 176–181.

4 *Tianmu Zhongfeng Heshang guanglu,* 11a: 8a; 32121a, also cited by Chün-fang Yü, "Chung-feng Ming-pen and Ch'an Buddhism in the Yüan," in *Yüan Thought: Chinese Thought and Religion under the Mongols,* edited by Hok-lam Chan and Wm. Theodore de Bary (New York: Columbia University Press, 1982), 441.

5 *Tianmu Zhongfeng Heshang guanglu,* 28:2b–3a; 32205b.

6 *Fofa jintang bian Z* 87, no. 1628, 444c24–445a12 and 446a7–11.

7 Amitābha's concern for sentient beings is like a mother thinking of her children.

8 *Tianmu Mingben Z* 70: 745a6–7. *Zhong* seems to be a mistake for *zhong.* Bodhidharma is buried at Mount Xionger.

9 Literally, "to occupy a stem." That is, they will be allotted their own flower in the pure land, into which they will be reborn.

## Bibliography

Shih, Heng-ching. *The Syncretism of Ch'an and Pure Land Buddhism.* New York: Peter Lang, 1992.

*Tianmu Mingben Chanshi zalu* (*ZL*). *Z* 70, no. 1402. Tokyo: Kokusho Kankōkai, [1975–1989].

*Tianmu Zhongfeng Heshang guanglu*. In *Zhonghua Dazang jing* 1:74. [Taibei]: Xiuding Zhonghua Dazang jing hui, 1965. Also in *Nihon kôtei Daizôkyô,* vols. 298–299. Kyoto: Zôkyô Shoin, 1902–1905.

Welter, Albert. *The Meaning of Myriad Good Deeds: A Study of Yung-ming Yen-shou and the Wan-shan t'ung-kuei chi*. New York: Peter Lang, 1993.

Yü, Chün-fang. "Chung-feng Ming-pen and Ch'an Buddhism in the Yüan." In *Yüan Thought: Chinese Thought and Religion under the Mongols,* edited by Hok-lam Chan and Wm. Theodore de Bary, 419–477. New York: Columbia University Press, 1982.

# V

# Ethical and Aesthetic Explications

## Overview

Buddha-fields or pure lands have been a platform for ethical discourses for a number of ancient and contemporary Buddhist preachers. Driven by a social concern to change and transform this world characterized by suffering into a realm that resembles a pure land, exegetes from China and Japan were keen to draw meaningful connections between this contaminated world of ours and Amitābha's pure land, demythologizing the latter in the process. The idea of a pure land immanent in this world dominates the intellectual lives of Japanese reformers, who find in it a perfect metaphor for social equality and nonviolence, and a source of inspiration for scholarly reflection, aesthetic representation, and faith as an interiorized form of cultivation bridging soteriology, ethical conduct, and society.

Jacques Fasan (chap. V.1) examines three pieces that encapsulate Kiyozawa Manshi's mature thoughts on ethics. The first selection, "The Cosmos as One Body," presents Kiyozawa's vision of all beings as interdependent parts of the one body of Amida Buddha. From this, Kiyozawa derives an ethic of personal responsibility for all things. The impossibility of enacting this ethic provides for a feeling of repentance, which in turn opens the gate to other-power faith. In the second essay, "The Coexistence of Freedom and Submission," Kiyozawa uses interdependence to wrestle with the notion of individual freedom. He concludes that freedom is a property of the whole, while individual existence entails submission to authority. In the last essay, "Peace and Comfort beyond Ethics," Kiyozawa again discusses the relationship between religion and ethics. He concludes that religion is in fact the only secure basis for ethical practice and not the other way around.

Ugo Dessì (chap. V.2) looks at the work of the Shin Buddhist (Ōtani-ha) thinker Hishiki Masaharu (b. 1950), which can be characterized as a critically oriented approach to Shin Buddhist ethics. Hishiki's discussion on *The Pure Land as a Principle of Criticism* (*Hihan genri to shite no jōdo*) admittedly operates within the framework provided by modern doctrinal studies' demythologization of the Pure Land. Hishiki, however, not only places emphasis on the nonsubstantial status of the Pure Land but also on its potential to provide a standard to measure the injustice of this world. In this sense, his thought is substantially related to the equalitarian dimension of the teachings and its wider implications for nonviolence.

Yanagi Sōetsu (1889–1961) was an art critic and the founder of the mingei (folk crafts) movement, which was destined to gain great popularity both in Japan and abroad. Yanagi's later aesthetic theory was deeply influenced by the Pure Land Buddhist tradition, and works such as *The Dharma Gate of Beauty* (*Bi no hōmon,* 1949) and *The Pure Land of Beauty* (*Bi no Jōdo,* 1962) clearly reflect this later development. This conception of art is grounded in the Fourth Vow of Amida Buddha, as found in one of the three main sutras of the Pure Land tradition, the *Daimuryōjukyō*, or Larger *Sukhāvatīvyūha sūtra*. Such ideas are to be found also in Yanagi's writing on the *Vow of Non-Discrimination between Beauty and Ugliness* (*Muu kōshu no gan*, 1957), examined and translated here by Elizabetta Porcu (chap. V.3), where Amida's Fourth Vow becomes the foundation for an explicitly "Eastern"—as opposed to a "Western"—conception of beauty and art.

Daniel Getz (chap. V.4) looks at Wang Rixiu's *Longshu's Discourse on Pure Land* (*Longshu jingtu wen*), a late twelfth-century Chinese Buddhist treatise, which sought to address a wide audience within contemporary Southern Song society on the urgent need to embrace Pure Land practice. While providing a clear summary of Pure Land belief and making an argument for the soteriological superiority of Pure Land practice over other Buddhist and non-Buddhist religious cultivations, Wang, who was trained in the Confucian classics and attained the *jinshi* degree, insists that Pure Land practice brings mundane as well as otherworldly benefits to those who embrace it. Getz seeks to highlight those passages where Wang integrates his Confucian sensibilities and values focused on the good of society and welfare in this world with the otherworldly aspiration to rebirth in Pure Land belief.

The lay Nichiren Buddhist leader Tanaka Chigaku (1861–1939) promulgated "Nichirenshugi" (Nichirenism), a rereading of the medieval Buddhist figure Nichiren geared to the practical realities of lay life and modern nation building. Nichiren had taught that exclusive devotion to the *Lotus Sūtra*, widely revered as the Buddha's highest teaching, would one day transform this world into a buddha-land. Tanaka drew on this idea to formulate a contemporary Lotus-based millennial vision in which Japan, newly reconfigured as a modern nation-state, would play the leading role. Tanaka's Japan-centered reading of Nichiren and the *Lotus Sūtra* helped to legitimize the country's militant imperialist ventures, even as his innovative proselytizing strategies inspired a range of lay Buddhist movements. The *Age of Unification,* taken from Tanaka's 1902 systematization of Nichirenshugi doctrine and translated here by Jacqueline Stone (chap. V.5), sets forth his early concept of a this-worldly buddha-land in which thought, religion, morality, society, and government would all be grounded in the *Lotus Sūtra.*

## Chapter 1

# Religion and Ethics in the Thought of Kiyozawa Manshi

Jacques Fasan

### Translator's Introduction

Kiyozawa Manshi (1863–1903) is one of the most influential modern thinkers of the largest Buddhist denomination in Japan, the Ōtani sect of True Pure Land (Shin) Buddhism. Kiyozawa is known for his attempts at institutional reform of the Ōtani, his philosophical writings, and his modern reformulation of Buddhism as an existential faith. In his own time, he was lauded in both the Buddhist world as well as in wider intellectual circles. Japan's most famous philosopher, Nishida Kitarō (1870–1945), praised Kiyozawa for his philosophical acumen, and the leading socialist of the day, Kōtoku Shūsui (1871–1911), mourned his passing in the pages of his *People's Newspaper.*[1] Interestingly, he may even have figured as the inspiration for a character in Natsume Sōseki's (1867–1916) novel *I Am a Cat.*[2]

Personally, compared to other well-known Buddhist reformers of his time, Kiyozawa presents an unusual figure. Unlike most Japanese Buddhist clerics, he was not born into a temple family, and he initially entered the priesthood solely for the pragmatic purpose of financing his education. Furthermore, unlike most of his fellow religious pupils, his primary studies were neither in Buddhist doctrine nor in Shin ritual but rather in Western philosophy. Finally, his own life was both tragic and tumultuous. His several attempts at administrative reform ultimately failed, and he received both censure (*jomei*) and the charge of heterodoxy (*ianjin*) from his head temple. He died at age forty-one of tuberculosis, but not before witnessing the death of his wife and oldest son.

## Kiyozawa's Life and Thought

Kiyozawa was born in 1863 into a lower-ranking samurai family outside of Nagoya in present-day Aichi Prefecture. His early education included studies in Confucian ethics and mathematics as well as foreign languages: some German and a solid grounding in English. Through his mother, Kiyozawa was also exposed to the basic teachings, scriptures, and practices of Shin Buddhism. This branch of Pure Land thought traces its origins back to the medieval reformer Shinran (1173–1262) who moved Pure Land teachings in Japan away from a focus on one's future rebirth to a renewed emphasis on realizing the mind of faith (*shinjin*) in the present moment. With the mind of faith, the individual believer is assured of salvation through Amida's grace. Due to this emphasis, for Shinran, the *nenbutsu* became not a means of salvation but rather an outward display of gratitude to Amida for one's emancipation.

Unable to continue his studies due to poverty, Kiyozawa eventually chose to enter the priesthood to become a cleric within the Ōtani branch of Shin. Kiyozawa excelled in his studies and was sent on a scholarship to study at what was to become Japan's premier institution of higher learning, Tokyo Imperial University. Here he majored in philosophy and the newly emergent discipline of the philosophy of religion, studying under the American Ernest Fenollosa (1853–1908). He was particularly drawn to the thought of Spinoza, Hegel, and the late nineteenth-century post-Hegelian thinker Rudolph Hermann Lotze (1817–1881).

Rather than pursue a promising academic career in the philosophy of religion, however, Kiyozawa chose to devote himself to ever-widening arenas of moral and religious reform, first himself, then his sect, and finally Japanese society at large. Beginning in the late 1880s, perhaps to set a moral example for his fellow clerics, he embarked on an increasingly severe program of personal ascetic self-cultivation. At one point Kiyozawa is reported to have been eating buckwheat gruel and pine resin, perhaps in imitation of indigenous traditions of mountain asceticism (*shugendō*). These practices contributed to a severe case of tuberculosis, to which he would eventually succumb.

Before his untimely death, however, he turned his focus upon reforming his own sect administration, spearheading the Shirakawa reform movement from 1896 to 1898. His calls for more intense religious training for clerics and for more autonomy for branch temples aroused intense opposition from the head temple. He was briefly removed from the rolls of active clergy in 1897 though reinstated the following year.[3]

From 1901 until his death in 1903, he led the spiritual activism movement (*seishinshugi undō*) for which he is most known. Through a journal, the *Spiritual World* (*Seishinkai*), as well as regular discussion groups throughout the country, Kiyozawa attempted to turn Japanese society away from a purely material focus on prosperity to a focus on the inner life of the spirit.

Kiyozawa's mature thought occurred at a time when Japan was ending a period of rapid importation of foreign technology and ideas and using these to create a modern nation-state based upon scientific reason, centralized administration, and aggressive capitalist development. Externally this led to war and victory over China in the first Sino-Japanese War (1894–1895), and internally it led to a state-sponsored program of national morality that emphasized obedience to authority and sacrifice to the state.

Kiyozawa's own relation to these historical trends is ambiguous. On the one hand, Kiyozawa created a modern system of Buddhist belief that systematically demythologized Pure Land doctrine and equated faith with the existential choice of the individual. He famously wrote, "We do not believe in the gods and buddhas because they exist. Rather, because we believe in them, the gods and buddhas exist."[4] In the Shirakawa movement, Kiyozawa also tried to loosen the virtual monopoly of power held by the head temple of his sect by advocating greater representation by local branch temples in decision making. Many have taken this emphasis on the individual in the religious sphere along with his push for sect administrative reform as at least a critique of the authoritarian nature of the Japanese state at this time. Kiyozawa, however, remained highly critical of those who would use Buddhism to call for more radical structural reforms within society. Against these, he writes, "Talk that Śākyamuni's teachings are for destroying social classes is misguided."[5] While not a strident supporter of Japanese nationalism like many of his peers, he supported hierarchies of class and obedience to authority, to the point of saying, "in times of national emergency, shoulder your rifle and set off for war."[6] It is thus difficult to draw a direct linkage between Kiyozawa's ideas and critiques of late Meiji society.

Regardless of Kiyozawa's relation to his own times, Kiyozawa's ideas have had a profound effect on both the politics and the doctrinal debates within his own sect. Kiyozawa's ideas have continued to be linked with calls for greater autonomy for both believers and local temples. It is in the area of Shin doctrine, however, that Kiyozawa has had the most lasting influence. Kiyozawa presents an idiosyncratic take on both Shin belief and traditional Pure Land teachings. This is due to his own training in Western philosophy, which provided the lens through which he viewed his own faith tradition. In discussing Kiyozawa's doctrinal understanding, it is useful to speak of two different periods. In the fairly brief decade of his active writing career (roughly from 1892 to 1903), it is possible to distinguish a turn from an emphasis on objective reason in his early writings to that of subjective experience and personal faith in his later essays.

The first period is represented by his maiden philosophical monograph, *The Skeleton of the Philosophy of Religion* (*Shūkyō tetsugaku gaikotsu*, 1892). Here Kiyozawa seeks to find a universal and rational definition of religion. He argues that religion is the "union of a finite with the Infinite."[7] Primarily under the influence of the Dutch philosopher Baruch Spinoza, Kiyozawa redefines Amida Buddha as the "Absolutely Infinite" (*zettai mugensha*) while individual sentient beings are finites (*yūgensha*). Salvation occurs through the awareness of one's identity as an interdependent element of the Infinite whole. Noticeably in Kiyozawa's formulation, Amida's personal, transcendent, and mystical qualities are absent. As the Absolutely Infinite, Amida is no longer an object of devotion, but rather a kind of rational postulate, a philosopher's god. Furthermore, rebirth in the pure land is not only de-emphasized (as in traditional Shin belief) but virtually absent. The emphasis is on the present awareness of one's essential identity with Amida.

In his later writings, primarily under the influence of German Idealism, Kiyozawa refines his understanding of the Absolutely Infinite. This change in understanding begins with *The Skeleton of the Philosophy of Other Power Faith* (*Tarikimon tetsugaku gaikotsu*) (1895) and culminates in his writings for the journal *The Spiritual World* from 1901 to 1903. He now speaks of the "cosmos as one body" (*banbutsu ittai*). This phrase is usually rendered as the "unity of all things" or the "oneness of the universe," but the Japanese term *ittai* can also mean "substance" or, more literally, "one body." In his earlier writings, Kiyozawa uses *ittai* to refer to the union between Infinite and finite. Here he embraces its more literal sense of a physical body. Whereas previously, Kiyozawa had spoken of the union of Infinite and finite as part to whole, much like pixels on a screen making up an image, here finites are in fact not truly separate but exist fundamentally as inseparable parts of the metaphysical body of the Infinite. Tellingly, he now uses the analogy of fingers on a hand to describe how finites relate to one another.[8] Like the coordinated activity of fingers on a hand, which respond to the actions of one mind, individual finites respond to the actions of the one will of the Absolutely Infinite. With this new conception and with Kiyozawa's increasingly desperate condition in regard to his tuberculosis, an element of fatalism beings to appear in his thought. As all is due to the workings of the one will, individual actions and situations are to a large degree givens that are not under human control. One's lot in life and occupation are gifts or decrees from Amida.[9]

In these later writings, to the degree that the individual is no longer in control of external circumstances, there is an increasing emphasis on the importance of spirit and will, what Kiyozawa terms "inner determination." Faith becomes the primary act of the individual will and becomes the basis not only for personal salvation but also for truth itself. The means of engendering this faith becomes a primary focus in Kiyozawa's later years.

He specifically distinguishes his own understanding of faith from that of secular morality. From his own early studies of Confucian texts to his ascetic regime as a young adult, Kiyozawa had consistently been concerned with the question of ethics. His concern was not so much about the content of ethics, as he remained essentially committed to a basic Confucian morality, but rather how to carry out its dictates. Many Buddhist modernizers, partly to curry favor with the Meiji state, had identified Buddhist teachings with the state's national morality. Kiyozawa strongly disagreed. He argues that faith begins where ethical practice ends, or rather, where one realizes that the dictates of morality are impossible to fulfill. It is the extreme discord that results from knowing what is good but being unable to carry it out that is the true doorway to religion.

Under the influence of the thirteenth century Shin text, *A Record in Lament of Divergences* (*Tannishō*), Kiyozawa begins to emphasize that faith can only truly arise for someone who has a radical sense of her own moral and personal failings. In the *Tannishō,* Shinran is recorded as presenting the doctrine that "the evil person is the proper object of Amida's vow" (*akunin shōki setsu*).[10] By this, Shinran had meant that the evil person is more likely to embrace true "other-power" precisely because it is the evil person who most clearly recognizes the inability to perform good actions and be saved by them. In contrast, rather than a negative statement meant to emphasize the inefficacy of "self-power," Kiyozawa sees the doctrine of *akunin shōki* as a positive injunction to develop an intense awareness of personal failings and the need for repentance. Thus, religious practice comes to entail not only an awareness that one's situation in life is largely beyond one's control, but further, an overriding emphasis on one's moral shortcomings and a resultant turn to Amida Buddha, who can relieve the individual of the concomitant psychological distress.

## The Translations

The three shorter pieces translated below are all taken from the journal *Spiritual World* and were published in the last years of Kiyozawa's life, between 1901 and 1903. Kiyozawa wrote a variety of short pieces for the journal, some taken from talks he had given. Together, these three encapsulate the various positions he explicated in the last years of his life and for which he is most well known. The first selection, "The Cosmos as One Body," presents Kiyozawa's vision of all beings as interdependent parts of the one body of Amida Buddha as the Absolutely Infinite.[11] From this, Kiyozawa derives an ethic of personal responsibility for all things. The impossibility of enacting this ethic provides for a feeling of repentance which in turn opens the gate to "other-power" faith.

In the second essay, "The Coexistence of Freedom and Submission," Kiyozawa uses interdependence to wrestle with the notion of individual freedom. He concludes that freedom and submission are both properties of the whole and that it is one-sided to emphasize one at the expense of the other. In the last essay, "Peace and Comfort beyond Ethics," Kiyozawa again discusses the relationship between religion and ethics. He concludes that religion is in fact the basis for ethics and not the other way around.

### Translations

## Essays on Religion and Ethics

Kiyozawa Manshi

### The Cosmos as One Body

The truth of the cosmos as one body has various explanations: idealism, pantheism, the Kegon teaching of the realm of nonobstruction between phenomena, the Tendai teaching of the middle way present in all things, the Yogācāra teaching that nothing exists apart from mind, or the Pure Land teaching that Amida's light shines throughout the ten directions.[12] To put it simply, though, we can say that the myriad things in the universe do not have separate, independent existence but exist interdependently and together make up one organism. For the time being, putting aside whatever importance this theory may have on purely academic grounds, I would like to speak a little bit about its implications for practice.

Even when we are not aware of the truth of the cosmos as one body, it is constantly acting upon us. We probably regard air and light, mountains and rivers, plants and animals as external things distinct from us. Yet we could not live without air or light. Our relations with mountains and rivers, plants and animals, or other people are not as direct, but when we see how they provide material for food, clothing, and shelter, it is clear that they are all connected with our existence. If we speak about our mental world, we obtain the majority of our thoughts and knowledge from people outside of us. Without these people, we could not exist.

In this manner, the truth of the cosmos as one body is always acting upon us. So, from our vantage point, we might say that all things exist for us. This is certainly not unreasonable. It is also clear that what we can say from our side, others can say as well. That is, from A's point of view, all the things in the universe exist for A, but from B's point of view, all things in the universe exist for B. C and D area also able to say the same thing. In other words, from the perspective of any one thing, everything else exists for it. Śākyamuni Buddha explained this as "The three worlds are all mine." With the mind of compassion for sentient beings, he further said, "All sentient beings are my children."[13]

I could express my intent still more in regard to property or offspring. All things are my possessions, and all living beings are my children. Therefore, I must cherish all things and treat all living things with tender care. If we truly cherish all things, we cannot harm them. If from our heart we treat all living things with tender care, we cannot cause them anguish or pain. It is here that a common morality arises, and the teaching of salvation occurs.

There are probably some people who will say that sages and saints could do this, and the truly magnanimous could accomplish it, but not an ordinary person. This is true. This is the attitude of a buddha. A buddha could do it, but we cannot easily attempt or realize this. However, we cannot say absolutely that there is no way to accomplish this. This is because we cannot be separated from the truth of the cosmos as one body which is our necessary foundation. However, the means and length of time to becoming a buddha will vary depending upon each of our different circumstances.

If we think about this from an actual psychological perspective, we feel we really cannot establish a spirit which cherishes all living beings as our children and maintains all things as our own. However, regardless of this, when we hear of the necessity of ethics, we believe it. When we hear the gospel of salvation, we give thanks. That is, in our breast, we know that we have a moral and religious nature. As we already have this nature, we cannot cultivate and nurture it and then abandon it half way without allowing this beautiful flower to come to full bloom. It is for this reason that while we listen to the teachings and admonitions of morality and religion, when we are unable to keep them, we feel a pain and agony in our breast which is difficult to explain. This is what is called the pain of conscience or the sense of sin. From the depths of our human nature an intense pain issues forth. Our nature is oppressed and resistance arises as it is unable to exhibit its proper function. The severity of the pain increases according to the strength of this resistance. You could say that this is the sign for the operations of our nature to eventually break through these obstacles and set out for the realm of freedom. This is the turn from morality to religion and arises through a process where the pangs of conscience grow severe and become an awareness of sin. This awareness of sin in turn induces the viewpoint of liberation.

There are scholars who say that the decrees of the gods and buddhas taught by followers of religion are simply the voices of conscience. These are the words of those who have yet to arrive at religion. When you have not yet attained religion, there is only morality, and that is all that one knows. So you know about the pain of conscience, but nothing about the salvation from it. You know that you must not commit evil, yet do not know a means to get rid of it. Therefore, it is in vain to complain about pain, in vain to speak only about evil. In the end, these are all words, and we cannot see any useful result.

Real religion is different. If it decries pain, it teaches the path of salvation. If it talks about sin, it imparts a means to extinguish it. Salvation through Amida Buddha has allowed us to understand this. Amida says, "Sentient beings, earnestly embrace the proper thought (chanting the *nenbutsu*). Come to me. Without regard for whether you are good or evil, wise or foolish, it is my duty to save all." For those who accept and believe in these welcome words, who among you feels pain, agony or despondency about whether you are good or evil, wise or foolish? Simply earnestly embrace the proper thought, revere the Buddha, and turn yourself over to him. If you do, at once the pain of conscience and sense of sin will dissipate like rapidly melting water. When we reach the path and cannot progress in ethical practice, this is because we try to construct morality merely through the power of our own words and actions. In the end, the flood of falsehoods, affectations, hypocrisies, and false morality is results from this. We think of morality as merely our own personal actions and take its results as a means to our own power and happiness. However, real morality does not arise from distinguishing self from other and the delusion of putting oneself above others. It is founded in the truth of the cosmos as one body and is caused by the true faith (the proper thought), which is based in equanimity and is free and without obstructions. The essence of this true faith is nothing other than Amida Buddha. Spurred on by the welcome words which arise from Amida Buddha's own resolute proper thought, the same proper thought arises within us. This is the essence of religion and the wellspring of morality.

### The Coexistence of Freedom and Submission

We love freedom, and in pursuing it, hate and despise submission, thinking that the two are mutually exclusive. Yet is this really the case? We live in this world but never in isolation. We always exist in mutual relations with other people and things. Freedom and submission have come to appear this way because we have this kind of existence. As a result, in order to occupy a position of freedom, others must fall into submission, while conversely, in order for others to take a position of freedom we must fall into submission. Consequently, in these circumstances, loving freedom and pursuing it while hating submission and despising it, we alone obtain complete freedom while all others are forced into nothing but submission. This must be called an attitude of tyranny and lording it over others. We must discard this attitude and try to obtain a correct understanding of freedom and submission.

We want freedom without causing others pain, and we hope for a form of submission in which we do not suffer. If we do not wish to inflict pain on others, we cannot obstruct their freedom in the slightest. Further, if we do not wish to suffer, others cannot be allowed to hinder our freedom. This being the case, between self and other, the scope of freedom must be limited. However, to speak of a "scope" or a "limit" to freedom clearly leads to a self-contradiction. We must find a way to escape this self-contradiction.

While setting our sights on freedom, we fell into a self-contradiction because we attempted to limit its scope. The reason for this was to remove the pain that results from infringing on each other's freedom. In order to escape from this self-contradiction, it is necessary for us to give some consideration to the issue of this pain.

First of all, what condition gives rise to this? The source for this is differentiating between the interests of self and other. If what was beneficial for me were beneficial for others, and if what was harmful for others were harmful for me, we would not sink into the pain of harming each other. Since my benefit is also that of others, when I gain a benefit, others do as well. Further, as another's loss is my loss, when I avoid loss, the other avoids loss too. That is, if we want to escape from the pain of mutually harming self and other, we must remove the opposition and contradiction between the interests of self and other. There is no choice but to find contentment at a place where there is sympathy between self and other (benefit and loss are mutual). We must arrive at the place where it is said, "We rejoice with all under heaven and grieve with all under heaven."[14]

"Rejoicing with all under heaven and grieving with all under heaven" is a grand statement. It seems that we cannot easily attempt this or realize it. However, the basis for this idea is that we are not entities that can be separated from each other. We are one activity which manifests out of "the cosmos as one body" from which we are constituted. Nevertheless, in reality when it comes to actually carrying this out, there are certainly differences for each in terms of depth or shallowness of degree and narrowness or broadness of expanse.

If we once reach a state of mind that "rejoices with all under heaven and grieves will all under heaven," a profound change in our attitude will arise. That is, in reaching this state, the consciousness of "the cosmos as one body" will increasingly become clearer. We will come to feel that self and other are merely two sides of the same thing. The actions of others do not exist in addition to mine nor do my actions exist in addition to those of others. My activities and those of others are absolutely one. Once we recognize this, our thinking in regard to freedom and submission will also undergo a radical shift. Though freedom and submission are normally taken as completely incompatible, we will come to understand that this is absolutely not the case. Freedom and submission are the active and passives sides of one substance. Since together they are the actions of the same substance, we cannot simply pursue one side and despise the other.

My opinion regarding the relationship between freedom and submission is roughly as I have stated above. However, there is still one more thing I would like to add. There is also a feeling of pleasure and pain in regard to freedom and submission. We feel pleasure with freedom and pain with submission. These feelings are compelling, especially when they are felt intensely. This is the basis for the distinction between freedom and submission and taking one and disregarding the other. However, feelings are frequently illusions that lead us astray. We have to struggle to grasp the truth.

Between the feelings related to freedom and submission, the sense of pleasure that accompanies freedom does not have any ill effects, yet the sense of pain that accompanies submission is an illusion that completely misguides us. This is because freedom and submission are the actions of one and the same substance. Their functions are interrelated and always appear together. Consequently, when we become conscious of the truth of the cosmos as one body, we escape from distinguishing between pleasure and pain. While this is the case, in practice we still will have these emotions, and if we are unable to free ourselves from the distinction, this is because our self-cultivation is insufficient. Nevertheless, we must not despair of realizing the harmony of freedom and submission.

In summary, freedom and submission are not incompatible. This opinion is rooted in the fallacy or delusion of being convinced that self and other are separate entities that have separate interests. However, if we arrive at the truth of "the cosmos as one body" and realize it, we understand that the interests of self and other are one. If we find peace in the state of mind that "rejoices with all under heaven and grieves with all under heaven," then we recognize that freedom and submission are the two necessary and interdependent dimensions of the actions of one and the same substance. Freedom is the active side and submission is the passive one. We must always be conscious of maintaining an attitude of equanimity.

## Peace and Comfort beyond Ethics

In the history of Japan, Taira Shigemori is often said to be a wise figure. However, from a religious perspective, he did not reach the ultimate position. He laments, "If I wish to be loyal, I cannot be filial. If I wish to be filial, I cannot be loyal. This is my dilemma," and prays for his own death.[15] Ethically, this does not seem particularly wise. However you look at it, it is truly pathetic that he has reached such a dilemma where he can do nothing but surrender to death. Shigemori fell into such anguish because he took the standpoint of ethics. In contrast, we take the standpoint of the great peace beyond ethics. Whatever situation we are in, we can live with composure. We have attained a superb state of mind which is content in the present.

There are many who have fallen into depression and have even come to seek their own deaths because, like Shigemori, they are fixed in an ethical standpoint and do not know the inconceivable power of Nyorai.[16] I personally have felt responsibility to such a degree that I would long ago have committed suicide, but I realized that toward all the events in the universe, I do not have responsibility for even one. Everything is directed by Nyorai. Saint Rennyo said that in Buddhism there is no ego.[17] For those who believe in the inconceivable power of Nyorai, every single action is due to him. So, the ego is not necessary. Since there is no ego, I do not have responsibility. If Saint Rennyo were to appear today and spoke in contemporary language, he would say, "Buddhism is about relying on the inconceivable power of Nyorai. You do not need to feel responsibility."

Those who have stolen feel constant worry and no matter how much they pretend to be fine, they always feel anguish. Though we say that this is my responsibility, or are unsatisfied about that, or feel that this was a big mistake in my life, Nyorai is vigorously at work. So, pain will not stop, yet we are unable to stop Nyorai's boundless efforts to bring about great peace of mind. We need to entrust all to Nyorai and submit to his guidance of things just as they are. If we do this, for the first time we will have the foundation of a peace beyond ethics. Saint Shinran expressed his own faith as, "I place my mind in the ground of the Buddha's Universal Vow and let my thoughts flow into the sea of the inconceivable Dharma!"[18] It is no coincidence that he also said, "I know nothing at all of good or evil."[19] So long as we completely abandon the ego and with all our heart cast ourselves into the sea of Nyorai, everything will come to be dependent upon his inconceivable power. We will see the distinction between good and evil as simply the actions of this inconceivable power.

If I speak like this, there will be some who will raise an objection such as the following. If you say that there is no ego, and Nyorai does everything while we rely on his inconceivable power, is it okay if I rise up and kill my parents? Is it okay if I feel emboldened and cause a huge riot? If I commit robbery, I can lay the blame on Nyorai. This is okay too? This is a huge misunderstanding, a self-contradiction. You cannot conclude that someone who is egoless would do things like kill and show off ostentatiously. Somebody who kills and does these other things is not lacking an ego, but is grandly asserting the ego. You cannot say such a person has become egoless and has become entrusted to Nyorai's inconceivable power.

A second type of objection will come up as well. For everything that is produced in the universe, sometimes this is Nyorai's doing and sometimes it is our doing. If Nyorai does it, there is no responsibility, but if what happens out of self-interest is not good, then what is the scope of Nyorai's actions and those of the self? It appears that there is some logic to this question, but it arises in the first place because there is no understanding of Nyorai's inconceivable power or because there is a lack of faith in its proof. In fact, the state of non-ego develops. For the person who entrusts all to Nyorai, every possible kind of work is Nyorai's work. Even in a dream it would not occur that this work is the individual's doing.

Given this, when it was said previously that one could kill his parents or commit robbery, I would say why can't this come from the ego? There is a slight misunderstanding that occurs here. In the universe, afternoon and evening, summer and fall, cannot occur in the same place at the same time. In a similar fashion, in our minds we cannot feel the behaviors of the ego and of Nyorai at the same time. When it is spring, the grass and trees turn green. With an unbroken view for thousands of miles, heaven and earth, mountains and rivers, all that is reflected in the eye is spring. There is nothing that is not tinged with the colors of spring. When it is fall, the trees and grasses wither, mountains and valleys and the deep woods all turn to fall. Exactly like this, when one returns to Nyorai, the ego is completely extinguished. Everything that happens in the universe is Nyorai's doing. Yet even after we have cut off our delusions, due to our remaining habits, when we forget Nyorai and return to the ego, everything is reflected in the eye of the ego and becomes an object of ego consciousness. Because of this, we begin to feel responsibility and to become mired in much suffering.

To give a rather simple example, a child is bringing a tray with food to a guest. His mother notices that the tray might fall, and patiently supports it from behind the child. The child thinks that he is carrying it, but when he looks over his shoulder and sees his mother, for the first time he becomes aware that his mother is helping him. When he forgets his mother and sees only himself, if he were to drop the tray, he would worry about what he was going to do and would feel responsible. However, when he knows his mother is helping him, his ego is completely effaced, and he relies on his mother's guidance.

For those who believe in Nyorai's inconceivable power, when one returns to the ego and becomes caught up in worry, one can quickly return back to Nyorai and the baggage of responsibility is taken away. When you feel cramped and have nowhere to turn, before Nyorai the entire universe of a billion worlds opens up. We unenlightened beings go back to the ego and are attacked by pain and melancholy. Yet, if we return to Nyorai, the ego is taken away, the light of his compassion shines forth, and we are enfolded in the lush green of spring. Suffering transforms into thanksgiving. People who have yet to discover the standpoint of the peace beyond ethics cannot say that this is pathetic or pitiable. We felt pity for Shigemori who made ethics his standpoint and ended up in such a dilemma. He had a struggle so painful that there was nowhere to go but death. What is truly sorrowful is not being able to enter into the vast world of Nyorai's inconceivable power.

There is no failure before those who know and believe in Nyorai's inconceivable power. Failure is not something that exists in the external world. Your mind determines failure. If you sink into the depths of despair, this is when there is failure. No matter what happens, Nyorai's guidance and encouragement lie before the person who acts through faith in what he has declared. There are no faults of your own. Socrates willingly took poison and accepted death. Saint Shinran was joyful with "profound gratitude for his teachers" and went into exile in high spirits.[20] This is the proof that if we do all before the inconceivable power, we cannot see any failure.

The previous year, when I paid a visit to the eminent Tendai cleric Kōkan at Seiraiji Temple in Tsu City, he had just fallen from a high place, broken his leg and was recuperating in bed. When I went to express my condolences, he said happily, "How fortunate that karma has brought about our meeting."

There is absolutely no failure before those who believe in the inconceivable power of the Absolutely Infinite. Sins and faults become the working of Nyorai's inconceivable power.

> Through the benefit of the unhindered light,
> We realize *shinjin* of vast, majestic virtues,
> And the ice of our blind passions necessarily melts,
> Immediately becoming the water of enlightenment.
>
> Obstructions of karmic evil turn into virtues;
> It is like the relation of ice and water:
> The more the ice, the more the water;
> The more obstructions, the more the virtues.[21]

These words express the intention of what I have said. It is said that worldly desires are at the same time *satori*, but this is not exactly what I am trying to express. Things that were the cause of grief until just now, at the same time immediately become great joy and thanksgiving if you turn to Nyorai. Saint Shinran praised Amida Buddha's Original Vow of "other-power," calling it the final teaching of the one vehicle. These words take reason to its final end.

## Notes

1 Miyakawa Tōru, "Kiyozawa Manshi to 'shūyō' shisō no tokushitsu" (Kyoto: Dōbōsha shuppan, 1991), 402.

2 Yasutomi Shinya, *Kiyozawa Manshi to ko no shisō* (Kyoto: Hōzōkan, 1999), 153–154.

3 For more on the Shirakawa movement, see Gilbert R. Johnston, "Kiyozawa Manshi's Buddhist Faith and its Relation to Modern Society" (PhD dissertation, Harvard University, 1972), 206–240.

4 Kiyozawa Manshi, *The Collected Works of Kiyozawa Manshi* (Tokyo: Iwanami Shoten, 2002–2003), 6:284.

5 Ibid., 7:271.

6 Ibid., 6:79.

7 Ibid., 1:142.

8 Ibid., 2:52.

9 Ibid., 2:124. A major influence on Kiyozawa at this point are the writings of the Greek Stoic philosopher Epictetus (55–135). Epictetus had been a slave and argued that true freedom arises from clearly distinguishing between what is in one's control and what is not. He argues that humans are most in control of their actions and the will, not externals such as occupation, health, or fortune. Epictetus, however, did not focus on religious faith as the primary act of the will as does Kiyozawa. Kiyozawa's *Rōsenki* (December fan) diaries are filled with passages from Epictetus.

10 The *Tannishō* is believed to have been written by Yuien, a disciple of Shinran. It is a short text that records Shinran's responses to certain misconceptions regarding his teachings. Kiyozawa's closest disciples popularized this text through their writings and speeches.

11 All three translations are taken from *The Collected Works of Kiyozawa Manshi*, vol. 6. "The Cosmos as One Body" (Banbutsu ittai), 12–14; "The Co-existence of Freedom and Submission" (Jiyū to fukujū to no sōun), 9–32; "Peace and Consolation beyond Ethics" (Rinri ijō no ani), 121–124.

12 Kiyozawa is here referring to key doctrines of various major schools of Mahāyāna Buddhism. The Kegon teaching of 事事無礙法界 (*jiji muge hokkai*) is literally "the non-obstruction between thing and thing in the dharma realm."

The Tendai teaching of 一色一香無非中道 (*isshiki ikkō muhi chūdō*) means that the Buddhist truth is present even within a single color or scent. The Yogācāra or consciousness-only school is represented with the teaching of 心外無別法 (*shinge mu beppō*) or "nothing exists apart from mind" while the Pure Land teaching of 光明遍照十方世界 (*kōmyō henshō jippō sekai*) in reference to Amida's light is taken from the *Pure Land Visualization Sūtra*.

13 These statements are taken from the third parables chapter of the *Lotus Sūtra*.

14 This is a paraphrase from *The Mencius*. "When a ruler rejoices in the joy of his people, they also rejoice in his joy; when he grieves at the sorrow of his people, they also grieve at his sorrow." James Legge, *The Chinese Classics, Part II: Mencius* (Boston: Houghton Mifflin Company, 1882), 30.

15 Japan's medieval epic, *The Tale of the Heike*, tells of the rise and ultimate fall of the Taira clan. Taira Shigemori is the conscience of his clan and is here remonstrating with his father, Taira Kiyomori, not to attack the emperor. His conflict results from the two opposing values, loyalty to the emperor and filial piety toward his father.

16 Nyorai is the Japanese rendering of Tathāgata, "thus come," an epithet of the historical Buddha.

17 Rennyo (1415–1499) is considered the second founder or "restorer" of Shin Buddhism.

18 Shinran, *Kyōgyōshinshō: On Teaching, Practice, Faith and Enlightenment*, trans. Inagaki Hisao (Berkeley, CA: Numata Center for Buddhist Translation and Research, 2003), 338.

19 Shinran, *The Collected Works of Shinran*, trans. Dennis Hirota et al. (Kyoto: Jodo shinshu Hongwanji-ha, 1997), http://shinranworks.com. This passage is from the postscript to the Tannishō.

20 In 1207, due to opposition from the established Buddhist sects, Shinran was forced into exile in Echigo Province while his teacher, Hōnen, was sent to Tosa Province.

21 Shinran, *Collected Works*. These passages are from *The Hymns of the Pure Land Masters*, no. 39 and 40.

## Bibliography

Fukushima Hirotaka and Akamatsu Tesshin, eds. *Shiryō Kiyozawa Manshi* (Research materials for Kiyozawa Manshi). 3 vols. Kyoto: Dōbōsha shuppan, 1991.

Johnston, Gilbert L. "Kiyozawa Manshi's Buddhist Faith and Its Relation to Modern Japanese Society." PhD dissertation, Harvard University, 1972.

Legge, James. *The Chinese Classics, Part II: Mencius.* Boston: Houghton Mifflin and Company, 1882.

Kiyozawa Manshi. *The Collected Works of Kiyozawa Manshi* (*Kiyozawa Manshi zenshū*). 9 vols. Tokyo: Iwanami Shoten, 2002–2003.

Miyakawa Tōru. "Kiyozawa Manshi to 'shūyō' shisō no tokushitsu" (The characteristics of Kiyozawa Manshi's notion of self-cultivation). In *Shiryō Kiyozawa Manshi: ronbun hen,* edited by Fukushima Hirotaka and Akamatsu Tesshin, 395–412. Dōbōsha shuppan, 1991.

Shinran. *The Collected Works of Shinran.* Translated by Dennis Hirota et al. Kyoto: Jodo shinshu Hongwanji-ha, 1997. http://shinranworks.com.

——. *Kyōgyōshinshō: On Teaching, Practice, Faith and Enlightenment.* Translated by Inagaki Hisao. Berkeley, CA: Numata Center for Buddhist Translation and Research, 2003.

Yasutomi Shinya. *Kiyozawa Manshi to ko no shisō* (Kiyozawa Manshi and the idea of the individual). Kyoto: Hōzōkan, 1999.

## Chapter 2

# The Pure Land and This World in Hishiki Masaharu's Shin Buddhist Ethics

Ugo Dessì

### Translator's Introduction

Until recently there has been a pronounced reluctance in non-Japanese scholarship to address the topic of social ethics in Shin Buddhism (Jōdo Shinshū). This is most probably due to the image of Shin Buddhism as a "Buddhism without precepts," and to the diffidence toward normative ethics found in mainstream doctrinal approaches within this tradition.

It was founder Shinran (1173–1262) who first emphasized the necessity of abandoning all "calculations" (*hakarai*) to access "other-power" (*tariki*), the salvific working of Amida Nyorai. From this perspective, intentional good acts are seen as manifestations of "self-power" (*jiriki*) obstructing the fundamental experience of *shinjin* and birth in Amida's Pure Land.[1] A careful reading of Shinran, however, reveals that such understanding of other-power did not imply the impossibility of moral action. He not only deplored the antinomian tendency of condoning evil (*zōaku muge*) but he also repeatedly recommended to his followers to respond in gratitude to the Buddha's benevolence (*hō-on*) by rejecting the evil of this world. Some passages of his work strongly discourage *kami* worship and suggest a critical attitude toward the interconnected system of rites and politics, and, perhaps most importantly for the future development of Shin Buddhism, he acknowledged the equality of all *nenbutsu* practitioners as "fellow companions" (*dōbō*), a point that was later emphasized by Rennyo (1415–1499).[2]

The Shin Buddhist tradition underwent important changes in the following centuries. Among these, one finds the adoption of an even more substantialized idea of the pure land, a more relaxed approach toward the worship of *kami*, the increasing absorption of elements of Confucian morality, and the elaboration of the *ōbō-buppō* (Imperial and Buddhist

Law) dialectic, which culminated in modern formulations of the *shinzoku nitai* (two truths) doctrine and the prescription for all practitioners to uncritically submit to the state and the existing social norms.[3] Still another important change at the beginning of the modern era was the demythologization of the concept of the Pure Land by the modern doctrinal studies initiated by Kiyozawa Manshi (1863–1903), which has exerted a considerable influence especially, but not only, upon the Ōtani branch of this denomination.[4]

Many of these themes can still be found interspersed in contemporary discussions on Shin Buddhist ethics. The idea that the pure land is not a distant abode in the afterlife but is immanent in the present world potentially implies the rethinking of one's religious commitment within society at large. The realization of *shinjin* may be understood as "peace of mind" (*anjin*), thus leading to a focus on the interiority of the practitioner rather than to interaction with the social sphere, but it can also be related to the ideal of compassionate behavior in response to Amida's call. The concept and practice of *dōbō* has deeply influenced the postwar reform movements within Shin Buddhism and their emphasis on nonviolence and peace and has inspired institutional action on behalf of discriminated minorities, such as the *hisabetsu burakumin* and former Hansen's disease patients. The exclusivist undertones of the Shin Buddhist tradition still reverberate in the present, as in the case of the critique of Western "humanism" as a manifestation of self-power. Moreover, some aspects of Shinran's thought, such as those implying contempt for *kami* worship, are seen by important sectors of Shin Buddhism as supportive of a critical attitude toward religiopolitical ideologies.[5]

The work of the Ōtani-ha thinker Hishiki Masaharu 菱木政晴 (b. 1950) can be broadly characterized as an example of this last critically oriented form of Shin Buddhist ethics. His discussion on "the Pure Land as a principle of criticism" (*Hihan genri to shite no jōdo* 批判原理としての浄土) admittedly operates within the framework provided by modern doctrinal studies' demythologization of the pure land. Hishiki, however, not only places emphasis on the nonsubstantial status of the pure land but also on its potential to provide a standard to measure the injustice of this world. In this sense, his thought is substantially related to the equalitarian dimension of the teachings and its wider implications for nonviolence.

Hishiki coined the expression "the Pure Land as a principle of criticism" in the late 1980s and ever since has illustrated his original approach in many books and articles written in Japanese. For him, despite the emphasis historically placed by Buddhism on individual suffering, the Buddha's awakening has actually more to do with social suffering, as is evident from basic expressions such as "You shall not slay, you shall not cause to slay" found in the *Dhammapada*. He laments, however, that the social implications of Buddhism were neglected throughout its development and transmission to East Asia, where it completed its transformation into the protector of the nation.

Hishiki highly values the figure of Shinran's master Hōnen (1133–1212) because he first questioned the intimate relationship between religious rituals and political power in medieval Japan by claiming that the selected practice of the *nenbutsu* alone was sufficient to achieve birth in the pure land. By doing so Hōnen (and Shinran) re-established a meaningful connection between soteriology and the social context. For Hishiki, however, their reference to the pure land as an otherworldly dimension meant the displacement of the solution to human problems in an ideal heavenly sphere and ended up in concealing the injustices of this world. In this sense, he claims, they reproduced the function of religion as an ideology of control, and their religious thought cannot serve, just as it is, to provide a religion of liberation (*kaihō no shūkyō*).

Another important point of reference for Hishiki is the concept of the Pure Land found in the writings of Kaneko Daiei (1881–1976), one of the leading exponents of modern doctrinal studies. According to Hishiki, however, Kaneko was unable to develop the critical potential of his demythologized idea of "the Pure Land as a concept" (*kannen to shite no jōdo*) and to relate it effectively to the social sphere. For this reason, Kaneko's thought remains confined to the level of subjective faith and is not sufficient to ground a theory and practice against discrimination and oppression.

According to Hishiki, what is needed is a different approach that accounts for both the lack of the dimension of the other in modern doctrinal studies and the possibility of taking the Pure Land as a principle of criticism. As the text translated for this anthology illustrates in detail, the first aspect is clarified in the discussion on the return to this world (*gensō*) to benefit other beings found in Shinran's *Kyōgyōshinshō*. According to Hishiki's interpretation, by responding to the call of Amida and uttering the *nenbutsu*, ordinary persons (*bonbu*) are not only assured of their birth in the pure land but also become able to benefit others. In this way, they can operate like bodhisattvas in this very world.

As for the aspect concerning the Pure Land as a principle of criticism, Hishiki thinks that the interpretive clue is offered by Amida's vows, and especially by the first four vows found in the *Muryōju-kyō* (*Sukhāvatīvyūha sūtra*). In Hishiki's interpretation, these vows illustrate as a whole no less than Amida's prominent concern for the establishment of a land where there is no discrimination and killing. More precisely, he distinguishes between the first and the second vows, focusing on hells (i.e., "bloodshed"), hungry ghosts (i.e., "poverty"), and animals (i.e., "submission"), and the third and the fourth vows, focusing on the shared features of humans and gods in the pure land (i.e. "equality").

For the Ōtani-ha thinker, it is only based on these assumptions that the pure land can work as a principle of criticism and a way to overcome the established dominant ideologies. In this sense, as he himself acknowledges, the concept of the Pure Land comes to play a role quite similar to that of the Kingdom of God found in Christianity, when this idea is interpreted as a standard for social justice.

Within Shin Buddhism this approach is quite significant and innovative because it contributes to an understanding of social ethics beyond the traditional characterization of morality as a response in gratitude to Amida. Similar views have been adopted by other Shin Buddhist thinkers such as Obata Bunshō, Honda Shizuyoshi, Anzai Kenjō, and Tamamitsu Junshō. Most of these thinkers have acknowledged Hishiki's impact upon their own work and have in turn exercised some influence on Hishiki's thought.

It is worth noting that the idea of the Pure Land as a principle of criticism is also deeply intertwined with social activism. For example, Hishiki and Anzai are well known in Japan for their leading roles in various lawsuits against government's attempts to revitalize wartime ultranationalism through the Yasukuni Shrine issue. In this connection, the high symbolic significance of such activism and intellectual endeavor can hardly be overlooked. In wartime Japan, various doctrines were elaborated within Shin Buddhism to support Japanese imperialism, including those establishing a connection between death on the battlefield, birth in the pure land, the *kokutai* (national polity), the emperor, and Amida. That the pure land and its virtues might represent a model for a peaceful coexistence and a just society is now one of the major concerns of Hishiki and other Shin Buddhist thinkers engaged in the theory and practice of the Pure Land as a principle of criticism.

This text has been edited by Hishiki for the specific purpose of this anthology and includes passages from his books *Kaihō no shūkyō e* (1998), *Hisen to Bukkyō* (2005), *Tada nenbutsu shite* (2009), and *Gokuraku no ninzū* (2012).

## Translation

### "The Pure Land as a Principle of Criticism"

Hishiki Masaharu

### "Liberation Shinshū" and "The Pure Land as a Principle of Criticism"

"The Pure Land as a principle of criticism" is what I have come to advocate as the basis of both my thinking and my social and religious activities. This idea does not consider Buddhism and Jōdo Shinshū as a retreat to the consolatory quietness of interiority or as an escape from the social reality of discrimination and violence. Rather, it emerges from the search for a critical approach to reality based on Buddhism.

From a broad perspective, my idea of "the Pure Land as a principle of criticism" has been influenced by Liberation Theology in Christianity, which indirectly suggests the possibility of a "Liberation Shinshū." From the perspective of the Shinshū tradition, I am indebted to the idea of "the Pure Land as a concept" illustrated by Kaneko Daiei in *Jōdo no kannen* and *Nyorai oyobi jōdo no kannen*.[6]

Kaneko's "Pure Land as a concept" diverges from the premodern mythological understanding of the pure land as a real afterlife abode. In contrast to that, he understood the pure land as a belief located in the interiority of the modern self, which places him in continuity with the modern doctrinal Jōdo Shinshū studies initiated by Kiyozawa Manshi.

For Kiyozawa, faith was an interiorized form of cultivation, but his interest in the social environment was rather weak. He focused on the suffering of the self and on the Buddha/Nyorai who achieved liberation from suffering but not on the pure land that provides the underlying environment. This probably reflects Kiyozawa's inability to thematize his own faith in critical relationship with the historical environment of the imperial state.

For Kaneko, the traditional style of faith as *anjin* ("peace of mind") that he had learned as a child implied that "Amida Buddha, who has nothing to do with us, takes us to some comfortable place without changing our mind."[7] In other words, it was a faith devoid of subjectivity and subordinated to an authority embellished with pompous rituals and complicated doctrines. The salvation fantasized in premodern Shinshū as "birth in the pure land in the afterlife" could not be clarified against the existence of the real world, and the assurance of salvation could only come from an external authority, which also implied an intimate relationship with the feudalistic system.

Since his youth (or, more precisely, since the time he became aware of Kiyozawa's modern doctrinal studies) Kaneko pushed away such superstitious conception of the pure land and came to focus on the problems of "the self and the Nyorai" and "the Buddha and the ordinary person." According to *Jōdo no kannen,* the discovery of the sinful and suffering self not only results in the devotion to the Buddha but also brings about the very manifestation of the Buddha. Kaneko explained this aspect with the following words: "It is not as if I understand that the Buddha is there from the beginning and I take refuge in him, but it is rather the attitude of taking refuge that is accompanied by the objective manifestation of the Buddha."[8] This understanding of the Nyorai encourages a critical approach to the self. And the self is in turn encompassed by social reality. This is what I mean by "the Pure Land as a concept."

However, this is not to say that Kaneko was able to articulate the critical potential of this idea. He referred to the metaphors of the "mirror" and "light" but it is not sufficient for reality to be "illuminated" to be understood critically. Kaneko's approach implies the acceptance rather than the criticism of reality, and therefore what he characterizes as "taking refuge in the Nyorai that is not the real self" (*bonbu*) can hardly take place.

The act of mirroring may refer to either the Nyorai illuminating the self or to the pure land illuminating social reality and the state, but there is a substantial difference between the reflection upon the inner self and that upon society. Whereas the reflection upon individual suffering can always start from the self as such, the precondition for a reflection upon the state and its discrimination and oppression cannot but be the actual encounter with the cries of those who have been subjected to such violence.

However, Kaneko was indifferent to this distinction and remained focused on the interior level. Therefore, although his "Pure Land as a concept" should potentially be able to provide a critique of the state, it ends up justifying and eventually dignifying its violence, thus degenerating in a sort of camouflage.

Kaneko's concept was at first ostracized as not consistent with the tradition, just to be rediscovered later as a useful tool to provide a solemn justification to the fascist state. I think that at the time the "concept of the Pure Land" was rejected by the religious institutions there was some concern that it might have been used as a critical principle, whereas when it was rediscovered what mattered most was its potential to serve as an ideology of control.

In my view, by developing Kaneko's thought into the "Pure Land as a principle of criticism" we can find a new standpoint on faith and practice that should be capable of approaching society in a critical way. I think that the "Pure Land as a principle of criticism" represents the core of Jōdo Shinshū. In the following, I will try to clarify the position of this idea in the religious philosophies of Shinran and Hōnen.

## What Is Pure Land Buddhism?

Buddhism is the religion of those who wish to overcome suffering after the example of Śākyamuni. According to the *Dhammapada,* the cause of suffering is craving (also called *bonnō*, worldly passions). Thus, the aim of the Buddha was the achievement of nirvana through the eradication of worldly passions.

It is essential that those who have achieved the goal of awakening can guide other people who are still trapped in *saṃsāra* toward the liberation from suffering. Achieving liberation is "benefiting oneself" (*jiri*), while guiding others is "benefiting them" (*rita*). Together they constitute the "perfection in the practices of improving oneself and bringing benefit to others" (*jiri rita enman*).

Śākyamuni was the only person credited to have been able to benefit others before having achieved final liberation. He alone was the Buddha, and the possibility for others to attain the "perfection in the practices of improving oneself and bringing benefit to others" remained at the level of mere rhetoric.

However, somewhere down the line a new movement emerged from within those who had realized the practical difficulty (or impossibility) of eradicating worldly passions. These practitioners were concerned with the search for an appropriate environment for the religious practice aimed at awakening. This was the beginning of Pure Land Buddhism, which teaches that it is possible to achieve awakening and become a buddha after being reborn in the pure land. One is first reborn there and can benefit oneself (*ōsō*); from there one can return to this world of suffering and benefit others by saving them (*gensō*).[9]

Pure Land Buddhism does not offer a solution to individual suffering. Rather, it represents a major transformation of Buddhism, since it understands social factors as the cause of suffering and indicates a path for social change. However, to the extent that the pure land remains an imaginary place, it cannot both inspire the solution to social problems and allow the complete liberation of the individual from worldly passions. Moreover, the act of benefiting oneself is commonly understood in traditional Pure Land Buddhism as taking place after death in the ideal environment established by Amida Nyorai. Thus, the possibility of benefiting others before birth in the pure land remains unreal.

## The Buddhism of Hōnen and Shinran: The Appearance of the Exclusive Practice of the *Nenbutsu*

In my view, the aim of Buddhism is the extinction of suffering. Pure Land Buddhism suggests that the problem of suffering should not be addressed as a spiritual matter but at the level of change in the social environment. The desired social environment is the peaceful and equalitarian environment envisioned by Amida Nyorai's vows in the *Larger Sūtra* and especially in the First Vow.

However, in the Pure Land Buddhist thought that developed in China, birth in the pure land was mainly conceived as the result of the extinction of worldly passions. The revolutionary thinker who radically altered this traditional view was Shinran's master, the Japanese monk Hōnen (1133–1212). In his *Senchakushū* Hōnen selected the utterance of the name of Amida Buddha as the ultimate path to attain birth in the Pure Land and discarded all other practices.

It was Hōnen's belief that since the aim (i.e., birth in the pure land) is the same for everyone, the means to achieve it should also be the same. At that time his standpoint was called the "exclusive practice of the *nenbutsu*" (*senju nenbutsu*). Such exclusive practice of the *nenbutsu* was not only oppressed by political power but also blamed and criticized by traditional Buddhism for being unorthodox. One of the most important reasons behind the compilation of Shinran's *Kyōgyōshinshō* was actually to provide an intellectual response to such criticism, and to clarify that the exclusive practice of the *nenbutsu* was the Buddhist path toward the perfection in the practices of improving oneself and bringing benefit to others. This aim was pursued by Shinran especially in the Chapter on Realization (*shōkan*) of the *Kyōgyōshinshō*.

The *Kyōgyōshinshō* includes six chapters (on Teaching, Practice, *Shinjin*, Realization, True Pure Land, and the Land of the Transformation Body), an introduction, an afterword, and another preface to the Chapter on

*Shinjin*. At the beginning of the Chapter on Teaching (*kyōkan*) we find the following sentence:

> Reverently contemplating the true essence of the pure land way, I see that Amida's directing of virtue to sentient beings has two aspects: the aspect for our going forth to the pure land and the aspect for our return to this world. In the aspect for going forth, there is the true teaching, practice, *shinjin*, and realization. To reveal the true teaching: It is the Larger *Sūtra* of the Buddha of Immeasurable Life.[10]

In other words, for Shinran, True Pure Land Buddhism (Jōdo Shinshū) is based on the two aspects of going forth and returning, and the first Chapter on Teaching deals with the former.

Similarly, at the beginning of the chapters on Practice and *Shinjin*, we find these two references to the aspect of going forth:

> Reverently contemplating Amida's directing of virtue for our going forth to the Pure Land, I find that there is great practice, there is great *shinjin*. The great practice is to say the Name of the Tathāgata of unhindered light.[11]

> Reverently contemplating Amida's directing of virtue for our going forth, I find there is great *shinjin*. Great *shinjin* is the superlative means for attaining longevity and deathlessness.[12]

Since the aspect of returning is introduced in a passage of the Chapter on Realization ("Second is Amida's directing of virtue for our return to this world. This is the benefit we receive, the state of benefiting and guiding others"),[13] we can assume that this was also the object of the remaining chapters on the true Pure Land and the land of the transformation body.

The opening paragraph of the Chapter on Realization reads as follows:

> To reveal, with reverence, the true realization: It is the wondrous state of perfect benefiting of others and the ultimate fruition of supreme nirvana. It arises from the Vow of necessary attainment of nirvana, also known as the Vow of realization of great nirvana. When foolish beings possessed of blind passions, the multitudes caught in birth-and-death and defiled by evil karma, realize the mind and practice that Amida directs to them for their going forth, they immediately join the truly settled of the Mahāyāna. Because they dwell among the truly settled, they necessarily attain nirvana.[14]

In the starting sentence, "To reveal . . . the ultimate fruition of supreme nirvana," there is no reference to either Amida's directing of virtue for going forth or Amida's directing of virtue for returning. However, in the chapters on teaching, practice, and *shinjin*, "Reverently contemplating the true essence of the Pure Land way" is related only to "the aspect of going forth." And the fulfillment of teaching, practice, and *shinjin*, that is, realization as the ultimate accomplishment of the true essence of the Pure Land way is inevitably the "perfection in the practices of both improving oneself and bringing benefit to others."

In other words, realization manifests the fulfillment of the two aspects of going forth and returning. Jōdo Shinshū (True Pure Land Buddhism) is just one of many Buddhist paths, but for Shinran it is the only true Buddhist path. The accomplishment of the Buddhist path encompasses by necessity the two aspects of benefiting oneself and benefiting others. This is why in the Chapter on Realization it is written that "the wondrous state of perfect benefiting of others" (benefiting others) is "the ultimate fruition of supreme nirvana" (benefiting oneself).

But how does birth in the pure land lead to benefiting oneself, that is, to the ultimate fruition of supreme nirvana? This aspect is illustrated by Shinran through reference to the Eleventh Vow of Amida that establishes the environment of the pure land. Here it is explained that those who are born in the pure land necessarily attain nirvana. The necessary attainment of nirvana and the supreme nirvana are the same thing.

Although reference is made in this passage to the fact that those who are born in the pure land are actually benefiting themselves, there is still no mention of the aspect of benefiting others. In the text of the *Kyōgyōshinshō* there are two expressions related to benefiting others: the first is "directing" and the second is the word "Mahāyāna" that precedes "the truly settled" (*shōjōju*).

"Directing" means to direct one's action and wish toward a certain aim. However, according to Shinran, "going forth and returning" is a gift bestowed to all beings by Amida Nyorai, who has established the pure land (the perfect manifestation of the Buddhist path) and has achieved the perfection in the practices of improving oneself and bringing benefit to others. This is the so-called directing by "other-power" (*tariki*). In other words, both birth in the pure land (*ōsō*) and influencing other beings (*gensō*) are directed by Amida Nyorai.

Historically, the idea of directing by other-power resulted from the deep realization that human beings are incapable of attaining the perfection in these two aspects of the Buddhist path (*ki no jinshin*) and that there is nonetheless inside us the aspiration to attain both (*hō no jinshin*). These two realizations are called the *ki* and *hō* aspects of deep faith (*kihō nishu no jinshin*).

Whereas the idea of the going forth and returning of other-power was first clarified by Donran, the concept of *kihō nishu no jinshin* was illustrated by Zendō (Shandao, 613–681). It was against the background of their thought that Shinran could affirm that "When foolish beings possessed of blind passions, the multitudes caught in birth-and-death and defiled by evil karma, realize the mind and practice that Amida directs to them for their going forth, they immediately join the truly settled of the Mahāyāna."[15]

In other words, ordinary persons defiled by evil karma who do not attempt to eradicate blind passions and do not pretend to have achieved this goal can attain the mind and practice of the going forth and returning, and thus immediately become members of the truly settled of the Mahāyāna.

The expression "truly settled" (*shōjōju*) means that "they are human beings whose attainment of buddhahood has been unmistakably determined," and that they are inhabitants of the pure land, the environment suitable for achieving awakening. The addition of "Mahāyāna" to this expression means that "like the bodhisattva in Mahāyāna Buddhism, although the attainment of buddhahood has been for them unmistakably determined, they resolutely remain in this world, and work for the salvation of all creatures who suffer because of discrimination, poverty, and war."

Moreover, as indicated by the Chapter on *Shinjin* ("Reverently contemplating Amida's directing of virtue for our going forth, I find there is great *shinjin*"), the mind of the going forth and returning is the true *shinjin* directed by Amida Nyorai. This *shinjin* does not arise from overexerting ourselves, nor is it something that we can get from a religious leader, who, excellent though he or she may be, remains all the same an ordinary person. Rather, it is just a response to the call of Amida Nyorai to recite the *nenbutsu* (Namu-Amida-Butsu).

The utterance of the *nenbutsu* is defined in the Chapter on Practice, in which it is written that "Reverently contemplating Amida's directing of virtue for our going forth to the pure land, I find that there is great practice, there is great *shinjin*. The great practice is to say the Name of the Tathāgata of unhindered light."

Therefore, the aforementioned passage, "When foolish beings . . . immediately join the truly settled of the Mahāyāna," can be explained as follows: "When foolish beings possessed of worldly passions, for whom the ideal of the Mahāyāna bodhisattva (the one who despite having achieved the perfection in the practices of improving oneself and bringing benefit to others and the status of Buddha, works for the exclusive benefit of others) is unachievable, respond to the call of Amida Nyorai and resolve to recite the *nenbutsu,* not only their birth in the pure land is determined ('truly settled'), but they are also qualified to devote themselves to benefiting others like the Mahāyāna bodhisattva."

It was Hōnen who first taught that the act of uttering without hesitation the Namu-Amida-Butsu is the sole and perfected practice for attaining birth in the pure land. Shinran clarified that this act is also a way of benefiting others.[16] I have already mentioned that the act of benefiting others appears in the Chapter on Realization, where it is written that

> Second is Amida's directing of virtue for our return to this world. This is the benefit we receive, the state of benefiting and guiding others. It arises from the Vow of necessary attainment of the rank of succession to buddhahood, also known as "the Vow of succession to buddhahood after one lifetime." It may further be called "the Vow of directing virtue for our return to this world." Since this Vow appears in the *Commentary on the Treatise,* I will not quote it here; see the passages from the *Commentary* [that follow].[17]

In my understanding, this passage means: "Second is Amida's directing of virtue for our return to this world. Practitioners of the selected practice of the *nenbutsu* acquire the ability to guide others through Amida Nyorai's Vow. This vow is the Vow of succession to buddhahood after one lifetime also known as the Vow of directing virtue for our return to this world, which is listed as the Twenty-Second Vow in the list of the forty-eight vows of Amida Nyorai found in the *Larger Sūtra.* I (Shinran) think that this Vow should better be called the Vow of directing of virtue for our return to this world. This understanding of the Vow is illustrated in Donran's *Ōjō-ronchū,* which is not fully cited here. Please refer to this work."

The understanding of the Twenty-Second Vow, which Shinran did not cite directly, is difficult. Was he really suggesting that we should read and understand the *Ōjō-ronchū* by ourselves? The text of the Twenty-Second Vow reads:

> May I not gain possession of perfect awakening if, once I have attained buddhahood, it is not the case that all the assemblies of bodhisattvas in the buddha-fields in the other nine regions of the universe gain rebirth in my land and there reach the culmination of the bodhisattva path, attaining without fail the stage in which only one birth separates them from full buddhahood—except for those who, because of the vows they took in the past to effortlessly bring all living beings to spiritual maturity, don the armor of the Great Vows, amass the roots of virtue, and liberate all these beings; and who, traveling freely to all buddha-lands cultivate the bodhisattva practice, honor with offerings all the buddhas, tathāgatas, in the ten regions of the universe, instruct and transform numberless living beings, as many as

> the sands of the Ganges, establishing them on the unsurpassable, correct, true Way; and who have gone beyond the ordinary and have manifested the conduct of all the stages of the bodhisattva practice, cultivating the virtues of the Bodhisattva Samantabhadra, the Universally Virtuous.[18]

In my understanding, this Vow can be paraphrased as follows: "Even though I succeed as an individual to awaken to the Dharma of the cessation of suffering, those engaged in the Buddhist path coming from different places to my Land (Amida's Land) for whom the achievement of buddhahood in the next lifetime has been determined, do not remain here but armored with Amida's Vow to save all human beings without discrimination they will study under the guide of many pioneers, receive practical training on how to build peace and equality, and guide countless human beings to the highest stage of independence. The Bodhisattva Samantabhadra is one of such human beings, and those who learn his virtues can without any need of inhabiting my land not only attain buddhahood but also reach any of the manifold directions. If all this will not take place, my individual awakening also cannot be meant to be a proper awakening."

From this vow it is clear that all those who inhabit the pure land are not enjoying the tranquility and happiness of the life in the other world. The vow also clarifies what is written at the beginning of the Chapter on Realization in the *Kyōgyōshinshō,* that is, that the realization of Jōdo Shinshū is not just the ultimate fruition of supreme nirvana (benefiting oneself) but also the realization of the wondrous state of benefiting others.

In other words, by uttering the Namu-Amida-Butsu, one says, "I agree with Amida's vow, I wish to be a member of Amida's Pure Land" right out loud. As already mentioned, Amida Nyorai's vows and his pure land envision a peaceful and equalitarian environment. This is especially evident in the First Vow, where the solemn promise is made by Amida that in the pure land there will not be any of the three evils, that is, hells (*jigoku*), hungry ghosts (*gaki*), and animals (*chikushō*). In modern language, this means the absence of oppression, discrimination, and violence.

Therefore, by uttering the Namu-Amida-Butsu one not only responds to the call of Amida and can embody the *ōsō* aspect related to birth in the pure land. Since this call can also be heard by other people, uttering the Namu-Amida-Butsu implies the *gensō* aspect (benefiting and guiding others) through the transmission to other human beings of its meaning: peace and equality in the pure land.

This is not to say that Amida's aspiration for peace and equality directly becomes our own. This transformation rather takes place through the working of the *ki* and *hō* aspects of deep faith (*kihō nishu no jinshin*) mentioned above: the very awareness of being an ordinary person subject to worldly passions (*ki no jinshin*)—for whom peace talk can be accompanied by the willingness to kill for the sake of oneself and one's country and for whom the opposition to domination can be accompanied by the willingness to dominate others—increasingly leads one to model one's own behavior after the true meaning of peace and equality expressed in Amida's vows (*hō no jinshin*).

That is, the uttering of the Namu-Amida-Butsu expresses our praise of Amida's vows that represents the perfection of our aspiration for peace and equality. And in this way it works as a direct criticism of the discrimination and slaughter in the real world. In other words, it represents the pure land as a principle of criticism.

## Notes

1 Cf. James Dobbins, *Jōdo Shinshū: Shin Buddhism in Medieval Japan* (Honolulu: University of Hawai'i Press, 1989). *Shinjin* implies being grasped by Amida's grace and being assured of birth in the pure land. Its meaning is close to "entrusting faith/heart" but is often left unchanged in English translations.

2 See Ugo Dessì, *Ethics and Society in Contemporary Shin Buddhism* (Berlin: Lit Verlag, 2007), 21–78. It is also worth mentioning here that Shinran's emphasis on the exclusive practice of the *nenbutsu* implied that other religious paths were ultimately unviable and inferior.

3 Cf. Minor Rogers and Ann T. Rogers, *Rennyo: The Second Founder of Shin Buddhism: With a Translation of His Letters* (Berkeley, CA: Asian Humanities Press, 1991).

4 See, for example, Yasutomi Shin'ya, *Kiyozawa Manshi to ko no shisō* (Kyoto: Hōzōkan, 1999). The Ōtani-ha is one of the two largest branches of Shin Buddhism, the other one being the Honganji-ha.

5 See Dessì, *Ethics and Society in Contemporary Shin Buddhism*, 79–140.

6 Kaneko Daiei, *Jōdo no kannen* (Kyoto: Bun'eidō, 1925); and Kaneko Daiei, *Nyorai oyobi jōdo no kannen* (Kyoto: Dōbōsha, 1927).

7 Cf. Kaneko Daiei, *Nyorai oyobi Jōdo no kannen*, 17.

8 Kaneko Daiei, *Jōdo no kannen*, p. 18.

9 The concepts of *ōsō* and *gensō* trace back to Donran's (C. Tanluan, 476–542) *Commentary on the Treatise on the Pure Land* (*Ōjō-ronchū*). They are directly related to the ideas of benefiting oneself (*jiri*) and benefiting others (*rita*) in

Tenjin's (Vasubandhu) *Treatise on the Pure Land* (the object of Tanluan's commentary) in connection to five forms of devotion to Amitābha, but this is a problem that cannot be discussed at length here.

10 Jōdo Shinshū Hongwanji-ha, *The Collected Works of Shinran,* vol. 1 (Kyoto: Jōdo Shinshū Hongwanji-ha, 1997), 7.

11 Jōdo Shinshū Hongwanji-ha, *The Collected Works of Shinran,* 13.

12 Jōdo Shinshū Hongwanji-ha, *The Collected Works of Shinran,* 79.

13 Jōdo Shinshū Hongwanji-ha, *The Collected Works of Shinran,* 158.

14 Jōdo Shinshū Hongwanji-ha, *The Collected Works of Shinran,* 355–356. [Translator's note] The translation has been modified here based on Hishiki's interpretation of this passage of the *Kyōgyōshinshō.*

15 Jōdo Shinshū Hongwanji-ha, *The Collected Works of Shinran,* 355–356.

16 The idea that the uttering of the *nenbutsu* may also be a way of benefiting others is suggested in Hōnen's *Senchakushū*. Cf. Hishiki Masaharu, *Tada nenbutsu shite: Shinran/Hōnen kara no hagemashi* (Tokyo: Hakutakusha, 2009).

17 Jōdo Shinshū Hongwanji-ha, *The Collected Works of Shinran,* 364.

18 Luis O. Gómez, trans., *The Land of Bliss: The Paradise of the Buddha of Measureless Light: Sanskrit and Chinese Versions of the Sukhāvathīvyūha Sutras* (Honolulu and Kyoto: University of Hawai'i Press and Higashi Honganji Shinshū Ōtani-ha, 1996), 168.

## Bibliography


Dessì, Ugo. *Ethics and Society in Contemporary Shin Buddhism*. Berlin: Lit Verlag, 2007.

Dobbins, James C. *Jōdo Shinshū: Shin Buddhism in Medieval Japan*. Honolulu: University of Hawai'i Press, 1989.

Gómez, Luis O., trans. *The Land of Bliss: The Paradise of the Buddha of Measureless Light: Sanskrit and Chinese Versions of the Sukhāvathīvyūha Sutras*. Honolulu and Kyoto: University of Hawai'i Press and Higashi Honganji Shinshū Ōtani-ha, 1996.

Hishiki Masaharu. *Gokuraku no ninzū: Takagi Kenmyō 'Yo ga shakaishugi' o yomu*. Tokyo: Hakutakusha, 2012.

———. *Hisen to Bukkyō: 'Hihan genri to shite no jōdo' kara no toi*. Tokyo: Hakutakusha, 2005.

——— *Kaihō no shūkyō e*. Tokyo: Ryokufū Shuppan, 1998.

———. *Tada nenbutsu shite: Shinran/Hōnen kara no hagemashi*. Tokyo: Hakutakusha, 2009.

Jōdo Shinshū Hongwanji-ha. *The Collected Works of Shinran.* 2 vols. Kyoto: Jōdo Shinshū Hongwanji-ha, 1997.

Kaneko Daiei. *Jōdo no kannen.* Kyoto: Bun'eidō, 1925.

——. *Nyorai oyobi jōdo no kannen.* Kyoto: Dōbōsha, 1927.

Rogers, Minor L., and Ann T. Rogers. *Rennyo: The Second Founder of Shin Buddhism: With a Translation of His Letters.* Berkeley, CA: Asian Humanities Press, 1991.

Yasutomi Shin'ya. *Kiyozawa Manshi to ko no shisō.* Kyoto: Hōzōkan, 1999.

# Chapter 3

# Toward a Pure Land Buddhist Aesthetics

## *Yanagi Sōetsu on the Vow of Non-Discrimination between Beauty and Ugliness*

Elisabetta Porcu

### Translator's Introduction

> Just as it would be a great oversight to omit the simple men of pure faith when considering religion, so also it would be only a partial view to leave out crafts of a corresponding nature in recording the history of art. I feel it is my special mission regarding the "Pure Land of Beauty" to cause folk-crafts, already accepted into Heaven and thereby "myōkō-hin," to be more deeply, more properly considered. It is because I feel this so strongly that I have taken up my pen and put together these thoughts though lying on a sickbed.
>
> —Yanagi Sōetsu, "The Pure Land of Beauty"[1]

In the 1920s a movement aimed at propagating an "art of the people" was developed in Japan. Its founder and leading exponent was the art critic Yanagi Sōetsu (1889–1961).[2] The *mingei* (folk crafts) movement, as it was called, was destined to gain great popularity both within Japan and abroad. While Yanagi, who was born into a wealthy Tokyo family and received an elitist education, first at the Gakushūin and then at Tokyo Imperial University, believed that fine arts were the expression of the high cultural level of a country, he also professed that the quality of life of a specific country is determined by the folk crafts.[3] Folk craft objects were defined by Yanagi and his followers as the work of unknown crafts-people, produced in large quantities, inexpensive, functional to every-day life, and closely linked to the region where they were manufactured.[4] Moreover, he clearly identifies "other-power," or *tariki* 他力, a fundamental concept in the Pure Land tradition, as a significant inspirational source of these "ordinary" but "wondrous" works.[5] In his words, "The beauty of folkcraft is the kind that comes from dependence on the Other Power."[6]

While Yanagi was influenced by a variety of sources, including European conceptions of arts, his later aesthetic theory is strongly informed by pure land motifs. In particular, it is grounded in the Fourth Vow of Amida Buddha, as found in one of the three main sutras of the Pure Land tradition, the *Daimuryōjukyō*, or Larger *Sukhāvatīvyūha sūtra*. The pure land is presented in this vow as the land where discrimination between beauty and ugliness vanishes. Yanagi, starting from this idea, argued that folk craft objects were indeed expressions of "true beauty," and he considered them the result of the working of other-power. He was thus able to develop what I called elsewhere a "*tariki* aesthetics," that is, a conception of beauty and the arts deeply inspired by Pure Land Buddhist teachings and where the idea of *tariki* plays a key role.[7]

Such a development of Yanagi's theory is clearly articulated in his postwar writings: *The Dharma Gate of Beauty* (*Bi no hōmon*, 1949), *The Pure Land of Beauty* (*Bi no Jōdo*, 1960), *The Vow of Non-Discrimination between Beauty and Ugliness* (*Muu kōshu no gan*, 1957), *The Compassionate Vow of a Buddhist Aesthetics* (*Bukkyō bigaku no higan*, 1958),[8] *The Dharma and Beauty* (*Hō to Bi*, 1961), *Namu Amida Butsu* (1955), and *Myōkōnin Inaba no Genza* (*The myōkōnin Inaba no Genza*).

Yanagi started to work on his ideas rooted in the Pure Land tradition after a "sudden self-realization"[9] that occurred during his stay in Toyama Prefecture at the Jōdo Shinshū Jōhana Betsuin. Toyama is one of the strongest areas of Jōdo Shinshū,[10] and much like the influence this location had on his friend and artist Munakata Shikō (1903–1975),[11] it played a role in Yanagi's later writings as well. In this context, in his attempt to create a religious theory applied to folk crafts, Yanagi deemed it necessary to find its validation in an "ultimate scriptural source" (*mujōna tenkyo*).[12]

In the first of these writings, *Bi no hōmon*, or "The Dharma Gate of Beauty," he recalls how, after a summer spent at Jōhana Betsuin immersed in the reading of the *Daimuryōjukyō*, he was deeply affected by the Fourth Vow and the idea of non-discrimination between beauty and ugliness. Yanagi considered it a fundamental stage in the development of his mature thought, "after many years of wandering in complicated ways," and the starting point of a religious explanation of the folk crafts rooted in "the Absolute Compassion of the Buddha."[13] Here, the spiritual character of folk crafts and their religious ground are closely connected to the conception of beauty as a "manifestation of the ultimate."[14] Moreover, because all things possess Buddha-nature, their purity transcends all contrasts such as that between beauty and ugliness and are of a non-dual nature.[15]

Yanagi did not limit his theory to the Fourth Vow, but incorporated ideas derived from later developments of the Pure Land teaching, in particular Jōdo Shinshū. For example, he considered "true beauty" as an expression of *jinen hōni* as taught by Shinran 親鸞 (1173–1262).[16] On another occasion, through a clear analogy with the term *myōkōnin* 妙好人,[17] he coined the word *myōkō-hin* 妙好品 (wondrous works) to indicate the beauty of folk craft objects and their privileged position in the Pure Land of Beauty.[18] Again, he paraphrased a well-known sentence in the third chapter of the *Tannishō* to claim that "'The genius can produce exceptional work, all the more so can the common man'—with the help of the Buddha."[19]

While Zen Buddhism was another source of inspiration for Yanagi,[20] he was eager to point out that rarely ugliness can be found in the folk crafts created by illiterate and ordinary people. In this regard, he made an interesting parallel between the difficult path toward enlightenment (based on "self-power," or *jiriki*), which can be followed only by a few monks, and the path of *tariki,* which is open to the many. In his words:

> How little fine work has come out of intellect, technique, and individuality. By contrast, how little evidence of ugliness there is to be found in those ordinary articles of folk life of the past? This is parallel with Buddhist experience, in which but few Zen monks, relying on their own endeavours, reach true Enlightenment. Whereas amongst the ranks of unlettered, good, simple men and women of Buddhist dependence on "other-power" (*tariki*) we find many of profound, humble faith.[21]

Yanagi claimed that his decision to build a theory based on a (Pure Land) Buddhist language was dictated by three main reasons: "First, I myself am a man of the East. Second, it is in Buddhism that Eastern thought has reached its deepest level. And third, it is in the Nenbutsu, or Jōdo, schools that the 'Other-power' way of viewing things is best represented."[22] These three elements are expressed in his aesthetic religious theory, what he called in the essay translated in this chapter a "religious gate of beauty" (*bi no shūmon*). His trajectory of thought, however, led him to the creation of a hierarchical theory centered on Japan and its folk crafts.[23] His theory of non-duality aimed at revealing "ultimate" beauty and was destined, in Yanagi's view, to become the "great gift" that the East could make to the West. This was because Western thought, dominated by logic and duality, prevented the Occident from discovering such "true" beauty.

In a later writing, *Bukkyō bigaku no higan,* or the *Compassionate Vow of a Buddhist Aesthetics,* "Occidental aesthetics" (*seiyō bigaku*) is contrasted to "Buddhist aesthetics" (*Bukkyō bigaku*), on which the *mingei* theory is founded. Yanagi's scheme presents opposite elements, such as difficult practices (*nangyō*) vs. easy practices (*igyō*), individuals (*kojin*) vs. all living beings (*shūjō*), self-power (*jiriki*) vs. other-power (*tariki*), and the distinction between beauty and ugliness (*bishū funbetsu*) vs. non-distinction between beauty and ugliness (*bishū mibun*).[24] He was in this way constructing a theory based on the overcoming of dualism and discrimination as expressed in one of Amida's vows, by means of a dualistic and discriminatory approach typical of cultural nationalist promotions of the uniqueness of Japan and its culture.[25]

In the translation that follows, which is part of the essay *The Vow of Non-Discrimination between Beauty and Ugliness* (*Muu kōshu no gan*),[26] Amida's Fourth Vow becomes the foundation for an explicitly "Eastern," as opposed to a "Western" conception of beauty and art. This essay follows the writing of *Bi no hōmon,* and the occasion to conceive it traced back, also in this case, to the summer spent by Yanagi in Toyama Prefecture in 1948. Among the aims of this essay is the quest for the meaning of beauty and its "essence." Also in this case, the answers need to be found, according to Yanagi, in the foundation of Amida's Fourth Vow and its intrinsic significance, in particular in the dissolution of the separation of beauty and ugliness.

"Non-duality" is the key term around which the essay revolves. Yanagi links this aspect to all forms of Buddhism, including Tendai, Zen, and Shingon, but it is in particular in the Pure Land *Daimuryōjukyō* that he finds the religious source and scriptural validation for his theory. What is expressed by the Fourth Vow goes, according to the founder of the *mingei* movement, against logic and common reasoning. Human beings think in dualistic terms and always differentiate between opposed terms, such as "good and evil" and "superior and inferior." For Yanagi, to aspire to "ultimate beauty" and the creation of a pure land unified by beauty means to overcome logical judgment—which constitutes the limit of all aesthetic theories—and thus to dissolve the opposition between "beauty and ugliness." This is, according to Yanagi, the special contribution (*tokubetsuna kōken*),[27] or in other words the "gift," that Japan through Buddhism can proudly offer to the West.[28]

There are various elements presented in this essay that can be found in others of his writings, in particular *Bi no hōmon* and *The Pure Land of Beauty*, or *Bi no Jōdo*, that was written about a decade later. What clearly emerges from Yanagi's later writings and his conception of art and aesthetics is the key role played by the Pure Land Buddhist teaching and the working of other-power in the creation of the folk crafts promoted as "ordinary" yet "wondrous" works, or *myōkō-hin*. At the same time, his apparently non-discriminatory and egalitarian theory was characterized by cultural nationalist traits that served to promote an exclusivist view of Japanese culture and spirituality and to validate Japan's privileged position both toward the West and the rest of the East.

This translation has been edited and some footnotes have been added for the purposes of this publication. I would like to thank my friend and colleague Kanno Rui for his precious comments.

## Translation

### *The Vow of Non-Discrimination between Beauty and Ugliness*

Yanagi Sōetsu

#### 1

There is no doubt that many people may find this title unusual. Its meaning appears mysterious to us. These words are frequently uttered simply by priests belonging to the Jōdo lineage during sutra recitation; however, I do not know if there are priests who have paid special attention to and reflected on the meaning of this vow.

The "Vow of non-discrimination between beauty and ugliness" (*muu kōshu no gan* 無有好醜の願) is the fourth of the wellknown forty-eight vows as they appear in the *Daimuryōjukyō* as translated by Kōsōgai (Saṃghavarman). Originally it derives from the phrase *ukōjusha* (if there are wondrous [things] and ugly [things]).

As you know, among the forty-eight vows made by Dharmakāra Bodhisattva to save all sentient beings (*shujōsaido*), the most well known is the 18th Vow, which is commonly called the "vow of birth through the *nenbutsu*" (*nenbutsu ōjō no gan*). We can say that the three main *nenbutsu* schools, Jōdoshū, Jōdo Shinshū, and Jishū, are all based on this 18th Vow.

As a matter of course, there are other significant vows too. For example, the 11th Vow, or *hisshi metsudo no gan* (the vow of necessary attainment of nirvana),[29] was particularly respected by Shinran *shōnin* and others. Moreover, Hōnen *shōnin* and others deeply speculated about the 19th Vow, or *raigō injō no gan* (the vow of Amida Buddha's coming to receive, or welcoming aspirants to the pure land).[30]

However, reading the forty-eight vows through the lenses of today's knowledge and experience, we may find some redundancies, parts that we would like to rewrite according to our present time and also parts that we no longer consider so important. At any rate, about two thousand years have passed since the completion of this sutra and I don't know whether it can be well suited to the present age just as it is. However, when reading it over carefully, I wonder if there are some vows that carry an unexpected deep truth among those that have not received much attention so far. Moreover, since the *Daimuryōjukyō* is a sutra on which the Pure Land school is primarily based, I wonder whether it might be also possible to newly rethink its unexpected truth from the perspective of other schools.

One day, when I was reading over again the 4th Vow, which is one of the vows left out from those acclaimed by many priests and religious scholars and simply just read aloud during sutra chanting, I found unexpectedly a very impressive part. At that moment, I was filled with admiration, and I hoped to write a piece about its meaning. The vow reads as follows:

> May I not gain possession of perfect awakening [*shōgaku*] if, once I have attained buddhahood, the humans and gods in my land are not the same in their appearance [*gyōshiki*] and are either beautiful or ugly [*kōshu*].[31]

The meaning of this vow is that "although I can attain buddhahood, if all the beings in the pure land are not of the same shape and form, and there is no distinction between beauty and ugliness, I will not become a buddha." The expression *shōgaku o toru* means to attain perfect enlightenment and become a buddha. As you know, this is one of the great vows pronounced by the Bodhisattva Dharmākara before becoming Amida Nyorai. This vow is called the "vow of non-discrimination between beauty and ugliness," since this implies the aspiration to a land [the pure land] where there is no distinction between beauty and ugliness.

The term *kōshu* corresponds to today's term *bishū* (beautiful or ugly), which appeared in old text, such as Huaigan's (Ekan) *Jōdo gungi ron* (Treatise on myriad doubts about the pure land), where it is called *keimu bishū no gan*. In particular, the truth that "in the pure land there is no distinction between beauty and ugliness" is mentioned here. Common interpretations have referred to a world where there is no discrimination regarding the body and appearance of people, big or small, superior or inferior, and that it is irrespective of one's own appearance. I would like to delve more deeply into its meaning and explore what is referred to as the compassionate vow[32] toward an ultimate world characterized by non-duality between beauty and ugliness.

The reason why I was deeply moved by this vow has been always the issue of addressing the problem of beauty, and furthermore: What is beauty? What is its essence? What makes things beautiful? Since I have turned my thoughts on these questions for many years, I think that times are ripe for me to pay attention to this vow that includes the two terms beauty (*bi*) and ugliness (*shū*). I still don't forget it. That summer at Jōhana Betsuin in the Etchū province[33] while I was reading the *Daimuryōjukyō* (Larger *Sukhāvatīvyūha sūtra*) something in the 4th Vow struck me. I still remember a thought that seemed like an eye-opening state of rapture.

If we read it, we may say that this vow is very simple, but the more I think about it the more I feel its deep intrinsic meaning, which includes the most profound answers to the question of beauty. From today onwards, aestheticians, historians, and [art] connoisseurs who deal with the issue of beauty should necessarily uncover the meaning of this vow and, on its basis, lay the foundation of a theory of beauty.

In the end, there is no doubt that the Dharma Gate of Beauty (*bi no hōmon*) can be built upon this vow. Exactly in the same way as the *nenbutsu* path (*nenbutsu mon*) developed into an independent school because there was the 18th Vow, I thus believe that the 4th Vow conceives the profound content on which the Religious Gate of Beauty (*bi no shūmon*) should be based. Therefore I would like to consider the "Vow of Non-Dualistic Beauty" (*fu ni bi no gan*) as the compassionate vow of the arts (*bijutsu no higan* 芸術の悲願). Truly, we can see here the "aspiration" for a Buddhist aesthetics. If we can clarify it properly, it will be possible to illuminate the truth that Western aesthetics has often being unable to reveal. I would like to find the roots of an aesthetic theory in the 4th Vow and, in the following, analyze its meaning as simply as I can.

## 2

In general terms, Buddhism—regardless of which school—teaches "emptiness" (*kū*) as its fundamental concept. However, due to the negative connotation of the term emptiness, which is generally prone to misunderstanding, it seems difficult for today's individuals to gain access to its true meaning. In particular, "thusness" (*nyo*), "as it is" (*soku*), and "within" (*naka*) are positing statements (*hyōsen*) each having a deep meaning. However, they are terms that are not immediately graspable to contemporary intellectuals. Such Buddhist terms are difficult to understand as they always overcome logic and demand another deep dimension.

But more than these, I deem the term "non-duality" (*funi*) as the most relevant. No matter what Buddhist teachings, in the last analysis the basic ideas return to "non-duality." The difference between schools lies only in the perspective from which "non-duality" is viewed. The Sanronshū term *chūgan* (contemplation of the middle way) is a non-dual contemplation. In the Tendai doctrine of *sandai en'yū kan,* or contemplation on the perfect interfusion of the triple truth,[34] the explanation of "middle" is indeed non-duality. Also the Shingon theory of *sokushin jōbutsu* (becoming Buddha in this very body) does not distance itself from the view of non-duality. In Zen Buddhism *shikan taza* (just sitting) and *jikishi ninshin* (directly pointing at people's minds) is nothing but mastering the state of non-duality. In Jōdoshū, the *nenbutsu zanmai* (mental absorption in the *nenbutsu*) too is in line with non-duality.

Now, various sutras that form the basis of different schools, in the last analysis all explain "emptiness" and "nothingness" (*mu*), but these are all doctrines (*hōmon*, "Dharma Gates") of non-duality (*funi no hōmon* 不二の法門). It is not only that the *Vimalakīrti sūtra* (*Yuimagyō*) provides a "Chapter on entering the Dharma Gate of non-duality" (*nyūfuni hōmon bon*), the Buddhist teaching itself is the gate of non-duality. This "non-twoness" can be substituted for the simple and affirmative word "one," but if we consider "one," it has meaning more in relation to the many and in comparison with the "two." Thus, as a term that dispels dualism, "non-twoness," that is, "not being two," is a much better way of saying it.

Indeed, as regards the idea of "non-duality," in the West there are insufficient signs of its development and we can say that it ripened for the first time in the East. Thus, this is what will become, in the future, the great ideological gift that the East will make to the West. The fact that in the West this concept did not develop so much might be because logic has always tended to be the basis of its thought. What I mean is that logic involves analyses and comparisons characterized by duality.

Now, "non-discrimination between beauty and ugliness" means, as this expression clearly hints, that in the pure land the dualistic idea of beauty and ugliness is unacceptable. This means that since the pure land is the land of non-duality, such distinction is excluded.

Since this vow, from the very beginning, refers to shape and form, that is, what we perceive as things with a tangible form, then, it inevitably refers to the problem about what kind of intrinsic value such beauty should have.

Now if we consider the general idea of the Buddhist teaching, it is in the nature of things that this Beauty ought to become a "Beauty of non-duality" (*funi no bi*). Therefore, "beauty versus ugliness" alone, that is, beauty that is dualistically fractioned, has no significant meaning in the pure land. This is because it ends up in relativity.

Hence, unsurprisingly, what should be called ultimate Beauty, or absolute Beauty, does not contain a separation between beauty and ugliness. This is because a dualistic dimension is not a part of it. If so, what we should call "Beauty of non-duality" is no doubt something that has the following properties. If we describe this intrinsic nature, it is immersed in the aforementioned "two" and it distances itself from the ideality of "non-duality." Then, if we try reluctantly to express the Beauty of "non-duality" in provisional words, this is how it will be: The "Beauty of non-duality" is

That which is not ugliness and is not beauty
That which precedes the separation of beauty and ugliness
That which combines beauty and ugliness
That which does not require ugliness to exist, it is beauty per se

In such a way, as a matter of course, the problem of transcending the gap between beauty and ugliness vanishes. In other words, "beauty and ugliness," "beauty or ugliness," "towards beauty rather than ugliness," and so on, as well as their characterization as opposing and competing elements are not to be found in the state of non-duality. If such opposition persists, the path toward the achievement of a "Beauty of non-duality" would be obstructed.

Cannot we say that the ultimate is not that which is divided into two or into many, but is a complete whole? Therefore, "not two-ness" has been called "emptiness," "nothingness," and *sabi,* as well as it has been referred to with words such as "within" (*naka*), "perfect" (*en*), "thusness" (*nyo*), and "as it is" (*soku*). Now, if we consider the arts and insist on the value of non-duality as their principle, we should not understand them as two different things in terms of beauty and ugliness. Indeed, the 4th Vow negates dualism in the world of art and aspires to non-duality.

Therefore, the "relativity between beauty and ugliness" must lead toward the negative "neither beauty nor ugliness." Again, it should return to a state when the separation of beauty and ugliness was not yet generated. Or this should turn to a "mutual identification of beauty and ugliness" and their complete interfusion (*en'yū*). Or else, it should manifest a state of "impartiality of beauty" (*bi ichiritsu*).

If we are unable to build the vow of non-discrimination between beauty and ugliness, it would be impossible to establish a pure land.[35] The pure land characteristic is "not-twoness," because it is not "two forms." The dimension of "two" and "not-two" is different, but trying to apply the logic of duality to the pure land is similar to attempting to see the light of the sun by turning on torches. Not only this though! Since it is a different dimension and not a mere difference in brightness, in the same way, it is as if the intensity of light would be measured with a scale.

## 3

The contents related to this vow are far away from the general idea of beauty. According to our common reasoning, beauty and ugliness are separated into two, which means that "choosing beauty is rejecting ugliness." In other words, if beauty and ugliness are kept in opposition, it is clear that beauty is not ugliness and ugliness is not beauty. Thus, to choose beauty and discharging ugliness becomes a necessary step for us. It is exactly as in the case of morality, if we separate our deeds into two, good and evil (*zen to aku*), to remove evil and pursue good can be considered the main duty of individuals. If we consider the theory of the separation between intrinsic goodness (*shōzen*) and evil by nature (*shōaku*) with regard to the characteristics of human beings, indeed this derives from people's way of thinking which separates things into two.

The fact that everything is divided into above and below, superior and inferior, is an urge of human beings' logic, and if this discrimination does not occur, due to loss of standards and lack of judgment, human thought would collapse into chaos.

The term distinction, as it clearly suggests, implies that we always separate things into two, and sets an alternative between this or that. It follows that our reply is either yes or no. All logic rules clearly reveal the relation between X and not X and the result is either affirmative or negative. According to the principle of excluded middle,[36] the existence of anything in between is impossible. If there was a middle, there would also be the issue of "middle or no-middle," and indeed it would not be possible to find a way out of the category "yes or no."

Therefore, we can say that the limit of all theories on beauty that are based on logical interpretations, as we can see today, derived from the conscious separation of beauty and ugliness.

Aesthetic theorists are those scholars who deal with the character of such a distinction. Art critics are those people who decide which work is beautiful and which is ugly. Artists are those who try to glorify beauty and masterfulness by fighting constantly against ugliness and unskillfulness. In other words, any of them does a job that lies within the world of the separation of beauty and ugliness.

Why do exceptional works diminish with the decline of times, while worthless objects profusely appear? This is because the contrast between beauty and ugliness has gradually become so intense that there have been people who, along the way, got tired and gave up. Moreover, the way toward beauty has become a quite rough path and en route people have got lost, stumbled, and have walked on the wrong path, making it difficult to reach the desired destination. Therefore only a small number of people can reach their destination. We glorify such people by calling them geniuses. However, the fact that we have to glorify the genius, on the other hand, tells us that there is a great number of ordinary people. This tragedy has become remarkable as the times progressed, and hasn't the distinction between beauty and ugliness become prominent and their discord sharpened? As everyone knows, today is the age of science, and with analytical knowledge being the principle for judgment, conflicts openly revealed, and society increasingly turned to be devoid of balance. As a result, according to "their appearance is not the same,"[37] discrimination between superior things and inferior things has become conspicuous.

Therefore, according to the claim that "there is beauty and ugliness," beautiful and unsightly things are opposed and this is this world's condition. Then sadly we can see the power of ugly things increasing day by day.

Thence, there must be people of good sense who cannot suppress their heart's desire to create in one way or another a pure land where ugliness vanishes, a land unified by beauty. Indeed, this aim and the efforts to reach it cannot be wrong. However, since such an effort always involves the subjugation of ugliness through beauty, the matter is not easy. Ugliness is a rather daunting thing and it is extremely difficult to control it, therefore we can see our ideals seemingly unlikely to be realized. It's not only this, but furthermore, ghastly and tasteless things are gradually increasing in this world to the extent that it is more likely to see the creation of a kingdom of ugliness rather than a kingdom of beauty and, in the end, we face a condition in which people who acclaim ugliness are increasing. The situation is precisely the same in the world of morality, too.

Despite the great number of men of high moral character, the fact that logicians have risen, and again, despite the strong demand for educational discipline, and even the establishment of a legal system, the result is that morality is collapsing, while crimes are increasing day by day. In particular, cities, which are the centers of culture, have the darkest sides. Unfortunately, the current situation is that those who plant seeds of evil gain force at a daily basis. Currently the fight between good and evil has come to a state that cannot be considered favorable to goodness. The same misfortune is hanging over in the world of beauty and ugliness. What is the underlying cause of such a misfortune? As long as we are caught and dominated by the duality between beauty and ugliness, and good and evil, will not such anguishes continue? If we say that this is the reality, that would be the end of the argument, but will it not be any way to cure this illness? I think it is the Vow of non-discrimination between beauty and ugliness that indeed offers the guiding principle to solve the issue of beauty and ugliness.

## Notes

1 Sōetsu Yanagi, "The Pure Land of Beauty," adapted by Bernard Leach, *The Eastern Buddhist New Series* 9, no. 1 (1976): 41, 18–41.

2 Another reading of 宗悦 is Muneyoshi.

3 Sōetsu Yanagi, *The Unknown Craftsman: A Japanese Insight into Beauty,* adapted by Bernard Leach (Tokyo: Kodansha International, 1972), 103.

4 See also the pamphlet of the Nihon Mingeikan (Japan Folk Crafts Museum) in Tokyo. Cf. Shinzō Ogyū, *Yanagi Muneyoshi no mingei to kyoshōtachi ten* (exhibition catalogue, Museum of Kyoto, Kyōto Bunka Hakubutsukan, Dec. 17, 2005–Jan. 29, 2006), 5. For a detailed analysis on Yanagi and Pure Land Buddhism, see Elisabetta Porcu, *Pure Land Buddhism in Modern Japanese Culture* (Leiden: Brill, 2008), 143–163; see also Ama Toshimaro, "Yanagi Muneyoshi to 'Shikishi wasan,'" in *Nenbutsu no kokoro: Rennyo to Honganji kyōdan* (Tokyo: Yomiuri Shinbunsha, 1991), 60–62; and Ama Toshimaro, "Bi no Jōdo o mezashite: Yanagi Muneyoshi to sono nakamatachi," in *Shinran to Rennyo* (Tokyo: Asahi Shinbunsha, 1992), 124–126. On the official website of the Nihon Mingeikan there is a clear reference to Yanagi's efforts to promote an original Buddhist aesthetics based on Amida's Primal Vow (*tariki hongan no shisō ni motozuku dokuzōtekina*

*bukkyō bigaku)* http://www.mingeikan.or.jp/about/yanagi-soetsu.html (English version at http://www.mingeikan.or.jp/english/about).

5 Yanagi, "The Pure Land of Beauty," 27, 40.

6 Yanagi, *The Unknown Craftsman,* 200.

7 See Porcu, *Pure Land Buddhism in Modern Japanese Culture.*

8 This has been also translated as "In Search of a Buddhist Aesthetics." I prefer here a translation more in line with the Buddhist term *higan.*

9 Sōetsu Yanagi, "The Dharma Gate of Beauty," trans. Bernard Leach, *The Eastern Buddhist New Series* 12, no. 2 (1979): 1–21, 2–3; and *Bi no hōmon,* 112.

10 This dates back to the time when Rennyo (1415–1499) moved to Yoshizaki in 1471. It was then that the Honganji developed into a powerful religious organization, playing also a very significant role in the uprisings in late medieval Japan, known as the *ikkō-ikki.* See Minor Rogers and Ann T. Rogers, *Rennyo: The Second Founder of Shin Buddhism. With a Translation of His Letters* (Berkeley, CA: Asian Humanities Press, 1991), 9–10.

11 See, in this regard, my analysis of Munakata's work in Porcu, *Pure Land Buddhism in Modern Japanese Culture,* 163–173.

12 Yanagi, "The Dharma Gate of Beauty," 2; *Bi no hōmon,* 111.

13 Yanagi, "The Dharma Gate of Beauty," 2–3.

14 Yanagi, "The Dharma Gate of Beauty," 4.

15 Yanagi, "The Dharma Gate of Beauty," 5.

16 See Yanagi, *Bi no hōmon,* 95; "The Dharma Gate of Beauty," 9.

17 Literally "wondrous people." The term refers to a specific category of fervent believers in Jōdo Shinshū, most of whom were illiterate. Asahara Saichi and Akao no Dōshu were among the most famous *myōkōnin.*

18 Yanagi, "The Pure Land of Beauty," 40–41; *Bi no hōmon,* 196–197.

19 Yanagi, "The Dharma Gate of Beauty," 16; *Bi no hōmon,* 104. The sentence of the Tannishō reads, "Even a good person attains birth in the Pure Land, so it goes without saying that an evil person will." See *The Collected Works of Shinran,* vol. 1 (Kyoto: Jōdo Shinshū Hongwanji-ha, 1997), 663.

20 See, for example, Yanagi, *The Unknown Craftsman,* 215; and "The Dharma Gate of Beauty," 9, 16. His view of both Zen and Shin Buddhism was greatly influenced by D. T. Suzuki, who was his English teacher at Gakushūin, and Nishida Kitarō, who was his German teacher. In this regard, see, for example, Shinzō Ogyū, "Yanagi Muneyoshi to mingei undō ni tsuite," 6, in Ogyū, *Yanagi Muneyoshi no mingei to kyoshōtachi ten,* 6–13. On the relationship between Yanagi and Suzuki, see also Mari Nakami, "Yanagi Muneyoshi to Suzuki Daisetsu. Kindai o meguru isō," in *Yanagi Muneyoshi to mingei undō,* ed. Kumakura Isao and Yoshida Kenji (Kyoto: Shibunkaku Shuppan, 2005), 52–70.

21 Yanagi, *The Unknown Craftsman,* 204.

22 Yanagi, "The Dharma Gate of Beauty," 3; *Bi no hōmon,* 113.

23 See Yuko Kikuchi, *Japanese Modernisation and Mingei Theory: Cultural Nationalism and Oriental Orientalism* (London and New York: Routledge Curzon, 2004); and Porcu, *Pure Land Buddhism in Modern Japanese Culture.*

24 See Yanagi, *Bi no hōmon,* 29.

25 See Porcu, *Pure Land Buddhism in Modern Japanese Culture.* On Yanagi's hierarchical evaluation of the folk art of minority groups and the Japanese colonies, see Kikuchi, *Japanese Modernisation and Mingei Theory.*

26 The translation refers to sections 1, 2, and 3 of this essay.

27 Yanagi, *Bi no hōmon,* 151.

28 See also Yanagi, *Bi no hōmon,* 151–153.

29 See *The Collected Works of Shinran,* vol. 1, 300; and *The Collected Works of Shinran,* vol. 2, 181.

30 See Hisao Inagaki, *A Dictionary of Japanese Buddhist Terms* (Kyoto: Nagata Bunshodo, 2003), 242; *The Collected Works of Shinran,* vol. 2, 327.

31 The Japanese in this essay reads, *Tatoi ware hotoke o etaran ni, kuni no naka no ninden, gyōshiki onaji karazu shite, kō to ju to areba, shōgaku o toraji* (Yanagi, *Bi no hōmon,* 121). English translation from Luis Gómez, *The Land of Bliss: The Paradise of the Buddha of Measureless Light: Sanskrit and Chinese Versions of the Sukhāvathīvyūha Sutras* (Honolulu and Kyoto: University of Hawai'i Press and Higashi Honganji Shinshū Ōtani-ha, 1996), 166.

32 Here, I translate *higan* in Buddhist terms, rather than "earnest desire" because of the context.

33 Today's Toyama Prefecture.

34 See also Inagaki, *A Dictionary of Japanese Buddhist Terms,* 49.

35 Here, I translate *shōgon suru* as "establish," but this is also closely related to the verb to adorn, decorate splendidly in Pure Land terms. See in this regard the term Shōgon Jōdo that means "a bodhisattva's establishment of a pure land adorned with glorious objects which are, in fact, embodiments of his meritorious acts." See Inagaki, *A Dictionary of Japanese Buddhist Terms,* 313.

36 *Principium tertii exclusi* is one of the three principles in classic logic that states that a proposition is either true or false.

37 *Gyōshiki onaji karazu* is a part of the 4th Vow.

## Bibliography

Ama Toshimaro. "Bi no Jōdo o mezashite: Yanagi Muneyoshi to sono nakamatachi." In *Shinran to Rennyo*, 124–126. Tokyo: Asahi Shinbunsha, 1992.

———. "Yanagi Muneyoshi to 'Shikishi wasan.'" In *Nenbutsu no kokoro: Rennyo to Honganji kyōdan*, 60–62. Tokyo: Yomiuri Shinbunsha, 1991.

*The Collected Works of Shinran* (CWS). 2 vols. Kyoto: Jōdo Shinshū Hongwanji-ha, 1997.

Gómez, Luis O., trans. *The Land of Bliss: The Paradise of the Buddha of Measureless Light: Sanskrit and Chinese Versions of the Sukhāvathīvyūha Sutras*. Honolulu and Kyoto: University of Hawai'i Press and Higashi Honganji Shinshū Ōtani-ha, 1996.

Inagaki, Hisao. *A Dictionary of Japanese Buddhist Terms*. Kyoto: Nagata Bunshodo, 2003.

Kikuchi, Yuko. *Japanese Modernisation and Mingei Theory: Cultural Nationalism and Oriental Orientalism*. London: Routledge Curzon, 2004.

Nakami, Mari. "Yanagi Muneyoshi to Suzuki Daisetsu. Kindai o meguru isō." In *Yanagi Muneyoshi to mingei undō*, edited by Kumakura Isao and Yoshida Kenji, 52–70. Kyoto: Shibunkaku Shuppan, 2005.

Ogyū, Shinzō. "Yanagi Muneyoshi to mingei undō ni tsuite." In *Yanagi Muneyoshi no mingei to kyoshōtachi ten*, 6–13. Ogyū Shinzō (editor-in-chief) (exhibition catalogue, Museum of Kyoto, Kyōto Bunka Hakubutsukan, Dec. 17, 2005–Jan. 29, 2006).

Porcu, Elisabetta. *Pure Land Buddhism in Modern Japanese Culture*. Leiden: Brill, 2008.

Rogers, Minor L., and Ann T. Rogers. Rennyo: *The Second Founder of Shin Buddhism. With a Translation of His Letters*. Berkeley, CA: Asian Humanities Press, 1991.

Yanagi, Sōetsu (Muneyoshi). *Bi no hōmon*. Tokyo: Iwanami Bunko, 1995.

———. "The Dharma Gate of Beauty." Translated by Bernard Leach. *The Eastern Buddhist New Series* 12, no. 2 (1979): 1–21.

———. "The Pure Land of Beauty." Adapted by Bernard Leach. *The Eastern Buddhist New Series* 9, no. 1 (1976): 18–41.

———. *The Unknown Craftsman: A Japanese Insight into Beauty*. Adapted by Bernard Leach. Tokyo: Kodansha International, 1972.

## Chapter 4

# A Confucian Pure Land?

## Longshu's Treatise on Pure Land *by Wang Rixiu*

Daniel Getz

### Translator's Introduction

Pure Land faith is commonly presented as a Buddhist soteriological path that promises the achievement of liberation and enlightenment through expedited rebirth in a pure idyllic Western realm created for the benefit of all beings by the Buddha Amitābha. The aspiration to rebirth in a world beyond the present, when viewed from the perspective of traditional Chinese culture, reinforced a long-standing characterization of Buddhism as an otherworldly orientation that stood in stark contrast to the values and institutions of Confucianism, which focused on the good order of the present world. This simplistic bifurcation of Buddhism and Confucian into otherworldly and this-worldly orientations, although given shape and bolstered by sporadic anti-Buddhist polemics down through history, actually obscures a much more complex and nuanced admixture of these two approaches within the Buddhist and Confucian traditions.

In the Chinese Pure Land tradition, this complex blending of orientations is evident in the *Longshu jingtu wen* 龍舒淨土文 (Longshu's treatise on Pure Land) by the Southern Song scholar Wang Rixiu 王日休 (d. 1173).[1] Written as a tract that, in turns both apologetic and evangelical, exhorts readers to embrace Pure Land faith, Wang's text reveals his deep commitment to Buddhism while often articulating that commitment in an idiom drawing inspiration from his roots as a Confucian scholar. The significance of the *Longshu jingtu wen*, then, lies not only in its ongoing historical influence as a complete argument for Pure Land faith, but also in its incorporation of Confucian values and sensibilities into Pure Land discourse. It is this "Confucian" version of Pure Land faith viewed in translated excerpts from the *Longshu jingtu wen* that is the concern of this chapter.

The sparse details of Wang's life that formed the backbone of his later Buddhist biographies are originally provided in a dedicatory preface of the *Longshu jingtu wen* by the famous Southern Song poet Zhang Xiaoxiang (1132–1169).[2] Wang's given name was Xuzhong, while his style name by which he is commonly known was Rixiu. He was a native of Shucheng in Longshu Prefecture located east of Chao Lake and south of the current Anhui provincial capital Hefei. He identified so closely with this native region that he became known as Layman Longshu, and he assigned this place name to the title of his most famous work, his treatise on Pure Land, in order to differentiate it from the host of other Pure Land works that already existed.[3]

The early period of Wang's life was evidently spent in intense learning, a fact implied by his attainment of the *jinshi* degree.[4] Not taking up the official position to which he was appointed, he continued to broadly read and to produce commentaries on the Confucian classics and other philosophical texts that amounted to several hundred thousand characters.[5] In his sixtieth year, he is recorded as observing, "This [study of the Confucian classics] is karma-generating behavior and not the ultimate teaching. I will turn to the Western Realm (Pure Land),"[6] and from this point on in his life he undertook an intensive recitation of Amitābha's name.

The reliability of this account, suggesting that Wang made a break with Confucian scholarship and that his conversion was precipitated by a turn to Pure Land faith, is called into question by abundant evidence in Wang's treatise that suggests a more nuanced and complicated explanation of this transition. In arguing for a consonance between Buddhist and Confucian teachings, Wang's treatise never suggests that he abandoned Confucian texts and teachings (nor does he advocate that his readers embrace such an approach). The treatise, in fact, has abundant references to Confucian texts and values suggesting Wang's ongoing connection with the Confucian tradition. His particular embodiment of the Confucian tradition blended with Buddhist belief provides an interesting counterbalance to the new Daoxue that was emerging in the twelfth century, most notably promoted by Wang's contemporary Zhu Xi (1130–1200).[7]

Further challenging the story of Wang's conversion is that his embrace of Pure Land belief appears to have taken place within the rich setting of twelfth-century Chan Buddhism. His text frequently cites scriptures and themes that preoccupied Chan Buddhists of his time, suggesting that he had been extensively exposed to Chan thought and practice well before his transformative leap to Pure Land practice. Perhaps the most important piece of evidence linking Wang to the Chan tradition was that no less a Chan luminary than Dahui Zonggao (1089–1163) provided a colophon for Wang's treatise, acknowledging the value of the text in promoting Pure Land belief.[8]

Wang's biographies emphasize that his turn to Pure Land practice involved a significant change in his life. He donned common garments, took up a vegetarian diet, undertook long journeys seeking to teach people, engaged in a thousand obeisances each day, and did not retire until midnight each evening.[9] Despite the intensity of this cultivation, he continued to immerse himself in scholarly work, reading extensively in Buddhist texts and engaging in critical textual work through the creation of new edition of the Larger *Sukhāvatīvyuha sūtra*.[10] His most important production, however, was the *Longshu jingtu wen*, which appeared in 1160.[11] This text, which sealed Wang's reputation in the history of Chinese Buddhism, not only reached a wide readership within decades of its publication, it also exerted an ongoing influence on the development of Pure Land Buddhism all the way down to the modern era. The text's popular dissemination is documented in the prefaces of the treatise as well as in Wang's biography included in Zongxiao's *Lebang wenlei* (Compendium of the Blissful Country), which was created just twenty-seven years after Wang's death in 1173. In the beginning of that biography, Zongxiao observed that Wang's treatise "is widely disseminated throughout the empire, and, among those practicing Pure Land, there is no one who has not read it."[12]

The extensive spread of this work from its beginnings was not an accident. From the text's continual exhortations calling upon readers to proselytize the Pure Land message, it is clear that Wang was driven by a sense of urgency in promoting Pure Land soteriology. He clearly intended his work for a broad audience, writing it in an accessible, straightforward style that shed the allusive pretensions found in works by his literati contemporaries. He further blended the Buddhist arguments in the text with the values and mindset of the society and culture of his time. He was also attuned to the power of print technology that was playing a crucial role in transforming Song society.[13] Throughout his work, he advocated the use of printing to spread the Pure Land message, and the dedicatory prefaces and colophons attached to the treatise make frequent reference to the printing of this work.[14] While it is clear that this work was quickly embraced by literary elites, Confucian and Buddhist alike, its spread through printing made it available to a wide audience within Song society.

Despite its importance and popularity, the *Longshu jingtu wen* in contemporary times has sometimes been presented in ways that have fostered misunderstandings with regard to its true nature. For example, the *Oxford Dictionary of Buddhism,* under the entry on Wang Rixiu, refers to this text as an anthology, suggesting that it represents a wide collection of excerpts and pieces on Pure Land and thus shares the same genre as Zongxiao's *Lebang wenlei.*[15] Even the entry in the *Busshō kaisetsu daijiten* (Dictionary of Buddhist texts) refers to Wang Rixiu as an editor (*henja*) suggesting that he edited or compiled this work.[16] Wang himself might have contributed to this impression in his opening comment in which he claims that he had thoroughly perused the Buddhist canon and the various biographies and annals so that there was not a character in the whole work that did not have a basis.[17] Adding to this impression is that the last two fascicles of the present twelve-fascicle work are a collation of miscellaneous works and passages on Pure Land. It is generally believed, however, that these two fascicles were not part of the original work but were added later.[18] For that reason, the current entry, which is only concerned with Wang Rixiu's original ten-fascicle text, refers to that text as the *Longshu jingtu wen,* rather than the current title within the Taishō canon *Longshu zengguang jingtu wen* (Longshu's expanded treatise on Pure Land), which alludes to this lengthened version containing the two-fascicle anthology.

The ten-fascicle *Longshu jingtu wen,* then, when looked at in its entirety represents not a scattered collection but a comprehensive, synthetic, popular treatise on Pure Land that had multiple aims: to persuade nonbelievers, to confirm believers in their faith, to explain Pure Land teaching, to set forth a program for practice, and to entreat practitioners of Pure Land to spread the Pure Land message. All this necessitated the adoption of multiple approaches addressing a plurality of audiences, while couching the entire work in a common idiom that appealed to native Chinese sensibilities.

The *Longshu jingtu wen* is organized into ten major topics, one for each fascicle, with each of these divided into further subsections, totaling 158 in all. His treatise begins with a consideration of the origins of faith, proceeds in the second fascicle to a survey of Pure Land doctrine, in the third to an entreaty to practice, and in the fourth to an examination of how to practice. The fifth fascicle is a biographical chapter, containing hagiographies of thirty eminent monastic and lay Pure Land practitioners whose lives gave testimony to the efficacy of Pure Land practice. The sixth fascicle identifies thirty-seven different states in life and occupations, for each of which Wang poses a unique set of ethical and cultivational responsibilities that an individual in that station must meet for rebirth in the pure land. The seventh fascicle is a cautionary chapter to Chan practitioners, providing biographies of figures recognized as reincarnations of previous Chan masters. Wang argues that these masters after their deaths had been reincarnated as famous contemporaries. The continuance of these former Chan masters within the prison of *saṃsāra* was because their Chan practice had not been accompanied by Pure Land cultivation. The eighth fascicle documents the efficacy of Pure Land practice in the present world through a series of tales. The ninth fascicle offers a discussion, progressing from shallow to deep, which documents how one can attain the highest level of rebirth. The tenth fascicle examines how Pure Land belief and practice are consonant with the highest truths of Buddhism.

Wang Rixiu's discussion throughout this tightly constructed and highly organized treatise reveals a merging of Buddhist and Confucian values, balancing the otherworldly focus of how to successfully attain rebirth in the Pure Land with the necessity of attending to the ethical demands of relationships and the quality of individual and societal life in this world. It is this assimilation of Confucian values and attention to societal order into Pure Land discourse that constitutes the focus of the translations in this entry. I wish to illustrate, through the evidence of the translated passages below, that Wang Rixiu's *Longshu jingtu wen* represents not just an eloquent and exhaustive exhortation for the practice of Pure Land, but in fact is an apologetic that specifically tethers the focus on Pure Land faith to the Confucian tradition. In this regard the text has a unique identity by offering a Pure Land perspective to the long tradition of Buddhist apologetics arguing for the fundamental consonance of Buddhism with the Confucian worldview and values. While this is a predominant feature of Wang's treatise, it should not be assumed that it is the only one. Any attempt to interpretively reduce Wang's work to a single message or approach would misrepresent his attempt through this work to reach out to the broadest audience possible.

Almost all the excerpts chosen for this entry reflect some dimension of the Confucian worldview and teaching that Wang draws into a relationship with Pure Land faith and practice. An exception to this is the preface, which contains no evident connection to Confucianism but has been included in this set of translations because it explains the meaning of the treatise's title and reveals Wang's declared option for stylistic simplicity as a way to ensure a wide audience.

The next two pieces represent the first and fourth of nine sections in Wang's first fascicle, which addresses the theme of awakening faith (*qixin* 起信) in Pure Land. In these two pieces, we can discern the essence of Wang's argument that Pure Land faith is not merely concerned with a future existence beyond the present life, but rather produces tangible benefits in the present life. In the first piece Wang identifies those benefits with upright moral conduct that shapes individuals into superior men (*junzi* 君子) and great worthies (*daxian* 大賢), cultivational goals set forth at the outset of the Confucian tradition by Confucius and Mencius.[19] Confucian moral axioms are identified in this first piece with the Buddhist principle of karma. Karma thereby becomes the foundational concept of the whole treatise, since both the moral actions along with their outcomes in the present world as well as the moral and religious actions that lead to rebirth in pure land turn on it. For Wang, there appeared to be no conceptual divide between Confucian morality and Buddhist precepts grounded in the cosmic principle of karma. In the second piece, Wang insists upon an identity between the aims of Confucian and Buddhist morality. This piece, with its copious citation of Confucian and Buddhist texts, reveals Wang's scholarly grounding in both textual traditions and his attempt to bring them together.

The next translated excerpt is the fifth subsection of nine in the third fascicle, which is concerned with calling for the universal cultivation of the pure land. This passage presents two allegories that suggest that preparation for things to come in no way impedes the responsibilities and work of the present. Through these allegories, Wang continues his attempt through the whole treatise to harmonize the demands of the otherworld with those of this world.

The next translated excerpt is the thirteenth subsection of fifteen in the fourth fascicle, which is dedicated to the issue of Pure Land cultivation. This passage contains an exhaustive list of deeds, the merit of which can be applied to rebirth in the Pure Land. These deeds, detailing the proper alignment of familial and societal relationships, in sum represent a synopsis of the Confucian moral agenda, which Wang now appropriates as means that lead to rebirth in the Pure Land.

The final translation entry is an extended translation from the first half of the sixth fascicle. In this section of his treatise, Wang entreats individuals in the context of their familial, occupational, or religious positions in Song society to embrace Pure Land faith.[20] Creating thirty-seven societal categories (of which the first sixteen are translated here), he addresses individuals in each, entreating them to first reflect on how they have been brought to their current station by their past karma and encouraging them either to apply the responsibilities of their current occupation or station to the attainment of pure land or to avoid the unwholesome aspect of their current status in hopes of achieving rebirth in the Pure Land. All are promised that reciting the name of Amitābha will gain them entrance to the Pure Land. But drawing upon the *Guan Wuliangshou Fo jing* (Visualization sūtra), which created a hierarchy of rebirth in the pure land by differentiating nine levels (divided into three grades, each with three levels),[21] Wang in an innovation not based upon the scripture suggests that rebirth at a particular level is dependent upon certain behaviors that are not mentioned in the scripture. Notably, in the section on filial sons, he inserts a Confucian requirement for rebirth, observing that being filial and caring for one's parents represent the most essential conditions for being born in the highest level of the highest grade.[22]

In organizing the social categories of the sixth fascicle into a hierarchy ranked from highest to lowest, Wang appears to correlate the individuals in descending categories with the attainment of increasingly lower levels of rebirth. Although this correlation requires further analysis, it is not improbable to suggest that Wang appeared to use the Buddhist doctrine of karma and the Pure Land teaching of grades of rebirth to confirm and solidify the social order of his time. In other words, Pure Land faith served to buttress the Confucian conception of society. Conversely, that Confucian vision of society in turn came to color how the Pure Land itself was portrayed in Wang's treatise.

## Translation

*Longshu jingtu wen,* Fascicle One

Wang Rixiu

## Preface

I have extensively read the Buddhist scriptures and various biographies and records, extracting their meaning to create a Pure Land treatise. There is not a single word here that is without basis. Please do not discount this teaching on account of this author's obscurity. I desire that all people come to a shared awareness of Pure Land. Therefore, the words of the treatise are straightforward and unembellished. I am from Longshu Prefecture. Since there is more than one Pure Land treatise being spread about today, I have adopted the name of this prefecture for the title so as to distinguish it from the others.

## Giving Rise to Faith (1)

Pure Land teaching is mostly manifested in daily practice, while its residual merit is manifest after this lifetime. The ignorant simply regard this teaching merely as an affair of the afterlife. They are entirely unaware that Pure Land teaching is of great benefit in the present life. How is this the case? It is because the Buddha's purpose in teaching people was nothing other than the promotion of goodness. How then is this different from the goal of Confucianism in teaching people? It differs only in name. Therefore, for those whose minds are set on Pure Land, what is manifest in their daily practice—the thoughts of the mind, the words of the mouth, and the actions of the body—is nothing other than goodness. Achieving goodness, they become superior men (*junzi*) and great worthies (*daxian*).[23] In the present lifetime people will respect them, the gods will protect them, good fortune and status will increase, and the length of their years will be extended. Therefore, who can say that there is no benefit in this life for those who follow the Buddha's words and set their minds on Pure Land?

Next are those gripped by karmic conditions and unable to singularly attend to Pure Land. Even these who half-heartedly attend to Pure Land can accordingly reduce evil conditions and increase good karmic conditions. Continuously reducing evil conditions must ultimately result in the elimination of evil. Continuously increasing good karmic conditions must ultimately result in the completion of goodness. Eliminating evil and completing goodness, how is this not to become a superior man? How is this not to become a great worthy? Therefore, who can say that there is no benefit in this life for those who follow the Buddha's words and set their minds on Pure Land?

Next are those unaware of the place of propriety and righteousness, oblivious to the fear of punishment, enthralled with power, and inclined to the use of force. Even if these half heartedly apply their minds to Pure Land, then they too will know to examine themselves and to assume blame. Although their actions cannot be brought entirely into accord with propriety and righteousness, they will indeed approximate propriety and righteousness. Although they cannot completely get beyond punishment, they will certainly distance themselves from punishment. Gradually they will be able to free themselves from the domain of small persons (*xiaoren*) and to take being superior men as their ultimate goal. The current age will most certainly view these ordinary individuals who are slightly versed in the Buddha's doctrine as good persons. This is the efficacy of Pure Land practice.

Therefore, who can say that there is no benefit in this life for those who follow the Buddha's words and set their minds on Pure Land? Some might say, "Is not following the words of Confucius and setting one's mind on Confucian teaching beneficial to the present life? Why is Pure Land necessary?" I say, "Confucianism is a this-worldly practice, not an otherworldly teaching. This-worldly practices cannot transcend the cycle of *saṃsāra*. Otherworldly practices directly extricate one from the cycle of *saṃsāra*. Pure Land is beneficial both in this lifetime and in the afterlife because it is concurrently an otherworldly practice."

## Giving Rise to Faith (4)

Confucians sometimes make light of the Buddhist teaching because followers of the Buddha lack conduct in accord with the precepts. Consequently, these Confucians do not believe in the Pure Land. This is not right. How can one make light of Laozi because Daoist practitioners are unseemly? Or how can they make light of Confucius because literati are unseemly? Wise persons are worthy in "not dismissing words on account of the speaker."[24] How then could they make light of a teaching because of the conduct of its followers? The teaching of the Śākyamuni has this-worldly doctrines (dharmas) and otherworldly doctrines (dharmas). The this-worldly doctrines that coincide with our Confucian teachings are beyond enumeration.

To raise in brief the most significant correspondences, the Buddha assiduously instructed the people of his age for no other purpose than to proscribe evil and exhort good. When have we Confucians not proscribed evil or not exhorted good?

Speaking in more detail, the Buddha regarded killing, stealing, and sexual misconduct as the three bodily karmas.[25] Confucius spoke of overcoming violence and doing away with killing.[26] The Poet of the *Book of Odes* stated that the virtue of King Wen extended to birds, beasts, and insects.[27] How is this not proscribing killing? There is indeed no need to talk about stealing here. Confucius said, "I have yet to witness the man who is as fond of virtue as he is of beauty in women."[28] The Poet mocked "those devoid of virtue who delight in sensuality."[29] How is this not proscribing sexual misconduct?

The Buddha held lying, idle talk, language that causes enmity, and abusive language as the four verbal karmas. Confucius declared, "I do not know how it is acceptable for a person to be untrustworthy in speech."[30] How is this not proscribing lying? Confucius also said, "Those with clever words and sycophantic manners are rarely humane."[31] How is this not proscribing idle talk? The *Book of Documents* says, "Do not appear to be agreeable while in my presence but upon leaving speak different words behind my back."[32] Is this not proscribing language that causes enmity? Abusive language refers to a voice of malicious anger; it does not quite reach the extreme of lewd language. Xunzi declared, "Words that injure people cut more deeply than spears and halberds."[33] Is this not proscribing a malicious and angry tongue?

The Buddha further regarded greed, anger, and delusion as the three mental karmas. Confucius said, "Think of righteousness when viewing gain."[34] This then is proscribing greed. He said, "Boyi and Shuqi did not think on old hurts."[35] This is proscribing anger. He said, "Encountering difficulties but not learning from them—the people regard this as inferior."[36] This then was proscribing delusion.

Speaking from this perspective, then, Confucianism and Buddhism have never been divergent. It is only that Confucianism is confined to this-worldly teachings, while Buddhism, in addition, has otherworldly teachings. Confucianism, confining itself to this-worldly teachings, therefore only speaks of one lifetime and traces it back to Heaven. Buddhism further has an otherworldly teaching and thus, aware of an accumulation of lifetimes, sees the beginning and the end of sentient beings' karma. It is here that these two traditions are not the same.

If you wish to know the strengths of Buddhism, then you must peruse the *Lengyan jing*,[37] the *Laṅkāvatāra sūtra*,[38] the *Yuanjue jing*,[39] and the *Wugaizhang Pusa suowen jing*.[40] Furthermore you should be familiar with the principle of the *Jin'gang jing*.[41] Those who are unable to do this, yet go on to deny the Buddhist teaching, are engaged in what Confucius referred to as "fabricating without knowing."[42] Shouldn't such behavior be proscribed? Since the suchness of reality described in these scriptures is truly the case, the Buddha, then, can be believed. How then could his words about Pure Land not be believed? Among the teachings on the other world, the Pure Land is the most essential. It is not acceptable for one not to strive for it.

## *Longshu jingtu wen,* Fascicle Three

### Universally Entreating Cultivation (5)

Consider for instance a man visiting a large city. He must first find a place to safely reside, and only then can he go out to conduct business. Thus when evening darkness arrives, he has a place to spend the night. Seeking out first a place to reside is a trope for cultivating Pure Land. The arrival of evening and night signifies the approach of death. Having a place to spend the night signifies being reborn in a lotus and not falling into inferior incarnations.

Then again, take for example going on long-distance trip during the spring months. A person must first prepare rain gear so that when a driving rain suddenly occurs, he will not have the misfortune of being drenched and uncomfortable. The prior preparation of rain gear is a trope for the cultivation of Pure Land. The sudden arrival of a driving rain signifies the imminent end of life. Not having the misfortune of being drenched and uncomfortable signifies avoiding submersion in inferior incarnations and subjection to manifold suffering and delusion. Furthermore, first seeking out a place to safely reside does not adversely affect one's conduct of business. The prior preparation of rain gear does not adversely affect one's carrying out a long journey. Just so, the cultivation of Pure Land does not hinder any worldly duties. Why do people not cultivate Pure Land?

One of my acquaintances during his lifetime frequently committed the transgression of killing fish. In his later years he developed an illness that resembled apoplexy (*zhongfeng*). Feeling compassion for his transgressions and the suffering from his illness, I went to see him. I entreated him to recite "Amituo Fo." He stubbornly refused to recite and only spoke with me about random matters. If it were not for an obstruction born of evil karma and a confused state of mind born of illness, how would he have been unable to turn his mind to reflection on goodness? What will happen once his eyes shut for good? Thus those who cultivate Pure Land should urgently turn back. People all know that in this world day must give way to night, and cold must give way to heat. These facts cannot be hidden. And yet if someone declares that life must give way to death, people would hold such talk to be taboo and be unwilling to speak openly about it. What a great cover-up this is! They are not aware that this entity called the self from the outset has never died. It departs only when karma has been extinguished. Therefore, one must cultivate Pure Land in order to seek rebirth in a lotus thereby acquiring a body with a pure spirit and life without limit so as to be free of all the sufferings and delusions of life and death.

## *Longshu jingtu wen,* Fascicle Four

### Methods of Cultivation (13)

You may take the merit acquired through the various reverential offerings to the Three Treasures—providing feasts for the *saṃgha* and making offerings to Buddhas, burning incense and offering flowers, reciting the Buddha's name, and performing repentance ceremonies—and direct it to your vow to be born in the Western Realm.

Or you may perform various this-worldly provisional good deeds for benefiting others—sons respecting and caring for parents; older brothers showing fraternal love to younger brothers; younger brothers honoring and obeying older brothers; women within the inner quarters spreading goodness throughout; clan members creating harmony among themselves; fellow villagers, neighbors, and in-laws greeting each other with propriety and exchanging goods with generosity; and for those serving the ruler, harboring loyalty to the nation; officials benefiting the people with humaneness and compassion; superiors creating security for those below; subordinates conscientiously serving those above; sometimes teaching and guiding the ignorant and misguided; or supporting and helping orphans and the weak; or providing aid in disasters; or giving assistance to the poor; or repairing bridges and wells; or dispensing medicine and distributing food; or reducing one's own emolument in order to benefit others; or, in collecting money, to forgive others their debt, resulting in one's own income becoming constrained; or entreating people to do good; or praising good to curb evil.

You may thus apply all of these this-worldly good deeds, performed with all of your might, to the vow for birth in Western Realm. While carrying out all these this-worldly beneficial deeds, no matter how large or small, no matter how many or few, if simply donating a single coin or a single cup of water to a person, or even performing the slightest good deed, you should also give rise to the intention: "May this merit be transferred to my vow for birth in the Western Realm." Persistently making this thought to be an unceasing one, so that thought after thought is upon birth in the Western Realm, will indeed result in rebirth in the highest grade.

## *Longshu jingtu wen,* Fascicle Six[43]

Those who cultivate Pure Land should perform good deeds according to their livelihood in order to enhance the merit gained from their cultivation. Therefore, the subsections of this chapter are entreaties specifically for this purpose. Those who are not literate should rely entirely upon compassionate gentlemen (*junzi*) who, giving rise to the bodhisattva mind, explain these passages to them. Those carrying out this act of giving in a significant way should order their approach by starting with the near and moving to the distant, or from the urgent to the less pressing. They should not be constrained by the loftiness or lowliness of a person's social standing.

### Entreating Literati[44]

Among literati, there are those who have not studied deeply and yet have directly achieved a degree in the civil service examinations (*deng gaoke*), while there are others who have deeply studied for a whole lifetime but have not been recommended to take the exam (*yüjian*). Is this not a case of a difference in karmic seeds planted in previous lives resulting in divergent karmic outcomes? Though the youthful attainment of success on exams requires merit to contribute to this momentary reward, this merit over time will be exhausted.

I respectfully entreat members of the younger generation, while being diligent in learning and conscientious in filial piety and fraternal love, to distantly reflect: "Who of my great and great-great grandparents is still alive? I will also heed this Way (Pure Land). After a long stretch of days and months, the accumulated merit from this practice will be significant, and at length I will achieve bliss."

With regard to those advanced in years, you should reflect: "All the events of my past are like a dream. Who is there that can avoid the passage of one day to another? How is it then acceptable for me not to urgently heed this Way (Pure Land)?"

If, irrespective of age, you are able to turn to the conversion of others, bringing them to mutually entreat and transform each other,[45] you will obtain good fortune in this life and rebirth at the highest grade in the next.[46]

## Entreating Gentlemen in Official Positions

Gentlemen in official positions (*youguan junzi* 有官君子) have all cultivated and planted good karma in previous lives, and therefore have received the reward of their current positions. This can be likened to planting in the spring, which brings harvest in the fall. If they had not cultivated good deeds, through what karmic condition could they then achieve this outcome? Yet this karmic reward itself will come to an end. If in cultivating good and carrying out every kind of saving deed through loving people and benefiting beings, these gentlemen further apply the merit from these actions to the Western Region, then they will directly escape *saṃsāra,* and their longevity and happiness will be without limit. How can worldly rewards compare with this?

If officials care deeply for the people and cannot bear to abandon them, what would prohibit them, after first being born in Pure Land and transcending the cycle of *saṃsāra,* from returning to this world and appearing in the form of a minister of state in order to accomplish a great benefit?[47]

If officials are able to turn to the conversion of others, bring them to mutually entreat and convert each other,[48] then, attaching great weight to their words, people will delight in following them. As indicated by the *Daci Pusa jie* (Gātha of the Bodhisattva of Great Compassion), they can avoid catastrophe and obtain prosperity in this world, and in the next life they will with certainty be reborn on the highest grade."[49]

## Entreating Clerks[50]

Clerks (*zai gongmenzhe*) should reflect on themselves, saying, "He (my supervisor) has an official post, while I am serving him. He is esteemed, while I am lowly. He is at rest, while I toil. In carrying out affairs, he is frequently delighted and without worry, while I encounter adversity and am reprimanded. I have come to this because my cultivation in previous lives did not match his. I alone must be careful and diligent in order to protect this current life. Deeds, no matter great or small, I will carry out properly as means to liberation. In the present, people will view my behavior with delight, and there will be no harm to me later. I will accumulate good karma without cease, and good fortune will reach to my sons and grandsons."

You should think, "For clerks, there is no doubt that the achievement of honor by sons and grandsons requires the ancestors (as clerks) to accumulate virtue and to make illustrious the Way of Heaven."

You should further constantly recite "Amituo Fo" and vow to be reborn in the World of Extreme Bliss (Pure Land). Furthermore you should turn to the conversion of others, bringing them to mutually entreat and convert each other. Not only will you obtain good fortune in this world, but in the next life you can achieve the highest level of the middle grade of rebirth in pure land.

## Entreating Physicians

Physicians should reflect on themselves, saying, "Human illness and suffering are not separate from me. Whoever comes summoning me, I will urgently go without delay. Or if they simply seek medication, I ought to immediately dispense it. I will not ask if those seeking my help are of high estate or low, nor will I make choices based on their poverty or wealth. If I single-mindedly take saving people as my motivation, seeking to connect them to the Dharma and to accumulate merit for myself, then in the invisible realm I will have beings protecting me. If, on the other hand, taking advantage of the dire circumstances of others, I avidly seek wealth and my motivation is not humane, then in the invisible realm there will be beings who will harm me."

Our township has a benevolent physician Zhang Yanming. When monks and adepts, poor literati, soldiers, officials, and ordinary poor people seek his treatment, he accepts money from none, yet sometimes conversely hands out money and rice. If people come summoning his help, even though they are extremely impoverished and lowly, he still goes to their aid. When the wealthy solicit medicine with money, he does not inquire how much they have, but out of necessity provides considerable medication in hope of guaranteeing a cure. He has never harbored a wish that they would come again bearing cash in search of medicine. When an illness is serious and he knows he cannot save the patient, he still administers a considerable amount of good medicine to put their mind at ease, and when they die, he is unwilling to collect money. I have associated with him for a long time and know well that in his practice of medicine he never speaks of money. He can be acclaimed as a first-class individual among physicians.

One day a conflagration in the middle of the city consumed the surroundings. In the smoke and ashes only his residence survived. In a pestilence that killed year-old calves, only those in his neighborhood survived intact. These are clearly efficacious signs that the gods are protecting and aiding him. His son studied and later attained first on the civil service exam. He has two or three grandsons who are imposing and stately in appearance. This further makes credible the claim that the Way of Heaven rewards the good. If he had been intent upon wealth and property, then considering that he would have lost these many blessings, what he would have gained could not have adequately compensated for what was lost. Should his fellow practitioners not mirror his example?

If you as a physician continually apply merit from such a mindset to Pure Land, then you will certainly be reborn at the highest level. If people are suffering from illness and you tell them about the pure land, then this can readily generate belief. If these people further make an expansive vow to broaden the spread of Pure Land teaching, then [later] either in seeking redemption for past offenses or a cure for their illness, they will most certainly achieve the aim of their vows. If their years allotted by Heaven are at an end, they can, through the power of this vow, be born in Pure Land. If you persist in converting others in this way, you will not only achieve a rebirth in the next life at the highest level, but in the present life others will indeed hold you in esteem and your karmic reward will be without limit, extending to your children and grandchildren.

## Entreating Monks

Monks should reflect on themselves, saying, "I am a person who has gone forth from home. Putting an end to the cycle of birth and death is a matter of apprehending my original state of enlightenment (*benfenshi*).[51] Not being able to do this, I have long been immersed in this world's dust. One day when the great limit (death) arrives, what will I have to rely upon? Although I have acquired good karma in this lifetime, I will not avoid continuing *saṃsāra*. When my good karmic recompense is exhausted, I will again fall back into the cycle of *saṃsāra*. It would be better that I practice Pure Land. Only when I have directly escaped *saṃsāra* and have met the Buddha Amitābha will my vocation of going forth from home be completed."

The Chan Masters Yongming Yanshou, Changlu Zongze, Wannian Fayi all practiced this Path (of Pure Land).[52] Moreover they turned to converting others, bringing them to mutually entreat and transform each other. How then to emulate these masters? Whenever you receive the donation of a single cash or the offering of a meal, in all instances you should speak to the donors about Pure Land in order to repay their virtue. Even if they do not believe, you have still made them aware of it. As their auditory sense base (*ergen*) gradually matures,[53] in time they will eventually come to belief. Even if it is a provisional belief, its benefit will be immense. If you frequently in this way convert people, you will be admired in this life. As your good karmic conditions become ever more manifest, you will further be able to single-mindedly visualize and in short order to see the true body of the Buddha.[54] After this karmic body ends, you will certainly be reborn in the highest level and become a nonretrogressing bodhisattva. An ancient saying states, "If you do not apply this [present] body to work for liberation in this very lifetime, then in what lifetime will you liberate this body?"[55] You must long reflect on the import of this, and you must not slack.

## Entreating Chan Practitioners

To achieve the great enlightenment through the practice of Chan, and thus directly escape the cycle of life and death, is indeed the superior way. But those arriving at this outcome number only two or three out of a hundred. Yet out of a thousand not a single one will be lost of those cultivating Pure Land. They will directly transcend the cycle of *saṃsāra* and make life and death one. I therefore desire to entreat monks, other than those with superior roots who are able to practice Chan, to cultivate Pure Land for brief periods each day. If you then achieve enlightenment through the practice of Chan, there will be nothing to keep you from transcending *saṃsāra,* traveling extreme distances to buddhalands and further going to see the Buddha Amitābha where you will do obeisance and honor him.

If [on the other hand] you have not yet attained the great enlightenment, and the number of your years suddenly comes to an end, you will temporarily pass through Pure Land where you will see the Buddha and hear the Dharma. What harm would there be then in not having achieved the great enlightenment? If, however, you don't practice Pure Land, you will not avoid going on in *saṃsāra*. Even figures like Qingcaotang, Chan Master Jie, and Zhenru Zhe all sank back into *saṃsāra*.[56] This is truly frightful! For a detailed account of their outcomes see Fascicle Seven of this work.

If a Chan master does not ignore this Way but makes progress in single-mindedly cultivating it and further turns to converting others, making them in turn entreat and convert each other, then others, regarding him as a renowned monk, will happily follow his words. He will bring benefit without end and he will most certainly be reborn in the highest level of the highest grade.

## Entreating Wealthy Persons

A wealthy person should reflect on himself, saying, "I am prosperous in this life all because in previous lives I cultivated seeds, just as the grain that is eaten this year is that which was planted last year. Raiment and food, wealth and status, and afterworld judgment all have a fixed amount. The combined amount from continuous past living also arrives naturally. The delay of its arrival can lengthen life, just like when water is shallow, its flow will be long. If I am frantically avaricious in seeking things, there is still just this amount. Thus, if I acquire something outside the [allotted] amount, then calamities will occur and I will depart this life, just as when water passes full, it spills over. I should live my life according to its allotment, not causing it to spill over. I should reduce my use of things to avert a spillover. [In this way] not only can I enjoy tranquility in this world, I can also plant future prosperity."

You should further reflect, "The prosperity of this world also has its end. If I apply merit to the Western Realm, then there will be no end to it. What is more, the wealth and prosperity of this world cannot bring about contentment in every respect. Only by keeping my thoughts on the Western Realm will I acquire happiness."

You as a merchant should further sponsor the printing and donation of Pure Land writings in order to widely encourage people, making them in turn entreat and convert each other. This is the planting of inexhaustible merit. In this world you can avert disaster and exorcise calamity; spirits and gods will honor and protect you. And after this life, you will certainly be reborn in the highest level of the highest grade.

## Entreating Greedy and the Miserly Persons

To acquire three thousand in cash from others but to regard it as paltry is greed. To spend two thousand but then to regard that amount as excessive is miserliness. The shortcomings of greed and miserliness are shared with all people and yet you are unaware of these shortcomings in yourself. If you can eliminate these, then you can become a worthy. In this way good deeds can all be accomplished while evil deeds can all be stopped. Why is this so? Because not being miserly with wealth is the doing of good, while being greedy involves the doing of evil.[57]

If through such conduct you cultivate Pure Land, then you most certainly will not be reborn on the lowest level. If you can further turn to converting others, making them in turn entreat and convert each other, then, because your heart is devoid of greed and miserliness, they will revere you even more and will gladly follow your attempts to transform them. The extent of those converted will be vast. What doubt will there be about being reborn at the highest level? A good karmic outcome in the present life will also be established and manifest. This outcome will be beyond description. Those cultivating themselves should be self-aware with regard to this.

## Entreating Filial Sons

Chan Master Changlu Zongze wrote the *Xiaoyou wen* (Treatise on filial piety and brotherly love) in 120 pieces.[58] The first hundred pieces, discussing happily serving and caring for one's parents, are concerned with this-worldly filial piety. The last twenty pieces, articulating entreating one's parents to practice Pure Land, are concerned with otherworldly filial piety. Thus the filial piety of this world is for one lifetime and is yet a lesser type of filial piety. The filial piety of the other world is never exhausted. Helping your parents be born in Pure Land where happiness and longevity are without limit, lasting for *kalpas* as many as the sands of the Ganges, is the greatest type of filial piety. What advantage is there if, when your parents are alive, you are unable to encourage them in the practice of Pure Land, only at a later time to grieve them and carry out rites to them in vain?

If further you are able to turn to converting others, and bring others in turn to entreat and convert each other, then the merit from this activity will enhance the good fortune and longevity of your parents and increase their karmic recompense. The Buddha does not obstruct the vows of sentient beings. This filial intention of yours will for certain be accomplished.

For those born in the highest rank of the highest grade, we must speak first of their being filial and caring for their parents. The reason I am able to promote this intention as being filial and caring is evident in the level of birth attained.

## Entreating Those Who Love Their Flesh and Blood

Those who love their flesh and blood should reflect on themselves, saying, "The Bodhisattva of Great Compassion (Daci Pusa) has a *gātha* that states,

> Mutual love and devotion for flesh and blood
> Have little hope that all will gather in old age.
> How many are those who perish in their prime?

Further are the infants and children whose lives are gone.
Entreat them to recite "Amituo Fo."
Then, being reborn on the seven-jeweled pond,
There will be a gathering that will never part
In a long life of happiness lasting ten thousand ages."[59]

If you are unable to do this and only provide clothing to adorn their bodies and exquisite food to delight their palate, one day you will be separated from them, powerless to do anything about it. Thus in this lifetime you should mutually entreat each other to recite the Buddha's name. If you are further able to turn to converting others, making them in turn to entreat and convert each other, this will not only bring about a love without end for your loved ones, it will further bring about a love without end for the loved ones of others. How could it be that their karmic recompense would be used up? You will certainly be reborn in the highest rank of the middle grade of Pure Land.

## Entreating [Married] Women

Married women should reflect on themselves, saying, "According to the word of the Buddha, those with strong passions will be given a woman's body. This already is unwholesome karma. If I don't not reflect on myself, but add jealousy and greed to my current plight, my karmic bonds will deepen and the outcome will be frightful. If I change my heart, repent, and put an end to negative thoughts; if I am humane and compassionate in dealing with maidservants and concubines, and gentle in decorum to those above and below me; if I frequently recite 'Amituo Fo' and make a vow: 'May my dark karma dissipate each day, and may my white karma grow by the day;' if I am pure in my present life, and am inwardly and outwardly serene, then after this lifetime, I will never again receive the body of a woman."

Perform recitation after recitation without cease. When your recitations naturally come to maturation, you will for certain be reborn in the World of Ultimate Bliss.

If you turn to converting your household, including maidservants, concubines, and clan relatives, your good karmic recompense will be inexhaustible. And you will certainly be reborn in the highest level. See Madame Jing Wang's biography in Fascicle Five where these outcomes are manifest.[60]

## Entreating Servants

Those who are servants should reflect on themselves, saying, "In previous lives I have not cultivated good karma and thus I have ended up poor and lowly. Others live in leisure, while I must toil. Others enjoy fine flavors, while I consume coarse grains. Others don garments both light and finely woven, while I wear clothes that are rough and inferior."

This is all due to karmic conditions generated in past lives. That which is past cannot be undone; from this point on, you should be mindful of goodness and amend your faults. You must be loyal and forthright, conscientious and diligent, carrying out your service with care, all of this in order to protect your current life and plant merit for your future.

You should constantly recite "Amituo Fo," performing recitation upon recitation without cease. When your recitations come to fruition, then you will with certainty be reborn in the Realm of Highest Bliss. Furthermore, if you convert fellow servants, making them mutually entreat other to change, then the good karmic outcomes that come from this will be without end, and you will with certainty be reborn in the highest rank in the middle grade of Pure Land.

## Entreating Farmers

Farmers should reflect on themselves, saying, "Despite the fact that farming is the foundation of all occupations, I have nevertheless killed and harmed the lives of numerous minute beings through plowing and planting."

Although this could not be helped, you should attempt to protect all beings to the degree that you are able, repent past misdeeds, constantly recite "Amituo Fo," and make a great vow, announcing, "After I have seen the Buddha and attained the Way, may I first save all the minute sentient beings whose lives I have taken since engaging in plowing and planting. Next, may I save all the sentient beings, both hated and loved."

Frequently producing this thought, perform recitation upon recitation without cease. When your recitations naturally come to maturation, you will with certainty be reborn in the Realm of Highest Bliss.

If you turn to converting others, making them entreat and convert each other, you will obtain karmic recompense in this life, and in the next you will be born in the highest level of the middle grade of pure land.

## Entreating Cultivators of Silk Worms

Those raising silk worms should reflect on themselves, saying, "Worms produce silken threads that are made into human clothing. This has been an enduring custom through the ages. And yet it too involves the killing of living beings." People of this age think that Bodhisattva Aśvaghoṣa found a justification for sericulture in the scriptures.[61] But the scriptures originally had no such teaching. There was only the teaching of the Buddha instructing his disciples not to clothe themselves with silk or to use leather for shoes, that is, things obtained through the taking of life. People have long engaged in raising silk worms for a living. How could they not be aware of its shamefulness?"

You should frequently repent, recite "Amituo Fo," and make a great vow, saying, "After I have seen the Buddha and attained the Way, may I save all those silk worms that whose lives I have taken since engaging in sericulture."

Perform recitation upon recitation without cease. When your recitations naturally come to maturation, you will for certain be reborn in the World of Ultimate Bliss.

If you turn to converting others, making them in turn entreat and convert each other, then in this world you will obtain happy recompense and after this life you will be reborn in the highest level of the middle grade of pure land.

## Entreating Merchants

Those who are merchants should reflect on themselves, saying, "If my life of selling things, albeit without deceit, involved bolts of silk obtained through the lives of silk worms, then I can not be said to be without blame. One day my life will be over, and I will depart following my karmic bonds. It would be better that I repent and carry out good deeds, making a living according to my allotted portion. If my fate is great wealth, then I will naturally and gradually acquire it; if my fate is to have little wealth, then the acquisition of more would further lead to loss. What is more, the allotment of wealth during a lifetime has a limit. If I hurriedly seek wealth and my allotment is filled, then I will come to a premature end. If I seek it gradually and it arrives late then my life will be lengthened." You must take care with this.

You should recite "Amituo Fo" and make a vow: "When I have seen the Buddha and attained the Way, may I first save all those with whom I have had dealings. Next, may I save both enemies and loved ones (*yuanqin*). And then, may I save all with whom I have had karmic links and those with whom I have had none."

In this way, perform recitation upon recitation without cease. When your recitations naturally come to maturation, you will for certain be reborn in the World of Ultimate Bliss.

If you turn to converting others, making them in turn entreat and convert each other, then in this world you will obtain happy recompense, and after this life you will certainly be born in the highest level of the middle grade of pure land.

## Entreating Craftsmen

Craftsmen should reflect upon themselves, saying, "Working as a craftsman, I have sometimes built houses for people and sometimes made furnishings for people's use. Though this is a wholesome occupation, yet because I did not cultivate seeds in previous lives, in this life, I am impoverished. The dwellings that I have built, other people occupy. The furnishings I have crafted, others use. If things were otherwise (and I had not engaged in this occupation), then I would be in want of clothing and food. I should follow my lot and do good deeds. When I am making things for other people, those things are nothing but the work that I am addressing at the moment, so I will apply my self assiduously." This also is a way of planting merit.

You should constantly recite "Amituo Fo." When you are wielding an axe, you should also single-mindedly, constantly recite [the name], performing recitation upon recitation without cease. When your recitations naturally come to maturation, you will for certain be reborn in the World of Ultimate Bliss.

If you turn to converting others, making them in turn entreat and convert each other, then in this world you will obtain happy recompense, and after this life be reborn in highest level of the middle grade of pure land.

## Notes

1 *Longshu zengguang jingtu wen* 龍舒增廣淨土文, *T.* 1970.

2 See *Longshu jingtu wen* 1, *T.* 1970.47.251b–c.

3 See Wang's preface to the *Longshu jingtu wen,* which is translated at the beginning of the excerpts below.

4 Wang is identified as as *jinshi* by Zongxiao, whose entry on Wang Rixiu in the *Lebang wenlei* represents the earliest known Buddhist Pure Land biography of Wang. See *Lebang wenlei* 3, *T.* 1969.47.196b, 29. Zongxiao's biography does not indicate when Wang attained the *jinshi* degree. Wang's biography in the *Jushi zhuan* 33 (*X.* 88.242b,12–13) states that he attained this during Gaozong's reign (1127–1162). This biography also observes that he did not take the official position to which he was appointed, a fact that can be inferred from the absence of official titles in references to Wang.

5 See Zhang Xiaoxiang's preface, *Longshu jingtu wen* 1, *T.* 1970.47.251c, 5–10. See also *Songren zhuanji ziliao suoyin,* 1.262. This work indicates that Wang produced a commentary on the *Yijing* and two on the *Spring and Autumn Annals.*

6 Zhang Xiaoxiang's preface, *Longshu jingtu wen* 1, *T.* 1970.47.251c, 7–8.

7 On developments within Song Confucianism, see Peter Bol, *"This Culture of Ours": Intellectual Transitions in T'ang and Song China* (Stanford, CA: Stanford University Press, 1994).

8 See Zonggao's colophon, *Longshu jingtu wen* 7, *T.* 1970.47.283b. This colophon is dated 1160. On the relationship between Chan and literati figures during the twelfth century, see Morten Schlutter, *How Zen Became Zen: The Dispute over Enlightenment and the Formation of Chan Buddhism in Song-Dynasty China* (Honolulu: University of Hawai'i Press, 2008), 55–77.

9 Zhang Xiaoxiang's preface, *Longshu jingtu wen* 1, *T.* 1970.47.251c, 8–10.

10 Wang Rixiu's redaction of this scripture is the *Foshuo Da Amituo jing, T.* 364.

11 1160 corresponds to the date (Shaoxing 30) found at the end of the tenth fascicle in two colophons by Zhou Kui and Miaoxi Laoren. *T.* 1970.47.283a, 25 and 283b, 8.

12 See Wang's biography in *Lebang wenlei* 3, *T.* 1969A.47.196c, 2.

13 On the complexities of the effects of print technology in Song society, see Susan Cherniack, "Book Culture and Textual Transmission in Sung China," *Harvard Journal of Asiatic Studies* 54, no. 1 (June 1994): 5–125.

14 See for example the preface by Lü Shishuo, *T.* 1970.47.251b, 6–9.

15 See item in Damien Keown, *Oxford Dictionary of Buddhism* (New York: Oxford University Press, 2003).

16 See *Bussho kaisetsu daijiten,* ed. Ono Gemmyō (Tokyo: Daitō shuppansha, 1932–1935, 1975–1978), 6.114c.

17 See Wang's preface translated below.

18 See *Bussho kaisetsu daijiten,* 6.115b.

19 The concept of *junzi* (superior man) as the ideal to which Confucius called his disciples appears throughout the *Analects.* Similarly the notion of *xian*

賢 as an ideal appears throughout the Mencius, with the concept of *daxian* (great worthy) being introduced in *Mencius*, 4 A.7.

20 This section of the text, which provides a window into how Wang as a Confucian and Buddhist viewed the society of his time, has attracted historians who have an interest in the nature of Song society. See for example Trevor Davis, "Pure Land and the Social Order in Twelfth-Century China: An Investigation of 'Longshu's Treatise on Pure Land'" (student work paper 1. http://elischolar.library.yale.edu/ceas_student_work/1). Davis' intensive study argues that the behaviors Wang advocated for social and moral inferiors tended to reinforce their debased position within Song society.

21 *See Foshuo Guan Wuliangshoufo jing, T.* 365.

22 *T.* 1970.47.271b, 3.

23 These are aims of Confucian cultivation set forth by Confucius and Mencius. See the discussion above.

24 *Analects*, 15.23.

25 See, for example, *Zengyi Ahan jing* 17, *T.* 125.2.816b.

26 *Analects*, 13.11.

27 See the preface to the *Lingtai* 靈臺poem in the *Maoshi zhengyi* 16.5.

28 *Analects*, 9.18; 15.13. Adapted from D. C. Lao.

29 See the preface to *Nüyue jiming* 女曰雞鳴poem in *Maoshi zhengyi* 4.3.

30 *Analects*, 2.22.

31 *Analects*, 1.3.

32 *Book of Documents*, *Yushu*, Yi and Ji.

33 *Xunzi*, *Rongru* 榮辱.

34 *Analects*, 16.10; 19.1.

35 *Analects*, 5.23.

36 *Analects*, 16.9.

37 Wang here is no doubt referring to the ten fascicle *Da Foding Rulai miyin xiuzheng liaoyi zhu pusa wanxing shou lengyan jing* (*T.* 945), which is commonly referred to as the *Shoulengyan jing* 首楞嚴經and which has incorrectly been assigned the Sanskrit title *Śuraṃgama sūtra*. This scripture, long judged to be a Chinese indigenous scripture, had a great influence in the development of the Chan tradition during the Song period. This should not be confused with the *Foshuo shoulengyan sanmei jing* (*Śuraṃgamasamādhi sūtra, T.* 642), which is indeed a translation from an Indic language by Kumārajīva and for which Sanskrit fragments survive. See Robert Buswell and Donald Lopez, eds., *The Princeton Dictionary of Buddhism* (Princeton, NJ: Princeton University Press, 2013), 873–874.

38 The *Laṅkāvatāra sūtra* had three translations in the Chinese, of which the one by Guṇabhadra (*T.* 670) played a significant role in the development of the Chan narrative in China. See Buswell and Lopez, *The Princeton Dictionary of Buddhism*, 466–467.

39 The *Yuanjue jing* is an indigenous Chinese scripture (*T.* 842) that promoted *Tathāgatagarbha* thought and was influential for the Tang dynasty Chan historian Zongmi (780–841). See Buswell and Lopez, *The Princeton Dictionary of Buddhism*, 1041.

40 This likely refers to *Chugaizhang Pusa suowen jing* (*T.* 489).

41 This presumably is referring to Kumārajīva's translation (*T.* 235), although there are five other Chinese translations (*T.* 220, 236–239). This text, like the others preceding it, held great importance within the Chan tradition.

42 *Analects*, 7.28.

43 For alternative translations of some of the following subsections in this fascicle, consult Davis, "Pure Land and the Social Order in Twelfth Century China," 45–58.

44 "Literati" here translates the Chinese *shiren* 士人, which in the Song had a broad reach that included students studying for the civil service exam, degree holders, and officials. Wang Rixiu in this section seems to focus the meaning of the term on the act of study, paying special attention to those who have studied but were not successful in their exams. Thus, this group is distinguished in terms of their obligations from those who have attained official positions. These latter are the subject of the next category.

45 The entreaty to convert others and in turn to spur them to entreat and convert others (轉以化人使更相勸化) is a formulaic expression that is found at the end of almost every category in this chapter of Wang's treatise. This activity of converting appears to be karmically linked by Wang with the level of pure land that one will attain. I am unclear with regard to whether this directive has scriptural origins and also as to the exact meaning of the expression *zhuan* 轉, a word that can mean "to turn" but can also be used to express an intensification of an activity through the expression "more and more." Despite these uncertainties, the intention of the formula remains clear: to promote widespread proselytization of Pure Land.

46 See the discussion of levels of rebirth in the introduction.

47 This passage is repeated in Fascicle Seven in the biography of Zeng Lu (Zeng Huai 1107–1175), a Southern Song minister of state regarded as a reincarnation of the Chan Master Qingcaotang. See *T.* 1970.47.275a,28.

48 I am reading the character *guan* 觀 (observe) in this title as *quan* 勸 (entreat).

49 The *Daci pusa jie* is a liturgical verse that Wang Rixiu includes in Fascicle Four of the *Longshu jingtu wen* (*T.* 1970.47.262a,3) and urges devotees to recite

once every morning. Wang refers to this as the *Daci Pusa zanfo chanzui huixiang fayuan* (The Bodhisattva of Great Compassion's gātha of praise, repentance, merit transfer, and vow). This verse, which has considerable liturgical significance in contemporary Chinese Buddhism, is found in *Nianfo chaotuo jiejing jing* (*X.* 13), a text whose provenance I have been unable to discover.

50 For this designation of subordinate functionaries working under the direction of officials (*zai gongmenzhe*) as "clerks," I am indebted to Davis' translation of this passage; "Pure Land and the Social Order in Twelfth Century China," 45.

51 This expression "*benfenshi*" 本分事, referring to one's original nature, is found throughout Chan literature. See *Foguang dacidian*, ed. Foguan dacidian bianxiu weiyuanhui (Taipei: Foguang chubanshe, 1988), 2.1960c.

52 Wang includes the biographies of Yanshou (904–975) and Zongze (fl. 1089) in the biographical section of his work. See *Longshu jingtu wen* 5, *T.* 46.268b. Fayi's (1084–1158) Pure Land activity is not evident in his biography (see *Da Ming gaoseng zhuan, T.* 50.926c) but his Pure Land devotion may have been assumed by Wang because Fayi was Zongze's student. Wang's contemporary, the Tiantai monk Zongxiao, in his *Lebang wenlei* (fasc. 3, *T.* 1969A.46.193c), accorded Zongze the honor of fifth patriarch of Lotus Society Patriarchs and also included Yenshou in his biographical section (fasc. 3, *T.* 1969A.46.195a).

53 The auditory sense base refers to the organ of hearing and also the capacity to hear. See *Foguang dacidian*, 3.2509b.

54 This is suggestive of the *Pratyutpannabuddhasaṃmukhāvasthitasamāhi sūtra* (*Banzhou sanmei jing*) that sets forth a visualization technique that leads to an ability to come into the presence of the visualized Buddha. See *T.* 418.

55 I have been unable to identify the source of this adage (此身不向今生度更向何生度此身), which is commonly cited in Chan and Pure Land sources.

56 Qingcaotang, Chan Master Jie, and Zhenru Zhe were Chan practitioners who were believed to have reincarnated as prominent Song literati. The stories of their reincarnations are related as cautionary tales for the practice of Pure Land in Fascicle 7 of *Longshu jingtu wen*. See *T.* 1970, 47a–c.

57 The logic of this passage (何則不吝財以為善不貪財以為惡故也 ) has eluded me. In order to make sense of it, I have eliminated the negative preceding.

58 This text is not extant. Changlu Zongze (fl. late eleventh and early twelfth centuries) was a Northern Song Chan Master renowned for his authorship of the *Chanyuan qinggui* (Rules of purity for the Chan monastery). He was also a promoter of *nianfo* practice.

59 Although this verse is associated with the Daci Pusa, whose liturgical *gātha* is cited above in the section for officials, this verse is clearly different from that *gātha*. The origins of this verse are unknown.

60 See *Longshu jingtu wen* 5, *T.* 1970, 269a–b.

61 Concerning the origins of the association of sericulture with Aśvaghoṣa, see Stuart Young, "For a Compassionate Killing: Chinese Buddhism, Sericulture, and the Silkworm God Aśvaghoṣa," *Journal of Chinese Religions* 41, no. 1 (2013): 25–48.

## Bibliography

### Primary Sources

*Analects*. ctext.org/Analects/zh.

*Banzhou sanmei jing*. *T.* 418.

*Foshuo Guan Wuliangshoufo jing*. *T.* 365.

Kong Yingda. *Maoshi zhengyi*. https://zh.wikisource.org/zh/毛詩正義.

Legge, James, trans. "The Shu King or Book of Historical Documents." In *The Chinese Classics*. Hong Kong: Chinese University Press, 1960.

*Mengzi*. ctext.org/Mengzi/zh.

*Nianfo chaotuo jiejing jing*. *X.* 13.

Peng Jiqing. *Jushi zhuan*. *X.* 1646.

Ruxing. *Da Ming gaoseng zhuan*. *T.* 2062.

Wang Rixiu. *Longshu zengguan jingtu wen*. *T.* 1970.

*Xunzi*. ctext.org/xunzi/zh.

*Zengyi Ahan jing*. *T.* 125.

Zongxiao. *Lebang wenlei*. *T.* 1969.

### Secondary Sources

Bol, Peter. *"This Culture of Ours": Intellectual Transitions in T'ang and Sung China*. Stanford, CA: Stanford University Press, 1994.

*Bussho kaisetsu daijiten*. Edited by Ono Gemmyō. Tokyo: Daitō shuppansha, 1932–1935, 1975–1978.

Buswell, Robert, and Donald Lopez, eds., *The Princeton Dictionary of Buddhism*. Princeton, NJ: Princeton University Press, 2013.

Cherniack, Susan. "Book Culture and Textual Transmission in Sung China." *Harvard Journal of Asiatic Studies* 54, no. 1 (June 1994): 5–125.

Davis, Trevor. "Pure Land and the Social Order in Twelfth Century China: An Investigation on 'Longshu's Treatise on Pure Land'" (2012). Student Work Paper 1. http://elischolar.library.yale.edu/ceas_student_work/1.

*Foguang dacidian* 佛光大辭典, 1st ed. Edited by Foguan dacidian bianxiu weiyuanhui. Taipei: Foguang chubanshe, 1988.

Keown, Damien. *Oxford Dictionary of Buddhism*. New York: Oxford University Press, 2003.

Mochizuki Shinkō. *Chūgoku jōdo kyōrishi*. Kyōtō: Hōzōkan, 1964 [1942].

Schlutter, Morten. *How Zen Became Zen: The Dispute over Enlightenment and the Formation of Chan Buddhism in Song-Dynasty China*. Honolulu: University of Hawai'i Press, 2008.

*Songren zhuanji ziliao suoyin*, 2nd ed. Edited by Chang Bide et al. Taipei: Dingwen shuju, 1987.

Young, Stuart. "For a Compassionate Killing: Chinese Buddhism, Sericulture, and the Silkworm God Aśvaghoṣa." *Journal of Chinese Religions* 41, no. 1 (2013): 25–48.

## Chapter 5

# Tanaka Chigaku on "The Age of Unification"

Jacqueline I. Stone

### Translator's Introduction

The medieval Japanese Buddhist teacher Nichiren (1222–1282) taught that the spread of faith in the *Lotus Sūtra* would one day transform this world into an ideal buddha-land. Several contemporary Buddhist movements deriving from the *Lotus Sūtra* and Nichiren's teachings have drawn on his vision in developing programs of social engagement: Sōka Gakkai and Risshō Kōseikai, two of Japan's largest lay Buddhist movements, are NGO members of the United Nations and are active in peace education and relief and welfare work; Sōka Gakkai also engages in politics at national and local levels. Nipponzan Myōhōji, a small Nichiren Buddhist monastic order known for its stance of absolute nonviolence, is especially committed to the antinuclear movement. These activities represent modern versions of engaged bodhisattva practice and are shared by other Buddhists, but for members of these particular groups, such endeavors have specific roots in the *Lotus Sūtra* and in Nichiren's teaching that the pure land is to be manifested here in this world.

This chapter introduces Tanaka Chigaku (1861–1939),[1] arguably the first person to put forth a modern *Lotus Sūtra*–based vision of a this-worldly pure land. Tanaka presents scholars of modern Buddhism with a complex interpretive challenge. On one hand, he was a learned and committed devotee who strove tirelessly to establish an active lay Buddhism and reform his inherited Nichiren tradition to meet modern needs. Yet at the same time, his concept of the buddha-land foregrounded elements that many Buddhists today, Nichiren Buddhists included, would strongly repudiate: Tanaka denied the legitimacy of other religions; argued for a merger of the *Lotus Sūtra* and government; and invested his own country, Japan, with a sacred status, elevating it above all other nations and ultimately supporting its imperialistic ventures. The question of how these troubling elements could coexist with universalistic Buddhist principles offers important insights into the historical and hermeneutical processes by which representations of religious ideals, including ideal buddha-lands, take shape.

## Who Was Tanaka Chigaku?

Tanaka was born into a staunch Nichiren Buddhist family, just a few years before the Meiji Restoration (1868) that marked Japan's transition from rule by hereditary shoguns to a modern nation-state. As a young man training for the Nichiren Buddhist priesthood, Tanaka was frustrated with the liberal stance of his seminary instruction. Buddhism in the late nineteenth century was under pressure from modernizing forces. Confucian and Shinto ideologues active in the new Meiji regime (1868–1912) condemned it as a superstitious holdover from the past, a drain on public resources, and a harmful foreign influence that had suppressed the native Japanese spirit. Buddhist leaders of all sects rallied to the challenge, seeking to reformulate their traditions in ways suited to a modernizing Japan. Many saw Buddhism's best hope of survival in interdenominational cooperation. They included leaders of the Nichiren sect, or Nichirenshū, who downplayed Nichiren's exclusivistic claim that only the *Lotus Sūtra* leads to liberation in the present, Final Dharma age. Tanaka, however, saw this accommodation as a betrayal of Nichiren's teaching. Eventually he abandoned his priestly training to become a lay evangelist, initiating a movement he called Nichirenshugi (Nichirenism). Nichirenshugi was not the traditional Nichiren Buddhism centered on temples and priests but a lay movement engaged with practical social realities. In 1880, Tanaka founded the Rengekai (Lotus Blossom Society) to propagate Nichirenshugi ideals. It was reorganized in 1884 as the Risshō Ankokukai (after Nichiren's famous treatise *Risshō ankoku ron*, Establishing the true Dharma and bringing peace to the land), and again in 1914 as the Kokuchūkai, or Pillar of the Nation Society (after Nichiren's words, "I will be the pillar of Japan"), as it is still called today. Tanaka called for a return to *shakubuku*, an aggressive mode of proselytizing that Nichiren had employed in asserting the unique efficacy of the *Lotus Sūtra*. The clause guaranteeing religious freedom included in the Meiji Constitution (promulgated 1889) had removed earlier strictures on proselytizing imposed by the preceding Tokugawa regime (1603–1868). For Tanaka, this made his own historical moment the ideal time to realize Nichiren's vision of worldwide propagation.

The Kokuchūkai never had more than about seven thousand members.[2] Nonetheless, Tanaka's influence far exceeded the modest size of his organization. Scholarly treatments of Tanaka often indicate the range of his appeal by listing his more famous associates, both committed followers and others who came for varying lengths of time within his orbit and drew on his message in differing ways. These included the scholar Anesaki Masaharu (1873–1949), instrumental in establishing the academic study of religion in Japan; the poet and author of children's literature Miyazawa Kenji (1896–1933); the literary figure Takayama Chōgyū (1871–1902); the Buddhist socialist and youth leader Seno'o Girō (1890–1961); Tanaka's close disciple General Ishiwara Kanji (1889–1949), operations officer of the Kwandung Army, whose role in the so-called Mukden Incident of 1931 committed Japan to armed invasion of Manchuria; and Inoue Nisshō (1886–1967), would-be radical social reformer and founder of the terrorist organization Ketsumeidan (League of blood). Tanaka's influence, however, went beyond such well-known individuals and helped shape the very contours of modern Japanese lay Buddhism. Tanaka struggled against perceptions of Buddhism as being chiefly for the ritual care of the dead. He initiated Buddhist wedding ceremonies and also devised rites for other major life passages.[3] Features of his organizational style influenced several subsequent lay Buddhist movements. Tanaka mobilized the resources of youth and women in his organization and made innovative use of print and visual media. But perhaps his most durable legacy was his conviction that, just as Nichiren had taught, this world could become the buddha-land, not as a distant ideal, but as a concrete, foreseeable reality. Viewed in retrospect, some aspects of his thinking, such as his militant nationalism, appear disturbingly flawed. But the ideal of lay bodhisattva practice and the goal of realizing the buddha-land that he espoused remain central to a number of contemporary Nichiren Buddhist movements, although now generally revised in accord with pacifist and universalist ideals.

## Background in the *Lotus Sūtra* and Nichiren

Tanaka's vision drew on a long tradition of *Lotus Sūtra* commentary and the teachings of Nichiren. The *Lotus* is a Mahāyāna scripture especially valued in East Asia for its teaching that all shall become buddhas. It presents itself as the Buddha's final statement; all his other, previous teachings were merely his "skillful means" to lead persons of differing religious capacities to the one buddha vehicle. Not only the Buddha's teachings but the great events of his life, including his awakening under the bodhi tree and his entry into final nirvana, were provisional teaching devices intended to guide the ignorant. In reality, Śākyamuni Buddha says, he has been awakened since the inconceivably distant past and ever since then has dwelt here in this world. Though deluded beings experience this world as a place of suffering, in reality it is the realm of the primordially awakened Buddha. East Asian exegetes developed this idea in terms of the non-duality of living beings and the land they inhabit (*eshō funi*): When one awakens to the buddhahood within oneself, one's surrounding world or environment becomes the pure land. Nichiren would greatly develop the implications of this idea.

Nichiren had originally trained in the Tendai (Tiantai) school, which accords the *Lotus Sūtra* a central place among the Buddha's teachings. Like many of his contemporaries, he believed himself to be living in the Final Dharma age (*mappō*), a period of decline said to have begun some two thousand years after the death of the historical Buddha, when human delusions are profound, misunderstandings of the Buddhist teachings proliferate, and awakening becomes increasingly difficult to achieve. In this age, Nichiren taught, only the *Lotus Sūtra* was profound and powerful enough to lead all beings to liberation; indeed, the Buddha had left it precisely for this evil era. Nichiren advocated a form of *Lotus* practice that, while grounded in sophisticated Mahāyāna teachings of non-duality, was at the same time accessible to all persons: chanting the *daimoku* or title of the sutra in the formula *Namu Myōhō-renge-kyō*.[4] For him, the title of the *Lotus* encapsulated the whole of the primordial Buddha's enlightenment; in chanting it, one simultaneously called forth buddhahood within oneself and manifested the buddha-land in one's surroundings.

Nichiren's approach to the *Lotus Sūtra* was fiercely exclusivistic. Now in *mappō,* he taught, other, incomplete teachings had lost their efficacy. To abandon the *Lotus* in favor of "lesser," provisional paths such as Zen, Pure Land, or the Esoteric teachings was to cast aside the one teaching that still led to awakening in the Final Dharma age, a misguided act that could only bring misery in both this life and the next. The disasters then confronting Japan—droughts, famine, epidemics, earthquakes, and the threat of invasion by the Mongols—were for Nichiren karmic retribution for neglect of the *Lotus Sūtra* and blind adherence to incomplete, provisional teachings. Conversely, he said, by embracing faith in the *Lotus Sūtra,* Japan would become an ideal realm. "Now you must quickly reform the faith you hold in your heart and direct it to the single good of the true vehicle," he urged. "If you do, the threefold world will all become a buddha-land, and how could a buddha-land ever decline?"[5] That this world is ultimately the buddha-land had long been recognized by Buddhist teachers as a truth one might realize subjectively through faith and practice. Nichiren, however, taught that as faith in the *Lotus Sūtra* spread, objective realities would actually change: people would enjoy harmony with nature, just rule, and freedom from catastrophes.

## Tanaka's Millennial Vision

For six centuries after Nichiren's death, the universal spread of the *Lotus Sūtra* remained for his followers a vague ideal, indefinitely deferred. But in the late nineteenth and early twentieth centuries, some Nichiren Buddhist figures, of whom Tanaka was most influential, began to re-envision it in concrete terms. Tanaka first articulated such a vision in his 1901 "Restoration of Our Sect" (Shūmon no ishin). This manifesto laid out a blueprint for reforming Nichiren Buddhism, along with a detailed fifty-year plan for world conversion to be implemented once those reforms had become reality. It reflects Tanaka's bombastic style, interweaving his evangelical fervor with innovative proselytizing strategies. Tanaka envisioned proselytizing throughout the country: by the roads, in halls and auditoriums, even at hot spring resorts. Laywomen would be organized into a nursing corps and charitable hospitals established, winning public respect through acts of practical compassion. The sect would operate a shipping fleet and establish colonies of Nichiren devotees in Hokkaido, Taiwan (then under Japanese rule), and other overseas countries as bases for world propagation. Its growing financial capital would contribute to the nation's wealth and power, and eventually Nichiren Buddhism would become the state religion. Tanaka expanded his vision in *An Overview of Nichirenshugi Doctrinal Studies* (*Nichirenshugi kyōgaku taikan*), a grand systematization of Nichiren's teaching based on Nichirenshugi principles, originally published in 1904–1913. A section of this latter work is translated here.

Tanaka shared some ground with a number of Buddhist reformers, such as his insistence that Buddhism must be relevant to realities of modern life. Like many government and intellectual leaders, he sought to purge society of ignorance and "superstition" that would retard modernization. To his mind, that included eliminating even from his own sect traditional elements of local religious culture that were now deemed irrational and at odds with modernity. And, though Tanaka's nationalism was inflected through his own particular reading of Nichiren, it was also part of an overriding concern with the nation, Japan, and its place in the world that structured the greater part of intellectual discourse and public endeavors at the time.

In other respects, however, Tanaka went against the current. His proposals for sectarian reform called on the various branches of Nichiren Buddhism to abandon their rivalries and unite, return to the rigorous practice of *shakubuku* that Nichiren had taught, and strive tirelessly to convert the world. This meant that he rejected the transsectarianism embraced by many Buddhist leaders of his time. Tanaka termed the future purified Nichiren Buddhism that he envisioned "Honge Myōshū," a name that resists concise translation. *Myō* ("subtle," "wonderful") is the first character of the *Lotus Sūtra*'s title; *myōshū* means the sect based on the Wonderful Dharma of the *Lotus*. *Honge*, a Buddhist technical term, refers to those bodhisattvas who were taught by the primordial Śākyamuni Buddha at the time of his original awakening in the inconceivably remote past. In the sutra's narrative, they emerge from beneath the earth at the Buddha's summons and receive his mandate to propagate the *Lotus* widely in an evil age following his nirvana. Nichiren spoke of himself as a forerunner preparing the way for these bodhisattvas, and his subsequent tradition often identified him as a manifestation of their leader, Bodhisattva Superior Conduct (Jōgyō). The name "Honge Myōshū" thus suggests the *Lotus Sūtra*'s promise of universal buddhahood while emphasizing Nichiren's mandate to spread faith in the *Lotus* in the Final Dharma age.

Tanaka also differed from other Buddhist reformers in his utter rejection of the religious-secular divide. In formulating policy toward Buddhism, Shinto, and other traditions, Meiji officials had appropriated a concept of religion shaped largely by Protestant Christianity, in which "religion" was understood to be a matter of private belief and confined to a personal, interior sphere. By this definition, the state could not legitimately intrude on individual faith commitments, but at the same time, religious bodies could not be allowed to influence the course of government. For Tanaka, however, Nichiren's teaching that the Wonderful Dharma of the *Lotus* encompasses all aspects of life and society was not simply a matter of individuals manifesting their faith in daily activities; Honge Myōshū, the reformed Nichiren sect, must actively guide, even subsume, the state. The unity of Buddhism and government, a major theme of the text translated here, set Tanaka and his followers radically apart from the secularizing spirit of the times.

## The Sacred Center and Japan's Global Role

As seen in the text that follows, Tanaka called for the building of a sacred center. Nichiren had taught that practice for the *mappō* era comprises "Three Great Secret Dharmas": the *daimoku*, or invocation of the *Lotus Sūtra*'s title; the object of worship (*gohonzon*), that is, the *maṇḍala* that Nichiren devised as a focus of practice for his followers, depicting in Chinese characters the *Lotus Sūtra* assembly or realm of the primordially awakened Buddha; and the ordination platform (*kaidan*). Nichiren established the first two himself but entrusted the realization of the ordination platform to his followers in the future. Superseding all other ordination platforms, it was to be the *honmon no kaidan*, the ordination platform based on the "origin teaching" (*honmon*), or latter fourteen chapters of the *Lotus Sūtra*, which reveal that the Buddha is always present in this world.

An "ordination platform" is a ritual space where the Buddhist precepts are conferred upon persons taking vows as monks or nuns. Nichiren, however, had taught that, now in *mappō*, the only valid precept is to embrace the *Lotus Sūtra*, and his intent regarding the future *kaidan* is not altogether clear. Nonetheless, the official ordination platforms in Japan in his time were state-sponsored, and Nichiren may well have seen the establishment of a *kaidan* as manifesting the traditional interdependent relationship of state and sangha in its ideal form, based on the *Lotus Sūtra*. Such a reading is suggested by "The Three Great Secret Dharmas" (*Sandai hihō shō*), cited here by Tanaka and the only writing in the corpus of works attributed to Nichiren to address the ordination platform in any detail.

After Nichiren's death, prospects for establishing such a *kaidan* seemed remote, and for centuries it remained an indefinite future goal. Many scholar-monks of the tradition interpreted the "ordination platform" in abstract terms (*ri kaidan*) to mean any place at all where a *Lotus* devotee might chant the *daimoku*. In the modern period, however, some Nichiren Buddhist leaders, most prominently Tanaka himself, began to re-envision the *kaidan* as a very real and not-too-distant possibility. For Tanaka, this was to be an actual edifice (*ji kaidan*) that would not only seal the unity of Buddhism and government, recast in modern terms, but also establish Japan as the world's spiritual center.

Japan's place in the world meant something quite different for Tanaka than it had for Nichiren. Nichiren had inherited from his Tendai forebears the idea that Japan had a particular karmic connection to the

*Lotus Sūtra*. For that very reason, he on one hand condemned Japan as a benighted country where people rejected the *Lotus*. But at the same time, he saw Japan as the place where the *daimoku* of the *Lotus Sūtra*, the true teaching for the Final Dharma age, was first destined to spread. From Japan, he said, it would rise, like the sun, and illuminate the world. Educated Buddhists in Nichiren's time were keenly conscious of living in a tiny archipelago on the easternmost periphery of the Buddhist world and in an age of decline. Nichiren's thinking about Japan as the birthplace of a new Buddhism uniquely suited to the *mappō* era was part of a larger move on the part of premodern Buddhist teachers across school and lineage boundaries to assert the legitimacy of Japanese Buddhism vis-à-vis that of India and China. Tanaka, however, read Nichiren's statements about Japan not in their historical context but in light of the country's geopolitical situation in the modern period, as Japan first struggled to establish itself as a developed nation able to hold its own against Western powers and then asserted itself as an imperial power in its own right.

Intellectuals of the day, drawing on Hegel and related thinkers, often conceived of nation-states not as human constructs but as ontologically real. Individual lives were held to derive meaning through their connection to the nation, and the universal truths of religion could have value for individuals only insofar as they could be grounded in the specifics of the country to which people actually belonged. The Christian leader Uchimura Kanzō (1861–1930) famously declared that he "loved two Js": Jesus, connecting him to the universal, and Japan, rooting him in the world. Tanaka, it has been observed, similarly cherished two Ns, Nichiren and Nippon (Japan), and sought to theoretize their relationship.[6] In the decades after completing his *Overview*, Tanaka devoted himself to elaborating a new branch of doctrinal studies that he called *kokutaigaku*, an interpretation from a Nichirenshugi perspective of the *kokutai*, the "national polity" or "national essence," a key term in political discourse of Japan's modern imperial period (1890–1945). In the excerpt translated here, Tanaka uses the term chiefly in the sense of polity and traces the relationship of government to religion over the course of Japan's history. Later, he would increasingly identify Japan's *kokutai* with the *Lotus Sūtra* itself. The modern Japanese state was not only to be based on the *Lotus Sūtra*, it was the vehicle by which the *Lotus Sūtra* would spread to the world.

Postwar critics have often charged Tanaka and other Nichirenshugi advocates with catering to an imperialist state by subordinating the dharma to the nation. Were the matter so simple, Tanaka would not present us with an interpretive challenge but could readily be dismissed as an eccentric chauvinist. The reality, however, was more complex. Tanaka was a serious Buddhist who saw the dharma—in particular Nichiren's teaching—as the only secure foundation on which an ideal nation could be established. He did not reinvent Nichiren Buddhism to serve the Japanese state so much as he enlisted the national ideology of his time to reassert to his contemporaries the truth claims of the Nichiren tradition. Yet his view of Japan as endowed with a sacred mission to unite the world through the *Lotus Sūtra* mapped smoothly onto Japan's armed expansion of empire in the mid-twentieth century and lent the imperial project a sacred legitimacy. Nichirenshugi adherents, and Nichiren Buddhists in general, were not necessarily any more committed to the imperial cause than the Buddhists of any other school; most religious organizations lent support to Japan's military ventures. But modern interpretations of Nichiren doctrine such as Tanaka's imbued public perceptions of the Nichiren tradition with a particularly nationalist coloration. During Japan's modern imperial period, this reading won sympathizers among intellectuals, officials, and military leaders, even outside Nichirenist circles. In the postwar era, however, Nichiren Buddhists seeking to frame their teaching in terms of contemporary liberal values have had to struggle against the fiercely nationalistic image of Nichiren forged by Tanaka and his sympathizers.

Tanaka Chigaku's case informs us that modernist visions of a this-worldly pure land do not emerge seamlessly from received Buddhist doctrine but are shaped by the needs of their creators and their historical circumstances. Doctrine is politically underdetermined, and how it will be appropriated for social agendas is often decided by external factors. Thus the *Lotus Sūtra*'s teaching that this world is not separate from the buddha-land has, within a historically short span of time, been invoked in ways that sacralized one nation above others, legitimizing its militant aims, and has also been enlisted in the service of universalist, postwar democratic visions of world peace.

The following excerpt from *Nichirenshugi kyōgaku taikan* is taken from a passage where Tanaka discusses the category of the "time," meaning the time when the *Lotus Sūtra* is destined to spread. Tanaka divides the Final Dharma age into three periods: (1) the age of establishment, when Nichiren appeared and declared his teaching; (2) the age of dissemination, when that teaching was spread and perpetuated through Nichiren Buddhist institutions; and (3) the coming age of unification, when, mediated by the merger of dharma and government and spearheaded by Japan, the world will be unified by faith in the *Lotus Sūtra* and the buddhahood of the land will be realized. The third section, on "the age of unification," has been translated here.[7]

## Translation

### "The Age of Unification"

Tanaka Chigaku

The last of the three periods of the Final Dharma age (*mappō*) will be the age of unification. In his "True Aspect of the Dharmas," [our founder Nichiren] declares [that someday the people of Japan will all chant the *daimoku* of the *Lotus Sūtra*,] "as surely as an arrow aimed at the earth cannot miss the mark."[8] In "On Practicing as the *Lotus Sūtra* Teaches," he cites "the golden words [of Zhiyi], 'The practice of the *Lotus Sūtra* is *shakubuku*, the refutation of provisional teachings,'"[9] asserting the principle by which this unification will surely be achieved. From a mundane perspective, the unification of religious thought at the national and global levels might appear to be an impossible dream, but such an attitude merely reflects one's own short-sightedness. The *Lotus Sūtra* itself says, "In the buddha lands of the ten directions, there is the dharma of only one vehicle," and "The worlds of the ten directions interpenetrated, forming a single buddha-land."[10] From the standpoint of the dharma, the age of unification is already a fact. From our standpoint, it is a precious edifice that we must build. And in terms of the non-duality of the dharma and ourselves, it is a reality that is approaching moment by moment.[11] When we advance a single step for the sake of the great dharma, then with that step, the ground of this age [of unification] unfolds before us; this is a certain thing. The buddhahood of the land (*kokudo jōbutsu*) to be realized in this age of unification is not like heaven or the pure land, which are never actually expected to appear before our eyes. We predict, envision, and aim for it as a future reality that we will definitely witness.

I will address this theme under three headings: the merger of Buddhism and government, the establishment of the ordination platform, and the unification of the world.

## The Merger of Buddhism and Government

First, the merger of Buddhism and government means the merging of the ruler's dharma (*ōbō*) and the buddha-dharma (*buppō*). This is the foremost requirement for world unification. It entails two aspects: first, subsuming government within the buddha-dharma, and second, applying the buddha-dharma to government.

"The Three Great Secret Dharmas" states:

> When the ruler's dharma becomes one with the buddha-dharma and the buddha-dharma is united with the ruler's dharma, and the ruler and his ministers all uphold the Three Great Secret Dharmas [of the origin teaching of the *Lotus Sūtra*], the bond that once existed in the past between the king Possessing Virtue (Utoku) and the monk Awakened Virtue (Kakutoku) will be restored in the future, in the polluted and evil Final Dharma age.[12] At that time, an imperial edict and official decree will be handed down, to seek out the most superior site, resembling the Pure Land of Sacred Eagle Peak [where the *Lotus Sūtra* was expounded], and erect the ordination platform there. You have only to await the time. This ordination platform will manifest in concrete form the dharma of the precepts [for the Final Dharma age] by which all people of the three countries [India, China, and Japan] and the entire world [Jambudvīpa] will perform repentance and eradicate their offenses.[13] Here too [the world-governing deities] Brahmā and Indra and the other gods will descend [to lend their protection].[14]

Before the entire world can be unified, the people of Japan must all convert [to the Wonderful Dharma], and on that basis, the merger of Buddhism and government must be achieved. In so doing, first government must be subsumed within Buddhism, and then Buddhism must be applied to government. If Buddhism were first merged with government without "awaiting the [proper] time," that would subordinate the transcendent dharma to worldly matters and end up in catering to political authority. In the merger of government with Buddhism (*ōbutsu myōgō*) that is to be achieved by the original disciples of the constantly abiding primordial Buddha of the *Lotus Sūtra*, the ruler's dharma must first be made to abide securely in the spirit of the buddha-dharma. Then, when the two have merged, the true Eagle Peak, the actual realm of Tranquil Light (*jakkō*), will manifest in this land.[15]

To illustrate: The buddha-dharma corresponds to "abstract principle" (*ri*), so it is like the mind. The ruler's dharma corresponds to "concrete actualities" (*ji*), so it is like the body.[16] From the standpoint of the buddha-dharma as principle, the truth that informs *Lotus*

*Sūtra*'s words about "the worlds of the ten directions interpenetrating to form a single buddha land" inherently encompasses the source of the ruler's dharma, just as our mind is naturally endowed with the buddha nature and has abided since the beginningless past. When we act in accordance with that buddha-nature in our thoughts, words, and actions, we directly realize buddhahood in this very body (*sokushin jōbutsu*). In like manner, when government is fully awakened to the spirit of the buddha-dharma and merges with it, then the "body" that is the ruler's dharma comes to possess the "mind" of the buddha-dharma, while the "mind" that is the buddha-dharma obtains the "body" of the ruler's dharma, and the buddhahood of the land will be manifested. This subsuming of government within Buddhism requires that the emperor take faith in the True Dharma and that the entire country come to accord with the one vehicle. It is our responsibility as Nichiren Buddhist practitioners to generate an atmosphere in which this can happen.

To sum up: The subsuming of government within the buddha-dharma means that the actual nation-state will achieve the ideal of [becoming] "indestructible as a diamond" (*kongō fue*), while the application of the buddha-dharma to government means that the ideal buddha-land of Tranquil Light will be manifested in this actual land.

Nonetheless, it would be appalling if this country were to merge with Buddhism as represented by the Nichiren sect in its current state, with its worship of foxes and badgers and other debased practices.[17] That is why the sect of the Wonderful Dharma brought by the Buddha's original disciples (Honge Myōshū) must steadily display its true worth from now on. It may actually be fortunate that a merger of government with Buddhism cannot take place at present. Were there a movement to make Nichirenshū as it is today our national religion, anyone with the slightest common sense and good conscience would have to oppose it for the sake of the nation and world civilization, to say nothing of the deleterious consequences such a move would have for Buddhism. To link to the project of world unification such barbarous practices as worshipping animals or shouting the *daimoku* in garbled form to the beat of hand drums[18] would be an absurdity on a grand scale. "Awaiting the time" in that fashion would be worse than futile. Those who would qualify as true followers of the Buddha's original disciples must undergo a great awakening in order to "await the time" in the correct way.

## Establishing the Ordination Platform

After the merger of Buddhism and government, the ordination platform must be erected. This will be the concrete manifestation of the precepts referred to in "The Three Great Secret Dharmas" quoted above. It means actually building the ordination platform where the people of all three countries and the entire world will perform repentance and eradicate their sins. The same writing says to "seek out the most superior site, resembling the Pure Land of Sacred Eagle Peak, and erect the ordination platform there." As these words indicate, this *kaidan* will be the sacred place that will gather the devotion of all people of the world. And if we turn to other [passages among our founder's teachings], we learn that it is to be established in our country.

For example, "The [Contemplation of the Mind and the] Object of Worship" says that [the Buddha's original disciples, the bodhisattvas who emerged from beneath the earth, will appear in the Final Dharma age and] "establish in this country the foremost object of worship in the world."[19] *Nikō's Record* states: "The 'originally innate Eagle Peak' refers to this Sahā world, and in particular, to the country of Japan. The 'subtlety of the original land' [of the primordial Buddha] indicated in the *Lotus Sūtra* refers to this Sahā world [and specifically] to the place where the great *maṇḍala* implicit in the 'Fathoming the Lifespan' chapter of the origin teaching will be established."[20] Elsewhere [our teacher Nichiren] refers to "Japan and all the world" or speaks of himself as "the pillar of Japan."[21] All such references secretly hint that Japan is the world center and the sacred ground where the ordination platform is to be established. In particular, Mount Fuji is called Great Sun Lotus King Mountain (Dainichirengeō-zan) and is deemed the most celebrated peak within the three countries. According to tradition, our founder buried a copy of the *Lotus Sūtra* there.[22] Thus it has already been established that the ordination platform should be erected here in Japan.

However, two great conditions must be fulfilled in order for that to take place. First, His Majesty the emperor, carrying on a single lineage unbroken through a myriad reigns, must convert to this great dharma [of the *Lotus*] and, as sponsor for the ordination platform, issue an edict that it be built. Second, a majority of the nation's people both high and low, of whatever class, must also convert to the great dharma. Now let us consider what is meant by these two conditions: the promulgation of an imperial edict and the conversion of the entire nation.

"The Three Great Secret Dharmas" says that "an imperial edict and official decree will be handed down." An "imperial edict" (*chokusen*) means the emperor's command establishing the ordination platform. "Official decree" (*migyōsho*) originally meant an order promulgated by the retired emperor, the regent, or the shogun; in the Kamakura period [1185–1333, when Nichiren lived], it meant an order of the Bakufu, that is, the shogunate or military government. In terms of the present era, we may consider "an official decree" to be a resolution of the National Diet. In order to obtain such a resolution from the Diet, we must first convert a majority of the people. That is, to create a trend of the times favorable to an "official decree," we must win the hearts of the entire populace to Nichirenism.

Our founder addressed himself to the Bakufu, rather than the imperial court, because in those days political power lay with the military government. Rather than placing priority on converting individual citizens, he directed his efforts toward the center of power and proclaimed his doctrine, admonishing the country's leaders [to support faith in the *Lotus Sūtra* alone] and urging that it be established as the national teaching. He did so because his was an age when politics and religion were united. Shallow-minded people dismiss his actions as collusion with political power, but that merely betrays their ignorance.

Government and religion ought to be one. Of course it would be undesirable either for government to be under the sway of an undeveloped religion or for religion to cater to government; both these cases are to be avoided. But to regard the unity of politics and religion as evil under any circumstances would be a grave misunderstanding. In the ancient past, the polity (*kokutai*) of our country of Japan was religious in nature; hence the expression "unity of rites and rule" (*saisei itchi*).[23] But with the passage of time, ideas about what constitutes the *kokutai* and what constitutes religion gradually separated. Confucian and Buddhist teachings entered the country [early on], and perhaps in that connection Prince Shōtoku (574–622), in addressing the three teachings, likened Shintō to the root, Confucianism to the flowers, and Buddhism to the fruit.[24] He said that although the three are different, they are all to be employed, thus expounding the unity of these three paths. He himself preached on the *Lotus, Queen Śrīmālā,* and *Humane Kings* sutras, designating these as the three scriptures for the protection of the nation and personally delivering lectures on them. In his seventeen-article constitution as well, he admonished that the three treasures [the Buddha, Dharma, and Sangha] were to be revered. All these acts of his express the ideal of the unity of government and religion. At a later point, the Great Teacher Dengyō [Saichō, 766/767–822, founder of the Japanese Tendai school] appeared and sought to unify religion and government by means of the *Lotus Sūtra*. Emperor Kanmu (r. 781–806) accepted his plan and strove to implement it. After the death of these two figures, however, a reversal of high and low occurred within the Buddhist teachings, so that they became spiritual poison for the nation.[25] From the period of Fujiwara rule through the struggle of the Minamoto and the Taira, the ascendancy of the Hōjō and then the Ashikaga military houses up until the time of total upheaval [in the late medieval period], Buddhism and the national polity coexisted in an orderly fashion; though minor conflicts broke out, there was no major revolt. But once a deviation occurred [within this coexistence], it acquired overwhelming momentum, and a succession of warlords battled to seize the nation's rule.[26] If one were to elaborate in detail on the relation of government and religion in terms of our national history, one would find clear evidence [to support my argument] and turn up many interesting matters, but I must defer such a discussion for another occasion.

In essence, the *kokutai* underwent its greatest disruption during the period of the Country at War. The first warlord to attempt to unify the country was Nobunaga (1534–1582). Nobunaga conceived of ruling the country by making use of religion, but he was unable to find anyone appropriate in the Buddhist world to serve as his tool. In the end, he mistook Christianity for a form of Buddhism and, placing his hopes in it, he struck a hard blow at the Nichiren and Jōdo Shin sects and also razed Mount Hiei and Mount Kōya, all of them powerful in the Buddhist world at the time.[27] In contrast, [his successor] Hideyoshi (1537–1598) discerned that Christianity would harm the nation and sought to eradicate it, replacing it with Buddhism [as a means to unify the realm] by such undertakings as the building of the Great Buddha [at Higashiyama in Kyoto]. But things did not go as he had hoped. Not only did Hideyoshi not positively establish a unity of government and religion, but in using religion to serve his ends, he failed to draw upon its better strands. Ieyasu (1542–1616), who followed him, wiped out the foreign religion and won the people's hearts. He protected all sects of Buddhism, beginning with the Pure Land sect, which was his family religion, and established a basis for making use of them [in governing the country].[28] But with respect to our sect, he attacked Nichiō and Nichikyō for upholding the principle of "neither receiving nor giving" (*fuju fuse*) and asserting that the *nenbutsu* leads to the Hell without Respite, and he forbade proselytizing based on doctrinal principles.[29] Thus inevitably he employed strategies for governance using religions that made the people stupid. Before Ieyasu died, the administrator of monks Tenkai (1536–1643) asked him, "Do you wish to be born in Amida Buddha's Land of Bliss? Or do you intend to remain in this realm and protect the nation?" Ieyasu replied that he had no desire to go to the Pure Land. In the end he decided that he personally would convert to the Tendai sect and protect the nation as the deity Tōshō Daigongen, which is how his mausoleum came to be established at Nikkō.[30] Such was his personal faith. In his ideas of government, however, he applied Confucian teachings but merely exploited Buddhism. Thus no teaching came into direct conflict with the power of the state but all submitted to its authority, as is presently the case. Religions that preached the principles of loyalty, filial conduct, integrity, and moral recompense according with one's deeds were all protected. Only Christianity and the Nichiren sect conflicted with Ieyasu's will and were proscribed throughout the country: Christianity, because its religious authority derived from foreign countries, and the Nichiren sect, because it sought to rectify government by means of religious truth.[31] However, Ieyasu never imagined the interpretation of the *kokutai* that would result from the combination of Confucian ideas about loyalty to the sovereign and the revival of Nativism (Kokugaku), such as that initiated by Tokugawa Mitsukuni (1628–1701).[32] In time, foreign countries sought trade treaties, the external threat posed by their demands aroused the people's self-awakening, and in the end the great work of the Imperial Restoration was accomplished, returning sovereignty to the emperor as in antiquity. At the beginning of the Meiji era (1868–1912), it briefly appeared that Shinto would become something like a national religion. But, apart from grassroots *kami* practices and some elements added on in later ages, Shintō has no religious aspects, no doctrine, and no articles of faith. Since it is no more than a custom of ancestor worship and stops at clarifying the *kokutai,* it was divorced from the realm of religion, and its religious strands came to be treated like Buddhism or Christianity.[33] The Constitution recognized citizens' freedom of religion, and a total separation of government and religion was thus achieved. The modern *kokutai* therefore has no connection to any religion but has come to be held supreme simply on its own merits.

The natural confluence of circumstances that has brought about this current state of affairs is truly advantageous for implementing our founder's teaching. It would create chaos if some mistaken religion of the present were to join forces with the imperial house and the state and become established as the national religion. But as long as the *kokutai* stands aloof from religion, natural selection, the struggle for survival of the fittest in the realm of religion, can proceed.[34] When at length the great religion has appeared whose influence will extend to all citizens as a whole, then at any time it can join together with the state and the imperial house. Honge Myōshū, our *Lotus* school of the Buddha's original disciples, is the teaching that carries this innate destiny and duty.

Therefore, for the present, rather than engage in public debates or petition the government, we should actively arouse public opinion. From a spiritual standpoint, we should bring about a great awakening at the source of popular thought, and from a practical standpoint, we should plan to nurture the power of our sect in terms of the wealth and military force that are a nation's real strength. Since debates are ultimately resolved by the power of finance or aggression, we should develop our influence to the point where it can sway national opinion even by such means. I have explained this ideal in concrete detail in my "Restoration of Our [Nichiren] Sect." The money to fund the building of the ordination platform and other endeavors, such as volunteer fleets to be maintained by the sect, are part of this design.[35] If matters can be implemented as I envision, then, when faced with a great conflict, such as the impending war with Russia, we should be able to launch three squadrons in the Japan Sea, the China Sea, and the Sea of Okhotsk respectively and also deploy a division of our followers in Siberia. When the priesthood in the Final Dharma age forgets the two great practical forces of financial power and military might and does nothing but preach sermons, then it becomes powerless to accomplish anything. [The imperative to concern ourselves with such matters] is a secret intent of the *Nirvāṇa Sūtra* and of [our founder's writings,] "The Object of Worship" and the "[*Risshō*] *ankoku ron*."[36] When our sect of the Wonderful Dharma borne by the original Buddha's disciples can implement this secret intent, our nation and society will come into their true life, and the conversion of the entire nation will come about of itself. Once it is clear that a majority of the country has converted, that will be the precise moment to petition the imperial household to make ours the state religion. At that time, the emperor will surely approve our petition and convene a special session of the Diet to deliver an edict mandating that article 27 [*sic*] of the Constitution, guaranteeing religious freedom, be revised, and a new system instituted with Honge Myōshū as the state religion.[37] If a two-thirds majority approves, [then the two conditions mentioned above,] the conversion of the entire nation and the promulgation of an imperial edict, will be realized, and the ordination platform can be established in actuality. The "time to be awaited" [referred to in "The Three Great Secret Dharmas"] is a time that we ourselves must create.

Under this newly established unity of government and religion, the *Lotus Sūtra*, that is, the wondrous principle that is the great truth of the one vehicle, shall manifest as the great power that is the nation. This tiny country of Japan, as the true Eagle Peak, the actual Land of Tranquil Light, will establish the ordination platform at Fuji as humanity's universal sacred place, becoming the holy nation where "all people of the entire world will perform repentance and eradicate their offenses." When one mentions the unity of government and religion, people today seem unable to conceive of it apart from the example of the Roman Catholic Church, but since "they who have not practiced cannot understand,"[38] theirs is an uninformed view. Originally speaking, Rome and Christianity had no special affinity or connection, and the Roman emperor in himself had no basis of moral authority. It would be a great mistake to compare that situation with our imperial house, which since its founding has upheld and transmitted the Way as its lifeblood. And, in terms of its teachings, Christianity contains no national elements pertaining to this world; thus it would also be wrong to compare it to the great ideal of a sacred country expressed in the ordination platform of the origin teaching. The Roman emperor, who had no basis in the Way, and Christianity, which had no foundational ideal of the nation, were brought together as an expedient. Thus in time, disputes broke out between the emperor and the pope, and all sorts of ecclesiastical abuses appeared. Now our country and Nichiren's Buddhism (Honge Myōshū) have an inherent affinity and bond: In the imperial house, there is the ideal of the imperishable Way, and in our sect, there is the doctrine that the land of the Wonderful Dharma will be manifested in actuality. With the sun as their common emblem, this country and this teaching will inevitably join together, sharing a destiny to save the people of the world.[39] The divine imperial ancestor [i.e., the sun goddess], manifesting the virtue that illuminates heaven and earth, declared, "My descendants shall rule over this land."[40] Our founder, as the savior for all people of the Final Dharma age, said, "I will be the pillar of Japan."[41] He also made reference to "Japan and all the world," and "the whole world, but specifically Japan," hinting at the profound relationship [between our country and the dharma]. Thus his words "You have only to await the time" resound in our ears.

Unless such unity of government and religion is achieved, it is pointless to ask which emperor will issue the edict or will he bestow the purple robe; or to think that if only one establishes close contact with the imperial household, one has made some great accomplishment; or to go around bragging about the Murakumo nuns' imperial pedigree, and the like.[42] Such actions represent an extremely narrow, low-level way of thinking that will only destroy the timing [of our undertaking] and the character of our sect. If the union of government and religion is not profoundly rooted throughout in the oneness of the *kokutai* and our fundamental teaching, it will be no more than a government strategy of exploiting religion or an incomplete joining of government and religion, or, as in the past, it will simply mirror the changing religious preferences of successive rulers. Compared to any of those, the complete separation of religion and government that we see today would be a far happier outcome both for our country and the world. But if we can realize the ordination platform in actuality by the proclamation of an imperial edict and the conversion of the entire nation, then the unification of the world will come about of itself.

## The Unification of the World

In the face of its seeming impossibility, people have always cherished the idea of unifying the world. Great religious leaders such as Śākyamuni and Jesus sought to accomplish it spiritually. Powerful statesmen such as Alexander and Napoleon tried to achieve it by force or by the power of diplomacy. However, force or diplomacy cannot readily accomplish it. Even if world unification should be realized temporarily through such means, it would soon dissolve, as we can learn by examining the history of great empires of the past. That said, it would also be difficult to accomplish world unification solely by the power of religion. Today, the various European nations are all Christian, but Christianity has merely produced ties among individuals. We cannot find anything in it that would serve as a point of unification among nations in religious terms. Must we then establish some sort of institution above nations that would unite them? Not necessarily. Today, joint undertakings in such arenas as international law, peace conferences, mail delivery systems, and the like are seeking commonalities across national boundaries. But they do not represent a unification of spirit and body, nor do they embody a religious ideal that can become the real power of the nation, and thus they cannot carry out the project of unifying the world. That task is none other than the establishment of the ordination platform of the origin teaching, the sacred mission of world unification, which will manifest the ideal world described in "On Practicing as the *Lotus Sūtra* Teaches":

> In that time, when the ruler, the people, and the various Buddhist schools all convert to the one vehicle, and the people all chant *Namu Myōhō-renge-kyō* as one, the wind will not thrash the branches nor the rain fall hard enough to erode the soil. The world will be as it was in the ages [of the ancient sage kings] Fuxi and Shennong. In this life, inauspicious disasters will be banished, and people will obtain the art of longevity. You will behold a time when the principle becomes manifest that persons and dharmas neither age nor die.[43]

For such unification to take place, some sort of standard or center is absolutely necessary. Force and diplomacy are responses geared to specific situations, so their results are bound to be temporary, and therefore they can never bring about true unification. Unification requires that which is constantly abiding and all-pervasive, bringing together all individuals and nations in the great ideal of the one vehicle, just like the string that holds together a necklace of pearls. What can serve as the center for that unification and generate the driving force to accomplish it is the great doctrine of the ordination platform of the origin teaching to be actualized in reality (*honmon ji no kaidan*). Where there is no ideal, there will be no unification. Honge Myōshū will unite the world by the teaching of the one buddha vehicle. Then all the various nations of the world, just as they are, will return to the single great ideal of the Wonderful Dharma. And, as the place of the ordination platform where that dharma has been established and is protected and upheld, our imperial nation will be revered; and our emperor, heir to a lineage unbroken throughout a myriad reigns, will receive the reverence of all humanity and nations as the protector of the way of antiquity and the foremost model for the world's leaders. Individuals and nations will each obtain their proper place and all alike return to the Great Way, enjoying the numinous blessings of humanity's original ground. This is the wondrous benefit to be conferred by our Honge Myōshū sect; it is the conversion of all under heaven and within the four seas to the Wonderful Dharma. It will entail the following five aspects: (1) unification of thought; (2) unification of religion; (3) unification of morality; (4) unification of society; and (5) unification of government.

In other words, in that age of world unification, thought, religion, morality, society, and government will all be unified in the *Sūtra of the Lotus*

*Blossom of the Wonderful Dharma*; all will steadily come to accord with the one vehicle. However, that does not mean that the ideas and cultural products of the world's nations will all become the same. Rather, these differing ideas and products, while each radiantly displaying its individual characteristics, will all have their point of unification in the Wonderful Dharma. Even when that dawn of world unification comes to pass, in the realm of thought [we will find varying attitudes]: there will be optimism; there will be pessimism; there will be prayers for the deceased. But in their essential points these varying outlooks will be unified. In any age, the vulgar masses and persons of education and refinement cannot possibly embrace the same views and spirit in all instances. In like manner, there will be people of varying religious temperaments, and they will not necessarily all come to embrace only the same elevated ideas. There will be those given to acts of religious charity, those who embrace lofty ideals of renunciation, and those who pray for peace and security in this world or for happiness in the future. But this diversity does not mean that the various religions and thought systems will be allowed to stand just as they are. We must seek out and establish their point of unification in the fundamental place to which they return. Reverence for the Wonderful Dharma is what unites all things at the center. Even more than the ethos of loyalty and filial piety that prevailed during the Tokugawa period, it will become a clear and profound way of thinking natural to ordinary citizens.

In this age of unification, morality, society, and government will be unified in the same manner as thought and religion, but there is no telling, specifically, what that unification will be like. When the time comes, assisted by the power of the Buddha's original disciples, the most perfect unification shall surely come about. Of course I have my own opinions on the matter, but to voice them now would just be foolish. I will leave it at simply asserting that this unification must take place.

## Notes

1 Names are given according to East Asian convention, with the surname first.

2 Ōtani Eiichi, *Kindai Nihon no Nichirenshugi undo* (Kyoto: Hōzōkan, 2001), 205–206.

3 Richard M. Jaffe, "Tanaka Chigaku and the Buddhist Clerical Marriage: Toward a Positive Appraisal of Family Life," in *Neither Monk nor Layman:*

*Clerical Marriage in Modern Japanese Buddhism* (Princeton, NJ: Princeton University Press, 2001), 165–188; Ōtani, *Kindai Nihon no Nichirenshugi undo,* 40–41.

4 *Myōhō-renge-kyō* (*Miaofa lianhua jing, Sūtra of the Lotus Blossom of the Wonderful Dharma*) is the title in Japanese pronunciation of Kumārajīva's famed 406 Chinese translation of the *Lotus Sūtra. Namu* is from Sanskrit *namo-* or *namas,* indicating praise, reverence, devotion, and the taking of refuge.

5 *Risshō ankoku ron*, in Risshō Daigaku Nichiren Kyōgaku Kenkyūjo, ed., *Shōwa teihon Nichiren Shōnin ibun* (hereafter *Teihon*) (Minobusan Kuonji: Minobuchō, Yamanashi Prefecture, 1952–1959, rev. ed. 1988), 1:226.

6 Nishiyama Shigeru, "Kindai no Nichirenshugi: 'Kennō' shinkō no keifu," *Nihon no bukkyō* 4 (1995): 228–240 (228–229). On Uchimura, see Hiroshi Miura, *The Life and Thought of Kanzō Uchimura, 1861-1930* (Grand Rapids, MI: Wm. B. Eerdmans, 1996).

7 The following selection has been translated and adapted from Tanaka Chigaku, *Nichirenshugi kyōgaku taikan,* 6 vols. (Tokyo: Kokusho Kankōkai, 1975), 4:2267–2280. This work was originally published from 1904–1913 in 5 volumes as *Honge Myōshu shikimoku kōgiroku* and retitled *Nichirenshugi kyōgaku taikan* in 1915. Based on a year-long series of lectures by Tanaka, it was edited by his disciple Yamakawa Chiō (1879–1956).

8 *Shohō jissō shō, Teihon* 1:727.

9 *Nyosetsu shugyō shō, Teihon* 1:733. The Chinese master Zhiyi (538–597) is considered the founder of the Tiantai school, and Nichiren regarded him as an important forebear. The statement quoted here appears in Zhiyi's *Fahua xuanyi, T.* 1716.33:792b. The *shakubuku* method aims directly at confronting and breaking attachment to inferior teachings. It stands in contrast to *shōju,* a mild method of leading others gradually without challenging their present views. Both terms occur in the Buddhist sutras, and commentators before Nichiren had linked *shakubuku* with the *Lotus Sūtra.* Today, the term is most often associated with the Nichiren tradition. See also George J. Tanabe Jr., "Tanaka Chigaku: The *Lotus Sutra* and the Body Politic," in *The Lotus Sutra in Japanese Culture,* ed. George J. Tanabe Jr. and Willa Jane Tanabe, 191–208 Honolulu: University of Hawai'i Press, 1989.

10 *Miaofa lianhua jing, T.* 262.9:8a; 52a. Tanaka slightly abridges the language of the second quote.

11 Literally, Tanaka begins this sentence, "In terms of ourselves and the dharma forming a single suchness (*ichinyo*)." Here and elsewhere, I have simplified some technical Buddhist terminology.

12 The *Mahāparinirvāṇa sūtra* tells how, in a prior age when the dharma was in decline, the monk Awakened Virtue alone correctly upheld the Buddha's teachings. When Awakened Virtue was attacked by corrupt monks, the

king, Possessing Virtue, defended him at the cost of his own life (*Da banniepan jing, T.* 374.12:383c–384a). For Nichiren, this story represented the ideal relationship between sangha and state, or Buddhism and worldly authority, in which the ruler would protect the true dharma to the utmost. He cites it at length in his *Risshō ankoku ron.*

13 "Offenses" here has traditionally been interpreted to mean rejecting or slighting the Wonderful Dharma of the *Lotus Sūtra.*

14 *Sandai hihō honjōji* (often abbreviated as *Sandai hihō shō*), *Teihon* 2:1864–65. Nichiren's authorship of this work has been questioned. In the postwar period, the controversy has centered on its incompatibility with modern notions of the separation of religion and state, and some scholars within the Nichiren tradition have argued that Nichiren never envisioned a state-sponsored *kaidan.* While the question of authorship continues to be disputed, since all official ordination platforms in Nichiren's time were state-sponsored, it would have been reasonable for him to have envisioned such a structure as the seal of official acceptance of his teaching. See entries for "kaidan," "sandai hihō," and "*Sandai hihō shō*" in Nichirenshū Jiten Kankō Iinkai, ed., *Nichirenshū jiten* (Tōkyō: Nichirenshū Shūmuin, 1981), 43d–47a, 130c–133c, 133c–134b; and Jacqueline I. Stone, "'By Imperial Edict and Shogunal Decree': Politics and the Issue of the Ordination Platform in Modern Lay Nichiren Buddhism," in *Buddhism in the Modern World: Adaptations of an Ancient Tradition,* ed. Steven Heine and Charles S. Prebish (New York: Oxford University Press, 2003), 196–197, and the sources cited there.

15 "Eagle Peak" (Gṛdhrakūṭa; Ryōjusen), a mountain near the city of Rājagṛha in the ancient Indian state of Magadha, is said to have been the site where the Buddha preached the *Lotus Sūtra.* It was later apotheosized as the ever-present pure land of the originally awakened Buddha. See Jacqueline I. Stone, "Realizing This World as the Buddha Land," in *Readings of the Lotus Sutra,* ed. Stephen F. Teiser and Jacqueline I. Stone (New York: Columbia University Press, 2009), 209–236.

16 *Ri* or "principle" corresponds to ultimate truth, while *ji* or "actuality" refers to the concrete particulars of the phenomenal world. In the Mahāyāna, the two are non-dually related, inseparable and interpenetrating; in the insight that all phenomena (*ji*) instantiate ultimate reality (*ri*), awakening is achieved. This way of thinking underlies key concepts such as the interconnection of all beings and the universal possibility of buddhahood. For Tanaka, *ji*, the realm of actuality, is represented by the nation-state. By grounding the state in the buddha-dharma or *ri*, he argues, the actual world will manifest its innate buddhahood.

17 Tanaka probably refers here to elements of local religious culture such as the exorcism of fox spirits, which were thought to cause illness and discord. Long-standing grassroots practices of this kind were carried out

across sectarian boundaries and often drew criticism from modernizers as well as outright government suppression. See James E. Ketelaar, *Of Heretics and Martyrs in Meiji Japan: Buddhism and Its Persecution* (Princeton, NJ: Princeton University Press, 1990), 50–52.

18 Tanaka refers to a traditional Nichiren Buddhist practice of chanting the *daimoku* to the beat of a hand-held fan-shaped drum (*uchiwa daiko*) while marching in procession, for example, when on pilgrimage or at festivals. During the Tokugawa period, such processions were common among Nichiren Buddhist lay or lay-oriented religious associations (*kō* or *kōchū*) and often drew considerable attention in the streets. Meiji government regulations at one point restricted possession of hand drums to one per each such group (see entry for "Kō" in Nichirenshū Jiten Kankō Iinkai, *Nichirenshū jiten*, 493b).

19 *Kanjin honzon shō, Teihon* 1:720.

20 *Onkō kikigaki* (aka *Nikō ki*), *Teihon* 3:2550. This work purports to be a record of Nichiren's oral teachings on the *Lotus Sūtra*, given to his closest disciples and recorded by Minbu Ajari Nikō. Most scholars now date it to later in the medieval period. "Origin teaching" (*honmon*) refers to the latter fourteen chapters of the *Lotus Sūtra*, which present Śākyamuni as the primordially awakened Buddha, in contrast to the first fourteen chapters, or "trace teaching" (*shakumon*), which depict him as a manifested "trace" or finite person in historical time. "Subtlety of the [Buddha's] original land" (*honkokudo myō*), the teaching that the primordially awakened Buddha dwells in this world, is one of ten "subtleties" or profound doctrines that Zhiyi identified in the origin teaching. Nichiren considered chapter 16, "Fathoming the Lifespan of the Tathāgata," to be the heart of the origin teaching; it formed his scriptural basis for the calligraphic *maṇḍala*, depicting the *Lotus* assembly on Eagle Peak as the ever-present realm of the primordial Buddha, which he inscribed as an object of worship for his followers. It was this ideal awakened buddha realm that Tanaka sought to actualize in the real world.

21 *Hōon shō, Teihon* 2:1248 ("Japan and all the world should make Lord Śākyamuni of the origin teaching their object of worship"). Nichiren's famous vow—"I will be the pillar of Japan, I will be the eyes of Japan, I will be the great ship of Japan"—appears in *Kaimoku shō, Teihon* 1:601.

22 The burying of sutras was conducted in premodern Japan as a devotional act, often with the aim of preserving the teachings throughout the Final Dharma age. Nichiren's own writings make no mention of him burying a copy of the *Lotus Sūtra* on Mount Fuji; an eighteenth-century biography, however, records a legend that in 1269 Nichiren buried there a copy of the *Lotus* he had personally inscribed, in order to plant karmic roots for the future spread of the *Lotus Sūtra* (*Kōso nenpu*, in Nichirenshū Zensho Shup-

pankai, ed., *Nichiren Shōnin denkishū* [Kyoto: Honmanji, 1974], 394). For Tanaka, Fuji (which he writes here with the homophonous characters for "non-duality") corresponded to "the most superior site, resembling the Pure Land of Sacred Eagle Peak" referred to in "The Three Great Secret Dharmas." In 1909, he began building a new Kokuchūkai headquarters close to Mount Fuji, in Miho in Shizuoka Prefecture. The top floor of this structure contained a room prepared to house the future imperial edict that would mandate the *kaidan*'s establishment (Ōtani, *Kindai Nihon no Nichirenshugi undō*, 152–154).

23 The slogan "unity of rites and rule" expressed the stance of those early Meiji Nativist ideologues who sought to restore the central position of the emperor as ritual mediator between the nation and the world of the gods, or *kami*, said to have obtained in Japan's ancient past. The "restoration" of this supposed unity formed the rationale for the Jingikan (variously translated as Ministry of Rites or Council of Divinities), which was established in 1868 but dismantled in 1872. See Ketelaar, *Of Heretics and Martyrs*, 87–96, and Helen Hardacre, *Shinto: A History* (New York: Oxford University Press, 2017), 359–368.

24 As regent for Empress Suiko (r. 592–628), Prince Shōtoku was an early and influential patron of Buddhism and a celebrated Japanese cultural hero. Many of the accomplishments credited to him, including his commentaries on the three sutras mentioned below, were probably the work of Korean immigrant scholars. The famous "tree metaphor" for the unity of the three teachings actually dates to Japan's medieval period and was attributed to Shōtoku retrospectively.

25 Tanaka here alludes to Nichiren's claim that devotion to the *Lotus Sūtra*, established by Saichō as the Buddha's supreme teaching, was later undermined by the rise of "lesser," provisional teachings such as Esoteric Buddhism, Pure Land, and Zen that were unsuited to the Final Dharma age. The next sentence, however, does not immediately follow through with this idea but returns to Tanaka's summary of the relation between government and religion in Japanese history.

26 This passage summarizes Tanaka's understanding of the relation of Buddhism and the polity up through the Sengoku ("country at war") era, roughly the late fifteenth through sixteenth centuries. The Fujiwara family dominated the court as regents to the emperor from around the mid-tenth through late eleventh centuries. The Minamoto and the Taira, two powerful warrior houses, battled for supremacy in the Genpei War (1180–1185); a Minamoto victory brought about the establishment of the first Bakufu, or shogunate, which soon came to be ruled by the Hōjō family based in Kamakura. Power shifted in 1333 to the Ashikaga shoguns, who were based in Kyoto. The decline over time of Ashikaga power opened the way to

protracted struggle among various warlords in the Sengoku era. Eventually Japan was united by the successive efforts of the so-called "three great hegemons"—Oda Nobunaga, Toyotomi Hideyoshi, and Tokugawa Ieyasu—whom Tanaka names below. Tanaka follows conventional usage in referring to major historical figures by their given names.

27 Mount Hiei and Mount Kōya are the headquarters respectively of the Tendai and Shingon schools of Buddhism. Nobunaga made concerted efforts to break the temporal power of late medieval Buddhist institutions.

28 Tanaka alludes to the early modern system of temple certification (*terauke seido*), which enlisted temples in the roles of census keeping and population oversight. Buddhist temples issued annual certificates attesting that patron households (*danka*) were temple families in good standing and did not espouse Christianity or other proscribed sects.

29 *Fuju fuse* ("neither receiving nor giving") denotes a movement within the Nichiren sect active in the late sixteenth through mid-seventeenth centuries. The term expresses a hard-line interpretation of Nichiren Buddhist commitment to the *Lotus Sūtra* alone as the only teaching efficacious in the Final Dharma age and means that Nichiren priests should neither accept offerings from nor perform ritual services for persons who are not *Lotus Sūtra* devotees, however powerful or high-ranking. Throughout the medieval period, based on this principle, Nichiren priests had often won exemption from the obligation to participate in official rituals along with priests of other sects. Matters changed in 1595, when Hideyoshi, in an attempt to display his authority, required that ten priests from each Buddhist sect participate together in a series of memorial rites for his deceased relatives, to be held before the "Great Buddha" image that Tanaka refers to above, which Hideyoshi had commissioned. Fearing punitive measures if they refused, most Nichiren sectarian leaders counseled compromise. Those constituting the minority *fuju fuse* faction, however, urged refusal and were prepared to risk their lives if need be to uphold the sole truth of the *Lotus Sūtra*. Busshōin Nichiō, a *fuju fuse* leader, and Jōrakuin Nichikyō were arrested and exiled in 1600 and 1609 respectively. See Stone, "Rebuking the Enemies of the *Lotus*: Nichirenist Exclusivism in Historical Perspective," *Japanese Journal of Religious Studies* 21, nos. 2–3 (1994): 231–259 (243–246).
*Nenbutsu* refers here to chanting the name of the Buddha Amida in hopes of birth in his pure land. "*Nenbutsu* leads to the Hell without Respite" is sloganized shorthand for Nichiren's opposition to the Pure Land teachings, which he criticized for setting aside the *Lotus Sūtra*–based principle of realizing buddhahood in this world in favor of the provisional doctrine of postmortem salvation in Amida's realm.

30 Tokugawa Ieyasu represents a paradigmatic instance of a warlord being posthumously apotheosized as a *gongen* ("avatar") or deity said to be a

manifestation of a buddha or bodhisattva. Ieyasu's tomb at the Tōshōgū shrine in Nikkō, where he was enshrined as Tōshō Daigongen ("great avatar illuminating from the east"), became the center of a nationwide network of Tōshōgū shrines. Tenkai (1536–1643), architect of the Tōshōgū cult, was a leading Tendai monk and advisor to Ieyasu.

31 Both Christianity and the Nichiren sect explicitly taught allegiance to a truth transcending the ruler's authority. Within the Nichiren sect, however, only the purist *fuju fuse* group was suppressed; other, conciliatory factions quickly reached a rapprochement with the Tokugawa regime.

32 Mitsukuni, lord of the Mitō domain, sponsored the compilation of a massive history of Japan (*Dai Nihonshi*) that stressed the centrality of the emperor. Emphasis on the emperor as the country's legitimate ruler, along with Nativist ideas about restoring the ways of ancient Japan, would become the ideological pillars of those who eventually overthrew the Tokugawa Bakufu and established the Meiji regime.

33 Tanaka presumably refers here to a legal distinction drawn by the Meiji government between Shinto-derived new religious movements (sometimes called "sect Shinto"), dating chiefly from the nineteenth century, that were officially registered as independent religious bodies, and the Shinto of government-administered shrines. The distinction was part of a larger move to define religion as a private matter and exclude it from public policy making. Tanaka's characterization here lends support to recent scholarship suggesting that so-called "state Shinto" in Japan's modern imperial period should be understood not as a national religion but as a form of the secular, albeit one with strong religious symbolism. See Jason A. Josephson, *Invention of Religion in Japan* (Chicago: University of Chicago Press, 2012), 132–163; and Jolyon B. Thomas, "Japan's Preoccupation with Religious Freedom" (PhD diss., Princeton University, 2014), 76–92, 395–402.

34 Evolutionary theory was appropriated in Japan for a range of intellectual, religious, and political agendas. See G. Clinton Godart, *Darwin, Dharma, and the Divine: Evolutionary Theory and Religion in Modern Japan* (Honolulu: University of Hawai'i Press, 2017). For Tanaka's interpretation in particular, see Yulia Burenina, "Kindai Nihon ni okeru Nichiren bukkyō no shūkyō shisōteki saikaishaku: Tanaka Chigaku to Honda Nisshō no 'Nichirenshugi' o chūshin toshite" (PhD diss., Ōsaka University, 2013), 65–78.

35 In the appendix to *Shūmon no ishin,* Tanaka offers detailed projections of the sect's capital, income, and expenditures over ten five-year periods, beginning from the implementation of his proposed sectarian reforms. He also outlines undertakings by which the sect would become a major social force, eventually dominating the national economy, infrastructure, and politics. He gives particular attention to the sect's building a fleet of ships that would promote trade, link settlements of devotees, and promote

proselytizing worldwide, and could also be armed and lent to the nation in times of emergency. The ordination platform was to be funded by life insurance policies held by Nichiren Buddhist adherents that would designate the future Honge Myōshū head temple, site of the *kaidan,* as beneficiary. See Tanaka, *Shūmon no ishin* (Tokyo: Shishiō Bunko, 1919), *furoku,* esp. 6–7.

36 This represents Tanaka's free interpretation. The *Mahāparinirvāṇa sūtra* permits arms to be borne in defense of the dharma; King Possessing Virtue's defense of the monk Awakened Virtue (see note 12 above) represents a case in point. Nichiren cites this episode in his *Risshō ankoku ron* but also makes clear his own stance that priests who distort the Buddhist teachings should be suppressed not by violence but by withdrawal of support. The issue of Buddhists raising arms or revenue to support their country's defense does not arise in either text. The reference to "The Object of Worship" is less clear still. Tanaka may have had in mind Nichiren's statement in that work that, in an age when *shakubuku* is necessary, the leaders of the bodhisattvas who are the Buddha's original disciples will appear as "wise kings who chastise foolish kings" (*Kanjin honzon shō, Teihon* 1:719). In context, the "wise king" probably referred to the Mongol ruler, since Nichiren saw the Mongol threat as Japan's deserved karmic retribution for rejecting the *Lotus Sūtra* in favor of provisional teachings. Tanaka, however, saw the "wise king" as that emperor of Japan who would one day subdue all nations and unite them in the one vehicle. See Nishiyama Shigeru, "Kindai no Nichirenshugi," 236–237.

37 The Meiji Constitutional guarantee of religious freedom actually appeared in article 28. In 1923, to begin implementing his goal of a government based on the *Lotus Sūtra,* Tanaka established a political party and ran candidates for local office. Though unsuccessful, this effort set a precedent for the postwar Sōka Gakkai's entry into electoral politics on a national scale (Ōtani, *Kindai Nihon no Nichirenshugi undo,* 297–299, 322–329).

38 Tanaka appropriates a quotation from the *Lotus Sūtra* (*Miaofa lianhua jing, T.* 262.9:10b). In context, the Buddha is saying that those who have not practiced and studied the dharma cannot understand how the buddhas employ a variety of skillful means in order to teach the one vehicle.

39 The names "Nichiren" and "Japan" (Nihon or Nippon; literally "sun origin") both begin with the character for "sun." Nichiren's name derives from the *Lotus Sūtra* passage, "Just as the light of the sun and moon can banish all shadows and obscurity, this person [who upholds the *Lotus*], in going about the world, can remove the darkness of living beings" (*T.* 262.9.52b). A flag with the rising sun disk was adopted as the Japanese national flag for merchant ships and for the navy in 1870.

40 According to ancient myth, Jinmu, a descendant of the sun goddess, became the first emperor of Japan, an event said to have occurred in 660 BC.

This passage marks an early instance of what later became a concerted effort on Tanaka's part to integrate national mythology into his interpretation of Nichiren's doctrine.

41 See note 21.

42 The purple robe was a mark of recognition bestowed by the emperor on eminent prelates. Murakumo Zuiryūji was an elite convent of the Nichiren sect near Kyoto, whose successive abbesses belonged to the imperial or regental families. Tradition attributes its founding to Hideyoshi's sister.

43 *Nyosetsu shugyō shō, Teihon* 1:733. The Mahāyāna expounds the conditioned, impermanent nature of both persons and dharmas, the momentary physical and mental elements that compose both individual persons and their environments. Nichiren's point is that all things, sentient and insentient, will manifest the constantly abiding Wonderful Dharma.

## Bibliography


Burenina, Yulia. "Kindai Nihon ni okeru Nichiren bukkyō no shūkyō shisōteki saikaishaku: Tanaka Chigaku to Honda Nisshō no 'Nichirenshugi' o chūshin toshite." PhD dissertation, Ōsaka University, 2013.

Godart, G. Clinton. *Darwin, Dharma, and the Divine: Evolutionary Theory and Religion in Modern Japan*. Honolulu: University of Hawai'i Press, 2017.

Hardacre, Helen. *Shinto: A History*. New York: Oxford University Press, 2017.

Jaffe, Richard M. "Tanaka Chigaku and the Buddhist Clerical Marriage: Toward a Positive Appraisal of Family Life." In *Neither Monk nor Layman: Clerical Marriage in Modern Japanese Buddhism*, 165–188. Princeton, NJ: Princeton University Press, 2001.

Josephson, Jason Ānanda. *The Invention of Religion in Japan*. Chicago: University of Chicago Press, 2012.

Ketelaar, James E. *Of Heretics and Martyrs in Meiji Japan: Buddhism and Its Persecution*. Princeton, NJ: Princeton University Press, 1990.

Lee, Edwin B. "Nichiren and Nationalism: The Religious Patriotism of Tanaka Chigaku." *Monumenta Nipponica* 30, no. 1 (1975): 19–35.

Miura, Hiroshi. *The Life and Thought of Kanzō Uchimura, 1861–1930*. Grand Rapids, MI: Wm. B. Eerdmans, 1996.

Nichirenshū Jiten Kankō Iinkai, ed. *Nichirenshū jiten*. Tokyo: Nichirenshū Shūmuin, 1981.

Nichirenshū Zensho Shuppankai, ed. *Nichiren Shōnin denkishū*. Kyoto: Honmanji, 1974.

Nishiyama Shigeru. "Kindai no Nichirenshugi: 'Kennō' shinkō no keifu." *Nihon no bukkyō* 4 (1995): 228–240.

Ōtani Eiichi. *Kindai Nihon no Nichirenshugi undo.* Kyoto: Hōzōkan, 2001.

Risshō Daigaku Nichiren Kyōgaku Kenkyūjo, ed. *Shōwa teihon Nichiren Shōnin ibun.* 4 vols. Minobu-chō, Yamanashi Prefecture: Minobusan Kuonji, 1952–1959, rev. ed. 1988.

Stone, Jacqueline I. "'By Imperial Edict and Shogunal Decree': Politics and the Issue of the Ordination Platform in Modern Lay Nichiren Buddhism. In *Buddhism in the Modern World: Adaptations of an Ancient Tradition,* edited by Steven Heine and Charles S. Prebish, 193–219. New York: Oxford University Press, 2003.

——. "Japanese *Lotus* Millennialism: From Militant Nationalism to Contemporary Peace Movements." In *Millennialism, Persecution, and Violence: Historical Cases,* edited by Catherine Wessinger, 261–280. Syracuse, NY: Syracuse University Press, 2000.

——. "Realizing This World as the Buddha Land." In *Readings of the Lotus Sutra,* edited by Stephen F. Teiser and Jacqueline I. Stone, 209–236. *Columbia Readings of Buddhist Literature.* New York: Columbia University Press, 2009.

——. "Rebuking the Enemies of the *Lotus*: Nichirenist Exclusivism in Historical Perspective." *Japanese Journal of Religious Studies* 21, nos. 2–3 (1994): 231–259.

Tanabe, George J., Jr. "Tanaka Chigaku: The *Lotus Sutra* and the Body Politic." In *The Lotus Sutra in Japanese Culture,* edited by George J. Tanabe Jr. and Willa Jane Tanabe, 191–208. Honolulu: University of Hawai'i Press, 1989.

Tanaka Chigaku. *Nichirenshugi kyōgaku taikan.* 6 vols. First published 1904–1913 in 5 vols. as *Honge Myōshu shikimoku kōgiroku.* Tokyo: Kokusho Kankōkai, 1975.

——. *Shūmon no ishin.* 1901. Ninth printing, Tokyo: Shishiō Bunko, 1919.

Thomas, Jolyon Baraka. "Japan's Preoccupation with Religious Freedom." PhD dissertation. Princeton University, 2014.

# VI

# Worlds beyond Sukhāvatī

## Overview

In its widest definition, Pure Land cosmology finds expression in a rich variety of conceptions about terrestrial and extraterrestrial lands portrayed in various apocalyptic traditions of Buddhism and in the writings of many religious traditions including Manicheism and Daoism. Superficially, Chinese Manichean hymns in praise of the realm of light would seem to have nothing to do with the Indo-Tibetan belief in Śambhala. Both are, however, linked to a universally shared vision and belief in ideal realms that believers may obtain access to through specific practices and aspirations. The ubiquitous proliferation of heavenly abodes in religious beliefs the world over both challenges and reinforces the uniqueness of Pure Land literature as a useful category to describe a cluster of heterogenous texts, practices, and beliefs. The presence of Chinese Daoist, Manichean, and Tibeto-Mongolian readings of pure lands modeled after the scriptures of Pure Land Buddhism reinforces the claim that Pure Land Buddhism was (and is) a distinct orientation with a succesful following of adherents.

The *Divine Scripture on the Rebirth in the Pure Land of the Lingbao Highest Cavern Mystery* (*Taishang dongxuan lingbao jingtu sheng shen jing*; hereafter *Jingtu sheng shen jing*), examined and translated by Henrik Sørensen (chap. VI.1), is a Daoist scripture composed by adherents of the Lingbao tradition sometime between the late sixth and the early seventh centuries. It is a classic example of a Daoist scripture, which has appropriated the salient features of the Buddhist Pure Land tradition and its scriptures. As such, its imagery and conceptualizations explicitly follow those of Buddhism. In contrast to the more exclusivist soteriological vision of the Buddhist Pure Land, however, what we see in Lingbao Daoism is closely related to the central practice of universal salvation, including the promulgation of an ordered society on the earthly plane. As such the scripture is a primary example of what one may refer to as "Buddho-Daoism."

Mānī (216–ca. 277 AD), the founder of Manichaeism, as well as his disciples laid special emphasis on proselytizing. During the translation process, Manichaean missionaries sought out religious analogies that could make their rather peculiar system more accessible to potential converts. They used Christian terminology in the West (Europe, Egypt), Zoroastrian in Iran, and Buddhist in the East (Central Asia, China). Given the popularity of texts describing Pure Lands in Tang China (AD 618–907), Manichaeans naturally applied the vocabulary surrounding this notion to describe the Manichaean Realm of Light, the goal of all Manichaean believers. Gábor Kósa (chap. VI.2) presents a fresh, annotated translation of a Chinese hymn (*In Praise of the Realm of Light; Tan mingjie*) from the Chinese Manichaean Hymnscroll from Dunhuang. This hymn consists of seventy-seven verses, four lines each, and has numerous parallels in other languages (Parthian, Sogdian, Uighur).

In Tibetan and Mongolian writings on Śambhala, especially those of the late nineteenth and twentieth centuries, different images of Śambhala emerge, differences that Vesna Wallace (chap. VI.3) examines. In some writings, it is a terrestrial pure land, the Buddhist tantric pure land of the human realm, which is intimately connected to the celestial Sukhavatī, and in some other writings, it is referred to as a celestial Sukhavatī. In yet other writings, similarly to other celestial pure lands, due to its tantric orientation, Śambhala is a place where the attainment of buddhahood is possible within a single lifetime and is thus more desirable than other pure lands. The production of various travel guides to Śambhala and rituals and prayers for rebirth in Śambhala proliferated especially in the early twentieth century in response to the perceived threat of the communist revolution, introduction of European scientific knowledge, and unstable socioeconomic conditions.

## Chapter 1

# The Divine Scripture on the Rebirth in the Pure Land of the Highest Cavern Mystery of Numinous Treasure

Henrik H. Sørensen

### Translator's Introduction

Heavens, paradises including the so-called "pure lands" (*jingtu*), occur in a wide number of Daoist scriptures representative of different traditions of that religion. In some cases these heavens have been modeled after those of Buddhism; in other cases they reflect a more distinct manner of conceptualization that reveal little or no influence from the Indian religion.[1]

During the second half of the Nanbeichao (386–581), a time when the Buddhist Pure Land tradition was gaining popularity and importance among Chinese believers, the scriptures of this tradition also came to the attention of Daoist practitioners, most notably those belonging to the Lingbao tradition.[2] Even though many of the early Lingbao scriptures, as well as some of those of the Shangqing revelations, refer to rebirth in the heavens as the result of good karma, none of them focus exclusively on the pure lands as afterlife destinations for the faithful. By the late sixth century, however, things began to change, undoubtedly due to influence from the Buddhist Pure Land tradition. One important scripture from this period, the *Benji jing* (Scripture on the fundamental boundary),[3] features a full chapter devoted to a discussion of pure lands largely modeled after the scriptures of Pure Land Buddhism. Most notable in this regard is the *Taishang dongxuan lingbao jingtu sheng shen jing* (The Divine Scripture on the rebirth in the Pure Land of the Highest Cavern Mystery of Numinous Treasure; hereafter *Jingtu sheng shen jing*).[4] As far as the Lingbao tradition goes, this is a relatively late scripture, probably dating from somewhere between the second half of the sixth century and the early seventh century. It thus does not appear in the earliest classification of the Lingbao scriptures.[5] Despite its importance as an example of what we may refer to as "Buddho-Daoism," this scripture has by and large avoided capturing the interest of the scholarly community.[6] It is, however, interesting for several reasons, not only because it documents the extent to which medieval Daoists borrowed from the scriptures of the Buddhist Pure Land tradition, but also because it provides us with an insight into those aspects that were unique to Daoism, as well as those Buddhist aspects that were significantly altered in the process of religious appropriation. Here it is also important to note that while earlier Daoist concepts on the pure lands had stipulated that there were five of them, one for each of the cardinal points and one in the center, the *Jingtu sheng shen jing* features as many as ten pure lands, thereby emulating a cosmological model following the time-honored Buddhist concept of the so-called "Buddha Realms of the Ten Directions" (*shifang fotu*).

Let us begin by looking at the most obvious borrowing from Buddhism. These include the overall concepts guiding the manner in which the pure lands of our text have been applied: (1) a paradise of nonreturn, the idea that having reached the paradise one will no longer return to be reborn in a woeful state, (2) the spirits in paradise living immersed in the Dao, that is, being continually exposed to Daoism, (3) the pure lands as destinations for the spiritually weak, (4) the pure lands as adorned by virtuous actions, (5) the overall structure and pseudo-geography of the pure lands, that is, physicality of the paradises. Further, the idea that the animals inhabiting the paradises are communicating the Daoist truth verbally to those reborn there has been taken directly from the Buddhist Pure Land tradition.

In addition to these more deep-seated Buddhist elements just listed, the *Jingtu sheng shen jing* features a number of more general or superficial conceptual appropriations as well as extensive terminological borrowing. The first of these involve, among other things, the idea of karmic retribution, the incorporation of certain classes of Buddhist divinities in its listing of gods, spiritual grading, the transposition and transformation of Buddhist divinities into Daoist ones, etc. The terminological aspects include the extensive use of the Buddhist "Dharma" (*fa*) to mean the Daoist teaching, the use of *kalpa* (*qie*) for cosmic cycle, *preta* (*e'gui*) for "hungry ghost," the "three paths" (*santu*), "five sufferings" (*wuku*), "six roots" (*indriya*) or "sense organs" (*liugen*), etc. We even encounter a passage that refers to the "invitation of Dharma-masters of great virtue (*dade fashi*),"[7] something that could as easily have been found in a Buddhist text.

Having surveyed the primary elements borrowed from Buddhism, let us now turn to those elements that are more distinctly Daoist in nature.

First, the paradises are permanent destinations. In contrast to the Buddhist notion of Sukhāvatī as a paradise of no return, but one in which those reborn there continue to evolve spiritually, the five pure lands discussed in the *Jingtu sheng shen jing* are understood as what may be referred to as "end stations." At least there is nothing in the text to indicate the belief in a continued process of spiritual refinement beyond the perpetual attendance in the congregation of the Heavenly Worthy presiding in the pure lands. In fact, three of the pure lands in the text are equated with the Sanqing, the Heavens of the Highest Purity, which, as their names indicate, are conceptualized as the highest and most sublime of the Daoist heavens.[8]

Second, rebirth in the pure lands is based on the accumulation of personal merit. In this regard, the *Jingtu sheng shen jing* stresses personal cultivation, sincerity, and a charitable disposition. Third, the importance of the materiality of the pure lands is stressed through extensive listings. This was possibly done to make the pure lands more attractive to the faithful. In any case this largely follows the same pattern for replicating the governing institutions of the human world in heaven as is common to Daoist cosmology.[9] And fourth, in addition to its borrowing of Buddhist terms and concepts, the scripture also features a more distinctly Daoist vocabulary and concepts such as the importance of virtue and conduct (*gongde*), which, although not unique to Daoism, has a special and time-honored place in that religion.

Then there are also a number of more general concepts such as the underlying five-fold structure based on the five agents, the Nine-Fold Mystery (*jiuxuan*), setting up yellow registers (*huanglu*),[10] the concept of "ghostly miasma" (*jingxie*), numinous things (*lingwu*), that is, objects imbued with cosmic power (*qi*) such as jades and divine fungi (*lingzhi*), etc., all of which have their origin in documented Daoist doctrine and belief. In addition we encounter numerological categories of various sorts as well as proper names that are typical of Daoism. The pure lands as described in this scripture are thus much more integrated into basic Daoist cosmology, the concepts of which permeate the text to a much greater extent than was the case with the previous scriptures under discussion.

Outside the more overt paradisal aspects described in the *Jingtu sheng shen jing*, the scripture also provides a detailed elaboration on the good deeds, the virtues (*gongde*) as it were, required of pious Daoists in order to qualify for rebirth in the pure lands. This involves practicing the Way, including prostrations, repenting sins, burning incense, reciting scriptures, copying scriptures, paying for scriptures to be taught, erecting altars, making statues of Daoist divinities, performing worship and rituals, supporting the Daoist and ordinary communities materially, repair temples, practice filial piety (*xiao*), liberating the living, etc. Especially the practice of charity (*shi*), the practice of which in our text has been modeled after the Buddhist *dāna,* is singled out as a qualifying factor for rebirth in the pure lands.

Although the pious elements in the scripture to some degree reflect the Buddhist *pāramitās* or perfections, there is an unusually high, if not overweening, concern with what we may call "good works" in our scripture. Furthermore, in contrast to the constant and selfless display of piety and charity required of Daoist believers, Buddhists aspiring to the pure land could qualify for rebirth on faith alone or by taking the shortcut of using spells (*dhāraṇī*).[11] None of this occurs in the *Jingtu sheng shen jing*.

Although the Buddhist Pure Land scriptures, which served as inspiration for the *Jingtu sheng shen jing,* provide many details on the geography of the pure land, our Daoist scripture goes into extreme detail in this regard. Not only does it describe the divine location of the paradises, it also describes the buildings, ponds, groves, plants, animals and semidivine beings who inhabit them. In effect the *Jingtu sheng shen jing* provides a comprehensive listing of everything in the paradises, a veritable, divine geographical and biological inventory, something that cannot be found to quite the same degree in the comparable descriptions of Buddhist pure lands.

Note on the translation and manner of organizing the text:

The Dunhuang manuscript from the Pelliot Collection, 2383 (hereafter P.), 2383 has served as the basis for the translation. Otherwise I have benefited greatly from the modern edited and punctuated versions of both *Chen Zuolong* and the *Zhonghua daozang.*

Square brackets represent my attempt at making the text more readable by inserting a word or small sentence, whenever I found it necessary.

All changes of characters in cases of copyist's mistakes have been duly noted.

The *inter alia* numbering corresponds to the lines of characters in the manuscript.

For practical reasons the scripture has been divided into the following seven parts:

Preamble
Beholding the Pure Lands
Causes for the Pure Lands
Conditions for Rebirth in the Pure Lands
Describing the Pure Lands
Further Descriptions of the Pure Lands
Conclusion

## Translation

### 太上洞玄靈寶淨土生神經 *Taishang dongxuan lingbao jingtu sheng shen jing* (The divine scripture on the rebirth in the Pure Land of the Highest Cavern Mystery of Numinous Treasure)

### [Preamble]

(1) Once the Heavenly Worthy of the Original Beginning (i.e., Yuanshi Tianzun), (2) was dwelling in the Dragon Net World in the realm of Fragrant Storage in the Hall of Nine Flower Clouds, seated on a great lotus flower, together with the holy assembly of the ten directions [consisting of] people from the limitless countries, (3) where he was speaking on the Daoist teaching (*fa*) to the great assembly over a period of one hundred days without getting up from his seat. Below and above heaven, whether they are with (4) or without consciousness,[12] limitless sentient beings, who surely all had left behind suffering, and seized the good opportunity [to hear the teachings], (5) awaken [to the fact] that their bodies are fleeting and false, impure and stinking filth, always impermanent.[13] By deeply entering the wondrous concentration (*samādhī*; *ruding*), they had rejected (6) all fetters,[14] whereby they were able to awaken to the True Way (*zhendao*). Reversing [evil] and giving rise to a mind of goodness, going single-mindedly forward, unassisted and sincere without (7) backsliding. The Heavenly Worthy of the Original Beginning, out of great compassion and kind view, level teaching[15] of transformation, (8) were all enlightened and liberated, understanding the constant sphere of the truth, and testified to the fruits of the nonactivity (*wuwei*).[16] The Heavenly Worthy Congealed Spirit Reaching Illumination (9) was about to return to the Hall of Constant Bliss and Blessings of Vacuous Quietude,

when suddenly there appeared from the World of Abundant Virtue (10) ten Flower Immortals (*huaxian*)[17] and others, 540 persons in all, who at that time, with their hands in supplication, together prostrated themselves on the ground and addressed (11) the Heavenly Worthy saying: "Each of us (lit. 'your disciples') have during innumerable *kalpas* revolved [in the sea] of birth and death (*saṃsāra*). Due to our good luck [brought about by] causes (12) and conditions we are [now] able to meet You. Today's blessings are truly without limit, (13) and cannot be fathomed. Despite the fact that all of us have received the category of immortal, the leakages (*lou*) of all [of us] are not [fully] exhausted, and we constantly fear (14) transmigration and being unable to escape life and death. In the course of [the next] ten thousand *kalpas*, the other Heavenly Worthies, did not know (15) when they were going to assemble again later. [Hence], we seek to consult [with you] in the meantime. Fearful to offend You to your face, (16) [kindly] uphold your vow of great compassion, asking you to please consent to look into this matter."

## [Beholding the Pure Lands]

The Heavenly Worthy said, "Even though all of you in successive *kalpas* have set your minds on (17) studying the way of immortality, you have not yet entered the Great Vehicle. Even though you have reached the position of immortals yet without mounting up to (18) the higher sphere, you certainly cannot escape birth and death.[18] As soon as you separate from me, [even in] ten thousand *kalpas* it will be difficult [for us] to meet [again].[19] As you now (19) have asked, [I can say] that this is exactly the right moment. You must simply calm your minds, do not be agitated and have no fear." At this (20) all the immortals bowed their heads and kowtowed. They then addressed the Heavenly Worthy, saying, "We must follow Your transformative teaching."[20] (21) Then they saw the realms in the Ten Directions, their men and women of purity, their future happiness and carefree behavior (lit. 'non-doing,' *wuwei*). After this they saw (22) the realms in the Ten Directions, their men and women stinking with filth, in the hundred extremities of grief and hatred and their lack of cultivation. [The immortals asked,] (23) "What performance of karmic practices [have the first ones done], in order to obtain this [state of] purity, the appearances of their [physical] shapes upright and correct? And what karmic practices [have the latter ones done], in order to receive this (24) stinking filth, troubled, repulsive and tied-up bodies? We humbly pray that You will bestow upon us your discriminating elucidation, little by little (25)."

The Heavenly Worthy addressed them, saying, "Sins and blessings are without entry (*wumen*). Only men make the designations 'good' and 'evil' retribution (*baodui*) (26) with their own bodies. If one cultivates good practices, then one will obtain [rebirth] in a pure land, the appearance of one's [physical] shape upright (27) and correct, receiving a lifespan that is long and extensive. If [on the other hand] one produces evil and make sins, it will cause one to dwell in a filthy land, the (28) appearance of one's [physical] shape ugly and crude. Their life spans cut short by injury. The causes and conditions of good and evil, it all depends on what the body does. (29) You should not think that it comes from something else. You should all listen attentively, to what I am now going to explain."

## [Causes for the Pure Lands]

(30) The Heavenly Worthy [again] addressed them, saying, "When ordinary people are born, and establish great virtue, cultivating all practices of [good] karma, (31) they will obtain rebirth in the pure land naturally and effortlessly in according with their past vows."

Of all the virtues in the world, (32) altogether there are five kinds, which, when brought together, constitute a gate of blessings:

The first is the virtue of discoursing on the Dharma. This means always with (33) the methods of the scriptures of the Three Caverns of the Heavenly Worthies, to teach and transform all sentient beings, well and ingeniously [employ] *upāya* (*fangbian*),[21] according to their root natures of, (34) higher, middling, and lower categories,[22] [including those] naturally endowed with consciousness, [whether] stupid or wise, astute or dull-witted, ordinary people, whether in extensive or abbreviated [form], (35) [whether through the use of] metaphor, example or sincere exhortation, whether causing them to become enlightened and enter true reality, seeing the worlds of men and gods, (36) protecting all, [or] through past veneration of the [Heavenly] Worthies, have obtained rebirth in all the heavens, or whether [by their own] intelligence and wisdom have become (37) great masters of the teaching (*fashi*).[23]

The second is the virtue of giving (*dāna*). This is explained as giving up one's body, life, and wealth, without grudge or being stingy. There are four kinds of conditions [in this regard as follows]:

(38) The first is the inner giving, which is explained as the head, eye marrow, brain, hand, foot, hair, (39) these may be used to give *dāna* to a starving eagle, a hungry tiger, poisonous snakes, cruel beasts, and all

types of strange things.[24] (40) [In these cases] one accords with their desires, so if they beg for a head one gives them one's head, if they beg for an eye one gives them an eye, if they beg for the body one gives them one's body, if they beg for a hand one gives them a hand [etc.]. (41) Without attachment and stinginess, one seeks to liberate sentient beings.

The second is the outer [form] of giving. It has an additional four conditions [as follows]:

(42) The first is the bestowal of compassion, which is explained as aiding [those who are suffering from] hunger, cold, old age and sickness, imprisoned persons, hungry dogs, the needy and poor, (43) greatly establish fields of compassion, [including] the bestowing of clothes and food, in accordance with what is needed, to be used as charity (*dāna*) (44) with which to help the people.

The second is the bestowal of the teaching (dharma; *fa*), which is explained as repairing buildings and founding numinous temples, making images and having scriptures copied, (45) streamers, flowers, bells, musical chimes, fragrant oils [and utensils to aid] the teaching, retreats (*zhai*)[25] for the sincere, the constantly dwelling, and for making offerings to the Three Jewels (*sanbao*)[26] (46) of all kinds of necessities.

The third is the bestowal of that which is difficult. This is what is meant by things such as countries, towns, wives and children, people and those things one loves the most, (47) including even [giving away] one's own life, which is the most difficult thing to do. [Doing so] will enable one to realize that all the ten thousand phenomena are impermanent (48), [including] wife, children, countries and towns, [all things which] for a short time, by relying on causes and conditions, come together, not lasting for a long time,[27] (49) [as] the enlightened body floating in the void, is fundamentally without self (*wuwo*).[28] Furthermore one's wife and children [also] depend on causes and conditions, (50) who [may therefore also] be used in the bestowal of charity, without giving rise to a feeling of grudge, but giving up what is difficult to part with, in a manner that cannot be imagined.

The fourth (51) is the bestowal of that which is easy. This is items such as carts, horses, slaves, clothes, foodstuffs, gold, silver, various types of silk, (52) rice, and utensils. All are things which we rely on, that are easy to part with. That which is "easy to bestow" (53) [should be given] widely and to all. Do not discriminate between holy and ordinary in regard to these four ones.

Furthermore, there are twenty kinds [of giving alms as follows]:

(54) The first, is giving one's body.
The second, is giving with force.[29]
The third, [is giving] (55) one's wife and children.
The fourth, is giving countries and towns.
The fifth, is giving gardens and residences.
The sixth, (56) is giving strong slaves.
The seventh, is giving carts and horses.
The eight, is giving clothes.
(57) The ninth, is giving utensils and things.
The tenth, is giving pearls and other precious things.
The eleventh, (58) is giving a mixture of the above.
The twelfth, is giving rice and barley
The thirteenth (59), is giving timber and wood,
The fourteenth, giving incense and oil.
The fifteenth, is giving foodstuffs,
The sixteenth, is giving music.
The seventeenth, (60) is giving with flowers and medicines, (61)
The eighteenth, is giving dharma robes.
The nineteenth, is giving the teaching (62).
The twentieth, is giving majestic force.[30]

These twenty ordinary things of giving, constitute the [discussion of the] gate of charity, which are explained as (63) performing charity (*bushi*), "widely" (*bu*) means encompassing all without being exhausted, and "bestowing" (*shi*) means giving to all. (64) Hence it is called giving.

The third [major cause (?)] is the establishment of virtue. This is explained as making buildings (65) in the past and future.[31] [As for] returning those things one relies on in the Three Worlds, there are fifteen types, (66) according to one's mental disposition [as follows]:

The first is making all numinous temples, following in the footsteps of the holy and true immortals, [such as] mysterious altars and pure[32] cottages, (67) halls, houses towers, pavilions, the master's rooms, large houses, platforms, trees, gardens complete all around, causing (68) them always to remain for eternal *kalpas*.

The second is making all images of the Heavenly Worthies in the three worlds and ten directions, (69) the class of the highest, holy, and true immortals, the Vajrapālas (*jingang*),[33] the jade lads and jade damsels, the spirit kings protecting the teaching, (70) by carving in gold, carved jade, bronze, iron, wood and stone, painted ornaments, and plaster. According with one's means, (71) one should adorn and decorate the images with the signs of goodness, perfect and complete, causing all to have faith.

The third is to make all (72) methods relating to the scriptures [such as] the seven sections of the Three Caverns (*sandong qibu*),[34] the accounts of the holy and true immortals, the methods of the talismanic charts (*futu*), the records, songs, (73) and hymns, [with their] paper, plain silk, slips (*jian*) tablets (*jie*), dyed paper (*zhuanghuang*), covers (*tao*), rollers (*zhu*), [all] compared and collated, corrected and authorized, circulating freely for study and recitation (74), the teaching which transforms men and gods.

The fourth is to make all screens and seats, great and small, high and low, according to the occasion. Adorn (75) them, by making use of the choicest materials.

The fifth is to make all the various streamers and flowers, [of materials such as] gold, silver, red jade, embroidered pictures, (76) sculpted engravings, knotted silk (*jilü*),[35] and weavings, in accordance with one's ability to be given as offerings to the Three Worthies.

The sixth (77) is to make all banners and streamers, lofty carts, and sedan chairs of the nine brilliances[36] and seven precious things, superior *zitan* (*sheng tan*)[37] that has been submerged in water, [all] essential, elegant, (78) delicate, and wonderful, and prepare them for the majestic rites.

The seventh is to make all incense burners, flower basins, and candle holders of (79) gold, silver, bronze, iron, jade stones, ceramic, glass, and wood, making use of what is at hand. One should not be concerned with the finer details (lit. "what is necessary"). The eighth, (80) those people who make all couches and seats, beautiful straw mats, when they are produced, they should all be well done.

The ninth (81) is to make all scriptural storages (*jingzang*), cases, document chests, painted and richly decorated, adorned in gold and silver, (82) [wherein] to place the precious scriptures, making sure that they not to become soiled.

The tenth is to make all [sorts of] fancy [ritual] robes of fabric, damask silk, (83) and beautiful cotton in three or five colors. Make sure that they are fragrant and clean, spreading them before the arranged seats.

(84) The eleventh is making all small tables, scripture stands (*jingjia*), and joined boards (*jiaxi* 夾膝) of fragrant sandal wood and similar woods, carved in high and low relief. (85) Each at a time, making offerings with scriptures and images, including to those who have left the family.

The twelfth (86) make all bells and chime stones, with gold, silver, bronze, and iron, jade stones and other types, great and small in accordance with the situation. (87) [Thereby] causing to have them sound day and night on a regular basis, far or near may go toward them. By greatly supplying implements for the [Daoist] teaching, for eternal *kalpa*s one makes fields of blessings.

(88) The thirteenth is to make all kinds of tools and utensils, [such as] basins, plates, trays, metal pots, brushes, bells, etc. (89) If one always provides offerings for the retreat whenever necessary, and without being stingy, [one will gain] a virtue that is hard to imagine.

(90) The fourteenth is to make all armrests, staffs, pitchers (*zaoguan*),[38] sitting mats, objects for retreats (*zhaiqi*) [such as] cloth wrappers (*jinpa*). To bestow them upon those who have left their homes (i.e., on Daoist monks and nuns), (91) [will result in] unlimited fields of blessings.

The fifteenth is to make all kinds of accoutrements for the faith, such as kerchiefs, headgear, shoes, sandals, clothes (92), bedding, corded beds, and such things, widely distributing it to those in the Ten Directions who have left their homes.

(93) These are the fifteen types of past and future virtue and lofty eminence [to be offered to the Daoist, monastic community].

The fourth [of the main categories] are the blessings from seeking to liberate others (lit. "to cross them over"). Instructing (94) all men and rulers, including the ordinary multitudes of reptiles, fish, birds, and [other] wild beasts—all that has blood that is in danger—all must be rendered (95) protection. Thereby one will establish fields of merit and certainly cause peace and tranquility, not allowing sadness and hatred, (96) the [ensuing] blessings will be limitless in a manner that cannot be imagined.

The fifth is the virtue of wisdom. This is explained as always with wisdom give peace (97) and happiness to all sentient beings, causing all men and gods to revert to the good Way, so that they may be eternally removed from the suffering hells, (98) and for a long time dwell in the blessed halls [of heaven]. Hence we call the one who does this for a virtuous person, and we call it virtue. To always practice this without being stingy is called merit (*gong*). (99) The merit [accumulated] during one *kalpa* is called virtue (*de*). These are the five.

Constantly give rise to the [following] sixteen prayers (*yuan*), as greatness (100) begins with a good heart:

The first is done on behalf of heaven and earth; pray that for eternal *kalpas* they will always be there.

The second is done on behalf of the sun and the moon; pray that (101) their light and brightness will spread extensively.

The third is to implore the stars and celestial bodies, praying that they will always comply with their proper divisions (i.e., follow their regular courses).

The fourth is for the mountains and seas; (102) pray that they will always control the discharges from their springs and sources.

The fifth is for the human sovereign, praying that for a long time he will maintain the realm and its territories.

The sixth is on behalf of those who assist the ruler, (103) praying that they will have prosperous positions and maintain the peace.

The seventh is for the Nine Mysteries; pray that they will enable us to be reborn in the pure land.

The eighth is for (104) one's parents; pray that they will always be guaranteed a godly age.

The ninth is for one's older brother; pray that he will practice benevolence and filial piety.

The tenth (105) is on behalf of one's older and younger sisters; pray that they will maintain purity and chastity.

The eleventh is on behalf of relatives and acquaintances; pray that all will be harmonious and reverential.

(106) The twelfth is on behalf of all under heaven; pray that all will enjoy peace and calm.

The thirteenth is for [those caught up in] the three evil paths (*santu*),[39] praying that they will be removed from sharp (107) poison (*chudu*).[40]

The fourteenth is to pray on behalf of everybody, that each will have a full life.

The fifteenth is for oneself, (108) praying that one will meet with the scriptures of the Way.

The sixteenth is for the Dharmadhātu (*fajie*),[41] praying that the [scriptures of] Three Caverns[42] will flow everywhere.

(109) If one is always able to practice without getting tired, causing all in past and future to seek refuge in and rise up to the pure land.

(110) As regards karmic cultivation, it is explained as always purifying the Three Karmas,[43] cleansing the Six Roots,[44] cultivating the Way reciting scriptures,[45] (111) upholding the retreat, prostrate, burn incense, make prayers, repent, burn lamps, respect the precepts, scatter flowers, and sincerely (112) redeem one's span of life. Do not kill, do not steal, do not be licentious, do not flatter, do not hate, do not bribe, do not covet, (113) do not desire, but always act on behalf of the realm's lords and the sovereigns of men, as well as for their spouses, the great ministers and rulers, all the princes (114), etc., the noble marquises,

and counts, [all] the humans under Heaven, [those in] the three evil paths and the five sufferings,[46] *pretas* (*e'gui*, hungry ghosts) and domestic animals. (115) Always prepare hundred seats,[47] for inviting all Dharma masters of great virtue (*dade fashi*), as well as the intelligent ones with a good disposition[48] (116), to discourse on the thirty-six sections of the worthy scriptures, the highest, wondrous excellence which makes all enlightened. (117) Day and night without ceasing [one should] burn incense, scatter flowers, and burn lamp with which to illumine the night, aiding Heaven's light at the road side, (118) dig wells, plant fruit trees, making houses, construct bridges [in order to] relieve those who suffer from [corvée] labor, original retribution (*yuanbao*) (119) that is one's obligation (?),[49] and by this one produces [good] karma. One practices it by attending to the suffering [of others], hence it is called "cultivating karma."

## [Conditions for Rebirth in the Pure Lands]

All the immortals (120) kowtowed and asked, saying, "Sentient beings of inferior and weak [disposition] may have insufficient strength to do this, could you kindly determine whether there is (121) an essential method [whereby] they may obtain, rebirth in the pure land?" "The Heavenly Worthy answered, saying, "If there are good men and good women, (122) who are only able to make an image in the likeness of my shape, discourse on and recite this scripture, make prostrations day and night, (123) and reflect on (i.e., the scripture) in their minds, then they will attain rebirth [there]. If they comply with the former injunctions to practice and do not commit any evils, all the gods will descend (124) to them while the bright sun illumines the sky (i.e., in broad daylight)." All the immortals then said, "Sentient beings are foolish and go astray in their desire for worldly things, (125) [consequently] they are unable to comply with the commands of Your teaching, and do not reflect on what will happen when they die. (126) What kind of virtue can be made [on their behalf]? And according to what prayer will they be reborn?" The Heavenly Worthy answered them, saying, "Correctly arrived (127) men and women, at the time of dying they must first repent the numerous grave transgressions they have committed in the course of their lifetime. (128) Next they must receive [the Daoist teaching] with sincerity and set up retreats for cultivating the Way, making images and copying scriptures, as well as all kinds of virtuous [activities], (129) widely giving to the permanently dwelling (*changzhu*),[50] making offerings to those who have left their homes, each one according to his or her means. It is only [important] that they do a lot of good. (130) On the day [of dying] they should close their eyes, and then they will be reborn in the pure land, so that they do not enter the three evil paths [of rebirth]. If somebody, after the end of their lives, on their behalf (131) sets up yellow registers, bright and true, [retreat] for the five purifications,[51] etc. for practicing the Way. From the passing of one day up to one hundred days, one (132) is making images, copying scriptures, lightening lamps, making prostrations day and night, (133) reciting the scriptures and repent, burning incense and scattering flowers. Moreover, at the time of birth [in one's family (?)] with clothes, beds, carriages, horses, (134) fine-looking slaves, gold, silver, pearls and jade, gauze silk, fine cotton, using their valuables, and dividing them into (135) seventeen parts, distributing one part to repair the numinous temples, [including] the mysterious altars, pure[52] huts (*qingshe*), halls, houses, (136) pagodas, rooms, verandas, chambers and kiosks; one part for making images of all the Heavenly Worthies, as well as the holy, true immortals; (137) one part for copying all the scriptures and their teachings; one part for all the constantly dwelling; one part for all the necessities for holding retreats (138); one part to be donated to all the sincere practitioners, as well as those staying in the mountains and forests studying the Way; one part to be used as offerings to those who have left their homes (139), such as necessary foodstuffs and medicines; one part for making all sounding bells; one part for making (140) all provisions and flowers [for ritual offerings]; one part for offering all screens and seats; one part with which to give fragrant oils; one part for giving (141) aid to imprisoned followers; one part to be given to all those who are needy, poor, old, and sick; one part for ransoming life (*shu shengming*);[53] (142) one part for bestowing fields of compassion; one part for maintaining and making bridges, roads, and paths; one part for the non-(143) obstruction of providing charity. In this manner are the [different] parts of charity with which one will obtain rebirth as a spirit in the pure land, [as well as] good fortune and divine protection (144) against all worldly calamities such as diseases. In the creation of all these fields of blessing, these are the primary ones (145) [the positive effects of which] cannot be imagined.

Now on behalf of you all, I will speak about the blessings and virtues of dwelling in the pure lands in the ten directions, the dwellings of virtue, (146) so that all men and women, in accordance with their prayers may go there for rebirth."

## [Describing the Pure Lands]

(147) The Heavenly Worthy said, "The Eastern Pure Land is the World of Benevolence and Love, it is adorned by blessings of virtue. (148) In terms of majestic wonder it is number one. Its precious platforms, precious halls, precious towers, and precious pavilions are all spontaneously manifested, and all are adorned with (149) nine-colored green jade, inside and outside the caves, in a manner that cannot be imagined. The Jade Precious Ruler, (150) the highest Heavenly Worthy always dwells in the Hall of Nine Bright Rarities seated on a nine-colored precious lotus, expounding on (151) the scriptures of the highest origin of the Three Caverns, the teaching of which transforms all in the realm.

"Moreover, there are the Perfected of Highest Compassion, (152) the Perfected Compassionate Kindness, the Perfected Sympathetic Compassion,[54] the Perfected Kind Love, the Perfected Compassionate Goodness, (153) the Perfected Compassionate Virtue, the Perfected Compassionate Light, the Perfected Compassionate Equality,[55] the Perfected Compassionate Enlightenment, (154) the Perfected Compassionate Succor, who constantly listen to the pleas and requests for [aiding] the suffering, leading sentient beings to salvation (*kaidu*).

"Moreover, there are also the Lad Nine Flowers, (155) the Lad Nine Brilliances, the Lad Nine Unities, the Lad Nine Forms, the Lad Nine Truths, (156) the Lad Nine Immortals, the Lad Nine Levels,[56] the Lad Nine Brightnesses, the Lad Nine Numinosities, (157) the Lad Nine Accomplishments, who constantly recite the scriptures and cultivate the Way, upholding the fasts and prostrate, addressing the people with advice.

"Moreover, there are (158) the Jade Lady Azure Flower, the Jade Lady Azure Palace, the Jade Lady Azure Essentials, the Jade Lady Azure Numinosity, (159) the Jade Lady Azure Lotus, the Jade Lady Azure Fungus, the Jade Lady Azure Light, the Jade Lady Azure Origin, (160) the Jade Lady Azure Brightness, the Jade Lady Azure City, who constantly scatter flowers, burn incense, chant singing in praise and admiration, while making offerings to (161) the Heavenly Worthies.

"Moreover, there is the Vajrapāla Good Power, the Vajrapāla Good Majesty, the Vajrapāla Good Victory, (162) the Vajrapāla Good Speed, the Vajrapāla Good Life, the Vajrapāla Good Transformation, the Vajrapāla Good Blessings, (163) the Vajrapāla Good Path, the Vajrapāla Good Patience, the Vajrapāla Good Kindness, who constantly protect the realm and territories, protecting the people, (164) overcoming *māras* and subduing demons, augmenting and extending their allocated number of years.

"Moreover, there is the Spirit King Benevolent Virtue, (165) the Spirit King Benevolent Determination, the Spirit King Benevolent Majesty, the Spirit King Benevolent Wisdom, the Spirit King Benevolent Profundity, the Spirit King Benevolent Victory, (166) the Spirit King Benevolent Favor, the Spirit King Benevolent Brightness, the Spirit King Benevolent Peace, the Spirit King Benevolent Respect, (167) who constantly overpower and cut off demonic essences, expelling turbid cravings, upholding and protecting this world, rubbing out the deviant demons (168).

"Moreover, there are also the Demon General Protector of the Realm, the Demon General Protector of [Human] Age, the Demon General Protector of Lifespan, (169) the Demon General Protector of Plans, the Demon General Protector of the People, the Demon General Protector of the Soil, the Demon General Protector of Victory, (170) the Demon General Protector of Majesty, the Demon General Protector of Accomplishment, the Demon General Protector of Faith, who constantly lead the cavalry of spirit immortals (171) nine myriads strong, keeping away and denouncing the gutter of misfortune, cleaning away bandits and invaders, aiding and protecting the people (172) [so that] the lifespans of the men and women of the realm will be greatly extended, without dying young. When men and women pass away, (173) their spirits will be reborn in the pure land where the host of holy ones will welcome them."

(174) The Heavenly Worthy said, "The South-eastern Pure Land is the World of Compassion and Harmony, adorned by blessings and virtues, (175) and in terms of majestic wonder it is number one. Its precious platforms, precious halls, precious towers, and precious pavilions are all spontaneously manifested, and all are (176) adorned with a single colored wall of jade, inside and outside the caves, in a manner that cannot be imagined. (177) The Heavenly Worthy, Well-Born Savior of Life, always dwells in the Hall of the Four Bright Treasures, sitting on a four-wheel flower seat, discoursing (178) on the highest scriptures of the Three Caverns, the teaching of which transforms those in the realm.

"Moreover, there are the Perfected Bright Superiority, (179) the Perfected Bright Kindness, the Perfected Bright Virtue, the Perfected Bright Path, the Perfected Bright Treasure, (180) the Perfected Bright Wisdom, the Perfected Bright Method, the Perfected Bright Jade, the Perfected Bright Marks, (181) the Perfected Bright Vacuity, who constantly listen to the the pleas for the relief from hardships, leading sentient beings to salvation.

"Moreover, there are the Lad True Unity, (182) the Lad True Numinosity, the Lad True Marks, the Lad True Vacuity, the Lad True Superiority,

(183) the Lad True Kindness, the Lad True Wisdom, the Lad True Boundary, the Lad True Origin, (184) the Lad True Path, who constantly recite the scriptures and cultivate the Way, upholding the retreat, prostrating and addressing the people with advice.

(185) "Moreover, there are the Jade Lady Flying in Vacuity, the Jade Lady Flying Fragrance, the Jade Lady Flying Mystery, Flying Cloud (186), the Jade Lady Flying Jade, the Jade Lady Flying Numinosity, the Jade Lady Flying Spouse, the Jade Lady Flying Flower, the Jade Lady Flying Canopy, (187) the Jade Lady Flying Azure, the Jade Lady Flying Gold, who constantly scatter flowers and burn incense, singing hymns, (188) and making offerings to the Heavenly Worthies.

"Moreover, there are also the Vajrapāla Roaming in the Mystery, the Vajrapāla Roaming in Vacuity, the Vajrapāla Roaming on High, (189) the Vajrapāla Roaming Truth, the Vajrapāla Roaming in Space, the Vajrapāla Roaming Cloud, the Vajrapāla Roaming Immortal, (190) the Vajrapāla Roaming Spirit, the Vajrapāla Roaming Far, the Vajrapāla Roaming Numinosity, who constantly protect the realm and its territories, (191) protecting the people, overcoming *māras* and subduing demons, augmenting and extending their allocated number of years.

"Moreover, there are also the Spirit King Wisdom Mountain, (192) the Spirit King Amassed Wisdom, the Spirit King Fruits of Wisdom, the Spirit King Bright Wisdom, the Spirit King Patient Wisdom, (193) the Spirit King Power of Wisdom, the Spirit King Majestic Wisdom, the Spirit King Distant Wisdom, the Spirit King Excelling Wisdom, the Spirit King Virtue of Wisdom, (194) who constantly overcome and cut off demonic essences, driving away pestilences, upholding and protecting the world, eliminating the deviant demons.

(195) "Moreover, there are the Demon General Pervading Brightness, the Demon General Pervading Profundity, the Demon General Penetrating Intelligence, (196) the Demon General Penetrating Heaven, the Demon General Penetrating the Numinous, the Demon General Penetrating Virtue, the Demon General Penetrating the Truth, (197) the Demon General Penetrating the Way, the Demon General Penetrating Kindness, the Demon General Penetrating Light, who constantly lead the cavalry of spirit immortals (198), 130,000 strong, keeping away and denouncing the gutter of misfortune, cleaning away bandits and invaders, aiding and protecting the people, [so that] the lifespans of the men and women of the realm (199) will be greatly extended, without dying young. When men and women pass away, (200) their spirits are reborn in the pure land where the host of holy ones will come to welcome them."

(201) The Heavenly Worthy said, "The Pure Land of the southern direction is the World of the Essential Teaching, it is adorned with blessings and virtue. (202) In terms of profound wonder, it is number one. Its precious platforms, precious halls, precious towers, and precious pavilions are all spontaneously manifested. All are adorned with (203) precious things in three colors of red, inside and outside the caves, in a manner that cannot be imagined. (204) The Heavenly Worthy Abstruse Truth of Ten Thousand Blessings, constantly dwell in the Hall of the Three Bright Lights, seated on a tricolored lotus flower, discoursing on (205) the highest scriptures of the Three Caverns, the teaching of which transforms those in this realm.

"Moreover, there are the Perfected Great Yang, the Perfected Great Brightness, (206) the Perfected Great Vacuity, the Perfected Great Origin, the Perfected Great Vacuity, the Perfected Great Brightness, (207) the Perfected Great Superiority, the Perfected Great Emperor, the Perfected Great Purity, the Perfected Great Unity, (208) constantly listening to the pleas for salvation from hardships, leading sentient beings to salvation.

"Moreover there are the Lad Fiery Light, (209) the Lad Fiery Superiority, the Lad Fiery Blaze, the Lad Fiery Relative, the Lad Fiery Flower, the Lad Fiery Jade, (210) the Lad Fiery Illumination, the Lad Fiery Mountain, the Lad Fiery Mirror, the Lad Fiery Dragon, (211) who constantly recite the scriptures and cultivate the Way, upholding the fasts, prostrating, addressing the people with advice.

"Moreover, there are (212) the Jade Lady Floating Vacuity, the Jade Lady Floating Fragrance, the Jade Lady Floating Cloud, the Jade Lady Floating Bride, (213) the Jade Lady Floating Numinosity, the Jade Lady Floating Mystery, the Jade Lady Floating Purity, the Jade Lady Floating Mist, the Jade Lady Floating Wheel, (214) the Jade Lady Floating Brightness, who constantly scatter flowers, burn incense, sing hymns, and make offerings to the Heavenly Worthies.

"Moreover, there are the (215) the Vajrapāla Solitary Vision, the Vajrapāla Solitary Position, the Vajrapāla Solitary Practice of the Golden Sword, (216) the Vajrapāla Solitary Wheel, the Vajrapāla Solitary Light, the Vajrapāla Solitary Sign, the Vajrapāla Solitary Power, (217) the Vajrapāla Solitary Brightness, the Vajrapāla Solitary Illumination, who constantly protect the realm and its territories, protecting the people, overcoming *māra*s and subduing demons, (218) augmenting and extending their allocated number of years.

"Moreover, there are the Spirit King Tablet[57] of Illumination, the Spirit King Tablet of Superiority, (219) the Spirit King Tablet of Vacuity, the Spirit King Tablet of Brightness, the Spirit King Tablet of Correctness, the Spirit King Tablet of Permission, (220) the Spirit King Tablet of Knowledge, the Spirit King Tablet of Wisdom, the Spirit King Tablet of Peace, the Spirit King Tablet of the Way, who constantly overcome and cut off demonic essences, (221) driving away pestilences, upholding and protecting the world, eliminating the deviant demons.

"Moreover, there are (222) the Demon General Great Strength,[58] the Demon General Great Wisdom, the Demon General Great Victory, the Demon General Great Majesty, the Demon General Great Brightness, (223) the Demon General Great Kindness, the Demon General Great Gathering, the Demon General Great Meaning, the Demon General Great Killer, (224) the Demon General Great Virtue, who constantly lead the cavalry of spirit immortals, keeping away and denouncing the gutter of misfortune (225), cleaning away bandits and invaders, aiding and protecting the people, [so that] the lifespans of men and women in the realm will be greatly extended, (226) without them dying young. When men and women pass away, in accordance with their prayers they will go for rebirth [in the pure land] where they will be welcomed by the host of holy ones."

(227) The Heavenly Worthy said, "The Southwestern Pure Land is the World of Majestic Template adorned by blessings and virtue. (228) In terms of majestic wonder it is number one. Its precious platforms, precious halls, precious towers, and precious pavilions are all spontaneously manifested, and all are (229) adorned with one-colored, yellow jade, inside and outside its caves, in a manner that cannot be imagined. [It is lorded over by] the Heavenly Worthy Great Numinous (230) Vacuous Sovereign, who constantly dwells in the Precious Hall of Yellow Jade, seated on a lotus flower with thousand petals (231) discoursing on the highest scriptures of the Three Caverns, the teaching of which transforms those in that realm.

"There are also the Perfected White Numinosity, (232) the Perfected Plain Flower, the Perfected Plain Virtue, the Perfected Plain Origin, the Perfected Plain Brightness, (233) the Perfected Plain Mystery, the Perfected Plain Cloud, the Perfected Plain Sincerity, the Perfected Plain Loyalty, (234) the Perfected Plain Reality, who constantly listens to pleas of deliverance from hardships, leading sentient beings to salvation.

"Moreover, there are the Lad Yellow Numinosity, (235) the Lad Yellow Superiority, the Lad Yellow Origin, the Lad Yellow Jade, the Lad Yellow Clouds, (236) the Lad Yellow Plainness, the Lad Yellow Constancy, the Lad Yellow Brightness, the Lad Yellow Flower, (237) the Lad Yellow Palace, who constantly recite the scriptures and cultivate the Way, upholding the retreat, prostrate, and address the people with advice.

(238) "Moreover, there are the Jade Lady Cloud of Flowers, the Jade Lady of Cloud Palace, the Jade Lady of Cloud Opening, (239) the Jade Lady Cloud Chamber, the Jade Lady Cloud Brilliance, the Jade Lady Cloud Platform, the Jade Lady Cloud Garment, the Jade Lady Cloud in Jade (240), the Jade Lady Cloud of Accomplishment, the Jade Lady Cloud Court Dust, who constantly scatter flowers and burn incense, sing hymns (241) and make offerings to the Heavenly Worthies.

"Moreover, there are the Vajrapāla Shaking Numinosity, the Vajrapāla Shaking Sword, (242), the Vajrapāla Shaking Banner, the Vajrapāla Shaking Halberd, the Vajrapāla Shaking Spirit, the Vajrapāla Shaking Mystery, (243), the Vajrapāla Shaking Emptiness, the Vajrapāla Shaking Demons, the Vajrapāla Shaking Sword, the Vajrapāla Shaking Cloud, who constantly protect the realm and its territories, (244) protecting its people by overcoming and subduing demons, and augmenting and extending their allocated spans of life.

"Moreover, there are the Spirit King Concealed Demon (245), the Spirit King Concealed Heterodoxy, the Spirit King Concealed Māra, the Spirit King Concealed Misfortune, the Spirit King Concealed Poison,[59] (246) the Spirit King Concealed Fault, the Spirit King Concealed Beast, the Spirit King Tiger, the Spirit King Concealed Dragon, the Spirit King Concealed Depravity (247), who constantly overpower and cut off heterodox essences, rejecting pestilences, upholding and protecting the realm, eliminating heterodox (248) demons.

"Moreover, there are the Demon General Majestic Crown, the Demon General Mountain Crown, the Demon General Ocean Crown, (249) the Demon General Martial Crown, the Demon General Animal Crown, the Demon General Evil Crown, the Demon General Jade Crown, (250) the Demon General Golden Crown, the Demon General Heavenly Crown, the Demon General Numinous Crown, who constantly lead the cavalry of spirit immortals (251), who constantly protect the realm and its territories, (252) protecting its people by overcoming and subduing demons, and augmenting and extending their allocated spans of life so that they do not die young. When men and women pass away (253) their spirits will be reborn in the pure land, where the crowd of holy ones will welcome them."

(254) The Heavenly Worthy said, "The Pure Land in the western direction is the World of Meaning of Consent, it is adorned by blessings and virtues. In terms of majestic (255) wonder it is number one. Its precious

platforms, precious halls, precious towers, and precious pavilions are all spontaneously manifested, and all are adorned with seven-(256) colored white jade, inside and outside the caves in a manner that cannot be imagined. (257) The Heavenly Worthy Highest Wonder Reaching the Extreme, constantly dwells in the Hall of Seven Precious Clouds, seated on a great, golden bed, discoursing on the highest scriptures (258) of the Three Caverns, the teachings of which transforms those in that realm.

"Moreover, there are the Perfected Precious Mystery, (259) the Perfected Precious Leader, the Perfected Precious Light, the Perfected Precious Love, the Perfected Precious Marks, the Perfected Precious Virtue, (260) the Perfected Precious Brilliance, the Perfected Precious Flower, the Perfected Precious Kindness, (261) the Perfected Precious Cloud, who constantly listens to pleas of deliverance from hardships, leading sentient beings to salvation.

"Moreover, there are the Lad Golden Light, (262) the Lad Golden Flower, the Lad Golden Leader, the Lad Golden Marks, the Lad Golden Cap, (263) The Lad Golden Seal, the Lad Golden Truth, the Lad Golden Hero, the Lad Golden Fungus, (264) the Lad Golden Fragrance, who constantly recite the scriptures and cultivate the Way, uphold the fasts, prostrate, addressing the people with advice.

(265) "Moreover, there are the Jade Lady Cavern Brightness, the Jade Lady Cavern Light, the Jade Lady Cavern Spirit, (266) the jade Lady Cavern Mystery, the Jade Lady Cavern Truth, the Jade Lady Cavern Immortal, the Jade Lady Cavern Void, the Jade Lady Cavern Numinosity, (267) the Jade Lady Cavern Flower, the Jade Lady Cavern Heaven, constantly scattering flowers and burning incense, singing hymns and making offerings to (268) the Heavenly Worthies.

"Moreover, there are the Vajrapāla Gazing at the Clouds, the Vajrapāla Gazing at the Mountains, the Vajrapāla Gazing at the Moon, (269) the Vajrapāla Gazing at the Distance, the Vajrapāla Gazing at the Sun, the Vajrapāla Gazing into Space, the Vajrapāla Gazing at the Immortals, (270) the Vajrapāla Gazing at Heaven, the Vajrapāla Gazing at the Wind, the Vajrapāla Gazing at the Vital Breath, who constantly protect the realm and its territories, (271) protecting the people by overcoming *māras* and subduing demons, augmenting and extending their allocated number of years.

"Moreover, there are the Spirit King Ascending the clouds, (272) the Spirit King Ascending the Wind, the Spirit King Ascending the Void, the Spirit King Ascending Dragon, the Spirit King Riding a Tiger (273) the Spirit King Riding the Sun, the Spirit King Riding the Moon, the

Spirit King Riding the Mist, the Spirit King Riding a Beast, the Spirit King Riding a Mountain, (274) who constantly overpower and cut off heterodox essences, rejecting pestilences, upholding and protecting the realm, eliminating heterodox (275) demons.

"Moreover, there are the Demon General Riding the Tiger, the Demon General Riding the Dragon, the Demon General Riding the Wind, (276) the Demon General Riding the Clouds, the Demon General Riding the Vital Breath, the Demon General Riding the Sun, the Demon General Riding the Moon, (277) the Demon General Riding in Space, the Demon General Riding Deviancy, the Demon General Riding in Heaven, who constantly lead the cavalry of spirit immortals (278) seventy myriads strong, keeping away and denouncing the gutter of misfortune (225), cleaning away bandits and invaders, aiding and protecting the people (279), [so that] the lifespans of men and women in the realm will be greatly extended, without them dying young. When men and women pass away (280), their spirits will be reborn in the pure land where they will be welcomed by the host of holy ones."

(281) The Heavenly Worthy said: "The Pure Land in the north-western direction is the World of Accomplished Transformation, it is adorned by blessings and virtue. (282) In terms of majestic wonder it is number one. Its precious platforms and precious halls, precious towers and precious pavilions are spontaneously produced, and all are adorned with (283) eight-colored pointed jade, inside and outside the caves, in a manner that cannot be imagined. There (284) the Heavenly Worthy Original Limit Great Flower constantly dwells in the Hall of Eight-fold Rosy Flowers, sitting on a dazzling, heavenly phoenix platform, expounding on the scriptures of the highest origin of the Three Caverns, (285), teaching and transforming those in that realm.

"Moreover, there are the Perfected Without Superior, (286) the Perfected Without Equal, the Perfected Non-Activity, the Perfected Nameless, the Perfected Fearless, (287) the Perfected Formless, the Perfected Signless, the Perfected Shapeless, the Perfected Flawless, (288) the Perfected Limitless, who constantly listen to the pleas of salvation from hardships, leading sentient beings to salvation.

"Moreover, there are the Lad Pure Numinosity, (289) the Lad Pure Brightness, the Lad Pure Vacuity, the Lad Pure Mystery, the Lad Pure Source, (290) the Lad Pure Penetration, the Lad Pure Superiority, the Lad Pure Cold, the Lad Pure Harmony, (291) the Lad Pure Truth, who constantly recite the scriptures and cultivate the Way, uphold the fasts, prostrate, and address the people with advices.

"Moreover, there are (292) the Jade Lady Original Numinosity, the Jade Lady Original Brightness, the Jade Lady Original Flower, the Jade Lady Original Truth, (293) the Jade Lady Original Chastity, the Jade Lady Original Leader, the Jade Lady Original Sovereign, the Jade Lady Original Superiority, (294) the Jade Lady Original Harmony, the Jade Lady of Original Beginning, who constantly scatter flowers and burn incense, singing hymns and (295) making offerings to the Heavenly Worthy.

"Moreover, there are the Vajrapāla Aroused Majesty, the Vajrapāla Aroused Martiality, the Vajrapāla Aroused Courage, (296) the Vajrapāla Aroused Power, the Vajrapāla Aroused Brightness, the Vajrapāla Aroused Mountain, the Vajrapāla Aroused Ocean, (297) the Vajrapāla Aroused Heaven, the Vajrapāla Aroused Kindness, the Vajrapāla Aroused Virtue, who constantly protect the realm and its territories, (298) protecting the people, by overcoming *māras* and subduing demons, augmenting and extending their allocated number of years.

"Moreover, there are the Spirit King Lofty Heaven, (299) the Spirit King Lofty Superiority, the Spirit King Lofty Brightness, the Spirit King High Vacuity, the Spirit King Lofty Numinosity, (300) the Spirit King Lofty Contemplation, the Spirit King Lofty Mountain, the Spirit King Lofty Profundity, the Spirit King Lofty Kindness, (301) the Spirit King Lofty Inspection, who constantly overpower and cut off heterodox essences, rejecting pestilences, upholding and protecting the realm, and eliminate heterodox (302) demons.

"Moreover, there are the Demon General Declaring the Way, the Demon General Declaring Brightness, the Demon General Declaring Majesty, the Demon General Declaring Power, (303) the Demon General Declaring Virtue, the Demon General Declaring Kindness, the Demon General Declaring the Profound, the Demon General Declaring Bravery, (304) the Demon General Declaring the Accomplishment of the Way, the Demon General Declaring War, who constantly lead the cavalry of spirit immortals, (305) and 120,000 man strong, keeping away and denouncing the gutter of misfortune, cleaning away bandits and invaders, aiding and protecting the people, [so that] the lifespans of men and women in the realm (306) will be greatly extended, without them dying young. When men and women pass away, their spirits will (307) reborn in the pure land, where the crowd of holy ones will welcome them."

(308) The Heavenly Worthy said, "The pure land in the northern direction is the World of Wisdom and Virtue. In terms of majestic wonder (309) it is number one. Its precious platforms, precious halls, precious towers, and precious pavilions are all spontaneously manifested, and all

are adorned with (310) five-colored dark jade, inside and outside the caves, in a manner that cannot be imagined. (311) The Heavenly Worthy Mysterious and Superior Jade Morning, always dwells in the Hall of Five Cloud Flowers, seated on a precious flower of five brightnesses, expounding on (312) the scriptures of the highest origin of the Three Caverns, teaching and transforming those in that realm.

"Moreover, there are the Perfected Mysterious Numinosity, (313) the Perfected Mysterious Oneness,[60] Perfected Mysterious Brightness, the Perfected Mysterious Virtue, the Perfected Mysterious Penetration, (314) the Perfected Mysterious Darkness, the Perfected Mysterious Superiority, the Perfected Mysterious Harmony, the Perfected Mysterious Enlightenment (315), who constantly listen to the pleas of salvation from hardships, leading sentient beings to salvation.

"Moreover, there are the Lad Moon Light, (316) the Lad Moon Marks, the Lad Moon Love, the Lad Moon Fragrance, the Lad Moon Superiority, (317) the Lad Moon Fullness, the Lad Moon Kindness, the Lad Moon Purity, the Lad Moon Brightness, (318) the Lad Moon Wisdom, who constantly recite the scriptures and cultivate the Way, uphold the fasts, prostrate, (319) addressing the people with advice.

"Moreover, there are the Jade Lady Fragrant Cloud, the Jade Lady Fragrant Marriage, the Jade Lady Fragrant Lamp, (320) the Jade Lady Fragrant Accumulation, the Jade Lady Fragrant Mountain, the Jade Lady Garden, the Jade Lady Fragrant Flower, (321) the Jade Lady Fragrant Forest, the Jade Lady Fragrant Light, the Jade Lady Fragrant Seal, who constantly scatter flowers,[61] burn incense, sing hymns, (322) and make offerings to the Heavenly Worthy.

"Moreover, there are the Vajrapāla Protecting Thoughts, the Vajrapāla Protecting the Body, the Vajrapāla Protecting the Law, (323) the Vajrapāla Protecting the Seal, the Vajrapāla Protecting the Span of Life, the Vajrapāla Protecting Vitality, (324) the Vajrapāla Protecting the Realm, the Vajrapāla Protecting the Altar, the Vajrapāla Protecting Incense, the Vajrapāla Protecting Goodness, who constantly (325) protect the realm and its territories, protecting the people by overcoming *māra*s and subduing demons, augmenting and extending their allocated number of years.

"Moreover, there are (326) the Spirit King Defending the Way, the Spirit King Defending the Seal, the Spirit King Defending the Dharma, the Spirit King Defending the Altar, (327) the Spirit King Defending Goodness, the Spirit King Defending Fragrance, the Spirit King Defending Protection, the Spirit King Defending the Clan, the Spirit King Defending

Virtue, (328)[62] the Spirit King Defending Guard, who constantly overpower and cut off heterodox essences, rejecting pestilences, upholding and protecting the realm (329), and eliminating heterodox demons.

"Moreover, there are the Demon General Overpowering Evil, the Demon General Overpowering Misfortune, the Demon General Overpowering Demons, (330) the Demon General Overpowering Army, the Demon General Overpowering *māras*, the Demon General Overpowering Wrong, the Demon General Overpowering Death, (331) the Demon General Overpowering Majesty, the Demon General Overpowering Spirit, the Demon General Overpowering Military Prowess, the Demon General Overpowering Force, who constantly lead (332) the cavalry of spirit immortals five myriads strong, keeping away and denouncing the gutter of misfortune, cleaning away bandits and invaders, aiding and (333) protecting the people [so that] the lifespans of the men and women of the realm will be greatly extended, and they will not die young. (334) When men and women pass away, their spirits will be reborn in the pure land, where the crowd of holy ones will welcome them."

(335) The Heavenly Worthy said, "The Northeastern Pure Land World of Stored Wisdom is adorned by blessings and virtue. In terms of majestic (336) wonder it is number one. Its precious platforms, precious halls, precious towers, and precious pavilions are all spontaneously manifested, and all are adorned with (337) ten-colored, mottled jade, inside and outside its caves, in a manner that cannot be imagined. (338) The Heavenly Worthy Saving Immortal and Superior Sage, constantly dwell in the Hall of Six United Preciousnesses, seated on the mysterious throne of the Six Unities, expounding on (339) the highest scriptures of the Three Caverns, teaching and transforming those in the realm.

"Moreover, there is the Perfected Ranked Love, (340) the Perfected Ranked Superiority, the Perfected Ranked Compassion, the Perfected Ranked Marks, the Perfected Ranked Brightness, (341) the Perfected Ranked Illumination, the Perfected Ranked Kindness, the Perfected Ranked Wisdom, the Perfected Ranked Contemplation, (342) the Perfected Ranked Enlightenment, constantly listening to pleas of salvation from hardships, leading sentient being to salvation.

"Moreover, there are (343) the Lad Aiding Suffering, the Lad Aiding Lifespan, the Lad Aiding Distress, the Lad Aiding Danger, (344) the Lad Aiding Hardships, the Lad Aiding Salvation, the Lad Aiding Goodness, the Lad Aiding Relief, (345) the Lad Aiding the Teaching, the Lad Aiding Protection, who constantly recite the scriptures and cultivate the Way, uphold the fasts, prostrate, (346) and address the people with advice.

"Moreover, there are the Jade Lady Hall of Blessings, the Jade Lady Blessings of Virtue, (347) Jade Lady Accumulated Blessings, the Jade Lady Complete Blessings, the Jade Lady Forest of Blessings, the Jade Lady Highest Blessings, the Jade Lady Blessings of Wisdom, (348) the Jade Lady Blessings of Kindness, the Jade Lady Mountain of Blessings, the Jade Lady Pure Blessings, who constantly scatter flowers and burn incense, (349) singing hymns and making offerings to the Heavenly Worthies.

"Moreover, there are the Vajrapāla Severing Heterodoxy, (350) the Vajrapāla Severing Desire, the Vajrapāla Severing Vision, the Vajrapāla Severing Fear, the Vajrapāla Severing Demons, the Vajrapāla Severing Doubt, (351) the Vajrapāla Severing Obstructions, the Vajrapāla Severing Uncertainty, the Vajrapāla Severing *māras*, (352) the Vajrapāla Severing Sword, who constantly protect the realm and its territories, protecting the people, overcoming *māras* and subduing demons, augmenting and (353) extending their allocated number of years.

"Moreover, there are the Spirit King Resisting Misfortune, the Spirit King Resisting Heterodoxy, the Spirit King Resisting Transgressions, (354) the Spirit King Resisting Evil Influences, the Spirit King Resisting Demons, the Spirit King Resisting Poison, the Spirit King Resisting Tigers, the Spirit King Resisting Beasts, (355) the Spirit King Resisting [Malevolent] Spirits, the Spirit King Resisting Invaders, who constantly overpower heterodox essences, rejecting pestilences (356), upholding and protecting the realm, and eliminating heterodox demons.

"Moreover, there is the Demon General Establishing Time, (357) the Demon General Setting Up Flags, the Demon General Establishing Bells, the Demon General Setting Up Drums, (358) the Demon General Establishing the Military, the Demon General Making Victory, the Demon General Making Talismans, the Demon General Setting Up Screens, (359) the Demon General Using Falcons, who constantly lead the cavalry of spirit immortals, 120,000 strong, keeping away and denouncing (360) the gutter of misfortune, cleaning away bandits and invaders, aiding and protecting the people [so that] the lifespans (361) of the men and women of the realm will be greatly extended, and they will not die young. When these men and women pass away, their spirits will be reborn in the pure land (362) where the host of holy ones will come and welcome them."

(363) The Heavenly Worthy said, "The Upper Pure Land is the Unlimited World, which is adorned by blessings and virtue. In terms of majestic (364) wonder it is number one. Its precious platforms, precious halls, precious towers, and precious pavilions are all spontaneously manifested, and all are adorned (365) with ten thousand kinds of adornments,

inside and outside the caves, in a manner that cannot be imagined. (366) The Heavenly Worthy Jade Vacuous Brilliance dwells in the Hall of Ten Thousand Treasures of Brightly Lit Clouds, sitting on ten thousand kinds of pure, precious (367) flowers, discoursing on the highest scriptures of the Three Caverns, teaching and transforming [those] in the realm.

"Moreover, there are (368) the Perfected Purple Space, the Perfected Purple Chamber, the Perfected Purple Platform, the Perfected Purple Profundity, (369) the Perfected Purple Yamen, the Perfected Purple Numinosity, the Perfected Purple Flower, (370) the Perfected Purple Yang, the Perfected Purple Purity, the Perfected Purple Origin, who constantly listen to pleas for the removal of hardships, (371) leading sentient being to salvation.

"Moreover, there are the Lad Superior Numinosity, the Lad Superior Mystery, the Lad Superior Origin, (372) the Lad Superior Space, the Lad Superior Vacuity, the Lad Superior Immortal, the Lad Superior Truth, the Lad Superior Wisdom, (373) the Lad Superior Signs, the Lad Superior Virtue, who constantly recite the scriptures and cultivate the Way, uphold the fasts, prostrate, (374) addressing the people with advice.

"Moreover, there are the Jade Lady Beautiful Flower, the Jade Lady Beautiful Cloud, the Jade Lady Beautiful Superiority, (375) the Jade Lady Beautiful Brightness, the Jade Lady Beautiful Vacuity, the Jade Lady Beautiful Light, the Jade Lady Beautiful Yang, (376) the Jade Lady Beautiful Mystery, the Jade Lady Beautiful Numinosity, the Jade Lady Beautiful Marks, who constantly scatter flowers and burn incense, singing hymns (377) and making offerings to the Heavenly Worthy.

"Moreover, there are the Self-So Vajrapāla, the Self-Knowing Vajrapāla, (378) the Self-Favoring Vajrapāla, the Self-Powered Vajrapāla, the Self-Wise Vajrapāla, the Self-Virtuous Vajrapāla, the Self-Enlightened Vajrapāla, the Self-Complete Vajrapāla, the Self-Pervading Vajrapāla, the (379) Self-Illuminating Vajrapāla, who constantly protect the realm and its territories (380), protecting the people, overcoming *māras* and subduing demons.

"Moreover, there are (381) the Spirit King Who Has Wisdom, the Spirit King Who Has Power, the Spirit King Who Has Kindness, the Spirit King Who Has Majesty, (382) the Spirit King Who Has Marks, the Spirit King Who Has Virtue, the Spirit King Who Has Numinosity, the Spirit King Who Has Respect, the Spirit King who Sees Spirits, (383) the Spirit King Who Has Penetration, who constantly overpower and cut off evil essences, drive away pestilences, protect (384) the realm, and eliminate the deviant *māras*.

"Moreover, there are the Demon General Heavenly Greatness, the Demon General Heavenly Power, (385) the Demon General Heavenly Majesty, the Demon General Heavenly Superiority, the Demon General Heavenly Penetration, the Demon General Heavenly Light, the Demon General Heavenly Wisdom, (386) the Demon General Heavenly Numinosity, the Demon General Heavenly Petal, the Demon General Heavenly Umbrella, who constantly lead the cavalry of spirit immortals, (387) divine persons and powerful beings (*lishi*),[63] hundred myriads strong, who protect the territories of the realm, eliminating heterodox essences, (388) and the men and women in the realm will enjoy lifespans like that of the gods. When these men and women pass away, their spirits will be reborn in the pure land (389) where the host of holy ones will come and welcome them."

(390) The Heavenly Worthy said, "The pure land in the lower direction is the World of Conveying Virtue, which is adorned with blessings. (391) In terms of majestic wonder it is number one. Its precious platforms, precious halls, precious towers and precious pavilions are all spontaneously manifested, (392) and all are adorned with the hundred precious things, inside and outside the caverns, in a manner that cannot be imagined. There the Heavenly Worthy Yellow Cave Abyss (393) constantly dwells in the Numinous Hall of Hundred Precious Vacuities and Brightnesses, seated on a lotus flower of a hundred transformations illuminating the cave, (394) discoursing on the highest scriptures of the Three Caverns, teaching and transforming those in the realm.

"Moreover, there are the Perfected Central Yellow, (395) the Perfected Central Brightness, the Perfected Central Heaven, the Perfected Central Flower, the Perfected Central Platform, (396) the Perfected Central Origin, the Perfected Central Immortal, the Perfected Central Numinosity, the Perfected Central Mystery, (397) the Perfected Central Luster, who constantly listen to the pleas for salvation from hardships, leading sentient beings to salvation.

"Moreover, there is the Lad Light and Brightness, (398) the Lad Light Flower, the Lad Light Marks, the Lad Light Kindness, the Lad Light Profundity, (399) the Lad Dazzling Light, the Lad Light Path, the Lad Light Numinosity, the Lad Light of Fullness, (400) the Lad Light Vacuity, who constantly recite the scriptures and cultivate the Way, uphold the fasts, prostrate, and address the people with advice.

(401) "Moreover, there are the Jade Lady Wondrous Fragrance, the Jade Lady Wondrous Flower, the Jade Lady Wondrous Numinosity, (402) the Jade Lady Wondrous Victory, the Jade Lady Wondrous Cloud, the Jade

Lady Wondrous Truth, the Jade Lady Wondrous Immortal, (403) the Jade Lady Wondrous Peace, the Jade Lady Wondrous Mystery, the Jade Lady Wondrous Moon, who constantly scatter flowers and burn incense and chant (404) hymns and make offerings to the Heavenly Worthy.

"Moreover, there are the Vajrapāla Fierce God,[64] the Vajrapāla Fierce Mouth, (405) the Vajrapāla Fierce Mountain, the Vajrapāla Fierce Domination, the Vajrapāla Fierce Wind, the Vajrapāla Fierce Numinosity, (406) the Vajrapāla Fierce Victory, the Vajrapāla Fierce Profundity, the Vajrapāla Fierce Excess, the Vajrapāla Fierce Canopy, who constantly (407) protect the realm, overcoming *māras* and subduing demons, augmenting and extending their allocated number of years.

"Moreover, there is the Spirit King, (408) Pacifying Sword, the Spirit King Pacifying Arrow, the Spirit King Pacifying Military, the Spirit King Pacifying Hoof, (409) the Spirit King Pacifying Strife, the Spirit King Pacifying Eagles, the Spirit King Pacifying Invaders, the Spirit King Pacifying Iron, the Spirit King Pacifying Tigers, (410) the Spirit King Pacifying Banner, who constantly overpower and cut off evil essences, rejecting pestilences, (411) upholding and protecting the world, and eliminating deviant *māras*.

"Moreover, there is the Demon General Encircling Heaven, the Demon General Encircling Halberd,[65] (412) the Demon General Encircling Iron, the Demon General Encircling Correctness, the Demon General Encircling Guard, (413) the Demon General Encircling Accomplishment, the Demon General Encircling Court, the Demon General Encircling Profundity, the Demon General Encircling Penetration, (414) who constantly lead the cavalry of spirit immortals, divine persons, and powerful beings, ten hundred myriads strong, (415) protecting the realm and its territories [against] hungry ghosts (*preta*) and destroying demonic essences. Men and women of this realm will accord with the end and beginning of the *kalpa*.[66] When [these] men (416) and women pass away, in accordance with their prayers go for rebirth [in the pure land]."

## [Additional Description of the Pure Lands]

(417) The Heavenly Worthy said, "The pure lands of the ten directions, their realms are adorned with the self-so power of blessings, their mountains, (418) forests, grasses, and trees, as well as their platforms, pavilions, halls and houses, are not the same as in the ordinary world. (419) Each of them has a Floating Cloud Temple, a Great Way Temple, a Displaying Longevity Temple, a Wanshou Temple, (420) a Prosperous Happiness

Temple, an Extensive Way Temple, a Reaching Truth Temple, a Prosperous Nation Temple, (421) a Commencing Holiness Temple, a Gathering of Numinosity Temple, an Offering Blessings Temple, (422) a Virtue of the Way Temple.

"Again, [there is also] a Purified Thought Tower, a Tower for Burning Incense, a Visiting Immortals Tower, (423) a Tower of Floating Through Space, a Tower of Four Brightnesses, a Tower of Nine Flowers, a Tower of Long Life, (424) a Tower of Fragrant Wind, a Tower of Penetrating Brightness, a Tower for Illuminating the Void, Tower of Firm Determination, (425) Tower of Pure Thoughts, Receiving the Truth Platform, Dancing Phoenix Platform, Flying Dragons Platform, Scattering Flowers Platform, (426) Platform of Connected Fragrance, Platform for Gathering the Sages, Vacuous Brightness Platform, Platform of Nine Brightnesses, (427) a Platform of the Six Unities, a Platform of Constant Numinosity, a Platform of Ten Thousand Blessings, a Platform for Recollecting the Truth, a Platform of Constant Numinosity, (428) a Platform of Coagulated Numinosity Pavilion, a Pavilion of Auspicious Egrets, a Pavilion of Flying Fragrance, a Pavilion for the Pure Truth, (429) a Pavilion for Accomplished Immortals, a Pavilion for Transforming the Living, a Pavilion of Peace and Longevity, a Pavilion for Protecting the Young, (430) a Long Life Pavilion, a Pavilion of Persistent Truth, a Pavilion for Knowing the Spirits, a Pavilion for Exercising the Mind, (431) a Palace of Eight Truths, a Palace of Ten Wheels, a Palace of Bright Light, a Palace of Cavern Yang, (432) a Palace of Azure Origin, a Palace of Jade Flowers, a Palace of Golden Essence, a Palace of Thriving Numinosity, (433) a Palace of Precious Fortune, a Palace of Spontaneity. [Then there is a] Hall of Ten Thousand Years, Hall of . . .[67] Hall of Cold Numinosity, (434) Hall of Purple Vapors, Hall of Virtues, Hall of Prosperous Holiness, Hall of Bliss, (435) Hall of Distant Strolling, Hall of a Thousand Fragrances, Hall of Hundred Precious Things, Hall of Pervading Divinity, (436) Hall of Bright Marks, Hall for Speaking the Dharma, Hall of Original Motion,[68] Hall for Welcoming the Truth, (437) Hall of Nine Harmonies, Hall of the Flower Moon, Hall of Ten Thousand Precious Things, Hall of the Ten Numinosities, (438) Hall of Constant Bliss, Hall of the Self-so, Hall of Fragrant Jade, Hall of Precious Jade, (439) Hall of Cavern Mystery, Hall of Ten Thousand Flowers, Chamber of Purple and Emerald, Chamber of Precious Lotus, (440) Chamber of Cloud Cliff, Chamber of Jade and Fungus, Chamber of the Purified Spirit, Chamber for Resting the Mind, (441) Chamber of Quiet Contemplation, Chamber of Successive **XXX**, Chamber of Bright Mystery, Chamber of Precious Life, (442) Chamber for Calming One's Will, Chamber for Extinguishing Thoughts (*mien-*

*ian*). All of these appear spontaneously, profoundly, and wonderfully adorned. (443) There is also a connecting wind, which makes [things] complete. There are also coagulating clouds, nine luminaries which illumine the caverns, seven (444) precious brightnesses, shifting by itself inside space, and a welcoming wind revolving on its own, which, according with the mind's thoughts (445), will come echoing one's position.

"Again, there are a Pool of Precious Lotuses, (446) a Pool of Floating Gold, a Pool of Pure Fragrance, Pool for Washing, Pool of Cherished Fragrance, Pool of Floating Fragrance, (447) a Pool of Pure Emptiness, a Pool of Shining Moon, a Pool of Cavern Heaven, Pool for Washing the Mind, a Pool of Cold Environment, (448) a Pool for Illuminating the Spirit Pool. All pervade the pure and bright caverns, always placid they do not run. (449) [Moreover] their banks are made of the seven precious things, and they are lined with golden sand.

"Again, there are a Water of Knowledge, Water of Washing Numinosity, Water of Cave Illumination (450), Water for Opening the Mind, Water of Abundant Space, Water Carrying Illumination, (451) Water that Constantly Turns, Water of Circular Brightness, Water of Streaming Fragrance, Water of Fragrant Mist, Water Illuminating the Mind, (452) Water of Divine Clarity, Water for Concentrating the Mind. All fragrant and beautiful, (453) constantly flowing day and night.

"Again, there are [grasses such as] Grass for Establishing Numinosity, Long Life Grass, Grass for Calming the Spirit Grass, (454) Grass for Protection the Year, Grass for Spirits and Immortals, Grass of Sweet Dew Grass, Grass of . . . ,[69] (455) Grass of Flower Mist, Grass of Intelligent Mind, Grass for Nourishing the Spirit, Grass of Harmonious Qi, (456) Grass without Sadness. All having gold and jade petals that do not fall and do not wither,[70] the dew held by the welcoming wind, carries a fragrance (457) that is spread [everywhere].

"Again, there are the Ring Net Petals, Elegant Lotus Petals, Distinguishing Fragrances Petals, (458) the Combined View Petals, the Fragrant Dew Petals, the Phoenix Head Petals, the Egret Heart Petals, (459) the Beautiful Dragon Petals, the Intelligent Magpie Petals, the Sounding Wind Petals, the Thousand Gold [Pieces] Petals, (460) the Nine Precious Petals. All bearing fruit in accordance with time, making nectar as one wishes, their flavors arranged on a thousand (461) plates, their shapes divided into ten thousand classes.

"Again there are Illumining Gold Flowers, Shining Jade Flowers, (462) Flying Fragrance Flowers, Floating Mist Flowers, Rising Cloud Flowers, Merging Dew Flowers, (463) Welcoming Wind Flowers, Shining Spirit

Flowers, Cavern Scene Flowers, Precious Light Flowers, (464) As You Wish Flowers, and Contemplating the Mind Flowers. All like gold and jade, illuminating the cavernous scenes with their streaming light, and growing where one dwells (465), their fragrance spreading for several li around.

"Again, there are Birds which Discourse on the Teaching,[71] (466) Birds of Equal Life, Birds of Harmonious Qi, Birds of the Same Heart, Birds Biting Incense, (467) Birds Coughing Up Jade, Birds Gargling Pearls, Birds of Jade Light, Birds of Golden Sparkles, Birds of Fragrant Feathers (468), Birds of Golden Wings, all have five colors, their feathers shining brightly.

"Again, there are (469) Opening Brightness Beasts, Golden Essence Beasts, Splitting Light Beasts, Jade-Faced Beasts, (470) Fragrant Spitting Beast, Drum Music Beasts, Chiming Bell Beast, Displaying Rarities Beast, (471) Scattering Flowers Beasts, Crying Numinous Beast, Dancing in Emptiness Beast, and Singing Immortal Beast. All [producing] sounds (472) that are harmonious and graceful, and when heard it releases peoples' hearts.

"Again, there is the Fragrance of a Thousand Combination, Fragrance of Ten Thousand Harmonies, (473) the Fragrance of One Hundred Harmonies, Fragrance of Ten Harmonies, Fragrance of the Spirit of Life, Fragrance for Recalling the Hun-Soul (*fanhun xiang*),[72] (474) Fragrance for Transforming Shapes, Fragrance of Flying Beauty, Fragrance of Coagulated Vacuity, Fragrance of Entangled Clouds, (475) Fragrance of Saving Life, Fragrance of Harmonious Bliss, Fragrance of Long Life.

"Again, there are famous Fragrant Trees, (476) Precious Vessel Trees, Sound of Music Trees, Garment Trees, Food Trees, (477) Fragrant Flower Trees, Seven Jewel Trees, Nine Lights Trees, Dragon Mist Trees, (478) Phoenix Cloud Trees, Beholding Rainbows Trees, and Splitting Gold Trees. (479) These trees are big, reaching to a height of thirty li, some twenty li, and the small ones ten li. None of them wither and do not fall, their flower petals (480) always blossoming. Famous/significant incense, precious utensils, music, clothes, foodstuffs, etc. All issue from (481) within the flowers, spontaneously and pure. All one needs to do is think of them, and they will appear.

"Again, there are phoenixes, imperial peacocks, (482) blue egrets, white magpies, serene and prosperous, which gather brightness, produce life, cuckoos, orioles, gold wings, and other such birds, (483) among them roosting birds, birds soaring and dancing, their cries and songs reciting sections of the Cavern [Scriptures] (*dongzhang*).

"Furthermore, there are divine dragons, (484) numinous tigers, *qilin*, wild beasts, heavenly deer warding off evil influences (*pixie*). Lions of golden essences sporting at will (485) among them, making the sound of bells and chime stones, spewing jade and holding pearls in their mouths (lit. biting pearls).

"Again, there are Thousand Petal Lotuses, (486) Nine Colored Lotuses, Hundred-Stem Lotuses, Thousand-Petal Lotuses, Fragrant Wind Lotuses, Sweet Dew Lotuses (487) with a circumference of three to five li, where accordingly [the inhabitants] dwell and are live. The men and women living inside this realm (488) have put an end to traveling afar, [and instead] listen to scriptures and discourses on the teaching, while naturally strolling about.

"Furthermore, there are heavenly flowers, heavenly (489) petals, heavenly fragrances, heavenly offerings, heavenly robes, heavenly music filling the empty sky, arriving in response to one's wish, (490) [bringing] peace and bliss to all sentient beings.

"Again, there are carriages and horse-drawn vehicles, all of which are made of the seven precious things emitting nine lights, (491) caused by wind (*yinfeng*) and driven by qi (*yuqi*) one's thoughts are born here and there.

"Again, there are male gods and goddesses, immortal lads and immortal damsels, (492) who cultivate the Way and recite the scriptures, sport in space from their abodes, scattering flowers and burning incense, and while flying listen to the teaching. (493)

"Again, there are heavenly kings and immortal lords (*bo*), well-versed in the virtue of the Way, [as well as] harmonious and refined people.

"Again, there are Heavenly Masters (*tianshi*)[73] (494) of the Taishang assisting the Heavenly Worthy, in teaching and transforming, by discoursing on the teaching, opening enlightenment without limit. (495) Men and women of the realm, constantly recite the scriptures, listen to the teaching, scatter flowers and burn incense, facing the Heavenly Worthy, seeking to consult him concerning (496) the Highest Way, golden appearance and jade-like looks, with signs of goodness, upright and refined, without any grief or sadness. With yellow gold (497) covering the ground, railings and steps of white jade, inside and outside brightly lit, all pure. (498) When men and women pass away, then they will go for rebirth [in the pure land] in accordance with their prayers."

## (499) [Conclusion]

The Heavenly Worthy (i.e., Congealed Spirit Reaching Illumination) [then] addressed all the immortals, saying, "As regards [experienced] evils and blessings, they are the results of retribution from former lifetimes (*suming*). [All] causes and conditions (*yinyuan*), (500) are affected by sentient beings. Just like images in a mirror, the shapes of which are seen according to their characteristics, one perceives them as good, ugly (501),[74] long, or short, always free of error. If one upholds the retreat, respect the precepts, sincerely cultivates the Way, recites the scriptures, prays (502) and repents, makes images and copies the scriptures, establishes the abstruse altars, repairs and maintains the numinous temples, (503) makes offerings to the Three Jewels, gives to the needy, liberates and redeems sentient beings, making all these virtuous acts, constantly practicing reverential faith, (504) purifying the six roots, overpowering and cutting off the mind of desire, without creating all evil [acts], having a true mind of recollection [then] in accordance with (505) one's prayers one will go for rebirth in the pure land of immediate bliss and nonactivity.

"If people [on the other hand] practices falsehood, kill sentient beings, (506) rob and steal, deviantly indulge in lewdness and licentiousness, are miserly, covetous, hateful, [behave] in a convoluted and stupid [manner], [use] elegant words [or] foolish words (507), lie, seek to hinder [other people], curse and spit, defer superficially to the Three Jewels, revile the text of the scriptures, (508) do not honor those who have left the family (i.e., Daoist priests), are unfilial as regards to the five relationships (*wuni*), create all kinds of evil karma, and who have no faith in good causes, (509) [then] one day, at the end of their lives, they will enter the nine-fold hells,[75] where they will receive all kinds of suffering for the duration of ten thousand *kalpas* sinking (510) and going under [in the sea of birth and death]. When afterwards they are reborn, they will dwell in a realm of filth (*huitu*),[76] their appearances and looks will be ugly and crude, the years of their lifespans will be short, they will suffer injury, (511) they will be deaf or blind and suffer from the six types of diseases, people with grievances will act against them with malice, [there will be] an abundance of beasts, [such as] tigers, foxes, thorns and brambles, poisonous plants, fetters (512), cangues, shackles, starvation and cold, surrounded by suffering and all kinds of evil conditions repressing one [such as] facing enemies, bitter grievances (513) and hateful hardships, all lasting a lifetime, day and night one is troubled by vexations without experiencing happiness or bliss, (514) revolving in *saṃsāra* for eternal *kalpas* without interruption. All this is obtained from sentient beings' karmic conditions. (515) I have now on your behalf discoursed on these causes and conditions. To all you men and women with a dedicated disposition, I urge you to diligently cultivate the good Way, (516) to be reborn as spirits in the pure lands, in accordance with your prayers and disposition of your hearts, so that forever you will not go wrong." (517)

[When] all the immortals and the others heard the Heavenly Worthy speak about the pure lands of the ten directions and the adornments of these realms and worlds, (518) they became very happy, jumped for joy, praised in unison the goodness [they had heard], kowtowed, and withdrew.

## Notes

1 For a comparative study of Buddhist and Daoist conceptions of heavens and the netherworld, see Xiao Dengfu, *Han Wei Liuchao fo dao liangjiao zhi tiantang diyu shuo* (Statements by two religions, Buddhism and Daoism During the Han, Wei and Six Dynasties concerning the Heavenly Halls and the Hells), *Daojiao yanjiu congshu* (Comprehensive collection of books for the Study of Daoism) 6 (Taibei: Xuesheng shuju, 1989). The concept of rebirth in early Daoism, the underlying notion for an afterlife in paradise, is explored in Stephen R. Bokenkamp, *Ancestors and Anxiety: Daoism and the Birth of Rebirth in China* (Berkeley: University of California Press, 2007). See also Friederike Assandri, "Examples of Buddho-Daoist Interaction: Conceptions of the Afterlife in Early Medieval Epigraphic Sources," *Electronic Journal of East and Central Asian Religions* (2013): 2–43.

2 For important contributions relating to this Daoist tradition, see Ōfuchi Ninji, *Dōkyō toso no kyōden* (Tokyo: Sōbunsha, 1997); and Stephen R. Bokenkamp, ed., *Early Daoist Scriptures* (Berkeley: University of California Press, 1997). See also Wang Chengwen, *Dunhuang gu Lingbao jing yu pu Tang daojiao* (The Old Lingbao Scriptures from Dunhuang and Daoism from the Jin to Tang [periods]), *Hualin boshi wenku* (Professor Hualin's treasury of writings) 3 (Beijing: Zhonghua shuju, 2002).

3 This extensive, but only partly extant scripture is an outstanding example of high-level integration of Buddhist and Daoist doctrine as formulated through the Lingbao tradition in the late Nanbeichao period. The discourses found in the sixth chapter evolves around the pure lands. Cf. Ye Guiliang, *Dunhuang ben Taixuan zhenyi benji jing - jixiao* (The Dunhuang version of the *Taixuan zhenyi benji jing*: Annotated and punctuated) (Chengdu: Sichuan chuban jituan Bashu shushe, 2010), 168–184.

4 Cf. P. 2383, P. 2401V, P. 4730. A modern edited version is contained in the Zhonghua daozang, 99.4, ed. Zhang Jiyu et al. (Beijing: Huaxia chubanshe, 2004), 241c–246a. A fascimile reproduction of P. 2383 can be found in Ōfuchi Ninji, *Tonkō dōkyo zurokuhen* (A Collation of the Daoist scriptures from Dunhuang with plates), 2 vols. (Tokyo: Kokubu shoten, 1979), 104–116. See also the *Zangwai daoshu* (Daoist books outside the Canon), vol. 21, ed. Hu Daojing, Lin Wangqing, and Chen Yaoqing (Chengdu: Ba Shu shushe 1992–1995), 124a–136a.

5 I date the text on the basis of its evolved conception of the pure lands, its vocabulary, including those words borrowed from Buddhism, the manner in which Daoism is described as a monastic organization together with all the related aspects of material culture, etc.

6 Ōfuchi, the pioneer on the study of the Lingbao tradition, has shown relatively little interest in those Lingbao scriptures that were greatly influenced by Buddhist thought. This also explains why he did not devote much attention to the *Jingtu sheng shen jing*, which is only provided with the briefest of descriptions in the *Tonkō dōkyo zurokuhen*. Cf. ibid., 77. Moreover, it is not even mentioned in his primary study, *Dōkyō toso no kyōden* (Daoism and its scriptural corpus) (Tokyo: Sōbunsha, 1997). Western scholarship has also largely ignored the scripture, which by the way was also excluded from the various studies by Stephen Bokenkamp, the pre-eminent specialist on the Lingbao tradition.

7 See Chen, *Dunhuang xue sanze xinji* (Taipei: Xinwen-feng chuban gongju, 1989), line 115, 455.

8 For information on the Sanqing Heavens and the related scriptures, see Xiao Dengfu, *Liuchao daojiao Shangqing pai yanjiu* (A Study of the Shangqing School of Six Dynasties' Daoism) (Wenlu chubanshe, 2005).

9 This is of course also the case with regard to the Daoist conceptions of the netherworld. See Henrik H. Sørensen, "The Meeting of Daoist and Buddhist Spatial Imagination: The Construction of the Netherworld in Medieval China," in *Locating Religions: Contact, Diversity and Translocality*, ed. Nikolas Jaspert (Leiden: Brill, 2017), 234–292.

10 Also written 黃籙. The Yellow Registers record the names of the deceased on whose behalf communal rites, later known as *huangly dajiao*, were performed. Our knowledge about how they were performed during the early Tang, that is, during the time the *Jingtu sheng shen jing* was written, remains spotty. It is clear, however, that it was a type of rite developed by the Lingbao tradition. For references to their performance during the pre-Tang and Tang periods, see *Yunji qiqian*, Zhonghua shuju edition (hereafter YJQQ), vol. 5, 2656–2661, 2685, 2693.

11 For Buddhist spells affording the faithful access to the pure land, see *T.* 1025.19, 724a; *T.* 1042.20, 34a; *T.* 1092.20, 307c, etc.

12 A structural concept found in the opening of many Buddhist sutras. Here it has been used in abbreviated form.

13 Here Chen has obviously misunderstood the syntax as well as the inner logic of the text. Cf. *Dunhuang xue sance xinji*, 448, line 5.

14 Buddhist term.

15 "Level" in the sense that it can be understood by people on all spiritual levels.

16 This probably refers to the movements of the Dao, when the world was first set in motion.

17 *Huaxian* 華仙 is a subcategory of immortals that appear in a number of Daoist scriptures including the celebrated *Duren jing* (Scripture on the salvation of mankind), *Zhentong daozang* (hereafter *DZ*) 1.1. For some reason they have not been graced with an entry in any of the major Daoist dictionaries.

18 This passage, in which the Heavenly Worthy chastises the Flower Immortals for their incomplete training and attainments, is reminiscent of the celebrated section in the *Saddharmapuṇḍarikā* where Buddha reveals the teaching of the One Vehicle, which arouses disbelief and suspicion in some of his followers. Cf. *T.* 262.9, 8bc.

19 This sentence is not entirely clear to me, but I trust that the gist of its intended meaning has nevertheless been conveyed.

20 Here there appears to be a lacunae in the text, probably a section in which the Heavenly Worthy, through his numinous powers, make the assembly behold the pure lands. We may infer this on the basis of the series of questions made to the Heavenly Worthy.

21 Yet another Buddhist concept ultimately based on the teaching of the Dual Truths (*erdi*).

22 This is also based on standard Buddhist concepts of ranking the spiritual potential of sentient beings. The most well-known in East Asia being the three categories of persons reborn in the pure land according to the *Sukhāvatīvyūha*. Cf. *T.* 360.12, 272b. For a translation of the relevant passage as found in this scripture, see Luis O. Gómez, trans., *The Land of Bliss: The Paradise of the Buddha of Measureless Light: Sanskrit and Chinese Versions of the Sukhāvatīvyūha Sutras* (Honolulu: University of Hawai'i Press, 1996), 187–188. There can be little doubt that the author (or authors) of the *Taishang dongxuan lingbao jingtu sheng shenjing* were familiar with this primary text of the Buddhist Pure Land tradition.

23 Exactly how all these forms of salvation refer to sentient beings of the three categories of spiritual maturity is unclear, as the text seemed to imply that all will eventually be saved. Perhaps the composer of the text did not quite grasp the underlying idea behind the three categories as applied in the Buddhist Pure Land tradition, which is directly related to the manner in which rebirth is attained in the pure land as based on karmic merit.

24 This constitutes a thinly veiled reference to the Buddhist *Jātaka* stories, such as the one on Prince Satī, etc. For a discussion of the presence of the *Jātakas* in Lingbao Daoism, See Stephen R. Bokenkamp, "The *Viśvantara-jātaka* in Buddhist and Daoist translation," in *Daoism in History: Essays in honour of Liu Ts'un-yan*, ed. Benjamin Penny (London: Routledge, 2006), 56–73.

25 Livia Kohn translates *zhai* in the Daoist communal context as "maigre feast," a ritual meal with formal offerings, but also indicates a wider usage

of the term. Cf. her *Cosmos and Community: The Ethical Dimension of Daoism* (Cambridge, MA: Three Pines Press, 2004), 44–45. See also Livia Kohn, *Monastic Life in Medieval Daoism: A Cross-Cultural Perspective* (Honolulu: University of Hawai'i Press, 2003), 124–126. My use of "retreat" here hinges on the fact that a *zhai* normally indicates a delineated period of intense practice involving several different including ritual performance, vegetarian meals, and meditation. The *Jingtu shengshen jing* refers broadly to *zhai,* therefore I prefer "retreat" rather than "maigre feast."

26 Obviously a borrowing from Buddhism. Here it stands for the Dao, the Daoist teaching (*fa* 法) and the community of practitioners.

27 This discourse on impermanence has a distinct Buddhist flavor with its straightforward rejection of material objects and application of the belief in natural causation, something that was not originally part of Daoist discourse.

28 This refers to the enlightened and fully liberated immortals, who have gone beyond the ordinary world. It also is a takeover from Buddhism.

29 This could also be interpreted as giving according to one's means.

30 A similar description of the practice of *dāna* can be found in the *Liudu jijing* (Scripture on the Six Liberations), *T.* 52.3, 1a; *Dānādhikāra sūtra, T.* 705.16, 813b, etc. For a structured list, cf. the *Dazhi du lun* (Mahāprajñāpāramitā treatise), *T.* 1509.25, 145a.

31 This sentence is out of place, and its appearance in the manuscript may have been caused by an error of copying.

32 The text reads *jing,* which must be a mistake for *qing,* "pure." These are cabins used for retreats.

33 This is a distinct Buddhist category of protectors usually associated with Esoteric Buddhism. They were evidently incorporated as a concept into the Daoist pantheon from the late sixth century onwards, and they occur as a named group in the *Yuanshi tianwang huanle jing* (Scripture on the happiness of the Heavenly Kings of the Primordial Commencement), said to date from the Tang dynasty. Cf. *DZ* 62.2, 27ab. For a discussion of this work see John Lagerwey, "*Yuanshi tianwang huanle jing,*" in *The Taoist Canon: A Historical Companion to the* Daozang, ed. Kristofer Schipper and Franciscus Verellen, 3 vols. (Chicago: University of Chicago Press, 2004), I.533.

34 This formal organization of the Daoist scriptures into a canon resembling that of the Buddhists dates from the first half of the fifth century CE. This fact alone of course places the *Jingtu shen sheng jing* well after this event. For a survey of the history of the early Daoist Canon, see Louis Komjathy, *Title Index to Daoist Collections* (Cambridge, MA: Three Pines Press, 2002), 1–3.

35 Could this be a form of embroidery in needle-loop technique?

36 These "nine brilliances" or splendors may refer to ornaments, perhaps emulating the nine luminaries in the sky?

37 This is an interesting early reference to the use of *zitan* wood for Daoist ritual implements.

38 A vessel similar to the *kuṇḍikā* used by Buddhist monks.

39 Rebirth as an animal, as a *preta,* and as a dweller in hell. These are standard types of rebirth as taught in Buddhism.

40 This is an ancient Chinese concept, which can at least be traced back to the Eastern Han. Cf. *Hou Han shu*, chap. 67, http://chinesenotes.com/houhanshu.html.

41 Here meaning the phenomenal world. Dharmadhātu being a name and concept borrowed from Buddhism.

42 Broadly understood as the Daoist scriptures, but here probably meaning more specifically the Lingbao tradition.

43 I.e. of body, speech, and mind. This, again, is a borrowed Buddhist concept.

44 The Six Roots, yet another Buddhist Abhidharma concept, are the sense organs: eye, ear, nose, tongue, skin, and mind.

45 This is a standard phrase, which occurs in a variety of Daoist texts and contexts.

46 Originally a Buddhist concept. The Five Sufferings are (1) birth, aging, sickness, and death, (2) separation from what one loves, (3) encounter with what one does not like, (4) being unable to get what one desires, (5) sufferings caused by the five *skandhas*. There are various related categories of five sufferings depending on religious context as well as scriptural tradition.

47 Undoubtedly this reflects a borrowing from a Buddhist scripture such as the *Renwang jing* (Scripture of the benevolent kings), where the "invitation of Dharma masters" also occurs. Cf. *T.* 245.8, 830a. Similar seats are also mentioned in other Buddhist scriptures.

48 This is a Daoist version of the Buddhist spiritual friend, the *kalyanamitra,* or "Good-knowing One."

49 Tentative translation.

50 This refers to the practitioners living in fixed temples. This concept originally derived from Buddhism.

51 The text has here *lian,* to practice, but this is most probably an error for *lian,* to melt, refine, or purify. The *Wulian zhai* (Retreat of the five purifications) is a well-known concept in Daoism. Cf. *Zhongguo Daojiao da cidian,* 516b.

52 Here the text has *jing* 精, which surely is a scribal error for *qing* 清 "pure."

53 This refers to the practice of paying for the release of animals that would otherwise be eaten, something the Daoists inherited from the Buddhists.

54 He also occurs in the Dunhuang manuscript P. 2582. See also Zheng Acai, "Beijing Gugong zang Dunhuang ben *Cishan xiaozi baoen chengdao jing* (The Dunhuang version of the *Cishan xiaozi baoen chengdao jing* in the collection of the Palace Museum in Beijing)," *Dunhuang xue* (Dunhuang Studies) 25 (2004): 543–558 (cf. esp. 545).

55 He also occurs in *DZ* 62.2.

56 The character 子 is missing in the manuscript.

57 The word used in the text is *zha* 札, which is the tablet on which officials before the Qing wrote missives and notes during court proceedings. Their occurrence in this relatively early text indicates that these tablets were adopted into Daoist ritual practice at an early stage in the religion's development, in any case, prior to the rise of the Tang dynasty.

58 This character would appear to be based on the Buddhist *vajrapāla* Mahābala, aka Ucchuṣma.

59 A protector-deity with the same name figures among the list of *vajrapāla*s in *DZ* 62.2, 27a.

60 This Perfected occurs in or is the primary hero of several canonical scriptures, including the *Dongxuan lingbao Xuanyi zhenren shuo shengye lunzhuan yinyuan jing* (Scripture of the Cavern Mystery of the Numinous Treasure spoken by the Perfected Xuanyi on the causes and conditions of revolving in Saṁsāra), *DZ* 1119.24; *Taishang xuanyi zhenren shuo quanjie falun miao jing* (Wondrous Scripture of the Highest Spoken by the Perfected Xuanyi on the exhortation of the Dharma Wheel of the Precepts), *DZ* 348.6; the *Taishang xuanyi zhenren shuo santu wuku quanjie jing* (Scripture of the Highest Spoken by the Perfected Xuanyi Warning against the Three Evil Paths and Five-Fold Sufferings), *DZ* 455.6, etc. This indicates, among other features, the *Jingtu sheng shen jing*'s relationship with the larger Daoist tradition.

61 The character 花 is missing in manuscript.

62 Chen has "修," which appears to be incorrect.

63 In Buddhism this category of protectors are known as *vīra* or *dvārapāla*. Obviously their presence in the scripture under consideration reflects yet another Daoist takeover of Buddhist demigods.

64 One missing character in Ms.

65 One missing character in Ms.

66 This may mean that their lives are as long as a *kalpa*. The concept of these extensive cycles was adapted by the Daoists from Buddhist texts quite early in Chinese history.

67 Here two characters are missing from the text.

68 The text distinguishes between *dian* 殿 "large hall," and *tang* 堂 "small hall," in accordance with Chinese architectural conventions. For convenience's sake, I shall refer to both of them as simply "halls."

69 One character missing.

70 The manuscript has here "*dong*" 洞, which is obviously a copyist's mistake.

71 This is undoubtedly a reference to the famous Dharma-teaching *kalaviṅka* birds from the *Sukhāvatīvyūha sūtra*. Cf. Gómez, *The Land of Bliss*, 84, 87, 104, etc.

72 One wonders what use this fragrance was to someone reborn in a paradise?

73 This constitutes a sure indicator of the scripture's sectarian affiliation.

74 According to Chan. Ms. has "短長."

75 This refers to the Avīci Hell of Buddhism.

76 In contrast to the pure lands of the righteous.

## Bibliography

### Text Collections and Reference Works

*Taishō shinshū daizōkyō*. Edited by Takakusu Junjirō et al. Tokyo: Taishō issaikyō kankōkai, 1924–1935.

*Zangwai daoshu*, 35 vols. Edited by Hu Daojing, Lin Wangqing, and Chen Yaoqing. Chengdu: Ba Shu shushe 1992–1995.

*Zhengtong Daozang*, 36 vols. Wenwu edition. Beijing: Wenwu chubanshe, 1988.

*Zhonghua daozang*, 49 vols. Edited by Zhang Jiyu et al. Beijing: Huaxia chubanshe, 2004.

### Primary Sources

*Sukhvatīvyūha sūtra*. *T*. 367. 12.

*Taishang dongxuan lingbao jingtu sheng shen jing*. P. 2383, P. 2401V, P. 4730. Modern redacted version. Chen Zulong, Dunhuang xue sanze xinji: 448–479.

*Taixuan zhenyi benji jing*. Modern redacted version. Ye Guiliang, Dunhuang ben Taixuan zhenyi benji jing - jixiao.

*Yunji qiqian*, 5 vols. Edited by Li Yongsheng. *Daojiao dianji xuankan*. Beijing: Zhonghua shuju, 2003.

### Secondary Sources

Assandri, Friederike. "Examples of Buddho-Daoist Interaction: Conceptions of the Afterlife in Early Medieval Epigraphic Sources." *Electronic Journal of East and Central Asian Religions* (2013): 2–43.

Bokenkamp, Stephen R. *Ancestors and Anxiety: Daoism and the Birth of Rebirth in China*. Berkeley: University of California Press, 2007.

——, ed. and trans. *Early Daoist Scriptures. With a Contribution by Peter Nickerson.* Berkeley: University of California Press, 1997.

——. "The *Viśvantara-jātaka* in Buddhist and Daoist translation." In *Daoism in History: Essays in honour of Liu Ts'un-yan,* edited by Benjamin Penny, 56–73. London: Routledge, 2006.

Chen Zulong. *Dunhuang xue sanze xinji*. Taipei: Xinwen-feng chuban gongju, 1989.

Gómez, Luis O. *The Land of Bliss: The Paradise of the Buddha of Measureless Light: Sanskrit and Chinese Versions of the Sukhāvatīvyūha Sūtra.* Honolulu: University of Hawai'i Press, 1996.

Huang, Shih-shan Susan. *Picturing the True Form: Daoist Visual Culture in Traditional China*. Harvard Asia Center, Cambridge, MA: Harvard University Press, 2012.

Kohn, Livia. *Cosmos and Community: The Ethical Dimension of Daoism.* Cambridge, MA: Three Pines Press, 2004.

——. *Monastic Life in Medieval Daoism: A Cross-Cultural Perspective*. Honolulu: University of Hawai'i Press, 2003.

Ōfuchi Ninji. *Dōkyō toso no kyōden*. Tokyo: Sōbunsha, 1997.

——. *Tonkō dōkyo zu rokuhen*, 2 vols. Tokyo: Kokubu shoten, 1979.

Sørensen, Henrik H. "The Meeting of Daoist and Buddhist Spatial Imagination: The Construction of the Netherworld in Medieval China." In *Locating Religions Contact, Diversity and Translocality*, edited by Reinhold Glei and Nikolas Jaspert, 234–292. Leiden: Brill, 2017.

Wang Chengwen. *Dunhuang gu Lingbao jing yu pu Tang daojiao*. Hualin boshi wenku 3. Beijing: Zhonghua shuju, 2002.

Xiao Dengfu. *Han Wei Liuchao fo dao liangjiao zhi tiantang diyu shuo*. Daojiao yanjiu congshu 6. Taibei: Xuesheng shuju, 1989.

——. *Liuchao daojiao Shangqing pai yanjiu*. Taibei: Wenlu chubanshe, 2005.

Ye Guiliang. *Dunhuang ben Taixuan zhenyi benji jing - jixiao*. Chengdu: Sichuan chuban jituan Bashu shushe, 2010.

Zheng Acai. "Beijing Gugong zang Dunhuang ben *Cishan xiaozi baoen chengdao jing* (The Dunhuang version of the *Cishan xiaozi baoen chengdao jing* in the collection of the Palace Museum in Beijing)." *Dunhuang xue* (Dunhuang Studies) 25 (2004): 543–558.

## Chapter 2

# A Manichaean Pure Land

## *The Buddhicized Description of the Realm of Light in the Chinese Manichaean* Hymnscroll

Gábor Kósa

### Translator's Introduction

Mānī (AD 216–ca. 277), the founder of Manichaeism, as well as his disciples, laid special emphasis on their missionary activity.[1] Manichaean missionaries translated their scriptures into the language of the targeted territory, and during this process they also sought out religious analogies that could make the complex Manichaean system more accessible to potential converts. They used Christian terminology in the West (Europe, Egypt), Zoroastrian in Iran, and Buddhist in the East (Central Asia, China).

After its arrival at the court of Empress Wu Zetian (r. 684–704) in AD 694, Manichaeism was basically a *religio licita* for some decades, then in 732 Emperor Xuanzong (r. 712–756) prohibited the Chinese citizens, though not the Iranian Sogdians residing in China, to practice the new religion. Later on, since the Uighur troops were instrumental in ending the An Lushan and Shi Siming (later Shi Chaoyi) uprising (AD 755–763), the subsequent Chinese emperors were compelled to allow the Manichaean Uighurs, as well as the Sogdians with them, to build Manichaean monasteries and spread their faith in China. Due to the defeat of the Uighur by the Kirghiz in 840, this external pressure ceased. Between AD 842 and 845 Emperor Wuzong (r. 840–846) vehemently persecuted Manichaeans as well as followers of other foreign religions. In order to avoid this harsh persecution in the north, some groups of Chinese Manichaeans fled to southeastern China, present-day Zhejiang and Fujian, where they survived for several more centuries.

Given the popularity of texts describing and images[2] depicting pure land(s) in Tang China (618–907 AD), Manichaeans applied notions in this set of scriptures to describe the Manichaean Realm of Light, the goal of all Manichaean believers. By applying compounds like *jile shijie* 極樂世界 (*H.* 328, *H.* 332: "the World of Utmost Bliss") or *(xin) jingtu* (新)淨土 (*H.* 041, *T.* 199: "[New] Pure Land"), the Manichaean translators made it explicit that they identify their Realm of Light with a pure land, although they did not wish to specify which pure land they meant. The Manichaean equation of the Realm of Light with a pure land was reinforced by two recently identified late Yuan, early Ming Manichaean paintings of the Realm of Light, which seem to imitate Buddhist depictions of pure lands.[3]

To summarize the Manichaean myth in a nutshell, two ontologically eternal and opposite principles, conceived as kingdoms, are postulated. The relationship between the Two Principles (the Realm of Light and the Kingdom of Darkness) evolves through the so-called Three Periods. After living side by side for a long period ("Initial Period"), Darkness attempts to attack the Realm of Light, the king of which, the Father of Greatness, sacrifices his Five Light Elements, which thus become mixed with Darkness. After a series of divine emanations, the Light swallowed and captured by the forces of the Darkness is retrieved through the creation and various operations of the universe, which works like a huge purifying machine ("Middle Period"). The engine of this purifying process is the community of the Manichaean believers, especially the "chosen ones," or elects, who are in turn helped by the "hearers" or auditors. After the mixed light, now purified, eventually returns to its original home, the universe collapses, and the Two Principles stay completely separated forever ("Last Period"), Darkness being bound in an eternal prison. Various divine emanations work actively in the process of rescuing light; thus a separate divine abode is created for them by one of the numerous members of the Manichaean pantheon, the Great Builder, at the beginning of this process.[4]

In order to safeguard the ultimate and inactive members of the Realm of Light (like the Father of Greatness, the Twelve Aeons, the Fragrant Air, or the Praiseworthy Earth), it is this separately created provisional state (*H.* 041: "New Pure Land," *H.* 143: *xin mingjie* 新明界 ["New Realm of Light"]) that serves as the resting place for both the active deities returning from the "battle" and for the light particles, including the human souls, liberated from the world after crossing the Pillar of Glory, the Moon and the Sun. In the eschatological future, this New Paradise will in some way coalesce with the "real," original Paradise, that is, the land of nirvana (*H.* 327: *niepan jie*). This concept of a twofold structure might have offered a distant analogy to the relation of the Buddhist pure land to the Buddhist nirvana, even if Chinese Manichaean scriptures, similarly to the Middle Iranian or the Coptic ones, apparently did not pay too much attention to the distinction between the temporary and the eternal realms and described both realms, with reason, in a similar vein.[5]

It is naturally hardly possible to assess the influence of Pure Land ideas on Manichaeism without defining the former. Without claiming expertise in Buddhist studies, here I endorse the stance according to which Pure Land ideas in China were not restricted to a special group of people, who would have been exclusively devoted to the cult of Amitābha, but I accept the opinion of those who think that these notions were part of the general Buddhist religious landscape. This stance was advocated by Gregory Schopen[6] and Gérard Fussmann[7] for India, Matthew T. Kapstein[8] for Tibet, and Todd T. Lewis[9] for Nepal. Compartmentalizing pure land as a clearly identifiable sect might be a retrospective view, which might have developed in Song China and in Japan.[10] To cite R. H. Sharf's succinct opinion: "Pure Land never existed at all as an independent exegetical tradition, much less an institution or sect, in T'ang or Sung China, and the same appears to be true of Tantra or Vajrayāna. These too are historiographic and bibliographic categories wielded by sectarian scholiasts long after the phenomena in question."[11] Or as the same author, also citing G. Schopen, states elsewhere,

> Chinese Buddhists, both monastic and lay, have, throughout their history, aspired to rebirth in the pure land, whether conceived of in metaphorical or in literal terms. The pure land is both a world of "ease and bliss" as well as a place wherein one may easily progress along the Buddhist path unencumbered by physical and mental impurities. To those born in the pure land, final liberation is assured. The aspiration to attain future birth in such a marvelous realm was not, of course, a uniquely Chinese development. Gregory Schopen has shown that the desire for rebirth in Sukhāvatī—the Land of Bliss—was an important aspect of Mahāyāna in India as well, although this realm was not necessarily associated with the cult of Amitābha. A careful reading of passages mentioning Sukhāvatī in a variety of early Mahāyāna scriptures reveals that "rebirth in *sukhāvatī* became a generalized religious goal open to the Mahāyāna community as a whole," and this development most likely occurred earlier than the second century A.D.[12]

G. Amstutz voiced a similar view: "There is no evidence that Pure Land led to the formation of distinct communities with an unusual character."[13] Or as Daniel A. Getz[14] formulated it, "An assessment of the various historical manifestations of Pure Land, however, reveals that for much of the history of Chinese Buddhism, Pure Land was not a distinct institutional entity with a self-conscious lineage or doctrinal system. Rather, until Southern Sung (1127–1279) Pure Land existed as one facet of religious life alongside others."

Thus here I will take a broader definition of pure land, which, however simplistic it may sound, designates any devotional aspiration to be reborn in a pure land as a Pure Land idea. Here I presume that this idea was present in Tang dynasty Buddhism without lending it a sectarian flavor, and it was this broadly defined idea of Pure Land that influenced Manichaeism during the Tang dynasty. A systematic comparison of the Manichaean material and the Buddhist Pure Land ideas would evidently involve the three major and the numerous other Pure Land sutras, but also parts of other scriptures like the *Avataṃsaka sūtra* or the sixth chapter of the *Lotus Sūtra.*[15]

Apparently neither Mānī nor his followers desired to treat other religious traditions and their scriptural corpus in a comprehensive manner, that is, they did not intend to discuss the general similarities and differences between their and others' religions. Instead, they focused on some details and picked up some major or minor motifs, based on which they could show conceptual equations between parts of their religion and those of the local belief system. Behind this practice was the deep-rooted belief that other major religious traditions, especially Zoroastrianism, Buddhism, and Christianity, are distorted versions of what Manichaeism represents in a pure form.

In China, Manichaeans concentrated on the central idea of pure land and equated it with the Manichaean Realm of Light. It is hard to discern any other major direct influence of Pure Land scriptures on the Chinese Manichaean corpus, and the explanation is self-evident: Manichaeans, for example, could not use the figure of Amitābha to denote the Father of Greatness, since these two figures are incompatible in many respects. Similarly, Manichaean scriptures mention pure land but never associate it with any direction, be it the west or other, since in Manichaeism there is only one single Realm of Light. Furthermore, directly attaining the Realm of Light was basically the privilege of the Manichaean *electi* ("priests"), who were practicing various types of austerities and were familiar with a complicated system of cosmogony and cosmology. Thus faith in itself did not suffice to assure redemption. Therefore, Manichaeans, *stricto sensu,* did not adopt the Pure Land doctrines, only some of their elements they could harmonize with their own teachings. This is exactly the same method that they applied in the case of Christianity and Zoroastrianism.

## Introduction to the Manichaean *Hymnscroll*

The *Hymnscroll* was one of the three major Chinese Manichaean manuscripts from Cave 17 of Dunhuang.[16] This manuscript was found by Aurel Stein in 1907 (S. 2659 [= Or. 8210], later included in the Taishō Canon as *T.* 2140: 1270b–1279c), but its Manichaean content was identified only in 1916 by Yabuki Keiki.[17] At present it is kept in the British Library. Paul Pelliot, who had become an expert on Manichaeism by that time, was engaged in other tasks, thus it was two German scholars who published the first translations of some hymns in 1926 and 1933. Later on, a full German translation was prepared by Helwig Schmidt-Glintzer in 1987.[18] The first and currently only complete English translation was published in 1943 by Tsui Chi, who was working from a microfilm version of the original and made use of the Taishō edition as well.[19] Unlike that of Waldschmidt and Lentz, Tsui Chi's translation did not contain commentaries, only some remarks by Henning. Waley and Campany prepared a new translation of a dozen of verses in Boyce's and BeDuhn's work, respectively.[20] In his comparative analysis, Bryder also translated some verses.[21] During the past decades, Lin Wushu and Rui Chuanming published critical editions of the text.[22]

The recto side of the manuscript basically contains Manichaean hymns translated from Parthian. The manuscript (1021 cm × 28.5 cm) also contains Buddhist texts like an excerpt from the *Da Tang xiyuji,* the *Wangsheng lizan wen,* and the *Shi'er guang lichan wen.*[23] Since the scroll becomes thin from column 91, the writing on the reverse side is almost always visible. According to the *communis opinio,* the Buddhist texts were written on the reverse side of the basically Manichaean scroll.[24] These Buddhist texts were most probably written by a certain Zhiyan 智儼 (tenth century), who, after returning from his pilgrimage to India in 924, placed the manuscript in Dunhuang.[25] The *Hymnscroll* is usually dated to the second half of the eighth century or the first part of the ninth century.[26] Based on the general presence of Buddhist terminology, Lin Wushu considered it to be the latest translation among the three Chinese Manichaean scriptures.[27] Based on the examination of the taboo characters, Yu Wanli argued that the translation was made during or after the reign of Daizong (r. 762–779), whose given name (Yu 豫) appears in nonstandard versions several times (*H.* 066, *H.* 071, *H.* 076, *H.* 118).[28] The postscript (*H.* 415–*H.* 422) explicitly informs us that the translator was a certain *Daoming* 道明.

The Manichaean hymns occupy 423 columns (hence abbreviated as numbers after "*H.*" = *Hymnscroll*), also comprising about 30 columns of titles or other liturgical instructions. There are three phonetically transcribed hymns of foreign texts (*H.* 001–*H.* 006, *H.* 154–*H.* 158, *H.* 176–*H.* 183), which are transcriptions of Middle Persian, Parthian, and Aramaic originals.[29] All the other hymns, as Daoming himself states in his postscript, are translations from a *fan* 梵 original, here definitely denoting a Middle Iranian idiom, most probably Parthian.

In Samuel N. C. Lieu's view, the title at the end of the manuscript (*Xiabu zan* 下部讚) may refer to the lower section of the Manichaean church, that is, the auditors ("laymen").[30] This would imply that although the scroll was in the possession of the elects ("priests"), the hymns themselves were probably sung at rituals where auditors were also present. *H.* 387, for example, instructs the users that every Monday (凡至莫日) the confessional text (懺悔願文) in question should be recited together with the auditors (與諸聽者). Moreover, the text begins by asking the auditors to kneel down: "You, auditors (汝等聽者), all should kneel down!" It is clear from these instructions that this particular text at least was indeed used by elects during the Monday ceremony of confession for the auditors. Similarly, another title (*H.* 410) explicitly says that the hymn in question was a confessional text for the auditors (此偈你逾沙懺悔文).

As for the genres in the collection, three technical words are applied in the titles of the various hymns: eulogy (*zan* 讚), praise (*tan* 歎), and *gāthā* (*ji* 偈). Most of the hymns have verses with four lines, written in a single column and separated by small gaps. Each "line" has seven characters (*qīyán*), reminiscent of the form widely used also in Buddhist works.[31]

Certain parts of the *Hymnscroll* have surviving parallels in Parthian, Middle Persian, Sogdian and Uighur. Henning discovered that *In Praise of the Realm of Light* (*H.* 261–*H.* 338), the focus of this contribution, is the translation of the first canto (*hnd'm*) of the Parthian *Huyadagmān*. Another hymn, the *Eulogy of the Five Lights* (*H.* 235–*H.* 260), has a relatively good Parthian analogy in prose (*The Sermon on the Soul, Gy'n wyfr's*).[32]

At present, it seems that the *Hymnscroll* was not a unique document, since further fragments, sometimes similar to the hymns of the *Hymnscroll,* have been also identified from the Turfan region.[33] One of these hymns (Ch. 258 R/I), for example, is a more succinct translation of a hymn in the *Hymnscroll* (*H.* 161-163). More unexpected was Chen Jinguo's and Lin Yun's discovery in 2009, which identified several Manichaean manuscripts in Xiapu (Fujian Province), which also contained several citations from the *Hymnscroll*.[34]

As mentioned above, Zhiyan wrote two Pure Land hymns on the verso side of the manuscript. Does this perhaps mean that he, perhaps inadvertently, considered the Manichaean hymns on the recto side as something similar to these two hymns? Or was it pure chance that for his completely different purpose he used a collection of hymns that contained repeated references to and also, as we will see soon, a complete hymn on the Realm of Light, identified as a pure land?[35]

The originally Parthian hymn was most probably written by Mār Ammō (AD third century), the most important Eastern missionary of Manichaeism, who established Parthian as a church language and who is himself credited with composing several hymns in this idiom.[36] Although the manuscript of the *Hymnscroll* has Wei Mao 未冒 as the author, it is generally agreed[37] that the intended first character must have been Mo 末, thus Mo Mao [Early Medieval Chinese: *mat maw*$^{h}$][38] would stand for Mār Ammō. On the other hand, in 1990 W. Sundermann reconstructed the name of Mār Xwaršēd-Wahman with the title *Huyadagmān* on a fragment (M233/R),[39] though this bishop is referred to as the one who had made the hymn publicly known and not as its author. W. Sundermann suggests that Mār Ammō was probably the author of the first canto, the one that is of interest to us here, and the said bishop added further cantos later on.[40] Mār Ammō as the author probably lent this canto such an importance that it is attested in various languages, while none of the other cantos survive in any non-Parthian idiom.[41]

In her translation of the fragmented first canto of the *Huyadagmān*, which is the Parthian original of the hymn translated below, Mary Boyce worked together with Sinologist Arthur Waley.[42] After the comparison of the Chinese and the Parthian versions, it is clear that in this hymn, the "translator" rendered two Parthian lines as four Chinese "lines" and expanded it to include Buddhist terminology, which was not part of the original.[43] N. Sims-Williams called the result of this process "a verbose Chinese paraphrase."[44]

As for the pure land influence on this specific hymn, G. Mikkelsen has shown that it shares several motifs with similar descriptions in major Pure Land scriptures.[45] On the other hand, the wording itself also owes a lot to a general Buddhist vocabulary, not only to that of the Pure Land scriptures defined in the narrow sense. Given that this hymn, like the others in the collection, is basically a translation from a non-Buddhist version, this feature is highly understandable. Even if Daoming had some freedom in rendering the Parthian original, he evidently did not wish to digress too much from it. Thus, although he frequently inserted Buddhist terms into the text, he also did his best to preserve the original Manichaean meaning. In some cases, what at first glance might seem like a Pure Land influence turns out to be already present in the Parthian original or even in the Coptic analogous texts, which indicates that Daoming was happy to find descriptions of a paradisiacal world similar to his own tradition.

Here I will present a fresh annotated translation of one of the Chinese hymns in this Manichaean collection ("In Praise of the Realm of Light," *Tan mingjie wen, H.* cols. 261–338), consisting of seventy-seven stanzas (one probably lost), four lines each. This hymn, uniquely, has numerous surviving parallels in some other languages: Parthian,[46] Sogdian,[47] and Uighur.[48] I give a prose rendition, as literal as possible. A. Waley opined that the hymn "lack[s] any poetical merit,"[49] which is definitely true for the translation presented here. Notes were added on some background information, especially on the Buddhist expressions in the Chinese text and the extant non-Chinese parallels.

## Translation

### *In Praise of the Realm of Light*

Mār Ammō

*H.* 261.
In praise of the Realm of Light
altogether 78 stanzas, (each) divided into four lines.
Composed by *mushe*[50] [teacher] Mār Ammō

*H.* 262. If our superior form[51] recognizes[52] the Light Honoured One,[53] with faith can we accept[54] the teachings on distinction.[55] The Great Saint[56] is the quintessence of all good deeds,[57] pray you send down your mercy[58] to make everybody joyous!

*H.* 263. (We) receive the Father's charitable thought by his sending a Light Envoy[59] (to us). He is able to cure our diseased soul,[60] to remove (our) topsy-turvy errors, as well as eliminate the bonds and fetters and the various afflictions,[61] to universally make (our) hearts and thoughts joyful and happy.[62]

*H.* 264. There is no darkness that will not become manifest, all will be brought to light, all the secrets will be revealed.[63] Aside from the good race,[64] who is able to comprehend the two great forces of the so-called Two Principles?[65]

*H.* 265. The first[66] (of the two principles) is without limit in height and width, light is everywhere, no dark place at all.[67] The buddhas[68] and light envoys reside within, which is the peaceful residence of the Light Honoured One.

*H.* 266. Pure[69] is the light all over the place, eternal joy[70] and tranquil extinction [*nirvāṇa*][71] without hindrance. Those (there) receive joy and happiness, without afflictions. If someone claims that there is suffering there, it is not this place.

*H.* 267. The Law halls[72] of the saints[73] are ornate and pure, and so are the monasteries[74] of the buddhas;[75] (they) constantly partake of joy and happiness[76] in the light.[77] If someone claims that there is sickness there, it is not this place.[78]

*H.* 268. Those getting to that country will not ever have sorrow and grief;[79] the saints are free,[80] all wander free from care,[81] never is one tortured, beaten, imprisoned, or bound.[82]

*H.* 269. Ornate[83] are the places there, all being pure. Wickedness and impurity do not exist (there) from the beginning; (it is) replete with joy and happiness, constant tranquility and ease. If someone claims that there is mutual fear there, it is not this place.

*H.* 270. Within the superior Realm of Light, the regions[84] are as numerous as grains of sand; they are spontaneously marvelous, ornate with jewels; the community of saints perpetually dwells within.

*H.* 271. In all these realms and regions, the diamond-jewel earth[85] penetrates and shines downwards, from infinite time, now and forever; even if somebody says so, no agitation or tremble[86] existed in this place.

*H.* 272. None of those saints are tainted by darkness[87] and desires,[88] (and since) they keep themselves at a great distance from being madly attached to male and female bodies, (how) could there be reincarnations[89] precipitating each other?

*H.* 273. The saints have a serene heart, all in harmony, how could weapons of divisions get there? They wander carefree without obstacles,[90] they do not desire lascivious acts.

*H.* 274. Ornate and pure are all the monastic places; there is no harm or conflict between them. Birth and death, destruction and impermanence, none of them exists in the Realm of Light.

*H.* 275. No grudging enemy invades its border,[91] there are no battle horses or armies guarding the frontier, no craving hearts[92] incited by the Demonic King;[93] none of these exists in the Realm of Light.

*H.* 276. The diamond-jewel earth is exceedingly marvelous; the immeasurable wonderful colors illuminate each other; all saints reside in peace without hindrance, removed from decay for good, without any anxiety.[94]

*H.* 277. The solemn countenance of the saints are most special;[95] (their) lights irradiate each other, their body being bright and crystalline. Even on the tip of their hair there is more light than the brilliance of a hundred thousand suns and moons.

*H.* 278. Light inside and outside, without dark shadow, their marvelous bodies constantly irradiate each other in myriad ways. On the Praiseworthy Diamond Earth they wander without having the tiniest weight.

*H.* 279. The famed robes[96] they wear are delightful, not made by hands they come to existence,[97] the robes of the saints are fresh and clean, they never get spoiled, no worms or earwigs (harm them).[98]

*H.* 280. In this realm famed flowers are collected, comparable to the subtle, wondrous, and upright marks, but their robes are even many times more adorned, immeasurably special and ornate is their color.

*H.* 281. The temples, monasteries, palaces, and pagodas, and also the marvelous treasures are accomplished (by themselves), and have no flaw or crack; the drinks and food, the various meals are all (made of) ambrosia;[99] the regions are rich, there is no hunger or famine there.

*H.* 282. The jeweled crown will never decay; once it is placed (on their head), it will never be removed.[100] The saints gather together and are eternally joyful; there is no misery or affliction[101] ever, no separation from each other.

*H.* 283. Green and lush is the headgear of flowers,[102] wonderfully ornate,[103] irradiating each other, fresh and never drooping or withering. The carnal tongue, if it wishes to praise, cannot comprehend them; their wondrous colors are without end, neither faint nor pale.[104]

*H.* 284. Light and constantly pure is the body of the saints, their hands and feet, limbs and joints have no obstructions; since they do not perform the deeds of birth and death, how could someone claim that they have fatigue and exhaustion?[105]

*H.* 285. Those saints are pure and detached, being constantly blissful in their person, their diamond body[106] never sleeps. Since they have no dreams and perverted ideas, how could someone claim that they have anxiety and fear?[107]

*H.* 286. The community of saints is constantly bright, all wondrous and wise. No forgetting or lack of remembrance ever existed there;[108] all the deeds and forms of the limitless worlds are visible as in a bright mirror.

*H.* 287. Sincere are the intentions in the saints' heart, no deceit or falseness ever existed there; the deeds of their body, mouth, and mind[109] are always pure; how could someone claim that they have deceitful speech?

*H.* 288. This world is replete with treasures; there is not a single deed that is not praiseworthy. The monasteries are vast and lack nothing, how could someone claim that poverty and suffering exist there?

*H.* 289. Greedy fire, flaming inflictions, and various sufferings,[110] the Realm of Light is eternal joy and void of all these. It is eternally detached from hunger and thirst, from inflicting and harming each other, there is no salty and bitter water there.[111]

*H.* 290. Fragrant and marvelous are the hundred creeks, the rivers and the seas, the water springs, and the water of life in (their) depth.[112] If (someone) enters them, he does not drift away, nor does he drown; there are no tides which would cause any harm.[113]

*H.* 291. The saints live in peace, in constant joy and happiness; their lands are praiseworthy, they do not mock each other. Sufferings arising from encountering hateful things[114] never existed there, and they do not slander each other while praising face to face.

*H.* 292. They are enthusiastically compassionate and sympathetic[115] toward each other, envy and wickedness never existed there. The speed of their steps is quicker than the wind; paralysis never impeded their four limbs.

*H.* 293. Swift are their divine feet like lightning, they can manifest themselves in all the ten directions without hindrance. It is difficult to describe their unique and miraculous form; disasters, diseases, and misfortune can never harm them.[116]

*H.* 294. Oppression, disasters, and hardships, fear and all the evil deeds, fights and attacks, harming and killing each other, these do not exist in the Realm of Light.

*H.* 295. There is no fear in the eternal peace of this world; the regions are ornate and pure, nothing that could hinder; the diamond-jewel earths have no boundaries; if someone speaks about decay and destruction, it is not this place.[117]

*H.* 296. In this place the jeweled trees[118] stand in rows;[119] the jeweled fruits are constantly growing, never do they wither. Their size is similar to each other, no worm eats them, (the trees are) green and lush, thriving by themselves.[120]

*H.* 297. Bitter and poisonous, sour and acrid, dark and black, the treasure fruit is not like this, it is fragrant and beautiful. It is not void inside and lavish outside, it is light on the surface and (also) within, having the taste of ambrosia.

*H.* 298. The root, the trunk, the branches, and the leaves of the jeweled tree are ambrosiac above and below throughout; its fragrance fills the world (the Realm of Light), the jeweled fruits shine on one another, constantly red and white.

*H.* 299. The gardens of that land are vast, adorned, and pure, wondrous fragrant air pervades the gardens.[121] Tiles, thorns,[122] and weeds, even if some claim, are nonexistent in this place.

*H.* 300. Those diamond earths are eternally glistening, shining, and brilliant inside and outside; there is nothing that cannot be seen. Jeweled earths laid on one another, regions without count, the gaze can penetrate all the details, they are all transparent and visible.

*H.* 301. The fragrant air pervades this world (the Realm of Light), it is purely one without mixture, the sea of souls;[123] it fills everything without hindrance, the saints wander in it, its fragrance is most miraculous.

*H.* 302. Like the law of emptiness, it has no alterations; the subtle and wondrous light clouds are without shadow and hindrance; clear, pure, without dust and shade, equally spread all over the various worlds.

*H.* 303. In that realm, there are myriad kinds of jeweled mountains,[124] million types of incenses emit their scent; the bodies are pure in the brilliance inside and outside, ambrosia fills and permeates it without boundaries.

*H.* 304. The pure streams from the fountainhead have no interruption; the flavor of the true ambrosia is neither muddy nor bitter.[125] The community of saints is fully fed, and lack nothing; it is not this place if there is thirst or need somewhere.

*H.* 305. Mildly blow the wondrous winds, all enjoyable; gently and pleasantly do they permeate the ten directions, lightly shaking the jeweled towers and the jeweled pavilions,[126] (thus) the small and large jeweled bells[127] constantly tinkle.

*H.* 306. Matchless is the bright and wondrous fire, its wondrous form is pure and cool, continuously does it shine; its brilliance persists all the time, never lighted or extinguished, its unique, extraordinary brilliance is hard to classify.

*H.* 307. Pure and void is the body of the fire, without poisonous heat; if one touches or enters it, he will not be burnt. That (fire) has no ash or soot; it is not this place if someone speaks of burning and scorching.

*H.* 308. The halls and palaces of that abode were not made firm by hands, they were not made by labor but were formed by themselves.[128] If someone speaks of construction, it is not this place.

*H.* 309. Those surging up from the jewel earth all have (the capacity of) seeing, hearing, and understanding, (thus) that they are able to see the unsurpassable King of Nirvana,[129] they praise, sing and extol the majesty of the Great Saint.[130]

*H.* 310. Never did that place have darkness or shadows, matchless light everywhere, inside and outside. All the figures are extremely exceptional and unique; those on the jewel earth are constantly fresh and lush.

*H.* 311. The bodily form of the saints is extremely exceptional and extraordinary; their height and width, their dignified countenance is really hard to fathom. They can penetrate down the jewel earth, there is no boundary for them; if you desire to know limitations, it is not the (proper) place.

*H.* 312. Treasurable are the wondrous bodies of those saints,[131] they have never suffered any disease, trouble, or disaster; strong and constantly peaceful, they never get feeble or old, they have no diminution, their body being always strong.

*H.* 313. Only the Great Saint knows (their) stature, how could an average person be able to estimate and describe it?[132] (Their) diamond body is inconceivable, only the saints can differentiate between their size or appearance.

*H.* 314. The appearance and countenance of the saints are rather subtle and wondrous, they emit light to infinite places, in (the past) without beginning, in the present and in the future eternity; if someone says here the body is corrupted, he speaks not of this place.

*H.* 315. (As for) the various sorts of humans and gods, saints and ordinary people (there), it is impossible[133] to praise them with carnal tongue. The various divine natures and forms are hard to fathom, and so is the diamond-jewel earth.

*H.* 316. Eternally blissful are the saints, never getting exhausted; they treasure the glory and splendor, are joyful forever; the form of their body is subtle and wondrous, always upright, it is indeed hard to express their adornment inside and outside.

*H*. 317. The brilliance of the saints is extremely unique and extraordinary, there is no interruption; they irradiate each other. The balanced heart of those saints is all in peace and harmony; if one mentions division or discord, these never existed here.

*H*. 318. Subtle and wondrous marks are on the dignified countenance of the saints; all dwell in the jeweled halls and pavilions of the monasteries. The intentions arisen, the thoughts initiated and all the conceptions of the heart are entirely and mutually irradiated and discerned, no doubt or error remains.

*H*. 319. All the saints and the other (inhabitants) of the Realm of Light, have a light and lively body without exhaustion or weight.[134] Their wondrous form wanders in all the shrines according to their thoughts; their intentions and manifested presence are entirely the same.

*H*. 320. The calm heart of the saints is constantly joyful; they perform their subtle and wondrous sounds without pause; they praise, revere, and laud without exhaustion, entirely praising the good deeds and majesty of the Light Worthy.[135]

*H*. 321. The wondrous sounds of eulogies and chants are all pleasing; their voice is pure and beautiful, all peaceful and quiet, above and below equally making wondrous sounds, which, without any interval, pervade the monasteries.

*H*. 322. The sounds performed are rather unique; they reciprocally[136] chant and praise each other all around, proclaiming the wondrous virtues. The saints, never tired, are joyful and happy forever, continuously dwelling in perpetual peace.

*H*. 323. No boundaries exist in the jewel earth of the light, this is not the (appropriate) place if you wish to find a precipice or a shore; it never had crowdedness or (needed) a place for shelter, everyone is free to wander in any place.

*H*. 324. With serene heart the saints are all in harmony, they never had divisions or fight for fame or profit.[137] Equality[138] and contentment everywhere, they dwell peacefully in their vast monasteries.

*H*. 325. Pure, wondrous, and ornamented are the monasteries; never was there any fear or difficulty (there); the large and small streets are wide and adorned,[139] wherever they want to wander, there will be peace and safety everywhere.

*H*. 326. As for the ugly, horrid faces and bodies of all the demons[140] and hungry ghosts, it is not this place if some would speak of their presence, (since they have never existed here) from the infinite (past), up to the present and (nor will they) in the future.

*H.* 327. Chickens, dogs, pigs, piglets, and other kinds (of animals) are all absent from the Realm of Nirvana.[141] It is not this place if some speaks about the various sounds made by the five kinds of animals.[142]

*H.* 328.[143] Dark shadows and earthly dust[144] does not exist in the World of Utmost Bliss;[145] the monasteries of the saints are clean, in this place there is no dimness or darkness.[146]

*H.* 329. Light fills and pervades everything,[147] long life eternally, peaceful forever; praise and joy never cease, the compassionate hearts are sincere and endlessly untroubled.[148]

*H.* 330. Constant happiness and joy never halt, the unrestrained and blissful bodies and minds (are enshrouded) by the (scent of) precious incenses. Not counting years, months, days or hours, why would one worry about the end of life and the three terminations?[149]

*H.* 331. The saints are free from birth and annihilation, the murderous demon of impermanence [death] does not attack (them). They do not commit fornication, have no unclean pregnancy; how could one claim that frenzy love exists (between them)?[150]

*H.* 332. Male and female bodies, which destruct and damage men and women, the impermanence of birth and death, the fruit of lustful desire, none of them exists in the Realm of Utmost Bliss, the places (here) are pure and void of any misery or disaster.

*H.* 333. The saints and worthies in the Realm of Light, they are far remote from conception, gathering or dispersal. The entire country is tranquil and peaceful, without any fear; it never had fright or dread, confusion or disorder.

*H.* 334. The many saints are transformed and manifested from the wondrous word of the living verb. Each manifestation is originally splendid, all of them look similar to one another, there is no difference in their appearance.

*H.* 335. The sizes of the countries are alike, no difference in the monasteries or the peaceful residences; each emit light without limit, their longevity is eternal, there is no (need to) note the years.

*H.* 336. Always peaceful and tranquil are the frontiers and the borderlands; the souls and the forms are equal, no difference in the earths (of the various countries). The [members of] the Three Constancies[151] and the Five Greatnesses[152] perpetually illuminate each other. If someone claims that there is darkness, (I say) it never existed here.

*H*. 337. This is called the Country of Eternal Bliss,[153] the original cause of existence[154] of the buddhas and the light envoys; the three miseries[155] and the eight difficulties[156] do not exist (here); birth, old age, disease, and death[157] do not follow each other.

*H*. 338. This is the single great force of the suchness,[158] revealed by Mānī,[159] the envoy of light. He was able to clarify the true way of the causes of existence, and this is how the saints all were able to achieve it.

## Notes

1 This chapter was written in the framework of a research project supported by the European Institutes for Advanced Study (EURIAS) Fellowship Programme. I also thank the Chiang Ching-kuo Foundation for International Scholarly Exchange (RG002-EU-13) and the Hungarian Academy of Sciences (MTA–ELTE–SZTE Silk Road Research Group, ELTE Eötvös Loránd University, Budapest, Hungary) for supporting my research. I am grateful to Gunner Mikkelsen for offering valuable pieces of advice.

2 Gunner B. Mikkelsen, "Sukhāvatī and the Light-World: Pure Land Elements in the Chinese Manichaean *Eulogy of the Light-World*," in *New Light on Manichaeism: Papers from the Sixth International Conference on Manichaean Studies*, ed. Jason BeDuhn (Leiden: Brill, 2009), 201. See, for example, Eileen Hsiang-Ling Hsu, "Visualization Meditation and the Siwei Icon in Chinese Buddhist Sculpture," *Artibus Asiae* 62, no. 1 (2002): 29, 9: "Toward the end of the sixth century, [as] the cult centered on Amitābha's Western paradise Sukhāvatī became increasingly popular, and eventually replaced the Maitreya cult as the dominant Buddhist school and thought"; "The most famous artworks created for this purpose are the depictions of Buddhist pure lands in the ancient cave temple site at Dunhuang, most of which date to the seventh and eighth centuries."

3 See Gábor Kósa, "The Sun, the Moon and Paradise: An Analysis of the Upper Section of the Chinese Manichaean Cosmology Painting," *Journal of Inner Asian Art and Archaeology* 6 (2015 [2011]): 171–193.

4 Mary Boyce, *The Manichaean Hymn-Cycles in Parthian* (Oxford: London Oriental Series, 1954), 15–23.

5 Boyce, *The Manichaean Hymn-Cycles*, 18–20. Also see Gábor Kósa, "The Manichaean 'New Paradise' in Text and Image," *Crossroads* [Studies on the History of Exchange Relations in the East Asia World] 13 (2016): 27–113.

6 Gregory Schopen, "Sukhāvatī As a Generalized Religious Goal in Sanskrit Mahāyāna Sūtra Literature," *Indo-Iranian Journal* 19, no. 3 (1977): 177–210.

7 Gérard Fussman, "La place des Sukhāvatī-Vyūha dans le bouddhisme indien," *Journal Asiatique* 287, no. 2 (1999): 523–586.

8 Matthew Kapstein, "Pure Land Buddhism in Tibet?" in *Approaching the Land of Bliss: Religious Praxis in the Cult of Amitābha,* ed. Richard Payne and Kenneth Tanaka (Honolulu: University of Hawai'i Press, 2004), 16–41.

9 Todd T. Lewis, "From Generalized Goal to Tantric Subordination: Sukhāvatī in the Indic Buddhist Traditions of Nepal," in *Approaching the Land of Bliss: Religious Praxis in the Cult of Amitābha,* ed. Richard K. Payne and Kenneth K. Tanaka (Honolulu: University of Hawai'i Press, 2004), 236–263.

10 Daniel A. Getz Jr., "T'ien-t'ai Pure Land Societies and the Creation of the Pure Land Patriarchate," in *Buddhism in the Sung,* ed. Peter N. Gregory and Daniel A. Getz Jr. (Honolulu: University of Hawai'i Press, 1999), 477; Robert H. Sharf, "On Pure Land Buddhism and Ch'an/Pure Land Syncretism in Medieval China," *T'oung Pao* (second series) 88, no. 4/5 (2002): 282–331.

11 Robert H. Sharf, *Coming to Terms with Chinese Buddhism: A Reading of the* Treasure Store Treatise (Honolulu: University of Hawai'i Press, 2002), 8.

12 Sharf, "On Pure Land Buddhism," 286.

13 Galen Amstutz, "The Politics of Pure Land Buddhism in India," *Numen* 45, no. 1 (1998): 76.

14 Getz, "T'ien-t'ai Pure Land Societies," 477.

15 In a previous work, I made an attempt to demonstrate the presence of some motifs from the Guanyin chapter of the *Lotus sūtra* in the first hymn of the *Hymnscroll*; see Gábor Kósa, "Buddhist Monsters in the Chinese Manichaean *Hymnscroll* and the *Pumen* Chapter of the *Lotus sūtra,*" *The Eastern Buddhist* 44 (2014): 27–76.

16 The present introduction basically follows Gábor Kósa, "Buddhist and Pseudo-Buddhist Motifs in the Chinese Manichaean *Hymnscroll,*" in *Frontiers and Boundaries—Encounters on China's Margins,* ed. Ildikó Bellér-Hann and Zsombor Rajkai (Wiesbaden: Harrassowitz, 2012), 50–53.

17 Yabuki Yoshiteru, *Manikyō to Tōyō no shoshūkyō.* (Tōkyō: Kōsei Publishing Co., 1988), 25 and 85; M. A. Stein, *Serindia: Detailed Report of Explorations in Central Asia and Westernmost China Carried Out and Described under the Orders of H.M. Indian Government by Aurel Stein,* vol. 2 (Oxford: Clarendon Press, 1921), 922; Ernst Waldschmidt and Wolfgang Lentz, "A Chinese Manichaean Hymnal from Tun-huang," *Journal of the Royal Asiatic Society* 58, no. 2 (1926): 117.

18 Ernst Waldschmidt and Wolfgang Lentz, "Die Stellung Jesu im Manichäismus," *Abhandlungen der königlichen preussischen Akademie der Wissenschaften* 4 (1926): 1–131; Ernst Waldschmidt and Wolfgang Lentz, *Manichäische Dogmatik aus chinesischen und iranischen Texten* (Berlin: Verlag der Akademie der Wissenschaften, 1933); Helwig Schmidt-Glintzer, trans. *Chinesische Manichaica. Mit textkritischen Anmerkungen und einem Glossar* (Wiesbaden: Otto Harrassowitz, 1987).

19 Samuel N. C. Lieu, "Manichaean Art and Texts from the Silk Road," in *Manichaeism in Central Asia and China* (Leiden: E. J. Brill, 1998), 51.

20 Tsui Chi, trans. "Mo Ni Chiao Hsia Pu Tsan: The Lower (Second?) Section of the Manichaean Hymns," *Bulletin of the School of Oriental and African Studies* 11 (1943): 199–208; Waley apud Boyce, *The Manichaean Hymn-Cycles*, pp. 67–77; Campany apud Jason D. BeDuhn, *The Manichaean Body in Disciple and Ritual* (Baltimore: Johns Hopkins University Press, 2000), 114–115, 303.

21 Peter Bryder, "Huyadagmān," in *Geng Shimin xiansheng 70 shouchen jinian* 70, ed. Ji Zengxiang (Beijing: Minzu Chubanshe, 1999), 252–275.

22 Lin Wushu, *Monijiao ji qi dongjian* (Beijing: Zhonghua Shuju, 1987), 234–264; Lin Wushu, *Monijiao ji qi dongjian* (Taibei: Shuxin Chubanshe, 1997), 287–316; Rui Chuanming, "Ru Hua Monijiao zhi 'fojiaohua' ji qi chuanbo—yi 'Xiabu zan Tan mingjie wen' wei li," *Chuantong Zhongguo yanjiu jikan* 5 (2008): 1–22. http://www.historicalchina.net/admin/WebEdit/ UploadFile/FragCM.pdf.

23 Waldschmidt and Lentz, "A Chinese Manichaean Hymnal from Tunhuang," 118; Gunner B. Mikkelsen, "Quickly Guide Me to the Peace of the Pure Land: Christology and Buddhist Terminology in the Chinese Manichaean *Hymnscroll*," in *The Chinese Face of Jesus Christ*, ed. Roman Malek (Sankt Augustin: Institut Monumenta Serica and China-Zentrum; Nettetal: Steyler Verlag, 2002), 220; Lin Wushu, "The Original Manuscript of a Chinese Manichaean Hymnal," in *The Manichaean NOYΣ. Proceedings of the International Symposium organized from the 31st of July to the 3rd of August 1991*, ed. Aloïs Van Tongerloo and Johannes van Oort (Lovanii: International Association of Manichaean Studies—Center of the History of Religions—BCMS (Louvain), 1995), 178–179; Lin, *Monijiao ji qi dongjian*, 239–240.

24 Lin, "The Original Manuscript," 179–180.

25 Lin, "The Original Manuscript," 180–181 and Mikkelsen, "Quickly Guide Me," 219–220.

26 Lionel Giles, *Descriptive Catalogue of the Chinese Manuscripts from Tunhuang in the British Museum* (London: Trustees of the British Museum, 1957), 229; eighth century, Gustav Haloun and Walter B. Henning, "The Compendium of the Doctrines and Styles of the Teaching of Mani, the Buddha of Light," *Asia Major* 3 (1952): 189 note 2; early ninth century, Waldschmidt and Lentz, "A Chinese Manichaean Hymnal from Tun-huang," 8; between 762–832, Lin, *Monijiao*, 216; Gunner B. Mikkelsen, "The Fragments of Chinese Manichaean Texts from the Turfan Region," in *Turfan Revisited—The First Century of Research into the Arts and Cultures of the Silk Road*, ed. D. Durkin-Meisterernst et al. (Berlin: Dietrich Reimer Verlag, 2004), 213; between 762–842 cf. Lin, "The Original Manuscript," 181.

27 Lin, *Monijiao*, 72.

28 Yu Wanli, "Dunhuang Monijiao 'Xiabu zan' xieben niandai xintan," *Dunhuang Tulufan yanjiu* 1 (1995): 37–46.

29 See e.g. Peter Bryder, *The Chinese Transformation of Manichaeism. A Study of Chinese Manichaean Terminology* (Löberöd: Plus Ultra, 1985), 47–62, Ma Xiaohe. "Monijiao 'Xiabu zan, Chusheng zanwen' xin kao," in *Monijiao yu gudai xiyu shi yanjiu* (Beijing: Renmin daxue chubanshe, 2008), 164–196; Ma Xiaohe, "Monijiao 'Xiabu zan, Chusheng zanwen' xu kao," in *Monijiao yu gudai xiyu shi* (Beijing: Renmin daxue chubanshe, 2008), 197–205; Yoshida Yutaka. "Manichaean Aramaic in the Chinese *Hymnscroll*," *Bulletin of the School of Oriental and African Studies* 46, no. 2 (1983): 326–331.

30 Lieu, "Manichaean Art," 50.

31 Waldschmidt and Lentz, "A Chinese Manichaean Hymnal from Tun-huang," 118; Mikkelsen, "Quickly Guide Me," 220.

32 Werner Sundermann, "Iranian Manichaean Texts in Chinese Remake. Translation and Transformation," in *Cina e Iran. Da Alessandro Magno alla Dinastia Tang,* ed. A. Cadonna and L. Lanciotti (Firenze: Leo S. Olschki Editore, 1996), 111–118.

33 Thomas Thilo, "Einige Bemerkungen zu zwei chinesisch-manichäischen Textfragmenten der Berliner Turfan-Sammlung," in *Ägypten—Vorderasien—Turfan. Probleme der Edition und Bearbeitung altorientalischer Handschriften,* ed. H. Klengel and W. Sundermann (Berlin: Akademie-Verlag, 1991); Mikkelsen, "The Fragments."

34 Chen Jinguo and Lin Yun, "Mingjiao de xin faxian—Fujian Xiapu xian Monijiao shiji bianxi," in *Bu zhi yu yi—Zhongyang meiyuan "yiwen ketang" mingjia jiangyan lu,* ed. Li Shaowen (Beijing: Beijing Daxue Chubanshe, 2010), 343–389.

35 G. Mikkelsen ("Quickly Guide Me," 221) suggests that Zhiyan simply reused the paper without heeding its contents.

36 J. P. Asmussen, "Mār Ammō," *Encyclopædia Iranica,* I/9 (1989): 979; available online at http://www.iranicaonline.org/articles/ammo-mar-mid, accessed on June 12, 2015; Claudia Leurini, "A New Manichaean Fragment Dedicated to Ammō," in *Proceedings of the 5th Conference of the Societas Iranologica held in Ravenna, 6-11 October 2003: Vol. 1. Ancient and Middle Iranian Studies,* ed. Antonio Panaino and Andrea Piras (Milano: Mimesis, 2006), 561–566.

37 Walter B. Henning, "Annotations to Mr. Tsui's Translation', app. to Tsui Chi, 'Mo Ni Chiao Hsia Pu Tsan: The Lower (Second?) Section of the Manichaean Hymns,'" *Bulletin of the School of Oriental and African Studies* 11 (1943): 216 note 6; Yoshida Yutaka, "Kanyaku Manikyō bunken ni okeru kanji onsha sareta chūsei irango ni tsuite," *Nairiku Ajia gengo no kenkyū* 2 (1986): § 10; Werner Sundermann, "Probleme der Edition iranisch-manichäischer Texte," in *Ägypten—Vorderasien—Turfan. Probleme der Edition und Bearbeitung altorientalischer Handschriften,* ed. H. Klengel and W. Sundermann (Berlin:

Akademie-Verlag, 1991), 110–111, Bryder, "Huyadagmān," 259–262, Gunner B. Mikkelsen, *Dictionary of Manichaean Texts. Vol. III. Texts from Central Asia and China. Part 4. Dictionary of Manichaean Texts in Chinese* (Turnhout: Brepols, 2006), 105 (2009), 206.

38 Edward G. Pulleyblank, *Lexicon of Reconstructed Pronunciation in Early Middle Chinese, Late Middle Chinese, and Early Mandarin* (Vancouver: University of British Columbia Press, 1991), 218, 209.

39 Werner Sundermann, *The Manichaean Hymn Cycles* Huyadagmān *and* Angad Rōšnān *in Parthian and Sogdian* (London: SOAS, 1990), 9; Sundermann, "Probleme der Edition," 110–111.

40 Sundermann, *The Manichaean Hymn Cycles,* 11, Sundermann, "Probleme der Edition," 111.

41 Sundermann, *The Manichaean Hymn Cycles,* 11.

42 Boyce, *The Manichaean Hymn-Cycles,* 67 note 1.

43 Cf. Bryder, *The Chinese Transformation,* 66.

44 Nicholas Sims-Williams, "A New Fragment from the Parthian Hymn-Cycle *Huyadagmān,*" in *Études irano-aryennes offertes à Gilbert Lazard,* ed. C.-H. de Fouchécour and Ph. Gignoux (Paris: Association pour l'avancement des études iråniennes, 1989), 322.

45 Mikkelsen, "Sukhāvatī and the Light-World."

46 Boyce, *The Manichaean Hymn-Cycles,* 66–77.

47 Sundermann, *The Manichaean Hymn Cycles.*

48 *H.* 326–331, Walter B. Henning, "A Fragment of the Manichaean Hymn-Cycles in Old Turkish," *Asia Major* (n.s.) 7 (1959): 122–124.

49 Waley's opinion cited in Boyce, *The Manichaean Hymn-Cycles,* 67 note 1.

50 After the head of the entire church, *mushe* (Middle Persian *hmwc'g*; Parthian *'mwcg*), i.e., teacher, is the second most important rank in the Manichaean church hierarchy. There were supposedly twelve teachers in the clergy, and the title is equally attested in the Western areas of Manichaeism (Greek διδάσκαλος; Latin *magister*; Arabic *al-mucallimūna*).

51 Given that the Chinese version completely lacks the reference to *hwydgm'n* ("fortunate"), which is the first word of the Parthian original (I/1), I presume that Daoming might have associated this word with *hwydgyft,* which can also mean "having a good form" (Desmond Durkin-Meisterernst, *Dictionary of Manichaean Texts. Vol. III.1. Dictionary of Manichaean Middle Persian and Parthian* (Turnhout: Brepols, 2004), 195), and thus he translated it as *shangxiang* 上相, "superior/excellent form." References to the Parthian original and its English translation are from Boyce, *The Manichaean Hymn-Cycles,* 66–77.

52 The Parthian (I/1) mentions "knew, understood" (*frwd'd,* Durkin-Meisterernst, *Dictionary of Manichaean Texts,* 157), a good equivalent of *wu* 悟.

53 *Mingzun* 明尊 designates the Father of Greatness, the king of the Realm of Light, also see *H.* 265. The expression resonates with *shizun* 世尊.

54 *Xinshou* 信受 is a common Buddhist compound that implies the faithful acceptance of a teaching. The Parthian original only has "accepted" (Durkin-Meisterernst, *Dictionary of Manichaean Texts,* 269: *pdgryft*); thus inserting "faith" was Daoming's contribution.

55 The otherwise Buddhist *fenbie shuo* 分別說 probably bears a surplus meaning in the Manichaean context, where distinguishing Light and Darkness is the ultimate goal of the religion; see e.g. another Manichaean text from Dunhuang, the so-called *Traité* cols. 65–66: "Those five light powers reside in a composite (i.e., mixed) body; therefore the good men [*electi*] distinguish the Two Powers (i.e., Light and Darkness) to make them distinct (其五明力住和合體。因彼善人銓簡二力，各令分別)." The Parthian original (*wcyhyšn*) simply says "teaching," "instruction," "interpretation" (Boyce, *The Manichaean Hymn-Cycles,* 66–67; Durkin-Meisterernst, *Dictionary of Manichaean Texts,* 338), although Daoming might have possibly associated this word with *wcyd* ("to discriminate"), which has the same meaning as *fenbie*. The Sogdian version has "holy word" (Sundermann, *The Manichaean Hymn Cycles,* 23).

56 Great Saint (*dasheng* 大聖), ultimately a Buddhist term, is used in connection with various members of the Manichaean pantheon. The Parthian original has *šhryd'r* ("sovereign").

57 Good deed (*shanye* 善業, also in *H.* 320) is a widely used Buddhist term (Sanskrit *kuśala, kuśalaṃkarma*). For the Buddhist terms here simply mentioned, see e.g. Charles A. Muller's Digital Dictionary of Buddhism, http://buddhism-dict.net/ddb/, accessed June 2015, the glossary in Luis O. Gómez, *The Land of Bliss: The Paradise of the Buddha of Measureless Light: Sanskrit and Chinese Versions of the Sukhāvativyūha Sutras* (Honolulu: University of Hawai'i Press, 1996), 280–333, or any other major Buddhist dictionary. One might wonder if Daoming perhaps tried to unfold the meaning of the Parthian *kyrbkr* (beneficent) here, which appears in the original (Boyce, *The Manichaean Hymn-Cycles,* 66–67).

58 The Parthian original has "show mercy to us" (*kr 'br 'm'h 'xšd'gyft*).

59 The fragmented Parthian original (I/2) only has "the envoy of the father" (*[fry]št[g] cy [pdr]*).

60 The Parthian original has "make the souls healthy" or "heal the souls" (*kryd gy'n'n dr wšt*). It is clear from this phrase that Chinese *xing* 性 ("nature") was used to render *gy'n,* i.e., "soul" in Parthian (Bryder, *The Chinese Transformation*, 68–70).

61 *Fannao* 煩惱 (also in *H.* 266) is the standard Chinese Buddhist equivalent of Sanskrit *kleśa*. The Parthian original of the long Chinese phrase simply has "removes sorrows" (*'zgyrwyd 'nd'[g]*).

62 "Receiving joy and happiness" (*de kuaile* 得快樂) is a Buddhist compound, among others also appearing in Pure Land sutras, e.g., *Fo shuo wuliang shou jing T.* 0360.12:0272a17. *Kuaile* is one the numerous possible Chinese translations of Sanskrit *sukha*.
The fragmented Parthian original has "gives joy to all" (*['w hrwyn dh]yd [š'd] yfṯ*), *pu* 普 being equivalent with *'w hrwyn* ("to all"), and *kuaile* 快樂 with *š'dyfṯ* ("joy" or "happiness").

63 The Sogdian version explicitly says that it will be the envoy who reveals these secrets: "Every hidden secrets thou revealest; thou un[veilest] the two powers [which] are hidden in this world" (Sundermann, *The Manichaean Hymn Cycles,* 23).

64 Good race (*shanzhong* 善種) alludes to those from the Realm of Light, basically the Manichaean believers.

65 *Liangzong* 兩宗 is obviously equivalent with the notion of the two eternal and antagonistic principles, otherwise called *erzong* 二宗 in Chinese Manichaeism.

66 Cf. the Sogdian version: "One [i.e. the First] is the Light Para[dise], without borders and [limits]." (N. Sims-Williams' interpretation apud Sundermann, *The Manichaean Hymn Cycles,* 23 note 12).

67 According to the Manichaean imagination, the Realm of Light is infinite "upwards" (height) and to the sides (width), but not "downwards." This partial infinity is especially detailed in Western descriptions of Manichaeism; see Byard Bennett, "*Iuxta unum latus terra tenebrarum*: The Division of Primordial Space in Anti-Manichaean Writers' Description of the Manichaean Cosmogony," in *The Light and the Darkness. Studies in Manichaeism and its World,* ed. Paul Mirecki and Jason BeDuhn (Leiden: Brill, 2001), 68–78. On the other hand, the Sogdian M178 mentions both the limitless height and depth of the Light Earth (Walter B. Henning, "A Sogdian Fragment of the Manichaean Cosmogony," *Bulletin of the School of Oriental and African Studies* 12 (1948): 307–308): "in *height it is beyond *reach (?), its *depth cannot be perceived" *(kyy 'ty-šyy wyy sk'wyẖ 'βy'p nyyst 'rṯyšyy xww n'ywk'wyy nyy "p'ṯ βwṯ).* M178 seems to preserve several analogies of this hymn (see Badri Gharib, "New Light on Two Words in the Sogdian Version of the Realm Light," in *Studia Manichaica. IV. Internationaler Kongress zum Manichäismus, Berlin, 14.–18. Juli 1997,* ed. Ronald E. Emmerick, Werner Sundermann, and Peter Zieme (Berlin: Akademie Verlag, 2000), 261–262; Rui, "Ru Hua Monijiao," 16–20.

68 The word buddha (*fó* 佛, also in *H.* 315, *H.* 337) is used to translate Parthian *bg* and Parthian / Middle Persian: *yzd* (god), and is mainly used to express

the idea of an emanated being, but in the Dunhuang manuscripts it is never used to refer to the originator of all these emanations, i.e., the king of the Realm of Light, the Father of Greatness (Bryder, *The Chinese Transformation,* 83). Although the word thus has a more general meaning of any deity, I preserve the translation "buddha," as it was evidently understood by the contemporary Chinese believers.

69 *Qingjing* 清淨 (also see *H.* 269, *H.* 284, *H.* 287, *H.* 302, *H.* 303, *H.* 325, *H.* 328, *H.* 332) is used in the sense of not being tainted by any earthly or evil defilement. In Buddhist texts it is used to translate Sanskrit *pariśuddhi, viśuddhi,* or *nirmala.*

70 *Changle* 常樂 (also in *H.* 285, *H.* 289, *H.* 316, *H.* 330, *H.* 337) is a frequently used Buddhist compound.

71 *Jimie* 寂滅 is a typical Buddhist term, also used in Pure Land scriptures (e.g., *Fo shuo wuliangshou jing, T.* 0360.12:0269c06, *T.* 0360.12:0274a10-11, *Fo shuo da Amituo jing, T.* 0364.12:0329c19).

72 Dharma halls (*fatang* 法堂) here naturally refer to celestial abodes.

73 The community of saints or multitude of saints (*shengzhong* 聖眾, also in *H.* 268, *H.* 270, *H.* 273, *H.* 277, *H.* 279, *H.* 284, *H.* 286, *H.* 301, *H.* 304, *H.* 311, *H.* 314, *H.* 316, *H.* 317, *H.* 320, *H.* 324, *H.* 334, *H.* 338) here seems to basically refer to the chosen ones (*electi*), who have already returned to the Realm of Light, though the compound itself is widely used in Buddhist scriptures.

74 The word for monastery here (*qielansuo* 伽藍所), an existing but not too frequently used Buddhist compound, comes from *sengqielanmo* 僧伽藍摩, a transcription of Sanskrit *saṅghārāma.* In this hymn, it appears in several other forms: *qielanchu* 伽藍處 (*H.* 274), *qielansi* 伽藍寺 (*H.* 324), or simply *qielan* 伽藍 (*H.* 288, *H.* 318, *H.* 321, *H.* 325, *H.* 328). The Buddhist scriptures usually apply the term *sengqielan* 僧伽藍, which, however, contains the character *seng* 僧 "(Buddhist) monk," and Daoming evidently tried to avoid this word. Accordingly, *seng* appears only once in the entire *Hymnscroll,* where its use was unavoidable, since the *triratna* is mentioned: "(the ignorant people) scold the buddha(s), destroy the law, and treat the true monks rudely [謗佛毀法慢真僧]" (*H.* 109). Interestingly, Daoming uses the expression "true monks," in this context, evidently referring to the Manichaean *electi*, as if indicating their difference from the Buddhist monks.

75 The Parthian original (I/6) mentions monasteries (*m'nyst'n*) and dwelling place or abode (*'r'm*).

76 *Changshou kuaile* 常受快樂 (or *heng shou kuaile* 恒受快樂) appears in several Buddhist texts.

77 The Parthian original only has "they are happy in the light" (*wyš[mnynd pd r]wšn*).

78 The Parthian version only has "they know no pain" (*drd ny z'n[ynd]*).

79 The Parthian original (I/7) only has "All who enter there, stay for eternity" (*hrw ky 'wwd 'dyhyn[d] [']wyštynd y'wyd'n*).

80 The reference to a state of freedom (*zizai* 自在) or unobstructed existence is a recurrent characteristic of those residing in the celestial realm.

81 Although *xiaoyao* 逍遙 (also in *H*. 273, *H*. 323) ultimately goes back to the Taoist concept of carefree wandering, famously described in the first chapter of the *Zhuangzi*, it is also frequently used in Buddhist texts.

82 The Parthian version only has "[Neither] blows nor torture [ever] overcome them" (*'wš'[n kd'c ny] trwyd ny j[xm] u dyjw'r*). The next ten strophes are missing in the Parthian.

83 *Zhuangyan* 莊嚴 (also see *H*. 280, *H*. 283, *H*. 316, *H*. 334) is a typically Buddhist term ("decorated, ornamented, adorned"), which, in a Buddhist context, translates, among others, Sanskrit *alaṃkāraka, vyūha, śobha,* or *śobhana;* see Stephen F. Teiser, "Ornamenting the Departed: Notes on the Language of Chinese Buddhist Ritual Texts," *Asia Major*, 3rd series, 22, no. 1 (2009): 201–237.

84 The various regions (*zhu guotu* 諸國土, also see *H*. 300, *H*. 335) denote the Aeons of Aeons, one of the so-called Five Greatnesses (Gharib, "New Light," 260).

85 This phrase (*jin'gang baodi* 金剛寶地, also see in *H*. 276, *H*. 295, *H*. 315; or the short version, *baodi* 寶地 in *H*. 300, *H*. 309, *H*. 310, *H*. 311, *H*. 323) appears in Buddhist texts as well (e.g., *Da fangguang huayanjing T.* 0278.09:0413a26). The meaning, however, is inherently Manichaean: it denotes the basis of the Realm of Light, of the so-called Three Constancies. The Sogdian text M178 also mentions diamond (Henning, "A Sogdian Fragment," 307–308): "its divine pavement is of the substance of diamond (*vajra*) that does not shake for ever" (*βγ'nyq pršprn '(β)jyr'ync kyy 'ty ''yqwn nyy 'βnwtyy*). Also see Sogdian M5271/r/10–11 with "Diamond Earth" (*βj(yr)nyẖ [ʾ](s)pndʾr(m)[t]*) (Elio Provasi, "The Diamond Earth. A Manichaean Sogdian Eulogy," in *Commentationes Iranicae. Сборник статей к 90-летию Владимира Ароновича Лившица* [The collection of articles on the 90th anniversary of Vladimir Aronovich Livshits], ed. Sergius Tokhtasev et Paulus Luria (Saint Petersburg: Nestor-Historia, 2013), 380), and the following Uighur passage (U262 [= T I D 20] /v/2–5; Provasi, "The Diamond Earth," 381; Peter Zieme, *Manichäisch-türkische Texte. Texte, Übersetzung, Anmerkungen* (Berlin: Akademie-Verlag, 1975), 31–32): "and besides, that light, gleaming, diamond-colored, blessed Land, which is the solid, firm, not-shaking, not-swaying seat and throne of all the gods."

86 See M178 above (Henning, "A Sogdian Fragment," 307–308, parallel pointed out by him in note 2): "that does not shake forever" (*kyy 'ty ''yqwn nyy*

*'βnwtyy)*, and Uighur *U.* 262 (above) *täprämäz kamšamaz* ("not-shaking and not-swaying"). Also see Augustine's description (Aug., *Contra Ep. Fund.* 13): "Thus his shining kingdoms are founded above the light and blessed land, in such a way that they cannot be moved or shaken by anyone" (ita autem fundata sunt eiusdem splendidissima regna supra lucidam et beatam terram, ut a nullo umquam aut moueri aut concuti possint), see Greg Fox, John Sheldon, trans., Samuel N. C. Lieu, comm., *Greek and Latin Sources on Manichaean Cosmogony and Ethics* (Turnhout: Brepols, 2010), 8–9.

87 "(Not) being tainted by darkness" ([*bu*] *ran wuming* [不]染无明) also appears in several Buddhist texts, though there *wuming* refers to *avidyā* and not the literal sense of the word used by the Manichaeans.

88 Lust or sexual desire (*yinyu* 婬慾, also in *H.* 273, *H.* 331) is a Buddhist term, far more frequently written as 婬欲 in Buddhist scriptures (and in *H.* 332 here).

89 *Lunhui* 輪迴 is a typical Buddhist notion, often appearing as *lunhui* 輪廻 or, more frequently, as *lunzhuan* 輪轉.

90 Hindrances or obstacles (*zhang'ai* 鄣礙 [also in *H.* 276, *H.* 293, *H.* 301], usually written as 障礙), or their lack, are widely used in Buddhist writings, prominently featuring in Huayan and Pure Land scriptures. Expressions like "removing all hindrances" (*jin chu yiqie zhu zhang'ai* 盡除一切諸障礙) are frequently followed by the motif of seeing Amitābha and rebirth at Sukhāvatī (*de wangsheng Anlecha* 得往生安樂剎), see e.g. *Avatamsaka sūtra, T.* 0293.10:0848a09-10, *Bangwen wenlei, T.* 1969A.47.0159b11.

91 Cf. Sogdian M178 (Henning, "A Sogdian Fragment," 307–308): "No enemy and no *injurer walk this Earth" (*nyy s'n 'ty-nyy (')wyjṯq'ryyẖ prywyδδ z'y 'nšprṯ*). Cf. Gharib, "New Light," 261 note 25.

92 *Tan'ai (xin)* 貪愛(心) is a widely used Buddhist term.

93 In Chinese Manichaeism, Mowang 魔王 is the personification of the ultimate evil principle, while in Buddhism "the king of *māras*" is more limited in power.

94 *Younao* 憂惱 (sorrow, anxiety, suffering, etc.) is a Buddhist compound, among others translating Sanskrit *śoka, duḥkha, durmanas, parikheda, saṃvega, upadrava.*

95 *Qite* 奇特, often applied in connection with appearance (also in *H.* 280, *H.* 293, *H.* 299, *H.* 306, *H.* 311), is basically a Buddhist word, the Chinese translation of Sanskrit *acintya, adbhuta,* or *āścarya.*

96 On the metaphor of robes in the *Hymnscroll*, see Johan Ferreira, "A Comparison of the Clothing Metaphor in the Hymn of the Pearl and the Chinese Manichaean Hymnscroll," in *Studia Manichaica. IV. Internationaler Kongress zum Manichäismus, Berlin, 14.-18. Juli 1997*, ed. Ronald E. Emmerick, Werner Sundermann, and Peter Zieme (Berlin: Akademie Verlag, 2000), 207–219.

97 Here the Parthian version (I/18) is close: "[The clothes which they wear none] had made by hand" (*[pdmwcn cy pdmwcynd kyc ny] (q)yrd pd dst*). Also see the Sogdian M178 (Henning, "A Sogdian Fragment," 308): "By supernatural power it (the Fragrant Air) shall, by itself, bring into being (create) the gods' marvel dress and garment, throne, diadem, and fragrant wreath, ornaments, and finery of all kinds."

98 The Parthian original, as I. D. Băncilă ("Ants, or Moths? Insects Not to Be Found in the Manichean Kingdom of Light, According to the Parthian *Huyadagmān* I.18," *ARCHÆVS. Studies in the History of Religions* XIII (2009): 189–198) argued, probably had "no moths are in them" (*[wy]w pd hwyn ny 's[t]*), M. Boyce originally restored "ant" (*[mr]w*) with a question mark (Boyce, *The Manichaean Hymn-Cycles*, 69).

99 *Ganlu* 甘露 (here mistakenly written as 甘路), also appearing in *H.* 297, *H.* 298, *H.* 303, *H.* 304, is a constant feature in the celestial realm and is associated with immortality. It is the translation of Sanskrit *amṛta* or *soma,* usually rendered with the Greek word *ambrosia*. The Sogdian M178 also mentions "ambrosial food" (*nwšynyy xwrṯ*), already pointed out by Henning ("A Sogdian Fragment," 308 note 5).

100 Crown is a general motif, the *Huyadagmān* also mentions it in other cantos; here I cite a Sogdian fragment from the fifth canto: "For all who are therein rejoice in eternal bliss and have a royal diadem on their head(s)" (*T.* II D 170, David N. MacKenzie, "Two Sogdian *Hwydgm'n* Fragments," in *Papers in Honour of Professor Mary Boyce*, II (*Acta Iranica* 25), ed. Jacques Duchesne-Guillemin and Pierre Lecoq (Leiden: Brill, 1985), 426).

101 *Ku'nao* 苦惱 is the Chinese translation of Sanskrit *duḥkha, dukha, kāraṇā,* or *kheda*.

102 In addition to the crown, the wreath is another symbol of the pure, redeemed state. Parthian "verdant garland" (*pwsg zrgwng*) and Sogdian "fragrant wreath" (M178 [Henning, "A Sogdian Fragment," 307–308]: *βwδ'ndc 'ps'k*) both indicate their being made of flowers, which is explicit in the Chinese version (*huaguan* 花冠), cf. Bryder, *The Chinese Transformation,* 65; Gharib, "New Light," 260 note 19. An excerpt from the Manichaean *Amatorium Canticum,* preserved in the ex-Manichaean Augustine's *Contra Faustum* (XV, 5–6), uses a similar image in connection with the Father of Greatness: "you describe the supreme reigning monarch, forever sceptre-bearing, crowned with floral wreaths [*floreis coronis cinctum*] and possessing a fiery countenance?" (Fox and Sheldon, *Greek and Latin Sources*, 20–21).

103 *Miao zhuangyan* 妙莊嚴, the Chinese translation of Sanskrit *su-maṇḍita* or *sv-alaṃkṛta,* frequently features in Buddhist texts.

104 The entire Parthian verse (I/22) is as follows: "Their verdant garlands never fade; they are wreathed brightly, in numberless colors" (*hwyn pwsg zrgwng*

*y'wyd'n ny wmysy(d) 'wd 'm(y')st pd nys'gyft pd 'n's'g gwng)*. See the exact parallel between Parthian "never fade" (*ny wmysyd*) and *bu danbo* 不淡薄 (Gharib, "New Light," 260 note 19).

105 The entire Parthian verse (I/23) is as follows: "Heaviness and drooping do not exist in their bodies, paralysis does not affect any of (their) limbs" (*gr'nyft 'w[d] 'mb'hg ny 'st pd hwyn (t)[nb'r] 'wd wyg'n ny 'h'z pd hrwyn hnd['m]*).

106 The compound *jin'gang zhi ti* 金剛之體, though relatively rarely, makes appearances in Buddhist texts as well.

107 The entire Parthian verse (I/24) is as follows: "heavy sleep never overtakes their souls. Deceptive dreams and delusions [are unknown among them]" (*gr'n xwmr 'by hwyn gryw'n ny g[yrwyd] 'wd xw(mr) d(r)'w'ng u wdybyšn [pd hwyn ny 'st]*). The Sogdian 18102/18152/v/1-3 says: "The heavy sleep does not seize their body and never ever do they see demonic dream visions" (Christiane Reck, "Reste einer Soghdischen Version von *Huyadagmān* I in der Form eines Responsoriums zwischen Erwählten und Hörer," in *Languages of Iran: Past and Present. Iranian Studies in Memoriam David Neil McKenzie*, ed. Dieter Weber (Wiesbaden: Harrassowitz, 2005), 160: "Der schwere Schlaf ergreift ihre Körper nicht und die dämonischen Traumvisionen sehen sie nie auf ewig"). The latter motif may refer to the fate of the *auditores*, who, unlike the *electi* in the paradise, are exposed to such visions, as described in the rather reliable *al-Fihrist* (W. Sundermann's suggestion apud Reck, "Reste," 155 note 13): "he [the Hearer] remains in the world like a man who sees horrible things in his dream"; see Bayard Dodge, trans., *The Fihrist of al-Nadim. A Tenth-Century Survey of Muslim Culture* (New York: Columbia Press, 1970), 796.

108 The Parthian original (I/25) has "[there is no forget]fullness in [their thought]" (*'wd fr'mw)štyft n[y 'st pd hwyn 'ndyšyšn]*).

109 *Shen, kou, yi ye* 身口意業 is a widely used Buddhist expression, and is the Chinese equivalent of Sanskrit *kāya-vāṅ-manas-karman*.

110 *Xinku* 辛苦 is a common Buddhist expression.

111 The Parthian equivalent (I/28) mentions hunger (*wšynd*), anguish (*'njwgyft*), and thirst (*tšyndyft*), an Uighur fragment (Ot. Ry. 1110 recto) mentions the lack of heat and cold, hunger and thirst, disease, aging, and death (Peter Zieme, "Die Preisung de Lichtreichs nach einem alttürkischen Fragment in London," in *Exegisti monumenta: Festschrift in Honour of Nicholas Sims-Williams*, ed. Werner Sundermann, Almut Hintze, and François de Blois (Wiesbaden: Harrassowitz, 2009), 595). The Coptic *Psalm-book* (65, 20–24) has an analogous description: "Thou hast reached the place wherein there is neither heat nor cold, where there is neither hunger nor thirst, and the . . . body. Thou art worthy of the Paradise of the Gods . . . not preventing thee from rejoicing and singing unto God (?)," see Charles R. C. Allberry, *A Manichaean Psalm-Book. Part II* (Stuttgart: W. Kohlhammer, 1938), 65.

112 A similar image can be found in Augustine's account: "the imaginary dwellings of the angels where the wholesome breeze blows and to fields which abound in sweet scent and hills and trees and seas and rivers which flow forever with sweet nectar [*maria et flumina, dulce nectar fluunt per cuncta saecula*]" (Fox and Sheldon, *Greek and Latin Sources,* 20–21).

113 The Parthian original (I/29) reads as follows: "[The waters] of all (its) lakes give out a [wondrous] fragrance. [Floods and] drowning are never [known among them]" (*['b] cy hrwyn zryh'n frbwy(d) ['škyft hynw'r u n](x)'b hmgyc [pd hwyn ny 'st]*).

114 *Yuanzeng huiku* 怨憎會苦 is a typical Buddhist phrase, the Chinese equivalent of Sanskrit *apriya-saṃprayoga-duḥkha.*

115 *Cibei* 慈悲 and *lianmin* 憐愍 are Buddhist expressions, translating, among others, Sanskrit *karuṇā* and *kṛpā.*

116 The much more concise Parthian (I/32) is as follows: "Their walk is quicker by far than lightning. In the bodies they possess, there is no sickness" (*['c] wrwc 'sk'dr hwyn cmg tyrgystr [pd] tnb'r cy d'rynd ywbhr 'ndr ny 'st*).

117 The Parthian version (I/34) has the following wording: "Fear and terror do not exist in those places, and . . . in those lands there is no destruction" (*['wd tr](s) u 's'w pd hwyn wy'g ny 'st u [....p]d hwyn zmyg wyg'n pd hwyn ny 'st*).

118 *Baoshu* 寶樹 (also in *H.* 298) is a frequent motif in Buddhist, especially Pure Land, sutras (e.g., *Fo shuo wuliang shou jing T.* 0360.12:0269a09, 270c13,15,17,20,22,24,26 passim). On the other hand, wonderful trees are also mentioned in the Coptic *Psalm-book* (136,45; 144,13): "Trees of fragrance"; "the blooming trees of the Land of Light" (Allberry, *A Manichaean Psalm-Book,* 136, 144).

119 This arrangement of the jeweled trees feature in several Buddhist scriptures, among others in the *Contemplation Sūtra* (*T.* 0365.12:0343a27), the *Lotus Sūtra* (*T.* 0262.09:0020c06), and various translations of the *Avatamsaka sūtra* (*T.* 0278.09:0680a17-18, 0697c25, 0730b11-12, 0756c16; *T.* 0279.10:0001c03, 0343a16, 0408a28-29).

120 The parallel text of the Sogdian M178, as already pointed out by Henning ("A Sogdian Fragment," 308 note 3), is as follows: "green fruit-bearing trees whose fruits never *drop, never rot, and never become wormed (*'ṯy wnd' βryyβrynyyṯ zrγwnyyt kyy 'tyšn xw βryy kδ'c nyy 'wryzt nyy pwst 'ṯy nyy kyrmnyy βwṯ*).

121 Fragrance is one of the constant characteristics of the Realm of Light (*H.* 290, *H.* 297, *H.* 298, *H.* 301, *H.* 303, *H.* 330). The third feature of the Realm of Light in an Uighur fragment (Or. 12452A/6) is "good odor" (Zieme, "Die Preisung de Lichtreichs," 588: *ädgü yid*), and the most probably Manichaean Or. 8212/84 has the phrase "sweet-smelling Paradise" (Sogdian *β(w)δ'nt'k rwyšn'γrδmnyh*, see Nicholas Sims-Williams, "The Sogdian fragments of the

British Library," *Indo-Iranian Journal* 18 (1976): 46–47). On this feature more generally, see Aloïs Van Tongerloo, "An Odour of Sanctity," in *Apocryphon Severini Presented to Søren Giversen*, ed. P. Bilde and H. K. Nielsen and J. P. Sørensen (Aarhus: Aarhus University Press, 1993), 245–256.

122 *Wali jingji* 瓦礫荊棘 appear in a handful of Buddhist texts (e.g., the *Lotus Sūtra, T.* 0262.09:0020c05 or the *Avataṃsaka sūtra, T.* 0279.10:0403b09).

123 On this special Manichaean compound, see Bryder, *The Chinese Transformation*, 69–70.

124 The Sogdian M178 (Henning, "A Sogdian Fragment," 307–308) has a parallel here: "adorned, graceful hills wholly covered with flowers, grown in much excellence" (*'rṯy yw pysṯyy 'xšnkt' γrṯ' wysp'sprγmyy rwsṯyẖ prw γrβ p'rγzy'*). The Coptic *Psalm-book* (136, 41–49) also mentions mountains: "Town of the godly. Citadel of the Angels. Habitation of the blessed. Fountain that gushes greatness. Trees of fragrance. Fountains filled with life. All the holy mountains. Fields that are green with life. Dew of ambrosia" (Allberry, *A Manichaean Psalm-Book,* 136). The Parthian Manichaean fragment M6232/R (Klimkeit 1993, 32–33) says: "The immortal, fragrant Breeze (Air) attends the gods together with the Earth and (its) trees. The source of Light, the blessed plants, the echoing, bright mountains of divine nature (are wonderful)." Another Parthian Manichaean text (M10, Klimkeit 1993, 44) has preserved the following description: "All the gods and inhabitants [of the Realm of Light], the mountains, trees and springs, the spacious and strong palaces and halls exulted at thy advent, Friend!" Mountains, enshrouded in colorful clouds, are also depicted on the recently identified Chinese Manichaean Realm of Light paintings. On the other hand, Buddhist pure lands are famously devoid of any mountain, e.g., *Fo shuo wuliangshou jing, T.* 0360.12:0270a13 (Gómez, *The Land of Bliss,* 176): "in this land there is no Mount Sumeru, or any of the other mountains or land features of a world system down to the ring of Diamond mountains. There are no great oceans, no small seas, no torrents, no canals, wells or valleys" (又其國土無須彌山及金剛圍一切諸山，亦無大海小海溪渠井谷).

125 M178 (Henning, "A Sogdian Fragment," 307–308, parallel pointed out by him in note 4): "springs flowing with ambrosia that fill the whole Paradise" (*x'xsryyṯ nwš'fṯ'kṯ kyy 'ṯy 'mbyrṯṯ w" 'nγṯṯc rwxšn'γrδmn*).

126 *Baolou* 寶樓 makes an appearance in several Buddhist scriptures, including the *Contemplation Sūtra* (*T.* 0365.12:0342c07) and the various translations of the *Avatamsaka sūtra*, the latter frequently conflating *baolou* 寶樓 and *baoge* 寶閣 as *bao louge* 寶樓閣 (e.g., *T.* 0278.09:0537b21). This latter example also has *baoling* 寶鈴 after mentioning *bao louge*.

127 *Baoling* 寶鈴 and *baoduo* 寶鐸 both appear in the *Avatamsaka sūtra* several times, although not following each other (e.g., *T.* 0279.10:0141b24, 0142b10).

128 The Sogdian M178 (Henning, "A Sogdian Fragment," 308) also mentions eternal habitats: "countless mansions and palaces, thrones and *benches that exist in perpetuity for ever and ever."

129 *Niepan wang* 涅槃王 refers to the Father of Greatness.

130 The Parthian original (I/48) says the following: "[Each who] ascends up to their land, and [who has the Knowledge, will praise] His manifestation, lauded and beneficent" (*[hrw ky] 'br hwy[n] zmyg snyd u z['nyd 'st'wyd 'w h](w) dydn 'st'[w'd]g u kyrb[kr]*).

131 The Parthian (I/51) simply says "precious are they" (*'rg'w 'hynd hwy(n)*).

132 The Parthian original (I/52) is again much simpler: "There is not one single man [who can tell their measure]" (*'wd 'ywyc mrdwh[m] pd m'n nyšhyd kw w'c'*).

133 A. Waley suggested that "certainly" should be read instead of "impossible" (apud Boyce, *The Manichaean Hymn-Cycles,* 75 note 3), which would thus make a contrast between the two parts of the verse. This possibility, however, though it may seem logical, is slightly contradicted by the fact that *po* 叵 is used in its normal meaning in *H.* 283, and the context is similar ("The carnal tongue, if it wishes to praise, cannot comprehend them, 肉舌欲歎叵能思). Moreover, there is nothing in the second part of the verse that would suggest a contrast.

134 The Parthian original (I/58) simply says: "[no] heavy bodies [are found] among [them]" (*gr'n tnb'r mdy'n [hwyn ny 'st]*).

135 The Parthian original (I/59) says: "They are joyous, (uttering) wonderful praises. They [continually] do reverence to the exalted and . . . [Lord]" (*['wd] (w)šmy(d ')štynd pd nys'g 's[t'wyšn hmyw] (p)d nm'c 'w hw bwrz u (s)[ ]*).

136 A. Waley (apud Boyce, *The Manichaean Hymn-Cycles,* 77 note 1) surmised that *bianhu geyang* 遍互歌揚 means "in antiphony their songs rise," but both the Parthian (Boyce, *The Manichaean Hymn-Cycles,* 76–77) and the Sogdian (Sundermann, *The Manichaean Hymn Cycles,* 22) say "they praise one another."

137 The first part is the same as 273a, while the second part is similar to 273b.

138 Equality and sameness is a recurrent feature in this description; see *H.* 296, *H.* 319, *H.* 334, *H.* 335 (cf. Gharib, "New Light," 262–263).

139 *Yanshi* 嚴飾 is used, for example, in the *Lotus Sūtra* (*T.* 0262.09:0020c04) to describe Guangming 光明 buddha's (Mahākāśyapa's) land called the "Luminous virtue" (*Guangde* 光德).

140 *Yiqie zhumo* 一切諸魔 makes a frequent appearance in Buddhist texts as well.

141 *Niepan jie* 涅槃界 is a Buddhist term, which here refers to the Manichaean Realm of Light.

142 The Uighur version has the following wording: "Barking of dogs, calls of birds, confusing and troublesome evil howling—they are not heard in (that)

land" (Henning, "A Fragment," 123). This distinction is epitomized by the elects' practice of not eating meat at all, since no substantial amount of light can be liberated from animals. The complete lack of animals is at variance with the usual description of Sukhāvatī, where various birds, though created by Amitābha, are present (*Fo shuo Amituo jing, T.* 0366.12:0347a12): "Moreover, Shariputra, in that land you will always see many flocks of rare and exquisite birds of many colors—white egrets, peacocks, parrots, shari and kalavinka birds, and those birds called 'Living-together.' Droves of these birds gather to sing with soothing, exquisite voices four times a day, exactly on the hour, day and night." Gómez, *The Land of Bliss,* 147). The presence of trees with the simultaneous exclusion of animals reflects the Manichaean view of the natural world: while plants are full of light particles, animals are predominantly seen as belonging to the sphere of the dark principle. Thus they hardly have any light in them, and consequently their presence in any form whatsoever in the Realm of Light is unwarranted.

143 As it is clear from an Uighur and a Parthian parallel in late Sogdian script, this stanza was preceded by another one omitted in the Chinese version and also in the Parthian version in Manichaean script, which explains the discrepancy between the seventy-eight stanzas mentioned in the subtitle and the surviving seventy-seven Chinese stanzas. Here I quote the Parthian version (TM 406a): "[Frightful] . . . does not exist [in their] land, and the searing wind does not prevail there" (Sims-Williams, "A New Fragment," 324). Also see Bryder, "Huyadagmān," 264–465.

144 *Chen'ai* 塵埃 is a widely used Buddhist term and translates the Sanskrit *rajas.*

145 *Jile shijie* 極樂世界 (also see *H.* 332) is the name of Sukhāvatī, featuring in a great number of Buddhist sutras, including the *Contemplation Sūtra* (*T.* 0365.12:341b29 / 341c20,c27 / 342c11, 343a16, etc.) and Xuanzang's translation of the Smaller *Sukhāvatīvyūha sūtra* (*T.* 0367.12:348c16,c17,c22,c23); see Mikkelsen, "Sukhāvatī and the Light-World," 204–205.

146 The Sogdian parallel (6386 in the Ōtani collection, Sundermann, *The Manichaean Hymn Cycles,* 22) says, "From all blackness [and] smoky [fogs their] dwelling place [is] free. And [there is no] darkness [therein]." The surviving part of the Uighur version (TM 278; Henning, "A Fragment," 123) is as follows: "From any darkness and fog . . . there is nothing within the pure abodes."

147 The Parthian version (I/68) has "all (is) full of Light" (*['wd] hmg pwr rwšn).*

148 The Uighur version says, "Full of Light is the(ir) 'Living Self'; ever in gladness and honor loving each other they are very beautiful" (Henning, "A Fragment," 123).

149 *Sanzhong* 三終 refers to three types of death by sickness, violence, and old age (Waley apud Boyce, *The Manichaean Hymn-Cycles,* 77 note 6; Mikkelsen,

*Dictionary,* 56). The Uighur version says, "They rejoice in gladness, they thrive on perfume (?). In days—there is no number of their 'Living Self' (=no limit in their lives)" (Henning, "A Fragment," 124).

150 A Sogdian fragment (TM 406a) preserved a more succinct version: "[Birth and death] do not exist [in] their land, nor the union of the bed of passion" (Sims-Williams, "A New Fragment," 324).

151 *Sanchang* 三常 is a Manichaean term, denoting the Father of Greatness, the Light Earth and the Fragrant Air.

152 *Wuda* 五大 is a Manichaean term that comprises the members of the *sanchang* (see previous note), plus the Twelve Aeons and the so-called Aeons of Aeons.

153 *Anleguo* 常樂國 is at first glance a Buddhist term, but it practically does not appear in any Buddhist scripture, the only early exception being the *Mahāprajñāpāramitaśāstra* (*Dazhidulun, T.* 1509.25.0080b22).

154 *Shengyuan* 生緣 is a Buddhist term, translating *jāti-pratyaya, utpanna-pratyaya,* here simply meaning the ultimate origin.

155 *Sanzai* 三災 (*tribhayāni*) is the three destructive calamities in Buddhist texts.

156 *Ba'nan* 八難 (*aṣṭa akṣaṇāḥ*) are the eight difficult states where it is difficult to hear about the dharma.

157 *Sheng, lao, bing, si* 生老病死 (*jāti-jarā-vyādhi-maraṇa*) are the four unavoidable afflictions in human life in Buddhism.

158 *Ruru* 如如 is a Buddhist term (*tathatā, tattva*), basically referring to the absolute, ultimate truth.

159 In the *Hymnscroll,* Mānī is consistently and uniquely called Mangni 忙儞, while in other sources the usual transcription of his name is Moni 摩尼.

## Bibliography

Allberry, Charles R. C. *A Manichaean Psalm-Book. Part II.* Manichaean Manuscripts in the Chester Beatty Collection, vol. II. Stuttgart: W. Kohlhammer, 1938.

Amstutz, Galen, "The Politics of Pure Land Buddhism in India." *Numen* 45, no. 1 (1998): 69–96.

Asmussen, J. P. "Mār Ammō." *Encyclopædia Iranica,* I/9 (1989): 979; available online at http://www.iranicaonline.org/articles/ammo-mar-mid. Accessed June 12, 2015.

Băncilă, I. D. "Ants, or Moths? Insects Not to Be Found in the Manichean Kingdom of Light, According to the Parthian *Huyadagmān* I.18." *ARCHÆVS. Studies in the History of Religions* XIII (2009): 189–198.

BeDuhn, Jason D. *The Manichaean Body in Disciple and Ritual.* Baltimore: Johns Hopkins University Press, 2000.

Bennett, Byard. "*Iuxta unum latus terra tenebrarum*: The Division of Primordial Space in Anti-Manichaean Writers' Description of the Manichaean Cosmogony." In *The Light and the Darkness. Studies in Manichaeism and its World,* edited by Paul Mirecki and Jason BeDuhn, 68–78. Leiden: Brill, 2001.

Boyce, Mary. *The Manichaean Hymn-Cycles in Parthian.* Oxford: London Oriental Series, 1954.

Bryder, Peter. *The Chinese Transformation of Manichaeism. A Study of Chinese Manichaean Terminology.* Löberöd: Plus Ultra, 1985.

——. "Huyadagmān." In *Geng Shimin xiansheng 70 shouchen jinian wenji* [Collected works in commemoration of the 70th birthday of Mr. Geng Shimin], edited by Ji Zengxiang, 252–275. Beijing: Minzu Chubanshe, 1999.

Chen Jinguo and Lin Yun. "Mingjiao de xin faxian—Fujian Xiapu xian Monijiao shiji bianxi" [New Manichaean siscoveries—an analysis of the relics of Manichaeism in Xiapu County, Fujian]. In *Bu zhi yu yi—Zhongyang meiyuan "yiwen ketang" mingjia jiangyan lu,* edited by Li Shaowen, 343–389. Beijing: Beijing Daxue Chubanshe, 2010.

Dodge, Bayard, trans. *The Fihrist of al-Nadim. A Tenth-Century Survey of Muslim Culture.* Vol. 2 (Records of Civilization; Sources and Studies 83) New York: Columbia Press, 1970.

Durkin-Meisterernst, Desmond. *Dictionary of Manichaean Texts. Vol. III.1. Dictionary of Manichaean Middle Persian and Parthian.* Turnhout: Brepols, 2004.

Ferreira, Johan. "A Comparison of the Clothing Metaphor in the Hymn of the Pearl and the Chinese Manichaean Hymnscroll." In *Studia Manichaica. IV. Internationaler Kongress zum Manichäismus, Berlin, 14–18. Juli 1997,* edited by Ronald E. Emmerick, Werner Sundermann, and Peter Zieme, 207–219. Berlin: Akademie Verlag, 2000.

Fox, Greg, and John Sheldon, trans., Samuel N. C. Lieu, introduction and commentary. *Greek and Latin Sources on Manichaean Cosmogony and Ethics.* Corpus Fontium Manichaeorum, Series Subsidia, 6. Turnhout: Brepols, 2010.

Fussman, Gérard. "La place des Sukhāvatī-Vyūha dans le bouddhisme indien." *Journal Asiatique* 287, no. 2 (1999): 523–586.

Getz, Daniel A., Jr. "T'ien-t'ai Pure Land Societies and the Creation of the Pure Land Patriarchate." In *Buddhism in the Sung,* edited by Peter N. Gregory and Daniel A. Getz Jr., 477–523. Honolulu: University of Hawai'i Press, 1999.

Gharib, Badri. "New Light on Two Words in the Sogdian Version of the Realm Light." In *Studia Manichaica. IV. Internationaler Kongress zum Manichäismus, Berlin, 14–18. Juli 1997,* edited by Ronald E. Emmerick, Werner Sundermann, and Peter Zieme, 258–269. Berlin: Akademie Verlag, 2000.

Giles, Lionel. *Descriptive Catalogue of the Chinese Manuscripts from Tunhuang in the British Museum.* London: Trustees of the British Museum, 1957.

Gómez, Luis O., trans., *The Land of Bliss: The Paradise of the Buddha of Measureless Light: Sanskrit and Chinese Versions of the Sukhāvativyūha Sutras.* Honolulu: University of Hawai'i Press, 1996.

Haloun, Gustav, and W. B. Henning. "The Compendium of the Doctrines and Styles of the Teaching of Mani, the Buddha of Light." *Asia Major* 3 (1952): 184–212.

Henning, Walter B. "Annotations to Mr. Tsui's Translation, app. to Tsui Chi, 'Mo Ni Chiao Hsia Pu Tsan: The Lower (Second?) Section of the Manichaean Hymns.'" *Bulletin of the School of Oriental and African Studies* 11 (1943): 216–219.

———. "A Fragment of the Manichaean Hymn-Cycles in Old Turkish." *Asia Major* (N.S.) 7 (1959): 122–124.

———. "A Sogdian Fragment of the Manichaean Cosmogony." *Bulletin of the School of Oriental and African Studies* 12 (1948): 306–318.

Hsu, Eileen Hsiang-Ling. "Visualization Meditation and the Siwei Icon in Chinese Buddhist Sculpture." *Artibus Asiae* 62, no. 1 (2002): 5–32.

Kapstein, Matthew. "Pure Land Buddhism in Tibet?" In *Approaching the Land of Bliss: Religious Praxis in the Cult of Amitabha* (Studies in East Asian Buddhism, 17), edited by Richard Payne and Kenneth Tanaka, 16–41. Honolulu: University of Hawai'i Press, 2004.

Kósa, Gábor. "Buddhist and Pseudo-Buddhist Motifs in the Chinese Manichaean *Hymnscroll*." In *Frontiers and Boundaries—Encounters on China's Margins,* edited by Ildikó Bellér-Hann and Zsombor Rajkai, 49–69. Wiesbaden: Harrassowitz, 2012.

———. "Buddhist Monsters in the Chinese Manichaean *Hymnscroll* and the *Pumen* Chapter of the *Lotus Sūtra*." *The Eastern Buddhist* 44 (2014): 27–76.

———. "The Manichaean 'New Paradise' in Text and Image." *Crossroads.* Studies on the History of Exchange Relations in the East Asia World 13 (2016): 27–113.

———. "The Sun, the Moon and Paradise: An Analysis of the Upper Section of the Chinese Manichaean Cosmology Painting." *Journal of Inner Asian Art and Archaeology* 6 (2015 [2011]): 171–193.

Leurini, Claudia. "A New Manichaean Fragment Dedicated to Ammō." In *Proceedings of the 5th Conference of the Societas Iranologica held in Ravenna, 6-11 October 2003: Vol. 1. Ancient and Middle Iranian Studies,* edited by Antonio Panaino and Andrea Piras, 561–566. Milano: Mimesis, 2006.

Lewis, Todd T. "From Generalized Goal to Tantric Subordination: Sukhāvatī in the Indic Buddhist Traditions of Nepal." In *Approaching the Land of Bliss: Religious Praxis in the Cult of Amitābha,* edited by Richard K. Payne and Kenneth K. Tanaka, 236–263. Honolulu: University of Hawai'i Press, 2004.

Lieu, Samuel N. C. "Manichaean Art and Texts from the Silk Road." In *Manichaeism in Central Asia and China,* 1–58. Leiden: E. J. Brill, 1998.

Lin Wushu. *Monijiao ji qi dongjian* [Manichaeism and its eastern expansion]. Beijing: Zhonghua Shuju, 1987.

———. *Monijiao ji qi dongjian* [Manichaeism and its eastern expansion]. Taibei: Shuxin Chubanshe, 1997.

———. "The Original Manuscript of a Chinese Manichaean Hymnal." In *The Manichaean NOYΣ. Proceedings of the International Symposium organized from the 31st of July to the 3rd of August 1991.* (Manichaean Studies 2), edited by Aloïs Van Tongerloo and Johannes van Oort, 177–181. Lovanii: International Association of Manichaean Studies—Center of the History of Religions—BCMS (Louvain), 1995.

Ma Xiaohe. "Monijiao 'Xiabu zan, Chusheng zanwen' xin kao [A New Study of the "Primeval Voice Eulogy" of the Manichaean Hymnscroll]." In *Monijiao yu gudai xiyu shi yanjiu* [Studies on Manichaeism and the ancient western regions], 164–196. Beijing: Renmin Daxue Chubanshe, 2008.

———. "Monijiao 'Xiabu zan, Chusheng zanwen' xu kao [A further study of the "Primeval Voice Eulogy" of the Manichaean Hymnscroll]." In *Monijiao yu gudai xiyu shi yanjiu* [Studies on Manichaeism and the ancient western regions], 197–205. Beijing: Renmin Daxue Chubanshe, 2008.

MacKenzie, David N. "Two Sogdian *Hwydgm'n* Fragments." In *Papers in Honour of Professor Mary Boyce*, II (Acta Iranica 25), edited by Jacques Duchesne-Guillemin and Pierre Lecoq, 421–428. Leiden: Brill, 1985.

Mikkelsen, Gunner B. *Dictionary of Manichaean Texts. Vol. III. Texts from Central Asia and China. Part 4. Dictionary of Manichaean Texts in Chinese.* Turnhout: Brepols, 2006.

———. "The Fragments of Chinese Manichaean Texts from the Turfan Region." In *Turfan Revisited—The First Century of Research into the Arts and Cultures of the Silk Road,* edited by D. Durkin-Meisterernst, S.-Ch. Raschmann, J. Wilkens, M. Yaldiz, and P. Zieme, 213–220. Berlin: Dietrich Reimer Verlag, 2004.

———. "Quickly Guide Me to the Peace of the Pure Land: Christology and Buddhist Terminology in the Chinese Manichaean *Hymnscroll.*" In *The Chinese Face of Jesus Christ,* edited by Roman Malek, 218–242. Sankt Augustin: Institut Monumenta Serica and China-Zentrum; Nettetal: Steyler Verlag, 2002.

———. "Sukhāvatī and the Light-World: Pure Land Elements in the Chinese Manichaean *Eulogy of the Light-World.*" In *New Light on Manichaeism: Papers from the Sixth International Conference on Manichaean Studies*, edited by Jason BeDuhn, 201–212. Leiden: Brill, 2009.

Provasi, Elio. "The Diamond Earth. A Manichaean Sogdian Eulogy." In *Commentationes Iranicae. Сборник статей к 90-летию Владимира Ароновича Лившица,* edited by Sergius Tokhtasev and Paulus Luria, 378–393. Saint Petersburg: Nestor-Historia, 2013.

Pulleyblank, Edward G. *Lexicon of Reconstructed Pronunciation in Early Middle Chinese, Late Middle Chinese, and Early Mandarin.* Vancouver: University of British Columbia Press, 1991.

Reck, Christiane. "Reste einer Soghdischen Version von *Huyadagmān* I in der Form eines Responsoriums zwischen Erwählten und Hörer." In *Languages of Iran: Past and Present. Iranian Studies in Memoriam David Neil McKenzie,* edited by Dieter Weber, 53–63. Wiesbaden: Harrassowitz, 2005.

Rui Chuanming. "Ru Hua Monijiao zhi 'fojiaohua' ji qi chuanbo—yi 'Xiabu zan Tan mingjie wen' wei li" [The Buddhisization of the Manichaeism upon its entrance and its spread—taking the "Eulogy on the Light World" of the *Hymnscroll* as an example]. *Chuantong Zhongguo yanjiu jikan* 5 (2008): 1–22. http://www.historicalchina.net/admin/WebEdit/UploadFile/FragCM.pdf.

Schmidt-Glintzer, Helwig, trans. *Chinesische Manichaica. Mit textkritischen Anmerkungen und einem Glossar.* Wiesbaden: Otto Harrassowitz, 1987.

Schopen, Gregory. "Sukhāvatī As a Generalized Religious Goal in Sanskrit Mahāyāna Sūtra Literature." *Indo-Iranian Journal* 19, no. 3 (1977): 177–210.

Sharf, Robert H. *Coming to Terms with Chinese Buddhism: A Reading of the* Treasure Store Treatise. Honolulu: University of Hawai'i Press, 2002.

——. "On Pure Land Buddhism and Ch'an/Pure Land Syncretism in Medieval China." *T'oung Pao* (second series) 88, no. 4/5 (2002): 282–331.

Sims-Williams, Nicholas. "A New Fragment from the Parthian Hymn-Cycle *Huyadagmān.*" In *Études irano-aryennes offertes à Gilbert Lazard* (Cahier de Studia Iranica 7), edited by C.-H. de Fouchécour and Ph. Gignoux, 321–331. Paris: Association pour l'avancement des études iràniennes, 1989.

——. "The Sogdian Fragments of the British Library." *Indo-Iranian Journal* 18 (1976): 43–82.

Stein, M. A. *Serindia: Detailed Report of Explorations in Central Asia and Westernmost China Carried Out and Described under the Orders of H.M. Indian Government by Aurel Stein.* Vol. 2. Oxford: Clarendon Press, 1921.

Sundermann, Werner. "Iranian Manichaean Texts in Chinese Remake. Translation and Transformation." in *Cina e Iran. Da Alessandro Magno alla Dinastia Tang,* edited by A. Cadonna and L. Lanciotti, 103–119. (Orientalia Venetiana 5.) Firenze: Leo S. Olschki Editore, 1996.

——. *The Manichaean Hymn Cycles* Huyadagmān *and* Angad Rōšnān *in Parthian and Sogdian.* London: SOAS, 1990.

——. "Probleme der Edition iranisch-manichäischer Texte." In *Ägypten—Vorderasien—Turfan. Probleme der Edition und Bearbeitung altorientalischer Handschriften,* edited by H. Klengel and W. Sundermann, 106–112. Berlin: Akademie-Verlag, 1991.

Teiser, Stephen F. "Ornamenting the Departed: Notes on the Language of Chinese Buddhist Ritual Texts." *Asia Major,* 3rd series, 22, no. 1 (2009): 201–237.

Thilo, Thomas. "Einige Bemerkungen zu zwei chinesisch-manichäischen Textfragmenten der Berliner Turfan-Sammlung." In *Ägypten—Vorderasien—Turfan. Probleme der Edition und Bearbeitung altorientalischer Handschriften,* edited by H. Klengel and W. Sundermann, 161–170. Berlin: Akademie-Verlag, 1991.

Tsui Chi, trans. "Mo Ni Chiao Hsia Pu Tsan: The Lower (Second?) Section of the Manichaean Hymns." *Bulletin of the School of Oriental and African Studies* 11 (1943): 174–215.

Van Tongerloo, Aloïs. "An Odour of Sanctity." In *Apocryphon Severini Presented to Søren Giversen,* edited by P. Bilde and H. K. Nielsen and J. P. Sørensen, 245–256. Aarhus: Aarhus University Press, 1993.

Waldschmidt, Ernst, and Wolfgang Lentz. "A Chinese Manichaean Hymnal from Tun-huang." *Journal of the Royal Asiatic Society* 58, no. 2 (1926): 116–122, 298–299.

——. *Manichäische Dogmatik aus chinesischen und iranischen Texten.* (Sonderausgabe aus den *Sitzungsberichte der Preussischen Akademie der Wissenschaften, Phil.-Hist. Klasse*) Berlin: Verlag der Akademie der Wissenschaften, 1933.

——. "Die Stellung Jesu im Manichäismus." *Abhandlungen der königlichen preussischen Akademie der Wissenschaften* 4 (1926): 1–131.

Yabuki Yoshiteru 矢吹慶輝. *Manikyō to Tōyō no shoshūkyō.* [Manichaeism and the Eastern Religions]. Tōkyō: Kōsei Publishing Co., 1988.

Yoshida Yutaka. "Kanyaku Manikyō bunken ni okeru kanji onsha sareta chūsei irango ni tsuite" [Remarks on the Manichaean Middle Iranian terms transcribed in Chinese script]. *Nairiku Ajia gengo no kenkyū* 2 (1986): 1–15.

——. "Manichaean Aramaic in the Chinese *Hymnscroll.*" *Bulletin of the School of Oriental and African Studies* 46, no. 2 (1983): 326–331.

Yu Wanli 虞萬里. "Dunhuang Monijiao 'Xiabu zan' xieben niandai xintan" [A New Research into the date of the manuscript of the Manichaean Hymnscroll of Dunhuang]. *Dunhuang Tulufan yanjiu* 1 (1995): 37–46.

Zieme, Peter. *Manichäisch-türkische Texte. Texte, Übersetzung, Anmerkungen.* Berlin: Akademie-Verlag, 1975.

——. "Die Preisung de Lichtreichs nach einem alttürkischen Fragment in London." In *Exegisti monumenta: Festschrift in Honour of Nicholas Sims-Williams,* edited by Werner Sundermann, Almut Hintze, and François de Blois, 587–596. Wiesbaden: Harrassowitz, 2009.

# Chapter 3

# Śambhala as a Pure Land

Vesna A. Wallace

## Translator's Introduction

The idea of a pure land or buddha-field (*buddhakṣetra*) as a place mentally created and presided over by a particular buddha within a certain world-system (*lokadhātu*) for those seeking a rebirth in the pure land in order to receive teachings and practice in the presence of a buddha is in most part applicable to various notions of the land of Śambhala. In a number of Tibetan and Mongolian sources, Śambhala is depicted as a unique pure land within the land of karma, or human realm, and is to some degree reminiscent of certain celestial pure lands, especially of Akṣobhya's eastern pure land, Abhirati. Both Śambhala and Abhirati resemble the improved versions of our world, in which human beings are born in the natural manner.[1] Moreover, in a number of Mongolian sources, Śambhala is explicitly referred to as a celestial Sukhāvatī, and yet it is also described as a geographical place.

The earliest notion of Śambhala as a pure locale appears in the Mahābhārata (3.188.89–93), where the village of Śambhala (*śambhala-grāma*) is referenced to as "a pure abode of *brāhmaṇas*," in which the *kalkī* Viṣṇu Yaśas is prophesied to arise as a universal emperor (*cakravartī*).[2] In the Indian Buddhist sources where the earliest references to Śambhala appear, namely, in the *Kālacakratantra* and its commentary, the *Vimalaprabhā*, Śambhala is more than a village. It is a vast kingdom with 960 million towns that was transformed into a Vajrayāna territory after thirty-five million of its brāhmaṇic sages abandoned the brāhmaṇic practices prescribed in the Vedas, such as sacrificial killing and the like, in consequence of receiving the Kālacakra initiation from the king Yaśas, an emanation of Mañjuśrī. If one considers the size of a territory that can accommodate 960 million towns, Śambhala appears to be more of a parallel universe than a restricted geographical region situated south of Kailāśa and north of Śītā River.

The earliest Buddhist references to Śambhala, preserved in the two aforementioned texts, lack an explicit mention of Śambhala as a Sukhāvatī. Nevertheless, one finds in these texts allusions to Śambhala as a pure land of the human realm, which is mentally brought into existence and governed by the emanations of great celestial bodhisattvas. According to the *Vimalaprabhā*, all the rulers of Śambhala—the fierce kings (*krodha-rāja*) of Śambhala, such as Yamāntaka and others, and bodhisattvas of the Tenth Stage (*bhūmi*), such as Kṣitigarbha and others—bear the thirty-two marks of a Great Man (*mahāpuruṣa-lakṣaṇa*) and the eighty minor marks. They are endowed with sovereignty (*aiśvarya*), the five extrasensory types of knowledge (*abhijñā*), and other supernatural abilities. Similar to Amitābha, who by means of his Enjoyment Body (*saṃbhogakāya*) teaches Dharma to those dwelling in his celestial Sukhāvatī, the kings of Śambhala teach Dharma to its inhabitants by means of their Emanation Bodies (*nirmāṇakāya*).[3] We are told this is so because even a single bodhisattva who is endowed with the ten perfections (*daśa-paramitā*), who has mastered the tenth stage and acquired the ten powers (*daśa-bala*), is able to teach Dharma to sentient beings in a single trichiliocosm by means of his numerous Emanation Bodies.[4] Puṇḍarīka, the author of the *Vimalaprabhā*, asserts that here in the land of karma, no one born from a woman's womb, with exception of the Lord Buddha, who mastered all twelve bodhisattva stages, bears the thirty-two marks of the Great Man.[5] This statement suggests that the bodhisattvic kings of Śambhala, who are endowed with the marks of the Great Man, are in fact the particular type of bodhisattvic buddhas. This idea seems to have been later supported in the *Padminīnāmapañjikā*[6] and in Buston's annotations to the *Kālacakratantra*.[7] Furthermore, in the *Vimalaprabhā*, Mañjuśrī Yaśas is explicitly referred to as a Bhagavān,[8] a designation reserved only for the buddhas.[9] The text also lays out certain similarities between the Buddha Śākyamuni and Sucandra, the king of Śambhala. Just like the Lord Buddha, who, having attained the twelve bodhisattva stages, was later born as the prince Siddhārtha from the womb of Mahāmāyā and as the son of the king Śuddhodhana for the sake of teaching Dharma in a buddha-field, so too did the Bodhisattva Vajrapāṇi, having attained the tenth stage, took birth from the womb of Vijayā as the prince Sucandra and as the son of Sūryaprabha, the king of Śambhala, in order to teach the *Paramādhibuddhatantra* for the sake of full and perfect awakening of its inhabitants. In the second year after the king Sucandra taught the *Paramādhibuddhatantra* in Śambhala's capital Kalāpa, he departed by means of his Enjoyment Body to the place (Aḍakavatī) from which he arrived to Śambhala by means of his Emanation Body.[10]

Similar views of the kings of Śambhala as enlightened beings reverberate through later Tibetan and Mongolian sources. The nineteenth-century text, the *Crystal Mirror* (*Bolur Toli*) composed by the Mongolian author Jambaldorj, reaffirms that the *kalkī* kings of Śambhala possess all the excellent qualities of those who have achieved bliss, inexhaustible wisdom, unimpeded mind, extrasensory perceptions, and magic powers.[11] According to another work composed by the Mongolian author Minjüür Dechin Shiirev, titled *The Jewel Steps of a Fortunate Disciple: A Prayer for a Sure Rebirth in the Land of Śambhala of the Great Siddhi, in the Land that Captivates a Person's Mind for a Definite Meeting with the Dharma of Raudra Kalkī*, even all the minor kings of Śambhala, who rule over the millions of its towns, are actual manifestations of the buddhas. The depiction of conditions in Śambhala found in Minjüür Dechin's work indirectly points to Śambhala as a special type of Sukhāvatī, as an esoteric Sukhāvatī of the human realm, or, as Minjüür Dechin calls it, "the place of the highest *siddhi*."[12] Referencing the three Tibetan sources—Vagindra's *Wish-Prayer for Śambhala*, the Second 'Jam dbyangs Bzhad pa's[13] *Response to Questions regarding Śambhala*, and Dkon mchog Darmabazar's *Composition on the Land of Śambhala* (eighteenth century)—Minjüür Dechin assures us that this is why even bodhisattvas in Sukhāvatī pray for their rebirth in Śambhala.[14] He thus implicitly tells us that a rebirth in the Vajrayāna-oriented Śambhala is more desirable than rebirth in any Sūtrayāna-oriented Sukhāvatī, where the long bodhisattva path is practiced.

According to Nāropā's *Paramārthasaṃgraha*, a commentary on the *Sekoddeśa*, the land of Śambhala is a place that was magically created by Vajrapāṇi.[15] This view was adopted by later Buddhist authors, one of whom was the early twentieth-century Mongolian scholar Ngag dbang rta mgrin bsrud (Agvaan Damdinsüren). His text, excerpts of which are cited in the second section of this chapter, titled *The Swift Path to Kalāpa: A Compilation of the Layout of Śambhala and Ritual Offering to The Dharma Kings and Kalkīs*, speaks of Śambhala as a place generated by the mind of the king Sucandra (Vajrapāṇi).[16] In yet another Mongolian source, *The Precious Crystal Stairway: Illuminating the Way to Śambhala, The Supreme and Glorious Abode for Accomplishing Siddhis*, composed by Shes rab rgya mtsho (Prajñāsāgara)[17] in 1921, Śambhala is spoken of as "a sublime *maṇḍala* of the earth, which is rotated by the Wheel of Dharma of the guaranteed Awakening, and celebrated by the illusory dance of the Sons of Jinas—the seven Dharma kings and twenty-five kalkīs."[18] Likewise, Minjüür Dechin Shiirev in his aforementioned work refers to Śambhala as "a land of Vajrapāṇi, the Lord of Secrets (Guhyapati), and as the marvelous Pure Land,"[19] where one can attain buddhahood within a single lifetime.[20] In these texts[21] we are told that everyone born in Śambhala is able to depart to the celestial Sukhāvatī at death. These texts, however, do not specify the celestial Sukhāvatī. Likewise, the inhabitants of the celestial Sukhāvatī, such as Nāgārjuna and Tsongkhapa, can descend to Śambhala, take on a physical form by entering their relics, and return to Sukhāvatī when their work is completed on the earth.

The explicit references to Śambhala as a celestial Sukhāvatī, or pure land, seem to be quite late. To my knowledge they appear primarily in the accounts of late nineteenth- and early twentieth-century Tibetan and Mongolian authors. Some among these scholars composed travel guides to Śambhala for those desiring to venture on a journey to geographical Śambhala as well as wish prayers, *sādhanas,* ritual texts, and transference of consciousness (*'pho ba*) practice guides for those aspiring to take rebirth in Śambhala. It is predominantly, but not exclusively, in these practice-oriented texts, some of which also contain detailed descriptions of Śambhala, its kings, and inhabitants, that both explicit references and implicit allusions to Śambhala as a Sukhāvatī are found. One of many examples of the identification of Śambhala with a celestial realm can be seen in the short verse of prayer composed by a Mongolian monk, Palden, in 1928, at the time of the persecution of Buddhist monks in Mongolia by soldiers of Mongolian People's Revolutionary Party. The prayer reads:

> Homage to the Guru!
> From now onward, may I achieve a fine body in Śambhala,
> The celestial realm of Khasarparṇadvīpa!
> And when my various appearances arise [there],
> May I attain the ability of being pierced with the sword of gnosis!
> *Oṃ āḥ hūṃ ho haṃ kṣa ma la va ra ya hūṃ phaṭ.*[22]

As in some Pure Land traditions, here too one who desires to reach Śambhala in the present life or to be born there is expected to generate faith, reflect on the relevant scriptures, recite prayers and mantras, and practice rituals and *sādhanas* focused on the layout and characteristics of Śambhala, its kings, and its human and nonhuman inhabitants. By means of these, the aspirant is to accumulate merit and purify sins in order to bring about the desired goal. Detailed descriptions of these practices can be found in various Tibetan and Mongolian guides to Śambhala and in practice-oriented texts outlining the methods for securing rebirth in that land.

The idea of the possibility of rebirth in Śambhala inspired the production of many prayers and rituals among Tibetan, Mongolian, and Buryat monks. This was the case especially during the period of political and social crises in the early twentieth century, in the wake of communist revolution and the percolation of European modernity and scientific knowledge into Inner Asia, which was seen as a threat to traditional Buddhist views and values and to the Buddhist tradition in general. Here is one example of such prayers written by the Eighth Bogdo Jebtsundamba (Ngag dbang blo bzang chos rje nyi ma bstan 'dzin dbang phyug, 1870–1924), the head of Mongolian state and church during that fraught period:

> A Prayer for Śambhala
> Homage to the feet of the Venerable Guru,
> Who, though after attaining the supreme state of the three perfect bodies,
> Became a supreme holder of the victory banner of the teaching
> Of the spontaneous Blo bzang, the Second Jina![23]
>
> May I and all other mother beings without exception,
> By the power of effort in pure, virtuous activity,
> Be born before too long in Śambhala of the northern direction
> And be also perfected in the practice of the Sons of the Jinas!
>
> After [you] assume the form of the fierce Hanumanda,
> When you thrust your sword into the heart of the enemies and obstructers, who violate pledges,
> May I also, being born in your retinue,
> Please you, O Protector!
>
> May all the transmigrating beings who make such aspirations
> Never be separated from the gracious Guru!
> Having eliminated the seeds of the two [types of] obscurations,
> May they bring to completion the two [types of] benefit and swiftly attain Perfect Buddhahood![24]

## Taking Rebirth in or Journeying to Śambhala

While some authors wrote shorter prayers for rebirth in Śambhala, others outlined more detailed practices leading to that goal. For instance, in his work mentioned above, Minjüür Dechin Shiirev lays out a program of practices necessary for rebirth in Śambhala. It begins with a prayer to the assembly of the buddhas and to the kings of Śambhala for their blessings. This is followed by a formal contemplation on karmic fruition, the accumulation of merit and gnosis, purification of obstacles, an expression of noble aspirations, and prayers for the purification of sins. The author assures the aspirant that if these three—accumulation of merit and gnosis, purification of obstacles, and generation of aspiration—are completed, then rebirth in Śambhala is certain. It is said that it is impossible to take rebirth in Śambhala for as long as one has not eliminated one's mental afflictions. The described practice involves mentally presenting offerings to the buddhas of the three times and ten directions and to the Buddha, Dharma, and to the Saṅgha of Śambhala, paying them homage with the body, speech, and mind and presenting them with various external offerings. The aspirant must generate the altruistic aspirations of a bodhisattva: to show compassion to all sentient beings in the future, turn the Wheel of Dharma, show kindness to all, and bring everyone to buddhahood. After that the aspirant is to engage in a five-fold practice that involves the *sādhana* focused on the structure of the land of Śambhala and on its kings, as well as recite the prayers for a guaranteed rebirth in Śambhala, for the encounter with Raudra Cakrī and his Dharma, and for attaining buddhahood.[25] For the aspirant who has successfully accumulated the aforementioned causes for rebirth in Śambhala, at death, when the clear light of death appears along with the dissolution of the four great elements, a stirring of subtle wind for rebirth in Śambhala occurs, immediately followed by the dissolution of the clear light of death. As soon as the *bar do* being of Śambhala is formed, a white light appears in the direction of Śambhala in the north. It is said, following the direction of that white light without fear, exhaustion, or mental shock, the *bar do* being reaches the land of the glorious Śambhala in a single moment.[26]

As seen in Tārānātha's (1575–1634) *Entrance to Kalāpa* (*Ka lā par jug pa*),[27] a translation of the fourteenth-century Nepalese text, *Kalāpāvatāra,* and in the Sixth Panchen Lama's (Blo bzang dpal ldan ye shes, 1738–1780) *Guide to Śambhala* (*Sham bha la'i lam yig*, 1775),[28] those intending to journey to Śambhala in the present life must already reach the state of advanced

Vajrayāna practitioners, who are accomplished in the *vidyā-mantras* (*rig sngags*), in order to stand a chance of physically reaching Śambhala. Before venturing on the perilous journey they must complete a propitiatory retreat on their tutelary deity and carefully examine their dreams for signs of permission. Their journey is a form of the pilgrimage to Śambhala, a process of purification during which they must recite many hundreds of thousands of different mantras, perform many *homa* rituals with fires made of various types of wood, offer *bali* cakes and numerous other offerings, and propitiate various deities in order to remove the dangers and obstacles to reaching Śambhala. In his concluding remarks to the *Guide to Śambhala*, the Sixth Panchen Lama points out that whether or not one travels to Śambhala, it is worthwhile making prayers for taking rebirth there. He himself composed the well-known *Prayer for Rebirth in Śambhala* (*Sham bha lar skye ba'i smon lam*),[29] which later circulated among different Mongolian ethnic groups in Tibetan and in its Mongolian versions.

According to the *Kālacakratantra*, geographical Śambhala is located within the land of karma (*karma-bhūmi*), which is situated on the seventh continent, or Jambudvīpa, in between the ocean of liquor and the salt ocean. The land of karma, where humans live, consists of twelve sections, each measuring twenty-five thousand leagues and having the shape of an eight-petaled lotus. Thus it measures altogether three hundred thousand leagues in circumference. In the center of one of the twelve sections of Small Jambudvīpa[30] is Mount Kailāśa, surrounded by snow mountains on all sides. The Kailāśa area, together with the surrounding snow mountains, occupies one-third of Small Jambudvīpa. Outside of the Kailāśa area, each of the section's eight petals has twelve principalities (*viṣaya*), making the entire section home of ninety-six principalities.[31] On the western side of Kailāśa, north of the Śītā River, is Śambhala, where there is the city of Kalāpa, residence of the excellent sages, or the kings of Śambhala, which is centrally located among ten million towns.[32] Ten million towns constitute one principality, and one hundred thousand towns constitute a prefecture (*maṇḍala*).[33]

While the *Kālacakratantra* and the *Vimalaprabhā* do not provide us with any further information, the later Tibetan and Mongolian sources on Śambhala give at times varied but always rich depictions of the layout of Śambhala, as well as descriptions of the wondrous life there, its natural environment, the appearance of its king and his palaces, and the attractive appearance of its inhabitants, their finery, and the like. The excerpts cited below, translated from the previously mentioned text composed in

Tibetan by the Mongolian author Agvaan Damdinsüren (Ngag dbang rta mgrin bsrud) in 1917 is one of many picturesque depictions of Śambhala and its wonders, which captivate imagination and are designed to arouse one's yearning to enter its portals.[34]

## Translation

### *The Swift Path to Kalāpa: A Compilation of the Layout of Śambhala and Ritual Offering to the Dharma Kings and* Kalkīs

Agvaan Damdinsüren

As for the northern Śambhala, in the center of Small Jambudvīpa there is Vajrāsana (Bodhgaya), the place where the buddhas of the Fortunate Era arrive. In the east is the five-peaked mountain (Wu-tai), which is an abode of Mañjuśrī. In the south is the Potala Mountain, an abode of Avalokiteśvara. In the west is Oḍḍiyāna, an abode of *ḍākiṇīs*. In the north is Śambhala, an abode of human *vidyādharas*. The fifth of those five abodes is the residence of the *kalkīs*, the Dharma kings. Moreover, corresponding to the three types of oceans, Small Jambudvīpa [measures] twenty-five thousand leagues from the south to the north and is divided into three regions. The northern section among those three regions is divided into six great territories;[35] and [it is said] in the great *Stainless Light Commentary* (*Vimalaprabhā*) that the fifth [territory] is Great China,[36] and the sixth [territory] is Himālaya. Thus, this [sixth section] belongs to the Himālayan [region]. Recalling the excellent qualities of the environment and inhabitants of Śambhala generates a strong aspiration to be born there. It is twenty-five thousand leagues from the south of Small Jambudvīpa to the north. One northern area is divided into three [parts], one of which is further divided into six parts, the fifth of which is Śambhala. In the core of its center there is the city of Kalāpa and the king's palace, which far surpasses even the mansion of [god] Indra. People born there are forever free from the [three] miserable destinations.

As for the layout of such a realm, the northern Śambhala is in the western part of the territory from the center of the Himālayas. This land [of Śambhala] is perfectly circular in the form of a lotus with its center and petals. Dividing this circle into three parts, the first part is the center, which measures one-third, and the second part comprises the petals. The center is a thousand leagues across. Each of the eight petals also measures a thousand leagues. The periphery of the center is ringed with one range of snow mountains; there is one range of snow mountains around the periphery of [all] eight petals, which is ringed by a second range of snow mountains. All the summits of the mountains are capped with snow and are bordered below by slate mountains, beneath which are rocky mountains, beneath which are grassy mountains, then forested mountains, mountains covered with fragrant trees, various flowers, and adorned with various medicinal herbs. All the valleys are exceptionally arrayed with lakes, ponds, pools, meadows, fruit trees, and various pleasure groves. They are vast in extent, filled with desirable things, pleasant, and serene. On the top of the core in the center, slightly higher than the petals, there is the king's palace, Kalāpa, made from five types of jewels and [measuring] twelve leagues [across]. In the center of the palace, the light that shines from the buildings where the *kalkī* king lives, which are made from emeralds, the finest crystals, and diamonds, overpowers even the light of the moon of the fifteenth lunar day (the full moon), and it cannot be outshone by the pale disc of the moon viewed above. Due to the light shining from the various mirrors on the walls of the mansion, the daytime and nighttime are indistinguishable. The thrones are made of gold from the Jambu River and inlaid with the finest jewels; the walls made of those same precious substances are superbly clear, like mirrors on which appear many spectacles of the reflections of animals as small as insects, including those under the water, from a distance of fifty leagues. Also, on the surface of the skylights are circular crystals through which one can see the mansions of the sun, moon, and stars, the gods, their pleasure gardens and walking paths, the twelve solar mansions, and so on, as if they were right in front of one. Around the thrones is a beautiful multicolored sandalwood floor, the pleasant fragrance of which spreads for a league. It is merely suggestive to describe the mats, cushions, and the like made of magnificent cotton and silk as worth ten billion coins of silver; in brief, if one were to estimate the value of each residence to be as that of a great ship filled to the brim with gold, what more needs to be said of everything else?

As for the appearance of the *kalkī*'s body, he has an artificial topknot made of dyed lion's mane and a cap made of gold from the Jambu River. As for the value of each of the jewels on the bracelets on his arms and legs, it is ten billion gold coins apiece. Due to the all-pervasive brilliance of each encrusted jewel and a combined luster of the white-tinged-with-red complexion of the *kalkī*'s body, it is difficult to bear its magnificence. He has a large retinue of ministers and generals, a vast retinue of queens, and a limitless array of mounts including *śarabhas,*[37] elephants, winged elephants, supreme steeds, chariots, palanquins, and so on. He possesses the "fortune of self and others" (*rang gzhan gyi 'byor ba*), wields the power of *vidyāmantra,* and has wealth and special foods offered [to him] by the *nāgas, asuras, rākṣas,* and *kinnaras* in his service, with which even [god] Indra cannot compete. The *kalkī* king has a very large retinue of queens, and when they give birth to their many male and female children, regardless of their seniority, a rain of white lotus flowers falls upon them. If for seven days after a son's birth, that [son's] body is invisible and becomes a jewel that radiates light, he is a *kalkī* king. As stated by Amoghāṅkuśa (Don yod lcags kyu) in the *Questions and Answers to Delight the Clear-Minded* (*Dris lan blo gsal dga' bskyed*):

> Whatever prince is born,
> He is a precious, radiant jewel
> That radiates light for seven days.
> He is a *kalkī* king.

Nevertheless, every one of these *kalkīs* is an Emanation [Body], so for seven days following their birth, the royal father grants empowerments in the *maṇḍala* and enthrones them as crown princes. Although there are many queens, that [son] is born as a *kalkī.* When a daughter of any one of the ninety-six minor kings of the periphery of Śambhala is born, a rain of water lilies descends. As a portent of a queen about to give birth [to a *kalkī* king], magnificent, never-before-seen lotus flowers grow in her home.

> When never-before-seen
> Flowers gloriously grow,
> In the home where they arise
> A king's queen is giving birth.

The king, together with the queen, owns the four kinds of treasures of the glorious Brahmā. Brahmā's four divisions [of treasures] are the four [pursuits of life]: sensual pleasure (*kāma*; *'dod pa ldan*), wealth (*artha*; *nor*), Dharma, and liberation (*mokṣa*; *thar pa*). The king and the queen do not age or become ill, and although they always delight in sensual pleasures, their virtue does not decrease. The four kinds [of the treasures of] Brahmā arise for all the kings who have accomplished *vidyāmantras.* Although no more than one or two heirs (*kulaputra*; *rigs sras*) are produced, many vajra-princesses are offered during the initiations held on the full moon of the third month each year.

On the northern side of Kalāpa,
The space-vajras are present everywhere.
There are eight thousand female demons
And many other powerful creatures.

On the outskirts of the northern periphery of the palace are ten million towns serving as female servants [to the palace]. Moreover, far to the north behind the palace is a crystal-like rocky mountain, whose form appears very clearly when viewed from afar, but when one is right in front of it, one cannot discern what it is, for it is extremely high. Its lower region is covered with a rich growth of *sāla* trees, juniper trees, and so on. The amazing mountain is inhabited by tens of thousands of bodhisattvas encircling the ten bodhisattvas—the Bodhisattva Bhadrapāla, Bodhisattva Meruśikharadhara, Bodhisattva Kṣitigarbha, Bodhisattva Mañjuśrī, Avalokiteśvara Halāhala, Ārya Tārā, Vajrapāṇi Guhyapati, Devī Keśinī,[38] Bodhisattva Parmārthasamudgata, and Bodhisattva Maitreya, [and others], some of whom are [standing] like statues and others sit cross-legged.

To the south of the palace is the great pleasure grove of the Malaya [mountains measuring] twelve leagues [across]. In the center is a complete body-speech-and-mind *maṇḍala* of the glorious Kālacakra. Mentally generated and erected by the king Sucandra, it is made of the five kinds of jewels, and [it measures] 412 cubits in each direction. There are many other marvelous *maṇḍalas* composed solely of precious substances, which were later created by other *kalkī* kings. To the east of that pleasure grove is the Upamānasa Lake (*Nye 'ba'i yid kyi mtsho*), similar to the moon on the eighth [day of the lunar month] and [measuring] twelve leagues [across]. To the west [of the pleasure grove] is Padma Lake, similar to a half moon and [measuring] twelve leagues [across], covered by lotus flowers, water lilies, and the like. All the humans, gods, and *nāgas* [residing there] delight and enjoy themselves with boats made of precious substances.

From the snow mountains surrounding the central city of Kalāpa up to the outer snow mountains is [a distance of] five hundred leagues, and the lay of the land is in the form of an eight-petaled lotus. The spaces between the petals are marked by water and snow. On each of the petals within that formation of eight petals are 120 million towns, totaling 960 million towns in all. Since there is one king for every ten million towns there are altogether ninety-six Dharma kings. For as long as the Buddha Śākyamuni's teaching persists for five thousand years, the royal succession will continue, and so the Dharma of Kālacakra will always be revealed. By and large, people who have achieved the *vidyā-mantra* included among the eight *siddhis* appear in each of the ninety-six minor kingdoms, and they hold in their hands a staff called "powerful mind." Thus, when these [kings] dispatch messengers, by pointing it with their hand, they instantly arrive in whatever place they have in mind. Due to the power of the *vidyā-mantra,* most Dharma practitioners appear to have their own *nāgas, asuras,* or others as their servants.

The two-storied houses of those towns, which are pleasant, are similar to Indian houses. Humans born there are very attractive, impressive, and youthful in appearance. According to the *Questions and Answers to Delight the Clear-Minded,* the weakest of them have the strength of two or three elephants, and if their strength is unimaginable, then what need to speak of the strong ones? The abundance of food, drink, ornaments, clothing, and the like is vast. These [humans] live under gentle laws, and there is no bondage, beating, and the like, and no illness, hunger at all. They have good natures, sharp faculties, and are naturally inclined to virtue. Most of them become buddhas in a single lifetime by way of any class of the *Unsurpassable Tantras* (*niruttara-tantra; bla med kyi rgyud*) such as the *Guhyasamāja, Cakrasaṃvara, Hevajra, Kālacakra,* and so on; also, many have attained *samādhi* and the like, as taught in the *Perfection of Wisdom Sūtra.* After the transference of consciousness at the time of death, even their servants who are householders without any practice go only to a pure land and never to miserable states of existence.

As for their clothing, the kings, having tied their styled hair on the tops of their heads, wear crowns decorated with the five symbols of the [buddha] families, and have the appearance of the *cakravartī* kings. By merely seeing them and touching them, fortunate ones are able to attain the excellent path. Men wear turbans, white or red robes, and the upper garments of householders; the women wear white or blue garments with jeweled designs. Even those with little wealth own around a hundred treasuries of precious substances. They worship and make immeasurable offerings to the *saṅgha* and the extraordinary representations of the [Buddha's] body, speech, and mind. The renunciates do not carry any necessities other than the three dharmic robes, begging bowls, and mendicant's staffs. They live with bare heads and feet, and they show great devotion for the *Vinaya* precepts.

They possess all the teachings of the Buddha and the commentaries in Jambudvīpa, ranging from the teachings on offering suitable water[39] in the tradition of the eighteen Vaibhāṣika schools up to the teachings of

Mahāyāna and the four classes of *tantras*. In particular, with the miraculous powers of the *vīras, ḍakinīs,* and *kalkī* kings, they adopt the teachings of the Jina Tsong kha pa and his spiritual sons, which are more widespread there than in Tibet. The *Emanated Dharma* (*Sprul pa'i chos*) states:

> Kalāpa, surrounded by 900 million towns,
> A region in which Ādibuddha's tradition prevails,
> Measures twelve leagues across.
> The lord of the supreme jeweled palace,
> The sons of the Jina, including Guhyādhipati,
> And the assembly of *krodhas,* including Yamāntaka,
> Are royal manifestations for the sake of transmigrating beings,
> And successively come as *kalkī* kings.

Then, in front of you, [visualize] the earth having the nature of various jewels, vast, very lovely, and even like the palm of your hand. It is beautified with trees made of various jewels and various rivers perfumed with *uragasāra* sandalwood and the like. The entire earth is covered by golden lattice filled with various jeweled lotuses, and the ground, intervening space, and the whole sky are completely and evenly engulfed by a bounty of pleasures to delight the senses, including divine parasols, victory banners, pennants, and canopies. In the center sits a palace, ablaze with seven kinds of jewels. Great light rays spread forth from it, expansively filling incalculable world systems. In its center is a great throne composed of various kinds of jewels and supported by eight large lions, resting on various kinds of jeweled lotuses. It is beautifully embellished with a vast, divine fabric, and is imbued with limitless excellent qualities, and so on.

The earthly Śambhala as a pure land of the human realm has a celestial Sukhāvatī as its prototype. Like a celestial Sukhāvatī, it exceeds in the beauty and magnificence of anything that one has seen. The aesthetic value of a physical world is not denied here. The beauty of Śambhala's nature, palatial structures, and residents and its structural and social orderliness and harmony convey its paradisiacal nature and articulate a longing for an idyllic Buddhist world. The earthly presence of this blissful world and the presence of celestial bodhisattvas who descend there make the ascendance to a celestial Sukhāvatī unnecessary if not unappealing. However, as seen in the travel guides to Śambhala, to those journeying to Śambhala in the present body, it is accessible only after numerous inner and outer dangers and distractions are overcome and after the terrifying river Śītā, which divides our world from the blissful land of Śambhala, is crossed. Hence, although already present on the earth, for those on this side of the river Śītā who are led by mental afflictions, Śambhala has not yet come.

In the narrative frameworks of the works mentioned above, descriptions of Śambhala as a Sukhāvatī, written in the expressive language that articulates the authors' feelings and attitudes, are not mediated by the buddhas. They communicate Śambhala's transcendent reality, which is both spatial and temporal, and esoteric in nature, not only in the sense of being the place dominated by Vajrayāna teachings, but also in the sense of being hidden. The notion of the existence of Śambhala, whether as a Sukhāvatī or as a geographical local, carries a strain of dualism: The world without mental afflictions and the world imbued with mental afflictions, the world of social justice and the unjust world, the world with optimal model of governance and that devoid of it, and so on.

## Notes

1 For the description of Abhirati, see the *Abhirativyūha sūtra* (*Akṣobhya Tathāgatasya Abhirativyūhanamamahāyānaratnakūṭa sūtra*) and Jan Nattier, "The Realm of Akṣobhya: A Missing Piece in the History of Pure Land Buddhism," *Journal of International Association of Buddhist Studies* 23, no. 1 (2000): 44–71.

2 According to the *Vimalaprabhā* commentary on the *Kālacakratantra*, there have been thirty-five million *brāhmaṇic* sages who have lived in the town of Kalāpa, the capital of Śambhala, but there have also been representatives of other castes there; see *Vimalaprabhāṭīkā of Kalkī Śrī Puṇḍarīka on Śrī Laghukālacakratantrarāja*, vol. 1, critically edited and annotated with notes by Jagannatha Upadhyaya (Sarnath, Varanasi: Central Institute of Higher Tibetan Studies, 1986), 22, 27.

3 *Vimalaprabhā* commentary on the *Kālacakratantra*, chap. 1, 22, 27.

4 *Vimalaprabhā* commentary on the *Kālacakratantra*, chap. 1, 23.

5 *Vimalaprabhā* commentary on the *Kālacakratantra*, chap. 1, 23.

6 *Padminī-nāma-pañjikā*, Peking edition, no. 2067, vol. 47.

7 Mkhas grub rje sees a difference between the Buddha, like Kālacakra, who attained all of the twelve stages and the tenth stage bodhisattvas.

8 *Vimalaprabhā* commentary on the *Kālacakratantra*, chap. 1, vol. 1, 30–31.

9 The same text informs us that just as the limitless buddhas teach mundane and transcendent Dharmas in the trichiliocosms or within their buddha-

fields by means of endless, illusory Emanation Bodies, so too do numerous sublime bodhisattvas, the masters of the ten perfections, ten powers, and ten stages (*daśa-bhūmi*), teach in trichiliocosms by means of their limitless Emanation Bodies.

10 *Vimalaprabhā* commentary on the *Kālacakratantra*, chap. 1, vol. 1, 23–24, 26. According to Nāropā's *Paramārthasaṃgraha*, 62, Aḍakavatī is to be understood as the tenth stage (*dharmameghā-bhūmi*).

11 Jambadorj, *Bolor Toly*, vol. 2, book 3 (Ulaanbaatar: Mongolian National University, Center for Mongolian Studies, 2006), 295.

12 *Khünii Oyunyg Barigch Oron, Deed Büteliin Shambalyn Orond Magadtai Törökh khiigeed Rigden Dagvyn Shashintai Magad Uirakhyn Erööl, Khuvytai Taviin Erdeniin Gishgüür Khemeekh Orshvoi* (2003), 19–22.

13 'Jigs med dbang po (1728–1791).

14 *Khünii oyunig barigch oron, deed büteeliin Shambalyn orond magadtai törökh khiigeed Rigden Dagvin shashintai magad uchrakhin erööl, khuvitai shaviin erdeniin gishgüür khemeekh orshvoi*, 2003, 25–27.

15 *The Sekoddeśaṭīkā by Nāropā*, 63, v. 10, *pada a*, cited from the *Root Tantra*.

16 *Shambha la'i zhing gi bkod pa'i 'don sgrigs chos rgyal rigs ldan rnams la mchod pa'i cho ga ka la par bgrod pa'i myur lam zhes bya ba bzhug so*, folio 8b, a xylographic copy from the private collection.

17 He was also popularly known as Gachoi Lam Damba Agramba.

18 *Grub pa'i gnas dpal ldan sham bha lar bsgrod ba'i lam gsal bar byed ba'i rin chen shel gyi them skas shes bya ba bzhugs so*, folio 2a, a xylographic copy from the private collection.

19 *Khünii Oyunyg Barigch Oron, Deed Büteliin Shambalyn Orond Magadtai Törökh khiigeed Rigden Dagvyn Shashintai Magad Uirakhyn Erööl, Khuvytai Taviin Erdeniin Gishgüür Khemeekh Orshvoi* (2003), 17.

20 Ibid., 27.

21 The Sixth Pan chen bla ma's *Guide to Śambhala*, the anonymous Mongolian text discovered in Buryatia and titled *This Is a Sūtra that Shows the Conditions of the Country of Śambhala, the Epoch of the Kings, and the Ways and Means of Travelling [There]*, and Jambadorj's *Crystal Mirror* (*Bolor Toly*, 1848) speak of predictions concerning Nāgārjuna and Tsong kha pa descending from Sukhāvatī to Śambhala, entering their relics, completing their task, and returning to Sukhāvatī.

22 *namo guru / deng dus nas bzung mi'i kha' spyod gling / shambha la'i rten bzang thob nas ni / rang gi snang bsna tshogs shar pa'i tshe / yes shes mtshon gyis 'begs pa'i nus thob shog / oṃ āḥ hūṃ ho haṃ kṣa ma la va ra ya hūṃ phaṭ /* According to the colophon, it was composed on the third day of the twelfth Mongolian month of the male Earth Dragon Year of the sixteenth cycle [of sixty years].

Translation from the Tibetan is my own. I am grateful to Mr. Erdbaatar Amgalan for sharing a copy of the text with me.

23 Blo bzang, the Second Jina is an appellation for Tsong kha pa Blo bzang grags pa (1357–1419).

24 *Shambha la'i smon tshig bzhugs so*, a xylograph, translated by me from Tibetan.

25 *Khünii Oyunyg Barigch Oron, Deed Büteliin Shambalyn Orond Magadtai Törökh khiigeed Rigden Dagvyn Shashintai Magad Uirakhyn Erööl, Khuvytai Taviin Erdeniin Gishgüür Khemeekh Orshvoi* (2003), 5–28.

26 Ibid., 50.

27 Rje bstun Tārānātha, *Dpal ldan ka lā par 'jug pa shes bya ba yul rnams kyi mchog tu gyur ba sham bha lar 'gro thsul gyi lam yig 'phags pa don yod lcags kyus gsung pa bzhugs so.*

28 The complete title of the text *is Grub pa'i gnas chen po sham bha la'i rnam bshad 'phags gyi rtogs brjod dang bcas pa.*

29 For a translation of the prayer and its bilingual version (Tibetan and Mongolian), see Charles Bawden, "The Wish-Prayer for Shambhala Again." *Monumenta Serica* 36 (1984–1985): 477–484.

30 According to Mkhas grub rje, *Dus 'khor ṭik chen* (TC 1075/5–1077/5), Small Jambudvīpa, which measures twenty-five thousand leagues, is divided into six equal sections: India, Tibet, Khotan, China, Great China, and Kailāśa. North of the Kailāśa section is Mount Meru, and south of it is the Śītā River. Śambhala's length from north to south is the same as that of Kailāśa, and it is surrounded by mountains on its periphery. It has the shape of a lotus having eight petals, and a pericarp that makes up one third of the land. See John Newman, "The Outer Wheel of Time: Vajrayana Buddhist Cosmology in the Kalacakra Tantra" (PhD diss., University of Wisconsin, 1987), 581.

31 See *The Sekoddeśaṭīkā by Nāropā* (*Paramārthasaṃgraha*), critical edition of the Sanskrit text by Francesco Sferra and critical edition of the Tibetan translations by Stefania Merzagora, Serie Orientale Roma, vol. 99 (Rome: Istituto Italiano per L'Aftica e L'Orient, 2006), 61, for mention of the ninety-six royal families of Śambhala.

32 See Ronald Davidson, "Hidden Realms and Pure Abodes: Central Asian Buddhism as Frontier Religion in the Literature of India, Nepal, and Tibet," *Pacific World: Journal of the Institute of Buddhist Studies*, third series, no. 4 (2002): 167, for his interpretation of the *Kālacakratantra*'s and the *Vimalaprabhā*'s discussions on the location of Śambhala.

33 See the *Kālacakratantra,* chap. 1, vs. 150–151, 153, and the *Vimalaprabhā* commentary on the *Kālacakratantra,* chap. 1, vs. 16–19, 71–72, 24.

34 I am grateful to Venerable Bulgan and Mr. Lhagvademchig Jadamba for providing me with a copy of the text.

35 According to Mkhas grub rje's commentary on the *Kālacakratantra, Dus 'khor ṭik chen* (TC 1075/5–1077/5), the six equal sections of Small Jambudvīpa are India, Tibet, Khotan, China, Great China, and Kailāśa. See Newman, "The Outer Wheel of Time," 581.

36 Mentioned in the *Vimalaprabhā* as Mahācīna.

37 The text reads: "*sha ra ṇa*" (*śaraṇa*), which is most likely a typographical error, since the word *śaraṇa* does not designate any type of conveyance of transportation, whereas *śarabha* often appears in Buddhist texts along with winged elephants and mythical beings serving as the means of transportation. *Śarabha* is a mythical animal, said to live in high snow mountains, have eight legs, and be stronger than a lion or an elephant.

38 Possibly the name of the goddess Umā.

39 Water for washing the mouth of a monk before and after taking food (*rung chu*).

## Bibliography

Bawden, Charles, R. "The Wish-Prayer for Shambhala Again." *Monumenta Serica* 36 (1984–1985): 453–510.

Davidson, Ronald, M. "Hidden Realms and Pure Abodes: Central Asian Buddhism as Frontier Religion in the Literature of India, Nepal, and Tibet." *Pacific World: Journal of the Institute of Buddhist Studies*, third series, no. 4 (2002): 153–181.

Jambadorj. *Bolor Toly*, vol. 1. Ulaanbaatar: Mongolian National University, Center for Mongolian Studies, 2006.

Minjüür Dechin Shiirev. *Khünii Oyunyg Barigch Oron, Deed Büteliin Shambalyn Orond Magadtai Törökh khiigeed Rigden Dagvyn Shashintai Magad Uirakhyn Erööl, Khuvytai Taviin Erdeniin Gishgüür Khemeekh Orshvoi*. Ulaanbaatar: Admon, 2003.

Mkhas grub rje. *Dus 'khor ṭik chen*. Mkhad grub dge legs dpal bzang: *Rgyud thams cad kyi rgyal po bcom ldan 'das dpal dus kyi 'khor lo mchog gi dang po'i sangs rgyas kyi trsa ba'i rgyud las phyung ba bsdud ba'i rgyud kyi 'grel chen rtsa ba'i rgyud kyi rjes su 'jug pa stong phrag bcu gnyis pa dri ma med pa'i 'od kyi rgya cher bshad pa de kho na nyid snang bar byed pa zhes bya ba*. In *Yab sras gsung 'bum*, Mkhas grub (Kha). Dharamsala: Tibetan Cultural Printing Press, 1983.

Nāropā. *Paramārthasaṃgrahanāmasekoddeśaṭīkā*. In *Sekoddeśaṭīkā of Naḍapāda*, edited by M. Carelli. Gaekwad's Oriental Series, no. 90. Baroda, 1941.

Nattier, Jan. "The Realm of Akṣobhya: A Missing Piece in the History of Pure Land Buddhism." *Journal of International Association of Buddhist Studies* 23, no. 1 (2000): 44–71.

Newman, John. "The Outer Wheel of Time: Vajrayana Buddhist Cosmology in the Kalacakra Tantra." PhD diss., University of Wisconsin, 1987.

Ngag dbang blo bzang chos rje nyi ma bstan 'dzin dbang phyug rje btsun dam pa. *Shambha la'i smon tshig bzhugs so*. Xylographic copy held in Mongolian National Library.

Ngag dbang rta mgrin bsrud. *Shambha la'i zhing gi bkod pa'i 'don sgrigs chos rgyal rigs ldan rnams la mchod pa'i cho ga ka la par bgrod pa'i myur lam zhes bya ba bzhug so*. Xylographic edition private collection.

*Padminī-nāma-pañjikā*. Peking edition, no. 2067, vol. 47.

Pan chen dpal ldan ye shes. *Sham bha la'i lam yig*. In *Gsung 'bum* of the Third Panchen bla ma dpal ldan ye shes. New Delhi: Private publishing by Gurudeva, 1975–1978. TBRC vol. no. 2225, work no. 2046.

*'Phags pa de bzhin gshegs pa mi 'khrugs pa'i bkod pa zhes bya ba theg pa chen po'i mdo* (*Akṣobhya Tathāgatasya Abhirativyūhanamamahāyānaratnakūṭa sūtra*). Derge/Tōhoku, no. 50.

Rje bstun Tārānātha. *Dpal ldan ka lā par 'jug pa shes bya ba yul rnams kyi mchog tu gyur ba sham bha lar 'gro thsul gyi lam yig 'phags pa don yod lcags kyus gsung pa bzhugs so*. In *Nang rig chos mdzod mun les sgron me shes bya ba bzhugs so*. Edited by Ven. Sungnyan Thupwang, Choejor Gyatso, and Rinchen Sang, 317–344. Snajauli, Shimla: Jonang Takten Phuntsok Chosling Cultural Society, Tibetan Buddhist Monastery, 2003.

*The Sekoddeśaṭīkā by Nāropā* (*Paramārthasaṃgraha*). Critical edition of the Sanskrit text by Francesco Sferra and critical edition of the Tibetan translations by Stefania Merzagora. Serie Orientale Roma, vol. 99. Rome: Istituto Italiano per L'Aftica e L'Orient, 2006.

*Shambal-yin orun-u baidal qaɣun-ud-un üy-e kiged zorčiqui-yin yosu arɣ-a ǰam noɣud-i üǰügülegsen sudur ene bolai*. Anonymous, manuscript copy in private collection.

*Shambald Zorchson Nuuts Temdeglel*. Translated from Tibetan by O. Sükhbaatar, D. Buyambasüren, and B. Batsanaa. Ulaanbaatar: Shambhal Niigemleg, 2005.

Shes rab rgya mtsho. *Grub pa'i gnas dpal ldan sham bha lar bsgrod ba'i lam gsal bar byed ba'i rin chen shel gyi them skas shes bya ba bzhugs so*. Xylographic edition in a private collection in Ulaanbaatar.

*Vimalaprabhāṭīkā of Kalkī Śrī Puṇḍarīka on Śrī Laghukālacakratantrarāja by Śrī Mañjuśrīyaśas*, vol. 1. Critically edited and annotated with notes by Jagannatha Upadhyaya. Sarnath, Varanasi: Central Institute of Higher Tibetan Studies, 1986.

# Contributors

**Michihiro Ama** is the Karashima Tsukasa associate professor of Japanese language and culture at the University of Montana. Previously, he taught as assistant professor of Japanese at the University of Alaska, Anchorage. He specializes in the study of modern Japanese Buddhism. His research interests include Buddhism and transnationalism, Buddhism in literature and film, Buddhism and language, Buddhism and gender and ethnicity, and Buddhism and law. He is the author of *Immigrants to the Pure Land: The Modernization, Acculturation, and Globalization of Shin Buddhism, 1898–1941* (2011).

**Anna Andreeva** specializes in the religious and cultural history of premodern Japan. Her main area of expertise is Japanese medieval religions, especially Esoteric Buddhism and kami worship; she is also working on her second book project about childbirth and women's health in medieval Japan. Anna Andreeva earned her PhD at University of Cambridge in 2007, and since then worked as a research fellow at Harvard, Cambridge, the International Research Center for Japanese Studies in Kyoto, and Heidelberg.

**James B. Apple** is an associate professor of Buddhist studies at the University of Calgary. He received his doctorate in Buddhist studies from the University of Wisconsin–Madison. He has published more than forty articles focusing upon the critical analysis of Mahāyāna sutras and topics within Indian and Tibetan Buddhist forms of Buddhism. His most recent books include *A Stairway Taken by the Lucid: Tsong kha pa's Study of Noble Beings* (2013) and *Stairway to Nirvāṇa* (2008).

**Clark Chilson** is an associate professor in the Department of Religious Studies at the University of Pittsburgh, where he teaches on religion in Asia and the relationship between Buddhism and psychology. He is the author of *Secrecy's Power: Covert Shin Buddhists in Japan and Contradictions of Concealment* (2014) and coeditor, with Paul Swanson, of the *Nanzan Guide to Japanese Religions* (2006). Between 2011 and 2014 he did three intensive Naikan retreats at a Naikan training center in Tokyo.

**Ugo Dessì** is Marie Skłodowska-Curie Fellow at Cardiff University, adjunct professor at the Institute for the Study of Religion, Leipzig University, and honorary research associate at the Department of Religious Studies, University of Cape Town. He has published widely on Shin Buddhism, including *Ethics and Society in Contemporary Shin Buddhism* (2007) and *The Social Dimension of Shin Buddhism* (2010). More recently, he has explored the topic of Japanese Buddhism, Shinto, and new religious movements within global dynamics in two monographs: *Japanese Religions and Globalization* (2013) and *The Global Repositioning of Japanese Religions: An Integrated Approach* (2017).

**Thomas Eijō Dreitlein** is professor of Esoteric Buddhist studies at Kōyasan University, Japan. He is working on English translations of the works of Kūkai and on studies of the content of the esoteric ritual manuals imported by Kūkai and how they developed into Japanese *shidai* in the Shingon tradition. He is a fully ordained priest of the Kōyasan Shingon-shū branch of Shingon Buddhism and is the only non-Japanese to have received Gakushu Kanjō, the highest *abhiṣeka* of Kōyasan. He has received and teaches the full transmission of the Shingon ritual practice lineages of Chūin-ryū, Sanbōin-ryū, and several others.

**Jacques Fasan** received his PhD in modern Japanese history from the University of Chicago. His research focuses on late Meiji and Taishō intellectual history. His work on Kiyozawa attempts to situate Kiyozawa within the mainstream of modern Japanese intellectual history by arguing that his religious thought attempted to provide an alternative to both Japanese nationalism and the theories of classical liberal political economy associated with thinkers such as Fukuzawa Yukichi.

**Daniel Getz** is an associate professor in the Department of Philosophy and Religious Studies at Bradley University. His research focuses on the Buddhism of the Song period, particularly as reflected in developments of the Tiantai tradition and in the diverse manifestations of Pure Land practice.

**Georgios T. Halkias** is an assistant professor and undergraduate program director at the Centre of Buddhist Studies at the University of Hong Kong. He earned his DPhil in Oriental studies at the University of Oxford and has held several research posts at the School of Oriental and African Studies, University of London, Warburg Institute, School of Advanced Study, University of London, and at Ruhr-Universität Bochum. He has published extensively on Indo-Tibetan Pure Land Buddhism and other topics. He is the author of *Luminous Bliss: A Religious History of Pure Land Literature in Tibet: With an Annotated Translation and Critical Analysis of the Orgyen-ling Golden Short Sukhāvatīvyūha-sūtra* (2013), and coeditor-in-chief of *The Oxford Research Encyclopedia of Buddhism*.

**Natasha Heller** is an associate professor in the Department of Religious Studies at the University of Virginia. She formerly taught at the University of California, Los Angeles, in the Department of Asian Languages and Cultures. Her earlier research has engaged the relationship between Buddhism and secular culture in China from the Tang dynasty through the Ming, and in 2014 she published a book-length study of an important Yuan dynasty monk titled *Illusory Abiding: The Cultural Construction of the Chan Monk Zhongfeng Mingben*. Presently her research focuses on contemporary Buddhism, and her current book project examines picture books published by Buddhist organizations in Taiwan.

**Charles B. Jones** earned a BA in music (1980) from Morehead State University, a master of theological studies (1988) from the Divinity School of Duke University, and a PhD in history of religions (1996) from the University of Virginia, with a specialization in East Asian Buddhism. He is currently an associate professor in the School of Theology and Religious Studies of the Catholic University of America and has published on Chinese Pure Land Buddhism, the history of Buddhism in Taiwan, interreligious dialogue, and the Jesuit missions in China during the late Ming and early Qing dynasties.

**Gábor Kósa** is an associate professor at the Department of Chinese Studies, Eötvös Loránd University (ELTE University), Budapest, and at present is the member of the MTA–ELTE–SZTE Silk Road Research Group at ELTE University. He graduated from the Department of Chinese Studies at ELTE, Budapest, where he earned his PhD in 2006. His major research interests include Chinese mythology, ancient Chinese shamanic-like practices, and Chinese Manichaeism.

**Ethan Lindsay** completed a PhD in the study of religion at Princeton University in 2012. His dissertation, "Pilgrimage to the Sacred Traces of Kōyasan: Place and Devotion in Late Heian Japan," examines the emergence of Mount Kōya as an increasingly popular site for pilgrimage, burial, and monastic practice in the eleventh and twelfth centuries. He is presently engaged in research on sacred places in medieval Japan, hagiography, and the intersections of Shingon Esoteric Buddhism and other forms of religiosity including Pure Land Buddhism and the cults of local deities.

**Richard D. McBride II** is an associate professor and chair of history at Brigham Young University–Hawaii. He earned a PhD in East Asian Languages and Cultures at UCLA (2001), specializing in Korean and Chinese Buddhism and early Korean history. He was a Fulbright Senior Researcher in Korea in 2007–2008. He is the author of *Domesticating the Dharma: Buddhist Cults and the Hwaŏm Synthesis in Silla Korea* (2008). He is the editor of *State and Society in Middle and Late Silla* (2010), the editor and primary translator of *Hwaŏm I: The Mainstream Tradition*, Collected Works of Korean Buddhism, volume 4 (2012), and the editor and translator of *Hwaŏm II: Selected Works*, Collected Works of Korean Buddhism, volume 5 (2012). His most recent work is *Doctrine and Practice in Medieval Korean Buddhism: The Collected Works of Ŭich'ŏn*, Korean Classics Library: Philosophy and Religion (2017). His current projects include a monograph titled *Aspiring to Enlightenment: Pure Land Buddhism in Silla Korea*.

**Ryan Richard Overbey** studies the intellectual and ritual history of Buddhism, with particular focus on early medieval Buddhist spells and ritual manuals. He studied at Brown University (AB in classics & Sanskrit and religious studies, 2001) and at Harvard University (PhD in the study of religion, 2010). He currently serves as the Robert H. N. Ho Family Foundation Assistant Professor in Buddhist Studies at Skidmore College.

**Richard K. Payne** is Yehan Numata Professor of Japanese Buddhist Studies at the Institute of Buddhist Studies, Berkeley. He is editor-in-chief of the Oxford Bibliographies Buddhism section, and coeditor-in-chief of the Oxford Research Encyclopedia Religion Buddhism section. He recently coedited, with Michael Witzel, *Homa Variations: The Study of Ritual Change across the* Longue Durée (2015). He is the founding chair of the Editorial Committee of the Pure Land Buddhist Studies Series, University of Hawai'i Press.

**Elisabetta Porcu** is a senior lecturer in Asian religions and the director of the Center for the Study of Asian Religions at the University of Cape

Town. Before moving to South Africa in 2014, she worked at universities in Japan, Germany, and Hawai'i. In addition to several articles and book chapters, she is the author of *Pure Land Buddhism in Modern Japanese Culture* (2008), "Pop Religion in Japan: Temples, Icons and Branding" (2014), and "Japanese Buddhisms in Diaspora" (2018). She is currently working on two monographs on Japanese religions and popular culture and on the Gion Festival in Kyoto. She is the founding editor of the *Journal of Religion in Japan* (Brill).

**Aaron P. Proffitt** received his PhD in Buddhist studies from the University of Michigan and currently works as an assistant professor of Japanese studies at the State University of New York (SUNY), Albany. His research focuses on the scholar-monk Dōhan (1179–1252), the diversity of Japanese Pure Land thought in the Kamakura period (1185–1333), and East Asian Buddhist theories of ritual speech (mantra, spells, etc.) and the afterlife. Proffitt is currently working on a book manuscript tentatively titled *Mysteries of Speech and Breath: Dōhan and Esoteric Pure Land Buddhism in Medieval Japan*.

**Fabio Rambelli** is professor of Japanese religions and International Shinto Foundation endowed chair in Shinto studies at the University of California, Santa Barbara. His research focuses primarily on the intellectual history of Shinto and the cultural analysis of the Esoteric Buddhist tradition in Japan. He is the author of *Buddhist Materiality* (2008), *Buddhism and Iconoclasm in East Asia* (with Eric Reinders, 2012), *A Buddhist Theory of Semiotics* (2013), and *Zen Anarchism* (2013), and the editor of *Buddhas and Kami in Japan* (with Mark Teeuwen, 2002) and *The Sea and the Sacred in Japan* (2018).

**Robert F. Rhodes** is a professor of Buddhist studies at Otani University in Kyoto, Japan. His research interests include Japanese Pure Land Buddhism and the Sino-Japanese Tiantai/Tendai tradition. He is the author of *Genshin's Ōjōyōshū and the Construction of Pure Land Discourse in Heian Japan* (2017). Together with Mark L. Blum, he has edited a collection of essays by modern Shin Buddhist thinkers titled *Cultivating Spirituality: A Modern Shin Buddhist Anthology* (2011).

**Jonathan A. Silk** received his PhD in Buddhist studies in 1994 from the University of Michigan. He has taught at Yale University and UCLA and is now professor in the study of Buddhism at Leiden University. He is the author of a number of books, including *Riven by Lust: Incest and Schism in Indian Buddhist Legend and Historiography* (2008), and is the general editor of Brill's *Encyclopedia of Buddhism* (2015–).

**Henrik H. Sørensen** is an independent scholar who has formerly taught at the University of Copenhagen and been a senior researcher at the National Museum in Denmark. He is currently the director of an independent research center, the Seminar for Buddhist Studies, affiliated with the University of Edinburgh through the publication of the electronic journal *Journal for the Study of East and Central Asian Religions* (*eJECAR*). His research interests include the relationship between religious practice and material culture in East Asia; Esoteric Buddhism; issues relating to the definition, textual history, and iconography of early Esoteric Buddhism in China; and the relationship and mutual influence of Buddhism and Daoism in medieval China. He was recently a research fellow at the KHK Research Project at Ruhr University, Germany (2011–2012), where he worked with Buddhist and Daoist interactions in medieval China. Since August 2017 he has been senior researcher at a five-year EU-sponsored project at Ruhr University concerning Buddhism on the Silk Road.

**Jacqueline I. Stone** is a professor of Japanese religions in the Religion Department at Princeton University. Her chief areas of focus are Japanese Buddhism of the medieval and modern periods. Among her research interests are death and dying in Buddhism, Buddhism and nationalism, and traditions of the *Lotus Sutra*, particularly Tendai and Nichiren. Her publications include *Original Enlightenment and the Transformation of Medieval Japanese Buddhism* (1999) and *Right Thoughts at the Last Moment: Buddhism and Deathbed Practices in Early Medieval Japan* (2016).

**Vesna A. Wallace** is a professor of religious studies in the Department of Religious Studies at the University of California in Santa Barbara. Her two areas of specialization are Indian Buddhism, particularly Mahāyāna and Vajrayāna traditions, and Mongolian Buddhism. She has authored and translated four books related to Indian Buddhism, three of which pertain to the Kālacakra tantric tradition in India, and she has published numerous articles on Indian and Mongolian Buddhism. She has also brought to press an edited volume on Mongolian Buddhism titled *Buddhism in Mongolian Culture, History, and Society* and is currently conducting research on the interplay between texts, images, and rituals in Mongolian Buddhism.

# Index

*Abhidharmakośa*, 195
*abhijñā* (extrasensory knowledge), 745
Abhirati, 6, 33, 70–84, 744
*abhiṣeka*, 227, 232
ablutions, 227–228, 234
Absolutely Infinite *(zettai mugensha)*, 557–562
Acalanātha Vidyārāja (Fudō Myōō), 61, 85
Accounts of auspicious responses accompanying birth in the Western Pure Land *(Wangsheng xifang jintu ruiyang zhuan)*, 459
Accounts of those from Mount Kōya who attained birth in a pure land, late twelfth century. See *Kōyasan ōjōden*
Achala, 176n15
Acharya, Diwakar, 79
*Achu fa* (Akṣobhya method), 224, 248n3
Aḍakavatī, 746
aesthetics: overview of, 551–553; translations, *Vow of Non-Discrimination between Beauty and Ugliness*, 587–601
*The Age of Unification*, 631–660; introduction, 553, 631–640; translation, 640–651
Agni, 85
Agvaan Damdinsüren (Ngag dbang rta mgrin bsrud), 746, 751. See also *The Swift Path to Kalāpa*
*aiśvarya* (sovereignty), 745
*ajikan* (Contemplation of the Letter A), 274
*Ajitasenavyākaraṇanirdeśa*, 514
Akamatsu, 502, 503, 523n4, 527nn18–19, 528n27
Ākāśagarbha, 229, 237–238
Akṣobhya (Buddha of the Eastern Pure Land; Ashuku), 6, 30, 33; cult of, 84–85; *homa* ritual, 79–114; importance of, 79–83; pure land of (Abhirati), 6, 33, 70–84, 744
Akṣobhya method *(Achu fa)*, 224, 248n3
*Akṣobhyavyūha*, 82, 112n30
*akunin shōki* doctrine, 558–559
*akunin shōki setsu* (evil person as object of Amida's vow), 558–559
Ama, Michihiro, 320, 379
Amaterasu, 351, 366–368
*Amerika bukkyō no shōrai. See* The Future of American Buddhism
Amida. *See* Amitābha
*Amidajō*, 273
*Amida-santai-setsu*, 274–275
*A-MI-TA* (name), 274–293
Amitābha (Amitāyus; Amida): contemplation of, 30, 115–138; cult of, 3, 6, 8–9, 14, 80–84, 269, 503; ethical discourses involving, 551; Japanese emperor as, 320, 349–378, 574; in Korea, 321, 420–451; in miracle tales, 478; *Namu Amidabutsu*, 30, 117–119, 271, 275; poetry dedicated to, 456, 496–539; pure land of, *See* Sukhāvatī; ritual practices involving, 29–30, 143–144; in Shin Buddhism, 396; in Tibet, 140, 143–144. See also *Quintessence of Amitābha*; in Vietnam, 15; visualizations, 157–158, 163–164. See also *Himitsu nenbutsu sho; Quintessence of Amitābha*; vows of, 552, 573–574, 588–590
*Amitābhā-hṛdaya-rāga-yamāri-sādhananāma.* See *Quintessence of Amitābha*
*Amitābha Sūtra.* See *Sukhāvatīvyūha sūtra*
*Amit'a-gyŏng*, 422–428
*A mi ta pur, namo a mi ta pur* (phrase), 502
Amitāyus. *See* Amitābha
*Amitāyus Ritual Manual (Wuliangshou yigui)*, 223–268; contents of, 226–231; introduction, 158, 223–231; China, 224–225; Japan, 225–226; translation,

232–247; introduction, 232–233; opening rituals, 233–242; main practice, 242–246; concluding rituals, 246–247
Amitāyus Tathāgata, *dhāraṇī* of, 224
*Amitāyus Visualization Sūtra*, 224–225, 231, 249n4, 249n6
*Amituo jing*. *See* Smaller *Sukhāvatīvyūha sūtra*
Amoghavajra, 59, 73n4, 73n11, 158, 224, 249n6. See also *Amitāyus Ritual Manual*
Amṛta-Kuṇḍalī ritual manual *(Ganlu Juntuli yigui)*, 223, 248n3, 250n8, 253n20, 253n23, 254n26
Amstutz, Galen, 3–4, 709–710
*Analects*, 625n19
*ānapāna* (counting breaths), 333–334
Andreeva, Anna, 30, 56
Anesaki Masaharu, 633
animals, mantras for, 330–331
*anjin* (peace of mind), 572
Annen, 60, 248n2, 271
Answers to Forty-Eight Questions about the Pure Land, 319, 322–348; introduction, 322–323; translation, 323–346; preface, 323–324; Question 1 (as the mind is pure...), 324–326; Question 2 (reputation and profit), 326; Question 3 (boddhisattva), 327; Question 4 (dreams), 327–328; Question 6 (dharma-body), 328–329; Question 7 (rebirth), 329–330; Question 9 *(nianfo)*, 330; Question 12 (animals), 330–331; Question 13 (enticements), 331–332; Question 15 (diversity of teaching), 332–333; Question 18 *(ānapāna)*, 333–334; Question 19 *(nianfo)*, 334–335; Question 20 (sickness of great delusion), 335; Question 24 (Tuṣita Heaven), 335–336; Question 26 (number of buddhas), 336–337; Question 27 (longevity of buddhas), 337–338; Question 28 (Utmost Bliss), 338–339; Question 30 (identical nature of buddhas), 339; Question 33 (purity), 339–340; Question 34 *(nianfo)*, 340; Question 36 *(nianfo)*, 340–341; Question 37 *(nianfo)*, 341–342; Question 39 (delusion), 342; Question 41 (women), 342–343; Question 43 (one mind), 343–344; Question 45 (dharma), 344; Question 46 (lotus calyx), 344–345; Question 47 *(saṃsāra)*, 345–346
Anuttarayoga *(bla na med pa'i rgyu)*, 162, 178n23, 180n39
Anyue Wofoyuan, 34
Anzai Kenjō, 574
*Aparimitāyurjñāna* sūtra, 502, 527nn18–19
Apparition de *Tsong-kha-pa*, 196
Apple, James, 158, 188
*araññavāsi* (forest dweller), 83
*argha*-water, 240–241, 246
Arguments of a rustic bowl *(Kibokuron)*, 64
arts, 15–16, 552, 587. *See also* aesthetics
*Ārya-Mañjuśrī-nāmāṣṭaśatakam*, 515
Ashuku. *See* Akṣobhya
*Ashu soku sai goma shiki shidai, Chūin*. See *Ritual Manual for the Protective Fire Offering devoted to Akṣobhya, Chūin Lineage*
An aspirational prayer for rebirth in Sukhāvāti *(Bde ba can du skye ba'i smon lam)*, 189
*Aspiration Prayer to the Pure Land Sukhāvatī (Rnam dag bde chen zhing gi smon lam)*, 141, 505
*Aṣṭasāh asrikāprajñāramitāsūtra* (Prajñāpāramitā sutra), 83
"as the mind is pure the land is pure," 324–326
*Atīśa and Tibet* (Chattopadhyaya), 175n8
Atīśa Dīpaṃkaraśrījñāna: biography of, 157, 159–162; texts, 159–160. See also *Quintessence of Amitābha*
Avalokiteśvara: in Kadampa School, 176n15; longevity of, 81; mantra of, 170, 227, 230–231, 242–244; as Regent of Sukhāvatī, 140, 143–144; Tibetan emperor as, 177n17
*Avataṃsaka-sūtra*, 424, 710
awakening, 5, 541–542, 607–611
awareness empowerments, 163, 178n24

*banbutsu ittai* (cosmos as one body), 557–558
*bar do* (intermediate state after death), 144, 749
Baso chöjé, 191
*bdag bskyed rim* (self-generation stage), 169–170, 181n43
*Bde ba can du skye ba'i smon lam* (An aspirational prayer for rebirth in Sukhāvāti), 189
*Bde ba can gyi smon lam dag zhing nye lam* (A shortcut to the Pure Land: A vow for the Land of Bliss), 505
*Bde ba can gyi zhing du bgrod pa'i myur lam gsal bar byed pa'i sgron me* (The clarifying lamp: A quick path for travel to the Land of Bliss), 505
*Bde ba can gyi zhing du skye ba 'dzin pa'i smon lam zhing mchog sgo 'byed* (Opening the door to the best land: A prayer to obtain birth in the Land of Bliss), 505
*Bde ba can gyi zhing du thogs pa med par bgrod pa'i myur lam* (An unhindered quick path to the Land of Bliss), 505
*Bde ba can gyi zhing las brtsams pa'i gtam dge ba'i lo tog spel byed dbyar skyes sprin chen glal ba'i sgra dbyangs* (A talk on the Land of Bliss: Thundering sound from the big bursting summer clouds which nourish the Crops of Good Qualities), 505
*Bde ba can gyi zhing sbyong ba'i dad pa gsal bar byed pa drang srong lung gi nyi ma* (The sun of the sage's instruction called clarification of faith [leading to] cultivation of the Land of Bliss), 505
*Bde chen zhing sgrub thabs*. See *Sādhana of the Pure Land Sukhāvatī*
*Bden pa gnyis la 'jug pa (Entry in the Two Truths; Satyadvayāvatāra)*, 161
*bde smon (demön)*, 140
beauty, 552, 588–590. *See also* aesthetics
Before Going to Be Reborn, Great Happiness Has Already Appeared, 487–491
*beikoku*, 382
*Benji jing* (Scripture on the fundamental boundary), 665
Bergen, Wesley, 12–13
Berkeley Buddhist Study Group, 382
*beyül (sbas yul)* (hidden valleys), 139
*Bhadrakalpika-sūtra*, 215n38
Bhagavān, 745
Bhairava (Yamāntaka), 166, 169–170, 180n40
*Bhaiṣajyaguru*, 519–520
Bhāviveka, 160
binding the earth, 228–229, 236–237
*Bi no hōmon (The Dharma Gate of Beauty)*, 552, 588–591
*Bi no Jōdo (The Pure Land of Beauty)*, 552
*bi no shūmon* (religious gate of beauty), 589
birth in a pure land at death *(ōjō)*, 458
*bishū funbetsu* (distinction between beauty and ugliness), 590
*bishū mibun* (non-distinction between beauty and ugliness), 590
*Bka' chems ka khol ma (Pillar Testament)*, 162, 174n3
*Bka' gdams glegs bam (Scriptures of the Kadampa)*, 151n13
*bka' gdams pa* (Kadampa School), 160, 176n15
*bla na med pa'i rgyu* (Anuttarayoga), 162, 178n23, 180n39
*Blaze of Reasoning (Tarkajvāla; Rtog ge 'bar ba)*, 160
*blo byong* (mind training) manuals, 160
Blo bzang chos kyi rgyal mthan, 505
Blo bzang dpal ldan ye shes (Sixth Panchen Lama), 749–750, 758n21
Blum, Mark, 3–4
*Bodaishinron*, 60, 64
*Bodaishinron hishaku (Secret Commentary* on the *Bodaishinron)*, 60
*bodhicitta*, 65, 117, 230–231, 321, 420, 424
*Bodhigarbhālaṅkāralakṣa-dhāraṇī* (Dhāraṇī of the Hundred Thousand Ornaments of the Essence of Awakening), 13
*bodhimaṇḍa*, 228–229, 238
*Bodhipathapradīpa (Lamp for the Path to Enlightenment; Byang chub lam gyi sgron ma)*, 159–160, 175n4

bodhisattva(s): presence in pure land, 3–4, 83, 327; who become buddhas, 80–83. See also *specific boddhisattva*
*Bodhisattvamaṇyāvalī (Byang chub sems nor bu'i 'phreng ba; Bodhisattva's Garland of Jewels)*, 160
*Bodhisattva's Garland of Jewels (Byang chub sems nor bu'i 'phreng ba; Bodhisattvamaṇyāvalī)*, 160
Bodhisattva Superior Conduct (Jōgyō), 636
Bogel, Cynthea, 57
*Bolur Toli (Crystal Mirror)*, 746, 758n21
*bonbu* (ordinary persons), 573
book, cult of, 13, 20n47, 21n50
Boyce, Mary, 711, 713
breath counting *(ānapāna)*, 333–334
Brief account of lectures *(Kakugenshō)*, 63
Bryder, P., 711
*bstan 'gyur* (Tengyur), 161–162, 170
buddha(s): bodhisattvas who become, 80–83; delusory, 342; identical nature of, 339; longevity of, 81, 337–338; number of, 111n12, 337; presence in pure land, 3–4, 83; pure lands associated with, 4, 14–15. See also *specific buddha*
Buddha Family, 227–231, 234–235
*buddhakṣetra* (buddha-field), 3, 6, 30, 744; purification of, 169. See also *specific pure land*
*buddhanusmṛti*, 4–5. See also *nenbutsu*
Buddha Realms of the Ten Directions *(shifang fotu)*, 666
'buddha-recollection practice, 8
Buddha's benevolence *(hō-on)*, 571
Buddhas of the Fortunate Aeon, 199
*Buddha's Salvation (Hotoke no kyūsai)*, 381
Buddhism: *versus* Confucianism, 602; cult in, 9–14, 79–86; genres in, 1–3, 14–16. See also *specific genre, such as Mahāyāna or Tantric*; geopolitical categories, 1–2, 16n2. See also *specific area, such as Japan or Tibet*; modernization of, 12, 319–320, 351, 382, 631–640; Pure Land, *See* Pure Land Buddhism
*Buddhism for Youth*, 380
Buddhist aesthetics *(Bukkyō bigaku)*, 590
Buddhist Churches of America (BCA), 111n7, 379–382
Buddhist Mission of North America (BMNA), 382
Buddho-Daoism, 663, 665–706
Buijnsters, Marc, 73n4
*Bukkyō bigaku* (Buddhist aesthetics), 590
*Bukkyō bigaku no higan (Compassionate Vow of a Buddhist Aesthetics)*, 588, 590
*bukkyōkai*, 382
*Busshi seikatsu (The Life of Buddhists)*, 381
*Busshō kaisetsu daijiten* (Dictionary of Buddhist texts), 605
Butön, 161, 176n14, 745
*Byang chub lam gyi sgron ma (Lamp for the Path to Enlightenment; Bodhipathapradīpa)*, 159–160, 175n4
Byang chub 'od (Jangchup Ö), 159
*Byang chub sems nor bu'i 'phreng ba (Bodhisattva's Garland of Jewels; Bodhisattvamaṇyāvalī)*, 160
*Byōchū shugyōki*, 274
*byōnin* (the sick), 397
*'byung ba lnga* (five elements), 170

Cakrasaṃvara, 161
calculations *(hakarai)*, 571
Campany, R., 711
Candrakīrti, 160, 514
canon, 501–504, 526n14
Carcikā (Carccā), 170, 181n44
Ceaselessly Reciting the Name of the Buddha, Ghosts Retreat and Illness Is Cured, 482–483
Chan-Pure Land traditions: Dzogchen (Great Perfection), 4; exoteric-esoteric divide, 19n29, 250n8; Li Yuansong on, 479; poetry, 540–548; Wang Rixiu on, 604–606, 618; Zhongfeng Mingben on, 456
chanting. *See* recitation
charity *(shi)*, 668
*Charyatantra* (Performance Tantra), 178n24
Chattopadhyaya, Alaka, 175n8
Chégompa (Lce sgom pa), 166
Chen Hailiang, 482

Chen Jinguo, 712
*Chen Zuolong*, 668
*Cherishing the Pure Land:* introduction, 540–544, 546; translation, 544–547
Chilson, Clark, 320, 396
Chinese Buddhism: canon, 502–504, 526n14; contemplative visualizations, 158, 163, 223–225; Daoism, 663, 665–706; doctrinal expositions, 322–348; ethical discourses, 551–552, 602–630; life-writing, 455–456, 458–459, 477–495; Manicheism, 663–664, 707–743; poetry, 456, 540–548; pure lands, 6; ritual practices, 33; Tang dynasty, *See* Tang Buddhism; Tibetan practices influenced by, 504
*Chos 'byung jin bris nor bu 'phreng ba (The Jewel Garland of Buddhist History)*, 161
Christianity, 5, 9–12, 18n19, 111n11, 636
Christmas, 320, 381, 391–392
Chu bzang bla ma Ye shes rgya mtsho, 505
Chūin-ryū schools, 253n20, 253n22
*Chūju kankyō no shi*, 252n13
churches, 10–12
Cintāmaṇicakra ritual manual. see *Ruyilun yigui*
The clarifying lamp: A quick path for travel to the Land of Bliss *(Bde ba can gyi zhing du bgrod pa'i myur lam gsal bar byed pa'i sgron me)*, 505
clerks, Longshu's entreaty to, 615–616
*Cloud of White Lotus Offerings*, 163
The Coexistence of Freedom and Submission: introduction, 551, 554–559; translation, 562–564
Collection of Essential Passages Concerning Birth into the Pure Land of Buddha Amida. See *Ōjōyōshū*
Collection of impressive teachings I heard *(Jūjūshinron uchigikishū)*, 60
*Collection of Instructions on the Middle Way (Dbu ma man ngag gi 'bum)*, 161
Collection of leaves gathered in stormy ravines *(Keiranshūyōshū)*, 64
*The Collection of the Shared Source of the Myriad Good Deeds (Wanshan tonggui ji)*, 541
colophon: *Longshu's Discourse on Pure Land*, 604, 625n8; *sādhana* of Amitābha, 144, 148–149
Commentary on the *Amitābha Sūtra Spoken by the Buddha*. See *Pulsŏl Amita-gyŏng so*
*Commentary on the Mahāvairocana Sūtra (Darijing shu, Dainichikyō sho)*, 59
Commentary on the *Sukhāvatīvyūhopadeśa (Wangsheng lun zhu)*, 321, 420, 423–428
Commentary on the Sūtra of Guiding Principle *(Liqujing shu, Rishushaku)*, 73n4
*Compassionate Vow of a Buddhist Aesthetics (Bukkyō bigaku no higan)*, 588, 590
Compendium of the Blissful Country *(Lebang wenlei)*, 604–605, 625n4
Compendium on the secret contemplation of Buddha. See *Himitsu nenbutsu sho*
*Composition on the Land of Śambhala*, 746
Confucianism: *versus* Buddhism, 602; *Longshu's Discourse on Pure Land*, 552, 602–630; in Shin Buddhism, 555, 558, 571, 632
*Consecration Scripture (Guanding jing)*, 29–30, 34, 50n5
*The Consecration Scripture Spoken by the Buddha on Being Reborn in Whichever of the Pure Lands of the Ten Directions You Wish*, 33–55; introduction, 33–35; translation, 36–49
contemplation: overview of, 157–158; gate of, 118–119. See also *nenbutsu*; translations: *Amitāyus Ritual Manual*, 223–268; *Himitsu nenbutsu sho*, 269–315; *Hundred Deities of Tuṣita*, 188–222; *Quintessence of Amitābha*, 159–187
Contemplation of the Letter A *(ajikan)*, 274
*Contemplation Sūtra*, 275, 341
cosmological locations for pure lands, 4, 8–9, 744–751
cosmos as one body *(banbutsu ittai)*, 557–558
The Cosmos as One Body: introduction, 551, 554–559; translation, 559–562
Council of Bsam yas, 506
craftsmen, Longshu's entreaty to, 624

*Crystal Mirror (Bolur Toli)*, 746, 758n21
Cực Lạc, 15
cult: in Pure Land Buddhism, 13–15, 79–86; as unit of study, 9–14
cultivation of the pure land, 607, 612–614
Cundī sūtra *(Zhunti jing)*, 224, 248n3, 249n7

*Dafangguang fo Huayan-jing Rufajie-pin dunzheng Piluzhena fashen zilun yujia yigui*, 249n6
*Dafangguang fo Huayan-jing Rufajie-pin sishierzi guanmen*, 249n6
*dag snang gter* (pure vision treasure), 141, 150n9
Dahui Zonggao, 541, 604
Daidenbōin, 57, 62
Daigoji, 63, 269
Daigo-ryū schools, 253n20
*Daijō mitsugonkyō* (Sūtra of the Mysterious Adornment of the Great Vehicle), 59
*daimoku* (invocation of *Lotus Sūtra*'s title), 634, 637–638
*Daimuryōjukyō. See* Larger *Sukhāvatīvyūha sūtra*
*Dai-Nihon kōtei shukusatsu daizōkyō*, 247n1
Daizong, 711
*Dai Zong chao zengsi Kong dabianzheng guangzhi sanzang heshang biaozhi ji*, 248n2
*Ḍākinī Vajrapañjara Tantra (Mkha' 'gro ma rdo rje gur gyi rgyud)*, 179n32
*Dam tshig thams cad bsdus pa (Summary of all Pledges; Sarvasamayasaṃgraha)*, 161
Dao'an, 502
Dao'ang, 335
Daochuo, 8
Daoism, 663, 665–706
Daoming, 712, 714
Daoxue, 603
*Darijing shu*, 73n12
*Darijing shu, Dainichikyō sho (Commentary on the Mahāvairocana Sūtra)*, 59
*daśa-bala* (ten powers), 745
*daśa-paramitā* (ten perfections), 745
*Dasheng miyan jing* (Sūtra of the Mysterious Adornment of the Great Vehicle), 59
*Da Tang xiyuji*, 711
*Da Tang zhenyuan xu kaiyuan shijiao lu*, 248n2
Davidson, Ronald, 3, 84, 174n3
*daxian* (great worthies), 607, 625n19
*Dbu ma man ngag gi 'bum (Collection of Instructions on the Middle Way)*, 161
death: intermediate state after *(bar do)*, 144, 749; sublimation of, 165–167
deathbed rituals *(rinjū gyōgi)*, 460
Dechen nyingpo, 197
defilment, 339–340
deity yoga *(lha'i rnal 'byor; devatāyoga)*, 164–165, 178n26
delusion, 335, 342
*demön (bde smon)*, 140
demythologization, 552, 556, 572–573
Denbōe, 56–57, 59
denomination, 10
desire: six heavens of, 195; sublimation of, 165–166, 179n32, 179n35
Dessì, Ugo, 551, 571
devotional activities: effectiveness of, 477. *See also* meditation; recitation; ritual practices
Dewai Dorjé, 194
Dga' ldan pa, 210n3
*dga' ldan yid dga' chos 'dzin* (Pleasant Doctrine-bearing Joyous Place), 197, 214n34
*dge lugs pa. See* Gelukpa School
*Dhammapada*, 573, 577
*dhāraṇī* (spells), 668
*dhāraṇī* of Amitāyus, 224, 230–231, 243–246
Dhāraṇī of the Hundred Thousand Ornaments of the Essence of Awakening *(Bodhigarbhālaṅkāralakṣa-dhāraṇī)*, 13
*The Dharma and Beauty (Hō to Bi)*, 588
dharma-body *(dharmakāya; hosshin; fashen)*: contemplation of, 118–119. See also *nenbutsu*; Mahāvairocana, 59, 67–72, 271, 276–297; nature of, 328–329
*The Dharma Gate of Beauty (Bi no hōmon)*, 552, 588–591
Dharmākara, 3, 275, 323, 396. *See also* Amitābha

*dharmakāya,* 19n29
Dharmarakṣita, 175n6
*Dhutaguṇanirdeśa,* 521
*dhūtaguṇas* (purification practices), 501, 504
Diamond-Vajra World (Kongōkai), 59
*A Diary of An Enemy Alien in Santa Fe and Lordsburg Internment Camps,* 379
Dictionary of Buddhist texts *(Busshō kaisetsu daijiten),* 605
Đi Dà Phật (Buddha Amitābha), 15
difficult practices *(nangyō),* 590
Dīpaṃkaraśrījñāna. *See* Atīśa Dīpaṃkaraśrījñāna
*Discourse on Ten Doubts about Pure Land,* 322
*Divine Scripture on the Rebirth in the Pure Land of the Lingbao Highest Cavern Mystery (Taishang dongxuan lingbao jingtu sheng shen jing),* 665–706; contents, 669; introduction, 663, 665–669; translation, 669–699; preamble, 669–670; beholding the pure lands, 670–671; causes for the pure lands, 671–677; conditions for rebirth in the pure lands, 677–678; describing the pure lands, 679–693; additional description of the pure lands, 693–697; conclusion, 697–699
Dkon mchog Darmabazar, 746
Dkon mchog tshul khrims (Könchok Tsültrim), 163
*Dmigs brtse ma* (Objectless Loving-Kindness Prayer), 191–193, 198, 212n18
*dōbō* (fellow companions), 571–572
doctrinal classification *(p'an'gyo; panjiao),* 420
Doctrinal essentials of the *Wuliangshou jing (Muryangsu-gyŏng chongyo),* 421–422
doctrine: overview of, 319–321; practice fused with, 542–543; privileging of, 2; translations: Answers to Forty-Eight Questions about the Pure Land, 322–348; The Future of American Buddhism, 379–395; *Naikan's Path,* 396–419; *Pulsŏl Amita-gyŏng so,* 420–451; The Role of Buddhism in Emperor Worship, 349–378
'Dod chags gshin rje gshe (Yamāntaka of Passion), 180n36
Dōhan, 158, 269–271. See also *Himitsu nenbutsu sho*
*Dōkyō toso no kyōden,* 700n6
Ḍombhīheruka, 176n14
Dpal yul (Payül) lineage, 142
dreams, 327–328, 477–478
dream-yoga meditation *(rmi lam),* 144, 146
Dreitlein, Thomas Eijō, 158, 223
Drepung Gomang, 195
Dreyfus, George, 190
Dromtön, 160
dualism, 590
*dug gsum* (three poisons), 169
Dülnakpa Palden Sangpo, 192, 199
Dunhuang: *Consecration Scripture,* 34, 50n8; *Divine Scripture on the Rebirth in the Pure Land of the Lingbao Highest Cavern Mystery,* 665–706; multilingualism of, 525n7; *In Praise of His Mighty Name,* 496–539; *In Praise of the Realm of Light,* 664, 707–743
*Dus 'khor ṭik chen,* 759n30
*Dus kyi 'khor lo rtsa rgyud (Kalachakra Tantra),* 161
Dzingji, 189
Dzogchen (the Great Perfection), 4

easy practices *(igyō),* 590
Eighteen Methods Recitation Sequence manuals *(Jūhachidō nenju shidai),* 225–226, 253n20
Eighth Bogdo Jebtsundamba (Ngag dbang blo bzang chos rje nyi ma bstan 'dzin dbang phyug), 748
8,000 Line Perfection of Wisdom Sutra, 112n30
*Ekādaśamukham,* 519
Eliot, Charles, 5–6
elites, privileging of, 2, 13–14, 16n4, 461–462
Emanation Bodies *(nirmāṇakāya),* 19n29, 745–746, 757n9
emperor worship, 177n17, 319–320, 349–378, 574
empowerment (initiation), 10, 144, 148, 163, 243
emptiness, dharma of, 344

Enchin, 248n2
Enchin faction, 116
End-Stage Nose Cancer Completely Cured through the Recitation of the Buddha's Name, 483–485
Enjoyment Body *(saṃbhogakāya)*, 745
the enlightened *(kaigoin)*, 397
enlightenment, 5, 59–60, 398
Ennin faction, 116, 248n2
Enryakuji, 115–116
enticements, 331–332
*Entrance to Kalāpa (Ka lā par jug pa)*, 749
*Entry in the Two Truths (Bden pa gnyis la 'jug pa; Satyadvayāvatāra)*, 161
Epictetus, 568n9
*eshō funi*, 634
Esoteric Buddhism: *versus* exoteric Pure Land, 8, 19n29, 250n8, 269; Japanese, *See* Shingon School; ritual practices, 30–31, 56–78; visualizations, 157–158; *Amitāyus Ritual Manual*, 223–268; *Quintessence of Amitābha*, 159–187
Essays on Religion and Ethics: introduction, 551, 554–559; translations: The Coexistence of Freedom and Submission, 562–564; The Cosmos as One Body, 559–562; Peace and Comfort Beyond Ethics, 564–568
*Essentials of Rebirth in the Pure Land.* See *Ōjōyōshū*
ethics: overview of, 551–553; translations: *The Age of Unification*, 631–660; Essays on Religion and Ethics, 559–568; *Longshu's Discourse on Pure Land*, 602–630; *The Pure Land as a Principle of Criticism*, 571–586
eulogy *(zan)*, 712
*Eulogy of the Five Lights*, 712
Eun, 248n2
Euro-American bias, 5, 9–14, 17n5, 17n7, 19n31, 111n8, 111n11, 636
evil, tendency to condone *(zōaku muge)*, 571
evil person as object of Amida's vow *(akunin shōki setsu)*, 558–559
Exalted Victory Banner (Maitreya's palace), 197
extraordinary signs *(isō)*, 458, 460
extrasensory knowledge *(abhijñā)*, 745

familial positions, Longshu's entreaties by, 607–608, 620–621
Fangshan, 34, 50n9
farmers, Longshu's entreaty to, 622
Fasan, Jacques, 551, 554
*fashen. See* dharma-body
Faure, Bernard, 11, 20n47
Fazhao, 8, 502
fellow companions *(dōbō)*, 571–572
A Felon Recollects the Buddha, and Amitābha Comes to Greet Him, 491–494
Feng Zizhen, 543–544
Fenollosa, Ernest, 555
filial piety *(xiao)*, 668
filial sons, Longshu's entreaty to, 620
Final Dharma *(mappō)* age, 632–660
finites *(yūgensha)*, 557–558
five elements *('byung ba lnga)*, 170
Fogelin, Lars, 16
Foguangshan, 479
folk crafts *(mingei)* movement, 552, 587, 590
forest dweller *(araññavāsi)*, 83
*Foshuo guan wuliangshou fo jing* (The scripture on the contemplation of the Buddha of Infinite Life spoken by the Buddha), 478
Fourth Vow of Amida Buddha, 552, 588–590
Fudō Myōō (Acalanātha Vidyārāja), 61, 85
*Fudō soku sai goma*, 85
Fukumoto, 398, 403
funereal rituals: in *Consecration Scripture*, 34, 36–49; pure lands in, 29–30; in Tibetan Buddhism, 7
Fussmann, Gérard, 709
The Future of American Buddhism *(Amerika bukkyō no shōrai)*, 379–395; introduction, 320, 379–382; translation, 383–394; implications for the future, 383–385; past and present, 385–387; the way it should be, 387–390; practice at home, 390–394

Gachoi Lam Damba Agramba (Prajñāsāgara; Shes rab rgya mtsho), 746, 758n17
*Gaṇḍavyūha,* 249n6
Ganden, 188
*Ganlu Juntuli yigui* (Amṛta-Kuṇḍalī ritual manual), 223, 248n3, 250n8, 253n20, 253n23, 254n26
*ganying* (sympathetic resonance), 477
*garbhakośadhātu maṇḍala,* 84–85
Garden of selflessness (Mugaen), 349
A garland of wish-fulfilling jewels, an extraordinary practice manual for the profound path of guru-yoga of the Sé tantric tradition *(Srad brgyud lugs kyi zab lam bla ma'i rnal 'byor thun mong ma yin pa'i khrid yig tsit ta ma ni'i phreng ba),* 196–197
gates of mindfulness, 117–118
*gāthā:* Manichean *Hymnscroll,* 712; *Wangsheng lun,* 321, 420, 423; *Wuliangshou yigui,* 229–230, 238, 252n15
Gautama Buddha, 381, 389, 392, 396
Gedün Lodrö, 214n34
Gelukpa School: on desire, 166; Kadampa in, 160; literature, 505; Tuṣita Heaven, 158, 188–222
*gen,* 56
Gendün drup, 192
*General Presentation of the Tantra Sets,* 180n41
genre, organization by, 1–3, 14–16
Genshin: biography of, 115–116; role of, 14, 60, 115; texts, 30, 459. See also *Ōjōyōshū*
*gensō* (return to this world), 573
gentlemen, Longshu's entreaty to, 615
geopolitical categories, 1–2, 16n2. See also *specific area, such as Japan or Tibet*
German Idealism, 557
Getz, Daniel, 552, 602, 710
ghostly miasma *(jingxie),* 667
gift *(tokubetsuna kōken),* 590
*gnam chos,* 141, 150n10, 151n13
Gnam chos Mi 'gyur rdo rje. *See* Migyur Dorje
*gnas mdo* (Nëdo) lineage, 141
*gnas skor* (pilgrimage sites), 139
*gohonzon* (object of worship), 637
*gokuraku* (Land of Utmost Bliss), 58, 338–339, 458. *See also* Sukhāvatī
*Gokuraku no ninzū,* 574
*gomitsu* (mystery of speech), 275
*gongan,* 544
Gorai Shigeru, 61
*Gorin kujimyō himitsushaku (Secret Commentary on the Five Wheels and Nine Syllables),* 58, 60, 64
*Goshūi ōjōden,* 459
*gotai tōchi* prostration, 117
government, religion and, 637–639, 641–642
the great matter of birth-and-death *(shengsi dashi),* 541
the Great Perfection (Dzogchen), 4
Great Prayer Festival, 190
*Great Treatise on the Stages of Mantra (Sngags rim chen mo),* 180n39
great worthies *(daxian),* 607, 625n19
greedy persons, Longshu's entreaty to, 619–620
Griffiths, Paul, 111n12
Grove of the Reclining Buddha (Anyue County), 34
*Gsang ba 'dus pa rtsa rgyud (Guhyasamāja Tantra),* 162, 177n16, 191, 192
Gsang phu ne'u thog (Sangphu Neuthok), 162
*gter ma* (treasure-text), 162
*Guanding jing.* See *Consecration Scripture*
*Guan-jing,* 249n4, 515, 519–520
*Guan Wuliangshoufo-jing* (Sūtra of contemplation on the Buddha of Immeasurable Life), 501, 608
*Guanzhi yigui,* 249n6
Guhyasamāja, 161
*Guhyasamāja Tantra (Gsang ba 'dus pa rtsa rgyud),* 162, 177n16, 191, 192
*Guide to Śambhala (Sham bha la'i lam yig),* 749–750, 758n21
*gumonjihō,* 56
Guozhen, 483
guru-yoga, 191–195, 198–199
Gyatso, Janet, 150n9
Gyeltsab Darma Rinchen, 190, 193

hagiographical writing, 141, 160. *See also* life-writing
*hakarai* (calculations), 571
Halkias, Georgios, 3–4, 31, 139, 157, 159, 521–522, 523n3, 526n17
Han Fujun, 487
Hansen's disease, 572
Hawaii, 380
Hayagrīva, 229, 239–240
Hayashima Daitetsu, 380
*Heart Sūtra,* 499
Heaven, Christian conceptions of, 9, 19n31
Heavens of the Highest Purity (Sanqing), 667
hell, 116
Heller, Natasha, 455–456, 477, 540
Henning, Walter B., 711, 712
Hevajra, 161
*Hevajra Tantra (Kye'i rdo rje'i rgyud),* 165
hidden valleys *(beyül; sbas yul),* 139
*Hihan genri to shite no jōdo.* See *The Pure Land as a Principle of Criticism*
*Himitsu giki,* 247n1
*Himitsu giki denju kuketsu,* 250n10
*Himitsu nenbutsu sho* (Compendium on the secret contemplation of Buddha), 269–315; introduction, 158, 269–275; description of Fascicle One, 273–275; manuscripts and editions, 272–273; translation, 276–297; on the name, 276–291; on the primal vow of calling the name, 291–293; on the *nenbutsu samādhi,* 293–295; on the ten-thought moments, 295–297
Hirosawa-ryū schools, 253n20
*hisabetsu burakumin,* 572
*Hisen to Bukkyō,* 574
Hishiki Masaharu, 551, 571–574. See also *The Pure Land as a Principle of Criticism*
*Hishō,* 226, 253n22
*Hizō hōken (The Jeweled Key to the Secret Treasury),* 60
Hōkō-in, 269
holidays, 320, 381, 391–392, 544
*homa* rituals, 29, 56, 79–114, 750
*Honchō shinshū ōjōden,* 459
Honda Shizuyoshi, 574
Hōnen: *jōdokyō,* 502; lineage, 7–8; *nenbutsu,* 117, 573, 578–584; religious quest, 5; *Senchaku hongan nenbutsu shū,* 270; Sukhāvatī, 140
*hongaku* (original enlightenment thought), 274
Honge Myōshū, 636
Hongyuan Temple, 479
*honmon* (origin teaching), 637
Honpa Hongwanji Mission (Hawaii), 380
*hō-on* (Buddha's benevolence), 571
Hōshō, 270
*hosshin. See* dharma-body
*Hō to Bi (The Dharma and Beauty),* 588
*Hotoke no kyōbō (The Teaching of Buddha),* 381
*Hotoke no kyūsai (Buddha's Salvation),* 381
*hrīḥ* mantra, 143–144, 146, 229–231, 242–243
*huanglu* (yellow registers), 667, 700n10
*huatou* (key phrase), 541
Huayan tradition, 424
Huiguo, 252n17
Huijian, 50n5
Huijing, 479. See also *Nianfo ganying lu*
Huiyuan, 14
Humanistic Buddhism, 479
*Hundred Deities of Tuṣita,* 188–222; introduction, 158, 188–199; characteristics of Tuṣita Heaven, 195–199; emergence of Tuṣita Heaven, 190–195; translation, 199–210
*Huyadagmān,* 712, 713
*Hymnscroll* (Manichean). See *In Praise of the Realm of Light*

*I Am a Cat,* 554
*igyō* (easy practices), 590
Immovable Lord of Wisdom (Acalanātha Vidyārāja; Fudō Myōō), 61, 85
Imperial and Buddhist Law *(ōbō-buppō),* 571–572
impermanence, dharma of, 344
Indhrabhūti, 176n14
Indian Buddhism: phases of, 159–160; pure lands in, 3–4, 6, 80–82, 744–746, 750; tantric practices, 176nn13–14. *See also*

Tantric Buddhism. *See also* Mahāyāna Buddhism
individual freedom, 551, 559, 562–564
individuals *(kojin)*, 590
Indrabhūti, 176n13
Infinite, 557–562
initiation (empowerment), 10, 144, 148, 163, 243
Inoue Nisshō, 633
*In Praise of the Realm of Light (Tan mingjie)*, 707–743; introduction, 664, 707–714; translation, 714–722
interviewer *(mensetsusha)*, 400
Ippen, 140
Ishiwara Kanji, 633
*isō* (extraordinary signs), 458, 460
Israelite rituals, 12–13
Itō Shōshin, 319–320, 349–350. *See also* The Role of Buddhism in Emperor Worship
*ittai*, 557–558
Iwazukō (say-nothing confraternity), 398

Jambaldorj, 746, 758n21
Jambudvīpa, 750
Jamgön Kongtrul Lodrö Thaye, 165
Jamyang Dewai Dorjé, 192, 195–197, 214n31
Jamyang Shepai Dorjé, 195
Jangchup Ö (Byang chub 'od), 159
Japan: modernization of, 551, 556, 632; Nichiren's thinking about, 637–639
Japanese Buddhism: aesthetics, 552, 587–601; canon, 501–502, 526n14; contemplative visualizations, 158, 163, 223–226; emperor worship, 319–320, 349–378, 574; Esoteric, *See* Shingon; ethical discourses, 551–601, 631–660; life-writing, 455, 457–476; ritual practices, 30, 33, 56–64, 115–138; Tibetan literature in, 505; in United States, 319–321, 379–395
Japanese Naikan Medical Association, 399–400
Japanese Spirit *(Nippon seishin)*, 350
Japan Naikan Association, 399
*The Jeweled Key to the Secret Treasury (Hizō hōken)*, 60
*The Jewel Garland of Buddhist History (Chos 'byung jin bris nor bu 'phreng ba)*, 161
*The Jewel Steps of a Fortunate Disciple: A Prayer for a Sure Rebirth in the Land of Śambhala of the Great Siddhi, in the Land that Captivates a Person's Mind for a Definite Meeting with the Dharma of Raudra Kalkī*, 746
Jey Yab Sey Sum, 193
Jiacai, 459
'Jigs med dam chos rgya mtsho, 215n38
*jile shijie* (World of Utmost Bliss), 708
*jinen hōni*, 589
*jingtu* (pure lands), 665
*Jingtu lun* (Treatise on the Pure Land), 459
*Jingtu sheng shen jing.* See *Divine Scripture on the Rebirth in the Pure Land of the Lingbao Highest Cavern Mystery*
*jingxie* (ghostly miasma), 667
Jingzong, 479
Jippan, 271, 274
*jiriki* (self-power), 571, 589–590
*jiuxuan* (Nine-Fold Mystery), 667
Jñānaguhyavajra, 161. *See also* Atīśa Dīpaṃkaraśrījñāna
Jñānapāda, 176n14
*jñānasattva* (wisdom beings), 143
Jñānashrī, 176n14
*jōdokyō*, 501–502
Jōdo Shinshū (True Pure Land Sect), 379, 502, 526n15, 588–589
Jōdo Shinshū Jōhana Betsuin, 588
Jōdo Shin tradition, 6
Jōdoshū (Pure Land Sect), 502
Jōgon, 247n1
Jōgyō (Bodhisattva Superior Conduct), 636
Jōhen, 270–271
Jokhang Temple, 162
Jones, Charles, 7, 319, 322, 526n17
*Jūhachidō kuketsu*, 252n17
*Jūhachidō nenju shidai* (Eighteen Methods Recitation Sequence manuals), 225–226, 253n20
*Jūhachidō nenju shidai Daishi Chūin*, 226, 253n20
*Jūhachidō sata*, 252n17
*Jūhachidō* template, 158, 223, 225–228. See also *Amitāyus Ritual Manual*

*Jūhachi geiin,* 252n19
*Jūjūshinron uchigikishū* (Collection of impressive teachings I heard), 60
*junzi* (moral conduct), 607–611, 625n19
*Jushi zhuan,* 625n4

Kadampa School *(bka' gdams pa),* 160, 176n15
*kaidan* (ordination platform), 637, 643–649
*kaigoin* (the enlightened), 397
*kaihō no shūkyō* (religion of liberation), 573
*Kaihō no shūkyō e,* 574
*kaikyōshi* (overseas minister), 379–380
*Kaiyuan shijiao lu,* 248n2
Kajihama Ryōshun, 505
Kakuban, 271; biography of, 56–57; intellectual impact of, 30, 58–61, 64; religious practice before and after, 61–64; texts, 57–58. See also *Short Meditation on the Pure Land, Mysteriously Adorned*; on *Wuliangshou yigui,* 252n17
*Kakugenshō* (Brief account of lectures), 63
Kakukai, 63, 270
*Kālacakratantra,* 744–745, 750, 757n2
*Kalachakra Tantra (Dus kyi 'khor lo rtsa rgyud),* 161
Kalāpa, 746, 750, 757n2
*Ka lā par jug pa (Entrance to Kalāpa),* 749
*Kalāpāvatāra,* 749
*kalkī* kings of Śambhala, 746, 750
Kalsang Gyatso, 192
*kami* worship, 571
Kaneko Daiei, 573
*kanhua,* 541–542
Kanjo, 56
*kannagara no michi* (Way of the Gods), 350
Kannon. *See* Avalokiteśvara
Kapstein, Matthew, 140, 709
karma, 607, 750
Karma Chagme (Karma chags med), 31, 141–142, 505–506
Karmic origins of construction and Esoteric practice at Kongōbuji *(Kongōbuji kenritsu shūgyō engi),* 61
Kawahara Ryūzō, 400
Kawakami Hajime, 349
*Keiranshūyōshū* (Collection of leaves gathered in stormy ravines), 64
Keisen, 461
Kenchō, 269
*kenmitsu nenbutsu,* 271, 299n26
*kenshūjo* (training centers), 400–401
Keō-in, 270
*Kexu ze xu,* 482
key phrase *(huatou),* 541
Khedrubje Gelek Pelzang, 190, 193
*Kibokuron* (Arguments of a rustic bowl), 64
Kingdom of Darkness, 708–709
kings of Śambhala, 745–746, 750
*Kinkai hatsueshō* (Short notes on arousing wisdom through the Diamond World), 64
Kirti Tshenshap Rinpoché, 181n43
Kita Chikushi, 461
Kiyozawa Manshi, 349, 551, 554–559, 572. *See also* Essays on Religion and Ethics
knowledge empowerments *(rig pa'i dbang lnga),* 163
Kōbō Daishi Kūkai. *See* Kūkai
Kōfukuji, 61–62, 461
*Kōjien,* 526n15
*Kojiki,* 350
*kojin* (individuals), 590
Kokuchūkai (Pillar of the Nation Society), 632–633
*kokutai* (national polity), 352, 574, 638
*kokutaigaku,* 638
Komatani, 398
Könchok Tsültrim (Dkon mchog tshul khrims), 163
Könchok Yarphel, 195
Kongōbuji, 57
*Kongōbuji kenritsu shūgyō engi* (Karmic origins of construction and Esoteric practice at Kongōbuji), 61
Kongōkai (Diamond-Vajra World), 59
Konkōji, 64
Korean Buddhism, 6, 247n1, 321, 420–451
*Koryo taejanggyong,* 247n1
Kósa, Gábor, 664, 707
Kōshū, 64
Kōtoku Shūsui, 349, 554
Kōyasan, 61–62, 270

*Kōyasan ōjōden* (Accounts of those from Mount Kōya who attained birth in a pure land, late twelfth century), 61, 457–476; introduction, 455, 457–462; translation, 463–474; Kiyohara Masakuni, 465–466; Kyōjin, 472–473; Kyōkai, 463–465; Kyōtoku, 470; Rentai, 468–470; Rinken, 473–474; Ryōzen, 471–472; Yuihan, 466–468
*krodha-rāja* (kings of Śambhala), 745–746, 750
Kūkai: *Chūju kankyō no shi,* 252n13; Esoteric Buddhism, 60, 158, 269–271; Jūhachidō, 225–226, 252nn17–18; Mount Kōya, 457; *Wuliangshou yigui,* 248nn2–3
Kumārajīva, 420–421
*kumitsu* (speech), 272
Kurodani Temple, 64
Kwan, Tai-wo, 82–84
*Kye'i rdo rje'i rgyud (Hevajra Tantra),* 165
*Kyōgyōshinshō,* 573
Kyōjin, 461, 472–473
Kyōkai, 61, 461, 463–465
Kyōtoku, 470

laity: folk crafts *(mingei)* movement, 552, 587, 590; *versus* monastics, 13–14, 636; on Mount Kōya, 462; *nenbutsu* practice, 573; *nianfo* practice, 542; social engagement, 631–635
*lakṣaṇa* (marks of the Buddha), 118–136
*Lalitavistara,* 197
Lalou, Marcelle, 523n4
Lama Umapa Tsöndrü Sengé, 189
*Lamp for the Path to Enlightenment (Bodhipathapradīpa; Byang chub lam gyi sgron ma),* 159–160, 175n4
Lamp for the three modes *(Nayatrayapradīpa),* 176n14
*lam rim* genre, 160
Land of Bliss. *See* Sukhāvatī
Land of Utmost Bliss *(gokuraku),* 58, 338–339, 458. *See also* Sukhāvatī
Larger *Sukhāvatīvyūha sūtra (Daimuryōjukyō; Muryōju-kyō; Wuliangshou jing),* 574, 588; Dharmākara story, 396; doctrinal approach, 423; in poetry, 501–504, 513–514; *Sukhāvatīvyūhopadeśa* (commentary), 321, 420, 423–428, 526n16; vows of Amida in, 552, 574, 590; Wang Rixiu's edition, 604; *Wuliangshou yigui,* 252n15
lauds of the names *(nāmasaṁgīti),* 525n9
Layman Longshu (Wang Rixiu), 552, 602–630. See also *Longshu's Discourse on Pure Land*
Lcang skya Ngag dbang blo bzang chos ldan dpal bzang po, 505
Lce sgom pa (Chégompa), 166
*Lebang wenlei* (Compendium of the Blissful Country), 604–605, 625n4
letter-disc, 231, 245–246
Lewis, Todd, 709
*lha'i rnal 'byor* (deity yoga; *devatāyoga),* 164–165, 178n26
Lha Lama Yéshé Ö, 159
Lhodrag Namkha Gyeltsen, 189
*Lianhe Bao,* 485
liberation-narrative *(rnam thar),* 141, 160. *See also* life-writing
Liberation Shinshū, 575–577
Lieu, Samuel N.C., 712
*The Life of Buddhists (Busshi seikatsu),* 381
life-writing: overview of, 455–456; translations: *Kōyasan ōjōden,* 457–476; *Nianfo ganying lu,* 477–495
Lindsay, Ethan, 455, 457
lineage, 9–14
Lingbao Daoism, 663, 665–706
*lingwu* (numinous things), 667
Lin Kanzhi, 485
Lin Wushu, 711
Lin Yun, 713
*Liqujing shu* (*Rishushaku,* Commentary on the Sūtra of Guiding Principle), 73n4
*Liqu shi,* 252n13
literati, Longshu's entreaty to, 614
living beings *(shūjō),* 590
Li Yuansong, 479
location of pure lands, 4, 8–9, 744–751
Lokakṣema, 250n10
Lokeśvara, 162, 177n16
long-life meditation, 144, 146
*Longshu's Discourse on Pure Land (Longshu jingtu wen),* 602–630; contents of,

606–607; introduction, 552, 602–608; translation, 608–624; fascicle one, 608–611; fascicle three, 612–613; fascicle four, 613–614; fascicle six, 614–624
*Longshu zengguang jingtu wen* (Longshu's expanded treatise on Pure Land). See *Longshu's Discourse on Pure Land (Longshu jingtu wen)*
Long *Sukhāvatīvyūha sūtra. See* Larger *Sukhāvatīvyūha sūtra*
Lord of the Assembly, 85
Losang gyeltsen sengé, 194
Lotus Blossom Society (Rengekai), 632
lotus calyx, 344–345
Lotus Family, 163, 180n41, 227–231, 235
*Lotus Sūtra,* 249n6, 552–553, 631–640, 652n4, 710. See also *The Age of Unification*
Lotze, Rudolph Hermann, 555
*Luminous Bliss* (Halkias), 521–522, 523n3, 526n17

Madhyamaka, 161
*Madhyamakāvatāra,* 514
Mahābhārata, 744
*mahāpuruṣa-lakṣaṇa* (marks of a Great Man), 745–746
Mahāsāṃghika, 160
Mahāsthāmaprāpta, 81
Mahāvairocana: dharma-body, 59, 67–72, 271; as Lord of the Assembly, 85; mandalas, 59, 63–70; pure land (Mysteriously Adorned), 30, 58. See also *Short Meditation on the Pure Land, Mysteriously Adorned*
*Mahāvairocanābhisaṃbodhi-sūtra,* 228, 349n5
*Mahāvairocana Sūtra,* 73n12
Mahāvihāra Vikramaśilā, 157, 159
*Mahāvyutpatti,* 520
Mahāyāna Buddhism: canon, 502–504, 526n14, 526nn16–17; *Lotus Sūtra,* 552–553, 631–640. See also *The Age of Unification*; pure lands in, 3–4, 6, 9, 15, 157, 163, 319; Akṣobhya, 79–82; Amitābha, *See* Sukhāvatī; Tibetan import of, 139; Tuṣita, 195, 198; *samādhi* of recollecting the buddha, 250n10; sutra structure, 423–424; Tibetan practices influenced by, 504
*Mahāyāna-saṃgraha,* 423
Maitreya, 6, 157; Exalted Victory Banner (palace), 197; Tuṣita Heaven, 6, 158, 188–222, 335–336, 458. See also *Hundred Deities of Tuṣita*; typology for myth of, 198
*Maitreyakṣetra,* 197
Maitreya-nātha, 189
*maṇḍala* (prefecture), 750
mandalas: Mahāvairocana, 59, 63–70; Nichiren, 637; Shingon, 84–85
Mānī, 664, 707
Manicheism, 663–664, 707–743
Mañjuśrī, 169, 180n40, 191, 503, 744–745
Mañjuśrīgarbha, 189, 193, 198
*Mañjuśrī-nāmasaṁgīti,* 503, 514–515
*Man ngag rin chen spungs pa'i dkar chag (Outline of the Jewel Mound of Instructions),* 166
mantras: *Amitāyus Ritual Manual,* 227–231, 234–247; for animals, 330–331; *homa* rituals, 86–110, 750; *nenbutsu,* See *nenbutsu*; poetry composed as, 498–499, 525n8; *sādhana* of Amitābha, 143–146
*mappō* (Final Dharma) age, 632–660
Mār Ammō, 713. See also *In Praise of the Realm of Light*
marks of a Great Man *(mahāpuruṣa-lakṣaṇa),* 745–746
marks of the Buddha *(lakṣaṇa),* 118–136
married women, Longshu's entreaty to, 621
Marvelous Array *(ngo mtshar rmad byung bkod pa),* 199, 215n38
Mār Xwaršēd-Wahman, 713
Masakuni, Kiyohara, 461–462, 465–466
Masatsugu, Michael, 382
McBride, Richard II, 321
medicine, 479, 616–617
meditation: *Amitāyus Ritual Manual,* 228, 230–231; *kanhua* approach to, 541–542; privileging of, 6, 12; in psychotherapy, 401–402; *sādhana* of Amitābha, 143–149. *See also* recitation; visualization

Meijaku, 56
*mensetsusha* (interviewer), 400
merchants, Longshu's entreaty to, 623–624
merit making, in *Consecration Scripture*, 34, 36–49
merit transference, gate of, 118
*Miaofa lianhua jing (Sūtra of the Lotus Blossom of the Wonderful Dharma; Myōhō-renge-kyō)*, 652n4
Migyur Dorje: biography of, 141–142; texts, 30–31. See also *Sādhana of the Pure Land Sukhāvatī*
*Mii ōjōden*, 475n7
Mikadoism, 349
Mikkelsen, G., 713
*Mikkyō daijiten*, 248n2, 253n20
Miller, W. Blythe, 11
Minami Chikushi, 461
mindfulness: gates of, 117–118; in psychotherapy, 401–402
mind training *(blo byong)* manuals, 160
Mind Treasury of Namchö Migyur Dorje. See *Sādhana of the Pure Land Sukhāvatī*
Mingben, Zhongfeng, 456, 540–544. See also *Cherishing the Pure Land*
Ming dynasty, 319
*mingei* (folk crafts) movement, 552, 587, 590
*Minglun yuekan*, 491
Minjüür Dechin Shiirev, 746–747, 749
Mi pham 'Jam dbyangs rnam rgyal rgya mtsho, 505
miracle tales. See *Nianfo ganying lu*
Mirouku. *See* Maitreya
miserly persons, Longshu's entreaty to, 619–620
*mishirabe*, 320–321, 397–403, 410–414
missionaries, 2, 379–380, 707
Mitsugon'in, 57–58
*mitsugon jōdo* (Pure Land of Mystical Splendor), 58–61, 64, 271
*Mitsugon jōdo ryakkan*. See *Short Meditation on the Pure Land, Mysteriously Adorned*
*mitsugon kaie* (secretly adorned ocean-assembly), 73n12
Mitsusada, Inoue, 459
Miwa-ryū, 63
Miyazawa Kenji, 633
*Mkha' 'gro ma rdo rje gur gyi rgyud (Ḍākinī Vajrapañjara Tantra)*, 179n32
Mkhas grub rje, 757n7, 759n30
*mkhas grup* (scholar-cum-adept; *paṇḍita-siddha*), 161
modernization: of Buddhism, 12, 319–320, 351, 382, 631–640; of Japan, 551, 556, 632
monasteries, 12–14. See also *specific monastery*
monastics: *versus* laity, 13–14, 636; Longshu's entreaty to, 617–618; as native informants, 17n7. See also *specific person*
*mondō* (question-and-answer) format, 273, 381
Mongolia, 664, 744–761
moral conduct *(junzi)*, 607–611, 625n19. *See also* ethics
mountain asceticism *(shugendō)*, 555
Mount Fudaraku (Potalaka), 458
Mount Hiei, 64
Mount Kailāśa, 750
Mount Kōya: esoteric practices, 158; Kakuban at, 56–58; life-writing, 455, 457–476; *nenbutsu hijiri* on, 61–63
Mount Negoro, 57–58, 62, 64
Mount Tianmu, 540
*mudrās*: *Amitāyus Ritual Manual*, 225, 227–231, 234–247; *homa* rituals, 86–110, 750; *Quintessence of Amitābha*, 173
*mugaai* (selfless love), 319, 349–350
Mugaen (Garden of selflessness), 349
Muksang *(rmugs sangs)*, 141
Munakata Shikō, 588
*Munayastava*, 515
Munetomo, Fujiwara no, 459
*Muryangsu-gyŏng chongyo* (Doctrinal essentials of the *Wuliangshou jing*), 421–422
*Muryōju-kyō*. *See* Larger *Sukhāvatīvyūha sūtra*
*Muryōju nyorai kangyō kuyō giki* (Ritual of contemplation and offerings to the Tathāgata Immeasurable Life), 73n4
*Muryōju nyorai kuyō sahō shidai*, 253n21
*Muu kōshu no gan*. See *Vow of Non-Discrimination between Beauty and Ugliness*

*Myōhō-renge-kyō (Miaofa lianhua jing, Sūtra of the Lotus Blossom of the Wonderful Dharma)*, 652n4
*myōko-hin* (wondrous works), 589, 591
*myōkōnin* (wondrous people), 589, 599n17
*Myōkōnin Inaba no Genza*, 588
Myōnin, 269
*myōshū*, 636
Mysteriously Adorned (pure land), 30, 58. See also *Short Meditation on the Pure Land, Mysteriously Adorned*
mystery of speech *(gomitsu)*, 275

Nāgārjuna, 5, 73n11, 176n14
*Naihanhō*, 403
*Naikan no Michi*, 402
Naikan psychotherapy, 319–321, 397–403, 414–418
*Naikan's Path*, 396–419; introduction, 320, 396–403; translation, 403–418; Yoshimoto's encounter with Shin Buddhism, 403–409; Yoshimoto's final *mishrabe*, 409–414; Yoshimoto's answers about Naikan, 414–418
*nāmasaṁgīti* (lauds of the names), 525n9
*Namchö*, 31, 141–144
Namchö Migyur Dorje: biography of, 141–142; texts, 30–31. See also *Sādhana of the Pure Land Sukhāvatī*
Namkha Gyeltsen, 189, 193
*Namu Amidabutsu*, 30, 117–119, 271, 275
*Namu Amida Butsu*, 588
*Namu Myōhō-renge-kyō*, 634
Nanbeichao, 665
*nangyō* (difficult practices), 590
*Nankai rurōki*, 270
Nara, 56
Nāropā, 746
narratives: attention to, 17n6; Genshin story, 115–116; miracle tales, See *Nianfo ganying lu*; Nāśa story, 35, 42–46. *See also* life-writing
Nāśa, 35, 42–46
national polity *(kokutai)*, 352, 574, 638
Natsume Sōseki, 554
Nattier, Jan, 6, 17n5, 33–34, 79–80, 112n28, 198
*Nayatrayapradīpa* (Lamp for the three modes), 176n14
near-death experiences, 477–478
Nëdo *(gnas mdo)* lineage, 141
*nenbutsu:* ethical aspects of, 555, 571–573, 578–584; *Himitsu nenbutsu shō*, 269–315; life-writing on, 459; *Ōjōyōshū*, 115–138; practices, 4–5, 29–30
*nenbutsu hijiri*, 61–62
*nenbutsu samādhi (nenbutsu sanmai)*, 275, 293–295
Nepal, 81
New Pure Land *(xin jingtu)*, 708
New Realm of Light *(xin mingjie)*, 708–709
Ngag dbang blo bzang chos rje nyi ma bstan 'dzin dbang phyug (Eighth Bogdo Jebtsundamba), 748
Ngag dbang rta mgrin bsrud (Agvaan Damdinsüren), 746, 751. See also *The Swift Path to Kalāpa*
Ngakpas, 174n3
*ngo mtshar rmad byung bkod pa* (Marvelous Array), 199, 215n38
*Ngo mtshar rmad byung bkod pa'i zhing gi bshad pa smon lam dang bcas pa rmad byung bkod par 'jug pa'i them skas*, 215n38
*nianfo*, 323–346, 455–456, 542–544
*Nianfo ganying jianwen ji* (Records of experiences of miraculous response from reciting the name of the Buddha), 485
*Nianfo ganying lu* (Records of the sympathetic resonance of recollecting the Buddha's name), 477–495; introduction, 455–456, 477–480; translations, 480–494; Ceaselessly Reciting the Name of the Buddha, Ghosts Retreat and Illness Is Cured, 482–483; End-Stage Nose Cancer Completely Cured through the Recitation of the Buddha's Name, 483–485; A Felon Recollects the Buddha, and Amitābha Comes to Greet Him, 491–494; Before Going to Be Reborn, Great Happiness Has Already Appeared, 487–491; With One Sound of Amitābha's Name, Children Avoid a Car

Accident, 485–486; Pursued by a Vengeful Spirit, Reciting the Buddha's Name Brings Down a Fever, 485–486; Recollecting the Buddha to Save One's Life, Radiating Light, 480–482
Nichiren, 631, 633–639
Nichirenshū, 632
Nichirenshugi (Nichirenism), 552–553, 631–639
*Nichirenshugi kyōgaku taikan* (An *Overview of Nichirenshugi Doctrinal Studies*), 635, 638–640
*Nihon Bukkyō tenseki daijiten*, 272
*Nihon ōjō gokurakuki* (A record of Japanese who attained birth in the Pure Land of Utmost Bliss), 459
*Nijūgo zammmai kakochō*, 116
*nijūgo zanmaie* (samādhi society of twenty-five), 14
Nine-Fold Mystery *(jiuxuan)*, 667
Ninnaji, 56–57, 59, 269, 461
*Nippon seishin* (Japanese Spirit), 350
Nipponzan Myōhōji, 631
*Niraupamya-stava*, 515
*nirmāṇakāya* (Emanation Bodies), 19n29, 745–746, 757n9
*nirvāṇa*, 165, 422, 634, 636, 709
Nisei Shin Buddhism, 382
Nishida Kitarō, 554
Nishi Honganji, 379, 380
Nishimoto Taikan, 398
non-duality, 590, 634
numinous things *(lingwu)*, 667
Nyingma School, 141–142, 162
Nyojaku, 460

Obata Bunshō, 574
Objectless Loving-Kindness Prayer *(Dmigs brtse ma)*, 191–193, 198, 212n18
object of worship *(gohonzon)*, 637
objects imbued with cosmic power *(qi)*, 667
*ōbō-buppō* (Imperial and Buddhist Law), 571–572
Occidental aesthetics *(seiyō bigaku)*, 590
occupational positions, Longshu's entreaties by, 607–608, 614–624
Odawara, 61–62
Ōe no Masafusa, 459
offerings: *Amitāyus Ritual Manual*, 228–230, 241–242, 246; *homa* rituals, 29, 56, 79–114, 750
Ōfuchi, 700n6
*ōjō* (birth in a pure land at death), 458
*ōjōden* genre, 455, 457–461
*Ōjōyōshū* (Essentials of Rebirth in the Pure Land), 115–138; introduction, 30, 115–119; role in praxis, 14, 30, 60, 459; translation, 119–136
*oṃ āḥ hrīḥ svāhā* mantra, 144, 146
*oṃ bhrūṃ svāhā* mantra, 144, 146
one mind, 343–344
Onjōji, 461
Onoda Shunzō, 505
Ono-ryū schools, 253n20
*On the Meaning of the Four Kinds of the Dharma Body (Shishu hosshin gi)*, 59
Opening the door to the best land: A prayer to obtain birth in the Land of Bliss *(Bde ba can gyi zhing du skye ba 'dzin pa'i smon lam zhing mchog sgo 'byed)*, 505
ordinary persons *(bonbu)*, 573
ordination platform *(kaidan)*, 637, 643–649
original enlightenment thought *(hongaku)*, 274
origin teaching *(honmon)*, 637
Orzech, Charles, 249n4, 249n7
Ōtani-ha, 551, 555, 572. *See also* Shin Buddhism
Ōtani (Shinshū) University, 349
other-power *(tariki)*, 571, 587–590
*Outline of the Jewel Mound of Instructions (Man ngag rin chen spungs pa'i dkar chag)*, 166
Overbey, Ryan, 29, 33
overseas minister *(kaikyōshi)*, 379–380
*An Overview of Nichirenshugi Doctrinal Studies (Nichirenshugi kyōgaku taikan)*, 635, 638–640
*Oxford Dictionary of Buddhism*, 605

Pabongkhapa Dechen Nyingpo, 191
*Padma thang yig*, 528n27
Padminīnāmapañjikā, 745

Palden, 747
Panchen Sonam Drakpa, 180n41
*paṇḍita-siddha* (*mkhas grup;* scholar-cum-adept), 161
*p'an'gyo* (*panjiao;* doctrinal classification), 420
Paramādhibuddhatantra, 745–746
*Paramārthasaṃgraha,* 746
*pāramitās* (perfections), 668, 745
*Pāramitāyāna* (Perfection Vehicle), 161
*parinirvāṇa:* Akṣobhya, 81; Amitābha, 34, 36
Parthian hymn. See *In Praise of the Realm of Light*
Payne, Richard, 30, 79
Payül (Dpal yul) lineage, 142
Peace and Comfort Beyond Ethics: introduction, 551, 554–559; translation, 564–568
peace of mind *(anjin),* 572
Pelliot, Paul, 711
perfections (*pāramitās*), 668, 745
Perfection Vehicle *(Pāramitāyāna),* 161
Performance Tantra *(Charyatantra),* 178n24
personal responsibility, ethics of, 559–562
personal spiritual orientations, 455–456. *See also* life-writing; poetry
*pha rol tu phyin pa drug* (six perfections; *ṣaṭpāramitā*), 169
*'Pho ba* text, 505
*phowa* (transference meditation), 144, 146–147
physicians, Longshu's entreaty to, 616–617
pilgrimage sites *(gnas skor),* 139
Pillar of the Nation Society (Kokuchūkai), 632–633
*Pillar Testament (Bka' chems ka khol ma),* 162, 174n3
Platonism, 9, 19n31
Pleasant Doctrine-bearing Joyous Place *(dga' ldan yid dga' chos 'dzin),* 197, 214n34
poetry: overview of, 455–456; translations: *Cherishing the Pure Land,* 540–544; *In Praise of His Mighty Name,* 496–539
Porcu, Elizabetta, 552, 587
Potalaka (Mount Fudaraku), 458
praise, gate of, 117
praise *(tan),* 712
praise literature *(stotra),* 499
*The Praise of the Name of the Tathāgata Amitābha,* 496–539; introduction, 456, 496–506; structure of, 500–501; translations, 506–513; appendix, 521–522; commentary, 513–521
Prajñāpāramitā sutra *(Aṣṭasāh asrikāprajñāramitāsūtra),* 83
Prajñāsāgara (Shes rab rgya mtsho; Gachoi Lam Damba Agramba), 746, 758n17
Prajñāśrījñānakīrti, 170
*Pratyutpannasamādhi-sūtra,* 250n10
*Prayer for Rebirth in Śambhala (Sham bha lar skye ba'i smon lam),* 750
prayers: *Hundred Deities of Tuṣita,* 158; *sādhana* of Amitābha, 144, 147–148. See also *specific prayer*
*The Precious Crystal Stairway: Illuminating the Way to Śambhala, The Supreme and Glorious Abode for Accomplishing Siddhis,* 746
primal vow, 275, 291–293
principalities *(viṣaya),* 750
*Principles of Buddhist Tantra,* 181n43
Proffitt, Aaron, 158, 269
profit-seeking, 326
proselytization, 604–605, 635, 664, 707
prostration, 117, 233–234, 247, 252n18
psychotherapy, 319–321, 397–403, 414–418
Puguang, 34, 36–49
*Pulsŏl Amita-gyŏng so* (Commentary on the *Amitābha Sūtra Spoken by the Buddha*), 420–451; introduction, 321, 420–428; translation, 429–441; narration of the Great Intent, 429–430; core teaching, 430–432; analysis of original text, 432–441
Puṇḍarīka, 745
*The Pure Land as a Principle of Criticism (Hihan genri to shite no jōdo),* 571–586; introduction, 551–552, 571–574; translation, 575–584; Liberation Shinshū, 575–577; Pure Land Buddhism, 577–578; *nenbutsu,* 578–584
Pure Land Buddhism: aesthetics, *See* aesthetics; buddha-fields, 3, 6, 30. See also *specific pure land*; canon, 501–504, 526n14; contemplation in, *See*

contemplation; cult in, 13–15, 79–86; definition of, 3–4; demythologization, 552, 556, 572–573; doctrine, *See* doctrine; ethics, *See* ethics; expansion of, 5–7, 15–16; as field of study, 7–9; marginalization of, 4–7, 80–82; organization of, 1–3, 14–16; other worlds, *See* worlds beyond Sukhāvatī; proselytization of, 604–605, 635, 664, 707; rituals in, *See* ritual practices; as social orientation, 455–456, 573–574. *See also* ethics; life-writing; poetry
Pure Land cultivation, 607, 612–614
Pure Land exceptionalism, 82, 111n7
*The Pure Land of Beauty (Bi no Jōdo)*, 552, 588, 591
Pure Land of Mystical Splendor *(mitsugon jōdo)*, 58–61, 64, 271
pure lands *(jingtu)*, 665
pure vision treasure *(dag snang gter)*, 141, 150n9
purification practices *(dhūtaguṇas)*, 501, 504
purity, 339–340
Pursued by a Vengeful Spirit, Reciting the Buddha's Name Brings Down a Fever, 485–486
*Pusa benye jing*, 51n11
*Pusa yingluo benye jing* (Sūtra on the original acts that serve as a bodhisattva's adornments), 423
*Putixin lun, Bodaishinron (The Treatise on the Mind Aspiring for Enlightenment)*, 59

*qi* (objects imbued with cosmic power), 667
*qixin* (awakening), 607–611
question-and-answer *(mondō)* format, 273, 381
*Questions about Pure Land*, 322
*Quintessence of Amitābha: Means for Realizing the Yamāntaka of Passion* ( *Amitābhā-hṛdaya-rāga-yamāri-sādhananāma)*: contents of, 168–170; introduction, 157–171; *sādhana* of deity yoga, 164–165; sublimation of death and desire, 165–167; summary, 168–171; translation, 171–174

Radich, Michael, 81
Rāhulagupta, 161
Raiyu, 64, 73n12, 252n17
Rambelli, Fabio, 163, 320, 349
Ratnākarashānti, 176n14
Rdo rje 'jigs byed (Vajrabhairava), 180n36
*rdo rje lus* (vajra body), 165
Realm of Light, 664, 708–709
recitation, 8; *Amitāyus Ritual Manual*, 227–231, 234–246; effectiveness of, 477, 608; *Lotus Sūtra*, 634, 637; *Namu Amidabutsu*, 30, 117–119, 271, 275; *nenbutsu*, See *nenbutsu*; *nianfo*, 323–346, 455–456, 542–544. See also *Nianfo ganying lu*; poetry intended for, 498–499. *See also* mantras
Recollecting the Buddha to Save One's Life, Radiating Light, 480–482
recompense body, 118–136
*A Record in Lament of Divergences (Tannishō)*, 558, 589
A record of Japanese who attained birth in the Pure Land of Utmost Bliss *(Nihon ōjō gokurakuki)*, 459
Records of experiences of miraculous response from reciting the name of the Buddha *(Nianfo ganying jianwen ji)*, 485
Records of rebirth at Kōyasan. See *Kōyasan ōjōden*
Records of the sympathetic resonance of recollecting the Buddha's name. See *Nianfo ganying lu*
relic, cult of, 13, 20n47, 21n50
religion: definition of, 557; ethics in, 551, 559, 564–568. *See also* ethics; government and, 637–639, 641–642
religion of liberation *(kaihō no shūkyō)*, 573
religious biographies, 455, 457–461. *See also* life-writing
religious gate of beauty *(bi no shūmon)*, 589
religious quest, 5
religious studies: cultural aspects of, 9–14; Euro-American bias in, 5, 9–14, 17n5, 17n7, 19n31, 111n8, 111n11, 636
Rendawa Zhonnu Lodro, 191
Rendōbō, Hōkyō, 62–64
Rengekai (Lotus Blossom Society), 632

Rennyo, 571, 599n10
Rentai, 461, 468–470
Renzen, 459
reputation-seeking, 326
response body, 118–136
*Response to Questions regarding Śambhala*, 746
Restoration of our Sect (Shūmon no ishin), 635
Returning to My Hometown of Hualian, 480
return to this world *(gensō)*, 573
Rhodes, Robert F., 30, 115
*rig pa'i dbang lnga* (knowledge empowerments), 163
*rig sngags (vidyā-mantras)*, 750
Rigzin Kunsang Sherab, 142
Rinchen Zangpo, 176n15
*rinjū gyōgi* (deathbed rituals), 460
Rinken, 461, 473–474
Rinpoche, 505
*Rishushaku* (*Liqujing shu*, Commentary on the Sūtra of Guiding Principle), 73n4
Risshō Ankokukai, 632
Risshō Kōseikai, 631
ritual area: inviting deity into, 229, 239; ordination platform *(kaidan)*, 637, 643–649; preparation of, 228–229, 236–237
*Ritual Manual for the Protective Fire Offering devoted to Akṣobhya, Chūin Lineage (Ashu soku sai goma shiki shidai, Chūin)*: introduction, 85–86; translation, 86–110
Ritual of contemplation and offerings to the Tathāgata Immeasurable Life *(Muryōju nyorai kangyō kuyō giki)*, 73n4
ritual practices: overview of, 29–31; effectiveness of, 477; translations: Akṣobhya *homa*, 79–114; *Consecration Scripture*, 29–30, 33–55; Mind Treasury of Migyur Dorje, 139–153; Mysteriously Adorned, 30–31, 56–78; *Ōjōyōshū*, 115–138. *See also* meditation; offerings; recitation
Riwo Ganden Nampar Gyelwé Ling, 190
Rixiu (Wang Rixiu), 552, 602–608. See also *Longshu's Discourse on Pure Land*
*rmi lam* (dream-yoga meditation), 144, 146
*rmugs sangs* (Muksang), 141
*Rnam dag bde chen zhing gi smon lam (Aspiration Prayer to the Pure Land Sukhāvatī)*, 141, 505
*Rnam dag bde chen zhing gi smon lam gyi 'byed 'grel bde chen zhing du bgrod pa'i them skas bzang po* (A wonderful staircase for ascension to the Land of Great Bliss: Commentary to a vow for the Land of Highest Bliss), 505
*rnam thar* (liberation-narrative), 141, 160. *See also* life-writing
The Role of Buddhism in Emperor Worship, 349–378; introduction, 319–320, 349–352; translation, 352–376; preface, 352–353; first chapter, 353–363; second chapter, 363–376
*Rōsenki*, 568n9
*Rtog ge 'bar ba (Blaze of Reasoning; Tarkajvāla)*, 160
Ruegg, David S., 13, 174n3
Rui Chuanming, 711
*Ruyilun yigui* (Cintāmaṇicakra ritual manual), 223; as basis for other ritual manuals, 225–226, 248n3, 253n20; Esoteric practice, 249n7, 250n8; ritual practices, 252n16, 253n23
Ryōgen, 116
Ryōjusen (Vulture Peak), 458
Ryōzen, 471–472
Ryūkan, 270

*Saddharmapuṇḍarīka*, 526n16
*sādhaka*, 167
*sādhana:* deity yoga, 164–165, 178n26; Śambhala, 749; Vajra-Yamāntaka, 169–170
*Sādhanamāla*, 178n26
*Sādhana of the Pure Land Sukhāvatī (Bde chen zhing sgrub thabs):* contents of, 142–144; introduction, 31, 139–144; translation, 145–149
*Sahō shidai*, 253n21
*Sahō-shū*, 253n22
Saichō, 248n2
Sainen, 461
Saisen, 56, 59, 73n12

Śaivism, 174n3
Sakai Toshihiko, 349
Śākyamuni: in emperor worship, 368–372; in Kadampa School, 176n15; in *Lotus Sūtra*, 634; *parinirvāṇa*, 34, 36–49; in Śambhala, 745; in Tuṣita Heaven, 197; in Vulture Peak, 458
*samādhi: Amitāyus Ritual Manual*, 224, 229–230, 238–240, 242–243; *Himitsu nenbutsu sho*, 275, 293–295; of recollecting the buddha, 224, 250n10
*Samādhirāja*, 520
samādhi society of twenty-five *(nijūgo zanmaie)*, 14
*samayas*, 227–231, 234–235
Samayavajra, 176n14
Śambhala, 664, 744–751. See also *The Swift Path to Kalāpa*
*saṃbhogakāya* (Enjoyment Body), 745
*sambogakāya*, 19n29
*Saṃdhinirmocana-sūtra*, 423
*saṃsāra*, 165, 169, 345–346, 396, 422, 458
Saṃtuṣita, 197
Sanbōin-ryū lineage, 253n22
*Sandai hihō shō (The Three Great Secret Dharmas)*, 637
*Sangaku-roku*, 248n2
*Sange ōjōki*, 459, 461
Sangphu Neuthok (Gsang phu ne'u thog), 162
*Sanjūjō sakushi*, 252n17, 252n19
Sanqing (Heavens of the Highest Purity), 667
Sanuki, 270
*saptāṅgavidhi* (Seven-Limbed Prayer; *yan lag bdun pa*), 192, 213n25
*Sarvasamayasaṃgraha (Summary of all Pledges; Dam tshig thams cad bsdus pa)*, 161
*Sar vatathāgatādhiṣṭhānasattvālokanabuddha kṣetrasandarśanavyūha-sūtra*, 519
*ṣaṭpāramitā* (*pha rol tu phyin pa drug*; six perfections), 169
*Satyadvayāvatāra (Entry in the Two Truths; Bden pa gnyis la 'jug pa)*, 161
*sbas yul* (*beyül*; hidden valleys), 139
Schleiermacher, Friedrich, 5
Schmidt-Glintzer, Helwig, 711
scholar-cum-adept *(mkhas grup; paṇḍita-siddha)*, 161
Schopen, Gregory, 33, 51n12, 163, 503, 709
The scripture on the contemplation of the Buddha of Infinite Life spoken by the Buddha *(Foshuo guan wuliangshou fo jing)*, 478
Scripture on the fundamental boundary *(Benji jing)*, 665
*Scriptures of the Kadampa (Bka' gdams glegs bam)*, 151n13
Second 'Jam dbyangs Bzhad pa', 746
*Secret Commentary on Mind as a Moon Disk (Shingachirin hishaku)*, 60
*Secret Commentary on the Bodaishinron (Bodaishinron hishaku)*, 60
*Secret Commentary on the Five Wheels and Nine Syllables (Gorin kujimyō himitsushaku)*, 58, 60, 64
secretly adorned ocean-assembly *(mitsugon kaie)*, 73n12
sects, 10–12
secularization, 636
Sé gyü dratsang, 192
*Seishinkai (Spiritual World)*, 556
*seishinshugi undō* (spiritual activism movement), 556
*seiyō bigaku* (Occidental aesthetics), 590
*Sekoddeśa*, 746
self-generation stage *(bdag bskyed rim)*, 169–170, 181n43
selfless love *(mugaai)*, 319
self-power *(jiriki)*, 571, 589–590
*Senchaku hongan nenbutsu shū*, 270
Sengé Tsé, 192
Seng ge'i nga ro (Siṃhasvara), 199
Sengyou, 50n5
Seno'o Girō, 633
*The Sermon on the Soul, Gy'n wyfr's*, 712
servants, Longshu's entreaty to, 622
Seven-Limbed Prayer *(saptāṅgavidhi; yan lag bdun pa)*, 192, 213n25
sexuality, in tantric practices, 165–166, 179n32, 179n35
sexual reversal, yoga of, 142
*sgrub thabs (sādhana)* of deity yoga, 164–165
*shakubuku*, 632, 636
*Sham bha la'i lam yig (Guide to Śambhala)*, 749–750, 758n21

*Sham bha lar skye ba'i smon lam (Prayer for Rebirth in Śambhala),* 750
Shandao, 8, 271, 479, 502
Shao Kang, 459
Sharf, Robert, 33, 477, 709
*shengsi dashi* (the great matter of birth-and-death), 541
Sherap Gyatso, 191
Sherap Sengé, 192
Shes rab rgya mtsho (Prajñāsāgara; Gachoi Lam Damba Agramba), 746, 758n17
*shi* (charity), 668
*Shi'er guang lichan wen,* 711
*shifang fotu* (Buddha Realms of the Ten Directions), 666
Shikoku, 270
Shin Buddhism, 117, 379–381; Essays on Religion and Ethics, 554–570; *Naikan's Path,* 396–419; Ōtani sect, 551, 555, 572; *The Pure Land as a Principle of Criticism,* 551–552, 571–586
*Shingachirin hishaku (Secret Commentary on Mind as a Moon Disk),* 60
Shingon School: contemplative practice, 274; cult figures, 84–86; founder of, 269; *homa* ritual, 29, 56, 79–114; *Jūhachidō* ritual, 158, 223, 225–226; life-writing, 457; mandalas, 84–85; pure lands in, 30, 56–63, 272; *samādhi* of recollecting the buddha, 250n10; Sanbōin-ryū lineage, 253n22
*shinjin,* 396–397, 571–572, 584n1
Shinkaku, 461
Shinmyō, 461
Shinran: *jinen hōni,* 589; *jōdokyō,* 502; *Kyōgyōshinshō,* 573; lineage, 7–8; *nenbutsu,* 117, 578–584; religious quest, 5; *shinjin,* 396, 555; Sukhāvatī, 140; *tariki,* 571
Shinshū (Ōtani) University, 349
Shinto, 350–351
*shinzoku nitai* (two truths) doctrine, 572
Shirakawa reform movement, 555–556
*Shishu hosshin gi (On the Meaning of the Four Kinds of the Dharma Body),* 59
*shittan* (Siddhaṃ), 272
*Sho-ajari shingon mikkyō burui sōroku,* 248n2
Shōchi-in, 269
*Shogiki ketsuei,* 250n10
*Shoki honjō roku,* 250n10
*Shōrai mokuroku,* 248n2
A shortcut to the Pure Land: A vow for the Land of Bliss *(Bde ba can gyi smon lam dag zhing nye lam),* 505
*Short Meditation on the Pure Land, Mysteriously Adorned (Mitsugon jōdo ryakkan),* 30, 56–78; introduction, 56–64; translation, 65–72
Short notes on arousing wisdom through the Diamond World *(Kinkai hatsueshō),* 64
Short *Sukhāvatīvyūha sūtra. See* Smaller *Sukhāvatīvyūha sūtra*
Shōyo, 461
*shugendō* (mountain asceticism), 555
*Shūi ōjōden,* 459, 461
*shūjō* (living beings), 590
Shukaku Hōshinnō, 269
*Shūkyō tetsugaku gaikotsu (The Skeleton of the Philosophy of Religion),* 557
Shūmon no ishin (Restoration of our Sect), 635
the sick *(byōnin),* 397
sickness of great delusion, 335
Siddhaṃ *(shittan),* 272
Silk, Jonathan, 456, 496
silk worm cultivators, Longshu's entreaty to, 623
Silla (Korea), 321, 420
Siṃhasvara (Tathāgata Seng ge'i nga ro), 199, 215n38
Sims-Williams, N., 713
Sinitic Buddhism, 321, 420–451
six perfections *(pha rol tu phyin pa drug; ṣaṭpāramitā),* 169
Sixth Panchen Lama (Blo bzang dpal ldan ye shes), 749–750, 758n21
*The Skeleton of the Philosophy of Other Power Faith ( Tarikimon tetsugaku gaikotsu),* 557
*The Skeleton of the Philosophy of Religion (Shūkyō tetsugaku gaikotsu),* 557
Smaller *Sukhāvatīvyūha sūtra (Amituo jing),* 321, 420–451, 501–504, 514; in poetry, 501–504, 514; in *Wuliangshou yigui,* 224–225, 251nn11–12
Small Jambudvīpa, 750, 759n30

*Snang ba mtha' yas kyi [zhing gi] yon tan la rnal 'byor pas bstod pa* (The Yogin's praise of the virtuous qualities of [the land of] Amitābha), 503
Snellgrove, David, 166, 175n4
*Sngags rim chen mo (Great Treatise on the Stages of Mantra),* 180n39
social orientation, 455–456, 573–574. *See also* ethics; life-writing; poetry
social positions, Longshu's entreaties by, 607–608, 614–624
Sōka Gakkai, 631
Songtsen Gampo, 140
Sørensen, Henrik, 663, 665
Soucy, Alexander, 15
sovereignty *(aiśvarya),* 745
speech *(kumitsu),* 272
Spinoza, Baruch, 557
spiritual activism movement *(seishinshugi undō),* 556
*Spiritual World (Seishinkai),* 556–557, 559
*spyan legs* (Sunetra), 215n38
*Srad brgyud lugs kyi zab lam bla ma'i rnal 'byor thun mong ma yin pa'i khrid yig tsit ta ma ni'i phreng ba* (A garland of wish-fulfilling jewels, an extraordinary practice manual for the profound path of guru-yoga of the Sé tantric tradition), 196–197
Śramaṇa Amoghavajra, 232
*śrāvakas,* 166
Śrīmitra, 50n5
Srong btsan sgam po, Emperor, 177n17
Stein, Aurel, 711
Stone, Jacqueline, 58, 553, 631
*stotra* (praise literature), 499
Strauch, Ingo, 79
stream, 11–12
Strickmann, Michel, 50n5
stupa, cult of, 13, 20n47, 21n50
*Subhāṣitaratnakoṣa,* 525n8
Substance of the Womb-store Realm *(Taizōkai sata),* 61
Sucandra, 745
suffering, dharma of, 344
Sukenaga, Fujiwara no, 460–461. See also *Kōyasan ōjōden*
Sukhāvatī (Land of Bliss): *versus* Abhirati, 82–84; in Chan-Pure Land traditions, 4; as goal of practice, 3, 7, 9, 14, 29, 319, 503; in Korea, 321, 420–451; life-writing about, 458; ritual practices involving, 29–55; Śambhala as, 744–751; in Tibet, 140. See also *Sādhana of the Pure Land Sukhāvatī*; *versus* Tuṣita Heaven, 198; visualizations involving, 158, 163, 189. See also *Amitāyus Ritual Manual; Himitsu nenbutsu sho; Quintessence of Amitābha*; worlds other than, *See* worlds beyond Sukhāvatī
Sukhāvatī triad, 15, 143–144
*Sukhāvatīvyūha,* 82–83, 163, 499, 528n28
*Sukhāvatīvyūha sūtra (Amitābha Sūtra):* Korean analysis of, See *Pulsŏl Amita-gyŏng so*; Longer, *See* Larger *Sukhāvatīvyūha sūtra*; in poetry, 501–504, 513–521; Smaller, *See* Smaller *Sukhāvatīvyūha sūtra*; ten-thought moments, 275
*Sukhāvatīvyūhopadeśa (Wangsheng lun),* 321, 420, 423–428, 526n16
*Summary of all Pledges (Sarvasamayasaṃgraha; Dam tshig thams cad bsdus pa),* 161
Summary of the stages of visualization according to « Opening the Door to the Best Land » *(Zhing mchog sgo 'byed kyi dmigs rim mdor bsdus),* 505
Sum pa mkhan po Ye shes dpal 'byor, 505
Sundermann, W., 713
Sunetra *(spyan legs),* 215n38
The sun of the sage's instruction called clarification of faith [leading to] cultivation of the Land of Bliss *(Bde ba can gyi zhing sbyong ba'i dad pa gsal bar byed pa drang srong lung gi nyi ma),* 505
Sūryaprabha, 745
*Susiddhikara,* 349n5
Sūtra of contemplation on the Buddha of Immeasurable Life *(Guan Wuliangshoufo-jing),* 501, 608
*Sūtra of the Lotus Blossom of the Wonderful Dharma (Myōhō-renge-kyō; Miaofa lianhua jing),* 652n4

Sūtra of the Mysterious Adornment of the Great Vehicle *(Dasheng miyan jing)*, 59
Sūtra on the original acts that serve as a bodhisattva's adornments *(Pusa yingluo benye jing)*, 423
*Suxidijielo gongyang fa*, 349n5
Suzuki, D. T., 397
*The Swift Path to Kalāpa: A Compilation of the Layout of Śambhala and Ritual Offering to The Dharma Kings and Kalkīs*, 744–761; introduction, 664, 744–751; translation, 751–757
sympathetic resonance *(ganying)*, 477

*Tada nenbutsu shite*, 574
Taikan-an, 397–398, 403–409
*Taishang dongxuan lingbao jingtu sheng shen jing*. See *Divine Scripture on the Rebirth in the Pure Land of the Lingbao Highest Cavern Mystery*
Taishō Canon, 247n1, 711
Taiwan, 455–456, 479
Taizōkai (Womb-Store World), 59
*Taizōkai sata* (Substance of the Womb-store Realm), 61
Takata, Tokio, 525n7
Takayama Chōgyū, 633
Takua Shōnin, 64
*Takushō*, 253n22
A talk on the Land of Bliss: Thundering sound from the big bursting summer clouds which nourish the Crops of Good Qualities, *(Bde ba can gyi zhing las brtsams pa'i gtam dge ba'i lo tog spel byed dbyar skyes sprin chen glal ba'i sgra dbyangs)*, 505
Tamamitsu Junshō, 574
Tameyasu, Miyoshi no, 459
*tan* (praise), 712
Tana Daishō, 320, 379–380. *See also* The Future of American Buddhism
Tanaka Chigaku, 552–553, 631–640. *See also* The Age of Unification
Tang Buddhism: *Amitāyus Ritual Manual*, 158, 223–268; Manicheism, 664, 707–743; Tuṣita Heaven, 335
Tanluan, 321, 420, 423–424, 502
*Tan mingjie*. See *In Praise of the Realm of Light*
*Tannishō (A Record in Lament of Divergences)*, 558, 568n10, 589
Tantric Buddhism: guru-yoga, 191–195, 198–199; *homa* ritual, 29, 56, 79–114; Indian arguments for, 176nn13–14; lineage in, 10; metonymic character of tantra, 84; pure lands in, 4, 7–10; *sādhana*, 143–144. See also *Sādhana of the Pure Land Sukhāvatī*; sexuality in, 165–166, 179n32, 179n35; Shingon tradition, *See* Shingon; in Tibet, 174n3, 176n14; visualizations, 157, 159–187, 191
Tārā, 176n15
Tārānātha, 749
*tariki* (other-power), 571, 587–590
*Tarikimon tetsugaku gaikotsu (The Skeleton of the Philosophy of Other Power Faith)*, 557
*Tarkajvāla (Blaze of Reasoning; Rtog ge 'bar ba)*, 160
Tashi khyil, 195
Tathāgata Seng ge'i nga ro (Siṃhasvara), 199, 215n38
*The Teaching of Buddha (Hotoke no kyōbō)*, 381
Tendai (Tiantai) School, 115–117, 274, 634
Tengyur *(bstan 'gyur)*, 161–162, 170
*tenmei kaigo* (enlightenment), 398
ten perfections *(daśa-paramitā)*, 745
ten powers *(daśa-bala)*, 745
ten-thought moments, 275, 295–297
testimonies. *See* life-writing
Thanksgiving, 320, 381, 391
theology: cultural aspects of, 9–14; Euro-American bias in, 5, 9–14, 17n5, 17n7, 19n31, 111n8, 111n11, 636
three-bodies schema (*trikāya* doctrine), 19n29
three disciplines *(trisaṃvara)*, 159–160
*The Three Great Secret Dharmas (Sandai hihō shō)*, 637
Three Periods, 708–709
three poisons *(dug gsum)*, 169
Three Teachings movement, 319
Thuken losang chökyi nyima, 192
Tianru Weize, 322
Tiantai (Tendai) School, 115–117, 274, 634
Tiantai Zhiyi, 322

Tibetan Buddhism: Chinese influences on, 504; lineage in, 11–12, 157; major transmissions in, 149n1; mystical side, 162; poetry, 456, 496–539; pure lands in, 4, 6, 7–9, 140, 528n28; ritual practices, 30–31, 139–153; Śambhala, 664, 744–761; schools in, 211n4; tantric practices, 174n3, 176n14; visualizations, 157–158; *Hundred Deities of Tuṣita,* 188–222; *Quintessence of Amitābha,* 159–187
Toba, 57
Tōdaiji, 461
Tōji, 57, 62
*tokubetsuna kōken* (gift), 590
Tomoe, 379–380
*Tonkō dōkyo zurokuhen,* 700n6
Tosotsu Heaven. *See* Tuṣita Heaven
training centers *(kenshūjo),* 400–401
transference meditation *(phowa),* 144, 146–147
transmigration, 116, 542
treasure-text *(gter ma),* 162
*Treatise on Birth in the Pure Land (Wangshenglun; Jingtulun),* 117
*The Treatise on the Mind Aspiring for Enlightenment (Putixin lun, Bodaishinron),* 59
Treatise on the Pure Land *(Jingtu lun),* 459
Trepiṭaka Bo Śrīmitra, 36
*trikāya* doctrine (three-bodies schema), 19n29
Tripiṭakamāla, 166, 176n14, 179n35
*tripiṭaka* teaching, 330
*trisaṃvara* (three disciplines), 159–160
Trisong Detsen, 139
Tsongkhapa Lozang Drakpa, 158, 160, 179n35, 180n39, 188–195, 198–199, 505–506
Tsui Chi, 711
Tuṣita Heaven, 6, 158, 188–222, 335–336, 458. See also *Hundred Deities of Tuṣita*
tutelary deity *(yi dam),* 164–165
Two Mandalas, 59
two truths *(shinzoku nitai)* doctrine, 572

Ucchuṣma ritual manual *(Wuchusemo yigui),* 223, 248n3
Uchimura Kanzō, 638
Uḍḍiyāna, 161
ugliness, 590
An unhindered quick path to the Land of Bliss *(Bde ba can gyi zhing du thogs pa med par bgrod pa'i myur lam),* 505
United States: Buddhism in, 319–321, 379–395; Naikan psychotherapy in, 401–402
*Upanisads,* 165
*uṣṇīṣa,* 118
Utmost Bliss, 338–339, 458. *See also* Sukhāvatī
Uttarakuru, 82

Vagindra, 746
Vāgīś varakīrti, 176n15
Vajrabhairava (Rdo rje 'jigs byed), 180n36
Vajrabodhi, 224
vajra body *(rdo rje lus),* 165
*vajradhātu maṇḍala,* 84–85
Vajra Family, 227–231, 235
Vajraghaṇṭapāda, 176n14
Vajrapāṇi (Vajragarbha), 143, 170, 193, 224, 227, 745–747
Vajrasattva, 169, 180n39
Vajraśekhara, 349n5
Vajra-Yamāntaka *sādhana,* 169–170
Vajrayāna, 157, 161–165, 174n3, 198, 744, 750
*Varṇārhavarṇa Stotra,* 515
vase empowerment ritual, 144, 148
Vasubandhu, 117, 321, 420, 423–424
veneration, gate of, 117
*vidyā-mantras (rig sngags),* 750
Vietnam, 15
Vijayā, 745
*Vimalakīrtinirdeśa sūtra,* 3
*Vimalaprabhā,* 744–745, 750, 757n2
virtues *(gongde),* 667–668
*viṣaya* (principalities), 750
Viṣṇu Yaśas, 744–745
visualization, 8; contemplative, *See* contemplation; effectiveness of, 477; marks of the Buddha, 118–136; *nenbutsu,* See *nenbutsu*; *sādhana,* 143–144. See also *Sādhana of the Pure Land Sukhāvatī*

*Visuddhimagga*, 520
vocalization. *See* recitation
A vow for the Land of Highest Bliss *(Rnam dag bde chen zhing gi smon lam)*, 141, 505
*Vow of Non-Discrimination between Beauty and Ugliness (Muu kōshu no gan)*, 552, 587–601; introduction, 552, 587–591; translation, 591–598
vows: of Amida, 552, 573–574, 588–590; gate of, 117; primal, 275, 291–293
Vulture Peak (Ryōjusen), 458

Waley, Arthur, 711, 713, 714
Wallace, Vesna, 664, 744
Wang Rixiu, 552, 602–608. See also *Longshu's Discourse on Pure Land*
*Wangsheng lizan wen*, 711
*Wangsheng lun (Sukhāvatīvyūhopadeśa)*, 321, 420, 423–428, 526n16
*Wangshenglun (Treatise on Birth in the Pure Land; Jingtulun)*, 117
*Wangsheng lun zhu* (Commentary on the *Sukhāvatīvyūhopadeśa*), 321, 420, 423–428
*Wangsheng xifang jintu ruiyang zhuan* (Accounts of auspicious responses accompanying birth in the Western Pure Land), 459
*Wanshan tonggui ji (The Collection of the Shared Source of the Myriad Good Deeds)*, 541
Wayman, Alex, 179n32, 180n39, 191
Way of the Gods *(kannagara no michi)*, 350
Way of the Kami, 350
wealthy persons, Longshu's entreaty to, 619
Wei Mao, 713
Western bias, 5, 9–12
Western Pure Land, 9
*The Wheel of Sharp Weapons*, 175n6
Where is the Living Buddha Amida?, 349–378; introduction, 319–320, 349–352; translation, 352–376; preface, 352–353; first chapter, 353–363; second chapter, 363–376
White Lotus Society, 14
Willemen, Charles, 79, 81–82
wisdom beings *(jñānasattva)*, 143
*Wish-Prayer for Śambhala*, 746
With One Sound of Amitābha's Name, Children Avoid a Car Accident, 485–486
Womb-Store World (Taizōkai), 59
women: exclusion from Mount Kōya, 462; in lay Buddhist movements, 633, 635; Longshu's entreaty to, 621; in pure land, 331–332, 342–343
A wonderful staircase for ascension to the Land of Great Bliss: Commentary to a vow for the Land of Highest Bliss *(Rnam dag bde chen zhing gi smon lam gyi 'byed 'grel bde chen zhing du bgrod pa'i them skas bzang po)*, 505
wondrous people *(myōkōnin)*, 589, 599n17
wondrous works *(myōko-hin)*, 589, 591
Wŏnhyo, 321, 420–422. See also *Pulsŏl Amita-gyŏng so*
World of Utmost Bliss *(jile shijie)*, 708
worlds beyond Sukhāvatī: overview of, 663–664; translations: *Divine Scripture on the Rebirth in the Pure Land of the Lingbao Highest Cavern Mystery*, 665–706; *In Praise of the Realm of Light*, 707–743; *The Swift Path to Kalāpa: A Compilation of the Layout of Śambhala and Ritual Offering to The Dharma Kings and Kalkīs*, 744–761
*Wo yuan nian mituo* (I vow to recite Amitābha's name), 483
*Wuchusemo yigui* (Ucchuṣma ritual manual), 223, 248n3
*Wuliangshou jing. See* Larger *Sukhāvatīvyūha sūtra*
*Wuliangshou yigui.* See *Amitāyus Ritual Manual*
Wu Yingbin, 346n1
Wu Zetian, Empress, 707
Wuzhen Monastery, 479
Wuzong, Emperor, 707

*Xiabuzan.* See *In Praise of the Realm of Light*
Xiangshan, 479
*xiao* (filial piety), 668
Xingyun, 479
*xin jingtu* (New Pure Land), 708
*xin mingjie* (New Realm of Light), 708–709
Xuanzong, Emperor, 707

*Xu Gaoseng zhuan,* 520
Xuzhong (Wang Rixiu), 552, 602–608. See also *Longshu's Discourse on Pure Land*

Yabuki Keiki, 711
Yamabe, Nobuyoshi, 16
Yamāntaka (Bhairava), 166, 169–170, 180n40
Yamāntaka of Passion ('Dod chags gshin rje gshed), 180n36
Yanagi Sōetsu, 552, 587–591. See also *Vow of Non-Discrimination between Beauty and Ugliness*
*yan lag bdun pa* (Seven-Limbed Prayer; *saptāṅgavidhi*), 192, 213n25
Yanshou, Yongming, 540–543
Yaśas, 744–745
Yasukuni Shrine, 574
Yasutane, Yoshishige no, 459–460
*Yellow Emperor's Classic of Internal Medicine,* 335
yellow registers *(huanglu),* 667, 700n10
Yeshé Gyeltsen, 158, 194. See also *Hundred Deities of Tuṣita*
*yi dam* (tutelary deity), 164–165
Yixing, 59, 73n12
Yogācāra, 423
yoga of sexual reversal, 142
The Yogin's praise of the virtuous qualities of [the land of] Amitābha *(Snang ba mtha' yas kyi [zhing gi] yon tan la rnal 'byor pas bstod pa),* 503
Yokawa, 115–116
Yoshimoto Ishin, 320–321, 397–398, 402. See also *Naikan's Path*
Yuan dynasty, 540
Yuanzhao, 271
Yu Chunxi, 322
Yūgen, Gochibō, 62–63
*yūgensha* (finites), 557–558
Yuien, 568n10
Yuihan, 461, 466–468
Yu Wanli, 711

*zan* (eulogy), 712
Zen Buddhism, 589
Zenrinji, 270
Zentsūji, 270
*zettai mugensha* (Absolutely Infinite), 557–562
Zhang Xiaoxiang, 603
Zhang Xiren, 480
Zhao Mengfu, 543–544
*Zhenyuan xinding shijiao lu,* 248n2
*Zhing mchog sgo 'byed kyi dmigs rim mdor bsdus* (Summary of the stages of visualization according to "Opening the Door to the Best Land"), 505
Zhi Qian, 51n11
Zhiyan, 711, 713
Zhiyi, 271
*Zhonghua daozang,* 668
Zhuhong, Yunqi, 14, 319, 322. *See also* Answers to Forty-Eight Questions about the Pure Land
*Zhunti jing* (Cundī sūtra), 224, 248n3, 249n7
Zhu Xi, 603
*zōaku muge* (tendency of condoning evil), 571
*Zoku honchō ōjōden,* 459
*Zoku senchaku mongi yōshō,* 270
Zongxiao, 604–605, 625n4, 625n8